ST▮▮▮▮▮▮▮ AS

C000262125

Devon

First published in 2003 by

Philip's, a division of
Octopus Publishing Group Ltd
2-4 Heron Quays, London E14 4JP

Second edition 2006
First impression 2006
DEVBA

ISBN-10 0-540-08847-1 (pocket)
ISBN-13 978-0-540-08847-8 (pocket)

© Philip's 2006

Ordnance Survey®

This product includes mapping data licensed from
Ordnance Survey® with the permission of the
Controller of Her Majesty's Stationery Office.
© Crown copyright 2006. All rights reserved.
Licence number 100011710.

Printed and bound in Spain
by Cayfosa-Quebecor

Contents

II   **Administrative and Postcode boundaries**

III **Key to map symbols**

IV   **Key to map pages**

VI   **Route planning**

1   **Street maps** at 1⅓ inches to 1 mile

150 **Street maps** at 2⅔ inches to 1 mile

261 **Street maps of Exeter and Plymouth city centres** at 5⅓ inches to 1 mile

264 **Index** of towns and villages

267 **Index** of streets, hospitals, industrial estates, railway stations, schools, shopping centres, universities and places of interest

Digital Data

The exceptionally high-quality mapping found in this atlas is available as digital data in TIFF format, which is easily convertible to other bitmapped (raster) image formats.

The index is also available in digital form as a standard database table. It contains all the details found in the printed index together with the National Grid reference for the map square in which each entry is named.

For further information and to discuss your requirements, please contact Philip's on 020 7644 6932 or james.mann@philips-maps.co.uk

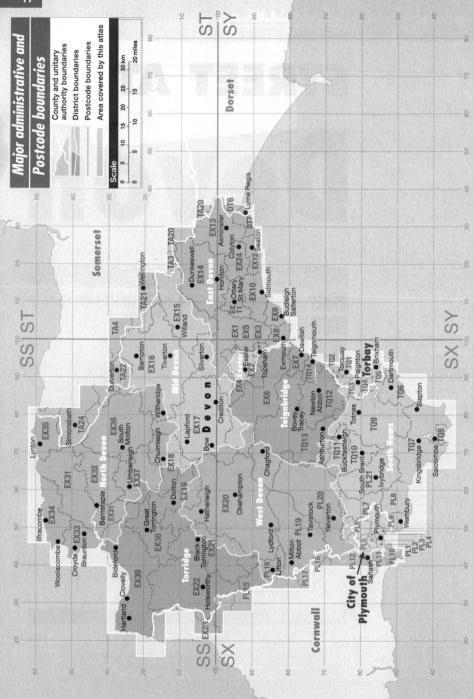

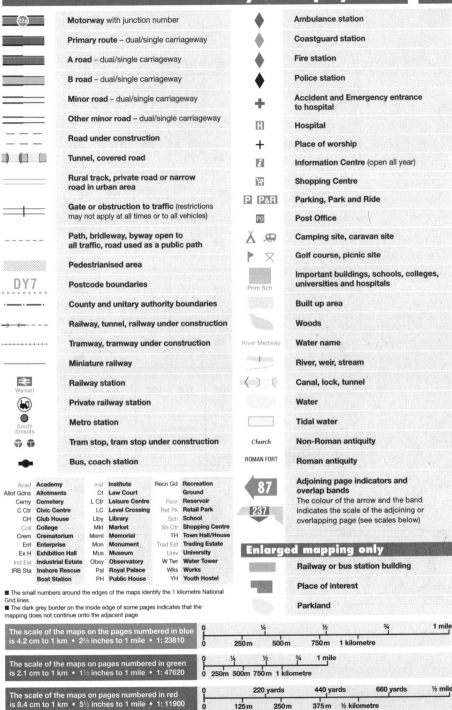

Symbol	Description
	Motorway with junction number
	Primary route – dual/single carriageway
	A road – dual/single carriageway
	B road – dual/single carriageway
	Minor road – dual/single carriageway
	Other minor road – dual/single carriageway
	Road under construction
	Tunnel, covered road
	Rural track, private road or narrow road in urban area
	Gate or obstruction to traffic (restrictions may not apply at all times or to all vehicles)
	Path, bridleway, byway open to all traffic, road used as a public path
	Pedestrianised area
DY7	Postcode boundaries
	County and unitary authority boundaries
	Railway, tunnel, railway under construction
	Tramway, tramway under construction
	Miniature railway
Walsall	Railway station
	Private railway station
South Shields	Metro station
	Tram stop, tram stop under construction
	Bus, coach station

Symbol	Description
◆	Ambulance station
◇	Coastguard station
◆	Fire station
◆	Police station
✚	Accident and Emergency entrance to hospital
H	Hospital
+	Place of worship
i	Information Centre (open all year)
🛒	Shopping Centre
P P&R	Parking, Park and Ride
PO	Post Office
Ⓧ 🚐	Camping site, caravan site
▶ ✕	Golf course, picnic site
Prim Sch	Important buildings, schools, colleges, universities and hospitals
	Built up area
	Woods
River Medway	Water name
	River, weir, stream
	Canal, lock, tunnel
	Water
	Tidal water
Church	Non-Roman antiquity
ROMAN FORT	Roman antiquity
87	Adjoining page indicators and overlap bands
237	The colour of the arrow and the band indicates the scale of the adjoining or overlapping page (see scales below)

Acad	Academy		Inst	Institute		Recn Gd	Recreation Ground
Allot Gdns	Allotments		Ct	Law Court			
Cemy	Cemetery		L Ctr	Leisure Centre		Resr	Reservoir
C Ctr	Civic Centre		LC	Level Crossing		Ret Pk	Retail Park
CH	Club House		Liby	Library		Sch	School
Coll	College		Mkt	Market		Sh Ctr	Shopping Centre
Crem	Crematorium		Meml	Memorial		TH	Town Hall/House
Ent	Enterprise		Mon	Monument		Trad Est	Trading Estate
Ex H	Exhibition Hall		Mus	Museum		Univ	University
Ind Est	Industrial Estate		Obsy	Observatory		W Twr	Water Tower
IRB Sta	Inshore Rescue Boat Station		Pal	Royal Palace		Wks	Works
			PH	Public House		YH	Youth Hostel

■ The small numbers around the edges of the maps identify the 1 kilometre National Grid lines
■ The dark grey border on the inside edge of some pages indicates that the mapping does not continue onto the adjacent page

Enlarged mapping only

Symbol	Description
	Railway or bus station building
	Place of interest
	Parkland

The scale of the maps on the pages numbered in blue is 4.2 cm to 1 km • 2⅔ inches to 1 mile • 1: 23810	0 ¼ ½ ¾ 1 mile / 0 250m 500m 750m 1 kilometre
The scale of the maps on pages numbered in green is 2.1 cm to 1 km • 1⅓ inches to 1 mile • 1: 47620	0 ¼ ½ ¾ 1 mile / 0 250m 500m 750m 1 kilometre
The scale of the maps on pages numbered in red is 8.4 cm to 1 km • 5⅓ inches to 1 mile • 1: 11900	0 220 yards 440 yards 660 yards ½ mile / 0 125m 250m 375m ½ kilometre

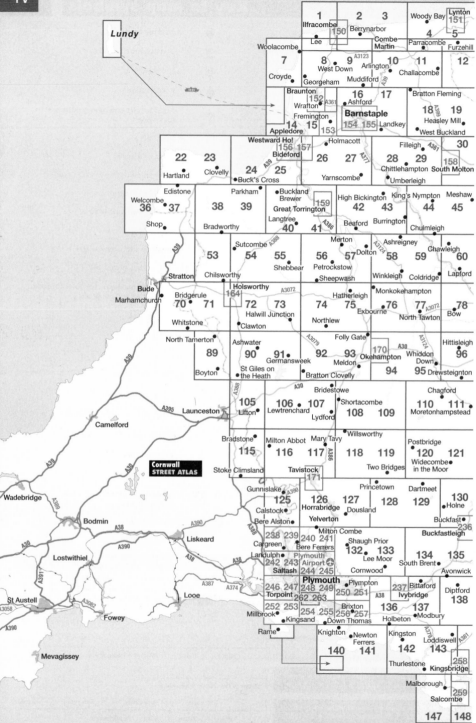

IV

Lundy

1 Ilfracombe
Woolacombe
Lee
150
2 Berrynarbor
3
Woody Bay
Lynton 151
5
Combe Martin
Parracombe
Furzehill
4

7
Croyde
8 West Down
Georgeham
9 A3123
Muddiford
Arlington
10
Challacombe
11
12

Braunton 152
Wrafton
Fremington
14 Appledore
A361
15 153
16 Ashford
17
Barnstaple 154 155
Landkey
Bratton Fleming
18
Heasley Mill
West Buckland
19

Westward Ho! 156 157
Bideford
Holmacott
26
27
Filleigh
28
Chittlehampton
Umberleigh
A361
29
South Molton
30
158

22
Hartland
23
Clovelly
24
Buck's Cross
25
Yarnscombe

Edistone
Welcombe
36 **37**
Shop
Parkham
38
39
Buckland Brewer
Great Torrington
Langtree
40
41
159
High Bickington
42 **43**
Beaford Burrington
King's Nympton
44
Chulmleigh
Meshaw
45

Bradworthy

53
Chilsworthy
Sutcombe
54
55
Shebbear
56
Petrockstow
Sheepwash
Merton
57
Dolton
Ashreigney
58
Winkleigh
59
Coldridge
Chawleigh
60
Lapford

Stratton
Bude
Marhamchurch
Bridgerule
70 **71**
Whitstone
164
Holsworthy
72
Halwill Junction
Clawton
73
A3072
74
Northlew
Hatherleigh
75
Exbourne
Monkokehampton
76
77 A3072
North Tawton
78
Bow

North Tamerton
89
Boyton
Ashwater
90
St Giles on the Heath
91
Germansweek
Bratton Clovelly
92
Meldon
93
Okehampton
94
170 A30
Folly Gate
Whiddon Down
95 Drewsteignton
Hittisleigh
96

Launceston
A395
105
Lifton
106
Lewtrenchard
107
Lydford
Bridestowe
Shortacombe
108
109
Chagford
110 **111**
Moretonhampstead

Camelford
Bradstone
115
Stoke Climsland
Milton Abbot
116
117 A386
Tavistock
171
Mary Tavy
Willsworthy
118
119
Two Bridges
Postbridge
120 **121**
Widecombe in the Moor

Cornwall STREET ATLAS

Gunnislake
125
Calstock
Bere Alston
A390
126
Horrabridge
Yelverton
127
Dousland
128
Princetown
129
Dartmeet
130
Holne
Buckfast
236

Wadebridge
Bodmin
A38
A390
Liskeard
A390
A38
238 239
Cargreen
242 243
Landulph
Saltash
240 241
Bere Ferrers
244 245
Plymouth Airport
Milton Combe
Shaugh Prior
132 133
Lee Moor
Cornwood
Buckfastleigh
134 135
South Brent
Avonwick

Lostwithiel
A38
A391
A387
A374
246 247
Torpoint
252 253
Millbrook
Kingsand
248 249
262 263
254 255
Down Thomas
Plympton
250 251
Brixton
256 257
Holbeton
Plympton
A38
237 Bittaford
Ivybridge
Modbury
136 137
Diptford
138

St Austell
A3058
A390
Fowey
Looe
Rame
Knighton
140
Newton Ferrers
141
Kingston
142
Loddiswell
143
Thurlestone
258
Kingsbridge

Mevagissey
Malborough
259
Salcombe
147 148

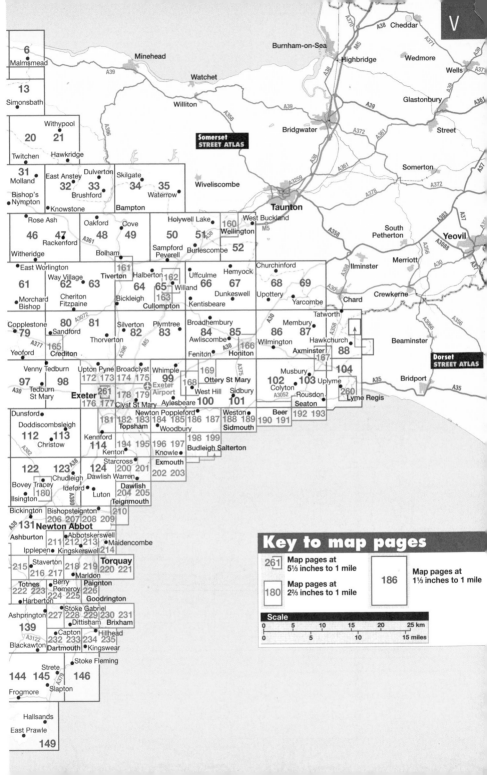

V

Cheddar
Burnham-on-Sea
Wedmore
Highbridge
Wells

6
Malmsmead

Minehead
Watchet
Williton

Glastonbury
Street

Somerset
STREET ATLAS

13
Simonsbath

Withypool
20 21

Twitchen
Hawkridge

Bridgwater
Somerton

31
Molland

East Anstey
32 33

Dulverton
Brushford

Skilgate
34

35
Waterrow

Wiveliscombe

Taunton

South
Petherton

Yeovil

Bishop's
Nympton

Knowstone

Bampton

Rose Ash
46 47
Rackenford

Oakford
48

Cove
49

Holywell Lake
50 51

West Buckland
Wellington
160

52

Ilminster
Merriott

Witheridge
Bolham

Sampford
Peverell
Burlescombe

Crewkerne

East Worlington
61

Way Village
62 63

Tiverton
161

Halberton
64 162
65 163
Willand

Uffculme
66 67

Hemyock

Churchinford
68 69

Chard

Morchant
Bishop

Cheriton
Fitzpaine

Bickleigh
Cullompton

Kentisbeare

Dunkeswell
Upottery

Yarcombe

Copplestone
79 80
Sandford

81

Silverton
82

Plymtree
83

Broadhembury
84 85
Awliscombe

Membury
86 87

Tatworth

Beaminster

Yeoford
165
Crediton

Thorverton

Feniton
Honiton
166

Wilmington

Hawkchurch
88
167
Axminster

Dorset
STREET ATLAS

Venny Tedburn
97 98

Upton Pyne
172 173
Exeter 261

Broadclyst
174 175

Whimple
99
168

Ottery St Mary
169

West Hill
Sidbury

Musbury
102 103
Colyton

Uplyme
104

Bridport

Dunsford
112 113

Doddiscombsleigh

Christow

Kennford
114

Clyst St Mary
176 177
178 179

Newton Poppleford
181 182 183 184 185 186 187
Topsham
Woodbury

Aylesbeare
100

Sidbury
101

Rousdon
Seaton

Weston
188 189
Sidmouth

Beer
190 191
192 193

Lyme Regis
260

Bovey Tracey
122 123
Chudleigh
Ideford
Ilsington 180

124
Starcross
Dawlish Warren
Luton
Dawlish
Teignmouth

Kenton
194 195
198 199
196 197
Knowle
Budleigh Salterton

Exmouth
202 203

Bickington
131 Newton Abbot
Bishopsteignton
206 207 208 209
210

Ashburton
211 212 213
Abbotskerswell
Maidencombe

Ipplepen
Kingskerswell
214

Staverton
215 216 217

218 219
Marldon
Torquay
220 221

Key to map pages

261 Map pages at
5⅓ inches to 1 mile

186 Map pages at
1⅛ inches to 1 mile

Totnes
222 223
Harberton

Berry
Pomeroy
224 225

Paignton
226
Goodrington

180 Map pages at
2⅔ inches to 1 mile

Ashprington
227
139

228 229 230 231
Stoke Gabriel
Dittisham
Brixham

Blackawton

Capton
232 233 234 235
Dartmouth
Hillhead
Kingswear

Scale

| 0 | 5 | 10 | 15 | 20 | 25 km |

| 0 | 5 | 10 | 15 miles |

Stoke Fleming
144 145 146
Frogmore
Strete
Slapton

Hallsands
East Prawle
149

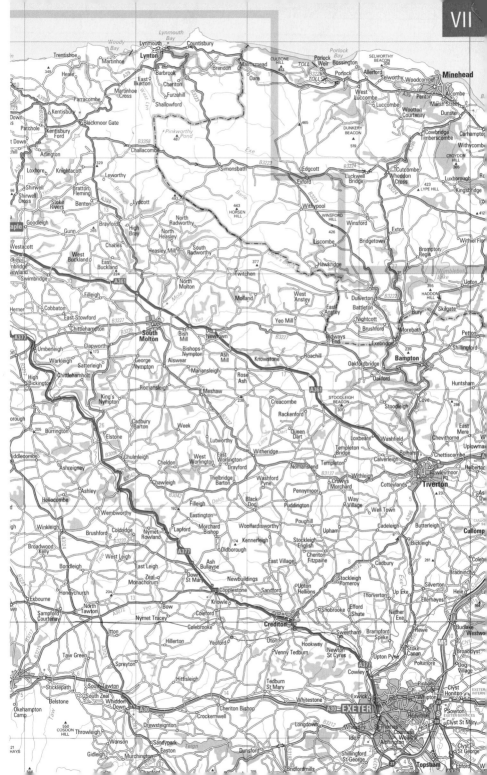

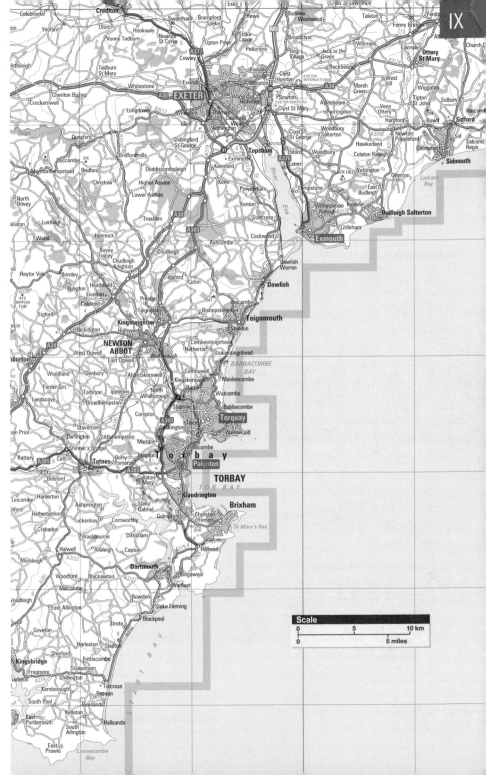

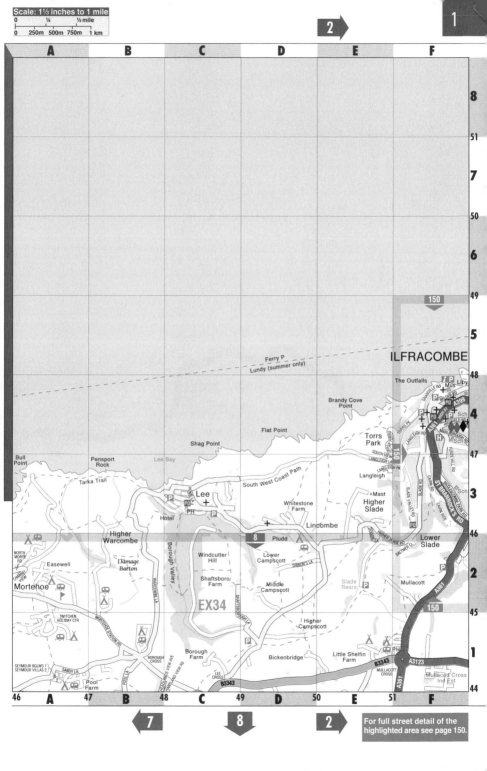

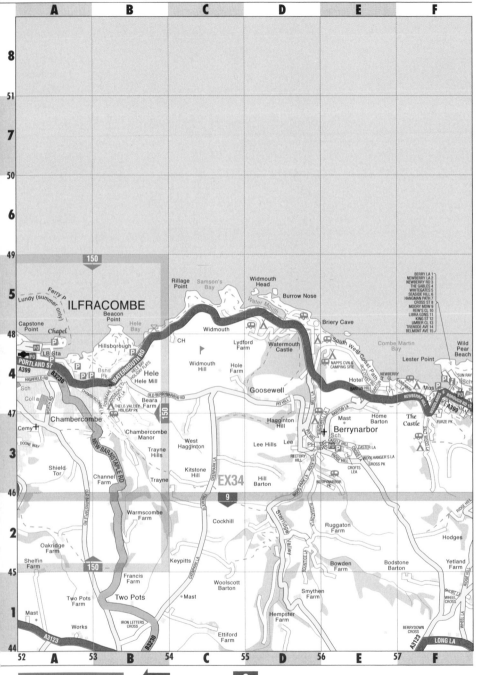

BERRY LA 1
NEWBERRY 2
NEWBERRY RD 3
THE GABLES 4
WHITEGATES 5
SEASIDE HILL 6
HANGMAN PATH 7
CROSS ST 8
MOORY MDW 9
REW'S CL 10
LIBRA GDNS 11
KING ST 12
LUMBER CL 13
TRENODE AVE 14
BELMONT AVE 15

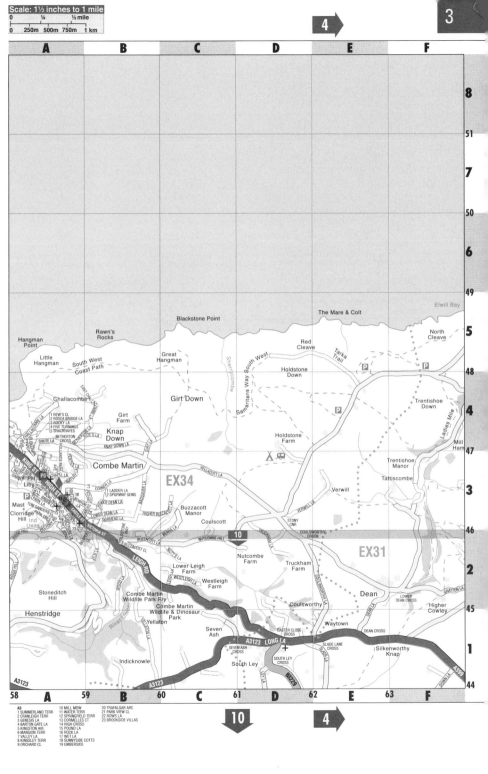

A   B   C   D   E   F

8
51
7
50
6
49
5
48
4
47
3
46
2
45
1
44

Elwill Bay

The Mare & Colt

North Cleave

Hangman Point

Rawn's Rocks

Blackstone Point

Red Cleave

Little Hangman

South West Coast Path

Great Hangman

Tarka Trail

Samaritans Way South West

Holdstone Down

P

P

Challacombe

1 REW'S CL
2 ROSEA BRIDGE LA
3 ROCKY LA
4 FIVE TURNINGS
5 SHACKHAYES

Girt Down

Trentishoe Down

Girt Farm

Ladies Mile

Knap Down

Holdstone Farm

KNAP DOWN LA

Combe Martin

Mill Ham

VELLACOTT LA

Trentishoe Manor

EX34

Verwill

Tattiscombe

PH

Liby

Buzzacott Manor

Coulscott

VERWILL LA

1 LADDER LA
12 SPURWAY GDNS

Mast

Clorridge Hill

STONY CNR

Ind Units

HIGHER BUZZACOTT

BEARA LA

NUTCOMBE HILL

COULSWORTHY CROOK

EX31

LOWER DEAN LA

BUZZACOTT LA

NUT'S LA

Nutcombe Farm

Truckham Farm

TRUCKHAM LA

Lower Leigh Farm

LEIGH RD

WESTLEIGH LA

Westleigh Farm

COULSWORTHY LA

Dean

GRATTON LA

LOWER DEAN CROSS

Stoneditch Hill

WOOLA LA

Combe Martin Wildlife Park Rly

Coulsworthy

DEAN LA

Higher Cowley

Henstridge

River Umber

Combe Martin Wildlife & Dinosaur Park

Yellaton

Waytown

DEAN CROSS

Silkenworthy Knap

VELLACOTT LA

Seven Ash

EASTER CLOSE CROSS

SLADE LANE CROSS

SLADE LA

A399

A3123

LONG LA

Indicknowle

SEVEN ASH CROSS

South Ley

SOUTH LEY CROSS

LEY LA

B3229

GORWILL LA

A3123

A3123

58   59   60   61   62   63

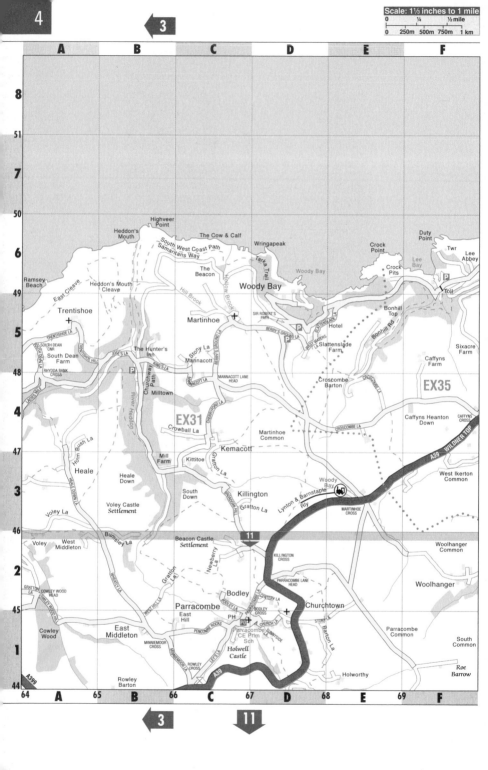

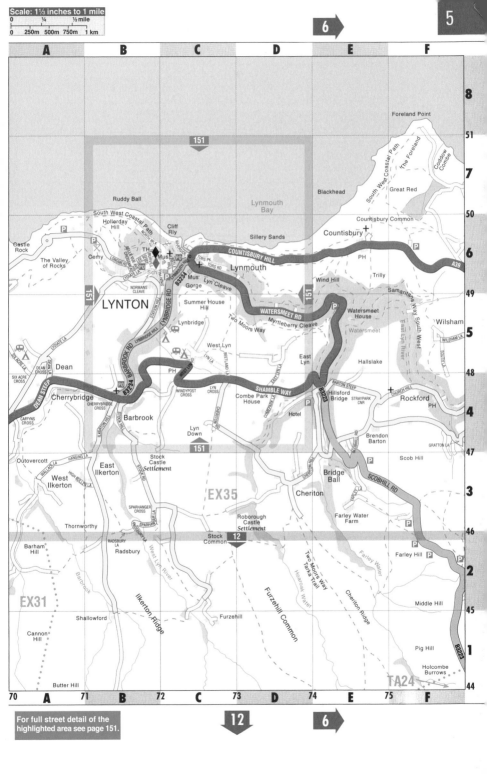

Scale: 1⅓ inches to 1 mile

| 0 | ¼ | ½ mile |
| 0 | 250m | 500m | 750m | 1 km |

A B C D E F

8

51

7

Foreland Point

The Foreland

Coddow Combe

Ruddy Ball

South West Coastal Path

Great Red

Blackhead

Lynmouth Bay

Countisbury Common

50

Castle Rock

Hollerday Hill

Cliff Rly

Sillery Sands

Countisbury

6

The Valley of Rocks

Cemy

TH

Mus

COUNTISBURY HILL

PH

A39

LYNTON

Lynmouth

Mus Gorge

Lyn Cleave

Wind Hill

Trilly

49

151

NORMANS CLEAVE

Summer House Hill

WATERSMEET RD

Samaritans Way South West

Wilsham

5

Lynbridge

Two Moors Way

Myrtleberry Cleave

Watersmeet House

East Lyn River

WILSHAM LA

West Lyn

East Lyn

Watersmeet

Hallslake

SOUTH LA

Dean

PH

SHAMBLE WAY

Barton Steep

48

SIX ACRE LA

LYDIATE LA

DEAN CROSS

Cherrybridge

Combe Park House

Hillsford Bridge

STRAYPARK CNR

Church Hill

Rockford

PH

4

CAFFYNS CROSS

Barbrook

Lyn Down

Hotel

GRATTON LA

47

Outovercott

East Ilkerton

Stock Castle Settlement

Bridge Ball

Scob Hill

SCOBHILL RD

3

West Ilkerton

WALLS LA

HIGH BULLEN LA

HANGING LA

Cheriton

Farley Water Farm

FARLEY LA

EX35

Thornworthy

SPARHANGER CROSS

Roborough Castle Settlement

46

Barham Hill

RADSBURY LA

Radsbury

West Lyn River

Stock Common

12

Farley Water

Farley Hill

2

EX31

Ilkerton Ridge

Shallowford

Furzehill

Furzehill Common

Two Moors Way Tarka Trail

Hoaroak Water

Cheriton Ridge

Middle Hill

45

Cannon Hill

Pig Hill

B3223

1

Butter Hill

Holcombe Burrows

TA24

44

70 A 71 B 72 C 73 D 74 E 75 F

For full street detail of the highlighted area see page 151.

12
6

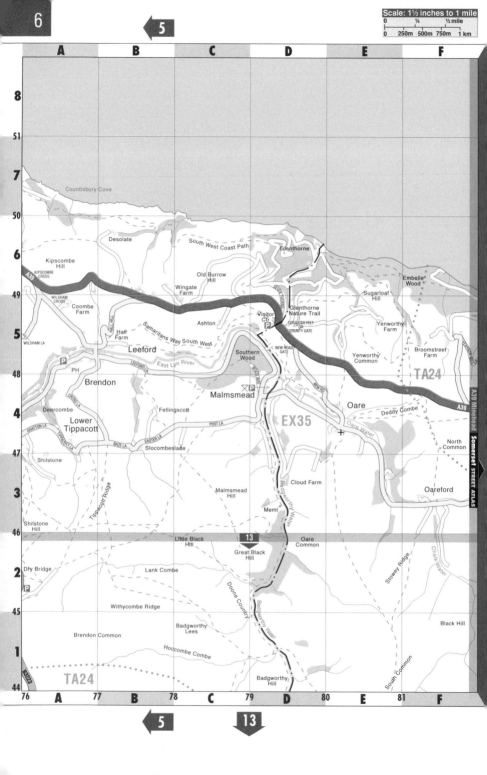

Scale: 1½ inches to 1 mile

0   ¼   ½ mile
0   250m 500m 750m 1 km

8

Mortehoe
Morte
Point
HEADLAND CT 1
KINEVOR CL 2
MORTEHOE STATION RD 3
ADA'S TERR 4
PH
PO
Cemy
Cart
Linhay
Her Ctr

45

Grunta
Beach
CASTLE
Grunta
Pool
ROCK
SHARP ROCK S
UPPER CLAYPARK 6
Hotel

7

Barricane
Beach
CROSSWAYS
CT
EX34
Woolacombe

44

Mem
ARLINGTON PL 1
THE GROVE 2
ARLINGTON RD 3
FROG ST 4
HUNTER LA 5
MILL LA 6
WEST RD 7
RAWNSLEY LA 8
FAIRHOLME RD 9
SPRINGFIELD RD 10
SANDY LANE CT 11
CLIFFSIDE 12
BEACH RD
BARTLE
SOUTH ST
Hotel

6

Dunes
CHALLACOMBE
HILL
Mill
Rock

43

Potter's
Hill

5

Morte
Bay
Woolacombe
Sand
Woolacombe
Down

42

4

Black
Rock
Putsborough
Sand
DOWN LA

41

Whiting
Hole
Long
Bar
Vention
Pickwell

South West Coast Path
Croyde
Hoe
Ramson La
CLIFTON
CT
Manor
House
Putsborough
PUTSBOROUGH RD

3

Baggy
Point
Middleborough
Hill
Middlehill La
New La
EX33

40

Croyde
Bay
Hotel
MOOR LA
Ora Hill
Croyde
North
Hole
Forda
Hill

2

Croyde Bay
CROYDE
CAMP
BELLWS
PENNY
HILL
PH
Mus
ST MARY'S RD
MILLERS
BROOK
Cross
South
Hole
Farm

Dunes
SANDY LA
CLOUTMAN'S LA
COTE LANE
COLE CLEAVE RD

39

B3231
SOMERTHING LA
Chapel
1 ORA STONE PK
2 BONNICOTT LA
3 LEADENGATE FIELDS
4 LEADENGATE CL
5 SANDY WAY
6 ST HELEN'S CL
7 HOME FARM CL
8 WATERY LA
9 MYRTLE FARM VIEW
10 SEA BIRDS PK
LONG LA

1

CROYDE RD
Saunton
Down
B3231

38

14

8

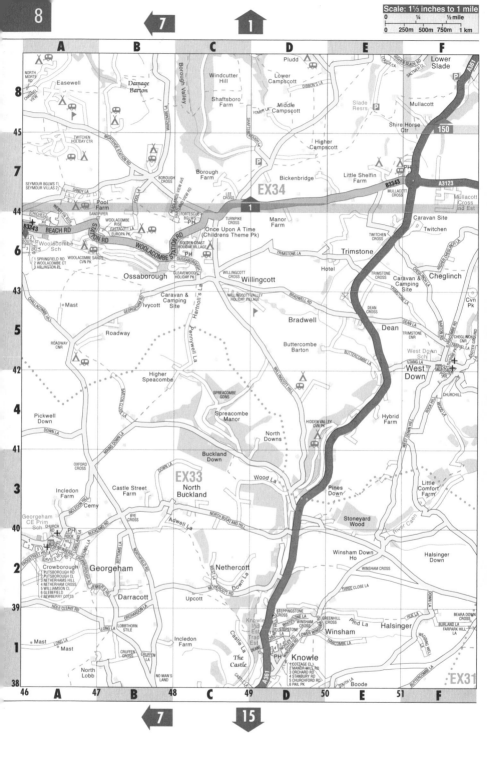

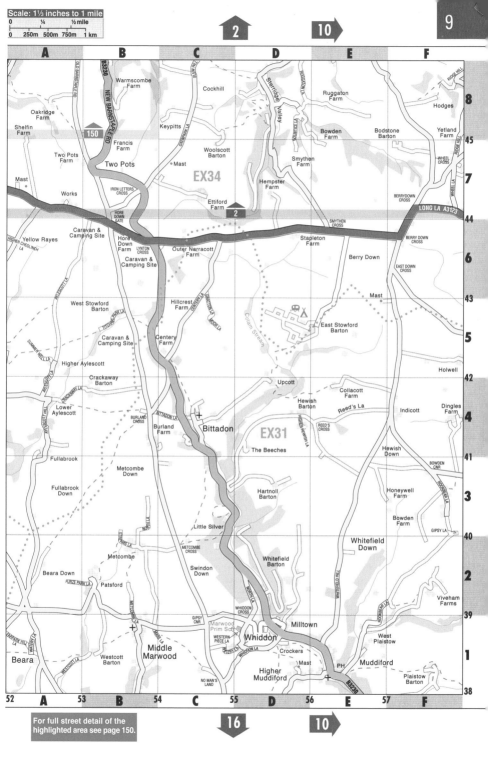

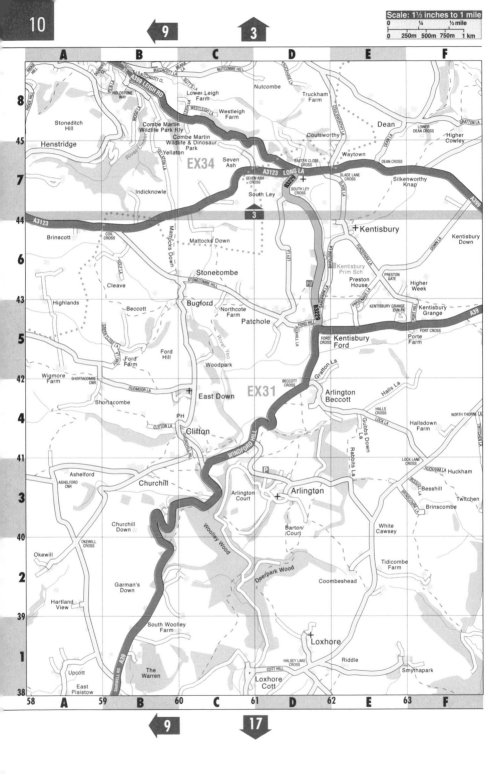

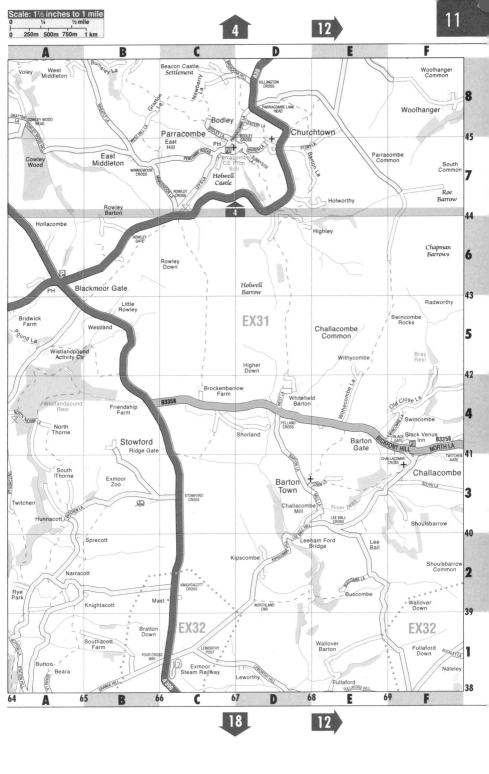

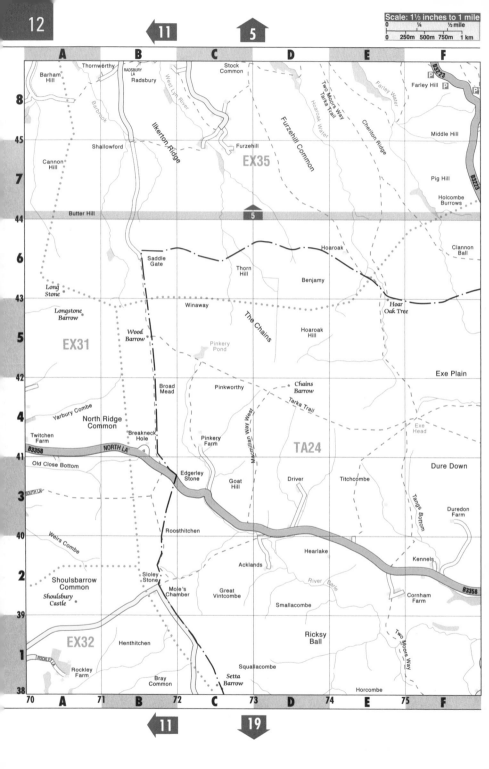

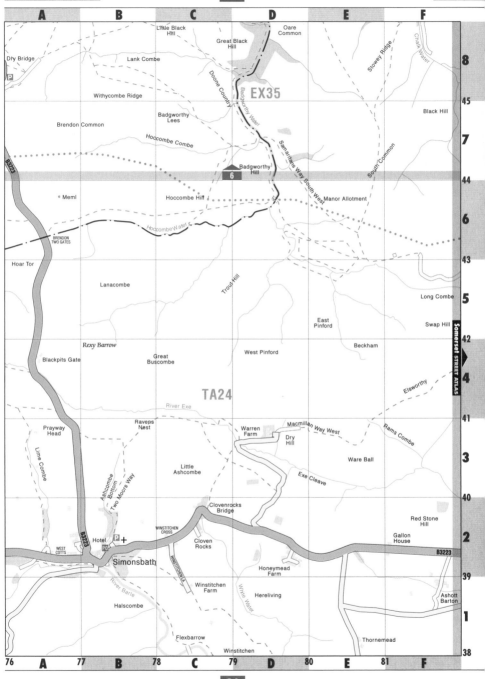

Scale: 1⅓ inches to 1 mile

0   ¼   ½ mile
0   250m 500m 750m 1 km

6

20

8
45
7
44
6
43
5
42
4
41
3
40
2
39
1
38

A   B   C   D   E   F

Dry Bridge

Little Black Hill

Great Black Hill

Oare Common

Stowey Ridge

Chalk Water

Lank Combe

Withycombe Ridge

Doone Country

EX35

Badgworthy Water

Black Hill

Brendon Common

Badgworthy Lees

Hoccombe Combe

Samaritans Way South West

South Common

Meml

Hoccombe Hill

Badgworthy Hill

6

Manor Allotment

Hoar Tor

Hoccombe Water

BRENDON TWO GATES

Lanacombe

Trout Hill

Long Combe

East Pinford

Swap Hill

Somerset STREET ATLAS

Rexy Barrow

West Pinford

Beckham

Blackpits Gate

Great Buscombe

TA24

Elsworthy

4

River Exe

Prayway Head

Raveps Nest

Warren Farm

Macmillan Way West

Rams Combe

Lime Combe

Dry Hill

Ware Ball

Ashcombe Bottom

Two Moors Way

Little Ashcombe

Exe Cleave

Clovenrocks Bridge

Red Stone Hill

WINSTITCHEN CROSS

Cloven Rocks

Gallon House

Hotel

WEST COTTS

B3223

Simonsbath

River Barle

Winstitchen Farm

White Water

Honeymead Farm

B3223

Hereliving

Ashott Barton

Halscombe

Flexbarrow

Winstitchen

Thornemead

76   A   77   B   78   C   79   D   80   E   81   F

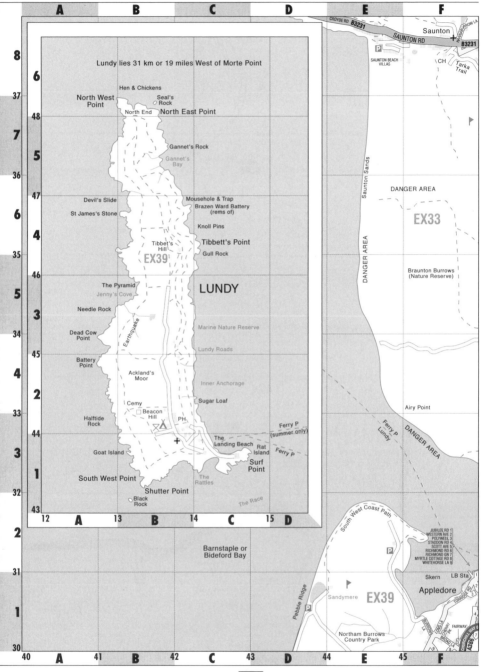

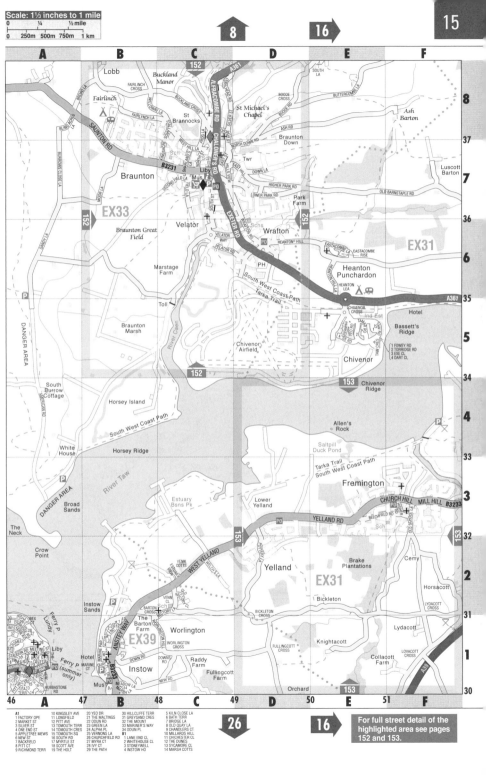

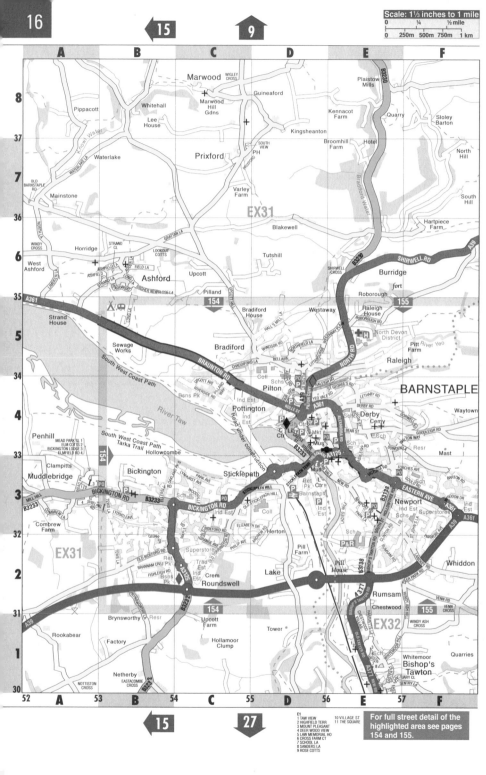

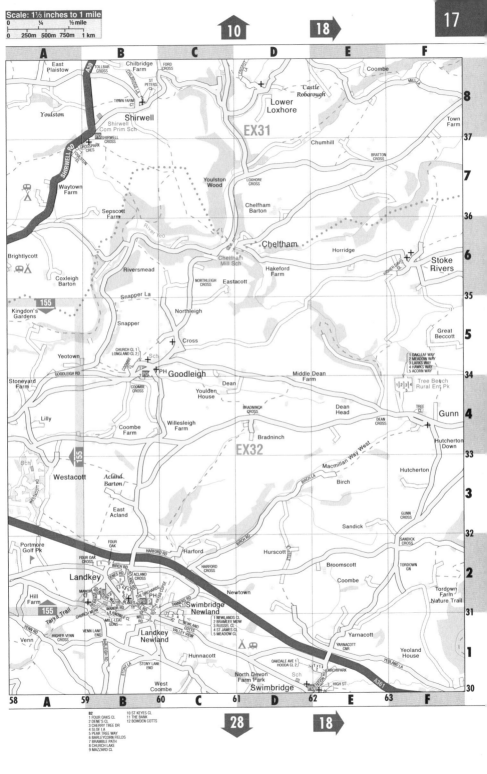

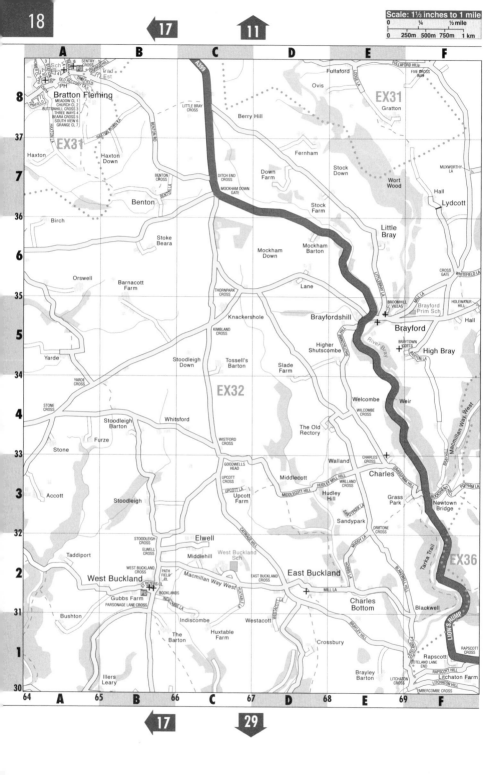

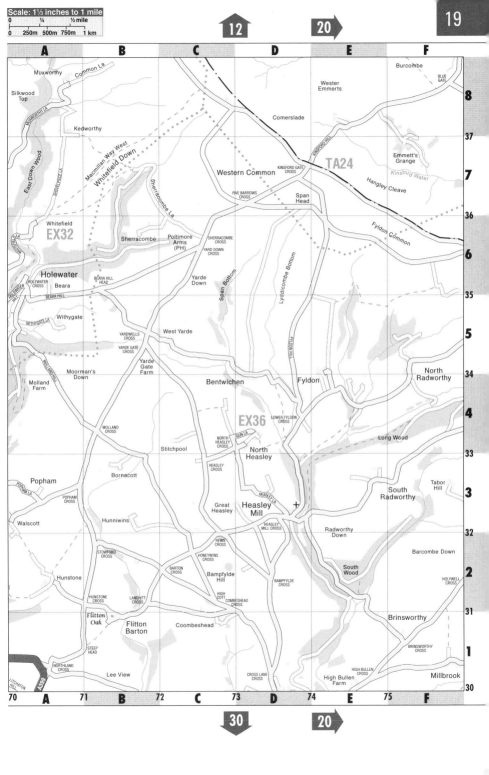

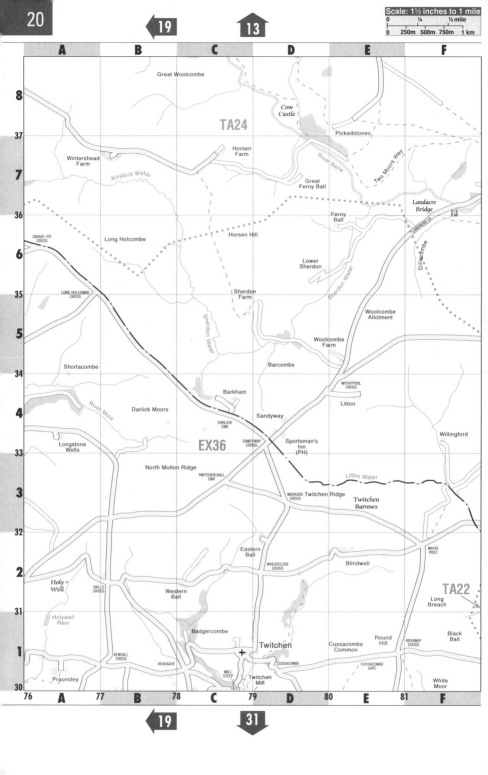

19

13

Scale: 1⅓ inches to 1 mile

0   ¼   ½ mile
0   250m 500m 750m 1 km

A   B   C   D   E   F

8

Great Woolcombe

37

TA24

Cow Castle

Pickedstones

Horsen Farm

River Barle

7

Wintershead Farm

Kinsford Water

Great Ferny Ball

Two Moors Way

Landacre Bridge

P

36

Ferny Ball

LANDACRE LA.

GRAVEL PIT CROSS

Long Holcombe

Horsen Hill

Lower Sherdon

Dillacombe

6

35

LONG HOLCOMBE CROSS

Sherdon Farm

Sherdon Water

Woolcombe Allotment

5

Shortacombe

Sherdon Water

Woolcombe Farm

34

Barcombe

WITHYPOOL CROSS

Barkham

River Mole

Darlick Moors

Litton

4

DARLICK CNR.

Sandyway

Longstone Wells

SANDYWAY CROSS

Sportsman's Inn (PH)

Willingford

EX36

33

North Molton Ridge

TWITCHEN BALL CNR.

Litton Water

3

MUDGATE CROSS

Twitchen Ridge

Twitchen Barrows

32

Eastern Ball

WHITE POST

2

WHEATCLOSE CROSS

Blindwell

TA22

Holy Well

BALLS CROSS

Western Ball

Long Breach

31

Holywell Resr

Black Ball

Badgercombe

Round Hill

RIDGWAY CROSS

1

Twitchen

Cussacombe Common

KENSALL CROSS

HEADGATE

CUSSACOMBE

CUSSACOMBE GATE

White Moor

Praunsley

MILL STEEP

Twitchen Mill

30

76   A   77   B   78   C   79   D   80   E   81   F

19

31

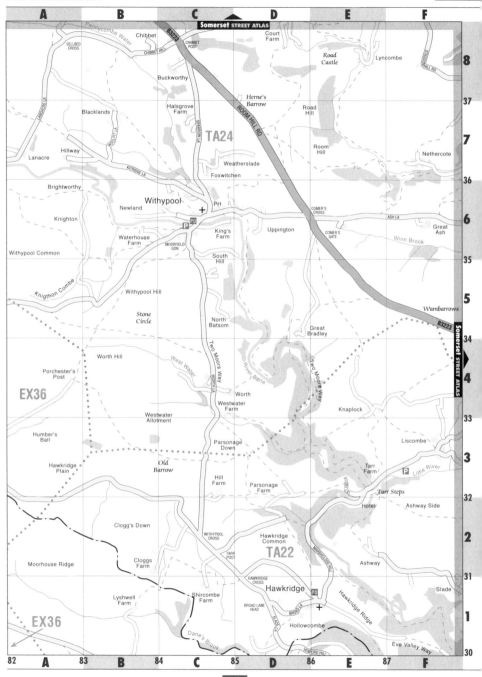

Scale: 1⅓ inches to 1 mile

0   ¼   ½ mile
0   250m 500m 750m 1 km

82   A   83   B   84   C   85   D   86   E   87   F

32

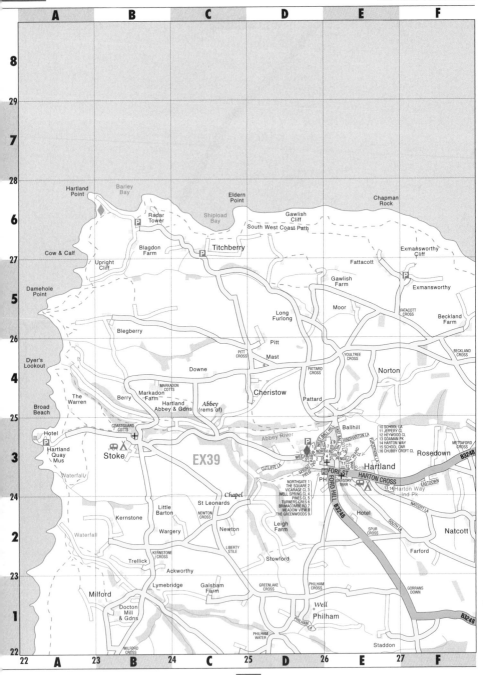

A   B   C   D   E   F

8

29

7

28

6

27

5

26

4

25

3

24

2

23

1

22

Hartland
Point

Barley
Bay

Radar
Tower

Eldern
Point

Chapman
Rock

Gawlish
Cliff

South West Coast Path

Shipload
Bay

Blagdon
Farm

Titchberry

Exmansworthy
Cliff

Cow & Calf

Upright
Cliff

Fattacott

Gawlish
Farm

Exmansworthy

Damehole
Point

Long
Furlong

Moor

FATACOTT
CROSS

Beckland
Farm

Blegberry

Pitt

PITT
CROSS

Mast

YOULTREE
CROSS

BECKLAND
CROSS

Dyer's
Lookout

Downe

PATTARD
CROSS

Norton

Cheristow

Pattard

Broad
Beach

The
Warren

Berry

MARKADON
COTTS

Markadon
Farm

Hartland
Abbey & Gdns

Abbey
(rems of)

COASTGUARD
COTTS

Hotel

Abbey River

Ballhill

WEST HARTLAND RD

HINDHARTLAND LA

Sch

METTAFORD
CROSS

Hartland
Quay
Mus

Stoke

EX39

NORTH RD

WEST ST

FITZGERALD RD

Sch

Hartland

Rosedown

B3248

Waterfall

CUTLIFFE LA

SPRING
FIELDS

PENGILLY RD

Sch

10 SCHOOL LA
11 JEFFERY CL
12 HEYWOOD CL
13 GOAMAN PK
14 HARTON WAY
15 SCHOOL CNR
16 CHUBBY CROFT CL

PH

GREGORY
TERR

HARTON CROSS

EASTDOWN

Chapel

St Leonards

NEWTON
CROSS

NORTHGATE 1
THE SQUARE 2
VICARAGE CL 3
WELL SPRING CL 4
PINES CRES 5
TURNERS CRES 6
BRIMACOMBE RD 7
MEADOW VIEW 8
THE GREENWOODS 9

FORD HILL

13 14 Harton Way
Ind Pk

NATCOTTLA

Little
Barton

Leigh
Farm

Hotel

SPUR
CROSS

SOUTH LA

Natcott

Kernstone

Wargery

Newton

LIBERTY
STILE

Stowford

Farford

Waterfall

KERNSTONE
CROSS

Trellick

Ackworthy

Lymebridge

Galsham
Farm

GREENLAKE
CROSS

PHILHAM
CROSS

GORRANS
DOWN

B3248

Milford

Docton
Mill
& Gdns

Well
Philham

PHILHAM
WATER

PHILHAM LA

Staddon

MILFORD
CROSS

22   A   23   B   24   C   25   D   26   E   27   F

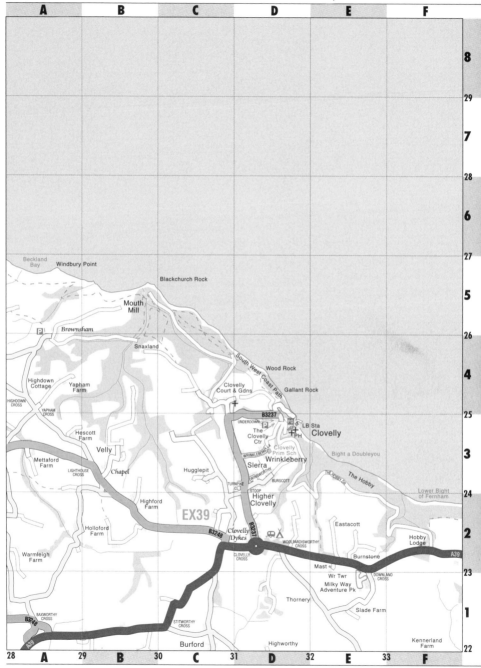

Scale: 1½ inches to 1 mile

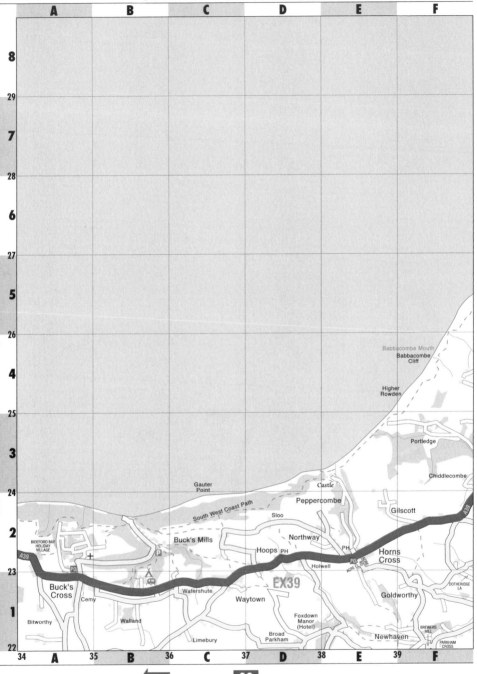

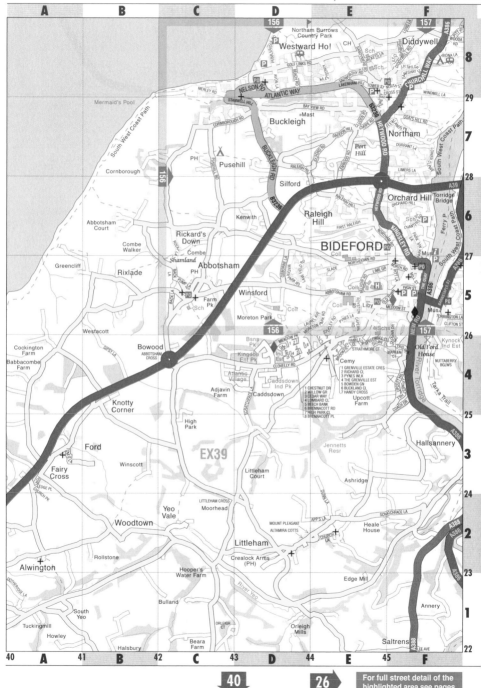

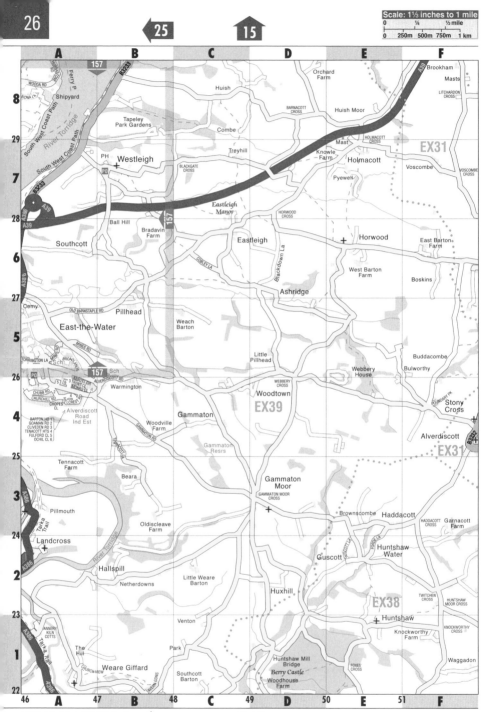

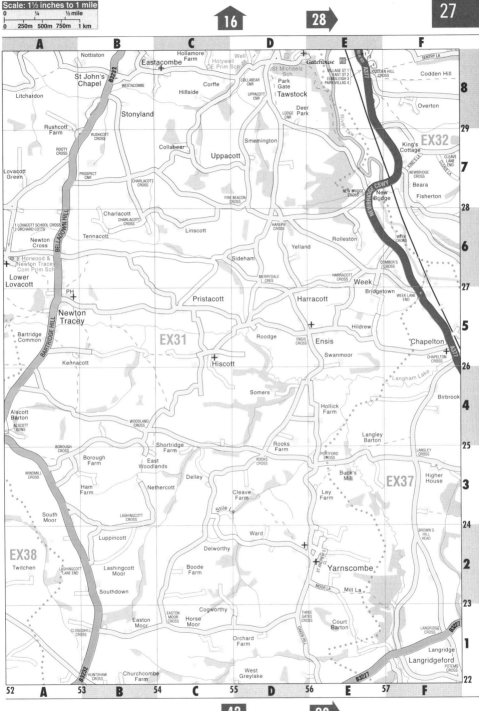

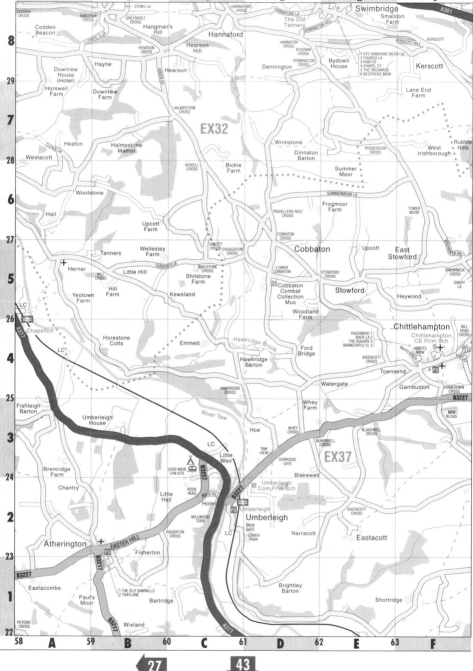

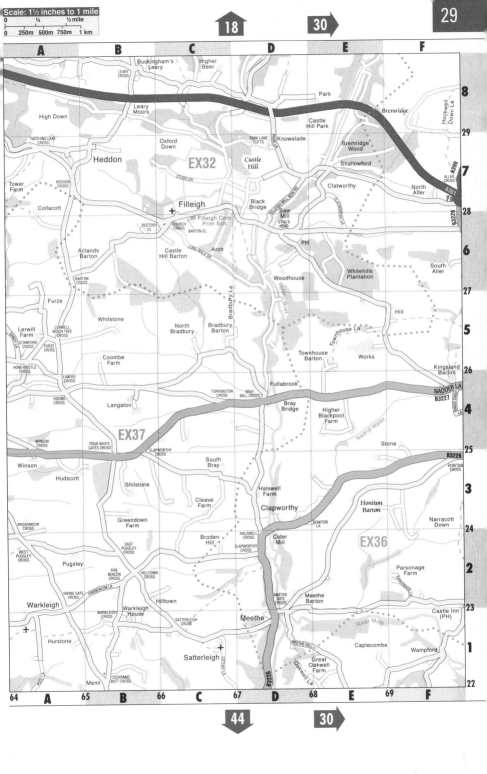

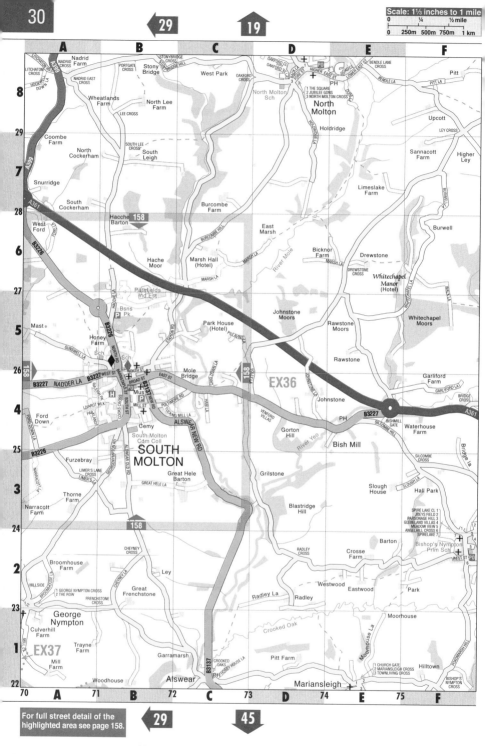

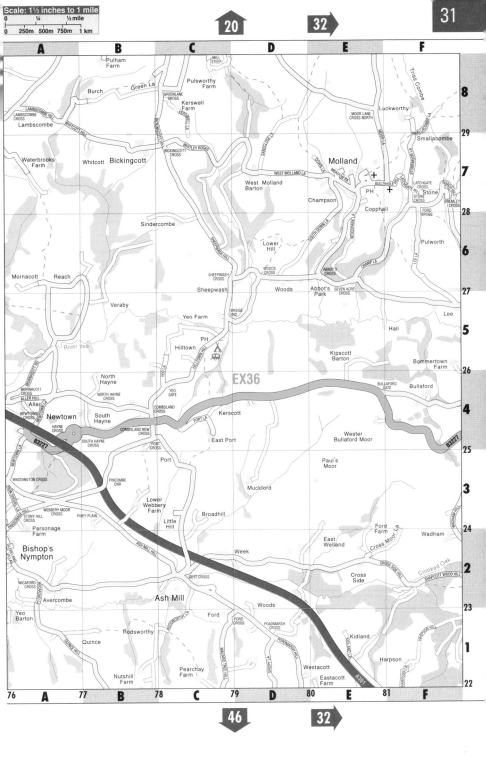

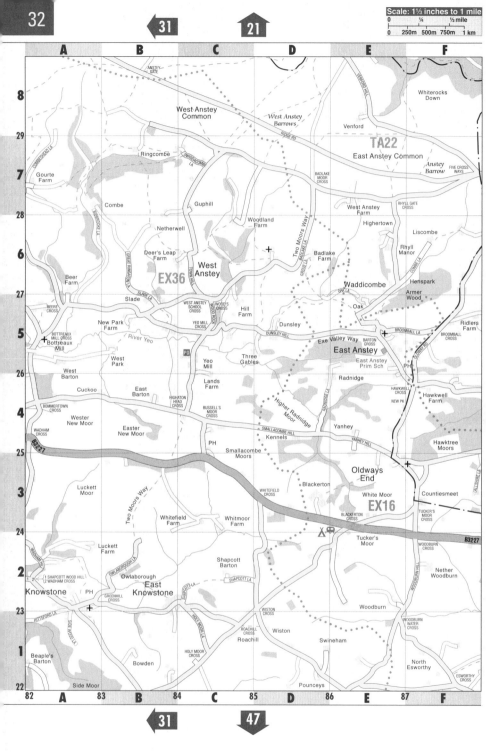

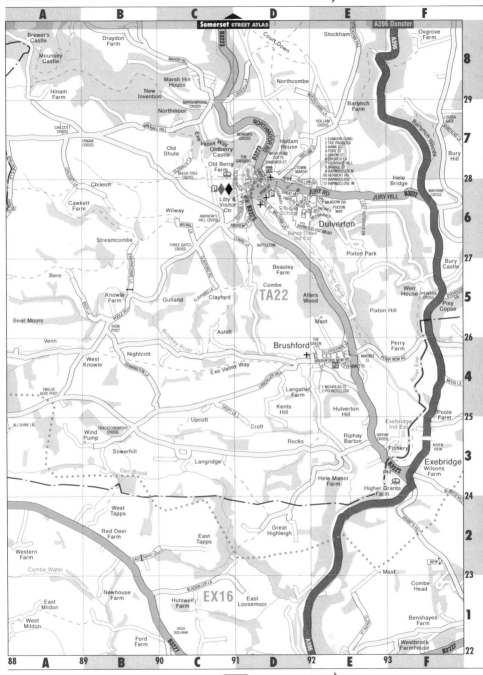

Scale: 1½ inches to 1 mile

0   ¼   ½ mile
0   250m 500m 750m 1 km

Somerset STREET ATLAS

A396 Dunster

A **B** **C** **D** **E** **F**

Brewer's Castle
Mounsey Castle
Draydon Farm
Hinam Farm
Marsh Hill House
New Invention
Northmoor
Northcombe
Stockham
Oxgrove Farm
Court Down
Marsh Hill
Marshbridge Cross
Northmoor Cross
Barlynch Farm
Louisa Gate
Chilcott Cross
Hinam Cross
Old Shute
Valley Way
Oldberry Castle
Old Berry Farm
Newgate Cross
Hollam Cross
Hollam House
Weir Head
Town Marsh
Barlynch Woods
Bury Hill
Chileott
Beech Tree Cross
The Gardens
Handver Ct
PH
Hele Bridge
Machine Cross
Cawkett Farm
Wilway
Andrew's Hill Cross
Streamcombe
Three Gates Cross
Knowle Farm
Gulland
Clayford
Clayford La
Clayford
Ashill
Beasley Farm
Combe
TA22
Allers Wood
Mast
Dulverton
Jury Hill
Jury Rd
Pixton Park
B3222
Weir House
Dyehouse Cross
Bury Castle
Pixy Copse
Bere
Beer Moors
Venn
Iron Post
Nightcott
West Knowle
Exe Valley Way
Brockey River
Brushford
The Green
Ellerslea
Brushford New Rd
Overdale Cl
Pixton Hill
Perry Farm
Pern New Rd
Moor La
River Exe
Twelve Acre Post
Trackfordmoor Cross
Wind Pump
Upcott
Croft La
Croft La
Croft
Langaller Farm
Kents Hill
Rocks
Hulverton Hill
Exebridge Ind Est
Poole Farm
Allshire La
Sowerhill
Langridge
Riphay Barton
Riphay Cross
Fishery
River View
Exebridge
Wilsons Farm
Den Brook
PH
Higher Grants Farm
B3222
West Tapps
Red Deer Farm
East Tapps La
East Tapps
Hele Manor Farm
Great Highleigh
Mast
New La
Combe Head
Western Farm
Combe Water
Newhouse Farm
Blackaller La
Hutswell Farm
EX16
East Loosemoor
Benshayes Farm
East Mildon
West Mildon
Ford Farm
B3221
High Bolham
A396
Westbrook Farmhouse
B3227

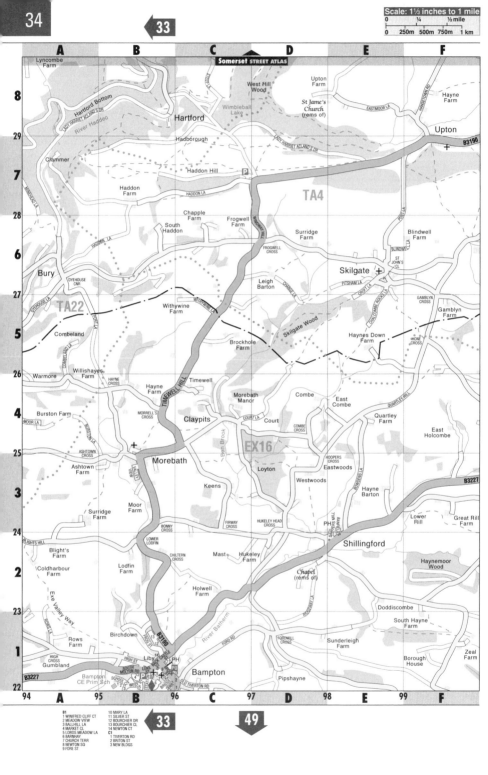

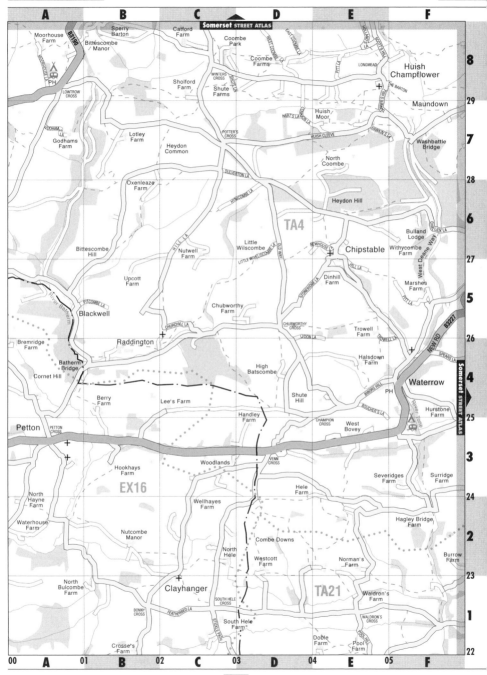

A   B   C   D   E   F

Moorhouse
Farm
B3190

Sperry
Barton

Catford
Farm

Coombe Park

8

Bittescombe
Manor

Coombe
Farms

EAST COOMBE LA
WEST COOMBE LA

Huish
Champflower
LONGMEAD
THE BARTON

LOWTROW
CROSS
PH

Sholford
Farm

Winters
Cross

Shute Farms

HART'S LA

Huish
Moor

HAWKINS LA

Maundown

29

GODHAM LA
Godhams
Farm

Lotley
Farm

Heydon
Common

Potter's
Cross

HUISH CLEEVE

North
Coombe

Washbattle
Bridge

7

DULVERTON LA

HUNICOMBE LA

28

Oxenleaze
Farm

Heydon Hill

TA4

6

DOCK LA

Bittescombe
Hill

Nutwell
Farm

Little
Wilscombe

LITTLE WILSCOMBE LA

OLD WAY
NEWHOUSE

Chipstable
Bulland
Lodge

Withycombe
Farm

WEST DEANE WAY

Upcott
Farm

Dinhill
Farm

HILL LA

Marshes
Farm

PITT LA

27

River Batherm

PITCOMBE LA

Blackwell

Chubworthy
Farm

CHURCH LA

SCRIDGE LA

Chubworthy
Cross

LYDON LA

Trowell
Farm

TROWELL LA

B3227
NEW RD

5

Bremridge
Farm

Raddington

Halsdown
Farm

SPEARS LA

Somerset STREET ATLAS

26

Batherm
Bridge
Cornet Hill

High
Batscombe

BIRDS HILL
PH

Waterrow

4

Berry
Farm

Lee's Farm

Handley
Farm

Shute
Hill

BOUCHER'S LA

River Tone

Hurstone
Farm

25

Petton
PETTON
CROSS

Champion
Cross

West
Bovey

Severidges
Farm

Surridge
Farm

3

Hookhays
Farm

Woodlands

VENN
CROSS

Hele
Farm

EX16

24

North
Hayne
Farm

Wellhayes
Farm

Hagley Bridge
Farm

2

Waterhouse
Farm

Nutcombe
Manor

Combe Downs

Norman's
Farm

Burrow
Farm

North
Hele

Westcott
Farm

23

North
Bulcombe
Farm

Clayhanger

FEATHERBED LA

SOUTH HELE
CROSS

TA21

Waldron's
Farm

BONNY
CROSS

STUCKLEY LA

WALDRON'S
CROSS

1

Crosse's
Farm

South Hele
Farm

Doble
Farm

POOL HILL

Pool
Farm

22

00   A   01   B   02   C   03   D   04   E   05   F

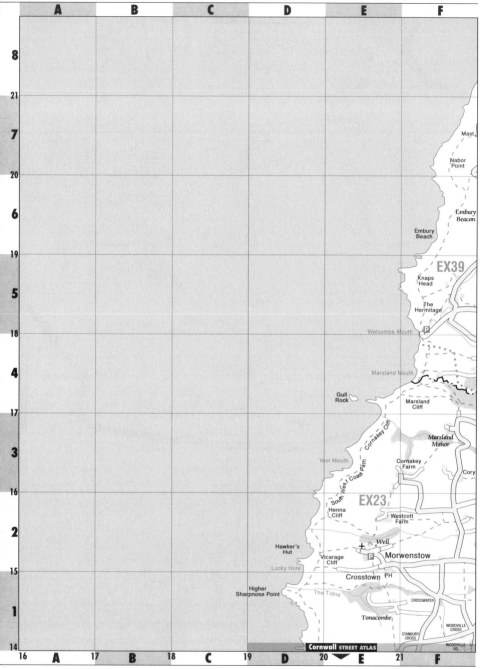

Mast

Nabor
Point

Embury
Beacon

Embury
Beach

EX39

Knaps
Head

The
Hermitage

Welcombe Mouth

Marsland Mouth

Gull
Rock

Marsland
Cliff

Cornakey Cliff

Marsland
Manor

Yeol Mouth

Cornakey
Farm

Cory

South West Coast Path

EX23

Henna
Cliff

Westcott
Farm

Hawker's
Hut

Well

Vicarage
Cliff

Morwenstow

Lucky Hole

Crosstown   PH

Higher
Sharpnose Point

The Tidna

CROSSWATER

Tonacombe

WOODVILLE
CROSS

STANBURY
CROSS

WOODVILLE
RD

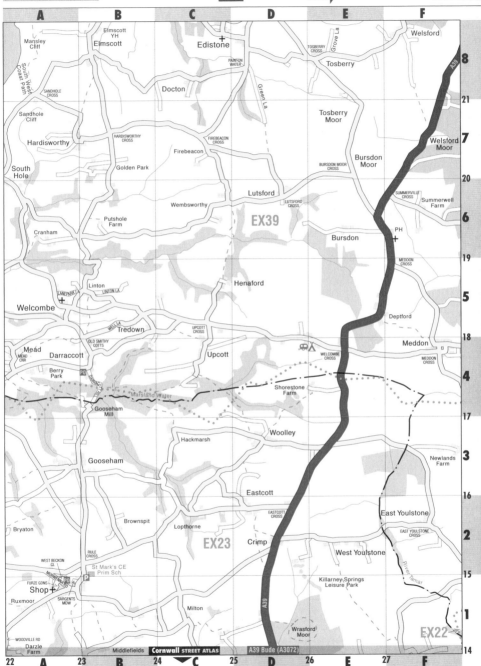

Scale: 1⅓ inches to 1 mile

0   ¼   ½ mile
0   250m 500m 750m 1 km

22   38

8
21
7
20
6
19
5
18
4
17
3
16
2
15
1
14

Mansley Cliff

South West Coast Path

SANDHOLE CROSS

Sandhole Cliff

Hardisworthy

South Hole

Elmscott YH
Elmscott

HARDISWORTHY CROSS

Golden Park

Putshole Farm

Cranham

Welcombe

LAMEPARK LA

Linton
LINTON LA

WELL LA

Tredown

OLD SMITHY COTTS

Mead
MEAD CNR

Darraccott

Berry Park

Gooseham Mill

Marsland Water

Gooseham

Bryaton

Brownspit

Ruxmoor

WEST BECKON CL

RULE CROSS

FURZE GDNS

Shop

SARGENTS MDW

WOODVILLE RD

Darzle Farm

Middlefields

Cornwall STREET ATLAS

Docton

Edistone

PAINTON WATER

Green La

Firebeacon

FIREBEACON CROSS

Wembsworthy

Lutsford

LUTSFORD CROSS

EX39

Henaford

UPCOTT CROSS

Upcott

Hackmarsh

Lopthorne

EX23

Crimp

EASTCOTT CROSS

Eastcott

Woolley

Shorestone Farm

WELCOMBE CROSS

Milton

St Mark's CE Prim Sch

Welsford

Tosberry

TOSBERRY CROSS

Grove La

Tosberry Moor

Bursdon Moor

BURSDON MOOR CROSS

Bursdon

PH

SUMMERVILLE CROSS

Welsford Moor

Summerwell Farm

MEDDON CROSS

Deptford

Meddon

MEDDON CROSS

Newlands Farm

East Youlstone

EAST YOULSTONE CROSS

West Youlstone

River Tamar

Killarney Springs Leisure Park

Wrasford Moor

EX22

A39

A39 Bude (A3072)

22   A   23   B   24   C   25   D   26   E   27   F

38

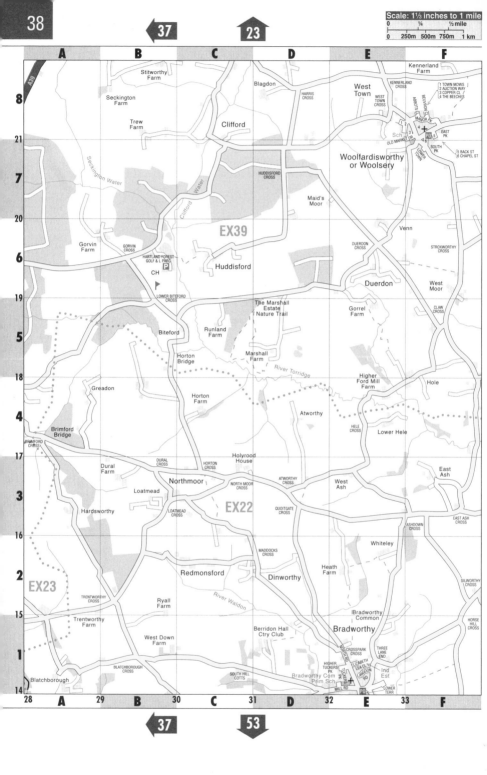

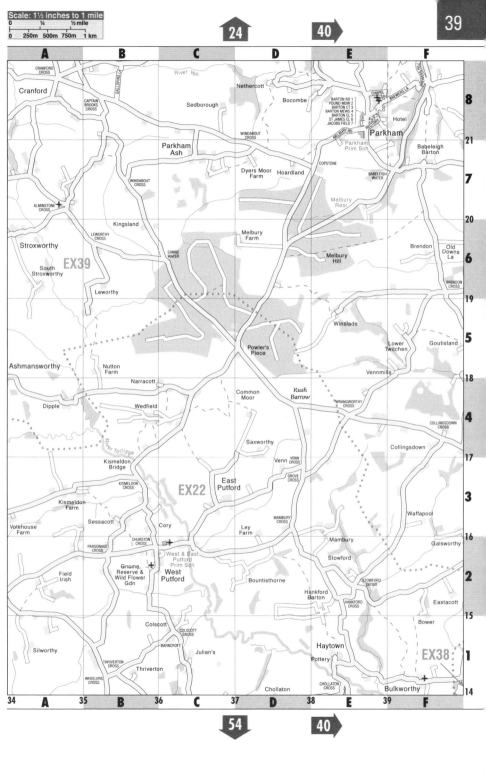

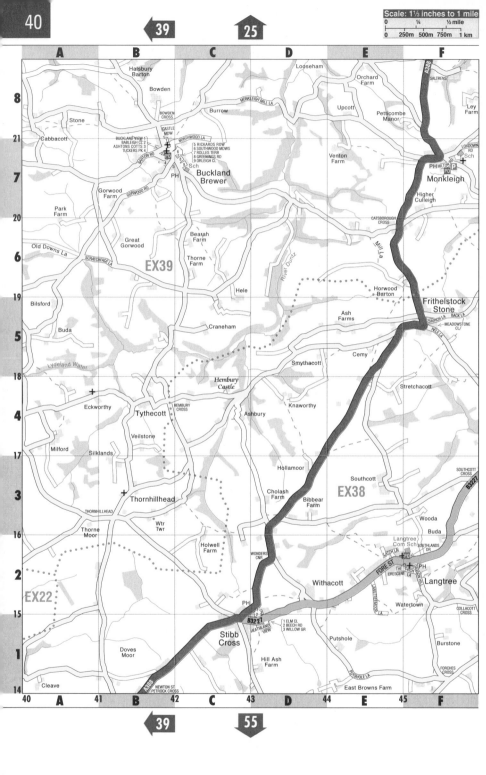

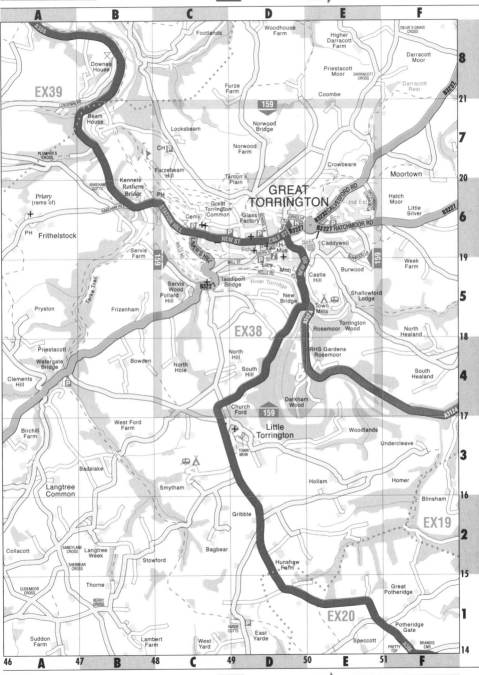

Scale: 1⅓ inches to 1 mile
0   ¼   ½ mile
0   250m 500m 750m 1 km

For full street detail of the highlighted area see page 159.

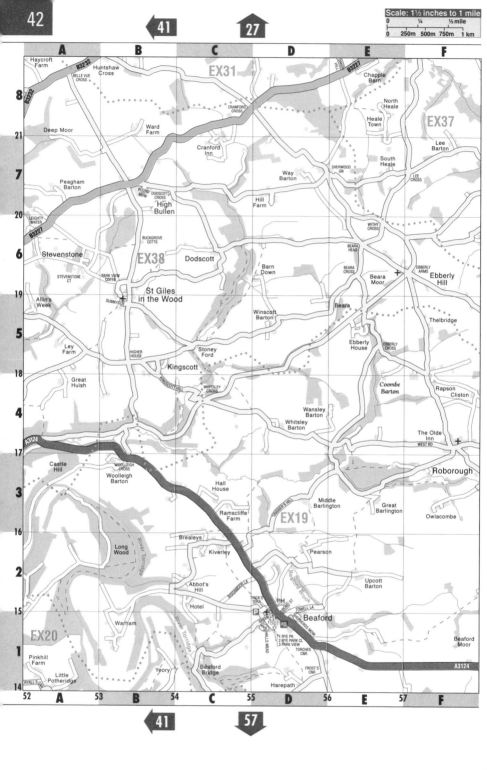

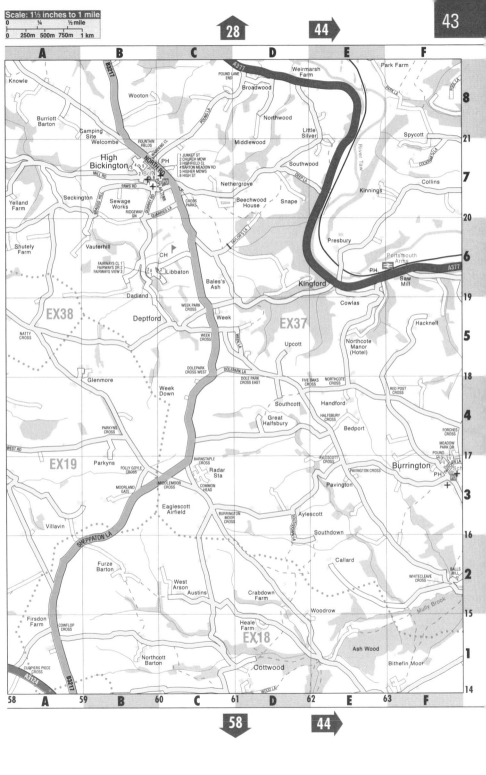

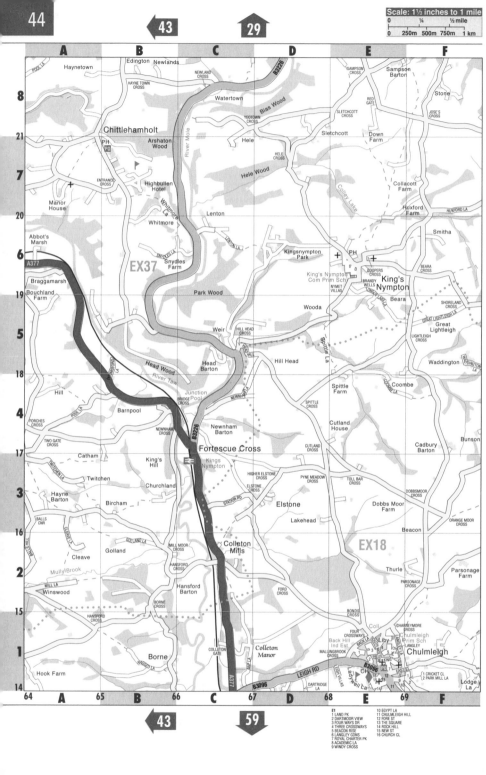

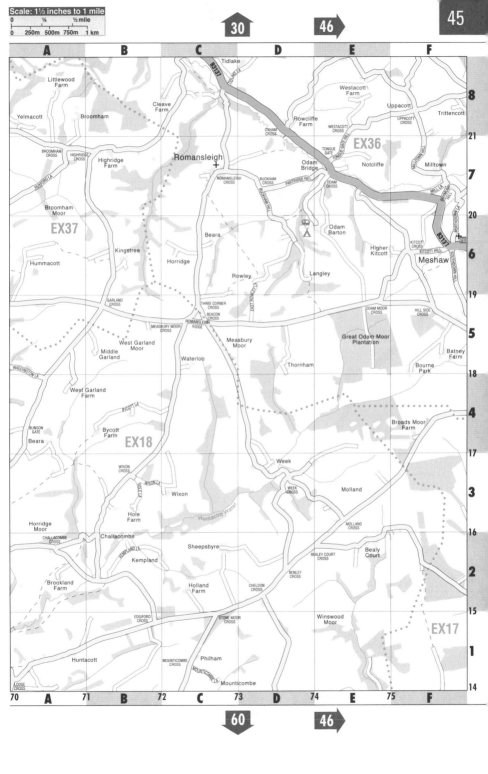

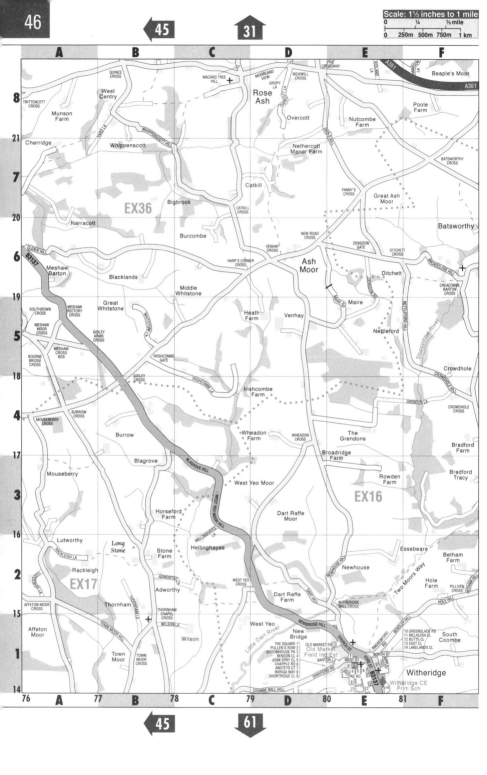

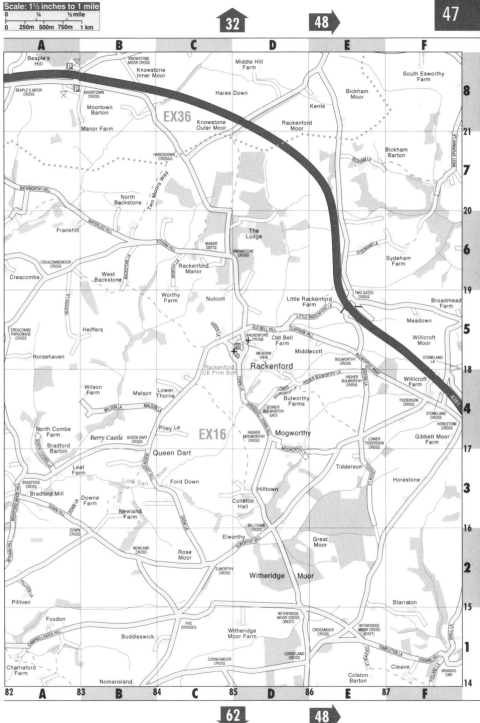

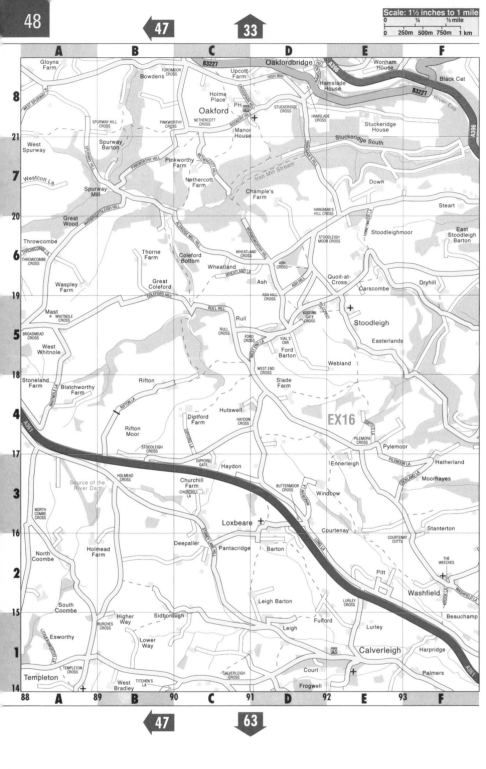

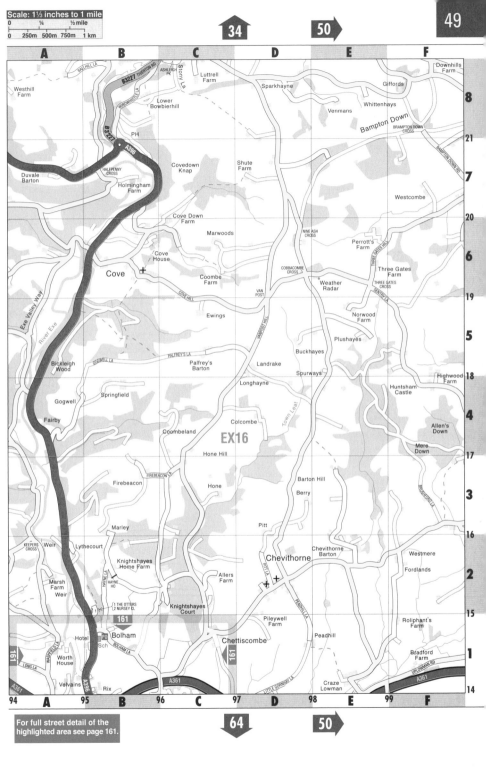

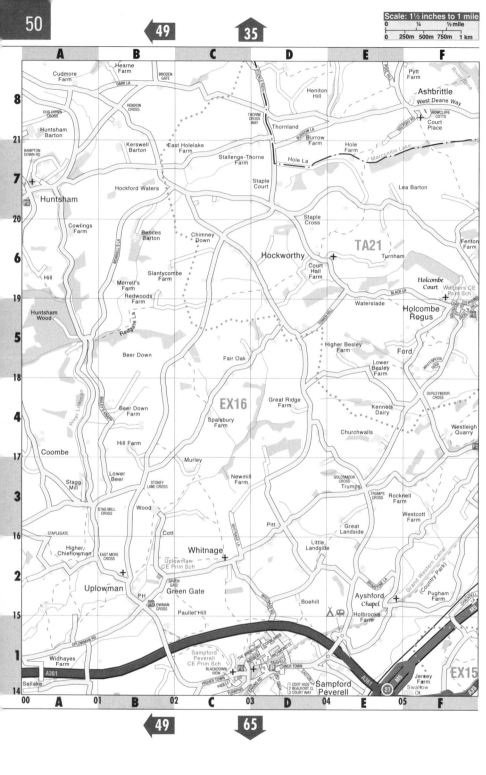

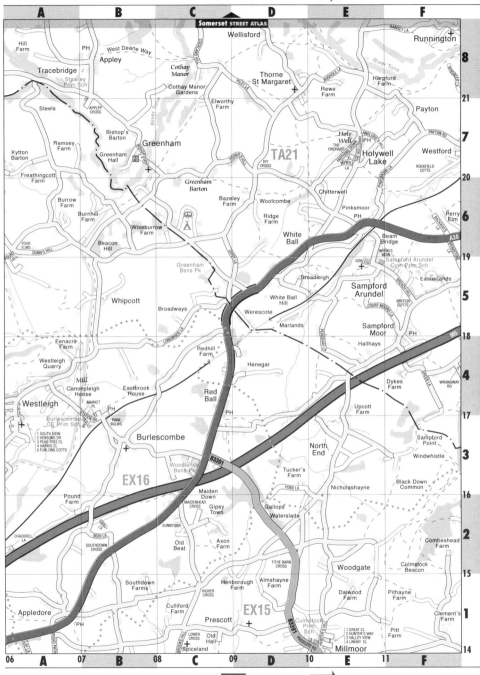

Somerset STREET ATLAS

Scale: 1½ inches to 1 mile

0   ¼   ½ mile
0   250m 500m 750m   1 km

Hill Farm
Tracebridge
Stawley Prim Sch
PH
West Deane Way
Appley
Cothay Manor
Wellisford
Runnington
River Tone
RAMSEY LA
PH

Steels
APPLEY CROSS
Bishop's Barton
Cothay Manor Gardens
Elworthy Farm
Thorne St Margaret
Rewe Farm
Harpford Farm
Payton
PAYTON RD

Ramsey Farm
Greenham Hall
Greenham
Holy Well
THE ORCHARD
Holywell Lake
Westford
ROCKFIELD COTTS

Kytton Barton
Freathingcott Farm
Greenham Barton
Bazeley Farm
IVY CROSS
MYRTLE LA
Chitterwell
Perry Elm

Burrow Farm
Burnhill Farm
Beacon Hill
Wiseburrow Farm
White Ball
Woolcombe
Ridge Farm
Pinksmoor
PH
Beam Bridge
WEEKES MDW
A38
Easterlands

FOUR ELMS
DUNN'S HILL
Greenham Bsns Pk
Broadleigh
GORLEGG
Sampford Arundel Com Prim Sch
BREECH HILL

Whipcott
Broadways
Werescote
White Ball Hill
Sampford Arundel
COURT MOORS LA
BREECH COTTS

Fenacre Farm
Redhill Farm
Marlands
Sampford Moor
PH
M5

Westleigh Quarry
Henegar
Hallays
Dykes Farm
WRANGWAY RD

Mill
Canonsleigh House
Eastbrook House
Red Ball
Upcott Farm
Sampford Point

Westleigh
MARKET
PARK BGLWS
PH
Windwhistle

Burlescombe OE Prim Sch
Burlescombe
North End
Black Down Common

1 SOUTH VIEW
2 HENSONS DR
3 PEAR TREE CL
4 HARRIS CL
5 FURLONG COTTS

EX16
B3391
Maiden Down
Tucker's Farm
POND LA
Nicholashayne

Pound Farm
MAIDENHEAD CROSS
Gipsy Town
Gallops
Waterslade
Combeshead Farm

CHACKRELL LA
BEER LA
SUNNYSIDE
Axon Farm
Woodgate
Culmstock Beacon

SOUTHDOWN CROSS
Old Beat
TITHE BARN CROSS
Dalwood Farm
Pithayne Farm

Appledore
Southdown Farms
Henborough Farm
Almshayne Farm
Clement's Farm

PH
Culliford Farm
HIGHER CROSS
Prescott
EX15
Culmstock Prim Sch
Pitt Farm

LOWER CROSS
Old Hall
Spiceland
B3391
Millmoor

1 GREAT CL
2 HUNTER'S WAY
3 VALLEY VIEW
4 LINHAY CL

TA21
TONE

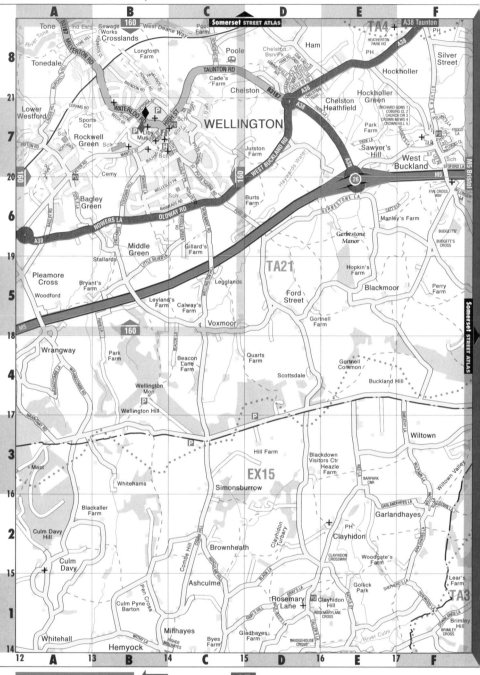

Scale: 1⅓ inches to 1 mile

| 0 | ¼ | ½ mile |

| 0 | 250m | 500m | 750m | 1 km |

Somerset STREET ATLAS

A **B** **C** **D** **E** **F**

Tone
Ind Ests
Sewage Works
West Deane Way
Pool Farm
TA4
A38 Taunton
PH

River Tone
Crosslands
Longforth Farm
Poole
Chelston Bsnr Pk
Ham
HEATHERTON PARK HO
PH

8

Tonedale
TAUNTON RD
Cade's Farm
Chelston
Hockholler

21

Lower Westford
CORAMS RD
WATERLOO RD
HIGH ST
WELLINGTON
Chelston Heathfield
Hockholler Green
Park Farm
ORCHARD GDNS 1
COBURG CL 2
CHURCH DR 3
CROWN MEWS 4
CROWN HILL 5

Sports Ctr
Liby Mus
Sawyer's Hill
West Buckland

7

Rockwell Green
Sch
Jurston Farm
WEST BUCKLAND RD
FIVE CROSS WAY

20

Cemy
Burts Farm
26
BUDGETT'S CROSS

6

Bagley Green
OLDWAY RD
Middle Green
Gillard's Farm
Gerbestone Manor
Manley's Farm
GERBESTONE LA
Perry Farm

Pleamore Cross
Stallards
Bryant's Farm
Legglands
Hopkin's Farm
Blackmoor

19

Woodford
NOWERS LA
Leyland's Farm
Calway's Farm
Ford Street
Gortnell Farm
TA21

5

A38
Voxmoor
Quarts Farm
Scottsdale
Gortnell Common
Buckland Hill

18

Wrangway
Park Farm
Beacon Lane Farm
Wellington Mon
Wellington Hill
Wiltown

4

Mast
Whitehams
Hill Farm
Blackdown Visitors Ctr
Heazle Farm
BARPARK CNR
Wiltown Valley

17

EX15
Simonsburrow
Garlandhayes

3

Blackaller Farm
Clayhidon Turbary
PH
Clayhidon
GARLANDHAYES LA

16

Culm Davy Hill
Brownheath
CLAYHIDON CROSSWAY
Woodgate's Farm

2

Culm Davy
Ashculme
Gollick Park
Lear's Farm
TA3

15

Pen Cross
Culm Pyne Barton
Rosemary Lane
Clayhidon Hill
ROSEMARYLANE CROSS
Brimley Hill
BRIMLEY CROSS

1

Whitehall
Hemyock
Millhayes
Byes Farm
Gladhayes Farm
BRIDGEHOUSE CROSS
River Culm

14

A **B** **C** **D** **E** **F**
12 13 14 15 16 17

For full street detail of the highlighted area see page 160.

51

67

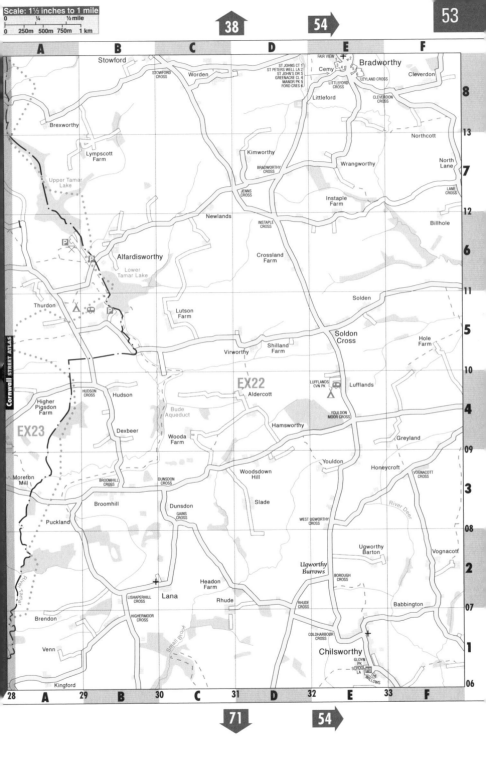

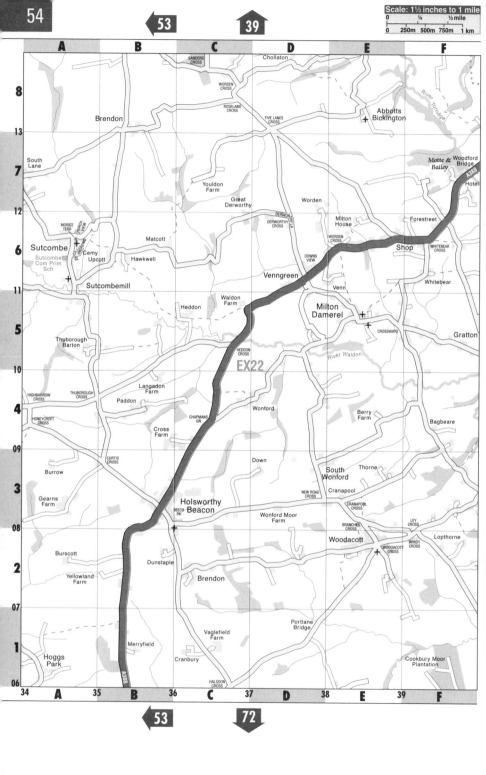

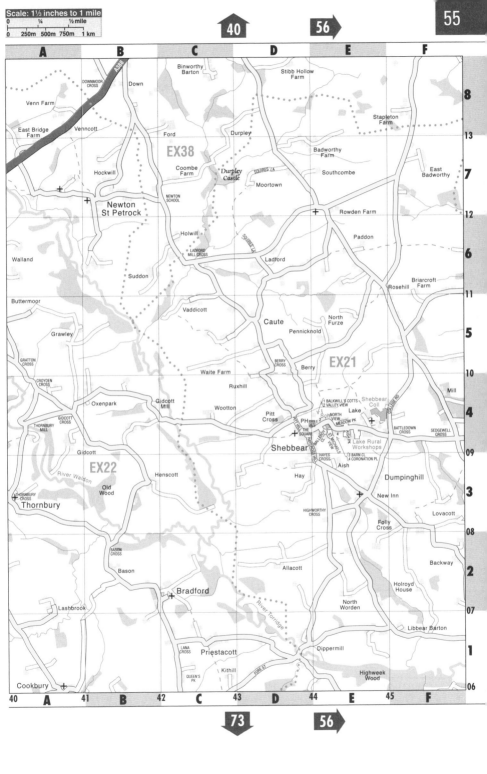

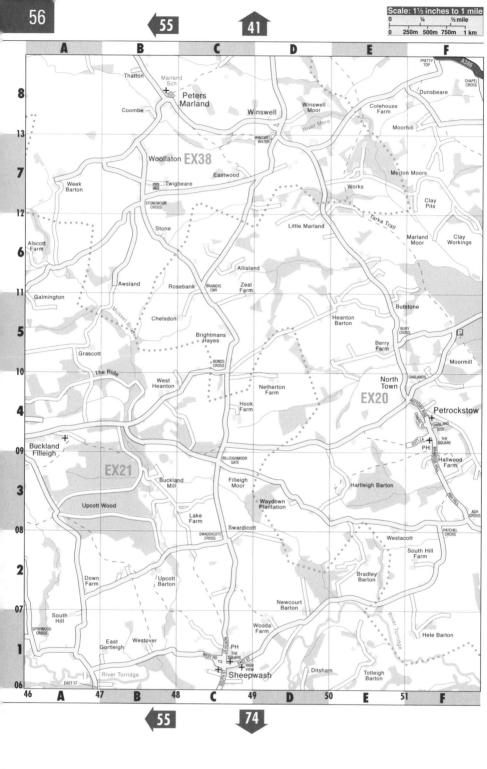

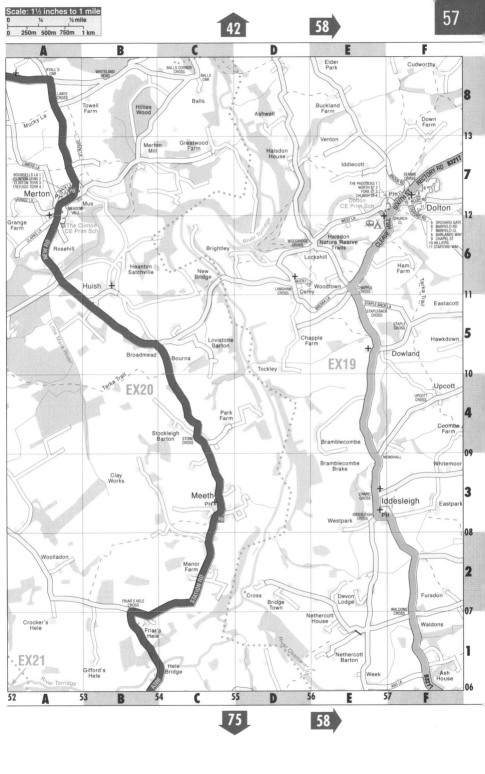

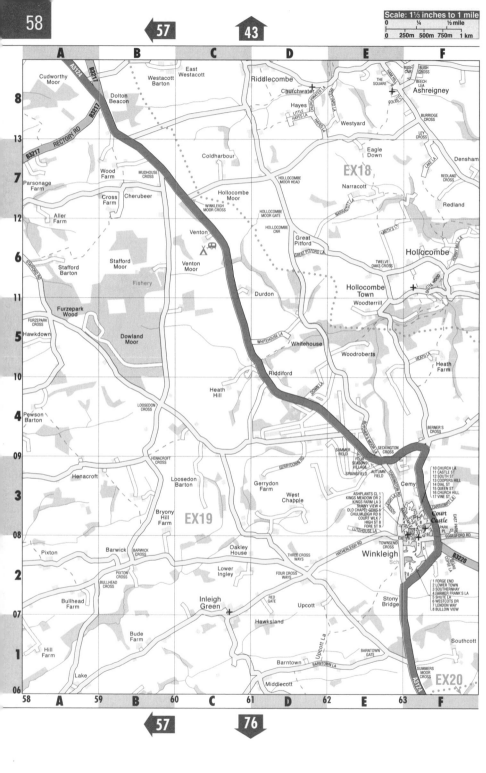

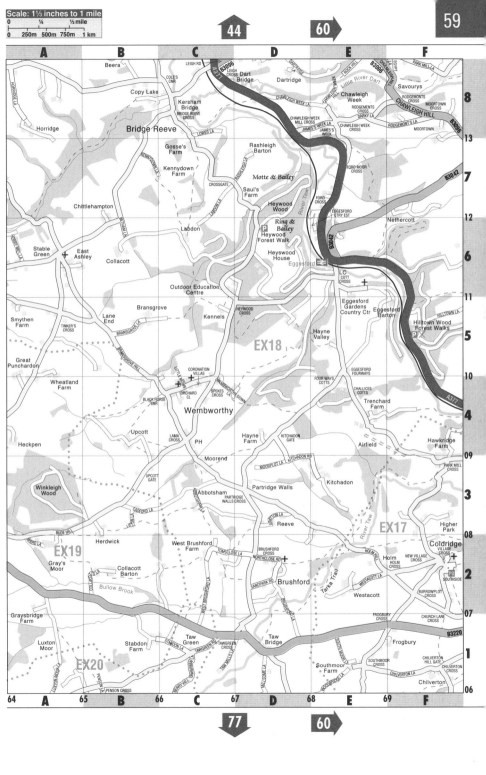

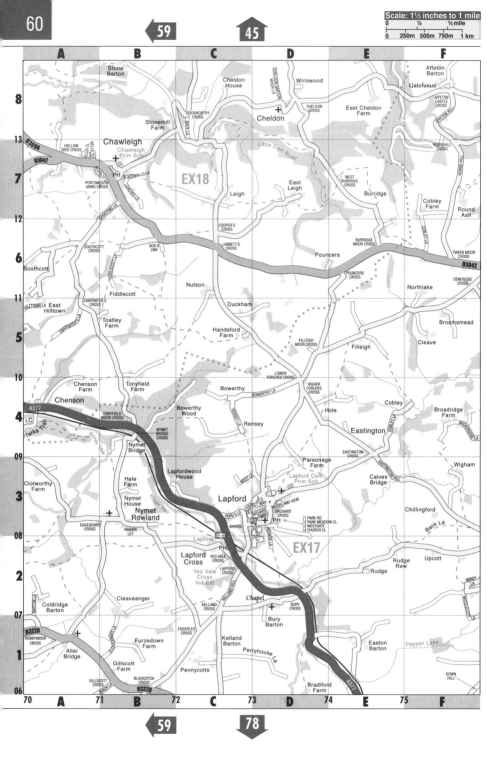

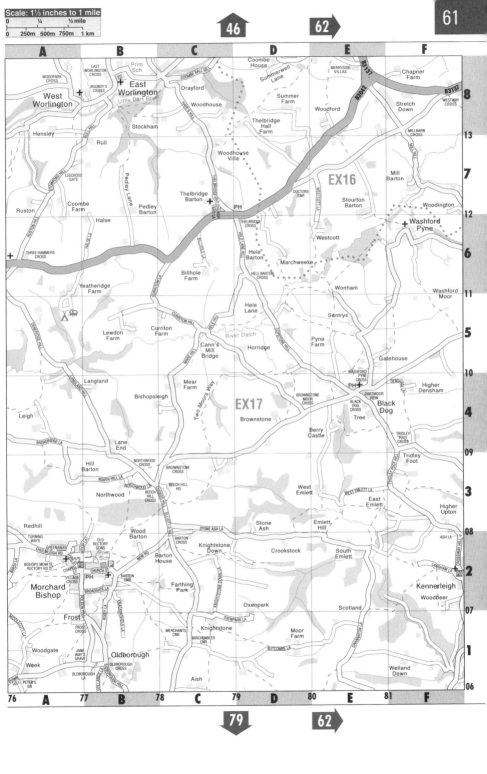

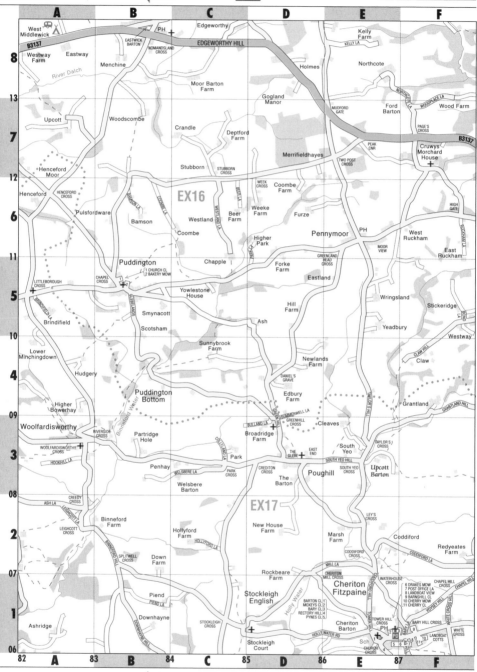

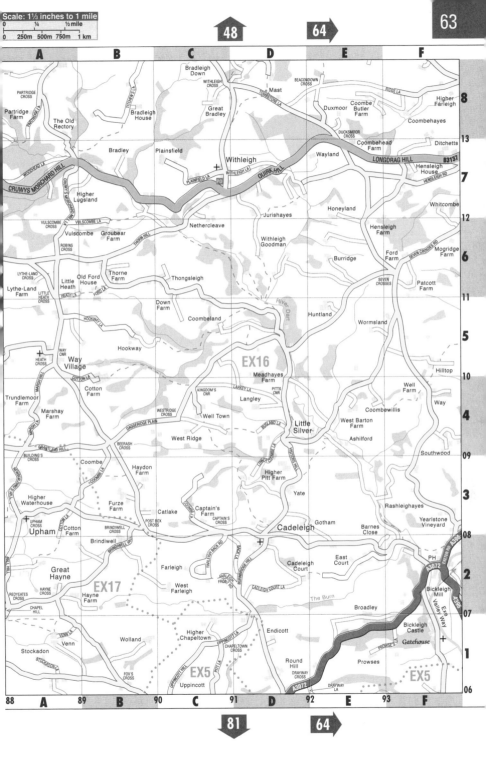

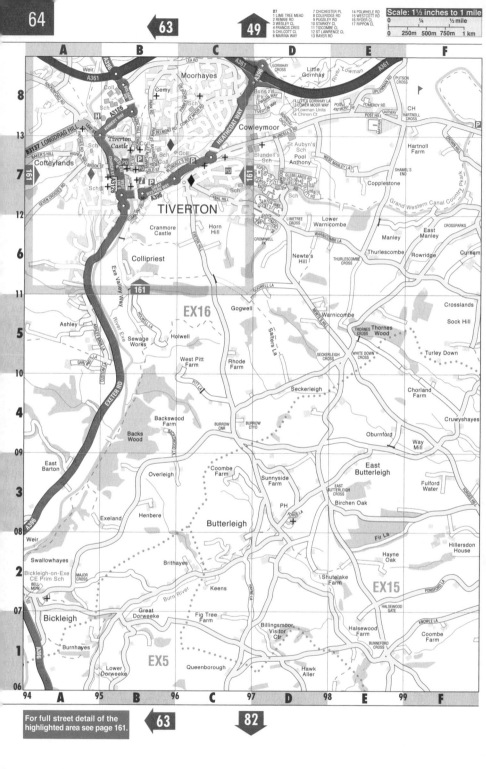

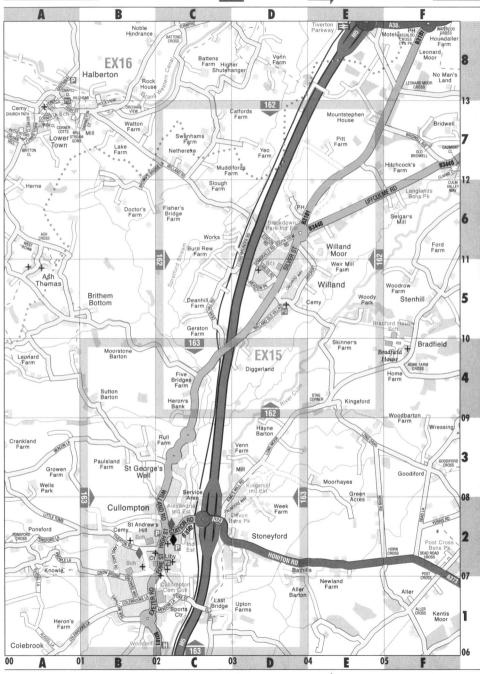

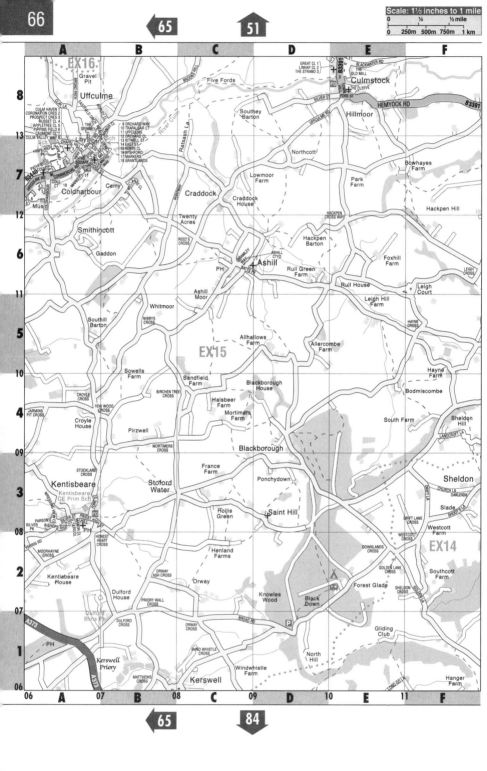

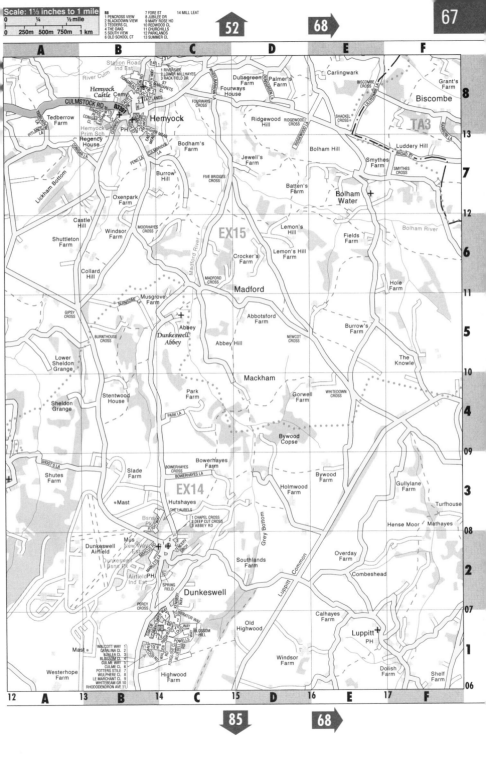

Somerset STREET ATLAS

TA20

DROVE WAY

WATERHAYNES LA

B3170

8

Stapley

ADDMBE CROSS

Willand

CHURCH RD

Royston House

Royston Water

Churchstanton Prim Sch

13

Paye Farm

Royston Rd

Robin Hood's Butts

Baker's Farm

BAKER'S CROSS

Higher Munty

Clivehayes Farm

BROAD ST

Redlane

RED LA

Churchinford

Martin's Farm

Brown Down Lodge

7

Wr Twr

TA3

MOOR LA

Fairhouse Farm

1 FAIRFIELD GN
2 WELLESLEY WAY
3 NEWBERRY'S PATCH
4 GILLARDS MEAD

Baker's Farm

12

Buttle's Farm

BUTTLE'S CROSS

BROOM'S LA

BUTTLE'S LA

South Down

KNAPPER'S WELL LA

Watchford Farm

BROADHEY'S HEAD BROWN DOWN LA

B3170

A303

Bolham River

Higher Southey Farm

Lower Southey Farm

LAMBPARK CT

Luxton

DENNINGTON LA

6

Middleton Barton

Southey Moor

Stout Farm

Higher Stout Farm

Knightshayne Farm

11

Valentine's Farm

Gotleigh Moor

BLOOM'S LA

Pamos Farm

Northam's Farm

STOUT CROSS

5

Smeatharpe

HOLEMORE CROSS

Middle Luxton

Hoemoor Farm

Knapp Farm

Cockhayes

Sweetlands Farm

10

MOONHAYES CROSS

Moonhayes

ELGOMBE LA

Highley Farm

Stopgate

STOPGATE CROSS

4

Riggle's Farm

Chapelhayes

Minson's Hill

TWISTGATE LA

Ullcombe

Twistgates Farm

Sandpit Hill

B3170

A303

09

RIGGLES CROSS

Beacon Hill

Tiphayes Farm

Beacon

3

Mattys Cross

Fair Oak Farm

Cleave Farm

TWISTGATE LA

Baxter's Farm

Rookery Farm

Newcott

08

Harvestwood Farm

Prim Sch

DANES CL

PIPERS PL

1 OAK TREE CL
2 MANOR GN

Preston Farm

Crinhayes Farm

Underdown Farm

A30

A303

2

Hilend Farm

Aller Farm

Upottery

PH

EX14

SANDY'S LA

Broadley Hill

Livenhayes Farm

07

Braddicksnap Hill

NEW RD

Bidwell Farm

Courtmoor Farm

Rosshayne Farm

ROSSHAYNE LA

Budgells Farm

POUND LA

Blackhayes Farm

1

Odle Farm

Spurtham Farm

Rawridge

VINEY LA

STOCKLAND HILL

Corrymoor Farm

BLACKHAYES LA

Rower Hill

Hartridge

HILLSIDE

OYTER GALE CL

Rawridge Farm

COTLEIGH CROSSING

A30

06

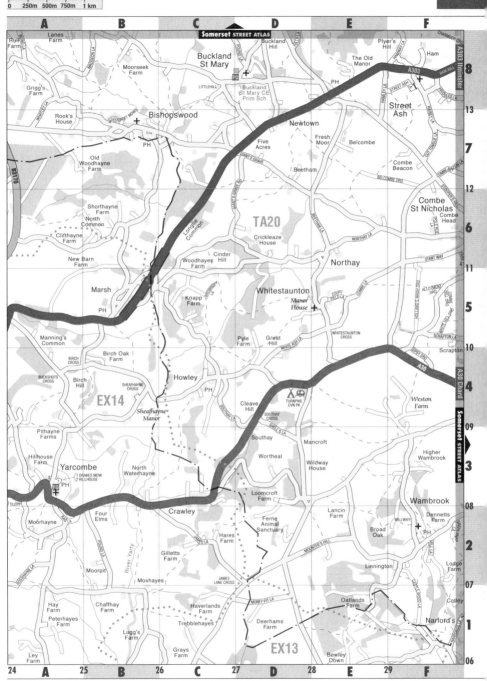

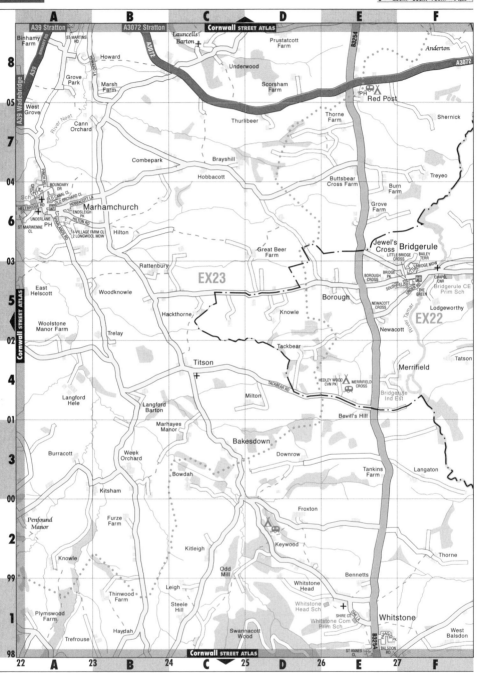

Scale: 1⅓ inches to 1 mile

| 0 | ¼ | ½ mile |
| 0 | 250m | 500m | 750m | 1 km |

A **B** **C** **D** **E** **F**

A39 Stratton · A3072 Stratton · **Cornwall** STREET ATLAS

Binhamy Farm
ST MARTINS RD
Howard
Launcells Barton
Underwood
Prustatcott Farm
Anderton

8

Grove Park
Marsh Farm
Scorsham Farm
Red Post
Shernick

05

West Grove
River Neet
Cann Orchard
Thurlibeer
Thorne Farm

7

Combepark
Brayshill
Hobbacott
Buttsbear Cross Farm
Burn Farm
Treyeo

04

BOUNDARY DR
OLD CANAL CL
OLD ORCHARD CL
HOBBACOTT LA
ENDSLEIGH PK
HILTON RD
Sch
HELEBRIDGE RD
Marhamchurch
Grove Farm
Jewel's Cross
Bridgerule

6

ST MARWENNE CL
UNDERLANE
PH
VILLAGE FARM CL
LONGWOOL MDW
Hilton
Great Beer Farm
LITTLE BRIDGE CROSS
BAILEY TERR
BRIDGE MDW
Bridgerule CE Prim Sch

03

Rattenbury
EX23
BRIDGE PK
BOROUGH CROSS
SOUTHFIELDS
UNDER RD
THE GREEN
CHAPEL CARR

East Helscott
Woodknowle
Hackthorne
Knowle
Borough
NEWACOTT CROSS
Lodgeworthy
EX22

5

02

Woolstone Manor Farm
Trelay
Tackbear
Newacott
Tatson

Titson
Merrifield

4

Langford Hele
Langford Barton
Milton
TACKBEAR RD
HEDLEY WOOD CVN PK
MERRIFIELD CROSS
Bridgerule Ind Est

01

Marhayes Manor
Bevill's Hill

Burracott
Week Orchard
Bakesdown
Downrow
Tankins Farm
Langaton

3

Bowdah

00

Penfound Manor
Kitsham
Froxton

Furze Farm
Keywood
Thorne

2

Knowle
Kitleigh
Bennetts

99

Leigh
Whitstone Head
Whitstone Head Sch

Thinwood Farm
Odd Mill
Whitstone Com Prim Sch
Whitstone

1

Plymswood Farm
Steele Hill
Swannacott Wood
SHIRE CT
BALSOON RD
West Balsdon

Trefrouse
Haydah
ST ANNES CL
B3254

98

Cornwall STREET ATLAS

22 **A** **23** **B** **24** **C** **25** **D** **26** **E** **27** **F**

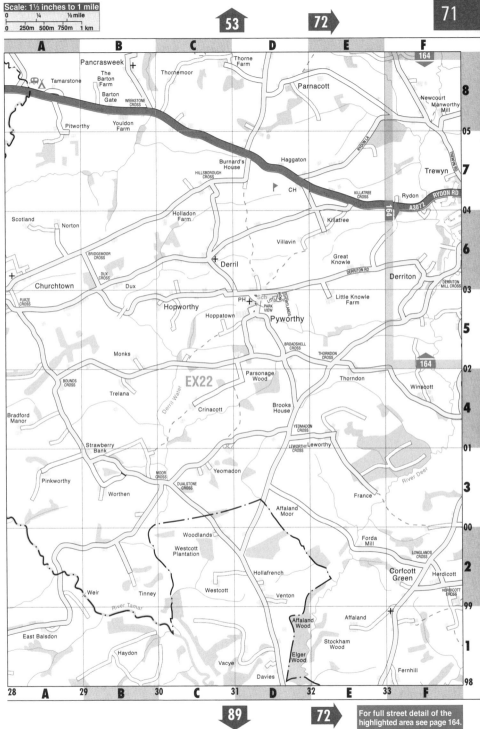

Scale: 1⅓ inches to 1 mile

0   ¼   ½ mile
0   250m 500m 750m 1 km

53
72
89
72

For full street detail of the highlighted area see page 164.

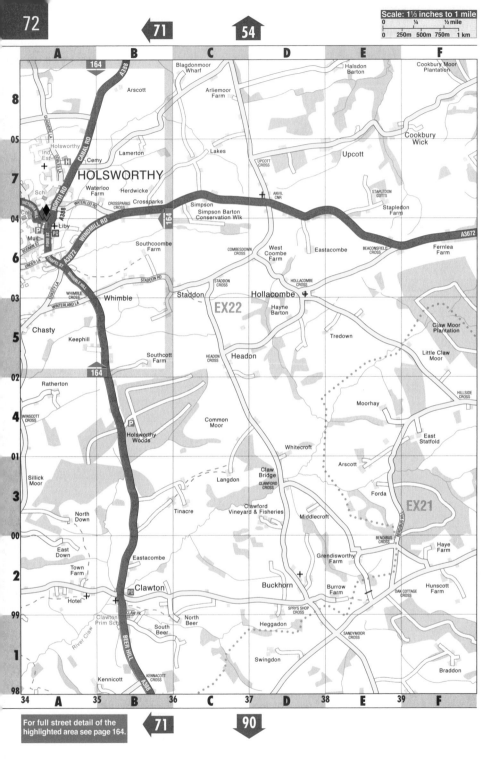

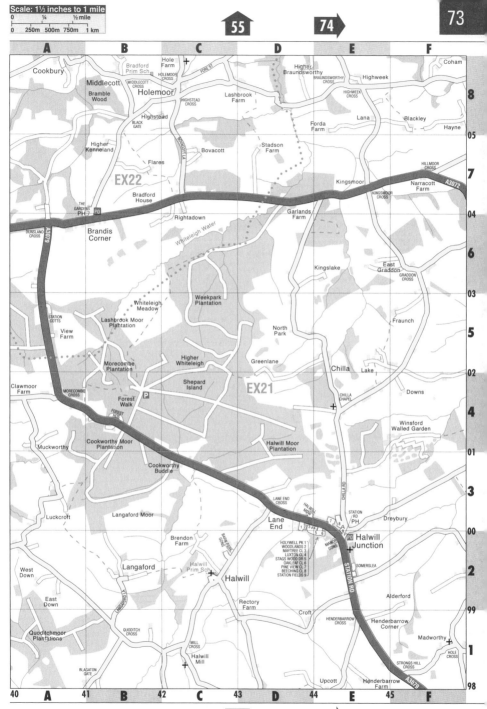

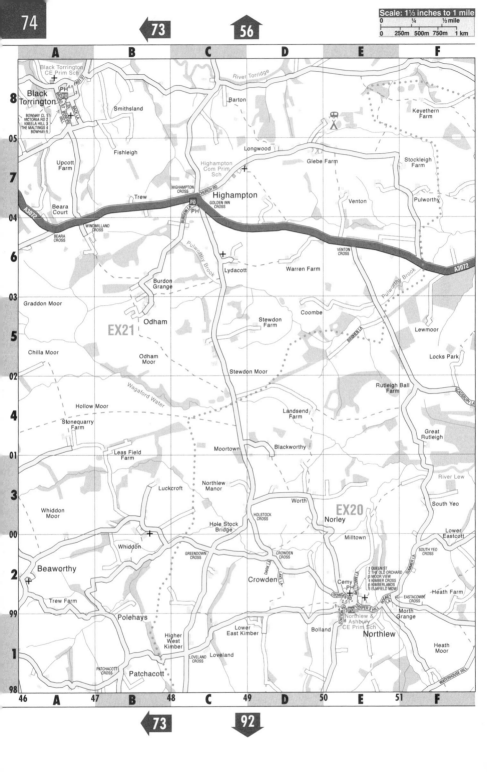

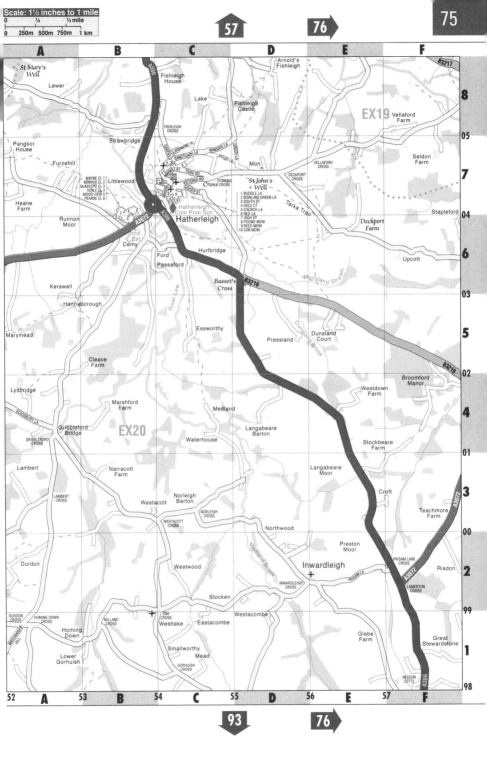

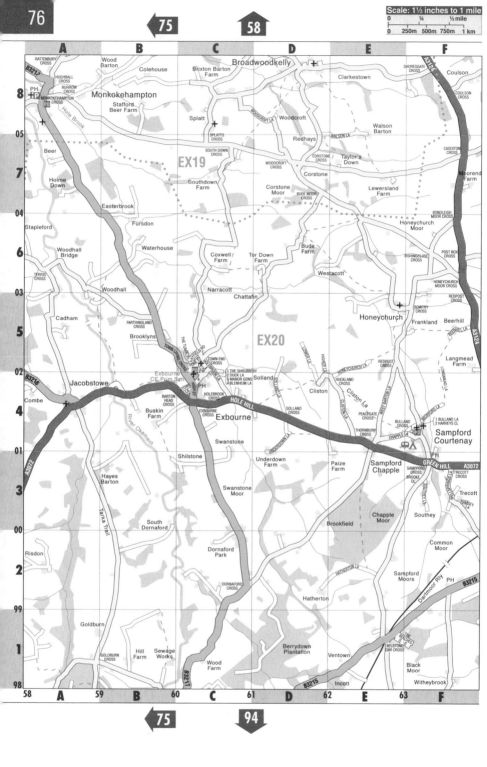

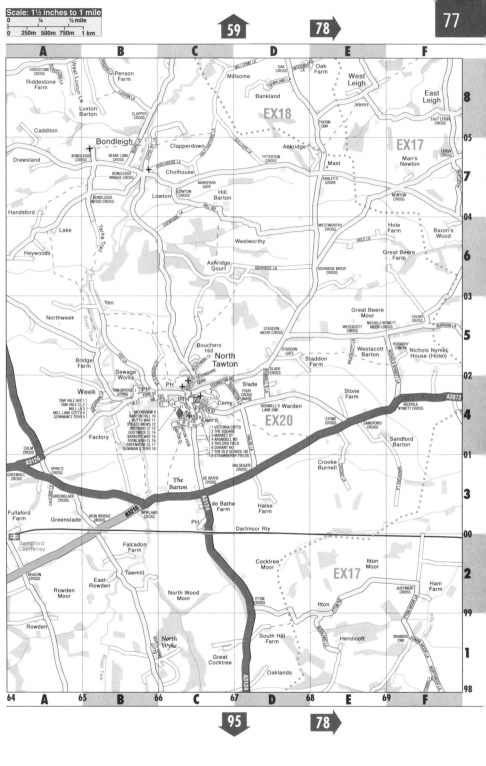

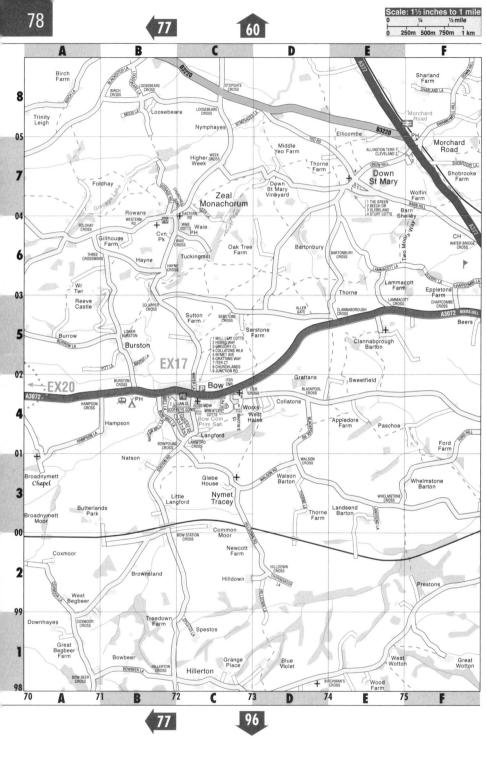

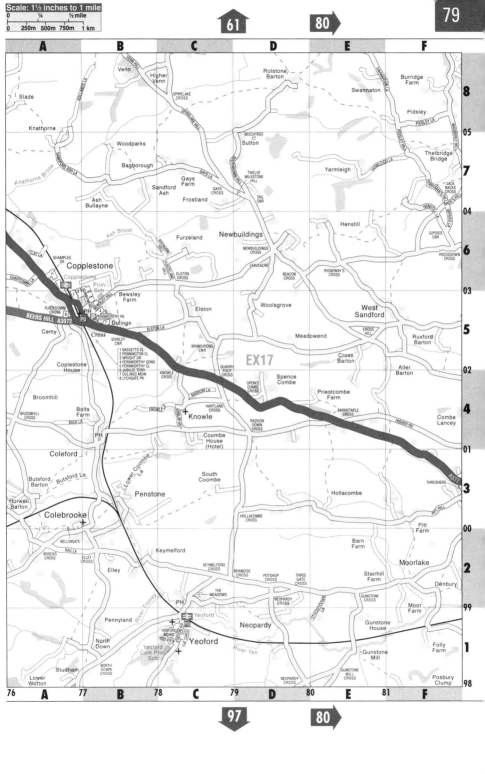

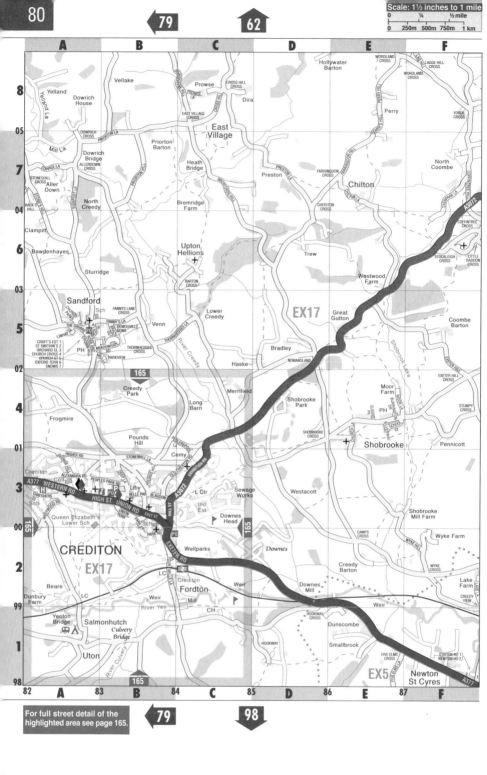

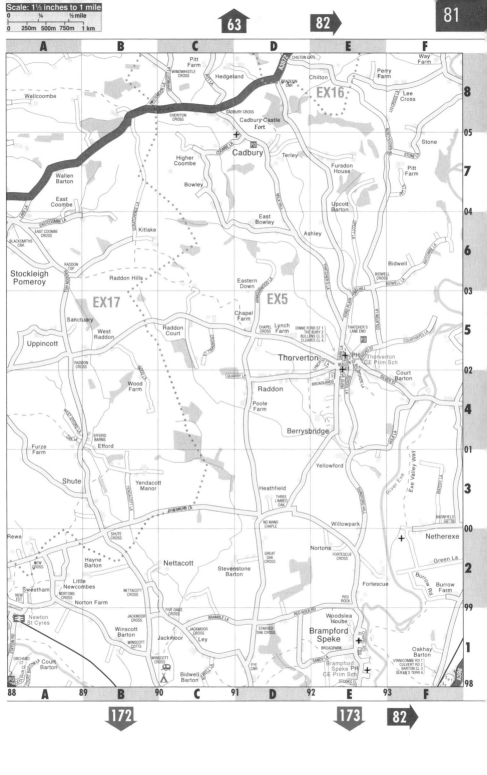

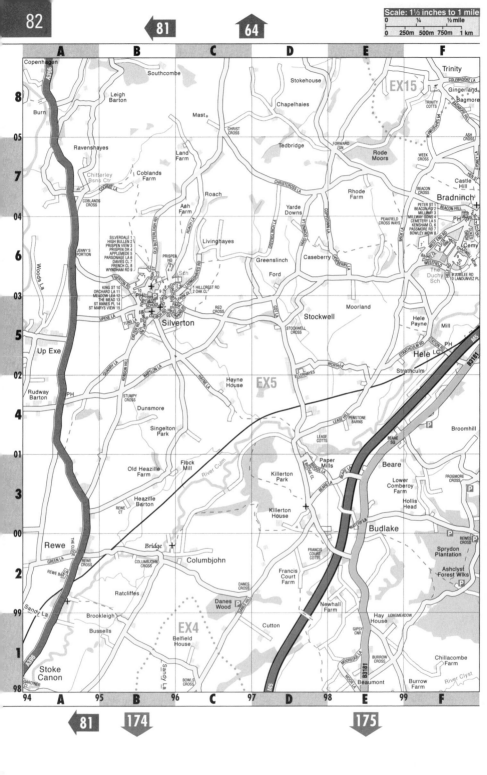

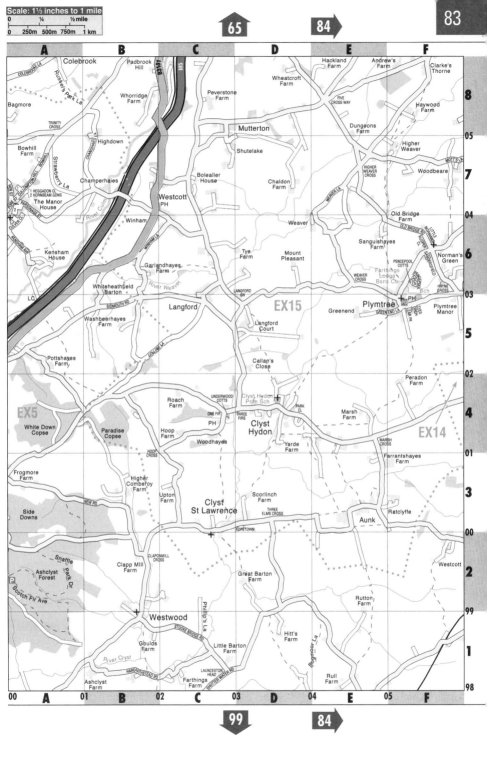

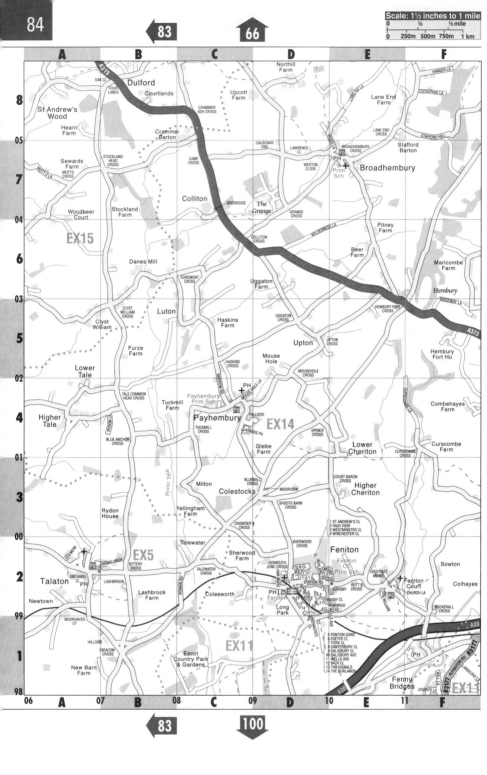

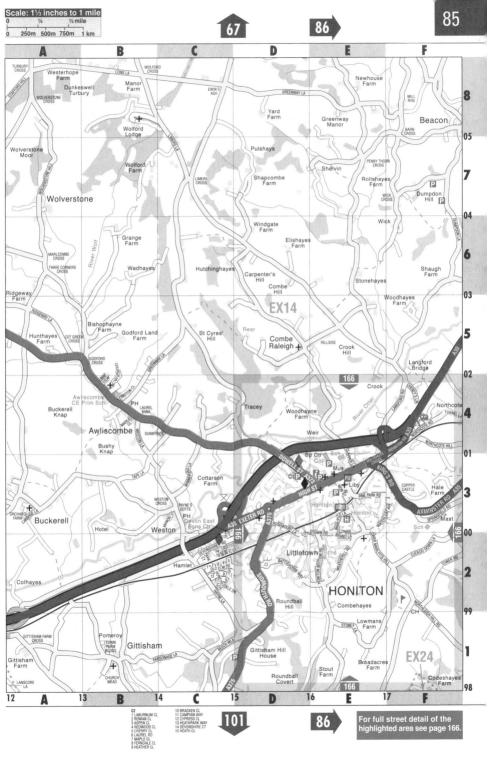

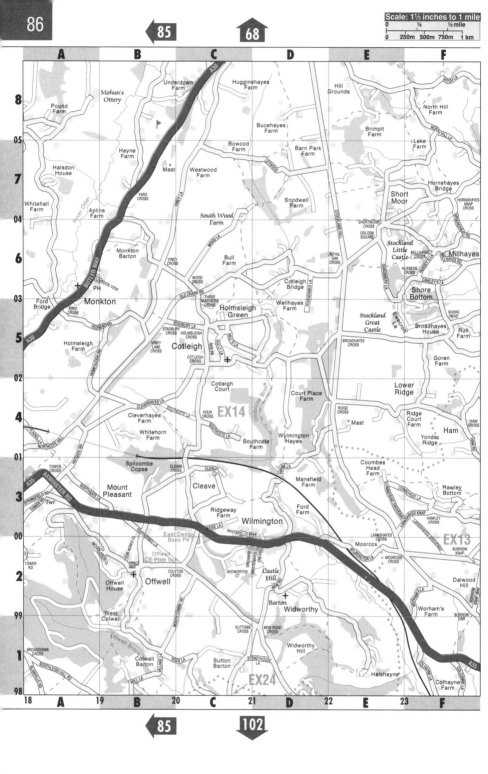

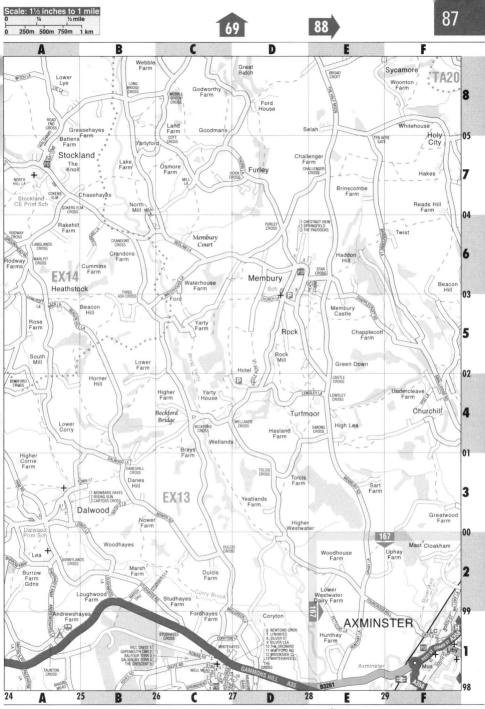

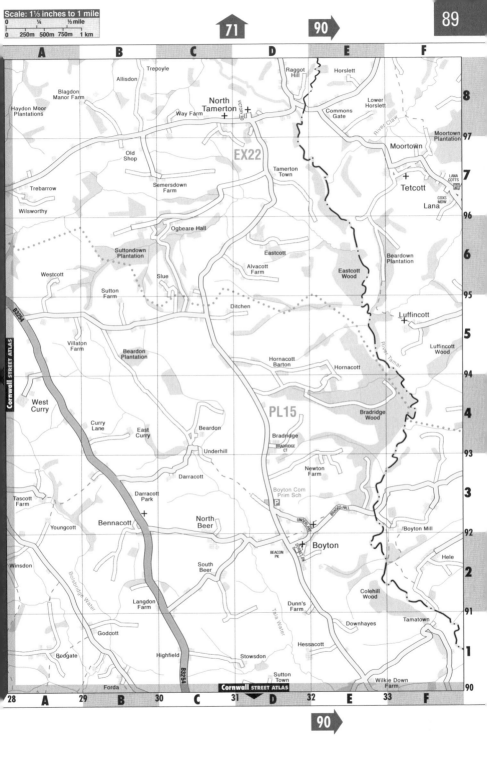

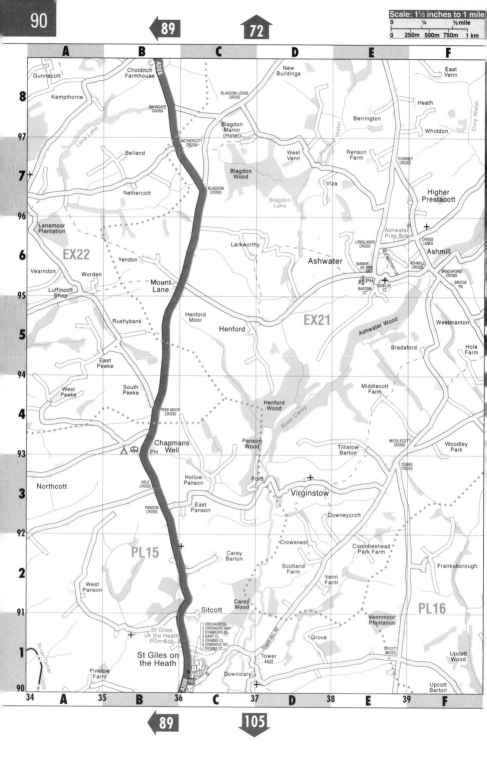

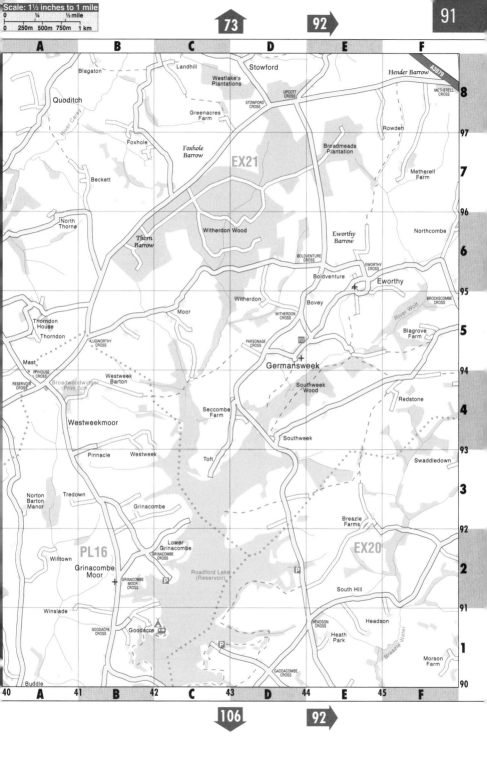

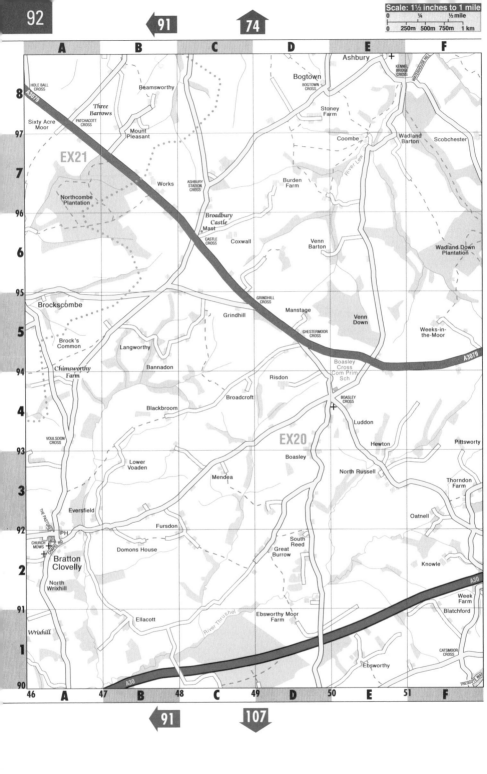

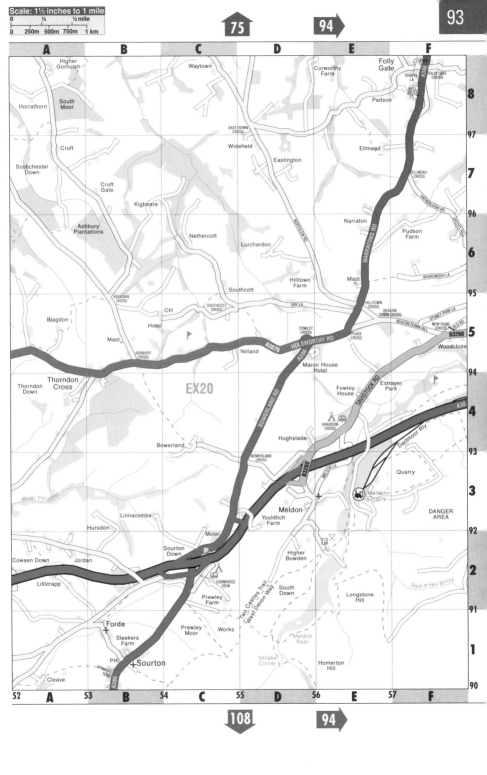

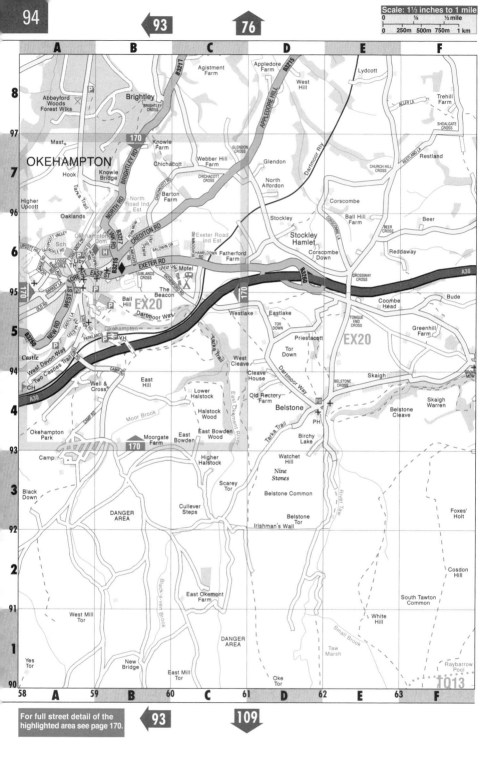

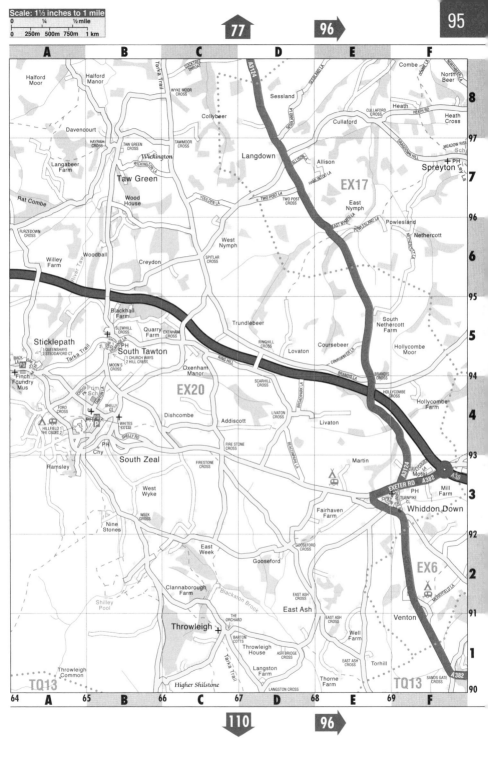

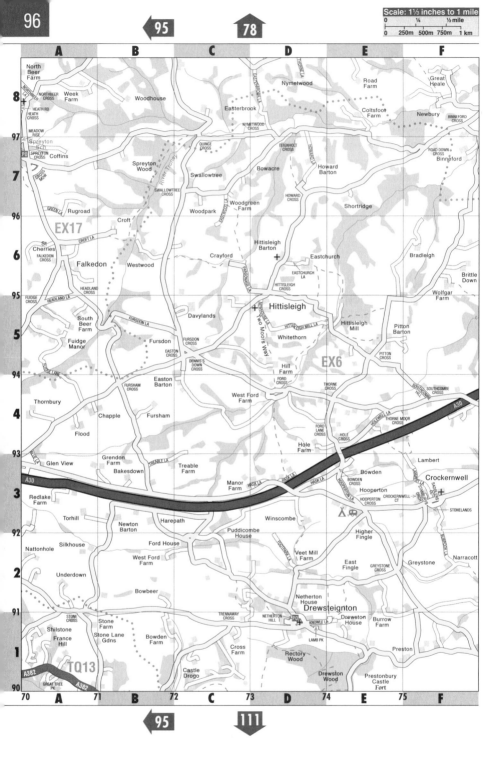

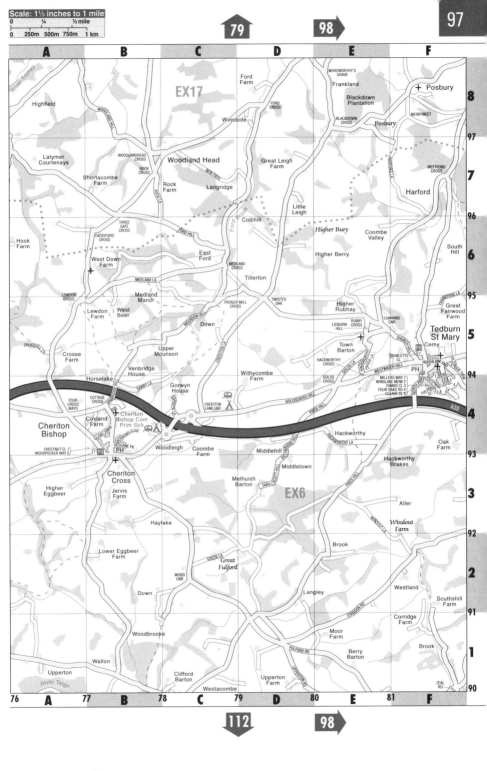

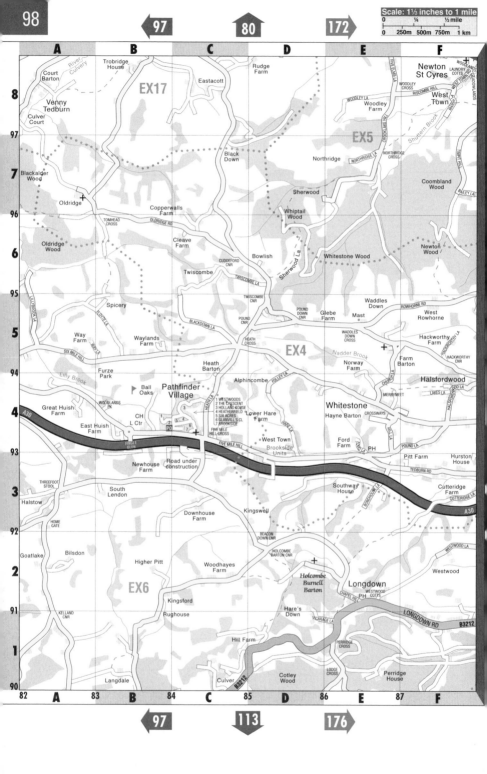

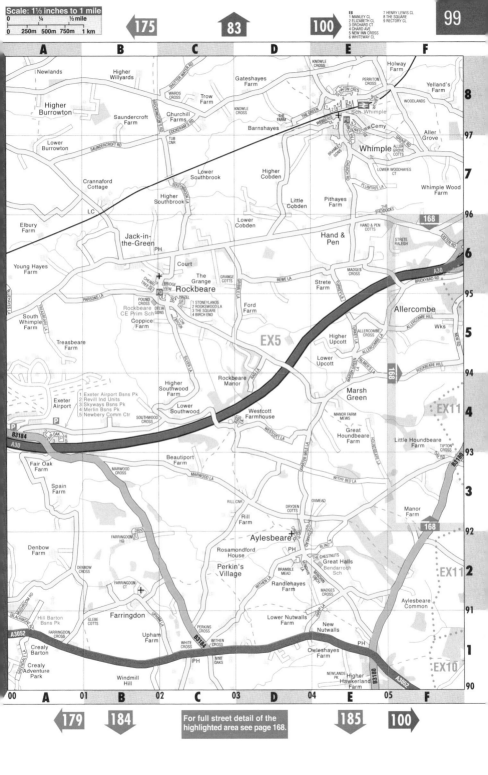

Scale: 1⅓ inches to 1 mile

0 ¼ ½ mile
0 250m 500m 750m 1 km

E8
1 MANLEY CL
2 ELIZABETH CL
3 ORCHARD CT
4 CHARD AVE
5 NEW INN CROSS
6 WHITEWAY CL

7 HENRY LEWIS CL
8 THE SQUARE
9 RECTORY CL

8
97
7
96
6
95
5
94
4
93
3
92
2
91
1
90

Newlands
Higher Willyards
Gateshayes Farm
Knowle Cross
Perriton Cross
Holway Farm
Yelland's Farm
Woodlands

Higher Burrowton
Saundercroft Farm
Wards Cross
Churchill Farms
Trow Farm
Knowle Cross
She Farm
The Green
Sinton Cres
Sch Whimple
Cemy

Lower Burrowton
Tub Cnr
Whimple
Aller Grove
Aller Grove Cotts

Crannaford Cottage
Lower Southbrook
Higher Cobden
Lower Woodhayes Ct

Higher Southbrook
LC
Higher Southbrook
Little Cobden
Pithayes Farm
Plumtree La
Whimple Wood Farm

Elbury Farm
Jack-in-the-Green
PH
Lower Cobden
Hand & Pen
Hand & Pen Cotts
168
Strete Ralegh
Exeter Rd

Young Hayes Farm
Court
The Grange
Grange Cotts
Rewe La
Strete Farm
Madges Cross
A30
Brickyard Rd
6

South Whimple Farm
Parsons La
Rockbeare
Pound Cross
Rockbeare CE Prim Sch
Delia Gdns
Hazel
1 Stoneylands
2 Rookswood La
3 The Square
4 Birch End
Ford Farm
Higher Upcott
Allercombe Hill
Allercombe
Wks
5

Treasbeare Farm
Coppice Farm
Higher Southwood Farm
Rockbeare Manor
Lower Upcott
Allercombe Rd
161
Rockbeare Hill
94

EX5
Marsh Green
EX11
4

Exeter Airport
1 Exeter Airport Bsns Pk
2 Revill Ind Units
3 Skyways Bsns Pk
4 Merlin Bsns Pk
5 Newbery Comm Ctr
Lower Southwood
Southwood Cross
Westcott Farmhouse
Westcott La
Manor Farm Mews
Great Houndbeare Farm
Little Houndbeare Farm
Tipton Cross
B3180
93

B3184
Oak
3 4 5
A30
Beautiport Farm
Marwood Cross
Marwood La
Withy Bed La
Manor Farm
3

Fair Oak Farm
Rill Cnr
Rill Farm
Dryden Cotts
Oxmead
168
92

Spain Farm
Farringdon Ho
Rosamondford House
Aylesbeare
PH
Great Halls
Bendarroch Sch
EX11
2

Denbow Farm
Denbow Cross
Farringdon Ct
Perkin's Village
Bramble Mead
The Chestnuts
Randlehayes Farm
Madges Cross

Hill Barton Bsns Pk
Glebe Cotts
Farringdon
Upham Farm
Perkins Cross
White Cross
Withen Cross
Lower Nutwalls Farm
New Nutwalls
PH
Aylesbeare Common
EX11
91

A3052
Crealy Barton
Crealy Adventure Park
PH
Nine Oaks
Windmill Hill
Owleshayes Farm
Newlands Pk
Higher Hawkerland Cross
B3180
A3052
EX10
1

For full street detail of the highlighted area see page 168.

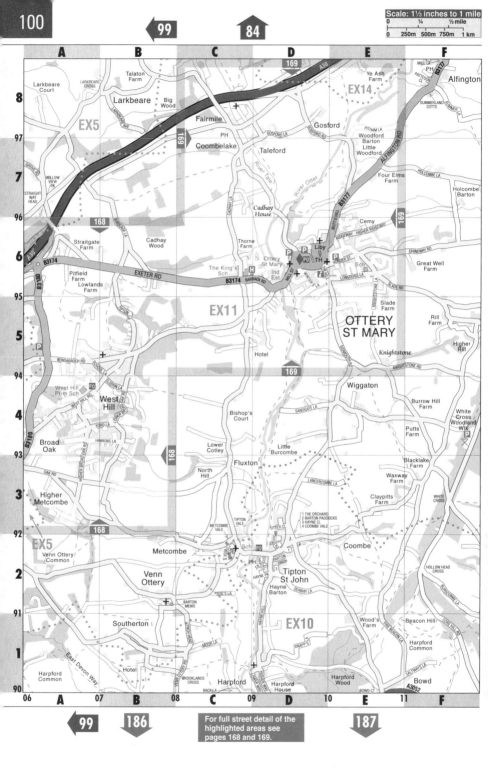

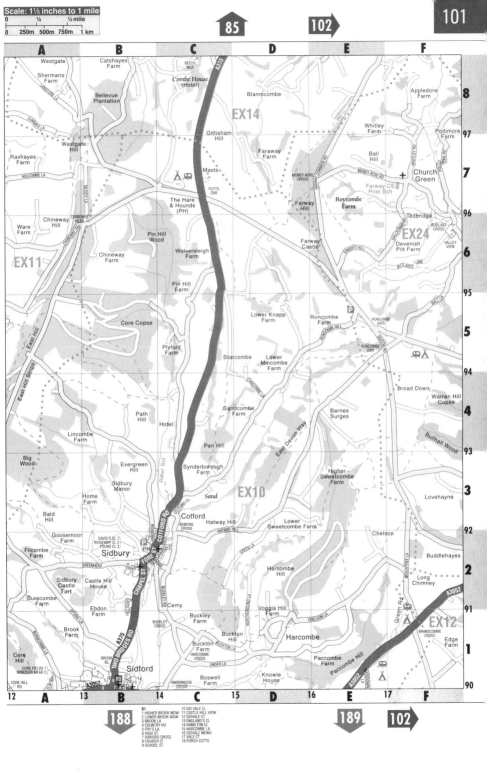

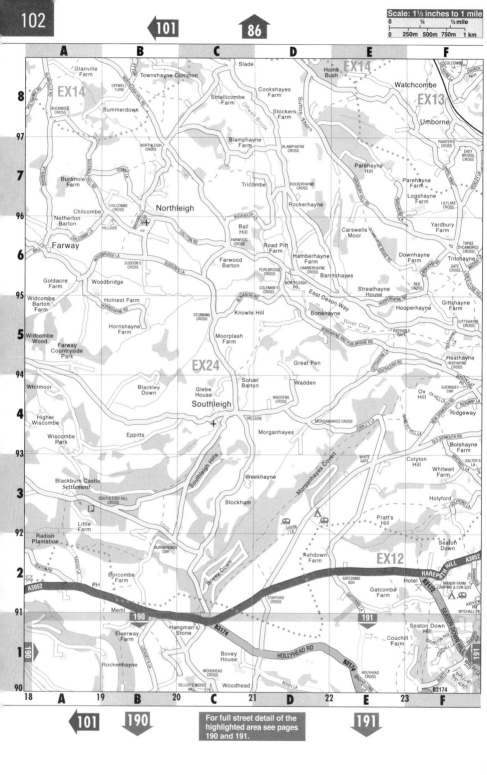

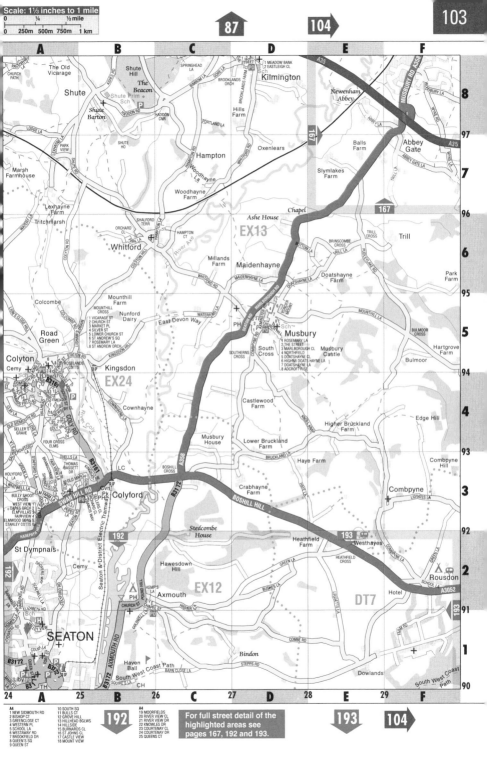

A4
1 NEW SIDMOUTH RD
2 BISHOP CT
3 GREENCLOSE CT
4 WESTERN PL
5 SCHOOL LA
6 WESTAWAY RD
7 BROOKFIELD DR
8 QUEEN'S SQ
9 QUEEN ST

10 SOUTH SQ
11 BULLS CT
12 GROVE HILL
13 HILLHEAD BGLWS
14 HILLSIDE
15 BURNARDS CL
16 ST JOHNS CL
17 CASTLE VIEW
18 MOUNT VIEW

A4
19 MOORFIELDS
20 RIVER VIEW CL
21 RIVER VIEW DR
22 KNOWLES DR
23 COURTENAY CL
24 COURTENAY DR
25 QUEENS CT

For full street detail of the
highlighted areas see
pages 167, 192 and 193.

8
97
7
96
6
95
5
94
4
93
3
92
2
91
1
90

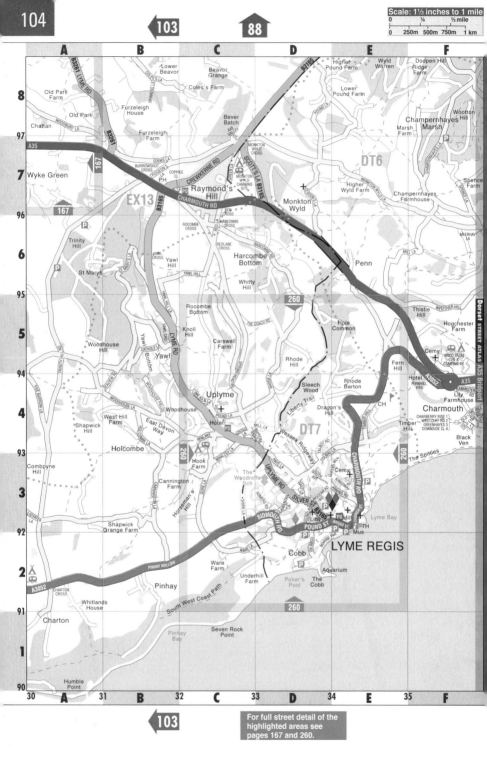

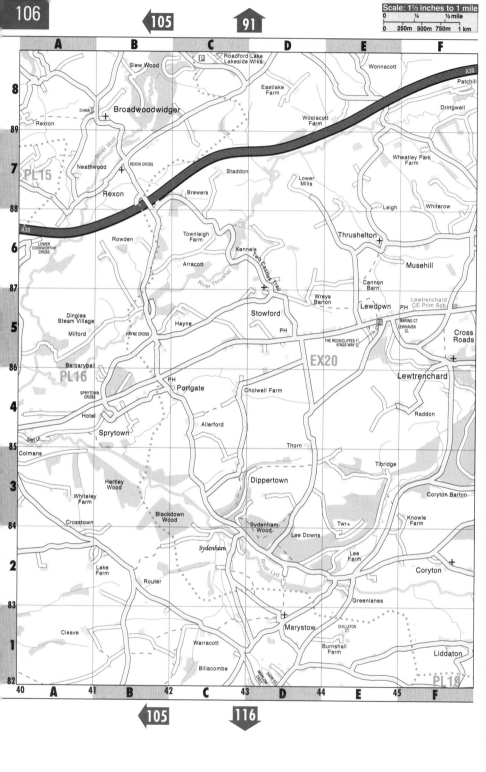

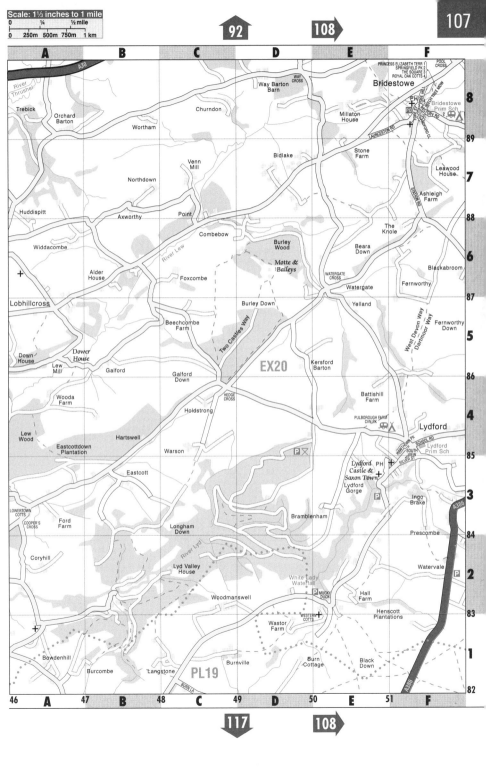

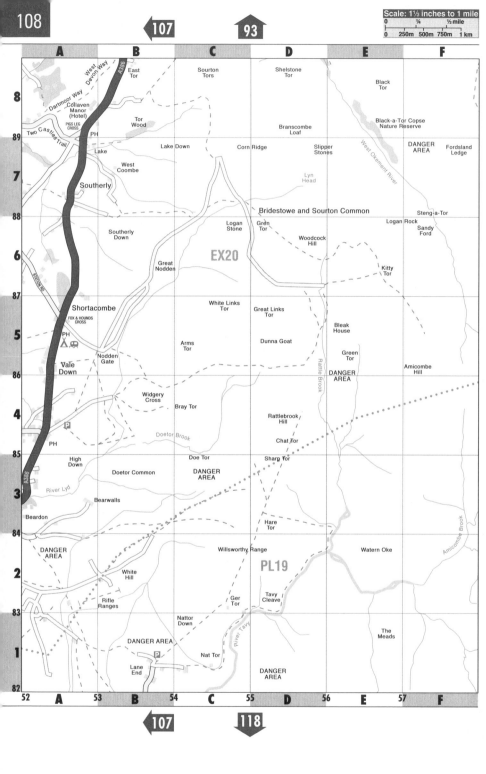

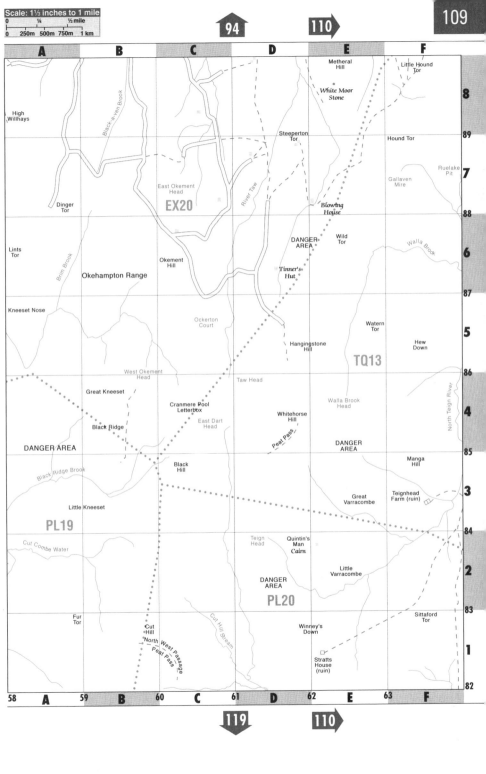

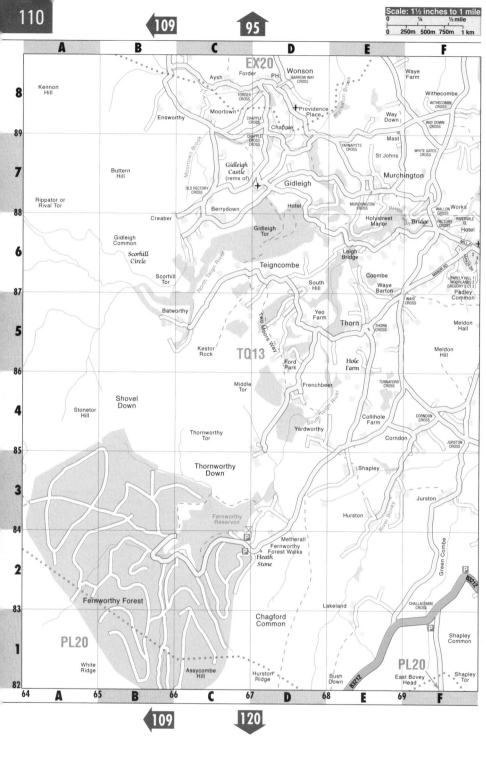

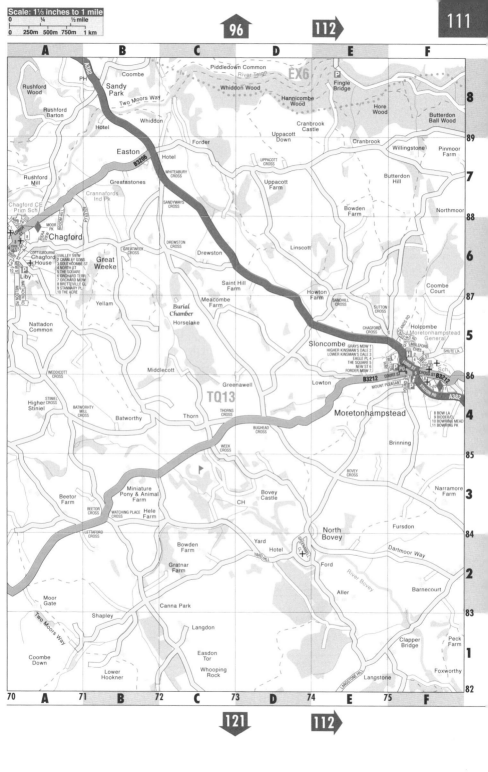

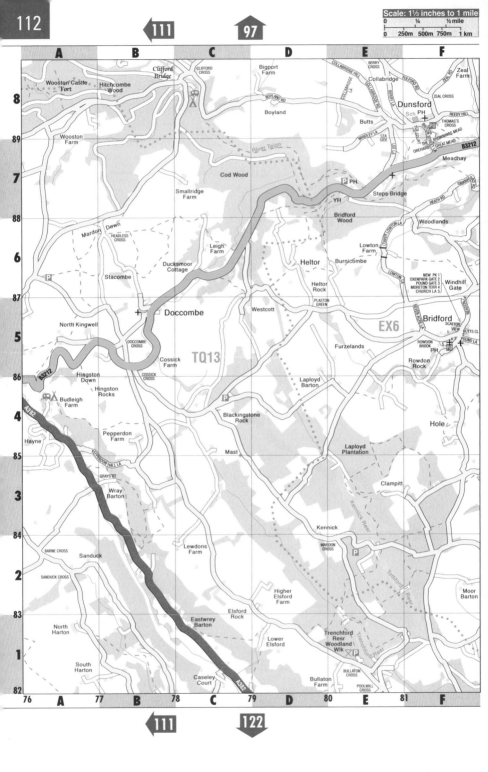

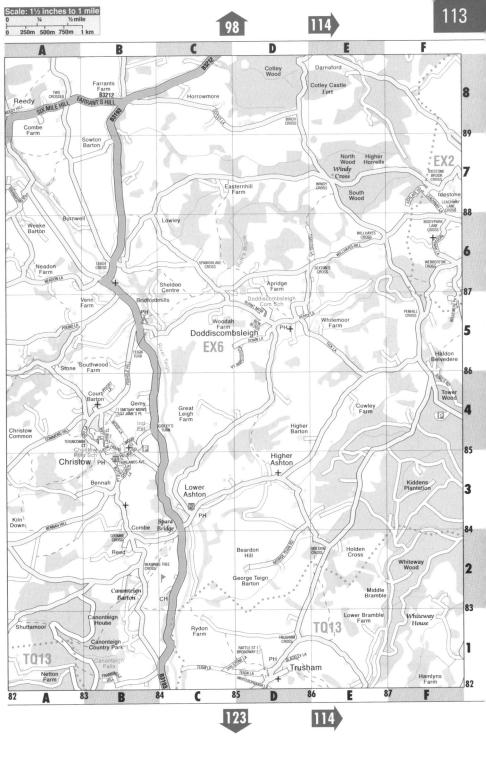

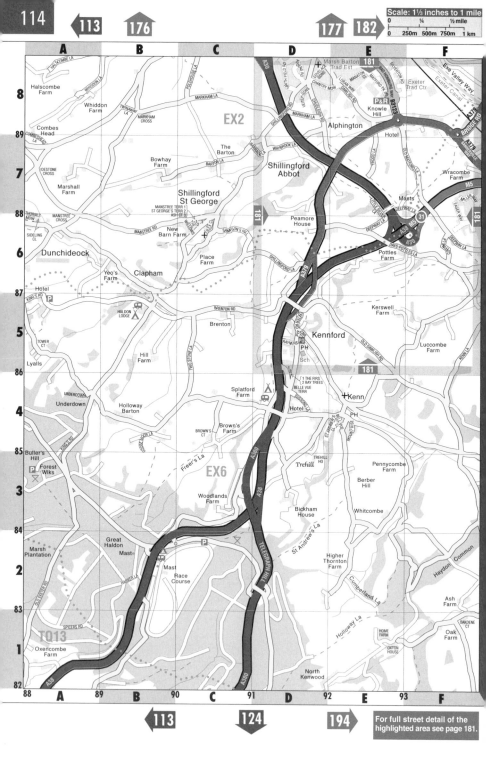

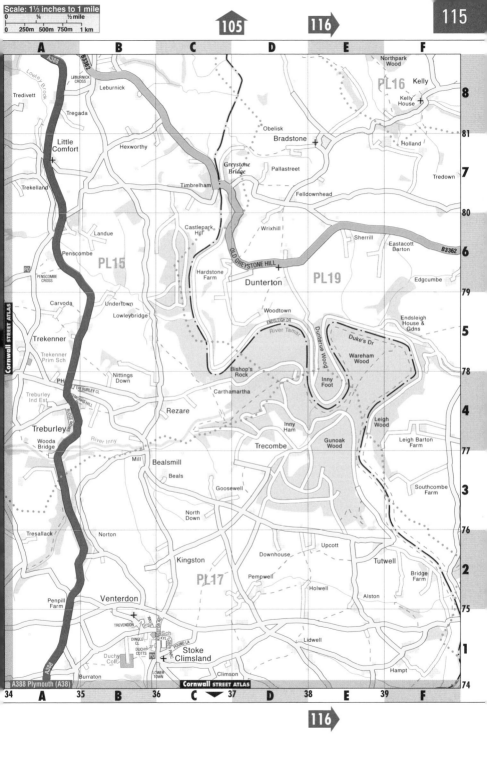

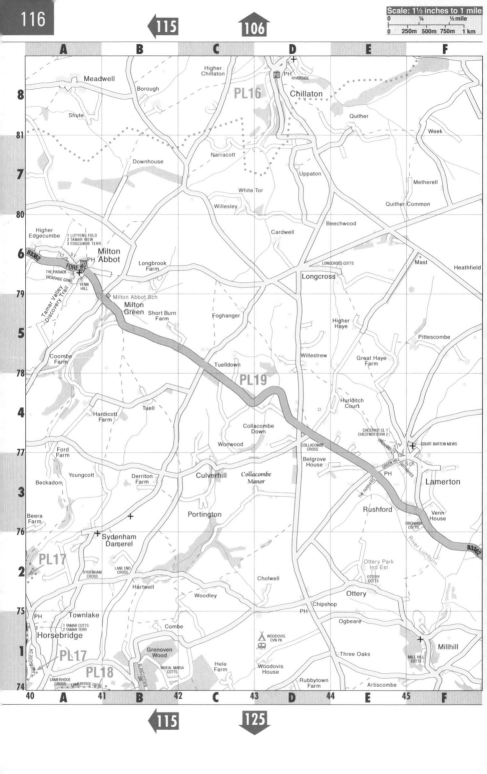

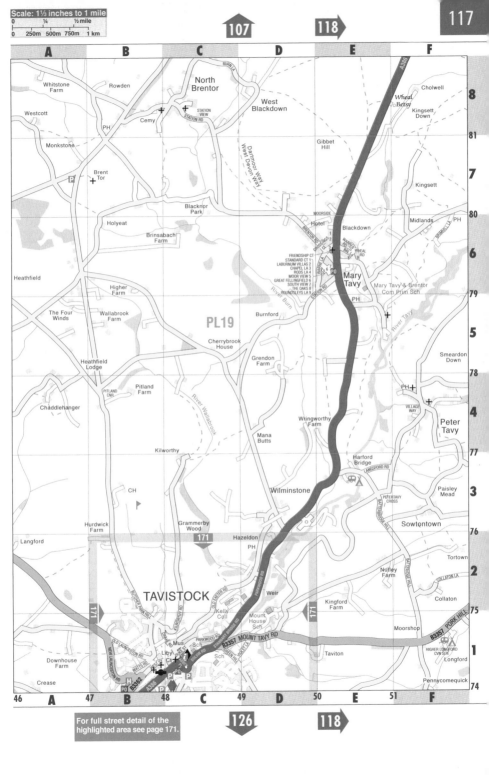

Scale: 1⅓ inches to 1 mile

0   ¼   ½ mile
0   250m 500m 750m 1 km

107   118

8
81
7
80
6
79
5
78
4
77
3
76
2
75
1
74

A   B   C   D   E   F

Whistone Farm
Rowden
North Brentor
West Blackdown
Cholwell
Wheal Betsy
Kingsett Down
Westcott
STATION VIEW
STATION RD
Cemy
PH
Monkstone
Gibbet Hill
Kingsett
Brent Tor
P
West Devon Way
Dartmoor Way
Blacknor Park
MOORSIDE
Hotel
Blackdown
Midlands
Holyeat
Brinsabach Farm
FRIENDSHIP CT
STANDARD CT 1
LABURNUM VILLAS 2
CHAPEL LA 3
RODS LA 4
MOOR VIEW 5
GREAT FELLINGFIELD 6
SOUTH VIEW 7
THE OAKS 8
ROUNDSLEYS LA 9
Heathfield
Higher Farm
WHARF RD
WHEAL RD
Mary Tavy
Mary Tavy & Brentor Com Prim Sch
The Four Winds
Wallabrook Farm
Burnford
STATION RD
River Burn
River Tavy
Smeardon Down
Heathfield Lodge
Cherrybrook House
Grendon Farm
PH
PITLAND CNR.
Pitland Farm
VILLAGE WAY
Chaddlehanger
River Wallabrook
Wringworthy Farm
Peter Tavy
Paisley Mead
CH
Mana Butts
Kilworthy
Harford Bridge
LANGSFORD RD
PETERTAVY CROSS
Hurdwick Farm
Grammerby Wood
Wilminstone
Sowtontown
Tortown
171
Hazeldon
PH
BATTERIDGE HILL
Langford
TAVISTOCK
Weir
Nutley Farm
COLLATON LA
Collaton
Kelly Coll
Mount House Sch
Kingford Farm
Moorshop
B3357 PORK HILL
171
171
OLD EXETER RD
PARKWOOD RD
HIGHER LONGFORD CVN SITE
Longford
B Mus
Liby
Sch
Taviton
B3357 MOUNT TAVY RD
Pennycomequick
Downhouse Farm
OLD LAUNCESTON RD
NEW LAUNCESTON RD
WATTS RD
PO
Crease
A386

PL19

For full street detail of the highlighted area see page 171.

46   47   48   49   50   51

A   B   C   D   E   F

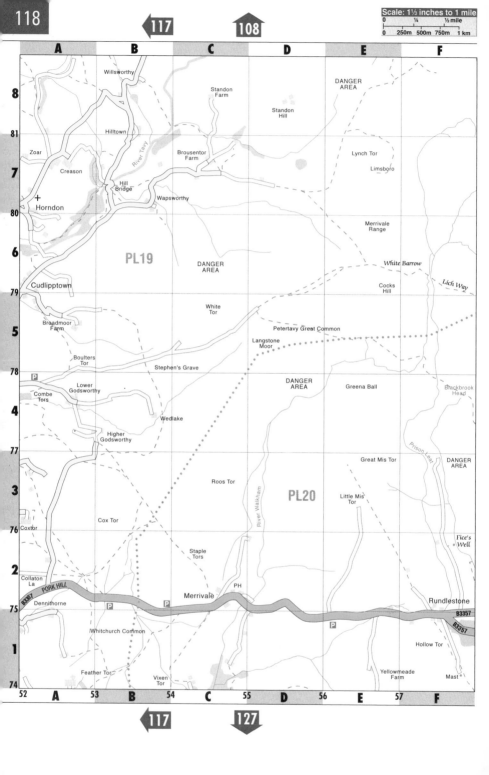

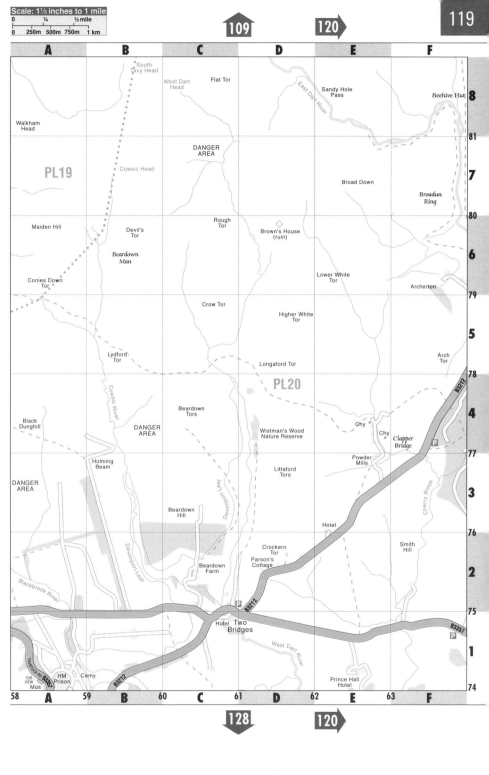

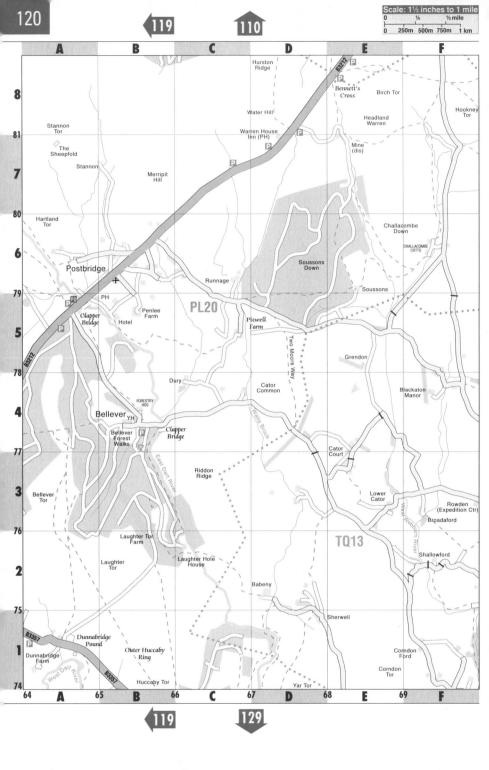

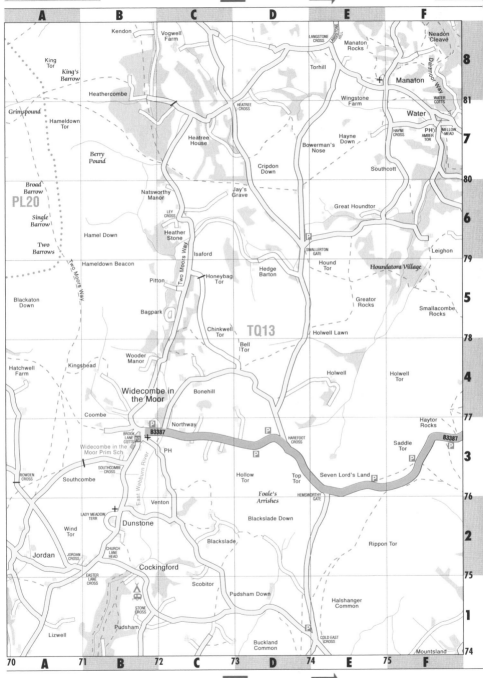

Scale: 1½ inches to 1 mile

111
122
130
122

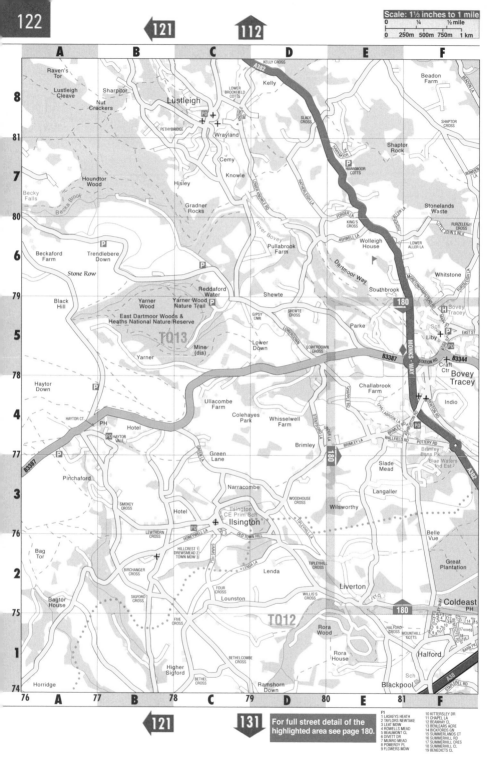

121
112

Scale: 1½ inches to 1 mile
0 ¼ ½ mile
0 250m 500m 750m 1 km

A B C D E F

8

81

7

80

6

79

5

78

4

77

3

76

2

75

1

74

Raven's Tor
Lustleigh Cleave
Nut Crackers
Sharpitor
Lustleigh
Wrayland
PETHYBRIDGE
LOWER BROOKFIELD COTTS
Kelly
KELLY CROSS
A382
SLADE CROSS
Shaptor Rock
Beadon Farm
SHAPTOR COTTS
Cerny
Knowle
Hisley
HAWKMOOR
HAWKMOOR COTTS
Houndtor Wood
Becky Falls
Becka Brook
Gradner Rocks
River Bovey
Pullabrook Farm
FORDER LA
King's Cross
ASHWELL LA
Wolleigh House
Stonelands Waste
FURZELEIGH CROSS
LOWER ALLER LA
Whitstone
Dartmoor Way
Southbrook
Beckaford Farm
Trendlebere Down
Stone Row
Black Hill
Yarner Wood
East Dartmoor Woods & Heaths National Nature Reserve
TQ13
Reddaford Water
Yarner Wood Nature Trail
Shewte
GIPSY CNR
SHEWTE CROSS
Parke
B3387
180
Bovey Tracey
Sch
Liby
EAST ST
Craft Ctr
B3344
Mine (dis)
Yarner
Lower Down
LOWERDOWN CROSS
LONGSDOWN
MONKS WAY
STATION RD
Haytor Down
HAYTOR CT
PH
Hotel
HAYTOR VALE
B3387
Pinchaford
GREEN LA
Green Lane
Ullacombe Farm
Colehayes Park
Whisselwell Farm
Brimley
CHAPPLE END
STRETCHER LA
TAVERN LA
BRIMLEY LA
BRIMLEY LA
WALLFIELD RD
POTTERY RD
Challabrook Farm
CHALLABROOK LA
Challabrook
A382
Indio
Slade Mead
Blue Waters Ind Est
Brimley Bsns Pk
Langaller
180
SMOKEY CROSS
LEWTHORN CROSS
Hotel
HONEYWELL LA
Ilsington CE Prim Sch
Ilsington
OLD TOWN HILL
Narracombe
WOODHOUSE CROSS
Wilsworthy
TIPLEYHILL LA
Belle Vue
Bag Tor
BIRCHANGER CROSS
HILLCREST 1
DREWSMEAD 2
TOWN MDW 3
SIGFORD CROSS
CHAGA HILL
LENDA LA
Lenda
TIPLEYHILL CROSS
WILLIS'S CROSS
Liverton
Great Plantation
Bagtor House
FIVE CROSS
FOUR CROSS
Lounston
TQ12
Rora Wood
180
Coldeast
PH
HALFORD CROSS
MOUNTHILL COTTS
Higher Sigford
BETHEL CROSS
BETHELCOMBE CROSS
Ramshorn Down
Rora House
Sch
Blackpool
Halford
A38
A382
Horridge

121
131

For full street detail of the highlighted area see page 180.

F1
1 LASKEYS HEATH
2 TAYLORS NEWTAKE
3 LEAT MDW
4 ROWELLS MEAD
5 BEAUMONT CL
6 DIVETT DR
7 MUNRO MEAD
8 POMEROY PL
9 FLOWERS MDW
10 KITTERSLEY DR
11 CHAPEL LA
12 BEANHAY CL
13 BENLEARS ACRE
14 BICKFORDS GN
15 SUMMERLANDS CT
16 SUMMERHILL RD
17 SUMMERHILL CRES
18 SUMMERHILL CL
19 BENEDICTS CL

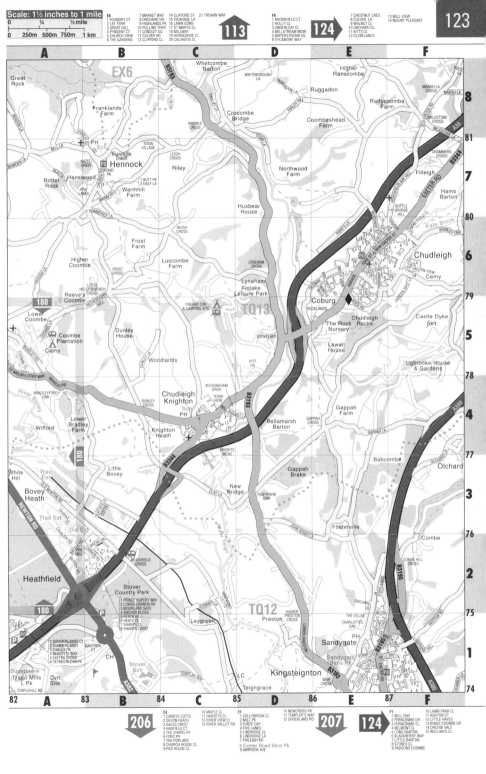

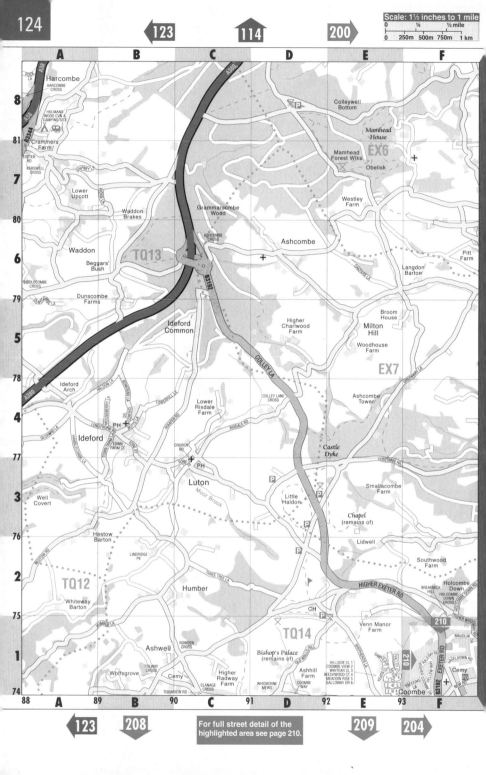

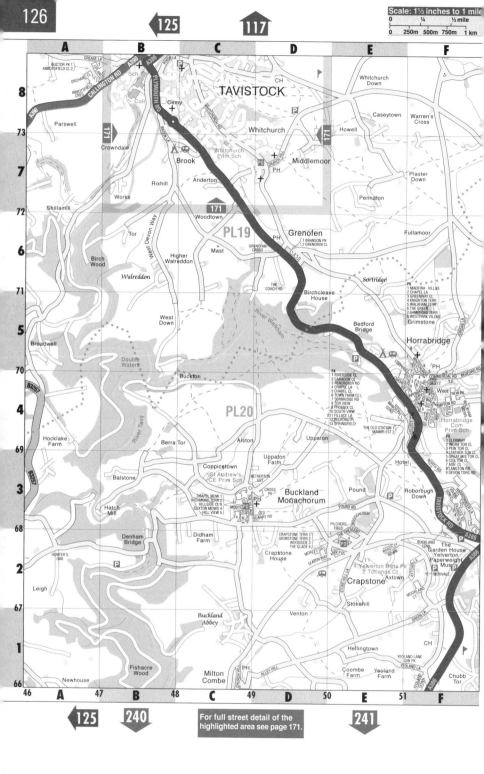

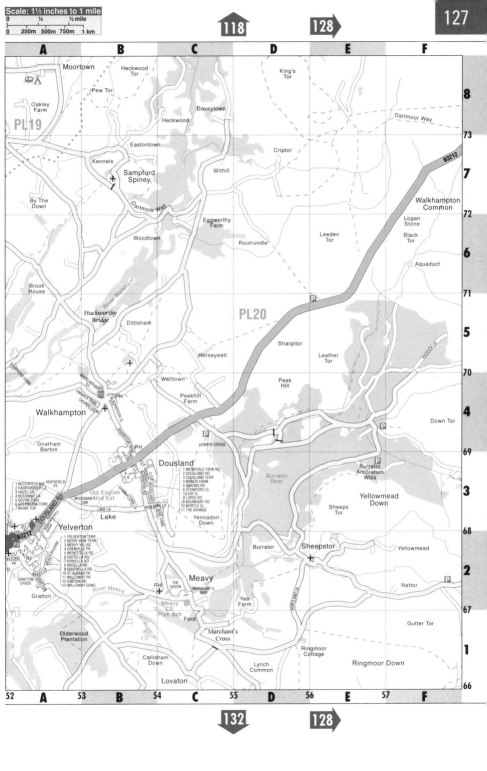

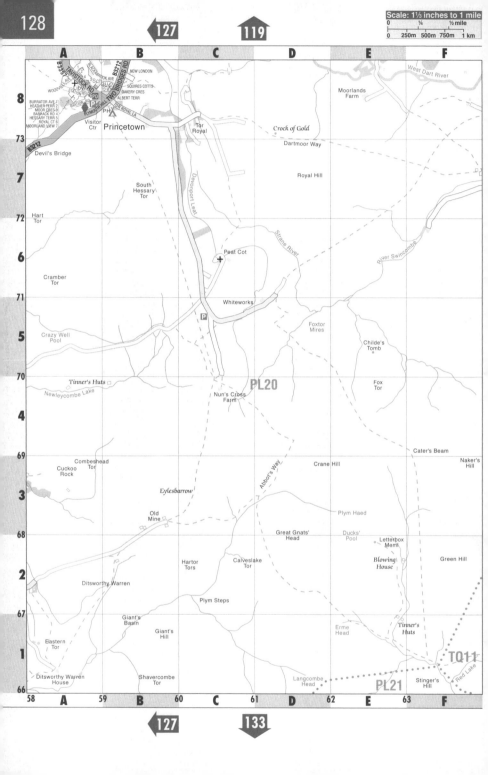

127
119

Scale: 1½ inches to 1 mile
0   ¼   ½ mile
0 250m 500m 750m 1 km

West Dart River

Moorlands Farm

Crock of Gold

Dartmoor Way

New London

Squires Cotts.
Oakery Cres
Albert Terr

Tor Royal

Royal Hill

BURRATOR AVE 1
HEATHER TERR 2
MOOR CRES 3
BARRACK RD 4
HESSARY TERR 5
ROYAL CT 6
MOORLAND VIEW 7

Visitor Ctr

Princetown

Devil's Bridge

South Hessary Tor

Hart Tor

Devonport Leat

Sherde River

River Swincombe

Peat Cot

Cramber Tor

Whiteworks

Foxtor Mires

Childe's Tomb

Crazy Well Pool

Fox Tor

Tinner's Huts

Nun's Cross Farm

PL20

Newleycombe Lake

Cater's Beam

Naker's Hill

Combeshead Tor

Cuckoo Rock

Abbot's Way

Crane Hill

Eylesbarrow

Plym Haed

Old Mine

Great Gnats' Head

Ducks' Pool

Letterbox Meml

Hartor Tors

Calveslake Tor

Blowing House

Green Hill

Ditsworthy Warren

Plym Steps

Giant's Basin

Giant's Hill

Erme Head

Tinner's Huts

TQ11

Eastern Tor

Ditsworthy Warren House

Shavercombe Tor

Langcombe Head

PL21

Stinger's Hill

Red Lake

127
133

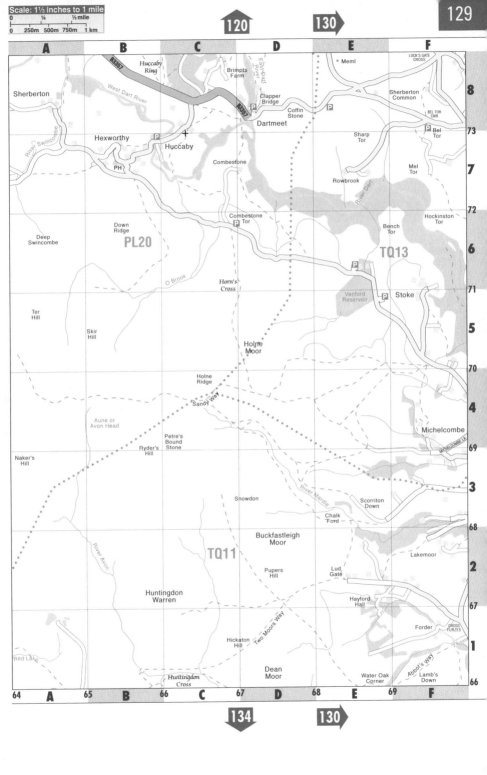

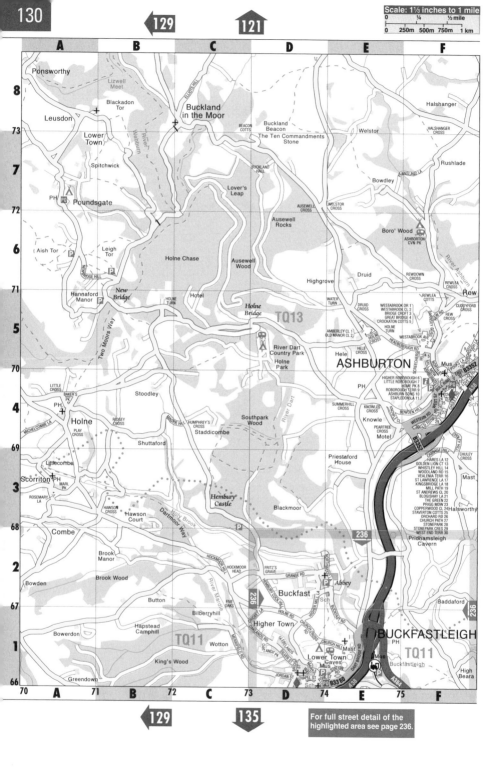

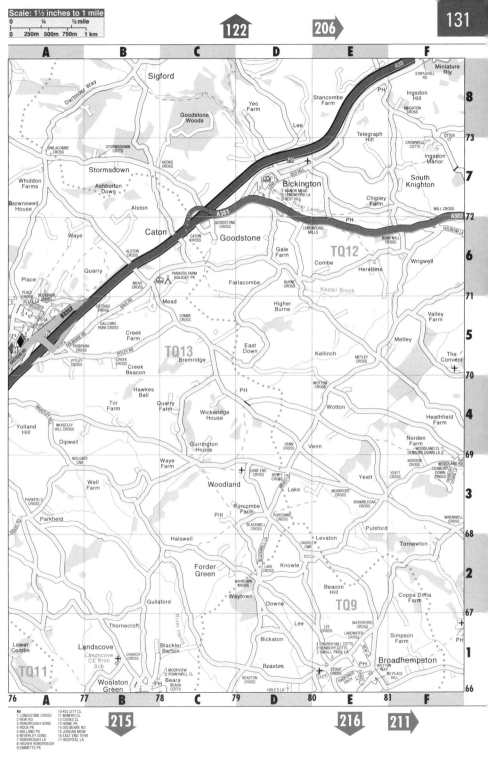

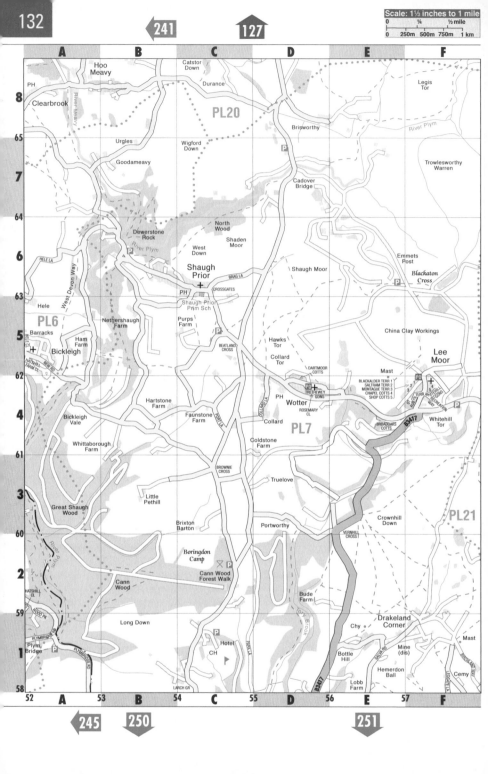

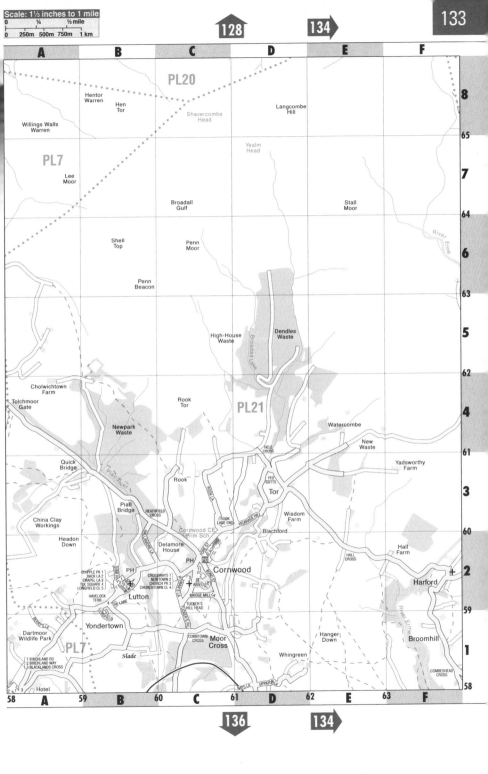

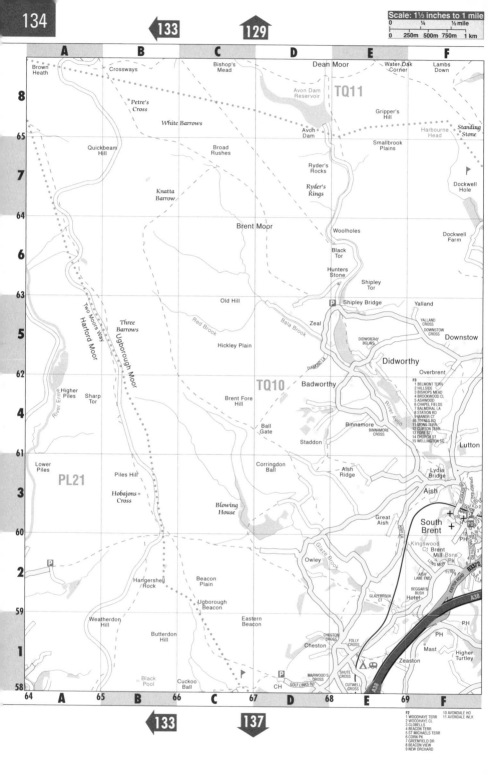

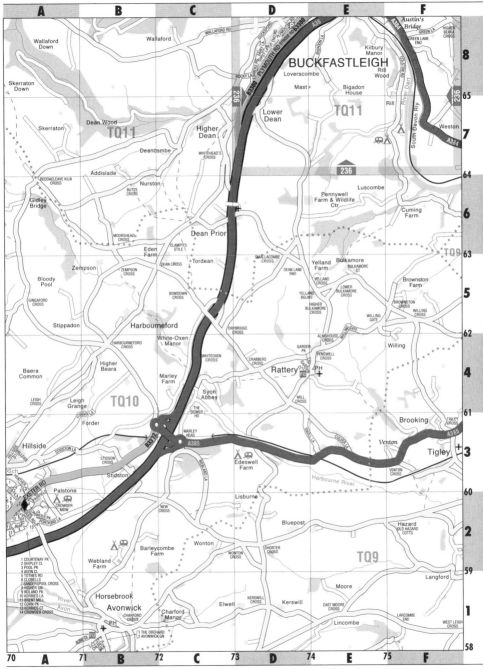

Scale: 1⅓ inches to 1 mile

0   ¼   ½ mile
0 250m 500m 750m 1 km

130   215

BUCKFASTLEIGH

Austin's Bridge
Higher Beara Cross
Green Lane End
GREEN LA

Kilbury Manor
Rill Wood
Loverscombe
Mast
Bigadon House
Rill
Weston
A384

TQ11

236

Wallaford Down
Wallaford
WALLAFORD RD

ROCKY LA

Skerraton Down

Dean Wood
TQ11
Higher Dean
Deancombe
WHITEHEAD'S CROSS

Skerraton

REDDACLEAVE KILN CROSS
Gidley Bridge
Addislade
BUTTS CROSS
Nurston
Lower Dean

Pennywell Farm & Wildlife Ctr
Luscombe
Cuming Farm

236

Dean Prior
MOORSHEAD CROSS
Eden Farm
CLAMPITS STILE
Tordean
DEAN CROSS
SMALLACOMBE CROSS
DEAN LANE END
Yelland Farm
Bulkamore
BULKAMORE GT
TQ9

Zempson
ZEMPSON CROSS
BOWDOWN CROSS
YELLAND CROSS
YELLAND BGLWS
LOWER BULKAMORE CROSS
Brownston Farm

Bloody Pool
GINGAFORD CROSS
HIGHER BULKAMORE CROSS
WILLING GATE
BROWNSTON CROSS
WILLING CROSS

Stippadon
Harbourneford
White-Oxen Manor
DRYBRIDGE CROSS
ALMSHOUSE CROSS
Willing

HARBOURNEFORD CROSS
WHITEOXEN CROSS
GARDEN PK
PENSWELL CROSS

Baera Common
Higher Beara
Marley Farm
CRABBERS CROSS
Rattery
PH

TQ10
LEIGH CROSS
Leigh Grange
Syon Abbey
MILL CROSS

Forder
THE DOWER HO
Brooking
TIGLEY CROSS
A385

Hillside
B3372
MARLEY HEAD
A385
Venton
Tigley

STIDSON LA
STIDSON CROSS
WEBLAND LA
CLEEVE LA
VENTON CROSS

Sch
Stidston
Edeswell Farm
Harbourne River

EXETER RD
Palstone
CROWDER MDW
PORTFORD LA
NEW CROSS
Lisburne
Bluepost
Hazard
OLD HAZARD COTTS

1 COURTENAY PK
2 SHIPLEY CL
3 POOL PK
4 AVON CL
5 TOTNES RD
6 CLOBELLS
7 SANDERSPOOL CROSS
8 HIGHER GN
9 NOLAND PK
10 KERRIES LA
11 BRENT MILL
12 CORN PK
13 KERRIES CT
14 CROWDER CROSS

Webland Farm
Barleycombe Farm
Wonton
WONTON CROSS
SHORTER CROSS
TQ9
Moore
Langford

River Avon
Horsebrook
Avonwick
CHARFORD CROSS
Charford Manor
Elwell
KERSWILL CROSS
Kerswill
EAST MOORE CROSS
LARCOMBE END
WEST LEIGH CROSS

1 THE ORCHARD
2 AVONWICK GN
PH
Lincombe

138   222

For full street detail of the highlighted area see page 236.

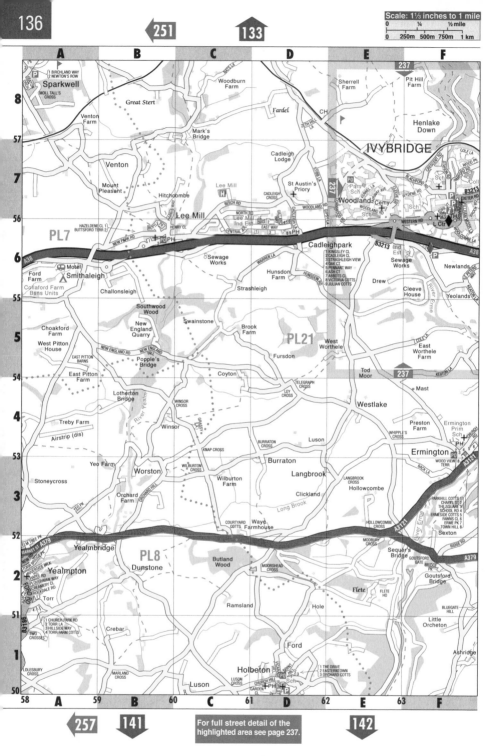

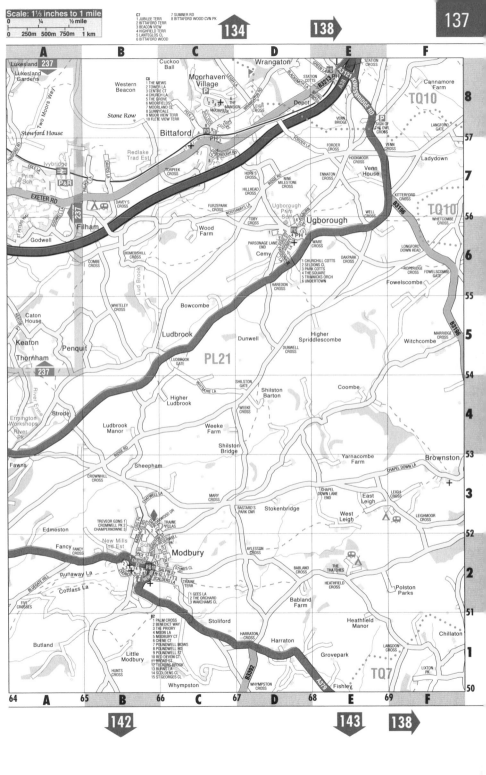

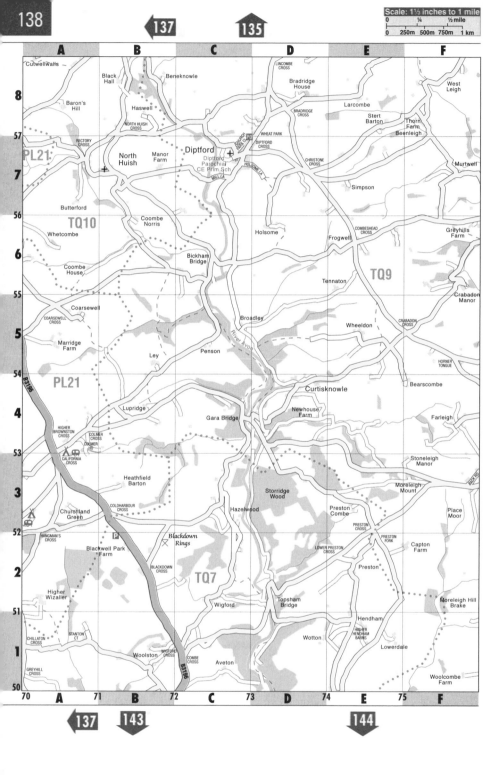

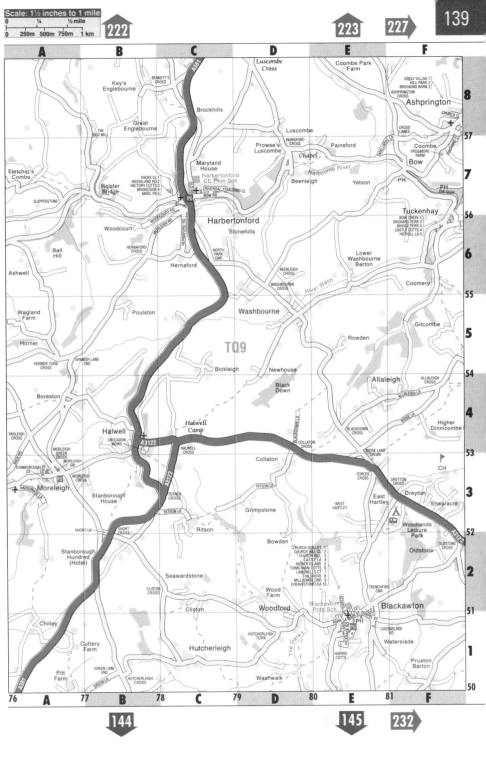

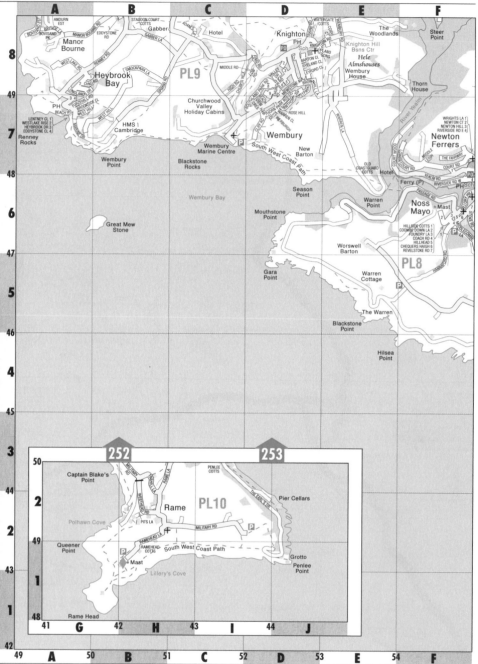

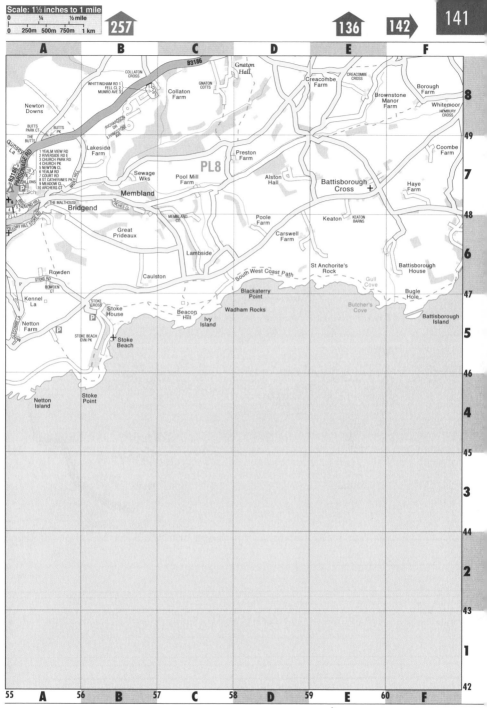

Scale: 1½ inches to 1 mile

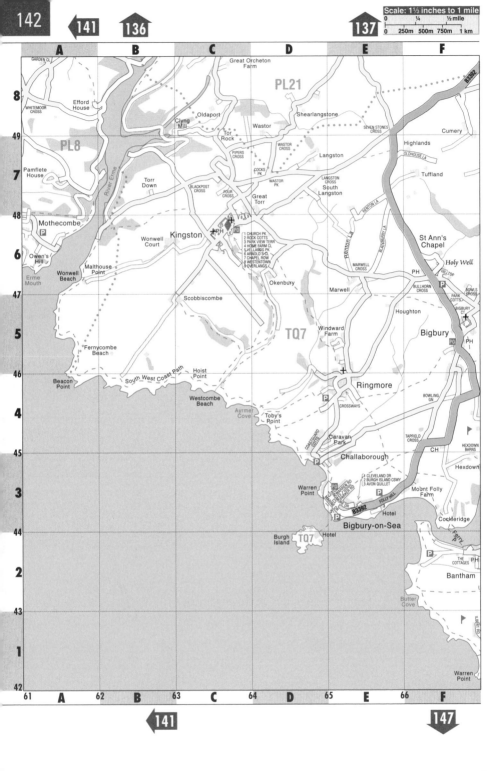

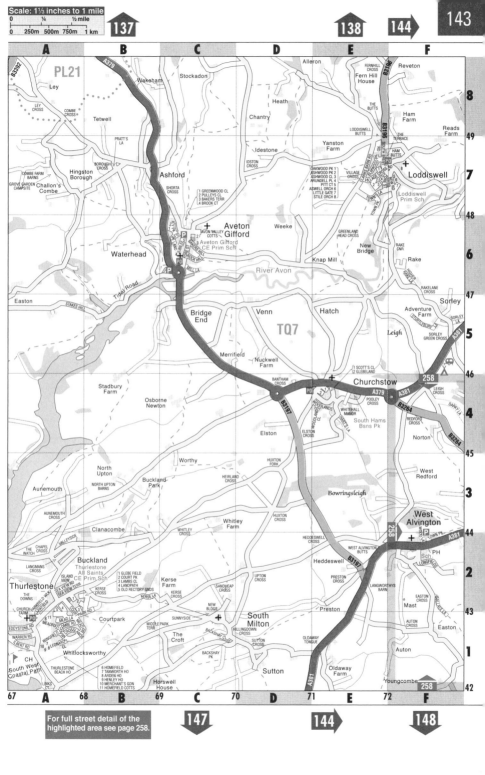

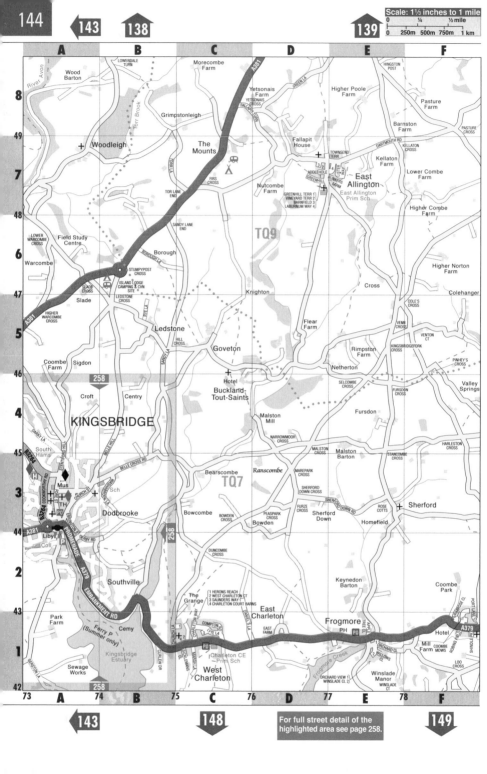

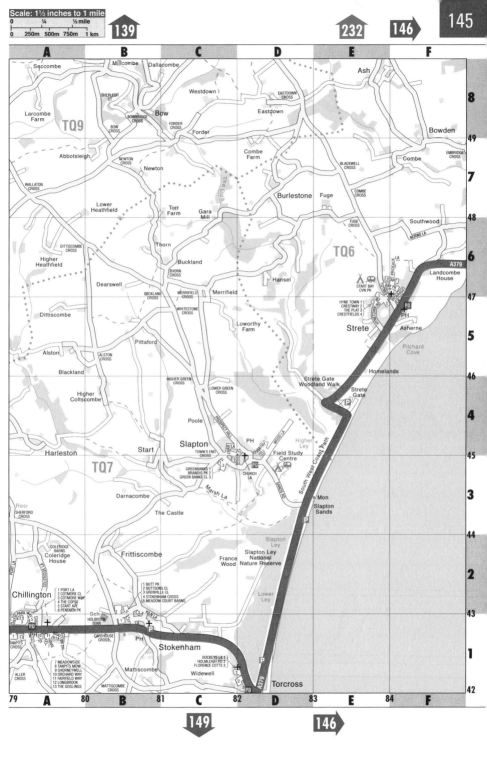

Scale: 1⅓ inches to 1 mile
0   ¼   ½ mile
0   250m 500m 750m 1 km

8

Worden

Venn

Thorn

TQ6

Lower
Week

Newfoundland
Cove

TQ6

Kingswear
Lookout
Sta

SW Coast Path

Inner Froward
Point

VENN
CROSS

POUNDHOUSE
CROSS

WEEKE HILL

REDLAP
CROSS

COMPASS COVE
COTTS

Blackstone
Point

DEER PARK

Poundhouse

Compass Cove

VENN PK 1
VENN WAY 2
GRATTON CL 3
VENN CL 4
BAY VIEW CL 5
BAY VIEW EST 6
HAREFIELD DR 7
GLEBE PK 8
RAVENSBOURNE LA 9

PH

Little
Dartmouth

49

Stoke
Fleming

Redlap
House

7

Stoke Fleming
Com Prim Sch

Hotel

Liby

Redlap
Cove

Dancing
Beggars

Combe
Point

MANOR CT 10
RECTORY LA 11
BAILEYS MDW 12

MILL LA

13 CHAPEL LA
14 STOKE HOUSE GDNS
15 WHITE LADIES
16 PENHILL CHALETS
17 BIDDERS WLK

Blackpool
Gardens

Sanders

Leonard's
Cove

48

BLACKPOOL HILL

NEW RD

LOVERSEAT

Blackpool

6

A379

Matthew's
Point

47

Forest
Cove

5

46

4

45

3

44

2

43

1

42

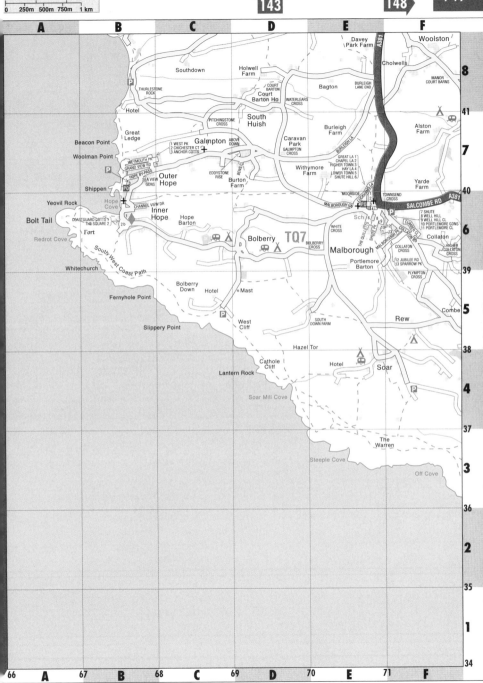

Woolston
Davey Park Farm
Cholwells
MANOR COURT BARNS
Southdown
Holwell Farm
Court Barton
Court Barton Ho
Bagton
BURLEIGH LANE END
THURLSTONE ROCK
Hotel
Waterlears Cross
PITCHINGSTONE CROSS
South Huish
Burleigh Farm
Alston Farm
Great Ledge
Beacon Point
Galmpton
ABOVE DOWN
Caravan Park
GALMPTON CROSS
Burleigh La
Woolman Point
1 WEST PK
2 CHICHESTER CT
3 ANCHOR COTTS
WEYMOUTH PK
GRAND VIEW RD
GREAT LA 1
CHAPEL LA 2
HIGHER TOWN 3
HAY LA 4
LOWER TOWN 5
SHUTE HILL 6
Yarde Farm
Shippen
HOPE RD BY PASS
SEA VIEW GDNS
Outer Hope
EDDYSTONE RISE
Burton Farm
Withymore Farm
TDWNSEND CROSS
SALCOMBE RD
A381
Yeovil Rock
CHANNEL VIEW DR
Hope Cove
Inner Hope
MALBOROUGH GN
MOORSIDE
Sch
Bolt Tail
COASTGUARD COTTS 1
THE SQUARE 2
Fort
Hope Barton
Bolberry
TQ7
White Cross
7 SHUTE
8 WELL HILL
9 WELL HILL CL
10 PORTLEMORE GDNS
11 PORTLEMORE CL
Collaton
Redrot Cove
Bolberry Cross
Malborough
COLLATON CROSS
HIGHER COLLATON CROSS
Whitechurch
Portlemore Barton
12 JUBILEE RD
13 SPARROW PK
Fernyhole Point
Bolberry Down
Hotel
Mast
PLYMPTON CROSS
South West Coast Path
Rew
Combe
West Cliff
SOUTH DOWN FARM
Slippery Point
Hazel Tor
Soar
Cathole Cliff
Hotel
Lantern Rock
Soar Mill Cove
The Warren
Steeple Cove
Off Cove

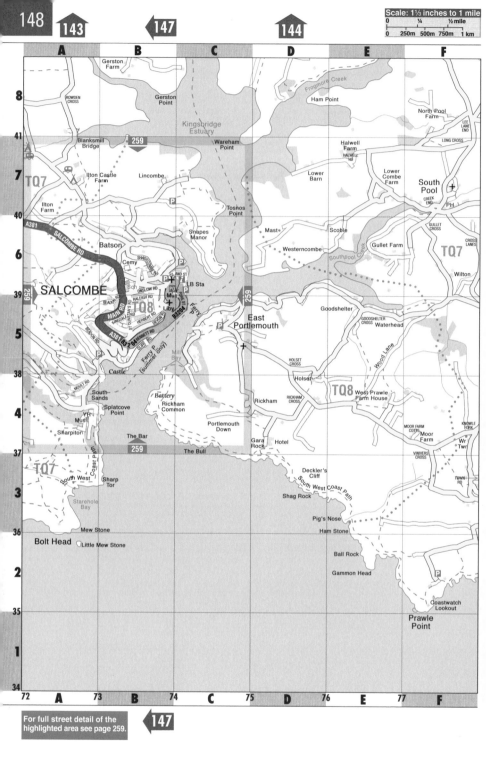

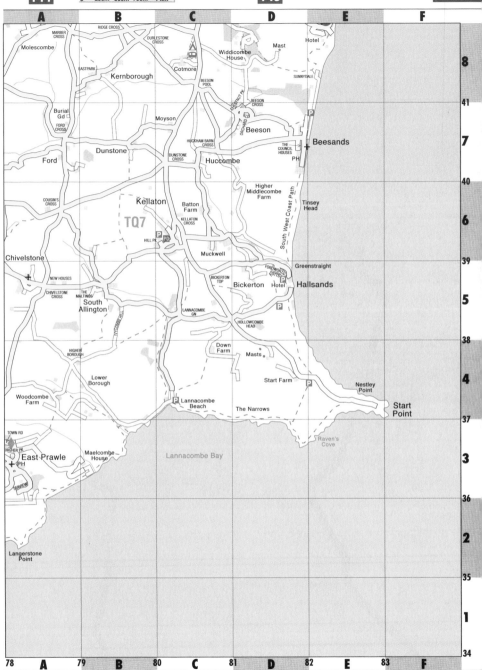

MARBER CROSS
RIDGE CROSS
Molescombe
DURLESTONE CROSS
Widdicombe House
Mast
Hotel
EASTPARK
Kernborough
Cotmore
BEESON POOL
SUNNYDALE
CHESTNUT PK
Burial Gd
Moyson
BEESON CROSS
FORD CROSS
ORCHARD
Beeson
Beesands
Dunstone
HUCKHAM BARN CROSS
THE COUNCIL HOUSES
Ford
DUNSTONE CROSS
Huccombe
PH
COUSIN'S CROSS
Higher Middlecombe Farm
Tinsey Head
Kellaton
Batton Farm
South West Coast Path
Chivelstone
TQ7
KELLATON CROSS
NEW HOUSES
HILL PK
TQ7
Muckwell
Greenstraight
FOREWINE'S COTTS
CHIVELSTONE CROSS
THE MALTINGS
BICKERTON TOP
Bickerton
Hotel
Hallsands
South Allington
LANNACOMBE GN
HOLLOWCOMBE HEAD
TYCOMBE RD
HIGHER BOROUGH
Down Farm
Masts
Woodcombe Farm
Lower Borough
Start Farm
Nestley Point
TOWN RD
LANNACOMBE BEACH
Lannacombe Beach
The Narrows
Start Point
HIGHER PK
Raven's Cove
East Prawle
PH
Maelcombe House
Lannacombe Bay
SEAVIEW
Langerstone Point

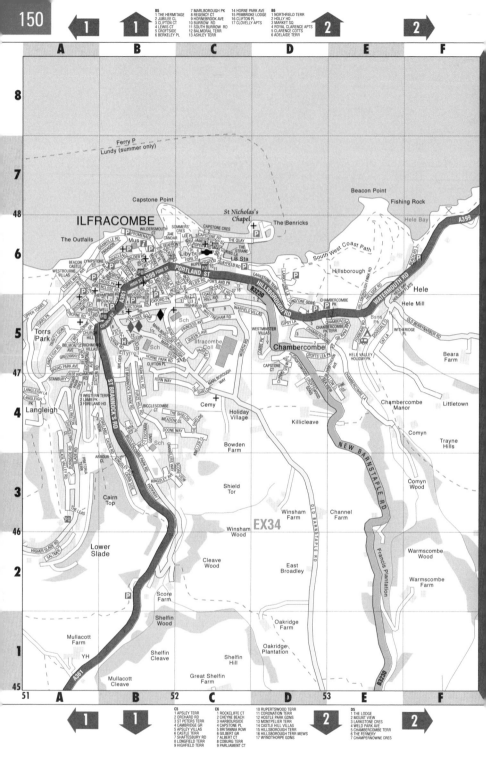

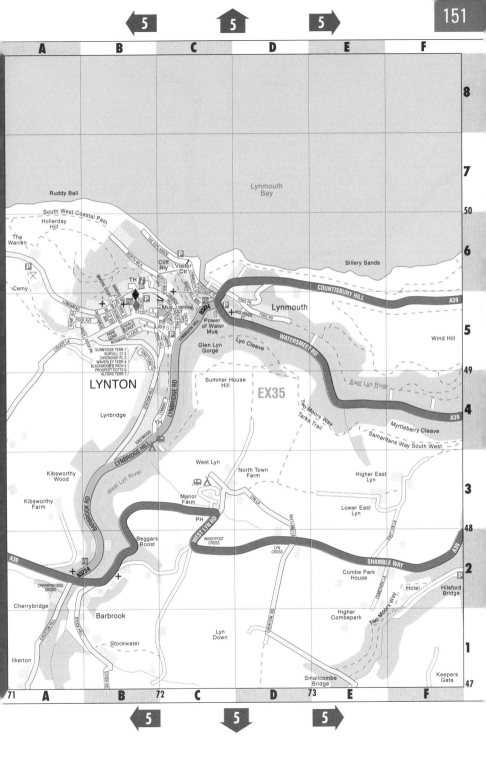

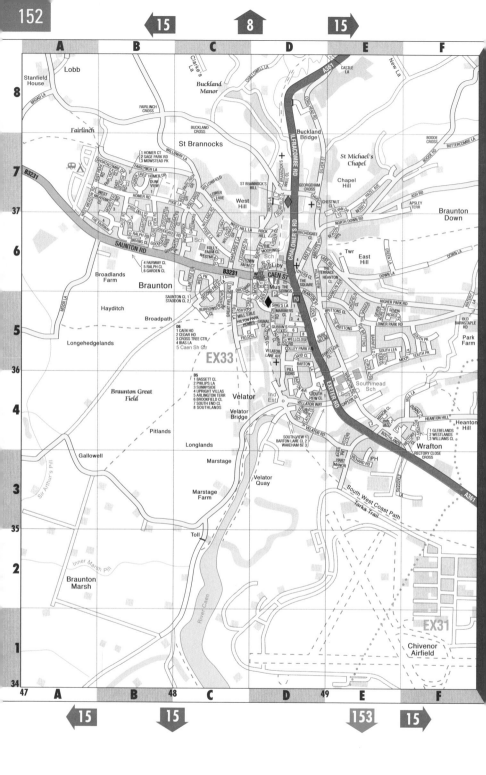

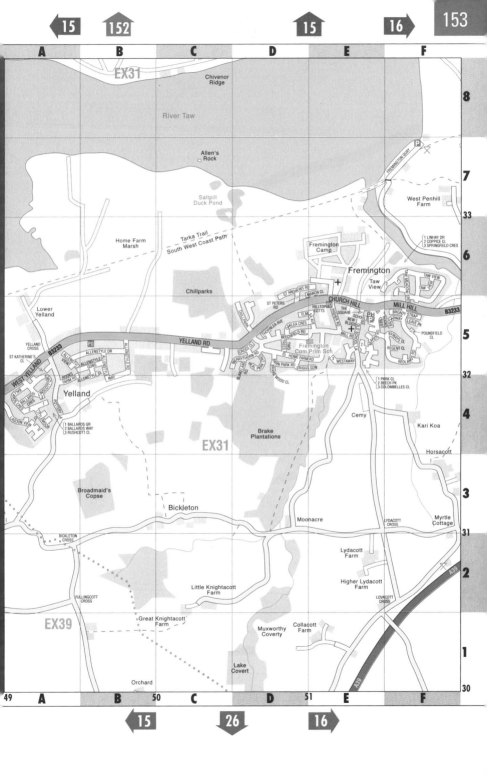

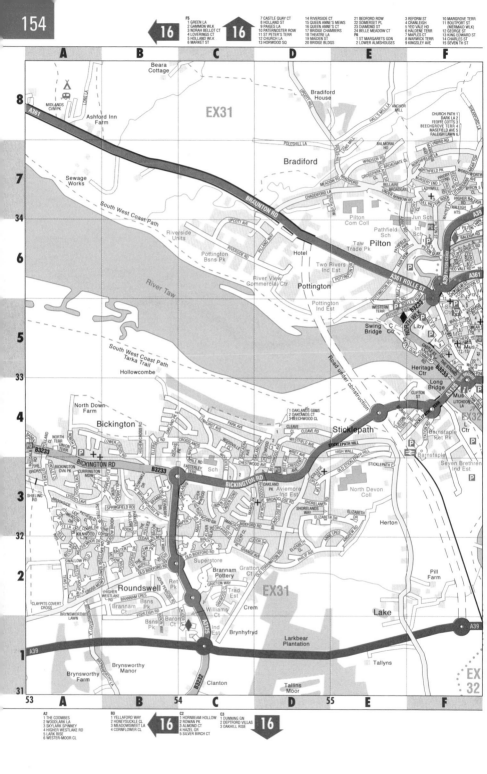

F5
1 GREEN LA
2 GAMMON WLK
3 NORAH BELLOT CT
4 LOVERINGS CT
5 HOLLAND WLK
6 MARKET ST

7 CASTLE QUAY CT
8 HOLLAND ST
9 PAIGES LA
10 PATERNOSTER ROW
11 ST PETER'S TERR
12 CHURCH LA
13 HORWOOD SQ

14 RIVERSIDE CT
15 QUEEN ANNE'S MEWS
16 QUEEN ANNE'S CT
17 BRIDGE CHAMBERS
18 THEATRE LA
19 THAIDEN ST
20 BRIDGE BLDGS

21 BEDFORD ROW
22 SOMERSET PL
23 DIAMOND ST
24 BELLE MEADOW CT

F6
1 ST MARGARETS GDN
2 LOWER ALMSHOUSES

3 REFORM ST
4 CRANLEIGH
5 YEO VALE HO
6 HALDENE TERR
7 MAPLES CT
8 WARWICK TERR
9 KINGSLEY AVE

10 MARGROVE TERR
11 BOUTPORT ST (MERMAID WLK)
12 GEORGE ST
13 KING EDWARD ST
14 CHARLES ST
15 SEVEN TH ST

CHURCH PATH 1
DARK LA 2
TEOFFE COTTS 3
BEECHGROVE TERR 4
MASEFIELD AVE 5
RALEIGH LAWN 6

A2
1 THE COOMBES
2 WOODLARK LA
3 SKYLARK SPINNEY
4 HIGHER WESTLAKE RD
5 LARK RISE
6 WESTER-MOOR CL

B3
1 YELLAFORD WAY
2 HONEYSUCKLE CL
3 MEADOWSWEET LA
4 CORNFLOWER CL

C2
1 HORNBEAM HOLLOW
2 ROWAN PK
3 ALMOND CT
4 HAZEL GR
5 SILVER BIRCH CT

C3
1 DUNNING GN
2 DEPTFORD VILLAS
3 OAKHILL RISE

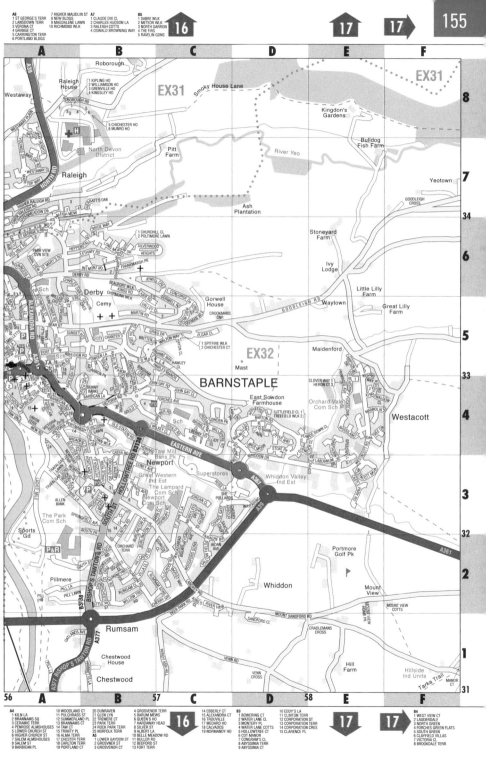

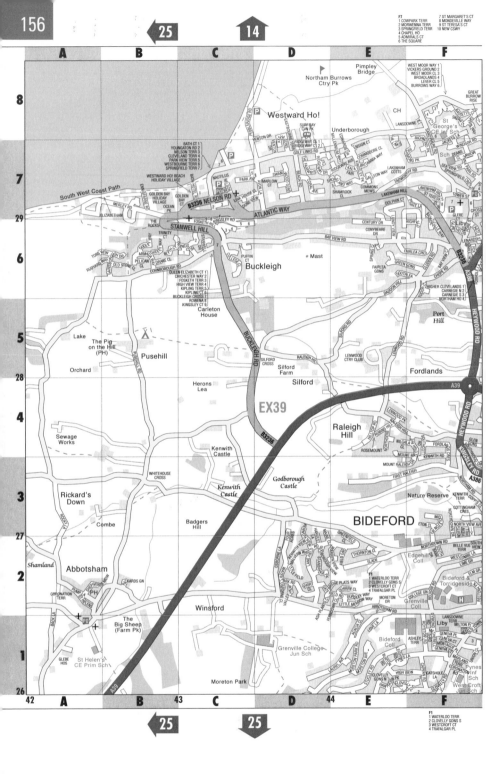

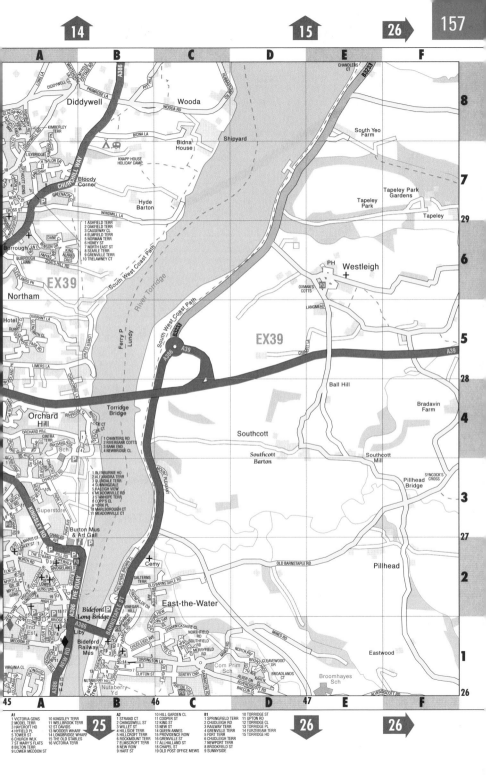

A   B   C   D   E   F

Diddywell

Wooda

Shipyard

South Yeo Farm

Knapp House Holiday Camp

Bidna House

Bloody Corner

Hyde Barton

Tapeley Park Gardens

Tapeley Park

Tapeley

1 ASHFIELD TERR
2 OAKFIELD TERR
3 CAUSEWAY CL
4 ELMFIELD TERR
5 NORMAN TERR
6 HONEY ST
7 NORTH EAST ST
8 SEARLE TERR
9 GRENVILLE TERR
10 TRELAWNEY CT

EX39

Northam

Westleigh

OXMAN'S COTTS

LANGMEAD

Hotel

Ferry P Lundy

EX39

South West Coast Path

River Torridge

Ball Hill

Bradavin Farm

Orchard Hill

Torridge Bridge

Southcott

Southcott Barton

Southcott Mill

SYNCOCK'S CROSS

Pillhead Bridge

1 CHANTERS RD
2 RIVERBANK COTTS
3 BANK END
4 NEWBRIDGE CL

1 GLENBURNIE HO
2 ALEXANDRA TERR
3 GLINDALE TERR
4 SUNNINGDALE
5 RALEIGH VIEW
6 MEADOWVILLE RD
7 STANHOPE TERR
8 CORY'S CL
9 YORK PL
10 MARLBOROUGH CT
11 MEADOWVILLE CT

Superstore

Burton Mus & Art Gall

Cerny

OLD BARNSTAPLE RD

Pillhead

SALTERNS TERR

East-the-Water

Bideford Long Bridge

MINES RD

Bideford Railway Mus

NORTH AV

CLEAVEWOOD DR

BROADLANDS CT

Broomhayes Sch

Eastwood

Com Prim Sch

Virginia CL

Nutaberry Yd

A1
1 VICTORIA GDNS
2 MODEL TERR
3 HAYCROFT HO
4 HYFIELD PL
5 TOWER ST
6 CHURCH WLK
7 ST MARY'S FLATS
8 BILTON TERR
9 LOWER MEDDON ST

10 KINGSLEY TERR
11 WELLBROOK TERR
12 ST DAVIDS
13 WOODER WHARF
14 LONGBRIDGE WHARF
15 THE OLD STABLES
16 VICTORIA TERR

A2
1 STRAND CT
2 CHINGSWELL ST
3 WILLET ST
4 HILLSIDE TERR
5 HILLCROFT TERR
6 ROCKMOUNT TERR
7 ELMSCROFT TERR
8 NEW ROW
9 HART ST

10 HILL GARDEN CL
11 COOPER ST
12 KING ST
13 NEW ST
14 QUEEN ANNES
15 PROVIDENCE ROW
16 GRENVILLE ST
17 ALLHALLAND ST
18 CHAPEL ST
19 OLD POST OFFICE MEWS

B1
1 SPRINGFIELD TERR
2 CHUDLEIGH RD
3 RAILWAY TERR
4 GRENVILLE TERR
5 FORT TERR
6 CHUDLEIGH TERR
7 NEWPORT TERR
8 BROOKFIELD ST
9 SUNNYSIDE

10 TORRIDGE ST
11 UPTON RD
12 TORRIDGE CL
13 TORRIDGE PL
14 FURZEBEAM TERR
15 TORRIDGE HO

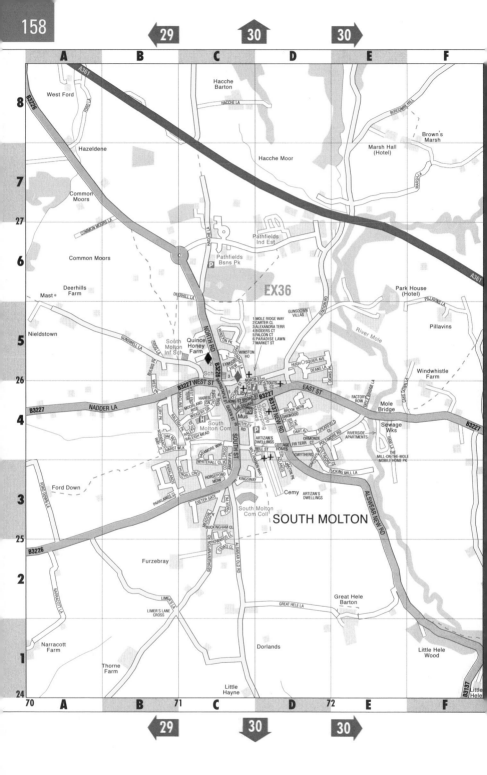

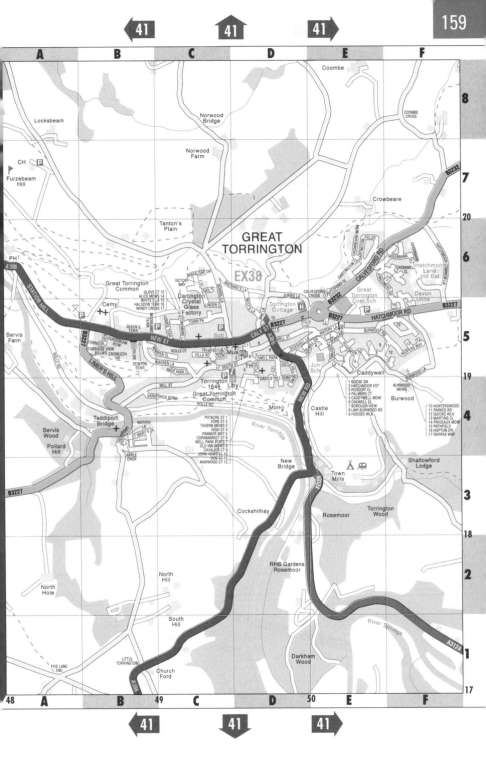

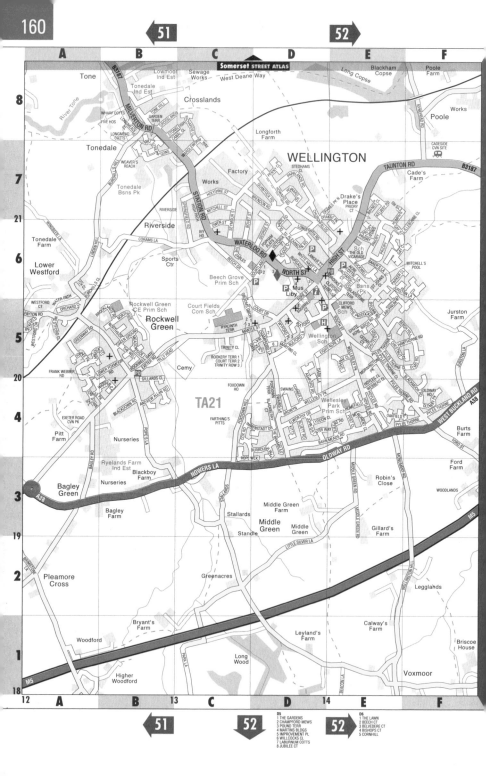

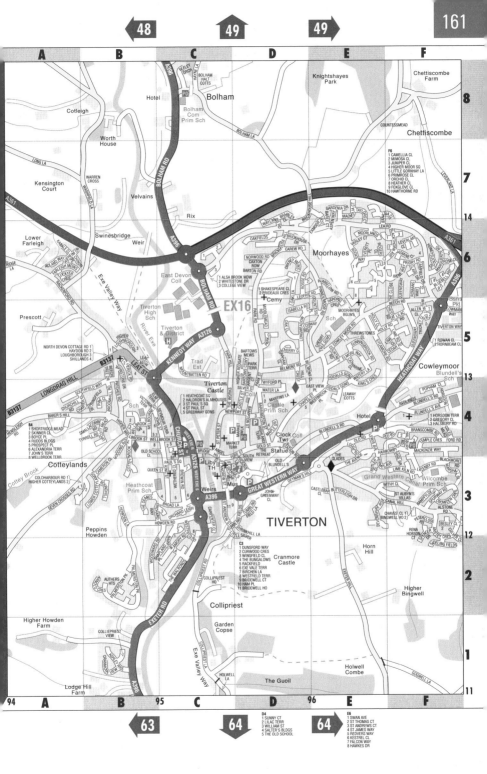

A   B   C   D   E   F

8

Chettiscombe Farm

Knightshayes Park

Hotel   Bolham

Bolham Halt Cotts

PD

Bolham Com Prim Sch

Cotleigh

COUNTESSMEAD

BOLHAM LA

Chettiscombe

Worth House

Long La

7

Kensington Court

WARREN CROSS

WASFIELD LA

Velvains

BOLHAM RD

A396

F6
1 CAMELLIA CL
2 MIMOSA CL
3 JUNIPER CL
4 HIGHER MOOR SQ
5 LITTLE GORNHAY LA
6 PRIMROSE CL
7 ORCHID CL
8 HEATHER CL
9 FOXGLOVE CL
10 HAWTHORNE RD

A361

Rix

14

Lower Farleigh

Swinesbridge   Weir

Exe Valley Way

River Exe

GARDENIA DR

WAYLAND

BRAMLA

A361

Moorhayes

6

Prescott

East Devon Coll

1 ALSA BROOK MDW
2 WHITESTONE DR
3 COLLEGE VIEW

NORWOOD RD
CAXTON ROW
BARTON RD
CAREW RD

OAKFIELDS

EX16

Cemy

1 SHAKESPEARE CL
2 PRIDEAUX CRES

Sch

MOORLANDS

A396

Bsns Pk
COWMAN WAY

NORTH DEVON COTTAGE RD 1
HAYDON RD 2
LOUGHBOROUGH 3
SHILLANDS 4

Tiverton High Sch

HIGHER

Tiverton & District

H

KENNEDY WAY

A3126

BOLHAM RD

ISABELLA ST

MOORHAYES BGLWS

THREESTONES

TIVERTON WAY

5

B3137

LONGDRAG HILL

Tiverton Castle

Trad Est

1 HEATHCOAT SQ
2 HALDRON'S ALMSHOUSES
3 ST PAUL'S SQ
4 ST PAUL ST
5 GREENWAY GDNS

Tiverton Castle Prim Sch

EAST VIEW

LEAWAY COTTS

Cowleymoor   Blundell's Sch

13

Cottey Brook

B4
1 SHORTRIDGE MEAD
2 SKINNER CL
3 BOYCE PL
4 RUDDS BLDGS
5 PROSPECT PL
6 ALEXANDRIA TERR
7 JOHN'S TERR
8 WELLBROOK TERR

Cotteylands

CHURCH ST

A3126

Liby
TH

Mus

Tiverton Castle

SILVER ST
WATER LA

NEWPORT ST

Coll

Clock Twr

OLD BLUNDELL'S

Coll
GOLD ST

Statue

BLUNDELL'S RD

1 HEATHCOAT SQ

Hotel

P

1 HORSDOM END
2 GREGORY CL
3 HALSBURY RD

BLUNDELL'S AVE

BRANSCOMBE

4

COLDHARBOUR RD 1
HIGHER COTTEYLANDS 2

Heathcoat Prim Sch

Queen St

Weirs

A396

GREAT WESTERN WAY

JOHN GREENWAY CL

THE CLADES
THE AVENUE

Grand Western Canal

Wilcombe Prim Sch

BLACKMORE

ALSTONE RD

3

Peppins Howden

ORCHARD LEIGH

HOWDEN RD

CAMPFIELD

BRINKHILL LA

TIVERTON

Cranmore Castle

CHAVES CL 1
BINGWELL HO 2

RENA HORSON

PEELING FIELDS

12

C3
1 DUNSFORD WAY
2 CURWOOD CRES
3 WINGFIELD CL
4 THE BUNGALOWS
5 RACKFIELD
6 EXE VALE TERR
7 BIRCHEN LA
8 WESTFIELD TERR
9 BRIDEWELL CT
10 HAM PL
11 BRIDEWELL HO

Horn Hill

2

AUTHERS HTS

PALMERSTON PK

COLLIPRIEST RD

Collipriest

Garden Copse

Higher Bingwell

Higher Howden Farm

EXETER RD

COLLIPRIEST VIEW

Exe Valley Way

HOLWELL LA

Holwell Combe

1

Lodge Hill Farm

A396

The Guoil

11

94   A   B   95   C   D   96   E   F

D4
1 SUNNY CT
2 LILAC TERR
3 WILLIAM ST
4 SALTER'S BLDGS
5 THE OLD SCHOOL

E6
1 SWAN AVE
2 ST THOMAS CT
3 ST ANDREWS CT
4 ST JAMES WAY
5 REDVERS WAY
6 KESTREL CL
7 FALCON WAY
8 HAWKES DR

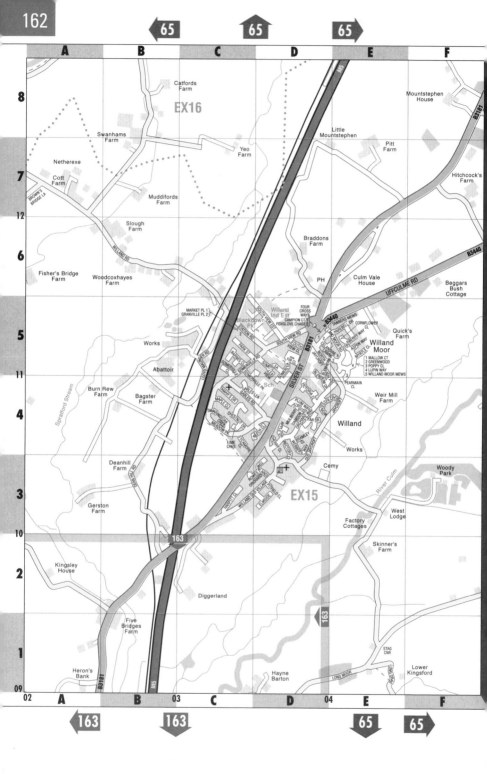

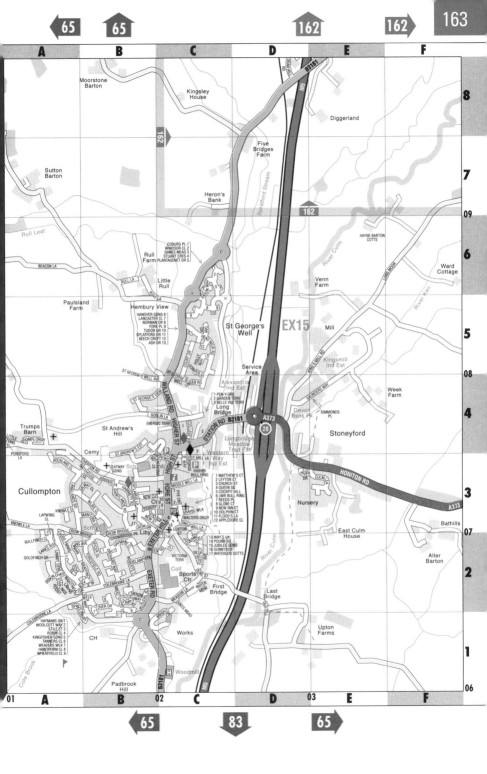

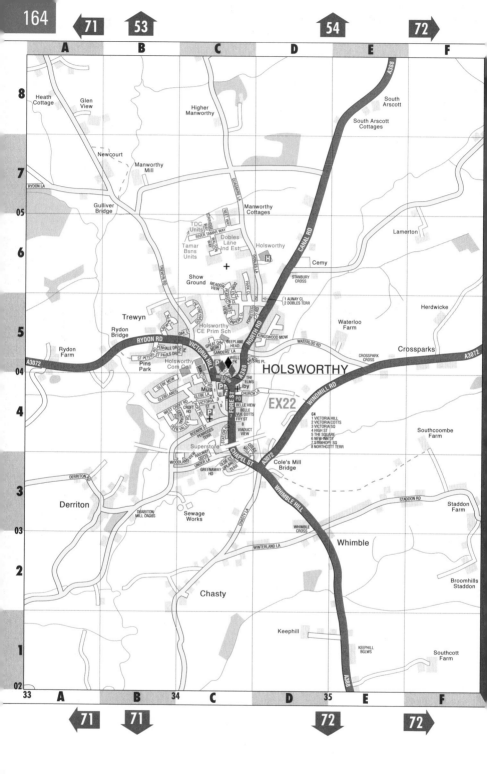

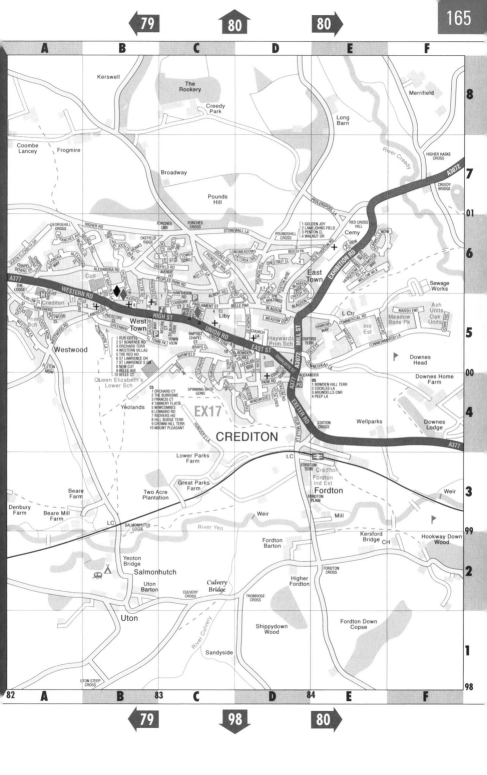

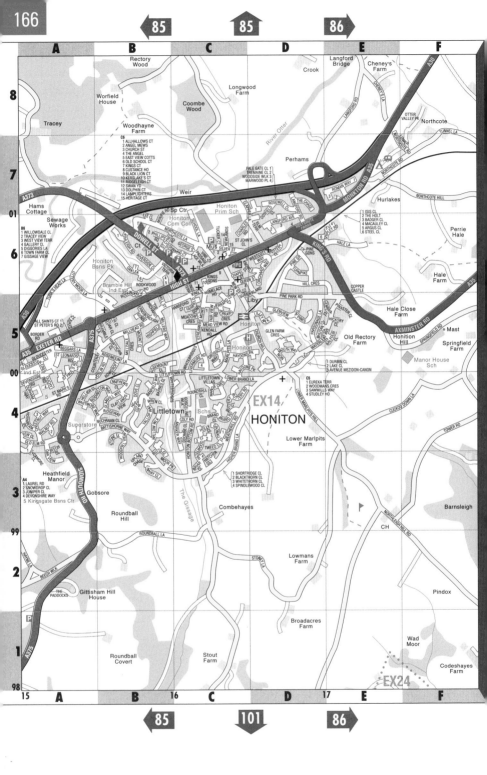

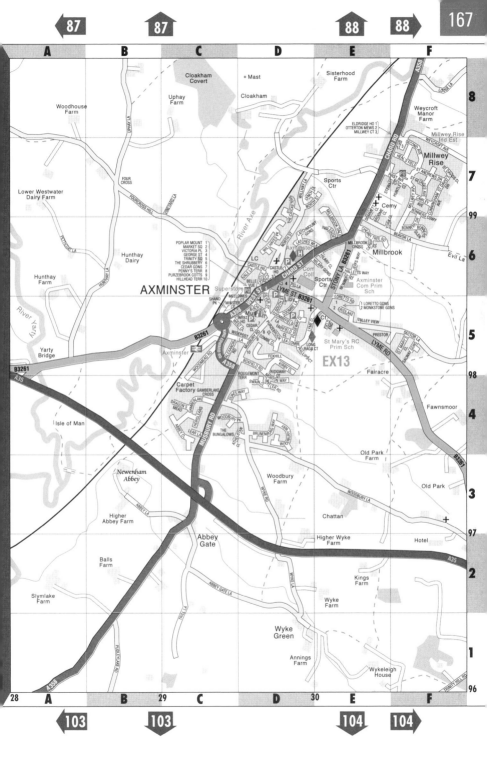

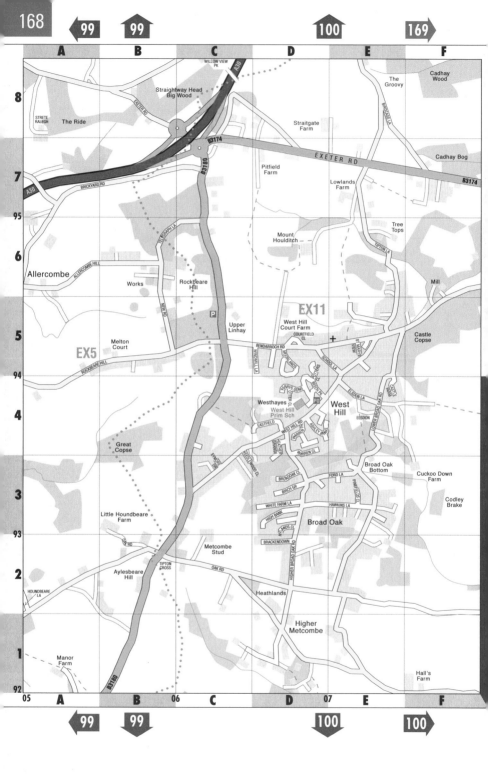

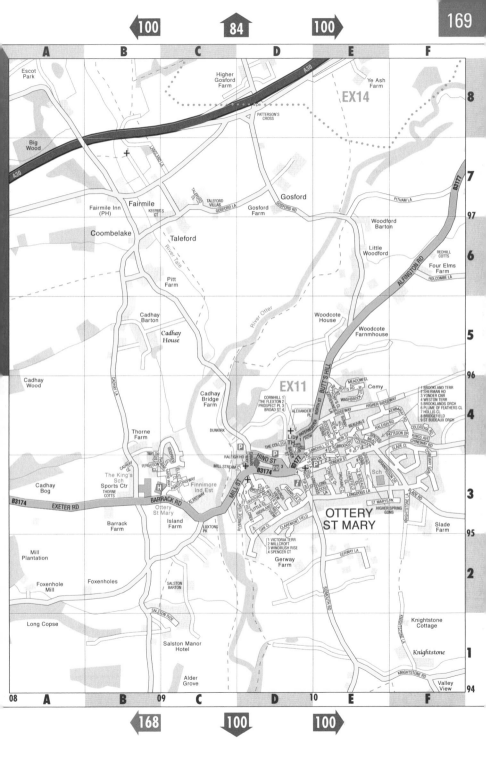

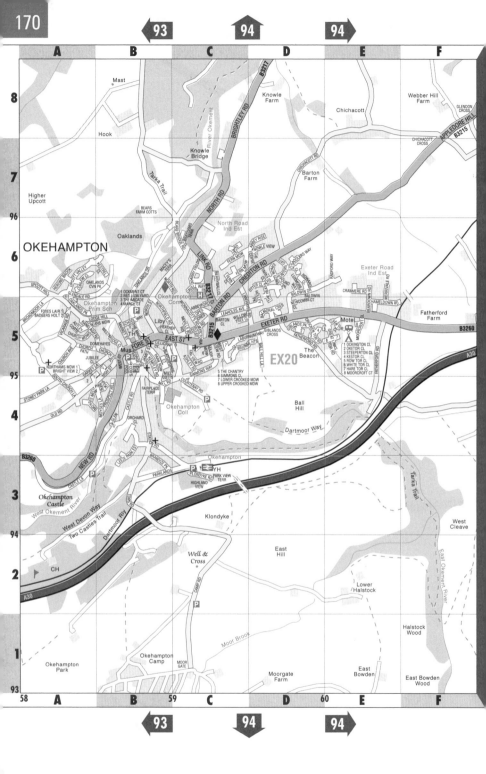

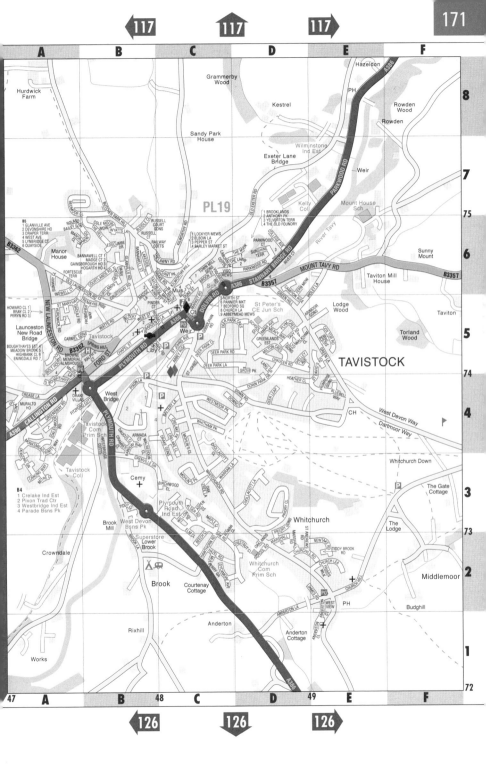

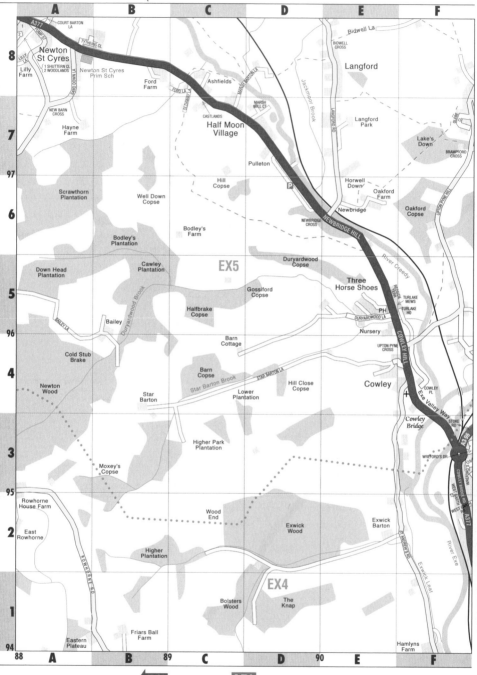

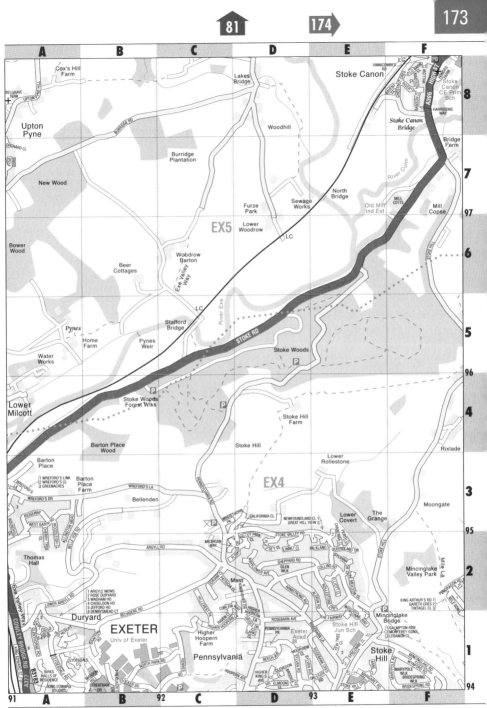

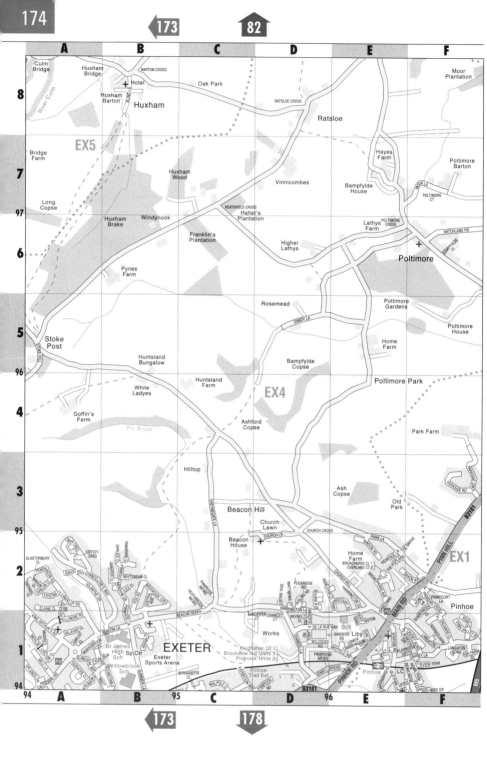

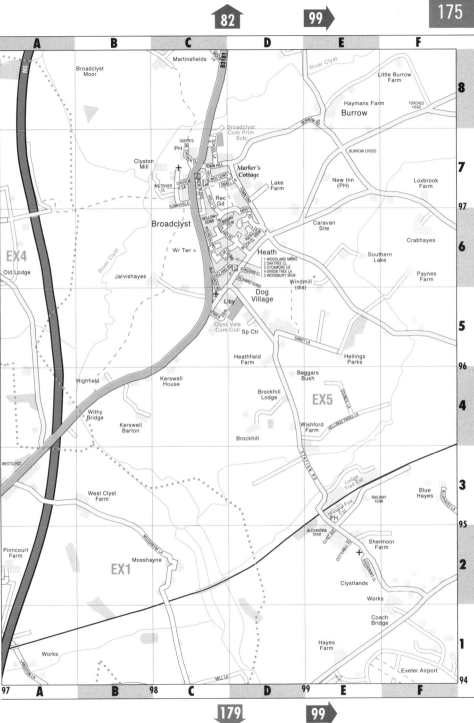

82   99

A   B   C   D   E   F

Martinsfields

Broadclyst
Moor

Little Burrow
Farm

River Clyst

8

Haymans Farm
Burrow

FORCHES
HEAD

Broadclyst
Com Prim
Sch

QUEEN'S
SQ

PH

BURROW RD

BURROW CROSS

7

Clyston
Mill

WILTSHIER
CL

Marker's
Cottage

Lake
Farm

New Inn
(PH)

Loxbrook
Farm

97

Broadclyst

Rec
Gd

SUNNYFIELD

WILLOW
GDNS

BROAD
VIEW

Caravan
Site

Crabhayes

6

Wr Twr

Heath

ELM CL

1 WOODLAND MEWS
2 OAKTREE CL
3 SYCAMORE CL
4 GREEN TREE LA
5 WOODBURY VIEW

Southern
Lake

Paynes
Farm

EX4

Old Lodge

Jarvishayes

River Clyst

P

SANDERS CL

ORCHARD GDNS

Liby

Windmill
(dis)

Dog
Village

5

Clyst Vale
Com Coll

Sp Ctr

SANDY LA

Hellings
Parks

96

Heathfield
Farm

Beggars
Bush

EX5

4

Highfield

Kerswell
House

Brockhill
Lodge

COUNCIL LA

HELLINGS PARKS LA

Withy
Bridge

Kerswell
Barton

Brockhill

Wishford
Farm

WESTCLYST

West Clyst
Farm

Lodge
Trad Est

Blue
Hayes

BLUEHAYES LA

3

RAILWAY
TERR

STATION RD

Happy Fox
PH

95

Pinncourt
Farm

EX1

Mosshayne

MOSSHAYNE LA

ALEXANDRA
TERR

CLYST RISE

COTTERELL RD

SHERCROFT CL

Shermoor
Farm

2

Clystlands

Works

Works

Coach
Bridge

1

Hayes
Farm

Exeter Airport

LANGATON LA

MILL LA

94

97   A   B   98   C   D   99   E   F

179   99

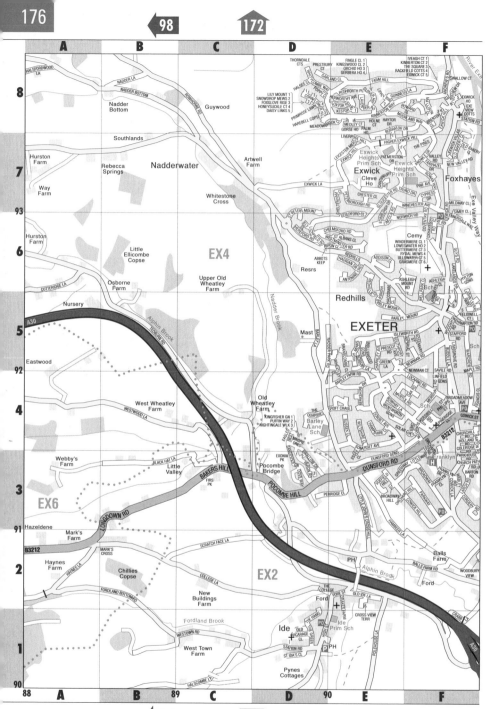

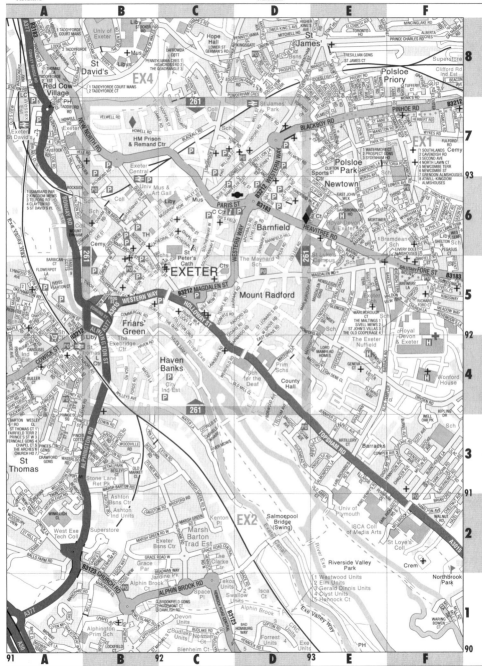

177

174

C8
1 MARK TWAIN HO
2 FLAYES ALMSHOUSES
3 PEEL ROW
4 ROYSTON CT

D5
1 NELSON WAY
2 WELLINGTON CL
3 THE SQUARE
4 ALEXANDER WLK
5 DRAKE AVE
6 MONTGOMERY RD

7 CROMWELL TERR
8 3RD AVE
9 MARLBOROUGH DR
10 BADGER CL

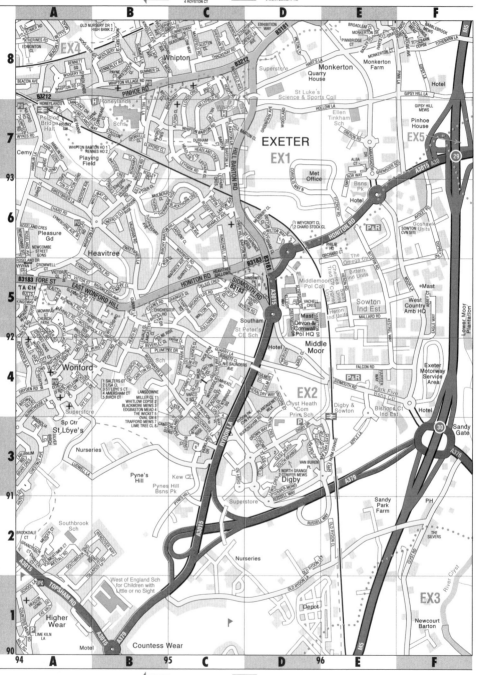

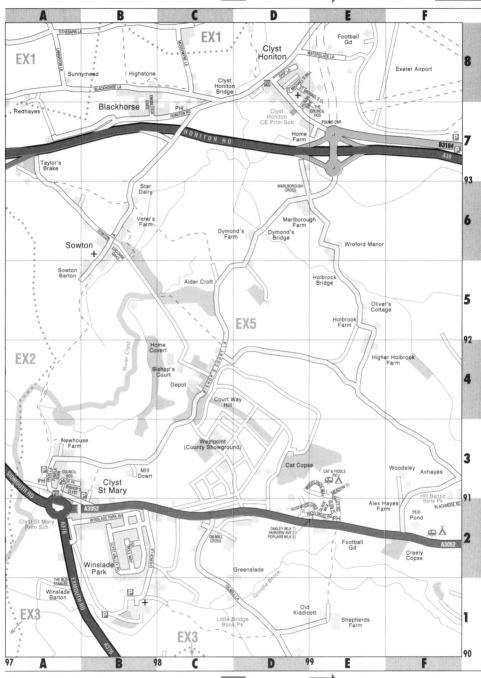

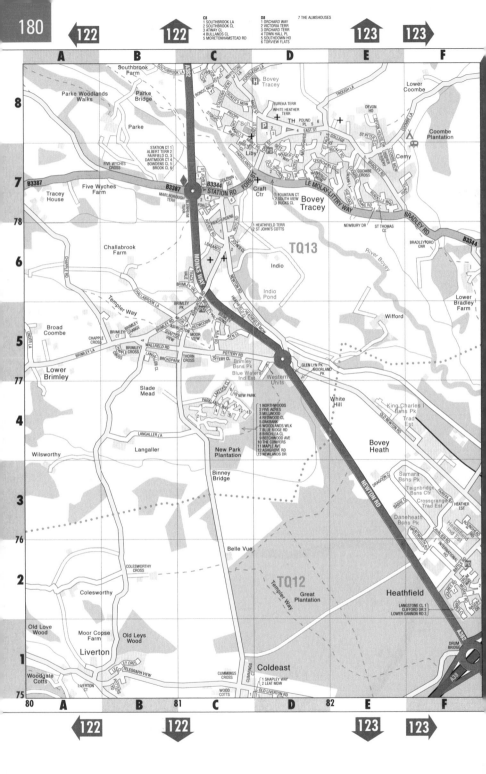

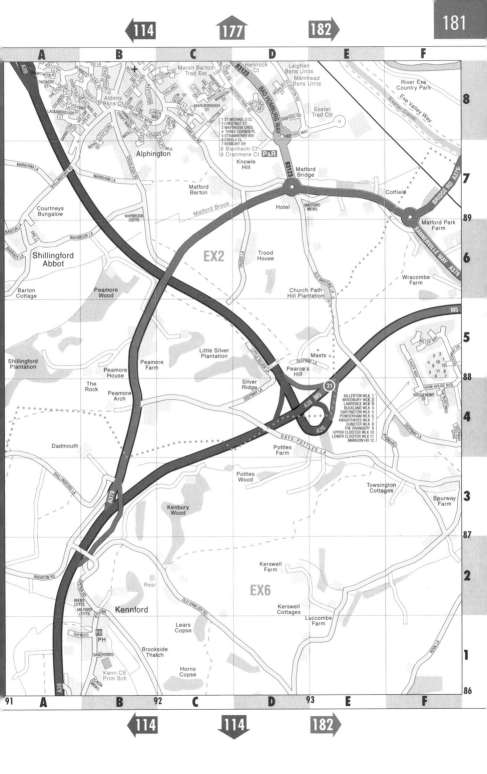

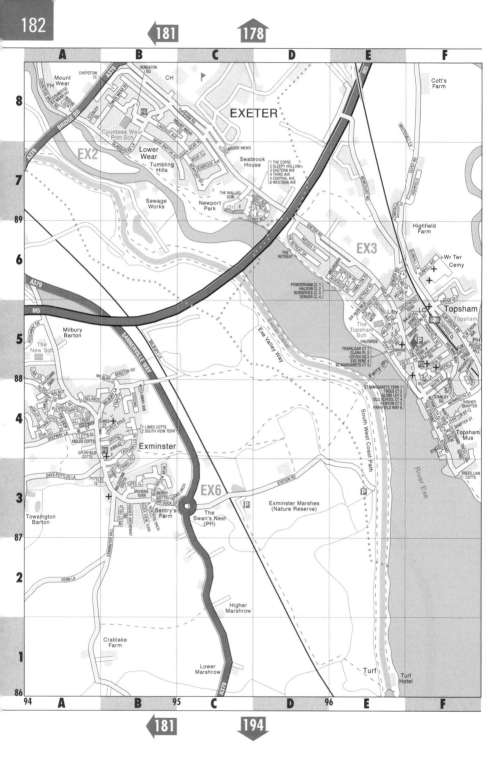

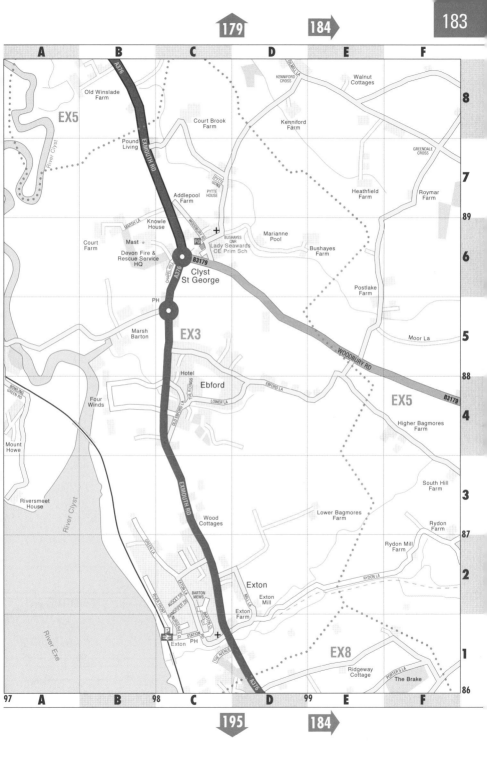

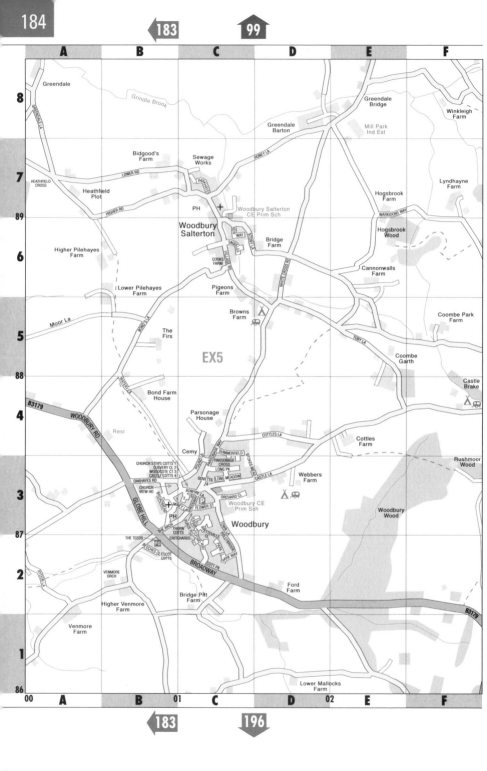

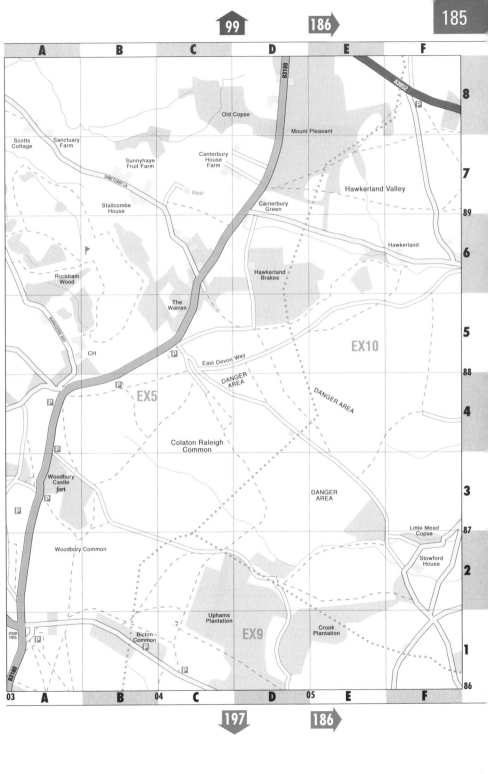

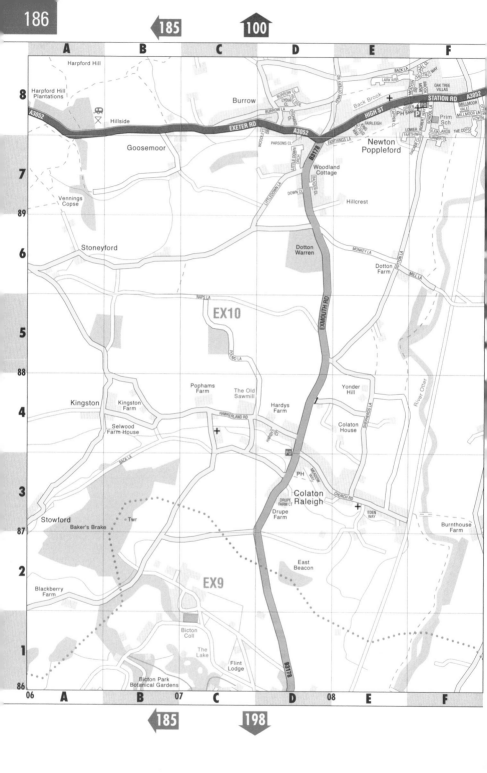

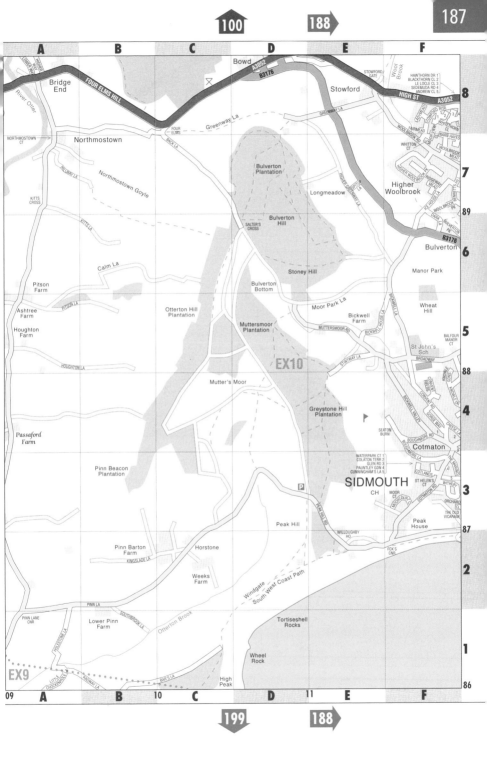

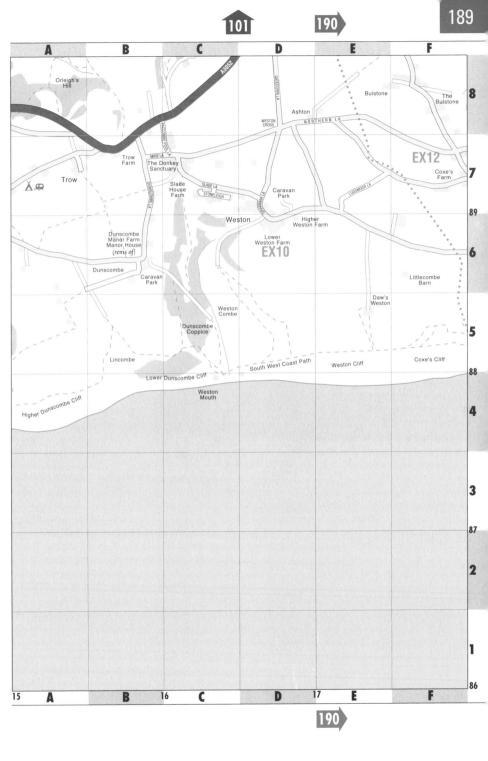

101
102

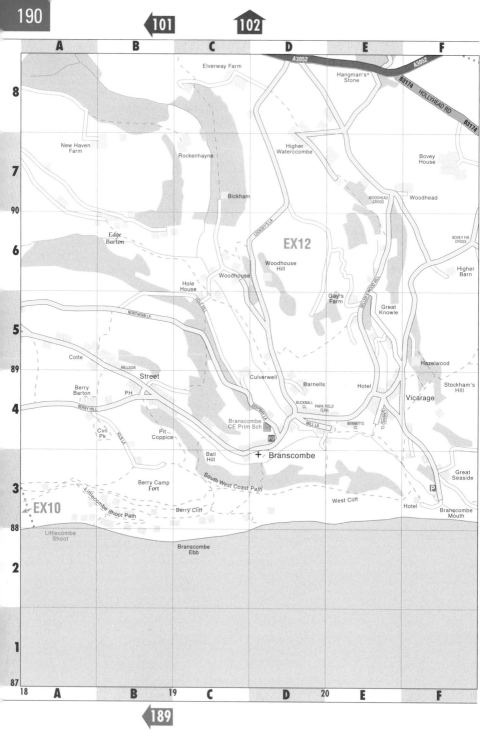

189

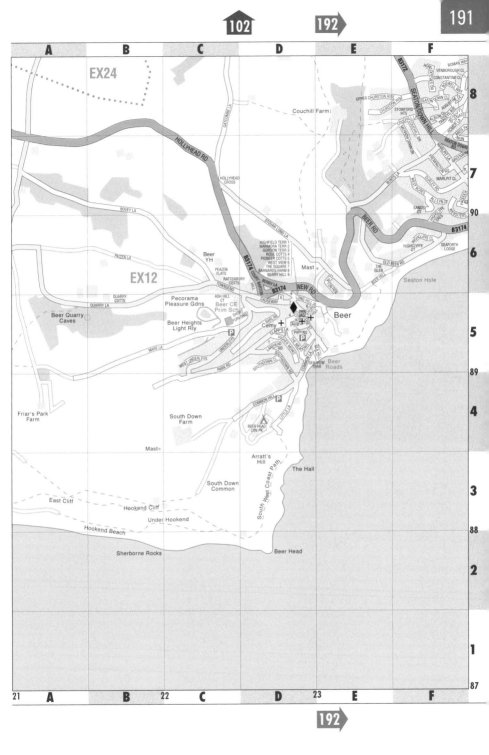

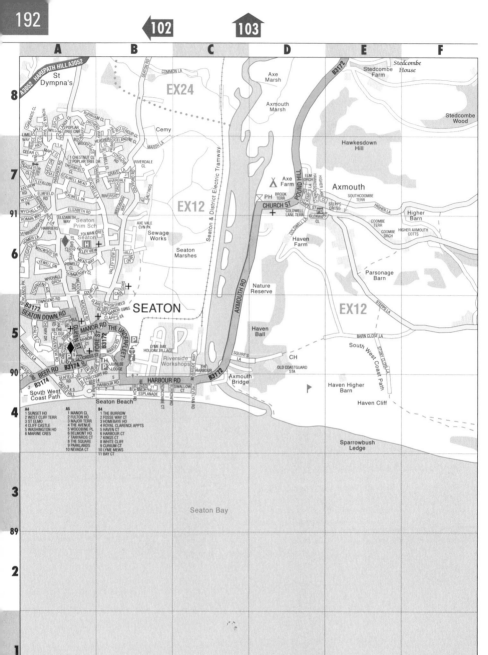

102
103
191

EX24

EX12

EX12

SEATON

Axe Marsh

Axmouth Marsh

Stedcombe Farm

Stedcombe House

Hawkesdown Hill

Axmouth

Stedcombe Wood

St Dympna's

Seaton Prim Sch

Sewage Works

Seaton Marshes

Nature Reserve

Haven Ball

Haven Farm

Parsonage Barn

Higher Barn

Higher Axmouth Cotts

South West Coast Path

Haven Higher Barn

Haven Cliff

Sparrowbush Ledge

Seaton Bay

Seaton Beach

South West Coast Path

Axmouth Bridge

Old Coastguard Sta

CHURCH ST

AXMOUTH RD

HARBOUR RD

SEATON DOWN RD

BEER RD

Axe Farm

A5
1 SUNSET HO
2 WEST CLIFF TERR
3 ST ELMO
4 CLIFF CASTLE
5 WASHINGTON HO
6 MARINE CRES

A5
1 MANOR CL
2 FULTON HO
3 MAJOR TERR
4 THE AVENUE
5 WOODBINE PL
6 BELMONT HO
7 TANYARDS CT
8 THE SQUARE
9 PARKLANDS
10 NEVADA CT

B4
1 THE BURROW
2 FOSSE WAY CT
3 HOMEBAYE HO
4 ROYAL CLARENCE APPTS
5 HAVEN CT
6 HARBOUR CT
7 KINGS CT
8 WHITE CLIFF
9 CURIUM CT
10 LYME MEWS
11 BAY CT

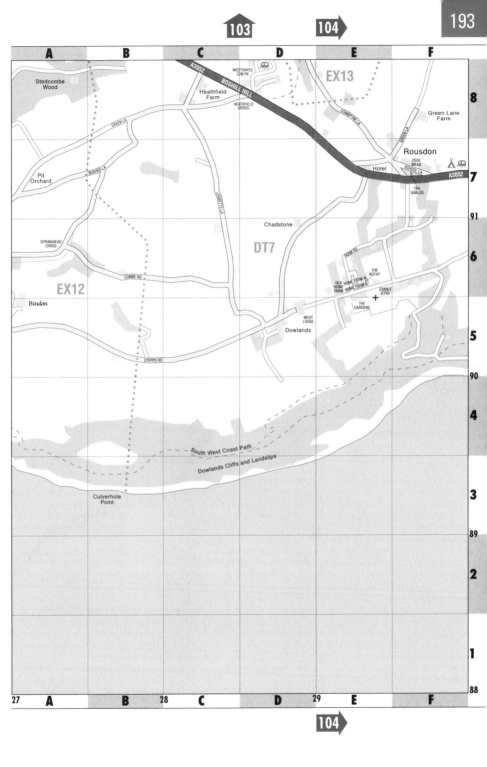

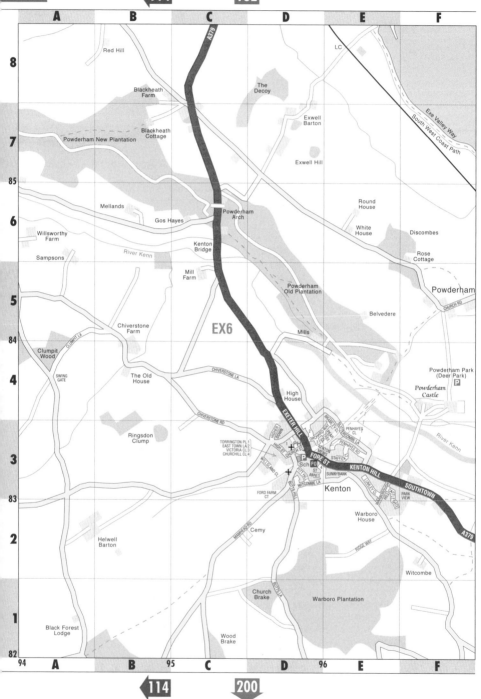

114
182

A · B · C · D · E · F

8

Red Hill

The Decoy

LC

Blackheath
Farm

Exwell
Barton

7

Blackheath
Cottage

Exe Valley Way

Powderham New Plantation

South West Coast Path

Exwell Hill

85

Round
House

6

Mellands

Powderham
Arch

White
House

Discombes

Gos Hayes

Willsworthy
Farm

Kenton
Bridge

River Kenn

Rose
Cottage

Sampsons

Mill
Farm

Powderham
Old Plantation

Powderham

5

EX6

Belvedere

CHURCH RD

84

Chiverstone
Farm

Mills

Clumpit
Wood

CLUMPIT LA

SWING
GATE

The Old
House

CHIVERSTONE LA

Powderham Park
(Deer Park)

4

High
House

Powderham
Castle

CHIVERSTONE RD

Ringsdon
Clump

River Kenn

EXETER HILL

BRACKET CL

PENHAYES
CL

ORCHARD WAY

COMBE LA

3

TORRINGTON PL 1
EAST TOWN LA 2
VICTORIA CL 3
CHURCHILL CL 4

PH

FORE ST

KENTON

STAFFICK

PENHAYES RD

CHURCH ST

HIGH ST

WILLS MEAD CL

P

Sch
PO

ST
ANNES

KENTON HILL

ELIM CL

SOUTHTOWN

83

FORD FARM
CT

BULLER RD

WITCOMBE LA

SUNNYBANK

Kenton

PARK
VIEW

A379

Warboro
House

2

MAMHEAD RD

Cemy

RIDGE WAY

Helwell
Barton

Witcombe

Church
Brake

SOUTH LA

Warboro Plantation

1

Black Forest
Lodge

Wood
Brake

82

94   A · B   95   C · D   96   E · F

114
200

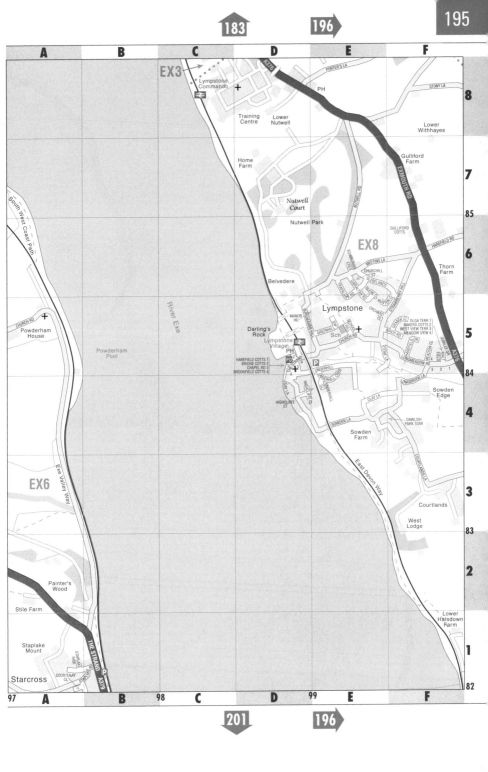

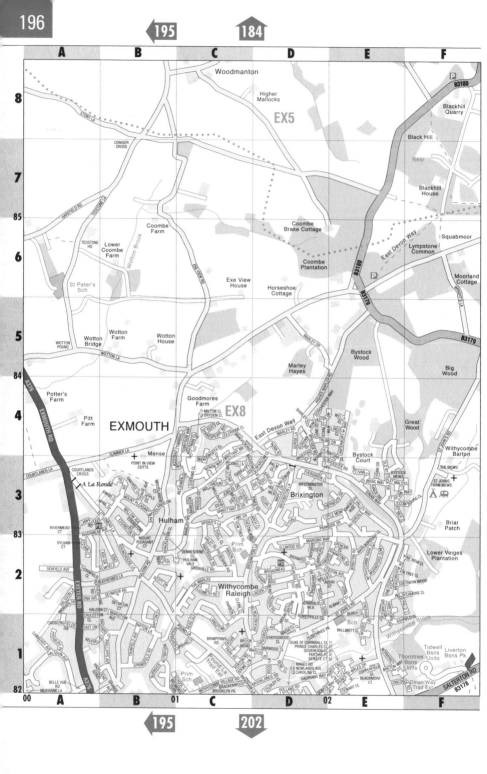

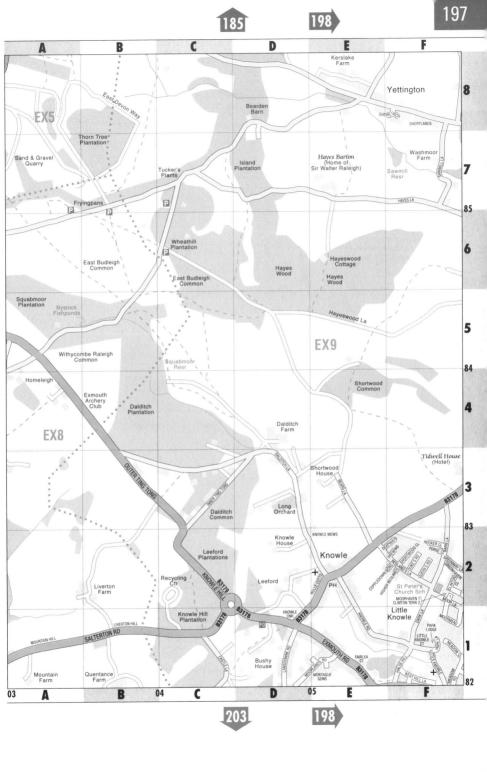

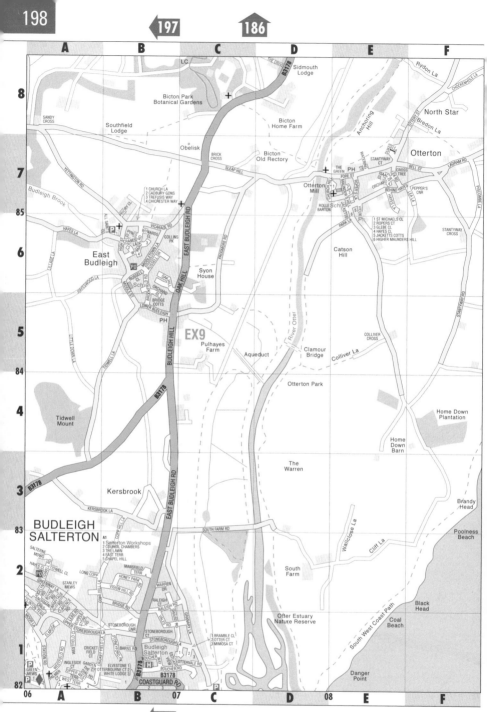

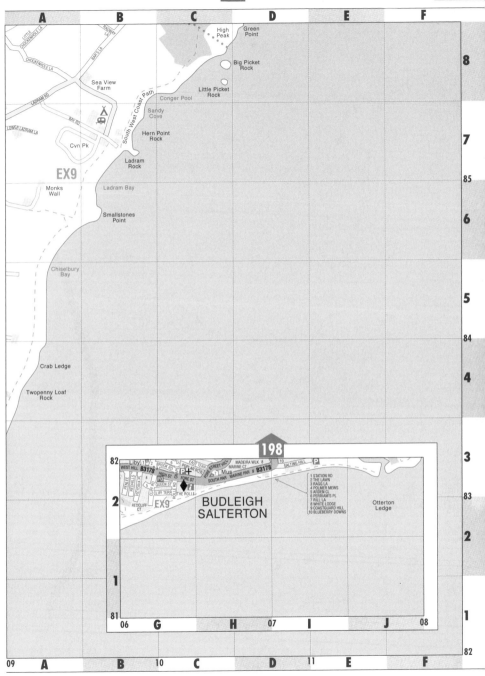

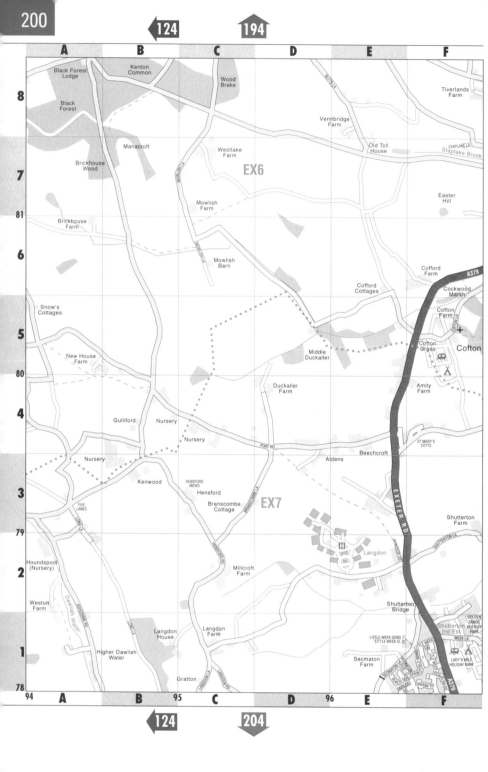

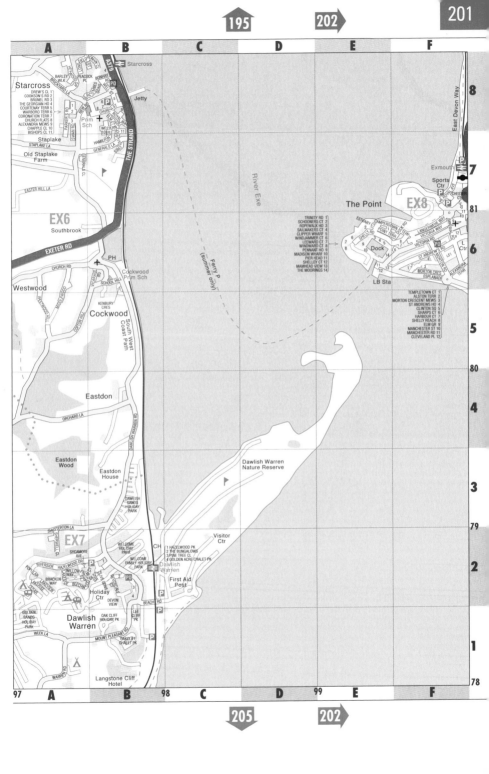

Starcross

Jetty

Starcross

DREW'S CL 1
COOKSON'S RD 2
BRUNEL RD 3
THE GEORGIAN HO 4
COURTENAY TERR 5
WARBORO TERR 6
CORONATION TERR 7
CHURCH FLATS 8
ALEXANDRA MEWS 9
CHAPPLE CL 10
BISHOPS CL 11

Staplake

STAPLAKE LA

Old Staplake Farm

Prim Sch

EXETER RD

EX6

Southbrook

PH

Church Rd

Cockwood Prim Sch

Westwood

KENBURY CRES

Cockwood

SCHOOL HILL

South West Coast Path

Eastdon

ORCHARD LA

Eastdon Wood

Eastdon House

Eastdon

SHUTTERTON LA

EX7

SYCAMORE AVE

WELCOME HOLIDAY PARK

WELCOME FAMILY HOLIDAY PARK

CH

Dawlish Warren

Visitor Ctr

1 HAZELWOOD PK
2 THE BUNGALOWS
3 PINE TREE CL
4 GOLDEN ACRE CHALET PK

First Aid Post

BEACH RD

Holiday Ctr

DEVON VIEW

GOLDEN SANDS HOLIDAY PARK

Dawlish Warren

OAK CLIFF HOLIDAY PK

WEEK LA

MOUNT PLEASANT

OAK CLIFF CHALET PK

Langstone Cliff Hotel

River Exe

Ferry P (summer only)

Dawlish Warren Nature Reserve

The Point

TRINITY RD 1
SCHOONERS CT 2
ROPEWALK HO 3
SAILMAKERS CT 4
CLIPPER WHARF 5
WINDJAMMER CT 6
LEEWARD CT 7
WINDWARD CT 8
PENNANT HO 9
MADISON WHARF 10
PIER HEAD 11
SHELLEY CT 12
MAMHEAD VIEW 13
THE MOORINGS 14

Dock

EX8

Exmouth

Sports Ctr

East Devon Way

LB Sta

TEMPLETOWN CT 1
ALSTON TERR 2
MORTON CRESCENT MEWS 3
ST ANDREWS HO 4
CLINTON SQ 5
SHARPS CT 6
HARBOUR CT 7
SHELLY REACH 8
ELM GR 9
MANCHESTER ST 10
MANCHESTER RD 11
CLEVELAND PL 12

MORTON CRES

ESPLANADE

VICTORIA WAY

LANGERWELE RD

81

80

79

78

8

7

6

5

4

3

2

1

97   98   99

A7
1 GEORGE ST
2 SHUTE MEADOW ST
3 CHARLES ST
4 STAPLES MEWS
5 GLENORCHY CT
6 ALBION CT
7 HENRIETTA PL
8 HENRIETTA RD
9 ALBION TERR
10 PALACE COTTS
11 ALL SAINTS MEWS

Works

EXMOUTH

EX8

Littleham

A6
1 CHAPEL ST
2 MAGNOLIA WLK
3 LOWER FORE ST
4 MARGARET ST
5 UNION ST
6 VICTORIA PL
7 HELENA PL
8 KING ST
9 UPPER CHURCH ST
10 MAGNOLIA HO
11 QUEEN ST
12 QUEEN'S CT
13 TOWER ST
14 CRITERION PL
15 CHAPEL HILL
16 BEACON HILL
17 ALEXANDRA TERR
18 LITTLE BICTON CT
19 THE OLD WEIGHBRIDGE
20 ST SAVIOURS HO
21 DRAY CT
22 ADMIRALS CT
23 PRINCES ST

B6
1 MONTPELLIER CT
2 ASHLEY HO
3 HIGHFIELD CT
4 HAMILTON CT
5 MAGNOLIA CT

PENCARWICK HO 1
ADELAIDE CT 2
LION HO 3
EXECLIFF 4

University of
Plymouth

The Maer

Maer
Farm

Green
Farm

Prattshayes
Farm

Sewage
Works

High Land
of Orcombe

South West Coast Path

Orcombe
Point

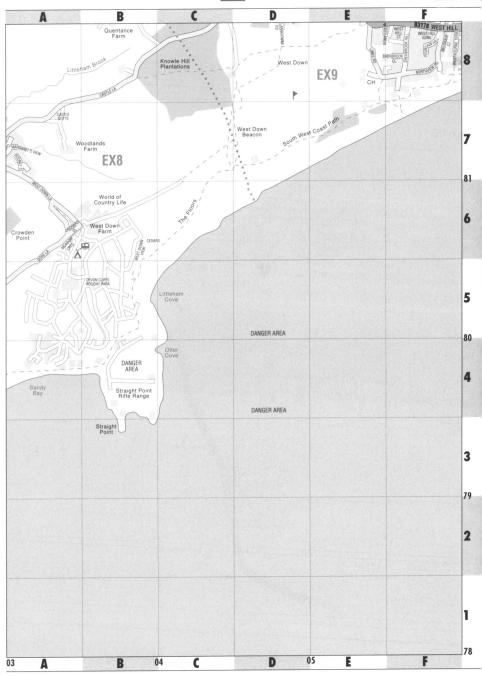

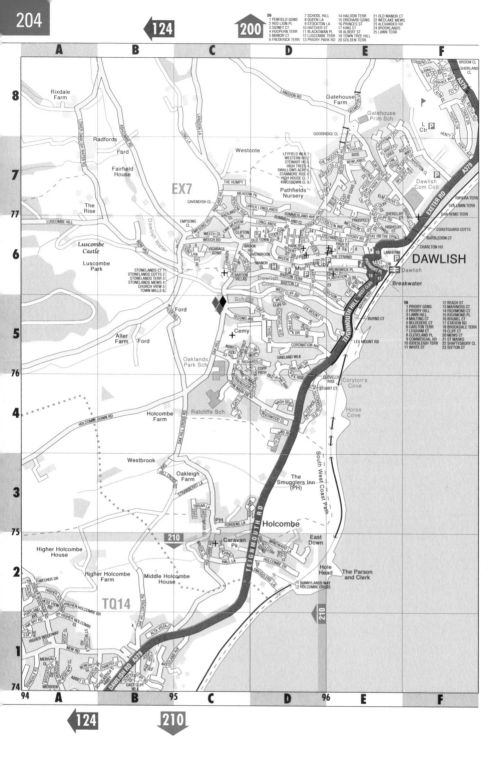

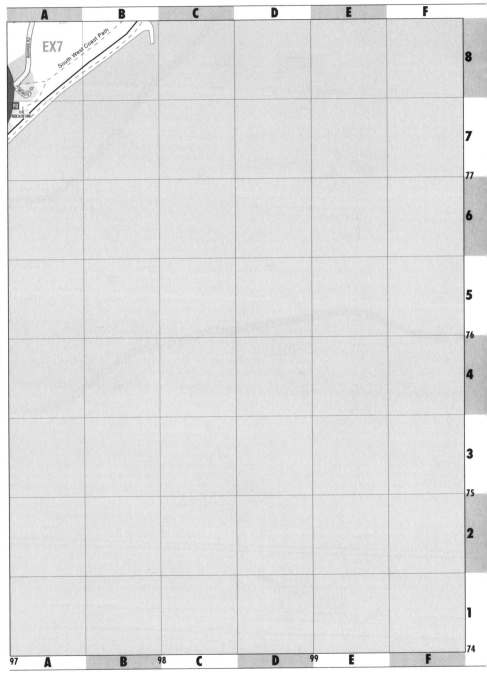

EX7

South West Coast Path

PO
THE
ROCKSTONE

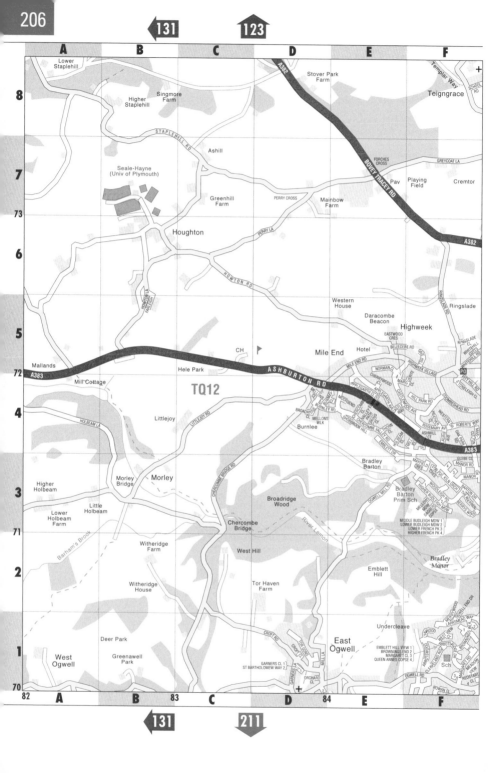

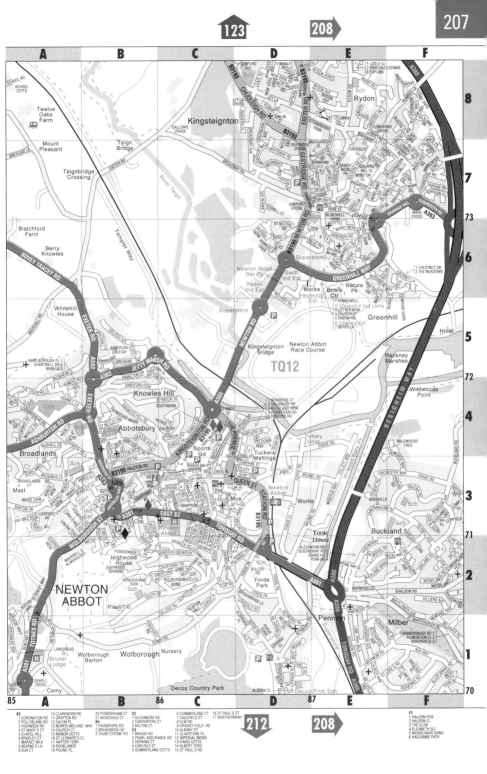

123
208
212
208

207
124

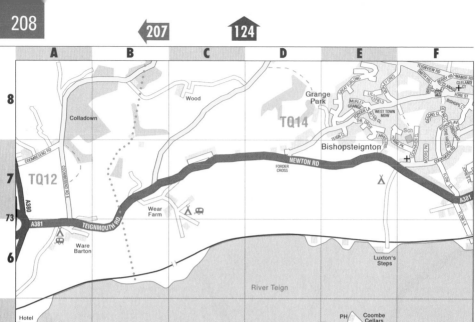

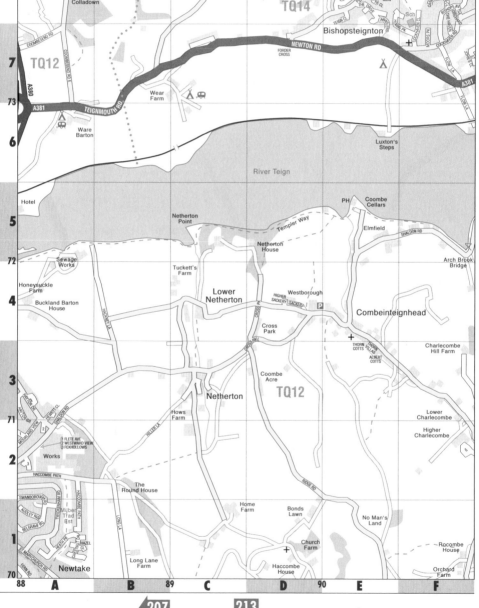

207
213

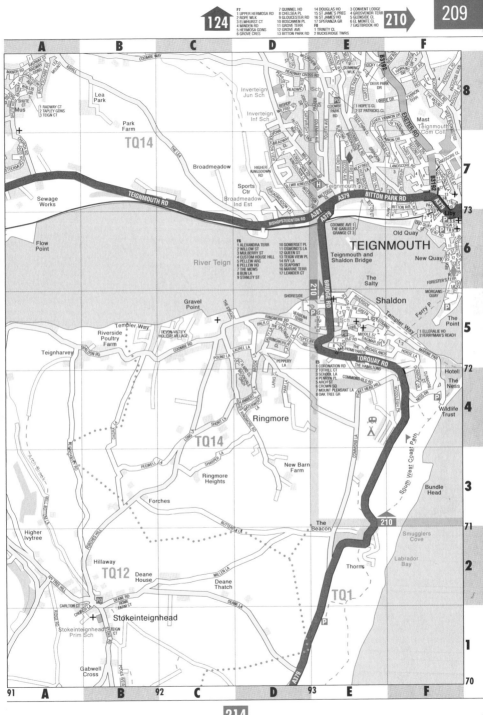

F7
1 UPPER HERMOSA RD
2 ROPE WLK
3 ELMHURST CT
4 MINDEN RD
5 HERMOSA GDNS
6 GROVE CRES

7 QUINNEL HO
8 CHELSEA PL
9 GLOUCESTER RD
10 BOSCAWEN PL
11 GROVE TERR
12 GROVE AVE
13 BITTON PARK RD

14 DOUGLAS HO
15 ST JAME'S PREC
16 ST JAMES HO
17 SPERANZA GR

F8
1 TRINITY CL
2 BUCKERIDGE TERR

3 CONVENT LODGE
4 GROSVENOR TERR
5 GLENSIDE CL
6 EL MONTE CL
7 EASTBROOK HO

F6
1 ALEXANDRA TERR
2 WILLOW ST
3 MULBERRY ST
4 CUSTOM HOUSE HILL
5 PELLEW ARC
6 PELLEW HO
7 THE MEWS
8 BUN LA
9 STANLEY ST
10 SOMERSET PL
11 OSMOND'S LA
12 QUEEN ST
13 TEIGN VIEW PL
14 IVY LA
15 SEAPOINT
16 MARINE TERR
17 LEANDER CT

E5
1 CORONATION RD
2 TOTHILL CT
3 SCHOOL LA
4 PENRYN PL
5 ARCH ST
6 CROWN SQ
7 MOUNT PLEASANT LA
8 OAK TREE GR

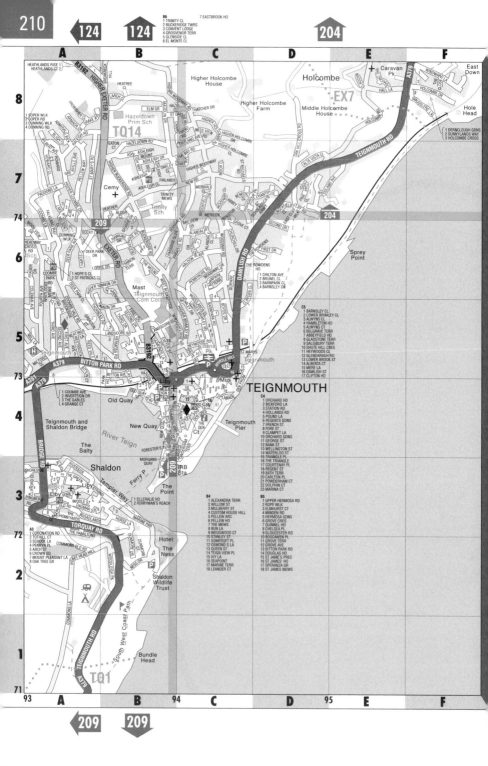

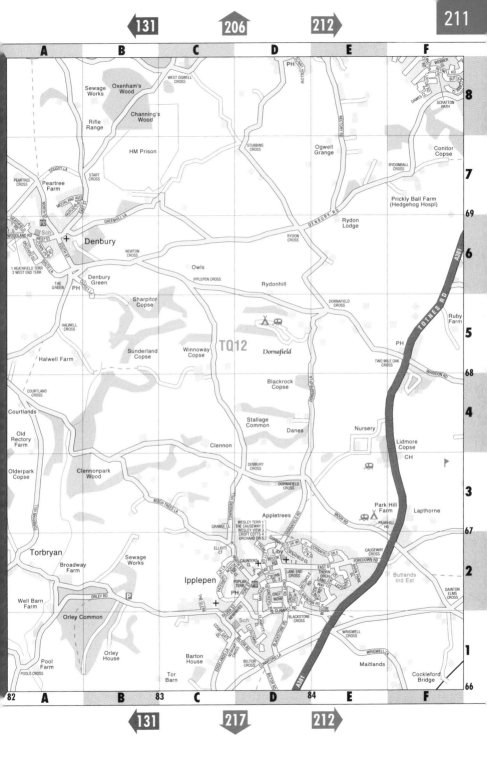

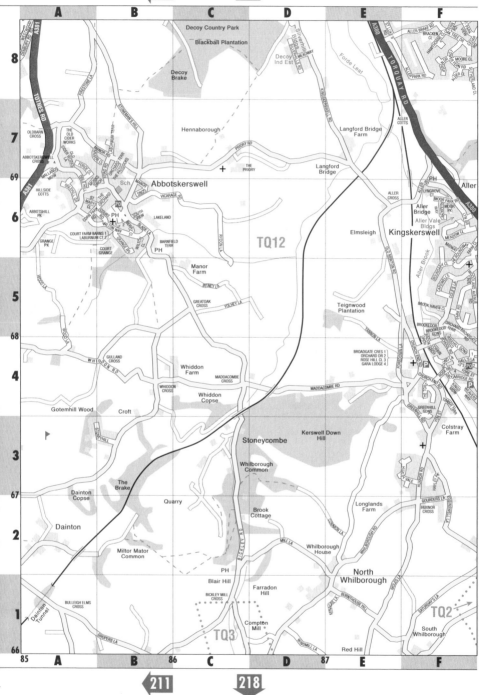

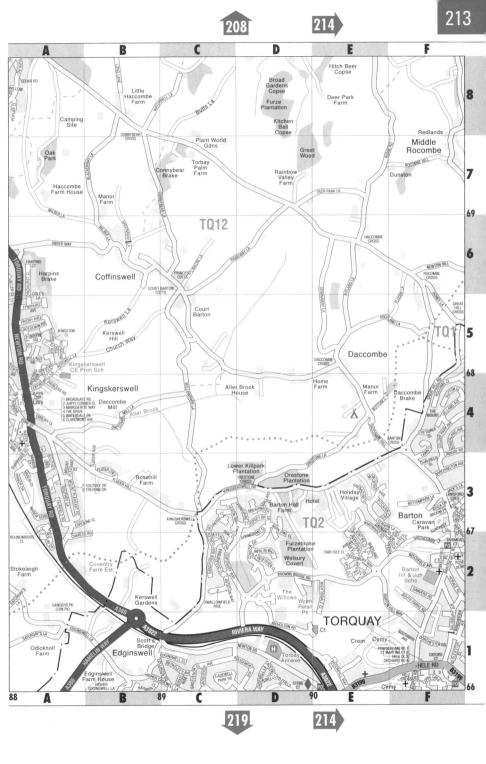

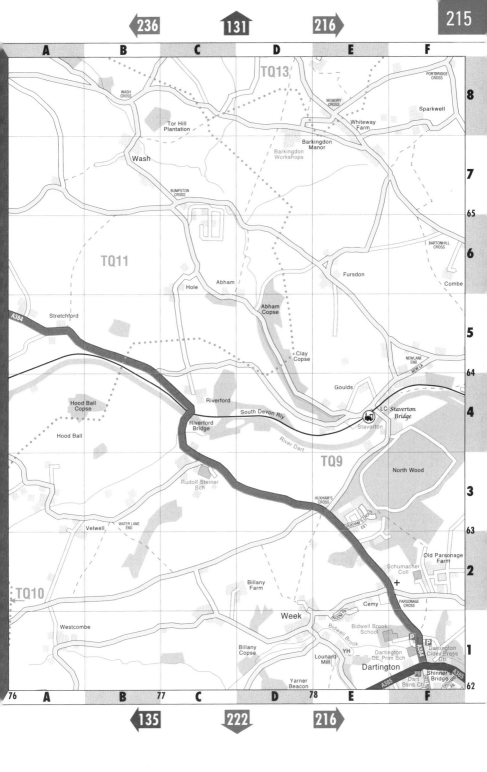

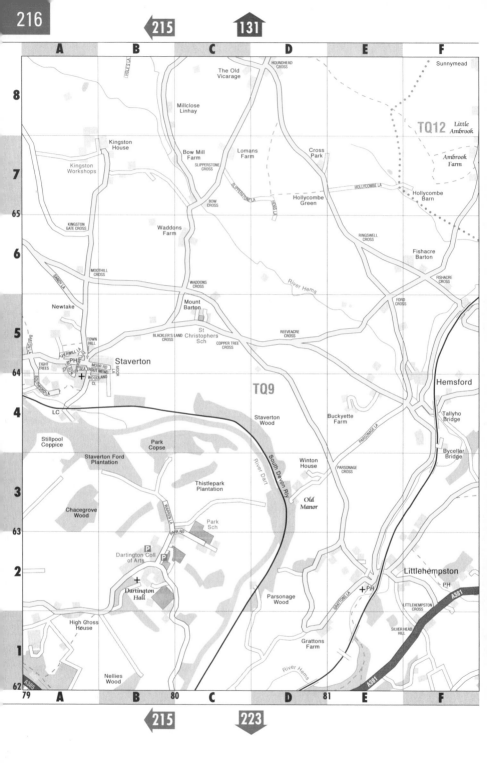

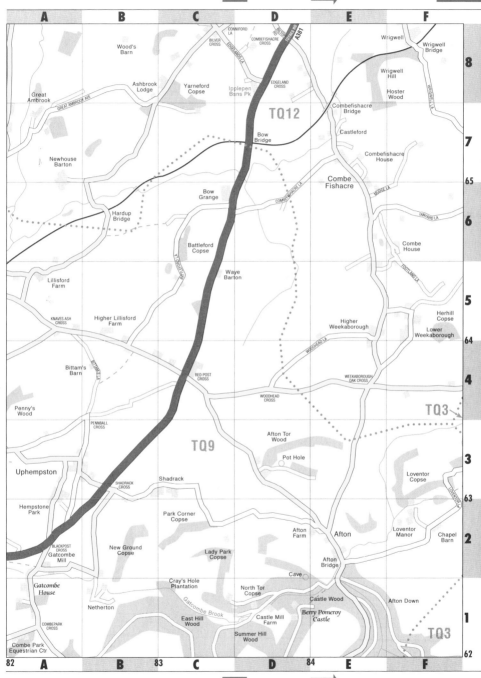

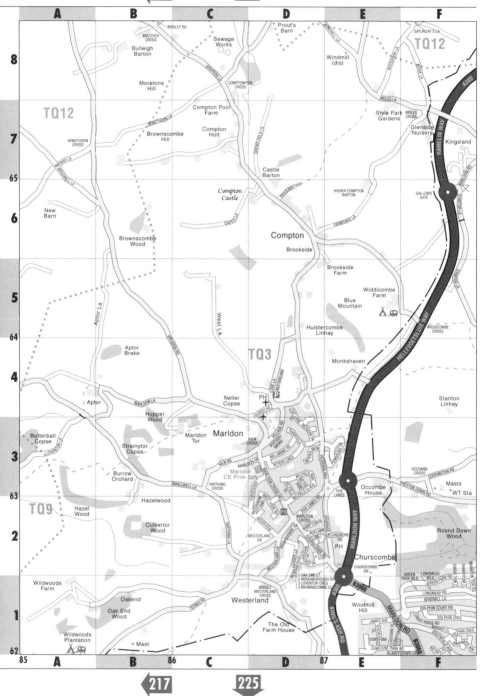

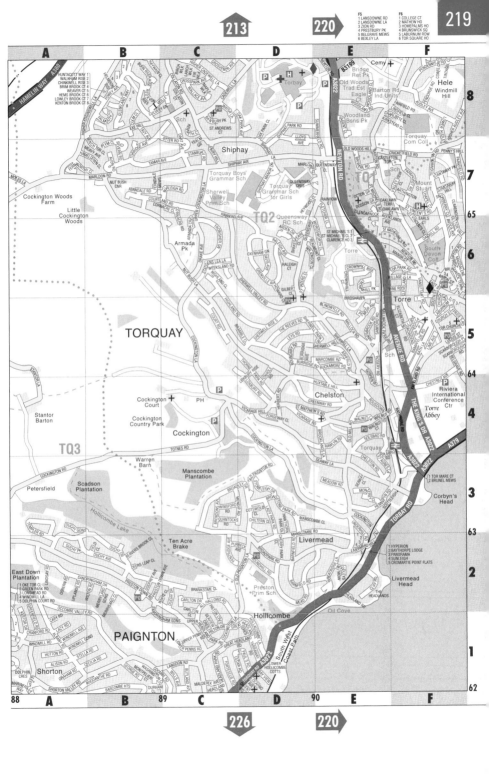

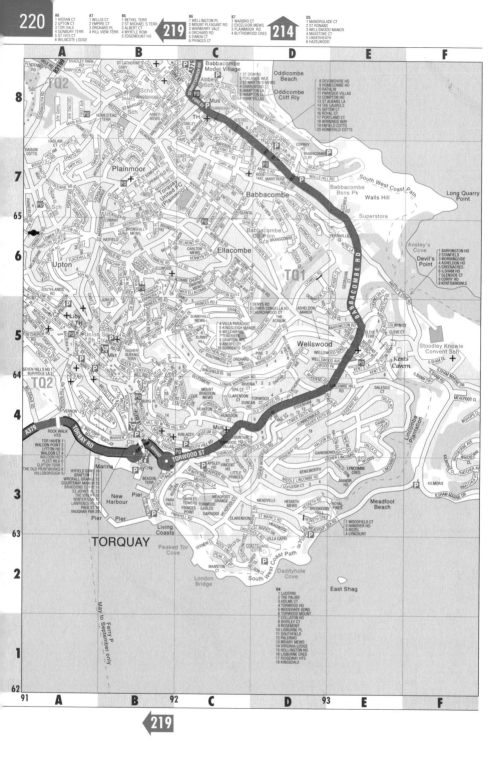

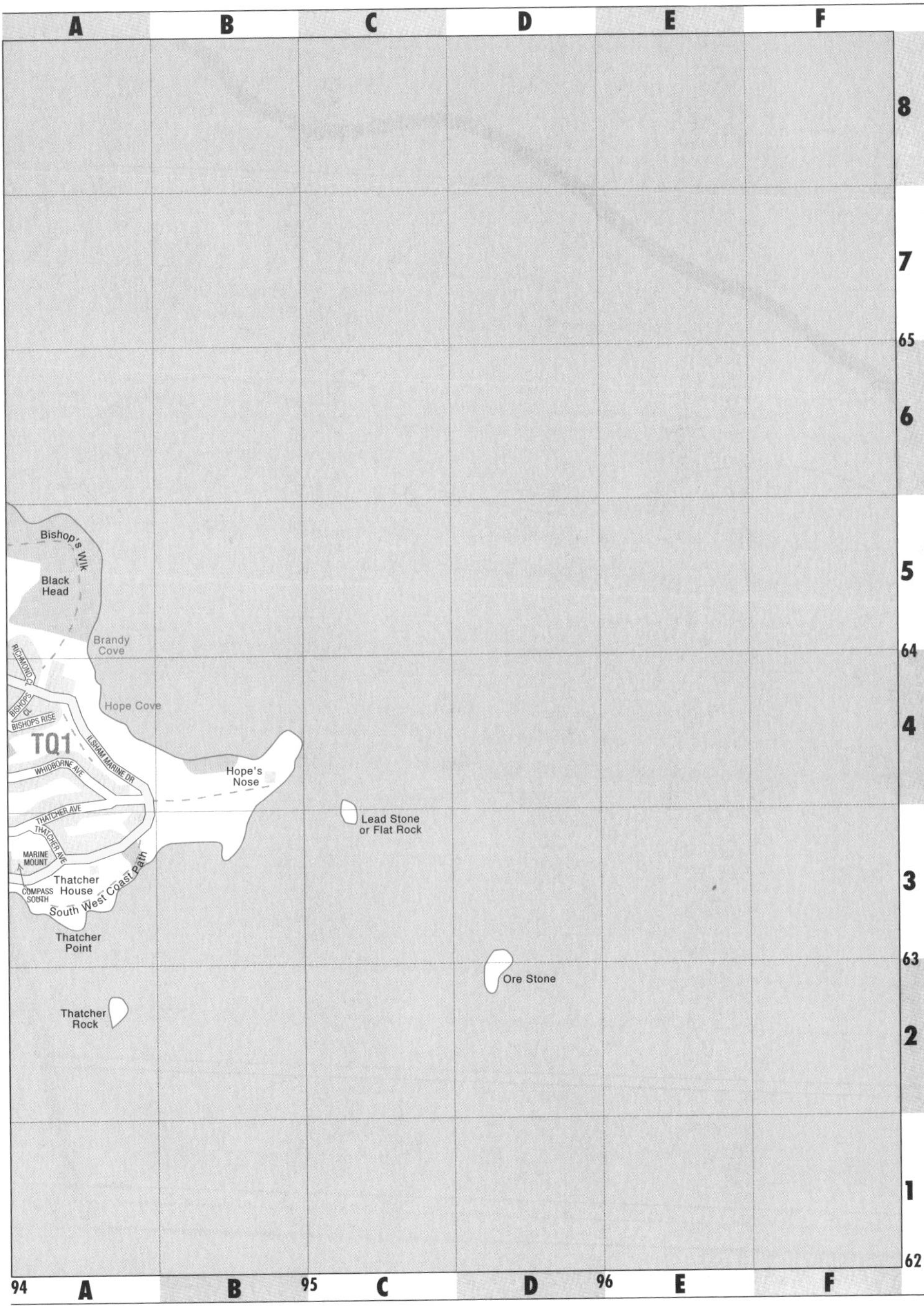
A
B
C
D
E
F
8
7
65
6
5
64
4
3
63
2
1
62
94
95
96
Bishop's Wlk
Black Head
Brandy Cove
Hope Cove
RICHMOND CL
BISHOPS CL
BISHOPS RISE
TQ1
ILSHAM MARINE DR
WHIDBORNE AVE
Hope's Nose
THATCHER AVE
THATCHER AVE
MARINE MOUNT
Thatcher House
COMPASS SOUTH
South West Coast Path
Thatcher Point
Thatcher Rock
Lead Stone or Flat Rock
Ore Stone

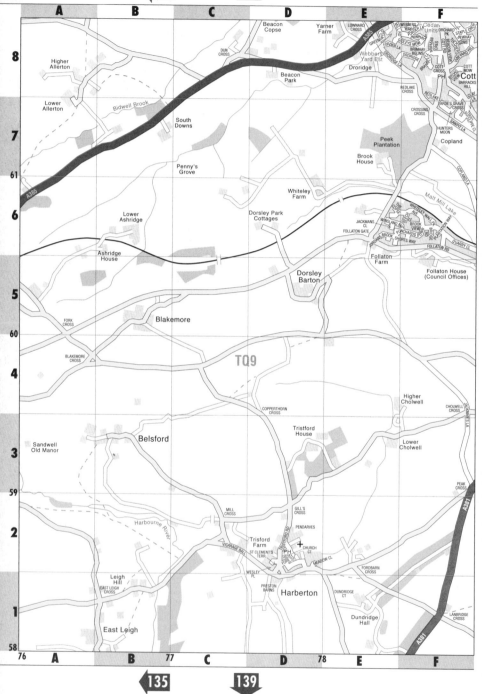

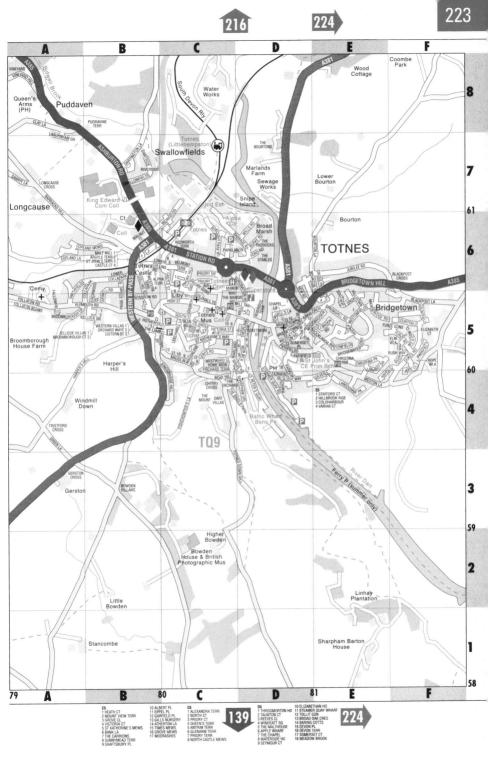

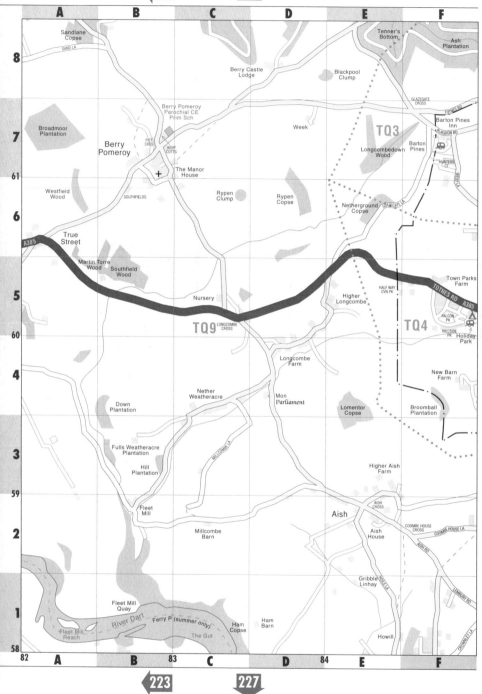

A B C D E F

8

Sandlane
Copse

SAND LA

Berry Castle
Lodge

Tenner's
Bottom

Ash
Plantation

GLAZEGATE
CROSS

Blackpool
Clump

Barton Pines
Inn

7

Broadmoor
Plantation

Berry Pomeroy
Parochial CE
Prim Sch

Week

TQ3

TOTNES RD

BLAGDON RD

Berry
Pomeroy

PITT
CRES

KEEP
COTTS

Longcombedown
Wood

Barton
Pines

BARTON CT

61

The Manor
House

HUNTER'S
CT

Westfield
Wood

SOUTHFIELDS

Rypen
Clump

Rypen
Copse

Netherground
Copse

GLAZEGATE LA

6

A385

True
Street

Martin Torre
Wood

Southfield
Wood

Nursery

Higher
Longcombe

HALF WAY
CVN PK

Town Parks
Farm

TOTNES RD

A385

5

TQ9

LONGCOMBE
CROSS

FALCON
PK

HILLSIDE
PK

Holiday
Park

TQ4

60

Longcombe
Farm

New Barn
Farm

4

Nether
Weatheracre

Mon
Parliament

Lomentor
Copse

Broomball
Plantation

Down
Plantation

MILLCOMBE LA

Higher Aish
Farm

3

Fulls Weatheracre
Plantation

Hill
Plantation

59

Fleet
Mill

Aish

AISH
CROSS

COOMBE HOUSE
CROSS

COOMBE HOUSE LA

Millcombe
Barn

Aish
House

AISH RD

COOMBE HOUSE LA

2

Gribble
Linhay

AISH LA

LEMBURY RD

Fleet Mill
Quay

River Dart

Ferry P (summer only)

Ham
Copse

Ham
Barn

CRIMPLE LA

1

Fleet Mill
Reach

The Gut

Howill

58

A B 83 C D 84 E F

82

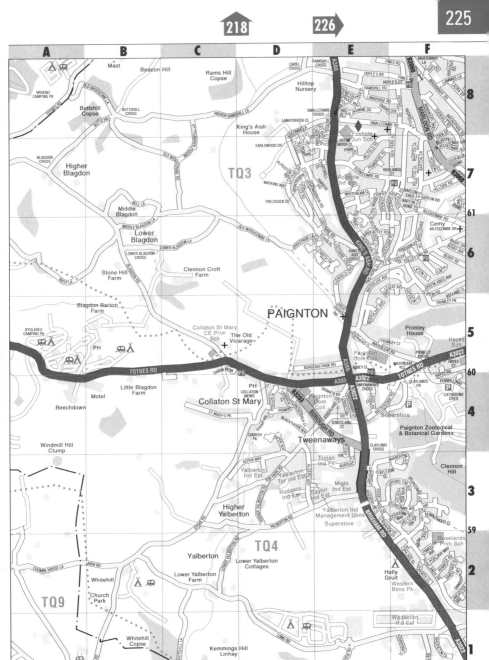

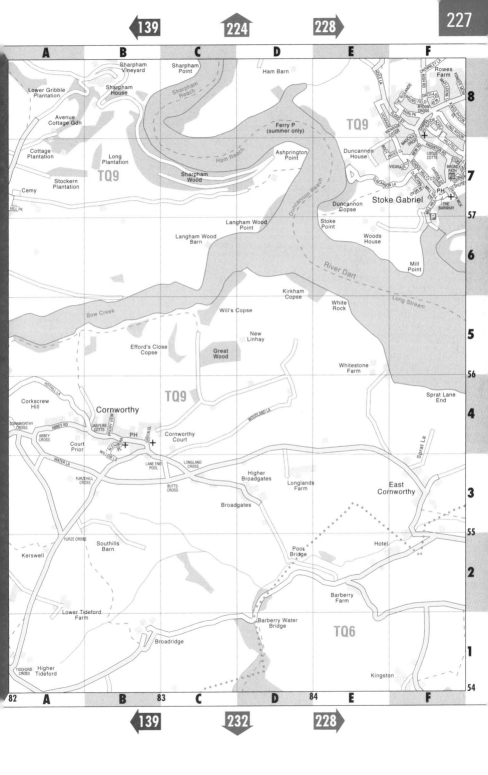

A B C D E F

8

Lower Gribble Plantation

Sharpham Vineyard

Sharpham Point

Sharpham House

Ham Barn

Rowes Farm

Avenue Cottage Gdn

Sharpham Reach

TQ9

Cottage Plantation

Long Plantation

Ferry P (summer only)

Duncannon House

TQ9

Sharpham Wood

Ham Reach

Ashprington Point

Stockern Plantation

Cemy

HILL PK

Langham Wood Point

Langham Wood Barn

Duncannon Reach

Stoke Gabriel

Stoke Point

Duncannon Copse

57

Woods House

Mill Point

6

River Dart

Bow Creek

Kirkham Copse

Long Stream

Will's Copse

White Rock

5

Efford's Close Copse

New Linhay

Great Wood

Whitestone Farm

56

Corkscrew Hill

TQ9

Sprat Lane End

4

Cornworthy

WOODLAND LA

Sprat La

CORNWORTHY CROSS

JASPERS COTTS

PH

Cornworthy Court

ABBEY CROSS

Court Prior

LANE END POOL

LONGLAND CROSS

Higher Broadgates

Longlands Farm

East Cornworthy

3

WATER LA

FURZEHILL CROSS

BUTTS CROSS

Broadgates

55

FURZE CROSS

Southills Barn

Poo Bridge

Hotel

2

Kerswell

Barberry Farm

Lower Tideford Farm

Barberry Water Bridge

TQ6

1

Broadridge

TIDEFORD CROSS

Higher Tideford

Kingston

54

82 A B 83 C D 84 E F

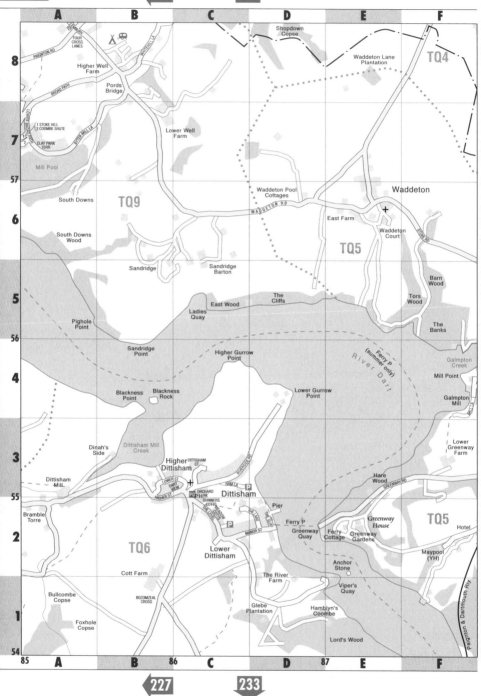

A B C D E F

8

7

57

6

5

56

4

3

55

2

1

54

85 86 87

TQ4

TQ9

TQ5

TQ6

TQ5

Shopdown Copse

Waddeton Lane Plantation

Waddeton

Waddeton Pool Cottages

WADDETON RD

East Farm

Waddeton Court

FOUR CROSS LANES

PAIGNTON RD

Higher Well Farm

WHITEHILL LA

BROAD PATH

Pords Bridge

Lower Well Farm

1 STOKE HILL
2 COOMBE SHUTE

STEKE MILL LA

CLAY PARK TERR

Mill Pool

South Downs

South Downs Wood

Sandridge

Sandridge Barton

Barn Wood

Tors Wood

The Banks

Pighole Point

East Wood

Ladies Quay

The Cliffs

Sandridge Point

Higher Gurrow Point

Lower Gurrow Point

Ferry P (summer only)

River Dart

Galmpton Creek

Mill Point

Galmpton Mill

Blackness Point

Blackness Rock

Lower Greenway Farm

Dinah's Side

Dittisham Mill Creek

Higher Dittisham

DITTISHAM CT

Hare Wood

GREENWAY RD

Dittisham Mill

LOWER ST
DART VIEW
HIGHER ST

ORCHARD CT
SHINNERS
SCOTES

Dittisham

IDAM LA

RIVERSIDE RD

Pier

Ferry P

Greenway Quay

Greenway House

Ferry Cottage

Greenway Gardens

TQ5

Hotel

Bramble Torre

Lower Dittisham

MANOR ST

THE LEVEL
THE QUAY

Cott Farm

BOZOMZEAL CROSS

The River Farm

Anchor Stone

Viper's Quay

Maypool (YH)

Bullcombe Copse

Foxhole Copse

Glebe Plantation

Hamblyn's Coombe

Lord's Wood

Paignton & Dartmouth Rly

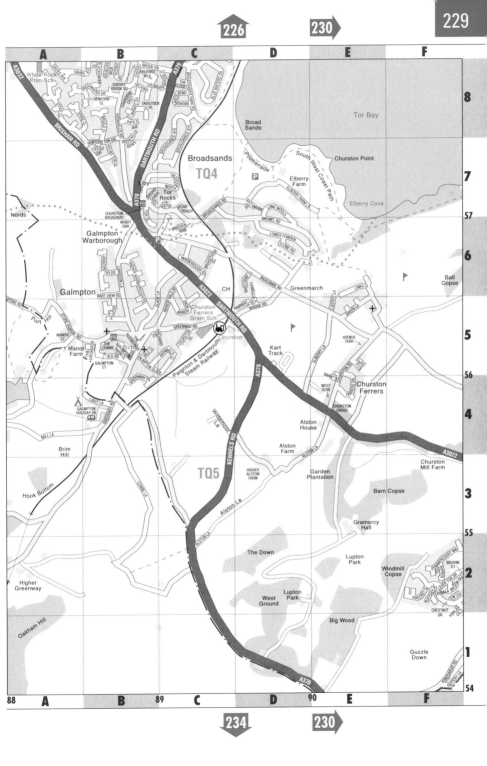

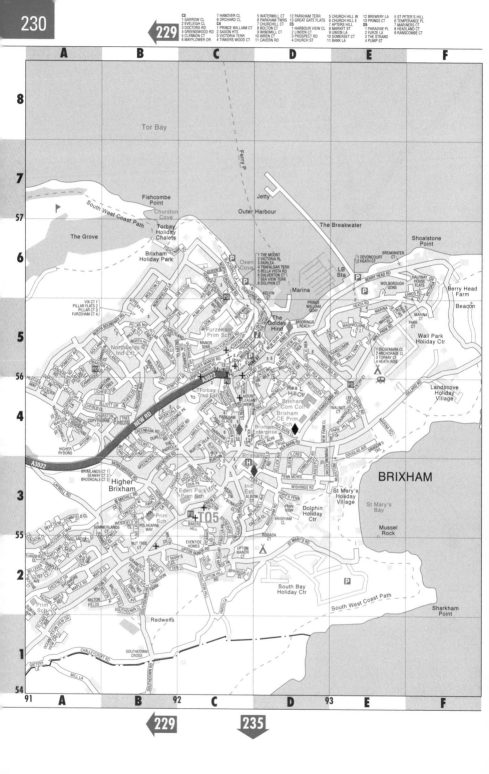

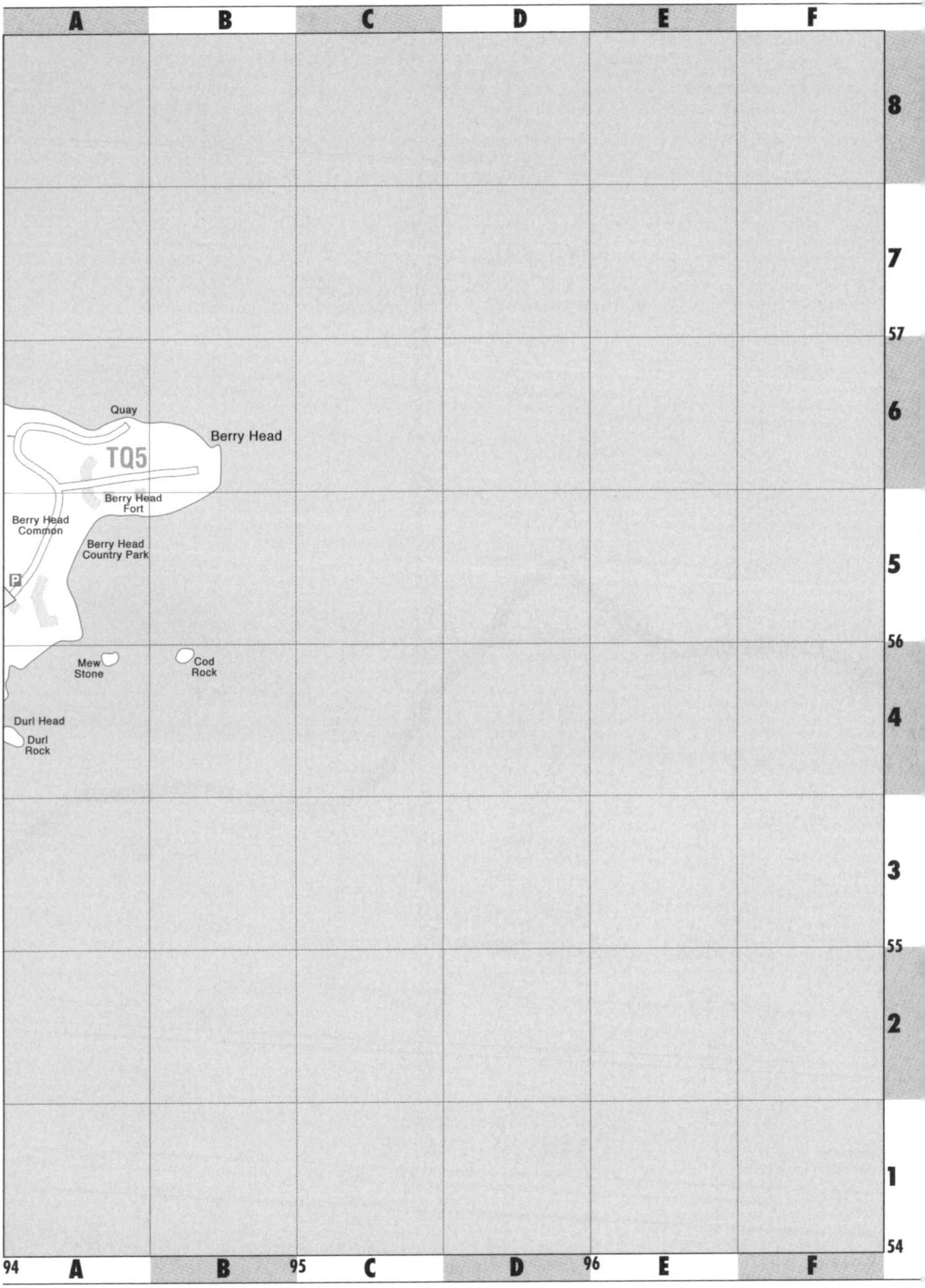

	A	B	C	D	E	F

8

7

6

Quay

TQ5

Berry Head

Berry Head
Fort

Berry Head
Common

Berry Head
Country Park

P

5

Mew
Stone

Cod
Rock

Durl Head

Durl
Rock

4

3

2

1

94	A	B	95	C	D	96	E	F

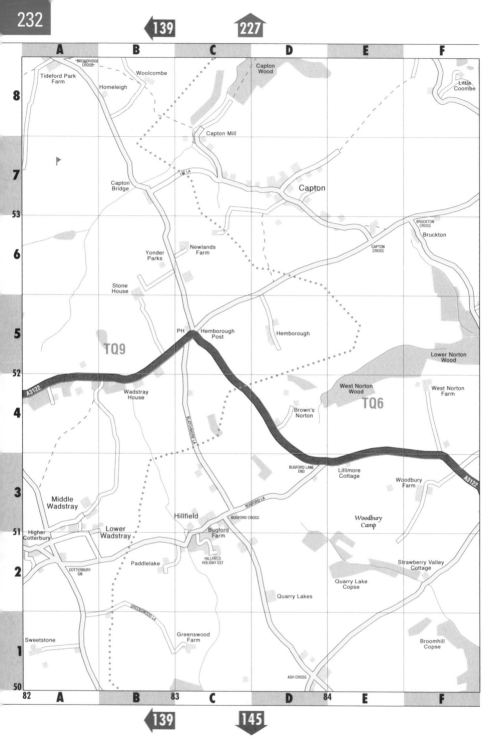

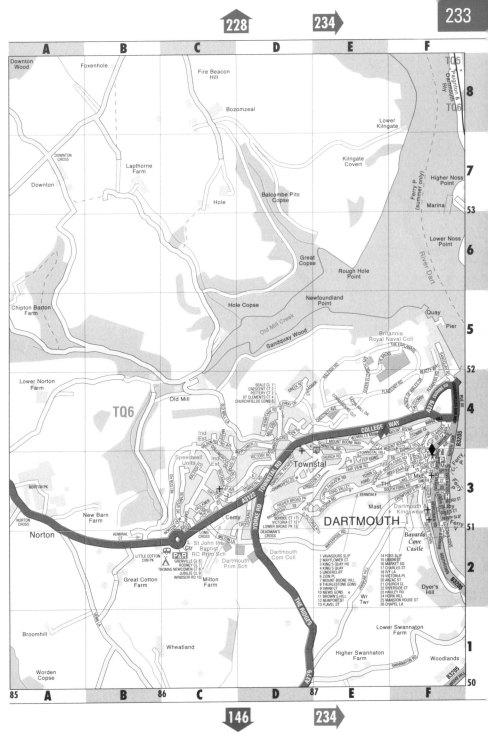

A   B   C   D   E   F

Downton
Wood

Foxenhole

Fire Beacon
Hill

Bozomzeal

Lower
Kilngate

8

Paignton &
Dartmouth
Rly

TQ6

Downton
Cross

Lapthorne
Farm

Kilngate
Covert

Higher Noss
Point

7

Downton

Hole

Balcombe Pits
Copse

Ferry P.
(summer only)

Marina

53

Chipton Barton
Farm

Great
Copse

Hole Copse

Rough Hole
Point

Newfoundland
Point

Lower Noss
Point

6

Quay

Pier

5

Lower Norton
Farm

Old Mill Creek

Sandquay Wood

Old Mill

Britannia
Royal Naval Coll

THE BACKS

THE ESPLANADE

Beatty Way

52

TQ6

SEALE CL 1
CRESCENT CT 2
POTTERY CT 3
ST CLEMENTS CT 4
CHURCHFIELDS GDNS 5

QUEEN ELIZABETH DR

COMMANDERS CUT

CLIFFE HILL

COLLEGE WAY

MOUNT BOONE

4

Ind
Est

Speedwell
Units

Ind
Est

VICTORY RD

Townstal

MOUNT BOONE WAY

TOWNSTAL RD

CHURCH RD

TOWNSTAL HILL

FAIR VIEW RD

RIDGE HILL

A379

FLAVEL ST

Dartmouth &
Kingswear

B3205

3

Norton
Pk

New Barn
Farm

A3122

YORKE RD

TOWNSTAL RD

Cemy

HIGHER BROAD PK

SCHOOL CT 11
VICTORIA CT 12
LOWER BROAD PK 13

FORD

DARTMOUTH

Mast

DARTMOUTH

51

Norton
Cross

Norton

ADMIRAL
CT

LONG
CROSS

St John the
Baptist
RC Prim Sch

DEADMAN'S
CROSS

Dartmouth
Com Coll

1 VAVASOURS SLIP
2 MAYFLOWER CT
3 KING'S QUAY HO
4 KING'S QUAY
5 UNDERCLIFF
6 ZION PL
7 MOUNT BOONE HILL
8 THURLESTONE GDNS
9 SWAIN CT
10 MEWS GDNS
11 BROWN'S HILL
12 NEWPORT ST
13 FLAVEL ST

14 FOSS SLIP
15 UNION ST
16 MARKET SQ
17 CHARLES ST
18 IVY LA
19 VICTORIA PL
20 ANZAC ST
21 CHURCH CL
22 RIVERSIDE CT
23 HAXLEY RD
24 HORN HILL
25 MANSION HOUSE ST
26 CHAPEL LA

Bayards
Cove
Castle

Dyer's
Hill

2

LITTLE COTTON
CVN PK

GRENVILLE CL 6
RODNEY CL 7
THOMAS NEWCOMEN CT 8
JUBILEE CL 9
WINDSOR RD 10

P&R

Milton
Farm

Dartmouth
Prim Sch

MILTON LA

Wr
Twr

B3205

Great Cotton
Farm

VERN LA

Broomhill

Wheatland

THE RIDGES

A379

Higher Swannaton
Farm

SWANNATON RD

Lower Swannaton
Farm

Woodlands

WEEKE HILL

1

Worden
Copse

50

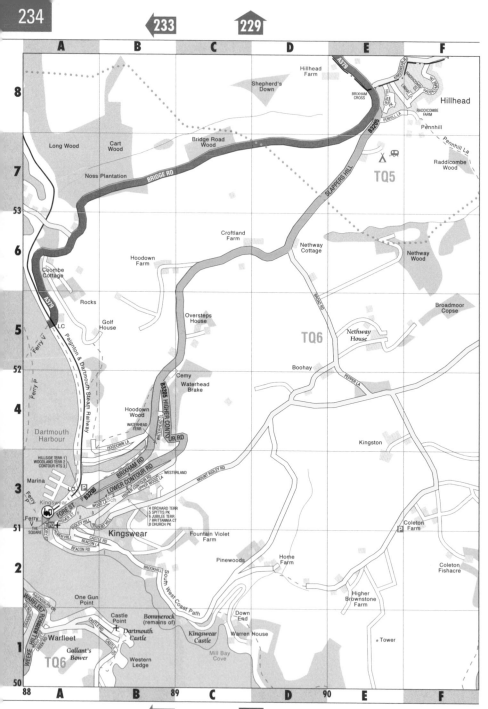

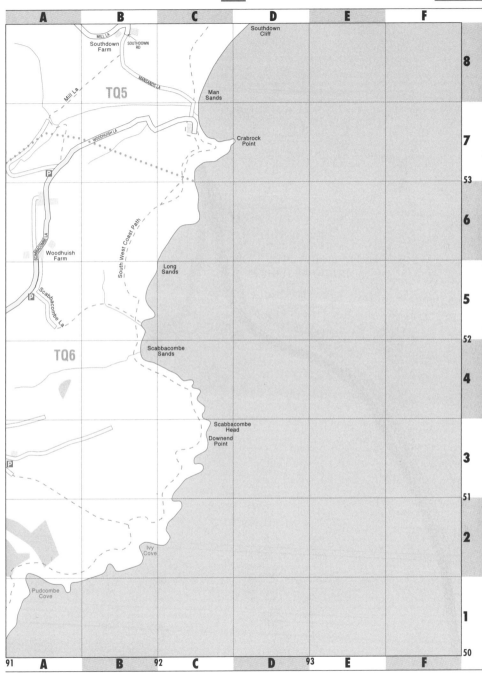

	A	B	C	D	E	F

8

Southdown
Cliff

MILL LA

Southdown
Farm

SOUTHDOWN
RD

MANSANDS LA

Mill La

TQ5

Man
Sands

7

WOODHUISH LA

Crabrock
Point

53

P

6

South West Coast Path

Woodhuish
Farm

Long
Sands

SCABBACOMBE LA

5

P

Scabbacombe La

52

TQ6

Scabbacombe
Sands

4

Scabbacombe
Head

Downend
Point

3

P

51

2

Ivy
Cove

Pudcombe
Cove

1

50

91	A	B	92	C	D	93	E	F

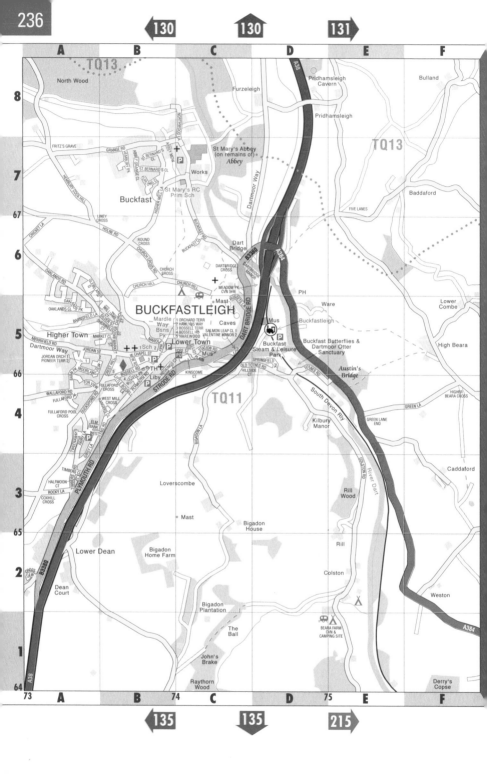

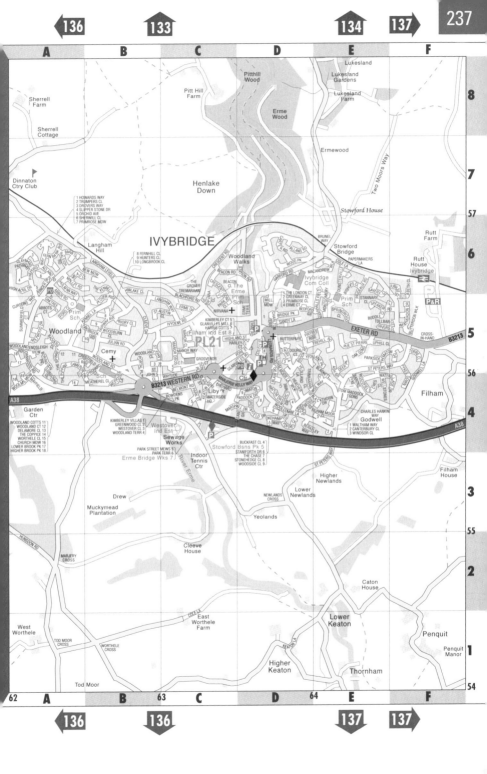

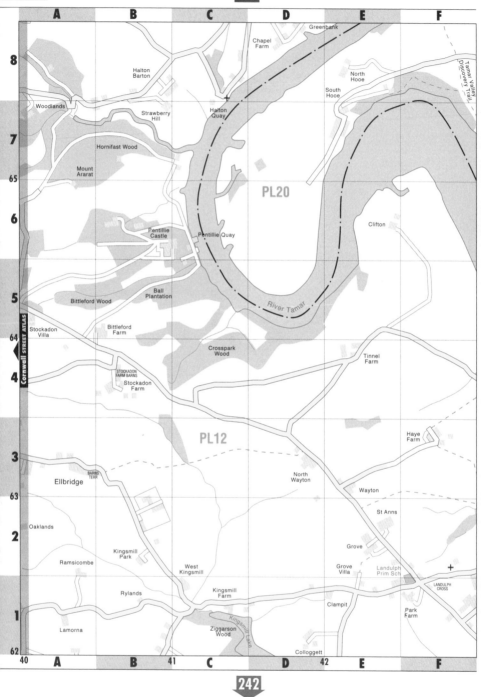

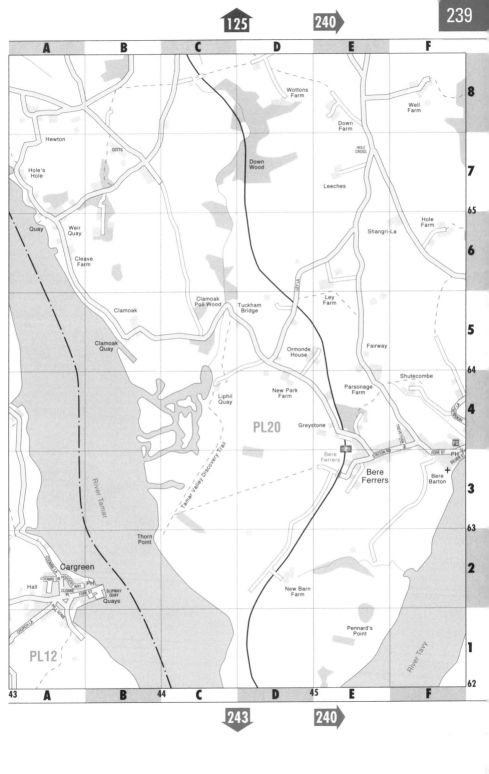

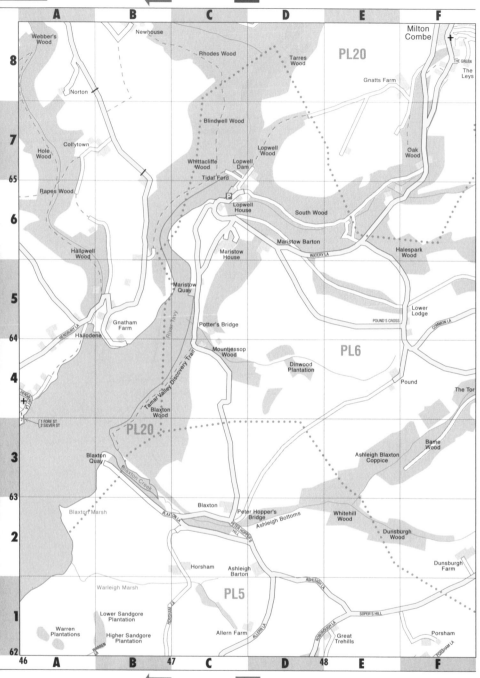

239
126

Milton Combe

PL20

THE GREEN

The Leys

Webber's Wood

Newhouse

Rhodes Wood

Tarres Wood

Gnatts Farm

Norton

Blindwell Wood

8

Hole Wood

Collytown

Lopwell Wood

Oak Wood

7

Whitttacliffe Wood

Lopwell Dam

65

Rapes Wood

Tidal Ford

P

Lopwell House

Hallowell Wood

South Wood

Maristow Barton

6

WATERY LA

Halespark Wood

Maristow House

Maristow Quay

Lower Lodge

5

HENSBURY LA

Gnatham Farm

Hallodene

POUND'S CROSS

COMMON LA

PL6

64

Potter's Bridge

River Tavy

Mountjessop Wood

Dinwood Plantation

Pound

The Tor

4

Tamar Valley Discovery Trail

Blaxton Wood

1 FORE ST
2 SILVER ST

PL20

Blaxton Quay

Ashleigh Blaxton Coppice

Barne Wood

3

Blaxton Creek

Blaxton

Peter Hopper's Bridge

Whitehill Wood

63

Blaxton Marsh

BLAXTON LA

Ashleigh Bottoms

Dunsburgh Wood

2

PETER HOPPER'S HILL

Dunsburgh Farm

Horsham

Ashleigh Barton

ASHLEIGH LA

Warleigh Marsh

PL5

HORSHAM LA

SOPER'S HILL

Lower Sandgore Plantation

ALLERN LA

Porsham

1

Warren Plantations

Higher Sandgore Plantation

Allern Farm

BOROUGH LA

Great Trehills

PORSHAM LA

62

46

A

B

47

C

D

48

E

F

239
244

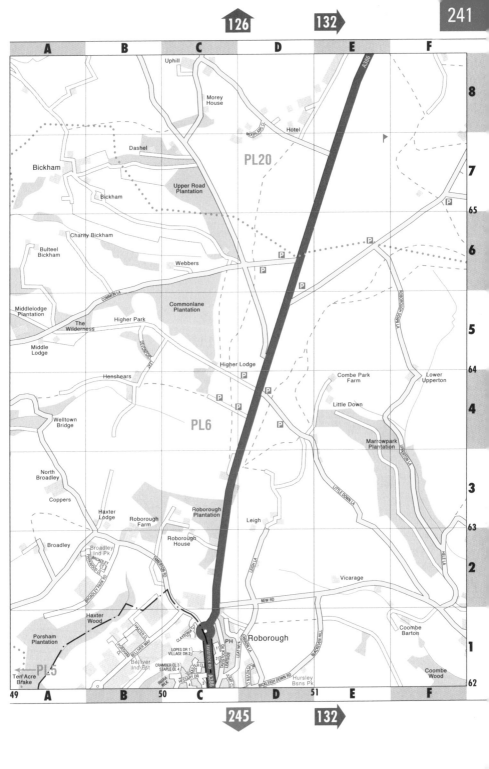

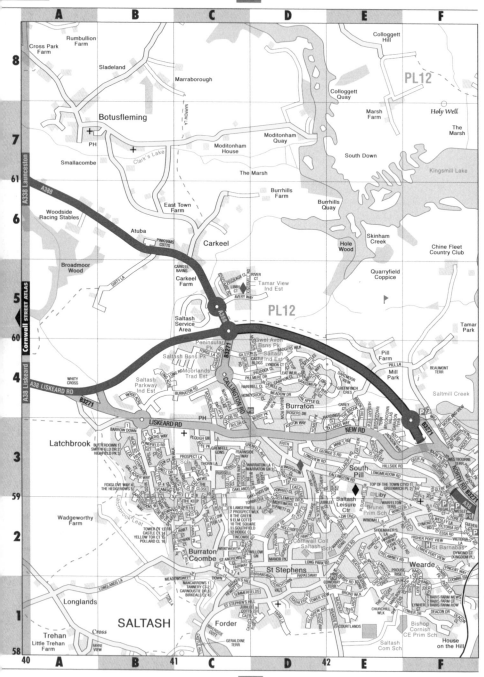

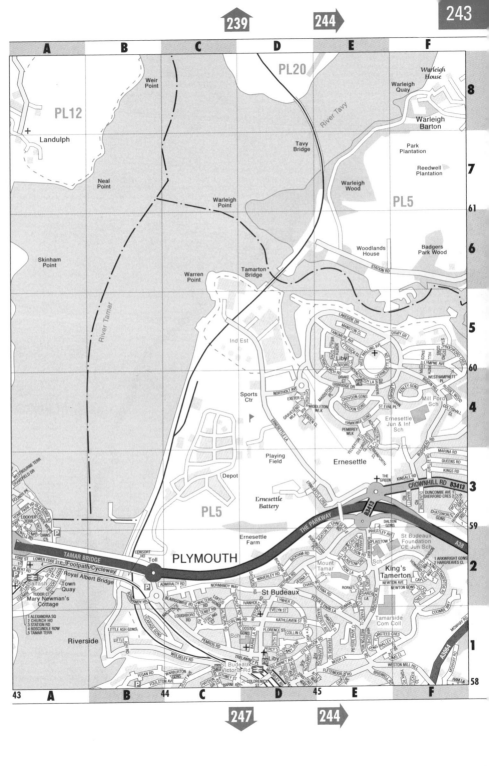

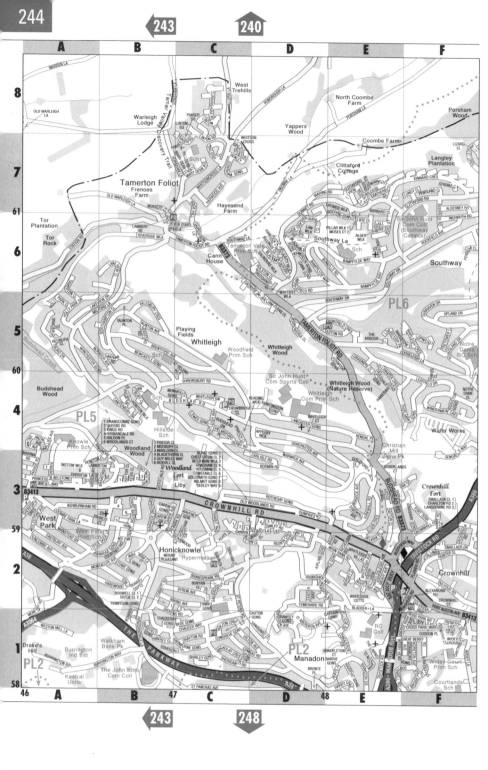

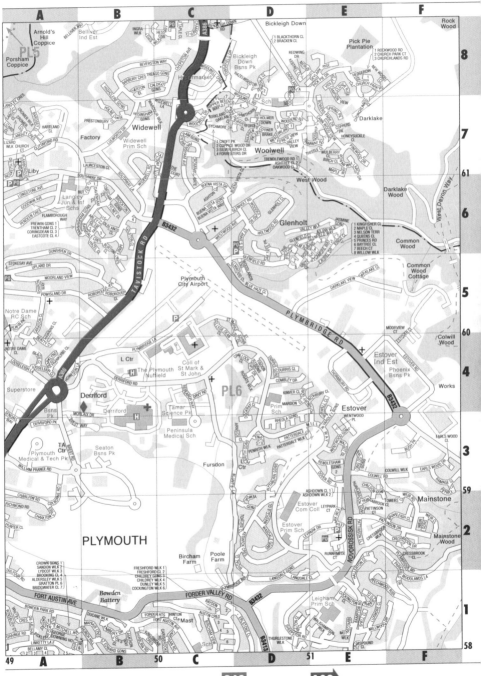

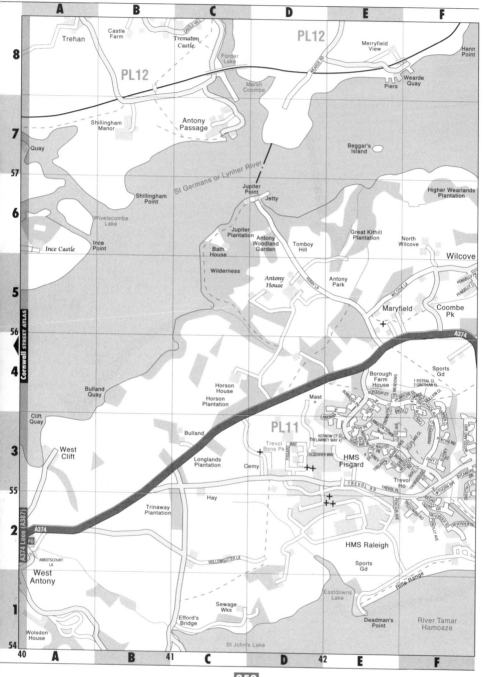

8

7

57

6

5

56

4

55

3

2

1

54

A   B   C   D   E   F

Trehan

Castle Farm

PL12

Shillingham Manor

Trematon Castle

CASTLE HILL

Forder Lake

Antony Passage

PL12

Merryfield View

Henn Point

MARSH RD

Marsh Coombe

Piers

Wearde Quay

Quay

St Germans or Lynher River

Shillingham Point

Beggar's Island

Jupiter Point

Jetty

Higher Wearlands Plantation

Wivelscombe Lake

Ince Castle

Ince Point

Jupiter Plantation

Bath House

Antony Woodland Garden

Tomboy Hill

Antony House

Wilderness

Great Kithill Plantation

FERRY LA

North Wilcove

Wilcove

Antony Park

WILCOVE LA

Maryfield

Coombe Pk

PENGELLY PK
PENGELLY CT

A374

Bulland Quay

Horson House

Horson Plantation

Mast

Borough Farm House

Sports Gd

1 FISTRAL CL
2 GWITHIAN CL

Clift Quay

West Clift

Bulland

Longlands Plantation

PL11

Trevol Bsns Pk

WAY

FISGARD

Cemy

KERNOW CT 3
THELAWNEY WAY 4

FROBISHER WAY

HMS Fisgard

Trevol Ho

Hay

Trinaway Plantation

A374 Looe (A387)

A374

PO

ABBOTSCOURT LA

West Antony

HOLLOWGUTTER LA

TREVOL RD

HMS Raleigh

Sports Gd

Wolsdon House

Efford's Bridge

Sewage Wks

St John's Lake

Eastdowns Lake

Deadman's Point

Rifle Range

River Tamar Hamoaze

A   B   C   D   E   F

40   41   42

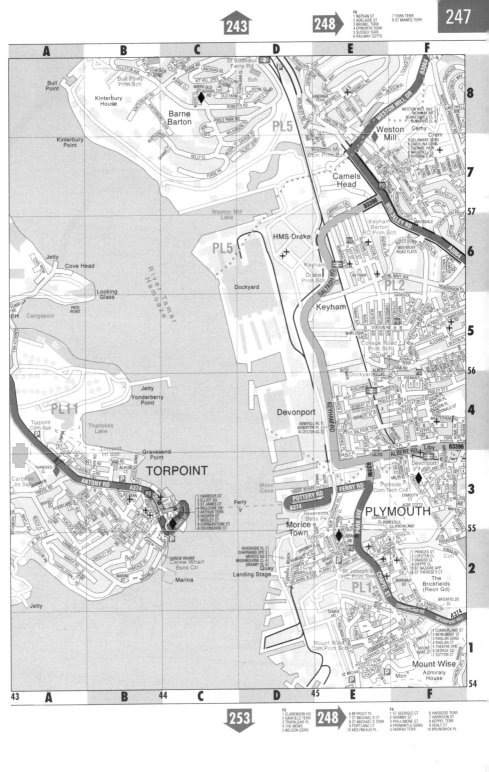

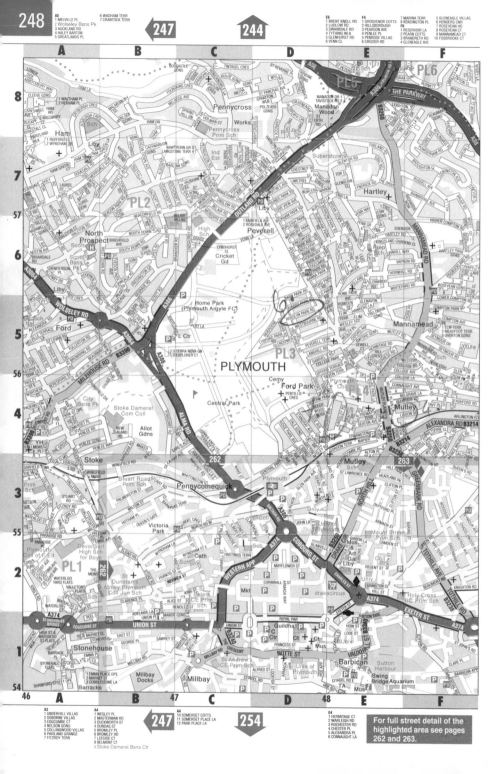

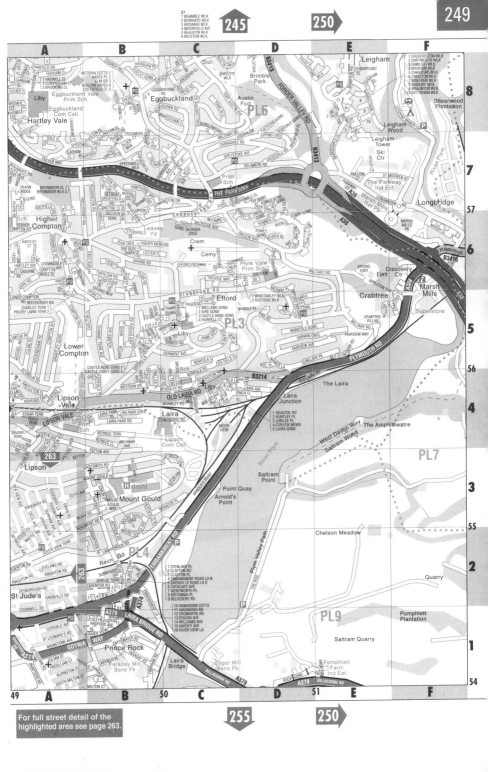

C7
1 BRAMBLE WLK
2 BOWHAYS WLK
3 BRISMAR WLK
4 MOORFIELD AVE
5 BEAUDYN WLK
6 BEESTON WLK

F8
1 CHURCHSTOW WLK
2 DARTMOUTH WLK
3 DAWLISH WLK
4 BROXHAM WLK
5 CHAGFORD WLK
6 CREDITON WLK
7 BIDEFORD WLK
8 BIGBURY WLK
9 BRAUNTON WLK
10 DITTISHAM WLK

Leigham

Shearwood Plantation

Eggbuckland Vale Prim Sch

Eggbuckland

Leigham Wood

Leigham Tower

Ski Ctr

Austin Fort

Hartley Vale

Eggbuckland Com Coll

Liby

PL6

The Parkway Ind Est

Longbridge

The Parkway

Prim Sch

Higher Compton

River Plym

Crem

Cemy

Plym View Prim Sch

Efford

Discovery Ctr

Marsh Mills

Lower Compton

Efford Pathway

Efford Fort

Crabtree

Superstore

PL3

1 WINSTANLEY WLK
2 RUDYERD WLK

1 WELLAND GDNS
2 AIRE GDNS
3 CASTLE BANK GDNS
4 HURRELL CT

Crabtree Villas

Liby

Fairview Way

Lower Compton

Sch

The Laira

Lipson Vale

Old Laira Rd

Laira

Liby

Laira Junction

PL7

Lipson Vale

Laira

Moor View

Lipson Com Coll

1 BEACON HO
2 HUNTLEY PL
3 JUBILEE PL
4 CURFEW MEWS
5 LAIRA GDNS

The Amphitheatre

West Devon Way

Saltram Wood

Lipson

River Plym

Saltram Point

Mount Gould

Mount Gould

Point Quay

Arnold's Point

Chelson Meadow

PL9

St Jude's

PL4

Recn Gd

1 STENLAKE PL
2 CLAYTON RD
3 CLAYTON PL
4 EMBANKMENT ROAD LA N
5 GRENVILLE ROAD LA S
6 CATHCART AVE
7 WENTWORTH PL
8 BRITANNIA PL
9 BELVEDERE RD

Quarry

Pomphlett Plantation

Prince Rock

10 HAWARDEN COTTS
11 CAVENDISH RD
12 CROMARTIE RD
13 RISDON AVE
14 WILLIAMS AVE
15 HARVEY AVE
16 RIVER VIEW LA

Saltram Quarry

Goynia Way

Sugar Mill Bsns Pk

Laira Bridge Rd

Laira Bridge

Pomphlett Farm Ind Est

Faraday Mill Bsns Pk

Billacombe Rd

For full street detail of the highlighted area see page 263.

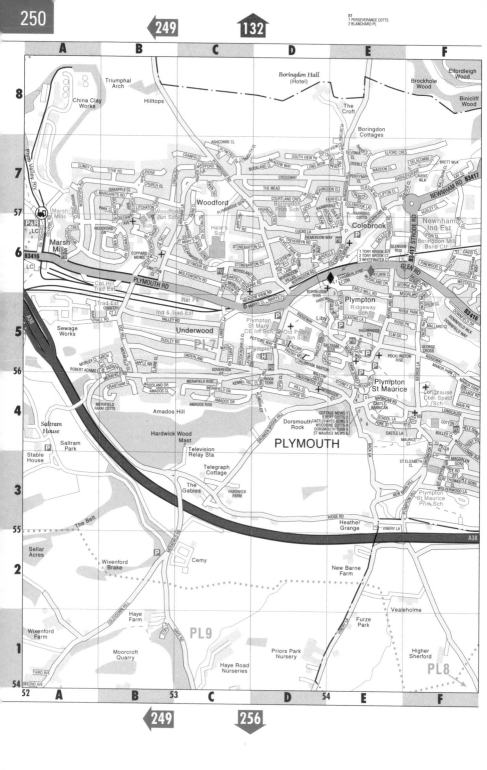

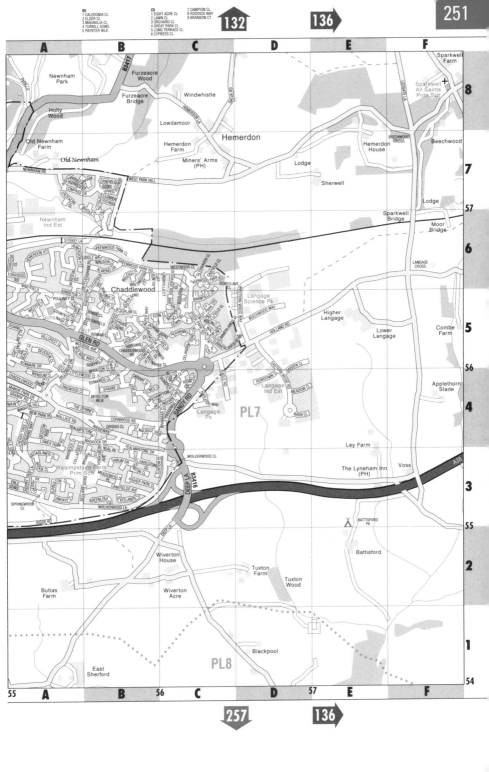

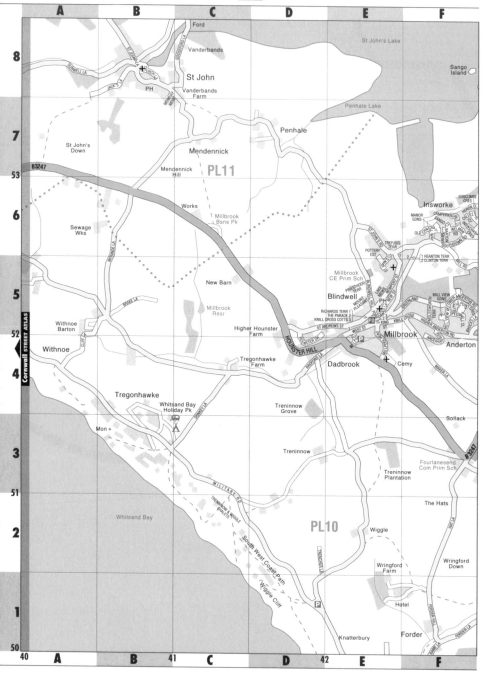

A   **B**   **C**   **D**   **E**   **F**

8

Ford

Vanderbands

St John's Lake

ST JOHN LA

JACK'S LA

PH

St John

Sango
Island

Vanderbands
Farm

7

Penhale Lake

St John's
Down

Penhale

Mendennick

B3247

53

Mendennick
Hill

PL11

Insworke

EDGCUMBE
CRES

6

Works

MANOR
GDNS

OLD RD

Sewage
Wks

Millbrook
Bsns Pk

TREFUSIS
TERR

POTTERY
EST

1 HEANTON TERR
2 CLINTON TERR

WITHNOE LA

BRAKE LA

New Barn

Millbrook
CE Prim Sch

PRIESTWOOD
TERR

MOUNT
PLEASANT

MILL VIEW
GDNS

5

Blindwell

PH

GREENLAND

Withnoe
Barton

Millbrook
Resr

RICHARDS TERR 1
THE PARADE 2
KNILL CROSS COTTS 3

KNILL CROSS

52

CLIFF LA

Higher Hounster
Farm

ST ANDREWS ST
WEST ST

Millbrook

Anderton

Withnoe

HOUNSTER HILL

DADBROOK

Dadbrook

Cemy

4

Tregonhawke
Farm

OPSTER DM

INSWORKE

Sollack

Tregonhawke

Whitsand Bay
Holiday Pk

DONKEY LA

Treninnow
Grove

B3247

3

Mon

MILITARY RD

Treninnow

Treninnow
Plantation

Fourlanesend
Com Prim Sch

51

The Hats

2

Whitsand Bay

TRENINNOW & WIGGLE
(PRIVATE)

PL10

Wiggle

Wringford
Farm

Wringford
Down

South West Coast Path

TRENCHER LA

Hotel

Forder

FORDER HILL

1

Wiggle Cliff

Knatterbury

Forder

FORE LA

50

40   **A**   **B**   41   **C**   **D**   42   **E**   **F**

Cornwall STREET ATLAS

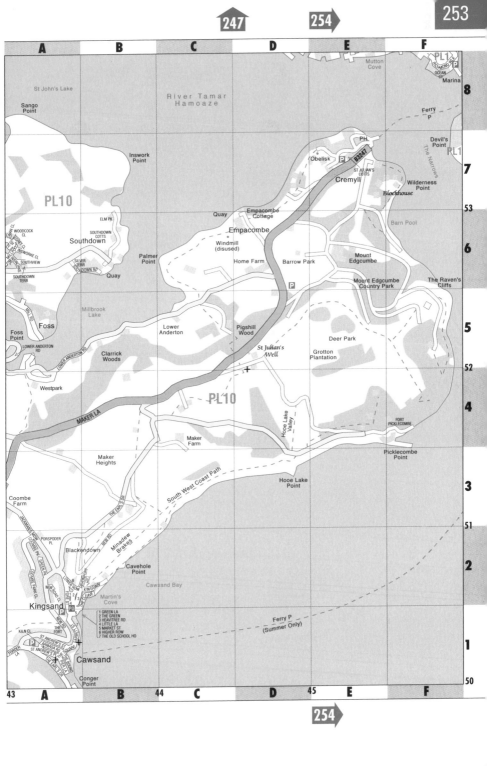

A   B   C   D   E   F

8
St John's Lake

Mutton Cove

PL1

Ferry
P

Sango
Point

River Tamar
Hamoaze

OCEAN

Marina

Devil's
Point

PL1

Inswork
Point

PH.

Obelisk
B3247

St Julian's
Cotts

The Narrows

7

53

PL10

ELM PK.

SOUTHDOWN
COTTS

Southdown

Quay

Empacombe
Cottage

Cremyll

Wilderness
Point

Blockhouse

Barn Pool

WOODCOCK
CL

SILVER
TERR
SOUTHDOWN RD

Palmer
Point

Quay

Empacombe

Windmill
(disused)

Home Farm

Barrow Park

Mount
Edgcumbe

6

SOUTHDOWN
TERR

Quay

P

Mount Edgcumbe
Country Park

The Raven's
Cliffs

Millbrook
Lake

Lower
Anderton

Pigshill
Wood

Deer Park

Foss
Point

Foss

LOWER ANDERTON
RD

Clarrick
Woods

St Julian's
Well

Grotton
Plantation

5

52

Westpark

MAKER LA

PL10

Hooe Lake
Valley

FORT
PICKLECOMBE

4

Maker
Farm

Picklecombe
Point

Maker
Heights

Hooe Lake
Point

3

Coombe
Farm

THE EARL'S DR

South West Coast Path

51

PORSPODER
PL

Blackendown

Minadew
Brakes

Cavehole
Point

Cawsand Bay

2

Kingsand

P

Martin's
Cove

1 GREEN LA
2 THE GREEN
3 HEAVITREE RD
4 LITTLE LA
5 MARKET ST
6 HIGHER ROW
7 THE OLD SCHOOL HO

Ferry P
(Summer Only)

1

KILN CL

THE
FORT

P

ST ANDREW'S ST

St Andrew's

Cawsand

Conger
Point

50

43   A   B   44   C   D   45   E   F

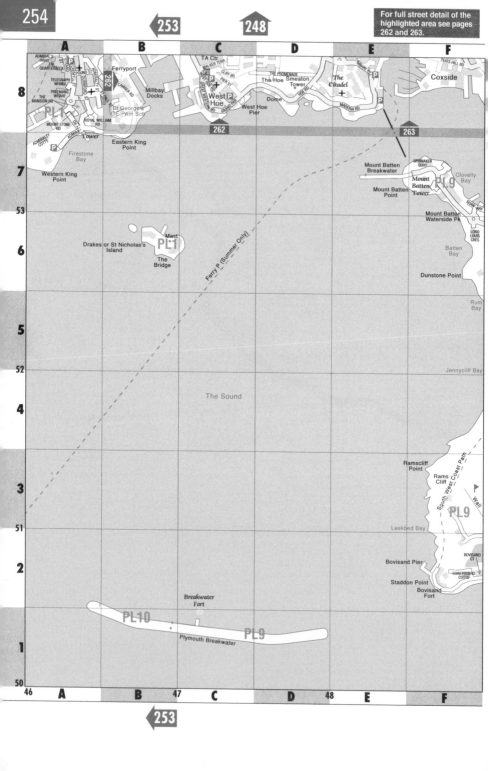

253
248

For full street detail of the highlighted area see pages 262 and 263.

A B C D E F

8

ADMIRAL'S HOUSE
THE QUARTERDECK
TELEGRAPH WHARF
FREEMANS WHARF
THE MANSION HO
PL1

Ferryport
CAMBER RD
Millbay Docks

St George's CE Prim Sch
MOUNT STONE RD
ROYAL WILLIAM RD
ADMIRALTY COTTS
Tower
P

TA Ctr
WALKER TERR
PIER ST
West Hoe
West Hoe Pier

THE PROMENADE
The Hoe
Smeaton Tower
Dome

HOE RD
MADEIRA RD
The Citadel

MOUNT WISE RD
Coxside
TEATS HILL RD

Eastern King Point

Firestone Bay

Western King Point

253

7

Mount Batten Breakwater
Mount Batten Point

SPINNAKER QUAY
Mount Batten Tower
PL9
Clovelly Bay

263

53

Mount Batten Waterside Pk
LORD LOUIS CRES

6

Drakes or St Nicholas's Island
Mast
PL1
The Bridge

Batten Bay

Dunstone Point

Rum Bay

5

Ferry P (Summer Only)

52

Jennycliff Bay

4

The Sound

3

Ramscliff Point
Rams Cliff
PL9
Well
South West Coast Path

51

Leekbed Bay

2

Bovisand Pier
Staddon Point
Bovisand Fort
BOVISAND CT
COASTGUARD COTTS

Breakwater Fort

PL10
PL9
Plymouth Breakwater

1

50

46 A B 47 C D 48 E F

253

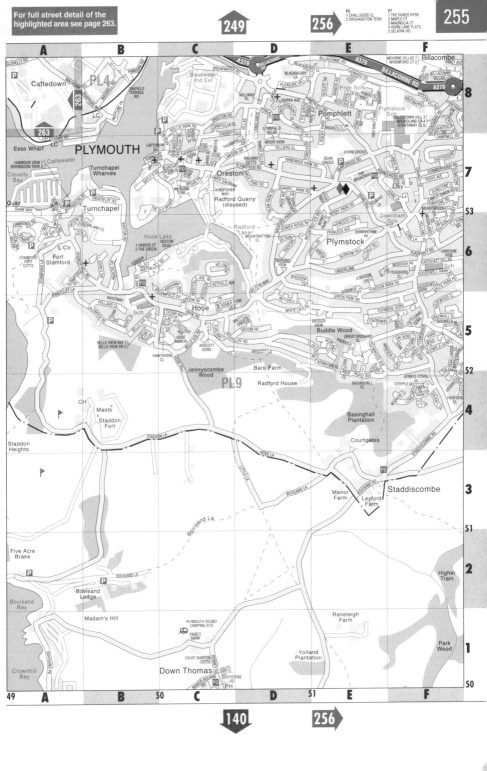

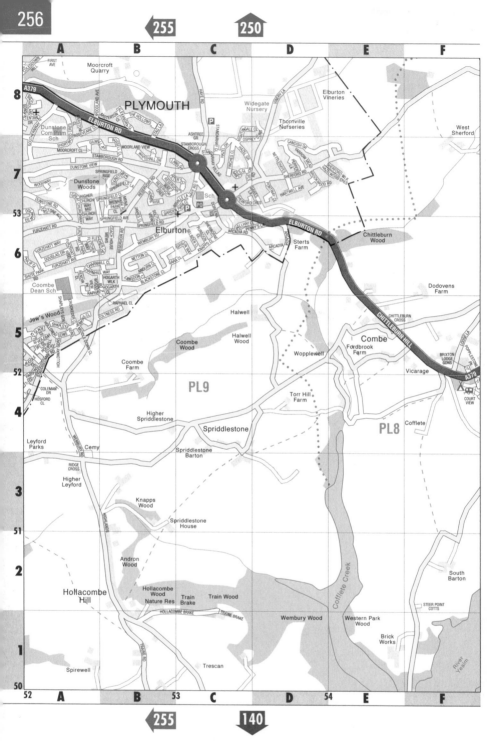

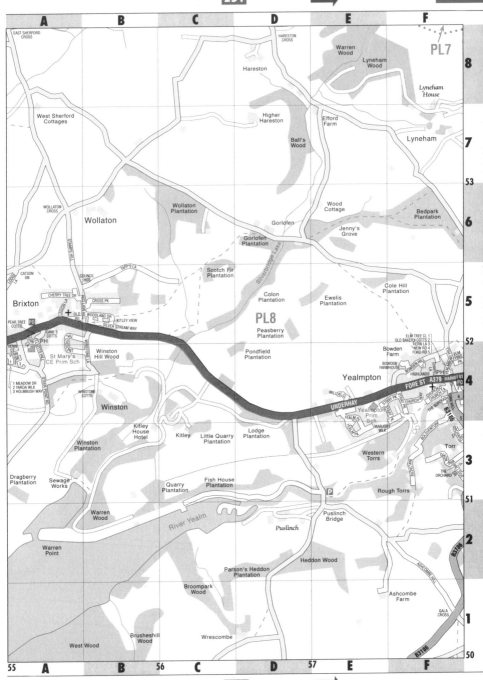

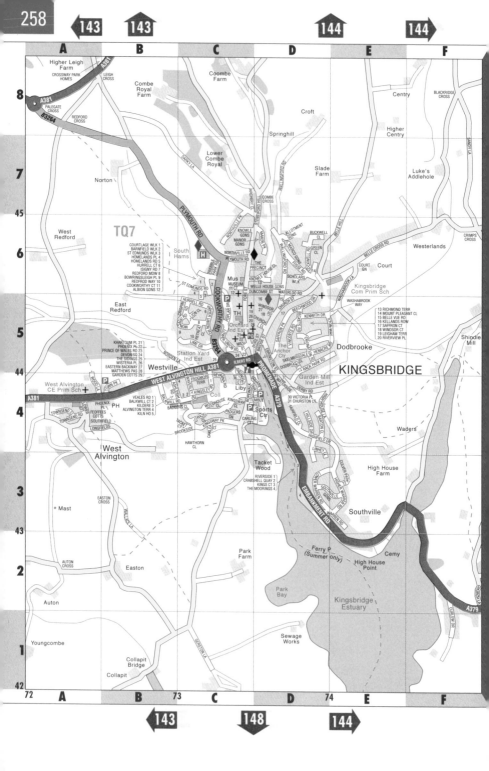

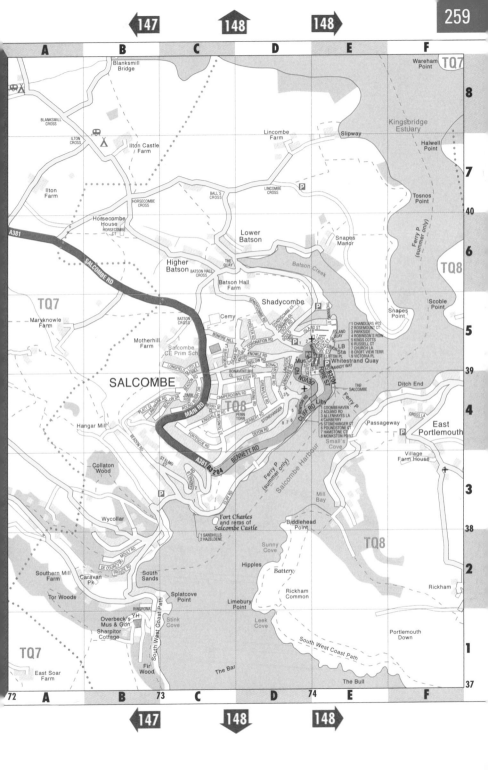

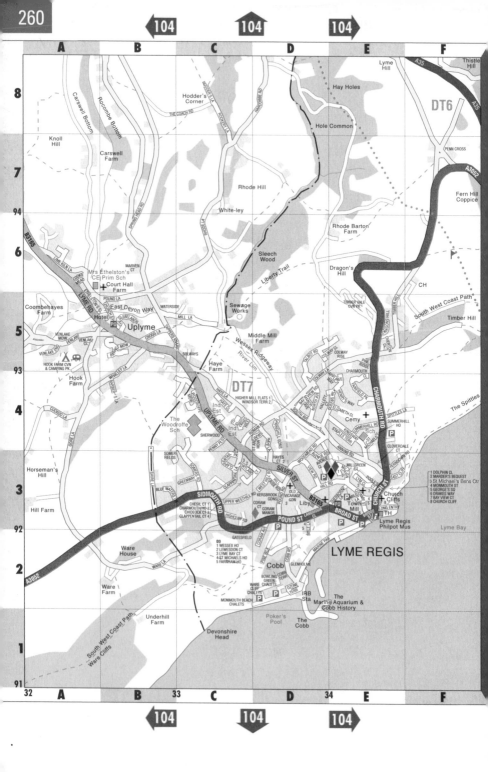

104
104
104

A B C D E F

8

Thistle Hill

Lyme Hill

A35

Hodder's Corner

Hay Holes

DT6

Knoll Hill

Carswell Bottom

Rocomba Bottom

THE COACH RD

Hole Common

PENN CROSS

7

Carswell Farm

Rhode Hill

A3052

Fern Hill Coppice

94

White-ley

Rhode Barton Farm

Sleech Wood

Dragon's Hill

CH

6

THE SILK LA

Marven Ct

Liberty Trail

South West Coast Path

Mrs Ethelston's CE Prim Sch

Court Hall Farm

Timber Hill

LYME RD

Coombehayes Farm

East Devon Way

WATERSIDE

Sewage Works

5

Uplyme

Middle Mill Farm

Wessex Ridgeway

River Lym

VENLAKE MDW

Hook Farm Cvn & Camping Pk

Haye Farm

DT7

Hook Farm

Higher Mill Flats 1
Windsor Terr 2

UPLYME RD

The Woodroffe Sch

Ind Est

Charmouth

4

Ind Est

Cemy

The Spittles

Sherwood

SOMERS FIELDS

93

92

91

Horseman's Hill

BLUE WATERS

GREENWAY

3

SIDMOUTH RD

CHESIL CT 1
CHARMOUTH HO 2
CHIDEOCK CT 3
CLAPPENTAIL CT 4

Hill Farm

HIGHCLIFF

UPPER WESTHILL

KERSBROOK GDNS

CORAM CT

CORAM MANOR

HAYES

SILVER ST

Libry

OLD VICARAGE GDN

Church Cliffs

Town Mill

B3165

BROAD ST

CHURCH ST

Church Cliffs

TH

Lyme Regis Philpot Mus

1 DOLPHIN CL
2 MARDER'S BEQUEST
3 ST MICHAEL'S Bsns Ctr
4 MONMOUTH ST
5 GEORGE'S SQ
6 DRAKES WAY
7 BAY VIEW CT
8 CHURCH CLIFF

2

Ware House

GATESFIELD

D3
1 WESSEX HO
2 LEWESDON CT
3 LYME BAY CT
4 ST MICHAELS HO
5 FARNHAM HO

POUND ST

MARINE PAR

Lyme Bay

LYME REGIS

Ware Farm

Cobb

GLENHOLME

A3052

WARE LA

BOWLING GREEN

TOWN GREEN

WARE CLIFF CHALETS

FOXLOW CT

IRB Sta

The Marine Aquarium & Cobb History

Underhill Farm

MONMOUTH BEACH CHALETS

Devonshire Head

Poker's Pool

The Cobb

1

South West Coast Path

Ware Cliffs

A B C D E F

32 33 34

104
104
104

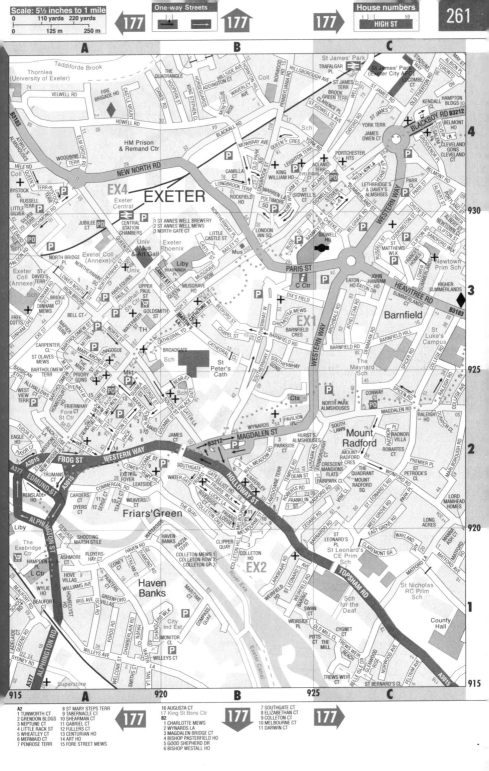

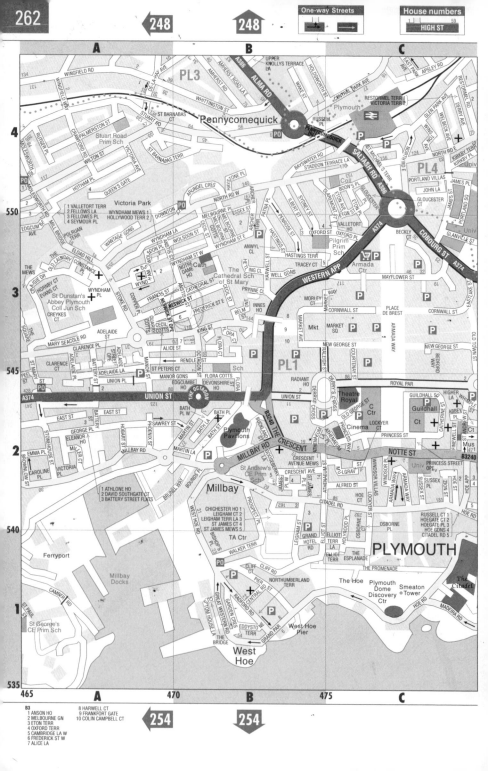

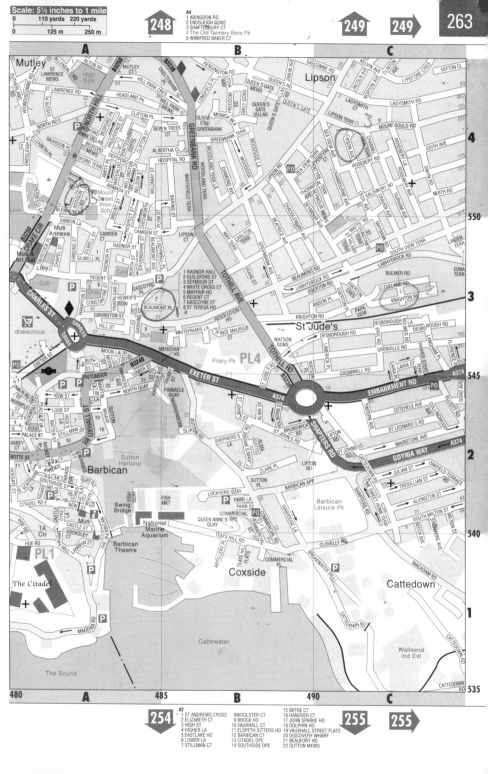

Index

Place name May be abbreviated on the map

Location number Present when a number indicates the place's position in a crowded area of mapping

Locality, town or village Shown when more than one place has the same name

Postcode district District for the indexed place

Page and grid square Page number and grid reference for the standard mapping

Church Rd **6** Beckenham BR2.........**53** C6

Public and commercial buildings are highlighted in magenta   Places of interest are highlighted in blue with a star*

Abbreviations used in the index

Acad	Academy	Comm	Common	Gd	Ground	L	Leisure	Prom	Promenade
App	Approach	Cott	Cottage	Gdn	Garden	La	Lane	Rd	Road
Arc	Arcade	Cres	Crescent	Gn	Green	Liby	Library	Recn	Recreation
Ave	Avenue	Cswy	Causeway	Gr	Grove	Mdw	Meadow	Ret	Retail
Bglw	Bungalow	Ct	Court	H	Hall	Meml	Memorial	Sh	Shopping
Bldg	Building	Ctr	Centre	Ho	House	Mkt	Market	Sq	Square
Bsns, Bus	Business	Ctry	Country	Hospl	Hospital	Mus	Museum	St	Street
Bvd	Boulevard	Cty	County	HQ	Headquarters	Orch	Orchard	Sta	Station
Cath	Cathedral	Dr	Drive	Hts	Heights	Pal	Palace	Terr	Terrace
Cir	Circus	Dro	Drove	Ind	Industrial	Par	Parade	TH	Town Hall
Cl	Close	Ed	Education	Inst	Institute	Pas	Passage	Univ	University
Cnr	Corner	Emb	Embankment	Int	International	Pk	Park	Wk, Wlk	Walk
Coll	College	Est	Estate	Intc	Interchange	Pl	Place	Wr	Water
Com	Community	Ex	Exhibition	Junc	Junction	Prec	Precinct	Yd	Yard

Index of localities, towns and villages

A

Abbey Gate 167 C2
Abbotsbury 207 B4
Abbotsham 156 A2
Abbotskerswell 212 B6
Abbotts Bickington 54 E8
Afton 217 E2
Aish Paignton 224 E2
  South Brent 134 F3
Albaston 125 C5
Alfardisworthy 53 B6
Alfington 100 F8
Allaleigh 139 E4
Allercombe 168 A6
All Saints 88 A4
Alphington 181 B7
Alston 88 A5
Alswear 30 C1
Alverdiscott 26 F4
Alwington 25 A2
Anderton 252 F4
Appledore Bideford 14 F1
  Uffculme 51 A1
Appley 51 B8
Arlingcott Beccott 10 D4
Arlington 10 D3
Ash 145 E8
Ashbrittle 50 F8
Ashburton 130 E5
Ashbury 92 E8
Ashcombe 124 D6
Ashculme 52 C1
Ashford Aveton Gifford . . . 143 C7
  Barnstable 66 D6
Ashill 66 D6
Ashmansworthy 39 A5
Ashmill 90 F6
Ash Mill 31 C2
Ashprington 139 F8
Ashreigney 58 F8
Ashridge 26 D6
Ash Thomas 65 A5
Ashwater 90 D6
Ashwell 124 B1
Atherington 28 A2
Aunk 83 E3
Aveton Gifford 143 C6
Avonwick 135 B1
Awliscombe 85 B4
Axminster 167 C6
Axmouth 192 E7
Aylesbeare 99 D2
Ayshford 50 E2

B

Babbacombe 220 D7
Badworthy 134 D4
Bagley Green 160 A3
Bakesdown 70 C3
Bampton 34 C1
Bantham 142 F2
Barbican 263 A2
Barbrook 151 B1
Barne Barton 247 C8
Barnfield 261 C3
Barnstaple 155 C4
Barton 213 F3
Barton Gate 11 E4
Barton Town 11 D3
Batsworthy 46 F6
Battisborough Cross 141 E7
Beacon 85 F8
Beacon Hill 174 C3
Beaford 42 D1
Bealsmill 115 C3
Beara 9 A1
Beare 82 E3
Beaston 131 D1
Beaworthy 74 A2
Beer 191 E5
Beesands 149 E7
Beeson 149 D7
Bellever 120 B4
Belsford 222 B3
Belstone 94 D4
Bennacott 89 B3
Benton 18 B7
Bentwichen 19 C4
Bere Alston 125 E1
Bere Ferrers 239 E3
Berrynarbor 2 E3
Berry Pomeroy 224 B7
Berrysbridge 81 E4
Bickerton 149 D5
Bickham 241 A7
Bickingcott 31 B7
Bickington Ashburton 131 D7
  Barnstable 154 B4
Bickleigh Plymouth 132 A5
  Tiverton 64 A1
Bickleton 153 C3
Bideford 156 E3
Bigbury 142 F5
Bigbury-on-Sea 142 E3
Birchill 88 A5
Biscombe 67 F8
Bish Mill 30 E4

Bishop's Tawton 16 F1
Bishops Nympton 31 A2
Bishopsteignton 208 E7
Bishopswood 69 C7
Bittadon 9 C4
Bittaford 137 C8
Blackawton 139 F2
Blackborough 66 D4
Black Dog 61 E4
Blackhorse 179 B7
Blackmoor 52 E5
Blackmoor Gate 11 A6
Blackpool 122 F1
Blackpool Corner 88 D1
Black Torrington 74 A8
Blackwell 35 B5
Blakemore 222 B5
Bodley 4 C2
Bogtown 92 D8
Boehetherick 125 B2
Bolberry 147 D6
Bolham 161 C8
Bolham Water 67 E7
Bondleigh 77 B7
Borne 44 B1
Borough 70 E5
Botusfleming 242 B7
Bovey Heath 180 E4
Bovey Tracey 180 D7
Bow Ashprington 139 F7
  Blackawton 145 B8
  Copplestone 78 C4
Bowd 100 F1
Bowden 145 F8
Bowood 25 B4
Boyton 89 E2
Bradfield 65 F4
Bradford 55 C2
Bradford 154 D7
Bradninch 82 F7
Bradstone 115 D7
Bradwell 18 F5
Bradworthy 38 E1
Brampford Speke 81 E1
Brandis Corner 73 B6
Branscombe 190 D3
Bratton Clovelly 92 A2
Bratton Fleming 18 A8
Braunton 152 B6
Brayford 18 E5
Brayfordshill 18 E5
Brendon Bradworthy 54 B8
  Holsworthy Beacon 54 C2
  Lynton 6 A4
Bridestowe 107 F8
Bridford 112 F5

Bridge Ball 5 E3
Bridge End Aveton Gifford 143 C5
  Newton Poppleford 187 A8
Bridgend 141 A7
Bridge-Reeve 59 B8
Bridgerule 70 F6
Bridgetown Launceston . . . 105 A8
  Totnes 223 F5
Brightley 94 B8
Brimley 88 D3
Brinsworthy 19 F1
Brithem Bottom 65 B5
Brixham 230 E3
Brixington 196 D3
Brixton 257 A5
Broadclyst 175 C6
Broadhembury 84 E7
Broadhempston 131 F1
Broadlands 207 A4
Broadley Hill 68 F2
Broad Oak 168 D3
Broadsands 229 C7
Broadwoodkelly 76 D8
Broadwoodwidger 106 B8
Brockfield 88 A8
Brockscombe 92 A5
Brook 171 B2
Brooking 135 F3
Broomhill 133 F1
Brownheath 52 C2
Brownston 137 F3
Brushford Bondleigh 59 D2
  Dulverton 33 D4
Buck's Cross 24 A1
Buck's Mills 24 C2
Buckerell 85 A3
Buckfast 236 B7
Buckfastleigh 236 C5
Buckhorn 72 D2
Buckland Newton Abbot . . 207 E2
  Thurlestone 143 B2
Buckland Brewer 40 C7
Buckland Filleigh 56 A4
Buckland Monachorum 126 D3
Buckland St Mary 69 C8
Buckland-Tout-Saints 144 C4
Buckleigh 156 D6
Budlake 82 E3
Budleigh Salterton 198 A2
Budford 10 C5
Bulkworthy 39 F1
Bulverton 187 F6
Burford 29 A2
Burlescombe 51 B3
Burlestone 145 D7

Burraton Ermington 136 D3
  Saltash 242 D4
  St Dominick 125 A2
Burraton Coombe 242 C2
Burridge 16 E6
Burrington 43 F3
Burrow Broadclyst 175 E8
  Newton Poppleford 186 C8
Burston 78 B5
Bury 34 A6
Butterleigh 64 C3

C

Cadbury 81 D7
Cadeleigh 63 D3
Cadleighpark 136 D6
Calstock 125 D3
Calverleigh 48 E1
Camels Head 247 E2
Capton 232 D7
Cargreen 239 A2
Carkeel 242 C6
Castle 88 D4
Caton 131 C6
Cattedown 263 C1
Caute 55 D5
Cawsand 253 B1
Chaddlewood 251 B6
Chagford 111 A6
Challaborough 142 E3
Challacombe 11 F3
Chamberombe 150 D5
Chapelton 27 F5
Chard Junction 88 E7
Chardstock 88 B7
Charles 18 E3
Charles Bottom 104 F4
Charmouth 104 A3
Charton 104 A1
Chasty 164 C2
Chawleigh 60 B7
Cheglinch 8 F6
Cheldon 60 D8
Chelfham 17 D6
Chelston Torquay 219 E4
  Wellington 52 B8
Chelston Heathfield 52 E7
Chenson 60 A4
Cheriston 22 D4
Cheriton 5 D3
Cheriton Bishop 97 A4
Cheriton Cross 97 B3
Cheriton Fitzpaine 62 E1
Cherrybridge 6 A4

Chestwood 155 B1
Chettiscombe 161 F8
Chevithorne 49 D2
Chilla 73 E5
Chillaton 116 D8
Chillington 145 A2
Chilson 88 C6
Chilson Common 88 D7
Chilsworthy Gunnislake 125 B7
  Holsworthy 53 E1
Chilton 80 E7
Chipstable 35 E6
Chittlehamholt 44 B8
Chittlehampton 28 F4
Chivelstone 149 A6
Chivenor 15 E5
Christow 113 A3
Chudleigh 123 F6
Chudleigh Knighton 123 C4
Chulmleigh 44 F1
Church Green 101 F7
Churchill Axminster 87 F4
  Barnstaple 10 B3
Churchinford 68 D7
Churchstow 143 E4
Churchtown Bridgerule 71 A6
  Parracombe 4 D2
Churscombe 218 E2
Churston Ferrers 229 E4
Clapham 114 B6
Clapworthy 29 D3
Clawton 72 B2
Clayhanger 35 C1
Clayhidon 52 E2
Claypits 34 C4
Clearbrook 132 A8
Cleave 86 C3
Clifford 38 C8
Clifton 10 C4
Clovelly 23 E3
Clyst Honiton 179 D8
Clyst Hydon 83 D4
Clyst St George 183 C6
Clyst St Lawrence 83 C3
Clyst St Mary 179 B3
Cobb 260 D2
Cobbaton 28 D5
Coburg 123 E5
Cockingford 121 B2
Cockington 219 C4
Cockwood 201 B5
Coffinswell 213 B6
Cofton 200 F5
Colaton Raleigh 186 D3
Coldeast 180 D1
Coldharbour 66 A7
Coldridge 59 F2
Colebrook Cullompton 65 A1
  Plymouth 250 E6
Colebrooke 79 A3
Coleford 79 A3
Collaton St Mary 225 C4
Colleton Mills 44 C2
Collipriest 161 C2
Colliton 84 C7
Columbjohn 82 C2
Colyford 103 B3
Colyton 103 A5
Combe Brixton 256 E5
  Buckfastleigh 130 A2
Combe Fishacre 217 E7
Combeinteignhead 208 E4
Combe Martin 3 B3
Combe Pafford 214 A1
Combe Raleigh 85 D5
Combe St Nicholas 69 F6
Combpyne 103 E2
Compton 218 D6
Cookbury 73 A8
Cookbury Wick 72 F8
Coombe Tipton St John 100 E2
  Tiverton 50 A4
Coombelake 169 B6
Copplestone 79 B6
Corfcott Green 71 F2
Cornwood 133 C2
Cornworthy 227 B4
Coryton Axminster 87 D1
  Lewtrenchard 106 F2
Cotford 101 C3
Cotmaton 187 F4
Cott 222 F8
Cotteylands 161 A3
Cottwood 43 D1
Countess Wear 178 B3
Countisbury 5 E6
Courshay 88 E3
Cove 49 B6
Cowley 172 E4
Cowleymoor 161 F5
Coxpark 125 A7
Coxside 263 B1
Crabtree 249 E5
Cradock 66 C7
Cranford 22 E6
Crapstone 126 E2
Crawley 69 C2
Crediton 165 D4
Cremyll 253 E2
Crimp 37 D2
Crockernwell 96 F3
Cross 7 F2
Crosslands 160 C8
Crossparks 164 F5
Cross Roads 106 F5
Crowden 74 D2
Crownhill 244 F2
Croyde 7 E2

Croyde Bay 7 D2
Cudlipptown 118 A6
Cullompton 163 A3
Culm Davy 52 A2
Culmstock 66 E8
Culverhill 116 C3
Curtisknowle 138 D4

D
Daccombe 213 E5
Dadbrook 252 E4
Dainton 212 A2
Dalwood 87 B3
Darracott 37 A4
Darracott 8 B2
Dartington 215 E1
Dartmeet 129 D8
Dartmouth 233 E3
Dawlish 204 F6
Dawlish Warren 201 A1
Dean Combe Martin 3 E2
  Lynton 5 A5
  West Down 8 E5
Dean Prior 135 C6
Denbury 211 B6
Deptford 43 B5
Derby 155 B6
Derriford 245 B4
Derriton 164 A3
Devonport 247 D4
Diddywell 157 B8
Didworthy 134 E5
Digby 178 D3
Dinworthy 38 D2
Dippertown 106 D3
Diptford 138 C7
Dittisham 228 C3
Doccombe 112 C5
Dodbrooke 258 E5
Doddiscombsleigh 113 C5
Dodscott 42 C6
Dog Village 175 D5
Dolton 57 F7
Dorsley Barton 222 D5
Dousland 127 C3
Dowland 57 F5
Down St Mary 78 E7
Downstow 134 F5
Down Thomas 255 C1
Drakeland Corner 132 E1
Drakewalls 125 C6
Drewsteignton 96 D2
Duerdon 38 E6
Dulford 84 B8
Dulverton 33 E6
Dumpinghill 55 F3
Dunchideock 114 A6
Dunkeswell 67 C2
Dunsford 112 F8
Dunstone Chillington 149 B7
  Widecombe in the Moor 121 B2
  Yealmpton 136 B2
Dunterton 115 D6
Duryard 173 A1
Dutson 105 A4

E
Eastacombe 27 C8
Eastacott 28 E2
East Allington 144 E7
East Anstey 32 E5
East Ash 95 D2
East Buckland 18 D2
East Budleigh 198 B6
East Butterleigh 64 E3
East Charleton 144 D1
Eastcott 37 D3
Eastdon 201 B4
East Down 10 C4
Eastern Town 188 B3
East Ilkerton 5 B3
Eastington 60 E4
East Knowstone 32 B2
Eastleigh 26 C6
East Leigh Haberton 222 B1
  Zeal Monachorum 77 F8
East Middleton 4 B1
East Ogwell 206 E1
Easton 111 B7
East Portlemouth 259 F4
East Prawle 149 A3
East Putford 39 C3
East Stowford 28 E5
East-the-Water 157 C2
East Town 165 E6
East Village 80 C8
East Worlington 61 B8
East Youlstone 37 F2
Ebberly Hill 42 F6
Ebford 183 C4
Edginswell 213 B1
Edistone 37 C8
Efford 249 C5
Eggbuckland 249 C8
Elburton 256 B6
Ellacombe 220 C6
Elmscott 37 B8
Elstone 44 D3
Elwell 18 C2
Ermington 136 F4
Ernesettle 243 E3
Estover 245 E4
Eworthy 91 E6
Exbourne 76 C4

Exebridge 33 F3
Exeter 261 B4
Exminster 182 B4
Exmouth 202 B7
Exton 183 D2
Exwick 176 E7

F
Fairmile 169 B7
Fairy Cross 25 A3
Falkedon 77 A6
Farringdon 99 B1
Farway 102 A6
Feniton 84 E2
Filham 237 F4
Filleigh 29 C7
Flitton Barton 19 B1
Fluxton 100 C3
Folly Gate 93 E8
Ford Bideford 25 B3
  Chillington 149 A7
  Holbeton 136 D1
  Holcombe Rogus 50 F5
Forda 93 B1
Forder 242 C1
Forder Green 131 C2
Fordlands 156 F5
Ford Park 248 D4
Ford Street 52 D5
Fordton 165 E3
Fortescue 188 D7
Fortescue Cross 44 C4
Foxhayes 176 F7
Friars' Green 261 A2
Frithelstock 41 A6
Frithelstock Stone 40 F5
Frittiscombe 145 B2
Frogmore 144 E1
Frost 61 A1
Furley 87 D7
Fyldon 19 D4

G
Galmpton Malborough 147 C7
  Paignton 229 A6
Galmpton Warborough 229 A6
Gammaton 26 C4
Gammaton Moor 26 D3
Garlandhayes 52 F2
Gatherley 105 D1
Georgeham 8 B2
George Nympton 30 A1
Germansweek 91 D5
Gidleigh 110 D7
Gilscott 24 E2
Gittisham 85 B7
Glenholt 245 D6
Goldworthy 24 F1
Goodleigh 17 C5
Goodrington 226 B2
Goodstone 131 C6
Gooseham 37 B3
Goosemoor 186 B7
Goosewell 2 D4
Gosford 169 D7
Goveton 144 C5
Grange Pk 208 D8
Gratton 54 F5
Great Hayne 63 A2
Great Torrington 159 D6
Great Weeke 111 B6
Green Gate 50 B2
Greenham 51 B7
Greenhill 207 E5
Grenofen 126 D6
Grinacombe Moor 91 B2
Gulworthy 125 E8
Gunn 17 F4
Gunnislake 125 D6
Guscott 26 E2

H
Haddacott 26 E3
Halberton 65 B8
Half Moon Village 172 C7
Halford 122 F1
Hallands 149 E5
Hallsannery 25 F3
Hallspill 26 B2
Halsfordwood 98 F4
Halsinger 15 F6
Halwell 139 B4
Halwill 73 C2
Halwill Junction 73 E2
Ham Axminster 86 F4
  Plymouth 248 A8
  Wellington 52 B8
Hampton 103 C7
Hand & Pen 99 C4
Hannaford 28 C8
Harberton 222 D1
Harbertonford 139 C6
Harbourneford 135 B5
Harcombe Chudleigh 124 A8
  Sidford 101 D1
Harcombe Bottom 104 D6
Hardisworthy 37 A7
Harewood 125 E4
Harford Cornwood 133 F7
  Tedburn St Mary 97 F7

Harleston 145 A4
Harpford 100 C1
Harrowbarrow 125 A4
Hartford 34 C8
Hartland 22 E3
Hartley 248 E7
Hartley Vale 249 A8
Hatch 143 E5
Hatherleigh 75 C6
Hawkchurch 88 E3
Hawkridge 21 D1
Haytown 39 E1
Headon 72 C5
Heale 4 A3
Heanton Punchardon 15 E6
Heasley Mill 19 D3
Heath 175 D6
Heathfield 180 F2
Heathstock 87 A6
Heavitree 178 B6
Heddon 29 B7
Hele Bradninch 82 F5
  Ilfracombe 150 F6
  Torquay 219 F8
Heltor 112 D6
Hemerdon 251 C7
Hemsford 216 F4
Hemyock 67 C8
Henford 90 C5
Hennock 123 B7
Henstridge 3 A1
Hexworthy 129 B7
Heybrook Bay 140 B8
Highampton 74 C7
High Bickington 43 B7
High Bray 18 F5
High Bullen 42 B7
Higher Ashton 113 D3
Higher Batson 259 C6
Higher Blagdon 225 A7
Higher Brixham 230 B3
Higher Burrowton 99 A8
Higher Cheriton 84 E3
Higher Clovelly 23 D2
Higher Compton 249 A6
Higher Dean 135 C7
Higher Gabwell 214 B7
Higher Keaton 237 D1
Higher Metcombe 168 D1
Higher Muddiford 9 D1
Higher Prestacott 90 F7
Higher Roscombe
  Barton 214 A6
Higher Slade 1 E3
Higher Tale 84 A4
Higher Town 236 A5
Higher Warcombe 1 B2
Higher Wear 178 A1
Higher Woolbrook 187 F7
Higher Yalberton 225 C3
Highweek 206 F5
Hillerton 78 C1
Hillfield 232 C3
Hillhead 234 F8
Hillmoor 66 E8
Hillside 135 A3
Hiscott 27 C5
Hittisleigh 96 D5
Hockholler 52 E8
Hockholler Green 52 E8
Hockworthy 50 D6
Hoggs Park 54 A1
Holbeton 136 D1
Holcombe Lyme Regis 104 B4
  Teignmouth 204 D3
Holcombe Rogus 50 F5
Holemoor 73 B8
Holewater 19 A6
Hollacombe 72 D6
Hollacombe Hill 256 A2
Hollicombe 219 D1
Hollocombe 58 F6
Hollocombe Town 58 E6
Holmacott 26 E7
Holmsleigh Green 86 C5
Holne 130 A4
Holsworthy 164 D5
Holsworthy Beacon 54 C3
Holy City 87 F7
Holywell Lake 51 E7
Honeychurch 76 E5
Honicknowle 244 B2
Honiton 166 D4
Hooe 255 C5
Hook 88 B8
Hoo Meavy 132 A8
Hoops 24 D2
Hopworthy 71 C5
Horndon 118 A7
Horns Cross 24 E2
Horrabridge 126 F5
Horsebridge 116 A1
Horsebrook 135 B1
Horwood 26 E6
Houghton 206 C6
Howley 69 C4
Huccaby 129 C7
Huccombe 149 C7
Huddisford 38 C6
Huish 57 B8
Huish Champflower 35 F8
Hulham 196 B3
Humber 124 C2
Huntsham 50 A7
Huntshaw 26 E1
Huntshaw Water 26 E2
Huxham 174 B8
Huxhill 26 D2

I
Iddesleigh 57 F3
Ide 176 D1
Ideford 124 A4
Ilfracombe 150 B6
Ilsington 122 C3
Ingleigh Green 58 C2
Inner Hope 147 C6
Instow 15 B1
Insworke 252 F6
Inwardleigh 75 E2
Ipplepen 211 C2
Ivybridge 237 C6

J
Jack-in-the-Green 99 B6
Jacobstowe 76 A4
Jewel's Cross 70 E6
Jordan 121 A2

K
Kellacot 105 F7
Kellaton 149 B6
Kelly 115 F8
Kemacott 4 C4
Kenn 114 E4
Kennerleigh 61 F2
Kennford 181 B2
Kentisbeare 66 A3
Kentisbury 10 E6
Kentisbury Ford 10 E5
Kenton 194 E3
Kernborough 149 B8
Kersbrook 198 B3
Kerscott 28 F8
Kerswell 66 C1
Keyham 247 E5
Killington 4 C3
Kilmington 103 D8
King's Nympton 44 E6
King's Tamerton 243 F2
Kingford 43 E6
Kingsand 253 A2
Kingsbridge 258 E5
Kingscott 42 B5
Kingsdon 103 B5
Kingskerswell 213 B4
Kingsteignton 207 C8
Kingston Bigbury 142 C6
  Colaton Raleigh 186 A4
  Stoke Climsland 115 C2
Kingswear 234 B2
Kitbridge 88 A6
Knap Down 3 B4
Knighton 140 D8
Knotty Corner 25 B4
Knowle Braunton 8 D1
  Budleigh Salterton 197 E2
  Copplestone 79 C4
Knowles Hill 207 B4
Knowstone 32 A2

L
Laira 249 C4
Lake Barnstaple 154 E2
  Yelverton 127 B3
Lamerton 116 F3
Lana Holsworthy 53 C2
  Tetcott 89 F7
Landcross 26 A2
Landkey 17 B2
Landkey Newland 17 B1
Landscove 131 B1
Landulph 243 A7
Lane End 73 D3
Langford 73 B2
Langbrook 136 D3
Langdown 95 D7
Langford
  Brampford Speke 172 E8
  Plymtree 83 C5
Langleigh 150 A4
Langridgeford 27 F1
Langtree 40 F2
Langtree Common 41 A3
Lapford 60 C3
Lapford Cross 60 C2
Larkbeare 100 B8
Launceston 105 B2
Lawhitton 105 B1
Ledstone 144 B5
Lee 1 C3
Leeford 6 B5
Lee Mill 136 C7
Lee Moor 132 F5
Leigham 249 E8
Leusdon 130 A8
Lewdown 106 E5
Lewtrenchard 106 F4
Liddaton 106 F1
Lifton 105 C4
Liftondown 105 B3
Lincombe 1 D3
Lipson 263 C4
Lipson Vale 249 A4
Little Comfort 115 A7
Littleham Bideford 25 D2
  Exmouth 202 F7
Littlehempston 216 F2
Little Knowle 197 F1

Little Silver . . . 63 D4
Little Torrington . . . 41 D3
Littletown . . . 166 B4
Livermead . . . 219 E2
Liverton . . . 180 A1
Lobb . . . 152 A8
Lobhillcross . . . 107 A5
Loddiswell . . . 143 F7
Longbridge . . . 249 F7
Longcause . . . 223 A7
Longdown . . . 98 C2
Longlands . . . 242 A1
Lovaton . . . 127 C1
Lower Ashton . . . 113 C3
Lower Batson . . . 259 D6
Lower Blagdon . . . 225 B6
Lower Brimley . . . 180 A5
Lower Cheriton . . . 84 E4
Lower Compton . . . 249 A5
Lower Dean . . . 236 A2
Lower Gabwell . . . 214 B8
Lower Holditch . . . 88 D5
Lower Keaton . . . 237 E1
Lower Lovacott . . . 27 A6
Lower Loxhore . . . 173 A4
Lower Milcott . . . 173 A4
Lower Netherton . . . 208 C4
Lower Ridge . . . 86 F4
Lower Slade . . . 150 B2
Lower Tale . . . 84 A5
Lower Tippacott . . . 6 A4
Lower Town Ashburton . . . 130 A7
  Buckfastleigh . . . 236 C5
  Halberton . . . 65 A7
Lower Wadstray . . . 232 B2
Lower Wear . . . 182 B7
Lower Westford . . . 160 A6
Lower Woolbrook . . . 188 A6
Loxbeare . . . 48 C3
Loxhore . . . 10 D1
Loxhore Cott. . . . 10 D1
Ludbrook . . . 137 C5
Luffincott . . . 89 F5
Luppitt . . . 67 E1
Luson . . . 136 C1
Lustleigh . . . 122 C8
Luton Payhembury . . . 84 B5
  Teignmouth . . . 124 C3
Lutsford . . . 37 D6
Lutton Cornwood . . . 133 B2
  South Brent . . . 135 F8
Luxton . . . 68 D6
Lydcott . . . 18 F7
Lydford . . . 107 F7
Lyme Regis . . . 260 E2
Lympstone . . . 195 E5
Lyneham . . . 257 F7
Lynmouth . . . 151 D5
Lynton . . . 151 B4

M

Mackham . . . 67 C4
Madford . . . 67 D6
Maidencombe . . . 214 D6
Maidenhayne . . . 103 F2
Mainstone . . . 245 F2
Malborough . . . 147 E6
Malmsmead . . . 6 C4
Manadon . . . 244 D1
Manaton . . . 121 F8
Mannamead . . . 248 F5
Manor Bourne . . . 140 A8
Marhamchurch . . . 70 A6
Mariansleigh . . . 30 D1
Marldon . . . 218 C3
Marsh . . . 69 B5
Marsh Green . . . 99 E4
Marsh Mills . . . 249 F6
Martinhoe . . . 4 C5
Marwood . . . 16 C8
Marystow . . . 106 D1
Mary Tavy . . . 117 E6
Maundown . . . 35 F7
Mead . . . 37 A4
Meadwell . . . 116 A8
Meavy . . . 127 C2
Meddon . . . 37 F4
Meeth . . . 57 C3
Meethe . . . 29 D1
Meldon . . . 93 D3
Membland . . . 141 B7
Membury . . . 87 D6
Merrifield . . . 70 F4
Merrivale . . . 118 C2
Merton . . . 57 A7
Meshaw . . . 45 F6
Metcombe . . . 100 B2
Metherell . . . 125 A4
Michelcombe . . . 129 F4
Middlecott . . . 73 B8
Middle Green . . . 160 D3
Middle Luxton . . . 68 C5
Middle Marwood . . . 9 B1
Middlemoor . . . 171 F2
Middle Moor . . . 178 D4
Middle Rocombe . . . 213 F7
Middle Wadstray . . . 232 A3
Middle Woolbrook . . . 188 A8
Milber . . . 207 F1
Mile End . . . 245 B3
Milford . . . 22 B1
Millbay . . . 262 B2
Millbrook Axminster . . . 167 E6
  North Molton . . . 19 F1
  Torpoint . . . 252 E4
Millhayes Hemyock . . . 52 C1

Honiton . . . 86 F6
Millhill . . . 116 F1
Millmoor . . . 51 E1
Milltown . . . 9 D1
Millwey Rise . . . 167 F7
Milton Abbot . . . 116 B6
Milton Combe . . . 126 C1
Milton Damerel . . . 54 D5
Milton Green . . . 116 B5
Milton Hill . . . 124 E5
Modbury . . . 137 C2
Mogworthy . . . 47 D4
Molland . . . 31 E7
Monkerton . . . 178 E8
Monkleigh . . . 40 F7
Monkokehampton . . . 76 B8
Monkton . . . 86 A5
Monkton Wyld . . . 104 D7
Moor Cross . . . 133 C1
Moorhaven Village . . . 137 C8
Moorhayes . . . 161 E6
Moorlake . . . 79 F2
Moortown Great Torrington . . . 41 F7
  Tavistock . . . 127 A8
  Tetcott . . . 89 F7
Morchard Bishop . . . 61 A2
Morchard Road . . . 78 F7
Morebath . . . 34 B3
Moreleigh . . . 139 A3
Moretonhampstead . . . 111 E4
Morice Town . . . 247 D3
Morley . . . 206 B3
Mortehoe . . . 7 F8
Morwellham . . . 125 E4
Morwenstow . . . 36 E2
Mothecombe . . . 142 A6
Mount Gould . . . 249 B3
Mount Lane . . . 90 B6
Mount Pleasant . . . 86 B3
Mount Radford . . . 261 C2
Mount Wise . . . 247 F1
Mouth Mill . . . 23 B5
Muddiford . . . 9 E1
Muddlebridge . . . 16 A3
Murchington . . . 110 F2
Musbury . . . 103 D5
Musehill . . . 106 F6
Mutley . . . 248 E4
Mutterton . . . 83 D8

N

Nadderwater . . . 176 B7
Narford's . . . 69 F1
Natcott . . . 22 F2
Neopardy . . . 79 D1
Nethercott . . . 81 F2
Netherexe . . . 81 F2
Netherton . . . 208 C3
Nettacott . . . 81 C2
Newbuildings . . . 79 D6
Newcott . . . 68 F3
Newhaven . . . 24 F1
Newport . . . 155 B3
Newtake . . . 208 A1
Newton Abbot . . . 207 A2
Newton Ferrers . . . 140 F7
Newton Poppleford . . . 186 E7
Newton St Cyres . . . 172 A8
Newton St Petrock . . . 55 B7
Newton Tracey . . . 27 A5
Newtown Buckland St Mary . . . 69 D7
  Exeter . . . 177 E6
  South Molton . . . 31 A4
New Town . . . 188 B4
Norley . . . 74 E3
Norris Green . . . 125 B4
Northam . . . 157 A6
Northay Axminster . . . 88 G3
  Chard . . . 69 E6
North Bovey . . . 111 E2
North Brentor . . . 117 C8
North Buckland . . . 8 C3
Northcott . . . 90 A3
North End . . . 51 E3
North Heasley . . . 19 D4
North Huish . . . 138 B7
Northleigh . . . 102 B7
Northlew . . . 74 E1
North Molton . . . 30 D8
Northmoor . . . 38 C3
Northmostown . . . 187 B7
North Prospect . . . 248 A6
North Radworthy . . . 19 F5
North Star . . . 198 F8
North Tamerton . . . 89 C8
North Tawton . . . 77 C5
North Town . . . 56 E4
Northway . . . 24 D2
North Whilborough . . . 218 A7
Norton Dartmouth . . . 233 A2
  Halwill . . . 22 E4
Noss Mayo . . . 140 F6
Nymet Rowland . . . 60 B3
Nymet Tracey . . . 78 C3

O

Oakford . . . 48 C8
Oakfordbridge . . . 48 D8
Oare . . . 6 C4
Oareford . . . 6 F3
Odham . . . 74 B5
Offwell . . . 86 B2
Okehampton . . . 170 A6
Olchard . . . 123 F3

Oldborough . . . 61 B1
Oldway . . . 226 A8
Oldways End . . . 32 E3
Orchard Hill . . . 157 A4
Oreston . . . 255 C7
Ossaborough . . . 8 B6
Otterton . . . 198 F7
Ottery . . . 116 E2
Ottery St Mary . . . 169 E3
Outer Hope . . . 147 C7

P

Paignton . . . 226 D6
Pancrasweek . . . 71 B8
Parkham . . . 39 E8
Parkham Ash . . . 39 C7
Parnacott . . . 71 D8
Parracombe . . . 4 C2
Patchacott . . . 74 B1
Patchole . . . 10 D5
Pathfinder Village . . . 98 C4
Payhembury . . . 84 C4
Payton . . . 51 F7
Penhale . . . 252 D7
Penhill . . . 16 A4
Penn . . . 104 E6
Penninn . . . 207 E1
Pennsylvania . . . 173 C1
Pennycomequick . . . 262 B4
Pennycross . . . 248 C8
Pennymoor . . . 62 D6
Penquit . . . 237 F1
Penstone . . . 79 B3
Peppercombe . . . 24 E2
Perkin's Village . . . 99 C2
Perry Street . . . 88 E8
Peter's Finger . . . 105 B7
Peters Marland . . . 56 C8
Peter Tavy . . . 117 F4
Petrockstow . . . 56 F4
Petton . . . 35 A3
Peverell . . . 248 D6
Philham . . . 22 D1
Pillhead . . . 157 F2
Pilton . . . 154 E6
Pinhay . . . 104 B2
Pinhoe . . . 174 F2
Plainmoor . . . 220 B7
Pleamore Cross . . . 160 A2
Plymouth . . . 262 C1
Plympton . . . 250 E5
Plympton St Maurice . . . 250 E4
Plymstock . . . 255 E6
Plymtree . . . 83 E5
Polehays . . . 74 B1
Polsloe Park . . . 177 E7
Polsloe Priory . . . 177 F8
Poltimore . . . 174 F6
Pomphlett . . . 255 E8
Ponsworthy . . . 130 A8
Poole . . . 160 F8
Popham . . . 19 A3
Portgate . . . 106 C4
Portington . . . 116 C3
Posbury . . . 97 F8
Postbridge . . . 120 A6
Pottington . . . 154 D6
Poughill . . . 62 D3
Poundsgate . . . 130 A7
Prescott . . . 51 C1
Preston . . . 226 B8
Priestacott . . . 55 E3
Prince Rock . . . 249 B1
Princetown . . . 128 B8
Pristacott . . . 27 C5
Prixford . . . 16 C7
Puddaven . . . 223 A8
Puddington . . . 62 B5
Puddington Bottom . . . 62 B4
Pusehill . . . 156 B5
Putsborough . . . 7 F3
Pyworthy . . . 71 D5

Q

Queen Dart . . . 47 C3
Quoditch . . . 91 A8

R

Rackenford . . . 47 D5
Raddington . . . 35 B4
Raddon . . . 81 D4
Raleigh . . . 155 A7
Raleigh Hill . . . 156 E4
Rame . . . 140 H2
Ratsloe . . . 174 D8
Rattery . . . 135 D4
Rawridge . . . 68 C1
Raymond's Hill . . . 104 C7
Red Ball . . . 51 C4
Red Cow Village . . . 177 A8
Redhills . . . 176 E5
Redlane . . . 86 C3
Redmonsford . . . 38 C2
Red Post . . . 70 E8
Reedy . . . 113 A8
Rew Ashburton . . . 130 F6
  Malborough . . . 147 F5
Rewe . . . 82 A2
Rexon . . . 106 B7
Rezare . . . 115 C4
Rickard's Down . . . 156 A3
Riddlecombe . . . 58 D8

Ringmore Bigbury-on-Sea . . . 142 E4
  Teignmouth . . . 209 D4
Riverside Plymouth . . . 243 A1
  Wellington . . . 160 B6
Rixlade . . . 25 B5
Road Green . . . 103 A5
Roborough
  Great Torrington . . . 42 F3
  Plymouth . . . 241 D1
Roborough Down . . . 126 F3
Rock . . . 87 D5
Rockbeare . . . 99 C6
Rockford . . . 5 F4
Rockwell Green . . . 160 B5
Romansleigh . . . 45 C7
Rosedown . . . 22 F3
Rosemary Lane . . . 52 D1
Roundswell . . . 154 B2
Rousdon . . . 193 F7
Royston Water . . . 68 F8
Rumsam . . . 155 B1
Rundlestone . . . 118 F2
Runnington . . . 51 F8
Rushford . . . 116 C3
Rydon . . . 207 E8

S

St Andrew's Wood . . . 84 A8
St Ann's Chapel
  Gunnislake . . . 125 B6
  Kingston . . . 142 F6
St Brannocks . . . 152 C7
St Budeaux . . . 243 D2
St David's . . . 177 B8
St Dominick . . . 125 A3
St Dympna's . . . 192 A8
St George's Well . . . 163 C5
St Giles in the Wood . . . 42 B6
St Giles on the Heath . . . 90 B1
Saint Hill . . . 66 D3
St James' . . . 177 D3
St John's Chapel . . . 27 B8
St John . . . 252 B7
St Jude's . . . 263 B3
St Loye's . . . 174 A1
St Marychurch . . . 214 C1
St Michaels . . . 226 A5
St Stephens . . . 242 D2
St Thomas . . . 177 A3
Salcombe . . . 259 B4
Salcombe Regis . . . 188 F6
Salmonhutch . . . 165 E2
Saltash . . . 242 B1
Saltrens . . . 25 F1
Sampford Arundel . . . 51 E5
Sampford Chapple . . . 76 E3
Sampford Courtenay . . . 76 F4
Sampford Moor . . . 51 E5
Sampford Peverell . . . 50 E1
Sampford Spiney . . . 127 B7
Sandford . . . 80 A5
Sandygate . . . 123 E1
Sandy Gate . . . 178 F3
Sandy Park . . . 111 B8
Satterleigh . . . 29 C1
Saunton . . . 14 F8
Sawyer's Hill . . . 52 E7
Scorriton . . . 130 A3
Seaton . . . 192 B5
Sector . . . 88 D3
Shadycombe . . . 259 D5
Shaldon . . . 210 A6
Shaugh Prior . . . 132 C6
Shebbear . . . 55 D4
Sheepstor . . . 127 E2
Sheepwash . . . 56 C1
Sheldon . . . 66 F3
Sherberton . . . 129 A8
Sherford . . . 144 F3
Shillingford . . . 34 E2
Shillingford Abbot . . . 181 A6
Shillingford St George . . . 114 C7
Shiphay . . . 219 C2
Shirwell . . . 17 B8
Shobrooke . . . 80 E4
Shop Kilkhampton . . . 37 C1
  Milton Damerel . . . 54 F6
Shore Bottom . . . 86 F6
Shortacombe . . . 108 A5
Short Moor . . . 86 E7
Shorton . . . 219 A1
Shute Kilmington . . . 103 A8
  Newton St Cyres . . . 81 A3
Sid . . . 188 C5
Sidbury . . . 101 C3
Sidford . . . 101 B1
Sidmouth . . . 188 C3
Sigford . . . 131 B8
Silford . . . 156 D4
Silver Street . . . 52 F8
Silverton . . . 82 B5
Simonsbath . . . 13 B2
Simonsburrow . . . 52 C3
Sitcott . . . 90 C2
Skilgate . . . 34 E6
Slapton . . . 145 C4
Slerra . . . 23 D3
Sloncombe . . . 111 E5
Smeatharpe . . . 68 B5
Smithaleigh . . . 136 A6
Smithincott . . . 66 A6
Soar . . . 147 E4
Soldon Cross . . . 53 E5
Sorley . . . 143 F5
Sourton . . . 93 B1
South Allington . . . 149 B5

South Brent . . . 134 F3
South Chard . . . 88 C8
South Common . . . 88 A4
Southcott . . . 157 D4
South Down . . . 66 C6
Southerly . . . 108 A7
Southerton . . . 100 B1
South Hole . . . 37 A7
South Huish . . . 147 D7
South Knighton . . . 131 F7
Southleigh . . . 102 C4
South Milton . . . 143 D1
South Molton . . . 158 D3
South Pill . . . 242 E3
South Pool . . . 148 F7
South Radworthy . . . 19 F3
South Tawton . . . 95 B5
Southville . . . 258 E3
Southway . . . 244 F6
South Wonford . . . 54 E3
South Zeal . . . 95 B3
Sowton . . . 179 B6
Sowtontown . . . 117 F3
Sparkwell . . . 136 A8
Spreyton . . . 95 F7
Spriddlestone . . . 256 C4
Sprytown . . . 106 B4
Staddiscombe . . . 255 F3
Staddon . . . 72 C6
Stapley . . . 67 E8
Starcross . . . 201 A8
Start . . . 145 B4
Staverton . . . 216 B5
Stevenstone . . . 42 A6
Stibb Cross . . . 40 C1
Sticklepath Barnstaple . . . 154 E4
  Okehampton . . . 95 A5
Stockland . . . 87 A7
Stockland English . . . 62 D1
Stockleigh Pomeroy . . . 81 A6
Stockley Hamlet . . . 94 C8
Stockwell . . . 82 D5
Stoford Water . . . 66 B3
Stoke Ashburton . . . 129 F5
  Hartland . . . 22 B3
  Plymouth . . . 248 A3
Stoke Canon . . . 173 E8
Stoke Climsland . . . 115 C1
Stoke Fleming . . . 146 B7
Stoke Gabriel . . . 227 F7
Stoke Hill . . . 173 E1
Stokeinteignhead . . . 209 B1
Stokenham . . . 145 C1
Stoke Post . . . 174 A5
Stoke Rivers . . . 17 F6
Stonecombe . . . 10 C6
Stonehouse . . . 248 A1
Stoneycombe . . . 212 D3
Stoneyford Cullompton . . . 163 D4
  Newton Poppleford . . . 186 A6
Stony Cross . . . 26 F4
Stonyland . . . 27 B8
Stoodleigh . . . 48 E5
Stopgate . . . 68 F4
Stormsdown . . . 131 B7
Stourscombe . . . 105 A2
Stowford Bradworthy . . . 53 B8
  Challacombe . . . 11 B4
  Chittlehampton . . . 28 E5
  Colaton Raleigh . . . 186 A3
  Halwill Junction . . . 91 D8
Stratton . . . 70 B5
Street . . . 187 E8
Street Ash . . . 69 F8
Strete . . . 145 E5
Stroxworthy . . . 39 A6
Sutcombe . . . 54 A6
Sutcombemill . . . 54 A6
Sutton . . . 143 D1
Swallowfields . . . 223 C7
Swimbridge . . . 17 D1
Swimbridge Newland . . . 17 C2
Sycamore . . . 87 B7
Sydenham Damerel . . . 116 B2

T

Talaton . . . 84 A2
Taleford . . . 169 C6
Tamerton Foliot . . . 244 B7
Tatworth . . . 88 C8
Tavistock . . . 171 C5
Taw Green . . . 95 B7
Tawstock . . . 27 D8
Tedburn St Mary . . . 97 F5
Teigncombe . . . 110 D6
Teigngrace . . . 206 F8
Teignmouth . . . 210 D4
Templeton . . . 48 A1
Tetcott . . . 89 F7
The Mounts . . . 144 C7
The Point . . . 201 E7
Thorn . . . 110 E5
Thornbury . . . 55 A3
Thorndon Cross . . . 93 A4
Thorne Moor . . . 105 E8
Thorne St Margaret . . . 51 D8
Thornham . . . 237 E1
Thornhillhead . . . 40 B3
Thorverton . . . 81 D5
Three Horse Shoes . . . 172 E6
Threshelton . . . 106 E6
Thurlestone . . . 143 A2
Tigley . . . 135 F3
Tilworth . . . 88 D3
Tinhay . . . 105 F4

Tipton St John........ 100 D2
Titchberry............. 22 C6
Titson................. 70 C4
Tiverton.............. 161 D3
Tone................. 160 A8
Tonedale............. 160 B7
Topsham.............. 182 F5
Tor.................. 133 D3
Torbryan............. 211 A2
Torcross............. 145 D1
Torpoint............. 247 C3
Torquay.............. 220 B2
Torre................ 219 F5
Torrs Park........... 150 A5
Tosberry.............. 37 E8
Totnes............... 223 E6
Townlake............. 116 A1
Townstal............. 233 D3
Tracebridge........... 51 A8
Treburley............ 115 A4
Trecombe............. 115 D4
Tregonhawke.......... 252 B4
Trehan............... 242 A1
Trekenner............ 115 A5
Trentishoe............. 4 A5
Trewyn............... 164 B5
Trimstone.............. 8 E6
Trinity............... 82 F8
Trow................. 189 A7
True Street.......... 224 A6
Trusham.............. 113 D1
Tuckenhay............ 139 F7
Tuckermarsh.......... 125 E2
Tudhay................ 88 C3
Turfmoor.............. 87 D4
Turnchapel........... 255 B7
Tutwell.............. 115 E2
Tweenaways........... 225 E4
Twitchen.............. 20 D1
Two Bridges.......... 119 C1
Two Pots.............. 2 B1
Tythecott............. 40 B4
Tytherleigh........... 88 C6

U

Uffculme.............. 66 A8
Ugborough............ 137 E6
Ullcombe.............. 68 D4
Umberleigh............ 28 D2
Umborne.............. 102 F8
Underwood............ 250 C5

Upcott Dolton......... 57 F4
  Holsworthy.......... 72 E7
Up Exe................ 82 A5
Upham................. 63 A3
Uphempston........... 217 A3
Uplowman.............. 50 B2
Uplyme............... 260 B5
Uppottery............. 68 C2
Uppacott.............. 27 D7
Uppincott............. 81 A5
Upton Payhembury..... 84 D5
  Skigate............. 34 F8
  Torquay............ 220 A6
Upton Hellions....... 80 C6
Upton Pyne.......... 173 A8
Uton................ 165 B1

V

Vale Down............ 108 A5
Velator.............. 152 C4
Velly................. 23 B3
Venn................. 143 D5
Venngreen............ 54 D6
Venn Ottery.......... 100 B2
Venny Tedburn......... 98 A8
Venterdon............ 115 B2
Venton................. 7 F3
Venton Drewsteignton. 95 F1
  Ivybridge.......... 136 B7
Vicarage............. 190 F4
Virginstow............ 90 D3
Voxmoor.............. 160 F1

W

Wadbrook.............. 88 C4
Waddeton............ 228 F6
Waddicombe........... 32 E6
Waddon............... 124 A6
Waggs Plot............ 88 B4
Walkhampton......... 127 A4
Wambrook............. 69 F3
Warfleet............. 234 A1
Warkleigh............. 29 A2
Warleigh Barton..... 243 F8
Wash................ 215 B7
Washbourne.......... 139 D5
Washfield............. 48 F2
Washford Pyne........ 61 F6
Watchcombe.......... 102 F8

Watcombe............ 214 B2
Water................ 121 F7
Waterhead........... 143 B6
Watermoor............ 35 F4
Waytown.............. 24 D1
Way Village........... 63 A5
Wearde.............. 242 F2
Weare Giffard......... 26 B1
Week Barnstaple....... 27 E6
  North Tawton........ 77 B4
  Totnes............. 215 D1
Welcombe............. 37 A5
Wellington........... 160 D7
Wellisford............ 51 D8
Wellswood........... 220 D5
Welsford.............. 37 F8
Wembury............. 140 D7
Wembworthy........... 59 C4
Westacott............ 155 F4
West Alvington...... 258 B4
West Anstey.......... 32 C6
West Buckland Barnstaple. 18 B2
  Wellington.......... 52 F7
West Charleton...... 144 C1
Westcott.............. 83 C7
West Curry............ 89 A4
West Down.............. 8 F5
Westerland.......... 218 D1
Western Common....... 19 D7
Western Town........ 188 A3
Westford.............. 51 F7
West Hill............ 168 E4
West Hoe............ 262 B1
West Ilkerton......... 5 A3
Westlake............. 136 E4
Westleigh Bideford... 157 E6
  Wellington.......... 51 A4
West Leigh............ 77 E8
West Ogwell......... 206 A1
Weston.............. 189 D6
Weston Mill......... 247 E8
Weston Town......... 189 D6
West Park........... 244 A3
West Putford......... 39 C2
West Sandford........ 79 E5
West Town Crediton.. 165 B5
  Newton St Cyres..... 98 F8
  Woolfardisworthy.... 38 E8
Westville............ 258 B5
Westward Ho!........ 156 D8
Westweekmoor........ 91 A4
Westwood Cockwood... 201 A6
  Crediton........... 165 A5

Whimple.............. 83 C1
West Worlington..... 61 A8
West Youlstone....... 37 E2
Weycroft............. 88 B2
Whiddon Barnstaple.. 155 D2
  Marwood............. 9 D1
Whiddon Down......... 95 F3
Whimble............. 164 E2
Whimple.............. 99 E7
Whipcott............. 51 B5
Whipton............. 178 C8
Whitchurch.......... 171 C6
White Ball........... 51 D6
Whitehall............ 52 A1
Whitestaunton....... 69 D5
Whitestone........... 98 E4
Whitford............ 103 B6
Whitleigh........... 244 C5
Whitnage............. 50 C2
Whitstone............ 70 E1
Widecombe in the
   Moor............. 121 B4
Widewell............ 245 B7
Widworthy............ 86 D2
Wiggaton............ 100 A4
Willand Taunton...... 68 B8
  Tiverton........... 162 E4
Willand Moor........ 162 E5
Willingcott........... 8 D6
Wilmington........... 86 D3
Wilminstone......... 117 D3
Wilsham............... 5 F5
Wiltown.............. 52 F3
Winkleigh............ 58 E2
Winsford............ 156 C2
Winsham............... 8 E1
Winslade Park....... 179 B2
Winston............. 257 B4
Winswell............. 56 D8
Withacott............ 40 D2
Witheridge........... 46 F1
Withleigh............ 63 D7
Withycombe Raleigh.. 196 C2
Withypool............ 21 C6
Wolborough......... 207 B6
Wollaton............ 257 B6
Wolverstone.......... 85 A7
Wonford............. 178 A4
Wonson.............. 110 D8
Wooda............... 157 C8
Woodacott............ 54 E2
Woodbury............ 184 C3
Woodbury Salterton.. 184 C6

Woodford Blackawton. 139 D2
  Plymouth........... 250 C7
Woodgate............. 51 E2
Woodland Ashburton.. 131 D3
  Ivybridge.......... 237 A5
Woodland Head........ 97 C7
Woodleigh........... 144 B7
Woodmanton......... 196 C8
Woodtown East-the-Water. 26 D4
  Fairy Cross......... 25 B2
Woody Bay............. 4 D6
Woolacombe........... 7 F7
Woolfardisworthy.... 62 A3
Woolfardisworthy or
   Woolsery.......... 38 E7
Woolhanger............ 4 F2
Woollaton............ 56 B7
Woolley.............. 37 D3
Woolston............ 147 F8
Woolston Green...... 131 B1
Woolwell............ 245 D7
Worlington........... 15 C1
Worston............. 136 B3
Wotter.............. 132 D4
Wrafton............. 152 F4
Wrangaton........... 137 D8
Wrangway............. 52 A4
Wrinkleberry......... 23 D3
Wyke Green.......... 167 D1

Y

Yalberton........... 225 C2
Yarcombe............. 69 A3
Yarnscombe........... 27 E2
Yawl................ 104 B5
Yealmbridge......... 136 A2
Yealmpton........... 257 E4
Yelland............. 153 A4
Yelverton........... 127 A3
Yeoford.............. 79 C1
Yettington.......... 197 F8
Yondertown.......... 133 B1

Z

Zeal Monachorum...... 78 C7

Index of streets, hospitals, industrial estates, railway stations, schools, shopping centres, universities and places of interest

3rd Ave 8 EX2 .... 178 D5

A

Abbeville Cl EX2........177 E3
Abbey Cl
  Axminster EX13........167 C4
  Bovey Tracey TQ13....180 C7
  Crapstone PL20.......126 E2
  Paignton TQ3.........225 E5
  Tatworth TA20.........88 D8
  Teignmouth TQ14......210 C7
Abbey Cross TQ9.......227 A4
Abbey Ct
  Exeter EX2............178 F5
  Plymouth PL1.........263 A2
Abbeydale EX10.........188 A3
Abbeyfield Ho 7 TQ14..210 C5
Abbeyford Ct EX20.....170 C5
Abbeyford Woods Forest
  Wilks EX20............94 A8
Abbey Gate La EX13....167 C4
Abbey Grange Cl TQ11..236 B7
Abbey La EX13..........167 B3
Abbey Mdw TQ11........236 B7
Abbeymead Mews PL19..171 C5
Abbey Mews
  Tatworth TA20.........88 D8
  Torquay TQ1..........220 B8
Abbey Pl
  Plymouth PL1.........262 C2
  Tavistock PL19.......171 C5
Abbey Rd
  Barnstaple EX31......154 E6
  Bovey Tracey TQ13....180 D6
  Cornworthy TQ9.......227 A4
  Dunkeswell EX14.......67 C2
  Exeter EX4...........177 F7
  Torquay TQ2..........220 A5
Abbey Rise
  Okehampton EX20......170 D6
  Tavistock PL19.......171 C5
Abbey Sch TQ1.........220 C8
Abbot Rd PL21.........237 A6
Abbotsbury Rd TQ12....207 B4
Abbotsbury Sch TQ12...207 D2
Abbotsbury Way PL2....247 F8
Abbots Cl
  Lee Mill PL21........136 D6
  Woolfardisworthy EX39..38 F8
Abbotscourt La PL11...246 A2

Abbot's Cross EX36.....31 E6
Abbots Ct PL21.......237 A5
Abbots Dr EX39.........26 A4
Abbotsfield Cl PL19...126 A8
Abbotsfield Cres PL19.126 A8
Abbotsham Cross EX39...25 C4
Abbotsham La EX18......59 C3
Abbotsham Rd EX39....156 E2
Abbots Keep EX4......176 D6
Abbotskerswell Cross
  TQ12................212 A7
Abbotskerswell Prim Sch
  TQ12................212 B6
Abbots Mdw EX37.......28 F4
Abbot's Rd EX4.......177 E8
Abbotsridge Dr TQ12..206 F1
Abbotswood
  East Ogwell TQ12....206 F1
  Kingsteignton TQ12..207 F8
Abbotts Hill EX33....152 D6
Abbotts Pk PL21......133 C2
Abbotts Rd PL3.......248 E6
Abbrook Ave 9 TQ12...123 E1
Abelia Cl TQ3........225 E8
Aberdeen Ave PL5.....244 D1
Aberfeldy TQ1........220 C5
Abingdon Rd 1 PL4...263 A4
Abney Cres PL6.......245 B6
Above Down TQ7.......147 D7
Above Town TQ6.......233 F2
Abscott La PL9.......255 C5
Abyssinia Cl 9 EX32..155 B3
Abyssinia Terr 8 EX32.155 B3
Acacia Cl
  Bideford EX39.......156 E1
  Kingsteignton TQ12..207 F6
Acacia Mews EX6......181 B1
Academic La EX18......44 E1
Acacia Rd TQ1........220 E4
Ackland Pk EX14.......84 D2
Acklington Pl PL5....243 E4
Acland Cross EX32.....17 B2
Acland Rd
  Broadclyst EX5......175 C6
  Exeter EX4..........261 C4
  Ivybridge PL21......237 A6
  Landkey EX32.........17 B2
  Salcombe TQ8........259 F8
Aclands EX36.........158 D3
Acland Terr EX4......261 C4
Acland Way EX16......161 A6

Acombe Cross TA3......68 B8
Acorn Way EX32........17 F4
Acre Cl EX39..........24 E2
Acre Cotts
  Plymouth PL1.......247 F3
  Wellington TA21....160 E6
Acre La TQ1..........220 E6
Acre Pl PL1..........247 F3
Acre EX39............24 E2
Acre The TQ13........111 A6
Adams Cl
  Plymouth PL5.......243 F1
  Torpoint PL11......246 F3
Adams Cres PL11......246 C3
Adam's La PL9........118 C8
Ada's Terr EX4.........7 F8
Adcroft Rise EX13....103 D5
Adder La EX31.........16 B6
Addington Ct EX4....261 B4
Addiscombe La EX6....113 D5
Addison Cl EX14......176 E6
Addison Rd
  Newton Abbot TQ12..207 E1
  Paignton TQ4.......226 A5
  Plymouth PL4.......263 A4
Addlehole TQ13.......144 D7
Adelaide Ct
  Exeter EX2.........261 A1
  Exmouth EX8........202 A5
Adelaide La PL1......262 A2
Adelaide Pl PL1......262 A3
Adelaide St
  2 Plymouth, Ford PL2.247 F5
  Plymouth PL1.......262 A3
Adelaide Street Ope PL1.262 A3
Adelaide Terr 6 EX34..150 B6
Adela Rd PL11........247 A3
Adelphi La TQ4.......226 C5
Adelphi Mans TQ4....226 C5
Adelphi Rd TQ4......226 C5
Adit La PL22.........242 E3
Adits The PL18.......125 D3
Adley La TQ13........111 B7
Admiral Ct TQ6......233 B2
Admirals Ct
  22 Exmouth EX8.....202 A6
  5 Northam EX39.....156 F7
Admiral's Hard PL1...254 A8
Admirals Wlk
  Exmouth EX8.......196 D2
  Teignmouth TQ14...210 A8
Admiralty Cotts PL1..254 A7

Admiralty Rd
  Plymouth, Millbay PL1.254 A8
  Plymouth, St Budeaux PL5.243 C2
Admiralty St
  Plymouth, Keyham PL2..247 E6
  Plymouth, Millbay PL1.254 A8
Adrian Cl EX39.......157 A4
Adworthy La EX17......46 B2
Affeton Castle Cross EX17.60 F8
Affeton Hill EX17.....60 E8
Affeton Moor Cross EX17..46 A2
Agaton Rd PL5.......243 E3
Aidan Ave EX32......155 C5
Ailescombe Dr TQ3...225 F6
Ailescombe Rd TQ3...225 F6
Ainslie Terr PL2....247 E7
Aire Gdns PL3.......249 B5
Airfield Ind Est EX14..67 B2
Aish Cross TQ9......224 E2
Aish La TQ10........134 E3
Aish Lane End TQ10...134 F2
Aish Pk EX21.........55 E4
Aish Rd
  Paignton TQ4......225 B2
  Stoke Gabriel TQ9..224 E2
Alamein Cl PL12.....242 E2
Alamein Rd PL12.....242 D2
Alandale Cl TQ14....210 C6
Alandale Rd TQ14....210 C6
Alansway EX11........169 C3
Ala Ronde EX8.......196 A3
Alba Ct EX1.........178 E7
Albany Ct EX8.......196 E2
Albany Ct TQ3.......226 B7
Albany Rd TQ3.......219 A1
Albany St
  10 Newton Abbot TQ12..207 C3
  Plymouth PL1......247 E2
Albemarle Villas PL1.247 E2
Alberta Cres EX4....177 F8
Alberta Ct TQ14....210 C5
Albert Cotts TQ12..208 E3
Albert Ct
  7 Ilfracombe EX34..150 C6
  3 Torquay TQ1....220 B5
Albertha Cl PL4....263 B4
Albert La 9 EX32....155 A5
Albert Pl
  Exmouth EX8.......202 A6
  10 Totnes TQ9....223 C5
Albert Rd
  Crediton EX17....165 C5

3rd – Ald

Albert Rd continued
  Plymouth PL2.......247 F3
  Saltash PL12.......243 A2
  Torquay TQ2........220 B5
Albert St
  18 Dawlish EX7....204 D6
  Exeter EX1.........261 C4
Albert Terr
  Bovey Tracey TQ13..180 C7
  Gunnislake PL18....125 C5
  14 Newton Abbot TQ12.207 C3
  Princetown PL20....128 B8
Albert Villas PL2...247 E4
Albion Cl EX12......191 F8
Albion Ct
  Brixham TQ5.......230 C3
  6 Exmouth EX8.....202 A7
  Torpoint PL11.....247 B3
Albion Dr PL2.......248 B7
Albion Gdns TQ7....258 C6
Albion Hill
  Exmouth EX8.......202 B7
  Newton Abbot TQ12..207 C3
Albion Pl
  Exeter EX4.........261 C4
  Exmouth EX8.......202 A7
  Plymouth PL11.....247 B3
Albion St
  Exeter EX4.........177 A5
  Exmouth EX8.......202 A7
  Teignmouth TQ14...210 A3
  West Albert EX4....202 A7
Alcester Cl PL2.....247 E4
Alcester St PL2.....247 F4
Aldborough Ct EX8...202 C6
Aidens Brks St EX2..181 B8
Aldens Rd EX2.......181 B8
Alder Cl
  Newton Abbot TQ12..212 F8
  Teignmouth TQ14...210 B7
Alder Glade EX31....154 C3
Alderney Rd PL6.....244 F7
Alder Rd PL19.......171 C3
Aldersley Wlk PL6...245 A1
Alderson Dr EX2.....178 D5
Alders Way TQ4......225 D3
Aldridge Mill Hill EX16..48 C6
Aldrin Rd EX4.......173 E2

Alexander Ct EX17 . . . . . 165 D4
Alexander Pl EX11 . . . . . 169 D4
Alexander Rd EX2 . . . . . 204 D6
Alexander Wlk **2** EX2 . . . 178 D5
Alexandra Cl
  Crediton EX17 . . . . . 165 A6
  Plymouth PL1 . . . . . 256 B8
Alexandra Ct **15** EX32 . . . 155 C6
Alexandra Dr PL20 . . . . . 125 F1
Alexandra Ho TQ12 . . . . . 207 E2
Alexandra La TQ1 . . . . . 220 B6
Alexandra Mews EX6 . . . 201 B8
Alexandra Pl
  Cornworthy TQ9 . . . . . 227 B4
  5 Plymouth PL4 . . . . . 248 E4
Alexandra Rd
  Axminster EX13 . . . . . 167 C5
  Barnstaple EX32 . . . . . 155 A5
  Crediton EX17 . . . . . 165 B6
  1 Newton Abbot TQ12 . . . 207 C2
  Plymouth, Crownhill PL6 . . . 244 F2
  Plymouth, Ford PL2 . . . . . 247 F5
  Plymouth, Mutley PL4 . . . 248 F4
  Torquay TQ1 . . . . . 220 B6
  Wellington TA21 . . . . . 160 D6
Alexandra Sq PL12 . . . . . 243 A2
Alexandra Terr
  Bideford EX39 . . . . . 157 A3
  Clyst Honiton EX5 . . . . . 175 E2
  Exeter EX4 . . . . . 177 E7
  Exmouth EX8 . . . . . 201 F6
  Newton Abbot TQ12 . . . . . 207 C2
  Plymouth PL2 . . . . . 247 F5
  South Molton EX36 . . . . . 158 C5
  1 Teignmouth TQ14 . . . 210 B4
  1 Totnes TQ9 . . . . . 223 C6
Alexandra Way EX17 . . . 165 A6
Alexandria Ind Est EX15 . . 163 D4
Alexandria Rd EX10 . . . 188 A6
Alexandria Terr **6** EX16 . . 161 B4
Alfington Rd
  Alfington EX11 . . . . . 84 F1
  Ottery St Mary EX11 . . . 169 F6
Alford Cl EX1 . . . . . 178 C7
Alford Cres EX1 . . . . . 178 B7
Alfred Pl PL2 . . . . . 247 F5
Alfred Rd PL2 . . . . . 247 F5
Alfred St PL1 . . . . . 262 C2
Alfriston Rd TQ3 . . . . . 225 D7
Alger Wlk PL6 . . . . . 244 E6
Alice La **7** PL1 . . . . . 262 B3
Alice Mews EX38 . . . . . 159 C5
Alice St PL1 . . . . . 262 A3
Alison Rd TQ3 . . . . . 219 A1
Allaleigh Cross TQ9 . . . . . 139 F4
Allaleigh La TQ9 . . . . . 139 F4
Allans Rd PL21 . . . . . 237 D6
Allaway EX10 . . . . . 188 B6
Allenby Rd PL2 . . . . . 248 A6
Allen Cl EX16 . . . . . 161 F5
Allendale Rd PL4 . . . . . 263 A4
Allenhayes La TQ8 . . . . . 259 D4
Allenhayes Rd TQ8 . . . . . 259 D4
Allenstyle Cl EX31 . . . . . 153 B5
Allenstyle Dr EX31 . . . . . 153 B5
Allenstyle Gdns EX31 . . . 153 B5
Allenstyle Rd EX31 . . . . . 153 B5
Allenstyle View EX31 . . . 153 A5
Allenstyle Way EX31 . . . 153 B5
Aller Brake Rd TQ12 . . . 212 F8
Aller Cl TQ12 . . . . . 213 A6
Allercombe Cross EX5 . . 99 E5
Allercombe Hill EX5 . . . 168 A6
Allercombe La EX5 . . . . . 99 E5
Aller Cotts TQ12 . . . . . 212 F7
Aller Cross
  Chillington TQ7 . . . . . 145 A1
  Kentisbeare EX15 . . . . . 65 F1
  Kingskerswell TQ12 . . . . . 212 E6
  South Molton EX36 . . . . . 29 F7
Allerdown Cross EX17 . . . 80 A7
Aller Gate EX17 . . . . . 78 D5
Aller Grove Cotts EX5 . . . 99 F7
Aller Hill
  Bishops Nympton EX36 . . . 31 A4
  Dawlish EX7 . . . . . 204 B5
Aller La EX20 . . . . . 94 F8
Aller Park Rd TQ12 . . . 212 E8
Aller Rd
  Dolton EX19 . . . . . 57 F7
  Kingskerswell TQ12 . . . . . 212 F6
Allerton Wlk PL6 . . . . . 249 B7
Aller Vale Bldgs TQ12 . . 212 F6
Allervale Cl EX2 . . . . . 178 B4
Alley Hill PL20 . . . . . 126 D1
Alleyn Ct EX12 . . . . . 191 F7
Alleyn Gdns PL3 . . . . . 248 E8
Allhalland St **7** EX39 . . . 157 A2
Allhallows Ct
  Exeter EX4 . . . . . 261 A2
  1 Honiton EX14 . . . . . 166 C6
Allhallows Mus EX14 . . . 166 C6
All Hallows Rd TQ13 . . . 219 C2
Allington Mead EX4 . . . 179 A3
Allington Terr EX17 . . . . . 78 F7
Allison La EX17 . . . . . 95 D7
Allotment Dro TA20 . . . . . 69 C5
Allotment Gdns TQ7 . . . 258 D6
All Saints CE Inf Sch
  EX10 . . . . . 188 B4
All Saints CE Prim Sch
  TA22 . . . . . 33 D6

All Saints CE Prim Sch
  (Marsh) TQ12 . . . . . 207 D3
All Saints CE Sch EX13 . . . 88 A4
All Saints Ct EX9 . . . . . 198 B6
All Saints Ct EX4 . . . . . 166 A5
All Saints Mews **11** EX8 . . 202 A7
All Saints Pk PL18 . . . . . 125 B5
All Saints' Rd EX10 . . . . . 188 A4
All Saints' Rd TQ1 . . . . . 220 C2
Allshire La EX16 . . . . . 32 F3
Alma Cl PL4 . . . . . 263 B2
Alma La EX10 . . . . . 188 C4
Alma Rd
  Brixham TQ5 . . . . . 230 C5
  Plymouth PL3 . . . . . 248 C4
Alma St PL4 . . . . . 263 B2
Alma Terr
  18 Barnstaple EX32 . . . 155 A4
  Gunnislake PL18 . . . . . 125 D6
Almeria Ct PL7 . . . . . 250 D4
Alminstone Cross EX39 . . 39 A7
Almond Cl **3** EX31 . . . . . 154 C2
Almond Dr PL7 . . . . . 251 B6
Almshouse Cross TQ10 . . . 135 E4
Almshouses **6** EX4 . . . . . 177 D8
Almshouses The 7
  TQ13 . . . . . 180 D8
Alpha Ctr TQ9 . . . . . 223 C6
Alpha Pl **24** EX39 . . . . . 15 A1
Alpha St EX1 . . . . . 177 F6
Alpha Terr TQ9 . . . . . 223 B6
Alphin Brook Ct EX2 . . . 177 C1
Alphin Brook Rd EX2 . . 177 C1
Alphington Prim Sch
  EX2 . . . . . 177 B1
Alphington Rd EX2 . . . . . 177 B3
Alphington St EX2 . . . . . 261 A1
Alpine Rd TQ1 . . . . . 220 B5
Alsa Brook Mdw EX16 . . 161 C6
Alscott Gdns EX31 . . . . . 27 A4
Alston Cross
  Ashburton TQ13 . . . . . 131 B6
  Slapton TQ7 . . . . . 145 B5
Alston Rd EX16 . . . . . 161 F3
Alston La TQ5 . . . . . 229 D4
Alston Terr EX8 . . . . . 201 F6
Alswear New Rd
  Alswear EX36 . . . . . 30 C1
  South Molton EX36 . . . . . 158 E3
Alswear Old Rd EX36 . . . 158 C2
Altamira EX3 . . . . . 182 F5
Altamira Cotts EX39 . . . . . 25 D7
Alta Vista Cl TQ14 . . . . . 210 D7
Alta Vista Rd TQ4 . . . . . 226 C4
Alton Pl PL4 . . . . . 248 E4
Alton Rd PL4 . . . . . 263 B4
Alverdiscott Rd EX39 . . . 26 B4
Alverdiscott Road Ind Est
  EX39 . . . . . 26 A4
Alver Gn EX39 . . . . . 157 D1
Alvington St PL4 . . . . . 263 C2
Alvington Terr TQ7 . . . . . 258 C4
Alwin Pk PL6 . . . . . 245 A5
Alwyns Cl **3** TQ14 . . . . . 210 C5
Alwyns Ct **4** TQ14 . . . . . 210 C5
Amacre Dr PL9 . . . . . 255 B6
Amados Cl PL7 . . . . . 250 B4
Amados Dr PL7 . . . . . 250 C4
Amados Rise PL7 . . . . . 250 C4
Ambassador Dr EX1 . . . . . 178 E2
Ambassador Ho TQ4 . . . 226 C5
Amberley Cl TQ13 . . . . . 133 B5
Amber Tor TQ13 . . . . . 121 F7
American Rd EX33 . . . . . 15 A4
Amersham Ct EX2 . . . . . 178 A4
Amherst Rd PL3 . . . . . 262 B4
Amherst Road La E PL3 . . 262 B4
Amity Pl PL4 . . . . . 263 A4
Amory Pl EX36 . . . . . 158 C4
Amory Rd
  Dulverton TA22 . . . . . 33 D6
  Tiverton EX16 . . . . . 161 C2
Amyas Way EX39 . . . . . 157 A6
Amyatt's Terr EX10 . . . . . 188 B3
Anchorage Cl TQ5 . . . . . 230 E5
Anchorage The TQ4 . . . . . 226 C5
Anchor Bldgs TQ12 . . . . . 123 B2
Anchor Cotts TQ7 . . . . . 147 B7
Anchor Ctr The TQ7 . . . . . 258 D5
Anchor Mall EX31 . . . . . 154 F5
Ander's La TA3 . . . . . 68 E8
Anderton Cl PL19 . . . . . 171 E1
Anderton Ct PL19 . . . . . 171 E2
Anderton La PL19 . . . . . 171 D2
Anderton Rise PL10 . . . 252 F4
Andor Ave TQ12 . . . . . 207 D7
Andrew Allan Rd TA21 . . 160 B4
Andrew Ct EX13 . . . . . 171 B4
Andrew Rd EX31 . . . . . 154 E2
Andrewshayes La EX13 . . . 87 A1
Andrew's Hill TA22 . . . . . 33 D6
Andrew's Hill Cross TA22 . . 33 C6
Andurn Cl PL9 . . . . . 256 B6
Andurn Est PL9 . . . . . 140 A8
Angel Hill EX16 . . . . . 161 C4
Angelhill Cross EX36 . . . . . 30 F7
Angel Mews **2** EX14 . . . 166 C6
Angel The **3** EX14 . . . . . 166 C6
Anne Cl EX4 . . . . . 173 E1
Anne Cres EX31 . . . . . 154 E3
Annery Kiln Cotts EX39 . . 26 A1
Anning Rd DT7 . . . . . 260 E4
Ann's Pl PL3 . . . . . 248 A4
Anson Ho **1** PL1 . . . . . 262 B3
Anson Pl
  Plymouth, Devonport
    PL2 . . . . . 247 F4
  Plymouth, St Jude's PL4 . . 263 C3

Anson Rd EX8 . . . . . 196 C2
Anstey Cres EX16 . . . . . 161 F3
Anstey Gate TA22 . . . . . 32 B8
Ansteys Cl TQ1 . . . . . 220 E5
Anstey's Cove Rd TQ1 . . 220 E6
Ansteys Ct EX16 . . . . . 46 E1
Anstey Way EX39 . . . . . 15 B1
Anstis Cl EX10 . . . . . 188 A7
Anstis St
  Plymouth PL1 . . . . . 262 A3
  Plymouth PL1 . . . . . 262 B3
Anthea Rd TQ3 . . . . . 226 B2
Anthony Pk EX19 . . . . . 171 D6
Anthony Rd EX1 . . . . . 177 F6
Antoine Cres EX4 . . . . . 176 E6
Antony Gdns PL2 . . . . . 248 C8
Antony House PL11 . . . . . 246 D5
Antony Rd PL11 . . . . . 247 B3
Antony Woodland Gdn
  PL11 . . . . . 246 D6
Antrim Terr **3** TQ9 . . . . . 223 C6
Anvil Cl EX22 . . . . . 72 D7
Anvil Ct PL17 . . . . . 115 B1
Anwyl Cl PL1 . . . . . 262 B3
Anzac Ave PL5 . . . . . 244 A4
Anzac St TQ6 . . . . . 233 F3
Applebee Way DT7 . . . . . 260 E4
Appleby Wlk PL5 . . . . . 244 D4
Apple Cl EX8 . . . . . 196 B3
Appledore Com Prim Sch
  EX39 . . . . . 15 A1
Appledore Hill EX20 . . . 170 F8
Apple Dr EX15 . . . . . 162 D4
Apple Farm Grange EX2 . . 178 E3
Applegarth Ave TQ12 . . 206 E4
Applegarth Cl TQ12 . . . 206 E4
Applehayes EX8 . . . . . 202 C5
Applehayes La EX15 . . . . . 52 F2
Applemede EX5 . . . . . 82 B6
Apple Orch EX8 . . . . . 159 B4
Appleton Tor Cl PL3 . . . 249 F5
Appletree Cl
  Barnstaple EX32 . . . . . 155 D4
  Uffculme EX15 . . . . . 66 A7
Apple Tree Cl
  Frogmore TQ7 . . . . . 144 E1
  Witheridge EX16 . . . . . 46 E1
Appletree Mews **5** . . . 15 A1
Apple Wharf **6** TQ9 . . . 223 D5
Appley Cross TA21 . . . . . 51 B7
App's La EX39 . . . . . 25 E2
April Cl EX8 . . . . . 196 B3
Apsley Ho TQ1 . . . . . 220 C3
Apsley Rd PL4 . . . . . 248 D4
Apsley Terr
  Braunton EX33 . . . . . 152 F7
  1 Ilfracombe EX34 . . . 150 C5
Apsley Villas **5** EX34 . . 150 C5
Apters Hill **7** TQ5 . . . . . 230 C5
Arbour Cl EX34 . . . . . 150 B3
Arbour The PL6 . . . . . 244 E5
Arcade Rd EX34 . . . . . 150 B6
Arcade The EX20 . . . . . 170 B5
Arcadia PL9 . . . . . 256 D6
Arcadia Rd PL9 . . . . . 256 C6
Arch Cotts TQ12 . . . . . 207 D7
Archer Pl PL1 . . . . . 262 B4
Archers Ct PL8 . . . . . 141 A7
Archer Terr PL1 . . . . . 262 B3
Archery Cl TQ7 . . . . . 258 C7
Arches The EX2 . . . . . 177 A4
Archibald Rd EX1 . . . . . 261 C3
Archipark EX32 . . . . . 17 E1
Arch St **3** TQ1 . . . . . 210 A3
Arch The EX5 . . . . . 184 B3
Archway Ave PL4 . . . . . 249 B3
Archway Dr TQ6 . . . . . 233 D4
Arcot Gdns EX10 . . . . . 188 B6
Arcot Pk EX10 . . . . . 188 B6
Arcot Rd EX10 . . . . . 188 B6
Arden Cl EX4 . . . . . 199 G2
Arden Dr TQ2 . . . . . 219 D6
Arden Gr PL2 . . . . . 248 C8
Arden Ho TQ7 . . . . . 143 A1
Ardennery Ct EX8 . . . . . 202 C5
Ardwyn TA21 . . . . . 160 D4
Arena Pk EX4 . . . . . 174 E1
Argent Ct EX16 . . . . . 161 D4
Argus Cl EX14 . . . . . 166 E6
Argyle Mews EX4 . . . . . 173 A1
Argyle Terr TQ9 . . . . . 223 B6
Argyll Rd EX4 . . . . . 173 B2
Arimoor Gdns PL19 . . . . . 171 E5
Ark Royal Cl PL5 . . . . . 247 D8
Arkwright Gdns PL5 . . . 243 F2
Arley Cl EX16 . . . . . 171 B4
Arlington Court EX31 . . . . 10 D3
Arlington Pl EX34 . . . . . 8 A6
Arlington Rd
  Plymouth PL4 . . . . . 248 F4
  Woolacombe EX34 . . . . . 7 F6
Arlington Terr **5** EX33 . . 152 D5
Armada Cl EX12 . . . . . 192 A7
Armada Ct PL19 . . . . . 171 B4
Armada Dr TQ14 . . . . . 210 A8
Armada Rd PL10 . . . . . 253 A1
Armada Rd EX4 . . . . . 263 A4
Armada Way
  Plymouth PL1 . . . . . 262 C2
  Plymouth PL1 . . . . . 262 C3
  Westward Ho! EX39 . . . . . 156 B6
Armourwood La EX5 . . . . . 81 D5
Armstrong Ave EX4 . . . . . 173 D2
Armytage Rd EX9 . . . . . 198 A2

Arnison Cl PL9 . . . . . 255 F5
Arnold Cres EX16 . . . . . 161 B2
Arnold's Cl TQ7 . . . . . 142 C6
Arnold's Point PL4 . . . . . 249 C3
Arnside Cl PL6 . . . . . 244 E5
Arran Cl TQ2 . . . . . 213 E2
Arscott Gdns PL9 . . . . . 255 C5
Arscott La PL9 . . . . . 255 D5
Arthington TQ1 . . . . . 219 F7
Art Ho **14** EX1 . . . . . 261 A2
Arthurs Cl EX8 . . . . . 196 D2
Arthur Terr PL11 . . . . . 247 B2
Artillery Ct EX2 . . . . . 177 E3
Artillery Pl PL4 . . . . . 263 B1
Artizan's Dwellings
  EX36 . . . . . 158 D4
Arun Cl PL3 . . . . . 249 C5
Arundel Cl EX2 . . . . . 181 B8
Arundel Cres PL1 . . . . . 262 B4
Arundell Cl PL16 . . . . . 105 E4
Arundell Gdns PL16 . . . 105 E4
Arundell Pl TQ7 . . . . . 143 E7
Arundell Rd EX20 . . . . . 77 C4
Arundells Cnr **3** EX17 . . 165 D5
Arundel Terr PL1 . . . . . 247 F4
Ascension Way TQ2 . . . . . 213 F2
Ascerton Cl EX10 . . . . . 188 B5
Ascerton Rd EX10 . . . . . 188 B5
Ashacre Cross TQ1 . . . . . 214 B6
Ashborton Cvn Pk TQ13 . . 130 F6
Ash Bridge Cross EX20 . . . 95 D1
Ashburn Cl EX31 . . . . . 16 B6
Ashburn Cl TQ13 . . . . . 130 F4
Ashburn Gdns TQ13 . . . 130 F5
Ashburnham Rd PL5 . . . 244 A3
Ashburn Wlk TQ4 . . . . . 229 B8
Ashburton & Buckfastleigh
  Hospl TQ13 . . . . . 131 A5
Ashburton Cl TQ13 . . . . . 180 C5
Ashburton Mus TQ13 . . 130 F4
Ashburton Prim Sch
  TQ13 . . . . . 130 F4
Ashburton Rd
  Bovey Tracey TQ13 . . . . . 180 C5
  Newton Abbot TQ12 . . . . . 206 D4
  Totnes TQ9 . . . . . 223 B7
Ashbury Cross EX20 . . . . . 93 B5
Ashbury Station Cross
  EX20 . . . . . 92 C7
Ash Cl **7** PL20 . . . . . 126 F3
Ashclyst Forest Wlks EX5 . . 82 F2
Ashclyst View EX5 . . . . . 175 D6
Ashcombe Cl PL7 . . . . . 250 C7
Ashcombe Cross EX7 . . . 124 C6
Ashcombe Hill PL8 . . . . . 257 F2
Ashcombe Rd EX7 . . . . . 204 B8
Ash Cross
  Bradninch EX5 . . . . . 82 F7
  Dartmouth TQ6 . . . . . 232 D1
  Halberton EX16 . . . . . 64 A5
  Oakford EX16 . . . . . 48 D6
  Petrockstow EX20 . . . . . 56 F3
Ash Ct
  Crediton EX17 . . . . . 165 C6
  Lee Mill PL21 . . . . . 136 D6
  Shillingford St George SX2 . . 114 C6
Ashculme Hill EX15 . . . . . 52 C2
Ashdown Cl PL6 . . . . . 245 E3
Ashdown Cross EX22 . . . . . 38 F3
Ashdown Wlk PL6 . . . . . 245 E3
Ash Dr EX15 . . . . . 163 C5
Asheldon Ho TQ1 . . . . . 220 E5
Asheldon Manor TQ1 . . . 220 D5
Asheldon Rd TQ1 . . . . . 220 E5
Ashelford Cnr EX31 . . . . . 10 A3
Ashery Dr PL9 . . . . . 255 C6
Ashes Rd
  Dalwood EX13 . . . . . 87 B1
  Shute EX13 . . . . . 103 B8
Ash Farm Cl EX1 . . . . . 174 F1
Ashfield Cl
  Ashford EX31 . . . . . 16 B6
  Exmouth EX8 . . . . . 196 E1
Ashfield La EX31 . . . . . 16 B6
Ashfield Rd TQ12 . . . . . 219 E5
Ashfield Terr EX39 . . . . . 157 A7
Ashford Cl PL3 . . . . . 249 A4
Ashford Cres PL3 . . . . . 249 A4
Ashford Hill PL4 . . . . . 249 A4
Ashford Rd
  Plymouth PL4 . . . . . 248 F4
  Topsham EX3 . . . . . 182 E5
  Wellington TA21 . . . . . 160 D4
Ash Gr
  Exmouth EX8 . . . . . 196 B2
  Ivybridge PL21 . . . . . 237 E5
  Plymouth PL2 . . . . . 247 F7
  Seaton EX12 . . . . . 192 A8
Ashgrove Rd TQ13 . . . . . 180 C4
Ash Hill
  Oakford EX16 . . . . . 48 D6
  Petrockstow EX20 . . . . . 56 F3
Ash Hill Cross EX16 . . . . . 48 B6
Ash Hill Rd TQ1 . . . . . 220 A6
Ashill TQ14 . . . . . 209 A8
Ashill Ctyd EX15 . . . . . 162 C6
Ash La
  Iddesleigh EX19 . . . . . 57 F1
  Withypool TA24 . . . . . 21 F6
  Woolfardisworthy EX17 . . . 62 A2
Ashlake Rd EX6 . . . . . 113 F7
Ash Leigh EX2 . . . . . 181 A8
Ashleigh CE Prim Sch
  EX32 . . . . . 155 A5
Ashleigh Cl
  Exeter EX4 . . . . . 176 F6

Ashleigh Cl continued
  Teignmouth TQ14 . . . . . 210 B7
  Torquay TQ2 . . . . . 213 F3
Ashleigh Cres EX32 . . . . . 155 B4
Ashleigh Ct TQ1 . . . . . 220 D3
Ashleigh Dr TQ14 . . . . . 210 B7
Ashleigh La PL5 . . . . . 240 D1
Ashleigh Mount TQ14 . . 210 B7
Ashleigh Mount Rd EX4 . . 176 F6
Ashleigh Pk
  Bampton EX16 . . . . . 49 C8
  Teignmouth TQ14 . . . . . 210 B7
Ashleigh Rd
  Barnstaple EX32 . . . . . 155 A5
  Exmouth EX8 . . . . . 202 C7
  Honiton EX14 . . . . . 166 B6
  Kingsbridge TQ7 . . . . . 258 B4
Ashleigh Rise TQ14 . . . . . 210 B7
Ashleigh Way
  Plymouth PL7 . . . . . 251 C4
  Teignmouth TQ14 . . . . . 210 B7
Ashley Back La EX16 . . . . . 64 A5
Ashley Brake EX11 . . . . . 168 D4
Ashley Cl EX15 . . . . . 66 B8
Ashley Cres EX10 . . . . . 188 A7
Ashley Ho **3** EX8 . . . . . 202 B6
Ashley Priors La TQ1 . . . 214 C4
Ashley Rd
  Okehampton EX20 . . . . . 170 C5
  Uffculme EX15 . . . . . 66 A7
Ashley Rise EX16 . . . . . 161 B1
Ashley Terr
  13 Bideford EX39 . . . . . 156 F1
  13 Ilfracombe EX34 . . . 150 B5
Ashley Way EX7 . . . . . 204 F7
Ashmead Gr EX33 . . . . . 152 C6
Ashmill Cl EX22 . . . . . 90 F6
Ashmill Ct TQ12 . . . . . 206 F4
Ash Mill Hill EX36 . . . . . 31 B2
Ashmore Ct EX2 . . . . . 261 A1
Ashplants Cl EX19 . . . . . 58 F3
Ash Plants Cl EX39 . . . . . 156 D2
Ashprington Cross TQ9 . . . 139 F8
Ash Rd
  Braunton EX33 . . . . . 152 F7
  Kingsteignton TQ12 . . . . . 207 E6
Ashridge Gdns
  Kingsteignton TQ12 . . . . . 207 F6
  Plymouth PL5 . . . . . 244 B2
Ashridge La EX20 . . . . . 77 D6
Ashridge Moor Cross
  EX20 . . . . . 77 E6
Ashton Bsns Ctr EX2 . . . 177 B2
Ashton Cl PL6 . . . . . 245 C6
Ashton Cross EX6 . . . . . 113 C5
Ashton Ct **10** TQ12 . . . . . 123 F1
Ashton Ind Units EX2 . . 177 B2
Ashton Rd EX2 . . . . . 177 B2
Ashtons Cotts EX39 . . . . . 40 B7
Ashton Terr TQ1 . . . . . 220 E5
Ashtown Cross EX16 . . . . . 34 A3
Ashtree Cl PL6 . . . . . 245 D8
Ashtree Gr PL9 . . . . . 256 C8
Ash Units EX17 . . . . . 165 F5
Ash Vale PL16 . . . . . 105 E4
Ashwater Prim Sch EX21 . . 90 F6
Ash Way TQ12 . . . . . 207 F1
Ashwell La TQ13 . . . . . 122 E6
Ashwood **3** TQ10 . . . . . 134 F3
Ashwood Cl
  Loddiswell TQ7 . . . . . 143 E7
  Plymouth PL7 . . . . . 251 B5
Ashwood Ct TQ12 . . . . . 207 E2
Ashwood Park Rd PL7 . . 251 C6
Ashwood Pk TQ7 . . . . . 143 E7
Ashwood Rd EX2 . . . . . 177 B3
Aspen Cl
  Exeter EX2 . . . . . 178 C4
  3 Honiton EX14 . . . . . 85 C2
  Tavistock PL19 . . . . . 171 C3
Aspen Dr TQ12 . . . . . 212 F8
Aspen Gdns PL7 . . . . . 251 B5
Aspen Way
  Paignton TQ4 . . . . . 225 D3
  Tiverton EX16 . . . . . 161 E7
Astley Corte EX20 . . . . . 170 A5
Astor Dr PL4 . . . . . 249 C3
Aswell Orch TQ7 . . . . . 143 F7
Athelstan Cl EX13 . . . . . 167 D4
Athelstan Rd EX1 . . . . . 261 C3
Athenaeum La PL1 . . . . . 262 B2
Athenaeum Pl PL1 . . . . . 262 C2
Athenaeum St PL1 . . . . . 262 B2
Atherton Pl PL2 . . . . . 247 E4
Atherton Way EX16 . . . . . 64 D7
Athlone Ho PL1 . . . . . 262 A2
Atkinson Cl EX4 . . . . . 174 A1
Atlantic Village EX39 . . . . . 25 D4
Atlantic Way EX39 . . . . . 156 D7
Attwill Ave EX2 . . . . . 178 A5
Atway Cl **7** TQ13 . . . . . 180 C8
Atwill-Kingdom Almshouses
  EX1 . . . . . 177 E6
Atwill's Almshouses EX4 . . 176 F7
Atworthy Cross EX22 . . . . . 38 D3
Auckland Rd **3** PL2 . . . 248 A5
Auction Way EX39 . . . . . 38 F8
Audley Cl EX20 . . . . . 188 A4
Audley Ave TQ2 . . . . . 219 F8
Audley Rise TQ12 . . . . . 208 A1
Augusta Ct EX2 . . . . . 261 A2
Augustine Cl EX12 . . . . . 191 F8
Auney Ct EX22 . . . . . 164 C5
Aune Cl TQ10 . . . . . 135 B1
Aunemouth Cross TQ7 . . 143 A3
Ausewell Cross TQ13 . . . 130 D7

Austin Cl EX4 . . . . 178 C8
Austin Ave PL2 . . . . 248 A6
Austin Cres PL6 . . . . 245 C1
Austin Farm Prim Sch
PL6 . . . . 249 C7
Authers Hts EX16 . . . . 161 B2
Austin Cross TQ7 . . . . 258 A2
Autumn Field EX19 . . . . 58 E3
Avalon Cl EX4 . . . . 174 A2
Aveland Rd TQ1 . . . . 220 C7
Avent Wlk PL7 . . . . 250 F7
Avenue Cl DT7 . . . . 260 D3
Avenue Cottage Gdn
TQ9 . . . . 227 A8
Avenue Ho EX17 . . . . 165 C6
Avenue Mezidon-Canon
EX14 . . . . 166 D5
Avenue Rd
Bovey Tracey TQ13 . . . . 180 C6
Ilfracombe EX34 . . . . 150 B6
Kingskerswell TQ12 . . . . 213 A5
Lyme Regis DT7 . . . . 260 D3
Torquay TQ2 . . . . 219 F5
Avenue Terr TQ5 . . . . 229 E5
Avenue The
Exton EX3 . . . . 183 C1
Newton Abbot TQ12 . . . . 207 D4
☑ Seaton EX12 . . . . 192 A5
Tiverton EX16 . . . . 161 E3
Avery Cl EX8 . . . . 196 D2
Avery Hill TQ12 . . . . 207 E8
Avery Way PL12 . . . . 242 C5
Aveton Gifford CE Prim Sch
TQ7 . . . . 143 C6
Aviemore Ind Est EX31 . . . 154 D3
Avoca Ave TQ1 . . . . 219 F6
Avocet Dr EX3 . . . . 183 C2
Avocet Rd EX2 . . . . 178 F6
Avon Cl
Plymouth PL3 . . . . 249 D6
South Brent TQ10 . . . . . 135 A2
Avondale Ho ☑ TQ10 . . 134 F2
Avondale Rd
Exeter EX2 . . . . 178 A5
Exmouth EX8 . . . . 202 D8
Avondale Wlk ☑ TQ10 . 134 F2
Avon La EX33 . . . . 156 D7
Avon Quillet TQ7 . . . . 142 E3
Avon Rd
Bideford EX39 . . . . 157 C1
Torquay TQ2 . . . . 219 F7
Avon Valley Cotts TQ7 . . . 143 C6
Avonwick TQ1 . . . . 220 C7
Avonwick Gn TQ10 . . . . . 135 B1
Avranches Ave EX17 . . . . 165 A6
Awliscombe CE Prim Sch
EX14 . . . . 85 B4
Axeford EX13 . . . . 249 D6
Axeford TA20 . . . . 88 E8
Axeford Mdws TA20 . . . . . . 88 E8
Axe Vale Cvn Pk EX12 . . . 192 B6
Axe Valley Cl EX13 . . . . . 104 C7
Axe Valley Com Coll The
EX13 . . . . 167 D6
Axeview Rd EX12 . . . . 192 A7
Axminster Com Prim Sch
EX13 . . . . 167 E6
Axminster Hospl EX13 . . . 167 D5
Axminster Mus EX13 . . . . 167 D5
Axminster Rd
Charmouth DT6 . . . . 104 F4
Honiton EX14 . . . . 166 F5
Musbury EX13 . . . . 103 D5
Offwell EX14 . . . . 86 A3
Tatworth TA20 . . . . 88 E5
Axminster Sta EX13 . . . . . 167 C5
Axmouth Rd EX12 . . . . . . 192 C5
Axtown La PL20 . . . . 126 F2
Aycliffe Gdns PL7 . . . . . . 251 A3
Aylesbury Cres PL5 . . . . . 244 B5
Aylescott Cross EX37 . . . . 43 E3
Aylescott Hill EX34 . . . . 9 A4
Aylescott La EX34 . . . . 9 A4
Ayleston Cross PL21 . . . . 137 C2
Ayleston Pk PL21 . . . . . . 137 C2
Aylwin Cl PL7 . . . . 250 E6
Ayres Cl EX39 . . . . 157 C1
Ayreville Rd PL2 . . . . 248 B7
Aysha Gdns EX39 . . . . . . 156 D8
Ayshford EX15 . . . . 66 A7
Azalea Cl EX14 . . . . 67 C1
Azes La EX32 . . . . 155 A5

B

Babbacombe Bsns Pk
TQ1 . . . . 220 E7
Babbacombe CE Prim Sch
TQ1 . . . . 220 D6
Babbacombe Cl PL6 . . . . 249 E8
Babbacombe Cliff TQ1 . . 220 D7
Babbacombe Downs Rd
TQ1 . . . . 220 D8
Babbacombe Model Village
TQ1 . . . . 220 C8
Babbacombe Rd TQ1 . . . 220 C6
Babbage Rd TQ9 . . . . 223 D6
Babbages EX31 . . . . 154 A4
Babblebrook Mews EX1 . 178 F8
Babeleigh Water EX39 . . . 39 E7
Baber Cl PL4 . . . . 125 A2
Babis Farm Cl PL12 . . . . 242 F1
Babis Farm Ct PL12 . . . . 242 F1
Babis Farm Mews PL12 . 242 F2
Babis Farm Row PL12 . . 242 F2
Babis Farm Way PL12 . . 242 F2

Babis La PL12 . . . . 242 F1
Babland Cross PL21 . . . . 137 D2
Bableigh Cross EX39 . . . . 40 B7
Bableigh Cross EX32 . . . . 28 B8
Bableigh Rd EX32 . . . . 17 B1
Babylon La EX5 . . . . 82 B5
Backfield ☑ EX39 . . . . 15 A1
Back Hill La PL12 . . . . . . 242 D2
Back Hill Ind Est EX18 . . . 44 E1
Back La
Abbotsham EX39 . . . . . . 156 A1
Bickleigh EX16 . . . . 63 D2
Black Torrington EX21 . . . 74 A8
Bradninch EX5 . . . . 82 E6
Chawleigh EX18 . . . . 60 C8
Chittlehampton EX37 . . . . 28 F4
Chulmleigh EX18 . . . . 44 E1
Colaton Raleigh EX10 . . 186 B3
Copplestone EX17 . . . . . . 79 A4
Ermington PL21 . . . . 136 F3
Frithelstock Stone EX38 . . 40 F5
Lutton PL21 . . . . 133 B2
Merton EX20 . . . . 57 A7
Newton Poppleford EX10 186 E8
North Molton EX36 . . . . . . 30 D8
Plymouth PL7 . . . . 250 E4
Sandford EX17 . . . . 80 A5
Sidmouth EX10 . . . . 187 C7
Sticklepath EX20 . . . . 95 A5
Stockland EX14 . . . . 87 A5
Back Rd
Crediton EX17 . . . . 79 F7
Sandford EX17 . . . . 80 A7
Back St
Bampton EX16 . . . . 34 B1
Modbury PL21 . . . . 137 B2
Woolfardisworthy EX39 . . . 38 F8
Backs The TQ6 . . . . 233 E5
Backstone La EX16 . . . . . . 47 B6
Backswood La EX16 . . . . . 64 B4
Backways La TA21 . . . . . . 51 F6
Backwells Mead EX24 . . . 102 B6
Badgaver La EX34 . . . . 3 B3
Badger Cl
Dartmouth TQ6 . . . . 233 D4
☑ Exeter EX2 . . . . 178 D5
Honiton EX14 . . . . 166 E7
Newton Poppleford EX10 186 D7
Paignton TQ3 . . . . 218 F1
Badgers Cl
Ivybridge PL21 . . . . 237 A5
Kingsbridge TQ7 . . . . . . 258 C4
Kingsteignton TQ12 . . . . 207 D8
Badgers Gn TQ7 . . . . 258 C4
Badger's Holt EX20 . . . . . 170 A5
Badger's Way TQ13 . . . . 180 D7
Badger's Wlk PL12 . . . . . 242 D4
Badger View PL9 . . . . . . 255 E5
Bad Homburg Way EX4 . 181 D8
Badlake Cl EX7 . . . . 204 C7
Badlake Hill EX7 . . . . 204 C7
Badlake La EX36 . . . . 32 D6
Badlake Moor Cross TA22 . 32 D7
Badon Cl EX4 . . . . 174 A2
Bagley La TA21 . . . . 160 A3
Bagmore Hill EX5 . . . . 82 F8
Bagshot Ave EX2 . . . . 177 D3
Bailey La EX5 . . . . 98 F7
Bailey's Knapp EX16 . . . . . 50 B4
Baileys Mdw TQ6 . . . . . . 146 B7
Bailey St EX4 . . . . 261 B3
Bailey Terr EX22 . . . . 70 F5
Bainbridge Ave PL3 . . . . 248 F7
Bainbridge Ct PL7 . . . . . . 250 E7
Baker Cl EX10 . . . . 188 A8
Bakers Cl PL7 . . . . 251 C5
Bakers Cotts EX8 . . . . . . 195 F5
Bakers Court La EX35 . . . 151 B5
Baker's Cross TA3 . . . . 68 A7
Bakers Ct EX35 . . . . 151 B5
Bakers Hill
Aveton Gifford TQ7 . . . . 143 C6
Brixham TQ5 . . . . 230 C3
Exeter EX2 . . . . 176 C3
Baker's Hill
Newton Abbot TQ12 . . . . 207 B3
Tiverton EX16 . . . . 161 A4
Bakers La
Churchinford TA3 . . . . 68 A7
Wellington TA21 . . . . . . 160 E6
Bakers Mead EX13 . . . . . . 87 A1
Baker's Pk TQ13 . . . . 130 A4
Bakers Pl PL1 . . . . 247 F1
Baker St EX2 . . . . 177 E5
Bakers Terr TQ7 . . . . 143 C6
Bakers View TQ12 . . . . . 207 A3
Bakery La EX8 . . . . 202 A7
Bakery Mdw EX16 . . . . 62 B5
Bakery Way EX32 . . . . 17 B2
Bala Brook Cl TQ5 . . . . . 229 F2
Baldwin Cl EX20 . . . . 170 D6
Baldwin Dr EX20 . . . . 170 D6
Balfour Cl EX39 . . . . 14 D6
Balfour Gdns EX10 . . . . . 188 A6
Balfour Manor Cl EX10 . . 188 A5
Balfour Manor Ct
Sidmouth EX10 . . . . 187 F5
Sidmouth EX10 . . . . 188 A5
Balfour Mews EX10 . . . . 188 A5
Balfours EX10 . . . . 188 A6
Balfour Terr
Kilmington EX13 . . . . 87 C1

Balfour Terr *continued*
Plymouth PL2 . . . . 247 E4
Balkwill Ct TQ7 . . . . 258 C4
Balkwill Rd TQ7 . . . . 258 B4
Balkwill's Cotts EX21 . . . . 55 E4
Bal La PL19 . . . . 82 B5
Balland La TQ13 . . . . 131 A5
Balland Pk ☑ TQ13 . . . . 131 A5
Ballards Cres EX31 . . . . . 153 A4
Ballards Gr EX31 . . . . 153 A4
Ballards Way EX31 . . . . . 153 A4
Balleroy Cl EX21 . . . . 55 E4
Ball Hill EX17 . . . . 63 A2
Ballhill La EX16 . . . . 49 B8
Ball Hill La EX20 . . . . 170 D5
Ball La EX24 . . . . 101 F5
Balls Cnr EX37 . . . . 44 A3
Balls Corner 57 C8
Balls Corner Cross EX37 . . 57 C8
Balls Cross EX36 . . . . 20 B2
Ball's Cross TQ8 . . . . 259 C7
Balls Farm Rd EX2 . . . . . 176 F2
Balls Hill EX37 . . . . 44 A2
Balmoral Ave PL2 . . . . . . 247 F5
Balmoral Cl TQ12 . . . . . . 207 E2
Balmoral Cres EX20 . . . . 170 D5
Balmoral Gdns EX3 . . . . 182 F5
Balmoral Ho EX31 . . . . . 154 E7
Balmoral Rd EX31 . . . . . . 16 A1
Balmoral Terr TQ12 EX34 . 150 B5
Balsdon Rd EX22 . . . . 70 E1
Baltic Wharf Bsns Pk
TQ9 . . . . 223 D4
Bampfylde Way PL6 . . . . 244 D6
Bampfylde Cl
Poltimore EX5 . . . . 174 F6
Tiverton EX16 . . . . 161 F3
Bampfylde Cross EX36 . . . 19 D2
Bampfylde Rd TQ2 . . . . . 219 F5
Bampfylde Way PL6 . . . . 244 E6
Bampton Cl TQ3 . . . . 218 D2
Bampton Down Rd EX16 . 49 F7
Bampton Prim Sch EX16 . 34 B1
Bampton Rd EX16 . . . . . . 245 E1
Bampton St EX16 . . . . . . 161 D4
Bamson La EX16 . . . . 62 B6
Banbury Pk TQ2 . . . . 219 C8
Banfield Way EX14 . . . . . 166 B4
Bank End EX39 . . . . 157 B4
Bank La
☑ Brixham TQ5 . . . . . . 230 C5
☑ Totnes TQ9 . . . . 223 C5
Bankland La EX20 . . . . 77 D8
Banksia Cl EX16 . . . . 161 E7
Bankside EX8 . . . . 196 C3
Bank Sq TA22 . . . . 33 D6
Bank St
Newton Abbot TQ12 . . . . 207 B3
☑ Teignmouth TQ14 . . 210 C4
Bank The ☑ EX17 . . . . . . 17 B2
Bannawell St PL19 . . . . . 171 B6
Bannawell St PL19 . . . . . 171 B6
Banner Ct ☑ TQ3 . . . . . 226 A6
Bantham Cross TQ7 . . . . 143 D4
Baptist Chapel Ct EX17 . 165 C5
Baptist St PL17 . . . . 125 D3
Bapton Cl EX8 . . . . 196 B2
Bapton La EX8 . . . . 196 B1
Barber's La
Uplyme DT7 . . . . 260 B4
West Buckland TA21 . . . . 52 F7
Barbican App PL4 . . . . . . 263 B2
Barbican Cl EX32 . . . . . . 155 A4
Barbican Ct
Exeter EX4 . . . . 177 A5
☑ Plymouth PL4 . . . . . 263 A2
Barbican La EX32 . . . . . . 155 A4
Barbican Leisure Pk PL4 263 C2
Barbican Pl ☑ TQ3 . . . . 155 A4
Barbican Rd
Barnstaple EX32 . . . . . . 155 A4
Plymouth PL7 . . . . 250 E4
Barbican Stps EX4 . . . . . 261 A2
Barbican Terr EX32 . . . . . 155 A4
Barbican The PL1 . . . . . . 263 A2
Barbican Theatre PL1 . . . 263 A1
Barbrook Rd EX35 . . . . . 151 B3
Barbury Cres PL6 . . . . . . 245 B8
Barchington Ave TQ2 . . . 213 F3
Barcombe Hts PL3 . . . . . 226 B8
Barcombe La TQ3 . . . . . . 226 B8
Barcombe Mews TQ3 . . . 226 B8
Barcombe Rd TQ3 . . . . . 226 B8
Barcote Wlk PL6 . . . . 249 C8
Bardsey Cl PL6 . . . . 245 A7
Barewell Cl TQ1 . . . . 220 B8
Barewell Rd TQ1 . . . . 220 B8
Barfield EX19 . . . . 57 F7
Barfield Rd EX19 . . . . 57 F7
Baring Cotts ☑ TQ9 . . . 223 D5
Baring Cres EX1 . . . . 177 E6
Baring Ct
Exeter EX2 . . . . 261 B1
Lewtrenchard EX20 . . . . 106 F5
Baring Flats EX1 . . . . 177 E6
Baring St PL4 . . . . 263 B4
Barker's Hill PL12 . . . . . . 242 C1
Barkers Way EX20 . . . . . . 77 C4
Barkingdon Workshops
TQ9 . . . . 215 D7
Barlands Way EX19 . . . . . 57 F7
Barle Cl EX2 . . . . 178 D4
Barle Ct EX16 . . . . 161 E7
Barley Cl EX15 . . . . 163 B2
Barley Farm Rd EX4 . . . . 176 E4
Barley La EX4 . . . . 176 D5

Barley Lane Sch EX4 . . . . 176 D4
Barley Market St PL19 . . 171 C6
Barley Mount EX4 . . . . . . 176 F5
Barley Wlk EX6 . . . . 201 A8
Barline EX12 . . . . 191 D5
Barlow Gdns PL2 . . . . . . 248 B7
Barlow Rd EX31 . . . . 155 A7
Barnacott Cross EX39 . . . . 26 D8
Barnardo Rd EX2 . . . . . . 261 C1
Barnards Farm EX12 . . . . 191 D5
Barnards Hill La EX12 . . . 192 A7
Barn Cl
Barnstaple EX32 . . . . . . 155 C3
Ivybridge PL21 . . . . 237 A6
Plymouth PL7 . . . . 251 D4
Shebbear EX21 . . . . 55 E4
Whiddon Down EX20 . . . . 95 F3
Barn Close La EX12 . . . . 192 E5
Barncroft EX22 . . . . 39 C1
Barn Cross EX14 . . . . 85 F3
Barn Cl TQ5 . . . . 229 E4
Barndale Cres PL6 . . . . . 245 B6
Barne Barton Prim Sch
PL5 . . . . 247 D8
Barne Cl PL5 . . . . 247 C8
Barne Cross TQ13 . . . . . 112 A2
Barne La PL5 . . . . 243 D1
Barne Rd PL5 . . . . 247 C8
Barnes Cl
Honiton EX14 . . . . 166 B4
Willand EX15 . . . . 162 C5
Barnes Close Mead TA22 . 33 D6
Barnes Mdw DT7 . . . . . . 260 B5
Barnfield
Crediton EX17 . . . . 165 C5
East Allington TQ9 . . . . . 144 D7
Barnfield Ave EX8 . . . . . . 202 D7
Barnfield Cl
Braunton EX33 . . . . 152 E5
Crediton EX17 . . . . 165 C5
Galmpton TQ5 . . . . 229 C5
Barnfield Cotts EX5 . . . . . 81 F3
Barnfield Cres EX1 . . . . . 261 B3
Barnfield Dr PL7 . . . . 251 C5
Barnfield Hill EX1 . . . . . . 261 C3
Barnfield Rd
Brixham TQ5 . . . . 230 D3
Exeter EX1 . . . . 261 B3
Exeter EX1 . . . . 261 C3
Paignton TQ3 . . . . 226 A7
Torquay TQ2 . . . . 219 D2
Barnfield Terr TQ12 . . . . 212 B6
Barnhay ☑ EX16 . . . . 34 B1
Barnhay The TQ9 . . . . . . 227 F7
Barn Hill EX17 . . . . 61 A3
Barnhill Rd TQ12 . . . . . . 213 A4
Barninghams Gdns PL6 . 245 E6
Barn La EX19 . . . . 197 F2
Barn Meads Rd TA21 . . . 160 E4
Barn Owl Cl TQ2 . . . . 213 D3
Barnpark Cl TQ14 . . . . . . 210 C6
Barn Park Cl TQ12 . . . . . 211 E2
Barn Park Gdns TQ3 . . . . 73 C2
Barnpark Rd TQ14 . . . . . 210 C6
Barn Park Rd
Fremington EX31 . . . . . . 153 D5
Plymouth PL3 . . . . 248 D6
Barnpark Terr TQ14 . . . . 210 C6
Barn Pk
Ashwater EX21 . . . . 90 E6
Buckfastleigh TQ11 . . . . 236 A5
Coldeast TQ12 . . . . 122 F1
Crediton EX17 . . . . 165 C5
Saltash PL12 . . . . 242 F3
Stoke Gabriel TQ9 . . . . . 227 F8
Wrafton EX33 . . . . 152 E3
Barn Rd TQ4 . . . . 226 C2
Barns Cl
Bradninch EX5 . . . . 82 F6
Kingsteignton TQ12 . . . . 207 E6
Barnsclose TA22 . . . . 33 D6
Barnsclose E Ind Est TA22 33 D6
Barnsclose W TA22 . . . . . 33 D6
Barnsey Gdns TQ13 . . . . 130 F5
Barnsfield La TQ11 . . . . . 236 A5
Barnshill Cl EX17 . . . . 62 F1
Barnsley Cl ☑ TQ14 . . . 210 C5
Barnsley Dr TQ14 . . . . . . 210 C6
Barns Rd EX9 . . . . 198 B1
Barnstaple C Ctr EX31 . . 154 E5
Barnstaple
Chittlehampton EX37 . . . . 28 E4
Plymouth PL6 . . . . 249 E7
Barnstaple Cross
Burrington EX37 . . . . 43 C3
Crediton EX17 . . . . 79 E4
Barnstaple Heritage Ctr
EX31 . . . . 154 F5
Barnstaple & N Devon Mus
EX32 . . . . 154 F4
Barnstaple Ret Pk EX31 . 154 F4
Barnstaple St
Bideford EX39 . . . . 157 B2
South Molton EX36 . . . . 158 C4
Winkleigh EX19 . . . . 58 F3
Barnstaple Sta EX31 . . . . 154 D6
Barns Terr PL12 . . . . 242 C1
Barnstone Ct EX2 . . . . . . 181 A8
Barntown EX39 . . . . 58 D1
Barntown La EX19 . . . . . . 58 D1
Barnwood Cl PL9 . . . . . . 255 E5
Barometer World & Mus
EX20 . . . . 57 A7
Baron Cl EX31 . . . . 154 B1
Barons Pyke PL21 . . . . . 237 E4

Barons Rd PL20 . . . . 127 B3
Baron Way EX31 . . . . 154 B1
Barossa Rd PL11 . . . . . . 247 B3
Barpark Cnr EX15 . . . . 52 E3
Barrack La EX2 . . . . 181 A6
Barrack Pl PL1 . . . . 248 A1
Barrack Rd
Exeter EX2 . . . . 177 E4
Ottery St Mary EX11 . . . 169 C3
Princetown PL20 . . . . . . 128 B8
Barracks Hill TQ4 . . . . . . 223 A7
Barracks Rd PL21 . . . . . . 137 B3
Barrack St PL1 . . . . 247 E2
Barradon Cl TQ2 . . . . 214 A4
Barrington Ct TQ4 . . . . . . 226 C5
Barrington Ho TQ1 . . . . . 220 E5
Barrington Rd EX10 . . . . 188 B4
Barrington Rd TQ1 . . . . . 220 C5
Barrington St EX16 . . . . . 161 D4
Barris EX17 . . . . 60 C3
Barrowdale Cl EX8 . . . . . 196 C3
Barrow Down EX12 . . . . . 242 B3
Barrow Way Cross EX20 . 110 D8
Bar's La EX9, EX10 . . . . . 199 B8
Bartholomew Rd PL2 . . . 248 B5
Bartholomew St E EX4 . . 261 A3
Bartholomew St W EX4 . 261 A2
Bartholomew Terr EX4 . . 261 A2
Barton Ave
Braunton EX33 . . . . 152 D4
Paignton TQ3 . . . . 225 F7
Plymouth PL2 . . . . 247 E5
Bartonbury Cross EX17 . . 78 E6
Barton Cl
Cheriton Fitzpaine EX17 . . 62 E1
Exton EX3 . . . . 183 C1
Filleigh EX32 . . . . 29 C6
Kingsbridge TQ7 . . . . . . 258 D4
North Tawton EX20 . . . . . 77 C4
Okehampton EX20 . . . . . 170 C5
Paignton TQ3 . . . . 225 F7
Parkham EX39 . . . . 39 E8
Plymouth PL7 . . . . 251 C5
Stoke Canon EX5 . . . . . . 81 F1
Wembury PL9 . . . . 140 D8
Barton Close La EX33 . . . 152 C4
Barton Cnr EX17 . . . . 61 B2
Barton Cotts EX20 . . . . . . 95 C1
Barton Cres
Dawlish EX7 . . . . 204 C6
Paignton TQ3 . . . . 225 F7
Barton Cross
East Anstey EX16 . . . . . . 32 E5
Filleigh EX32 . . . . 29 A6
Heasley Mill EX36 . . . . . . 19 C2
Instow EX39 . . . . 15 B2
Morchard Bishop EX17 . . . 61 C2
Poltimore EX5 . . . . 174 B8
Sandford EX17 . . . . 80 C5
Torquay TQ3 . . . . 213 F4
Barton Ct
☑ Exeter EX1 . . . . 90 E6
Exeter EX1 . . . . 178 C7
Parkham EX39 . . . . 39 E8
Sidmouth EX10 . . . . 188 A3
Barton Dr
Newton Abbot TQ12 . . . . 206 F3
Paignton TQ3 . . . . 225 F7
Barton Gate La EX34 . . . . . 3 A3
Barton Gdns TQ3 . . . . . . 225 F7
Barton Head Cross EX20 . 76 C4
Barton Hill
Berrynarbor EX34 . . . . 2 E4
Daccombe TQ1, TQ12 . . 214 A6
Dawlish EX7 . . . . 204 D6
North Tawton EX20 . . . . . 77 C4
Bartonhill Cross TQ9 . . . 215 F6
Barton Hill Rd TQ2 . . . . . 213 F2
Barton Ho TQ2 . . . . 26 A4
Barton Inf Sch TQ2 . . . . . 213 F2
Barton Jun Sch TQ2 . . . . 213 F2
Barton La
Barton Town EX31 . . . . . . 11 D3
Berrynarbor EX34 . . . . 2 E4
Braunton EX33 . . . . 152 D5
Brayford EX32 . . . . 18 F4
Dolton EX19 . . . . 57 D4
Lapford EX17 . . . . 60 A2
Shillingford Abbot EX2 . . 114 C7
Staverton TQ9 . . . . 216 A5
Witheridge EX16 . . . . 46 E1
Barton Lane Cl EX33 . . . 152 D4
Barton Meadow Rd EX37 . 43 B7
Barton Mews
Exeter EX3 . . . . 183 C1
Millbrook PL10 . . . . 252 F6
Parkham EX39 . . . . 39 E8
Venn Ottery EX11 . . . . . 100 B2
Barton Orch EX10 . . . . . . 100 D2
Barton Paddocks EX10 . . 100 D2
Barton Rd
Barnstaple EX32 . . . . . . 155 C4
Buckland Brewer EX39 . . 40 B7
Okehampton EX20 . . . . . 170 C5
Paignton TQ3 . . . . 225 F7
Parkham EX39 . . . . 39 E8
Plymouth PL9 . . . . 255 B6
Tiverton EX16 . . . . 161 D6
Torquay TQ1, TQ2 . . . . . 219 F7
West Down EX34 . . . . 8 E5
Woolacombe EX34 . . . . . . 8 F5
Barton Rd Ind Units TQ2 219 E8

Barton Rise EX14 . . . . .84 E2
Barton St EX20 . . . . .77 C4
Barton Steep EX35. . . . . .5 E4
Barton Terr EX7. . . . . .204 D6
Barton The TA4 . . . . .35 E8
Barton Tors EX39 . . . . . . .157 C1
Barton View EX20. . . . . . . .77 C4
Barton Villas EX7. . . . . . . .204 C6
Bartows Cswy EX16. . . . . . .161 D5
Bartows Mews EX16 . . . . . .161 D5
Bartridge Hill EX31 . . . . . . .27 A5
Barum Arc EX32 . . . . .155 A5
Barum CI TQ3 . . . . .226 C7
Barum Mews ⑤ EX32 . . . . .155 A5
Barwick Cross EX19. . . . . . .58 B2
Bary CI EX17 . . . . .62 F1
Bary Hill Cross EX17 . . . . . .62 F1
Bary La EX17 . . . . .62 F1
Bascombe CI TQ5 . . . . .229 D6
Bascombe Rd TQ5 . . . . .229 D6
Basinghall CI PL9. . . . . .255 E5
Basket Ope PL4 . . . . .263 A2
Bason Cross EX22. . . . . .55 B2
Bassett CI ① EX33 . . . . . . .152 D5
Bassetts CI
Copplestone EX17 . . . . .79 A5
Northam EX39 . . . . .156 F8
Bassetts Farm Prim Sch
EX8. . . . . .196 E1
Bassetts Gdns EX8 . . . . . . .196 D2
Bastard's La EX36. . . . . . . .159 D6
Bastard's Park Cnr PL21 .137 D3
Batcombe La EX5. . . . . .81 F6
Bate CI EX2 . . . . .177 A1
Bateman's Cross EX13 . . . . .88 E7
Bath CI EX14 . . . . .84 D2
Bath Ct EX39 . . . . .156 C7
Bathern Rd EX17 . . . . .178 D4
Bath Hotel Rd EX39. . . . . .156 C7
Bath La
Plymouth PL1. . . . . .262 B2
Torquay TQ2. . . . . .219 F5
Bath Meadow Dr TA22 . . . .33 E6
Bath PI
Ilfracombe EX34 . . . . .150 B6
Plymouth PL1. . . . . .262 B2
Bath PI W PL1. . . . . .262 B2
Bath Rd EX8. . . . . .202 A6
Bath St PL1 . . . . .262 B2
Bath Terr
⑥ Instow EX39. . . . . .15 B1
⑲ Teignmouth TQ14 . . . . .210 C4
Batson Cross TQ8 . . . . .259 C5
Batson Gdns TQ4 . . . . .226 B4
Batson Hall Cross TQ8 . . . .259 C6
Batson La EX16. . . . . .46 F7
Batsworthy Hill EX16. . . . . .47 A7
Battens EX14 . . . . .87 A7
Battens Cross EX16 . . . . . . .65 C8
Batterbridge Hill PL19 . . . .117 E3
Batteridge Hill PL19 . . . . . .117 F2
Battershall CI PL9 . . . . .255 F5
Batter St PL4 . . . . .263 A2
Battersway Rd TQ4. . . . . . .225 E4
Battery La PL19 . . . . .171 C4
Battery St PL1. . . . . .262 A2
Battery Street Flats PL1. .262 A2
Battisford Pk PL7 . . . . .251 E3
Battishorne Way EX14. . . . .166 B4
Battledown Cross EX21 . . . .55 F4
Battleford La TQ9 . . . . .217 C5
Battle Rd TQ12. . . . . .180 F2
Battle St EX15 . . . . .52 E1
Battledon TA2 . . . . .33 D6
Batt's La EX11 . . . . .169 D3
Batts Pk EX15 . . . . .66 C6
Batworthy Mill Cross
TQ13 . . . . .111 A4
Bavent CI EX5 . . . . .173 F8
Baxter CI EX2 . . . . .178 D3
Baxworthy Cross EX39 . . . .23 A1
Bayard's Cove TQ6. . . . . . .233 F3
Bayard's Hill TQ6 . . . . .233 F3
Bayclose La EX14. . . . . .10 D6
Bay Ct ⑪ EX12 . . . . .192 B4
Baydon CI PL6. . . . . .245 C1
Bayly Fort Mans TQ1 . . . . .220 A4
Bayly's Rd PL9. . . . . .255 B7
Baymount Rd TQ3. . . . . . . .226 A7
Baynes CI TA21 . . . . .160 E7
Bay Rd EX9 . . . . .199 A7
Bayside La PL9 . . . . .140 A8
Bayswater Rd PL2 . . . . .262 B4
Baythorpe Lodge TQ2 . . . .219 E2
Baytor Ind Est TQ12. . . . . .225 E3
Baytree CI PL6. . . . . .245 D6
Baytree Gdns PL2 . . . . .248 A7
Bay Trees EX6 . . . . .114 D4
Bay View TQ3. . . . . .219 D1
Bay View CI TQ6 . . . . .146 B7
Bay View Ct
Lyme Regis DT7. . . . . .260 E3
Northam EX39 . . . . .156 F6
Bay View Dr TU4. . . . . .210 C6
Bay View Est TQ6 . . . . .146 B7
Bay View Farm Cvn &
Camping Site EX33 . . . . . . .7 E1
Bay View Rd
Lyme Regis DT7. . . . . .260 D4
Northam EX39 . . . . .156 E6
Woolacombe EX34. . . . . .7 E4
Baze La EX35. . . . . .6 B4
Bazley Sq EX1 . . . . .178 E8
Beach Rd
Croyde EX33 . . . . .7 D2

Beach Rd continued
Dawlish Warren EX7 . . . . . .201 B2
Heybrook Bay PL9 . . . . . . .140 A7
Ilfracombe EX34 . . . . .150 F6
Paignton TQ4 . . . . .226 C6
Seaton EX12 . . . . .192 B4
Torquay TQ1. . . . . .220 D7
Westward Ho! EX39 . . . . . .156 D7
Woolacombe EX34. . . . . .8 A6
Beach St ② EX7 . . . . .204 E6
Beach View Cres PL9. . . . .140 D7
Beacon Ave EX4 . . . . .178 A8
Beacon Castle EX34. . . . . .150 A6
Beacon CE Prim Sch The
EX8. . . . . .202 A6
Beacon Cotts TQ13. . . . . . .130 C8
Beacon Cross
Bradninch EX5. . . . . .82 F7
Copplestone EX17 . . . . .79 D6
North Tawton EX20 . . . . . . .77 A2
Romansleigh EX36. . . . . . . .45 C5
Talaton EX5. . . . . .54 B1
Beacon Down Ave PL2 . . . .248 B7
Beacon Down Cross EX6 . . .98 D2
Beacondown Cross EX16 . .63 E8
Beacon Down Cross EX20 .93 E5
Beacon Down Hill EX20 . . .93 F5
Beaconfield Rd PL2 . . . . . .248 B7
Beacon Heath EX4 . . . . . . .174 C1
Beacon Hill
Bradninch EX5. . . . . .82 F7
⑯ Exmouth EX8 . . . . .202 A6
Torquay TQ1. . . . . .220 B3
Beacon Hill La EX14 . . . . . .87 A5
Beacon Ho PL3. . . . . .249 D4
Beacon Hts EX33 . . . . .152 E6
Beacon La
Cullompton EX15. . . . . .65 A3
Exeter EX4. . . . . .178 A8
Hennock TQ13 . . . . .123 A7
Kingswear TQ6. . . . . .234 A2
Wellington TA21. . . . . .52 C4
Beaconpark La EX20. . . . . . .95 D3
Beacon Park Rd PL2 . . . . .248 B7
Beacon Pk PL15 . . . . .89 D2
Beacon PI EX8. . . . . .202 A6
Beacon Quay TQ1. . . . . . . .220 B3
Beacon Rd
Bradninch EX5. . . . . .82 F7
⑧ Horrabridge PL20. . . . . .126 F4
Kingswear TQ6. . . . . .234 A2
Beacon Rise EX14 . . . . .44 E1
Beaconsfield Cross EX22 . .72 E6
Beacon Terr
④ South Brent TQ10. . . . . .134 F2
Torquay TQ1. . . . . .220 B3
Beacon The EX8 . . . . .202 A6
Beacon View
⑤ Bittaford PL21 . . . . . . .137 C7
Dartington TQ9 . . . . .222 F8
⑧ South Brent TQ10. . . . . .134 F2
Beadon Dr TQ8 . . . . .259 C4
Beadon La TQ13 . . . . .123 A8
Beadon Rd
Salcombe TQ8 . . . . .259 B4
Salcombe TQ8 . . . . .259 C4
Beaford Com Prim Sch
EX19. . . . . .42 D1
Bealey Court Cross EX18. .45 C2
Bealswood CI PL18 . . . . . .125 D6
Bealswood Rd PL18. . . . . .125 D6
Beanhay CI ⑫ TQ12. . . . . .122 F1
Beans Mdw EX20 . . . . .170 A5
Beaple's Moor Cross
EX36. . . . . .47 A8
Beara Cotts TQ13 . . . . .131 C1
Beara Cross
Bratton Fleming EX31. . . . . .18 A8
Highampton EX21 . . . . .74 A6
King's Nympton EX37 . . . . . .44 F6
Roborough EX38 . . . . .42 A5
Beara Down Cross EX31. . . .8 F1
Beara Farm Cvn & Camping
Site TQ11 . . . . .236 E1
Beara Head EX38 . . . . .42 E6
Beara Hill EX32 . . . . .30 E7
Beara Hill Head EX36 . . . . .19 B6
Beara La
Bratton Fleming EX31. . . . . .18 A8
Combe Martin EX34. . . . . . . .3 C3
Beardown Rd EX20. . . . . . .170 E5
Beards Rd EX31. . . . . .153 E5
Beare Bridge Rd EX20. . . .170 C6
Beare Copse La EX19 . . . . .58 F2
Beare La
Beare EX5 . . . . .82 E3
Bondleigh EX20 . . . . .77 B7
Beare Lane Cross EX20. . . .77 A7
Beare Sq EX5 . . . . .82 E4
Beare's La ⑬ TQ12 . . . . . .207 B3
Bearne's Prim Sch TQ12 .207 C3
Bearsdown CI PL6. . . . . . . .249 C8
Bearsdown Rd PL6. . . . . . . .249 C8
Bears Farm Cotts EX20. . .170 B7
Bear St
Barnstaple EX32 . . . . .155 A5
Exeter EX1. . . . . .261 B2
Beaston Cross TQ9 . . . . . . .131 D1
Beatland Cross PL7 . . . . . .132 C5
Beatlands Rd EX10. . . . . . .188 B4
Beatrice Ave
Plymouth, Keyham PL2 . . . .247 E5
Plymouth, St Jude's PL4 . . .263 B3
Saltash PL12 . . . . .242 C2
Beatrice Gdns PL12 . . . . . .242 E1

Beattie Rd PL5 . . . . .247 B8
Beatty CI PL6. . . . . .245 A4
Beatty Way TQ6. . . . . .233 F4
Beauchamp Cres PL2 . . . . .248 C7
Beauchamp Rd PL2 . . . . . .248 C7
Beaudyn Wlk ⑤ PL6 . . . . .249 C7
Beaufort CI EX16 . . . . .50 D1
Beaufort Ct EX2 . . . . .261 A1
Beaufort Ho ⑤ PL4 . . . . . .263 A2
Beaufort Rd EX2. . . . . .261 A1
Beaufort Wlk EX32. . . . . . .155 B6
Beauly CI PL7 . . . . .251 A5
Beaumaris Gdns PL3. . . . . .248 F8
Beaumaris Rd PL3 . . . . . . .248 F7
Beaumont Ave PL4. . . . . . .263 A3
Beaumont CI
⑤ Coldeast TQ12 . . . . . . .122 F1
Torquay TQ2. . . . . .219 D6
Beaumont PI PL4 . . . . .263 A3
Beaumont Rd
Newton Abbot TQ12. . . . . .207 C3
Plymouth PL4. . . . . .263 A3
Beaumont St PL2 . . . . .248 A5
Beaumont Terr PL12 . . . . . .242 F4
Beauvale CI EX11. . . . . . . .169 E4
Beavers Brook CI TQ3 . . . .219 B2
Beavor La EX13. . . . . .167 F6
Beaworthy CI EX2. . . . . . . .177 A3
Beccott Cross EX31. . . . . . . .10 C1
Becket Rd TQ13. . . . . .180 E7
Beckets Rd TQ7 . . . . .258 D5
Beckford CI PL7 . . . . .251 A5
Beckford Cross EX13. . . . . . .87 C4
Beckham La EX36 . . . . .31 E2
Becklake CI EX31 . . . . .154 A2
Beckly Ct PL1 . . . . .262 C3
Becky Falls TQ13. . . . . .122 A7
Bede Gdns PL5 . . . . .244 C1
Bedford CI PL18 . . . . .125 C6
Bedford Cotts PL20 . . . . . .126 F4
Bedford Flats EX10 . . . . . .188 B3
Bedford Gr PL21. . . . . .237 D5
Bedford Mews PL4. . . . . . .263 A4
Bedford Park Villas PL4 . .263 A4
Bedford Pk
⑩ Bere Alston PL20. . . . . .125 E1
Plymouth PL4. . . . . .263 A4
Bedford PI
⑥ Bere Alston PL20. . . . . .125 E1
⑨ Horrabridge PL20. . . . . .126 F4
Bedford Rd
Horrabridge PL20. . . . . . . .126 F4
Plymouth PL9. . . . . .255 E8
Torquay TQ1. . . . . .220 D8
Bedford Row ② EX31 . . . .154 F5
Bedford Sq
Sidmouth EX10 . . . . .188 B3
Tavistock PL19. . . . . .171 C5
Bedford St
⑤ Barnstaple EX32 . . . . . .155 A5
Bere Alston PL20. . . . . . . .125 E1
Exeter EX1. . . . . .261 B3
Plymouth PL2. . . . . .247 F5
Bedford Terr PL4 . . . . .263 A4
Bedford Units PL18 . . . . . .125 C5
Bedford Villas ⑦ PL20 . . .125 E1
Bedford Way PL1 . . . . .262 C3
Bedland's La EX13 . . . . .87 C6
Bedlem's La EX13 . . . . .197 F2
Beech Ave
Exeter EX4. . . . . .173 D1
Plymouth PL4. . . . . .263 C2
Bedford Way TQ3 . . . . .218 B3
Beech Bank EX39 . . . . .25 D4
Beech CI
Barnstaple EX31 . . . . .154 B2
Broadclyst EX5 . . . . .175 D6
Honiton EX14. . . . . .166 A4
Tavistock PL19. . . . . .171 C2
Torpoint PL11 . . . . .247 A3
Totnes TQ9. . . . . .222 F6
Willand EX15 . . . . .162 D4
Beech Croft EX15. . . . . . . .163 C5
Beechcroft Rd
Plymouth, Beacon Park
PL2 . . . . .248 B7
Plymouth, Lower Compton
PL3 . . . . .249 A6
Beech Ct
Plymouth PL6. . . . . .245 D5
② Wellington TA21 . . . . . .160 D6
Beech Dr
Down St Mary EX17. . . . . . .78 E7
Ipplepen TQ12. . . . . .211 E2
Beeches CI EX5. . . . . .184 B2
Beeches The
Okehampton EX20 . . . . .76 E1
Woolfardisworthy EX39. . . .38 F8
Beechfield Ave
Torquay TQ2. . . . . .213 F2
Yelverton PL20. . . . . .127 A3
Beechfield Gr PL3 . . . . .248 E6
Beechfield PI TQ2 . . . . . . .213 F2
Beechfield Rd EX13 . . . . . .153 D5
Beech Gr
Barnstaple EX31 . . . . .154 F7
Wellington TA21. . . . . .160 C6
Beech Grove Prim Sch
TA21. . . . . .160 C6
Beech Grove Terr EX31 . . .154 F7
Beech Hill EX31. . . . . .160 F5
Beech Hill Cross EX17. . . . .61 B3
Beech Hill Ho EX17 . . . . . . .61 C3
Beeching CI EX31. . . . . .73 E3
Beech La EX31. . . . . .88 E1
Beech Lea EX18 . . . . .58 F8

Beech Pk
Crediton EX17 . . . . .165 D6
Fremington EX31. . . . . . . .153 E5
Holsworthy Beacon EX22 . . .54 C3
West Hill EX11. . . . . .168 D4
Beech Rd
Lee Mill PL21. . . . . .136 C7
Stibb Cross EX38. . . . . .40 D1
Beech Tree Cross TA22 . . . .33 C7
Beechtree La EX10, E12 . .101 F2
Beech Tree Mdw EX20. . . .107 F8
Beech Trees La TQ12 . . . . .211 C3
Beechway EX8. . . . . .202 A8
Beech Wlk EX14 . . . . .85 C1
Beechwood Ave
Barnstaple EX31 . . . . .154 D4
Bovey Tracey TQ13. . . . . . .180 C4
Newton Abbot TQ12. . . . . .207 E1
Plymouth PL4. . . . . .248 D8
Beechwood CI EX31. . . . . .154 D4
Beechwood Cres PL7 . . . . .251 F7
Beechwood Cross PL7 . . . .251 F7
Beechwood Ct TQ14 . . . . . .124 E1
Beechwood Dr TQ7 . . . . . . .258 D5
Beechwood Rd TQ13 . . . . .123 E6
Beechwood Rise PL6 . . . . .245 E1
Beechwood Terr PL4 . . . . . .248 D8
Beechwood Way PL7. . . . . .251 D5
Beeley Orch EX16 . . . . .161 C8
Beenleigh Cross TQ9 . . . . .139 D6
Beersah Cross EX16. . . . . . .63 B4
Beer CE Prim Sch EX12 . .191 C5
Beer Cross EX20. . . . . .94 E6
Beer Cross EX36. . . . . .32 A5
Beer Head Cvn Pk EX12 . .191 D4
Beer Heights Light Rly
EX12 . . . . .191 C5
Beer Hill
Clawton EX22 . . . . .72 B1
Seaton EX12 . . . . .191 E6
Beer La EX36 . . . . .18 E2
Beer La EX36 . . . . .32 A4
Beerhill La EX20 . . . . .76 F5
Beer La
Burlescombe EX16. . . . . . . .51 B2
Dulverton TA22 . . . . .33 D5
Puddington EX16. . . . . .62 C6
Zeal Monachorum EX17. . . .78 C7
Beer Quarry Caves EX12 .191 A5
Beer Rd EX12. . . . . .191 E6
Beers Cotts EX6 . . . . .181 B2
Beers Hill EX17 . . . . .79 A5
Beer Youth Hostel EX12 . .191 C6
Beesands TQ7 . . . . .149 E7
Beeson Cross EX39 . . . . . . .22 F3
Beeson Pool TQ7 . . . . .149 E8
Beeston Wlk ⑥ PL6. . . . . .249 C7
Beetham La TA20 . . . . .69 E6
Beetland La EX35 . . . . .151 D2
Beetor Cross TQ13 . . . . . . .131 B3
Beggar's Bush TQ10. . . . . .134 F2
Beggars La EX14 . . . . .85 A7
Behind Hayes EX9 . . . . . . .198 E7
Bekhams Tree Cross
EX6. . . . . .113 B2
Belair Rd PL2. . . . . .248 C7
Belair Villas PL2 . . . . .248 C7
Belcombe Dro TA20. . . . . . .69 E7
Belfield Ave TQ3. . . . . .218 D3
Belfield CI TQ3 . . . . .218 D3
Belfield Rd TQ3 . . . . .218 D3
Belfield Rise TQ3 . . . . .218 D3
Belfield Way TQ3 . . . . .218 D3
Belgrave Ct EX9 . . . . .203 F8
Belgrave La EX4 . . . . .248 F4
Belgrave Mews ⑤ TQ2. . .219 F5
Belgrave Rd
Exeter EX1. . . . . .261 C3
Newton Abbot TQ12. . . . . .207 F1
Plymouth PL4. . . . . .248 F4
Torquay TQ2. . . . . .219 F5
Belgrave Terr
⑥ Teignmouth TQ14 . . . . .210 C5
Upton Pyne EX5. . . . . .173 A8
Beliers Hill EX31 . . . . .27 A6
Bellaire EX31 . . . . .154 E7
Bellaire Dr EX31. . . . . .154 E7
Bellamarsh La TQ13 . . . . . .123 C4
Bellamy CI PL7. . . . . .251 A5
Bella Vista Rd TQ5 . . . . . . .230 C6
Bell CI PL7. . . . . .251 A4
Bell Ct EX4 . . . . .261 A3
Belle Acre CI PL3 . . . . .248 F6
Belle Ave EX17. . . . . .165 B5
Belle Cross Rd TQ7 . . . . . .258 E6
Belle CI EX17 . . . . .165 B5
Belle Hill TQ7. . . . . .258 E6
Belle Isle Dr EX2 . . . . .261 C1
Belle Meadow Ct ②
EX32. . . . . .154 F5
Belle Meadow Rd ⑯
EX32. . . . . .155 A5
Belle Par EX17. . . . . .165 D5
Bellever CI PL20 . . . . .128 B8
Bellever Forest Wlks
PL20. . . . . .120 B4
Bellever Tor Dr TQ5 . . . . . .229 F2
Belle View EX17 . . . . .164 C4
Belle View Terr TA20 . . . . . .69 C6
Belle Vue
Axminster EX13 . . . . .167 D6
Chawleigh EX18. . . . . .60 A7
Belle Vue Ave
Lynton EX35. . . . . .151 B5
Plymouth PL9. . . . . .255 B5
Belle Vue CI EX4 . . . . .173 A1
Belle Vue Cotts EX22. . . . .164 C4
Belle Vue Cross EX38. . . . . .42 A8

Belle Vue Dr PL9. . . . . .255 B5
Belle Vue Rd
Exeter EX4. . . . . .173 A2
Exmouth EX8 . . . . .202 A8
Kingsbridge TQ7 . . . . .258 D5
Paignton TQ4 . . . . .226 C5
Plymouth PL9. . . . . .255 C5
Saltash PL12 . . . . .242 F2
Belle Vue Rise PL9. . . . . . .255 B5
Bellevue Sq PL11 . . . . .247 B2
Belle Vue Terr
Bideford EX39. . . . . .156 F2
Cullompton EX15. . . . . . . .163 C4
Gunnislake PL18 . . . . .125 D6
Kennford EX6. . . . . .114 D4
Bellingate EX17 . . . . .79 A2
Bellingham Cres PL7. . . . . .251 C4
Belliver Ind Est PL6. . . . . .241 B1
Belliver Way PL6 . . . . .241 B3
Bell La
Hennock TQ13 . . . . .123 A7
Paignton TQ3 . . . . .225 B7
Bell Mdw EX16 . . . . .64 A2
Bellrock CI TQ2 . . . . .214 B3
Bells CI EX18 . . . . .60 A7
Bell St EX9 . . . . .198 F7
Belmont EX32 . . . . .155 A5
Belmont Ave
Combe Martin EX34. . . . . . . .2 F4
Ilfracombe EX34 . . . . .150 A5
Belmont CI
④ Kingsteignton TQ12 . . .123 F1
Tiverton TQ12 . . . . .161 D5
Belmont Ct ⑥ PL3 . . . . . . .248 A4
Belmont Ho
Exeter EX4. . . . . .261 C4
⑥ Seaton EX12. . . . . .192 A5
Belmont PI PL3 . . . . .248 A4
Belmont Rd
Barnstaple EX32 . . . . .155 B6
Brixham TQ5 . . . . .230 C4
Exeter EX1. . . . . .261 C4
Ilfracombe EX34 . . . . .150 A5
Ivybridge PL21 . . . . .237 C4
Tiverton EX16 . . . . .161 D5
Torquay TQ1. . . . . .220 C6
Belmont St PL1. . . . . .262 B3
Belmont Terr
Exmouth EX8 . . . . .196 C1
⑪ South Brent TQ10. . . . . .134 F3
Belstone Cnr EX5 . . . . .244 A3
Belstone Cnr Cross EX20. .76 E1
Bel Tor Cnr TQ13. . . . . .129 F8
Beltor Cotts TQ12. . . . . . . .211 D1
Belvedere CI PL3 . . . . .182 E6
Belvedere Ct
⑤ Dawlish EX7 . . . . .204 E6
⑧ Wellington TA21 . . . . . .160 D6
Belvedere Pk EX2 . . . . .113 F5
Belvedere Rd
Exmouth EX8 . . . . .202 A7
Ilfracombe EX34 . . . . .150 B6
Newton Abbot TQ12. . . . . .206 C5
Plymouth PL4. . . . . .249 B2
Belvidere Rd EX4 . . . . .173 B2
Belworthy CI PL18 . . . . .168 D5
Bendarroch Rd EX11. . . . . .168 D5
Bendarroch Sch EX5 . . . . . .99 E2
Bendbow Rise EX4 . . . . . . .176 F5
Bendibus Hill EX21 . . . . . . .72 E3
Bendle La EX36. . . . . .30 E8
Bendle Lane Cross EX36 . .30 E8
Bendles EX16. . . . . .46 E1
Benedict CI TQ14 . . . . .210 C7
Benedicts CI ⑩ TQ12 . . . .122 F1
Benedict Way ② PL21. . . .137 B2
Ben Jonson CI TQ2 . . . . . . .219 C6
Benjamin Acre ⑬ TQ12 . .122 F1
Benley Cross EX18 . . . . .45 D2
Bennah Hill EX6 . . . . .113 A3
Bennetts La PL12. . . . . . . .242 F3
Bennett CI EX2 . . . . .181 B8
Bennett Rd TQ8 . . . . .259 D3
Bennetts CI EX12 . . . . .190 E4
Bennetts Hill EX10 . . . . . . .187 F7
Bennett Sq EX4 . . . . .178 A8
Bennett St PL1 . . . . .247 E1
Benson CI EX4. . . . . .46 E1
Benson Dr EX39 . . . . .157 A6
Benton Cross EX32. . . . . . . .18 B7
Benton La EX32 . . . . .18 A8
Benton Rd EX31 . . . . .18 B8
Ben Venue CI TQ1 . . . . .220 C5
Berachah Rd TQ1 . . . . .220 B6
Bere Alston Prim Sch
PL20. . . . . .125 E1
Bere Alston Sta PL20 . . . . .125 E2
Berea Rd TQ1 . . . . .220 C6
Bere Ferrers Sta PL20. . . . .239 E3
Bere Hill EX17 . . . . .204 B6
Beresford St PL2 . . . . .248 A4
Berkeley Ave ⑦ TQ2 . . . . .213 C1
Berkeley CI ⑥ EX34. . . . . .150 B5
Berkeley Rise TQ2 . . . . . . .213 C1
Berkeley Way PL21. . . . . . .237 D4
Berkshire Dr
Exeter EX4. . . . . .176 E4
Plymouth PL2. . . . . .247 F5
Bernadette CI EX4 . . . . . . .174 C1
Berner's Cross EX19 . . . . . .58 F4
Bernice CI PL4 . . . . .249 B4

Bernice Terr PL4........249 B4
Berretts Way TQ12......123 A1
Berrow Park Rd PL3....248 E6
Berry Ave TQ3..........225 F6
Berryball Cl EX20......170 C6
Berrybrook Mdw EX6...182 B3
Berry Cl
  Abbotskerswell TQ12...212 B6
  Exmouth EX8..........202 E8
  Salcombe TQ8.........259 C4
Berry Cotts EX6.........182 B3
Berry Cross
  Dunsford EX6..........112 E8
  Langtree EX38..........41 B1
  Shebbear EX21..........55 D5
Berrydown Cross EX34....2 F1
Berry Down Cross EX34...9 F6
Berry Dr TQ3...........226 A6
Berry Head Country Pk
  TQ5.................231 A5
Berry Head Gdns PL6....244 E1
Berry Head Rd TQ5.....230 E6
Berry Hill
  Beer EX12............191 D5
  Bishopsteignton TQ14..208 F8
  Branscombe EX12.......190 A4
  North Tawton EX20......59 C1
Berry La
  Axminster EX13.........88 F3
  Bow EX12.............191 D6
  Combe Martin EX34......2 F4
  Dunsford EX6..........112 E8
  Kingsteignton TQ12....207 E6
Berry Mdw TQ12........207 E6
Berrynarbor CE Prim Sch
  EX34................2 E3
Berrynarbor Pk EX34......2 E3
Berry Park Cl PL9.......255 E6
Berry Park Rd PL9......255 E7
Berry Pk PL12..........242 D4
Berry Pomeroy Castle
  TQ9.................217 D1
Berry Pomeroy Parochial CE
  Prim Sch TQ9.........224 B7
Berry Rd
  Barnstaple EX32.......155 C4
  Braunton EX33.........152 E7
  Paignton TQ3.........225 F6
Berry's Ground La EX31...4 C5
Berry's La PL7..........133 A1
Berry Sq TQ4...........226 C6
Berrys Wood TQ12......206 F3
Berthon Rd PL5.........247 C8
Berwick Ave PL5........244 E3
Besigheim Way TQ12....207 F4
Besley Cl EX10..........56 C4
Besley Ct EX2...........177 B3
Besshill La EX31........10 F3
Bestridge Mdw EX32.....28 E8
Best's La EX38.........159 D5
Betham Hill EX16........46 F2
Betham La EX14.........59 B6
Bethelcombe Cross
  TQ12................122 C1
Bethel Cross TQ12......122 C1
Bethel Terr [1] TQ1.....220 B5
Betjeman Wlk PL5.......244 C3
Betjemen Dr EX8........196 C3
Betony Rise EX2........178 C3
Betton Way TQ13.......111 F5
Bettys Mead EX4........178 A8
Beuvron Cl EX39.........38 F8
Bevan Rd EX32.........155 A5
Beverley Cl EX2........155 A5
Beverley Gdns [1] TQ13.131 A5
Beverley Rd PL3........249 C4
Beverley Rise TQ5......230 B4
Beverley Way TQ12.....207 A2
Beverston Way PL6......245 B8
Bevil Cl EX39..........157 A1
Beweys Pk PL12........242 C2
Bewhay Gdns TQ9.......222 F8
Bewsley Hill EX17.......79 B5
Bexley La [6] TQ2......219 F5
Beyrout Pl [6] PL1......247 F3
Bhutan Cl EX14........166 D5
Bias La [8] EX33.......152 D6
Bibors Hill TA4.........35 E4
Bicclescombe Ct EX34..150 B4
Bicclescombe Gdns
  EX34...............150 A4
Bicclescombe Park Rd
  EX34...............150 A4
Bickell Cross EX32......28 C6
Bickern Rd PL11........247 B3
Bickerton Top TQ7......149 C5
Bickford La [2] EX14.....61 A4
Bickfords Gn [4] TQ12..122 F1
Bickham La EX16.........47 E7
Bickham Park Rd PL3...248 D7
Bickham Rd PL5........243 D2
Bickingcott Cross EX36...31 C7
Bickingcott Hill EX36....31 C8
Bickington Cvn Pk EX31.154 A3
Bickington Lodge EX31...16 A3
Bickington Rd EX31....154 C3
Bickland Castle EX16....63 F1
Bickleigh Cl
  Exeter EX4...........174 D2
  Plymouth PL6.........245 A1
Bickleigh Down Bsns Pk
  PL6................245 D8
Bickleigh Down CE Prim Sch
  PL6................245 D8
Bickleigh Down Rd PL6.241 D1
Bickleigh Mill Watermill &
  Craft Ctr EX16........63 F2

Bickleigh-on-Exe CE Prim
  Sch EX16.............64 A2
Bickleton Cross EX31...153 A2
Bickley Mill Cross TQ12.212 C1
Bickley Rd TQ12........212 C2
Bickwell House La EX10.187 E5
Bickwell La EX10.......187 F5
Bickwell Valley EX10...187 F4
Bickwill Cross EX36......46 D8
Bicton Cl PL6..........245 D1
Bicton Coll EX9.........186 C1
Bicton Park Botanical Gdns
  EX9................198 C8
Bicton Pl
  Exeter EX1...........177 F6
  Exmouth EX8.........202 A6
Bicton St
  Barnstaple EX32......155 A5
  Exmouth EX8.........202 A6
Bicton Villas EX8.......202 B6
Bidbrooke La EX36.......32 A6
Biddacott Cross EX37....28 E4
Biddamoor La EX14.......42 C2
Bidder Cl TQ13........111 F4
Bidders Cl TQ6........146 B7
Bidders Ct EX36.......158 C4
Bidders Wlk TQ6.......146 B7
Biddick Dr PL2.........247 F6
Biddicombe Cross
  TQ13...............124 A6
Biddypark La EX2.......113 F6
Bideford Bay Holiday Village
  EX39................24 A2
Bideford Coll EX39.....156 E1
Bideford Railway Mus
  EX39................157 B1
Bideford & Torridgeside
  Hospl EX39..........156 F2
Bideford Wlk PL6......249 E8
Bidmead Cl EX8........202 E7
Bidna La EX39.........157 B8
Bidwell Brook Dr TQ4..226 C1
Bidwell Brook School
  TQ9................215 F1
Bidwell Cross
  Langford EX5.........172 E8
  Thorverton EX5........81 E6
Bidwell La
  Brampford Speke EX5...81 C1
  Thorverton EX5........81 F6
Bidwell Wlk TQ4.......226 B1
Biera View TQ13.......111 A6
Bigadon La TQ11......236 D4
Bigbury Cl TQ7.........142 F5
Bigbury Way TQ2.......214 B2
Bigbury Wlk PL6.......249 E8
Biggin Hill PL5........243 F4
Big Sheep (Farm Pk) The
  EX39................156 B1
Bilbie Cl EX15.........163 B3
Bilbury St [1] PL4.......263 A3
Bilcombe Rd PL6.......249 E1
Billacombe Villas PL9..255 F8
Bill Douglas Centre Mus The
  ....177 B8
Billhole La EX17.........61 C6
Billings Cl PL6.........244 D6
Billingsmoor Visitor Ctr
  EX15................64 D1
Billington Cl PL6.......249 E7
Bilton Terr [8] EX39....157 A1
Biltor Rd TQ12.........211 D1
Bilver Cross TQ12......217 C8
Bimbom La EX13.......103 C8
Bindon Rd EX4........174 E2
Binford Cl EX1.........178 B6
Bingfield Cl TQ1.......220 C5
Bingham Cres EX32....155 B4
Bingwell Ho EX16......161 F3
Binhamy Rd EX23.......70 A8
Binkham Hill PL20.....127 A3
Binnamore Cross TQ10.134 E4
Binneford Cross EX17....96 F8
Binneford Hill EX17......62 B2
Bircham View PL6......245 C1
Birchanger Cross TQ13.122 B2
Birch Cl PL6...........245 E7
Birch Cross
  Doddiscombsleigh EX6.113 D8
  Yarcombe EX14........69 A4
  Zeal Monachorum EX17..78 B8
Birchen End EX5.........99 C5
Birchen La
  Highampton EX20, EX21..74 E5
  [7] Tiverton EX16.....161 C3
Birchen Tree Cross EX15..66 C4
Birches The PL6.......245 D6
Birchfield Ave TQ12....248 B6
Birch Gr EX11.........168 D3
Birchill Cross EX13.....88 A6
Birch La
  Barnstaple EX31......154 C2
  Landkey EX32..........17 D3
  Morchard Bishop EX17...61 A2
  Zeal Monachorum EX17..78 A8
Birchland Rd PL7......133 A1
Birchland Way PL7.....136 A8
Birchlea TQ13.........180 C4
Birchman's Cross EX17..78 E1
Birchpark La EX20.......77 B4
Birch Pond Rd PL9.....255 D2
Birch Rd
  Landkey EX32..........17 B2

Birch Rd continued
  Landkey EX32..........17 D2
  Lympstone EX8........195 F5
  Newton Abbot TQ12...207 F1
  Wellington TA21.......160 E5
Birch Wlk TQ2.........219 C8
Birchwood Cl
  Tavistock PL19........171 C3
  Totnes TQ9...........223 B5
Birchwood Gdns PL7....251 A7
Birchwood Rd EX8......196 D2
Birchy Barton Hill EX1..178 B6
Birchy La EX13........168 E8
Birdshaven TQ2........219 E5
Birdswell La EX34.......2 D3
Birkbeck Cl PL7........250 E7
Birkdale Cl PL12.......242 C2
Birkett Cl EX2.........178 C4
Birks Halls of Residence
  EX4................173 A1
Biscombe Cross TA3.....67 E8
Biscombe Gdns PL12...243 A2
Bishmill Gate EX36......30 E4
Bishop Cornish CE Prim Sch
  PL12...............242 F1
Bishop Ct [2] EX24....103 A4
Bishop Dunstan Sch
  TQ12...............207 B2
Bishop Pasterfield Ho [4]
  EX2................261 B2
Bishops Ave TQ14.....208 F8
Bishops Cl
  Ivybridge PL21.......237 E6
  Saltash PL12.........242 E3
  Starcross EX6........201 B4
  Torquay TQ1.........221 A4
Bishop's Clyst EX5.....179 A3
Bishops Court Ind Est
  EX2................178 E4
Bishop's Court La EX5..179 C4
Bishops Ct
  Bishopsteignton TQ14..208 F8
  [4] Wellington TA21...160 D6
Bishop's Hill TA21.......51 B7
Bishops Mdw EX17......61 A2
Bishops Mead [3] TQ10.134 F3
Bishops Nympton EX36...31 C1
Bishop's Nympton Cross
  EX36...............30 F1
Bishop's Pl
  Paignton TQ3.........226 B6
  Plymouth PL1........262 B1
Bishops Rise
  Kentisbeare EX15......66 A3
  Torquay TQ1.........221 A4
Bishop's Tawton Prim Sch
  EX32...............16 E1
Bishop's Tawton Rd
  Barnstaple EX32......155 B2
  Bishop's Tawton EX32..16 E1
Bishopsteignton Mus of
  Rural Life TQ14.....209 A8
Bishopsteignton Rd
  TQ14...............209 D6
Bishopsteignton Sch
  TQ14...............208 F8
Bishop Westall Ho [6]
  EX2................261 B2
Bishop Westall Rd EX2..178 A2
Bishop Wilfrid Rd TQ14.209 D8
Bitney La TQ12.........212 C5
Bittadon La EX31.........9 C4
Bittaford Terr [2] PL21..137 C7
Bittaford Wood [6] PL21.137 C7
Bittaford Wood Cvn Pk [8]
  PL21...............137 C7
Bittam's La TQ9.......217 B4
Bittern Ind Units EX2..178 E5
Bittern Rd EX2........178 E6
Bittery Cross EX5.......84 B2
Bitton Ave TQ14.......210 B5
Bitton Ct TQ14........210 C4
Bitton Park Rd [1] TQ14.210 B5
Blachford Cl PL21......133 C2
Blachford Rd PL21.....237 C5
Blackabrook Ave PL20..128 A8
Blackacre Rd EX24......102 C6
Blackalder Terr PL7.....132 F4
Blackaller La EX16.......33 C1
Blackall Rd EX4........261 B4
Black-a-tor Copse Nature
  Reserve EX20.........108 E8
Blackawton Prim Sch
  TQ9................139 E2
Blackball La TQ5......230 C6
Blackberry Ct PL9.....255 E8
Blackberry Ct TA21....160 D4
Blackberry La
  Bigbury TQ7..........142 E6
  Plymouth TQ9........255 E8
Blackberry Way [6] TQ12.123 F1
Blackboy Rd EX1.......177 E7
Blackbrook Ave TQ4....226 B1
Blackbrook La PL20....127 B4
Blackbrook Wlk TQ4....226 B1
Blackditch Cross EX17...60 B1
Blackditch La EX17......78 B8
Black Dog Cross EX17...61 E4
Blackdown Bsns Pk
  TA21...............160 C6
Blackdown Cross
  Cornworthy TQ9......139 E4
  Loddiswell TQ7.......138 B2
  Tedburn St Mary EX4...97 E8
Blackdown La
  Halwell TQ9..........139 D4
  Tedburn St Mary EX4...98 C5
Blackdown Pk EX15....162 C5

Blackdown Rd TA21....160 B4
Blackdown View
  [2] Hemyock EX15.....67 B8
  Sampford Peverell EX16.50 C1
Blackdown Visitors Ctr
  EX15...............52 D3
Blackenway La TQ12...213 B7
Blackerton Cross EX16...32 E3
Blackett Cl PL21......237 E4
Blackeven Cl PL6......241 D1
Blackeven Hill PL6.....241 E1
Blackfriars La PL1.....263 A2
Black Gate
  Challacombe EX31......11 F4
  Holemoor EX22........73 B8
Blackgate Cross EX39....26 C7
Blackhall Gdns PL6....244 D6
Black Hat La EX6.......176 B3
Blackhaven Cl TQ4.....229 B8
Blackhayes La EX14......68 F1
Black Horse Cnr EX18...59 C4
Blackhorse La EX5.....179 B8
Black La
  Hemyock EX15........52 D2
  Holcombe Rogus EX16...50 E6
Blackler's Land Cross
  TQ9................216 B5
Blackley La TQ13.......67 F8
Black Lion Ct [9] EX14..166 C6
Blackmoor Rd TQ10....160 F4
Blackmoor's Path EX35.151 B5
Blackmore Cres PL6....244 D6
Blackmore Ct EX8......196 E1
Blackmore Dr EX10....188 B4
Blackmore Mews EX2..178 C4
Blackmore Rd
  Exeter EX5...........99 A1
  Tiverton EX5........161 F3
Blackmore CE Prim Sch
  TQ12...............122 F1
Blackpool Cl EX4.......78 D4
Blackpool Gdns TQ6....146 A6
Blackpool Hill TQ6.....146 A6
Blackpool Rd EX17......78 D4
Blackpool Valley Rd TQ6.146 A7
Blackpost Cross
  Kingston TQ7.........142 C7
  Totnes, Littlehempston
    TQ9...............217 A2
  Totnes TQ9..........223 F6
Blackpost La TQ9......223 F5
Blackridge Cross TQ7..258 F8
Blacksmith La TQ10....137 D8
Blacksmiths Cnr EX17...81 A6
Blackstone Cl PL9......255 B8
Blackstone Cross TQ12.211 D1
Blackstone Rd PL2.....211 D1
Blackswan Pl [11] EX7..204 D6
Blackthorn Ave EX16...161 F6
Blackthorn Cl
  Honiton EX14........166 C4
  Plymouth, Honicknowle
    PL5...............244 B3
  Plymouth, Woolwell PL6.245 D8
  Sidmouth EX10........187 F8
Blackthorn Cres EX1...178 C5
Blackthorn Dr PL21....237 E4
Blackthorn Way TQ4....225 D4
Black Torrington CE Prim
  Sch EX21............74 D8
Blackwalls La EX18......60 B7
Blackwater La EX13......88 F3
Blackwater Rd EX15.....66 B8
Blackwell Cross
  Broadhempston TQ13..131 D3
  Strete TQ6..........145 E7
Blackwell La TQ13.....131 D2
Bladder La PL5........244 E2
Bladon Cl TQ12........207 D1
Blagaton Gate EX21.....73 B1
Blagdon Cl EX17.......165 D5
Blagdon Ct EX17.......165 D5
Blagdon Cross
  Ashwater EX21........90 C7
  Paignton TQ3.........225 A7
Blagdon Lodge Cross
  EX21...............90 C8
Blagdon Rd TQ3.......225 B6
Blagdon Rise EX17.....165 D6
Blagrove Hill EX17......46 C3
Blagrove Rd PL5.......243 C2
Blair Rd PL21.........237 D5
Blake Cl TQ1..........220 B8
Blake Gdns PL5........243 D2
Blakeland Rd EX31.....153 D5
Blakemore Cross TQ9..222 A4
Blakes Hill Rd EX32.....17 B2
Blakewell Cross
  Chittlehampton EX37....28 E3
  Landkey EX32.........28 D3
Blakewell Hill EX32......18 E2
Blakey Down La TQ3...218 F1
Blamphayne Cross EX24.102 C7
Blanchard Pl [2] PL7...250 E7
Blanchdown Dr PL18....125 C7
Blandford Rd PL3......249 C6
Blangy Cl EX20........162 C7
Blanksmill Cross TQ7...259 A8
Blatchborough Cross
  EX22...............38 B1
Blatchcombe Dr TQ3...225 F7
Blatchcombe Rd TQ3...225 E6
Blatchfords Ct EX20....170 B5
Blatchmore La TQ6.....232 C4
Blaxton La PL5........240 C2
Blenheim Cl
  Newton Abbot TQ12...207 A5
  Torquay TQ1.........220 E4

Blenheim Cl continued
  Willand EX15.........162 D5
Blenheim Ct
  Exeter EX2..........177 C1
  Willand EX15.........162 D5
Blenheim Dr EX15......162 D4
Blenheim La EX20.......76 C4
Blenheim Rd
  Exeter EX2..........177 B2
  Plymouth PL4........263 A4
Blenheim Terr TQ13....180 C7
Bligh Cl TQ14.........210 A8
Blights Hill EX16, TA22...33 F3
Blind Acres La EX33....15 A8
Blind La
  Aylesbeare EX5........99 E2
  Buckland St Mary TA20..69 A8
  Huxham EX5..........174 B8
Blindwell Ave TQ12....207 F7
Blindwell Farm Cotts
  TQ12...............207 E7
Blindwell Hill TQ10....252 E5
Blindwell La TA4........34 E6
Blindwylle Rd TQ2.....219 E5
Blogishay La TQ13.....130 F4
Bloomball Cl PL3.......249 B6
Blossom Cl EX14........67 C1
Blossom Hill EX14......67 C1
Blue Anchor Cross EX14.84 B4
Blue Ball TQ9.........223 C5
Bluebell Ave EX16.....161 F6
Bluebell Cl
  Saltash PL12.........242 D4
  Seaton EX12.........192 B7
Bluebell Rd PL13.......67 C1
Bluebell Way
  Launceston PL15......105 A2
  Tavistock PL19........171 E4
Blueberry Downs EX9...199 I2
Blue Cedar Ct EX8.....202 B6
Blue Gate TA24........19 F8
Bluegate Hill PL21.....137 A2
Bluehayes La
  Clyst Honiton EX5....175 F3
  Rockbeare EX5........99 A5
Blue Haze Cl PL6.......245 D5
Blue Ridge Rd TQ13....180 C4
Bluett Rd TA21........160 D4
Blue Waters Dr
  Lyme Regis DT7.......260 B3
  Paignton TQ4........229 C8
Blue Waters Ind Est
  TQ12...............180 C5
Blundell's La PL9......161 F4
Blundell's Rd
  Tiverton, Cowleymoor
    EX15..............64 D8
  Tiverton EX16........161 F4
Blundell's Sch EX16....161 F4
Blunt's La PL6.........245 C3
Blyth Ct EX9..........156 B6
Blythswood Cres [4] TQ3.220 B7
Boarden Barn EX8......202 B6
Boasley Cross EX20......92 E4
Bockland Cl EX15......163 A3
Boconnic La PL20......127 A3
Bodley Cl EX1.........178 B7
Bodley La EX31..........4 C2
Bodmin Rd PL5........244 D3
Bodmin St EX22........164 C4
Body Hayes Cl TQ9....227 F7
Body's Ct PL18........125 C6
Bogtown Cross EX20....92 D8
Bolberry Cross TQ7....147 E6
Boldventure PL8.......257 F3
Boldventure Cross EX21.91 A5
Bolham Halt Cotts EX16.161 D8
Bolham Prim Com Sch
  EX16...............161 C8
Bolham Rd EX16.......161 C7
Bolt House Ct PL19....171 A5
Bolton Cl [8] TQ5......230 C4
Bolton St TQ5.........230 C4
Bommertown Cross EX36.32 A4
Bonair Cl TQ5.........230 C3
Bonaventure Cl TQ8....259 D5
Bonaventure Rd TQ8...259 D5
Bondhouse La EX6.......98 E3
Bond La EX16..........62 F7
Bondleigh Bridge Cross
  EX20...............77 B7
Bondleigh Cross EX20...77 B7
Bondleigh Moor Cross
  EX20...............76 F6
Bondleigh Wood Cross
  EX20...............77 B7
Bonds Cross
  Chulmleigh EX18.......44 E1
  Petrockstow EX20......56 C5
Bonds Mdw TQ13......180 C8
Bond St
  Beaford EX19..........42 D2
  Cornwood PL21.......133 C2
  Plymouth PL6........244 E6
Bonehayne and Purlbridge
  Rd EX24............102 C5
Bone Mill Cross TQ12..131 F6
Bonfire Cross EX10.....101 C3

Bonfire Hill
Black Torrington EX21 . . . . . 74 A8
Salcombe TQ8 . . . . 259 C5
Bonfire La EX5 . . . . 184 C3
Bonhay Cl EX6 . . . . 201 B8
Bonhay Rd
Exeter EX4 . . . . 177 A6
Starcross EX6 . . . . 201 B8
Boniford Cross EX14 . . . . . . 87 A4
Bonners Cswy EX13 . . . . . . 167 F7
Bonners Dr EX13 . . . . 167 F6
Bonners Glen EX13 . . . . . . 167 F6
Bonnicott La EX33 . . . . 7 D1
Bonnington Gr EX1 . . . . . . 177 F6
Bonny Cross
Clayhanger EX16 . . . . 35 B1
Morebath EX16 . . . . 34 B3
Bonville Cl EX1 . . . . 178 B7
Bonville Cres EX16 . . . . 64 D7
Bonville Rd PL6 . . . . 244 E6
Boobery EX15 . . . . 50 D1
Boode Cross EX33 . . . . 152 F7
Boode Rd EX33 . . . . 152 F7
Booklands EX32 . . . . 18 B2
Boon's Pl PL1 . . . . 262 C4
Booth Way EX8 . . . . 196 B2
Borden Gate EX16 . . . . 50 B8
Border Rd EX14 . . . . 166 A5
Boringdon Ave PL5 . . . . . . 247 D8
Boringdon Cl PL7 . . . . 250 D7
Boringdon Hill PL7 . . . . . . 250 D7
Boringdon Mill Bsns Ctr
PL7 . . . . 250 F6
Boringdon Pk PL21 . . . . . . 237 A5
Boringdon Prim Sch
PL7 . . . . 250 F6
Boringdon Rd
Plymouth, Plympton PL7 . . 250 D6
Plymouth, Turnchapel PL9 . 255 A7
Boringdon Terr
Plymouth, Plympton PL7 . . 250 D6
Plymouth, Turnchapel PL9 . 255 A7
Boringdon Villas PL7 . . . . . 250 D6
Borne Cross EX37 . . . . 44 B2
Borough Cl TQ14 . . . . 225 E3
Borough Cross
Aveton Gifford TQ7 . . . . . . 143 B7
Bridgerule EX22 . . . . 70 E5
Chilsworthy EX22 . . . . 53 E2
Newton Tracey EX31 . . . . . . 27 A3
Woolacombe EX34 . . . . 1 B1
Borough Ct PL11 . . . . 246 E4
Borough La TQ9 . . . . 144 B6
Borough Park Rd
Paignton TQ3 . . . . 225 C6
Totnes TQ9 . . . . 223 C6
Borough Pk PL11 . . . . 246 E4
Borough Rd
Combe Martin EX34 . . . . 2 F4
Great Torrington EX38 . . . . 159 C5
Paignton TQ4 . . . . 225 E4
Torquay TQ1 . . . . 214 B1
Borough The PL8 . . . . 257 F4
Borough View EX38 . . . . . . 159 C5
Borrowdale Cl PL6 . . . . . . 244 D5
Boscastle Gdns PL2 . . . . . 248 C8
Boscawen Pl
Plymouth PL2 . . . . 247 E4
10 Teignmouth TQ14 . . . . 210 B5
Boscundle Row PL12 . . . . . 243 A2
Boshill Hill
Axmouth EX17 . . . . 193 C8
Colyford EX17, EX12 . . . . . 103 E3
Bossell Ho TQ11 . . . . 236 B5
Bossell Pk TQ11 . . . . 236 B5
Bossell Rd TQ11 . . . . 236 B5
Bossell Terr TQ11 . . . . 236 B5
Bosuns Point TQ4 . . . . 226 C4
Boswell Cl PL5 . . . . 244 B2
Boswell's La EX20 . . . . 77 D4
Boswell's Lane End EX20 . . 77 D4
Boswell Way EX12 . . . . . . 191 F8
Bothy The DT7 . . . . 193 E6
Bottle Bridge Hill TQ13 . . 123 F7
Bottle Pk PL21 . . . . 136 B6
Bottom La EX13 . . . . 103 D6
Bottompark La TQ2 . . . . . 213 F3
Bottoms La EX33 . . . . 8 B2
Bottom's La TQ12 . . . . . . 213 E4
Bottreaux Mill Cross
EX36 . . . . 32 A5
Boucher Rd EX9 . . . . 198 B1
Boucher's La TA4 . . . . 35 E4
Boucher Way EX9 . . . . 198 B1
Bouchiers Cl EX20 . . . . 77 C5
Boughmore La EX10 . . . . . 187 F3
Boughmore Rd EX10 . . . . . 187 F4
Boughthayes Est PL19 . . . 171 A5
Boulden Cl PL7 . . . . 251 C5
Boulter Cl PL7 . . . . 241 C1
Boundary Cl TQ12 . . . . . . 212 F5
Boundary Dr EX23 . . . . 70 A6
Boundary Pk
Bideford EX39 . . . . 26 F4
Seaton EX12 . . . . 192 A8
Bounds Cross EX22 . . . . . . 71 A4
Bounds Pl PL1 . . . . 262 B2
Bound The PL10 . . . . 253 A1
Boundy's Cross EX17. . . . . . 61 B8
Bounsells La EX20 . . . . 57 A7
Bountice La EX34 . . . . 2 D2
Bourchier Cl 13 EX16 . . . . . 34 B1

Bourchier Dr 12 EX16 . . . . . 34 B1
Bourne Bridge Cross
EX36 . . . . 46 A5
Bourne Cl PL3 . . . . 249 D6
Bourne Rd TQ5 . . . . 229 F2
Bourne Rd TQ12 . . . . 213 A5
Bourn Rise EX4 . . . . 174 D2
Bourton La TQ9 . . . . 223 E6
Bourton Rd TQ9 . . . . 223 E6
Bourtons The TQ9 . . . . . . 223 D7
Boutport St (Mermaid Wlk)
11 EX31 . . . . 154 F6
Boutport St EX31 . . . . 154 F5
Bovacott La EX22 . . . . 73 C7
Bovemoor's La EX2 . . . . . . 178 A4
Bove Park Rd TQ2 . . . . . . 214 A4
Bovet St TA21 . . . . 160 C6
Bovey Cross
Broadhempston TQ13 . . . . 131 D3
Moretonhampstead TQ13 . 111 E3
Bovey Fir Cross EX12 . . . . 190 F6
Bovey La
Beer EX12 . . . . 191 B7
Broadhempston TQ12,
TQ13 . . . . 131 D3
Bovey Tracey Hospl
TQ13 . . . . 180 D8
Bovey Tracey Prim Sch
TQ13 . . . . 180 C8
Bovey Tracey Rd TQ12 . . . 206 E7
Boville La PL9 . . . . 256 C2
Bovisand Ct PL9 . . . . 254 F2
Bovisand Est PL9 . . . . 140 A8
Bovisand La
Down Thomas PL9 . . . . . . 255 B2
Staddiscombe PL9 . . . . . . 255 D3
Bovisand Pk
Down Thomas PL9 . . . . . . 255 A1
Heybrook Bay PL9 . . . . . . 140 A8
Bovisand Rd PL9 . . . . 255 E3
Bow Beer Cross EX17 . . . . . 78 A1
Bowbeer La EX17 . . . . 78 B1
Bowbridge Cross TQ9 . . . . 145 B8
Bow Com Prim Sch EX17 . . 78 C4
Bow Creek TQ9 . . . . 139 F6
Bow Cross
Blackawton TQ9 . . . . 145 B8
Staverton TQ9 . . . . 216 C7
Bowd Ct EX10 . . . . 100 E1
Bowden Cnr EX31 . . . . 9 F3
Bowden Cotts 12 EX32 . . . . 17 B2
Bowden Cross
Buckland Brewer EX39 . . . . 40 B8
Drewsteignton EX6 . . . . . . 96 E3
Kingsbridge TQ7 . . . . 144 C3
Bowden Farmhouse PL8 . . 257 F4
Bowden Hill EX39 . . . . 25 E4
Bowden Hill
Ashburton TQ13 . . . . 130 F4
Crediton EX17 . . . . 165 D5
Newton Abbot TQ12 . . . . . 207 C2
Yealmpton PL8 . . . . 257 F4
Bowden Hill Terr 11
EX17 . . . . 165 D5
Bowden House & British
Photographic Mus
TQ9 . . . . 223 C2
Bowden La TQ13 . . . . 123 A7
Bowden Park Rd PL6 . . . . 245 A1
Bowden Pillars TQ9 . . . . . 223 B3
Bowden Rd TQ12 . . . . 211 E2
Bowdens Cl TQ13 . . . . 180 C7
Bowdens La
Ideford TQ13 . . . . 124 B4
Shillingford EX16 . . . . 34 E3
Bowdens Pk PL21 . . . . 237 D4
Bowdown Cross TQ10 . . . . 135 C5
Bowe Ct EX1 . . . . 177 E6
Bowerhayes Cross EX14 . . . 67 C3
Bowerhayes La EX14 . . . . . 67 C3
Bowering Cl 1 EX32 . . . . . 155 B3
Bowerland Ave TQ2 . . . . . 213 F4
Bowerland Cross EX20 . . . . 93 D4
Bowerland Rd EX20 . . . . . . 93 D4
Bowers Park Dr PL6 . . . . . 245 E7
Bowers Rd EX2 . . . . 248 B5
Bowerthy La EX17 . . . . 60 D4
Bowhay EX21 . . . . 74 A8
Bowhay Cl EX21 . . . . 74 A8
Bowhay La
Combe Martin EX34 . . . . . . 3 A3
Exeter EX4 . . . . 176 E4
Bowhays Wlk 2 PL6 . . . . 249 C7
Bowhill EX5 . . . . 83 A7
Bowhill Prim Sch EX4 . . . . 176 F4
Bow La TQ13 . . . . 111 F4
Bowley Mdw EX5 . . . . 82 F6
Bowling Gn TQ7 . . . . 142 F4
Bowling Green Chalets
DT7 . . . . 260 D2
Bowling Green La
Combe Martin EX34 . . . . . . 3 A3
Hatherleigh EX20 . . . . 75 B7
Bowling Green Rd EX3 . . . 183 A4
Bowls Cross
Bigbury TQ7 . . . . 142 F5
Stoke Canon EX4 . . . . 82 C1
Bow Mill La EX17 . . . . 78 B4
Bowpound Cross EX17 . . . . 78 B7
Bow Rd TQ9 . . . . 139 C7
Bowring Cl EX1 . . . . 178 B7
Bowring Mead TQ13 . . . . . 111 F4
Bowring Pk TQ13 . . . . 111 F4
Bowringsleigh Pl TQ7 . . . . 258 C5
Bow Station Cross EX17 . . . 78 C2
Boxfield Rd EX13 . . . . 167 D5
Boxhill Cl PL5 . . . . 244 B3

Boxhill Gdns PL2 . . . . 248 C8
Box's Cnr EX18 . . . . 60 B6
Boyce Pl 3 EX16 . . . . 161 B4
Boyds Dr TQ14 . . . . 210 C5
Boyce Cl EX16 . . . . 65 A7
Boyland Rd EX6 . . . . 112 D8
Boyne Rd EX9 . . . . 198 A2
Boyton Com Prim Sch
PL15 . . . . 89 D3
Bozomzeal Cross TQ6 . . . . 228 B1
Bracken Cl
10 Honiton EX14 . . . . 85 C2
Newton Abbot TQ12 . . . . . 212 F8
Plymouth PL6 . . . . 245 D8
Brackendale EX8 . . . . 196 C4
Brackendown EX11 . . . . . . 168 D2
Bracken Rise TQ4 . . . . 229 C6
Bracken Way EX7 . . . . 201 A2
Brackenwood EX8 . . . . . . 196 C1
Braxken Cl EX31 . . . . 154 B2
Braddaford Cross 90 F6
Braddons Cliffe TQ1 . . . . . 220 B4
Braddons Hill PL7 . . . . . . 250 B7
Braddons Hill Rd E TQ1 . . 220 B4
Braddons Hill Rd W TQ1 . . 220 B4
Braddons St TQ1 . . . . 220 B4
Bradfield Cl PL6 . . . . 245 E1
Bradfield House Sch EX15 . 65 F4
Bradfield Rd EX4 . . . . 174 D1
Bradford Cl
Exmouth EX8 . . . . 196 C3
Plymouth PL6 . . . . 249 B7
Bradford Cross EX16 . . . . . 47 A3
Bradford Moor Hill EX16 . . 47 A3
Bradford Prim Sch EX22 . . 73 B8
Bradham Ct EX8 . . . . 202 D8
Bradham La EX8 . . . . 202 D8
Bradiford Cross EX31 . . . . . 154 E7
Bradiford La
TQ12 . . . . 206 E3
Bradley Ct 6 TQ12 . . . . . 207 B3
Bradleyford Cnr TQ13 . . . 180 F6
Bradley La TQ12 . . . . 207 A3
Bradley Manor TQ12 . . . . 206 F2
Bradley Park Rd TQ12 . . . 214 B1
Bradley Rd
Bovey Tracey TQ13 . . . . . 180 E7
Newton Abbot TQ12 . . . . . 207 A1
Plymouth PL4 . . . . 248 F4
Bradman Way EX2 . . . . . . 177 C2
Bradninch Cross EX32 . . . . 17 D4
Bradninch Pl EX4 . . . . 261 B3
Bradridge Cross TQ9 . . . . 138 D8
Bradridge Ct PL15 . . . . . . 89 D7
Bradwell EX34 . . . . 150 A5
Bradwell Rd EX34 . . . . 8 C1
Bradworthy Com Prim Sch
EX22 . . . . 38 E1
Bradworthy Cross EX22 . . . 53 D7
Brady Cl EX17 . . . . 80 B5
Braemar Cl PL7 . . . . 251 C4
Braeside Mews TQ4 . . . . . 226 C4
Braeside Rd
Paignton TQ4 . . . . 226 C4
Torquay TQ2 . . . . 214 A4
Braggs Hill PL15 . . . . 89 C3
Braggs' Hill EX37 . . . . 43 B7
Brag La PL7 . . . . 132 C6
Brahms Way EX32 . . . . . . 155 C5
Brakefield TQ10 . . . . 135 A2
Brake Ho TQ12 . . . . 207 B3
Brake La PL10 . . . . 252 B5
Brake Rd PL5 . . . . 244 E2
Brakeridge Cl TQ5 . . . . . . 229 C6
Brake Wood Cl EX31 . . . . . 153 D5
Bramble Cl
Budleigh Salterton EX9 . . . 198 C1
Dartington TQ9 . . . . 222 F8
Plymouth PL3 . . . . 249 B7
Plymouth, Woolwell PL6 . . 245 D8
Torquay TQ2 . . . . 219 D5
Bramble Hill Ind Est
EX14 . . . . 166 B6
Bramble La
Brampford Speke EX5 . . . . 81 C1
Crediton EX17 . . . . 165 E6
Honiton EX14 . . . . 166 B5
Bramble Mead EX5 . . . . . . 99 D2
Brambleoak Cross TQ12 . . 131 E3
Bramble Path 7 EX32 . . . . 17 B2
Brambles The TA21 . . . . . 160 D4
Bramble Wlk
Barnstaple EX31 . . . . 154 B3
1 Plymouth PL6 . . . . 249 C7
Bramdean Sch EX1 . . . . . . 177 F6
Bramfield Pl PL6 . . . . 249 D7
Bramley Ave EX1 . . . . 178 C6
Bramley Cl
Kenton EX6 . . . . 194 E3
Tiverton EX16 . . . . 161 D7
Willand EX15 . . . . 162 D4
Bramley Gdns EX5 . . . . 99 E7
Bramley Mdw EX32 . . . . . . 17 C2
Bramley Rd EX32 . . . . 155 C4
Bramley Way EX15 . . . . 66 C6
Brampford Cross EX5 . . . . 172 F7
Brampford Speke CE Prim
Sch EX5 . . . . 81 C1
Brampton Down Cross
EX16 . . . . 49 F8
Branches Cross EX22 . . . . . 54 E3
Brancker Rd PL2 . . . . 248 C6
Brand Cl EX14 . . . . 166 C4
Brandiron Cross EX6 . . . . . 123 B7
Brandirons Cnr EX17 . . . . . 79 C5

Brandis Cnr
Little Torrington EX20 . . . . 41 F1
North Tawton EX17 . . . . . . 77 F1
Petrockstow EX20 . . . . 56 C5
Rackenford EX16 . . . . 47 F1
Brandis Cross EX20 . . . . . . 95 E4
Brandise Cross EX17 . . . . . . 79 C2
Brandise Hill EX20 . . . . 56 F3
Brandis La EX20 . . . . 95 E4
Brandis Pk TQ7 . . . . 145 C3
Brandize Pk EX20 . . . . 170 B3
Brandon Rd PL3 . . . . 248 F6
Brand Rd EX14 . . . . 166 C4
Brandreth Rd 3 PL3 . . . . 248 F6
Brandy Wells EX37 . . . . 44 C6
Branksome Cl TQ3 . . . . . . 219 C2
Brannam Cres EX31 . . . . . 154 B2
Brannam Ct EX31 . . . . 154 B2
Brannam Pottery EX31 . . . 154 B2
Brannams Cl EX32 . . . . . . 155 A4
Brannams Ct EX32 . . . . . . 155 A4
Brannams Sq EX32 . . . . . . 155 A4
Branscombe CE Prim Sch
EX12 . . . . 190 D4
Branscombe Cl
Colyford EX24 . . . . 103 A3
Exeter EX4 . . . . 176 E5
Torquay TQ2 . . . . 220 D6
Branscombe Cross EX10 . . 101 F1
Branscombe Gdns PL5 . . . 244 A3
Branscombe Rd EX10 . . . . 200 C3
Branscombe Rd EX14 . . . . 161 F4
Bransgrove Hill EX18 . . . . . 59 B5
Bransgrove La EX18 . . . . . . 59 B5
Branson Cl 9 PL7 . . . . . . 251 C5
Branson Pk PL19 . . . . 126 A6
Brantwood Cl TQ4 . . . . . . 226 A3
Brantwood Cres TQ4 . . . . 226 A3
Brantwood Dr TQ4 . . . . . . 226 A3
Bratton Cross EX31 . . . . . . 17 E7
Bratton Fleming Com Prim
Sch EX31 . . . . 18 A8
Braunsworthy Cross
EX21 . . . . 73 E8
Braunton Mus EX33 . . . . . 152 D6
Braunton Rd EX31 . . . . . . 154 D7
Braunton Sch & Com Coll
EX33 . . . . 152 E4
Braunton Wlk PL6 . . . . . . 249 E8
Bray Cl
Burlescombe EX16 . . . . 51 B3
Tavistock PL19 . . . . 171 A5
Brayford Cl PL5 . . . . 244 B3
Brayford Prim Sch EX32 . . 18 F5
Brayhams Terr EX20 . . . . . 170 C6
Bray Hill EX32 . . . . 18 F3
Brayley Hill EX32 . . . . 18 E7
Bray Mill Cross EX37 . . . . . 29 D4
Brays Cl EX17 . . . . 165 C5
Braytown Cotts EX32 . . . . . 18 F5
Breach Hill TA21 . . . . 51 F5
Breaka La EX19 . . . . 57 F5
Breakneck Cross EX37 . . . . 28 F5
Breakneck Hill
Chittlehampton EX37 . . . . . 28 F5
Teignmouth TQ14 . . . . . . 124 F2
Breakwater Cl TQ5 . . . . . . 230 E6
Breakwater Ind Est PL9 . . 255 C8
Breakwater Rd PL9 . . . . . 255 C8
Breakwater Rd EX9 . . . . . . 198 A1
Brean Down Cl PL3 . . . . . 248 A6
Brean Down Rd PL3 . . . . . 248 A7
Brecon Cl
Bideford EX39 . . . . 157 D1
Paignton TQ4 . . . . 229 A7
Plymouth PL3 . . . . 249 A7
Breech Cotts TA21 . . . . 51 F5
Bremley Cross EX36 . . . . . . 31 F7
Brendon Cross EX39 . . . . . . 39 F6
Brendon Hill EX17 . . . . 79 C6
Brendon Rd TA21 . . . . 160 D7
Brendons Ave TQ2 . . . . . . 219 C3
Brendon Two Gates TA24 . 13 A6
Brennacott Pl EX39 . . . . . . 25 D4
Brennacott Rd EX39 . . . . . 25 D4
Brent Cl EX5 . . . . 184 C3
Brentford Ave PL5 . . . . . . 244 B5
Brent Hill PL8 . . . . 136 D1
Brent Knoll Rd 1 PL3 . . . 248 E6
Brent Mill TQ10 . . . . 135 A2
Brent Mill Bsns Pk TQ10 . 134 F2
Brenton Rd EX6 . . . . 114 C5
Brentor Cl EX4 . . . . 176 E8
Brentor
Mary Tavy PL19 . . . . 117 D6
Plymouth PL4 . . . . 249 B2
Brent Rd 1 TQ3 . . . . 226 B6
Brent To PL19 . . . . 117 B7
Brent Rd PL6 . . . . 245 A3
Brest Way PL6 . . . . 245 A3
Bretonside PL4 . . . . 263 A2
Breton Way EX8 . . . . 196 E1
Bretteville Cl
Chagford TQ13 . . . . 111 A6
Woodbury EX5 . . . . 184 C3
Brett Wlk 1 PL7 . . . . 250 F7
Brewer Rd EX32 . . . . 155 C4
Brewers Hill EX39 . . . . 39 F5
Brewers La EX39 . . . . 25 D4
Brewery La
12 Brixham TQ5 . . . . 230 C5
Exeter EX4 . . . . 177 F5
Sidmouth EX10 . . . . 188 B5

Briar Cres EX2 . . . . 177 F2
Briardale Rd PL2 . . . . 247 F6
Briarleigh Cl PL6 . . . . 245 F2
Briar Rd PL3 . . . . 248 F7
Briars Row PL12 . . . . 242 D4
Briar Tor PL20 . . . . 127 A3
Briary La TQ1 . . . . 220 B5
Briary Mews 3 TQ1 . . . . . 220 D4
Brick Cross EX9 . . . . 198 C7
Brickfields Cl PL1 . . . . 247 F1
Brickhouse Dr EX16 . . . . . 161 D6
Brickhouse Hill EX16 . . . . 161 A6
Brickyard La EX16 . . . . . . 161 A8
Brickyard Rd EX5 . . . . 168 A7
Bridespring Rd EX4 . . . . . 173 F1
Bridespring Wlk EX4 . . . . 173 F1
Bridestowe Prim Sch
EX20 . . . . 107 F8
Bridewell Ct 23 EX16 . . . . 161 C2
Bridewell Ho 11 EX16 . . . 161 C2
Bridford Rd EX2 . . . . 177 C2
Bridge Bldgs 12 EX11 . . . 154 F5
Bridge Chambers 17
EX31 . . . . 154 F5
Bridge Cl EX5 . . . . 82 D3
Bridge Cotts
Chard Junction TA20 . . . . . 88 C8
East Budleigh EX9 . . . . . . 198 B5
4 Exeter EX4 . . . . 177 D8
Lympstone EX8 . . . . 195 D5
Bridge Croft TQ13 . . . . . . 130 F5
Bridge Cross
Bishops Nympton EX36 . . . 30 F4
Fortescue Cross EX37 . . . . 44 B4
Bridge Ct EX4 . . . . 261 A3
Bridge End EX36 . . . . 31 C5
Bridgefield EX11 . . . . 169 E4
Bridge Hill EX3 . . . . 182 F5
Bridgehill Garth EX3 . . . . 182 F5
Bridge Ho 1 TQ12 . . . . . . 207 C3
Bridgehouse Cross EX15 . . 52 D1
Bridge La
Budlake EX5 . . . . 82 D3
7 Instow EX39 . . . . 15 B1
Bridgeland St EX39 . . . . . 157 A2
Bridge Mill La PL21 . . . . . 133 C2
Bridgemoor Cross EX22 . . . 71 B6
Bridgend Hill PL8 . . . . 141 A7
Bridge Pk
Ashwater EX21 . . . . 90 F6
Bridgerule EX22 . . . . 70 F5
Ermington PL21 . . . . 136 F2
Ivybridge PL21 . . . . 237 D5
Bridge Plats Way EX39 . . 156 E2
Bridge Rd
Budleigh Salterton EX9 . . . 198 B2
Churston Ferrers TQ5 . . . . 229 D5
Exeter EX2, EX6 . . . . 182 A8
Exmouth EX8 . . . . 202 A8
Kingswear TQ5, TQ6 . . . . 234 B7
Teignmouth TQ14 . . . . . . 210 A3
Torquay TQ2 . . . . 219 F5
Totnes TQ9 . . . . 222 F6
Bridge Reeve Cross EX18 . 59 C8
Bridge Ret Pk TQ2 . . . . . . 219 E8
Bridgericke CE Prim Sch
EX22 . . . . 70 E4
Bridgeside TQ9 . . . . 139 C7
Bridge St
Bideford EX39 . . . . 157 A1
Buckfastleigh TQ11 . . . . . 236 B5
Dulverton TA22 . . . . 33 D6
Hatherleigh EX20 . . . . 75 C7
Ipplepen TQ12 . . . . 211 D2
Kingsbridge TQ7 . . . . 258 D5
Lyme Regis DT7 . . . . 260 E3
Sidbury EX10 . . . . 101 B2
Tiverton EX16 . . . . 161 C4
Uffculme EX15 . . . . 66 A7
Bridges The PL12 . . . . 242 E1
Bridge Terr
Ashprington TQ9 . . . . 139 F6
Bampton EX16 . . . . 34 B1
Bridge The PL1 . . . . 262 B1
Bridgetown TQ9 . . . . 223 D5
Bridgetown Ct TQ9 . . . . . 223 D6
Bridgetown Hill TQ9 . . . . 223 C6
Bridge View EX5 . . . . 99 C6
Bridgewater Gdns TQ9 . . . 223 D5
Bridgwater Cl PL6 . . . . . . 245 B1
Bridle Cl
Paignton TQ4 . . . . 229 B8
Plymouth PL7 . . . . 251 B7
Bridle Path The TQ9 . . . . . 223 C4
Bridle Way PL12 . . . . 242 D4
Bridwell Ave EX5 . . . . 65 F7
Bridwell Cl PL5 . . . . 247 E8
Bridwell La N PL5 . . . . . . 247 E8
Bridwell Rd PL5 . . . . 247 E8
Brightley Cross EX20 . . . . . 94 B8
Brightley Rd EX20 . . . . . . 170 C8
Bright View EX20 . . . . 170 C6
Brimacombe Rd EX39 . . . . 22 E3
Brim Brook Ct TQ2 . . . . . 219 B8
Brimford Cross EX38 . . . . . 38 A4
Brimhay TQ9 . . . . 222 F8
Brimhay Bglws TQ9 . . . . . 222 F8
Brim Hill TQ1 . . . . 214 C5
Brimhill Cl PL7 . . . . 251 B3
Brimhill La PL19 . . . . 117 F6
Brimlands TQ5 . . . . 230 B4
Brimlands Ct TQ5 . . . . . . 230 B4
Brimley Bsns Pk TQ13 . . . 180 C5
Brimley Cl TQ13 . . . . 123 F6
Brimley Cross
Bovey Tracey TQ13 . . . . . 180 B5
Hemyock TA3 . . . . 52 F1

Brimley Ct TQ13 . . . . 180 B5
Brimley Dr TQ14 . . . . 210 C5
Brimley Gdns TQ13 . . . . . . 180 C5
Brimley Grange TQ13 . . . . 180 B5
Brimley Halt TQ13 . . . . 180 C5
Brimley Hill EX13 . . . . 88 D2
Brimley Pk TQ13 . . . . 180 C5
Brimley Rd
  Axminster EX13 . . . . 88 D3
  Bovey Tracey TQ13 . . . . . . 180 B5
Brimley Vale TQ13 . . . . 180 C6
Brimpenny Rd EX8 . . . . 196 C1
Brimstone La
  Rockwell Green TA21 . . . . . 160 A2
  Sampford Arundel TA21 . . . . 51 F6
  Sampford Peverell EX16 . . . 50 E2
Brindlefield La EX17 . . . . 62 A5
Brindiwell Cross EX17 . . . . . . 63 B3
Brindiwell Hill EX17 . . . . 63 B2
Brinkburn Ct EX10 . . . . 188 A3
Brinscombe Cross EX13 . . . 103 E6
Brinscombe La
  Arlington EX31 . . . . 10 F3
  Membury EX13 . . . . 87 E6
Brinsworthy Cross EX36 . . . 19 F1
Briseham Cl TQ5 . . . . 230 D3
Briseham Rd TQ5 . . . . 230 D3
Brismar Wlk 8 TQ6 . . . . . . 249 C7
Britannia Ave TQ6 . . . . 233 C3
Britannia Pl PL4 . . . . 249 B2
Britannia Row 5 EX34 . . . 150 C6
Britannia Royal Naval Coll
  TQ6 . . . . 233 F5
Britannia Way EX39 . . . . . . 156 E7
Briton St 2 EX16 . . . . 34 C1
Briton Streetlane EX16 . . . 112 F7
Brittannia Ct TQ6 . . . . 234 B3
Brittany Rd EX8 . . . . 196 C4
Britten Dr
  Barnstaple EX32 . . . . 155 B5
  Exeter EX2 . . . . 178 B5
Britton Cl EX16 . . . . 65 A7
Brittons Cl EX13 . . . . 152 E5
Brittons The EX33 . . . . 152 E5
Briwere Rd TQ1 . . . . 219 E7
Brixham CE Prim Sch
  TQ5 . . . . 230 D4
Brixham Com Coll TQ5 . . 230 D4
Brixham Cross TQ5 . . . . . . 234 E8
Brixham Enterprise Est
  TQ5 . . . . 230 D4
Brixham Heritage Mus
  TQ5 . . . . 230 C5
Brixham Hospl TQ5 . . . . . . 230 C4
Brixham Rd
  Kingswear TQ6 . . . . 234 B3
  Paignton TQ4 . . . . 225 E3
Brixham Wlk PL6 . . . . 249 E8
Brixington Com Prim Sch
  EX8 . . . . 196 C2
Brixington Dr EX8 . . . . 196 C2
Brixington La EX8 . . . . 196 C2
Broadacre Dr TQ5 . . . . 230 D5
Broad Cl
  Crediton EX17 . . . . 165 A6
  North Molton EX36 . . . . 30 D4
Broadclose Hill EX16 . . . . . 46 F6
Broadclose Rd EX31 . . . . . 154 D3
Broad Croft Prim Sch
  EX5 . . . . 175 C7
Broad Croft EX13 . . . . 87 E8
Broaddown Cross EX14 . . . 86 A1
Broadfield Rd EX32 . . . . . . 155 B4
Broadfields Rd EX2 . . . . . . 178 C5
Broadgate
  Barnstaple EX31 . . . . 154 E7
  Exeter EX1 . . . . 261 A3
Broadgate Cl
  Barnstaple EX31 . . . . 154 E7
  Braunton EX33 . . . . 152 D6
Broadgate Cres TQ12 . . . . 212 F4
Broadgate La EX17 . . . . 61 B2
Broadgate Rd TQ12 . . . . . . 212 F4
Broadhayes Cross EX14 . . . 86 E5
Broadhembury Cross
  EX14 . . . . 84 E7
Broadhembury Prim Sch
  EX14 . . . . 84 E7
Broad La
  Appledore EX39 . . . . 14 F1
  Braunton EX33 . . . . 152 A8
  Hawkridge TA22 . . . . 21 D1
  Tiverton EX16 . . . . 161 C3
Broadland Gdns PL9 . . . . . 256 A8
Broadland La PL9 . . . . 255 F8
Broadlands
  Bideford EX39 . . . . 157 D1
  Northam EX39 . . . . 156 F8
  Teignmouth TQ14 . . . . 210 A3
  Thorverton EX5 . . . . 81 E4
Broadlands Ave TQ12 . . . . 207 A3
Broadlands Cl PL7 . . . . 251 A3
Broadlands Cts
  Bideford EX39 . . . . 157 D1
  Newton Abbot TQ12 . . . . . 207 A3
Broadlands Rd EX2 . . . . . . 226 A4
Broad Lane Head TA22 . . . 21 D1
Broadleaf Cl EX11 . . . . 178 E8
Bradley Ct PL6 . . . . 241 B2
Bradley Cl TQ2 . . . . 219 C3
Bradley Ind Pk PL6 . . . . . . 241 B2
Bradley Park Rd PL6 . . . . . 241 B2
Broadmead
  Exmouth EX8 . . . . 196 D2

Broadmead *continued*
  Woodbury EX5 . . . . 184 B3
Broadmead Bglws EX32 . . 155 C2
Broadmead Cross EX16 . . . 48 A5
Broademede Ct TQ12 . . . . 207 D2
Broadmead Gdns EX35 . . . 151 B5
Broadmeadow Ave EX4 . . 176 F4
Broadmeadow Ind Est
  TQ14 . . . . 209 D7
Broadmeadow La TQ14 . . 209 D7
Broadmeadow View
  TQ14 . . . . 209 D7
Broadmoor Cross EX37 . . . 29 A2
Broadmoor La EX20 . . . . . . 170 A5
Broadoak Cl EX11 . . . . 168 D3
Broad Oak Cres 13 TQ9 . . 223 D5
Broadoak Hill EX31 . . . . 4 C3
Broadoaks Cotts PL7 . . . . 132 E4
Broadpark
  Bovey Tracey TQ13 . . . . . . 180 B5
  Bampford Speke EX5 . . . . . 81 E1
  Dartmouth TQ6 . . . . 233 D3
Broad Park Ave EX34 . . . . 150 A5
Broad Park Cl EX33 . . . . 7 E2
Broad Park Cres EX34 . . . 150 A4
Broad Park La EX20 . . . . . . 95 D4
Broadpark Rd
  Paignton TQ3 . . . . 226 A7
  Torquay TQ2 . . . . 219 D2
Broad Park Rd
  Bere Alston PL20 . . . . 125 E2
  Exmouth EX8 . . . . 196 C1
  Plymouth PL3 . . . . 248 D6
Broadparks Ave EX4 . . . . . 174 E2
Broadparks Cl EX4 . . . . . . 174 E2
Broad Path
  Stoke Gabriel TQ9 . . . . . . 228 A8
  Uffculme EX15 . . . . 66 A8
Broad Pk PL9 . . . . 255 C7
Broad Rd
  Kerswell EX15 . . . . 66 C1
  Kingswear TQ6 . . . . 234 D5
Broad Reach TQ4 . . . . 229 C7
Broadridge Cl TQ12 . . . . . 206 D4
Broadridge Cross TQ9 . . . 232 A8
Broadridge La EX17 . . . . . . 61 A4
Broadsands Ave TQ4 . . . . 229 C7
Broadsands Bend TQ4 . . . 229 C8
Broadsands Ct TQ4 . . . . . . 229 B7
Broadsands Park Rd
  TQ4 . . . . 229 C8
Broadsands Rd TQ4 . . . . . 229 C7
Broadshell Cross EX22 . . . 71 D5
Broad St
  Black Torrington EX21 . . . . 74 A8
  Churchinford TA3 . . . . 68 A7
  Ilfracombe EX34 . . . . 150 C6
  Lyme Regis DT7 . . . . 260 E3
  11 Modbury PL21 . . . . 137 B2
  South Molton EX36 . . . . . . 158 C4
Broadstone TQ6 . . . . 233 F4
Broadstone Park Rd
  TQ6 . . . . 219 D3
Broad View
  Broadclyst EX5 . . . . 175 C6
  Dartington TQ9 . . . . 222 F8
Broadway
  Exeter EX2 . . . . 176 F3
  Fremington EX31 . . . . 153 F5
  Sidmouth EX10 . . . . 187 F5
  Trusham TQ13 . . . . 113 D1
  Woodbury EX5 . . . . 184 C2
Broadway Ave TQ12 . . . . . 207 D7
Broadway Hill EX2 . . . . . . 176 E3
Broadway La EX33 . . . . 7 D3
Broadway Rd TQ12 . . . . . . 207 D7
Broadways Head EX14,
  TA20 . . . . 68 F6
Broadway The
  Exmouth EX8 . . . . 202 E8
  Plymouth PL9 . . . . 255 E7
Broad Wlk PL12 . . . . 242 E1
Broadwoodwidger Prim Sch
  PL16 . . . . 91 A4
Broady Strap EX31 . . . . . . 153 F5
Brock Ho 9 PL4 . . . . 263 A2
Brockhole La EX13, TA20 . . 88 B7
Brockhurst Pk TQ3 . . . . . . 218 D2
Brockington's Rd EX5 . . . . 99 C8
Brockley Rd EX2 . . . . 177 A2
Brockscombe Cross EX21 . 91 F5
Brocks Cross EX17 . . . . 79 A2
Brocks La PL10 . . . . 252 F5
Brockton Gdns PL6 . . . . . . 245 B6
Brodick Cl EX4 . . . . 173 D1
Bromhead Cl PL6 . . . . 249 A8
Bromley Ho 6 PL2 . . . . . . 248 A4
Bromley Pl 5 PL2 . . . . 248 A4
Bronescombe Ave TQ14 . 209 A8
Bronshill Ho TQ1 . . . . 220 B6
Bronshill Mews TQ1 . . . . . 220 B6
Bronshill Rd TQ1 . . . . 220 B6
Bronte Pl PL5 . . . . 244 D1
Brook Cl
  Bovey Tracey TQ13 . . . . . . 180 C7
  Exeter EX1 . . . . 178 B8
  Holcombe EX7 . . . . 210 E8
  Plymouth PL7 . . . . 251 A3
  Sidford EX10 . . . . 101 B1
Brook Cross
  Aveton Gifford TQ7 . . . . . . 143 C6
  Barnstaple EX31 . . . . 154 B3
Brookdale EX13 . . . . 169 E4
Brookdale Ave EX14 . . . . . 150 A5
Brookdale Cl TQ5 . . . . 230 B4

Brookdale Ct
  Brixham TQ5 . . . . 230 B4
  Exeter EX2 . . . . 178 A2
Brookdale Pk TQ5 . . . . 230 B4
Brookdale Terr
  8 Barnstaple EX32 . . . . . . 155 B4
  18 Dawlish EX7 . . . . 204 E6
Brookdown Terr PL12 . . . . 242 E3
Brookdown Villas PL12 . . . 242 E3
Brooke Ave EX2 . . . . 177 F3
Brooke Cl
  Saltash PL12 . . . . 243 A2
  Sampford Courtenay EX20 . 76 F3
Brookedor TQ12 . . . . 212 F5
Brookedor Gdns TQ12 . . . 212 F5
Brooke Rd EX16 . . . . 46 E1
Brookesby Hall TQ1 . . . . . 220 D3
Brookfield EX39 . . . . 25 E4
Brookfield Cl
  8 Braunton EX33 . . . . 152 D5
  Kingsteignton TQ12 . . . . . 207 E7
  Paignton TQ3 . . . . 226 C8
  Plymouth PL7 . . . . 251 B5
Brookfield Cotts EX8 . . . . 195 D5
Brookfield Cl 1 TQ13 . . . . 123 F6
Brookfield Dr
  7 Colyton EX24 . . . . 103 A4
  Teignmouth TQ14 . . . . 210 C7
Brookfield Gdns EX22 . . . 177 B1
Brookfield Ho TQ1 . . . . . . 226 C8
Brookfield Pl EX34 . . . . . . 150 B5
Brookfield Rd EX9 . . . . . . 198 B6
Brookfield St 8 EX39 . . . . 157 B1
Brook Green Terr EX4 . . . . 261 C4
Brook Haven Cl TQ12 . . . . 212 F5
Brookhayes Cl EX8 . . . . . . 202 B8
Brookhill TQ6 . . . . 234 B2
Brook Ho EX7 . . . . 204 C6
Brooking Barn TQ9 . . . . . . 139 F8
Brooking Cl PL6 . . . . 249 A8
Brookingfield Cl PL7 . . . . . 250 C5
Brooking Way PL12 . . . . . . 242 C3
Brook La
  Calverleigh EX16 . . . . 48 F2
  Shaldon TQ14 . . . . 209 D5
  3 Sidford EX10 . . . . 101 B1
  Tavistock PL19 . . . . 171 B2
Brooklands
  24 Dawlish EX7 . . . . 204 D6
  Tavistock PL19 . . . . 171 D6
  Totnes TQ9 . . . . 223 D5
Brooklands Cross EX10 . . 100 C1
Brooklands Ct TQ2 . . . . . . 244 E3
Brooklands Farm Cl
  EX13 . . . . 103 D8
Brooklands La TQ2 . . . . . . 219 E4
Brooklands Orch
  Kilmington EX13 . . . . 103 D8
  Ottery St Mary EX11 . . . . . 169 E4
Brooklands Rd
  Exmouth EX8 . . . . 196 D1
  Rockwell Green TA21 . . . . 160 A5
Brookland Terr EX11 . . . . . 169 E3
Brook Lane Cotts TQ13 . . 121 B3
Brookleigh Ave EX1 . . . . . 178 B5
Brooklyn Pk EX8 . . . . 196 C1
Brook Mdw
  Exmouth EX8 . . . . 196 C1
  Newton Poppleford EX10 . 186 F8
  South Molton EX36 . . . . . . 158 D4
Brook Orch TQ12 . . . . 212 F4
Brook Rd
  Budleigh Salterton EX9 . . 199 G2
  Cullompton EX15 . . . . 163 B2
  Dolton EX19 . . . . 57 F7
  Ipplepen TQ12 . . . . 211 D2
  Ivybridge PL21 . . . . 237 D5
Brooks Hill EX15 . . . . 66 C8
Brookside
  Barnstaple EX31 . . . . 154 A3
  Broadhembury EX14 . . . . . . 84 C7
  Kingsbridge TQ7 . . . . 258 C4
  Pathfinder Village EX6 . . . . 98 C4
  Sidmouth EX10 . . . . 188 A7
Brookside Cl
  Heybrook Bay PL9 . . . . . . 140 A7
  Kilmington EX13 . . . . 87 C1
  Teignmouth TQ14 . . . . 210 A5
Brookside Cres EX4 . . . . . 174 B2
Brookside Ind Units EX4 . 174 D1
Brookside Units EX4 . . . . . 98 D4
Brookside Villas 23 EX34 . . 3 A3
Brooks Pl TA21 . . . . 160 E6
Brook St
  Bampton EX16 . . . . 34 B1
  Dawlish EX7 . . . . 204 D6
  Ottery St Mary EX11 . . . . . 169 D3
  Slapton TQ7 . . . . 145 C3
  Tavistock PL19 . . . . 171 C6
Brook Terr EX12 . . . . 192 D7
Brook The PL21 . . . . 242 E4
Brookvale Orch TQ14 . . . . 209 D4
Brook View TQ9 . . . . 222 F6
Brookway EX1 . . . . 178 C7
Brook Way TQ12 . . . . 211 D2
Brookwood Cl 4 TQ13 . . . 124 F3
Brookwood Rd PL9 . . . . . . 256 D7
Broomball Cross EX14 . . . . 32 F5
Broomball La EX16 . . . . 32 E5
Broomborough Ct TQ9 . . . 223 B5
Broomborough Dr TQ9 . . . 223 A5
Broom Cl
  Dawlish EX7 . . . . 204 F8
  Exeter EX4 . . . . 178 A5
Broome Cl EX13 . . . . 167 E6
Broomfield Dr PL9 . . . . 255 C5
Broomham Cross EX37 . . . 45 A7
Broomhayes Sch EX39 . . . 157 E1

Broom Hill
  Chagford TQ13 . . . . 111 A6
  Saltash PL12 . . . . 242 D2
Broomhill Cross
  Chilsworthy EX22 . . . . 53 B3
  Copplestone EX17 . . . . 77 A4
Broomhill Rd EX16 . . . . . . 161 B4
Broomhill Villas EX32 . . . . 18 E5
Broomhouse La EX14 . . . . 112 F7
Broomhill Way TQ2 . . . . . . 213 E5
Broomhouse La EX8 . . . . . . 46 E1
Broomhouse Pk EX16 . . . . 46 E1
Broom La EX13 . . . . 88 C5
Broom Pk
  Dartington TQ9 . . . . 215 E1
  Plymouth PL9 . . . . 255 D5
  Torquay TQ2 . . . . 213 F3
Broom's La TA13 . . . . 68 C7
Broughton Cl PL3 . . . . 248 F7
Brow Hill TQ12 . . . . 206 F1
Brown Down La TA20 . . . . . 68 F7
Browne Memorial
  Almshouses PL19 . . . . 171 A5
Brownhill La PL9 . . . . 140 D8
Brownhills Rd TQ12 . . . . . 207 A3
Brownie Cross PL7 . . . . . . 132 C3
Browning Cl EX2 . . . . 178 A4
Browning Rd PL2 . . . . 248 A5
Brownings End TQ12 . . . . 206 F1
Brownings Mead EX6 . . . . 112 F7
Brownings Wlk TQ12 . . . . 206 F1
Brownlands Cl EX10 . . . . . 188 C5
Brownlands Rd EX10 . . . . . 188 C5
Brownlees EX6 . . . . 182 A4
Brownlow St PL1 . . . . 262 A2
Brown's Bridge La EX15 . . 65 B7
Browns Bridge Rd TQ2 . . 213 D2
Brownscombe Cl TQ3 . . . 218 D2
Brown's Cl EX6 . . . . 182 A4
Brownsey La TA20 . . . . 69 C5
Brown's Hill TQ6 . . . . 233 F3
Brown's Hill Head EX37 . . 27 F2
Brownstone Cross EX17 . . 61 C3
Brownstone Moor Cross
  EX17 . . . . 61 D4
Brownston St 2 PL21 . . . 137 B2
Broxfords Hill EX7 . . . . 80 C7
Broxton Dr PL9 . . . . 249 E1
Bruckland La EX12, EX13 . 103 D3
Bruckton Cross TQ6 . . . . . 232 F6
Brunel Ave
  Plymouth PL2 . . . . 247 F5
  Torquay TQ2 . . . . 214 B4
Brunel Cl
  Exeter EX4 . . . . 177 A7
  Teignmouth TQ14 . . . . 210 C6
Brunel Ct 16 EX7 . . . . 204 E6
Brunel Lodge Hospl
  TQ12 . . . . 207 A1
Brunel Mews TQ12 . . . . . . 219 F4
Brunel Prim Sch PL12 . . 242 E2
Brunel Rd
  Newton Abbot TQ12 . . . . . 207 B3
  Paignton TQ4 . . . . 229 D6
  Saltash PL12 . . . . 242 C4
  Starcross EX6 . . . . 201 A8
Brunel Terr 3 PL2 . . . . . . 247 F5
Brunel Way
  Ivybridge PL21 . . . . 237 E6
  Plymouth PL1 . . . . 262 A2
  Saltash PL12 . . . . 242 A4
Brunnicks Way EX12 . . . . . 167 D4
Brunswick Pl
  Dawlish EX7 . . . . 204 E6
  10 Plymouth PL2 . . . . 247 F4
Brunswick Rd PL4 . . . . 263 B2
Brunswick Sq 4 TQ1 . . . . 219 F6
Brunswick St
  Exeter EX4 . . . . 177 A5
  Teignmouth TQ14 . . . . 210 C4
Brunswick Terr TQ1 . . . . . 219 F6
Brushford La
  Chevithorne EX16 . . . . 49 F3
  Chulmleigh EX18 . . . . 59 D7
Brushford New Rd TA22 . . 33 E4
Brynmoor Cl PL3 . . . . 249 A7
Brynmoor Pk PL3 . . . . 249 A6
Brynmoor Wlk PL3 . . . . . . 249 A6
Brynsworthy La EX31 . . . . 154 A1
Brynsworthy Lawn EX31 . . 154 A2
Brynsworthy Pk EX31 . . . . 154 B3
Bubrook La EX6 . . . . 96 F2
Buchanan Cl EX14 . . . . . . 166 B4
Buckerell Cross EX14 . . . . 84 F2
Buckerell Rd EX2 . . . . 177 E3
Buckeridge Ave TQ14 . . . . 210 B6
Buckeridge Rd TQ14 . . . . 210 B6
Buckeridge Twrs 2
  TQ14 . . . . 210 C6
Buckfast Abbey EX11 . . 236 C7
Buckfast Butterflies &
  Dartmoor Otter Sanctuary
  TQ11 . . . . 236 D5
Buckfast Cl
  Buckfast TQ11 . . . . 236 C6
  Ivybridge PL21 . . . . 237 D4
  Plymouth PL2 . . . . 248 A8
Buckfastleigh Prim Sch
  TQ11 . . . . 236 B5
Buckfastleigh Sta TQ11 . . 236 D6
Buckfast Rd TQ11 . . . . . . 236 C6
Buckfast Steam & Leisure Pk
  TQ11 . . . . 236 D5
Buckham Cross EX36 . . . . 45 D7
Buckham Hill EX36 . . . . . . 45 B6
Buckhouse La EX24 . . . . . 102 C7

Buckingham Cl
  Exmouth EX8 . . . . 202 E7
  South Molton EX36 . . . . . . 158 C3
Buckingham Orch TQ12 . . 123 C4
Buckingham Pl PL5 . . . . . . 243 E2
Buckingham Rd EX2 . . . . . 178 D3
Buckland Abbey PL20 . . . 126 C1
Buckland Brake TQ12 . . . . 207 E2
Buckland Brewer Com Prim
  Sch EX39 . . . . 40 C7
Buckland Cross
  Bideford EX39 . . . . 25 E4
  Plymouth PL7 . . . . 250 D7
Buckland Cross
  Braunton EX33 . . . . 152 C8
  Slapton TQ7 . . . . 145 C6
Buckland Hall TQ13 . . . . . 130 D7
Buckland Rd
  Georgeham EX33 . . . . 8 B3
  Newton Abbot TQ12 . . . . . 207 F4
Buckland St Mary CE Prim
  Sch TA20 . . . . 69 D8
Buckland St PL1 . . . . 262 B2
Buckland Terr PL20 . . . . . 126 F2
Buckland View
  Buckland Brewer EX39 . . . 40 B7
  Newton Abbot TQ12 . . . . . 207 D4
Buckland Wlk EX6 . . . . . . 181 F5
Buckleigh Cross EX39 . . . 156 C6
Buckleigh Rd EX39 . . . . . . 156 C5
Buckley Cross EX10 . . . . . 101 C1
Buckley Rd EX10 . . . . 101 C2
Buckley St TQ8 . . . . 259 E5
Bucknall Cl EX12 . . . . 190 D4
Bucknill Cl EX6 . . . . 182 A4
Bucknole Cross EX14 . . . . 102 A8
Bucknole Hill Rd EX24 . . . 102 A7
Bucks Cl TQ13 . . . . 180 D7
Buckshots Cross EX10 . . . 69 A4
Buckwell Cl EX15 . . . . 163 C1
Buckwell Cl TQ7 . . . . 258 D6
Buckwell Rd TQ7 . . . . 258 D6
Buckwell St PL1, EX24 . . . 263 A2
Buctor Pk PL19 . . . . 126 A8
Buddle Cl
  Ivybridge PL21 . . . . 237 E5
  Plymouth PL9 . . . . 256 A5
  Tavistock PL19 . . . . 171 B6
Buddle La
  Exeter EX4 . . . . 176 F5
  Hatherleigh EX20 . . . . 75 C7
Bude Hill EX19 . . . . 59 A3
Bude Moor Cross EX19 . . . 76 D7
Bude St
  Appledore EX39 . . . . 15 A1
  Exeter EX4 . . . . 261 B3
Budge Mdws PL15 . . . . . . 115 A4
Budgetts TA21 . . . . 52 F6
Budgett's Cross TQ12 . . . . 52 F6
Budlake Cross EX24 . . . . . 101 F6
Budlake Rd EX2 . . . . 177 C1
Budlake Units EX2 . . . . . . 177 C1
Budleigh Cl
  Plymouth PL9 . . . . 255 F5
  Torquay TQ2 . . . . 220 D6
Budleigh Hill EX9 . . . . 198 B5
Budleigh Salterton Hospl
  EX9 . . . . 198 B1
Budshead Dr PL6 . . . . 244 C4
Budshead Rd PL5 . . . . 244 C4
Budshead Way PL5 . . . . . . 244 E2
Budshead Cross PL6 . . . . 245 D6
Buena Vista Cl PL6 . . . . . . 245 D6
Buena Vista Dr PL6 . . . . . 245 C6
Buena Vista Gdns PL6 . . . 245 C6
Buena Vista Way PL6 . . . . 245 C6
Bugford Cross TQ6 . . . . . . 232 C3
Bugford La TQ6 . . . . 232 D3
Bugford Lane End TQ6 . . . 232 D3
Bughead Cross TQ13 . . . . 111 D4
Bughole La TA21 . . . . 51 E8
Building's Cross EX17 . . . 63 A4
Bulford TA21 . . . . 160 D5
Bulford La TA21 . . . . 160 D5
Bulgis Pk PL6 . . . . 158 B5
Bull Cl EX31 . . . . 154 F5
Bulleid Cl PL2 . . . . 247 F7
Bulleigh Cross TQ12 . . . . 218 B8
Bulleigh Elms Cross
  TQ12 . . . . 212 A1
Bullens Cl EX5 . . . . 81 E4
Bullen St EX5 . . . . 81 E4
Buller Cl
  Plymouth PL7 . . . . 250 F4
  Torpoint PL11 . . . . 247 A3
Buller Ct EX2 . . . . 177 A4
Buller Pk PL12 . . . . 242 D3
Buller Rd
  11 Barnstaple EX32 . . . . . 155 A5
  Crediton EX17 . . . . 165 B6
  Exeter EX4 . . . . 177 A5
  Newton Abbot TQ12 . . . . . 207 D2
  Torpoint PL11 . . . . 247 A3
Buller's Hill Forest Wlks
  EX6 . . . . 114 A3
Bullfinch Cl EX15 . . . . 163 A2
Bullhead Cross EX19 . . . . . 58 B2

Bull Hill
Barnstaple EX31 . . . . .154 F7
Bideford EX39 . . . . 157 A1
Bullhorn Cross TQ7 . . . . . .142 F6
Bull Meadow Rd EX2 . . . . .261 B2
Bullow View EX19 . . . . .58 F2
Bull Point Prim Sch PL5 .247 B8
Bull Ring TQ13 . . . . .130 F4
Bulls Ct 11 EX24 . . . . 103 A4
Bull's La TA20 . . . . .88 C8
Bully Shoot Cross EX24 . 103 A3
Bulmer Rd PL4 . . . . 263 C3
Bulmoor Cross EX13 . . . . 103 F5
Bulteel Gdns PL6 . . . . . . .244 E7
Bulverton Pk EX16 . . . . . .187 F6
Bulworthy Cross EX16 . . . .47 E5
Bulworthy Knap EX16 . . . .47 E5
Bumpston Cross TQ11 . . . 215 C7
Bungalows The
Axminster EX13 . . . . 167 C4
Dawlish Warren EX7 . . . . .201 B2
Bunkers Farm TQ9 . . . . . .144 E7
Bun La 8 TQ14 . . . . 210 B4
Bunneford Cross EX15 . . . .64 E1
Bunn Rd EX8 . . . . 196 D4
Bunson Gate EX18 . . . . .45 A4
Bunting Cl
Newton Abbot TQ12 . . . . . .207 A1
Teignmouth TQ14 . . . . 210 A5
Buntings The EX13 . . . . . 181 F4
Bunts La EX12 . . . . 191 F7
Bunyan Cl PL5 . . . . 244 C2
Burch Cl EX8 . . . . .196 E2
Burches Cross EX16 . . . . . .48 A1
Burch Gdns EX7 . . . . 200 E1
Burchills Cl TA21 . . . . 160 A6
Burchill's Hill TA21 . . . . .160 B7
Burcombe Hill EX36 . . . . .158 E8
Burdon La EX21 . . . . .74 C7
Burgage TA21 . . . . .160 D6
Burgh Island Cswy TQ7 . .142 E3
Burgmanns Hill EX8 . . . . 195 D5
Burke Rd TQ9 . . . . .223 D6
Burland Cross EX31 . . . . 9 B4
Burland La EX33 . . . . .8 F1
Burlands The EX14 . . . . . . .84 D2
Burleigh La
Malborough TQ7 . . . . .147 E2
Plymouth PL3 . . . . 248 D7
Burleigh Lane End TQ7 . .147 E8
Burleigh Manor PL3 . . . . 248 D7
Burleigh Park Rd PL3 . . . .248 D6
Burleigh Rd TQ2 . . . . 219 C2
Burlescombe CE Prim Sch
EX16 . . . . .51 B3
Burlington Cl EX32 . . . . . .155 B3
Burlington Gr EX32 . . . . . .155 B2
Burnard Cl PL6 . . . . .244 E7
Burnards Cl 15 EX24 . . . . 103 A4
Burnards Field Rd EX24 . .103 A4
Burnbridge Hill EX16 . . . . .63 D2
Burne Cross TQ12 . . . . . . 131 D6
Burnett Cl PL12 . . . . 178 C3
Burnett Cl PL12 . . . . .242 D2
Burnett Rd PL6 . . . . .248 F8
Burnham Ct EX12 . . . . . . 192 A8
Burnham Ct TQ12 . . . . . . .207 E7
Burnham Park Rd PL3 . . .248 D6
Burniston Cl PL7 . . . . 251 A3
Burniston Ct PL7 . . . . 251 A3
Burn La
Lydford PL19 . . . . 107 C1
North Brentor PL19 . . . . . . 117 C8
Burnley Cl TQ12 . . . . 206 D8
Burnley Rd TQ12 . . . . 206 D4
Burn River Rise TQ2 . . . . 219 B8
Burns Ave
Exeter EX2 . . . . .177 F3
Plymouth PL5 . . . . 244 C2
Burns Ct EX7 . . . . 204 E5
Burnside EX8 . . . . 196 B1
Burnside Rd EX34 . . . . . . 150 A3
Burns La 13 PL21 . . . . . . 137 B2
Burnsome La EX14, EX15 . .67 B5
Burnthouse Cross EX14 . . .67 B5
Burnthouse Hill TQ12 . . .212 E1
Burnthouse La EX2 . . . . . .177 F3
Burnt Mdw EX6 . . . . 113 D5
Burraton Com Prim Sch
PL12 . . . . 242 C3
Burraton Cross PL21 . . . . 136 D4
Burraton Rd PL12 . . . . . . .242 C4
Burrator Arboretum Wlks
PL20 . . . . .127 E3
Burrator Ave PL20 . . . . . . 128 A8
Burrator Dr EX4 . . . . .176 E8
Burrator Rd PL20 . . . . . . .127 B3
Burrator Ave TQ2 . . . . . . .219 D5
Burridge Cross EX18 . . . . .58 F8
Burridge La TQ2 . . . . 220 A5
Burridge Moor Cross
EX18 . . . . .60 E6
Burridge Rd
Torquay TQ2 . . . . 219 D5
Upton Pyne EX5 . . . . .173 B8
Burrington CE Primary Sch
EX37 . . . . .43 F3
Burrington Dr PL7 . . . . . . 250 E4
Burrington Ind Est PL5 . . 244 A1
Burrington Moor Cross
EX37 . . . . .43 C3
Burrington Rd PL5 . . . . . .244 A1
Burrington Way PL5 . . . . .244 B1

Burrough Lawn EX39 . . . .157 A6
Burrough Rd EX39 . . . . . . 157 A6
Burrough Way TA21 . . . . .160 D4
Burrow Cl EX10 . . . . 186 D8
Burrow Cnr
Butterleigh EX16 . . . . .64 C4
Dalwood EX13 . . . . .86 F2
Burrow Cross
Budlake EX5 . . . . .82 E1
Burrow EX5 . . . . .175 E7
Meshaw EX17 . . . . .46 A4
Monkokehampton EX19 . . .76 A8
Burrow Ctyd EX16 . . . . . . .64 C4
Burrowe The 2 EX17 . . . . 165 C5
Burrow Farm Gdns EX13 . .87 A2
Burrow Hill PL9 . . . . 255 E6
Burrow Knap EX13 . . . . . . .87 A2
Burrow Knap Way EX13 . . .86 F2
Burrow La
Ashbrittle TA21 . . . . .50 D8
Bow EX17 . . . . .78 A5
Newton Poppleford EX10 . .186 D8
Burrowplot Cross EX17 . . .59 F2
Burrow Rd
Burrow EX5 . . . . .175 E8
10 Ilfracombe EX34 . . . . .150 B5
Seaton EX12 . . . . .192 B4
Burrows Cl EX33 . . . . 152 C5
Burrows Close La EX33 . . .15 A7
Burrowshot Cross EX13 . .104 B7
Burrows La EX39 . . . . .14 F1
Burrows Pk EX33 . . . . 152 C5
Burrows Way EX39 . . . . . .156 D8
Burrow The 11 EX12 . . . . .192 B4
Burscombe La EX10 . . . . .101 A1
Burscott EX39 . . . . .23 D3
Bursdon Moor Cross
EX39 . . . . .37 E7
Bursledon Ct EX7 . . . . . . .204 F6
Burston Cross EX17 . . . . . .78 B4
Burston La EX16 . . . . .34 A4
Burton Cl PL6 . . . . .245 B6
Burton Mus & Art Gallery
EX39 . . . . .157 A2
Burton Pl TQ5 . . . . .230 C4
Burton Rd EX39 . . . . 156 E1
Burton St TQ5 . . . . 230 C3
Burton Villa Cl TQ5 . . . . . .230 C4
Burvill St EX35 . . . . .151 B5
Burwell Cl PL6 . . . . 245 E4
Burwell La EX36 . . . . .30 F7
Burwood La EX38 . . . . 159 F5
Burwood Mews EX38 . . . . .159 F5
Burwood Rd EX38 . . . . 159 F5
Bury Cross
Lapford EX17 . . . . .60 D2
Petrockstow EX20 . . . . .56 F5
Bury Rd TQ12 . . . . .207 B4
Bury The EX5 . . . . .81 E5
Buscombe La EX31 . . . . . . .11 E2
Bushayes Cnr EX3 . . . . . . 183 C6
Bush Cnr EX18 . . . . .58 F8
Bush Cross EX18 . . . . .58 F8
Bushell Rd TQ12 . . . . 207 A4
Bushes La EX12, DT7 . . . . 193 B7
Bushmead Ave TQ12 . . . . 213 A5
Bush Pk PL6 . . . . 245 F3
Bushy La EX16 . . . . .48 A4
Bussell's Moor Cross
EX36 . . . . .32 C4
Butcher Park Hill PL19 . . .117 B7
Butcher's Moor La EX19 . .58 E4
Butchers Row EX31 . . . . . .154 F5
Butcombe La EX17 . . . . . . .61 D1
Bute Rd PL4 . . . . 249 A4
Butlakes La EX24 . . . . 101 F6
Butland Ave TQ3 . . . . 219 C1
Butland Rd TQ12 . . . . 207 D8
Butlands Ind Est TQ12 . . .211 F2
Butler Cl
Plymouth PL6 . . . . 245 B6
Tiverton EX16 . . . . .161 E3
Butler Way EX14 . . . . .86 A6
Buttercombe Cl TQ12 . . . .211 F8
Buttercombe La
Braunton EX33 . . . . .15 E8
Knowle EX31, EX34 . . . . . . .8 F1
West Down EX34 . . . . .8 E5
Buttercup Cl EX12 . . . . . . 192 B8
Butterdon Wlk PL21 . . . . 237 F5
Butterdown PL12 . . . . 242 B3
Butterfly La TQ12 . . . . . . .209 C2
Butterlake TQ3 . . . . .218 D3
Butterleigh Dr EX16 . . . . .161 E3
Buttermere CE EX14 . . . . . 176 F5
Buttermoor Cross EX16 . .48 D3
Butterpark PL21 . . . . 237 D5
Buttery Cl EX14 . . . . 166 C4
Buttery Rd EX14 . . . . .166 C4
Buttgarden St EX39 . . . . . .157 A1
Buttle's Cross TA3 . . . . . . .68 C7
Buttle's La TA3 . . . . .68 B6
Buttonhill Cross EX31 . . . .11 A8
Butt La EX31 . . . . .11 A1
Butt Park Rd PL5 . . . . . . .244 B3
Butt Parks EX17 . . . . 165 D4
Butt Pk
Hennock TQ13 . . . . 123 B7
Stokenham TQ7 . . . . .145 B1
Butts Cl
Bradford EX6 . . . . 112 F5
Chawleigh EX18 . . . . .60 B7
Honiton EX14 . . . . .166 B4
Witheridge EX16 . . . . .46 E1
Butts Cross
Buckfastleigh TQ11 . . . . . 135 B6
Cornworthy TQ9 . . . . .227 C3
Butts Ct EX2 . . . . .178 A5

Buttsford Terr PL21 . . . . .136 B6
Butts Hill
Kenton EX6 . . . . .194 D3
Paignton TQ3 . . . . .225 B8
Butt's Hill EX11 . . . . .169 E4
Buttshill Cross TQ3 . . . . . 225 B8
Butts La
Christow EX6 . . . . 113 A3
Ideford TQ13 . . . . 124 B4
Kenton EX6 . . . . 194 D1
Starcross EX6 . . . . .200 D8
Buttsons Cl TQ7 . . . . .145 B1
Butts Park Ct PL8 . . . . . . .141 A7
Butts Pk PL8 . . . . 141 A7
Butts Rd
Colyton EX24 . . . . .103 A4
Loddiswell TQ7 . . . . .143 E8
Newton Ferrers PL8 . . . . . 141 A7
Butts Way EX20 . . . . .77 C4
Buzzacott Cl EX34 . . . . .3 B2
Buzzacott La EX34 . . . . .3 B2
Byard Cl PL5 . . . . .243 E1
Bycott La EX18 . . . . .45 B4
Bydown Cross EX32 . . . . . .28 D8
Bye Cross EX33 . . . . .8 B3
Byes Cl EX10 . . . . 188 C8
Byeside Rd EX10 . . . . 188 C8
Byes La EX10 . . . . 188 D8
Bygones Mus TQ1 . . . . . . 220 C8
Byland Rd PL3 . . . . .249 A6
Byron Ave PL5 . . . . 244 C2
Byron Ct EX31 . . . . 154 F7
Byron Rd
Exeter EX2 . . . . 178 C5
Torquay TQ1 . . . . 220 A8
Byron Way EX8 . . . . .196 C3
Byslades Camping Pk
TQ4 . . . . .225 A5
Bystock Cl EX4 . . . . .261 A4
Bystock Mews EX8 . . . . . .196 E3
Bystock Rd EX8 . . . . 196 D4
Byter Mill La TQ9 . . . . . . .228 A7
Byways Cl EX31 . . . . 153 F5

C

Cabbage Hill TQ13 . . . . . . 130 F4
Cabbage La EX14 . . . . .85 A3
Cabot Cl PL12 . . . . .242 E2
Cabourg Cl TQ8 . . . . .259 D5
Cadbury Cross EX17 . . . . . .81 C8
Cadbury Gdns EX9 . . . . . .198 B6
Caddiford Cross EX17 . . . . .97 B6
Caddiford Cross EX20 . . . .76 F7
Caddsdown Ind Pk EX39 . .25 D4
Caddywell La EX38 . . . . . .159 E5
Caddywell Mdw EX38 . . . .159 E5
Cadeside Cvn Site TA21 . .160 F7
Cadewell Cres TQ2 . . . . . 213 D1
Cadewell La EX19 . . . . .59 B3
Cadewell Park Rd TQ2 . . .213 C1
Cadford La EX19 . . . . .59 B3
Cadhay House EX11 . . . . .169 B5
Cadhay La EX11 . . . . 169 B4
Cadlake La EX20 . . . . .77 A3
Cadleigh Cl PL21 . . . . 136 D6
Cadleigh Court La EX21 . . .63 D2
Cadleigh Cross PL21 . . . . 136 D7
Cadleigh La PL21 . . . . 136 D6
Cadover Cl PL6 . . . . .245 A1
Cadway Cl EX11 . . . . 169 B3
Cadwell Rd TQ3 . . . . 226 B7
Caen Com Prim Sch
EX33 . . . . .152 D6
Caen Field EX33 . . . . .152 D6
Caen Gdns EX33 . . . . 152 D6
Caen Ho 7 EX33 . . . . .152 D6
Caen Sh Ctr 5 EX33 . . . . .152 D6
Caen St EX33 . . . . 152 D6
Caernarvon Gdns PL2 . . . .248 B7
Caffyns Cross EX35 . . . . . . .5 A4
Cairn Rd EX34 . . . . 150 B4
Cairn Side EX34 . . . . 150 B3
Cake Down La EX36 . . . . .158 E4
Calder Cl PL3 . . . . 249 B6
Caldicot Gdns PL6 . . . . . . 245 C8
Caledonia Cl PL7 . . . . 251 B5
Calf St EX38 . . . . 159 C5
California Cl EX4 . . . . 173 D3
California Cross PL21 . . . .138 A3
California Gdns PL3 . . . . . 249 D6
Caller's La EX15 . . . . .52 D1
Callington Rd
Saltash PL12 . . . . 242 E3
Tavistock PL19 . . . . 171 A4
Calstock Com Prim Sch
PL18 . . . . 125 D3
Calstock Rd PL18 . . . . 125 D6
Calstock Sta PL17 . . . . . . 125 D3
Calthorpe Rd EX4 . . . . 177 F8
Calvados 18 EX32 . . . . . . 155 A5
Calvados Cl 20 TQ13 . . . .123 E6
Calvados Pk TQ13 . . . . . . 207 F7
Calverleigh Cross EX16 . . .48 C1
Calvesford Cross EX38 . . .159 E5
Calvesford Rd EX38 . . . . . .159 E6
Calvez Cl PL10 . . . . 253 A1
Cambercombe Terr 2
EX34 . . . . .150 D5
Camber Rd PL1 . . . . .262 A1
Camborne Cl PL5 . . . . 244 A5
Camborne Cres TQ4 . . . . .229 B8

Cambrian Cl TQ4 . . . . 225 D4
Cambridge Gr 4 EX34 . . .150 C5
Cambridge La W 5 PL1 . .262 B3
Cambridge Rd
Brixham TQ5 . . . . 230 A4
Plymouth PL2 . . . . .247 F5
Torquay TQ1 . . . . .214 B1
Cambridge St 4 EX4 . . . . 177 A5
Cambridge Terr EX16 . . . .188 B4
Camden Cl PL4 . . . . 263 A3
Camden Rd TQ1 . . . . 220 B5
Camden St PL4 . . . . .263 A3
Came Cross EX14 . . . . .84 C7
Camellia Cl
Churston Ferrers TQ5 . . . .229 D5
11 Tiverton EX16 . . . . . . 161 F6
Camelot Ct EX4 . . . . .174 A1
Cameron Cl EX16 . . . . 161 B3
Cameron Dr PL21 . . . . 237 A5
Cameron Way PL6 . . . . . . .245 B1
Camfield Dr EX16 . . . . . . .161 F6
Camilla Ct EX4 . . . . .261 B4
Camilla Terr PL2 . . . . 248 D7
Campbellhayes Hill EX16 . .47 A1
Campbell Rd PL9 . . . . 255 F7
Camp Cross PL15 . . . . 105 E7
Camperdown Rd TQ8 . . . .259 C4
Camperdown St PL2 . . . . .247 F4
Camperdown Terr EX8 . . .201 F6
Camperknowle Cl PL10 . .252 F6
Campian Way 11 EX14 . . . .85 C2
Campion Cl
7 Plymouth PL7 . . . . . . .251 C5
Saltash PL12 . . . . 242 D4
Campion Ct
Torquay TQ1 . . . . .214 B1
Willand EX15 . . . . 162 D5
Campion Dr EX32 . . . . . . .155 E5
Campion Gdns EX2 . . . . . 178 C3
Campion Rise PL19 . . . . . .171 D6
Campion View PL6 . . . . . . 245 E8
Camp Rd EX20 . . . . 170 C2
Camps Cross EX17 . . . . . . .80 E2
Canaan Way EX11 . . . . . . .169 D3
Canada Hill Com Prim Sch
TQ12 . . . . 206 F1
Canal Cl TA21 . . . . .160 B8
Canal Hill EX16 . . . . 161 F3
Canal Rd
Holsworthy EX22 . . . . 164 D6
Tavistock PL19 . . . . 171 B5
Canberra Cl EX4 . . . . 173 E2
Candar The EX34 . . . . 150 B6
Candish Dr PL9 . . . . .256 D7
Candys Cotts 1 TQ13 . . . . 123 C4
Canefields Ave PL7 . . . . . .251 B3
Cane's Cotts PL8 . . . . 257 A5
Canhaye Cl PL7 . . . . 251 A3
Cann Gdns PL6 . . . . .244 D6
Cannington La EX17 . . . . . 104 B3
Cannon Rd TQ12 . . . . 123 B2
Cannon St PL1 . . . . .247 E3
Canns Water EX39 . . . . .39 C6
Cann Wood Forest Wlk
PL7 . . . . 132 C2
Cann Wood View PL6 . . . .245 E7
Canons Cl TQ14 . . . . 208 F8
Canons Way PL19 . . . . 171 A3
Canonteign Cty Pk EX6 . .113 B1
Canonteign Falls EX6 . . . .113 B1
Canon Way EX2 . . . . .181 B8
Canterbury Cl
Feniton EX14 . . . . .84 D2
Ivybridge PL21 . . . . .237 E2
Canterbury Dr PL5 . . . . . .244 B4
Canterbury Rd EX4 . . . . . .176 E7
Canterbury Way EX8 . . . . 196 E4
Capel La EX8 . . . . .202 F8
Capern Cl EX33 . . . . 152 E4
Capern Rd EX39 . . . . 156 F1
Capper Cl EX10 . . . . .186 E8
Capstone Cres EX34 . . . . .150 C6
Capstone Pl 4 EX34 . . . . .150 C6
Capstone Rd EX34 . . . . . . 150 C5
Captain Brooks Cross
EX39 . . . . .39 B8
Captain's Cross EX16 . . . . .63 C3
Captains Gdns PL5 . . . . . .244 E1
Captains Rd TQ12 . . . . . . .207 D8
Capton Cross TQ6 . . . . . . 232 E6
Caradon Cl PL6 . . . . .245 A5
Caradon Ct 2 PL20 . . . . . 126 F4
Caradon View EX17 . . . . . .61 A2
Carbeile Jnr Sch PL11 . . .247 A3
Carbeile Rd PL11 . . . . 247 A2
Carberry Tq8 . . . . .259 D4
Carberry Ave EX8 . . . . . . 196 A1
Carders Ct EX2 . . . . .261 A2
Cardiff Cl PL7 . . . . .251 B4
Cardigan Rd PL6 . . . . 245 C1
Cardinal Ave PL5 . . . . 244 D8
Carehouse Cross TQ7 . . . .145 B1
Careswell Ave PL2 . . . . . . .247 F8
Carew Ave PL5 . . . . .244 B3
Carew Gdns
Newton Abbot TQ12 . . . . . 207 F3
Plymouth PL5 . . . . 244 B3
Saltash PL12 . . . . 242 D3
Carew Gr PL5 . . . . .244 B3
Carew Ho EX16 . . . . 161 D6
Carew Terr PL11 . . . . .247 B2
Carew Wharf PL11 . . . . . .247 C2
Carew Wharf Bsns Ctr
PL11 . . . . 247 C2
Carey Cl PL12 . . . . .242 E3
Carey Rd TQ6 . . . . .233 C3
Carhaix Way EX7 . . . . 204 F8

Carisbrooke Rd PL6 . . . . . 245 C1
Carkeel Barns PL12 . . . . . 242 C5
Carlile Rd
Brixham TQ5 . . . . 230 A5
Exeter EX2 . . . . 178 A5
Carling Ct TQ7 . . . . 258 C4
Carlisle St PL5 . . . . 244 D3
Carlisle St 4 TQ12 . . . . . . 207 C3
Carlton Cl
Paignton TQ3 . . . . .219 C2
Plymouth PL3 . . . . 249 B5
Carlton Ct TQ12 . . . . 209 B2
Carlton Dr TQ3 . . . . .219 C2
Carlton Hill EX8 . . . . 202 A5
Carlton Mews TQ1 . . . . . . 220 C6
Carlton Pl 20 TQ14 . . . . . 210 C4
Carlton Rd
Exeter EX2 . . . . .178 B4
Torquay TQ1 . . . . 220 C6
Carlton Terr
18 Barnstaple EX32 . . . . .155 A4
6 Dawlish EX7 . . . . .204 E6
Plymouth, Lipson PL4 . . . .263 B3
Plymouth, Weston Mill PL5 .247 E8
Carlyle Ave EX32 . . . . 155 A6
Carlyon Cl
Exeter EX1 . . . . 178 A6
Torpoint PL11 . . . . .246 F4
Carlyon Gdns EX1 . . . . . . 178 A6
Carmarthen Rd PL4 . . . . . 249 B2
Carmel Gdns PL19 . . . . . . 171 A5
Carnegie N EX39 . . . . .156 F6
Carnegie S EX39 . . . . 156 F6
Carnock Rd PL2 . . . . 248 D8
Carnoustie Dr PL12 . . . . . 242 C2
Carolina Gdns PL2 . . . . . .247 F7
Caroline Cl
Exmouth EX8 . . . . .196 D1
Kingskerswell TQ12 . . . . . .213 A3
Caroline Pl PL1 . . . . .262 A2
Carousel Ct EX4 . . . . 177 A4
Carpenter Cl
Exeter EX4 . . . . 261 A3
Tiverton EX16 . . . . .161 C3
Carpenter Rd PL9 . . . . . . .255 F8
Carpenter's Cross EX16 . . .60 A5
Carpenters Ct 2 TQ12 . . . 207 C2
Carpenter's La EX16 . . . . . .60 A5
Carradale Rd PL6 . . . . 249 C7
Carrington Terr 2 EX32 . .155 A6
Carrington La EX19 . . . . . .58 F3
Carrions The 8 TQ9 . . . . . 223 C5
Carrisbrooke Way PL12 . . 242 B2
Carr La TQ7 . . . . .145 C4
Carroll Rd PL5 . . . . 244 C2
Carron La PL6 . . . . .241 D1
Carswells TQ12 . . . . 212 F5
Carter Ave EX8 . . . . .202 A8
Carter Cl EX36 . . . . 158 C5
Carter Rd PL21 . . . . 237 D6
Carters Cross EX13 . . . . . . .87 A3
Cartwright Cres TQ4 . . . . 209 D8
Cary Ave TQ1 . . . . .220 B7
Cary Castle TQ1 . . . . 220 B8
Cary Par TQ2 . . . . 220 B4
Cary Park Rd TQ1 . . . . . . 220 C7
Cary Rd
Paignton TQ3 . . . . .219 A1
Torquay TQ2 . . . . 220 A4
Caseberry La EX5 . . . . .82 E6
Case Gdns EX12 . . . . .192 B6
Cassiobury Way TQ2 . . . . 213 E2
Castlands EX5 . . . . .172 C7
Castle Acre Gdns PL3 . . . .249 B5
Castle Bank Gdns PL3 . . .249 B5
Castle Barbican PL7 . . . . .250 E4
Castlebar Cl EX16 . . . . . . .161 E3
Castle Bldgs PL12 . . . . . . 242 D4
Castle Carey Gdns PL3 . . .249 B5
Castle Cir TQ1 . . . . 220 A5
Castle Circus Ct TQ1 . . . . 220 A5
Castle Cotts
Exmouth EX8 . . . . .203 A7
Tuckenhay TQ9 . . . . .139 F6
Wellington TA21 . . . . .52 D8
Woodbury EX5 . . . . 184 C3
Castle Cross
Axminster EX13 . . . . .88 D4
Bratton Clovelly EX20 . . . . .92 C5
Membury EX13 . . . . .87 E4
Castle Ct
Saltash PL12 . . . . 242 C2
Torquay TQ1 . . . . 220 C7
Totnes TQ9 . . . . .223 B6
Castle Down Sch EX8 . . . .202 F7
Castle Dyke La PL1 . . . . . .263 A2
Castle Farm EX11 . . . . . . 168 E4
Castle Gate EX6 . . . . 194 E3
Castlehayes Gdns PL7 . . . .250 E4
Castle Hill
Axminster EX13 . . . . 167 D6
Bradworthy EX34 . . . . .2 E3
Ilfracombe EX34 . . . . .150 C6
Lynton EX35 . . . . .151 C5
Saltash PL12 . . . . 242 C1
Seaton EX12 . . . . .192 A4
Castle Hill Ave EX34 . . . . .150 C6
Castle Hill Gdns EX38 . . . 159 D5
Castle Hill View EX16 .101 B1
Castle Hill Villas 14
EX34 . . . . .150 C6
Castle Ho EX13 . . . . .167 D6
Castle Hts EX35 . . . . 151 C5
Castle La
Blackawton TQ9 . . . . .139 E2
Budleigh Salterton EX9 . . .197 C1

Castle La continued
Exmouth EX8, EX9 . . . . . . .203 B8
Okehampton EX20. . . . . . . .170 A3
Paignton TQ3 . . . . .218 C6
Plymouth PL7. . . . . .250 E4
Torquay TQ1. . . . . .220 B5
Woodbury EX5. . . . . .184 D3
Castle Mdw EX39 . . . . .40 B8
Castlemead Cl PL12. . . . . . .242 D3
Castlemead Dr PL12. . . . . . .242 D3
Castle Park Rd EX32. . . . . .155 E3
Castle Mount EX4. . . . . .261 A4
Castle Pk EX15 . . . . .67 B8
Castle Prim Sch The
  EX16. . . . . .161 D4
Castle Quay EX31 . . . . .154 F5
Castle Quay St [7] EX31 .154 F5
Castle Rd
  Dartmouth TQ6 . . . . .234 B1
  Kingswear TQ6. . . . . .234 B1
  Okehampton EX20 . . . . . .170 B4
  Torquay TQ1. . . . . .220 B5
  Tiverton EX16 . . . . .52 D8
Castle Rise
  Plymouth PL3. . . . . .249 B4
  Saltash PL12 . . . . .242 D1
Castle Rock EX34 . . . . .7 F7
Castle St
  Axminster EX13. . . . . .167 D6
  Bampton EX16. . . . . .34 B1
  Barnstaple EX31. . . . . .154 F5
  Combe Martin EX34. . . . . . . .3 A3
  Exeter EX4. . . . . .261 B3
  Great Torrington EX38. . . .159 D5
  Northam EX39 . . . . .156 F6
  Plymouth PL1. . . . . .263 A4
  Tiverton EX16 . . . . .161 D4
  Totnes TQ9 . . . . .223 C6
  Winkleigh EX19 . . . . .58 F3
Castle Terr [17] EX34 . . . .150 C5
Castleton Cl PL3. . . . . .249 A4
Castleton Tor TQ1. . . . . . . .219 F7
Castle View
  [17] Colyton EX24 . . . . . . .103 A4
  Saltash PL12 . . . . .242 D1
Castle Way TQ12. . . . . .206 F4
Castlewood Ave TQ12 .206 F4
Castle Wood La TA20. . . . . .69 F1
Castor Cl TQ5. . . . . .230 D3
Castor La TQ4 . . . . .226 B1
Castor Rd TQ5. . . . . .230 C3
Catalina Cl EX14. . . . . .67 C1
Catalina Villas PL9 . . . . . . .255 A6
Cater Rd EX32. . . . . .155 B4
Cat & Fiddle Pk EX5 . . . . . .179 E3
Catharine Ct EX16 . . . . . . .161 E5
Cathcart Ave PL4 . . . . .249 B2
Cathedral Cl EX1 . . . . .261 B3
Cathedral Sch The
  Exeter EX2. . . . . .261 B2
  Exeter EX4. . . . . .261 A3
Cathedral St PL1 . . . . .262 B3
Cathedral Yd EX1 . . . . .261 B3
Catherine Cres TQ4 . . . . . .225 F4
Catherine St
  Exeter EX1. . . . . .261 B3
  Plymouth PL1. . . . . .262 C2
Cath of St Mary & St
  Boniface PL1 . . . . .262 B3
Cathole La D17. . . . . .104 B5
Catkill Cross EX36. . . . . . . .46 C7
Cat La EX34 . . . . .150 E5
Catmoor Cross EX13. . . . . . .88 A5
Catnip Cl EX14. . . . . .167 E6
Caton Cross TQ12. . . . . . . .131 C6
Catriage Hill EX32 . . . . .18 C2
Catsborough Cross EX39. .40 E6
Catshole La EX34 . . . . .156 F1
Catsmoor Cross EX20. . . . . .92 F1
Catson Gn PL8. . . . . .257 A5
Cattedown Rd PL4. . . . . . .263 C1
Catterick Cl PL5. . . . . .243 E5
Cattewater Rd PL4. . . . . . .249 B1
Catt's La TA21. . . . . .52 E6
Caulston Cl EX8 . . . . .196 A2
Caulfield Ct [7] TQ12 . . . .207 C3
Caumont Cl EX15 . . . . .65 F7
Caunters Cl TQ12 . . . . .211 D2
Causeway EX12 . . . . .191 D5
Causeway Cl EX39 . . . . . . .157 A7
Causeway Cross TQ12. . . . .45 A2
Causeway End EX14. . . . . . .84 D7
Causeway The TQ12. . . . . .211 D2
Causey Gdns EX1. . . . . . . .174 F1
Causey La EX1. . . . . .174 F1
Cavalier Ct EX38 . . . . .159 D5
Cavalier Rd TQ12 . . . . .180 F3
Cavell Way EX20. . . . . .170 C6
Cavendish Cl EX7. . . . . . . .204 C7
Cavendish Pl EX35. . . . . . .151 B5
Cavendish Rd
  Exeter EX1. . . . . .177 F6
  Plymouth PL4. . . . . .249 B1
Cavern Rd
  [11] Brixham TQ5. . . . . . . .230 C4
  Torquay TQ1. . . . . .220 B5
Cavie Cres EX33 . . . . .152 B6
Cavie Rd EX33 . . . . .152 B6
Cawley's La EX14 . . . . .167 F7
Cawley's La EX14 . . . . .86 F6
Caxton Gdns PL5 . . . . .244 C1
Caxton Row EX16 . . . . .161 D6
Cayley Way PL5. . . . . .243 F7
Cayman Cl TQ2 . . . . .213 E3
Cecil Ave
  Paignton TQ3 . . . . .226 B8
  Plymouth PL4. . . . . .263 C4
Cecil Cotts PL1 . . . . .262 A3

Cecilia Rd TQ3. . . . . .219 B1
Cecil Mews TQ3 . . . . .226 B7
Cecil Rd
  Exeter EX2. . . . . .177 A4
  Paignton TQ3 . . . . .226 B7
Cecil St PL1. . . . . .262 B3
Cedar Ave EX7. . . . . .201 A2
Cedar Ave PL9 . . . . .255 C5
Cedar Cl
  Axminster EX13. . . . . .167 D5
  Exmouth EX8 . . . . .196 D3
  Honiton EX14. . . . . .166 B5
  Seaton EX12 . . . . .192 A7
  Torquay TQ14. . . . . .210 D7
  Torpoint PL11 . . . . .246 F2
Cedar Court Rd TQ1 . . . . . .220 B7
Cedarcroft Rd PL2 . . . . . . .248 B7
Cedar Ct
  Saltash PL12 . . . . .242 F2
  Wellington TA21. . . . . . . .160 E5
Cedar Dr PL11. . . . . .246 F2
Cedar Gdns EX13 . . . . .167 D5
Cedar Ho [2] EX33. . . . . . .152 D6
Cedar Rd
  Newton Abbot TQ12. . . . .212 F8
  Paignton TQ3 . . . . .219 C1
  Tiverton EX16 . . . . .161 F5
Cedars EX8. . . . . .203 B6
Cedars Pk EX31. . . . . .154 B4
Cedars Rd
  Exeter EX2. . . . . .261 B2
  Torquay TQ1. . . . . .220 D5
Cedar Units TQ9 . . . . .222 F8
Cedar Way
  Bideford EX39. . . . . .25 D4
  Brixham TQ5 . . . . .230 A2
Celandine Cl EX12 . . . . . . .192 B7
Celandine Gdns PL7 . . . . . .251 C5
Celandine Lawns EX15 .162 D5
Celia Cres EX4. . . . . .174 A2
Cembra Cl EX14 . . . . .174 A2
Cemetery La EX5. . . . . .82 F6
Cemetery Rd PL18. . . . . . . .125 C5
Centenary Way TQ2 . . . . . .213 C2
Centery La
  Bittadon EX31 . . . . .9 C5
  Parracombe EX31. . . . . .4 D2
Central Ave
  Stoke Gabriel TQ9 . . . . . .227 F8
  Exeter,
    EX2 . . . . .182 D7
  Exeter, Whipton EX4 . . . .174 B2
  Holsworthy EX22. . . . . . . .164 B4
  Lee Mill PL21. . . . . .136 C6
  Paignton TQ3 . . . . .226 B7
Central Park Ave PL4 . . . . .262 C4
Central Rd PL1 . . . . .262 B1
Central Station Chambers
  EX4. . . . . .261 A3
Centre Ct [3] PL21. . . . . . .137 C8
Centry Ct TQ5 . . . . .230 E4
Centry Rd TQ5 . . . . .230 E4
Centurion Ho [13] EX1. . . . .261 A2
Century Dr EX39. . . . . .156 E6
Ceramic Terr [3] EX32. . . .155 A4
Chackrell La EX16. . . . . .50 F2
Chaddiford La EX31 . . . . . .154 D7
Chaddlewood Ave PL4 . . . .263 B3
Chaddlewood Cl PL7. . . . . .251 A4
Chaddlewood Ho PL7. . . . .251 B5
Chaddlewood Inf Sch
  PL7. . . . . .251 A5
Chaddlewood Prim Sch
  PL7. . . . . .251 A5
Chad Rd PL9 . . . . .140 A8
Chaffcombe Cross EX17. . .78 F5
Chaffcombe La EX17. . . . . .79 A6
Chaffinch Dr EX15. . . . . . . .163 B2
Chagford CE Prim Sch
  TQ13. . . . . .111 A7
Chagford Cross TQ13. . . . .111 E5
Chagford Wlk PL6 . . . . .249 E8
Chains Rd EX16. . . . . .50 D1
Chalcombe Rocks La TA4. .34 E5
Chalfield Cl TQ2 . . . . .213 F3
Challabrook La TQ13. . . . . .180 B6
Challacombe Cotts PL20 .120 F6
Challacombe Cross
  Chagford TQ13. . . . . .110 F2
  Challacombe EX31. . . . . . . .11 F3
  Chulmleigh EX18 . . . . .45 A2
Challacombe Hill EX34 . . . .7 A6
Challacombe Hill Rd EX34. .7 F6
Challenger Cross EX13 . . . .82 F2
Challeycroft Rd TQ5. . . . . .230 A1
Challgood Cl [2] PL9 . . . . .255 F5
Challgood Rise PL9. . . . . . .255 F5
Challices Cotts EX18 . . . . . .59 E4
Challick La EX14. . . . . .35 F6
Challock Cl PL6. . . . . .245 D4
Challowell La EX33 . . . . .15 D2
Chaloner's Rd EX33 . . . . . .152 D6
Chamberlain La EX34. . . . .150 E4
Chamberlaine Manor
  EX34. . . . . .150 C5
Chambercombe Park Rd
  EX34. . . . . .150 E5
Chambercombe Pk EX34 .150 E5
Chambercombe Pk Terr
  EX34. . . . . .150 D5
Chambercombe Rd
  EX34. . . . . .150 D5
Chamberlain Rd EX2 . . . . .261 A1
Chamberlayne Dr PL7. . . . .250 E6
Chambers Cl EX10 . . . . . . .188 A8
Champernhayes La DT6. .104 F7
Champernowne PL21 . . . . .137 F7

Champernowne Cres [4]
  EX34. . . . . .150 D5
Champford La TA21 . . . . . .160 D5
Champford Mews [2]
  TA21. . . . . .160 D5
Champion Cross TA4 . . . . . .35 E3
Chancel Ct EX4 . . . . .174 D1
Chancel La EX4 . . . . .174 D1
Chancellor's Way EX4 . . .174 A2
Chandlers Ct [4] EX39 . . . .15 B1
Chandlers Hts TQ8. . . . . . .259 D5
Chandlers' La EX10 . . . . . .188 B5
Chandlers Way EX34 . . . . .150 B3
Chandlers Wlk EX2 . . . . . .261 A1
Change La EX4. . . . . .34 D6
Channel Park Ave PL3 . . . .249 B5
Channel Sch (Language)
  EX34. . . . . .150 B4
Channel View
  Ilfracombe EX34 . . . . .150 D5
  Woolacombe EX34. . . . . . . .1 A2
Channel View Dr TQ7. . . .147 B6
Channel View Terr PL4 . . .263 C4
Channon Rd PL21. . . . . . . .242 C4
Chanter Ct EX2 . . . . .178 A2
Chanter's Hill EX32 . . . . . .155 B5
Chanters Rd EX39. . . . . . . .157 A3
Chantry Ave EX39. . . . . . . .157 A3
Chantry Cl TQ14 . . . . .210 D7
Chantry Ct PL7 . . . . .250 B5
Chantry Hill TQ7 . . . . .145 D4
Chantry Mdw EX2. . . . . . . .181 B8
Chantry The EX2. . . . . .170 C5
Chapel Cl
  Gunnislake PL18 . . . . .125 B5
  Halberton EX16. . . . . .65 A8
  [5] Horrabridge PL20. . . .126 F4
  Petrockstow EX20 . . . . . . .56 F4
Chapel Cnr EX22. . . . . .70 F5
Chapel Cotts PL7 . . . . .132 F4
Chapel Cross
  Dunkeswell EX14 . . . . .67 C2
  Iddesleigh EX19 . . . . .57 E3
  Petrockstow EX20 . . . . . . .56 F8
  Puddington EX16. . . . . .62 B5
  Thorverton EX5 . . . . .81 D5
  Thurlestone TQ7 . . . . .143 A2
Chapel Ct
  Exeter EX4. . . . . .177 A4
  [5] Newton Abbot TQ12 . .207 B3
  Swimbridge EX32 . . . . .28 E8
  Torquay TQ1. . . . . .219 F7
Chapel Down La PL21 . . . .137 F3
Chapel Down Lane End
  PL21. . . . . .137 E3
Chapeldown Rd PL11. . . . .247 A2
Chapel Downs Dr EX17. . .165 A6
Chapel Downs Rd EX17 . . .165 A6
Chapel Fields [6] TQ10 . . .134 F3
Chapel Hill
  [5] Budleigh Salterton
    EX9 . . . . .198 A1
  Cheriton Fitzpaine EX17. . .62 F1
  Clyst St George EX3 . . . . .183 C6
  [15] Exmouth EX8 . . . . . . .202 A6
  Longdown EX6. . . . . .98 E2
  [16] Newton Abbot TQ12 . .207 B3
  Uffculme EX15. . . . . .66 A7
Chapel Hill Cross EX17. . . .62 F1
Chapel Mdw EX39. . . . . . . .156 F7
Chapel Knap EX13, EX24 .102 F7
Chapel La
  [11] Coldeast TQ12 . . . . . .122 F1
  Combe Martin EX34. . . . . . .3 A3
  Folly Gate EX20 . . . . .93 D4
  [4] Horrabridge PL20. . . .126 F4
  Lutton PL21. . . . . .133 B2
  Malborough TQ7 . . . . .147 E6
  Mary Tavy PL19 . . . . .117 E6
  Ottery St Mary EX11 . . . .169 E4
  Stoke Fleming TQ6. . . . . .146 B7
  Totnes TQ9. . . . . .223 D5
  Yealmpton PL8. . . . . .257 F4
Chapel Mdw TQ13 . . . . . . .126 C3
Chapel Rd
  Brampford Speke EX5. . . .81 E1
  Bratton Clovelly EX20 . . . .92 A2
  Exeter EX2. . . . . .177 B1
  Lympstone EX8 . . . . .195 D5
  Newton Abbot TQ12. . . . .207 D3
  Parkham EX39 . . . . .39 E8
  Plymouth PL9. . . . . .255 C6
  Sidmouth EX10. . . . . .188 B3
  Yealmpton PL8. . . . . .136 A2
Chapel Row EX17. . . . . .142 C6
Chapelry The [5] TQ13 . . .123 C4
Chapel St
  Axmouth EX12 . . . . .192 D7
  [2] Bere Alston PL20 . . . .125 E1
  [13] Bideford EX39. . . . . . .157 A1
  Blackawton TQ9 . . . . .139 E1
  Braunton EX33. . . . . .152 D5
  Buckfastleigh TQ11 . . . . .236 B5
  Budleigh Salterton EX9 . .199 G2
  Dolton EX19. . . . . .57 F7
  Dulverton TA22 . . . . .33 D6
  Ermington PL21. . . . . .136 F4
  Exeter EX1. . . . . .261 B3
  [6] Exmouth EX8 . . . . . . .202 A6
  Gunnislake PL18. . . . . . . .125 D6
  Holsworthy EX22. . . . . . . .164 C3
  Honiton EX14. . . . . .166 C6
  Lifton PL16. . . . . .105 E4
  Morchard Bishop EX17. . . .61 A2
  Plymouth, Mount Wise PL1 .247 E2
  Plymouth PL4. . . . . .263 A3

Chapel St continued
  Sidbury EX10 . . . . .101 B2
  Sidmouth EX10. . . . . .188 B3
  Tavistock PL19. . . . . .171 B5
  Tiverton EX16 . . . . .161 B4
  Woolfardisworthy EX39. . . .38 F7
Chapel The [1] TQ9 . . . . . .223 D5
Chapelton Cross EX37. . . . .27 F5
Chapelton Sta EX37. . . . . . .28 A4
Chapeltown Cross EX5 . . . .63 C1
Chapel Way PL3 . . . . .249 A6
Chapman Ct PL12. . . . . . . .242 B3
Chapmans Gn EX22 . . . . . . .54 C4
Chapmans Ope PL1 . . . . . .247 D2
Chapple Cl EX6. . . . . .201 B8
Chapplecroft Rd EX13. . . . .87 E5
Chapple Cross
  Bovey Tracey TQ13. . . . . .180 B5
  Chagford TQ13. . . . . .110 D8
  Dolton EX19. . . . . .57 E6
Chapple Cross Cross
  TQ13 . . . . .110 D7
Chapple La TQ20. . . . . .76 E4
Chapple Rd
  Bovey Tracey TQ13. . . . . .180 A6
  Witheridge EX16. . . . . .46 E1
Charberry Rise DT6 . . . . . .104 F4
Chard Ave EX5 . . . . .99 E8
Chard Barton PL5. . . . . . . .244 B3
Chard Rd
  Axminster EX13. . . . . .88 B4
  Exeter EX1. . . . . .178 A6
  Plymouth PL5. . . . . .243 D2
Chard St
  Axminster EX13. . . . . .167 D6
  Chardstock EX13 . . . . .88 B7
Chard Stock Cl EX1 . . . . . .178 D6
Charfield Dr PL6. . . . . .249 A8
Charford Cross TQ10. . . . .135 B1
Charlacott Cross
  Newton Tracey EX31. . . . .27 B6
  Newton Tracey EX31. . . . .27 B7
Charlemont Rd TQ14 . . . . .210 B8
Charles Ave EX39 . . . . .157 A2
Charles Cross
  East Buckland EX32. . . . . .18 E3
  Plymouth PL4. . . . . .263 A3
Charles Dart Cres EX32 .155 B6
Charles Hankin Way
  PL21. . . . . .237 E4
Charles Hudson La [2]
  EX31. . . . . .155 A7
Charles Rd
  Honiton EX14. . . . . .166 C6
  Kingskerswell TQ12. . . . . .213 A2
Charles St
  [14] Barnstaple EX32 . . . . .154 F6
  Dartmouth TQ6 . . . . .233 F3
  [15] Exeter EX4. . . . . .261 A2
  Plymouth PL1. . . . . .263 A3
Charles Terr PL3. . . . . .249 A6
Charleston CE Prim Sch
  TQ7 . . . . .144 C1
Charleton Court Barns
  TQ7 . . . . .144 C1
Charleton Way TQ7 . . . . . .144 C1
Charlotte Cl TQ2. . . . . .219 F8
Charlotte Ct TQ2 . . . . .214 B1
Charlotte Mews [2] EX2 .261 B2
Charlottes Oak TQ12 . . . . .123 C1
Charlotte St
  Crediton EX17 . . . . .165 D5
  Plymouth PL2. . . . . .247 E4
Charlton Cres PL6 . . . . . . .245 E4
Charlton Ho EX7. . . . . .204 F6
Charlton Rd EX2. . . . . .245 A3
Charlton Terr PL21 . . . . . . .237 D5
Charlwood Ct TQ1 . . . . . . .220 B6
Charmoor Dro TA20 . . . . . . .69 F8
Charmouth Cl
  Lyme Regis DT7. . . . . .260 E4
  Torquay TQ1. . . . . .220 C3
Charmouth Ho DT7 . . . . . .260 C3
Charmouth Rd
  Lyme Regis DT7 . . . . .260 E4
  Raymond's Hill EX13. . . . .104 C7
Charneymore Cross EX18. .44 E1
Charnhill Cl PL9 . . . . .256 A6
Charnhill Way PL9 . . . . . . .256 A6
Charnley Ave EX4 . . . . .176 E5
Charter Cl EX16. . . . . .161 B4
Charton Cross DT7. . . . . . .104 A2
Chartwell Cl TQ3. . . . . . . .225 E7
Chartwell Dr TQ12 . . . . . . .207 A4
Charwell Mdw EX5. . . . . . . .82 F6
Chase The
  Honiton EX14. . . . . .166 D7
  Ivybridge PL21 . . . . .237 D4
Chasty La EX22 . . . . .164 C3
Chatham Cl EX8 . . . . .196 B4
Chatsworth Gdns PL5 . . . .243 F3
Chatsworth Rd TQ1. . . . . . .220 B6
Chatto Rd TQ1. . . . . .220 A7
Chatto Way TQ1 . . . . .220 B7
Chaucer Ave EX2 . . . . .177 F3
Chaucer Prim Sch PL5 . . .244 C2
Chaucer Rd PL19 . . . . .171 D5
Chaucer Way EX2 . . . . .177 F4
Chaucer Way PL5. . . . . . . .244 C2
Chaves Cl EX16 . . . . .161 F3
Chawleigh Cl PL18 . . . . . . .125 C5
Chawleigh Hill EX18 . . . . . .59 F8
Chawleigh Prim Sch EX18 60 B7
Chawleigh Week Cross
  EX18 . . . . .59 E8
Chawleigh Week La EX18 .59 D8

Chawleigh Week Mill Cross
  EX18. . . . . .59 D8
Cheavestone Lea TQ9 . . . .139 E1
Checkridge La EX13. . . . . . .88 D2
Chedworth St PL4 . . . . .263 A3
Cheeke St EX1. . . . . .261 C3
Cheese La EX10. . . . . .187 F4
Cheglinch Cnr EX34. . . . . . . .8 F5
Cheglinch La EX34 . . . . .8 F6
Cheldon Barton Moor La
  EX18. . . . . .60 D8
Cheldon Cross
  Chawleigh EX18. . . . . .60 D8
  Chulmleigh EX18 . . . . .45 D2
Chelfham Mill Sch EX32. . .17 C6
Chelfham Senior Sch
  PL20. . . . . .125 C3
Chelmer Cl PL7. . . . . .251 A5
Chelmsford Pl PL5 . . . . . . .244 C4
Chelmsford Rd EX4 . . . . . .176 E6
Chelsea Pl [8] TQ14. . . . . .210 B5
Chelsea Trad Ctr EX2. . . . .178 E5
Chelson Gdns PL6 . . . . . . .245 E3
Chelson La EX10 . . . . .101 E1
Chelston Bsn Pk TA21. . . . .52 D8
Chelston Rd
  Newton Abbot TQ12. . . . .207 B4
  Torquay TQ2. . . . . .219 E3
Chelston Terr TA21. . . . . . . .52 D8
Cheltenham Cl PL3 . . . . . .263 B4
Cheltenham Pl PL5 . . . . . .263 B4
Chene Ct [7] PL21. . . . . . . .137 B2
Cheney's La EX14. . . . . . . .166 E8
Chepstow Ave PL6 . . . . . . .245 C8
Chepstow Cl EX2 . . . . .182 B8
Chequers Haigh PL8 . . . . .140 F6
Chercombe Bridge Rd
  TQ12 . . . . .206 C3
  [1] Newton Abbot TQ12 . .206 C4
Chercombe Valley Rd
  TQ12 . . . . .206 E4
Cheriswood Ave EX8 . . . . .196 D1
Cheriswood Cl EX8 . . . . . .196 D1
Cheriton Bishop Com Prim
  Sch EX6. . . . . .97 B4
Cheriton Cross
  Cadbury EX5. . . . . .81 C8
  Chilton EX17 . . . . .80 D7
Cheriton Fitzpaine Prim Sch
  EX17. . . . . .62 F1
Cheriton Hill EX35 . . . . .5 D3
Cheriton Mill Cross EX17. .62 F2
Cheriton Rd EX35. . . . . . . .151 D1
Cherry Arbour TQ12 . . . . .155 C3
Cherrybridge Cross
  EX35. . . . . .151 A2
Cherry Brook Dr TQ4. . . . .229 A3
Cherry Brook Sq TQ4 . . . .229 A3
Cherry Brook Wlk TQ4 . . .226 B1
Cherry Cl
  Cheriton Fitzpaine EX17 . .62 F1
  Exmouth EX8 . . . . .196 C3
  [8] Honiton EX14. . . . . . . .85 C2
  Tiverton EX16 . . . . .161 B5
  Willand EX15 . . . . .162 D4
Cherry Cross TQ9 . . . . .223 C4
Cherryford La EX31. . . . . . . .4 C4
Cherry Gdns
  Crediton EX17 . . . . .165 C5
  Exeter EX2. . . . . .178 A4
  Paignton TQ3 . . . . .226 A7
Cherry Gr EX32. . . . . .155 C2
Cherry Mdw EX17. . . . . .62 F1
Cherry Park Cl TQ12 . . . . .219 D2
Cherry Pk
  Appledore EX39. . . . . .14 F1
  Plymouth PL7. . . . . .251 A3
Cherry Tree Cl
  Exeter EX4. . . . . .173 A2
  Kingskerswell TQ12. . . . . . .99 B6
Cherry Tree Dr
  Brixton PL8 . . . . .257 A5
  [3] Landkey EX32. . . . . . . .17 B2
Cherry Tree Gdns EX16. . .161 E5
Cherry Tree La PL7. . . . . . .251 A4
Cherry Tree Rd EX13 . . . . .167 E6
Cherrywood Cl TQ12 . . . . .206 E4
Cheshire Dr PL6 . . . . .244 D6
Cheshire Rd EX8 . . . . .196 C2
Chesil Ct DT7 . . . . .260 C3
Chesnut Cl PL7 . . . . .242 D4
Chester Cl EX4. . . . . .176 E7
Chester Ct EX8 . . . . .201 F7
Chesterfield Rd PL3. . . . . .249 B4
Chestermoor Cross EX20. .92 D1
Chester Pl [4] PL4. . . . . . .248 E4
Chester Terr [13] EX32. . . .155 A4
Chesterton Cl PL5. . . . . . . .244 C3
Chestnut Ave
  Cullompton EX15. . . . . . . .163 C2
  Dartmouth TQ6 . . . . .233 C4
  Exeter EX2. . . . . .178 A3
  Plymouth PL9. . . . . .255 C6
  Torquay TQ2. . . . . .219 F4
Chestnut Cl
  Barnstaple EX33. . . . . . . .152 E6
  Cheriton Bishop EX6 . . . . .97 B4
  Crediton EX17 . . . . .165 D6
  Exmouth EX8 . . . . .196 C3
  Lamerton PL19 . . . . .116 E4
  Seaton EX12 . . . . .192 A7
  Tavistock PL19. . . . . .171 D2
  Torpoint PL11 . . . . .246 F3

Chestnut Cl continued
Wellington TA21..........160 E5
Chestnut Cres
7 Chudleigh TQ13........123 F6
Stoke Canon EX5........173 F8
Chestnut Ct EX2........181 B8
Chestnut Dr
Bideford EX39........25 D4
Brixham TQ5........230 A2
Kingsteignton TQ12....207 F6
Newton Abbot TQ12....208 A1
Willand EX15........162 C4
Chestnut Mews EX14....84 E2
Chestnut Pk TQ7........149 D7
Chestnut Prim Sch TQ5..230 A2
Chestnut Rd
Plymouth PL3........248 D7
Tiverton EX16........161 F5
Chestnuts The EX5........99 D2
Chestnut Terr PL19........116 E3
Chestnut Wlk EX13........87 D6
Chestnut Way
Honiton EX14........166 A4
Newton Poppleford EX10..186 F8
Chestnut Wlk EX7........204 C5
Cheston Cross TQ10....134 E1
Chestwood Ave EX31....154 C3
Chestwood Cl EX31....154 D4
Chestwood Villas EX32....16 E1
Cheyne Beach 2 EX34..150 C6
Cheynegate La EX4........174 C3
Cheyne Rise EX4........174 D2
Cheyney Cross EX36........30 B2
Cheyney La EX36........30 B2
Chibbet Hill TA24........21 B8
Chibbet Post TA24........21 C8
Chichacott Cross EX20..170 F7
Chichacott Rd EX20....170 D7
Chichester Cl
Barnstaple EX32........155 B2
Exmouth EX8........202 C8
Ilfracombe EX34........150 A4
1 Instow EX39........15 B1
Chichester Cres
Barnstaple EX32........155 B2
Saltash PL12........242 E1
Chichester Ct
Barnstaple EX32........155 C5
Horrabridge PL20........126 F4
Outer Hope TQ7........147 B7
Chichester Ho
Barnstaple EX31........155 B8
Exeter EX2........178 B5
Plymouth PL1........262 B2
Chichester Mews EX1..261 B3
Chichester Pk EX34........8 A6
Chichester Rd 7 EX16...64 D7
Chichester Rd EX32....155 B2
Chichester Way
East Budleigh EX9........198 B6
Newton Abbot TQ12....207 F3
Westward Ho! EX39....156 C6
Chideock Ct DT7........260 C3
Chilbridge La EX31........17 B8
Chilcombe Cross EX24..102 B7
Chilcombe La EX24....102 A6
Chilcote Cl TQ1........220 C8
Chilcott Cl 5 EX16.......64 D7
Chilcott Cross TA22........33 A7
Chilcott La TA22........33 A7
Childrey Gdns PL6........245 C1
Childrey Wlk PL6........245 C1
Chilla Chapel EX21........73 E4
Chilla Rd EX21........73 E3
Chillaton Cross TQ7....138 A1
Chillaton Ct PL16........106 E6
Chillpark EX31........153 D5
Chill Pits La EX13........88 B8
Chiltern Cl TQ2........219 D3
Chiltern Cross EX16....34 B2
Chilton Ave TQ14........210 C6
Chilton Cl PL6........249 B7
Chilton Gate EX16........81 D8
Chilton La EX17........80 E7
Chilverton Cross EX17....59 F1
Chilverton Hill Gate EX17 59 F1
Chilverton La EX17........59 F1
Chineway Gdns EX11....169 F3
Chineway Head EX11...101 B6
Chineway Hill EX11....101 A6
Chineway Rd EX11....100 F6
Chingswell St 2 EX39..157 A2
Chinkwell Rise TQ2....219 D7
Chinon Ct EX16........64 D8
Chinon Pl EX16........161 A6
Chinston Ct EX14........85 B4
Chipmunk Wlk EX32....155 B6
Chipple Pk PL21........133 B2
Chircombe La EX39....157 A4
Chiseldon Farm TQ5....230 B2
Chiseldon Hill TQ5....230 C2
Chiseldon Ho EX4........173 A1
Chitterley Bsns Ctr EX5..173 A2
Chittlebum Cross PL8..256 E5
Chittleburn Hill PL8....256 E5
Chittlehampton CE Prim Sch
EX37........28 F4
Chivelstone Cross TQ7..149 A5
Chivenor Ave PL5........243 D4
Chivenor Cross EX31....15 C5
Chiverstone La EX6....194 C4
Chiverstone Rd EX6....194 C4
Chockenhole La EX9....199 A8
Chockland Rd TQ12....123 E1
Cholhouse La EX20........77 C7

Chollacott Cl PL19........171 C4
Chollacott La PL19........171 D3
Chollaton Cross EX22........39 E1
Cholwell Cross TQ9........222 F4
Chope Rd EX39........156 F6
Chopes Cl EX39........26 A4
Chough Cl PL15........105 A2
Christ Cross EX5........82 C8
Christcross La EX5........82 D7
Christian Mill Bsns Pk
PL6........244 E4
Christina Par TQ9........223 F5
Christina Pl TQ9........223 E5
Christone Cross TQ9....138 D7
Christow Com Sch EX6..113 B4
Christow Rd EX2........177 B2
Chrystel Cl EX10........100 D2
Chubb Dr PL3........248 A8
Chubb Rd EX39........26 A4
Chubby Croft Cl EX39....22 E3
Chubs Cross EX20........77 F5
Chubworthy Cross TA4..35 D5
Chudleigh Ave EX39....157 B1
Chudleigh CE Com Prim Sch
TQ13........123 C6
Chudleigh Knighton CE Prim
Sch TQ13........123 C4
Chudleigh Rd
2 Bideford EX39........157 B1
Exeter EX2........181 B7
Kingsteignton TQ12....207 D8
Plymouth PL4........249 A4
Chudleigh Terr 6 EX39..157 B1
Chudley Cl EX8........196 D1
Chuggaton Cross EX37....28 C5
Chuley Cross TQ13....130 F3
Chuley Hill TQ13........130 F4
Chuley Rd TQ13........130 F4
Chulmleigh Hill EX18....44 E1
Chulmleigh Prim Sch
EX18........44 E1
Chulmleigh Rd
Morchard Bishop EX17....61 A2
Winkleigh EX19........58 F3
Church Cl
Ashprington TQ9........139 F8
Aylesbeare EX5........99 D2
Bratton Fleming EX31....18 A8
Broadclyst EX5........175 C7
Dartmouth TQ6........233 F3
Dolton EX19........57 F6
Goodleigh EX32........17 B5
Kingsbridge TQ7........258 D5
Lapford EX17........60 D3
Plymouth PL7........250 B7
Puddington EX16........62 B5
Totnes TQ9........223 C5
Yealmpton PL8........257 F4
Church Cliff DT7........260 E3
Church Cross
Buckfastleigh TQ11....236 B6
Cheriton Fitzpaine EX17....62 E1
Exeter EX4........174 D3
Filleigh EX32........29 C6
Sandford EX17........80 A5
Church Cross Rd TQ11...236 B6
Church Ct
Harberton TQ9........222 D2
Kingsteignton TQ12....207 E6
4 Newton Abbot TQ12..207 B3
Plymouth PL6........245 A7
Church Dr TA21........52 F7
Church End Rd TQ12..212 F4
Church Farm TQ7........143 A1
Churchfield Rd 20 EX39..15 A1
Church Fields TA21....160 D8
Churchfields Dr TQ13..180 D7
Churchfields Gdns TQ6..233 D3
Churchfields W TQ6...233 D3
Church Flats EX6........201 B8
Churchford Rd EX33....8 D1
Church Gate EX36........30 E1
Church Gr EX32........155 B3
Church Hill
Awliscombe EX14........85 B4
Beer EX12........191 D5
Blackawton TQ9........139 E1
Brendon EX35........5 F4
Buckfastleigh TQ11....236 B6
Calstock PL18........125 E3
Exeter EX4........174 E2
Fremington EX31........153 E5
Holbeton PL8........136 D1
Honiton EX14........166 D5
Ilfracombe EX34........150 A5
Kingswear TQ6........234 A2
Lynton EX35........151 C5
Marldon TQ3........218 D4
Milton Combe PL20....126 C1
Musbury EX13........103 D5
Otterton EX9........198 D7
Plymouth PL6........245 B1
Tavistock PL19........171 E2
Teddburn St Mary EX6....97 F5
Winkleigh EX19........58 F3
Church Hill Cl TQ9....131 E1
Church Hill Cotts TQ9..131 E1
Church Hill Cross EX20....94 E7
Church Hill E 6 TQ5....230 C5
Church Hill La EX33........8 D1
Church Hill Rd PL9....255 A6
Church Hill W 5 TQ5....230 C5
Church Ho
Exeter EX2........177 A4
Saltash PL12........243 A2

Church House Cl 8
TQ13........123 C4
Churchill EX34........8 F4
Churchill Ave EX7....204 D5
Churchill Cl
Barnstaple EX32........155 B6
Kenton EX6........194 D3
Churchill Cotts PL21....137 D6
Churchill Cres EX36....158 C3
Churchill Ct
7 Brixham TQ5........230 C4
Lympstone EX8........195 E6
Churchill Dr
Crediton EX17........165 B6
Teignmouth TQ14....210 C6
Churchill Gdns EX17....78 C7
Churchill Hill EX31........10 C4
Churchill La
Barnstaple EX34........88 A5
Calverleigh EX16........48 C3
Chipstable TA4........35 C5
Churchill Rd
Bideford EX39........26 A4
Exeter EX2........176 F4
Exmouth EX8........196 D2
Tavistock PL19........171 D2
Tiverton EX16........161 A4
Churchills 11 EX15........67 B8
Churchills The TQ12....207 A4
Churchill Way
Appledore EX39........14 F1
Northam EX39........157 A7
Plymouth PL3........248 E6
Churchill Wlk PL12....242 E1
Church La
Alfington EX11........84 F1
12 Barnstaple EX32....154 F5
Bideford EX39........25 E2
4 Bittaford PL21........137 C8
Bridford EX6........112 F5
Broadclyst EX5........175 C7
Calstock PL18........125 D3
Cargreen PL12........239 A1
Christow EX6........113 B3
Clyst St Mary EX5........179 B2
Crediton EX17........165 D5
Dulverton TA22........33 D6
East Budleigh EX9....198 B6
Exeter, Heavitree EX2....177 F5
Exeter, Pinhoe EX4....174 D2
Feniton EX14........84 E2
Frithelstock Stone EX38....40 F5
Great Torrington EX38...155 C7
Hatherleigh EX20........75 C7
Holsworthy EX22........164 C4
Kingsbridge TQ7........258 F2
Langtree EX38........40 F2
Membury EX13........87 D5
Modbury PL21........137 B2
Parracombe EX31........4 D1
Salcombe TQ8........259 E5
Sheldon EX14........80 B6
Shobrooke EX17........80 E4
Slapton TQ7........145 D3
St John PL11........252 B8
Stokeinteignhead TQ12...209 B2
Swimbridge EX32........28 E8
Tavistock PL19........171 C5
Torquay TQ2........219 F5
Whitestone EX4........98 E4
Winkleigh EX19........58 F3
Yealmpton PL8........257 F4
Church Lake 8 EX32....17 B2
Churchlands EX17........78 C4
Churchlands Cl PL6....245 E7
Churchlands Rd PL6...245 E8
Church Lane Cross EX17..78 C4
Church Lane Head TQ13..121 B2
Church Live PL19........171 E2
Church Mdw
High Bickington EX37....43 B7
Ivybridge PL21........237 A4
Landkey EX32........17 B2
Church Mdws
Bratton Clovelly EX20....92 A2
Okehampton EX20....170 A5
Church Mead EX14........85 B1
Church Mews TQ12....207 B3
Church Park Cl TQ9....138 C7
Church Park Ct PL6....245 E8
Church Park Rd
Newton Ferrers PL8....141 A7
Plymouth PL6........245 E8
Church Park EX17........80 A5
Church Path
Ashburton TQ13........130 F4
Barnstaple EX31........154 F7
Exeter EX1........178 A5
Halberton EX16........65 A7
Okehampton EX20....170 A5
6 Paignton TQ3........226 B6
Shute EX13........102 F8
Church Path Rd EX2....176 F3
Church Pl
Bideford EX39........25 A3
Cornwood PL21........133 C2
Horrabridge PL20........126 F4
Kingston TQ7........142 C6
Kingswear TQ6........234 B3
Newton Ferrers PL8....141 A7
Paignton TQ3........225 D4
Church Pool EX34........8 F5
Church Quillet TQ9....139 E1
Church Rd
Bishopsteignton TQ14..209 A7
Churchinford TA3........68 C8
Cockwood EX6........201 A6

Church Rd continued
Colaton Raleigh EX10..186 E3
Dartmouth TQ6........233 E3
Ermington PL21........136 F4
Exeter, Alphington EX2..177 B1
Exeter, St Thomas EX2..177 A4
Exmouth EX8........202 A7
Georgeham EX33........8 A2
Hennock TQ13........123 B7
Highampton EX21........74 C7
Ideford TQ13........124 B4
Ilfracombe EX34........150 B6
Kenton EX6........194 F5
Luton TQ13........124 C4
Lympstone EX8........195 E5
Newton Abbot TQ12....207 C2
Plymouth, Plympton PL7..250 F4
Plymouth, Plymstock PL9..255 F7
Saltash PL12........242 D2
Silverton EX5........82 B5
Stoke Fleming TQ6....146 B8
Torquay, Barton TQ2....214 A3
Torquay, St Marychurch
TQ1........220 B8
Wembury PL9........140 D8
Whimple EX5........99 E7
Church Row La PL5....244 C6
Church St Mews 4 TQ3..226 B6
Church Side EX5........179 D7
Church St
Axminster EX13........167 D5
Axmouth EX12........192 D7
Bradninch EX5........83 A7
Braunton EX33........152 D7
4 Brixham TQ5........230 C5
Buckfastleigh TQ11....236 B5
Calstock PL18........125 D3
Colyton EX24........103 A5
Combe Martin EX34........3 A3
Crediton EX17........165 D5
Cullompton EX15........163 C3
Dawlish EX7........204 C6
Dolton EX19........57 F7
Exeter EX2........177 F5
Exmouth EX8........202 A7
8 Honiton EX14........166 C6
Ilfracombe EX34........150 B5
Kenton EX6........194 F5
Kingsbridge TQ7........258 D5
Kingsteignton TQ12....207 E6
Lyme Regis DT7........260 E3
Modbury PL21........137 B2
Morchard Bishop EX17....61 A2
Okehampton EX20....170 B5
Paignton TQ3........226 B6
Plymouth PL3........248 A4
Salcombe TQ8........259 E5
Sandford EX17........80 A5
Sidbury EX10........101 C2
8 Sidford EX10........101 B1
Sidmouth EX10........188 B3
14 South Brent TQ10....134 F3
South Molton EX36....158 C4
Starcross EX6........201 B8
Tiverton EX16........161 C4
Torquay TQ2........220 B5
Uplyme DT7........260 B5
Witheridge EX16........46 E1
Churchstanton Prim Sch
TA3........68 B8
Church Steps Cotts EX5..184 B3
Church Stile EX6........182 B4
Churchstow Wlk PL6....249 E8
Church Terr
7 Bampton EX16........34 B1
Exeter EX1........177 F5
Churchtown Cl PL21....133 C2
Churchtown Vale PL12..242 D1
Church View
Bideford EX39........26 A1
6 Chudleigh TQ13....123 E6
Dawlish EX7........204 C6
Kingsteignton TQ12....207 E6
Ottery St Mary EX11....169 D3
St Dominick PL12........125 A2
Sutcombe EX22........54 A6
Walkhampton PL20....127 A4
Church View Ho EX5....184 B3
Churchward Rd TQ3....226 B7
Churchwater La EX18....58 D8
Churchway TQ1........220 C7
Church Way
Newton Abbot TQ12....207 E1
Plymouth PL5........247 E8
Yealmpton PL8........257 F4
Church Wlk
Avonwick TQ10........135 B1
6 Bideford EX39........157 A1
Stoke Gabriel TQ9........228 C7
Wembury PL9........140 C8
Church Wlk
Churchwood Ct TQ1....220 C5
Churchyard La EX17....61 C7
Churscombe Gn TQ3....218 E2
Churscombe Pk TQ3....218 D2
Churscombe Rd TQ3....218 D2
Churston Broadway TQ4..229 B7
Churston Cl TQ5........229 C5
Churston Cross
Churston Ferrers TQ5...229 E4
West Putford EX22........39 B2
Churston Ct TQ7........258 D4
Churston Ferrers Gram Sch
TQ5........229 C5
Churston Rd TQ5........229 E5
Churston Rise EX10....191 F8
Churston Sta TQ5........229 C5
Churston Way TQ5....230 B4

Chute St EX1........261 C4
Cinders La TQ6........146 B7
Cintra Terr EX39........157 A4
Cistern St TQ9........223 B5
Citadel Ope 12 PL1....263 A2
Citadel Rd PL1........262 C2
Citadel Rd E PL1........263 A2
Citadel The PL1........263 A1
City Arch EX1........261 A2
City Bsns Pk EX3........248 A4
City Ind Est EX2........261 B1
City Mus & Art Gal PL4..263 A3
City Mus & Art Gal Annexe
PL4........263 A3
Claddon La TQ1, TQ2....214 A5
Clampet La TQ14........210 C4
Clampits Stile TQ11....135 C6
Clanage Cl TQ12........211 D1
Clampitt Rd TQ12........211 D2
Clampits EX15........163 B2
Clanage Cross TQ14....124 C1
Clanage St TQ14........208 F8
Clannaborough Cross
EX17........78 E5
Claponmill Cross EX5....83 B2
Clappentail Cl DT7....260 C4
Clappentail La DT7....260 C3
Clappentail Pk DT7....260 C3
Clapperbrook La EX2...177 B1
Clapper Cross
Bondleigh EX20........77 B8
Zeal Monachorum EX17..78 B5
Clapper La EX14........166 C7
Clapp's La
Beer EX12........191 D5
Seaton EX12........192 B5
Clapworthy Cross EX36..29 D2
Clara Pl EX3........182 E5
Claredale Rd EX8........202 B6
Clare Dr EX16........161 F6
Claremont Ave TQ12....213 A4
Claremont Field EX11..169 D3
Claremont Gr
Exeter EX1........261 C1
Exmouth EX8........202 B7
Claremont La EX8........202 C7
Claremont Pl EX20........75 C7
Claremont St PL1........262 C4
Clarence Cotts 8 EX34..150 B6
Clarence Ct PL1........262 A3
Clarence Hill TQ6........233 F4
Clarence Pl TQ6........219 E6
Clarence Rd
18 Barnstaple EX32....155 B3
Exeter EX4........261 C4
Plymouth, Morice Town
PL2........262 A3
Plymouth, Stonehouse PL1..262 A3
Clarence Rd
Budleigh Salterton EX9..198 B2
6 Exeter EX4........177 A5
Exmouth EX8........202 A7
Torpoint PL11........247 B3
Clarence St TQ6........233 F4
Clarendon Cl TQ1........220 C3
Clarendon Ho TQ1........219 F6
Clarendon Ho TQ1........220 C4
Clarendon Ho 1 PL1....247 F3
Clarendon Rd
Ipplepen TQ12........211 D2
16 Newton Abbot TQ12..207 B3
Clare Pl PL4........263 B2
Clare St PL21........237 C4
Claridge The TQ3........226 C8
Clarke Cl EX15........65 F7
Clarke Ctr The EX2....177 C2
Clarke Mead EX2........178 C4
Clarks Barn Rd TQ7....143 E7
Clarks La EX20........57 A6
Clatworthy La EX22........29 E6
Claude Dix Cl 1 EX31..155 A7
Claw Cross EX39........38 F5
Clawford Cross TQ22....72 D3
Clawford Vineyard &
Fisheries EX22........72 D3
Claw Hill EX16........62 F4
Claw Pk EX22........62 A5
Clawton Prim Sch EX22..72 B1
Clayfield Villas 8 EX32..155 B4
Clayford La TA22........33 C5
Clayford Rd TA22........33 C5
Clayhidon Crossway EX15..52 E2
Clay La
Chudleigh Knighton
TQ13........123 C3
Colyton EX24........103 A4
Copplestone EX17........79 A6
Dartington TQ9........223 A8
Lympstone EX8........195 E4
Teignmouth TQ14........210 B5
Uffculme EX15........66 A8
Clayland Cross TQ4....225 E4
Claylands Dr TQ4........225 E4
Clayland Cross EX14....166 B4
Claymans Pathway PL21..237 A6
Claypark Hill CU15........47 D5
Clay Park Terr TQ9....228 A7
Claypits Covert Cross
EX31........154 A2
Claytonia Cl PL6........241 C1
Clayton Pl PL4........249 B2
Clayton Rd
Exeter EX4........177 A7
Plymouth PL4........249 B2
Clearbrook Ave PL5....243 E1
Clear View PL12........242 E3
Cleaveanger La EX17....78 B4

Cleave Cl
  Barnstaple EX31 .... 154 D4
  Tedburn St Mary EX6 ..... 97 F4
Cleave Cross EX14 ......86 C3
Cleave Hill
  Dolton EX19 .... 57 E6
  Meshaw EX36 .... 46 A6
Cleave La
  Bishop's Tawton EX32 ... 27 F7
  Burrington EX37 .... 44 A2
  Chapelton EX32 .... 28 A7
  Wilmington EX14 ......86 C3
Cleaveland Rise TQ12 ... 206 F1
Cleave Lane End EX32 ... 27 F7
Cleave Pk EX31 .... 153 F5
Cleave Rd EX31 .... 154 D4
Cleaves Cl EX5 .... 81 E5
Cleave The PL10 .... 253 B2
Cleavewood Dr EX39 .. 157 D1
Cleavewood Holiday Pk
  EX34 .... 8 C6
Cleeve Ct EX2 .... 237 B5
Cleeve Gdns PL2 ...... 248 A8
Cleeve The PL15 .... 66 E8
Clegg Ave PL11 .... 246 E3
Cleland Ct TQ14 ...... 208 F8
Clement Rd PL7 .... 251 B5
Clement's La EX32 ..... 28 B8
Clennon Ave TQ4 ...... 226 B4
Clennon Ct
  [5] Brixham TQ5 .... 230 C3
  Torquay TQ2 .... 214 A2
Clennon Dr TQ4 .... 226 B4
Clennon Gdns TQ4 .... 226 B4
Clennon Hts TQ4 ...... 226 B4
Clennon La TQ2 .... 214 A2
Clennon Pk TQ4 .... 226 B4
Clennon Rise TQ4 ..... 226 B4
Clennon Summit TQ4 .. 226 B4
Clennon Valley Ct TQ4 . 226 B4
Clerk Cl EX8 .... 196 C2
Cleve Ct TQ1 .... 220 E5
Clevedon Ho EX10 ..... 188 C5
Clevedon Park Ave PL2 . 248 B6
Clevedon Pk EX10 ..... 188 C5
Cleve Terr TQ1 .... 220 E5
Cliff Bastin Cl EX2 .... 178 C4
Cliff Castle [4] EX12 ... 192 A4
Cliff Ct
  [10] Dawlish EX7 .... 204 E6
  Plymouth PL1 .... 262 B1
Cliffden Cl TQ14 ...... 210 C5
Cliff Ho TQ4 .... 226 D5
Cliff La PL10 .... 252 A5
Cliff Mews TQ4 .... 226 D5
Clifford Ave TQ12 ..... 123 E1
Clifford Cl
  [13] Chudleigh TQ13 .... 123 E6
  Exeter EX1 .... 178 B7
  Kingsteignton TQ12 .... 207 E7
  Plymouth PL5 .... 243 E2
Clifford Cross EX16 ... 210 A3
Clifford Dr TQ12 ...... 180 F2
Clifford Gdns EX17 .... 165 D5
Clifford Mews TA21 ... 160 E6
Clifford Rd EX4 .... 177 F8
Clifford Rd Ind Est EX4 . 177 F8
Clifford St
  [1] Chudleigh TQ13 ..... 123 E6
  Kingsteignton TQ12 .... 207 E7
Clifford Terr TA21 ..... 160 E6
Cliff Park Ave TQ4 .... 226 C3
Cliff Park Rd TQ4 ..... 226 C3
Cliff Rd
  Budleigh Salterton EX9 . 199 G2
  Paignton TQ4 .... 226 D5
  Plymouth PL1 .... 262 B1
  Salcombe TQ8 .... 259 C3
  Sidmouth EX10 .... 188 C3
  Teignmouth TQ14 ..... 210 D7
  Torquay TQ2 .... 219 E2
  Wembury PL9 .... 140 D7
Cliffside EX34 .... 7 F6
Cliffside Rd TQ1 ...... 220 C8
Cliff Terr EX9 .... 199 G2
Cliff View Terr PL18 ... 125 D6
Clifton Ave PL7 .... 250 E7
Clifton Bank [5] TQ3 .. 226 A6
Clifton Ct
  Croyde EX33 .... 7 E3
  Exeter EX1 .... 177 E7
  [3] Ilfracombe EX34 .... 150 B5

Clifton Gdns TQ3 ...... 226 A6
Clifton Gr TQ3 .... 226 A6
Clifton Hill EX1 .... 177 E7
Clifton Ho [17] TQ14 .. 210 C5
Clifton La EX31 .... 10 B4
Clifton Pl
  Dawlish EX7 .... 204 C6
  [16] Ilfracombe EX34 ... 150 B5
  Plymouth PL4 .... 263 A4
  Salcombe TQ8 .... 259 E5
Clifton Rd
  Exeter EX1 .... 261 C3
  Paignton TQ3 .... 226 A6
Clifton Rise TQ3 ...... 226 A6
Clifton St
  Barnstaple EX31 ...... 154 F4
  Bideford EX39 .... 157 B1
  Exeter EX1 .... 177 E6
  Plymouth PL4 .... 263 A4
Clifton Terr
  Barnstaple EX31 ...... 154 E4
  [16] South Brent TQ10 .. 134 F3
  Torquay TQ1 .... 220 B4
Climsland Rd TQ4 ..... 226 A5
Clinton Ave
  Exeter EX4 .... 177 E8
  Plymouth PL4 .... 249 A4
Clinton CE Prim Sch The
  EX20 .... 57 A6
Clinton Gdns EX20 .... 57 A7
Clinton Rd EX32 ...... 155 B3
Clinton Rise EX12 ..... 191 E6
Clinton Sq EX8 .... 201 F6
Clinton St EX4 .... 177 A5
Clinton Terr
  [11] Barnstaple EX32 ... 155 B3
  Budleigh Salterton EX9 . 198 A2
  Great Torrington EX38 .. 159 B5
  Merton EX20 .... 57 A7
  Millbrook PL10 .... 252 F6
Clipper Quay EX2 ..... 261 B1
Clipper Wharf EX8 .... 201 E6
Cliston Ave EX8 .... 196 E2
Cliston TQ9 .... 139 C2
Cliston La EX20 .... 76 E4
Clittaford Rd PL6 ..... 244 F7
Clittaford View PL6 ... 244 E7
Cliveden Rd EX39 ..... 26 A4
Cloake Pl PL12 .... 239 A2
Clobells [3] TQ10 ..... 134 F2
Cloggshill Cross EX31 . 27 B1
Cloister Rd EX4 .... 177 F7
Clonway [1] PL20 ..... 126 F3
Close The
  [14] Bere Alston PL20 .. 125 E1
  Brixham TQ5 .... 230 C6
  Holcombe EX7 .... 210 F8
  Paignton TQ4 .... 229 C8
  Rewe EX5 .... 82 A2
  Saltash PL12 .... 242 C3
  Seaton EX12 .... 192 A5
  Tiverton EX16 .... 161 F6
Cloutman's La EX33 .... 7 E2
Clovelly Apts [8] EX34 . 150 B5
Clovelly Cl EX39 ...... 156 E1
Clovelly Court & Gdns
  EX39 .... 23 D4
Clovelly Cross EX39 ... 23 D2
Clovelly Ctr The EX39 . 23 D3
Clovelly Gdns N EX39 . 156 E1
Clovelly Gdns S [2] EX39. 156 F1
Clovelly Prim Sch EX39 . 23 D3
Clovelly Rd
  Bideford EX39 .... 25 D4
  Plymouth PL4 .... 263 C1
Clovelly Rise
  Dawlish EX7 .... 204 D5
  Paignton TQ3 .... 225 E6
Clovelly Road Ind Est
  EX39 .... 25 D4
Clovelly View PL9 ..... 255 A7
Clover Ave EX4 .... 176 E8
Coverdale Ct DT7 ..... 260 E3
Clover Dr EX15 .... 163 B2
Clover Rise PL8 ...... 245 E8
Clover Way EX32 ...... 155 E4
Clover Wlk PL12 ...... 242 C3
Clowance Cl PL1 ...... 247 F1
Clowance La PL1 ...... 247 E1
Clowance St PL1 ...... 247 F1
Cluden Rd EX3 .... 156 F6
Cludens Cl EX2 .... 181 B8
Clumpit La EX14 ...... 194 A4
Clydesdale Ct EX5 .... 173 A1
Clydesdale Rd EX4 .... 173 A1
Clyde St PL2 .... 247 F5
Clyst Ave
  Brixham TQ5 .... 230 A2
  Clyst Honiton EX5 .... 175 C2
Clyst Halt Ave EX2 .... 178 E3
Clyst Heath EX2 ...... 178 D3
Clyst Heath Com Prim Sch
  EX2 .... 178 D3
Clyst Honiton CE Prim Sch
  EX5 .... 179 D7
Clyston Hydon View
  EX5 .... 83 D4
Clyst Rd
  Exeter EX3 .... 178 F2
  Topsham EX3 .... 182 F7
Clyst St Mary Prim Sch
  EX5 .... 179 A2
Clyst Units EX2 .... 177 D1
Clyst Vale Com Coll EX5. 175 D5
Clyst Valley Rd EX5 ... 179 B2
Clyst William Cross EX15. 84 B5
Coach Dr EX39 .... 25 F4

Coach Ho The
  Grenofen PL19 .... 126 D6
  Paignton TQ3 .... 226 C7
Coach House Mews PL9. 256 B6
Coach Pl TQ12 .... 207 C2
Coach Rd
  Newton Abbot TQ12 ... 207 B1
  Noss Mayo PL8 .... 140 F6
  Silverton EX5 .... 82 B6
Coach Rd The DT7 ..... 260 C8
Coarsewell Cross PL21. 138 A5
Coastguard Cotts
  Challaborough TQ7 .... 142 D4
  Dawlish EX7 .... 204 F6
  Down Thomas PL9 ..... 254 F2
  Inner Hope TQ7 .... 147 B6
  Stoke EX39 .... 22 B3
  Torquay TQ1 .... 220 D2
Coastguard Hill EX9 ... 199 H2
Coastguard Rd EX9 ... 198 B1
Coates Rd EX2 .... 178 B5
Cobbacombe Cross EX16. 49 D6
Cobbaton Combat Collection
  Mus EX37 .... 28 D5
Cobbaton Cross EX37 . 28 D6
Cobbett Rd PL5 .... 244 B2
Cobb La PL5 .... 255 F6
Cobblestone La PL1 ... 248 A1
Cobb Rd DT7 .... 260 D2
Cobb Terr DT7 .... 260 D2
Cobb The DT7 .... 260 D1
Cob Castle TA21 ...... 52 D8
Coblands Cross EX5 ... 82 A7
Cobley La
  Bideford EX39 .... 26 C6
  Lapford EX17 .... 60 E4
  West Worlington EX17.. 60 F4
Cob Mdw EX20 .... 75 C7
Cobourg St PL1 ...... 262 B3
Coburg Cl TA21 ...... 52 F7
Coburg Rd
  Cullompton EX15 ..... 163 C6
  Torquay TQ1 .... 220 B4
Coburg Rd EX10 ...... 188 A3
Coburg Terr
  [8] Ilfracombe EX34 .... 150 C6
  Sidmouth EX10 .... 188 A3
Cockeram's Rd EX5 ... 99 C8
Cockhaven Cl TQ14 ... 208 F7
Cockhaven Rd TQ14.. 208 F7
Cockington Cl PL6 .... 245 E1
Cockington Ctry Pk TQ2. 219 B4
Cockington La
  Paignton TQ4 .... 219 C1
  Torquay TQ2 .... 219 C1
Cockington Prim Sch
  TQ2 .... 219 F5
Cockington Rd TQ3 ... 219 A3
Cockington Wlk PL6 .. 245 C1
Cockland Hill TA21 .... 51 C8
Cockland La EX16 ..... 48 F3
Cockles La [2] EX17 ... 165 D5
Cockles Rise EX17 .... 165 D5
Cockpit Hill EX15 ..... 163 B3
Cockrams Butt Cross
  EX37 .... 29 B1
Cockram's La EX37 .... 43 F7
Cockspark La EX14 .... 84 F8
Cocks Pk TQ7 .... 142 D7
Cocktree Throat EX20 . 95 C8
Cockwood Prim Sch EX6 201 B6
Codden Cross EX32 ... 28 A8
Coddiford Cross EX17 . 62 E2
Coddiford Hill EX17 ... 62 E1
Coddiford La EX17 .... 62 F2
Codrington St EX1 .... 261 C3
Coffins La EX6 .... 181 F4
Coffinswell La TQ12 ... 213 A4
Coffintree Cross EX17 . 80 F6
Coffintree Hill EX17... 80 F7
Cofton Hill EX6 .... 201 A5
Cofton La EX6 .... 200 F5
Cofton Rd EX2 .... 177 D1
Coil Cross EX31 ...... 10 B6
Coker Ave TQ2 .... 214 A4
Cokers Elm EX14 ..... 87 A7
Cokers Elm Cross EX14. 87 A7
Colands Ct EX2 ...... 181 A8
Colaton La EX5 .... 181 E5
Colaton Terr
  Sidmouth EX10 .... 187 F4
  Sidmouth EX10 .... 188 A4
Colborne Rd PL6 ..... 245 A2
Colcombe La
  Dalwood EX13 .... 86 F1
  Shute EX13 .... 102 F8
Colcombe Rd EX24 ... 103 A5
Cold East Cross TQ13 . 121 C1
Coldharbour
  Bideford EX39 .... 157 A2
  [3] Totnes TQ9 .... 223 C5
  Uffculme EX15 .... 66 A7
Coldharbour Cross
  Chilsworthy EX22 ..... 53 E1
  Loddiswell PL21 ...... 138 B3
Coldharbour Mill Mus
  EX15 .... 66 A7
Coldharbour Rd EX4 .. 161 A3
Coldrenick St PL5 .... 243 D1
Coldwell La EX12 ..... 192 D6
Coldwell Lane Terr
  EX12 .... 192 D7
Colebrooke La EX15.. 65 A1
Colebrook La PL7 ..... 250 E7
Colebrook Rd
  Plymouth, Plympton PL7. 250 E6
  Plymouth, St Budeaux PL5. 243 D1

Coleford Hill EX16 ....48 B6
Cole La
  Ivybridge, Higher Keaton
   PL21 .... 237 C1
  Ivybridge PL21 .... 237 E6
Coleman Ave TQ4 ..... 210 A5
Coleman Dr PL9 ...... 255 F4
Colemans Cross PL15 . 105 B5
Coleman's Cross EX24 . 102 D6
Cole Moore Mdw PL19 . 171 B6
Coleridge Ave PL6 .... 244 F2
Coleridge Barns TQ7 . 145 A2
Coleridge Cl EX8 ..... 196 C4
Coleridge Ct TQ7 ..... 145 A2
Coleridge La TQ7 ..... 145 A2
Coleridge Rd
  Exeter EX2 .... 176 F4
  Ottery St Mary EX11 .. 169 F4
  [8] Tiverton EX16 ...... 64 D7
Coles Cl EX17 .... 78 C3
Coles Cnr EX18 .... 59 C8
Coles Cotts PL9 ...... 255 C1
Coles Ct TQ9 .... 144 F5
Coles Ct EX18 .... 58 E8
Coles Ct TQ6 .... 233 F3
Colesdown Hill PL9 ... 250 B1
Coles La TQ12 .... 212 F5
Coles Mead EX16 .... 161 F4
Coles Mill Cl EX22 ... 164 C4
Coles's La EX13 ...... 104 A5
Colesworthy Cross TQ12. 180 B2
Coley Cl EX16 .... 245 B6
Colhayne La
  Dalwood EX13 .... 86 F1
  Shute EX13 .... 102 F8
Colin Campbell Ct [10]
  PL1 .... 262 B3
Colin Rd TQ3 .... 226 C7
Collabear Cnr EX31 ... 27 D8
Collabridge Hill EX6 .. 112 E8
Collabridge La EX6 ... 112 E8
Collabridge Rd EX6 ... 112 E8
Collacombe Cross PL19. 116 D4
Collacott Cross EX38 .. 40 F2
Collacotts La EX19 ... 59 B2
Collaford Farm Bsns Units
  PL7 .... 136 A6
Collapark TQ9 .... 223 B6
Collard La PL7 .... 132 D4
Collaton Cross
  Halwell TQ9 .... 139 C4
  Malborough TQ7 ..... 147 F6
  Yealmpton PL8 .... 141 B8
Collaton Ct TQ2 ...... 214 A2
Collaton Ct [7] TQ1 .. 220 D4
Collaton La PL19 ..... 117 F2
Collaton Mews TQ4 .. 225 D8
Collaton Rd
  Malborough TQ7 ..... 147 F6
  Torquay TQ2 .... 219 C8
Collaton St Mary CE Prim
  Sch TQ3 .... 225 C5
Collatons Wlk EX17 .. 78 C4
Coll Ct EX15 .... 66 A7
College Ave
  Exeter EX2 .... 261 C2
  Plymouth PL3 .... 248 E5
  Tavistock PL19 .... 171 D6
College Cl
  Barnstaple EX31 ...... 154 D3
  [1] Torquay TQ1 .... 219 F6
College Dean Cl PL6 .. 245 C5
College Gn
  Bideford EX39 .... 156 F2
  Uffculme EX15 .... 66 A7
College La
  Clyst Hydon EX5, EX15 . 83 B5
  Ide EX2 .... 176 C2
  Plymouth PL4 .... 248 F4
College Park Pl PL3 .. 248 E5
College Rd
  Cullompton EX15 ..... 163 C4
  Exeter EX1 .... 261 C3
  Newton Abbot TQ12 ... 207 C2
  Plymouth PL2 .... 247 E5
College Road Prim Sch
  PL2 .... 247 E5
College The
  Exeter EX2 .... 176 D2
  Ottery St Mary EX11 .. 169 D4
College View
  Plymouth PL3 .... 248 E4
College Way TQ6 ..... 233 E4
Colleton Cl EX8 ...... 202 C8
Colleton Cres EX2 .... 261 B2
Colleton Ct [9] EX2 .. 261 B2
Colleton Gate EX2 ... 44 C1
Colleton Gr EX2 ...... 261 B1
Colleton Hill EX2 ..... 261 B1
Colleton Mews EX2 .. 261 B2
Colleton Row EX2 .... 261 B1
Colleton Way EX8 .... 202 C8
Collett Way TQ12 .... 207 E3
Colley Cres EX2 ...... 261 B1
Colley End Pk TQ3 ... 226 A5
Colley End Rd TQ3 ... 226 A5
Colley La TQ13 ...... 124 D4
Colley Lane Cross TQ13. 124 D4
Colley Park Rd EX33 . 152 D5

Colliepriest View EX16 . 161 B1
Colliers Cl [5] PL9 .... 140 D8
Collin Cl PL5 .... 243 D1
Collingsdown Cross EX39. 39 F4
Collingwood Ave PL4 . 263 C2
Collingwood Cl
  Dartmouth TQ6 .... 233 C3
  Torquay TQ1 .... 220 C2
Collingwood Rd
  Dartmouth TQ6 .... 233 C3
  Paignton TQ4 .... 226 A5
  Plymouth PL1 .... 248 A3
Collingwood Villas [5]
  PL1 .... 248 A3
Collins Pk EX9 .... 198 B6
Collins Rd
  Exeter EX4 .... 173 E2
  Totnes TQ9 .... 223 B6
Colliepriest Ho EX16 .. 161 C2
Colliepriest La EX16 .. 161 C1
Colliepriest Rd EX16 .. 161 C2
Colliton Cross EX14 .. 84 C6
Colliver Cross EX9 .... 198 E5
Coll of St Mark & St John
  PL6 .... 245 C4
Collybank La EX17.... 62 C3
Collybear Cross PL21.. 138 A4
Colmer Cross PL21 ... 138 A4
Colmer Rd PL8 .... 138 A4
Colne Gdns PL3 ...... 249 B5
Colombelles Cl EX31.. 153 E5
Colscott Cross EX22 .. 39 C1
Colston Cl PL6 .... 245 B6
Colston Cross EX13 .. 88 B4
Colston La EX16 ..... 47 E1
Colston Rd TQ11 ..... 236 E3
Coltishall Cl PL5 ..... 244 B6
Coltness Rd PL9 ..... 256 B5
Coltsfield Cl PL6 ..... 249 B8
Columbjohn Cross EX5. 82 B2
Colvin Cl EX2 .... 202 D7
Colway Cl DT7 .... 260 D5
Colway Rd TQ14 ..... 124 B1
Colway La
  Chudleigh TQ13 ...... 123 F6
  Lyme Regis DT7 ...... 260 D4
Colway Rise DT7 ..... 260 E5
Colwill Rd PL6 .... 245 E3
Colwill Wlk PL6 ...... 245 F3
Colwyn Ct TQ1 ...... 220 E5
Colwyn Rd PL11 ..... 247 A3
Colyford Rd EX12 .... 192 B7
Coly Rd
  Colyton EX24 .... 103 A4
  Honiton EX14 .... 166 C4
Colyton Cl EX2 ...... 86 C2
Colyton Gram Sch EX24. 103 A3
Colyton Hill EX13, EX24. 103 A4
Colyton Prim Sch EX24. 103 A4
Colyton Rd
  Colyton EX13, EX24 ... 103 A6
  Northleigh EX24 ...... 102 C6
Coly Vale EX24 ...... 103 A4
Combas La EX33 ..... 7 E2
Combe Beacon La TA20. 69 F7
Combe Cl EX13 ...... 167 D5
Combe Cross
  Ashburton TQ13 ...... 131 C5
  Aveton Gifford PL21... 143 A8
  Ivybridge PL21 .... 137 B6
  Kingsbridge TQ7 ..... 258 D7
  Loddiswell TQ7 ...... 138 C1
  Shillingford EX16 .... 34 D4
  Strete TQ6 .... 145 E7
Combe Dean Cl PL6 .. 245 C5
Combefishacre Cross
  TQ12 .... 217 D8
Combefishacre La TQ9,
  TQ12 .... 217 D6
Combe Hayes EX10 .. 188 B8
Combehead Droveway
  EX13 .... 86 E3
Combehead La EX13 . 86 F3
Combe Hill EX15 ..... 52 C2
Combe Hill Cross TQ12. 123 F2
Combe Hill Dro TA20 . 69 F5
Combe La
  Dulverton TA22 ...... 33 D6
  East Anstey TA22 .... 32 F6
  Galmpton TQ5 .... 229 B3
  Northleigh EX24 ..... 102 B7
  Trew Sawton EX17 ... 77 F1
  Spreyton EX17 .... 95 F3
  Torquay TQ2 .... 214 A1
  Whitestaunton TA20... 69 E5
Combeland La EX17 .. 78 C4
Combe Martin Prim Sch
  EX34 .... 2 F4
Combe Martin Wildlife &
  Dinosaur Pk EX34 ... 3 C2
Combe Martin Wildlife Park
  Rly EX34 .... 3 C2
Combe Moor La EX17 . 77 F1
Combe Pafford Sch TQ2. 214 B3
Combepark Cross TQ9 . 217 A1
Combe Pk EX34 ...... 150 D5
Combe Rd
  Axmouth EX12, DT7... 193 B6
  Torquay TQ2 .... 214 B2
Comber's Cross EX14 . 86 A5
Combesdown Cross EX22. 72 C6
Combeshead Cross
  Cornwood PL21 ...... 133 F1
  Diptford TQ9 .... 138 C6
  Heasley Mill EX36 ... 19 C2

Combeshead La
Dunchideock EX2. . . . . 114 A7
West Anstey EX36. . . . . .32 A7
Combley Dr PL6 . . . . 245 D4
Combpyne La D17, EX13 . 193 E8
Combpyne Rd EX13 . . . . . 103 D5
Combrew La EX31 . . . . .16 A3
Combsland Cross EX36. . . .31 B4
Combsland New Cross
EX36. . . . . .31 B4
Comburg Cl EX8 . . . . 196 E3
Comepark La EX35. . . . . . . 151 E2
Comer's Cross TA24. . . . . . .21 E6
Comer's Gate TA24. . . . . . .21 E6
Comers La EX34 . . . . 3 B3
Comilla Cl EX8 . . . . 196 C3
Commanders Cut TQ6. . . 233 E4
Commercial Ope PL4 . . . . 263 B2
Commercial Pl PL4 . . . . . . 263 B1
Commercial Rd
Barnstaple EX31 . . . . 154 F5
Calstock PL18 . . . . 125 D3
Crediton EX17 . . . . 165 C5
8 Dawlish EX7 . . . . 204 E6
Exeter EX2. . . . . 261 A2
Horrabridge PL20 . . . . 126 F4
Paignton TQ4 . . . . 226 B6
Plymouth PL4. . . . . 263 B2
Uffculme EX15. . . . . .66 A7
Commercial St
Gunnislake PL18 . . . . 125 D6
Plymouth PL4. . . . . 263 B2
Commin's Rd EX1. . . . . 177 F7
Commodore Cl EX39 . . . . 156 E7
Common Head EX37 . . . . . .43 C3
Common Hill EX12. . . . . . 191 D4
Common La
Beer EX12 . . . . 191 D5
Huish Champflower TA4. . . .35 D7
Kingskerswell TQ12 . . . . . 212 E2
Milton Combe PL6 . . . . . . 241 B5
Seaton EX24 . . . . 192 B8
Commonmarsh La EX17. . 165 C5
Common Moors La EX36 158 A6
Commons Hill EX6. . . . . . 113 A4
Commons La TQ14. . . . . . 210 A2
Commons Mews EX36. . . 156 E7
Commons Old Rd
Shaldon TQ14. . . . . 210 A3
Shaldon TQ14. . . . . 210 A3
Community College The
EX18. . . . . .44 E1
Compass Dr PL7. . . . . 251 A7
Compass Quay EX2. . . . . . 261 B1
Compass South TQ1 . . . . 221 A3
Compton Ave PL3. . . . . . . 249 A5
Compton Castle TQ3 . . . . 218 C6
Compton CE Prim Sch
PL3. . . . . 249 A6
Compton Ho TQ1 . . . . 220 C7
Compton Knoll Cl PL3 . . 249 A6
Compton Leigh PL3. . . . . 249 A6
Compton Park Rd PL3 . . . 248 F5
Compton Pl TQ1 . . . . 214 B1
Compton Vale PL3 . . . . . . 249 A5
Comptonpool Cross TQ3 218 C8
Compton Rd TQ7 . . . . 144 C1
Compton Vale PL3 . . . . . . 249 A5
Concorde Dr TQ2 . . . . 155 C5
Concorde Rd EX8 . . . . 196 F1
Condor Dr TQ2 . . . . 213 D2
Conduit Sq **11** TQ13. . . . 123 E6
Coney Ave EX24 . . . . 155 B3
Coney Ct EX2. . . . . 261 A1
Coneypark La EX34 . . . . . . .3 A3
Congella Rd TQ1. . . . . 220 C6
Congram's Cl **7** EX32. . . 155 B3
Congreve Gdns PL5. . . . . . 244 C1
Conifer Cl EX15. . . . . 163 C5
Conifer Mews EX2 . . . . . . 178 D3
Conifers The
Bovey Tracey TQ13. . . . . . 180 C4
Torquay TQ2 . . . . 214 B3
Conigar Cl EX15 . . . . .67 B8
Conigar La EX15. . . . . .67 A7
Coniger Cross EX8. . . . . . . 196 B7
Coniston Cl TQ5 . . . . 230 A2
Coniston Gdns PL6 . . . . . . 244 F4
Coniston Rd TQ12 . . . . . . 211 F8
Connaught Ave PL4 . . . . . 248 F4
Connaught Cl EX10 . . . . . 188 A4
Connaught La **10** PL4 . . . 248 E4
Connaught Rd EX10. . . . . 188 A4
Conniford La TQ12 . . . . . 211 D1
Connybear Cross TQ12 . . 213 B8
Connybear La TQ12 . . . . . 213 C7
Conqueror Dr PL5 . . . . . . 244 E1
Conrad Ave EX4 . . . . 178 B8
Conrad Rd PL5 . . . . 244 D1
Consort Cl PL3 . . . . 248 E7
Consort Ho PL5. . . . . 243 B2
Constable Cl PL5. . . . . 244 D3
Constance Pl PL1. . . . . 262 A3
Constantine Cl EX12 . . . . 191 F8
Constantine St **9** PL4. . . 263 A3
Constitution Hill EX32. . . 155 B4
Contour Hts TQ6. . . . . 234 A3
Convent Cl
Barnstaple EX32. . . . . 155 C2
Saltash PL12. . . . . 242 E3
Convent Fields EX10 . . . . 187 F4
Convent Lodge **3** EX10 210 B6
Convent Rd EX10 . . . . 187 F4
Conway Cres **2** TQ4 . . . . 226 A5
Conway Ct EX1 . . . . 261 C2
Conway Gdns PL2 . . . . 248 B7
Conway Ho **4** TQ3. . . . . . 226 A5
Conway Rd TQ4. . . . . 226 B5
Conybeare Cl EX4. . . . . . . 178 B7
Conybeare Dr EX39 . . . . . 156 C5
Conyngham Ct PL6 . . . . . 249 A8
Cooban Ct PL6 . . . . 249 A8
Cook Ct PL12 . . . . 242 B3
Cooke Dr TQ12 . . . . 211 E2
Cooks Cl
12 Ashburton TQ13 . . . . 131 A5
Kingsteignton TQ12. . . . . 207 F7
Cooks Cross EX36 . . . . . . 158 C3
Cooks La EX13 . . . . 104 B7
Cooksley Ct PL1 . . . . 263 A1
Cooks Mead DT7 . . . . 260 A6
Cookson's Rd EX16 . . . . . 201 A8
Cookworthy Cl TQ7 . . . . . 258 C6
Cookworthy Moor Forest Wlk
EX21 . . . . .73 B4
Cookworthy Rd
Kingsbridge TQ7 . . . . 258 C5
Plymouth PL2. . . . . 247 F6
Coombe Ave TQ14 . . . . . . 210 A5
Coombe Ball Hill
East Worlington EX17. . . . .61 C8
Witheridge EX16. . . . . .46 D1
Coombe Cl
Bovey Tracey TQ13. . . . . . 180 C2
Dartmouth TQ6 . . . . 233 F4
Goodleigh EX32. . . . . .17 B5
Honiton EX14. . . . . 166 C4
Coombe Cross
Bovey Tracey TQ13. . . . . . 180 C2
Christow EX6. . . . . 113 B2
Goodleigh EX32. . . . . .17 B4
Great Torrington EX38. . . 159 F8
Coombe Dean Sch PL9. . 256 A6
Coombe Down La PL8 . . . 140 F6
Coombe Dr PL12. . . . . 239 A2
Coombefield La EX13 . . . 167 D5
Coombehaven TQ9 . . . . . 226 C7
Coombe Hill EX14 . . . . . . .47 F1
Coombe House Cross
TQ9 . . . . 224 F2
Coombe House La TQ9 . . 225 A2
Coombe La
Axminster EX13 . . . . 167 C5
Bicklegh EX16. . . . . .63 C3
Bovey Tracey TQ13. . . . . . 180 F8
Cadbury EX5. . . . . .81 C7
Cargreen PL12 . . . . 239 A2
Cheriton Fitzpaine EX16,
EX17. . . . . .63 B3
Chulmleigh EX18. . . . . . . .44 E4
Plymouth PL5. . . . . 244 D7
Puddington EX16. . . . . . . .62 B6
Silverton EX5. . . . . .82 B7
Teignmouth TQ14 . . . . . . 210 A7
Coombe Mdw TQ13 . . . . 180 E7
Coombe Mdws TQ7 . . . . . 144 F1
Coombe Orch EX14 . . . . . 192 E6
Coombe Park Cl PL10. . . 253 A2
Coombe Park La PL5. . . . 244 A3
Coombe Park Rd TQ14 . . 210 A6
Coombe Pk
Cawsand PL10. . . . . 253 A2
Saltash PL12. . . . . 242 F2
Coombe Rd
Dartmouth TQ6 . . . . 233 F4
Paignton TQ3 . . . . 219 C1
Saltash PL12. . . . . 243 A2
Shaldon TQ14. . . . . 209 C5
Coombesend Rd
Kingsteignton TQ12 . . . . 207 F7
Coombesend Rd E TQ12. 208 A7
Coombeshead Coll TQ12 207 A4
Coombeshead Rd TQ12. . 206 F4
Coombe Shute TQ9 . . . . . 227 F7
Coombe St
Exeter EX1. . . . . 261 B2
Lyme Regis DT7 . . . . 260 E3
Coombes The **1** EX31. . . 154 A2
Coombe Terr EX12 . . . . . . 192 E6
Coombe The
Dartmouth TQ6 . . . . 233 F4
Galmpton TQ5 . . . . 229 B5
Coombe Vale EX10 . . . . . 100 D2
Coombe Vale Rd TQ14. . . 210 A5
Coombe View
Plymouth PL2. . . . . 247 F7
Teignmouth TQ14. . . . . . . 124 C1
Coombe Way
Bishopsteignton TQ14 . . 209 B8
Plymouth PL5. . . . . 243 F1
Coopers Cross EX37 . . . . . .44 C6
Cooper's Cross
Chawleigh EX18. . . . . .60 C6
Lydford EX20. . . . . 107 A3
Coopers Dr EX31 . . . . 154 B2
Coopers Hill EX19 . . . . . . .58 F3
Cooper St **11** EX39. . . . . 157 A2
Coot Hide EX16. . . . . .50 D1
Copland La TQ9 . . . . 223 A6
Copland Mdws TQ9. . . . . 223 B6
Copleston Rd PL6. . . . . . . 244 E5
Copley Cl TQ3 . . . . 225 F6
Copley Dr EX31 . . . . 154 D3
Coppard Mdws PL7. . . . . 250 B6
Copper Beech Way PL6 . 245 C7
Copper Castle EX14 . . . . 166 C6
Copper Cl EX39. . . . . .38 F8
Copperfield Cl EX8 . . . . . 196 E1
Copperfields PL20 . . . . . . 126 E5
Copper Pk PL6 . . . . 245 E7
Copperthorn Cross TQ9 . 222 D4
Copper Tree Cross TQ9 . 216 C5
Copperwood Cl TQ13. . . 130 F4
Copp Hill La EX9. . . . . 198 A2
Coppice Cl
Barnstaple EX32. . . . . 155 B3
Fremington EX31. . . . . . . 153 F6
Raymond's Hill EX13. . . . 104 B7
Coppice Gate EX32 . . . . . 155 C3
Coppice Gdns PL5. . . . . . . 244 E2
Coppice La EX17. . . . . .80 A7
Coppice The
Dawlish EX7. . . . . 204 D4
Ivybridge PL21. . . . . 237 A4
Coppice Wood Dr PL6 . . 245 C7
Coppledown Gdns EX9. . 197 F2
Copplestone Dr EX4 . . . . 173 A1
Copplestone Prim Sch
EX17. . . . . .79 B5
Copplestone Rd EX9 . . . . 198 A1
Copplestone Sta EX17. . . .79 A6
Copp Path EX7 . . . . 204 C5
Copp's Cl EX39 . . . . 157 A3
Copse Cl PL7. . . . . 250 D4
Copse Hill La EX20. . . . . . .77 B7
Copse Pl PL7 . . . . 250 D4
Copse The
Barnstaple EX31 . . . . 154 B3
Chillington TQ7 . . . . 145 A1
Exeter EX2. . . . . 182 C7
Exmouth EX8 . . . . 196 E2
Newton Poppleford EX10 .186 F8
Okehampton EX20. . . . . . 170 D6
Totnes TQ9. . . . . 222 E6
Copsey La TQ12. . . . . 211 B6
Copstone EX39 . . . . .39 E7
Copstone Hill EX17 . . . . . .61 D5
Copthorne Gdns PL9 . . . . 255 F5
Copydown La EX5 . . . . . . .82 D6
Copythorne Cl TQ5. . . . . 230 A4
Copythorne Pk TQ5 . . . . 230 A4
Copythorne Rd TQ5 . . . . 230 A4
Coral Ave EX39 . . . . 156 D7
Coram Ave DT7 . . . . 260 D2
Coram Ct DT7. . . . . 260 D3
Coram Manor DT7 . . . . . . 260 D3
Corams La TA21 . . . . 160 D6
Cordery Rd EX2. . . . . 176 F3
Corea Terr PL1. . . . . 248 A2
Core Fields EX10 . . . . 188 B8
Core Hill Rd EX10. . . . . . . 100 F1
Coreway EX10 . . . . 188 B8
Corfe Cl PL21. . . . . 237 D4
Corfe Ave PL3 . . . . 248 F8
Corfe Cres TQ2 . . . . 213 F1
Corilhead Rd EX33 . . . . . 152 D8
Coringdean Cl PL6. . . . . . 245 B6
Coriolis Way N EX1 . . . . . 178 D7
Cormelles Ct **3** EX34 . . . . 3 A3
Cormorant Cl TQ2 . . . . . 213 D3
Cornacre Cl TQ2 . . . . 219 C7
Cornacre Rd TQ2 . . . . 219 C7
Cornborough Rd EX39 . . 156 B6
Cornbrook Rd EX14 . . . . . 65 A7
Corner Brake PL6. . . . . 245 D7
Corner TA21 . . . . 160 D4
Corner Cotts EX14. . . . . . .65 A7
Corner La
Combe Martin EX34. . . . . .3 B3
Halberton EX16. . . . . .65 A7
Cornermoor Cross EX16. .47 C1
Cornerstone Ct PL11. . . . 247 B3
Cornfield Gdns PL7. . . . . 251 B7
Cornfield La TQ12 . . . . . . 214 B2
Cornflower Cl
4 Barnstaple EX31 . . . . 154 B3
Willand EX15. . . . . 162 E5
Cornflower Hill EX4. . . . . 176 D8
Cornhill
Hemyock EX15. . . . . .67 B8
Ottery St Mary EX11. . . . 169 D4
5 Wellington TA21 . . . . . 160 D6
Cornlands EX10. . . . . .50 D1
Cornmarket St EX38 . . . . 159 D5
Corn Mill Cres EX2 . . . . . 177 A1
Corn Park Rd TQ12 . . . . . 212 A6
Corn Pk TQ10 . . . . 134 F2
Cornridge View EX20. . . . .93 C2
Corntown Cross PL21. . . 133 C1
Cornwall Beach PL1 . . . . 247 D2
Cornwall Coll Saltash
PL12. . . . . 242 D2
Cornwall St
Bere Alston PL20. . . . . . . 125 E1
8 Exeter EX4 . . . . 177 A5
Plymouth, Morice Town
PL1. . . . . 247 D2
Plymouth PL1. . . . . 262 C3
Cornwood CE Prim Sch
PL21. . . . . 133 C2
Cornwood Rd
Ivybridge PL21. . . . . 237 A5
Plymouth PL7. . . . . 251 B4
Cornworthy Cl PL2. . . . . . 248 A7
Cornworthy Cross TQ9 . . 227 A4
Coronation Ave EX7. . . . . 204 D5
Coronation Cres EX15. . . .66 A7
Coronation Pl
Plymouth PL1. . . . . 247 E8
Shebbear EX21. . . . . .55 E4
Coronation Rd
Bideford EX39 . . . . 156 F1
Exeter EX2. . . . . 178 A4
Kingsbridge TQ7 . . . . 258 D5
Kingsteignton TQ12. . . . . 207 E7
1 Newton Abbot TQ12. 207 B3
Salcombe TQ8 . . . . 259 D5
Coronation Rd continued
1 Teignmouth TQ14 . . . . 210 A3
Totnes TQ9. . . . . 223 D6
Coronation St EX32 . . . . 154 F6
Coronation Terr
Abbotsham EX39. . . . . . . 156 A2
1 Ilfracombe EX34 . . . . 150 C6
Starcross EX6. . . . . 201 B8
Coronation Villas EX12 . 191 D6
Coronella Rd PL2. . . . . . . 248 B7
Coronet Cl EX2 . . . . 178 D3
Corporation Cres **14**
EX32. . . . . 155 B3
Corporation Rd PL2. . . . . 248 D7
Corporation St **12** EX32. 155 B3
Corporation Terr **13**
EX32. . . . . 155 B3
Corry Ho TQ1. . . . . 220 E5
Corscombe La EX20. . . . . .94 E6
Corsham Cl PL6 . . . . 245 B6
Corsham Rd TQ4. . . . . . . 226 A5
Corstone Cross EX19. . . . .76 D7
Cory Ct PL9 . . . . 140 E8
Coryton Cl EX7. . . . . 204 E6
Coryton La EX13 . . . . .87 C1
Cosdon Pl PL6. . . . . 244 F1
Cosgates Feet or County
Gate EX35. . . . . .4 D6
Cossick Cross TQ13 . . . . . 112 B5
Costly St PL21 . . . . 237 D5
Cosway Rd EX16 . . . . 161 D5
Cotehele Ave
Plymouth, Keyham PL2 . . 247 F5
Plymouth, Prince Rock PL4 263 C2
Cotehele Dr TQ3 . . . . 225 D7
Cotehele Ho PL12. . . . . . . 125 C3
Cotehele Quay Mus
PL12. . . . . 125 C3
Cotehele View PL18 . . . . 125 D3
Coteland La EX32. . . . . . . .18 F1
Coteland Lane End EX32 .18 F1
Cotfield Cl EX14 . . . . 166 D7
Cotfield St EX2 . . . . 177 C3
Cotford Cl EX10 . . . . 101 C3
Cotford Rd EX10. . . . . 101 C3
Cot Green Cross EX14 . . . .85 B5
Cothay La EX37. . . . . .29 C1
Cothay Manor Gardens
TA21. . . . . .51 C8
Cot Hill PL7 . . . . 250 B5
Cot Hill Trad Est PL7. . . . 250 B6
Cot La EX5. . . . . .82 C8
Cotlands EX10 . . . . 187 F3
Cotleigh Cross EX14 . . . . .86 C5
Cotleigh Crossing EX14 . .68 C1
Cotley La EX6 . . . . 113 C8
Cot Manor **6** EX32 . . . . 155 B3
Cotmaton Rd EX10. . . . . . 187 F3
Cotmore Cl
Brixham TQ5 . . . . 230 A2
Chillington TQ7 . . . . 145 A1
Cotmore Way TQ7 . . . . . . 145 A1
Cotswold Cl TQ2 . . . . 219 D3
Cottage Cl EX33 . . . . .8 D1
Cottage Cross
Ashburton TQ13. . . . . 131 B5
Cheriton Bishop EX6. . . . .97 B4
Cottage Homes EX36. . . 158 D4
Cottage La TA22 . . . . .33 D6
Cottage Mews PL7. . . . . . 250 E4
Cottages The TQ7 . . . . . . 142 F2
Cott Cross
Ash Mill EX36. . . . . .31 C2
Chawleigh EX18. . . . . .59 E6
Dartington TQ9 . . . . 222 F8
Cottey Brook EX16. . . . . . 161 B4
Cottey Cres EX16 . . . . 174 A2
Cottey Mdw TQ7 . . . . 207 E6
Cott Hill EX31 . . . . .10 D1
Cottingham Cres EX39. . 156 F3
Cottington Ct EX10 . . . . 188 A4
Cottington Mead
Sidmouth, Lower Woolbrook
EX10. . . . . 188 B6
Sidmouth, Weston Town
EX10. . . . . 188 A4
Cottisbourne TQ13. . . . . 111 A6
Cott La
Croyde EX33. . . . . .7 E1
Petrockstow EX20. . . . . . . .56 F4
Cott Pk EX5 . . . . 184 C4
Cott Rd TQ9 . . . . 222 F8
Cotts Cotts EX16. . . . . . . .26 D1
Cotthayne La EX24. . . . . . 102 E5
Cottishill Dr EX12 . . . . . . 191 F8
Cotuhill EX12. . . . . 191 F8
Coulsdon Rd EX10. . . . . . 188 B6
Coulson Cross EX20. . . . . .76 F8
Coulsworthy Crook EX34. .3 D2
Coulsworthy La EX34. . . . .3 E2
Council Chambers **2**
EX39. . . . . 198 A1
Council Hos
Brixton PL8 . . . . 257 B5
Clyst St Mary EX5 . . . . . . 179 A3
Council Hos The EX5. . . . 179 E7
Council Houses The
TQ7 . . . . 149 D7
Council La EX5 . . . . 175 E4
Countessmead EX16. . . . 161 F8
Countess Pl EX16. . . . . . . 161 F8
Countess Wear Ho EX2. . 182 A8
Countess Wear Prim Sch
EX2. . . . . 182 B8
Countess Wear Rd EX2. . 182 A8
Counties Cres EX6. . . . . . 201 B7
Countisbury Hill EX35. . . 151 E5
Country Ho **8** EX10. . . . 101 B1
County Cl PL7. . . . . 251 A5
Couper Mdws EX2 . . . . . . 178 D3
Coursebeer La EX20 . . . . .95 E5
Court Barton Cross EX14. .84 E3
Court Barton TQ7 . . . . . . 147 D8
Court Barton Cotts
Coffinswell TQ12 . . . . 213 C6
Down Thomas PL9 . . . . . . 255 C1
Court Barton Hill EX12 . 191 D6
Court Barton La EX5 . . . . 172 A8
Court Barton Mews PL19 116 F4
Court Dr
Cullompton EX15. . . . . . . 163 C5
Wellington TA21. . . . . 160 D5
Courtenay EX14. . . . . 166 A5
Courtenay Cl
2 Colyton EX24 . . . . . . 103 A4
Starcross EX6. . . . . 201 B8
Courtenay Cotts EX16. . . .48 F2
Courtenay Dr **24** EX24. . 103 A4
Courtenay Gdns
Exeter EX2. . . . . 181 A8
Newton Abbot TQ12. . . . . 207 C2
Courtenay Manor TQ1. . 220 C4
Courtenay Park Rd TQ12 207 D3
Courtenay Pk TQ1 . . . . . . 135 A3
Courtenay Pl **17** TQ14 . . 210 C4
Courtenay Rd
Exeter EX2. . . . . 177 B3
Newton Abbot TQ12. . . . . 207 C2
Okehampton EX20. . . . . . 170 C4
Paignton TQ4 . . . . 226 C2
Courtenay St
Newton Abbot TQ12. . . . . 207 B3
Plymouth PL1. . . . . 262 C3
Salcombe TQ8 . . . . 259 D5
Courtenay Terr EX6 . . . . 201 B8
Court Farm Barns PL21 . 212 B6
Courtfield TQ9 . . . . 223 F5
Courtfield Cl EX11 . . . . . 168 D5
Courtfield Rd PL3 . . . . .62 A1
Courtfield Rd PL3. . . . . . . 248 F5
Court Fields Com Sch
TA21. . . . . 160 C5
Court Gate Cl TQ12 . . . . 211 C1
Court Gn TQ7. . . . . 258 E6
Court Grange TQ12 . . . . . 212 B6
Courthayes La EX5. . . . . . .81 F5
Courtis Gdns EX17. . . . . . 165 D5
Court La
Morebath EX16. . . . . .34 D4
Seaton EX24 . . . . 192 A6
Courtlage Wlk TQ7 . . . . . 258 C6
Courtland Cres PL7. . . . . . 250 D7
Courtland Cross TQ12 . . 211 A4
Courtland Rd
Paignton TQ3 . . . . 226 B7
Torquay TQ2 . . . . 219 B7
Wellington TA21. . . . . 160 D6
Courtlands PL12 . . . . 242 E1
Courtlands Cross EX8 . . . 196 A3
Courtlands La EX8 . . . . . . 195 F3
Courtlands Rd
Newton Abbot TQ12. . . . . 207 D2
Tavistock PL19 . . . . 171 B6
Courtlands Sch PL6. . . . . 244 F1
Court Moors La TA21. . . . .51 E5
Courtney Ho PL5 . . . . 244 B2
Courtney Rd EX16 . . . . . . 161 C5
Court Park Rd TQ7. . . . . . 143 A1
Court Pk TQ7 . . . . 143 A2
Court Rd
Abbotskerswell TQ12. . . . 212 B6
Newton Ferrers PL8 . . . . . 140 F7
Torquay TQ2 . . . . 219 C5
Court St TQ13 . . . . 111 F4
Court Terr TA21 . . . . 160 C5
Court The
Dunsford EX6. . . . . 112 F8
Plymouth PL6. . . . . 245 C7
Saltash PL12. . . . . 242 C2
Court View PL8 . . . . 256 F4
Court Wik EX16. . . . . .58 D1
Court Wlk EX19 . . . . .58 F3
Court Wood PL8 . . . . 140 E7
Courtyard Cotts PL21 . . . .36 C3
Cousens Ct EX7 . . . . 204 F8
Cousin's Cross TQ7 . . . . . 149 A6
Cove Hill EX16. . . . . .49 C6
Cove Mdw PL11. . . . . 247 A6
Coventry Cl EX14. . . . . . . .84 D2
Coventry Farm Est TQ12. 213 B2
Coventry Rd EX4 . . . . 176 F6
Coverdale Pl PL5 . . . . 244 C1
Coverdale Rd
Exeter EX2. . . . . 177 B3
Paignton TQ3 . . . . 226 B6
Cow Down Rd TA20. . . . . .88 F8
Cowdray Ct PL12. . . . . . . 242 E2
Cowdray Terr PL12. . . . . . 242 E2
Cowflop Cross EX18 . . . . .43 A1
Cowick Hill EX2 . . . . 176 F3
Cowick La EX2 . . . . 176 F3
Cowick Rd EX2 . . . . 177 A3
Cowick St EX4. . . . . 177 A4
Cow La EX34 . . . . 150 B5

Cowley Bridge Rd Bsns Pk
EX4 . . . . .173 A1
Cowley Hill EX5 . . . . .172 F4
Cowley Moor Rd EX16 . .161 E5
Cowley Pl EX5 . . . . .172 F5
Cowley Rd PL5 . . . . .244 D3
Cowley Wood Head EX31 . . .4 A2
Cowley Wood Rd EX31 . . . .4 A2
Cownhayne La EX24 . . . .103 B4
Cowpark Terr **1** EX39 . .156 F7
Cowper Ave EX2 . . . . . . .177 F3
Coxhill Cross TQ11 . . . . .236 A3
Coxley La PL13 . . . . .102 F7
Coxmoor Cross EX17 . . . .78 A1
Coxmoor La EX17 . . . . . . .78 A2
Cox Rd TA21 . . . . .160 C4
Cox's Cl PL6 . . . . .245 B1
Cox Mdw EX22 . . . . .89 F7
Cox Tor Cl **6** PL20 . . . .126 F3
Cox Tor Rd PL19 . . . . . . .171 E5
Coypool Rd PL7 . . . . .250 A6
Coysh Sq EX3 . . . . .182 E5
Crabadon Cross TQ9 . . . .138 F5
Crabbers Cross TQ10 . . .135 D4
Crabb La EX2 . . . . .177 A2
Crabbs Cl PL15 . . . . .90 C1
Crabshell Quay TQ7 . . . .258 D4
Crabtree Cl PL3 . . . . .249 E5
Crabtree Villas PL3 . . . . .249 E5
Crackaway La EX4 . . . . .9 A4
Crackston Cl PL7 . . . . . . .250 A5
Cradlemans Cross EX32 . .155 E1
Craig Ct EX10 . . . . .188 C4
Craigie Dr PL1 . . . . .262 A3
Craigmore Ave PL2 . . . . .247 F5
Cramber Cl
Roborough PL6 . . . . . . .245 C8
Tavistock PL19 . . . . . . .171 A4
Crammer Ash Cross EX15 . .84 C8
Crammers Cross TQ13 . .123 F7
Crampit La EX39 . . . . . . .157 E5
Cramp La EX36 . . . . .31 E6
Cranapool Cross EX22 . . . .54 E3
Cranbourne Ave PL4 . . . .263 C4
Cranbrook Rd EX2 . . . . . .178 A5
Cranford Cl EX20 . . . . . . .107 F8
Crandons Cross EX14 . . . .87 B6
Cranes La EX9 . . . . .198 B6
Cranfield PL7 . . . . .250 C7
Cranford Ave EX8 . . . . . .202 D6
Cranford Cl EX8 . . . . . . .202 C6
Cranford Cross
Great Torrington EX38 . . . .42 C8
Woolfardisworthy EX39 . . .39 A8
Cranford Ho EX8 . . . . . . .202 C6
Cranford Rd TQ3 . . . . . . .219 A1
Cranford View EX8 . . . . .202 C6
Cranishaies La EX5 . . . . . .83 B7
Cranleigh **2** EX32 . . . .154 F6
Cranleigh Terr **2** EX34 . . .3 A3
Cranley Gdns TQ13 . . . . .111 A6
Cranmere Ct EX2 . . . . . . .181 C8
Cranmere Rd
Okehampton EX20 . . . . .170 E6
Plymouth PL3 . . . . .249 A6
Cranmore View EX16 . . .161 B1
Crannafords Ind Pk
TQ13 . . . . .111 B7
Crantock Terr **7** PL2 . .248 A5
Craon Gdns EX20 . . . . . .170 D6
Crapstone Terr PL20 . . . .126 E2
Crashaw Cl PL5 . . . . .244 D3
Craven Ave PL4 . . . . .263 C4
Crawford Gdns EX2 . . . . .177 A3
Crawford Rd PL1 . . . . . . .262 A4
CRC Units EX2 . . . . .177 D1
Creacombe Barton Cross
EX16 . . . . .46 F6
Creacombemoor Cross
EX16 . . . . .47 A6
Creacombe Parsonage Cross
EX16 . . . . .47 A5
Crealy Adventure Pk EX5 . .99 A1
Creamery Cl PL8 . . . . . . .136 A2
Crease La PL19 . . . . .171 A4
Crediton Cross EX17 . . . . .62 D3
Crediton Hospl EX17 . . . .165 A6
Crediton La EX6 . . . . .97 C5
Crediton Lane End EX6 . . .97 C4
Crediton Rd
Okehampton EX20 . . . . .170 C5
Okehampton EX20 . . . . .170 D6
Crediton Sta EX17 . . . . . .165 E3
Crediton Wlk PL6 . . . . . . .249 E8
Creedy Bridge EX17 . . . . .165 F7
Creedy Cross EX17 . . . . . .62 A2
Creedy Rd
Crediton EX17 . . . . .165 D5
Plymouth PL3 . . . . .249 C5
Creedy View EX5 . . . . .80 F2
Creek Cross TQ13 . . . . . .131 B5
Creek End TQ7 . . . . .148 F4
Creek Rd TQ6 . . . . .233 D4
Creely Cl EX2 . . . . .181 C8
Crelake Cl PL19 . . . . .171 C4
Crelake Ind Est **1** PL19 .171 B4
Crelake Pk PL19 . . . . . . .171 C4
Cremyll Rd PL11 . . . . . . .247 B2
Cremyll St PL1 . . . . .254 A8
Crescent Ave
Barnstaple EX31 . . . . . .154 D3
Plymouth PL1 . . . . .262 B2
Crescent Ct TQ6 . . . . . . .233 D4
Crescent Gdns PL21 . . . .237 C6

Crescent Mansions Flats
EX2 . . . . .261 C2
Crescent Rd PL21 . . . . . .237 C6
Crescent The
Brixton PL8 . . . . .257 A5
Crapstone PL20 . . . . . . .126 E3
Exmouth EX8 . . . . .202 E8
Gunnislake PL18 . . . . . .125 D6
Kilmington EX13 . . . . . . .87 C1
Langtree EX38 . . . . .40 E2
Lifton PL16 . . . . .105 E4
Pathfinder Village EX6 . . .98 B4
Plymouth PL1 . . . . .262 B2
Cresents Gdns PL21 . . . .237 C6
Cressbrook Cl PL6 . . . . .245 F2
Cressbrook Dr PL6 . . . . .245 F2
Cressbrook Wlk PL6 . . . .245 E2
Cresswell Cl TQ12 . . . . . .213 A5
Crest Hill TQ11 . . . . .236 B5
Cresthill Rd PL2 . . . . .248 B7
Crestway TQ6 . . . . .145 E5
Crewkerne Rd EX13 . . . .104 C7
Crewkerne Turning EX13 . .88 C6
Creykes Ct PL1 . . . . .262 A3
Cricket Cl EX18 . . . . .44 F1
Cricket Pk EX23 . . . . .70 A6
Cricketers St EX13 . . . . .167 D7
Cricketfield Cl TQ13 . . . .123 F6
Cricket Field Cir EX9 . . . .198 A1
Cricket Field La EX9 . . . .198 A1
Cricketfield Rd TQ1, TQ2 .219 F7
Cricket Field Rd **9**
TQ12 . . . . .207 C3
Cricket La TQ11 . . . . .236 A6
Cridlake EX13 . . . . .167 E5
Crimps Cross TQ7 . . . . . .258 C5
Crispin Rd TQ7 . . . . .258 C5
Critchards EX5 . . . . .184 C2
Criterion Pl **14** EX8 . . .202 A6
Crocadon Mdws TQ9 . . . .139 B4
Crockaton Cotts TQ13 . . .130 F5
Crocken Tor Rd EX20 . . . .170 D5
Crockernwell Ct EX6 . . . . .96 F3
Crocker's Row PL18 . . . . .125 D6
Crockers Way PL15 . . . . . .90 C1
Crockwells Cl EX6 . . . . . .182 B3
Crockwells Rd EX6 . . . . . .182 B4
Croft Chase EX4 . . . . . . .176 E4
Croft Cl EX12 . . . . .206 D1
Croft Cotts TQ12 . . . . . . .211 D2
Croft Ct TQ2 . . . . .220 A5
Croft Ho EX22 . . . . .220 A5
Croft Orch TQ12 . . . . . . .211 D2
Croft Pk PL6 . . . . .245 C7
Croft Rd
East Ogwell TQ12 . . . . .206 D1
Holsworthy EX22 . . . . . .164 C4
Ipplepen TQ12 . . . . . . .211 D2
Salcombe TQ8 . . . . .259 D5
Torquay TQ2 . . . . .220 A5
Croft's Est EX17 . . . . .80 A5
Croftside **5** EX34 . . . .150 B5
Crofts Lea EX34 . . . . .2 E3
Crofts Lea Pk EX34 . . . . .150 D5
Croftswood EX34 . . . . . .150 D5
Croftswood Gdns EX34 . .150 D4
Croft The EX20 . . . . .95 A4
Croft View Terr TQ8 . . . . .259 E5
Crogg La DT7 . . . . .260 B5
Croker's Mdw TQ13 . . . . .180 C8
Crokers Way TQ12 . . . . . .211 D2
Cromartie Point Flats
TQ2 . . . . .219 E2
Cromartie Rd PL4 . . . . . .249 B1
Cromer Cl PL6 . . . . .245 A7
Cromer Wlk PL6 . . . . . . .245 A7
Cromlech Ho EX38 . . . . .159 B5
Cromwell Cotts TQ12 . . . .131 F7
Cromwell Ct EX1 . . . . . . .178 A5
Cromwell Gate PL6 . . . . .245 C7
Cromwell Pk
Modbury PL21 . . . . .137 B3
Tiverton EX16 . . . . .161 E6
Cromwell Rd PL4 . . . . . . .263 C3
Cromwells Mdw EX17 . . .165 A6
Cromwells Way TQ13 . . .180 C8
Cromwell Terr **7** EX2 . .178 D5
Crookeder Cl PL9 . . . . . . .256 A5
Crooked Oaks EX36 . . . . .30 C1
Crooke La EX20 . . . . .77 E3
Crooklake Hill EX5 . . . . . .98 E8
Crookmans Cnr EX32 . . . .15 A4
Croscombe La EX35 . . . . . .4 E4
Cross Cl EX31 . . . . .153 D5
Crosscut Way EX14 . . . . .166 C5
Cross Farm Ct **6** EX32 . .16 E1
Cross Furzes TQ11 . . . . .181 A8
Crossgate EX18 . . . . .59 C7
Cross Gate EX22 . . . . .18 F6
Crossgates PL7 . . . . .132 C6
Cross Gn PL15 . . . . .105 A2
Crossgrange Trad Est
TQ12 . . . . .180 F3
Cross Hill
Combeinteignhead TQ12 .208 D3
Crediton EX17 . . . . .79 E5
East Village EX17 . . . . . .80 C8
Plymouth PL2 . . . . .247 E4
Cross Hill Cross EX17 . . . .80 C8

Crosshill La EX6 . . . . .97 A5
Crossing Cross TQ9 . . . . .222 F7
Crossingfields Dr EX8 . . .196 A1
Crossings Cl PL19 . . . . . .117 E6
Cross-in-Hand PL21 . . . .237 F5
Cross La
Berrynarbor EX34 . . . . . .2 E3
Brendon EX35 . . . . .6 A4
East Portlemouth TQ8 . . .259 F4
Crossland La EX14 . . . . . .68 C2
Crosslands
Barnstaple EX31 . . . . . .154 C4
Thurlestone TQ7 . . . . . .143 A1
Wellington TA21 . . . . . . .160 B8
Cross Lane Cross EX36 . . .19 D1
Cross Lanes
Ashprington TQ9 . . . . . .139 F8
Ashwater EX21 . . . . .90 F6
South Pool TQ7 . . . . . . .148 F6
Crossley Cl TQ12 . . . . . . .207 E2
Crossley Moor Rd TQ12 . .207 E7
Cross Mdw EX17 . . . . .96 A7
Cross Mdws EX31 . . . . . .154 A2
Crossmead EX5 . . . . .151 B5
Crossmoor Cross EX16 . . .47 E1
Cross Moor La EX36 . . . . .31 E2
Crosspark Ave TQ2 . . . . .219 C8
Cross Park Ave PL6 . . . . .244 F1
Cross Park Cl EX31 . . . . .154 E7
Crosspark Cross EX31 . . . .17 A7
Crosspark Cross
Bradworthy EX22 . . . . . .38 E1
Holsworthy EX22 . . . . . .164 E5
Crosspark Hill EX16 . . . . .48 C8
Cross Park Way
Plymouth PL6 . . . . .244 F1
Wembury PL9 . . . . .140 D8
Crossparks
Dartmouth TQ6 . . . . . . .233 D3
Tiverton EX16 . . . . .64 F6
Cross Parks
Cullompton EX15 . . . . . .163 A2
High Bickington EX37 . . . .43 C7
Cross Park Way PL6 . . . . .244 F1
Cross Pk
Berrynarbor EX34 . . . . . . .2 E3
Brixham TQ5 . . . . .230 B3
Brixton PL8 . . . . .257 B5
Buckland Monachorum
PL20 . . . . .126 D3
Combeinteignhead TQ12 .208 D4
Ilfracombe EX34 . . . . . .150 B6
South Zeal EX20 . . . . . . .95 A4
Totnes TQ9 . . . . .223 E6
Cross Side Hill EX36 . . . . .31 F2
Cross St
Barnstaple EX31 . . . . . .154 F5
Combe Martin EX34 . . . . .2 F4
Lynton EX35 . . . . .151 B5
Moretonhampstead TQ13 .111 F5
Northam EX39 . . . . .157 A7
Seaton EX12 . . . . .192 A5
Cross Terr PL18 . . . . .125 C5
Cross The
Kilmington EX13 . . . . . . .87 D1
St Dominick PL12 . . . . .125 A2
Cross Tree EX9 . . . . .198 E2
Cross Tree Ctr **3** EX33 .152 D6
Cross View
Buckfastleigh TQ11 . . . .236 A2
Exeter EX2 . . . . .177 B1
Cross View Terr EX2 . . . .176 E2
Crosswater EX23 . . . . .36 F1
Crossway
Paignton TQ4 . . . . .226 C2
Plymouth PL7 . . . . .250 D7
Crossway Ave PL4 . . . . . .249 B3
Crossway Cross EX20 . . . .94 E6
Crossway Hill EX17 . . . . . .61 F2
Crossway Park Homes
TQ7 . . . . .258 A8
Crossways
Cornwood PL21 . . . . . . .133 C2
Milton Damerel EX22 . . . .54 E5
Paignton TQ4 . . . . .226 B6
Ringmore TQ7 . . . . .142 E4
Tatworth TA20 . . . . .88 D8
Whitestone EX4 . . . . .98 E4
Crossways Ct EX14 . . . . .166 C5
Crowbeare Mdw EX38 . . .159 E6
Crowborough Rd EX33 . . . .8 A2
Crow Bridge EX15 . . . . . .163 B3
Crowbridge Pk PL5 . . . . .163 B2
Crowden Cres EX16 . . . . .161 F3
Crowden Cross EX20 . . . . .74 D2
Crowden Rd EX20 . . . . . . .74 E2
Crowder Mdw TQ12 . . . . .135 A2
Crowder Pk TQ10 . . . . . . .135 A2
Crowder's Cross EX14 . . . .84 C3
Crowdhole Cross EX16 . . .46 F4
Crowdhole Hill EX16 . . . . .46 F4
Crow Gn EX15 . . . . .163 B3
Crow La EX16 . . . . .45 B8
Crown and Anchor Way **5**
TQ3 . . . . .226 B6
Crowndale Ave PL4 . . . . .249 A6
Crown Gdns PL4 . . . . . . .245 A1
Crown Hill
Halberton EX16 . . . . .64 F7
West Buckland TA21 . . . . .52 F7
Crownhill Cross PL21 . . . .137 B3
Crownhill Ct
Plymouth PL6 . . . . .244 F2
Crediton EX17 . . . . .219 E6
Crownhill Fort PL6 . . . . . . .63 F7
Crownhill Fort Rd PL6 . . .244 F3

Crownhill La EX5 . . . . .81 C5
Crownhill Pk TQ2 . . . . . . .219 E6
Crownhill Rd PL5 . . . . . . .244 C3
Crown Hill Rise TQ2 . . . . .219 E6
Crown Hill Terr **2** EX17 .165 C5
Crownley La PL12 . . . . . .242 F5
Crownley La TQ9 . . . . . . .227 F8
Crown Mews TA21 . . . . . .52 F7
Crown Sq EX17 . . . . .210 A3
Crown Way EX2 . . . . .178 D3
Crow Pk PL3 . . . . .248 F5
Crowther's Hill TQ6 . . . . .233 F3
Croyde Gem Rock & Shell
Mus EX33 . . . . .7 E2
Croyden Cross EX22 . . . . .55 A4
Croyde Rd EX33 . . . . .7 D1
Croyde Sands Bglws EX33 . .7 D2
Croydon Gdns PL5 . . . . . .243 E4
Croylands Ct EX8 . . . . . . .202 C6
Croyle Cross EX15 . . . . . .66 A4
Crozier Rd **1** PL4 . . . . .248 F4
Cruel Cross TQ7 . . . . .225 D8
Cruffen Cross EX33 . . . . . . .8 B1
Cruffen La EX33 . . . . .8 B1
Cruwys Morchard Hill
EX16 . . . . .63 A7
Cruwy's Morchard Mill La
EX16 . . . . .63 A7
Crystal Cl TQ4 . . . . .226 C2
Cuckoo Down La EX14 . . .166 E4
Cuckoo Hill EX14 . . . . . . .61 C3
Cuckoo La DT7 . . . . .260 A4
Cuckoo's La EX32 . . . . . . .28 C6
Cuddeford Cnr EX4 . . . . . .98 C6
Cuddenhay La EX17 . . . . .46 A2
Cuddyford Cross TQ13 . . .130 F5
Cudemoor Cross EX38 . . . .41 A1
Cudhill Rd TQ5 . . . . .230 B4
Cudmore Pk EX16 . . . . . . .64 D6
Cuffe Rd PL3 . . . . .248 C4
Culbin Gn PL6 . . . . .249 D7
Culdrose Cl PL5 . . . . .243 E4
Cullaford Cross EX17 . . . . .95 E8
Cullompton Com Coll
EX15 . . . . .163 C2
Cullompton Hill EX5 . . . . .83 A7
Culmbridge La EX15 . . . . .67 B7
Culm Cl
Exeter EX2 . . . . .178 D4
Torquay TQ2 . . . . .219 B8
Culm Cross EX20 . . . . . . .77 A4
Culme Rd PL3 . . . . .249 A5
Culme Way EX14 . . . . .67 C1
Culm Gr EX2 . . . . .178 D4
Culm Haven EX15 . . . . . . .66 A7
Culm Lea EX15 . . . . .163 E3
Culmstock Prim Sch EX15 .51 E1
Culmstock Rd EX15 . . . . .67 B8
Culm Valley Way EX15 . . .65 F7
Culver Cl
Bradninch EX5 . . . . .83 A6
Plymouth PL6 . . . . .249 A6
Tiverton EX16 . . . . .161 F3
Culver Ct PL12 . . . . .242 F2
Culverdale TQ9 . . . . .223 E4
Culver Gdns EX10 . . . . . .188 B4
Culver Ho **2** TQ13 . . . .123 E6
Culver La EX15 . . . . .37 F8
Culver Park Cl TQ8 . . . . .258 E3
Culver Rd PL12 . . . . .242 F2
Culvert Rd EX5 . . . . .81 F1
Culver Way PL6 . . . . .249 A6
Culverwood Cl PL7 . . . . . .251 C6
Culvery Cl EX5 . . . . .184 C3
Culvery Ct EX17 . . . . .165 C2
Culvery Gn TQ2 . . . . .219 B8
Cumber Cl
Brixham TQ5 . . . . .230 B5
Malborough TQ7 . . . . . .147 F6
Cumber Dr TQ5 . . . . .230 B5
Cumberland Cl EX8 . . . . .202 D8
Cumberland Gn TQ5 . . . .230 B5
Cumberland Rd PL1 . . . . .247 E2
Cumberland St PL1 . . . . .247 E2
Cumberauld TQ1 . . . . . . .220 D4
Cummings Cross TQ12 . . .180 C1
Cummings Ct TQ12 . . . . .180 C1
Cummins Cnr EX6 . . . . . . .97 E5
Cummins La EX14 . . . . . . .87 B6
Cundy Cl PL7 . . . . .250 A7
Cunliffe Ave PL9 . . . . . . .255 A6
Cunningham Ave EX13 . .167 F7
Cunningham Rd
Exmouth EX8 . . . . .196 D2
Plymouth PL5 . . . . .244 B6
Cunningham's La EX10 . .187 F3
Cunningham Way PL12 . .242 D3
Cuppers Piece Cross
EX19 . . . . .43 A1
Curium Ct **9** EX2 . . . . .192 B4
Curledge St TQ4 . . . . . . .226 B5
Curledge Street Prim Sch
TQ4 . . . . .226 B5
Curlew Cl EX20 . . . . .170 A6
Curlew Dr
Kingsbridge TQ7 . . . . . .258 F1
Torquay TQ2 . . . . .213 C6
Curlew Mews PL3 . . . . . .249 C4
Curlew Way EX4 . . . . . . .173 C2
Currington Mdw EX31 . . .154 A3
Curriton Hill EX17 . . . . . . .61 C5
Curriton La EX17 . . . . .61 B4

Curscombe Cross EX14 . . .84 F4
Curscombe La EX14 . . . . .84 F4
Cursons Way PL21 . . . . . .237 A5
Curtis Cross EX22 . . . . . . .54 B3
Curtis St PL1 . . . . .247 E1
Curve Acre EX33 . . . . . . .152 E5
Curwood Cres **2** EX16 . .161 C2
Cussacombe Cross EX36 . . .20 D1
Cussacombe Gate EX36 . . .20 E1
Custacon Ho **8** EX14 . .166 C6
Custom House Hill **4**
TQ14 . . . . .210 B4
Custom House La PL1 . . .262 B1
Custom La EX16 . . . . .64 B4
Cuthays La EX13 . . . . .88 B1
Cuthbert Cl TQ1 . . . . . . .214 A1
Cutland Cross EX18 . . . . . .44 C4
Cutliffe La EX39 . . . . .22 D3
Cutteridge La EX4 . . . . . .176 A6
Cut Tongue La TA20 . . . . .69 F7
Cutwell Cross TQ10 . . . . .134 E1
Cuxton Mdws PL20 . . . . .126 C3
Cygnet Cl EX2 . . . . .261 C1
Cygnet Units EX2 . . . . . .178 E5
Cypress Cl
12 Honiton EX14 . . . . . .85 C2
6 Plymouth PL7 . . . . .251 C5
Torquay TQ2 . . . . .220 A5
Cypress Dr EX4 . . . . .176 F7
Cyprus Rd EX4 . . . . .202 B6
Cyprus Terr EX32 . . . . . .155 B3

D

Dabby La EX6 . . . . .97 B4
Daccabridge Rd TQ12 . . .212 F4
Daccombe Cross TQ12 . . .213 E5
Daccombe Mill TQ2, TQ12 .213 E4
Daccombe Mill La TQ12 . .213 B4
Daddon Hill EX39 . . . . . .156 E6
Daddyhole Rd TQ1 . . . . . .220 E4
Daggeridge Plain EX16 . . .63 B4
Daggers Copse TQ12 . . . .206 A5
Dagmar Rd EX8 . . . . .202 A6
Dagmar St TQ12 . . . . . . .210 A3
Dagra La TQ13, TQ14 . . .209 B4
Daimonds La TQ14 . . . . .210 B5
Dainton Elms Cross
TQ12 . . . . .211 F2
Dainton Mews TQ4 . . . . .226 B5
Dairs Orch TA20 . . . . .88 C8
Dairy Cl EX6 . . . . .182 B3
Dairy Hill TQ7 . . . . .258 C4
Dairy La PL21 . . . . .237 D5
Daison Cotts TQ1 . . . . . . .220 A7
Daison Cres TQ1 . . . . . . .220 B8
Daisy Links EX4 . . . . .176 D8
Dalbury Cl TQ1 . . . . .207 C4
Daldtich La EX9 . . . . .197 D3
Dale Ave PL6 . . . . .249 C7
Dale Gdns PL4 . . . . .248 D4
Dale Rd PL4 . . . . .248 D4
Daleside Cl TQ1 . . . . .220 E4
Daleside Rd EX4 . . . . . . .173 C1
Daleswood Rd PL9 . . . . . .171 A4
Dalton Gdns PL5 . . . . . . .243 E3
Dalverton Ct TQ5 . . . . . . .230 D4
Dalwood La EX13 . . . . . . .87 B3
Dalwood Prim Sch EX13 . .87 A3
Dame Hannah Rogers' Sch
PL21 . . . . .237 B5
Damerel Cl PL1 . . . . .247 F2
Damson Cl EX15 . . . . . . .162 D4
Danby Heights Cl TQ1 . . .220 E4
Danby La EX8 . . . . .202 A7
Danby Terr EX8 . . . . .202 A7
Dandy La EX4 . . . . .174 D5
Dane Ct EX39 . . . . .157 A6
Danethorpe Bsns Pk
TQ12 . . . . .180 F3
Danes Cl EX14 . . . . .68 C2
Daneshay EX39 . . . . .157 A6
Danes Hill EX4, EX5 . . . . .82 C4
Daneshill Cross EX13 . . . .87 B3
Danes Mead EX15 . . . . . .163 C6
Danes' Rd EX4 . . . . .261 B4
Daneswáy EX4 . . . . .174 E2
Daniel's Grave EX16 . . . . .62 D4
Daniel's La
Broadhempston TQ9 . . . .131 C1
West Charleton TQ7 . . . .144 C1
Danum Dr PL7 . . . . .251 B3
Danvers Rd TQ2 . . . . . . .213 F2
Daphne Cl TQ12 . . . . . . .213 A1
D'arcy Ct TQ12 . . . . .207 C4
Dares Orch EX24 . . . . . . .103 A3
Darkey La
Lifton PL16 . . . . .105 E4
Okehampton EX20 . . . . .170 A5
Dark La
Barnstaple EX31 . . . . . .154 F7
Budleigh Salterton EX9 . .197 F1
Hockworthy EX16 . . . . . .50 B8
Modbury PL21 . . . . .137 B3
Northlew EX20 . . . . .74 D2
Sidmouth EX10 . . . . . . .187 F6
Thorverton EX5 . . . . .81 E5
Wellington TA21 . . . . . . .160 D5
Darklake Cl PL6 . . . . .245 E5
Darklake La PL6 . . . . .245 E5
Darklake View PL6 . . . . . .245 E5
Dark Street La PL7 . . . . . .250 E4

Darky La
Chulmleigh EX18 . . . . .59 E8
Kingsbridge TQ7 . . . . 258 C7
Darlick Cnr EX36 . . . . .20 C4
Darnell Cl EX10 . . . . .188 B6
Darracott Cross EX38 . . . . . .41 E8
Darracott Hill EX39 . . . . . .37 B4
Darran Cl TQ12 . . . . .207 F7
Darran Rd TQ12 . . . . .207 F7
Dart Ave TQ2 . . . . .219 C2
Dartbridge Cross TQ11 . . .236 C6
Dartbridge Manor TQ11 . .236 C6
Dart Bridge Rd TQ11 . . . . .236 C5
Dart Bsns Ctr TQ9 . . . . . . .215 F1
Dart Cl
Braunton EX31. . . . . .15 E5
Plymouth PL3 . . . . .249 D7
St Giles on t H PL15 . . . . . .90 C1
Dart Hill EX16 . . . . .46 D2
Dartington CE Prim Sch
TQ9 . . . . .215 F1
Dartington Cider Press Ctr
TQ9 . . . . .215 F1
Dartington Cl EX38 . . . . . . .159 E6
Dartington Coll of Arts
TQ9 . . . . .216 B2
Dartington Crystal Glass
Factory EX38. . . . . .159 C5
Dartington Fields EX38 . . .159 E6
Dartington Hall TQ9 . . . . . .216 B2
Dartington La TQ9 . . . . . . .223 B7
Dartington Wlk
Exminster EX6. . . . . .181 F5
Plymouth PL6. . . . . .249 E8
Dartmeet PL20. . . . . .129 D8
Dartmeet Ave PL3 . . . . .249 B6
Dartmoor Cotts PL7. . . . . .132 D4
Dartmoor Ct TQ13 . . . . . . .180 C5
Dartmoor Prison Mus
PL20. . . . . .119 A1
Dartmoor's Miniature Pony &
Animal Farm TQ13. . . . . .111 B3
Dartmoor View
Chulmleigh EX18 . . . . .44 E1
Plymouth PL4. . . . . .249 C3
Saltash PL12 . . . . .242 E4
Woolfardisworthy EX17. . . .61 E4
Dartmoor Wildlife Pk
PL7. . . . . .133 A1
Dartmouth Castle TQ6 . . . .234 B1
Dartmouth Com Coll
TQ6 . . . . .233 D2
Dartmouth Hill TQ6 . . . . . .146 B7
Dartmouth & Kingswear
Hospl TQ6. . . . . .233 F3
Dartmouth Mus TQ6 . . . . . .233 F3
Dartmouth Prim Sch
TQ6 . . . . .233 D2
Dartmouth Rd
East Allington TQ9 . . . . . .144 E7
Paignton TQ4, TQ5 . . . . . .226 C3
Stoke Fleming TQ6 . . . . . .146 B8
Dartmouth Wlk PL6. . . . . . .249 E8
Darton Gr TQ9 . . . . .227 F7
Dart Pk EX36 . . . . .158 D4
Dartridge La EX18 . . . . . . .44 D1
Dartside TQ9 . . . . .223 B7
Dart View TQ6 . . . . .228 C3
Dart View Rd TQ5 . . . . .229 B6
Dart Villas TQ9 . . . . .223 C4
Darwin Cres PL3. . . . . .249 D5
Darwin Ct 11 EX2 . . . . .261 B2
Dashley Cnr TQ9 . . . . .131 D2
Dashpers TQ5 . . . . .230 B3
Daucus Cl PL9 . . . . .171 B4
Davenham Cl PL6. . . . . .245 B6
Daveycourt La EX20. . . . . . .95 F3
Davey's Cross PL21 . . . . . . .137 B7
David Cl
Braunton EX33. . . . . .152 D5
Plymouth PL7. . . . . .250 F6
David Rd TQ3. . . . . .226 A7
David's Cl PL10. . . . . .101 B2
David's Hill EX33 . . . . .8 A2
Davids La PL21 . . . . .137 B7
David Southgate Ct PL1. .242 B1
Davies Ave TQ4 . . . . .229 A8
Davies Cl EX5. . . . . .82 B6
Davis Ave TQ2 . . . . .219 D6
Davy Cl TQ6 . . . . .233 C3
Davy Cl PL11 . . . . .246 F3
Davy Rd PL6. . . . . .245 C4
Dawes Cl TQ12. . . . . .211 F8
Dawes Ct TQ4 . . . . .226 B5
Dawes La
Millbrook PL10. . . . . .252 E5
Plymouth PL9. . . . . .256 D7
Dawlish Com Coll EX7 . . . .204 F7
Dawlish Com Hospl EX7. .204 D6
Dawlish Mus EX7 . . . . .204 E6
Dawlish Park Terr EX8 . . .195 F4
Dawlish Rd
Exeter EX2 . . . . .181 C8
Teignmouth TQ14. . . . . . . .210 C6
Dawlish Sands Holiday Pk
EX7. . . . . .201 B3
Dawlish St 10 TQ14 . . . . . . .210 C5
Dawlish Sta EX7 . . . . .204 E6
Dawlish Warren Nature
Reserve EX7 . . . . .201 D3
Dawlish Warren Rd EX6. . .201 B4
Dawlish Warren Sta EX7 .201 B2
Dawlish Warren Visitor Ctr
EX7. . . . . .201 C2
Dawlish Wlk PL6. . . . . .249 E8

Dawn Cl EX1 . . . . .178 A6
Daws Ct PL12. . . . . .243 A2
Daws Mdw TQ12. . . . . .207 E6
Dawson Cl PL5 . . . . .243 E1
Daymond Rd PL5 . . . . .243 D2
Days-Pottles La EX6,
EX2. . . . . .181 D4
Dayton Cl PL1. . . . . .244 E3
Deacon Cl EX2 . . . . .181 B8
Deacon Dr PL12 . . . . .242 F1
Deacons Gn PL19 . . . . .171 A3
Dead La EX15. . . . . .65 F2
Deadman's Cross TQ6. . . .233 D2
Dead Road Cross EX15. . . .65 F2
Dean Cross
Combe Martin EX31. . . . . . . .3 E1
Gunn EX32. . . . . .17 E4
Lynton EX35. . . . . .5 A5
Plymouth PL9. . . . . .255 E7
South Brent TQ10 . . . . . . .135 C5
West Down EX34. . . . . .8 E5
Dean Cross Rd PL9 . . . . . . .255 E7
Deane Cl EX33. . . . . .8 D1
Deane La TQ12 . . . . .209 B2
Deane Rd TQ12 . . . . .209 B2
Deanes The EX16. . . . . .161 B3
Deane Way TA20. . . . . .88 D8
Dean Hill PL9. . . . . .255 E7
Dean Hill Rd EX15 . . . . . . .162 B3
Dean La
Combe Martin EX31. . . . . . . .3 E1
Lynton EX35. . . . . .5 A5
West Down EX34. . . . . .8 F5
Dean Lane End TQ10 . . . . .135 D5
Dean Park Rd PL9 . . . . .255 D7
Dean Rd PL7 . . . . .250 D6
Deans Cl
Bishopsteignton TQ14 . . . .208 F8
Northam EX39 . . . . .156 F7
Deans La EX36. . . . . .158 D5
Deans Mead EX10 . . . . . . .188 A5
Deans Pk EX36 . . . . .158 D5
Dean St
Crediton EX17 . . . . .165 D5
Exeter EX2. . . . . .261 B2
Dean Steep EX35 . . . . .5 A8
De Bathe Cross EX20. . . . . .77 C3
Debden Cl PL5 . . . . .243 D4
De Brionne Hts EX20. . . . .170 C5
Deckport Cross EX20. . . . . .75 D7
De Courcy Rd TQ8 . . . . . . .259 B2
Decoy Ctry Pk TQ12 . . . . . .207 C1
Decoy Ind Est TQ12 . . . . . .212 D8
Decoy Prim Sch TQ12 . . . .207 D1
Decoy Rd TQ12 . . . . .207 D1
Deeble Cl PL7 . . . . .250 E7
Deep Cut Cross EX14 . . . . .67 C2
Deep Dene Cl TQ5 . . . . . . .230 A3
Deepdene Pk EX2. . . . . . . .177 E4
Deep La
Crediton EX17 . . . . .165 C6
High Bickington EX37 . . . . .43 D7
Plymouth PL7. . . . . .251 C3
Deeplane Head EX22. . . . . .164 C5
Deepway Ct EX6 . . . . .182 A4
Deepway Gdns EX6 . . . . . . .181 F4
Deepway La
Branscombe EX12 . . . . . . .190 D4
Exeter EX2. . . . . .181 D4
Exminster EX6. . . . . .182 A4
Deepways EX9 . . . . .197 F2
Deer Leap PL19 . . . . .171 D4
Deer Park Ave TQ14. . . . . .210 A6
Deer Park Cl
Tavistock PL19 . . . . .171 C5
Teignmouth TQ14. . . . . . . .210 A6
Deer Park Cres PL19 . . . . .171 C5
Deer Park Dr
Plymouth PL7. . . . . .249 D7
Teignmouth TQ14. . . . . . . .210 A6
Deer Park La
Daccombe TQ12. . . . . .213 E7
Teignmouth TQ14. . . . . . . .171 C5
Deer Park Rd
Barnstaple EX32 . . . . .155 C2
Newton Abbot TQ12. . . . . .207 D1
Stoke Fleming TQ6 . . . . . .146 B8
Tavistock PL19 . . . . .171 C5
Deer Pk
Ivybridge PL21 . . . . .237 E5
Saltash PL12 . . . . .242 F3
Deers Leap Cl TQ3 . . . . . . .219 A6
Deer Valley Rd EX22 . . . . .164 C4
Deer Wood View 4 EX32. .16 E1
Defoe Cl PL5 . . . . .244 C1
Delacombe Cl PL7 . . . . .250 B6
De-La-Hay Ave PL3 . . . . . .262 A4
Delamere Rd PL6 . . . . .249 D7
Delamore Cl PL21. . . . . . . .237 A5
Delamore Gdns PL21. . . . .247 F7
Delaware Com Prim Sch
PL18. . . . . .125 C5
Delaware Cotts PL18. . . . .125 C5
Delaware Ct PL18. . . . . . . .125 C5
Delaware Gdns PL18. . . . .125 C5
Delaware Rd PL18 . . . . . . .125 D5
Delderfield Gdns EX38 . . .159 E6
Delgany Villas EX5 . . . . . . .99 C5
Delius Cres EX2 . . . . .178 C5
Dell The
Plymouth PL7. . . . . .250 B6
Tavistock PL19 . . . . .171 A5
Delve's Grave Cross EX38 .41 F4
Demuville Gdns EX17. . . . . .80 B6
Denbigh Terr EX10. . . . . . . .188 B5
Denbow Cross EX5. . . . . . . .99 C3

Den Brook Cl TQ1. . . . . . .220 D6
Denbury Cross TQ12 . . . .211 D3
Denbury Ct EX2. . . . . .181 D8
Denbury Down Cross
TQ12 . . . . .131 F3
Denbury Down La TQ12 . .131 F3
Denbury Prim Sch TQ12 . .211 A6
Denbury Rd TQ12 . . . . . . .211 E6
Denby Ho TQ4 . . . . .226 C5
Den Cres TQ14. . . . . .210 C4
Dencroft La EX14 . . . . .87 A5
Dendy Rd TQ4 . . . . .226 B6
Dene Cl EX8. . . . . .196 D1
Deneridge Cross EX17 . . . .60 F6
Deneridge Hill EX17 . . . . . .61 A5
Dene's Cl 2 EX32 . . . . .17 B2
Denes Rd EX32. . . . . .17 B2
Dengie Cl PL7 . . . . .251 B5
Denham Cl PL5 . . . . .244 C2
Dening Ct EX8. . . . . .202 B8
Denise Cl EX2 . . . . .181 B8
Denmark Rd
Exeter EX1, EX2. . . . . .261 C3
Exmouth EX8 . . . . .202 D8
Denmark Way EX15. . . . . . .66 A7
Dennadene Cl EX8 . . . . . . .196 B3
Dennington Cross EX32 . . .28 D8
Dennington Hill EX32 . . . .28 D8
Dennington La
Churchinford EX14. . . . . . . .68 F6
Dulverton TA22 . . . . .33 B4
Dennis Cl PL5 . . . . .247 C7
Dennis's Down Cross EX6 .96 C5
Dennysmead Ct EX4 . . . . .173 A1
Den Prom TQ14. . . . . .210 C4
Den Rd TQ14 . . . . .210 C4
Densdon Gate EX16. . . . . . .46 E6
Densham La EX17. . . . . .61 F4
Den The TQ14. . . . . .210 C4
Denton Cl EX8 . . . . .182 E6
Denver Rd EX32 . . . . .182 E6
Denys Rd
Torquay TQ1. . . . . .220 C5
Totnes TQ9 . . . . .223 C5
Deptford Pl PL4 . . . . .263 A4
Deptford Villas 2 EX1 . .154 C3
Derby Rd
Barnstaple EX32 . . . . .155 B6
Kingsbridge TQ7 . . . . .258 D4
Plymouth PL5. . . . . .244 C4
Derick Rd EX16. . . . . .161 B5
Derncleugh Gdns EX7. . . .210 F8
Derrell Rd TQ4. . . . . .226 A4
Derriford Bsns Pk PL6 . . .245 A4
Derriford Hospl PL6 . . . . . .245 B4
Derriford Pk PL6 . . . . .245 A4
Derriford Rd PL6. . . . . .245 B5
Derrton Mill Cross EX22 164 B3
Derriton Rd EX22 . . . . .71 E6
Derry Ave PL4 . . . . .262 B2
Derry's Cross PL1. . . . . . . .262 B2
Derwent Cl PL3 . . . . .249 C5
Derwent Rd TQ1 . . . . .220 B7
Derworthy Cross EX22 . . . .54 D6
Derworthy La EX22 . . . . . . .54 D6
Desborough La PL4 . . . . . .263 C3
Desborough Rd PL4. . . . . .263 C3
De Tracey Pk TQ13 . . . . . . .180 D7
Devon Cl PL7. . . . . .251 A5
Devon Bsns Pk EX15 . . . . .163 D4
Devon Cliffs Holiday Pk
EX8. . . . . .203 B5
Devon & Cornwall Pol HQ
(Middlemoor) EX2 . . . . .178 D5
Devoncourt TQ5 . . . . .230 E6
Devoncourt Rd EX8 . . . . . .201 B2
Devon Cres PL1 . . . . .262 A3
Devon East Bsns Ctr EX15 85 C3
Devon Guild of Craftsmen
TQ13 . . . . .180 D7
Devon Heath 2 TQ13 . . . . .123 C4
Devon Ho TQ13 . . . . .180 E8
Devon Pk Dr TQ13 . . . . . . .180 E8
Devon Pl 1 TQ9 . . . . .223 D5
Devonport High Sch for Boys
PL1. . . . . .248 A2
Devonport High Sch for Girls
PL2. . . . . .248 C6
Devonport Hill
Cawsand PL10 . . . . .253 A2
Plymouth PL9. . . . . .247 F1
Devonport Leat PL6. . . . . .241 B5
Devonport Rd PL3 . . . . . . .247 F3
Devonport Sta PL1 . . . . . .247 E2
Devon Rd
Exeter EX4 . . . . .177 F8
Salcombe TQ8 . . . . .259 D4
Devonshire Ct
10 Honiton EX14. . . . . .85 C2
Tavistock PL19 . . . . .171 A4
Devonshire Ho
Plymouth PL1. . . . . .262 B2
2 Tavistock PL19 . . . . . . .171 B5
Devonshire Pk EX39 . . . . . .157 A1
Devonshire Pl PL4. . . . . . . .177 D8
Devonshire Rise EX16. . . . .161 C3
Devonshire Way 4 EX14 .164 A4
Devon Sq
Kingsbridge TQ7 . . . . .258 C5
Newton Abbot TQ12. . . . . .207 C3
Devons' Rd TQ1. . . . . .220 C7
Dolphin Cl
Lyme Regis DT7. . . . . .260 E3

Devon Terr
Plymouth PL3. . . . . .248 E5
16 Teignmouth TQ9 . . . . .223 D5
Devon Tors PL20. . . . . .127 A3
Devon Tors Rd 9 PL20. . .126 F3
Devon Units
Exeter EX2. . . . . .177 C1
Great Torrington EX38. . . .159 F6
Devon Valley Holiday Village
TQ14 . . . . .209 C5
Devon View EX7 . . . . .201 B2
Dewberry Dr EX31 . . . . . . .154 B3
Deyman's Hill EX16. . . . . . .161 D3
Dial Ho The EX9 . . . . .198 A1
Dial St EX19 . . . . .58 F3
Diamond Ave PL4. . . . . .263 B4
Diamond La TQ10 . . . . .134 D5
Diamond Rd EX2. . . . . .261 A1
Diamond St 23 EX32 . . . . .154 F5
Diana Cl PL1 . . . . .106 A8
Diane Cl EX8 . . . . .196 D4
Dibbon's La EX34 . . . . .1 D2
Dickens Dr EX2 . . . . .177 F3
Dickens Rd PL5. . . . . .244 B1
Dickers Terr TQ12 . . . . . . .207 E7
Dickiemoor La PL5 . . . . . . .244 C2
Dickna St PL15 . . . . .90 C1
Dick Pym EX2 . . . . .178 C4
Dick's Hill EX36. . . . . .46 E8
Dickshill La EX38 . . . . .159 D5
Diddywell Cl EX39 . . . . . . .157 A8
Didworthy Bglws TQ10 . . .134 E5
Dieppe Cl PL1 . . . . .247 F2
Digby Dr EX2. . . . . .178 D3
Digby Gr PL5 . . . . .243 F5
Digby Rd TQ14 . . . . .210 C4
Digby & Sowton Sta EX2 .178 E4
Diggerland EX15. . . . . .155 B2
Diggories La 5 EX14 . . . .166 B6
Dillons PL8 . . . . .141 A7
Dillybridge Hill EX6. . . . . . .97 D4
Dinan Way EX8 . . . . .196 E3
Dinan Way Trad Est EX8 .196 F3
Dince Hill Cl EX5 . . . . .99 E7
Dingle Cl PL17. . . . . .115 B1
Dingle Rd
Plymouth, North Prospect
PL2. . . . . .248 A6
Plymouth, Plympton PL7 . .250 C6
Dingles Steam Village
PL16. . . . . .106 A5
Dingwall Ave PL5 . . . . .244 E3
Dinham Cres EX4 . . . . .261 A3
Dinham Rd EX4. . . . . .261 A3
Dinne Ford St EX5 . . . . .81 E5
Dinnicombe Cross EX14 . . .86 C3
Dipford Gate EX36 . . . . . . .44 E6
Dipford Cl TQ12 . . . . .48 C4
Dipford Cross TQ9 . . . . . . .223 A6
Dipford Parochial CE Prim
Sch TQ9 . . . . .138 C7
Dirty La EX38 . . . . .242 B5
Discovery Wharf 7 PL4 . .263 A2
Distine Cl PL3 . . . . .249 D7
Ditch End Cross EX32 . . . . .28 C7
Ditchett Cross EX14 . . . . . .86 E6
Dittiscombe Cross TQ9 . . .145 A6
Dittisham Wlk PL6 . . . . . . .249 E8
Ditton Ct PL6. . . . . .249 E8
Divett Dr 6 TQ12. . . . . . . .122 F1
Dixon Pl PL2 . . . . .247 F4
Dixon Rd PL3. . . . . .247 F4
Dixon Terr PL8 . . . . .140 F7
Dix's Field EX1 . . . . .261 B3
Doatlands Cl EX13. . . . . . . .103 D5
Doatshayne La
Musbury EX13 . . . . .103 D6
Musbury, Maidenhayne
EX13 . . . . .103 D5
Dobbin Arch TQ12 . . . . . . .212 F4
Dobbs Moor Cross EX18 . . .44 F3
Dobles Cl EX22 . . . . .164 C6
Dobles La EX22 . . . . .164 C6
Dobles Lane Ind Est
EX22. . . . . .164 D5
Dobles Terr EX22 . . . . .164 D5
Doccombe Cross TQ13 . . . .112 B4
Dockeys La TQ7 . . . . .145 D1
Dockray Cl PL6 . . . . .245 D6
Dock Rd EX8 . . . . .201 F6
Dockworthy Cross EX18. . .60 C8
Dockyard PL2 . . . . .247 E4
Docton Mill & Gdns EX39 .22 F3
Doctors Cnr EX16 . . . . .61 D7
Doctors Rd 3 TQ5. . . . . . .230 C3
Dodbrooke Ct TQ7 . . . . . . .258 D5
Doddiscombe Sch
TQ13 . . . . .112 E2
Doddridge Cl PL9. . . . . .255 F6
Doddscott Cross EX18 . . . .59 C2
Doe Cl EX38 . . . . .159 D5
Dog Down Cross EX14 . . . . .50 A4
Doggie La EX34 . . . . .1 B8
Dohm Cl PL6 . . . . .249 C8
Dokkum Rd EX17 . . . . .165 C4
Dolbeare Rd 2 TQ13 . . . . .130 F4
Dolbeare Rd EX5 . . . . .99 E8
Dole Park Cross East
EX37. . . . . .43 D5
Dolepark Cross West
EX37. . . . . .43 C5
Dolphin Cl continued
Plymouth PL9. . . . . .255 F6
Dolphin Court Rd
Paignton TQ3 . . . . .218 F1
Plymouth PL9. . . . . .255 F6
Dolphin Cres TQ3 . . . . .218 F1
Dolphin Ct
Brixham TQ5 . . . . .230 C6
Cullompton EX15. . . . . . . .163 C3
13 Honiton EX14. . . . . . . .166 C6
Northam EX39 . . . . .156 E7
22 Teignmouth TQ14 . . . .210 C4
Dolphin Ho 18 PL4. . . . . . .263 A2
Dolphin Sch The EX8. . . . .202 B6
Dolphin Sq
Bovey Tracey TQ13. . . . . . .180 C7
Plymouth PL9. . . . . .255 F6
Dolphin St EX24 . . . . .103 A5
Dolton CE Prim Sch EX19 .57 F2
Dolvin Rd PL19 . . . . .171 C5
Domehayes EX20. . . . . .170 B5
Dommett Cl EX13. . . . . .167 E7
Donkey La
Malborough PL10. . . . . . . .252 C4
Ugborough PL21 . . . . .137 D6
Donkey Sanctuary The
EX10. . . . . .189 B7
Donnington Dr PL3 . . . . . .249 C7
Doomsford La EX37 . . . . . . .44 B5
Doone Way EX34 . . . . .150 B4
Dorchester Ave PL5. . . . . .244 D4
Dorchester Gr TQ2 . . . . . . .213 F1
Dorchester Way EX14 . . . .196 D4
Dorena Rd PL9 . . . . .256 C7
Doriam Cl EX4. . . . . .173 C2
Dormy Ave PL3 . . . . .248 F5
Dornafield Cl TQ12. . . . . . .211 D2
Dornafield Cross
Abbotskerswell TQ12. . . . .211 D3
Ipplepen TQ12 . . . . .211 D3
Dornafield Dr E TQ12 . . . .211 D2
Dornafield Dr W TQ12 . . . .211 D2
Dornafield La TQ12 . . . . . . .211 E4
Dornafield Rd TQ12 . . . . . .211 D3
Dornaford Cross EX20. . . . .76 C2
Dorridge Gate EX37. . . . . . .28 B5
Dorset Ave EX4. . . . . .176 E4
Dorset Pk PL15 . . . . .89 D2
Dorsmouth Terr PL7 . . . . .250 E4
Dosson Gr TQ1 . . . . .219 E7
Dotheridge La EX39. . . . . . .25 A1
Dotton Cl EX1 . . . . .178 D6
Dotton La EX10 . . . . .186 E6
Doughy La TQ12 . . . . .211 A7
Douglas Ave
Brixham TQ5 . . . . .230 E4
Exmouth EX8 . . . . .202 C6
Douglas Dr PL9 . . . . .256 A5
Douglas Ho PL3 . . . . .210 B5
Douglass Rd PL3 . . . . .249 A4
Douro Ct PL21. . . . . .237 D5
Dousland Ho PL20 . . . . . . .127 A3
Dousland La PL20 . . . . .127 A3
Dousland Terr PL20 . . . . . .127 A3
Dove Cl
Cullompton EX15. . . . . . . .163 A2
Dovedale Cl EX34 . . . . .150 E5
Dovedale Rd PL2 . . . . .248 B6
Dove Gdns PL3 . . . . .249 D7
Dove La PL6 . . . . .245 E3
Dover's Hill EX17 . . . . .80 A4
Dove Way EX2 . . . . .176 D3
Dowell St EX14 . . . . .166 B6
Dowell Ct EX14 . . . . .166 B6
Dowel Dr PL21 . . . . .137 C7
Dower Ho The TQ10 . . . . . .135 C4
Dower Rd TQ1 . . . . .220 D7
Downash La EX13. . . . . .88 E3
Downash Way EX13 . . . . . .213 C5
Newton Poppleford
EX10. . . . . .186 D7
Down Cl EX33 . . . . .242 C2
Down End EX17 . . . . .165 F5
Downeshead La EX17 . . . . .59 E2
Downfield Cl TQ5 . . . . .230 A3
Downfield Dr PL7 . . . . .250 F5
Downfield Way PL7 . . . . . . .250 F5
Downfield Wlk PL7 . . . . . . .250 F5
Downgate Gdns PL2. . . . . .248 D8
Downgate La EX14. . . . . . . .86 C3
Downhayes Rd EX39 . . . . .255 F7
Downhayne Brake Rd
EX24. . . . . .102 F7
Downhayne Hill EX24 . . . . .102 F4
Down Hill
Morchard Bishop EX17 . . . .78 F8
Morchard Road EX17 . . . . .47 A3
Down La
Braunton EX33. . . . . .152 C6
Doddiscombsleigh EX6 . . .113 D5
Georgeham EX33 . . . . .8 A4
Kenwick EX23 . . . . .10 F6
Knowle EX33. . . . . .8 B3
Newton St Cyres EX5 . . . . .81 F7
Rackenford EX16 . . . . .46 E7
Winkleigh EX19 . . . . .58 D4
Downlea Cross EX39. . . . . . .37 A3
Downlands Cross EX15. . . . .66 E2
Downlands La TA3. . . . . .68 E2
Downlea PL19 . . . . .171 D4
Downmoor Cross EX38 . . . .55 B5

Down Park Dr PL19 ..... 171 D4
Down Rd
  Instow EX39 .... 15 B1
  Plymouth PL7 .... 251 C5
  Tavistock PL19 .... 171 D4
Down St Mary Vineyard
  EX17 .... 78 D7
Downside Ave PL6 ...... 249 C7
Downside Cl DT6 .... 104 F4
Downs Rd EX39 .... 15 C1
Downs The TQ7 .... 143 A2
Downstow Cross TQ10 .. 134 F5
Downs View LT2 .... 54 D6
Down The PL20 .... 125 F1
Downton Cl PL1 .... 262 A4
Downton Cross TQ6 ..... 233 A7
Down View Rd TQ12 .... 211 A6
Dowrich Cross EX17 ...... 80 A7
Dracaena Ave EX1 .... 154 C4
Dragdown Hill EX1 .... 95 F7
Dragon Hill EX38 .... 40 F2
Dragons Hill EX7 .... 260 E5
Dragon's Mead EX13 .... 167 C4
Dragon's Tail TQ5 .... 230 E4
Dragoon Cl TQ12 .... 180 E3
Drake Ave
  [5] Exeter EX2 .... 178 D5
  Teignmouth TQ14 .... 210 A8
  Torquay TQ2 .... 219 C6
Drake Cir PL1, PL4 .... 263 A3
  drakecircus Sh Ctr PL1.. 263 A3
Drake Cl EX39 .... 156 B6
Drake Ct
  Plymouth, Ernesettle
  PL5 .... 243 E4
  Plymouth, St Jude's PL4 . 263 B3
Drake Dr TQ4 .... 226 B2
Drakefield Dr PL12 .... 243 A3
Drake Gdns PL19 .... 171 C4
Drake La TQ13 .... 180 E7
Drake Prim Sch PL2 ..... 247 E6
Drake Rd
  Bovey Tracey TQ13 ...... 180 E7
  Newton Abbot TQ12 .... 207 F3
  Salcombe TQ8 .... 259 C5
  Tavistock PL19 .... 171 C6
Drakes Ave
  Exmouth EX8 .... 202 D8
  Sidmouth EX10 .... 188 C8
Drake's CE Prim Sch
  EX9 .... 198 B6
Drakes Cl PL6 .... 244 F4
Drakes Cres TA20 .... 188 D8
Drakes Ct TQ1 .... 220 B8
Drakes Pk TA21 .... 160 D7
Drakes Pk N TA21 .... 160 D7
Drakes Rd EX4 .... 177 A4
Drake's Rd TQ4 .... 225 E4
Drakes Way DT7 .... 260 E3
Drake Villas PL19 .... 171 A4
Drakewalls Gdns PL18 .. 125 C5
Drakewalls Pl PL18 ...... 125 C5
Drake Way PL9 .... 255 E7
Drapers Cl EX34 .... 3 B3
Draper Terr [3] PL19 .... 171 B5
Drax Gdns PL6 .... 248 E8
Draycott Cl EX2 .... 178 A4
Dray Ct [3] EX8 .... 202 A6
Drayford Rd EX16 .... 46 E1
Drayton Rd PL5 .... 244 C1
Drayway Cross EX16 ...... 63 D1
Drayway La EX16 .... 63 A1
Drew's Cl EX6 .... 201 A8
Drews Field La TQ3 ...... 218 F7
Drewsmead TQ13 .... 122 C3
Drew St TQ5 .... 230 C3
Drewston Cross TQ13 ... 111 C6
Drewstone Cross EX36 ... 30 E6
Dreys Ct EX1 .... 177 E6
Dreyton Cross TQ9 ...... 139 F3
Drift La EX14 .... 66 F3
Drift Lane Cross EX14 .... 66 F3
Drift The TA20 .... 88 E8
Drive The
  Bishopsteignton TQ14 .. 208 E8
  Brixham TQ5 .... 230 C2
  Dawlish EX7 .... 204 E6
  East Budleigh EX9 ...... 198 D8
  Exeter EX5 .... 99 B3
  Holbeton PL8 .... 136 D1
  Kingskerswell TQ12 .... 213 A4
  Plymouth PL3 .... 248 E7
Droridge TQ9 .... 222 F8
Droridge La TQ9 .... 222 F8
Drovers Way
  Ivybridge PL21 .... 237 A6
  Seaton EX12 .... 192 B8
Drove Way TA3 .... 68 C8
Druid Cross TQ13 .... 130 E5
Drum Bridge TQ12 .... 180 F1
Drummond Cl PL2 .... 247 F7
Drummond Pl PL1 .... 247 F3
Drum Way TQ12 .... 180 F2
Drunken Bridge Hill PL7 . 250 D4
Drupe Farm Ct EX10 .... 186 D3
Drybridge Cross TQ10 .. 135 C5
Dryburgh Cres PL2 ...... 248 A8
Dryden Ave PL5 .... 244 C1
Dryden Cl EX8 .... 196 C4
Dryden Cotts EX5 .... 99 D2
Dryden Rd PL7 .... 177 F4
Dryfield EX6 .... 182 B4

Dry La
  Christow EX6 .... 113 B4
  Okehampton EX20 .... 93 D5
Drymung Hill EX36 .... 45 F7
Dualstone Cross EX22 .. 71 C3
Dubbs Cross EX21 .... 90 E3
Ducane Wlk PL6 .... 245 B1
Duchy Ave TQ3 .... 219 B2
Duchy Coll PL17 .... 115 B1
Duchy Dr TQ3 .... 219 B2
Duchy Gdns TQ3 .... 219 B2
Duchy Pk TQ3 .... 219 A2
Duchy Rd EX14 .... 166 A4
Duchy Sch The EX5 .... 82 F6
Duck La EX20 .... 76 C5
Ducksmoor Cross EX16 .. 63 E8
Ducks Orch EX6 .... 182 B3
Duckspond Rd TQ11 .... 236 A4
Duckworth St [3] EX2 .... 261 A3
Duckworth St [3] PL2 ... 248 A4
Ducky Row PL17 .... 125 A4
Dudley Gdns PL6 .... 249 B8
Dudley Rd PL7 .... 250 B5
Dudley Way EX39 .... 156 B6
Dudmoor La EX31 .... 10 B4
Duerdon Cross EX39 ...... 38 E6
Duke Of Cornwall Cl
  EX8 .... 196 E1
Dukes Cl
  Otterton EX9 .... 198 E7
  Paignton TQ3 .... 225 E6
Dukes Cres EX8 .... 196 E1
Dukes Dr PL19 .... 125 E4
Dukes Mead EX15 .... 163 C2
Dukes Orch EX5 .... 82 F6
Dukes Rd EX9 .... 197 F2
Dukes Ryde The [1] PL9 . 255 F7
Duke St
  Cullompton EX15 .... 163 C2
  Dartmouth TQ6 .... 233 F3
  Kingsbridge TQ7 .... 258 D5
  Plymouth PL1 .... 247 E2
  South Molton EX36 .... 158 C4
  Tavistock PL19 .... 171 C6
Dulcis Cross EX13 .... 87 C2
Dulford Bsns Pk EX15 .... 66 A1
Dulford Cross EX15 .... 66 B1
Dulings Mdw EX17 .... 79 B5
Duloe Gdns PL2 .... 248 C8
Dulverton La TA4 .... 35 D7
Dulverton Mid & Com Sch
  TA22 .... 33 D6
Dumfries Ave PL5 .... 244 D3
Dumpdon La EX14 .... 85 F6
Dumpdon View EX14 ..... 86 A6
Duncan Ho PL1 .... 220 C4
Duncannon La TQ9 ...... 227 E7
Duncannon Mead TQ9 .. 227 F7
Duncan St PL1 .... 247 E1
Dunclair Pk PL3 .... 249 F5
Duncombe Ave PL5 ..... 244 A2
Duncombe Cross TQ9 .. 144 C2
Duncombe St TQ7 .... 258 D6
Dun Cross TQ9 .... 222 C8
Dundas St [4] PL2 .... 248 A4
Dundonald St TQ2 ...... 247 F4
Dundridge Ct TQ9 ...... 222 E1
Dunes The [2] EX39 .... 15 B1
Dune View
  Braunton EX33 .... 152 B7
  Westward Ho! EX39 .... 156 D7
Dune View Rd EX33 ..... 152 B6
Dunheved Rd PL17 ...... 125 A4
Dunkeswell Airfield EX14 . 67 B2
Dunkeswell Bsns Pk EX14 .67 B2
Dunkeswell Meml Mus
  EX14 .... 67 B3
Dunkirk EX11 .... 169 C4
Dunley Cross TQ13 ...... 123 B4
Dunley La TQ13 .... 123 B5
Dunmere Wlk PL6 .... 245 C1
Dunmore Cl TQ14 .... 210 B2
Dunmore Dr TQ14 .... 210 B2
Dunmore Rd Ho PL6 .... 244 D7
Dunning Ct EX14 .... 166 A6
Dunning Gn [8] EX31 ... 154 C3
Dunning Rd TQ14 .... 210 A7
Dunning Wlk
  Teignmouth TQ14 .... 210 A6
  Teignmouth TQ14 .... 210 A7
Dunn La EX39 .... 25 E2
Dunns Cl EX33 .... 152 F4
Dunn's Hill TA21 .... 51 A6
Dunraven [20] EX32 ..... 155 A4
Dunraven Dr PL6 .... 245 A6
Dunrich Cl EX2 .... 261 C2
Dunscombe La
  Chudleigh TQ13 .... 124 A5
  Sidmouth EX10 .... 189 B7
Dunsdon Cross EX22 .... 53 C3
Dunsford Com Prim Sch
  EX6 .... 112 F8
Dunsford Gdns EX4 ..... 176 E3
Dunsford Hill EX5 .... 81 E3
Dunsford Rd EX2 .... 176 E3
Dunsford Way [1] EX16 . 161 C2
Dunsgreen La EX17 .... 67 D8
Dunsland Cross EX22 .... 73 A6
Dunstey Hill EX16, EX36 .. 32 C5
Dunster Cl PL7 .... 251 C4
Dunsterville Rd PL21 ... 237 E6
Dunster Wlk EX6 .... 181 F5

Dunstone Ave PL9 .... 256 A7
Dunstone Cl
  Plymouth PL9 .... 218 E1
  Plymouth PL9 .... 255 F7
Dunstone Com Prim Sch
  PL9 .... 256 A8
Dunstone Cross TQ7 ... 149 C7
Dunstone Dr PL9 .... 255 F7
Dunstone La PL9 .... 256 B7
Dunstone Park Rd TQ3 . 218 E1
Dunstone Rd
  Plymouth, Plymstock PL9 .255 F7
  Plymouth, St Budeaux PL5. 243 F3
Dunstone Rise TQ3 ...... 218 E1
Dunstone View PL9 ...... 256 A7
Duntz Hill PL16 .... 105 E4
Dunvegan Cl EX4 .... 177 A8
Dunwell Cross PL21 .... 137 D5
Dural Cross EX22 .... 38 B3
Durant House LT20 .... 77 C4
Durban Rd PL3 .... 248 D5
Durbin Cl EX14 .... 166 D5
Durdon Cross EX20 .... 75 A1
Dure La EX36 .... 30 E8
Durham Ave PL4 .... 263 C4
Durham Cl
  Exeter EX1 .... 178 C7
  Exmouth EX8 .... 196 D4
  Paignton TQ3 .... 219 B1
Durham Way EX4 .... 166 A4
Durleigh Rd TQ5 .... 230 B4
Durlestone Cross TQ7 .. 149 B8
Durleymoor Cross EX16 . 50 F4
Durley Rd EX12 .... 191 F7
Durnford St PL1 .... 248 A1
Durnford Street Ope
  PL1 .... 248 A1
Durrant Cl
  Northam EX39 .... 157 A5
  Plymouth PL1 .... 247 E3
Durrant La EX39 .... 157 A5
Durris Cl PL6 .... 245 D4
Durris Gdns PL6 .... 245 D4
Dursley Way EX39 .... 156 E2
Durwent Cl PL9 .... 255 A6
Duryardwood La EX5 ... 172 E5
Dux Cross EX22 .... 71 B6
Duxford Cl PL5 .... 243 E5
Dyehouse Cnr TA22 ...... 34 A6
Dyehouse Cross TA22 ... 33 F5
Dyehouse La TA22 .... 34 A5
Dyers Cl
  Braunton EX33 .... 152 D6
  West Buckland TA21 .... 52 F7
Dyers Ct EX2 .... 261 A2
Dyke Hill Terr TA20 .... 88 D8
Dymond Ct (Kingdom Pl)
  PL12 .... 242 F7
Dymond Rd PL9 .... 156 F1
Dynevor Ct PL3 .... 248 F7

E

Eager Way EX6 .... 181 F5
Eagle Cl TQ12 .... 123 E1
Eagle Cotts EX4 .... 177 A5
Eagle Ct TQ2 .... 219 E8
Eagle Hurst Ct [5] EX10 .188 A4
Eagle Hurst Lodge [4]
  EX10 .... 188 A4
Eagle Pl TQ13 .... 111 F5
Eagle Rd PL7 .... 251 C4
Eaglescott Airfield EX37 . 43 C3
Eagles Nest EX2 .... 176 D4
Eaglewood Cl TQ2 ...... 213 C2
Earl Richard's Rd N EX2 . 178 E4
Earl Richard's Rd S EX2 . 177 F2
Earl's Acre PL3 .... 248 C4
Earls Ct TQ1 .... 219 F6
Earl's Dr The
  Cawsand, Kingsand PL10 .253 B3
  Cawsand PL10 .... 253 A1
  Rame PL10 .... 140 I2
Earls Mill Rd PL7 .... 250 E6
Earls Wood Cl PL6 ...... 245 F3
Earlswood Dr TQ3 .... 225 D7
Earls Wood Dr PL6 ...... 245 F3
Eastacombe Cross
  Barnstaple EX31 .... 16 B1
  Northlew EX20 .... 74 E2
Eastacombe Rise EX31 .. 15 E6
Eastacott Cross EX37 .... 28 E2
Eastacott La EX34 .... 8 B7
East Allington Prim Sch
  TQ9 .... 144 D7
East Anstey Prim Sch
  EX16 .... 32 E5
East Ash Cross
  Bradworthy EX22 .... 38 F3
  Whiddon Down EX20 .... 95 D2
  Whiddon Down EX20 .... 95 E1
East Ave EX1 .... 177 F6
East Ball Hill EX39 .... 22 E3
Eastbourne Terr EX39 .. 156 D7
Eastbrook Ho [7] TQ14 .. 210 B6
East Buckland Cross
  EX32 .... 18 D2
East Budleigh Rd
  Budleigh Salterton EX9 . 198 B3
  East Budleigh EX9 ...... 198 C6
Eastbury Ave PL5 .... 244 A2
East Butterleigh Cross
  EX15 .... 64 E3

East Challacombe La EX34 .3 B4
Eastchurch La EX6 .... 96 D6
East Cliff EX39 .... 46 E1
East Cliff DT7 .... 260 E3
East Cliff Cl EX7 .... 204 E7
East Cliff Gdns EX7 ..... 204 E7
East Cliff Rd EX7 .... 204 E7
East Cliff Wlk TQ14 .... 210 D7
East Coombe Cross EX17 .81 A6
Eastcoombe La EX17 ..... 81 A6
East Coombe La TA4 ..... 35 D8
Eastcote Cl PL6 .... 245 B6
Eastcott Cross EX23 ..... 37 D2
East Dartmoor Woods &
  Heaths National Nature
  Reserve TQ13 .... 122 B5
East Devon Bsns Pk EX14 .86 C3
East Devon Coll EX16 .. 161 C6
East Devon Coll (Annexe)
  EX16 .... 161 D4
Eastdown EX20 .... 22 F3
Eastdown Cross TQ9 ... 145 D8
East Down Cross
  Combe Martin EX34 .... 9 F6
  Okehampton EX20 .... 93 D8
East Dr EX8 .... 196 A1
Eastella Rd PL20 .... 127 A2
East End EX17 .... 62 D3
East Farm [13] EX13, EX13 .131 A5
Easterbrook La EX6 ...... 96 D8
Easter Close Cross EX31 . 3 D1
Easter Cl EX31 .... 154 E2
Easterdown Cl PL9 ...... 255 F7
Easterfield La TQ1 ...... 214 C2
Easter Ground La EX34 .. 8 F5
Easter Hill EX37 .... 28 E2
Easter Hill La EX6 .... 201 A7
Easter La
  Berrynarbor EX34 .... 2 E3
  Lower Tippacott EX35 ..... 6 B4
Easter Lane Cross TQ13 . 121 B2
Easterley Terr EX31 ..... 154 C3
Eastern Ave
  Barnstaple EX32 .... 155 C4
  Exeter EX2 .... 182 C7
East Mead EX15 .... 67 B8
East Meadow Rd EX33 . 152 B7
East Mere Cross EX16 .... 50 B2
East Moore Cross TQ9 . 135 E1
Eastmoor La TA4 .... 34 E8
East Nymph La EX17 .... 95 E6
Easton Cross
  Hittisleigh EX6 .... 96 C5
  West Alvington TQ7 .... 258 B3
Easton La EX16 .... 50 D1
Easton Moor Cross EX31 . 27 C1
East Pafford Ave TQ2 .. 214 B3
Eastpark TQ7 .... 149 B8
East Park Ave PL4 ...... 262 C4
East Park Cl EX19 .... 58 F3
East Park Rd EX32 ...... 155 D4
East Pitton Barns PL7 .. 136 A5
East Pk EX39 .... 38 F8
East Pugsley Cross TQ9 . 29 B2
East Ridge View EX39 .. 157 B1
East Rowley La EX36 .... 45 D5
East Sherford Cross PL8 .257 A8
East St
  Ashburton TQ13 .... 130 F5
  Bishop's Tawton EX32 .. 74 A8
  Black Torrington EX21 .. 74 A8
  Bovey Tracey TQ13 ..... 180 D8
  Braunton EX33 .... 152 D6
  Chittlehampton EX37 ... 28 F4
  Chulmleigh EX18 .... 44 E1
  Crediton EX17 .... 165 D5
  Denbury TQ12 .... 211 A7
  Great Torrington EX38 .. 159 D5
  Ipplepen TQ12 .... 207 C3
  Newton Abbot TQ12 .... 170 C5
  Okehampton EX20 ...... 170 C5
  Plymouth PL1 .... 262 A2
  Sheepwash EX21 .... 56 C1
  Sidmouth EX10 .... 188 B3
  South Molton EX36 .... 158 D4
  Torquay TQ2 .... 219 F6
  Uffculme EX15 .... 66 A7
East Tapps La EX16 ...... 33 B2
East Terr EX9 .... 199 H2
East-the-Water Com Prim
  Sch EX39 .... 157 C1

East Town La EX14 ...... 194 D3
East View Cotts [5] EX14. 166 C6
East View Pl EX16 .... 161 C4
East Village Cross EX17 .. 80 C8
East Way PL21 .... 136 D6
Eastwick Barton EX16 .. 62 B8
Eastwood Wd Hill EX2 .. 178 B5
Eastwoods EX31 .... 151 B4
Eastwood Cl PL6 .... 249 A6
Eastwood La EX16 .... 96 C7
East Worlington Cross
  EX17 .... 61 B8
East Worlington Prim Sch
  EX17 .... 61 B8
East Youlstone Cross
  EX23 .... 37 F2
Easy Bridge Cross EX13 . 102 F7
Eaton La TQ12 .... 123 B7
Eaton Ct TQ14 .... 210 B7
Eaton Hall EX1 .... 261 C3
Eaton Hall Dr TQ6 ...... 233 E4
Eaton Pl TQ4 .... 226 B5
Ebberley Lawn EX32 ... 155 A5
Ebberly Arms EX38 .... 42 F6
Ebberley Cross EX19 .... 42 E5
Ebberly Ct [4] EX32 .... 155 A5
Ebenezer Rd TQ3 .... 226 A5
Ebford La EX3 .... 183 D4
Ebrington Rd EX2 .... 177 B7
Ebrington St
  Kingsbridge TQ7 .... 258 D5
  Plymouth PL4 .... 263 A3
Eddy's La [1] EX32 ...... 155 B3
Eddystone Cl
  Heybrook Bay PL9 ...... 140 A7
  Plymouth PL3 .... 249 C6
Eddystone Rd
  Down Thomas PL9 ...... 255 C1
  Thurlestone TQ7 .... 143 A1
Eddystone Rise TQ7 .... 147 D7
Eddystone Terr PL1 ..... 262 B1
Eden Cl TQ5 .... 230 C3
Eden Gr TQ3 .... 225 F7
Eden Park Prim Sch
  TQ5 .... 230 C3
Eden Pk TQ5 .... 230 C3
Edenside PL3 .... 248 F6
Edenvale Rd TQ3 .... 225 F8
Eden Way EX10 .... 186 E3
Edgar Terr PL4 .... 249 A4
Egbaston Mead EX2 ... 178 C4
Edgcumbe Ave PL1 ..... 262 A3
Edgcumbe Cl PL18 ..... 125 D6
Edgcumbe Cres PL10 .. 252 F6
Edgcumbe Ct [3] PL3 .. 248 A3
Edgcumbe Dr PL19 .... 171 B6
Edgcumbe Ho PL1 ...... 262 B2
Edgcumbe Park Rd PL3 . 248 D6
Edgcumbe Rd
  Saltash PL12 .... 242 C5
  St Dominick PL12 ...... 125 A2
Edgcumbe St PL1 .... 248 A1
Edgcumbe Terr
  [13] Bere Alston PL20 .. 125 E1
  Milton Abbot PL19 ..... 116 A6
Edgecombe Way PL18 .. 125 B5
Edgehill Coll EX39 ...... 156 F2
Edgeland Cross TQ12 .. 217 D8
Edgelands La TQ12 ..... 211 C1
Edgeley Rd TQ2 .... 214 A2
Edgemount Ho [5] PL3 . 220 B5
Edgerley Cross EX17 ..... 60 C1
Edgerton Park Rd EX4 . 177 D8
Edgeworthy Hill EX16 ... 62 C8
Edgiford Cross EX18 ..... 45 B1
Edginswell Cl TQ2 ...... 213 C1
Edginswell La TQ2, TQ12 . 213 A1
Edinburgh Cres EX8 ... 195 E6
Edinburgh Dr EX4 ...... 176 E6
Edinburgh Rd TQ5 ..... 230 D3
Edinburgh St PL1 .... 247 E1
Edith Ave PL4 .... 263 C4
Edith St PL5 .... 243 D1
Edmonton Cl EX4 .... 178 A8
Edmund St EX2, EX4 ... 261 A2
Edna Terr PL4 .... 263 C3
Edwards Cl PL7 .... 251 B4
Edwards Cres PL12 .... 242 C2
Edwards Dr
  Plymouth PL7 .... 251 B5
  Westward Ho! EX39 .... 156 E7
Edwards Rd PL13 .... 90 C1
Edward the Peacemaker
  (Statue) EX16 .... 161 C4
Edwin Rd EX2 .... 177 B3
Effingham Cres PL3 .... 248 D7
Efford Barns EX17 .... 81 B4
Efford Cres PL3 .... 249 B6
Efford Fort PL3 .... 249 B5
Efford La PL3 .... 249 B5
Efford Pathway
  Plymouth PL3 .... 249 C6
  Plymouth PL3 .... 249 C5
Efford Rd EX17 .... 80 E7
Efford Rd PL3 .... 249 B6
Efford Wlk PL3 .... 249 B6
Egerton Cres PL4 .... 263 C3
Egerton Pl PL4 .... 263 C3
Egerton Rd
  Plymouth PL4 .... 263 C3
  Torquay TQ1 .... 220 C5
Eggbuckland Com Coll
  PL6 .... 249 A8
Eggbuckland Rd PL3 ... 249 C6

Eggbuckland Vale Prim Sch
PL6 . . . . 249 A8
Eggesford Cross EX17 . . . . 60 A3
Eggesford Ctry Est EX18 . . 59 D6
Eggesford Fourways EX18 59 E5
Eggesford Gardens Cntry Ctr
EX18 . . . . 59 E6
Eggesford Rd EX18 . . . . 58 F3
Eggesford Sta EX18 . . . . 59 E6
Egg Moor La EX13 . . . . 88 A7
Egham Ave EX2 . . . . 177 D3
Egremont Cross EX14 . . . . . . 84 C6
Egremont Rd EX8 . . . . 202 A7
Egret Cl PL10 . . . . 253 A6
Egypt La EX18 . . . . 44 E1
Eiffel Pl 11 TQ9 . . . . 223 C5
Eight Acre Cl 1 PL7 . . . . 251 C5
Eight Acre La TA21 . . . . 160 E5
Eight Trees TQ9 . . . . 216 A5
Elaine Cl
  Exeter EX4 . . . . 174 A2
  Plymouth PL7 . . . . 250 B5
Elba Cl TQ4 . . . . 226 C7
Elberry Farm La TQ4 . . . . . . 229 D7
Elberry La TQ5 . . . . 229 E5
Elbow La PL19 . . . . 171 C6
Elburton Prim Sch PL9 . . . . 256 F2
Elburton Rd PL9 . . . . 256 B8
Eldad Hill PL1 . . . . 262 A3
Elderberry Way EX15 . . . . . . 162 E5
Elder Cl 2 PL7 . . . . 251 B5
Elder Gr EX17 . . . . 165 E6
Eldertree Gdns EX4 . . . . 177 A7
Eldridge Ho PL13 . . . . 167 F7
Eleanor Ho PL1 . . . . 262 A2
Elford Cres PL7 . . . . 250 E7
Elford Dr PL9 . . . . 255 C7
Elford Pk PL20 . . . . 127 A2
Elgar Cl
  Barnstaple EX32 . . . . 155 C5
  Exeter EX2 . . . . 178 C5
Elgin Cres PL5 . . . . 244 E3
Elim Cl EX10 . . . . 188 B5
Elim Ct PL3 . . . . 248 E5
Elim Terr PL3 . . . . 248 E5
Elim Villas EX10 . . . . 188 B5
Eliot St PL5 . . . . 247 E8
Elizabethan EX9 . . . . 156 B7
Elizabethan Ct 8 EX2 . . . . 261 B2
Elizabethan Ho 10 TQ9 . . 223 D5
Elizabethan House (Mus) The
  PL1 . . . . 263 A2
Elizabeth Ave
  Brixham TQ5 . . . . 230 A1
  Exeter EX4 . . . . 177 E8
Elizabeth Cl
  Barnstaple EX31 . . . . 154 D2
  Ivybridge PL21 . . . . 237 F5
  Lyme Regis DT7 . . . . 260 E4
  2 Whimple EX5 . . . . 99 E8
Elizabeth Ct
  2 Plymouth PL1 . . . . 263 A2
  Torquay TQ2 . . . . 219 F5
  Totnes TQ9 . . . . 223 F5
Elizabeth Dr EX31 . . . . 154 D3
Elizabeth Lea Cl EX22 . . . . . 38 E1
Elizabeth Pl PL4 . . . . 263 A4
Elizabeth Rd
  Exmouth EX8 . . . . 196 C2
  Seaton EX12 . . . . 192 A7
Elizabeth Sq 4 TQ12 . . . . . 207 F2
Elizabeth Way EX12 . . . . 192 A6
Elkins Hill TQ5 . . . . 230 D5
Ellacombe Church Rd
  TQ1 . . . . 220 C6
Ellacombe Rd TQ1 . . . . 220 B6
Ellacombe Sch TQ1 . . . . 220 B6
Ellards Cl EX2 . . . . 177 E3
Ellen Tinkham Sch EX1 . . 178 E7
Ellerhae Ho TQ14 . . . . 210 B3
Ellerhayes EX5 . . . . 82 D4
Ellersdown La TA22 . . . . 33 E4
Ellerslie Rd EX31 . . . . 154 B4
Ellesmere TQ1 . . . . 220 C4
Ellesmere Rd TQ1 . . . . 220 C5
Elley Cross EX17 . . . . 79 B2
Elliot Cl
  Barnstaple EX32 . . . . 155 C4
  Ottery St Mary EX11 . . . . . . 169 C3
Elliot Ho EX2 . . . . 261 B2
Elliot Plain TQ11 . . . . 236 C5
Elliots Hill TQ13 . . . . 130 C8
Elliot Sq PL11 . . . . 247 B3
Elliot St PL1 . . . . 262 B1
Elliott Cl
  Exeter EX4 . . . . 173 E2
  Saltash PL12 . . . . 242 D2
Elliott Ct TQ12 . . . . 211 C2
Elliott Terr PL1 . . . . 262 C1
Elliott Gr TQ5 . . . . 230 B4
Elliott Rd PL4 . . . . 249 B1
Elliott Terrace La PL1 . . . . 262 C1
Elliotts Hill PL8 . . . . 257 A4
Elliott's Hill EX17 . . . . 61 C3
Elliott Way EX2 . . . . 178 D5
Elmdale Cross EX20 . . . . . . 93 F7
Ellwood Cl TQ1 . . . . 220 B6
Ellwood Rd EX8 . . . . 196 D2
Elm Bank TQ1 . . . . 220 B6
Elmbank Gdns 3 TQ4 . . . . 226 A5
Elmbank Rd TQ4 . . . . 226 A5
Elmbridge Gdns EX4 . . . . . . 177 A8
Elm Cl
  Broadclyst EX5 . . . . 175 C6
  Stibb Cross EX38 . . . . 40 D2

Elm Cl continued
  Tavistock PL19 . . . . 171 C3
Elm Cotts
  Barnstaple EX31 . . . . 16 A3
  Saltash PL12 . . . . 242 C3
Elm Cres PL3, PL4 . . . . 249 A4
EIMCroft PL2 . . . . 248 B7
Elm Ct EX6 . . . . 201 B8
Elmdale Rd EX39 . . . . 157 A3
Elmdon Cl EX4 . . . . 173 D1
Elm Dr TQ12 . . . . 207 F7
Elm Farm La EX4 . . . . 103 A3
Elmfield Cres EX8 . . . . 196 B2
Elmfield Mdw EX20 . . . . . . 74 E1
Elmfield Rd
  Barnstaple EX31 . . . . 16 A3
  Seaton EX12 . . . . 192 A7
Elmfield Terr EX39 . . . . 157 A7
Elm Gr
  Bideford EX39 . . . . 156 F2
  Exmouth EX8 . . . . 201 F6
Elm Grove Ave EX3 . . . . 182 F5
Elm Grove Cl EX7 . . . . 204 E4
Elm Grove Dr EX7 . . . . 204 E7
Elm Grove Gdns EX3 . . . . . 182 F5
Elm Grove Rd
  Dawlish EX7 . . . . 204 E7
  Exeter EX4 . . . . 261 A4
  Topsham EX3 . . . . 182 F5
Elmhirst Dr TQ9 . . . . 223 C5
Elmhurst Ct 3 TQ14 . . . . . 210 B5
Elm La EX5 . . . . 202 F7
Elmlea Ave EX31 . . . . 153 E5
El Monte Cl 6 TQ14 . . . . . 210 B6
Elm Orch EX12 . . . . 192 D7
Elmsworthy Way EX16 . . . . 161 E5
Elm Pk
  Millbrook PL10 . . . . 253 B6
  Paignton TQ3 . . . . 225 F6
Elm Rd
  Brixham TQ5 . . . . 230 A2
  Exmouth EX8 . . . . 202 C7
  8 Newton Abbot TQ12 . . . . 207 C3
  Plymouth, Glenholt PL6,PL5 245 D6
  Plymouth, Mannamead PL4 248 F4
  Elmscott YN EX2 . . . . 37 B8
Elmscroft Terr 7 EX39 . . . 157 A2
Elmside
  Budleigh Salterton EX9 . . . 198 A1
  Exeter EX4 . . . . 177 E7
  Willand EX15 . . . . 162 D3
Elmside Cl EX4 . . . . 177 E7
Elm Terr PL21 . . . . 237 E8
Elmsleigh Pk TQ4 . . . . 226 B5
Elmsleigh Rd TQ4 . . . . 226 B5
Elms The
  Colyford EX24 . . . . 103 A3
  Holsworthy EX22 . . . . 164 C4
  Plymouth PL3 . . . . 248 A3
Elm Terr
  Honiton EX14 . . . . 166 D6
  1 Plymouth PL3 . . . . 248 F5
  Tiverton EX16 . . . . 161 B4
Elm Tree Cl PL8 . . . . 257 F4
Elm Tree Pk TQ6 . . . . 136 A2
Elm Units EX2 . . . . 177 D1
Elm Villas EX24 . . . . 103 A3
Elm Way EX10 . . . . 101 A1
Elm Wlk TQ9 . . . . 223 F5
Elmwood Ave TQ12 . . . . 206 E4
Elmwood Cl PL6 . . . . 245 D5
Elmwood Cres EX7 . . . . 204 E4
Elmwood Gdns EX24 . . . . . 103 A3
Elmwood Pk TQ7 . . . . 143 E2
Elphinstone Rd PL2 . . . . . . 248 C7
Elsdale Rd TQ4 . . . . 226 A4
Elsdon EX11 . . . . 168 E4
Elsdon La EX11 . . . . 168 E4
Elsdon's La DT6 . . . . 104 D7
Elspeth Sitters Ho 11
  PL4 . . . . 263 A2
Elston Cross
  Churchstow TQ7 . . . . 143 D4
  Copplestone EX17 . . . . 79 C6
Elstone Cross EX18 . . . . . . 44 C3
Elston La EX17 . . . . 79 B5
Elston Mdw EX17 . . . . 165 A5
Elton Rd EX4 . . . . 177 E8
Elvestone EX9 . . . . 198 B1
Elvis Rd EX8 . . . . 202 D7
Elwell Cross EX32 . . . . 18 B2
Elwell Rd PL12 . . . . 243 A4
Elwick Gdns PL3 . . . . 249 B5
Elworthy Cross EX16 . . . . . . 47 C2
Elworthy Dr TA21 . . . . 160 D4
Elworthy Hill EX16 . . . . 47 D2
Elwyn Rd EX8 . . . . 202 C6
Ely Cl
  Exeter EX4 . . . . 176 D6
  Feniton EX14 . . . . 84 D2
Elysian Cl EX36 . . . . 158 D5
Elysian Fields EX10 . . . . . . 188 B5
Embankment La PL4 . . . . . 249 B2
Embankment Rd
  Kingsbridge TQ7 . . . . 258 D3
  Plymouth PL4 . . . . 249 B2
Embankment Road La N
  PL4 . . . . 249 B2
Embercombe Cross EX32 . 18 F1
Embleford Cres TQ13 . . . . . 111 F5
Emblett Dr TQ12 . . . . 206 E4
Emblett Hill View TQ12 . . 206 F1
Embridge Cross TQ6 . . . . . 145 F7

Embridge Hill TQ6 . . . . 146 A7
Embury Cl TQ12 . . . . 213 A4
Emily Gdns PL4 . . . . 263 B4
Emmanuel Cl 1 EX4 . . . . . 177 A5
Emmanuel Rd 2 EX4 . . . . . 177 A5
Emma Pl PL1 . . . . 248 A1
Emma Place Ope PL1 . . . . . 248 A1
Emmasfield EX8 . . . . 202 D7
Emmetts Pk 9 TQ13 . . . . . 131 A5
Emperor Way EX1 . . . . 178 E2
Empire Ct 2 TQ1 . . . . 220 A7
Empire Rd TQ1 . . . . 220 A7
Empsons Cl EX7 . . . . 204 C6
Empsons Hill EX7 . . . . 204 C6
Emsfield Cl EX41 . . . . 178 B6
Endsleigh Cres EX5 . . . . . . 179 B7
Endsleigh Dr PL9,PL19 . . . 115 D5
Endsleigh Gdns 4 PL4 . . . 263 A4
Endsleigh House & Gdns
  PL19 . . . . 115 F5
Endsleigh Park Rd PL3 . . . 248 D6
Endsleigh Pk EX23 . . . . 70 A6
Endsleigh Pl PL4 . . . . 263 A4
Endsleigh Rd PL9 . . . . 255 C7
Endsleigh View PL21 . . . . . 237 A5
Energic Terr EX15 . . . . 163 C4
Enfield Cl EX17 . . . . 165 A5
Enfield Cotts TQ1 . . . . 220 D7
Enfield Rd TQ1 . . . . 220 C7
England's Cl 8 EX10 . . . . . 101 B1
Eningdale Rd PL19 . . . . 171 A4
Ennaton Cross PL21 . . . . . 137 E7
Ennerdale Gdns PL6 . . . . . 244 E5
Ennerdale Way EX4 . . . . . . 176 F6
Ennisfarne Rd EX39 . . . . . . 156 B7
Ensign Ct EX39 . . . . 156 F2
Ensis Cross EX31 . . . . 27 D5
Entrance Cross EX37 . . . . . 44 B7
Epping Cres PL6 . . . . 249 D7
Epworth Terr 4 PL2 . . . . . . 247 F5
Erica Dr TQ2 . . . . 213 F3
Eric Rd
  Calstock PL18 . . . . 125 E3
  Plymouth PL4 . . . . 263 C3
Erith Ave PL2 . . . . 247 F2
Erle Gdns PL7 . . . . 250 F3
Erlstoke Cl PL6 . . . . 245 C5
Erme Bridge Wks PL21 . . 237 C4
Erme Ct PL21 . . . . 237 D5
Erme Dr PL21 . . . . 237 D5
Erme Gdns PL3 . . . . 249 C5
Erme Pk PL21 . . . . 136 F3
Erme Prim Sch The
  PL21 . . . . 237 D5
Erme Rd PL21 . . . . 237 D5
Ermeside Cotts PL21 . . . . 136 F4
Erme Terr PL21 . . . . 237 D5
Ermington Prim Sch
  PL21 . . . . 136 F4
Ermington Terr PL4 . . . . . . 248 E4
Ermington Workshops
  PL21 . . . . 137 A4
Ernborough Ct EX2 . . . . . . 261 C2
Ernesettle Com Prim Sch
  PL5 . . . . 243 F4
Ernesettle Cres PL5 . . . . . . 243 F4
Ernesettle Gn PL5 . . . . 243 F4
Ernesettle La PL5 . . . . 243 D4
Ernesborough Gdns EX14 . 166 B5
Escot Cotts PL5 . . . . 184 B2
Escot Ctry Pk & Gdns
  EX11 . . . . 84 C1
Eskill Pl EX38 . . . . 159 C6
Esmonde Gdns PL5 . . . . . . 247 B8
Esplanade
  Exmouth EX8 . . . . 202 A5
  Seaton EX12 . . . . 192 A4
  Teignmouth TQ14 . . . . 210 C4
Esplanade The
  Dartmouth TQ6 . . . . 233 F5
  Plymouth PL1 . . . . 262 C1
  Sidmouth EX10 . . . . 188 B3
  Woolacombe EX34 . . . . 7 F7
Essa Rd PL12 . . . . 242 F2
Essex Cl PL4 . . . . 262 B4
Essex St PL1 . . . . 262 B4
Essington Cl EX8 . . . . 196 B3
Essington La EX20 . . . . 77 C4
Essington Rd EX20 . . . . 77 C4
Estover Cl PL6 . . . . 245 F5
Estover Com Coll PL6 . . . . 245 D2
Estover Ind Est PL6 . . . . . . 245 E5
Estover Rd PL6 . . . . 245 F4
Estuary Bsns Pk EX31 . . . . 15 C3
Estuary Ct EX8 . . . . 201 E6
Estuary View
  Budleigh Salterton EX9 . . . 198 B1
  Northam EX39 . . . . 157 A8
  Yelland EX31 . . . . 15 C2
Esworthy Cross EX16 . . . . . 32 F1
Ethelston's Cl DT7 . . . . 260 A5
Ethelwynne Brown Cl
  EX39 . . . . 157 B2
Eton Ave PL1 . . . . 262 C4
Eton Cl EX39 . . . . 156 F3
Etonhurst Cl EX2 . . . . 178 D3
Eton Pl PL1 . . . . 262 C4
Eton St PL1 . . . . 262 C4
Eton Terr 3 PL1 . . . . 262 B3
Eugene Rd TQ3 . . . . 226 C8
Eureka Terr
  Bovey Tracey TQ13 . . . . 180 D8
  1 Honiton EX14 . . . . 166 C5
Europa Pk EX34 . . . . 8 B6
Evans Ct PL1 . . . . 262 A3

Evans Pl PL2 . . . . 248 B5
Eveleigh Cl 2 TQ5 . . . . 230 C3
Eveleighs Ct EX4 . . . . 261 B4
Evelyn Pl PL4 . . . . 263 A4
Evelyn St PL5 . . . . 243 D1
Evenden Ct PL11 . . . . 247 A3
Eventide Homes TQ5 . . . . . 230 C2
Everest Dr EX12 . . . . 192 A7
Everett Pl EX16 . . . . 161 E6
Evergreen Cl EX8 . . . . 196 D3
Evett Cl EX8 . . . . 202 E8
Evran Dr EX8 . . . . 196 E3
Ewart's Ash EX14 . . . . 85 C8
Eworthy Cross EX21 . . . . . . 91 E6
Exbourne CE Prim Sch
  EX20 . . . . 76 C4
Exbourne Cross EX20 . . . . 76 C4
Excalibur Cl EX4 . . . . 174 A1
Excelsior Mews 2 TQ1 . . 220 B7
Exchange St PL1 . . . . 263 A2
Exebridge Ctr The EX4 . . . 261 A1
Exebridge Ind Est TA22 . . 33 F3
Exe Cl EX31 . . . . 15 E5
Execliff EX8 . . . . 202 A5
Exe Dene EX3 . . . . 182 E5
Exe Gdns PL3 . . . . 249 C7
Exe Hill TQ2 . . . . 219 B8
Exe St
  Exeter EX4 . . . . 261 A3
  Topsham EX3 . . . . 182 F5
Exeter Acad EX4 . . . . 173 D1
Exeter Airport EX5 . . . . 99 A4
Exeter Airport Bsns Pk
  EX5 . . . . 99 A4
Exeter Bsns Ctr EX2 . . . . . 177 C2
Exeter Central Sta EX4 . . 261 A4
Exeter Cl
  Feniton EX14 . . . . 84 D2
Exeter Coll PL5 . . . . 243 D4
Exeter Coll EX4 . . . . 177 A7
Exeter Coll (Annexe)
  EX4 . . . . 261 A3
Exeter Coll Bishop Blackall
  Annex EX4 . . . . 261 B4
Exeter Cross
  Coldeast TQ12 . . . . 123 A1
  Sidmouth EX10 . . . . 188 B6
Exeter Foyer EX2 . . . . 261 A2
Exeter Gate EX4 . . . . 158 C3
Exeter Hill
  Cullompton EX15 . . . . 163 B2
  Kenton EX6 . . . . 194 D3
  Shobrooke EX17 . . . . 80 F5
  Tiverton EX16 . . . . 161 E2
Exeter Hill Cross EX17 . . . 80 F4
Exeter Nuffield Hospl The
  EX2 . . . . 177 E4
Exeter Phoenix EX1 . . . . . . 261 B3
Exeter Rd
  Braunton EX33 . . . . 152 E4
  Chudleigh TQ13 . . . . 123 F7
  Crediton EX17 . . . . 165 D4
  Cullompton EX15 . . . . 163 B2
  Dawlish EX7 . . . . 200 E3
  Exmouth EX8 . . . . 196 A2
  Exmouth EX8 . . . . 202 A7
  Honiton EX14 . . . . 166 B5
  Ivybridge PL21 . . . . 237 E5
  Kennford EX6 . . . . 181 A2
  Kingsteignton TQ12 . . . . . . 207 D8
  Newton Abbot TQ12 . . . . . . 207 B5
  Okehampton EX20 . . . . 170 D5
  Ottery St Mary EX11 . . . . . . 169 A3
  Rockwell Green TA21 . . . . . 160 B5
  Silverton EX5 . . . . 82 B5
  South Brent TQ10 . . . . 135 A3
  Teignmouth TQ14 . . . . 210 B6
  Tiverton EX16 . . . . 64 B4
  Topsham EX2, EX3 . . . . 182 D6
  West Hill EX11 . . . . 168 E7
  Whiddon Down EX20 . . . . . 95 F3
  Whimple EX5 . . . . 168 B8
  Winkleigh EX19 . . . . 58 F2
Exeter Road Bsns Pk 8
  TQ12 . . . . 123 E1
Exeter Road Com Prim Sch
  EX8 . . . . 202 A7
Exeter Road Cvn Pk
  TA21 . . . . 160 A4
Exeter Road Ind Est
  EX20 . . . . 170 E6
Exeter St David's Sta
  EX4 . . . . 177 A7
Exeter Sch EX2 . . . . 177 E5
Exeter St
  North Tawton EX20 . . . . 77 C4
  Plymouth PL4 . . . . 263 A3
  Plymouth PL4 . . . . 263 B2
  Exeter Trad Ctr EX2 . . . . . . 181 E8
  Exe Units EX2 . . . . 177 D1
Exe Vale Rd EX30 . . . . 160 A4
Exe Vale Terr 6 EX16 . . . . 161 C3
Exe View EX6 . . . . 194 D6
Exe View Cotts EX4 . . . . . . 176 F6
Exe View Rd EX30 . . . . 160 A4
Exhibition Rd EX17 . . . . . . 165 C6
Exhibition Way EX4 . . . . . . 178 D8
Exminster Hill EX6 . . . . . . 182 C2
Exminster Marshes (Nature
  Reserve) EX6 . . . . 182 D3
Exminster Prim Sch EX6 182 A4
Exmoor Cl EX16 . . . . 161 E6
Exmoor Gdns TA22 . . . . 33 D6
Exmoor National Park Visitor
  Ctr EX35 . . . . 151 C6

Exmoor Steam Railway
  EX32 . . . . 11 C1
Exmoor View EX36 . . . . 158 C5
Exmoor Zoo EX31 . . . . 11 B3
Exmouth Com Coll EX8 . . 202 B8
Exmouth Ct
  Exmouth EX8 . . . . 202 B6
  Plymouth PL1 . . . . 247 F3
Exmouth Express Miniature
  Rly EX8 . . . . 203 A5
Exmouth Hospl EX8 . . . . . 202 B7
Exmouth Rd EX8 . . . . 202 A7
Exmouth Rd
  Budleigh Salterton EX9 . . . 197 E1
  Clyst St Mary EX5 . . . . 179 A1
  Exton EX3 . . . . 183 C3
  Lympstone EX8 . . . . 195 F7
  Newton Poppleford EX10 . 186 D5
  Plymouth PL1 . . . . 247 F3
Exmouth Sta EX8 . . . . 201 F7
Exonia Pk EX2 . . . . 176 D3
Explorer Ct PL2 . . . . 248 B5
Exton Gdns EX3 . . . . 183 C2
Exton Rd EX2 . . . . 177 C3
Exton Sta EX3 . . . . 183 C1
Exwick Ct EX4 . . . . 176 F8
Exwick Heights Prim Sch
  Exeter EX4 . . . . 176 E7
Exwick Hill EX4 . . . . 176 F7
Exwick Ho EX4 . . . . 176 F8
Exwick La EX4 . . . . 176 D7
Exwick Rd EX4 . . . . 176 F7
Exwick Villas EX4 . . . . 176 F7
Eyewell Gn EX12 . . . . 192 A6
Eymore Dr EX11 . . . . 168 C3
Eyrecourt Rd EX12 . . . . 192 A4

F

Factory Cotts TQ9 . . . . 139 C7
Factory Cross TQ13 . . . . . . 110 F6
Factory La TA20 . . . . 88 D8
Factory Ope 1 EX39 . . . . . 15 A1
Factory Row
  South Molton EX36 . . . . 158 E4
  Torquay TQ2 . . . . 220 A5
Fairacre Ave EX2 . . . . 155 C2
Fairfax Gdns EX2 . . . . 177 B2
Fairfax Pl TQ6 . . . . 233 F3
Fairfax Rd TQ12 . . . . 180 F3
Fairfax Terr 5 PL2 . . . . 247 F4
Fairfax Way EX38 . . . . 159 F5
Fairfield
  Bratton Fleming EX31 . . . . 18 A8
  Ilfracombe EX34 . . . . 150 C5
  Plymouth PL7 . . . . 250 E7
  Samford Peverell EX16 . . . 50 D1
  South Brent TQ10 . . . . 135 A2
Fairfield Ave
  Exeter EX4 . . . . 178 C8
  Plymouth PL2 . . . . 248 C7
Fairfield Cl
  Axminster EX13 . . . . 167 D5
  Bovey Tracey TQ13 . . . . 180 C7
  Exmouth EX8 . . . . 202 B6
  Kingsbridge TQ7 . . . . 258 F8
Fairfield Gdns EX14 . . . . . . 166 C5
Fairfield Gn TA3 . . . . 68 D7
Fairfield Pk DT7 . . . . 260 E4
Fairfield Rd
  Crediton EX17 . . . . 165 C6
  Exeter EX2 . . . . 181 B8
  Exmouth EX8 . . . . 202 B5
  Kingskerswell TQ12 . . . . . . 213 A3
  Torquay TQ2 . . . . 219 F8
Fairfield Terr
  Exeter EX2 . . . . 177 A4
  Newton Abbot TQ12 . . . . . . 207 C3
Fairfield Way TQ7 . . . . 145 A1
Fairhazel Dr EX4 . . . . 176 F7
Fairholme Rd EX34 . . . . 7 F6
Fair Isle Cl TQ2 . . . . 213 E2
Fairlands Ave EX6 . . . . 113 B3
Fairlawn Ct EX10 . . . . 188 B5
Fairlawns Pk TQ4 . . . . 226 B2
Fairlea TQ5 . . . . 230 C6
Fairlea Cl EX7 . . . . 200 F1
Fairlea Cres EX39 . . . . 156 E6
Fairlea Cl EX9 . . . . 197 E1
Fairlea Rd EX7 . . . . 200 F1
Fairleigh EX10 . . . . 186 E8
Fairlinch Cross EX33 . . . . . 152 A3
Fairlynch Cl EX33 . . . . 152 B7
Fairlynch Gr EX33 . . . . 152 C7
Fairlynch La EX33 . . . . 152 B7
Fairlynch Mus EX9 . . . . 199 H2
Fairmead EX10 . . . . 187 F8
Fairmead Ct TQ2 . . . . 213 F2
Fairmead Mews PL12 . . . . 242 C3
Fairmead Rd PL12 . . . . 242 C2
Fair Oak Cl EX5 . . . . 99 A4
Fairpark Cl EX2 . . . . 261 C2
Fairpark Rd EX2 . . . . 261 B2
Fairplace Terr EX20 . . . . . . 170 B5
Fairview TQ12 . . . . 223 D4
Fair View
  Barnstaple EX31 . . . . 154 E6
  Bradworthy EX22 . . . . 53 E8
  Exeter EX4 . . . . 103 A3
Fairview Ave
  Clyst St Mary EX5 . . . . 179 D2
  Plymouth PL5 . . . . 249 D5
Fair View La EX24 . . . . 103 A3
Fairview Rd TQ12 . . . . 211 A2

Fair View Rd
Dartmouth TQ6 . . . . .233 E3
Honiton EX14 . . . . .166 C5
Fairview Terr EX1 . . . . . . .174 F1
Fair View Terr EX8 . . . . . .202 B7
Fairview Way PL3 . . . . . . .249 E5
Fairwater Cl TQ12 . . . . . . .207 F7
Fairwaters TQ12 . . . . .207 E8
Fairway
Appledore EX39 . . . . .14 F1
Saltash PL12 . . . . .242 C2
Tiverton EX16 . . . . .64 E8
Fairway Ave PL21 . . . . . . .237 D5
Fairway Cl
Braunton EX33 . . . . .152 B6
Churston Ferrers TQ5 . . . .229 D5
Fairways Ct EX37 . . . . .43 B6
Fairways Dr EX37 . . . . .43 B6
Fairways The EX39 . . . . . .156 D7
Fairways View EX37 . . . . . .43 C6
Fairway The
Braunton EX33 . . . . .152 B6
Exeter EX4 . . . . .173 E1
Newton Ferrers PL8 . . . . . .140 F7
Falcon Cl EX2 . . . . .177 E6
Falcon Cl EX36 . . . . .158 C4
Falcon Pk TQ4 . . . . .224 F5
Falcon Rd EX2 . . . . .178 E4
Falcon Units TQ12 . . . . . .207 A3
Falcon Way EX1 . . . . .161 E6
Falkedon Cross EX17 . . . . .96 A6
Falkland Cl EX4 . . . . .173 E2
Falkland Dr TQ12 . . . . . . .207 F8
Falkland Rd TQ2 . . . . .219 F5
Falkland Way TQ14 . . . . . .210 A6
Fallapit Turn TQ9 . . . . . . .144 C8
Falloway Cl TQ2 . . . . .214 A2
Fallowfield Cl TQ12 . . . . . .207 F3
Fallowfields TQ9 . . . . .223 A5
Fallow Fields EX32 . . . . . .155 C2
Falmouth Cl TQ2 . . . . .219 B8
Fanny's Cross PL16 . . . . . .137 A2
Fanny's Cross EX36 . . . . . . .46 E7
Fanny's La EX17 . . . . .80 B5
Fannys Lane Cross EX17 . . .80 B5
Fanshawe Way PL9 . . . . . .255 C6
Faraday Ho EX1 . . . . .177 C6
Faraday Mill Bsns Pk
PL4 .249 B1
Faraday Rd PL4 . . . . .249 B1
Faraday Rd PL4 . . . . .249 B3
Farleigh TQ12 . . . . .206 B5
Farleigh Back Rd EX16 . . . .63 C2
Farleigh Cross TQ9 . . . . . .139 A4
Farleigh Front Rd EX16 . . .63 C2
Farleigh Mdws EX16 . . . . .161 A3
Farley Hill TQ13 . . . . .123 D8
Farley La EX35 . . . . .5 E3
Farley's Grave EX20 . . . . . .77 E7
Farm Cl
Exeter EX2 . . . . .178 C4
Kingskerswell TQ12 . . . . . .212 F6
Plymouth PL7 . . . . .250 C7
Farmer Frank's La EX19 . . .58 F2
Farm Hill EX4 . . . . .176 E8
Farmhouse Ave EX1 . . . . . .178 F8
Farm House Rise EX6 . . . .181 F4
Farm La
Plymouth PL5 . . . . .244 B2
Saltash PL12 . . . . .242 D1
Farm Rd D77 . . . . .193 E6
Farm The EX5 . . . . .99 D8
Farm Way EX14 . . . . .84 D2
Farmyard La TQ3 . . . . .218 E6
Farnham Ho 5 D77 . . . . . .260 D3
Farnham Terr 4 TQ3 . . . .226 B7
Farney Cl PL6 . . . . .245 B6
Farpark Hill La EX31 . . . . . .9 E4
Farrant Ct EX10 . . . . .188 A6
Farrant's Hill EX6 . . . . .113 B8
Farriel La EX34 . . . . .8 F5
Farriers Cotts PL7 . . . . . . .250 E7
Farriers The PL19 . . . . . . .116 E4
Farrington Cross
Chilton EX17 . . . . .80 C7
Exeter EX5 . . . . .99 A1
Farrington Ct EX5 . . . . .99 B2
Farrington Hill EX17 . . . . . .80 C7
Farrington Ho EX5 . . . . .99 B2
Farthing Cross TQ3 . . . . . .218 C3
Farthing Down TA21 . . . . . .51 E7
Farthing La TQ3 . . . . .218 C2
Farthing Lake Cross EX32 . .29 A7
Farthingland Cross EX20 . .76 B5
Farthings La EX10 . . . . . . .186 E7
Farthings Lodge Bsns Ctr
EX15 . . . . .83 E6
Farthing's Pitts TA21 . . . . .166 C4
Far View Rd EX20 . . . . . . .170 C5
Farway CE Prim Sch
EX24 . . . . .101 F7
Farway Common Rd EX14,
EX24 . . . . .101 E7
Farway Countryside Pk
EX24 . . . . .102 A5
Farwell Rd TQ9 . . . . .223 B6
Farwood Cross EX24 . . . . .102 C6
Fatacott Cross EX39 . . . . . .22 F5
Fatherford Rd EX20 . . . . . .170 D5
Faulkner Cl TQ6 . . . . .233 C3
Fawns Cl PL21 . . . . .136 F4
Fay Rd EX7 . . . . .204 E6
Fayre View PL12 . . . . .242 B1
Fearnside Way PL12 . . . . . .242 C3
Featherbed La
Clayhanger EX16 . . . . .35 C1
Exmouth EX8 . . . . .196 B2
Monkton EX14 . . . . .86 D6

Featherbed La *continued*
Offwell EX14 . . . . .86 B2
Featherstone Rd EX8 . . . . .196 A2
Federation Rd PL3 . . . . . . .249 C4
Fegan Rd PL5 . . . . .243 B1
Felixwell Ct EX4 . . . . .176 F5
Fell Cl PL8 . . . . .141 B8
Fellows PI PL1 . . . . .248 A2
Fellows La PL1 . . . . .262 A4
Feltrim Ave EX2 . . . . .261 C1
Feniton CE Prim Sch
EX14 . . . . .84 E2
Feniton Gdns EX14 . . . . . . .84 D2
Feniton Sta EX14 . . . . .84 D2
Fenten Pk PL12 . . . . .242 F3
Feoffe Cotts EX31 . . . . . . .154 F7
Feoffees Cotts TQ7 . . . . . .258 A4
Ferguson Cl EX11 . . . . . . .169 B3
Fernbank Ave PL21 . . . . . .237 A6
Fern Cl
Brixham TQ5 . . . . .230 D4
Okehampton EX20 . . . . . . .170 C6
Plymouth PL7 . . . . .251 B3
Ferncombe Cl 3 TQ12 . . .123 F1
Ferncombe Dr 2 TQ12 . . .123 F1
Ferndale Cl PL6 . . . . .233 E3
Ferndale Ave PL2 . . . . .247 E7
Ferndale Cl
8 Honiton EX14 . . . . .85 C2
Plymouth PL6 . . . . .245 D8
Ferndale Gdns EX2 . . . . . .177 A4
Ferndale Mews TQ2 . . . . .219 B7
Ferndale Rd
Exeter EX2 . . . . .177 A4
Plymouth PL2 . . . . .247 F7
Teignmouth TQ14 . . . . .210 B6
Torquay TQ2 . . . . .219 B7
Ferndown Cl EX39 . . . . . . .156 E2
Ferndown Rd D77 . . . . . . .260 E3
Ferne Animal Sanctuary
TA20 . . . . .69 D2
Fernhill Cl PL21 . . . . .237 B5
Fernhill Cross TQ7 . . . . . .143 E8
Fernhill Hts DT6 . . . . .104 F4
Fernicombe Rd TQ3 . . . . . .225 E7
Fernleigh Cl EX20 . . . . .77 C4
Fernleigh Rd PL3 . . . . .248 F5
Fernleigh Terr PL18 . . . . . .125 B5
Fern Mdw
Okehampton EX20 . . . . . . .170 C6
Tavistock PL19 . . . . .171 D6
Fernpark Cl EX2 . . . . .177 E2
Fern Pk EX34 . . . . .150 B5
Fern Rd TQ12 . . . . .207 F1
Fern Way EX4 . . . . .150 B4
Fernworthy Cl
Copplestone EX17 . . . . .79 B5
Torquay TQ2 . . . . .219 A7
Fernworthy Forest Walks
TQ13 . . . . .110 D2
Fernworthy Gdns EX17 . . . .79 B5
Fernworthy Pk EX17 . . . . . .79 B5
Ferrers Gn TQ5 . . . . .229 E4
Ferrers Rd PL5 . . . . .243 E1
Ferry La PL11 . . . . .246 D5
Ferryman's Reach TQ14 . .210 B3
Ferry Rd
Plymouth PL1 . . . . .247 E3
Topsham EX3 . . . . .182 E5
Ferry Slip TQ6 . . . . .233 F3
Ferry St PL11 . . . . .247 C3
Feversham PI PL7 . . . . . . .251 B6
Fiddlecott La EX18 . . . . .60 B6
Field Cl
Braunton EX33 . . . . .152 C5
Paignton TQ3 . . . . .219 B2
Field End
Axminster EX13 . . . . .167 C5
Bideford EX39 . . . . .156 E2
Field La
Ashford EX31 . . . . .16 B6
Braunton EX33 . . . . .152 C5
Filham Ind Est PL21 . . . . . .237 D5
Filham Moor Cl PL21 . . . . .237 E4
Fillace La PL19 . . . . .126 F4
Fillace Pk EX20 . . . . .189 D8
Filleigh Com Prim Sch
EX32 . . . . .29 C6
Filleigh Mill New Rd
EX32 . . . . .29 D7
Filleigh Moor Cross EX17 . .60 D5
Filleighmoor Gate EX17 . . .56 C3
Filham Moor La PL21 . . . . .237 D5
Filmer Way EX2 . . . . .177 B3
Fincer Dr PL21 . . . . .237 A6
Finch Cl PL3 . . . . .249 D4
Finches Cl PL9 . . . . .256 C7
Fir Cl
Honiton EX14 . . . . .166 B5
Willand EX15 . . . . .162 D5
Fircroft Rd PL2 . . . . .248 B7
Firebeacon Cross EX39 . . . .37 C7
Fire Beacon Cross
Bishop's Tawton EX31 . . . . .27 D7
Chittlehampton EX37 . . . . . .29 B2

Firebeacon La
Bolham EX16 . . . . .49 C3
Chittlehampton EX37 . . . . . .29 B2
Fire Beacon La EX10 . . . . .100 E1
Fire Brigade Hos EX4 . . . .261 A4
Firestone Cross EX20 . . . . .95 C3
Fire Stone Cross EX20 . . . .95 C4
Firestone La TQ12 . . . . . . .212 A8
Firlands TQ14 . . . . .210 B7
Firlands Rd TQ2 . . . . .214 A2
Firleigh Rd 7 TQ12 . . . . .123 E1
Firs Cross TQ9 . . . . .144 C7
Firs Gr EX32 . . . . .155 B5
Firs Pk EX2 . . . . .176 C3
First Ave
Axminster EX13 . . . . .167 F7
Dawlish EX7 . . . . .204 D5
Exeter, Countess Wear
EX2 .182 D7
Exeter, Heavitree EX1 . . . .177 F6
Plymouth, Billacombe PL9 .255 F8
Plymouth, Stoke PL1 . . . . .248 A2
Teignmouth TQ14 . . . . .210 A5
Torquay TQ1 . . . . .220 A8
First Dr
Teignmouth TQ14 . . . . .210 B5
Torquay TQ1 . . . . .210 D6
Firs The
4 Barnstaple EX32 . . . . . .155 B5
Kennford EX6 . . . . .114 D4
Wilmington EX14 . . . . .86 D2
First Raleigh EX39 . . . . . . .156 E3
Fir Terr EX36 . . . . .158 D4
Fir Tree Cl EX8 . . . . .196 C2
Firtree Rise PL21 . . . . .237 D5
Firway Cross EX16 . . . . .34 C3
Fir Wlk TQ2 . . . . .219 C8
Fisgard Way PL11 . . . . . . .246 D3
Fishacre Cl TQ3 . . . . .225 E8
Fishacre Cross TQ9 . . . . . .216 F6
Fishchowter's La TQ9 . . . .223 C4
Fishcombe Rd TQ5 . . . . . . .230 B6
Fisher Rd
Newton Abbot TQ12 . . . . . .207 B3
Plymouth PL2 . . . . .248 A5
Fisher's Hill TA21 . . . . .51 D7
Fishers Mead TA22 . . . . . . .33 D6
Fisher St TQ4 . . . . .226 B5
Fisherton Cross EX37 . . . . .28 C2
Fishingclose Cross EX20 . . .76 F6
Fishleigh Cross EX20 . . . . .75 C8
Fishleigh Rd EX31 . . . . . . .154 B2
Fish Mkt PL4 . . . . .263 B2
Fish Quay PL4 . . . . .263 A2
Fistral Cl PL11 . . . . .246 F4
Fitzford Cotts PL19 . . . . . .171 B4
Fitzroy Rd
Exeter EX1 . . . . .178 E6
Plymouth PL1 . . . . .248 A3
Fitzroy Terr 7 PL1 . . . . . .248 A3
Five Acres TQ13 . . . . .180 C4
Five Barrow La EX13 . . . . .104 A4
Five Barrows Cross EX36 . .19 D7
Five Bridges Cross EX15 . . .67 C7
Five Cross TQ12 . . . . .122 C1
Five Crosses
Modbury PL21 . . . . .137 A2
Rackenford EX16 . . . . .47 C1
Five Crossway EX36 . . . . . .46 D8
Five Cross Way
Brayford EX13 . . . . .18 F8
Plymtree EX15 . . . . .83 E8
West Buckland TA21 . . . . . . .52 F6
Five Cross Ways TA22 . . . . .32 F7
Five Elms Cross EX5 . . . . . .80 E1
Five Elms La EX5 . . . . .80 E1
Five Hos TA21 . . . . .160 B8
Five Lane End EX38 . . . . . .159 A1
Five Lanes
Buckfastleigh TQ13 . . . . . .236 E7
Dawlish EX7 . . . . .200 A3
Hennock TQ13 . . . . .123 B7
4 Kingsteignton TQ12 . . .123 E1
Marldon TQ3 . . . . .218 E3
Five Lanes Cross EX22 . . . .54 D8
Five Oaks TQ13 . . . . .218 D2
Five Mile Hill EX6 . . . . .98 C7
Five Mile Hill Cross EX6 . . .98 C4
Five Oaks TQ11 . . . . .130 C2
Five Oaks Cross
Brampford Speke EX5 . . . . .81 C1
Burrington EX37 . . . . .43 D4
Five Turnings EX34 . . . . .3 A4
Five Wyches Cross TQ13 .180 B7
Flagstaff Rd TQ6 . . . . .233 E4
Flamborough Rd PL6 . . . . .245 A7
Flamborough Way PL6 . . .245 A6
Flamsteed Cres PL5 . . . . . .243 E1
Flavel PI TQ6 . . . . .233 F3
Flavel St TQ6 . . . . .233 F3
Flayes Almshouses 2
EX4 .178 C8
Fleet St
Plymouth PL2 . . . . .247 E6
Torquay TQ1, TQ2 . . . . .220 B4
Fleet Walk Sh Ctr TQ2 . . .220 B4
Fleet Wlk TQ2 . . . . .220 B4
Fleming Ave EX10 . . . . . . .188 C8
Fleming Way EX2 . . . . .177 E4
Flemons Ct 6 TQ4 . . . . . .226 A5
Fletcher Cl TQ2 . . . . .219 E7
Fletcher Cres PL9 . . . . .256 B6
Fletcher Way PL9 . . . . .256 A6
Flete PL21 . . . . .136 E2
Flete Ave TQ12 . . . . .207 F2
Flete Cl TQ12 . . . . .207 F2
Flete Ho PL21 . . . . .136 E2
Fletemoor Rd PL5 . . . . .243 E1

Flete View Terr 10 PL21 .137 C8
Flexapark EX34 . . . . .3 A3
Flexton The EX1 . . . . .169 D4
Flightway EX14 . . . . .67 B3
Floaters Rd TQ6 . . . . .233 F4
Flood's La EX15 . . . . .163 B3
Flood St TQ9 . . . . .227 F8
Flora Cotts PL1 . . . . .262 B2
Flora Ct PL1 . . . . .262 B3
Flora St PL1 . . . . .262 B2
Florence Cotts TQ7 . . . . . .145 D1
Florence PI
Newton Abbot TQ12 . . . . . .207 D1
Plymouth PL4 . . . . .263 C3
Florence St PL5 . . . . .243 D1
Florida Dr EX4 . . . . .173 D2
Florida Gdns PL3 . . . . .249 C6
Florida Rd TQ1 . . . . .220 A6
Flowerpot La EX4 . . . . .177 A5
Flowers Mdw 1 TQ12 . . . .122 F1
Flower St EX5 . . . . .184 C3
Flow La TQ14 . . . . .208 F7
Floyd Cl PL2 . . . . .247 F7
Floyers-Hay Ct EX2 . . . . . .261 A1
Floyte La EX6 . . . . .98 B5
Fluder Cres TQ12 . . . . .213 B3
Fluder Hill TQ12 . . . . .213 B3
Fluder La TQ12 . . . . .213 F5
Fluder La TQ12 . . . . .213 B3
Fluder Rise TQ12 . . . . .213 B3
Foldhay Cross EX17 . . . . . . .78 A6
Foliot Ave PL2 . . . . .248 A6
Foliot Rd PL2 . . . . .248 A6
Follafield Pk TQ5 . . . . .230 B2
Follaton Bglws TQ9 . . . . . .223 A5
Follaton Gate TQ9 . . . . . . .222 E6
Follaton Rd TQ9 . . . . .222 F6
Follett Rd
Tiverton EX16 . . . . .64 D7
Topsham EX3 . . . . .182 E5
Folley La EX4 . . . . .98 D4
Folly Cross TQ10 . . . . .134 E1
Folly Farm Cl EX33 . . . . . .152 C6
Folly Gate Cross EX20 . . . . .93 F8
Folly Goyle Cross EX19 . . . .43 B3
Folly Hill TQ7 . . . . .142 C8
Folly La
Buckland St Mary TA20 . . . .69 D8
South Molton EX36 . . . . . . .30 D4
Football La TQ12 . . . . .207 E8
Footland La
Daccombe TQ12 . . . . .213 F5
Ipplepen TQ12 . . . . .217 F5
Footland Rd TQ4 . . . . .226 A4
Footpark La EX6 . . . . .96 C2
Forbes Cl TQ12 . . . . .180 F2
Forcefield Rd EX15 . . . . . .163 B2
Forces Cross TQ9 . . . . .139 E3
Forches Ave EX32 . . . . . . .155 C4
Forches Cnr EX17 . . . . .165 C6
Forches Cross
Burrington EX37 . . . . .43 F4
Crediton EX17 . . . . .165 C6
Langtree EX38 . . . . .40 F1
Newton Abbot TQ12 . . . . . .206 E7
Forches Cross Com Prim Sch
EX32 . . . . .155 C4
Forches Green Flats 4
EX32 . . . . .155 B4
Forches Head EX5 . . . . . . .175 B4
Forches Hill TQ12 . . . . .209 B2
Ford TQ6 . . . . .233 E3
Fordbarn Cross TQ9 . . . . . .222 E2
Ford Cl PL21 . . . . .237 A5
Ford Cres EX22 . . . . .53 E8
Ford Cross
Ash Mill EX36 . . . . .31 D1
Chawleigh EX18 . . . . .59 E7
Chulmleigh EX18 . . . . .44 D2
Ford TQ7 . . . . .149 A7
Hittisleigh EX6 . . . . .96 D4
Kentisbury EX31 . . . . .10 D5
Molland EX36 . . . . .31 F7
Monkton EX14 . . . . .86 A5
Oakford EX16 . . . . .48 D5
Shirwell EX31 . . . . .17 C8
South Zeal EX20 . . . . .95 B8
Staverton TQ9 . . . . .216 E5
South Molton EX17 . . . . . . .97 D8
Ford Down La EX36 . . . . . .158 A3
Forde Abbey & Gardens
TA20 . . . . .88 F8
Forde Cl
Abbotskerswell TQ12 . . . . .212 A7
Newton Abbot TQ12 . . . . . .207 D3
Forde Cross EX17 . . . . .80 F8
Forde Gdns TQ12 . . . . .207 D1
Forde La EX38 . . . . .26 E2
Fordens La EX7 . . . . .204 C3
Forde Pk TQ12 . . . . .207 D2
Forder Cross
Bishopsteignton TQ14 . . . .208 A8
Bovey Tracey TQ13 . . . . . . .122 F3
Cawsand PL10 . . . . .252 F6
Dartington TQ9 . . . . .222 E8
Dartington TQ9 . . . . .222 E8
South Brent TQ10 . . . . .135 B4
Ugborough PL21 . . . . .137 D7
Forder Way TQ13 . . . . .123 B6
Forder Valley Rd PL6 . . . . .249 D8

Ford Hill
Bow EX17 . . . . .78 F4
Cheriton Bishop EX6, EX17 . .97 C5
Hartland EX39 . . . . .22 E3
Kentisbury EX31 . . . . .10 D5
Plymouth PL2 . . . . .248 A5
Thorverton EX5 . . . . .81 E6
Fordisbaies La EX5, EX15 . .82 F6
Ford La
Cheriton Fitzpaine EX16 . . .63 B6
Clifton EX31 . . . . .10 B5
South Molton EX36 . . . . . . .158 A8
West Hill EX11 . . . . .168 E3
Whitestone EX4 . . . . .98 C4
Ford Leat
EX6 .176 B2
Fordlands Cres EX39 . . . . .156 F4
Fordlands Rd TQ13 . . . . . . .111 F5
Ford Lane Cross EX6 . . . . . .96 D4
Fordmill Cross EX16 . . . . . .34 D1
Fordmoor Cross EX18 . . . . .59 F7
Ford Orch 50 D1
Ford Park La PL4 . . . . .248 E4
Ford Park Rd PL4 . . . . .248 D4
Ford Pk 8 TQ13 . . . . .123 C4
Ford Plain EX5 . . . . .81 E5
Ford Prim Sch PL2 . . . . . . .248 A5
Ford Rd
Abbotskerswell TQ12 . . . . .212 B7
Bampton EX16 . . . . .34 C1
Tiverton EX16 . . . . .64 D7
Totnes TQ9 . . . . .223 D6
Wembury PL9 . . . . .140 D8
Yealmpton PL8 . . . . .136 A2
Fords Rd EX2 . . . . .261 A1
Ford St
Moretonhampstead
TQ13 . . . . .111 F5
Tavistock PL19 . . . . .171 B5
Wellington TA21 . . . . .160 F4
Fordton Cross EX17 . . . . . .165 E2
Fordton Ind Est EX17 . . . . .165 E3
Fordton Plain EX17 . . . . . . .165 E3
Fordton Terr EX17 . . . . .165 D3
Ford Valley TQ6 . . . . .233 E3
Fordworth Cotts TQ7 . . . . .149 D5
Foredown La TQ12 . . . . . . .212 E4
Foredown Rd TQ12 . . . . . . .211 E2
Foreland Ho EX34 . . . . .150 A4
Foreland View EX34 . . . . . .150 B4
Fore St
Aveton Gifford TQ7 . . . . . . .143 C6
8 Bampton EX16 . . . . .34 B1
Beer EX12 . . . . .191 D5
Bere Alston PL20 . . . . .125 E1
Bere Ferrers PL20 . . . . .239 F3
Bishopsteignton TQ14 . . . .208 F8
Bovey Tracey TQ13 . . . . . . .180 D7
Bradninch EX5 . . . . .82 F6
Bridestowe EX20 . . . . .107 F8
Brixham TQ5 . . . . .230 C5
Buckfastleigh TQ11 . . . . . .236 E5
Budleigh Salterton EX9 . . .199 G2
Calstock PL18 . . . . .125 D3
Cargreen PL12 . . . . .239 A2
Cawsand PL10 . . . . .253 A2
Chudleigh TQ13 . . . . .123 E6
Chulmleigh EX18 . . . . .44 E1
Cornwood PL21 . . . . .133 C2
Cullompton EX15 . . . . .163 C3
Culmstock EX15 . . . . .66 E8
Dartmouth TQ6 . . . . .234 A3
Dolton EX19 . . . . .57 F7
Dulverton TA22 . . . . .33 D6
Exbourne EX20 . . . . .76 C5
Exeter EX4 . . . . .261 A2
Exeter, Heavitree EX1 . . . .177 F5
Exmouth EX8 . . . . .202 A6
Great Torrington EX38 . . . .159 D5
Gunnislake, Albaston PL18 .125 C5
Gunnislake PL18 . . . . .125 D6
Harberton TQ9 . . . . .222 D2
Hartland EX39 . . . . .22 E3
7 Hemyock EX15 . . . . .67 B8
Holbeton PL8 . . . . .136 D1
Holcombe Rogus TA21 . . . .50 F5
Holemoor EX22 . . . . .73 C8
Holsworthy EX22 . . . . .164 C4
Ide EX2 . . . . .176 E2
Ideford TQ13 . . . . .124 B4
Ilfracombe EX34 . . . . .150 C6
Ipplepen TQ12 . . . . .211 D2
Ivybridge PL21 . . . . .237 D5
Kentisbeare EX15 . . . . .66 A3
Kenton EX6 . . . . .194 D3
Kingsbridge TQ7 . . . . .258 C6
Kingskerswell TQ12 . . . . . .213 A4
Kingsteignton TQ12 . . . . . .207 E7
Langtree EX38 . . . . .40 E2
Lifton PL16 . . . . .105 E4
Loddiswell TQ7 . . . . .143 E7
Luton TQ13 . . . . .124 C3
Millbrook PL10 . . . . .252 E5
Milton Abbot PL19 . . . . . . .116 A6
Morchard Bishop EX17 . . . .61 A2
Moretonhampstead TQ13 . .111 F5
Northam EX39 . . . . .156 F6
North Molton EX36 . . . . . . .30 D8
North Tawton EX20 . . . . . . .77 B4
Okehampton EX20 . . . . . . .170 B5
Otterton EX9 . . . . .198 E7
Plymouth, Devonport PL1 . .247 C2
Plymouth, Plympton PL7 . .250 E4

Fore St *continued*
Plymouth, Tamerton Foliot
PL5 . . . .**244** B6
Salcombe TQ8 . . . .**259** E4
Saltash PL12 . . . .**242** F7
Seaton EX12 . . . .**192** B5
Shaldon TQ14 . . . .**210** A3
Shebbear EX22 . . . .**55** D1
Sidbury EX10 . . . .**101** B2
Sidmouth EX10 . . . .**188** B3
Silverton EX5 . . . .**82** B5
1 South Brent TQ10 . . . .**134** F3
South Tawton EX20 . . . . . .**95** B5
Tatworth TA20 . . . .**88** D8
8 Teignmouth TQ14 . . . .**210** C4
Tiverton EX16 . . . .**161** D4
Topsham EX3 . . . .**182** F5
Torpoint PL11 . . . .**247** B3
Torquay, Barton TQ2 . . . .**214** A2
Torquay, St Marychurch
TQ1 . . . .**220** B8
Totnes TQ9 . . . .**223** C5
Uffculme EX15 . . . .**66** A7
Ugborough PL21 . . . .**137** D6
Wellington TA21 . . . .**160** D6
Winkleigh EX19 . . . .**58** F3
Witheridge EX16 . . . .**46** E1
Yealmpton PL8 . . . .**257** F4
Fore Ave PL2 . . . .**248** C7
Foresters Rd
Holsworthy EX22 . . . .**164** C5
Plymouth PL9 . . . .**255** D7
Forester's Terr TQ14 . . . .**210** B4
Forest Hill EX39 . . . .**25** F4
Forest Hos EX21 . . . .**73** B4
Forest Rd TQ12 . . . .**220** A7
Fore Street Ctr EX4 . . . . . .**261** A2
Fore Street Hill EX9 . . . . .**199** H2
Fore Street Mews 16
EX4. . . . .**261** A2
Forest Ridge Rd TQ3 . . .**218** F1
Forestry Hos PL20 . . . . . .**120** B4
Foretown EX15 . . . .**83** D3
Forge Cl EX9 . . . .**197** F2
Forge End EX19 . . . .**58** F2
Forge La
Butterleigh EX15 . . . .**64** D3
Saltash PL12 . . . .**242** C4
Forge Pl TQ13 . . . .**180** C7
Forges Hill EX15 . . . .**64** F3
Forge Way EX15 . . . .**163** C3
Forgeway Cl TQ2 . . . .**219** D4
Fork Cross TQ9 . . . .**222** A5
Forresters Dr PL6 . . . . . .**245** D7
Forrest Units EX2. . . . . . .**177** D1
Forster Rd TQ8 . . . .**259** D5
Forsythia Dr PL12 . . . . . .**242** C3
Fort Austin Ave PL6 . . . .**245** C1
Fortescue Bglws EX34 . . . .**8** C6
Fortescue Cl EX33 . . . . . .**152** E5
Fortescue Cross EX5 . . . . .**81** E2
Fortescue Pl PL3 . . . .**249** A6
Fortescue Rd
Barnstaple EX32 . . . .**155** B2
Exeter EX2 . . . .**177** B3
Ilfracombe EX34 . . . .**150** B6
Paignton TQ3 . . . .**219** C4
Salcombe TQ8 . . . .**259** C4
Sidmouth EX10 . . . .**188** D7
Fort Hill EX2 . . . .**155** B5
Forth Gdns PL3 . . . .**249** D6
Fort Hill Dr EX32 . . . .**155** B5
Fortmead Cl EX34 . . . . . .**155** A5
Forton Rd EX8 . . . .**196** C1
Fort Picklecombe PL10 . .**253** F4
Fort St EX32 . . . .**155** A4
Fort Terr
16 Barnstaple EX32 . . . . .**155** A4
5 Bideford EX39 . . . . . .**157** B1
Plymouth PL6. . . . .**244** F3
For The PL10 . . . .**253** A1
Fortune Way TQ1 . . . .**220** B7
Forward Gn EX5 . . . .**82** E7
Fosbrooke Ct 10 PL3 . . .**248** F5
Fosketh Hill EX39 . . . . . .**156** C6
Fosketh Terr TR19 . . . . . .**156** C6
Fosse Rd TQ7 . . . .**258** D6
Fosseway Cl EX13 . . . . . .**167** D5
Fosse Way Ct 2 EX12 . . .**192** B4
Foss Slip TQ6 . . . .**233** F3
Foss St TQ6 . . . .**233** F3
Fosterlea EX15 . . . .**163** B3
Foulston Ave PL5 . . . . . .**247** B8
Foundry Ct 9 TQ13 . . . .**123** E6
Foundry La PL8. . . . .**140** F6
Fountain Ct TQ13 . . . . . .**180** D7
Fountain Fields EX37 . . . .**43** B7
Fountain Hill EX9 . . . . . .**203** F8
Fountain Ho TQ1 . . . .**220** C4
Fountains Cres PL2 . . . . .**248** C8
Fouracre Cl EX4 . . . .**174** A1
Four Acres EX39 . . . .**156** D2
Four Acres Cl EX14 . . . . . .**86** B2
Fouracre Way TQ12 . . . . .**207** F8
Four Cross
Axminster EX13 . . . .**167** B4
Ilsington TQ12 . . . .**122** C2
Kingston TQ7 . . . .**142** C2
Wilmington EX14 . . . .**86** C4
Four Cross Elms EX24 . . .**103** A4
Fourcross Hill EX33 . . . .**187** B7
Four Cross Lanes TQ9 . .**228** B4

Four Cross Way EX32 . . . . .**11** C1
Four Crossways EX18 . . . .**44** E1
Four Cross Ways
Cheriton Bishop EX6 . . . . .**97** A4
North Tawton EX20 . . . . . .**77** D4
Witland PL5 . . . .**162** D5
Winkleigh EX19 . . . .**58** D2
Four Elms
Holcombe Rogus TA21 . . . .**51** A6
Sidmouth EX10 . . . .**187** C8
Four Elms Hill EX10 . . . . .**187** B8
Four Firs EX5. . . . .**185** A1
Four Lanes EX5. . . . .**84** B8
Fourlanesend Com Prim Sch
PL10 . . . .**252** F3
Four Mills La EX17 . . . . .**165** D4
Four Oak EX32. . . . .**17** B2
Four Oak Cross EX32. . . . .**17** B2
Four Oaks Cl 1 EX32 . . . .**17** B2
Four Oaks Rd EX6 . . . .**97** F4
Four Seasons Village
EX19. . . . .**58** E3
Fourth Ave TQ14 . . . .**210** A6
Four Ways Cotts EX18. . . .**59** E4
Four Ways Cl EX15 . . . . . .**67** C8
Four Ways Dr EX18 . . . . . .**44** E1
Four White Gates Cross
EX37. . . . .**29** B4
Fowelscombe Gate PL21. .**137** F6
Fowey Ave TQ2 . . . .**219** B8
Fowey Cl EX1. . . . .**177** F7
Fowey Gdns PL3 . . . .**249** D6
Fowey Rd EX31 . . . .**15** E5
Fowler Cl EX6 . . . .**182** A4
Fowley Cross EX20. . . . . . .**93** D5
Foxbeare Rd EX34 . . . . . .**150** E5
Fox Cl
Okehampton EX20 . . . . . .**170** D6
Rockwell Green TA21. . . . .**160** A6
Foxdown Hill TA21 . . . . . .**160** C4
Foxdown Rd TA21. . . . . . .**160** C4
Foxdown Terr TA21. . . . . .**160** D4
Foxes' Cross EX38 . . . . . .**26** E1
Foxes Lair EX20. . . . .**170** A6
Fox Field Cl PL3 . . . .**249** C5
Foxglove Chase EX15 . . .**162** D5
Foxglove Cl
Barnstaple EX32 . . . .**155** E4
Dunkeswell EX14 . . . .**67** C1
Launceston PL15 . . . .**105** A2
3 Tiverton EX16. . . . . . .**161** F6
Foxglove Rd EX12 . . . . . .**192** B7
Foxglove Rise EX4 . . . . . .**176** D8
Foxglove Way PL12 . . . . .**242** B3
Foxhayes Rd EX4 . . . .**176** F6
Foxhill EX13 . . . .**167** D5
Fox Hill EX39 . . . .**156** F6
Foxhole Hill EX6 . . . .**113** B4
Foxhole Inf Sch TQ3. . . . .**225** E7
Foxhole Jun Sch TQ3 . . . .**225** E8
Foxhole La EX39 . . . .**156** F6
Foxhole Rd
Paignton TQ3 . . . .**225** F7
Torquay TQ2. . . . .**219** D5
Foxhole Wik EX8 . . . .**202** D4
Foxhollows TQ12. . . . . . .**208** A2
Fox & Hounds Cotts
EX20. . . . .**108** A5
Foxlands Wlk TQ1. . . . . .**220** C8
Foxley Cres TQ12 . . . . . .**206** F3
Fox Rd EX4 . . . .**174** B2
Fox's Cnr EX10 . . . .**187** F2
Fox's Cross EX17 . . . .**63** B1
Foxtor Rd EX4 . . . .**244** B3
Fox Tor Cl TQ4 . . . .**229** B2
Foxtor Rd EX4 . . . .**176** E8
Foxwell La TQ12 . . . .**207** A4
Foxwood Gdns
Plymouth, Plymstock PL9 . .**255** F5
Plymouth, Southway PL6. . .**244** E5
Foyle Cl PL7 . . . .**251** A5
Frances Homes EX1 . . . . .**261** C3
Francis Cl EX4 . . . .**176** F4
Francis Court Cotts EX5. . .**82** D2
Francis Cres 4 EX31. . . . .**16** A2
Francis Ct
7 Crediton EX17 . . . .**165** C5
Exeter EX2. . . . .**177** E5
Francis Dr EX39 . . . .**156** C6
Francis St PL1. . . . .**262** A3
Francis Way EX24. . . . . . .**103** B3
Franeth Cl TQ12 . . . .**207** D8
Frankford La EX4 . . . .**43** B3
Frankfort Gate 9 PL1. . .**262** B3
Franklea Cl EX11 . . . .**169** D3
Franklin St EX2. . . . .**261** B2
Franklyn Ave EX33 . . . . .**152** E6
Franklyn Cl EX2 . . . .**176** F3
Franklyn Dr EX2 . . . .**176** F3
Franklyn Hospl EX2 . . . . .**176** F3
Franklyns PL6. . . . .**245** A4
Franklyns Cl PL6. . . . . . .**245** A4
Frankmarsh Pk EX32 . . . .**155** B5
Frankmarsh Rd EX32 . . . .**155** B6
Frankmills Hill EX6 . . . . .**113** B1
Frank Webber Rd TA21. . .**160** A5
Fraser Dr TQ14 . . . .**210** A6
Fraser Pl PL5. . . . .**244** C7
Fraser Rd
Exmouth EX8 . . . .**196** D2
Plymouth PL5. . . . .**244** C7
Fraser Sq PL5 . . . .**244** C7
Frederick St E PL1. . . . . .**262** B3
Frederick St W 6 PL1. . .**262** B3
Frederick Terr 6 EX7 . . . .**204** D6
Fredington Gr PL2 . . . . . .**248** B6
Free Cotts EX4 . . . .**261** A3
Freedom Sq PL4. . . . .**263** B4

Freelands Cl EX8 . . . . . .**202** D8
Freemans Wharf PL1. . . .**254** A8
Freestone Rd TQ12. . . . .**207** D8
Fremantle Gdns 4 PL2 . .**247** F4
Fremantle Pl PL2 . . . . . .**247** F4
Fremington Com Prim Sch
EX31. . . . .**153** D5
Fremington Quay EX31. . .**153** F7
Fremington Rd EX12 . . . .**191** F7
French Cl EX5 . . . .**82** B6
French St 7 TQ14 . . . . . .**210** C4
Frenchstone Cross EX36 . .**30** B2
Fresham Ave PL6 . . . .**245** C7
Fresham Gdns PL6 . . . . .**245** C7
Freshford Cl PL6. . . . . . .**245** C1
Freshford Wlk PL6. . . . . .**245** C1
Freshwater Dr TQ4. . . . .**229** B8
Frewin Gdns PL6 . . . . . .**245** B6
Frewins PL6 . . . .**197** F2
Friars' Gate EX2 . . . .**261** B2
Friar's Hele Cross EX20 . .**57** B2
Friars' La PL1 . . . .**263** A2
Friars Lodge EX2 . . . . . .**261** B2
Friars Wlk PL19. . . . .**171** C2
Friars' Wlk EX2 . . . .**261** B2
Friary Pk PL4. . . . .**263** B3
Friary St PL4 . . . .**263** B3
Friendship Ct PL19 . . . . .**117** E6
Friernhay Ct EX4 . . . .**261** A2
Friernhay St EX4 . . . .**261** A2
Frith Rd PL22 . . . .**242** D3
Fritz's Grave TQ11. . . . . .**236** A7
Frobisher App PL5. . . . . .**244** D2
Frobisher Cl TQ14. . . . . .**210** A8
Frobisher Dr PL12 . . . . . .**242** E2
Frobisher Gn TQ2 . . . . . .**219** C6
Frobisher La TQ8 . . . . . .**259** C5
Frobisher Rd EX8 . . . . . .**196** C2
Frobisher Way
Paignton TQ4 . . . .**226** B2
Tavistock PL19 . . . .**171** B5
Torpoint PL11 . . . .**246** D3
Frogbury Cross EX17 . . . .**59** F1
Froggy Mill Cross EX6 . . .**97** C5
Frog La
Braunton EX33. . . . .**152** D7
Clyst St Mary EX5 . . . . . .**179** A3
Holcombe Rogus TA21 . . . .**50** F5
South Molton EX36 . . . . .**158** B5
Frogmore Ave
Plymouth PL6. . . . .**249** B7
Plymouth PL6. . . . .**249** C7
Frogmore Cross EX5 . . . . .**82** F3
Frogmore Ct PL6. . . . . . .**249** B7
Frogmore Farm TQ9 . . . .**139** F7
Frogmore Rd PL6 . . . . . .**198** C6
Frogmore Terr TQ7 . . . . .**258** C4
Frogs La TA21 . . . .**52** F7
Frog St
Bampton EX16. . . . .**34** B1
Exeter EX1, EX2. . . . .**261** A2
Woolacombe EX34 . . . .**7** F6
Frogstreet Hill EX33 . . . . .**8** A2
Frogwell Cross TA4 . . . . .**34** D6
Fromne Cl PL7 . . . .**251** A4
Frontfield Cres PL6. . . . .**244** E5
Frost Cross
Bovey Tracey TQ13. . . . . .**123** B6
Morchard Bishop EX17 . . . .**61** B1
Frost's Cnr EX19. . . . .**42** D1
Froude Ave TQ2. . . . .**214** B3
Froude Rd TQ8 . . . .**259** B2
Fry's La 8 EX10 . . . .**101** B3
Fry St EX22. . . . .**164** C4
Fuge Cross TQ6 . . . .**145** E6
Fuidge Cross EX17. . . . . .**96** A5
Fuidge La EX17 . . . .**96** A5
Fulda Cres EX17 . . . .**165** D4
Fulford Cl
Bideford EX39 . . . .**26** A4
Tedburn St Mary EX6. . . . .**97** F4
Fulford Dr EX15. . . . .**163** B2
Fulford Rd
Cheriton Bishop EX6 . . . . .**97** D1
Dunsford EX6. . . . .**112** F8
Exeter EX1. . . . .**177** F7
Fulford Way EX5. . . . . . .**184** C2
Fullaford Cross TQ11. . . .**236** B4
Fullaford Hill EX18. . . . . .**18** E8
Fullaford Rd TQ11 . . . . . .**236** A4
Fullaford Pool Cross
TQ11 . . . .**236** A4
Fullers Ct 12 EX2 . . . . . .**261** A2
Fullerton Rd PL2 . . . .**248** A5
Fullingcott Cross EX39. . .**153** A2
Fulton Cl TQ12. . . . .**211** D2
Fulton Ho 2 EX12 . . . . . .**192** A5
Furland Cl PL9 . . . .**255** C5
Furley Cross EX13 . . . . . .**87** D6
Furlong Cl TQ11 . . . .**236** B7
Furlong Cotts EX16 . . . . .**51** A4
Furneaux Ave PL2 . . . . . .**248** B5
Furneaux Rd PL2 . . . .**248** B6
Furness Cl TQ4 . . . .**226** A2
Furrough Cross TQ1 . . . .**220** C8
Furrough Ct TQ1. . . . . . .**220** C8
Fursdon Cl PL9 . . . .**256** C6
Fursdon Cross
East Allington TQ7 . . . . . .**144** E4
Hittisleigh EX6. . . . .**96** C5
Fursdon House EX5. . . . . .**81** E7
Fursdon La EX6 . . . .**96** B5
Furse Pk PL5 . . . .**247** C2
Fursham Cross EX6 . . . . .**96** B4
Furzeacre Cl PL7 . . . .**251** C5
Furzebeam Row EX38. . . .**159** B5
Furzebeam Terr 14 EX39. .**157** B1
Furzebrook EX11 . . . .**169** E4

Furze Cap 3 TQ12. . . . . .**123** E1
Furze Cross
Bridgerule EX22. . . . .**71** A5
Chittlehampton EX37. . . . . .**29** A5
Cornworthy TQ9 . . . .**227** A2
Kingsbridge TQ7 . . . .**144** D3
Furzedown Cross
Copplestone EX17 . . . .**79** A5
Taw Green EX20 . . . .**95** A6
Furzedown Rd TQ12. . . . .**213** A5
Furze Gdns
Shop EX23 . . . .**37** A1
Totnes TQ9. . . . .**223** F5
Furzegood TQ3 . . . .**218** D3
Furzeham Ct TQ5 . . . . . .**230** B5
Furzeham Pk TQ5 . . . . . .**230** B5
Furzeham Prim Sch TQ5 . .**230** C5
Furzehatt Ave PL9 . . . . . .**256** A6
Furzehatt Park Rd PL9 . . .**256** A6
Furzehatt Rd PL9 . . . .**255** F6
Furzehatt Rise PL9 . . . . . .**256** A6
Furzehatt Villas PL9 . . . . .**255** F6
Furzehatt Way PL9 . . . . . .**256** A6
Furzehill EX10 . . . .**101** B2
Furzehill Cross TQ9 . . . . .**227** B3
Furzehill Rd
Heybrook Bay PL9 . . . .**140** A7
Plymouth PL4 . . . .**248** F4
Rousdon DT7 . . . .**193** E5
1 Wellington TA21 . . . . .**160** D5
Furze Hill Rd EX34 . . . . .**150** B4
Furze La 2 TQ5 . . . .**230** D5
Furzeland Hill EX17 . . . . .**79** C6
Furzeleigh Cross TQ13 . . .**122** F6
Furzeleigh La TQ13 . . . . .**180** D8
Furzepark Cross
Bittaford PL21 . . . .**137** C7
Dolton EX19. . . . .**58** A5
Furzepark La
Hartland EX39 . . . .**22** E3
Kentisbury EX31 . . . .**10** E6
Furze Park La EX31 . . . .**9** B2
Furze Park Rd EX31. . . . . .**18** A8
Furze Pk EX34 . . . .**2** F3
Furze Rd
Totnes TQ9. . . . .**223** F5
Woodbury EX5. . . . .**184** C3
Fyldon Hill EX36 . . . .**19** D5

G

Gabber La PL9. . . . .**140** B8
Gable Pk TQ1. . . . .**220** C6
Gables Lea EX15. . . . .**162** C4
Gables Rd EX15. . . . .**162** C4
Gables The
Combe Martin EX34. . . . . . .**2** F4
Exmouth EX8 . . . .**202** D6
Rousdon DT7 . . . .**193** F7
Teignmouth TQ14. . . . . . .**210** A5
Wellington TA21. . . . .**160** C6
Gabriel Ct 11 EX2 . . . . . .**261** A2
Gabriels Wharf EX2 . . . . .**177** C3
Gabwell Hill TQ1, TQ12 . .**214** C7
Gabwell La TQ12 . . . .**214** C7
Gaddacombe Cross EX20 . .**91** D1
Gainsborough Cl TQ1 . . . .**220** E4
Gainsborough Dr EX39 . . .**156** B6
Gainsborough Ho
Exeter EX1. . . . .**177** E6
Tavistock PL19 . . . .**171** B6
Gains Cross EX22 . . . .**53** C3
Gala Cross PL8 . . . .**257** F1
Galahad Cl EX4 . . . .**174** A1
Gale Rd TQ13 . . . .**131** B5
Gales Crest 3 TQ13 . . . . .**123** C4
Galileo Cl PL7 . . . .**250** E6
Gallacher Way PL12. . . . .**242** B3
Galleon Way EX39 . . . . . .**156** E7
Gallery Cl 4 EX14 . . . . . .**166** B6
Galloping La EX9 . . . .**39** B8
Gallops The PL12 . . . . . .**242** D4
Galloway Dr TQ14 . . . . . .**124** E1
Gallows Cross TQ12 . . . .**207** C8
Gallows Gate TQ3. . . . . .**218** F6
Gallows Park Cross
TQ13 . . . .**131** B5
Galmpton CE Prim Sch
TQ5 . . . .**229** B5
Galmpton Cross TQ7. . . .**147** D2
Galmpton Ct TQ5 . . . . . .**229** B5
Galmpton Farm Cl TQ5. . .**229** B5
Galmpton Glade TQ5. . . .**229** B5
Galmpton Holiday Pk
TQ5 . . . .**229** A2
Galmpton Rise EX4 . . . . .**173** E1
Galpin St PL21 . . . .**137** C2
Galsworthy Cl PL5. . . . . .**244** C2
Galsworthy Sq EX4 . . . . .**178** C8
Galva Rd
Hemerdon PL7 . . . .**251** C8
Sparkwell PL7 . . . .**132** E1
Gamberlake EX13 . . . . . .**167** C4
Gamberlake Cross EX13. .**167** C4
Gamblyn Cross TA4 . . . . .**34** F5
Gammaton Moor Cross
EX39. . . . .**26** D3
Gammaton Rd EX39 . . . . .**26** B4
Gammons Hill EX13 . . . . .**87** D1
Gammon Wlk 2 EX31. . . .**154** F5
Ganders Pk (Cvn Pk)
TQ2 . . . .**213** A2
Gandy St EX4 . . . .**261** A3
Ganges Rd PL2 . . . .**248** A5
Ganna Park Rd PL3. . . . . .**248** D6
Gapemouth Cross EX33 . . .**8** C1
Gappah Cross TQ13 . . . . .**123** E4
Gappah La TQ13 . . . .**123** E4

Gara Cl PL9 . . . .**256** B6
Gara Lodge TQ12 . . . . . .**212** F4
Gard Cl TQ2 . . . .**214** A3
Garden Cl
Braunton EX33. . . . .**152** B6
Exeter EX2. . . . .**178** C4
Holbeton PL8 . . . .**142** A8
Plymouth PL7. . . . .**251** D5
Rattery TQ10 . . . .**135** D4
Garden Cotts TQ7 . . . . . .**258** C5
Garden Cres PL1. . . . . . .**262** B1
Garden Ct EX9. . . . .**198** A1
Garden House Yelverton
Paperweight Ctr The
PL20. . . . .**126** F2
Gardenia Dr EX16. . . . . . .**161** E7
Garden La PL19. . . . .**171** B5
Garden Mill Ind EstTQ7. . .**258** D4
Garden Park Cl TQ3 . . . . .**256** C7
Garden Pk TQ10 . . . .**135** D4
Garden Rd TQ1 . . . .**220** B6
Garden Spot La TQ13 . . . .**123** F6
Garden St EX2 . . . .**247** E4
Gardens The
6 Chudleigh TQ13 . . . . .**123** E6
Dunterton TA22 . . . .**33** D7
Holemoor EX22 . . . .**73** B7
Rousdon DT7 . . . .**193** E5
1 Wellington TA21 . . . . .**160** D5
Garden Terr
Cullompton EX15 . . . .**163** C4
Tavistock PL19 . . . .**160** B7
Garden Village PL9 . . . . .**255** F8
Gardiner Cl EX5 . . . .**82** A1
Gards La PL5 . . . .**243** E2
Gareth Cres EX4 . . . .**173** F2
Garfield Pl 11 TQ9 . . . . .**223** C5
Garfield Rd TQ4 . . . .**226** C6
Garfield Terr PL2. . . . . . .**248** A3
Garland Cl EX4 . . . .**176** E8
Garland Cross EX37 . . . . .**45** B5
Garlandhayes La EX15 . . . .**52** E2
Garland Rd EX16. . . . .**64** A5
Garlic Rea TQ5 . . . .**230** D5
Garliford La EX36. . . . . . .**30** F4
Garners Cl TQ12 . . . .**206** D1
Garners La TQ12 . . . .**206** D1
Garratt Cl EX8 . . . .**196** C3
Garratt St PL1 . . . .**262** A3
Garrick Cl PL5. . . . .**244** C2
Garrison Cl PL1. . . . .**247** E1
Garrow Cl 1 TQ5 . . . .**230** C3
Garston Ave TQ12 . . . . . .**207** B4
Garston Cl PL9 . . . .**256** A8
Garth Rd TQ2 . . . .**214** A2
Gascoyne Cl PL4. . . . . . .**263** A3
Gascoyne Pl PL4. . . . . . .**263** A3
Gashay La EX13. . . . .**88** A3
Gashouse La PL4 . . . .**263** B2
Gasking St PL4 . . . .**263** A3
Gas La EX38 . . . .**159** D5
Gatcombe Ash EX12 . . . .**102** E2
Gatcombe La
Beer EX12 . . . .**191** C8
Seaton EX12. . . . .**102** E2
Gate Cl EX13 . . . .**88** E3
Gate Cross EX24 . . . .**102** F6
Gatedown La
Salcombe Regis EX10 . . . .**101** E1
Sidmouth EX10 . . . .**189** D8
Gate Field Rd EX39 . . . . .**156** E7
Gatehouse Cl
Cullompton EX15 . . . .**163** B3
Dawlish EX7. . . . .**204** E7
Gatehouse Hill EX7 . . . . .**204** E7
Gatehouse Prim Sch
EX7. . . . .**204** E8
Gatehouse Rise EX7 . . . .**204** E7
Gater La EX1 . . . .**261** B2
Gates Field PL7 . . . .**250** D7
Gate Tree Cl TQ12 . . . . . .**207** F7
Gattery La TQ5 . . . .**229** F1
Gavel The EX36 . . . .**158** D4
Gaverick Ct TQ12 . . . . . .**123** B1
Gay Cl TA21 . . . .**160** E6
Gaydon St EX32. . . . .**155** A5
Gays Cross EX17 . . . .**79** C5
Gay's La EX17 . . . .**79** C7
Gaze Hill TQ12 . . . .**206** F5
Gdynia Way PL4 . . . .**263** C2
Geasons La PL7. . . . .**250** E5
Gees La PL21 . . . .**137** C2
Generals Cl EX6 . . . .**201** A7
Generals La EX6. . . . . . .**201** B7
Genesis La 3 EX34 . . . . . .**3** A3
Geneva Cl EX2. . . . .**177** E4
Geneva Ct
Bideford EX39 . . . .**156** F1
Exeter EX4. . . . .**177** E4
Geneva Pl EX39 . . . .**156** F1
Gennys Cl PL18 . . . .**125** B6
Gentian Cl TQ3 . . . .**218** D2
George Ave PL7 . . . .**250** F6
George Cross PL7. . . . . . .**250** F5
George Downing Ho
PL6 . . . .**245** A1
Georgeham CE Prim Sch
EX33 . . . .**8** A2
Georgeham Cross EX33 . .**152** D7
Georgeham Rd
Croyde EX33 . . . .**7** F2
Woolacombe EX34 . . . .**8** B5
George Hill EX17 . . . .**165** B6
George Ho EX17 . . . .**165** A6
George La
Kilmington EX13 . . . .**87** C1
Plymouth PL7. . . . .**250** F5

George Nympton Cross
EX36 .... 30 A2
Georgenympton Rd
EX36 .... 158 C2
George Pl PL1 .... 262 A2
George Rd TQ3 .... 219 B1
Georges Cl EX1 .... 178 B6
George Shopping Mews
EX36 .... 158 C4
George Sq PL1 .... 247 F1
George's Sq DT7 .... 260 E3
George St
Axminster EX13 .... 167 D6
12 Barnstaple EX32 .... 154 F6
Exeter EX1 .... 261 A2
1 Exmouth EX8 .... 202 A7
Honiton EX14 .... 166 C6
Newton Abbot TQ12 .... 207 B3
Okehampton EX20 .... 170 B5
Plymouth PL1 .... 247 F1
11 Teignmouth TQ14 .... 210 C4
Wellington TA21 .... 160 D6
George Teign Rd EX6 .... 113 D2
Georgia Cres PL3 .... 249 C6
Georgian Ct TQ1 .... 220 E6
Georgian Ho The EX6 .... 201 B8
Gerald Dinnis Units EX2 .... 177 D1
Geraldine Terr PL12 .... 242 C1
Gerbera Ho EX4 .... 176 E8
Gerbestone La TA21 .... 52 E6
Gerrydown Rd EX19 .... 58 D3
Gerston Cross TQ9 .... 223 A3
Gerston La TQ7 .... 258 C1
Gerston Pl 8 TQ3 .... 226 B6
Gerston Rd TQ4 .... 226 B6
Gervase Ave EX2 .... 261 A1
Gerway La EX11 .... 169 E2
Gestridge Cross TQ12 .... 207 D7
Gestridge Rd TQ12 .... 207 D7
Giant's Grave TA20 .... 69 D7
Giant's Grave Rd TA20 .... 69 D7
Gibb Hill PL21 .... 133 B2
Gibbon La PL4 .... 263 A3
Gibbons St PL4 .... 263 A3
Giblands Cross EX20 .... 170 D5
Giblands Pk EX20 .... 170 D5
Gibraltar Rd EX8 .... 195 E6
Gibson Cl EX8 .... 196 E1
Gibson Ct TQ4 .... 226 A1
Gibson Dr TQ4 .... 226 A1
Gibson Gdns TQ4 .... 226 A1
Gibson Rd TQ4 .... 226 A1
Gidcott Cross EX22 .... 55 A4
Gidley Arms Cross EX36 .... 46 A5
Gidley Cross EX36 .... 46 B4
Gidleys Mdw TQ9 .... 222 F8
Gidley's Turn EX6 .... 113 C4
Gifford Pl PL3 .... 248 D4
Gifford Terrace Rd PL3 .... 248 E5
Gilbert Ave
Exeter EX2 .... 178 C4
Teignmouth TQ14 .... 210 A7
Gilbert Cl TQ2 .... 219 D6
Gilbert Ct PL7 .... 251 B6
Gilbert Gr 6 EX34 .... 150 C6
Gilbert La PL2 .... 248 C5
Gilbert Rd TQ12 .... 207 E3
Gilbert Way TQ4 .... 226 A3
Gilchrist Way EX10 .... 188 C5
Gillard Rd TQ5 .... 230 F4
Gillards Cl TA21 .... 160 B4
Gillards Mead TA3 .... 68 D7
Gillard Way PL21 .... 136 D6
Gill Pk PL3 .... 249 B5
Gillscott Cross EX17 .... 60 B1
Gill's Cross TQ9 .... 222 D2
Gills Nursery 13 TQ9 .... 223 C5
Gilly's Wlk PL18 .... 125 C5
Gilpin Cl EX7 .... 204 F8
Gilston Rd PL12 .... 242 D4
Gilwell Ave PL9 .... 256 B7
Gilwell Pl PL4 .... 263 A3
Gilwell St PL4 .... 263 A3
Gingaford Cross TQ10 .... 135 A5
Gipsies Cnr EX17 .... 79 F6
Gipsies La EX17 .... 79 F6
Gipsy Cnr
Bovey Tracey TQ13 .... 122 D5
Budlake EX5 .... 82 E1
Whiddon EX31 .... 9 C1
Gipsy Cross EX15 .... 67 A5
Gipsy Dro TA20 .... 69 F4
Gipsy Hill La EX1 .... 178 F8
Gipsy Hill Mews EX1 .... 178 F7
Gipsy La
Bideford EX39 .... 25 B4
Bittadon EX31 .... 9 F3
Buckfastleigh TQ11 .... 236 A4
Exeter EX1 .... 178 F8
Exmouth EX8 .... 202 B8
Ilfracombe EX34 .... 150 D5
Ivybridge PL21 .... 136 D7
Sampford Arundel TA21 .... 51 D5
Girt La EX34 .... 3 B4
Gissage Hill EX17 .... 78 B7
Gissage View 7 EX14 .... 166 B6
Gissons EX6 .... 182 B4
Gissons La EX6 .... 114 D4
Gittisham Cl EX1 .... 178 D6
Gittisham Farm Cross
EX14 .... 85 A1
Gittshayne Cross EX24 .... 102 F5
Glade Cl PL6 .... 245 A4
Glades The EX16 .... 161 E3
Glade The PL20 .... 126 E2
Glade Wlk EX5 .... 179 E2
Gladstone Pl 11 TQ12 .... 207 C3
Gladstone Rd EX1 .... 177 E6
Gladstone Terr
8 Teignmouth TQ14 .... 210 C5
Wellington TA21 .... 160 E6
Glanville Ave 1 PL19 .... 171 B5
Glanville Rd
Offwell EX14 .... 102 A8
Tavistock PL19 .... 171 B6
Glanvilles Mill PL21 .... 237 D5
Glanvilles Rd PL21 .... 237 D5
Glanville St PL1, PL4 .... 262 C3
Glanville Terr PL12 .... 242 F3
Glanvill's Cl EX6 .... 98 C4
Glanvill Way EX14 .... 166 B4
Glascott Cl EX20 .... 75 B6
Glasshouse La EX2 .... 182 B7
Glastonbury Cl EX4 .... 174 A2
Glave Saunders Ave EX2 .... 178 C4
Glazebrook Ct TQ10 .... 134 E2
Glazegate Cross TQ3 .... 224 F7
Glazegate La TQ3, TQ4,
TQ9 .... 224 E6
Glazon Way EX39 .... 157 A8
Glebe Ave PL12 .... 242 F3
Glebe Cl
Exmouth EX8 .... 202 F7
Lympstone EX8 .... 195 E6
Newton Abbot TQ12 .... 206 F3
Otterton EX9 .... 198 E7
Upton Pyne EX5 .... 172 F7
Glebe Cotts EX5 .... 99 B1
Glebe Ct EX39 .... 156 F6
Glebefield EX33 .... 8 A2
Glebe Field TQ7 .... 143 A2
Glebefields EX39 .... 156 F6
Glebe Hos EX39 .... 156 A1
Glebe La EX22 .... 164 C4
Glebeland
Churchstow TQ7 .... 143 E4
Down St Mary EX17 .... 78 E7
Glebe Land TQ7 .... 143 C6
Glebelands
Buckfastleigh TQ11 .... 236 A6
Cheriton Bishop EX6 .... 97 B4
12 Chudleigh TQ13 .... 123 F6
Exminster EX6 .... 182 A4
Holsworthy EX22 .... 164 B4
Lympstone EX8 .... 195 E6
Newton Poppleford EX10 .... 186 F8
Puddington EX16 .... 62 B5
Sidmouth EX10 .... 188 A4
Wrafton EX33 .... 152 E4
Glebelands Rd EX16 .... 64 D7
Glebelands The DT7 .... 260 B5
Glebeland Villas EX36 .... 31 A2
Glebeland Way TQ2 .... 219 B8
Glebe Mdw EX22 .... 164 B4
Glebe The
Ipplepen TQ12 .... 211 C2
Poughill EX17 .... 62 D3
Thorverton EX5 .... 81 E4
Glenarm Terr 6 TQ9 .... 223 C6
Glenavon Rd PL3 .... 248 E5
Glenburn Cl PL3 .... 248 E7
Glenburnie Ho EX39 .... 157 A3
Glenburnie Rd EX39 .... 157 A3
Glencarnock Cl TQ1 .... 219 E7
Glen Cl
Clyst St Mary EX5 .... 179 E2
Sidmouth EX10 .... 188 A3
Glencoe EX2 .... 177 E5
Glendale Rd EX20 .... 170 A6
Glendale Terr EX39 .... 157 A3
Glendaragh Rd 12 TQ14 .... 210 C5
Glendon Cross EX20 .... 170 F8
Glendower Rd PL3 .... 248 D5
Gleneagle Ave 4 PL3 .... 248 F6
Gleneagle Rd PL3 .... 248 F6
Gleneagle Villas 5 PL3 .... 248 F6
Glen Farm Cres EX14 .... 166 D5
Glenfield Cl PL6 .... 245 D6
Glenfield Rd
Bideford EX39 .... 157 A4
Plymouth PL6 .... 245 D5
Glenfield Way PL6 .... 245 E6
Glengarth Cl EX39 .... 157 A5
Glen Gdns EX39 .... 156 F4
Glenholme DT7 .... 260 D2
Glenholt Cl PL6 .... 245 D6
Glenholt Rd PL6 .... 245 D6
Glenhurst Rd 5 PL3 .... 248 E6
Glen Isla EX10 .... 188 B3
Glen Lyn 21 EX32 .... 155 A4
Glen Lyn Gorge EX35 .... 151 C5
Glen Lyn Pk TQ13 .... 180 D5
Glenmore Ave PL2 .... 247 F5
Glenmore Rd
Brixham TQ5 .... 230 C4
Exeter EX2 .... 178 A5
Glennaven Cl PL7 .... 251 C6
Glenorchy Ct 5 EX8 .... 202 A7
Glen Park Ave PL4 .... 262 C4
Glen Park Prim Sch PL7 .... 251 B5
Glen Rd
Paignton TQ3 .... 226 B7
Plymouth, Mannamead PL3 .... 248 F5
Plymouth, Plympton PL7 .... 250 F6
Sidmouth EX10 .... 188 A3
Glenside Cl 5 TQ14 .... 210 B6
Glenside Ct TQ1 .... 220 E5
Glenside Rise PL7 .... 250 E6
Glen The
Beer EX12 .... 191 E6
3 Newton Abbot TQ12 .... 207 F2
Okehampton EX20 .... 170 B4
Glenthorne Cl TQ1 .... 220 D4
Glenthorne Nature Trail Gate
EX35 .... 6 D5
Glenthorne Rd EX4 .... 173 A1
Glentor Rd PL3 .... 248 E7
Glentorr Rd EX39 .... 157 A3
Glenview EX14 .... 166 D5
Glenwater Cl EX12 .... 192 D6
Glen Wlk EX4 .... 173 D2
Glenwood Rd PL3 .... 248 E6
Glenwood Rise EX2 .... 261 C1
Globe Ct EX15 .... 163 C3
Globefield EX3 .... 182 F5
Globe Hill EX5 .... 184 B3
Globe La EX3 .... 182 F4
Globe Ley EX3 .... 182 F5
Gloster Rd EX32 .... 155 A4
Gloucester Cl
Honiton EX14 .... 166 A5
Torquay TQ2 .... 213 F1
Gloucester Cres EX14 .... 166 A5
Gloucester Ct PL1 .... 262 C4
Gloucester Pl PL1 .... 262 C4
Gloucester Rd
Exeter EX4 .... 176 E7
Exmouth EX8 .... 196 E3
Newton Abbot TQ12 .... 207 C3
9 Teignmouth TQ14 .... 210 B5
Glove Ct EX38 .... 159 C5
Gloyn Pk EX22 .... 53 E1
Glynsmead TA20 .... 88 C8
Gnaton Cotts PL8 .... 141 C8
Gnome Reserve & Wild
Flower Gdn EX22 .... 39 B2
Goad Ave
Plymouth PL4 .... 263 C2
Torpoint PL11 .... 246 E3
Goad Cl PL11 .... 246 F3
Goaman Pk EX39 .... 22 E3
Goaman Rd EX39 .... 26 A4
Goats Hill Rd EX39 .... 157 A6
Goblin Hill EX17 .... 79 C4
Goblin La EX15 .... 163 C4
Godborough View EX39 .... 156 D2
Godding Gdns PL6 .... 244 E6
Godford Cross EX14 .... 85 B5
Godfrey Ave TQ3 .... 219 B2
Godfrey Cl EX11 .... 169 C3
Godfreys Gdns EX17 .... 78 C4
Godhams La TA4 .... 35 A7
Godolphin Cl EX5 .... 81 A1
Godolphin Ho PL19 .... 171 C5
Godwell La PL21 .... 237 F5
Gogwell La
Cove EX16 .... 49 B5
Tiverton EX16 .... 161 F1
Goldburn Cross EX20 .... 76 B1
Golden Acre Chalet Pk
EX7 .... 201 B2
Golden Bay Ct EX39 .... 156 C7
Golden Bay Holiday Village
EX39 .... 156 B7
Golden Cl TQ5 .... 230 B2
Golden Coast Holiday Village
EX34 .... 8 C6
Golden Hind The TQ5 .... 230 D5
Golden Inn Cross EX21 .... 74 C7
Golden Joy EX17 .... 165 D6
Golden La EX14 .... 66 F2
Golden Lane Cross EX14 .... 66 E2
Golden Lion Ct TQ13 .... 130 F4
Golden Park Ave TQ2 .... 213 F4
Golden Sands Holiday Pk
EX7 .... 201 A1
Golden Square EX14 .... 86 E6
Golden Terr 20 EX7 .... 204 D6
Goldfinch Cl PL15 .... 105 A2
Goldfinch Gr
Cullompton EX15 .... 163 A2
Saltash PL12 .... 242 D4
Golds Cross EX6 .... 97 E4
Goldscross Hill EX6 .... 97 D4
Golds La EX6 .... 97 E5
Goldsmith Gdns PL5 .... 244 D3
Goldsmiths La EX13 .... 88 A4
Goldsmith St
Exeter EX4 .... 261 A3
Exeter, Heavitree EX1 .... 177 F6
Goldsmoor Cross EX16 .... 50 E3
Gold St
Ottery St Mary EX11 .... 169 D4
Tiverton EX16 .... 161 D4
Golf Links Rd
South Brent TQ10 .... 134 D1
Westward Ho! EX39 .... 156 D7
Golland La EX37 .... 44 B2
Gollands TQ5 .... 230 B5
Gollands Cl TQ5 .... 230 A5
Gollands La
Copplestone EX17 .... 79 B8
Morchard Bishop EX17 .... 61 B1
Golvers Hill Cl TQ12 .... 207 E7
Golvers Hill Rd TQ12 .... 207 E7
Goodacre Cross PL16 .... 91 B1
Goodeve Cl PL9 .... 255 E6
Goodgates Cl EX33 .... 152 C6
Goodgates Cres EX33 .... 152 B6
Goodgates Gr EX33 .... 152 B6
Goodgates Pk EX33 .... 152 C6
Goodgates Rd EX33 .... 152 B6
Goodiford Cross EX15 .... 65 F3
Gooding Rise EX16 .... 161 B4
Goodleigh CE Prim Sch
EX32 .... 17 B5
Goodleigh Cross EX32 .... 155 F7
Goodleigh La EX19 .... 58 E3
Goodleigh Rd EX32 .... 155 D5
Goodridge Cl EX7 .... 204 E8
Goodrington Orch Cvn Pk
TQ4 .... 226 C2
Goodrington Rd TQ4 .... 226 B1
Goodrington Sands Sta
TQ4 .... 226 C4
Goodshelter Cross TQ8 .... 148 E5
Good Shepherd Dr 5
EX2 .... 261 B2
Goodstone Cross TQ12 .... 131 C6
Goodstone Way TQ4 .... 225 F3
Goodwells Head EX32 .... 18 C3
Goodwin Ave PL6 .... 245 A6
Goodwin Cres PL2 .... 248 A6
Goodwood Park Rd
EX39 .... 157 A5
Gooseberry La PL1 .... 262 B2
Gooseford Cross EX20 .... 95 D2
Gooseford La PL11 .... 252 C8
Goose Gn EX38 .... 159 E5
Goose Moor La EX6 .... 114 B4
Goosewell Hill PL6 .... 249 C8
Goosewell Park Rd PL9 .... 255 F6
Goosewell Prim Sch PL9 .... 255 F6
Goosewell Rd PL9 .... 255 F5
Goosewell Terr PL9 .... 255 F6
Gora La EX34 .... 8 A6
Gordon Ct PL12 .... 242 D2
Gordon Rd
Exeter EX1 .... 177 E7
Topsham EX3 .... 182 E6
Gordon's Pl EX1 .... 177 F5
Gordon Terr
Beer EX12 .... 191 D5
Plymouth PL4 .... 248 E4
Gore La
Exmouth EX8 .... 202 E4
Kilmington EX13 .... 103 C8
Uplyme DT7 .... 260 A4
Gorfin Cl EX8 .... 202 E8
Gorhuish Cross EX20 .... 75 C1
Gorlegg TA21 .... 51 E5
Gornhay Cross EX16 .... 64 D8
Gornhay Orch EX16 .... 64 D8
Gorrans Down EX39 .... 22 F1
Gorse Ho EX4 .... 176 E8
Gorse La EX8 .... 196 D4
Gorse Way
Ivybridge PL21 .... 237 E4
Sidmouth EX10 .... 187 F4
Gorsey Cl PL5 .... 244 E2
Gorvin Cross EX39 .... 38 B6
Gorway TQ14 .... 210 C6
Gorwell Rd EX32 .... 155 C5
Gorwood Rd EX39 .... 40 B7
Gorwyn La EX6 .... 97 C4
Gosceline Wlk EX14 .... 166 C4
Gosford La EX11 .... 169 C7
Gosford Rd EX11 .... 169 D7
Goshawk Units EX2 .... 178 F6
Goshen Rd TQ2 .... 219 E4
Goslings The TQ7 .... 145 A1
Goss Mdw EX17 .... 78 C4
Gostwick Cl EX20 .... 77 C4
Goswela Cl PL9 .... 255 F5
Goswela Gdns PL9 .... 255 F5
Gothic Rd TQ12 .... 207 B2
Gould Cl EX32 .... 155 B4
Gould Rd
Barnstaple EX32 .... 155 C4
Salcombe TQ8 .... 259 D5
Gourders La TQ12 .... 212 F2
Goutsford Gate PL21 .... 136 F2
Govers Mdw EX24 .... 103 A4
Govetts EX5 .... 184 C3
Gower Ridge Rd PL9 .... 255 D6
Gowman's Terr EX20 .... 77 B4
Goyle Acre La EX13 .... 87 D4
Grace Par EX2 .... 177 B2
Grace Rd Central EX2 .... 177 C2
Grace Rd W EX2 .... 177 B2
Grace Road S EX2 .... 177 D1
Graddon Cross
Black Torrington EX21 .... 73 F6
Okehampton EX20 .... 93 E4
Grafton Ct TQ1 .... 220 B4
Grafton Hts TQ1 .... 220 C5
Grafton Rd
Exeter EX4 .... 173 B1
11 Newton Abbot TQ12 .... 207 B3
Plymouth PL4 .... 248 E4
Torquay TQ1 .... 220 B4
Grafton Terr TQ1 .... 220 B4
Graham Cl EX16 .... 161 D5
Graham Rd TQ3 .... 219 A1
Grainger Cl EX2 .... 178 C5
Grainge Rd PL6 .... 245 A1
Gramercy Fields TQ5 .... 230 B2
Grammar La EX10 .... 189 D7
Grampian Cl TQ4 .... 225 D4
Granary La EX9 .... 198 C1
Granby Ct PL1 .... 247 E2
Granby Gn PL1 .... 247 E2
Granby Pl PL1 .... 247 E2
Granby St PL1 .... 247 E2
Granby Way PL1 .... 247 E2
Grand Hotel Rd PL1 .... 262 B1
Grandison Ave TQ14 .... 209 A8
Grandisson Ct EX2 .... 178 A2
Grandisson Dr EX11 .... 169 F3
Grand Par PL1 .... 262 B1
Grand View Rd TQ7 .... 147 B7
Grand Western Canal
(Country Pk) EX16 .... 50 F2
Grand Western Canal Ctry Pk
EX16 .... 64 F7
Grange Ave
Barnstaple EX31 .... 154 C2
Exmouth EX8 .... 202 B8
Paignton TQ4 .... 226 B2
Grange Bglws EX39 .... 157 B1
Grange Cl
Bratton Fleming EX32 .... 18 A8
Exmouth EX8 .... 202 B8
Ipplepen TQ12 .... 211 C3
Lympstone EX8 .... 195 F5
Newton Abbot TQ12 .... 207 D1
Wellington TA21 .... 160 E5
Grange Cotts EX5 .... 99 C6
Grange Cross EX14 .... 84 D7
Grange Ct
4 Barnstaple EX32 .... 155 A6
Teignmouth TQ14 .... 210 A5
Grange Dr TQ14 .... 210 B6
Grange Heights Cl TQ4 .... 226 A1
Grange Hill EX32 .... 18 B8
Grange Hts TQ4 .... 226 A2
Grange La EX20 .... 57 A7
Grange Pk TQ12 .... 212 A6
Grange Rd
Abbotskerswell TQ12 .... 212 B6
Bideford EX39 .... 157 B1
Buckfast TQ11 .... 236 B7
Paignton TQ4 .... 226 B2
Plymouth PL7 .... 251 A4
Torquay TQ1 .... 220 C5
Yelverton PL20 .... 126 F3
Grange The
Braunton EX33 .... 152 E5
Dousland PL20 .... 127 B3
Grange View TQ4 .... 226 A2
Grantham Cl PL7 .... 250 B4
Grantland Hill EX16, EX17 .... 63 A4
Grantlands EX15 .... 66 A7
Grantley Gdns PL3 .... 249 A5
Grant's Hill EX16, TA22 .... 33 F2
Granville Ave EX32 .... 154 F6
Granville Pl EX15 .... 162 C5
Granville Rd EX34 .... 150 B6
Gras Lawn EX2 .... 177 E4
Grasmere Cl
Plymouth PL6 .... 244 E5
Torquay TQ2 .... 214 B2
Grasmere Ct EX4 .... 176 F5
Grassendale Ave PL2 .... 247 F7
Grass La PL2 .... 248 C6
Grasslands Dr EX1 .... 178 F8
Grassmere Way PL12 .... 242 D4
Grasspark Hill EX32 .... 18 E3
Grass Rd TQ13 .... 131 A3
Grassy La PL8 .... 136 C4
Grattan La EX31 .... 16 B6
Grattans Way EX17 .... 78 C4
Gratton Cl TQ6 .... 146 B8
Gratton Cross
Shebbear EX22 .... 55 A5
Yelverton PL20 .... 127 A2
Gratton Ct EX31 .... 154 C2
Gratton Dr TQ7 .... 145 A1
Gratton La
Bittadon EX31 .... 9 C5
Chulmleigh EX18 .... 59 D3
Combe Martin EX31 .... 3 F2
Lower Tippacott EX35 .... 6 A4
Yelverton PL20 .... 127 A2
Gratton Pl PL6 .... 245 A1
Grattons Dr EX35 .... 151 B5
Grattons La TQ9 .... 216 E2
Gratton Way EX31 .... 154 C2
Gravel La EX12 .... 192 B7
Gravel Pit Cross EX36 .... 20 A6
Gravel Wlk EX15 .... 163 C3
Gravesend Gdns PL11 .... 247 B3
Gravesend Wlk PL5 .... 243 D4
Graybridge Rd PL20 .... 126 F4
Gray Cres PL5 .... 247 C8
Graynfylde Dr EX39 .... 157 B2
Grays Ct TQ13 .... 112 B3
Gray's Hill EX15 .... 52 D1
Gray's La EX15 .... 52 D1
Grays Mdw TQ13 .... 111 F5
Great Ambrook Ave
TQ12 .... 217 A7
Great Berry Rd PL6 .... 244 F1
Great Bridge TQ13 .... 130 F5
Great Burrow Rise EX39 .... 156 F8
Great Churchway PL9 .... 256 A7
Great Cl EX15 .... 51 E1
Great Fellingfield PL19 .... 117 E6
Great Field Gdns EX33 .... 152 C5
Greatfield Rd PL3 .... 249 B7
Great Furlong TQ14 .... 208 E8
Great Gate Flats 13 TQ5 .... 230 C4
Great Headland Cres
TQ3 .... 219 D1
Great Headland Rd TQ3 .... 219 C1
Great Hele La EX36 .... 158 D2
Great Hill 3 TQ13 .... 123 E6
Great Hill Cross TQ1 .... 213 F5
Great Hill Rd TQ2 .... 213 F4
Great Hill View EX4 .... 173 E2
Great La TQ7 .... 147 E6
Greatlands Cres PL2 .... 248 A6
Greatlands Pl 5 PL2 .... 248 A5
Great Lightleigh La EX18 .... 44 F5
Great Links Tor Rd EX20 .... 170 E5
Great Mdw TA22 .... 33 D6
Great Mead EX6 .... 112 F7
Great Mis Tor Cl 5 PL20 .... 126 F3
Greatoak Cross TQ12 .... 212 C5
Great Oak Cross EX5 .... 81 D2
Great Oak Mdw EX22 .... 164 C5
Great Orchard Cl PL9 .... 255 E5
Great Park Cl 4 PL7 .... 251 C5
Greatpark La TQ3 .... 225 D6
Great Parks Rd TQ3 .... 225 E5

Great Pitford La EX18 58 D6
Great Rea Rd TQ5 230 D5
Great Ringaton La EX36 32 B6
Great Tor Cl TQ3 218 F1
Great Torrington Bluecoat CE Inf Sch EX38 159 C5
Great Torrington Com Sch & Sports Coll EX38 159 E5
Great Torrington Jun Sch EX38 159 E5
Great Tree Pk TQ13 96 A1
Greatweek Cross TQ13 111 B6
Great Western Cl TQ4 226 C4
Great Western Ind Est EX32 155 B3
Great Western Rd
12 Paignton TQ4 226 B6
Plymouth PL1 262 B1
Great Western Way
EX16 161 D3
Great Woodford Dr PL7 250 B6
Greatwood Terr EX3 182 F5
Grebe Cl PL7 250 F5
Grecian Way EX2 178 C4
Greebys The TQ3 226 A6
Greenacre EX33 152 C6
Greenacre Cl
Bradworthy EX22 53 E8
Northam EX39 157 A7
North Tawton EX20 77 C4
Greenacres
Exeter EX4 173 A3
Plymouth PL9 255 F8
Torquay TQ1 220 E5
Greenacres Cl EX14 84 D1
Greenaway EX17 61 A2
Greenaway Ho EX22 164 C3
Greenaway La TQ12 213 B6
Greenaway Rd TQ12 207 A4
Greenawell Cl TQ13 111 D2
Greenbank
Great Torrington EX38 159 F6
Plymouth PL4 263 B4
Green Bank EX10 186 E8
Greenbank Ave
Kingsteignton TQ12 207 D8
Plymouth PL4 263 B3
Greenbank Cl EX38 159 F6
Greenbank Rd
Barnstaple EX32 155 C4
Brixham TQ5 230 B4
Plymouth PL4 263 B4
Greenbanks TQ7 145 C3
Green Banks Cl TQ7 145 C3
Greenbank Terr
Plymouth PL4 263 B4
Yelverton PL20 127 A3
Green Cl
Cornworthy TQ9 227 B4
Exmouth EX8 202 C8
Kingsbridge TQ7 258 D6
Greenclose Ct 3 EX24 103 A4
Green Close La EX31 10 B5
Greenclose Rd EX34 150 B6
Greendale Cross EX5 183 F7
Greendale La
Exeter EX5 99 A1
Woodbury Salterton EX5 184 A8
Greendale Rd PL2 248 A7
Greendown Cross EX20 74 C2
Green End La EX15 83 F5
Greenfield Cl EX39 156 E2
Greenfield Dr
Ivybridge PL21 237 D4
7 South Brent TQ10 134 F2
Greenfield Rd
Paignton TQ3 219 A1
Saltash PL12 242 D2
Greenfield Terr TA20 88 D8
Greenfinch Cres PL12 242 E4
Greenford Villas EX2 261 A1
Green Gables EX10 188 A4
Green Gate EX16 50 B2
Green Gdns EX39 156 E6
Greenham Bsns Pk TA21 51 C5
Greenhaven EX9 197 F2
Greenhayes
Charmouth DT6 104 F4
Dartington TQ9 222 E8
Greenhays Foot EX13 88 B6
Greenhead EX10 101 B2
Greenhill
East Allington TQ9 144 D7
Kingsteignton TQ12 207 E6
Green Hill
Lamerton PL19 116 E3
Poughill EX16, EX17 62 D3
Sampford Courtenay EX20 76 F3
Tavistock PL19 171 D5
Greenhill Ave
Exmouth EX8 202 C7
Lympstone EX8 195 E5
Greenhill Cl PL9 255 F5
Greenhill Cross
East Knowstone EX36 32 B2
Knowle EX33 8 E1
Poughill EX17 62 D3
Sampford Chapple EX20 77 A3
Greenhill Gdns TQ12 212 F4
Greenhill Ind Units TQ12 207 E6
Greenhill La TQ12 211 B6
Greenhill Rd
Kingskerswell TQ12 212 F4
Kingsteignton TQ12 207 E6
Greenhill Terr TQ9 144 D7
Greenhill Way TQ12 207 E6
Greenings Rd EX39 40 C7
Green Knap La TA20 69 F2
Green La
23 Appledore EX39 15 A1
Axmouth EX12, DT7 193 B8
1 Barnstaple EX31 154 F5
Beaford EX19 42 D1
Bittaford TQ10 137 E8
Blackawton TQ9 139 B1
Braunton EX33 152 E6
Buckfastleigh TQ11 236 F4
Cawsand PL10 253 A2
Chard Junction TA20 88 D7
Chardstock EX13 88 B7
Cheriton Bishop EX6 97 C2
Churston Ferrers TQ5 229 E5
Colyford EX24 103 A3
East Allington TQ9 144 D8
Exeter EX4 176 E5
Exton EX3 183 B2
Hatherleigh EX20 75 D7
Ilsington TQ13 122 C4
Merton EX20 57 A7
Molland EX36 31 B8
Rackenford EX16 47 C5
Raymond's Hill EX13 104 C7
Rewe EX5 82 F1
Rousdon DT7 193 F8
Sampford Arundel TA21 51 F4
Sidbury EX10 101 D2
Southleigh EX24 102 D3
Spreyton EX17 96 A7
Swimbridge EX32 28 B8
Tavistock PL19 171 E5
Totnes TQ9 223 A4
Yelverton PL20 126 F1
Greenlake Cross EX39 22 D1
Greenland PL10 252 F5
Greenland Head Cross
Churchstow TQ7 143 E6
Pennymoor EX16 62 E6
Greenlands Ave TQ3 225 F6
Greenlands Est PL19 171 D5
Greenlane Cross EX36 31 C8
Green Lane End
Blackawton TQ9 139 B1
Buckfastleigh TQ11 236 E4
Green Lanes Sh Ctr EX31 154 F5
Greenlees Dr PL7 251 B3
Greenmeadow Dr EX31 155 A7
Green Mews EX9 198 A1
Green Mount EX10 188 C6
Greenover Cl TQ5 230 B3
Greenover Rd TQ5 230 B3
Greenpark Ave EX1 178 D7
Green Park Ave PL4 248 D4
Greenpark Rd EX8 196 D2
Green Park Rd
Paignton TQ3 218 F1
Plymouth PL9 255 E5
Green Park Way TQ7 145 A1
Green Park Wlk TQ3 218 F1
Green Pk PL10 253 A2
Greenslade Cross EX20 77 A3
Greenslade Rd
Blackawton TQ9 139 E1
Witheridge EX16 46 E1
Greenslinch La EX5 82 D6
Greensway Rd PL19 171 A4
Greenswood La TQ6 232 B1
Greenswood Rd 4 TQ5 230 C3
Green The
Ashburton TQ13 130 F4
Bridgerule EX22 70 F5
Brushford TA22 33 E4
Cawsand PL10 253 A2
Denbury TQ12 211 A6
Down St Mary EX17 78 E7
Exmouth EX8 202 F8
6 Horrabridge PL20 126 F5
Ide EX2 176 D1
Meavy PL20 127 C2
Milton Combe PL20 240 F8
Otterton EX9 198 E7
Plymouth, Ernesettle PL5 243 E3
Plymouth, Hooe PL9 255 B6
Saltash PL12 242 C3
Teignmouth TQ14 210 A3
Whimple EX5 99 E8
Green Tree La EX5 175 D6
Greenway
Crediton EX17 165 B5
Exeter EX2 176 F3
Halberton EX16 65 A8
Lyme Regis DT7 260 C3
Seaton EX12 191 F7
Woodbury EX5 184 C3
Greenway Ave PL7 250 B6
Greenway Cl
3 Horrabridge PL20 126 F5
Ivybridge PL21 237 D5
Torquay TQ2 214 A1
Greenway Gdns
Galmpton TQ5 228 E2
Tiverton EX16 161 C4
Torquay TQ2 214 A2
Greenway La
Ashcombe EX7 124 F5
Awliscombe EX14 85 B5
Beacon EX14 85 D8
Budleigh Salterton EX9 198 A2
Sidmouth EX10 187 E8
Torquay TQ1 220 B8
Greenway Pk TQ5 229 B4
Greenway Rd
Galmpton TQ5 229 B4
Greenway Rd *continued*
Paignton TQ5 228 E3
Rockwell Green TA21 160 A5
Torquay, Chelston TQ2 219 E4
Torquay, St Marychurch TQ1 220 B8
Greenways EX34 150 A5
Greenwich Pl PL12 242 F3
Greenwood Cl
Aveton Gifford TQ7 143 C6
Ivybridge PL21 237 C5
Greenwood Dr EX2 178 D5
Greenwood Park Cl PL7 251 B6
Greenwood Park Rd PL7 251 B6
Greenwoods The EX39 22 E3
Gregory Cl
Bow EX17 78 C4
Tiverton EX16 161 F4
Gregory's Ct TQ13 110 F6
Gregory's Mdw PL15 105 A2
Gregory Terr EX39 22 E3
Grenadier Rd EX1 178 E7
Grenadine Cl TQ2 213 E3
Grendon Almshouses
EX1 177 E6
Grendon Bldgs 2 EX1 261 A2
Grendon Ct TQ14 210 A5
Grendon La EX16 46 E4
Grendon Rd EX1 177 E6
Grenfell Ave PL12 242 D3
Grenfell Gdns PL12 242 C3
Grenofan Cross PL19 126 D6
Grenofen Cl PL19 126 D6
Grenville Ave
Exeter EX4 178 D8
Teignmouth TQ14 210 A7
Torquay TQ2 219 D6
Grenville Cl
Dartmouth TQ6 233 D3
Newton Abbot TQ12 207 E3
Stokenham TQ7 145 B2
Grenville Coll EX39 156 F2
Grenville College Jun Sch EX39 156 D1
Grenville Ct PL7 251 C6
Grenville Dr PL19 171 B3
Grenville Estate Cres
EX39 25 E4
Grenville Est The EX39 25 E4
Grenville Ho EX31 155 A8
Grenville Pk PL20 127 A2
Grenville Rd
Exmouth EX8 196 C2
Plymouth PL4 263 C3
Salcombe TQ8 259 D4
Grenville Road La S PL4 249 B2
Grenville St 16 EX39 157 A2
Grenville Terr
4 Bideford EX39 157 B1
Northam EX39 157 A7
Grenville Way TQ4 226 B3
Gresham Cl PL5 244 C7
Greycoat La TQ12 206 F7
Greyfriars Rd EX4 177 F8
Greyhill Cross TQ7 138 A1
Greysand Cres 31 EX39 15 A1
Greysholt Cross EX32 28 B8
Greystoke Ave PL6 249 D7
Greystone Cross EX6 96 E2
Greystone Way TQ1 220 C7
Gribble Cl EX32 155 C4
Gribbleford Cross EX20 75 A4
Gribble La EX5 99 D6
Gribblemead EX24 103 A4
Grieg Dr EX32 155 C5
Griffin Way PL9 256 C6
Griggs Cl
Northam EX39 157 A6
Plymouth PL7 251 B4
Griggs Gdn EX31 153 D5
Grigg's La EX10 188 D7
Grimspound TQ13 121 A7
Grimspound Cl PL6 249 E8
Grimstone Terr PL20 126 E2
Grinacombe Cross PL16 91 B2
Grinacombe Moor cross
PL16 91 B2
Grindhill Cross EX20 92 D5
Grindle Way EX5 179 B2
Grizedale Rd PL6 249 D7
Gronau Cl EX14 166 C4
Grooms Orch TA21 160 C5
Gropers La
Ipplepen TQ3, TQ12 218 C8
North Whilborough TQ12 212 B1
Gropy La
Ash Mill EX36 31 D1
South Molton EX36 46 D8
Grosvenor Ave TQ2 213 C1
Grosvenor Cl TQ2 213 C1
Grosvenor Cotts 1 PL4 248 F4
Grosvenor Ct
3 Barnstaple EX32 155 A5
Ivybridge PL21 237 C5
Grosvenor Pl EX1 261 C4
Grosvenor Rd
Paignton TQ4 226 B5
Plymouth PL6 244 F2
Grosvenor St 2 EX32 155 A5
Grosvenor Terr
4 Barnstaple EX32 155 A5
Paignton TQ4 226 B5
4 Teignmouth TQ14 210 B6
Groundhead Rd EX14 86 F6
Grove Ave 12 TQ14 210 B5
Grove Cl 3 TQ9 223 C5
Grove Cres 6 TQ14 210 B5
Grove Cross EX22 39 D3
Grove Ct
Dawlish EX7 204 F6
Teignmouth TQ14 210 C6
Grove Garden Campsite
TQ7 143 A7
Grove Hill
12 Colyton EX24 103 A4
Topsham EX3 182 F5
Grove Ho EX3 182 F5
Grove La EX36 32 D6
Grove Mdw EX20 94 F5
Grove Mews 16 TQ9 223 C5
Grove Pk
Tavistock PL19 171 D5
Torpoint PL11 246 E3
Grove Prim Sch The TQ9 223 C5
Grove Rd EX5 99 F7
Groves The PL21 237 C6
Grove Terr 11 TQ14 210 B5
Grove The
5 Bittaford PL21 137 C8
Blackawton TQ9 139 E1
Exeter EX4 174 E2
Paignton TQ4 225 E4
Plymouth, Plymstock PL9 255 D8
Plymouth, Stoke PL3 248 A4
Sidmouth EX10 188 B4
Totnes TQ9 223 C5
Woolacombe EX34 7 F6
Gubbin's La EX33 152 D5
Guernsey Cnr EX24 102 F4
Guestland Rd TQ1 220 C7
Guildford Cl
Exeter EX4 176 E6
Plymouth PL5 244 E3
Guildford St PL4 263 A3
Guildhall Sh Ctr EX4 261 A3
Guildhall Sq PL1 262 C2
Guildhall Yd TQ9 223 C5
Guinea St EX1 261 A2
Guinevere Way EX4 174 A1
Guinness La EX4 176 E8
Gulland Cross TQ12 212 B4
Gullet Cross TQ7 148 F6
Gulliford Cotts EX8 195 F6
Gulliver La EX20 77 D7
Gullyhole Hill EX36 31 F7
Gully La EX14 86 C5
Gully Shoot EX24 103 A3
Gulway Mead TA20 88 D8
Gulworthy Cotts PL19 125 E7
Gulworthy Cross PL19 125 E7
Gulworthy Prim Sch PL19 125 E7
Gun La EX36 19 D4
Gunn Cross EX32 17 F3
Gunnislake Prim Sch PL18 125 C6
Gunnislake Rural Workshops PL18 125 C6
Gunnislake Sta PL18 125 C5
Gunsdown Villas EX36 158 D5
Gunstone Cross EX17 79 E2
Gunstone Mill Cross EX17 79 E1
Gunswell La EX36 158 B5
Gurnard Wlk PL3 249 C6
Gurney Cl PL11 246 F3
Gurneys The TQ3 226 A5
Guscott La EX38 26 E2
Gussiford La EX8 202 B6
Guy Miles Way PL5 244 B3
Guys Rd EX4 176 F6
Gwel Avon Bsns Pk PL12 242 D4
Gwen Dr PL7 250 C7
Gwithian Cl PL11 246 F4
Gwyn Rd PL4 263 C4
Gwythers EX36 158 D4

H

Hacche La EX36 158 C6
Haccombe Cl EX4 176 E5
Haccombe Cross TQ12 213 E6
Haccombe Path TQ12 208 A2
Hacker Cl EX10 186 F7
Hackney La
Kingsteignton TQ12 207 F6
Newton Abbot TQ12 208 B4
Hackpen Cross Way EX15 66 D4
Hackworthy Cnr EX4 98 F5
Hackworthy Cross EX6 97 E5
Hackworthy Cross La EX6 97 E5
Hackworthy La
Nadderwater EX4 98 F5
Tedburn St Mary EX6 97 E4
Haddacott Cross EX38 26 F3
Haddington Rd PL2 247 F4
Haddon Cnr EX13 103 C8
Haddon Ct 2 TQ3 226 B7
Haddon La TA4 34 C7
Haddon Rd EX13 103 B8
Hadfield Ct 4 TQ13 123 C4
Hadrian Dr EX4 176 E6
Hadrians Way EX8 196 D1
Halberton Prim Sch EX16 65 A7
Halcyon Ct PL2 248 A6
Halcyon Rd
Newton Abbot TQ12 207 B3
Plymouth PL2 248 A6
Haldene Terr 6 EX32 154 F6
Haldon Ave TQ14 210 C6
Haldon Belvedere EX6 113 F5
Haldon Cl
2 Newton Abbot TQ12 207 F2
Topsham EX3 182 E6
Torquay TQ1 220 E4
Haldon Ct EX8 196 B2
Haldon La TQ13 124 B4
Haldon Lodge EX6 114 B5
Haldon Pl PL5 244 A3
Haldon Rd
Exeter EX4 177 A6
Torquay TQ1 220 D4
Haldon Rise 1 TQ12 207 F2
Haldon Terr 14 EX7 204 D6
Haldon View TQ13 123 F6
Haldon View Terr EX2 177 F5
Haldron's Almhouses
EX16 161 C4
Hale La EX14 166 E6
Haley Barton 4 PL2 248 A5
Haley Cl EX8 196 C2
Half Farthing La EX20 77 C7
Halfmoon Ct TQ11 236 A3
Half Moon The EX13 87 E8
Halford Cross TQ12 122 E1
Halfpenny Cross EX16 49 B7
Halfsbury Cross EX37 43 E4
Half Way Cvn Pk TQ4 224 E5
Halfway House Flats
TQ5 230 F6
Hallamore La PL21 133 B2
Hall Cross PL21 133 E2
Hallerton Cl PL6 245 E2
Hallett Cl PL12 242 B3
Hallett Ct DT7 260 D4
Halletts Way EX13 167 E6
Halley Gdns PL5 243 E1
Hall Hill EX35 6 B5
Hall La EX7 210 E8
Halls Cross EX31 10 E4
Hall's La TQ12 212 F4
Hall's Mill La EX31 154 E8
Hallswell Ct TQ4 226 B6
Halmpstone Cross EX32 28 C7
Halsbury Rd EX16 161 F4
Halscombe La EX2 176 C1
Halsdon Ave EX8 196 A1
Halsdon Cross EX22 54 C1
Halsdon La EX8 196 A2
Halsdon Nature Resrve Trails EX19 57 E6
Halsdon Rd EX8 202 A7
Halsdon Terr EX38 159 C5
Halsegate Cross EX20 77 D3
Halse Hill EX9 197 F1
Halse La
North Tawton EX20 77 D4
West Worlington EX17 61 B6
Halses Cl EX4 176 D8
Halsewood Gate EX15 64 E2
Halsey Lake Cross EX31 10 D1
Halsfordwood La EX4 98 F4
Halshanger Cross TQ13 130 F8
Halsteads Rd TQ2 214 A2
Halswell Cross EX36 29 D2
Halwell Cross
Denbury TQ12 211 A5
Halwell TQ9 139 C4
Halwell Ho TQ7 148 E7
Halwill Mdw EX21 73 D3
Halwill Prim Sch EX21 73 C2
Halyards EX3 182 E5
Hambeer La EX2 176 E3
Hamberhayne Cross
EX24 102 D6
Hamble Cl PL3 249 D7
Hamblecombe La TQ13 124 A4
Hambleton Ho 4 TQ14 210 C5
Hambleton Way TQ4 226 A2
Ham Butts TQ7 143 F7
Ham Cl PL2 248 B8
Ham Cross EX13 86 F4
Ham Dr PL2 248 B8
Hameldown Cl TQ2 219 B7
Hameldown Rd EX20 170 E5
Hameldown Way TQ12 207 D4
Hamelin Way TQ2, TQ3 219 A8
Ham Gn PL2 248 A7
Ham Green Ct PL2 248 A7
Ham Green La PL2 248 A7
Ham Hill
Ashreigney EX18 58 E8
Street Ash TA20 69 F8
Ham Ho PL2 248 A8
Hamilton Ave EX2 177 F2
Hamilton Cl
Bideford EX39 25 E4
14 Sidford EX10 101 B1
Hamilton Ct 4 EX8 202 B6
Hamilton Dr
Exeter EX2 178 D5
Newton Abbot TQ12 207 B5
Hamilton Gdns PL4 248 D4
Hamilton Gr EX6 201 B7
Hamilton La EX8 202 C7
Hamilton Rd
Exmouth EX8 202 D7
Topsham EX3 182 E6
Hamiltons The TQ14 210 A3
Ham La
Colyton EX24 103 A4
Dittisham TQ6 228 C3
Plymouth PL2 248 A8
Shaldon TQ14 209 D4
Sidmouth EX10 188 B3
South Molton EX36 158 E4
Hamley La TA20 69 E8
Hamlin Gdns EX1 178 A7
Hamlin Ho EX1 178 A7
Hamlin La EX1 178 A7
Hamlintoo La EX17 95 E7
Hamlyns Way TQ11 236 B5
Hammett Rd EX15 163 B3

Hammetts La
Barnstaple EX32 155 B1
Bishop's Tawton EX32 16 E1
Hammond Croft Way
EX2 181 B8
Hamoaze Ave PL5 247 D8
Hamoaze Pl PL1 247 D2
Hamoaze Rd PL11 247 B2
Hampden Pl EX2 261 A1
Ham Pl 10 EX6 161 C3
Hampshire Cl EX4 176 E4
Hampson Cross EX17 78 A4
Hampson La EX17 78 A4
Hampton Ave TQ1 220 C8
Hampton Bldgs EX4 261 C4
Hampton Ct EX13 103 C6
Hampton La
Torquay TQ1 220 C8
Whitford EX13 103 C6
Hampton Rd
Newton Abbot TQ12 207 C3
Whitford EX13 103 C7
Hampton St PL4 263 A3
Ham Rd
Dalwood EX13 87 A3
Wellington TA21 52 D8
Hamslade Cross EX16 48 D8
Hamslade Hill EX16 48 D8
Hams The EX2 176 D1
Hamstone Ct TQ8 259 D4
Hanaford La TA20 69 F4
Hancock Cl PL16 244 D6
Hancock's Devon Cider Mill
EX36 29 D2
Hand & Pen Cotts EX5 99 E6
Handy Cross EX39 25 E4
Hanger La EX14 84 F8
Hanging La EX35 5 A3
Hangman Path EX34 2 F6
Hangman's Cross PL21 138 A2
Hangman's Hill EX14 84 E5
Hangman's Hill Cross
EX16 48 E7
Hankford Cross EX22 54 C2
Hannaburrow La EX33 14 F8
Hannaford Cross EX32 28 D8
Hannaford La EX32 28 D8
Hannaford Rd
Lifton PL16 105 E3
Noss Mayo PL8 140 F5
Hannaton Cross EX32 28 D8
Hanover Cl
7 Brixham TQ5 230 C3
Exeter EX1 177 F6
Plymouth PL3 249 B5
Hanover Ct
Dulverton TA22 33 D7
Exeter EX2 181 C8
10 Plymouth PL1 263 A2
Hanover Gdns EX15 163 C5
Hanover Ho TQ1 220 D3
Hanover Rd
Exeter EX1 177 F6
Plymouth PL3 249 C4
Hansetown Rd TA4 34 F8
Hansford Cross
Ashreigney EX18 44 A1
Burrington EX37 44 B2
Hansford Ct EX14 166 C5
Hansford Way EX11 169 C3
Hanson Pk EX39 157 A4
Happaway Cl TQ2 214 A2
Happaway Rd TQ2 214 A2
Harberton Cl TQ4 225 E3
Harbertonford CE Prim Sch
TQ9 139 C7
Harbour Ave
Plymouth, Camels Head
PL5 247 E8
Plymouth PL4 263 A2
Harbour Ct
Exmouth EX8 201 F6
8 Seaton EX12 192 B4
Harbour Ave TQ4 225 E3
Harbourneford Cross
TQ10 135 B4
Harbour Rd EX12 192 B4
Harbourside 8 EX34 150 C6
Harbour St PL11 247 B3
Harbour The EX12 192 C5
Harbour View
Plymouth PL9 255 A7
Saltash PL12 242 E2
Harbour View Cl 1 TQ5 230 C5
Harcombe Cross
Chudleigh TQ13 124 A8
Raymond's Hill EX13 104 C6
Sidbury EX10 101 C1
Harcombe Fields EX10 188 D8
Harcombe La EX10 188 D8
Harcombe La E EX10 188 E8
Harcombe Rd
Raymond's Hill DT7 104 D6
Uplyme DT7 260 D8
Hardaway Head 7 EX32 155 A5
Harden Ho TQ3 225 E7
Harding Cres EX16 161 E5
Hardings Ct PL12 242 E3
Hardisworthy Cross EX39 37 B7
Hardwick Farm PL7 250 C3
Hardy Cl TQ1 220 C2
Hardy Cres PL5 244 E1
Hardy Rd EX2 178 D5
Hardys Ct EX10 186 D4
Harebell Cl PL12 242 D4
Harebell Copse EX4 176 D8
Harebell Dr EX15 162 E5
Haredon Cross PL21 137 D6

Harefield Cl EX4 177 A8
Harefield Cotts EX8 195 D5
Harefield Dr
Lympstone EX8 195 F5
Stoke Fleming TQ6 146 B7
Harefield Rd EX8 195 F6
Harefoot Cross TQ13 121 D3
Hare La EX4 98 D4
Harepath Hill EX12 192 A8
Harepath Rd EX12 192 A7
Harepathstead Rd EX5 83 B1
Harepie Cross EX31 27 D6
Haresdown Cross EX36 47 C7
Hares Gn EX32 158 C4
Hares La TQ13 130 F4
Hareston Cl PL7 251 B3
Hareston Cross PL8 257 D8
Harestone Cross EX13 88 B7
Hare Tor Cl EX20 170 E5
Harewood TQ11 236 B5
Harewood Cl PL7 250 E5
Harewood Cres PL5 244 B2
Harewood Rd PL18 125 D3
Harford Cross EX32 17 C2
Harford La EX6, EX17 97 F7
Harford Rd
Ivybridge PL21 237 D6
Landkey EX32 17 B2
Hargood Terr 6 PL2 247 F4
Hargreaves Cl PL5 243 F2
Harker La EX6 114 B2
Harletch Cl PL3 249 A7
Harlequins EX4 261 A3
Harleston Cross TQ7 144 F4
Harley Ct PL21 237 D5
Harlington Ct TQ12 207 C4
Harman Wlk EX32 155 C5
Harnorlen Rd PL2 248 D7
Haroldsleigh Ave PL5 244 E2
Harper's Hill
Northlew EX20 74 C2
Totnes TQ9 223 A5
Harpins Ct TQ12 213 A6
Harpitt Cl EX15 162 C3
Harp La EX5 99 E2
Harp's Corner Cross EX36 46 C6
Harpson Rd EX36 31 F1
Harpson La
Bishops Nympton EX36 31 F1
South Molton EX36 46 F8
Harracott Cross EX31 27 E6
Harraton Cross PL21 137 D1
Harriers Cl EX12 192 A6
Harrier Way EX2 178 E4
Harriet Gdns PL7 250 B6
Harringcourt Rd EX4 174 E2
Harrington Dr EX4 174 E2
Harrington Gdns EX4 174 E1
Harrington La EX4 174 D2
Harris Cl EX16 51 A4
Harris Cotts
Blackawton TQ9 139 E1
Ivybridge PL21 237 C5
Harris Cross EX39 38 D8
Harris Ct PL9 255 B6
Harrison St 7 PL2 247 F4
Harrisons Way EX5 173 B8
Harris Way PL21 136 B6
Harrowbarrow Sch PL17 125 A4
Harrowbeer La PL20 126 F3
Harrowby Cl EX16 161 F4
Hartland Abbey & Gdns
EX39 22 C3
Hartland Cl PL6 245 A7
Hartland Cross EX17 79 C4
Hartland Forest Golf & L
Parc EX39 38 B6
Hartland Prim Sch EX39 22 D4
Hartland Quay Mus EX39 22 A3
Hartland Tor Cl TQ5 230 A2
Hartland View Rd EX4 8 C6
Hartley Ave PL3 249 A6
Hartley Ct PL3 249 A6
Hartley Park Gdns PL3 248 F6
Hartley Rd
Exmouth EX8 202 A6
Paignton TQ2 226 A5
Plymouth PL3 248 E6
Hartleys The EX8 202 A6
Hart Manor EX33 152 E3
Hartnoll Cross EX16 64 E8
Harton Cross EX39 22 E3
Harton Way EX39 22 E3
Harton Way Ind Pk EX39 22 E3
Hartop Rd TQ1 214 B1
Hartop Rd TQ1 214 B1
Harts Cl
Exeter EX1 178 E8
Teignmouth TQ14 210 A6
Hart's La
Churchstow TQ7 143 E4
Exeter EX1 178 D8
Huish Champflower TA4 35 D7
Hart St 9 EX7 157 A2
Hartwell Ave PL9 256 D7
Harvest La EX39 156 D2
Harvey Ave PL4 249 B1
Harveys Cl
11 Chudleigh Knighton
TQ13 123 C4
Sampford Courtenay EX20 76 F4
Harvey St PL1 247 B3
Harwell Ct 8 PL1 262 B3
Harwell St PL1 262 B3
Harwood Ave PL5 244 C7
Harwood Cl EX8 196 D1
Haskins Cross EX14 84 C5
Hask La EX6 96 D3

Haslam Ct TQ1 220 A7
Haslam Rd TQ1 220 A7
Hastings St PL1 262 B3
Hastings Terr PL1 262 B3
Haswell Cl PL6 249 A8
Hatchcombe La TQ2 213 F2
Hatcher Cl EX14 166 C3
Hatcher St 10 EX7 204 D6
Hatchland Rd EX4 174 F6
Hatchmoor Common La
EX38 159 F6
Hatchmoor Est EX38 159 E5
Hatchmoor Ind Est EX20 75 B6
Hatchmoor Lane Ind Est
EX38 159 F6
Hatchmoor Rd EX38 159 F5
Hatfield TQ1 220 B6
Hatfield Rd TQ1 220 B6
Hatherdown Hill TQ12 124 A1
Hatherleigh Com Prim Sch
EX20 75 C7
Hatherleigh La TQ13 122 D7
Hatherleigh Rd
Exeter EX2 177 A2
Okehampton EX20 93 F7
Winkleigh EX19 58 E2
Hatherton La EX20 76 E2
Hat La PL10 252 F2
Hatshill Cl PL6 132 A2
Hatshill Farm Cl PL6 132 A3
Hatway Hill EX10 101 C3
Hauley Rd TQ6 233 F3
Havelock Rd TQ1 214 B1
Havelock Terr
Lutton PL21 133 B2
Plymouth PL2 247 F3
Haven Banks EX2 261 B1
Haven Cl EX2 261 A1
Haven Ct 5 EX12 192 B4
Haven Rd EX2 261 A1
Haven The TQ14 209 F7
Havenview Rd EX12 192 A5
Have's Hill EX17 61 C8
Hawarden Cotts PL4 249 B1
Hawcombe La EX33 8 E1
Haweswater Cl PL6 244 E4
Hawkchurch CE Prim Sch
EX13 88 E3
Hawkchurch Cross EX13 88 E3
Hawkchurch Rd EX13 88 E3
Hawkerland Rd EX10 186 C4
Hawkers Ave PL4 263 A2
Hawkers La PL3 248 E5
Hawkesdown Cl EX12 192 D7
Hawkes Dr 8 EX16 161 E6
Hawkins Ave TQ2 219 C7
Hawkins Cl PL6 245 A5
Hawkins Dr TQ12 210 B6
Hawkins La EX11 168 E3
Hawkin's La TA4 35 E7
Hawkins Rd TQ12 207 F3
Hawkmoor Cotts TQ13 122 B7
Hawkmoor Hill EX13, DT6 88 H2
Hawkmoor Pk TQ13 122 B7
Hawkridge Cross
Hawkridge TA22 21 D1
Umberleigh EX37 28 C4
Hawkridge Rd EX31 15 E5
Hawks Pk PL12 242 C2
Hawks Way EX32 17 F4
Hawkwell Cross EX16 32 F4
Hawley Cl EX32 155 C5
Hawley Cross EX13 86 F3
Hawley Manor EX32 155 C5
Hawson Cross TQ11 130 B3
Hawthorn Ave
Ilfracombe EX34 150 D5
Torpoint PL11 246 F3
Hawthorn Cl
Cullompton EX15 163 B2
Honiton EX14 166 B5
Kingsbridge TQ7 258 C4
Plymouth, Hooe PL9 255 C5
Plymouth, Woolwell PL6 245 D7
Hawthorn Dr
Sidmouth EX10 187 F8
Wembury PL9 140 D7
Hawthorne Cl TQ12 212 F8
Hawthorne Rd
10 Tiverton EX16 161 F6
Wellington TA21 160 F5
Hawthorn Gr
Exmouth EX8 196 E1
Plymouth PL2 248 C7
Hawthorn Park Cl TQ2 219 D3
Hawthorn Park Rd PL9 140 D7
Hawthorn Pk
Bideford EX39 156 E1
Lydford EX20 107 F4
Hawthorn Rd
Barnstaple EX32 154 C2
Crediton EX17 165 C5
Exeter EX2 177 F3
Tavistock PL19 171 D4
Hawthorns PL12 242 D2
Hawthorn Way
Exeter EX2 181 A8
Plymouth PL3 249 B7
Haxter Cl PL6 241 B1
Haxton Down La EX31 18 B8
Haxton La EX31 18 A8
Haycroft Ho 3 EX39 157 A1
Haycross Hill EX21 55 D4
Haydn Cl EX32 155 C5
Haydon Cross EX16 48 C4

Haydon Gr PL5 243 C1
Haydon Rd EX16 161 B5
Haydons Pk EX14 166 C5
Haye Cl DT7 260 C4
Haye La
Colyford DT7, EX13 103 D3
Lyme Regis DT7 260 D4
Haye Rd PL7, PL9 250 C1
Haye Rd S PL9 256 C7
Hayes Barton EX9 197 E7
Hayes Barton Ct EX4 177 A5
Hayes Cl
Budleigh Salterton EX9 198 A2
Otterton EX9 198 E7
Totnes TQ9 223 E4
Hayes Copse EX32 17 B2
Hayes Cross EX21 55 E3
Hayes Ct
Lyme Regis DT7 260 D3
Paignton TQ4 225 F5
Hayes Gdns
Plymouth PL9 256 A4
Hayes La
Ashreigney EX18 58 D8
East Budleigh EX9 198 A6
Otterton EX9 198 E7
Hayes Pl PL6 249 B8
Hayes Rd
Paignton TQ3, TQ4 226 A5
Plymouth PL9 255 C7
Hayes Sch TQ4 225 F5
Hayes The TQ5 229 E5
Hayeswood La EX9 198 A6
Hayfield Rd EX20 76 C5
Hay La TQ7 147 E6
Hayle Ave TQ4 229 B8
Hayley Pk TQ12 212 F3
Haymans Cl EX15 163 B2
Haymans Gn EX15 163 B2
Hayne Barton Cotts
EX15 163 E6
Hayne Cl
Exeter EX4 178 A7
Tipton St John EX10 100 D2
Hayne Cross
Ashill EX15 66 F5
Bishops Nympton EX36 31 A4
Cheriton Fitzpaine EX17 63 A2
Lewtrenchard EX20 106 B5
Lustleigh TQ13 121 F7
Moreton EX16 34 B4
Plymtree EX15 83 F6
Zeal Monachorum EX17 78 B6
Hayne Hill EX10 100 D2
Hayne Ho EX16 49 B2
Hayne La
Bolham EX16 49 B2
Butterleigh EX15 64 C2
Honiton EX14 85 C2
Silverton EX5 82 C4
Wilmington EX14 86 D3
Hayne Pk
Barnstaple EX32 155 B4
Tipton St John EX10 100 D2
Hayne Town Cross EX37 44 B8
Hayrish Cross EX20 95 B7
Haystone Pl PL1 262 B4
Haytor Cl
Plymouth PL5 244 B3
Teignmouth TQ14 210 D8
Haytor Ct TQ13 122 A4
Haytor Dr
Exeter EX4 176 E7
Ivybridge PL21 237 D4
Newton Abbot TQ12 208 A3
Haytor Gr TQ12 208 A3
Haytor Pk TQ12 207 E2
Haytor Rd TQ1 220 B7
Haytor Terr 17 TQ12 207 B3
Haytor Vale EX20 122 B4
Haytown Pottery EX22 39 E1
Haywain Cl TQ2 213 B1
Haywards Prim Sch
EX17 165 D5
Hazel Ave EX13 152 E7
Hazel Cl
Kingsbridge TQ7 258 C4
Newton Abbot TQ12 208 A1
Newton Poppleford EX10 186 F8
Plymouth PL6 245 B6
Seaton EX12 192 A7
Hazel Gr
Exeter EX1 177 F2
Tavistock PL7 171 C2
Hazeldene Cl EX8 196 C1
Hazeldene Gdns EX8 196 A1
Hazeldown Prim Sch
TQ14 210 A8
Hazeldown Rd TQ14 210 B7
Hazel Dr PL9 256 C7
Hazelmead Rd EX5 179 E2

Headgate EX36 20 B1
Head Hill EX18, EX37 44 C5
Headingley Cl EX2 178 A6
Headland Cl EX1 178 C7
Headland Cres EX1 178 C7
Headland Cross EX17 96 A6
Headland Ct
8 Brixham TQ5 230 D5
Woolacombe EX34 7 F8
Headland Gr TQ3 219 C1
Headland La EX7 178 A4
Headland Park Rd TQ3 219 C1
Headland Pk PL4 263 A4
Headland Rd TQ2 219 E2
Headlands The TQ2 219 E2
Headlands View Ave EX34 1 B1
Headless Cross TQ13 112 B6
Headon Cross EX22 72 C5
Headson Cross EX20 91 E1
Headstock Rd TA20 88 E7
Headway Cl TQ14 209 D8
Headway Cross Rd TQ14 209 D8
Headway Rise TQ14 209 D8
Head Weir Rd EX15 163 C5
Heale Down La EX31 4 A3
Heal Park Cres EX31 153 D5
Heal's Field EX13 167 F7
Healy Cl 9 PL2 247 F4
Healy Pl PL2 247 F4
Heanton Cl EX33 152 E6
Heanton Ct TQ1 220 C4
Heanton Hill EX33 152 F4
Heanton Hill La EX31 15 E6
Heanton Lea EX31 15 E6
Heanton St EX33 152 D5
Heanton Terr PL10 252 E6
Heard Ave EX8 202 E8
Heard Cl EX39 22 E3
Hearl Rd PL12 242 B3
Hearson Cross EX32 28 B8
Heasley Cross EX36 19 C3
Heasley La EX36 19 D3
Heasley Mill Cross EX36 19 D3
Heathayne Cross EX24 102 F5
Heathayne La EX24 102 F5
Heathbrook Mews EX4 174 C2
Heath Cl
Heathfield TQ12 123 B2
15 Honiton EX14 85 C2
Heathcoat Fst Sch EX16 161 B3
Heathcoat Prim Sch
EX16 161 B3
Heathcoat Sq EX16 161 C4
Heathcoat Way EX16 161 F5
Heath Comm EX13 87 E6
Heath Cross
Cheriton Fitzpaine EX16 63 A5
Spreyton EX17 96 A8
Tedburn St Mary EX4 98 C5
Heath Ct
Brixham TQ5 230 E6
1 Totnes TQ9 223 C5
Heather Cl
Exeter EX1 178 B6
10 Honiton EX14 85 C2
Newton Abbot TQ12 206 F4
Okehampton EX20 170 B5
Seaton EX12 192 B7
Tavistock PL19 171 D4
8 Tiverton EX16 161 F6
Heather Dr
Exeter EX1 176 F2
Ivybridge PL21 237 D4
Heather Grange EX14 168 D4
Heather Pk TQ10 135 A3
Heathers The
Okehampton EX20 170 D6
Plymouth PL6 245 D7
Heatherton Park Ho TA4 52 E8
Heather Way TQ5 230 A4
Heather Wlk PL21 237 D4
Heathfield TQ12 180 C5
Heathfield Cotts TQ12 123 B3
Heathfield Cross
Axmouth DT7 193 D8
Cornwood PL21 133 B3
Modbury PL21 137 E2
Poltimore EX4 174 C7
Woodbury Salterton EX5 184 A7
Heathfieldlake Hill TQ13 123 F7
Heathfield Mdw TQ13 180 D5
Heathfield Pk PL20 127 A3
Heathfield Rd
Bideford EX39 157 C1
Denbury TQ12 211 A6
Plymouth PL4 249 B3
Heathfield Terr
Bovey Tracey TQ13 180 C6
Denbury TQ12 211 A6
Heath Hill TQ12 123 B2
Heath La
Cheriton Fitzpaine EX16 63 A6
Hollacombe EX19 58 F5
Tedburn St Mary EX4, EX6 98 C4
Heathlands TQ14 210 A8
Heathlands Rise TQ14 210 A8
Heathpark Ind Est EX14 166 A5
Heathpark Way 13 EX14 85 C2

Heath Pk
Brixham TQ5 . . . .**230** E5
Newton Abbot TQ12 . . . . . **208** A1
Heath Rd
Brixham TQ5 . . . .**230** E5
Dunsford EX6 . . . .**112** F7
Exeter EX2 . . . .**178** B5
Spreyton EX17 . . . .**95** F8
Heath Rise TQ5 . . . .**230** E5
Heath Terr PL18 . . . .**125** C5
Heatree Cl TQ14 . . . .**210** E8
Heatree Cross TQ13 . . . . .**121** D7
Heaviside Cl TQ2 . . . .**214** B3
Heavitree Gallows EX1 . . .**178** C5
Heavitree Pk EX1 . . . .**178** A5
Heavitree Rd
Cawsand PL10 . . . .**253** A2
Exeter EX1 . . . .**177** E6
Heddeswell Cross TQ7 . . .**143** E2
Heddon Cross
Heddon EX32 . . . .**29** A7
Milton Damerel EX22 . . . . . .**54** C5
Hederman Cl EX5 . . . .**82** B5
Hedge Cross EX20 . . . .**107** C4
**Hedgehog Hospl (Prickly Ball
Farm)** TQ12 . . . .**211** F7
Hedgend Rd EX14 . . . .**86** B5
Hedgerow Cl
Crediton EX17 . . . .**165** E6
Plymouth PL6 . . . .**245** E8
Hedgerows The PL12 . . . . .**242** B3
Hedingham Cl PL7 . . . .**251** C4
Hedingham Gdns PL6 . . . . .**245** B7
Hedley Wood Cvn Pk
EX22 . . . .**70** E4
Heggadon Cl EX5 . . . .**83** A7
Heiffers La EX16 . . . .**47** A5
Heirland Cross TQ7 . . . .**143** D3
Hele Almshouses PL9 . . . .**140** E8
Hele Barton Cross EX17 . . .**61** D6
Hele Cl
Barnstaple EX32 . . . .**154** A3
Bickleigh PL6 . . . .**132** A5
Torquay TQ2 . . . .**213** F11
Hele Cross
Ashburton TQ13 . . . .**130** E5
Bradworthy EX22 . . . .**38** E4
Cornwood PL21 . . . .**133** D4
King's Nympton EX37 . . . .**44** D7
St Giles on t H PL15 . . . .**90** B3
Torquay TQ2 . . . .**213** F11
Hele Gdns PL7 . . . .**251** A4
Hele Hill EX14 . . . .**61** C5
Hele La
Barnstaple EX31 . . . .**154** A3
Frithelstock Stone EX38 . . . .**40** F5
Roborough PL6 . . . .**241** F2
Shaugh Prior PL6, PL7 . . . . .**132** A6
Hele Lane Hill EX17 . . . .**61** D6
Hele Mill EX34 . . . .**150** E5
Helena Pl EX8 . . . .**202** A6
Helens Mead Cl TQ2 . . . . . .**214** A4
Helens Mead Rd TQ2 . . . . . .**214** A4
Hele Rd
Bradninch EX5 . . . .**82** F6
Exeter EX4 . . . .**261** A4
Kingsteignton TQ12 . . . .**123** E1
Torquay TQ2 . . . .**213** F11
Hele Rise EX31 . . . .**154** A3
Hele's Sch PL7 . . . .**250** C6
Hele's Terr PL4 . . . .**249** B2
Hele Valley Holiday Pk
EX34 . . . .**150** E5
Helford Dr TQ4 . . . .**229** B8
Helford Wlk TQ4 . . . .**229** B8
Helgan Dr TQ3 . . . .**225** E8
Hellevoetsluis Way TQ3 . . .**218** F4
Hellier Cl EX14 . . . .**166** A4
Hellinghayes La EX16 . . . . . .**46** C3
Hellings Gdns EX5 . . . .**175** C7
Hellings Parks La EX5 . . . .**175** E4
Helmdon Rise TQ2 . . . .**219** B8
Helston Cl TQ3 . . . .**225** F7
Hembury Cock Hill TQ11 . .**236** A7
Hembury Cotts TQ9 . . . . . .**131** E1
Hembury Cross
Holbeton PL8 . . . .**141** F8
Stibb Cross EX38 . . . .**40** C4
Hembury Fort Cross EX14 .**84** E5
Hembury Pk TQ11 . . . .**236** B7
Hemerdon House PL7 . . . . .**251** E7
Hemerdon Hts PL7 . . . .**251** A6
Hemerdon La PL7 . . . .**251** C8
Hemerdon Way PL7 . . . .**250** D6
Hems Brook TQ12 . . . .**219** B8
Hems La TQ9 . . . .**216** D7
Hemsworthy Gate TQ13 . . .**121** E3
Hemyock Castle EX15 . . . . . .**67** B8
Hemyock Prim Sch EX15 . . .**67** B8
Hemyock Rd EX15 . . . .**66** E8
Henacre Rd TQ7 . . . .**258** D5
Henacroft Cross EX19 . . . . . .**58** B3
Henbury Cl TQ1 . . . .**220** B6
Henceford Cross EX17 . . . . .**62** A6
Henderbarrow Cross
EX21 . . . .**73** E1
Henders Cnr PL3 . . . .**248** F6
Henderson Pl PL2 . . . .**247** F6
Hendon Cross EX16 . . . .**30** B8
Hendwell Cl PL6 . . . .**244** E6
Heneaton Sq EX2 . . . .**182** B8
Henlake Cl PL21 . . . .**237** B6

Henley Cl EX13 . . . .**88** B7
Henley Dr PL5 . . . .**244** C7
Henley Ho TQ7 . . . .**143** A1
Henley Rd EX8 . . . .**202** C7
Hennapyn Rd TQ2 . . . .**219** E3
Hennock Com Prim Sch
TQ13 . . . .**123** B7
Hennock Ct EX2 . . . .**181** D8
Hennock Rd TQ4 . . . .**225** F2
Hennock Rd Central EX2 .**177** C1
Hennock Rd N EX2 . . . .**177** D1
Hennock Rd N EX2 . . . .**177** C2
Henrietta Pl 7 EX8 . . . .**202** A7
Henrietta Rd 8 EX8 . . . .**202** A7
Henry Cl PL21 . . . .**136** B6
Henry Lewis Cl 7 EX5 . . . . .**99** E8
Henry's Way DT7 . . . .**260** E4
Hensbury La PL20 . . . .**239** F7
Hensford Mews EX7 . . . . . .**200** C3
Hensford Rd EX7 . . . .**200** C2
Hensleigh Dr EX2 . . . .**177** E5
Hensleigh Rd EX16 . . . .**63** F7
Hensons Dr EX16 . . . .**51** A3
Hen St EX5 . . . .**83** A7
Henstill La EX17 . . . .**79** F7
Henty Ave EX7 . . . .**204** F7
Henty Cl EX7 . . . .**204** F8
Heppenstall Rd EX32 . . . . . .**155** B6
Heraldry Way EX2 . . . .**178** D4
Herbert Ho TA22 . . . .**33** D6
Herbert Pl PL2 . . . .**247** E4
Herbert Rd
Exeter EX1 . . . .**177** F7
Salcombe TQ8 . . . .**259** D4
Torquay TQ2 . . . .**219** D4
Herbert St PL2 . . . .**247** E4
Hercules Rd EX1 . . . .**178** D6
Herdicott Cross EX22 . . . . . .**71** F2
Hereford Cl EX8 . . . .**196** D4
Hereford Rd
Exeter EX4 . . . .**176** D6
Plymouth PL5 . . . .**244** B5
Heritage Cl PL12 . . . .**242** C3
Heritage Ct 11 EX14 . . . . . .**166** C6
Heritage Way EX10 . . . .**188** B8
Hermes Ave EX16 . . . .**161** E3
Hermitage Ct 11 PL4 . . . . . .**248** E4
Hermitage Rd
Dartmouth TQ6 . . . .**233** D4
Ilfracombe EX34 . . . .**150** B6
Plymouth PL3 . . . .**248** E5
Hermitage The 11 EX34 . . .**150** B5
Hermosa Gdns 5 TQ14 . . .**210** B5
Hermosa Rd TQ14 . . . .**210** B5
Hernaford Cross TQ9 . . . . .**139** B6
Hernaford Rd TQ9 . . . .**139** B6
Hern La PL8 . . . .**257** F4
Heron Cl PL10 . . . .**252** F6
Heron Ct
Barnstaple EX32 . . . .**155** E4
Exmouth EX8 . . . .**202** C6
Heron Ind Units EX2 . . . . . .**178** E5
Heron Rd
Exeter, Middle Moor EX2 . . .**176** D3
Exeter, Sowton EX2 . . . .**178** E5
Honiton EX14 . . . .**166** B4
Herons Brook EX20 . . . .**170** A6
Herons Reach TQ7 . . . .**144** C1
Heron Way
Cullompton EX15 . . . .**163** B2
Torquay TQ2 . . . .**213** C3
Herschel Gdns PL5 . . . .**243** E1
Herschell Rd EX4 . . . .**177** E8
Hertland Wlk PL2 . . . .**248** A7
Hescane Pk EX6 . . . .**97** B4
Hesketh Cres TQ1 . . . .**220** D3
Hesketh Mews TQ1 . . . .**220** D3
Hesketh Rd TQ1 . . . .**220** D3
Hessary Dr PL6 . . . .**241** C1
Hessary Terr PL20 . . . .**128** A8
Hessary View
Saltash PL12 . . . .**242** E4
Tavistock PL19 . . . .**171** B6
Hestow Rd TQ12 . . . .**123** F1
Hetling Cl PL1 . . . .**262** B3
Hewer's Row PL4 . . . .**263** A3
Hewett Cl TQ12 . . . .**208** A3
Hewitt Cl PL12 . . . .**242** C1
Hexdown Barns TQ7 . . . . . .**142** F3
Hexham PL7 . . . .**248** A8
Hexton Hill Rd PL9 . . . .**255** B6
Hexton Quay PL9 . . . .**255** C6
Hexworthy Ave EX4 . . . .**176** E8
Heybrook Ave PL5 . . . .**243** D1
Heybrook Dr PL9 . . . .**140** A7
Heydon's La EX10 . . . .**188** A4
Heyswood Ave EX32 . . . . . .**155** C2
Heywood Cl
Hartland EX39 . . . .**22** E3
Torquay TQ2 . . . .**219** E7
Heywood Cross EX18 . . . . . .**59** D5
Heywood Dr EX6 . . . .**201** A8
Heywood Rd TQ12 . . . .**207** F6
Heywood Forest Wlk
EX18 . . . .**59** D6
Heywood Rd EX39 . . . .**156** F5
Heywoods Cl TQ14 . . . .**210** C5
Heywoods Rd TQ14 . . . .**210** C5
Hibernia Terr PL5 . . . .**247** E8
Hickory Cl EX14 . . . .**166** E5
Hickory Dr PL7 . . . .**251** B5
Hick's La PL4 . . . .**263** A2
Hidden Valley Cvn Pk EX34 .**8** D4
Hides Rd EX10 . . . .**188** C8
Hidewood La EX15 . . . .**52** F1
Hierns La EX34 . . . .**150** C6
High Acre Dr PL21 . . . .**237** A6
Highampton Com Prim Sch
EX21 . . . .**74** C7

Highampton Cross EX21 . . .**74** C7
Highaton Head Cross
EX36 . . . .**32** C4
High Bank
Exeter EX4 . . . .**178** B8
West Hill EX11 . . . .**168** D3
Highbank Cl PL19 . . . .**171** A4
Highbarrow Cross EX22 . . . .**54** A4
High Bickington CE Prim Sch
EX37 . . . .**43** B7
High Bolham EX16 . . . .**33** C1
Highbridge Ct PL7 . . . .**250** E5
High Bullen EX5 . . . .**82** B6
High Bullen Cross EX36 . . . .**19** E1
High Bullen La EX35 . . . .**5** B3
Highbury Cres PL7 . . . .**250** D7
Highbury Hill EX39 . . . .**157** A8
Highbury Pk EX8 . . . .**196** A1
Highbury Rd
Barnstaple EX32 . . . .**155** C3
Torquay TQ1 . . . .**220** B6
High Cl TQ13 . . . .**180** E7
Highclere Gdns PL6 . . . .**245** B8
Highcliff Ct EX7 . . . .**204** E6
Highcliffe Cl
Lympstone EX8 . . . .**195** D4
Seaton EX12 . . . .**191** F6
Highcliffe Cres EX12 . . . . . .**191** F6
Highcliffe Ct EX8 . . . .**195** D4
Highcliffe Mews TQ4 . . . . .**226** C4
Highcliff Rd DT7 . . . .**260** C3
Highclyffe Ct EX12 . . . .**191** F6
High Cott EX36 . . . .**19** C2
High Creek Cross EX10 . . . .**188** F8
Highcroft EX4 . . . .**173** A1
High Cross
Bampton EX16 . . . .**34** A1
14 Combe Martin EX34 . . . . . .**3** A3
High Cross Ho TQ9 . . . .**216** A1
Highcross Rd EX4 . . . .**177** C8
Highdown Cross EX39 . . . . . .**23** A4
Higher Aboveway EX6 . . . .**182** B3
Higher Aller La TQ13 . . . . . .**180** E6
Higher Alston Farm TQ5 . .**229** D3
Higher Anderton Rd
PL10 . . . .**252** F5
Higher Audley Ave TQ2 . . .**219** F8
Higher Axmouth Cotts
EX12 . . . .**192** F6
Higher Barley Mount
EX4 . . . .**176** E5
Higher Beara Cross
EX34 . . . .**236** F4
Higher Bedlands EX9 . . . . .**197** F2
Higher Bibbery TQ13 . . . . . .**180** E7
Higher Borough TQ7 . . . . . .**149** A4
Higher Brand La EX14 . . . .**166** C4
Higher Brimley Rd TQ14 . .**210** C5
Higher Broad Oak Rd
EX11 . . . .**168** D2
Higher Broad Path TQ9 . . .**223** D3
Higher Brook Mdw 11
EX10 . . . .**101** B1
Higher Brook Pk PL21 . . . . .**237** A5
Higher Brownston Cross
PL21 . . . .**138** A4
Higher Buckeridge Rd
TQ14 . . . .**210** B7
Higher Budleigh Mdw
TQ12 . . . .**206** F3
Higher Bulkamore Cross
TQ10 . . . .**135** E5
Higher Bull Ring EX15 . . . . .**163** C3
Higher Bulworthy Cross
EX16 . . . .**47** A4
Higher Bulworthy La
EX16 . . . .**47** A4
Higher Buzzacott La EX34 . .**3** B1
Higher Cadewell La TQ2 .**219** D8
Higher Cheglinch La EX34 . .**8** F6
Higher Church St 8
EX32 . . . .**155** A4
Higher Churchway PL9 . . . .**256** A7
Higher Clevelands EX36 . .**156** F6
Higher Collaton Cross
TQ14 . . . .**147** F6
Higher Compton Barton
TQ3 . . . .**218** E6
Higher Compton Rd PL3 . .**248** F6
Higher Contour Rd TQ6 . .**234** B3
Higher Coombe Dr TQ14 .**210** A7
Higher Coombes TA20 . . . . .**88** D8
Higher Copythorne TQ5 . .**230** A4
Higher Cotteylands EX16 .**161** B3
Higher Cross EX15 . . . .**51** C1
Higher Cross Rd EX31 . . . .**154** B3
Higher Davis Cl EX32 . . . . . .**17** F6
Higher Dean TQ11 . . . .**135** C7
Higher Dean La EX34 . . . .**3** B3
Higher Doats Hayne La
EX13 . . . .**103** D5
Higher Down EX6 . . . .**194** D3
Higher Downs Rd TQ1 . . . .**220** C8
Higher Dr EX7 . . . .**204** F8
Higher East St EX36 . . . .**30** D8
Higher Edginswell La
TQ2 . . . .**219** B8
Higher Efford Rd PL3 . . . . .**249** B5
Higher Elmwood EX31 . . . .**154** C3
Higher Elstone Cross
EX18 . . . .**44** D3
Higher Erith Rd TQ1 . . . . . .**220** D4
Higher Exeter Rd TQ14 . . .**124** E2
Higher Ewrick Hill EX4 . . .**176** E7
Higher Forches Cross
EX17 . . . .**78** E7
Higher Fortescue EX10 . . .**188** D7
Higher French Pk TQ12 . . .**206** F3

Higher Furzeham Rd
TQ5 . . . .**230** C6
Higher Gn TQ10 . . . .**135** A2
Higher Green Cross TQ7 .**145** C4
Higher Greenway La
EX10 . . . .**187** E7
Higher Gunstone EX39 . . .**157** A2
Higher Haske Cross
EX17 . . . .**165** F7
Higher Hendham Barns
TQ7 . . . .**138** E1
Higher Hewish La EX31 . . . .**9** D4
Higher Hill View EX10 . . . .**188** A5
Higher Ho EX38 . . . .**42** B5
Higher Holcombe Cl
TQ14 . . . .**210** C7
Higher Holcombe Dr
TQ14 . . . .**210** C8
Higher Holcombe Rd
TQ14 . . . .**210** C8
Higher Hoopern La EX4 .**173** C1
Higher Island TQ9 . . . .**139** E2
Higher Kelly PL18 . . . .**125** D3
Higher King's Ave EX4 . . . .**177** D8
Higher Kingsdown Rd
TQ14 . . . .**209** D7
Higher Kinsman's Dale
TQ13 . . . .**111** F5
Higher La
Axmouth EX12 . . . .**192** E7
Plymouth PL1 . . . .**262** C2
Sampford Courtenay EX20 . . .**76** D5
Higher Lane EX12 . . . .**192** D7
Higher Ley EX17 . . . .**60** B3
Higher Lincombe Rd
TQ1 . . . .**220** E3
Higher Longford Cvn Site
PL19 . . . .**117** F1
Higher Loughborough
EX16 . . . .**161** B5
Higher Manor Rd TQ5 . . . .**230** C5
Higher Manor Terr 11
TQ3 . . . .**226** A5
Higher Marley Rd EX8 . . . .**196** D4
Higher Mauldin St 7
EX32 . . . .**155** A6
Higher Maunders Hill
EX9 . . . .**198** E7
Higher Mdws
Beer EX12 . . . .**191** D5
High Bickington EX37 . . . . . .**43** B7
Higher Mead EX15 . . . .**67** B8
Higher Mill Flats DT7 . . . . .**260** D4
Higher Millhayes EX15 . . . . .**52** B1
Higher Mill La
Buckfast TQ11 . . . .**236** B7
Cullompton EX15 . . . .**163** C3
Higher Mogworthy Cross
EX16 . . . .**47** D4
Highermoor Cross EX22 . . . .**53** B1
Higher Moor Sq 4 EX16 .**161** F6
Higher Mowles PL3 . . . .**249** B6
Higher Newclose La EX36 . .**16** B6
Higher Park Cl PL7 . . . .**251** B3
Higher Park Rd EX33 . . . . . .**152** E5
Higher Penn TQ5 . . . .**230** D3
Higher Pk TQ7 . . . .**149** A3
Higher Polsham Rd TQ3 . .**226** B7
Higher Port View PL12 . . . .**242** F2
Higher Preston Cross
TQ12 . . . .**123** D1
Higher Queens Terr TQ1 .**220** B5
Higher Rake La TQ7 . . . .**143** F6
Higher Raleigh Rd EX31 . .**155** A7
Higher Ramshill La TQ3 . .**225** C8
Higher Ranscombe Rd
TQ5 . . . .**230** D4
Higher Rd
Crediton EX17 . . . .**165** B6
Fremington EX31 . . . .**153** E5
Woodbury Salterton EX5 . . .**184** B7
Higher Redgate EX16 . . . . . .**161** D5
Higher Ridgeway EX11 . . . .**169** E4
Higher Ringmore Rd
TQ14 . . . .**209** D4
Higher Roborough 8
TQ13 . . . .**131** A5
Higher Row PL10 . . . .**253** A2
Higher Rydons TQ5 . . . .**230** A4
Higher Sackery TQ12 . . . . .**208** D4
Higher Shapter Cl EX3 . . . .**182** F4
Higher Shapter St EX3 . . . .**182** F4
Higher Slade Rd EX34 . . . .**150** A2
Higher Spring Gdns
EX11 . . . .**169** E3
Higher St
Brixham TQ5 . . . .**230** C5
Cullompton EX15 . . . .**163** C4
Dartmouth TQ6 . . . .**233** F3
Dittisham TQ6 . . . .**228** B2
Hatherleigh EX20 . . . .**75** C7
Kingswear TQ6 . . . .**234** A3
Higher Stert Terr PL4 . . . . .**263** C3
Higher Summerlands
EX1 . . . .**261** C3
Higher Tamar Terr PL18 . .**125** D7
Higher Town
Malborough TQ7 . . . .**147** E6
Sampford Peverell EX16 . . . .**50** C1
Higher Tuckers Pk EX22 . . .**38** E1
Higher Union La TQ2 . . . . .**220** A5
Higher Union Rd TQ7 . . . . .**258** C5
Higher Venn Cross EX32 . . .**17** A1
Higher Warberry Rd
TQ1 . . . .**220** D5
Higher Warborough Rd
TQ5 . . . .**229** B6

Higher Warcombe Cross
TQ7 . . . .**144** A5
Higher Warren Rd TQ7 . . .**258** E3
Higher Way EX10 . . . .**187** A8
Higher Wear Rd EX2 . . . . . .**182** C7
Higher Weaver Cross
EX15 . . . .**83** E7
Higher Wellbrook St
EX16 . . . .**161** B4
Higher Westlake Rd
4 Barnstaple EX31 . . . . . .**154** A2
Barnstaple EX31 . . . .**154** B2
Higher Westonfields
TQ9 . . . .**223** E5
Higher Woodfield Rd
TQ1 . . . .**220** D3
Higher Woodford La
PL7 . . . .**250** C7
Higher Woodway Cl
TQ14 . . . .**210** C7
Higher Woodway Rd
TQ14 . . . .**210** B8
Higher Woolbrook Pk
EX10 . . . .**187** F7
Higher Yalberton Rd
TQ4 . . . .**225** D3
Higher Yannon Dr TQ14 . .**210** A6
Highfield
Honiton EX14 . . . .**166** B5
Lapford EX17 . . . .**60** D3
Northam EX39 . . . .**156** F6
Sidmouth EX10 . . . .**188** A5
Topsham EX3 . . . .**182** F7
Highfield Cl
Barnstaple EX32 . . . .**155** B4
Brixham TQ5 . . . .**230** A4
High Bickington EX37 . . . . . .**43** B7
Plymouth PL3 . . . .**249** C5
Highfield Cres TQ3 . . . .**225** E6
Highfield Ct 3 EX8 . . . .**202** B6
Highfield Dr
Kingsbridge TQ7 . . . .**258** D4
Wembury PL9 . . . .**140** D8
Highfield Gdns EX34 . . . .**3** A3
Highfield La EX8 . . . .**202** B6
Highfield Pk PL12 . . . .**242** B3
Highfield Prim Sch PL3 . . .**249** C5
Highfield Rd
Dunkeswell EX14 . . . .**67** C1
Ilfracombe EX34 . . . .**150** C5
Highfield Terr
Beer EX12 . . . .**191** D5
2 Bishop's Tawton EX32 . . .**16** E1
4 Bittaford PL21 . . . .**137** C7
9 Ilfracombe EX34 . . . .**150** C5
High Gate EX16 . . . .**62** F6
Highglen Dr PL7 . . . .**251** B7
Highgrove Pk TQ14 . . . .**210** C7
High House La EX7 . . . .**204** E7
High House Rd TQ7 . . . .**258** D4
Highland Cl TQ2 . . . .**219** C6
Highland Pk EX15 . . . .**66** A7
Highland Rd TQ2 . . . .**219** C5
Highlands
Ottery St Mary EX11 . . . . . .**169** D3
Wembury PL9 . . . .**256** B3
Yealmpton PL8 . . . .**257** F4
Highlands Pk 9 TQ13 . . . . .**123** E6
Highland Terr
Tiverton EX16 . . . .**161** D4
Uffculme EX15 . . . .**66** A7
Highland View EX20 . . . . . .**170** C3
High Mdw EX10 . . . .**188** B7
High Mdws EX4 . . . .**176** E8
High Moor Visitor Ctr
PL20 . . . .**128** A8
High Park Cl EX19 . . . .**25** D4
High Path TA21 . . . .**160** C7
High Rd PL9 . . . .**140** C8
Highridge Cross EX37 . . . . .**45** B7
High St
Bampton EX16 . . . .**34** B1
Barnstaple EX31 . . . .**154** F5
Bideford EX39 . . . .**157** A2
Budleigh Salterton EX9 . . . .**199** G2
Chagford TQ13 . . . .**111** A6
Clovelly EX39 . . . .**23** D3
Combe Martin EX34 . . . .**3** A3
Crediton EX17 . . . .**165** C5
Cullompton EX15 . . . .**163** C3
Dawlish EX7 . . . .**204** E6
Dulverton TA22 . . . .**33** D6
East Budleigh EX9 . . . .**198** B6
Exbourne EX20 . . . .**76** C4
Exeter EX4 . . . .**261** B3
Exmouth EX8 . . . .**202** A6
Great Torrington EX38 . . . . .**159** C5
Halberton EX16 . . . .**65** A7
Hatherleigh EX20 . . . .**75** C7
Hemyock EX15 . . . .**67** B8
High Bickington EX37 . . . . . .**43** B7
Holsworthy EX22 . . . .**164** C4
Ide EX2 . . . .**176** D1
Ilfracombe EX34 . . . .**150** B6
Kentisbeare EX15 . . . .**66** A3
Kenton EX6 . . . .**194** D3
Newton Poppleford EX10 . . .**186** B8
North Tawton EX20 . . . .**77** C4
Okehampton EX20 . . . .**170** B5
3 Plymouth PL1 . . . .**262** A3
Plymouth, Stonehouse PL1 .**248** B3
Sidford EX10 . . . .**188** B8
Sidmouth EX10 . . . .**188** B4
Silverton EX5 . . . .**82** B6
Stoke Canon EX5 . . . .**173** F8
Swimbridge EX32 . . . .**28** E8
Topsham EX3 . . . .**182** F5

High St *continued*
Totnes TQ9 223 C5
Uffculme EX15 66 A7
Wellington TA21 160 E6
Winkleigh EX19 58 F3
Highstead Cross EX22 73 C8
High Street Prim Sch PL1 248 A2
High Street & Waterloo Street Flats PL1 248 A1
High Trees EX7 204 E7
High View
Bideford EX39 156 E1
Feniton EX14 84 E2
Sheepwash EX21 56 C1
High View Gdns EX8 202 B7
High View Terr EX39 156 C6
High Wall EX31 154 E4
High Way EX16 48 D8
Highweek Com Prim Sch TQ12 207 A3
Highweek Cross EX21 73 E8
Highweek Rd
Newton Abbot TQ12 207 A4
3 Newton Abbot TQ12 207 B3
Highweek St TQ12 207 B3
Highweek Village TQ12 206 F5
Highweek Way TQ12 207 B3
Highwell Rd EX12 192 A5
Highwood Grange TQ12 207 B2
Highworthy Cross EX21 55 E3
Hilary Cl EX13 167 E6
Hilary Gdns EX13 167 E6
Hill Barton Bsns Pk
Clyst St Mary EX5 179 F2
Exeter EX5 99 A1
Hill Barton Cl EX1 178 C7
Hill Barton La EX1 178 C7
Hill Barton Rd EX2 178 C7
Hillbrook Rd TQ9 223 E5
Hillbrook Rise 2 TQ9 223 E5
Hill Budge Terr 8 EX17 165 C5
Hill Cl
Exeter EX4 173 D1
Plymouth PL7 250 D4
Hillcliffe Terr 30 EX39 15 A1
Hill Cres EX14 166 D6
Hillcrest
Ilsington TQ13 122 C3
Oakford EX16 48 D5
Ottery St Mary EX11 169 D3
Hill Crest
Exminster EX6 182 A4
Kilmington EX13 87 C1
Plymouth PL3 248 E5
South Tawton EX20 95 B5
Tiverton EX16 161 D5
Hillcrest Cl
Plymouth PL7 251 A5
9 Wembury PL9 140 D8
Hillcrest Dr PL7 251 A4
Hillcrest Pk EX4 173 C2
Hillcrest Rd
Barnstaple EX32 155 B2
Bideford EX39 26 A4
Silverton EX5 82 C6
Hillcroft Terr 5 EX39 157 A2
Hill Cross
Cobbaton EX32 28 B5
Kingsbridge TQ7 144 B5
Hilldale Rd PL9 255 E6
Hilldean Cl PL5 244 C7
Hilldown TQ9 223 E5
Hilldown Cross EX17 78 D2
Hilldown La EX17 78 D2
Hilldown Rd EX17 78 C3
Hill Dr EX8 196 B3
Hilldrop Terr TQ1 220 B5
Hiller La TQ12 208 B2
Hillerton Cross EX17 78 B1
Hillesdon Rd TQ1 220 B4
Hillfield
South Zeal EX20 95 A4
Stoke Gabriel TQ9 227 F7
Hillfield Holiday Est TQ6 232 C2
Hill Garden Cl 10 EX39 157 A2
Hill Gdns PL12 239 A2
Hillhead
Colyton EX24 103 A4
Halberton EX16 65 A7
Noss Mayo PL8 140 F6
Hill Head EX37 28 F4
Hillhead Bglws 13 EX24 103 A4
Hillhead Cross PL21 137 D7
Hill Head Cross
Chittlehampton EX37 28 F4
King's Nympton EX37 44 C5
Hillhead Pk TQ5 234 E8
Hillhead Terr EX13 167 D5
Hillhouse EX14 69 A3
Hilliers EX19 57 F7
Hillingdown Cross TQ7 143 D1
Hillington EX34 150 A4
Hill La
Chipstable TA4 35 C6
Exeter EX1 178 B7
Plymouth PL3 248 F7
Waterrow TA4 35 E5
Whitestone EX4 98 E4
Hillmans Rd TQ12 207 D2
Hillmoor Cross EX21 73 F7
Hill Park Cl TQ5 230 E4
Hill Park Cres PL4 263 A4
Hill Park Mews PL4 263 B4
Hill Park Rd
Brixham TQ5 230 E4
Newton Abbot TQ12 206 F4
Torquay TQ1 220 A7
Hill Park Terr TQ4 226 C5
Hill Path PL5 243 F5
Hill Pk
Ashprington TQ9 139 F8
Kellaton TQ7 149 C6
Hill Rd
Bondleigh EX20 77 C7
Lyme Regis DT7 260 D3
Newton Abbot TQ12 207 B2
Hillrise TQ5 229 B5
Hill Rise EX1 178 C7
Hill Rise Rd DT7 260 D3
Hillsborough
2 Plymouth PL4 248 F4
Torquay TQ1 220 B4
Hillsborough Ave EX4 261 B4
Hillsborough Cross EX22 71 C7
Hillsborough Park Rd EX34 150 E5
Hillsborough Rd EX34 150 D5
Hillsborough Terr 15 EX34 150 C6
Hillsborough Terr Mews 16 EX34 150 C6
Hillsdunne Rd PL3 248 E6
Hillside
Bittaford PL21 137 C8
Branscombe EX12 190 B5
14 Colyton EX24 103 A4
George Nympton EX36 30 A2
Honiton EX14 85 E5
Newton Poppleford EX10 186 D8
Northleigh EX24 102 B6
Payhembury EX14 84 C4
Rawridge EX14 68 C1
Sidbury EX10 101 B2
South Brent TQ10 135 A3
Southleigh EX24 102 C4
Talaton EX5 84 B1
Hillside Ave
Exeter EX4 261 B4
Plymouth PL4 248 D4
Saltash PL12 242 F3
Hillside Cl
Buckland Monachorum PL20 126 C3
South Brent TQ10 135 A3
Teignmouth TQ14 124 E1
Hillside Cotts
Abbotskerswell TQ12 212 A6
Noss Mayo PL8 140 F6
Hillside Cres PL9 255 F8
Hillside Cross EX21 72 F4
Hill Side Cross EX36 45 F5
Hillside Ct TQ11 236 C5
Hillside Dr
Kingsbridge TQ7 258 D4
Yealmpton PL8 257 F3
Hillside Ind Units EX32 155 F1
Hillside Pk TQ4 224 F5
Hillside Rd
Brixham TQ5 230 C4
Ilfracombe EX34 150 E5
Paignton TQ3 225 F7
Saltash PL12 242 E3
Sidmouth EX10 188 C4
Hillside Sch PL5 244 B4
Hillside Terr
4 Bideford EX39 157 A2
Kingswear TQ6 234 A3
2 Paignton TQ3 226 A6
Hillside Way PL8 136 A2
Hill's La EX14 86 C5
Hill St PL4 263 A3
Hills The EX10 188 B5
Hills View
Barnstaple EX32 155 A5
Braunton EX33 152 D6
Hill The EX13 87 C1
Hilltop TQ7 142 F6
Hilltop Cotts EX31 153 E5
Hill Top Crest PL5 243 E2
Hilltop Rd EX39 156 E4
Hilltown Cross
Chittlehampton EX37 29 B2
Okehampton EX20 93 E5
Rackenford EX16 47 D2
Hilltown Hill EX36 31 C5
Hilltown La EX18 59 F5
Hilltown Wood Forest Wlks EX18 59 F5
Hill View
Buckland Monachorum PL20 126 C3
Ottery St Mary EX11 169 D3
Sidmouth EX10 188 B5
Hill View Terr 4 TQ1 220 A7
Hillway La EX10 187 A7
Hillyfield Rd EX1 178 C7
Hilly Gardens Rd TQ1 214 B1
Hilly Head TA21 160 B5
Hillymead EX12 192 B6
Hilton Ave PL5 244 D1
Hilton Cres TQ3 219 C1
Hilton Dr TQ3 219 C1
Hilton Park Homes EX33 152 C5
Hilton Rd
Marhamchurch EX23 70 A6
Monkleigh EX39 40 F7
Newton Abbot TQ12 207 C3
Hinam Cross TA22 33 B7
Hindharton La EX39 22 E3
Hind St
Bovey Tracey TQ13 180 D8
Ottery St Mary EX11 169 D3
Hingston Ct PL6 249 A8
Hingston Post TQ9 144 E8
Hingston Rd TQ1 220 C7
Hinton Ct PL6 245 C1
Hirmandale Rd PL5 243 F3
Hittisleigh Cross EX6 96 D6
Hittisleigh Mill La EX6 96 D5
Hittsford La EX36 32 A1
Hobart St PL1 262 A2
Hobbacott La EX23 70 A6
Hobbs Cres PL12 242 C3
Hobb's Hill EX33 7 E2
Hobbs La EX32 18 E2
Hobbs Way EX17 78 B4
Hobby Dr The EX39 23 E3
Hobby House La EX36 30 C1
Hobbymoor Cross EX17 60 A1
Hockmoor Head TQ11 130 C2
Hockmoor Hill TQ11 130 C2
Hodder's La DT7 260 C8
Hodders Way PL12 239 A2
Hodge Cl PL12 242 C2
Hodges Wlk EX38 159 E5
Hodson Cl TQ3 225 F7
Hoe App PL1 262 C2
Hoe Ct PL1 262 C2
Hoegate Ct PL1 262 C2
Hoegate Pl PL1 262 C2
Hoegate St PL1 263 A2
Hoe Gdns PL1 262 C2
Hoe Rd PL1 262 C1
Hoe St PL1 262 C2
Hoe The PL1 262 C1
Hofheim Dr EX16 161 A6
Hogarth Cl PL9 256 B6
Hogarth Ho PL19 171 B6
Hogarth Wlk PL9 256 B6
Hoile La TQ9 224 E1
Hoker Rd EX2 178 A5
Holbeam Cl TQ12 206 E4
Holbeam La
Bickington TQ12 131 F6
Newton Abbot TQ12 206 A4
Holbeton Sch PL8 136 D1
Holborn Pl PL7 250 E6
Holborn Rd TQ5 230 C6
Holborn St PL4 263 B2
Holbrook Terr TQ7 145 B1
Holcombe Barton Cnr EX6 98 D2
Holcombe Cross EX7 210 F8
Holcombe Down Cross TQ14 124 F2
Holcombe Down Rd EX7, TQ14 204 A4
Holcombe Dr
Holcombe EX7 210 F8
Plymouth PL9 255 F5
Holcombe La
Ottery St Mary EX11 100 F7
Uplyme DT7 104 B4
Holcombe Rd EX7, TQ14 210 E8
Holcroft Cl PL12 242 D2
Holden Cross EX6 113 E2
Holdridge La EX36 30 D8
Holdstone Way EX34 3 B2
Holdsworth St PL4 262 B4
Hole Ball Cross EX21 92 A8
Holebay Cl PL9 256 A5
Holebrook Cross EX20 76 C4
Holebrook La EX20 76 C5
Hole Cleave Rd EX33 8 A1
Hole Cross
Halwill EX21 73 F1
Hittisleigh EX6 96 E4
Yelverton PL20 239 E7
Hole Ct EX20 75 C7
Hole Hill
Branscombe EX12 190 C5
Exbourne EX20 76 C4
Witheridge EX16 46 F2
Hole La
Chulmleigh EX18 45 B3
Combe Martin EX31 10 B6
Croyde EX33 7 F1
North Tawton EX20 77 E6
Holemoor Cross EX22 73 C8
Holemore Cross EX14 68 C5
Hole's La
Broadhempston TQ9 131 D1
Staverton TQ9 216 B8
Holestone La EX10 187 A1
Holewater Cross EX32 19 A6
Holewater Hill EX32 19 A6
Holewell La EX6 96 E4
Hollacombe Brake PL9 256 C1
Hollacombe Cross
Holsworthy EX22 72 D6
Yeoford EX17 79 D3
Hollacombe La TQ3 219 D1
Hollam Cross TA22 33 E7
Hollam Dr TA22 33 D6
Hollam La TA22 33 D7
Hollamoor View EX31 154 B3
Hollam Way TQ12 207 F8
Holland Cl EX31 154 A4
Holland Copse EX6 98 C4
Holland Rd
Exeter EX2 176 F4
Exmouth EX8 196 D1
Plymouth, Chaddlewood PL7 251 D5
Plymouth, Peverell PL3 248 E6
Plymouth, Plymstock PL9 255 F6
Holland's La TA4 35 E8
Hollands Park Ave EX34 3 A3
Hollands Rd 4 TQ14 210 C4
Holland St 8 EX31 154 F5
Holland's Wash Dro TA20 69 F5
Holland Wlk 5 EX31 154 F5
Holley Cl EX6 182 A4
Holley Pk EX20 170 D6
Holleys Cl TA20 88 D8
Hollies The EX31 154 B3
Hollingarth Way EX15 67 B8
Hollington Ho 15 TQ1 220 D4
Hollis Cl EX11 169 E4
Hollocombe Cnr EX18 58 D6
Hollocombe Moor Gate EX18 58 D7
Hollocombe Moor Head EX18 58 D7
Holloway Gdns PL9 256 A5
Holloway St EX2 261 B2
Holloway The TA21 51 E7
Hollowcombe Cross PL21 136 E3
Hollowcombe Head TQ7 149 D5
Hollowgutter La PL11 246 C2
Hollow Hayes PL6 249 B8
Hollow Head Cross EX10 100 F2
Hollow La EX1 178 E7
Hollow Pits Ct EX2 181 B8
Hollows The
Exmouth EX8 202 B7
Plymouth PL9 256 B8
Hollow Tree Cross EX18 60 A7
Hollowtree Ct 5 EX32 155 B3
Hollowtree Rd EX32 155 B3
Holly Cl
Broadclyst EX5 175 C7
2 Chudleigh TQ13 123 F6
Honiton EX14 166 C4
Tiverton EX16 161 E5
Hollycombe Cross EX20 95 E4
Hollycombe La TQ9 216 E7
Hollycroft Rd PL3 249 A7
Holly Ct PL6 249 E7
Hollyford La EX17 62 C2
Hollyhead Cross EX12 191 C7
Hollyhead Rd EX12 191 B8
Holly Ho 2 EX34 150 B6
Hollymount Cl EX8 196 C3
Holly Park Cl PL5 244 A5
Holly Park Dr PL5 244 B5
Holly Rd
Exeter EX2 177 F3
Tiverton EX16 161 E5
Holly Villas TQ9 139 F8
Hollywater Cl TQ1 220 D5
Holly Water Rd EX17 62 E1
Holly Way EX15 163 C5
Holly Wlk EX8 196 D3
Hollywood Terr PL1 262 A3
Holmacott Cross EX39 26 E7
Holman Cl EX7 204 F8
Holman Ct PL2 248 C8
Holmans Bldgs PL1 247 D2
Holmans Mdw PL15 105 B1
Holmans Wood Cvn & Camping Site TQ13 124 A8
Holman Way
Ivybridge PL21 237 A6
Topsham EX3 182 F5
Holmbush Way PL8 257 A4
Holm Cross EX17 59 F2
Holmdale EX10 188 B4
Holmead Cross EX16 48 B3
Holme Ct 3 TQ1 220 D4
Holmer Down PL6 245 D7
Holmes Ave PL3 249 B5
Holmes Rd TQ12 180 F2
Holm Hill EX17 59 E2
Holmleigh Rd TQ7 145 D1
Holmsleigh Cross EX14 86 C5
Holmwood Ave PL9 255 E5
Holne Chase PL6 245 B7
Holne Cross TQ13 130 E5
Holne Ct EX4 176 E8
Holne Moor Cl TQ3 225 E7
Holne Rd TQ11 236 B6
Holne Rise EX2 178 B4
Holne Turn
Ashburton TQ13 130 E5
Holne TQ13 130 B5
Holset Cross TQ8 148 D5
Holsome La TQ9 138 D7
Holstock Cross EX20 74 D3
Holsworthy CE Prim Sch EX22 164 C5
Holsworthy Com Coll EX22 164 C5
Holsworthy Hospl EX22 164 D6
Holsworthy Mus EX22 164 C4
Holsworthy Rd EX20 93 D5
Holt The
19 Appledore EX39 15 A1
Honiton EX14 166 E7
Holtwood Dr PL21 237 A5
Holtwood Rd PL6 245 D6
Holway TA20 88 D8
Holwell Cl PL9 256 A5
Holwell La EX16 64 B5
Holwell Rd TQ5 230 B4
Holwill Dr EX38 159 D5
Holwill Tor Wlk TQ4 225 F3
Holy Cross RC Prim Sch PL4 263 A3
Holyford La
Colyford EX24 102 F3
Colyford EX24 103 A4
Holy Moor Cross EX36 32 C1
Holy Moor La EX36 32 C1
Holyoake St TA21 160 C7
Holyrood Pl PL1 262 C2
Holyshute Cross EX14 166 D6
Holywell CE Prim Sch EX31 27 D8
Holywell Cross EX36 19 F2
Holywell Pk EX21 73 D3
Homebaye Ho 3 EX12 192 B4
Homebourne Ho TQ4 226 C5
Home Cl
Brixham TQ5 230 C3
Chillington TQ7 145 A1
Homeclose La EX13, TA20 88 A8
Homeclyst Ho EX2 261 A1
Homecombe Ho TQ1 220 C8
Homecourt Ho EX4 261 A2
Homedown Cross EX37 28 F4
Home Farm EX6 114 E1
Home Farm Cl
Croyde EX33 7 E2
Kingston TQ7 142 C6
Home Farm Cross EX15 65 F4
Home Farm Ct TQ12 209 B2
Home Farm N DT7 193 E6
Home Farm Rd
Fremington EX31 153 D5
Plymouth PL9 255 E8
Home Farm S DT7 193 E6
Homefield
Thurlestone TQ7 143 A1
Wellington TA21 160 E4
Homefield Cl EX11 169 E3
Homefield Cotts
Thurlestone TQ7 143 A1
Torquay TQ1 220 D7
Homefield Rd EX1 177 F6
Home Gate EX6 98 A3
Home La EX34 1 C3
Homelace Ho EX14 166 C7
Homelands Pl TQ7 258 C6
Homelands Prim Sch TQ1 220 B8
Homelands Rd TQ7 258 C6
Home Mdw TQ9 223 C5
Homemeadows Ho EX10 188 B5
Homepalms Ho 3 TQ1 219 F6
Home Park Ave PL3 248 E6
Home Park (Plymouth Argyle FC) PL2 248 C5
Home Park Rd PL12 243 A3
Home Pk
Ashburton TQ13 130 F5
Plymouth PL2 247 F4
Homer Cl EX31 18 A8
Homer Cres EX33 152 B7
Homer Ct EX33 152 B7
Homer Dr EX33 152 B7
Homer La
Seaton EX12 191 F8
Seaton EX12 192 A6
Homer Park La S PL9 255 C5
Homer Pk
Plymouth PL9 255 C5
Saltash PL12 242 D3
Homer Rd EX33 152 B7
Homer Rise PL9 256 B7
Homers Cl TQ12 207 D6
Homers Cres TQ12 207 D6
Homershill Cross PL21 137 B6
Homers La TQ12 207 D6
Homesleigh Rd EX14 86 A5
Homestead Rd TQ1 220 A8
Homestead Terr TQ1 220 A8
Home Sweet Home Terr PL4 263 C2
Hometeign Ho TQ12 207 D4
Hometor Ho EX8 202 A8
Homeyards The TQ14 210 A3
Homing Down Cross EX20 75 A1
Honcray PL9 255 D8
Hone Cross EX16 34 F5
Honest Heart Cross EX15 66 A3
Honestone St EX39 157 A1
Honeybeetle Cross EX37 29 A5
Honeychurch La EX20 76 E5
Honeychurch Moor Cross EX20 76 F6
Honeycroft Cross EX22 54 A4
Honey Ditches Dr EX12 191 F8
Honey La
Daccombe TQ1, TQ12 213 F5
Exeter EX1 174 F2
Woodbury Salterton EX5 184 D7
Honeylands Childrens Ctr (Hospl) EX4 178 B7
Honeylands Dr EX4 178 A7
Honeylands Way EX4 178 A7
Honeymoor La EX16 48 E7
Honey Park Rd EX9 198 B2
Honey St EX39 157 A7
Honeysuckle Cl
2 Barnstaple EX31 154 B3
Paignton TQ3 225 E8
Plymouth PL6 245 E7
Saltash PL12 242 D4
Tiverton EX16 161 F6
Honeysuckle Ct EX4 176 D8
Honeysuckle Dr EX14 85 C2
Honeywell TQ12 207 E6
Honeywell Cl EX32 155 B2
Honeywell La TQ13 122 C3
Honeywell Rd TQ12 207 E6
Honeywins Cross EX36 19 C2
Honicknowle PL5 244 B2
Honicknowle Gn PL5 244 B2
Honicknowle La PL5 244 B1
Honicombe Cnr PL17 125 B5
Honicombe Manor Holiday Village PL17 125 B5
Honicombe Pk PL17 125 B5

Honiton Bottom Rd
EX14..................................**166** C4
Honiton Bsns Pk EX14 ....**166** B6
Honiton CI PL5 ....**244** B3
Honiton Com Coll EX14 . **166** C6
Honiton Cross EX36........**29** F3
Honiton Hospl EX14........**166** C5
Honiton La EX36................**29** E3
Honiton Prim Sch EX14 . **166** C6
Honiton Rd
Blackhorse EX5 ....**179** C7
Cullompton EX15 ....**163** E3
Exeter EX1.........................**178** C5
Honiton Sta EX14............**166** C5
Honiton Wlk PL5 ....**244** B4
Honors Farm EX5 ....**173** F8
Hooda CI EX32.....................**17** E1
Hoodown La TQ6.............**234** B4
Hooe Hill PL9 ....**255** C5
Hooe La PL9......................**255** D3
Hooe Manor PL9..............**255** C5
Hooe Prim Sch PL9.........**255** B5
Hooe Rd PL9 ....**255** C5
Hook Cross EX13 ....**87** D7
Hooker CI EX9 ....**197** F2
Hook Farm Cvn & Camping
Pk DT7 ....**260** A5
Hookhill La EX17 ....**62** A3
Hookhills Dr TQ4 ....**226** C1
Hookhills Gdns TQ4.........**229** B7
Hookhills Gr TQ4 ....**226** C1
Hookhills Rd TQ4 ....**226** B1
Hookmoor Cross PL21 ....**137** C7
Hooksbarry Ave PL7........**251** B3
Hooks Cross TQ12 ....**131** C7
Hookway EX17.....................**80** D1
Hookway Cross EX5...........**80** D1
Hookway La EX16...............**63** B5
Hookwell Down La EX36 . **30** A8
Hoop Cross EX15................**83** B4
Hooperhayne Rd EX24 ...**102** E5
Hoopern Ave EX4.............**173** D1
Hoopern La EX4................**177** C8
Hoopern St EX4................**261** B4
Hoopern Terr 4 EX7 ....**204** D6
Hoopers Cross EX16.........**34** D3
Hoopers La PL18...............**125** C6
Hooper St PL11.................**247** C3
Hoopers Way EX38...........**159** F5
Hooperton Cross EX6 ....**96** E3
Hooperton La EX6..............**96** E3
Hope By-Pass TQ7............**147** B7
Hope CI TQ9......................**223** F5
Hope Rd EX2 ....**178** A5
Hope's CI TQ14 ....**210** A6
Hope Wlk TQ9 ....**223** F5
Hopkins Ct 8 TQ12 ....**207** C3
Hopkins La TQ12 ....**207** C3
Hopperstyle EX31............**154** B3
Hopton CI PL6 ....**248** F8
Hopton Dr EX38 ....**159** F5
Horace Rd TQ2 ....**213** F2
Hore Down Gate EX34......**9** B6
Hore's Cross PL21 ....**137** D7
Horestone Cross EX16 .....**47** F4
Hornapark CI PL16..........**105** E3
Hornbeam CI
Honiton EX14.....................**166** A4
Tiverton EX16 ....**161** F5
Hornbeam Gdns EX5.........**83** A7
Hornbeam Hollow 1
EX31....................................**154** C2
Hornbrook Gdns PL6......**244** D6
Hornby CI PL5...................**262** A3
Hornby St 2 PL2 ....**247** F4
Hornchurch La PL5..........**243** E4
Hornchurch Rd PL5 ....**243** E4
Horn Cross
Kentisbeare EX15................**65** F2
Plymouth PL9....................**255** F5
Horn Cross Rd PL9..........**255** F7
Hornbrook Ave 9 EX34 **150** B5
Horne Park Ave 14 EX34 **150** B5
Horne Park Rd EX34 ......**150** B5
Horne Rd EX34 ....**150** B5
Horner Tongue TQ9 ....**138** A5
Horner Turn Cross TQ9 ...**139** A5
Horn Hill TQ6...................**233** F3
Horn La
Brixton PL8 ....**257** A5
Plymouth PL9....................**255** F5
Horn Lane Flats 4 PL9 ..**255** F7
Horn Rd EX15 ....**65** E2
Hornshayes Knap Cross
EX14...
Hornshayne Rd EX24.....**102** B5
Horns Pk TQ14 ....**208** E7
Horrabridge Com Prim Sch
PL20...................................**126** F4
Horridge La EX18 ....**59** A8
Horsey Mill La EX18........**158** F6
Horsdon Rd EX16..............**161** F4
Horsdon Terr EX16..........**161** F4
Horsecombe Cross TQ8 ..**259** B7
Horseguards EX4..............**261** B4
Horse Hill EX17...................**60** F7
Horsehill Cross EX17........**60** F7
Horse Hill Cross EX22 ....**38** F1
Horse La TQ14.................**210** B3
Horsepond Mdw EX36....**158** C3
Horsepool St TQ5............**230** B3
Horseshoe Bend TQ4......**226** C2
Horseshoe CI 10 TQ13 ...**123** E6

Horsham La
Plymouth, Honicknowle
PL5...................................**244** C2
Plymouth, Tamerton Foliot
PL5...................................**244** C2
Horslears EX13 ....**167** C4
Horswell CI PL7 ....**251** B5
Horton Cross EX22............**38** C3
Horwood Cross EX39........**26** D7
Horwood & Newton Tracey
Com Prim Sch EX31........**27** A6
Horwood Sq 18 EX31......**154** F5
Hosegood Way TQ12.......**207** D7
Hosford CI PL9 ....**256** A4
Hoskings Ct TQ11............**236** B5
Hospital Hill PL4 ....**204** D6
Hospital La
7 Ashburton TQ13 ....**131** A5
Exeter EX1.........................**178** C8
Hospital Rd PL4 ....**263** B4
Hostle Park Gdns 12
EX34...................................**150** C6
Hostle Park Rd EX34.......**150** C6
Hostle Pk EX34 ....**150** C6
Hotham PI PL1 ....**262** A4
Hothill La
Ashprington TQ9 ....**139** F6
Cornworthy TQ9...............**227** A4
Houghton La EX10 ....**187** A5
Houldsworth Rd PL9 ....**255** C7
Houndbeare La EX5..........**99** E4
Houndhead Cross TQ9 ...**216** D8
Houndiscombe Rd PL4...**248** E4
Hound Tor CI TQ4 ....**229** B7
Hounster Dr PL10.............**252** D4
Hounster Hill PL10..........**252** D4
Housman CI PL5................**244** D3
Hove Villas EX2................**261** A1
Howard Ave EX32............**155** B4
Howard CI
Exeter EX4.........................**176** F8
Okehampton EX20 ....**170** D6
Plymouth PL5....................**243** F2
Saltash PL12 ....**242** D3
Tavistock PL19 ....**171** A5
Teignmouth TQ14 ....**210** A7
Torquay TQ2......................**219** D6
Howard Cross EX16...........**96** D7
Howard Ct TQ14 ....**210** A7
Howard La
Hittisleigh EX6...................**96** D7
Marhamchurch EX23 ....**70** B8
Howard Rd
Plymouth PL5....................**255** E8
Wellington TA21................**160** D7
Howards CI EX36 ....**158** C2
Howards Way
Ivybridge PL21 ....**237** A6
Newton Abbot TQ12.........**207** F4
Howarth CI EX10 ....**188** A8
Howden La EX16...............**161** B3
Howden Rd EX16 ....**161** C3
Howell Rd
Exeter EX4.........................**177** A7
Exeter EX4.........................**261** A4
Howeson La PL6...............**245** A4
How St PL4 ....**263** A2
Howton La TQ12 ....**206** B5
Howton Rd TQ12 ....**206** C6
Hoxton Rd TQ1 ....**220** B5
Hoyles Ct TQ1 ....**162** E4
Hoyle's Ct TQ3 ....**225** F8
Hoyles Rd TQ1..................**160** E4
Hoyle's Rd TQ3 ....**225** E8
Hubbastone Rd EX39......**157** C8
Huccaby CI TQ5................**229** F2
Huckham Barn Cross
TQ7.....................................**149** C7
Huckham La EX31 ....**10** F8
Huckland Cross EX20.......**76** D4
Huddisford Cross EX39 ....**38** D7
Hudley Mill Hill EX32 ....**18** D3
Hudson Cross EX22 ....**53** B4
Hue La EX33........................**8** F1
Hughball Cross EX19.........**76** A8
Hughes Ave EX32.............**155** B3
Hugh Squier Ave EX36 ...**158** D5
Huish Cleeve TA4 ....**35** E7
Huish Cross TQ13 ....**123** C6
Huishlane End EX6............**97** F5
Hukeley Head Cross EX16 **34** D3
Hulham La EX8 ....**196** B2
Hulham Vale EX8 ....**196** C2
Hulk La EX6........................**81** F4
Humber CI PL3 ....**249** D6
Humber La TQ12, TQ14 ..**124** B1
Hume Ave EX35 ....**151** A5
Hummingbird CI EX1......**174** E1
Humphery's Cross TQ13 .**130** C4
Humphreys Rd TA21.......**160** E7
Humphries Pk EX8 ....**196** D1
Humpy The EX7 ....**204** C7
Hungerford Rd PL2.........**248** B5
Hungry Fox Est EX5........**175** E3
Huniver's La EX17 ....**165** C4
Hunivers PI EX17 ....**165** D4
Hunsdon Ct TQ1 ....**220** C4
Hunsdon Rd
Ivybridge PL21 ....**237** A2
Lee Mill PL21....................**136** D6
Torquay TQ1......................**220** C4
Hunstone Cross EX36 ......**19** B2
Huntacott Way TQ12 ......**219** B8
Hunter CI PL6 ....**244** F2
Hunter La EX34 ....**7** F6
Hunters CI PL21 ....**237** B5
Hunters Ct TQ3 ....**224** F7
Hunters Gate EX20..........**170** D6

Hunter's Hill EX15.............**51** E1
Hunters Moon TQ9...........**222** F7
Hunters Moon Touring Pk
EX13....................................**88** E1
Hunters's Oak PL20.........**126** A2
Hunters Tor Dr TQ4 ....**229** B7
Hunter's Way EX15............**51** E1
Hunterswell Rd TQ12......**207** A3
Hunterswood EX38..........**159** F5
Hunthay La EX13..............**167** B6
Huntingdon Gdns PL5 ....**244** D4
Huntley CI EX13 ....**167** F7
Huntley La EX13 ....**88** A8
Huntley PI PL3..................**249** C4
Hunton CI EX8 ....**195** F5
Hunts Cross PL21 ....**137** B1
Huntshaw Cross EX31......**27** B1
Huntshaw Moor Cross
EX38....................................**26** F2
Hurdwick Rd PL19 ....**171** A5
Hurrabrook CI PL6...........**245** E2
Hurrabrook Gdns PL6 ....**245** E2
Hurrell CI PL6 ....**244** D6
Hurrell Ct
Kingsbridge TQ7 ....**258** C5
Plymouth PL3....................**249** C5
Hurrell Rd TQ7.................**258** C5
Hursley Bsns Pk PL6 ....**241** D1
Hurst Ave EX2...................**178** B4
Hurst CI PL9 ....**255** F5
Hurst's Almshouses EX2 **261** C2
Husseys Cross EX14 ....**86** F6
Hussey's La EX14 ....**86** F6
Hutcherleigh Cross TQ9 **139** B1
Hutcherleigh Turn TQ9 ..**139** D1
Hutchings CI PL6 ....**244** D6
Hutchings Mead EX1.......**178** F8
Hutchings Way TQ14......**209** D8
Hutchins Rd EX14 ....**86** A4
Hutton Rd TQ3 ....**219** A1
Huxford La EX37 ....**44** F7
Huxham CI PL6.................**249** A8
Huxham Rd TQ3...............**211** A4
Huxham's Cross TQ9 ....**215** E3
Huxham's Cross Est TQ9 **215** E3
Huxley CI PL7 ....**250** F7
Huxley Vale TQ12 ....**212** F3
Huxnor Cross TQ12 ....**212** F2
Huxnor Rd TQ12 ....**212** F3
Huxtable Hill TQ2 ....**219** E4
Huxton La EX32..................**18** C2
Huxton Cross TQ7 ....**143** D3
Huxton Fork TQ7 ....**143** D3
Hyacinth Terr TA21 ....**160** C5
Hyde Park Jun & Inf Sch
PL3......................................**248** E5
Hyde Park Rd PL3 ....**248** E5
Hyde Rd TQ4 ....**226** B6
Hyfield Gdns TQ1............**220** B4
Hyfield PI 4 EX39 ....**157** A1
Hylands CI EX11 ....**168** D3
Hylton Gdns EX4..............**176** F6
Hynetown Rd TQ6 ....**145** E5
Hyne Town Rd TQ6..........**145** E5
Hynicombe La TA4 ....**35** D6
Hyperion Rd TQ2 ....**219** E2

I

Ian Hay CI EX39................**157** C1
Ibex CI EX39........................**15** A1
Ice House La EX10............**187** F7
Icy Pk TQ7.........................**143** C6
Iddesleigh Cross EX19 .....**57** E3
Iddesleigh Rd EX4 ....**177** E8
Iddesleigh Terr 10 EX7 ..**204** E6
Ide La EX2.........................**177** A1
Ide Prim Sch EX2.............**176** E1
Idestone Brook Cross
EX2......................................**113** F7
Idestone Cross EX2 ....**114** A7
Idewell Rd TQ2.................**214** B2
Idston Cross TQ7 ....**143** D7
Ilbert Cotts PL7................**250** E4
Ilbert Rd
Kingsbridge TQ7 ....**258** C5
Thurlestone TQ7 ....**143** A1
Ilbert St PL1 ....**262** B4
Ilex CI
Exeter EX4.........................**174** B2
Shillingford St George EX2 **114** C6
Ilfracombe CE Jun Sch
EX34...................................**150** C5
Ilfracombe Coll EX34 .....**150** C5
Ilfracombe Inf Sch EX34 **150** B5
Ilfracombe Mus EX34......**150** B6
Ilfracombe Rd
Braunton EX33..................**152** D7
West Down EX33 ....**8** F5
Ilkerton Hill EX35............**151** A1
Ilsham CE Prim Sch TQ1 **220** E5
Ilsham CI TQ1...................**220** F5
Ilsham Cres TQ1...............**220** F4
Ilsham Ho TQ1..................**220** E5
Ilsham Marine Dr TQ1....**221** A4
Ilsham Rd TQ1 ....**220** D5
Ilsington CE Prim Sch
TQ13...................................**122** C3
Ilton Cross TQ7 ....**259** A2
Ilton Way TQ7 ....**258** D5
Immenstadt Dr TA21 ......**160** D4
Imperial Bldgs TQ12.......**207** D8
Imperial Ct
Lynton EX35.....................**151** C5
Torquay TQ1......................**220** C7
Imperial Mews 12 TQ12 **207** C3
Imperial Rd EX38 ....**201** F6
Imperial St EX4 ....**176** F5

Improvement PI 5 TA21 **160** D5
Ince CI PL11......................**246** F4
Inchcoulter EX8...............**202** C5
Inchkeith Rd PL6.............**244** F7
Incledon Hill EX33.............**8** A3
Indicombe La EX32...........**18** B2
Indio Rd TQ13 ....**180** C6
Ingleside EX13.................**167** E6
Ingleside Ct EX9..............**198** A1
Ingra Rd PL3.....................**249** A6
Ingra Tor CI 2 PL20........**126** F3
Ingra Wlk PL6 ....**245** B8
Innerbrook Rd TQ2 ....**219** E5
Inner Ting Tong EX9........**197** C3
Innes Ho PL1 ....**262** B3
Instaple Cross EX22 ....**53** D6
Instow Com Prim Sch
EX39.....................................**15** C2
Instow Ho 4 EX39...........**15** B1
Instow Signal Box Mus
EX39.....................................**15** B1
Instow Wlk PL5................**244** A3
Inswell Ct PL19 ....**171** A6
Insworke CI PL10.............**253** A6
Insworke Cres PL10........**252** F6
Insworke PI PL10.............**253** A6
International Ho TQ12 ....**180** F2
Inverdene PL3 ....**248** D5
Invertelgn Dr TQ14 ....**210** A5
Invertelgn Inf Sch EX14 **209** D8
Invertelgn Jun Sch
TQ14 ....**209** D8
Inwardleigh Cross EX20 ...**75** D2
Iolanthe Dr EX4 ....**174** A2
Iona Ave EX8 ....**196** A2
Ipplepen Bsns Pk TQ12 .**217** D8
Ipplepen Cross TQ12 .....**211** C6
Ipplepen Prim Sch TQ12 **211** D1
Ipplepen Rd TQ3 ....**218** C4
Ipswich CI PL5 ....**244** C4
Irene Way EX16................**161** F6
Iris Ave EX2......................**261** A1
Irishcombe Gate EX36......**46** B5
Irishcombe La EX36...........**46** C4
Iron Bridge EX4...............**261** A3
Iron Bridge Cross EX20 ....**77** B3
Iron Letters Cross EX4 ....**2** B1
Iron Mine La PL20 ....**127** B3
Iron Post TA22...................**33** B5
Iron Shovel La EX36..........**31** A3
Irsha St EX39.....................**15** A1
Irving CI EX33 ....**152** B6
Isaac CI EX9......................**198** E7
Isaacs Rd TQ2..................**214** A2
Isabella Rd EX16 ....**161** D5
Isambard Ct TQ2..............**214** B3
Isambard Par EX4 ....**177** A7
ISCA Coll of Media Arts
EX2......................................**177** D1
Isca Ct EX2 ....**177** D1
Isca Rd
Exeter EX4.........................**261** A1
Exmouth EX8 ....**202** C5
Isigny Rd TQ7...................**258** C5
Isis CI EX14.......................**166** F7
Island Lodge Camping & Cvn
Site TQ7 ....**144** B6
Island Quay TQ8 ....**259** E5
Island St TQ8 ....**259** E5
Island View TQ7 ....**143** A2
Isleworth Rd EX4.............**176** F5
Iter Cnr EX17 ....**78** C4
Iter Cross EX17 ....**78** C4
Iter Ct EX17 ....**78** C4
Iter Pk EX17 ....**78** C4
Itton Cross EX20 ....**77** D2
Itton Moor La EX17 ....**77** F2
Ittron Rd EX17 ....**77** E2
Ivanhoe Rd PL5 ....**243** D2
Ivatt Rd TQ6 ....**233** C3
Iveagh Ct EX4...................**176** F8
Ivybridge Com Coll PL21 **237** D6
Ivybridge Com Woodland
PL21...................................**237** D6
Ivybridge Sta PL21 ....**237** F6
Ivy CI
Exeter EX2.........................**178** A4
Sidmouth EX10 ....**188** B7
Ivycombe Hill TQ7...........**149** B5
Ivy Cotts PL18 ....**125** C6
Ivy Cross TQ21 ....**51** D7
Ivy Ct 28 EX39 ....**15** A1
Ivydale EX36 ....**158** D3
Ivydale Rd PL4.................**248** F4
Ivydene Rd PL21 ....**237** C5
Ivy Ho TA21......................**160** C6
Ivyhouse Cross PL16 ....**91** A4
Ivy La
Dartmouth TQ6 ....**233** F3
18 Teignmouth TQ14.......**210** B4
Ivy Tree Hill TQ12 ....**209** A2

J

Jack Backs Cross EX17.....**79** F7
Jack Bears Ho 10 TQ4....**226** B6
Jacketts La EX34 ....**156** F7
Jacketts EX9.....................**198** E7
Jacketts Cotts EX9..........**198** E7
Jackmans CI TQ9 ....**222** E6
Jackman's La TQ9 ....**222** F4
Jackman's Mdw PL10......**253** A3
Jackmoor Cross
Brampford Speke EX5 ....**81** C1
Newton St Cyres EX5..........**81** B1
Jack's La
St John PL11 ....**252** B8

Jack's La continued
Torquay TQ2......................**213** F3
Jackson CI PL5 ....**247** F8
Jackson PI PL2 ....**247** F4
Jackson Way PL12...........**242** E3
Jacobs Field EX39..............**39** E8
Jacob's Pool EX20 ....**170** B5
Jacolind Wlk TQ5.............**230** D5
Jago Ave PL11..................**247** B3
James Ave TQ3.................**218** E1
James CI PL9.....................**256** B6
James Ct EX4 ....**264** B3
James La EX14...................**69** C2
James Lane Cross EX13 ...**69** C2
James Owen Ct EX4 ....**261** C4
James Rd PL19 ....**171** E2
James St
Plymouth, Mount Wise
PL1....................................**247** E1
Plymouth PL4....................**262** C4
James's Week EX18............**59** E8
James's Week La EX18......**59** E8
Jane Way's Grave EX17 ...**61** B1
Jardine Pk EX2 ....**178** C4
Jarmins Pit Cross EX15 ...**66** A4
Jarvis CI EX8 ....**202** E7
Jasmine CI EX16..............**161** F6
Jasmine Gdns
Plymouth, Chaddlewood
PL7....................................**251** B5
Plymouth, Glenholt PL6...**245** E8
Jasmine Gr TQ3 ....**225** E8
Jaspers Cotts TQ9 ....**227** B4
Jawbone Hill TQ6.............**233** E2
Jaycroft EX15....................**162** E4
Jays Cross PL15 ....**105** B6
Jean Cres PL3 ....**249** B6
Jedburgh Cres PL2 ....**248** A8
Jeffery CI
Hartland EX39 ....**22** E3
Plymouth PL6....................**244** D6
Jefford Ho EX4 ....**173** A1
Jeffs Way EX13 ....**167** E6
Jellicoe Rd PL5 ....**244** E1
Jellicoe Villas TQ9 ....**223** B5
Jenker's Hill EX33 ....**8** B2
Jenkins CI PL9 ....**256** A5
Jennifer CI EX2 ....**177** E3
Jenns Cross EX22..............**53** D7
Jennycliff La PL9 ....**255** A6
Jennys Combe CI PL9 .....**255** F4
Jenny's Portion EX5 ....**82** A6
Jenwood Rd EX14 ....**67** B1
Jephson Rd PL4 ....**249** B3
Jericho St EX5 ....**81** E5
Jerrard CI EX14 ....**166** C5
Jerrard Cres EX14 ....**166** C5
Jesmond Rd EX1 ....**177** E7
Jessops PL7 ....**250** D7
Jesu St EX11 ....**169** D3
Jetty Marsh Rd TQ12......**207** B5
Jewell Cres EX32 ....**155** C6
J.H.Taylor Dr EX39 ....**157** A7
Jingles La EX32................**155** A4
Jinkin Ave PL4..................**263** B4
Joan Spry CI EX16............**46** E1
Jobbie's La EX24 ....**102** E4
Jocelyn Mead EX17..........**165** B4
Jocelyn Rd EX9 ....**198** A2
Jockey Hill EX17 ....**165** C6
Joeys Field EX36................**30** F3
John Acres La TQ12 ....**123** D3
John Gay CI EX32 ....**155** C4
John Gay Rd EX32 ....**155** C4
John Greenway CI EX16 .**161** D3
John Grinter Way TA21 ..**160** D4
John Hannam Ho EX1 ....**261** C3
John Howe CI EX38 ....**159** C5
John Kitto Com Coll The
PL5......................................**244** B1
John La PL4.......................**262** C4
John Levers Way EX4......**176** F5
John Nash Dr EX7 ....**204** C4
John Penrose Rd EX31....**154** B2
John Smale Rd EX31.......**154** C4
Johnson CI 2 PL20..........**125** C1
Johnson Rd EX31 ....**154** C2
John Sparke Ho 17 PL1 .**263** A2
John St
Exeter EX1, EX4................**261** A2
Plymouth PL1....................**247** E3
Tiverton EX16 ....**161** C4
John's Terr 7 EX16 ....**161** B4
Johnstone Dr EX16 ....**161** B5
Johnstone La EX36............**30** D4
Jones's Hill EX33 ....**7** F2
Jonida CI TQ1 ....**220** A7
Jordan CI EX32 ....**155** C3
Jordan Cross TQ13..........**121** A2
Jordan Dr TQ14................**209** D8
Jordan La PL20 ....**126** F5
Jordan Orch TQ11............**236** A5
Jordans Brook TQ9..........**222** E6
Jordans La EX36...............**30** D4
Jose's Cross EX37..............**44** F8
Jose's La EX31...................**154** C6
Joslin CI TQ12 ....**207** D8
Joslin Rd EX14 ....**166** B5
Joy St EX31 ....**154** F5
Jubilee CI
Dartmouth TQ6 ....**233** C3
2 Lewtrenchard EX6........**182** A4
2 Ilfracombe EX34 ....**150** B5
Ivybridge PL21 ....**237** F6
Okehampton EX20 ....**170** B5
Saltash PL12 ....**242** D2

Jubilee Cotts PL12......242 C1
Jubilee Ct
  Ashwater EX21...........90 E6
  Exeter EX4.............261 A3
  Torquay TQ1..........220 B5
  🔳 Wellington TA21....160 D5
Jubilee Dr
  Exmouth EX8..........196 C3
  🔳 Hemyock EX15......67 B8
Jubilee Gdns
  Cullompton EX15......163 C2
  North Molton EX36......30 D8
  Sidmouth EX10.........188 C8
Jubilee Gr EX8........195 F5
Jubilee Lodge EX12...192 B5
Jubilee Pl PL3........249 C4
Jubilee Rd
  Appledore EX39.........14 F1
  Bradninch EX5..........82 F6
  Exeter EX1............177 E7
  Malborough TQ7.......147 F6
  Newton Abbot TQ12...207 B2
  Totnes TQ9............223 E6
Jubilee St TQ7.........143 C6
Jubilee Terr
  🔳 Bittaford PL21......137 C7
  Copplestone EX17.......79 B5
  Kingswear TQ6.........234 B3
  Paignton TQ3...........226 A6
  Plymouth PL4..........249 C2
Julian Cotts PL21......136 D6
Julian Rd PL21.........237 B5
Julian St PL4...........263 C2
Julian Wlk PL6.........245 E6
Jump Cl PL6............241 C1
Junction Rd EX17.......78 C4
Juniper Cl
  Exeter EX4.............174 B2
  🔳 Honiton EX14......166 A4
  🔳 Tiverton EX16.......161 F6
Juniper Ct EX31........154 C3
Juniper Way PL7.......251 B5
Junket St EX37..........43 B7
Jupes Cl EX6...........182 B3
Juries La EX38.........159 D6
Jurston Cross TQ13....110 F4
Jurston La
  Wellington TA21.......160 E6
  Wellington TA21.......160 F5
Jury Hill TA21..........33 E6
Jury Pk EX36..........158 B4
Jury Rd TA22...........33 E6
Jurys Cnr TQ12........213 A4
Jurys Corner Cl TQ12..213 A4
Justment Cross EX17....77 F2

K

Kabale Cl EX16.........161 A6
Kala Fair EX39.........156 E7
Karen Cl EX39.........157 D1
Katherines La EX11....169 E4
Kathleaven St PL5.....243 D1
Kay Cl
  Exmouth EX8..........202 C8
  Plymouth PL7..........250 F7
Keals Croft EX35.......151 B5
Keatings La TQ14......210 A5
Keaton Barns PL8......141 E6
Keaton La PL21........237 D1
Keaton Rd PL21.......237 C4
Keats Cl
  Exmouth EX8..........196 C4
  Teignmouth TQ14......124 E1
Keat St PL2...........247 E4
Kedlestone Ave PL5...244 A3
Keep Cotts TQ4........224 B7
Keepers Cross EX16.....49 A2
Keeper's Ct EX11......169 B7
Keep Gdns The TQ6...233 E3
Keephill Bglws EX22...164 F4
Keep La TQ9...........233 E4
Keep The PL12.........242 C2
Kellacott Cross PL16...105 F7
Kelland Cl EX43.......226 A5
Kelland Cnr EX6........98 A1
Kelland Cross EX17.....60 C2
Kelland Hill EX17.......60 C2
Kellands Row TQ7.....258 D5
Kellaton Cross
  East Allington TQ9.....144 E7
  Kellaton TQ7...........149 C6
Kellett Cl 🔟 TQ13....131 A5
Kellock Dr TQ9........223 B5
Kelly Cl
  Plymouth PL5..........247 C7
  Torquay TQ1..........220 C2
Kelly Coll PL19.........171 D7
Kelly Cross TQ13......122 D8
Kelly La EX16...........62 E8
Kelvin Ave PL4........263 C4
Kelvin Ct
  Brixham TQ5..........230 D5
  Torquay TQ1..........214 C1
Kelway Rd TA21.......160 E7
Kemmings Cl TQ4.....225 F1
Kemp Cl TQ2..........247 F6
Kempland La EX18.....45 B2
Kempley Rd EX20......170 B5
Kemp's La EX12........192 D7
Kemps Way TA22......33 C6
Kempton Terr PL11....247 B2
Kemyell Pl PL2........247 E4
Kenbury Cres EX6.....201 B6
Kenbury Dr EX2........181 C8
Kendall Cl EX4.........261 C4

Kendal Ho EX14.......166 C5
Kendal Pl PL5.........244 E4
Kenilworth Rd EX4....261 C4
**Kenilworth TQ1........220 D3
Kenilworth Rd PL2....248 B7
Kenley Gdns PL5......243 F4
Kenmare Dr PL7.......251 A5
Kennacott Cross EX22..72 B1
Kennaway Rd EX11....169 F4
Kenn CE Prim Sch EX6..181 B1
Kenn Cl PL5...........244 B3
Kennedy Way
  Dunkeswell EX14........67 C2
  Tiverton EX16..........161 C5
Kennel Bridge Cross EX20..92 E8
Kennel Hill PL7.........250 D4
Kennel Hill Cl PL7.....250 C4
Kennel La
  Georgeham EX33.........8 A2
  Ivybridge PL21.........237 B5
Kennels Rd TQ5.......229 C4
Kennerland Cross EX39..38 C8
Kennerley Ave EX4....178 B8
Kennet Cl PL3.........249 B6
Kenneth Ct TQ2.......219 C8
Kennford Cross EX1....177 B3
Kennford Cross EX5...183 D8
Kenn La
  Exeter EX6............181 F1
  Exminster EX6.........182 A2
Kennydown La EX18....59 B7
Kensall Cross EX36.....20 B1
Kensey Cl TQ1.........220 E6
Kensham Ave EX5......83 A6
Kensham Cl EX5........82 F6
Kensington Pl 🔳 PL4..248 F4
Kensington Rd PL4....263 B4
Kenson Hill EX5........82 B5
Kent Cl EX12..........178 A4
Kentisbeare CE Prim Sch EX15..........66 A3
Kentisbury Grange Cvn Pk EX31............10 E5
Kentisbury Prim Sch EX31............10 E6
Kenton Brook Ct TQ2..219 B8
Kenton Hill EX6.......194 D4
Kenton Mews EX6.....194 D3
Kenton Pl EX2.........177 C2
Kenton Prim Sch EX6..194 D3
Kent Rd
  Plymouth PL2.........247 F5
  Tatworth TA20.........88 D8
Kent's Bglws TA20.....88 D8
Kents Cavern TQ1.....220 E5
Kents Cl
  Tatworth TA20.........88 C8
  Uffculme EX15..........66 A7
Kent's Cotts TA20......88 D8
Kents La TA20.........88 D8
Kent's La TQ1.........220 E5
Kent's Orch TA20......88 D8
Kent's Rd TQ1.........220 E5
Kenwith Dr TQ7.......258 D5
Kenwith Rd EX39.....156 F4
Kenwith Terr EX39....156 F3
Kenwith View EX39....156 D2
Kenwyn Rd TQ1.......220 C6
Kenyon Ct EX3........182 F5
Keppel Pl PL2.........247 E4
Keppel St PL2.........247 F4
Keppel Terr 🔳 PL2....247 F4
Kernou Rd TQ4........226 C6
Kernow Cl PL11.......246 E3
Kernow Pl PL11.......246 E3
Kernstone Cross EX39..22 B2
Kerria Cl TQ3.........225 E8
Kerries Cl TQ10.......135 A2
Kerries La TQ10......135 A2
Kerries Rd TQ10......135 A2
Ker St the PL1........247 E2
Kersbrook Gdns DT7...260 D4
Kersbrook La EX9.....198 A3
Kerscott Cross TQ13..124 A7
Kerscott Hill EX32.....28 F8
Kerse Cross
  Thurlestone, South Milton TQ7............143 C2
  Thurlestone TQ7.......143 B2
Kerse La TQ7.........143 B2
Kerslake's Ct 🔟 EX14..166 C6
Ker St PL1...........247 E1
Kerswell Cross TQ13..124 A7
Kerswell La
  Kingskerswell TQ12...213 A5
  Molland EX36..........31 C8
Kerswill Cross TQ9...135 D1
Kerswill Rd EX4......176 F4
Kestell Rd EX10.......188 C4
Kestor Cl EX20.......170 D5
Kestor Dr
  Exeter EX4............176 E8
  Paignton TQ3.........219 A1
Kestral Units PL5.....244 A1
Kestrel Cl
  Okehampton EX20.....170 B6
  Plymouth PL6.........245 D8
  🔳 Tiverton EX16.....161 E6
Kestrel Ct 🔟 TQ1...220 C8
Kestrel Way
  Barnstaple EX32......155 E5
  Exeter EX2...........178 E5
Keswick Cres PL6.....245 D2
Keverel Rd EX8.......196 A1
Kew Cl EX3...........178 C3
Keyberry Cl TQ12....207 D1

Keyberry Pk TQ12....207 D1
Keyberry Rd TQ12....207 D1
Keyes Cl EX2..........247 F2
Keyham Barton RC Prim Sch PL2................247 E6
Keyham Ct PL2.......247 E6
Keyham Rd PL2.......247 E6
Keyham St PL5........247 E8
Keyham Sta PL2......247 E6
Keymelford Cross EX17..79 C2
Keysfield Rd TQ4.....226 C5
Khartoum Pl TQ7.....258 C5
Khyber Cl PL11.......247 A3
Kiddicott EX17.......165 B5
Kidland La
  Bishops Nympton EX36...31 E1
  South Molton EX36.....46 E8
Kidwelly Cl PL7.......251 C4
Kiel Pl PL3...........249 D5
Kieran Ct 🔳 TQ1.....220 A6
Kigbeare Cross EX20..93 B5
Kilbarran Rise EX4...177 A8
Kildare TQ7..........258 C4
Killarney Springs Leisure Pk EX23............37 E1
Killatree Cross EX22...71 E7
Killerton Cl 🔳 TQ3..226 B7
Killerton Ho EX5.......82 D3
Killerton Wlk EX6.....181 C5
Killigrew Ave PL12....242 D1
Killington Cross EX31...4 D2
Kilmington Prim Sch EX13.................103 D8
Kilmore TQ1...........220 F3
Kilmore TQ1..........220 F3
Kiln Cl
  Bovey Tracey TQ13....180 C5
  Cawsand PL10.........253 A1
  Plymouth PL5.........247 C8
Kiln Close La 🔳 EX39..15 B1
Kiln Cross TQ3.......218 D3
Kilnford Rd TQ12....207 F7
Kiln Ho TQ7..........258 C4
Kiln La
  🔳 Barnstaple EX32...155 A4
  Branscombe EX12......190 B4
  Combe Martin EX34.....3 B2
  Stokenham TQ7........145 B1
  Kiln Orch TQ12........206 F3
  Kiln Path TQ5.........230 C4
Kiln Rd
  Bovey Tracey TQ13....180 C5
  Marldon TQ3...........218 C3
Kilnwood Pk EX31.....154 A3
Kilworthy TQ1........220 C6
Kilworthy Hill PL19...171 C6
Kilworthy Rd PL19....171 C6
Kimber Cross EX20.....74 E2
Kimberlands EX20......74 E2
Kimberley Cl PL7.......237 D5
Kimberley Pk EX39....157 A7
Kimberley Rd EX2.....261 B2
Kimberley Terr EX39..157 A8
Kimberley Villas PL21..237 C4
Kimberly Dr PL6......245 B1
Kimbland Cross EX32..185 C5
Kincraig EX8.........202 C6
Kinevor Cl EX34........7 F8
King Alfred Dr EX9...157 A6
King Alfred Way EX10..186 A8
King Arthur's Rd EX4...174 A1
King Charles I Bsns Pk TQ12................180 E4
King Charles Way EX10..188 B8
Kingdom Mews EX4...177 A7
Kingdom's Cnr EX16...63 C4
Kingdon Ent Pk EX39..25 D4
King Edward Rd
  Axminster EX13.......167 C5
  Saltash PL12..........242 F2
King Edward St
  🔳 Barnstaple EX32...154 F6
  Exeter EX4............173 A1
King Edward Studios EX4................173 A1
King Edward VI Com Coll TQ9..................223 B7
King Edward VI Com Coll (Kennicott Ho) TQ9...223 B6
King Edward VI Com Coll (The Mansion) TQ9....223 C6
Kingfisher Cl
  Plymouth PL6.........245 E6
  Torquay TQ2..........213 D2
Kingfisher Dr
  Barnstaple EX32......155 E4
  Exeter EX4............173 D2
Kingfisher Gdns EX15..163 B2
Kingfisher Rd EX32...176 D3
Kingfisher Way PL9...255 C7
King Henry's Rd EX2..177 E3
Kingsacre EX33.......152 C6
Kingsacre Com Sch EX33................152 C6
Kingsale Rd TQ8.......259 C4
King's Ash Cross TQ3..225 E6
King's Ash Rd TQ3...225 E6
Kings Ave
  Ottery St Mary EX11..169 F4
  Paignton TQ3.........226 C7
Kingsbridge TQ7.......220 B8
Kingsbridge Com Coll TQ7................258 E6
Kingsbridge Com Prim Sch TQ7...............258 E6
Kingsbridgefork Cross TQ9................144 E5

King St continued
  Tavistock PL19........171 B6
  Tiverton EX16.........161 C3
  Torpoint PL11.........247 C3
King's Tamerton Rd PL5..243 F2
Kingsteignton Rd TQ12..207 C4
King Stephen Cl EX4...261 B4
Kings Terr EX14......166 C6
Kingston Ave 🔳 EX4...3 A3
Kingston Cl
  Kingskerswell TQ12...213 A5
  Plymouth PL7.........251 A5
Kingston Dr PL7......251 B5
Kingston Gate Cross TQ9................216 A6
Kingston La TQ6.....233 E3
Kingston Rd
  Exmouth EX8.........202 C7
  Stoke Climsland PL17..115 C1
Kingston Workshops TQ9................216 A7
Kingswater Ct TQ5...230 C5
Kingsway
  Cawsand PL10.........253 B2
  Exeter EX2...........177 F5
  Lyme Regis DT7.......260 E4
  South Molton EX36...158 C3
  Teignmouth TQ14.....209 D7
Kings Way EX20......106 E5
Kingsway Ave TQ6...226 A1
Kingsway Cl
  Kingsbridge TQ7......258 C4
  Paignton TQ4.........226 A1
Kingsway Dr TQ4....226 A1
Kingsway Gdns PL6...244 F3
Kingsway Pk TQ7.....258 C4
Kingswear Cres PL6...245 D3
Kingswear Lookout Sta TQ6................146 F8
Kingswear Prim Sch TQ6................234 B3
Kingswear Rd TQ6...234 B3
Kingswear Sta TQ6...234 A3
Kingswood Cl EX4....176 E8
Kingswood Ct
  Paignton TQ4.........226 C5
  South Brent TQ10....134 F2
Kingswood Mdw EX22..164 D5
Kingswood Park Ave PL3................248 D6
Kingswood Rd PL18...125 D6
King William Ho EX4..261 B4
King William St EX4..261 A4
Kinlacey Ct TQ1.....220 C4
Kinnard Cres PL6.....244 F7
Kinnerton Ct EX4.....176 E8
Kinnerton Way EX4...176 E8
Kinross Ave PL4......249 A4
Kinsale Rd PL5.......243 F3
Kinscome Ct TQ11...236 C5
Kinsford Gate Cross EX36...............19 D7
Kinsford Hill TA24....119 C1
Kinterbury St PL1....247 E2
Kinterbury Terr PL5..247 B8
Kintyre Cl PL2........213 E2
Kinver Cl PL6.........245 D4
Kipling Cl EX39......156 C6
Kipling Dr EX2.......177 F4
Kipling Gdns PL5....244 D2
Kipling Rd EX8......188 A5
Kipling Terr EX39....156 C6
Kipscombe Cross EX35...6 A6
Kipscombe Hill EX31...11 D2
Kirby Cl EX13........167 D5
Kirby Pl PL4.........262 C4
Kirby Terr PL4.......262 C4
Kirkdale Gdns PL2....248 B7
Kirkella Rd PL20.....127 A2
Kirkham Cl 🔳 TQ3...226 A7
Kirkham House Mus TQ3................226 B6
Kirkham St 🔳 TQ3...226 B7
Kirkland Cl PL6......245 C7
Kirkstall Cl PL2......248 A8
Kirkstead Cl TQ2.....219 E8
Kirkwall Rd PL5......244 E3
Kirton La EX16.......47 C4
Kirton Pl PL3........249 B5
Kirtons Rd TQ12....214 B7
Kismeldon Cross EX22..39 B3
Kissing Gate Cross EX16..48 D5
Kitchadon Gate EX18..59 D3
Kitchadon Rd EX18...59 D3
Kitcott Cross EX16....45 F6
Kitcott Hill EX36.....45 F6
Kit Hill Cres PL5.....247 C8
Kitley View PL8.....257 B5
Kitley Way PL5......243 D1
Kitridge La TA24.....21 B7
Kits Cl 🔳 TQ13.....123 F6
Kitter Dr PL9.........256 A5
Kitterford Cross PL21..137 F7
Kittersley Dr 🔟 TQ12..122 F1
Kittiwake Dr TQ2...213 E2
Kitts TA21..........160 D4
Kitts Cross EX10.....187 A7
Kitts La EX10.........187 B6
Kitwell St EX15........66 A7
Klondyke Rd EX20....170 C3
Knackershole La EX17..61 B3
Knacker's Hole La TA3...68 D6
Knap Cross EX34......136 C4
Knap Down La EX34....3 B4

Knapp Hill EX10 . . . . 188 A5
Knapp House Holiday Camp
EX39 . . . . 157 B7
Knapp Park Rd TQ4 . . . . . . 226 C2
Knapps Cl PL9 . . . . 256 C6
Knapp's La EX10 . . . . 100 D1
Knaves Ash Cross TQ9 . . 217 A5
Kneela Hill EX21 . . . . 74 A8
Kneele Gdns PL3 . . . . 248 E8
Kneller Cl EX34 . . . . 150 C4
Knick Knack La TQ5 . . . . . 230 C3
Knightacott Cross EX32 . . 11 C2
Knighthayes Wlk EX6 . . . . 181 F5
Knightley Rd EX2 . . . . 177 E3
Knighton Cross TQ12 . . . . 131 F8
Knighton Hill Bsns Ctr
PL9 . . . . 148 E8
Knighton Rd
Plymouth PL4 . . . . 263 C3
Wembury PL9 . . . . 140 D8
Knighton Terr **4** PL20 . . . 126 F5
Knights Cres EX2 . . . . 178 D3
Knights Field Way EX39 . 157 A8
Knightshayes Court EX16 . .49 C2
Knight's La EX11 . . . . 88 A4
Knights Mead TQ13 . . . . . . 123 C4
Knights Rd TA21 . . . . 52 D8
Knightstone Down La
EX17 .61 C2
Knightstone La
Ottery St Mary EX11 . . . . . 169 F3
Ottery St Mary, Wiggaton
EX11 . . . . 169 F1
Knightstone Rd EX11 . . . . 169 F1
Knightswood EX15 . . . . . . 163 C2
Knill Cross PL10 . . . . 252 E5
Knill Cross Cotts PL10 . . 252 E5
Knockworthy Cross EX38 . 26 F1
Knoll Knap EX13 . . . . 103 E4
Knoll The PL7 . . . . 250 B6
Knowland Cl PL1 . . . . 247 F3
Knowle Ave PL2 . . . . 247 E6
Knowle Cl
Ashburton TQ13 . . . . 130 E4
Cullompton EX15 . . . . 163 A3
Honiton EX14 . . . . 166 C6
Landkey EX32 . . . . 17 B2
Knowle Cnr EX9 . . . . 197 D1
Knowle Cross
Copplestone EX17 . . . . 79 C4
Hennock TQ13 . . . . 123 C8
Whimple EX5 . . . . 99 E8
Knowle Ct TQ8 . . . . 259 D5
Knowle Dr
Exeter EX4 . . . . 176 F7
Sidmouth EX10 . . . . 188 A4
Knowle Fork TQ7 . . . . 148 F4
Knowle Gdns
Combe Martin EX34 . . . . .3 A3
Kingsbridge TQ7 . . . . 258 C6
Sidmouth EX10 . . . . 188 A4
Knowle Grange **1** EX10 . 188 A4
Knowle Hill EX9 . . . . 197 C2
Knowle Ho (Fire Service HQ)
EX3 . . . . 183 B6
Knowle House Cl TQ7 . . . 258 D6
Knowle Ind Est EX33 . . . . . .8 D1
Knowle La
Butterleigh EX15 . . . . 64 F1
Copplestone EX17 . . . . 79 C4
Drewsteignton EX6 . . . . .96 D3
Knowle Mews EX9 . . . . 197 E2
Knowle Prim Sch PL5 . . . 244 A4
Knowle Rd
Knowle EX9 . . . . 197 E1
Lustleigh TQ13 . . . . 122 C8
Salcombe TQ8 . . . . 259 D5
Knowles Cross TQ13 . . . . 130 E4
Knowles Dr **2** EX24 . . . . 103 A4
Knowle Hill Rd TQ12 . . . . 207 B4
Knowles Hill Sch
Newton Abbot TQ12 . . . . . 207 A4
Newton Abbot TQ12 . . . . . 207 B4
Knowle Terr PL20 . . . . 127 B4
Knowle View EX20 . . . . 170 D6
Knowstone Cross EX16 . . .47 D6
Knowstone Moor Cross
EX36 .47 B8
Kyl Cober Parc PL17 . . . . 115 C1
Kynance Cl PL11 . . . . 246 F4
Kynock Ind Est EX39 . . . . .25 F4

L

Labbett's Cross EX18 . . . . .60 C6
Laboon La EX18 . . . . 59 C7
Laburnham Gr TQ9 . . . . . . 223 A7
Laburnum Cl
Exmouth EX8 . . . . 196 D3
1 Honiton EX14 . . . . .85 C2
Laburnum Cotts
Tavistock PL19 . . . . 171 C6
7 Wellington TA21 . . . . . 160 D5
Wellington TA21 . . . . 212 B6
Laburnum Dr
Barnstaple EX32 . . . . 155 E3
6 Wembury PL9 . . . . 140 D8
Laburnum Rd
Exeter EX2 . . . . 177 F3
Newton Abbot TQ12 . . . . . 207 E1
Wellington TA21 . . . . 160 E5
Laburnum Row **5** TQ2 . . 219 F6
Laburnum St TQ2 . . . . 219 F5
Laburnum Terr TQ12 . . . . 212 B7

Laburnum Villas PL19 . . . 117 E6
Laburnum Way
East Allington TQ7 . . . . 144 E7
Okehampton EX20 . . . . 170 C5
Lace Wlk EX14 . . . . 166 C6
Lacey Ho **7** TQ3 . . . . 226 B6
Lackaborough Ct EX2 . . . 181 A8
Lacy Rd TQ3 . . . . 219 A1
Ladder La EX34 . . . . 3 B3
Ladford Mill Cross EX21 . .55 C6
Ladies Mile EX31 . . . . 4 A4
Ladies' Mile EX32 . . . . 155 A3
Ladram Rd EX9 . . . . 199 A8
Lady Harriet Acland's Dr
TA22 .34 A8
Ladymead EX10 . . . . 187 F8
Lady Meadow Terr TQ13 . 121 B2
Lady Modifords CE Prim Sch
PL20 . . . . 127 B4
Lady Park Rd TQ2 . . . . 219 D3
Lady Seawards CE Prim Sch
EX3 . . . . 183 C6
Lady's Mile Holiday Pk
EX7 . . . . 200 F1
Ladysmith Cl PL4 . . . . 263 C4
Ladysmith Inf Sch EX1 . . 177 F7
Ladysmith Jun Sch EX1 . 177 F7
Ladysmith Rd
Exeter EX1 . . . . 177 F7
Plymouth PL4 . . . . 263 C4
Lady St TA22 . . . . 33 D7
Lady Victoria's Dr TA22 . . .33 E6
Ladywell EX31 . . . . 154 F7
Ladywell Pl PL4 . . . . 263 B3
Lafrowda Cott EX4 . . . . . . 177 C8
Lagge Hill Cross EX17 . . . 80 F8
Lag Hill EX17 . . . . .62 F1
Lagoon View EX31 . . . . 153 A4
Laira Ave TQ1 . . . . 220 A6
Laira Bridge Rd PL4 . . . . . 249 B1
Laira Gdns PL3 . . . . 249 C4
Laira Green Prim Sch
PL3 . . . . 249 C4
Laira Park Cres PL4 . . . . . 249 B4
Laira Park Pl PL4 . . . . 249 B4
Laira Park Rd PL4 . . . . 249 B4
Laira Pl PL4 . . . . 263 C2
Laira St PL4 . . . . 263 C3
Laity Wlk PL6 . . . . 244 D6
Lake Ave TQ14 . . . . 210 A4
Lake Cl EX14 . . . . 166 D5
Lake Cross TQ9 . . . . 131 D2
Lake La
Ashreigney EX18 . . . . 58 F7
Dousland PL20 . . . . 127 B3
Newton St Cyres EX5 . . . . . .96 F2
Northlew EX20 . . . . 74 D2
Stockleigh Pomeroy EX17 . .81 A7
Lakeland TQ12 . . . . 212 B6
Lakelands Cl EX16 . . . . .46 E1
Lakelands Dr EX4 . . . . 176 F6
Lake Mews EX10 . . . . 252 E5
Lakenham Cotts EX39 . . . 156 E7
Lakenham Hill EX39 . . . . . 156 F7
Lake Rd PL9 . . . . 255 B6
Lakerise EX7 . . . . 201 A2
Lake Rural Workshops
EX21 . . . . 55 E4
Lakes Cl TQ5 . . . . 230 A5
Lakes Cross EX20 . . . . 57 A8
Lakes Ct EX10 . . . . 188 B3
Lakeside
Salcombe TQ8 . . . . 259 D5
Tavistock PL19 . . . . 171 B6
Lakeside Ave EX2 . . . . 182 B8
Lakeside Cl TQ13 . . . . 180 C4
Lakeside Dr PL5 . . . . 243 E5
Lakes La EX4 . . . . .98 F4
Lakes Rd TQ5 . . . . 230 A4
Lake St TQ6 . . . . 233 F3
Lakeview EX7 . . . . 201 A2
Lake View Cl PL7 . . . . 165 E6
Lake View Cl PL5 . . . . 244 B6
Lakeview Dr PL5 . . . . 244 B5
Lakewater Cross TQ9 . . . 131 E1
Lalebrick Rd PL9 . . . . 255 B5
Lamacraft Cl EX7 . . . . 204 F8
Lamacraft Dr EX4 . . . . 178 A7
Lama Cross EX18 . . . . .59 C4
Lamaton Pk EX36 . . . . 158 D3
Lambert Cl EX7 . . . . 204 F8
Lambert Cross EX20 . . . . . 75 A3
Lambert La EX6 . . . . 96 F2
Lambert Rd PL5 . . . . 244 B6
Lambert's La TQ14 . . . . . . 209 D4
Lambhay Hill PL1 . . . . 263 A1
Lambhay St PL1 . . . . 263 A1
Lamb Park Cl **10** TQ12 . . 123 F1
Lambpark Ct TA3 . . . . 68 C6
Lamb Pk
Chagford TQ13 . . . . 111 A6
Drewsteignton EX6 . . . . 96 D1
Ilfracombe EX34 . . . . 150 A4
Lambs Cl TQ7 . . . . 143 A2
Lambscombe Cross EX36 . 31 A8
Lambscombe Hill EX36 . . .31 A8
Lamb The TQ9 . . . . 223 B5
Lamerghs Field EX17 . . . . 165 D6
Lamerhooe Cross PL19 . . 116 A1
Lamerhooe Dr PL19 . . . . . 116 A1
Lamerton CE Prim Sch
PL19 . . . . 116 E3
Lamerton Cl PL5 . . . . 244 B3
Lamerton Cross EX20 . . . . 75 F2
Lammacott Cross EX17 . . .78 E5
Lammacott La EX17 . . . . . . 78 E6
Lammas La TQ3 . . . . 226 A8
Lamorna Pk PL11 . . . . 246 E4

Lampard Com Sch The
EX32 . . . . 155 C3
Lamplighters **14** EX14 . . 166 C6
Lamplough Rd EX8 . . . . . . 196 A3
Lana Cotts EX22 . . . . 89 F7
Lana Cross EX22 . . . . 55 C1
Lanbridge Cross TQ9 . . . . 222 F1
Lancaster Cl
Cullompton EX15 . . . . 163 C5
Exeter EX2 . . . . 178 B5
Lancaster Dr TQ4 . . . . 226 A2
Lancaster Gdns PL5 . . . . . 244 D4
Lancaster Rd TQ4 . . . . 226 C5
Lancelot Rd EX4 . . . . 174 A2
Lancercombe La EX10 . . . 100 D3
Lancer Cl TA21 . . . . 160 D6
Lanchitt Cross EX36 . . . . . .19 B2
Lancock St TA21 . . . . 160 A5
Landboat Cotts EX17 . . . . 62 F1
Landboat View EX17 . . . . . 62 F1
Landcroft La EX15 . . . . .66 A1
Lander Rd PL12 . . . . 242 F3
Landhayes Rd EX4 . . . . . . 176 D8
Landkey Prim Sch EX32 . . 17 B2
Landkey Rd EX32 . . . . 155 C2
Landlord's Hill TA21 . . . . . .51 E7
Landmark Rd TQ8 . . . . 259 B4
Landpath TQ7 . . . . 143 A2
Land Pk EX18 . . . . 44 E1
Landrake Cl PL5 . . . . 247 C8
Landscore EX17 . . . . 165 B5
Landscore Cl
Crediton EX17 . . . . 165 B5
Teignmouth TQ14 . . . . 210 A5
Landscore Prim Sch
EX17 . . . . 165 A5
Landscore Rd
3 Exeter EX4 . . . . 177 A5
Teignmouth TQ14 . . . . 210 B5
Landscove CE Prim Sch
TQ13 . . . . 131 B1
Landsend La EX17 . . . . 78 E3
Lands Pk PL9 . . . . 255 F7
Lands Rd
Brixham TQ5 . . . . 230 F6
Exeter EX4 . . . . 174 D1
Landulph Cross PL12 . . . 238 F1
Landulph Gdns PL5 . . . . . 247 C8
Landunvez Pl EX5 . . . . .82 F6
Landuph Prim Sch PL12 . 238 F1
Lane Cross EX22 . . . . 53 F7
Lane End La **1** EX39 . . . . 15 F8
Lane End Cross
Broadhembury EX14 . . . . . .84 E8
Broadhempston TQ13 . . . 131 D3
Halwill EX21 . . . . 73 D3
Horsebridge PL19 . . . . 116 B2
Ipplepen TQ12 . . . . 211 D2
Lane End Rd EX32 . . . . 155 D4
Lane End Pool TQ9 . . . . . . 227 B3
Lane Field Rd EX39 . . . . . . 156 D2
Lane Head Cl EX33 . . . . .7 E2
Lanehead Rd EX12 . . . . . . 191 D5
Lanepark La EX39 . . . . .37 A5
Lane The
Dittisham TQ6 . . . . 228 D2
Lutton PL21 . . . . 133 B2
Plymouth PL7 . . . . 250 D6
Langaford La EX21 . . . . . . .73 B2
Langage Cross PL7 . . . . . . 251 F6
Langage Ind Est PL7 . . . . 251 D4
Langage Pk PL7 . . . . 251 C4
Langage Science Pk
PL7 . . . . 251 D5
Langaller Cl TQ13 . . . . 180 B5
Langaller Hill TA22 . . . . . . .33 D4
Langarron Pk EX32 . . . . . 155 B5
Langaton Gdns EX1 . . . . . 174 F1
Langaton La EX1 . . . . 175 A1
Langbrook Cross PL7 . . . 136 E3
Langdale Cl PL6 . . . . 245 D1
Langdale Gdns PL6 . . . . . 245 D1
Langdon Cross TQ21 . . . . 137 F1
Langdon Ct PL9 . . . . 256 B6
Langdon Down Way
PL11 . . . . 246 E3
Langdon Fields TQ5 . . . . . 229 B6
Langdon Hosp EX7 . . . . . 200 E2
Langdon La
Dawlish EX7 . . . . 204 C8
Galmpton TQ4, TQ5 . . . . . 229 B6
Langdon Rd
Bradworthy EX22 . . . . 38 E1
Dawlish EX7 . . . . 204 D8
Paignton TQ3 . . . . 219 C1
Langdons Way TQ10 . . . . . 88 C8
Langdown Way EX8 . . . . . 201 F6
Langerwell Cl PL12 . . . . . 242 C3
Langerwell La PL12 . . . . . 242 C3
Langford Ave EX14 . . . . . . 166 D6
Langford Cres TQ2 . . . . . . 213 F3
Langford Cross EX17 . . . . . 78 C4
Langford Gate PL21 . . . . . 137 F8
Langford Gn EX15 . . . . .83 D5
Langford Rd
Honiton EX14 . . . . 166 D7
Honiton EX14 . . . . 166 E7
Langford EX5 . . . . 172 E7
Lang Gdns PL18 . . . . 125 D3
Lang Gr
Plymouth PL6 . . . . 256 C2
Tavistock PL19 . . . . 171 D5
Langham Cross PL19 . . . . 116 F3
Langham La EX17 . . . . 61 F2
Langham Levels PL21 . . . 237 B6

Langham Pl PL4 . . . . 263 C3
Langham Way PL21 . . . . . 237 C5
Langhill Rd PL3 . . . . 248 D5
Langland Hill EX17 . . . . . . .61 A4
Langlands Bsns Pk EX15 . .65 F6
Langlands Cl TQ4 . . . . 225 E4
Langlands Cross EX14 . . . .87 A6
Langlands Rd EX15 . . . . . 163 A3
Langleigh La EX34 . . . . . . 150 A4
Langleigh Pk EX34 . . . . . . 150 A4
Langleigh Rd EX34 . . . . . . 150 A5
Langley Cl EX18 . . . . .44 E1
Langley Ave TQ5 . . . . 230 C4
Langley Cl
Brixham TQ5 . . . . 230 C4
Plymouth PL6 . . . . 245 A7
Langley Cres PL6 . . . . 244 F7
Langley Cross EX37 . . . . . .27 F3
Langley Gdns EX18 . . . . . . 44 E1
Langley Jun & Inf Scns
PL6 . . . . 245 A6
Langley La EX18 . . . . .44 E1
Langman Cl **7** EX20 . . . . 125 E1
Langmans Cross TQ7 . . . 143 A2
Langmead EX39 . . . . 157 E5
Langmead Cl PL6 . . . . 249 C8
Langmead Rd PL6 . . . . . . 249 C8
Langmoor Cl DT7 . . . . 260 D3
Langmoor La EX13 . . . . . . .88 D2
Langmoor La EX16 . . . . . . 249 A7
Langridge Cross EX37 . . . .27 F1
Langridge Rd TQ3 . . . . . . 225 E8
Langsfield EX33 . . . . .7 D1
Langsford Rd PL19 . . . . . . 117 E3
Langs Rd TQ3 . . . . 226 C8
Langston Cross
Kingston TQ7 . . . . 142 D7
Modbury, Brownston EX20 . .95 D1
Langstone Cl
Heathfield TQ12 . . . . 180 F2
Torquay TQ1 . . . . 220 D6
Langstone Cross TQ13 . . 121 E8
Langstone Dr EX8 . . . . 196 C1
Langstone Hill
Lustleigh TQ13 . . . . 121 E8
Moretonhampstead TQ13 . 111 E1
Langstone Rd PL2 . . . . 248 C7
Langstone Terr PL2 . . . . . 248 C7
Langton Rd **8** PL20 . . . . 126 F3
Langtree Com Sch EX38 . . 40 F2
Langtreemoor La EX38 . . .40 E2
Lang Way TQ12 . . . . 211 E2
Langwells Ct TQ9 . . . . 139 E1
Langworthys Barn TQ7 . . 143 E2
Lanherne EX7 . . . . 204 E6
Lanhydrock Cl TQ3 . . . . . . 225 D8
Lanhydrock Rd PL4 . . . . . 249 B2
Lannacombe Gn TQ7 . . . . 149 C5
Lanscore Cl EX14 . . . . 101 A8
Lanscore La EX14 . . . . 101 A8
Lansdowne EX2 . . . . 178 B4
Lansdowne La **2** TQ2 . . . 219 F5
Lansdowne Pk
Northam EX39 . . . . 156 F8
Totnes TQ9 . . . . 223 E4
Lansdowne Rd
Budleigh Salterton EX9 . . 197 D1
Plymouth PL6 . . . . 244 F2
1 Torquay TQ2 . . . . 219 F5
Lansdowne Terr
Bideford EX39 . . . . 156 F1
Exeter EX2 . . . . 261 B2
Lansdown Terr **2** EX32 . 155 A6
Lanteglos Cl **5** PL21 . . . 137 C7
Lapford Com Prim Sch
EX17 . . . . 60 D3
Lapford Cross EX17 . . . . . . 60 C2
Lapford Sta EX17 . . . . 60 A2
Lapthorn Cl PL9 . . . . 255 C7
Lapwing Cl EX15 . . . . 163 A3
Larch Cl
Exmouth EX8 . . . . 196 D3
1 Honiton EX14 . . . . 166 A4
Larch Dr PL6 . . . . 245 E7
Larch Gr PL7 . . . . 132 C1
Larch Rd EX2 . . . . 176 F3
Larch Wlk TQ2 . . . . 219 C8
Larcombe End TQ9 . . . . . . 135 F1
Larkbeare Ave EX5 . . . . . . 100 B8
Larkbeare Cross EX5 . . . . 100 B8
Larkbeare Rd EX2 . . . . 261 B1
Lark Cl EX4 . . . . 173 D1
Larkey La EX16 . . . . .63 D4
Larkhall Rise PL3 . . . . 249 B5
Larkham Cl PL7 . . . . 251 C6
Larkham La PL7 . . . . 251 C6
Lark Hill PL2 . . . . 248 A6
Lark Rise
6 Barnstaple EX31 . . . . 154 A2
Newton Poppleford EX10 . 186 E8
Larks Cl TQ14 . . . . 209 D4
Larkshayes Cross EX13 . . .86 E3
Larkshayes Droveway
EX13 . . . . 86 F3
Larkshayes Knap EX13 . . .86 E3
Larksmead Cl TQ12 . . . . . 207 A1
Larksmead Way TQ12 . . . 207 A1
Larks Rise EX15 . . . . 163 A2
Larkstone Cres EX34 . . . . 150 D5
Larkstone Gdns EX34 . . . 150 D5
Larkstone La EX34 . . . . . . 150 D6
Larkstone Terr EX34 . . . . . 150 D6
Larks Way EX32 . . . . 17 F4
Lashbrook EX5 . . . . .84 B2
Lashingcott Cross EX31 . . 27 B3

Lashingcott Lane End
EX31 . . . . 27 B2
Laskeys Heath **1** TQ12 . . 122 F1
Laskeys La EX10 . . . . 188 C4
Latches Wlk EX11 . . . . 167 D6
Latchgate Cross EX36 . . . .31 F7
Latchgate Hill EX36 . . . . . .31 F7
Latch La EX38 . . . . .40 E2
Latchmount Gdns EX13 . 167 D6
Latham Cl PL6 . . . . 249 A7
Latimer Cl PL7 . . . . 251 B5
Latimer Rd EX4 . . . . 178 A8
Latimer Wlk PL6 . . . . 244 E7
Lauderdale **8** EX32 . . . . . 155 B4
Lauderdale Dr EX32 . . . . . 155 B4
Lauder La EX31 . . . . 154 C1
Launceston Cl PL6 . . . . . . 245 B7
Launceston Head EX5 . . . .83 C1
Launceston Rd EX20 . . . . 107 E8
Laundry Cotts EX5 . . . . . . .98 F8
Laura Ave TQ3 . . . . 226 B8
Laura Gr TQ3 . . . . 226 A8
Laura Pl **1** TQ3 . . . . 226 A6
Laurel Ave EX39 . . . . 156 E1
Laurel Bank EX14 . . . . 188 C4
Laurel Cl PL2 . . . . 248 A4
Laurel Dene PL2 . . . . 248 A7
Laurel Dr PL6 . . . . 245 E5
Laurel La TQ14 . . . . 209 D5
Laurel Rd
Exeter EX2 . . . . 177 F3
1 Honiton EX14 . . . . 166 A4
Plymouth PL2 . . . . 248 A7
Laurel Rise EX8 . . . . 202 D8
Laurels The
Barnstaple EX31 . . . . 154 B2
Dunkeswell EX14 . . . . .67 C3
Gunnislake PL18 . . . . 125 B5
Sidmouth EX10 . . . . 188 A5
Torquay TQ1 . . . . 220 D8
Laureston Rd TQ12 . . . . . 207 C2
Laurie Ave TQ12 . . . . 206 F4
Lauriston Cl TQ2 . . . . 220 A5
Lavender Cl TQ5 . . . . 230 A4
Lavender Rd EX4 . . . . 176 E8
Lavington Cl PL7 . . . . 251 B5
Lavinia Dr PL7 . . . . 250 C5
Law Memorial Ho **5**
EX32 . . . . .16 E1
Lawn Cl
2 Plymouth PL7 . . . . 251 C5
Torquay TQ2 . . . . 213 F4
Lawn Dr TQ3 . . . . 123 E6
Lawn Gdns **16** TQ3 . . . . . 123 E6
Lawn Hill **3** EX7 . . . . 204 E6
Lawn Rd EX4 . . . . 202 A7
Lawns End TQ1 . . . . 208 E8
Lawns The
Plymouth PL5 . . . . 244 E4
Torpoint PL11 . . . . 247 A4
Lawn Terr **25** EX7 . . . . . . 204 D6
Lawn The
3 Budleigh Salterton
EX9 . . . . 198 A1
Tavistock PL19 . . . . 171 D6
1 Wellington TA21 . . . . . 160 D6
Lawn Vista EX10 . . . . 188 B5
Lawrence Ave EX4 . . . . . . 177 A4
Lawrence Cl EX14 . . . . .84 D7
Lawrence Pl TQ12 . . . . 220 B4
Lawrence Rd PL9 . . . . 255 A6
Lawrence Wlk EX6 . . . . . . 181 F5
Lawson Gr PL9 . . . . 255 C7
Lax Wlk PL6 . . . . 244 D6
Laxton Ave EX1 . . . . 178 C6
Layne Cl EX6 . . . . 113 B4
Layne Fields EX6 . . . . 113 B4
Laywell Cl TQ5 . . . . 230 B2
Laywell Rd TQ5 . . . . 230 A3
Lazenby Rd EX16 . . . . 161 F3
Leaches La EX18 . . . . 60 B7
Leachway La EX2 . . . . 113 F7
Leachway Lane Cross
EX2 . . . . 113 F7
Lea Combe EX13 . . . . 167 D5
Leadengate Cl EX33 . . . . . . 7 E1
Leadengate Fields EX33 . . .7 D1
Leader La TQ12 . . . . 218 D2
Leaholes Ave EX20 . . . . . . 170 C5
Lea La EX9 . . . . 199 F7
Lea Rd TQ13 . . . . 180 C6
Lea Mount Cl EX7 . . . . 204 A8
Lea Mount Dr EX7 . . . . . . 204 A8
Lea Mount Dr EX7 . . . . . . 204 D5
Lea Mount Rd EX7 . . . . . . 204 E5
Leander Ct **18** TQ14 . . . . 210 C5
Leander Way PL5 . . . . 244 D2
Leanway PL12 . . . . 242 E2
Lea Rd
Otterton EX9 . . . . 198 E7
Tiverton EX16 . . . . 161 F6
Torquay TQ2 . . . . 214 B3
Lear La EX13 . . . . .87 F5
Lear Pk EX15 . . . . .83 F5
Lears La TQ13 . . . . 123 F6
Leary Cross EX32 . . . . .29 B8
Lease Cotts EX5 . . . . .82 D4
Lease Hill EX5 . . . . .82 D4
Lea Side EX6 . . . . 112 F8
Leas Rd EX9 . . . . 198 A1
Leas The EX34 . . . . 150 A3
Leat Cl PL20 . . . . 127 B3
Lea Terr EX39 . . . . .15 A1
Leatfield Dr PL6 . . . . 244 F4
Lea The TQ14 . . . . 209 C7
Leatherby Cl PL6 . . . . 244 E6
Leather Tor Cl **4** PL20 . . 126 F3

Leat Mdw
3 Coldeast TQ12 . . . . .122 F1
Tiverton EX16 . . . . .161 B5
Leat Rd PL16 . . . . .105 F3
Leatside
Exeter EX2 . . . . .261 A2
Roborough PL6 . . . . .241 C1
Leatside Ho TQ12 . . . . . . .207 A3
Leat St EX16 . . . . .161 B5
Leat View PL12 . . . . .242 B3
Leatway Gdns EX15 . . . . . .163 B3
Leat Wlk
Plymouth PL3 . . . . .248 C6
Roborough PL6 . . . . .241 D1
Saltash PL12 . . . . .242 D4
Lea Vale Rd TQ12 . . . . . . .207 A3
Leaveacre EX17 . . . . .79 D6
Leaves Yd PL3 . . . . .249 B7
Lea View EX15 . . . . .162 D5
Leaway Cotts EX16 . . . . . .161 E4
Leaze Rd TQ12 . . . . .207 D8
Lebanon Cl EX4 . . . . .173 E1
Leburnick Cross PL15 . . . . .115 B8
Ledgate La PL7 . . . . .251 F8
Ledsgrove TQ12 . . . . .211 E2
Ledstone Cross TQ7 . . . . . .144 B5
Lee Ave EX39 . . . . .25 F1
Lee Ball Cross EX31 . . . . . . .11 E3
Lee Ball Hill EX31 . . . . .11 D3
Leechwell La TQ9 . . . . .223 C5
Leechwell St TQ9 . . . . .223 B5
Lee Cl EX14 . . . . .166 B6
Lee Cliff Pk EX7 . . . . .201 B1
Lee Cross
Broadhempston TQ9 . . . . . .131 E1
Great Torrington EX37 . . . . .42 F7
North Molton EX36 . . . . . . .30 B8
Woolacombe EX34 . . . . .1 C1
Leecross Gate EX17 . . . . . . .61 A7
Leecross La EX5 . . . . .193 B5
Lee Ct TQ5 . . . . .230 E4
Leeford La EX35 . . . . .6 B5
Lee La
Bishops Nympton EX36 . . . . .31 F6
Dartmouth TQ6 . . . . .232 C7
Dunsford EX6 . . . . .112 E7
Lee Lane End TQ7 . . . . .148 F8
Lee Mill Host Pl PL21 . . . . .136 C7
Lee Mill Ind Est PL21 . . . . .136 C6
Lee Pk TA21 . . . . .52 F7
Lee Rd EX35 . . . . .151 B5
Leeside Ct 7 PL2 . . . . .248 A4
Lees Mdw EX5 . . . . .84 A2
Lee Terr 2 TQ13 . . . . .123 E6
Leeward Ct EX8 . . . . .201 E6
Leeward La TQ2 . . . . .213 E3
Leeze Park Est EX20 . . . . . .170 B4
Leggetts La DT7 . . . . .193 C7
Legion La PL8 . . . . .257 A5
Legion Way EX2 . . . . .177 B2
Legis Wlk PL6 . . . . .245 B8
Leicester Mead EX4 . . . . . .176 E7
Leigham Ct
7 Dawlish EX7 . . . . .204 E6
Plymouth PL1 . . . . .262 B2
Leigham Manor Dr PL6 . . . .245 E1
Leigham Prim Sch PL6 . . . .245 E1
Leigham St PL1 . . . . .262 B1
Leigham Terr TQ7 . . . . . . .258 C5
Leigham Terr La PL21 . . . . .262 B2
Leighan Bsns Units EX2 . . .181 D8
Leigh Cl PL21 . . . . .137 C8
Leighcot Cross EX17 . . . . . .62 A2
Leighcott La EX17 . . . . .62 A2
Leigh Cross
Ashill EX15 . . . . .66 F6
Bittaford PL21 . . . . .137 D8
Bridford EX6 . . . . .113 B6
Chulmleigh EX18 . . . . .59 C8
Hennock TQ13 . . . . .123 C7
Kingsbridge TQ7 . . . . .258 A8
Modbury PL21 . . . . .137 F3
South Brent TQ10 . . . . .135 A4
Zeal Monachorum EX17 . . . . .77 F7
Leigh Ct PL6 . . . . .249 A8
Leigh Dene Cl EX2 . . . . . . .177 E4
Leigh La
Bittaford PL21 . . . . .137 C8
Combe Martin EX34 . . . . .3 C2
Roborough PL6 . . . . .241 D2
Leighmoor Cross PL21 . . . .137 E3
Leighon Rd TQ3 . . . . .226 C7
Leigh Rd
Bideford EX39 . . . . .156 E1
Chulmleigh EX18 . . . . .44 D1
Combe Martin EX34 . . . . .3 B2
Leighton Rd PL3 . . . . .248 F8
Leighton Terr 3 EX16 . . . . .161 D4
Leighty Water EX38 . . . . . . .42 A6
Leigh Villas EX38 . . . . .44 E1
Leland Gr PL21 . . . . .237 D4
Le Locle Cl EX10 . . . . .187 F8
Le Marchant Cl EX14 . . . . . .67 B1
Lembury Rd TQ9 . . . . .225 E1
Le Molay-Littry Way
TQ13 . . . . .180 E7
Lemonford La TQ12 . . . . . .131 D7
Lemonford Mills TQ12 . . . .131 D6
Lemon Pl TQ12 . . . . .207 C3
Lemon Rd TQ12 . . . . .207 C3
Lenards Rd EX39 . . . . .156 F6
Lenda La TQ12 . . . . .122 C2
Lendon Way EX19 . . . . .58 F2
Lennard Rd 6 EX17 . . . . . .165 C5
Lennards Ct EX10 . . . . .188 B3
Lennox Ave EX10 . . . . .188 B4
Lentney Cl PL9 . . . . .140 A8

Lenton La EX37 . . . . .44 C6
Lenwood Ctry Club EX39 . .156 E5
Lenwood Pk EX39 . . . . .156 E4
Lenwood Rd EX39 . . . . .156 E5
Leofric Rd EX16 . . . . .161 D6
Leonard Moor Cross EX15 . .65 F8
Leonards Cl TQ7 . . . . .143 A1
Leonards Rd PL21 . . . . .237 D5
Lerwell Beech Tree Cross
EX37 . . . . .29 A5
Leslie Rd EX8 . . . . .202 A8
Lester Cl PL3 . . . . .249 B6
Lestock Cl EX8 . . . . .202 F7
Lethaby Rd EX32 . . . . .155 B6
Lethbridge Rd EX2 . . . . . . .178 B4
Lethbridge's & Davey's
Almshouses EX1 . . . . . .261 C4
Letheren 's La EX20 . . . . . . .77 B5
Lettaford Cross TQ13 . . . . .111 B3
Level The TQ6 . . . . .228 C2
Lever Cl EX39 . . . . .156 F8
Leverlake EX16 . . . . .161 F6
Leverlake La EX16 . . . . .161 F7
Lewdon Cross EX6 . . . . .97 A5
Lewesdon Ct 2 DT7 . . . . . .260 D3
Lewes Gdns PL5 . . . . .244 C4
Lewhaven Cl EX20 . . . . .106 E5
Lewis Ave EX16 . . . . .161 E4
Lewis Cres EX2 . . . . .178 D3
Lewis Cl 4 EX34 . . . . .150 B5
Leworthy Cross
Holsworthy EX22 . . . . .71 D4
Woolfardisworthy EX39 . . . . .39 B6
Leworthy Hill EX31 . . . . . . .11 D1
Leworthy Post EX32 . . . . . . .11 C1
Lewsley Cross EX13 . . . . . . .87 E4
Lewsley La EX13 . . . . .87 E4
Lewthorn Cross TQ13 . . . . .122 B3
Lewtrenchard CE Prim Sch
EX20 . . . . .106 F5
Lexhayne La EX13 . . . . .103 A7
Leyburn Rd EX2 . . . . .226 A4
Ley Cl TQ12 . . . . .180 B1
Ley Cres TQ12 . . . . .180 B1
Ley Cross
Ashreigney EX18 . . . . .58 F8
Aveton Gifford PL21 . . . . . .143 A8
Ermington PL21 . . . . .136 D4
Holsworthy Beacon EX22 . . . .54 F3
North Molton EX36 . . . . . . .30 F8
Widecombe in the Moor
TQ13 . . . . .121 C6
Leyfield Vllas EX7 . . . . .204 E7
Leyford Cl PL9 . . . . .140 D8
Ley La
Bere Ferrers PL20 . . . . .239 D6
Kentisbury EX31 . . . . .10 D6
Kingsteignton TQ12 . . . . . .207 D8
Ley La Cross TQ12 . . . . . . .207 D8
Leyland Cross EX22 . . . . . . .53 E8
Ley Meadow Dr EX31 . . . . .154 A3
Leypark Cl EX1 . . . . .178 C7
Leypark Cres EX1 . . . . .178 C7
Leypark Ct PL6 . . . . .245 E2
Leypark Rd EX1 . . . . .178 C7
Leypark Wlk PL6 . . . . .245 E2
Ley's Cross EX17 . . . . .62 E2
Ley's La EX31 . . . . .4 C1
Leys Rd TQ2 . . . . .219 D5
Leyton Ct EX15 . . . . .163 C3
Leywood EX14 . . . . .86 D7
Libby Ct PL12 . . . . .242 C5
Liberator Way EX14 . . . . . . .67 C1
Liberty Stile EX39 . . . . .22 C2
Libra Gdns EX3 . . . . .2 F4
Lichfield Ave TQ2 . . . . .214 A1
Lichfield Cl TQ5 . . . . .230 A4
Lichfield Dr TQ5 . . . . .230 A4
Lichdon Hill EX6 . . . . .176 D6
Liddle Way PL7 . . . . .251 B6
Lidford Tor Ave TQ4 . . . . . .225 F3
Lidyates La DT7, EX13 . . . . .103 F3
Liffey Rise EX4 . . . . .176 E8
Lifton Com Prim Sch
PL16 . . . . .105 E4
Liftondown Cross PL16 . . . .105 C4
Lifton La EX19 . . . . .59 B3
Lifton Rd PL4 . . . . .263 A3
Lighthouse Cross EX39 . . . . .23 B3
Light La TQ5 . . . . .229 B4
Lightleigh Cross EX18 . . . . . .44 F5
Lilac Cl PL9 . . . . .255 C5
Lilac Rd
Exeter EX2 . . . . .177 F3
Tiverton EX16 . . . . .161 F5
Lilac Terr 2 EX16 . . . . .161 D4
Lilian Cl EX17 . . . . .78 B4
Lillage La EX9 . . . . .198 A6
Lillebonne Cl TA21 . . . . . . .160 F6
Lilley Wlk EX14 . . . . .166 D5
Lillicrap Ct EX20 . . . . .170 B5
Lillybrook La EX6 . . . . .98 A5
Lillycombe La TA3, EX15 . . . .67 E8
Lilly La EX5 . . . . .172 A8
Lilybridge EX39 . . . . .157 A2
Lily Cl EX39 . . . . .157 A7
Lilylake Cross EX24 . . . . . . .102 F7
Lily Mount EX4 . . . . .176 D8
Lime Ave TQ2 . . . . .219 F5
Lime Cl
Broadclyst EX5 . . . . .175 C6
Tiverton EX16 . . . . .161 F5
Lime Cres EX15 . . . . .162 C4
Lime Gr
Bideford EX39 . . . . .156 F2

Lime Gr continued
Exminster EX6 . . . . .182 A5
Exmouth EX8 . . . . .196 C3
Kingsbridge TQ7 . . . . .258 C5
Limegrove Rd EX4 . . . . .176 F5
Limehayes Rd EX20 . . . . . . .170 C5
Limekiln La EX31 . . . . .16 A6
Lime Kiln La
Exeter EX2 . . . . .178 A1
Uplyme DT7 . . . . .260 A6
Lime Kiln Rd EX16 . . . . .161 F3
Lime Rd EX16 . . . . .161 F5
Limerick Pl PL4 . . . . .263 C3
Limers Cross
Chittlehampton EX37 . . . . . .29 A4
Wolverstone EX14 . . . . .85 C7
Limer's Hill EX38 . . . . .159 B5
Limers La
Merton EX20 . . . . .57 A7
Northam EX39 . . . . .157 A5
Wolverstone EX14 . . . . .85 C7
Limer's Lane Cross EX36 . . .158 B2
Limers Lane Cross EX36 . . . .158 B2
Limes Cotts EX6 . . . . .182 A4
Limes Ct EX6 . . . . .182 A4
Lime St TQ13 . . . . .111 F5
Limes The PL6 . . . . .244 F2
Lime Tree Cl EX2 . . . . .178 C1
Lime Tree Cross EX16 . . . . . .64 D6
Limetree Gr EX33 . . . . .152 E6
Lime Tree Mead 8 EX16 . . .64 D7
Limetree Rd PL3 . . . . .248 D7
Lime Tree Wlk TQ12 . . . . . .207 E1
Lime Way EX12 . . . . .192 A7
Linacre La TQ12 . . . . .213 C6
Linacre Rd TQ2 . . . . .213 F4
Lincoln Ave PL4 . . . . .263 C4
Lincoln Cl
Exmouth EX8 . . . . .196 E4
Feniton EX14 . . . . .84 D2
Lincoln Gn TQ2 . . . . .214 A1
Lincoln Rd EX4 . . . . .176 E6
Lincombe Cross
Diptford TQ9 . . . . .138 D8
Salcombe TQ8 . . . . .259 D7
Lincombe Dr TQ1 . . . . .220 E3
Lincombe Hill Rd TQ1 . . . . .220 E4
Linden Cl
Barnstaple EX31 . . . . .154 C3
Braunton EX33 . . . . .152 D6
Exmouth EX8 . . . . .196 D2
Great Torrington EX38 . . . . .159 C5
Linden Ct 2 TQ5 . . . . .230 C5
Linden Gdns EX11 . . . . .169 E3
Linden Hill TA21 . . . . .160 A6
Linden Rd
Cullompton EX15 . . . . .163 C4
Dawlish EX7 . . . . .204 D5
Linden Terr
Newton Abbot TQ12 . . . . . .207 A3
Plymouth PL4 . . . . .263 C3
Lindfield Cl TQ2 . . . . .219 F8
Lindisfarne Way TQ2 . . . . . .213 E2
Lindridge Cl 6 TQ12 . . . . . .123 E1
Lindridge Hill TQ12 . . . . . .123 F1
Lindridge La 6 TQ12 . . . . . .123 E1
Lindridge Pk TQ12 . . . . . . .124 B2
Lindridge Rd TQ1 . . . . .220 B4
Lindsay Rd TQ3 . . . . .219 A2
Lindthorpe Way TQ5 . . . . . .230 B4
Liney Cross TQ11 . . . . .236 A6
Linfield Gdns EX4 . . . . .176 F4
Linhay Bsns Pk TQ13 . . . . .131 A5
Linhay Cl
Brixham TQ5 . . . . .234 F8
Honiton EX14 . . . . .166 B3
Millmoor EX15 . . . . .51 E1
Linhay Dr EX31 . . . . .153 F6
Linhay Pk EX17 . . . . .80 A5
Linhey Cl TQ7 . . . . .258 D4
Linkadells PL7 . . . . .250 C5
Linketty La PL7 . . . . .250 D5
Linketty La E PL6 . . . . .245 A1
Linketty La W PL6 . . . . . . .244 F8
Linkhay TA20 . . . . .88 D8
Linkhay Cl TA20 . . . . .88 D8
Link House Cl EX39 . . . . . . .156 C7
Link Rd EX20 . . . . .170 C6
Links Cl
Churston Ferrers TQ5 . . . . .229 C6
Exmouth EX8 . . . . .202 C8
Links Ct TQ7 . . . . .143 A1
Links Rd EX9 . . . . .203 E8
Links The
Northam EX39 . . . . .157 A8
Torquay TQ1 . . . . .214 C1
Linnet Cl EX4 . . . . .173 D2
Linnet Ct EX2 . . . . .178 D3
Linnet Dene EX15 . . . . .163 A2
Linscott Cres EX13 . . . . . . .153 A4
Linton Cl PL5 . . . . .244 C5
Linton La EX39 . . . . .37 B5
Linton Rd PL5 . . . . .244 C7
Linton Sq PL5 . . . . .244 C7
Lion Cl TQ2 . . . . .258 C5
Lion Ho EX8 . . . . .202 A7
Lion's Close Hill EX24 . . . . .103 A5
Lions Mill EX31 . . . . .154 E7
Lion's Rump EX32, EX36 . . . .18 F1
Lippell Dr PL9 . . . . .255 E6
Lipson Ave PL4 . . . . .263 B4
Lipson Com Coll PL4 . . . . . .249 C4
Lipson Ct PL4 . . . . .263 B3
Lipson Rd PL4 . . . . .263 B4
Lipson Sports Ctr PL4 . . . . .249 C4
Lipson Terr PL4 . . . . .263 B3
Lipson Vale PL4 . . . . .249 A4

Lipson Vale Prim Sch
PL4 . . . . .249 A4
Lipstone Cres PL4 . . . . .263 C4
Lisa Cl EX2 . . . . .178 A4
Lisburne Cres 10 TQ1 . . . . .220 D4
Lisburne Pl 10 TQ1 . . . . . . .220 D4
Lisburne Sq TQ1 . . . . .220 D4
Liscawn Terr PL11 . . . . .247 B3
Liscombe Cl PL18 . . . . .125 D7
Lisham's Drain EX24 . . . . . .103 A5
Lishaperhill Cross EX22 . . . .53 B2
Liskeard Rd PL12 . . . . .242 B3
Lisson Gr PL4 . . . . .248 F4
Lister Cl
Exeter EX2 . . . . .177 E4
Plymouth PL7 . . . . .250 F6
Lister Way TQ9 . . . . .144 E7
Litchardon Cross EX31 . . . . .26 F8
Litchaton Cres PL7 . . . . . . .250 B7
Litchaton Cross
East Buckland EX32 . . . . . . .18 F1
North Molton EX36 . . . . . . .30 A8
Litchaton Hill
East Buckland EX32 . . . . . . .18 F1
North Molton EX36 . . . . . . .30 A8
Litchaton Way PL7 . . . . . . .250 B7
Litchaton Cross EX32 . . . . . .154 F4
Litchdon St EX32 . . . . .155 A4
Litchfield Cl PL7 . . . . .251 B6
Litebury Rd EX16 . . . . .64 D7
Litlabourne EX31 . . . . .154 F7
Little Ash Gdns PL5 . . . . . . .243 B1
Little Ash Rd PL5 . . . . .243 B1
Little Barton 7 TQ12 . . . . .123 F1
Little Bicton Cr 18 EX8 . . . .202 A6
Little Bicton Pl EX8 . . . . . . .202 A6
Littleborough Cross EX17 . .62 A5
Little Bossell La TQ11 . . . . .236 B4
Little Bray Cross EX32 . . . . .18 C8
Little Bridge La EX32 . . . . . .18 E6
Little Bridge Bsns Pk
EX5 . . . . .179 D1
Little Bridge Cross EX22 . . .70 F5
Little Bridge Mdw EX22 . . . .70 F5
Little Butts PL9 . . . . .255 E6
Little Castle St EX4 . . . . . . .261 B3
Little Chockenhole La
EX9 . . . . .199 A8
Little Cl
Kingsteignton TQ12 . . . . . .207 E8
Ottery St Mary EX11 . . . . . .169 D3
Little Cotton Cvn Pk
TQ6 . . . . .233 C2
Little Cross TQ13 . . . . .130 A4
Little Dock La PL5 . . . . .244 B2
Little Down La EX6 . . . . . . .202 F7
Littledown La EX10 . . . . . . .186 D7
Little Down La
East Budleigh EX9 . . . . .198 A5
Roborough PL6 . . . . .241 E8
Little Down Orch EX10 . . . . .186 D7
Little Esworthy La EX16 . . . .48 A1
Little Fancy Cl PL6 . . . . .245 C7
Littlefield TQ14 . . . . .208 E8
Little Field EX39 . . . . .156 D2
Littlefield Dr
Barnstaple EX32 . . . . .155 D4
Torquay TQ2 . . . . .213 D1
Littlefields Ct EX22 . . . . . . .192 A7
Littleford Cross EX22 . . . . . .53 E8
Little Gate TQ7 . . . . .143 F7
Littlegate Rd TQ3 . . . . .226 B6
Little Gornhay La
Chevithorne EX16 . . . . .49 D1
Tiverton EX16 . . . . .64 D8
5 Tiverton EX16 . . . . .161 F6
Littleham CE Prim Sch
EX8 . . . . .202 F7
Littleham Cross
Bideford EX39 . . . . .25 C2
Exmouth EX8 . . . . .202 D7
Littleham Rd EX8 . . . . .202 E7
Little Hayes La EX18 . . . . . . .58 D8
Little Hayes La EX16 . . . . . . .63 A6
Little Heath Cross EX16 . . . .63 A6
Little Helstonbench Cross
TQ13 . . . . .123 B6
Littlehempston Cross
TQ9 . . . . .216 F2
Little Hill TQ8 . . . . .259 C5
Little Hill Cl TQ12 . . . . .123 F1
Little Hill TQ12 . . . . .123 F1
Little John's Cross Hill
EX2 . . . . .176 F3
Little John's Wlk TQ13 . . . .122 F6
Littlejoy Rd TQ12 . . . . .206 C4
Little Knowle EX9 . . . . .197 F1
Little Knowle Ct EX9 . . . . . .197 F1
Little La
Beer EX12 . . . . .191 D4
Cawsand PL10 . . . . .253 A2
Staddiscombe PL9 . . . . . . .255 D3
Little Mdw
Exmouth EX8 . . . . .196 E3
Pyworthy EX22 . . . . .71 D5
Little Mdws EX18 . . . . .59 C4
Littlemead La EX8 . . . . .196 B2
Little Meadow Way EX39 . .156 C2
Littlemoor Cl EX31 . . . . . . .153 A4
Little Normans EX15 . . . . . . .83 F6
Little Park Rd TQ3 . . . . .226 A6
Little Point Cres PL10 . . . . .252 F5
Little Princes TQ1 . . . . .220 C3
Little Queen St EX4 . . . . . . .261 B3
Little Rackenford La EX16 . .47 E5
Little Rack St 4 EX1 . . . . . . .261 A2
Little Raddon Cross EX17 . . .80 F6
Little Roborough TQ13 . . . .130 F5

Little Silver
Exeter EX4 . . . . .261 A4
Tiverton EX16 . . . . .161 D3
Little Silver La
Exeter EX2 . . . . .181 D5
Wellington TA21 . . . . .160 D2
Little Tons EX15 . . . . .65 A2
Littleton Pl PL2 . . . . .247 F4
Little Torrington EX38 . . . . .159 B1
Littletown Prim Sch
EX14 . . . . .166 C4
Littletown Rd EX14 . . . . . . .166 B4
Littletown Villas EX14 . . . . .166 C4
Littleway EX2 . . . . .176 F3
Little Week Cl EX7 . . . . .200 F1
Little Week Gdns EX7 . . . . .200 F1
Little Week La EX7 . . . . .200 F1
Little Week Rd EX7 . . . . . . .200 F1
Little Wiveliscombe La
TA4 . . . . .35 D6
Littlewood Cl PL7 . . . . .251 A4
Livarot Wlk EX36 . . . . .158 B4
Livaton Cross EX20 . . . . .95 D4
Livermead Hill TQ2 . . . . . . .219 E2
Livermore Rd EX14 . . . . . . .166 C5
Liverpool Hill EX4 . . . . .176 E7
Liverton Bsns Pk EX8 . . . . . .196 F1
Liverton Cl EX8 . . . . .202 E8
Liverton Cl TQ12 . . . . .180 A1
Liverton Hill EX18 . . . . .197 B1
Livery Dole Almshouses
EX2 . . . . .177 E5
Living Coasts TQ1 . . . . .220 B3
Livingshayes Rd EX5 . . . . . . .82 C6
Livingstone Ave EX8 . . . . . .141 B8
Livingstone Rd TQ14 . . . . . .210 C6
Livonia Rd EX10 . . . . .188 B6
Lixton Pk PL21 . . . . .137 F1
Lizard Cl PL6 . . . . .244 F7
Lizard Wlk PL6 . . . . .245 A7
Lloyd Ave TQ2 . . . . .219 D7
Lloyd Maunder Rd EX15 . . .162 C5
Lloyds Cres EX1 . . . . .178 C8
Lloyds Ct EX1 . . . . .178 C8
Loatmead Cross EX22 . . . . . .38 B3
Lobbthorn Stile EX33 . . . . . . .8 B1
Locarno Ave TQ3 . . . . .219 D1
Locarno Rd EX4 . . . . .176 F4
Lockeridge Rd PL20 . . . . . . .125 E1
Lockfield Ct EX2 . . . . .177 B1
Lockington Ave PL3 . . . . . . .248 F7
Lock La EX31 . . . . .10 E4
Lock Lane Cross EX31 . . . . . .10 F3
Locks Cl
Braunton EX33 . . . . .152 D5
Torquay TQ1 . . . . .220 D7
Locksey's La EX12 . . . . .190 D6
Lock's Gate Cross TQ13 . . .129 F8
Locks Hill TQ1 . . . . .220 D7
Locksley Cl
Exeter EX2 . . . . .182 A8
Torquay TQ1 . . . . .220 A7
Locksley Grange TQ1 . . . . . .220 A7
Locks Wlk PL1 . . . . .247 E1
Lockyer Ave EX10 . . . . .188 C8
Lockyer Cres EX16 . . . . .161 A6
Lockyer Ct PL1 . . . . .262 C2
Lockyer Mews PL19 . . . . . . .171 C6
Lockyer Rd PL3 . . . . .248 E5
Lockyers Quay PL4 . . . . . . .263 B2
Lockyer St PL1 . . . . .262 C2
Lockyer Terr PL12 . . . . .243 A3
Loddiswell Butts TQ7 . . . . .143 E8
Loddiswell Prim Sch
TQ7 . . . . .143 F7
Lodge Cl TA21 . . . . .160 D6
Lodge Cnr EX31 . . . . .27 D8
Lodge Cross
Chulmleigh EX18 . . . . .45 A1
Plymouth PL6 . . . . .98 E1
Lodge Gdns PL6 . . . . .244 E3
Lodge Hill
Exeter EX4 . . . . .177 A8
Okehampton EX20 . . . . . . .170 B5
Lodge La
Axminster EX13 . . . . .88 B2
Bratton Fleming EX31 . . . . . .18 E8
Bruton PL8 . . . . .256 F5
Shute EX13 . . . . .103 A8
Lodge Rd EX16 . . . . .161 E4
Lodge The EX17 . . . . .165 A6
Lodge Trad Est EX16 . . . . . .175 E3
Lofoten Cl PL1 . . . . .247 E2
Loftus Gdns PL5 . . . . .243 C2
Logan Rd TQ3 . . . . .226 C7
Logan Way EX15 . . . . .162 D5
Lolesbury Cross PL8 . . . . . .136 A1
Lollabury Rd PL12 . . . . .242 E3
Lombard Cl EX39 . . . . .25 D4
London Ct TQ2 . . . . .237 D5
London Inn Sq EX1 . . . . . . .261 B3
Longacre PL7 . . . . .250 B7
Long Acre Cl TQ2 . . . . .242 B4
Long Acre EX5 . . . . .261 C2
Long Barton 6 TQ12 . . . . . .123 F1
Longbridge Cl PL6 . . . . .249 F6
Long Bridge Cross EX31 . . . .87 B8
Longbridge Meadow Trad Est
EX15 . . . . .163 D4
Longbridge Rd
Plymouth, Laira PL3 . . . . . .249 C4
Plymouth, Longbridge PL6 . .249 E7
Longbridge Wharf 14
EX39 . . . . .157 A1
Longbrook TQ7 . . . . .145 A1

Longbrook Barton PL7 . . . . 250 D5
Longbrook Cl PL21 . . . . 237 B5
Longbrook La EX8 . . . . 195 F4
Longbrook Rd PL21 . . . . . . 237 B5
Longbrook St
Exeter EX4 . . . . 261 B4
Plymouth PL7 . . . . 250 F4
Longbrook Terr EX4 . . . . . . 261 B4
Longcause PL7 . . . . 250 F4
Longcause Com Specl Sch
PL7 . . . . 250 F4
Longcause Cross TQ9 . . . . 223 A7
Longcombe Cross TQ9 . . . . 224 C5
Long Copp EX9 . . . . 198 A2
Longcroft Ave TQ5 . . . . 230 B3
Longcroft Dr TQ5 . . . . 230 B3
Long Cross
Dartmouth TQ6 . . . . 233 C3
South Pool TQ7 . . . . 148 F7
Longcross Cotts PL19 . . . . 116 C6
Longdogs Cl EX11 . . . . 169 E3
Longdogs La EX11 . . . . 169 E3
Long Down Gdns PL6 . . . . . 245 E3
Longdown Rd EX2, EX6 . . . 176 B3
Long Drag EX15 . . . . 65 C3
Longdrag Hill EX16 . . . . . . 161 A4
Long Entry DT7 . . . . 260 C3
Longfield
[11] Appledore EX39 . . . . . . 15 A1
Lutton PL21 . . . . 133 B1
Longfield Ave TQ12 . . . . . . 207 F8
Longfield Cl
Braunton EX33 . . . . 152 E5
Lutton PL21 . . . . 133 B2
Longfield Dr TQ8 . . . . 259 C5
Longfield Est EX6 . . . . 201 A8
Longfield Pl PL4 . . . . 263 B4
Longfields TQ7 . . . . 258 A4
Longfield Terr [8] EX34 . . . 150 C5
Longfield Villas PL9 . . . . . 255 D8
Longford Cross TQ12 . . . . 207 E8
Longford Down Head
PL21 . . . . 137 F6
Longford La TQ12 . . . . 207 E8
Longford Pk TQ12 . . . . 207 E8
Longforth Rd TA21 . . . . . . 160 D6
Long-Go La EX14 . . . . 84 E8
Long Hill EX12 . . . . 191 D5
Long Holcombe Cross
EX36 . . . . 20 A6
Long La
Appledore EX39 . . . . 14 F1
Ashford EX31 . . . . 16 B6
Barnstaple EX31 . . . . 154 A8
Calverleigh EX16 . . . . 48 D2
Combe Martin EX31, EX34 . . 3 C1
Dawlish EX7 . . . . 200 B1
Exmouth EX8 . . . . 202 C6
Georgeham EX33 . . . . 8 B1
Newton Abbot TQ12 . . . . 208 B1
Northam EX39 . . . . 157 A8
Shaldon TQ14 . . . . 209 C4
Tiverton EX16 . . . . 161 A7
Wolverstone EX14 . . . . . . 85 B8
Longland Cl EX32 . . . . 17 B5
Longland Cross TQ9 . . . . . 227 C3
Longland La EX33 . . . . 8 A2
Longlands
Dawlish EX7 . . . . 204 D6
Plymouth PL9 . . . . 255 D8
Longlands Cross
Ashwater EX21 . . . . 90 E6
Corfcott Green EX22 . . . . . 71 F2
Longlands Dr PL9 . . . . 140 A8
Longlands La PL12 . . . . . . 242 B1
Long Ley PL3 . . . . 249 B6
Long Mdw
Plymouth PL7 . . . . 250 D7
South Brent TQ10 . . . . . . 134 F2
Longmead
Hemyock EX15 . . . . 67 B8
Huish Champflower TA4 . . . 35 E8
Lynton EX35 . . . . 151 A5
Longmead Cl TQ1 . . . . 160 B8
Longmead Cotts TA21 . . . . 160 B8
Longmead La EX20 . . . . . . 76 F4
Longmeadow
Budlake EX5 . . . . 82 E1
Tiverton EX16 . . . . 161 D5
Long Meadow EX5 . . . . . . 184 C3
Longmeadow Cl PL7 . . . . . 250 E7
Long Meadow Dr EX32 . . . 155 B6
Longmeadow Rd
Lympstone EX8 . . . . 195 F5
Saltash PL12 . . . . 242 E3
Longmeadows EX17 . . . . . 165 D6
Longmead Rd TQ3 . . . . . . 218 F1
Longmead Wlk TQ3 . . . . . 218 F1
Long Moor
Cullompton EX15 . . . . . . 163 F6
Willand EX15 . . . . 162 E1
Long Orch PL20 . . . . 125 E1
Long Park Cl PL9 . . . . 255 F5
Long Park Dr PL6 . . . . 245 D7
Longpark Hill TQ1 . . . . . . 214 C6
Long Park Rd PL12 . . . . . . 242 D2
Long Pk
Ashburton TQ13 . . . . 131 A5
Modbury PL21 . . . . 137 B3
Woodbury EX5 . . . . 184 C3
Longpot La EX31 . . . . 17 D8
Long Ragg Ct EX13 . . . . . . 167 D5
Long Rd
Paignton TQ4 . . . . 225 D1

Long Rd continued
Saltash PL12 . . . . 242 B4
Long Rowden PL3 . . . . 248 E6
Long Rydon TQ9 . . . . 227 F8
Longstone Ave PL6 . . . . . . 245 A6
Longstone Cross [1]
TQ13 . . . . 131 A5
Longstone Rd TQ4 . . . . . . 225 E4
Long Terrace Cl [5] PL7 . . 251 C5
Longthorn Rd TQ13 . . . . . 124 B4
Longview Rd PL12 . . . . . . 242 D3
Longview Terr PL3 . . . . . . 249 B7
Long Walk Dr EX2 . . . . 29 C6
Longwood Cl PL7 . . . . 251 A4
Longwood La TA21 . . . . . . 51 C4
Longwool Mdw EX23 . . . . 70 A6
Long Wools TQ4 . . . . 229 D7
Lonsdale Rd
Exeter EX1 . . . . 178 B5
Newton Abbot TQ12 . . . . 207 D2
Loo Cross TQ7 . . . . 144 F1
Looe Rd EX4 . . . . 177 A7
Looe St PL4 . . . . 263 A2
Lookout Cotts EX31 . . . . . . 16 B6
Loosecall La TA22 . . . . 33 D8
Loosebeare Cross
Zeal Monachorum EX17 . . 78 B8
Zeal Monachorum EX17 . . 78 C8
Loosebeare La EX17 . . . . 78 B8
Looseland Cross EX19 . . . . 58 B4
Looseland Cross EX16 . . . . 47 D1
Looseleigh Cl PL6 . . . . . . 245 A4
Looseleigh La PL6 . . . . . . 244 F5
Lopes Cres EX20 . . . . 170 C5
Lopes Dr PL6 . . . . 241 C1
Lopes Rd
Dousland PL20 . . . . 127 B3
Plymouth PL2 . . . . 248 B6
Lopwell Cl PL6 . . . . 244 F5
Loram Way EX2 . . . . 181 C8
Lord Louis Cres PL9 . . . . . 254 F6
Lord Mamhead Homes
EX2 . . . . 177 E4
Lords Meadow La [5]
EX16 . . . . 34 B1
Lords Pl TQ1 . . . . 220 B6
Lords Way EX2 . . . . 178 C4
Loretto Gdns EX13 . . . . . . 167 C5
Loretto Rd EX13 . . . . 167 E5
Loring Rd TQ8 . . . . 259 D4
Lorrie Dr TQ14 . . . . 210 B6
Lorrimore Ave PL2 . . . . . . 247 F5
Lotherton Cl PL7 . . . . 251 B3
Lotus Cotts TQ9 . . . . 227 F7
Loughboro Rd PL5 . . . . . . 243 C1
Loughborough EX16 . . . . . 161 B5
Loughwood La EX13 . . . . . 87 B2
Louisa Gate TA22 . . . . 33 F7
Louisa Pl EX8 . . . . 202 A5
Louisa Terr EX8 . . . . 202 A5
Louise Terr EX38 . . . . 159 C5
Louis Way EX14 . . . . 67 C1
Louvigny Cl EX14 . . . . 84 E2
Louville Cl TQ4 . . . . 226 C2
Lovacott Cross EX31 . . . . . 153 F2
Lovacott School Cross
EX31 . . . . 27 A6
Love La
Ashburton TQ13 . . . . 130 F4
Bickington TQ12 . . . . 131 D7
Bideford EX39 . . . . 156 E1
Colyton EX24 . . . . 103 A4
Marldon TQ3 . . . . 218 D4
Saltash PL12 . . . . 242 E2
Lovelace Cres EX8 . . . . . . 202 D8
Lovelace Gdns EX2 . . . . . 182 B8
Loveland Cross EX20 . . . . . 74 C1
Love Lane Cl TQ3 . . . . 218 D4
Lovell Cl EX8 . . . . 196 C3
Lovell Rd PL3 . . . . 248 F6
Loventor Cres TQ3 . . . . . . 218 D2
Loventor La TQ3, TQ9 . . . . 217 F3
Loveridge La TA20 . . . . 88 D8
Lovering Cl EX8 . . . . 196 C3
Loverings Ct [4] EX31 . . . 154 F5
Low Brook EX5 . . . . 99 C2
Lower Albert St EX1 . . . . . 261 C3
Lower Aller La TQ13 . . . . . 122 E6
Lower Almshouses [2]
EX31 . . . . 154 F6
Lower Anderton Rd PL10 . 252 F5
Lower Argyll Rd EX4 . . . . 173 A2
Lower Audley Rd TQ2 . . . . 219 F8
Lower Ave EX1 . . . . 177 E6
Lower Biteford Cross
EX39 . . . . 38 B6
Lower Blagdon Cross
TQ3 . . . . 225 B6
Lower Blagdon La TQ3 . . . 225 C6
Lower Brand La EX14 . . . . 166 C4
Lower Brimley Cl [2]
TQ14 . . . . 210 C5
Lower Brimley Rd TQ14 . . 210 C5
Lower Broad Oak Rd
EX11 . . . . 168 E4
Lower Broad Path TQ9 . . . 228 A7
Lower Broad Rd TQ6 . . . . . 233 D8
Lower Brookfield Cotts
TQ13 . . . . 122 C8
Lower Brook Mdw [2]
EX10 . . . . 101 B1
Lower Brook Rd PL21 . . . . 237 A5
Lower Brook St [13] TQ14 . 210 C5
Lower Budleigh EX9 . . . . . 198 B5
Lower Budleigh Mdw
TQ12 . . . . 206 F3

Lower Bulkamore Cross
TQ10 . . . . 135 E5
Lower Bulworthy Gate
EX16 . . . . 47 D4
Lower Bulworthy La EX16 . 47 D4
Lower Burston EX17 . . . . . 78 B5
Lower Burwood Rd EX38 . 159 C5
Lower Cannon Rd TQ12 . . 123 B2
Lower Church St
[5] Barnstaple EX32 . . . . . 155 A4
Colyton EX24 . . . . 103 A5
Lower Cl EX16 . . . . 65 A7
Lower Claypark EX34 . . . . . 7 F7
Lower Cleave
Braunton EX33 . . . . 152 C7
Northam EX39 . . . . 157 B5
Lower Cloister Wlk EX6 . . 181 F5
Lower Cobbaton EX37 . . . . 28 C5
Lower Collapark TQ9 . . . . 223 B6
Lower Collins Rd TQ9 . . . . 223 B6
Lower Compton Rd PL3 . . 248 F5
Lower Congella Rd TQ1 . . 220 C6
Lower Contour Rd TQ6 . . . 234 B3
Lower Cookworthy Cross
PL16 . . . . 106 A6
Lower Coombe La EX16 . . . 63 F4
Lower Coombe Rd TQ12 . . 207 F7
Lower Coombe St EX1 . . . 261 A2
Lower Coombses TA20 . . . 88 D8
Lower Cotteylands EX16 . . 161 B3
Lower Court Rd PL8 . . . . . 140 F7
Lower Crooked Mdw
EX20 . . . . 170 C5
Lower Cross EX16 . . . . 51 C1
Lower Cross Rd EX31 . . . . 154 B4
Lowerdale Turn TQ9 . . . . . 144 B8
Lower Dawlish Water Rd
EX7 . . . . 204 A7
Lower Dean Cross EX31 . . . 3 F2
Lower Dean La EX34 . . . . . . 3 B3
Lowerdown TQ13 . . . . 122 D5
Lower Dr EX7 . . . . 204 F8
Lower Duck St EX36 . . . . . 182 B3
Lower East St EX36 . . . . . . 30 E8
Lower Ellacombe Church Rd
TQ1 . . . . 220 C6
Lower Erith Rd TQ1 . . . . . 220 D4
Lower Fairview Rd TQ6 . . 233 E3
Lower Farm Rd PL7 . . . . . 251 A4
Lower Farthings EX10 . . . 186 F8
Lower Fern Rd TQ12 . . . . . 212 F8
Lower Forches Cross
EX17 . . . . 60 D4
Lower Fore St
[3] Exmouth EX8 . . . . . . 202 A6
Saltash PL12 . . . . 243 A2
Lower Fowden TQ4 . . . . . . 229 D6
Lower Foxmoor Rd TA21 . 160 B5
Lower French Pk TQ12 . . . 206 F4
Lower Fyldon Cross EX36 . 19 C4
Lower Gaydon St [1]
EX32 . . . . 155 A5
Lower Green Cross TQ7 . . 145 C4
Lower Griggs EX10 . . . . . 188 D7
Lower Gunstone EX39 . . . 157 A2
Lower Harrington La
EX4 . . . . 174 C1
Lower Hill Barton Rd
EX1 . . . . 178 C6
Lower Hollicombe Cotts
TQ3 . . . . 219 D1
Lower Kelly PL18 . . . . 125 D3
Lower King's Ave EX4 . . . 177 D8
Lower Kingsdown Rd
TQ14 . . . . 209 D7
Lower Kinsman's Dale
TQ13 . . . . 111 F5
Lower Knowle Rd TQ13 . . 122 D7
Lower La
Chulmleigh EX18 . . . . 59 C8
Dalwood EX13 . . . . 87 B2
Ebford EX3 . . . . 183 C4
[6] Plymouth PL1 . . . . . . 263 A2
Sampford Courtenay EX20 78 D6
Lower Ladram La EX9 . . . 199 A7
Lower Lodfin EX16 . . . . . . 34 B2
Lower Lowton La EX16 . . . 112 C6
Lower Manor Rd TQ5 . . . . 230 C5
Lower Marlpits Hill
EX14 . . . . 166 D4
Lower Meadow Rise
EX7 . . . . 204 C6
Lower Meddon St [9]
EX39 . . . . 157 A1
Lower Millhayes EX15 . . . . 67 C8
Lower Mill La EX15 . . . . . 163 C3
Lower Moor EX32 . . . . 155 D4
Lower Moor Way EX15 . . . . 64 D8
Lower Northcote Rd
EX14 . . . . 166 E7
Lower North St EX4 . . . . . 261 A3
Lower Park EX37 . . . . 28 D2
Lower Park Dr PL9 . . . . . . 255 C6
Lower Park Rd EX33 . . . . . 152 E5
Lower Penns Rd TQ3 . . . . 219 C1
Lower Pk [2] TQ3 . . . . 226 A7
Lower Polsham Rd TQ3 . . 226 C7
Lower Port View PL12 . . . 242 F2
Lower Preston TQ12 . . . . . 123 D1
Lower Preston Cross
TQ9 . . . . 138 E2
Lower Raleigh Rd EX31 . . 155 A7
Lower Rd EX5 . . . . 184 B7
Lower Rea Rd TQ5 . . . . . . 230 D5
Lower Ridings PL7 . . . . . . 251 B7
Lower Row PL10 . . . . 253 A2
Lower St German's Rd
EX4 . . . . 177 C8

Lower Saltram PL9 . . . . . . 255 C7
Lower Shapter St EX3 . . . 182 F4
Lower Shirburn Rd TQ1 . . 220 A7
Lowerside PL2 . . . . 248 A8
Lower St
Chagford TQ13 . . . . 111 A6
Dartmouth TQ6 . . . . 233 F3
Dittisham TQ6 . . . . 228 B3
Plymouth PL4 . . . . 263 A3
West Alvington TQ7 . . . . . 258 A4
Lower Summerlands
EX1 . . . . 261 C3
Lower Tamar Terr PL18 . . 125 D7
Lower Terr EX22 . . . . 38 E1
Lower Thurlow Rd TQ1 . . 220 A6
Lower Tidderson Cross
EX16 . . . . 47 E4
Lower Town
Halberton EX16 . . . . 65 A7
Malborough TQ7 . . . . 147 E6
Sampford Peverell EX16 . . 50 D1
Stoke Climsland PL17 . . . 115 C1
Winkleigh EX19 . . . . 58 F2
Woolfardisworthy EX39 . . 38 F7
Lowertown Cotts TQ9 . . . 223 C6
Lower Union La TQ2 . . . . . 220 B5
Lower Union Rd TQ7 . . . . 258 C5
Lower Warberry Rd TQ1 . . 220 C4
Lower Warcombe Cross
TQ7 . . . . 144 A6
Lower Warren Rd TQ7 . . . 258 D3
Lower Way EX10 . . . . 187 A8
Lower Wear Rd EX2 . . . . . 182 B8
Lower Westlake Rd
EX31 . . . . 154 A2
Lower Wheathill EX10 . . . 188 B8
Lower Winsham Rd EX33 . . 8 E1
Lower Woodfield Rd
TQ1 . . . . 220 C4
Lower Woodhayes Ct EX5 . 99 F2
Lower Yalberton Rd TQ4 . 225 C2
Lowley Brook Ct TQ2 . . . . 219 B8
Lowseater Ho EX4 . . . . . . 176 F6
Lowley Brook Ct TQ2 . . . . 219 B8
Lowman Rd EX16 . . . . 50 B2
Lowman Units EX16 . . . . . . 64 D8
Lowman Way EX15 . . . . 64 D8
Lowmoor Ind Est TA21 . . 160 B8
Lownard Cross TQ9 . . . . . 222 E8
Low Rd PL9 . . . . 140 D8
Lowton Cross EX20 . . . . . . 77 D7
Lowton La EX16 . . . . 112 E6
Lowtrow Cross TA4 . . . . . . 35 A8
Loxbury Rd TQ2 . . . . 219 D4
Loxbury Rise TQ2 . . . . 219 D5
Loxdown Rd EX39 . . . . 41 A7
Loxhore Cross EX31 . . . . . 17 D7
Lucas Ave EX4 . . . . 177 D8
Lucas La PL7 . . . . 250 D6
Lucas Terr PL4 . . . . 249 B2
Lucerne [1] TQ1 . . . . 220 D4
Lucius St TQ2 . . . . 219 F5
Luckham's La TQ7 . . . . . . 147 E6
Lucky La EX2 . . . . 261 B2
Lucombe Ct EX4 . . . . 261 C4
Lucombe Oaks EX5 . . . . . 179 B6
Ludbrook Gate PL21 . . . . 137 C5
Ludlow Rd [2] PL3 . . . . . . 248 E5
Ludwell La EX2 . . . . 178 A3
Lufflands Cvn Pk EX22 . . . 53 E4
Lugsmoor La EX10 . . . . . . 189 E7
Lugworthy Cross EX21 . . . 91 B5
Lukesland Gardens PL21 237 E8
Luke St EX14 . . . . 84 B1
Lulworth Cl TQ4 . . . . 225 F2
Lulworth Dr PL6 . . . . 245 B7
Lumley Cl EX6 . . . . 194 D3
Lummaton Cross TQ2 . . . 214 A2
Lummaton Pl TQ2 . . . . . . 214 B1
Lundy Cl
Barnstaple EX32 . . . . 155 C5
Plymouth PL6 . . . . 244 F7
Lundy View EX39 . . . . 156 E6
Lurley Cross EX16 . . . . 48 E2
Luscombe Cl
Ipplepen TQ12 . . . . 211 D1
Ivybridge PL21 . . . . 237 A4
Luscombe Cres TQ3 . . . . . 225 E6
Luscombe Terr [2] EX7 . . 204 D6
Luson Cross PL8 . . . . 136 C1
Lustleigh Cl EX2 . . . . 181 C8
Lusways Ct EX10 . . . . 188 C4
Lutehouse La EX19 . . . . . . 58 E3
Lutsford Cross EX39 . . . . . 37 D6
Lutterburn St PL21 . . . . . 137 D6
Lutyens Dr TQ3 . . . . 225 D7
Lutyens Fold PL19 . . . . . . 116 A6
Luxmore Cl PL6 . . . . 245 E1
Luxmore Way EX20 . . . . . 170 D6
Luxton Cl EX21 . . . . 73 E3
Luxton Ct EX15 . . . . 163 C3
Luxton La EX20 . . . . 77 B8
Luxton Moor La EX20 . . . . 59 A1
Luxton Rd TQ12 . . . . 211 F8
Luxtons PK EX11 . . . . 169 C2
Lwr Bull Ring EX15 . . . . . 163 C3
Lych Cl PL9 . . . . 255 A6
Lychgate Pk EX17 . . . . 79 A5
Lydacott Cross EX31 . . . . 153 F3
Lydcot Wlk PL6 . . . . 245 A1
Lyddicleave EX31 . . . . 154 A3
Lyddon Cl TA21 . . . . 160 D4

Lydford Castle & Saxon Town
EX20 . . . . 107 E3
Lydford Cl PL21 . . . . 237 D4
Lydford Gorge EX20 . . . . . 107 E3
Lydford Ho TQ12 . . . . 207 F4
Lydford Park Rd PL3 . . . . 248 D5
Lydford Prim Sch EX20 . . 107 F4
Lydgates Rd EX12 . . . . . . 192 A6
Lyd Gdns PL19 . . . . 171 D5
Lydia Cl EX10 . . . . 186 D8
Lydiate La EX35 . . . . 5 A5
Lydia Way PL4 . . . . 263 B4
Lydon La TA4 . . . . 35 D5
Lydwell Park Rd TQ1 . . . . 220 E5
Lydwell Rd TQ1 . . . . 220 D6
Lye La EX14 . . . . 87 A8
Lym Cl DT7 . . . . 260 D3
Lyme Bay Ct [3] DT7 . . . . 260 E3
Lyme Bay Holiday Village
EX12 . . . . 192 B5
Lyme Bay Rd TQ14 . . . . . 210 C7
Lymebourne Ave EX1 . . . . 178 A6
Lymebourne La EX10 . . . . 188 B6
Lymebourne Ho EX10 . . . 188 B6
Lymebourne Pk EX10 . . . 188 B6
Lyme Cl EX13 . . . . 167 D5
Lyme Mews [10] EX12 . . . 192 B4
Lyme Regis Sch
Axminster EX13 . . . . 167 E5
Uplyme DT7 . . . . 104 B5
Lyme Regis Ind Est DT7 . 260 C4
Lyme Regis Philpot Mus
DT7 . . . . 260 E3
Lyme St EX13 . . . . 167 D6
Lyme View Cl TQ1 . . . . . . 220 D7
Lyme View Rd TQ1 . . . . . 220 D7
Lymington Rd TQ1 . . . . . . 220 A6
Lympne Ave PL5 . . . . 243 F5
Lympstone CE Prim Sch
EX8 . . . . 195 E5
Lympstone Commando Sta
EX8 . . . . 195 C8
Lympstone Ct EX4 . . . . . . 150 B6
Lympstone Village Sta
EX8 . . . . 195 D5
Lynbridge Ct [5] PL19 . . . 171 B5
Lynbridge Hill EX35 . . . . 151 B3
Lynbridge Rd EX35 . . . . . 151 C4
Lynbro Rd EX31 . . . . 154 F7
Lynch Cl
Axminster EX13 . . . . 167 D7
Thorverton EX5 . . . . 81 E5
Lynch Head TQ10 . . . . . . 100 C1
Lyncombe Cl EX4 . . . . . . 173 E1
Lyncombe Cres TQ1 . . . . 220 E3
Lyncourt TQ1 . . . . 220 D3
Lyndale Rd TQ12 . . . . 207 D8
Lyndhurst Ave TQ12 . . . . 213 A5
Lyndhurst Cl
Kingskerswell TQ12 . . . . 213 A6
Plymouth PL2 . . . . 248 C6
Lyndhurst Rd
Exeter EX4 . . . . 177 E5
Exmouth EX8 . . . . 202 A8
Plymouth PL2 . . . . 248 C6
Lyndon Ct PL12 . . . . 242 D4
Lyndrick Rd PL3 . . . . 248 E7
Lyneham Cross TQ13 . . . 123 B6
Lyn Gr TQ12 . . . . 212 F6
Lyngrove Ct TQ12 . . . . . . 212 F6
Lynhayes EX13 . . . . 87 C1
Lynher Ct PL12 . . . . 242 F1
Lynher Dr PL12 . . . . 242 F1
Lynher St PL5 . . . . 243 D2
Lynhurst Ave EX1 . . . . . . 154 C4
Lyn La EX35 . . . . 151 D3
Lynmouth Ave TQ4 . . . . . 225 F2
Lynmouth Cl PL7 . . . . . . 250 C7
Lynmouth Hill EX35 . . . . 151 C5
Lynton & Barnstaple Rly
EX31 . . . . 4 D3
Lynton CE Prim Sch
EX35 . . . . 151 C5
Lynton Cross EX34 . . . . 9 B6
Lynton & Exmoor Museum
EX35 . . . . 151 C5
Lynton & Lynmouth Cliff
Rlwy EX35 . . . . 151 C6
Lynton YH EX35 . . . . 151 C4
Lynway
Lynton EX35 . . . . 151 C5
Lynway Ct TQ1 . . . . 220 A7
Lynwood TQ12 . . . . 206 F1
Lynwood Ave
Exeter EX4 . . . . 177 A5
Plymouth PL7 . . . . 250 B6
Lyte La TQ7 . . . . 144 C1
Lyte's Rd TQ5 . . . . 230 D4
Lythe-Land Cross EX14 . . . 63 A6
Lytton Ho TQ7 . . . . 220 A4

M

Mabel Pl TQ4 . . . . 226 B5
MacAdam Rd PL4 . . . . . . 263 C1
MacAndrew Wlk PL21 . . . 237 E6
MacAulay Cres TQ12 . . . . 207 F6
MacAuley Cl EX14 . . . . . . 166 E6
Macey St PL11 . . . . 247 C3
Macey's Terr EX20 . . . . . . 170 B6
Machine Cross TA22 . . . . . 33 F6
Mackenzie Pl PL5 . . . . . . 243 C2
Mackenzie Way EX16 . . . 161 F4

Mackrell's Almshouses
TQ12 . . . . 207 A2
Maclins Cl EX36 . . . . . . 158 C4
Macwood Dr EX12 . . . . 192 A6
Madagascar Cl EX8 . . . . 202 E8
Maddacombe Cross
TQ12 . . . . 212 C4
Maddacombe Rd TQ12 . . 212 D4
Madden Rd PL1 . . . . . . 247 F2
Maddock Cl PL7 . . . . . . 251 A4
Maddock Dr PL7 . . . . . . 251 B4
Maddocks Cross EX22 . . . 38 D2
Madeira Cl EX8 . . . . . . 202 B5
Madeira Ct EX8 . . . . . . 202 B5
Madeira Pl PL1 . . . . . . 263 A1
Madeira Villas
Exmouth EX8 . . . . . . 202 A7
Horrabridge PL20 . . . 126 F5
Madeira Wlk EX9 . . . . . 199 H2
Madford Cross EX15 . . . . 67 C6
Madge Ct PL19 . . . . . . 171 B6
Madge La PL19 . . . . . . 171 B6
Madgeon La TA20 . . . . . 69 B8
Madges Cross
Aylesbeare EX5 . . . . . . 99 E2
Rockbeare EX5 . . . . . . 99 E6
Madicks Orch TQ9 . . . . 227 F8
Madison Ave EX1 . . . . . 178 A6
Madison Cl EX5 . . . . . . 173 F8
Madison Wharf EX8 . . . 201 E6
Madrepore Rd TQ1 . . . . 220 B4
Maer Bay Ct EX8 . . . . . 202 B5
Maer La EX8 . . . . 202 C5
Maer Rd EX8 . . . . 202 C5
Maer Top Way EX31 . . . 155 A7
Maer Vale EX8 . . . . 202 C6
Magdala Rd EX31 . . . . . 154 A3
Magdalen Bridge Ct
EX2 . . . . 261 B2
Magdalen Court Sch
EX2 . . . . 177 E5
Magdalen Cl TQ9 . . . . . 223 C5
Magdalene Lawn
EX32 . . . . 155 A6
Magdalene Rd TQ1 . . . . 220 A6
Magdalen Gdns
Exeter EX2 . . . . 177 E5
Plymouth PL2 . . . . . . 250 F3
Magdalen Rd EX2 . . . . . 261 C2
Magdalen St EX1, EX2 . . 261 B2
Magnolia Ave
Exeter EX2 . . . . 178 A3
Exmouth EX8 . . . . . . 202 E8
Magnolia Cl
Barnstaple EX32 . . . . 155 E4
Plymouth PL9 . . . . . . 251 B5
Magnolia Cl
Exmouth EX8 . . . . . . 202 B6
Plymouth PL9 . . . . . . 255 F7
Tiverton EX16 . . . . . . 161 E7
Magnolia Ho EX8 . . . . . 202 A6
Magnolia Wlk EX8 . . . . 202 A6
Magpie Cres EX2 . . . . . 176 D4
Magpie Hill TQ13 . . . . . 130 C4
Maida Vale Terr PL4 . . . 248 F4
Maidencombe Cross
TQ1 . . . . 214 C6
Maidencombe Ho TQ1 . . 214 C4
Maidenhayne La EX13 . . 103 D6
Maidenhead Cross EX16 . . 51 C2
Maiden St EX31 . . . . . . 154 F5
Maidenway La TQ3 . . . . 225 F8
Maidenway Rd TQ3 . . . . 225 F8
Maidenwell Rd PL7 . . . . 250 C5
Main Ave TQ1 . . . . 220 A8
Maine Cl EX39 . . . . 156 D2
Maine Gdns PL2 . . . . . . 247 F7
Main Rd
Exeter EX4 . . . . 174 E2
Salcombe TQ8 . . . . . . 259 C4
Mains Down La EX33 . . . . 8 A4
Main St TQ9 . . . . 139 E1
Mainstone Ave PL4 . . . . 263 C2
Maire Rd EX36 . . . . 46 E5
Maitland Dr PL3 . . . . . . 248 F8
Major Cross EX16 . . . . . 64 A2
Majorfield Rd EX3 . . . . . 182 F5
Major's Mdw EX20 . . . . 170 C5
Major Terr EX12 . . . . . . 192 A5
Maker La PL10 . . . . 253 B4
Maker Rd PL11 . . . . 247 A2
Maker View PL3 . . . . . . 248 B4
Malborough Gn TQ7 . . . 147 E6
Malborough Pk TQ7 . . . 147 F6
Malborough with South
Huish CE Prim Sch
TQ7 . . . . 147 E6
Malden Cl EX10 . . . . . . 188 B7
Malden La EX10 . . . . . . 188 B8
Malden Rd EX10 . . . . . . 188 C8
Malderek Ave TQ3 . . . . 219 C1
Mallands Mdw TQ12 . . . 212 A7
Mallard Cl
Plymouth PL7 . . . . . . 250 F5
Torquay TQ2 . . . . 213 D3
Mallard Rd EX2 . . . . . . 178 E5
Mallett La EX32 . . . . . . 155 A5
Mallingbrook Cross EX18 . 44 E1
Mallison Cl EX4 . . . . . . 176 F8
Mallock Rd TQ2 . . . . . . 219 E5
Mallocks Cl EX10 . . . . . 100 D3
Mallow Ct EX15 . . . . . . 162 D5
Malmesbury Cl PL2 . . . . 248 B8
Malory Cl PL5 . . . . 244 D2
Maison La EX16 . . . . . . 47 B4
Malston Cross TQ7 . . . . 144 D4

Malt Field EX8 . . . . 195 F5
Malthouse The
Bridgend PL8 . . . . . . 141 A7
Totnes TQ9 . . . . 223 D5
Malting Ct EX7 . . . . . . 204 E6
Maltings The
Appledore EX39 . . . . . 15 A1
Black Torrington EX21 . 74 A8
Crediton EX17 . . . . . . 165 D5
Exeter EX2 . . . . 177 F5
South Allington TQ7 . . 149 B5
Malt Mill TQ9 . . . . 223 B6
Malvern Gdns EX2 . . . . 178 A4
Malvernleigh TQ1 . . . . . 220 B8
Malvern Rd PL2 . . . . . . 248 B8
Malvern Way EX39 . . . . 156 D2
Mambury Cross EX22 . . . 39 D3
Mamhead Bsns Units
EX2 . . . . 181 D8
Mamhead Forest Wlks
EX6 . . . . 124 E7
Mamhead Rd
Exeter EX2 . . . . 178 C4
Kenton EX6 . . . . 194 C2
Mamhead View EX8 . . . 201 E6
Manadon Cl PL5 . . . . . . 244 E1
Manadon Dr PL5 . . . . . . 244 E1
Manadon Hill PL5, PL6 . . 244 F1
Manadon Vale Prim Sch
PL5 . . . . 248 E8
Manaton Cl EX2 . . . . . . 181 C8
Manaton Ct EX2 . . . . . . 181 C8
Manaton Tor Rd TQ3 . . 218 F1
Manby Gdns PL5 . . . . . . 243 F5
Manchester Rd EX8 . . . . 201 F6
Manchester St EX8 . . . . 201 F6
Mandrake Cl EX2 . . . . . 177 B1
Mandrake Rd EX2 . . . . . 177 A1
Manifold Gdns PL3 . . . . 249 D5
Manitoba Gdns EX15 . . . 163 B3
Manley Cl EX5 . . . . 99 E2
Manleys La EX14 . . . . . . 67 B2
Manna Ash Ct EX2 . . . . 261 C1
Mannacott La EX31 . . . . 4 C4
Mannacott Lane Head
EX31 . . . . 4 C4
Mannamead Ave PL3 . . . 248 F6
Mannamead Ct PL3 . . . . 248 F6
Mannamead Rd PL3 . . . 248 F6
Manning Ave EX15 . . . . 163 A2
Mannings Mdw TQ13 . . 180 D7
Mannings Way EX31 . . . 154 F7
Manor Ave
Lyme Regis DT7 . . . . . 260 D4
Paignton TQ3 . . . . . . 226 C8
Manor Bend TQ5 . . . . . . 229 C5
Manor Bourne Rd
Down Thomas PL9 . . . 255 C1
Heybrook Bay PL9 . . . 140 A8
Manor Cl
Abbotskerswell TQ12 . . 212 A7
Awliscombe EX14 . . . . 85 C3
Barnstaple EX31 . . . . 154 C3
Dawlish EX7 . . . . 204 D6
Fremington EX31 . . . . 153 C6
Ivybridge PL21 . . . . . 237 C5
Kingskerswell TQ12 . . 213 A3
Seaton EX12 . . . . 192 A5
Sidmouth EX10 . . . . . 188 A5
Tavistock PL19 . . . . . 171 A6
Uffculme EX15 . . . . . . 66 B8
Wrafton EX33 . . . . . . 152 E4
Manor Cotts
Newton Abbot TQ12 . . 207 B3
Rackenford EX16 . . . . . 47 C6
Manor Court Barns TQ7 . 147 F8
Manor Cres
Honiton EX14 . . . . . . 166 C4
Paignton TQ3 . . . . . . 226 C8
Manor Ct
Barnstaple EX32 . . . . 155 F1
Dawlish EX7 . . . . 204 D6
Galmpton TQ5 . . . . . . 229 A4
Kingskerswell TQ12 . . 213 A3
Landkey EX32 . . . . 17 B2
Paignton TQ3 . . . . . . 226 C7
Seaton EX12 . . . . 192 A5
South Brent TQ10 . . . 134 F3
Stoke Fleming TQ6 . . . 146 B7
Totnes TQ9 . . . . 219 F6
Manor Dr
Chagford TQ13 . . . . . 110 F6
Ivybridge PL21 . . . . . 237 C5
Kingskerswell TQ12 . . 213 A3
Manor East PL20 . . . . . 126 E4
Manor Farm EX20 . . . . . 127 B3
Manor Farm Camping & Cvn
Site EX12 . . . . 102 F2
Manor Farm Cl TA20 . . . 69 A8
Manor Farm Mews EX5 . . 99 E4
Manor Gdn TQ1 . . . . . . 220 E3
Manor Gdns
Abbotskerswell TQ12 . . 212 B6
Exbourne EX20 . . . . . . 76 C5
Halwill Junction EX21 . . 73 E2
Horrabridge PL20 . . . . 126 E4
Kingsbridge TQ7 . . . . 258 D6
Kingskerswell TQ12 . . 213 A3
Millbrook PL10 . . . . . 252 A6
Paignton TQ3 . . . . . . 226 C8
Plymouth PL1 . . . . . . 262 B2
Seaton EX12 . . . . 192 B5
Manorglade Ct TQ1 . . . 220 D5
Manor Gn EX14 . . . . 68 C2
Manor Ho
Lympstone EX8 . . . . . 195 D5
Torquay TQ1 . . . . 220 E3

Manor Ho The TQ9 . . . . 223 C6
Manor House Sch EX14 . 166 F5
Manor La PL3 . . . . 249 D5
Manor Mead TQ12 . . . . 131 D7
Manor Mill Rd EX33 . . . . 8 D1
Manor Park Cl PL7 . . . . 250 F5
Manor Park Dr PL7 . . . . 251 A4
Manor Pk
Ashwater EX21 . . . . . . 90 E6
Barnstaple EX31 . . . . 154 C3
Bradworthy EX22 . . . . 53 E8
Clyst St Mary EX5 . . . 179 A3
Dousland PL20 . . . . . 127 B3
Kingsbridge TQ7 . . . . 258 D6
Saltash PL12 . . . . 242 D2
Woolfardisworthy EX39 . 38 F8
Manor Prim Sch PL21 . . 237 C5
Manor Rd
Abbotskerswell TQ12 . . 212 B7
Bishopsteignton TQ14 . 208 F8
Chagford TQ13 . . . . . 110 F6
Exeter EX4 . . . . 177 A5
Landkey EX32 . . . . 17 B2
Newton Abbot TQ12 . . 206 F3
Paignton TQ3 . . . . . . 226 C8
Plymouth PL9 . . . . . . 255 A6
Seaton EX12 . . . . 192 A5
Sidmouth EX10 . . . . . 188 A3
Tavistock PL19 . . . . . 171 B6
Torquay TQ2 . . . . 220 C8
Manor St
Dittisham TQ6 . . . . . . 228 D2
Plymouth PL1 . . . . . . 262 A3
Manor Terr
Brixham TQ5 . . . . 230 C5
Paignton TQ3 . . . . . . 226 A5
Manor Vale Rd TQ5 . . . . 229 C5
Manor View TQ12 . . . . 207 A3
Manor Way
Ivybridge PL21 . . . . . 237 C5
Instow EX39 . . . . 15 B1
Mansands La TQ5 . . . . . 235 B8
Mansbridge Rd TQ9 . . . 223 E5
Manscombe Cl TQ2 . . . 219 D3
Manscombe Rd TQ2 . . . 219 D3
Mansfield Rd EX4 . . . . . 177 E8
Mansfield Terr EX9 . . . . 198 B2
Mansion Ho EX6 . . . . . . 181 F5
Mansion Ho The PL1 . . . 254 A8
Mansion House St TQ6 . 233 F3
Mansion Terr EX34 . . . . . 3 A3
Manston The PL21 . . . . 137 C8
Manston Cl PL5 . . . . . . 243 C5
Manston Ct TQ1 . . . . . . 220 C2
Manstone Ave
Sidmouth EX10 . . . . . 188 A7
Sidmouth EX10 . . . . . 188 B7
Manstone Cl EX10 . . . . 188 B7
Manstone La EX10 . . . . 188 B7
Manstone Mead EX10 . . 188 B8
Manstone Workshops
EX10 . . . . 188 B7
Manston Rd EX1 . . . . . . 177 E7
Manston Terr EX2 . . . . . 177 E5
Manstree Cross EX2 . . . 114 A6
Manstree Rd EX2 . . . . . 114 A6
Manstree Terr EX2 . . . . 114 C6
Mantle Gdns PL5 . . . . . 247 D8
Mantle St TA21 . . . . . . 160 C5
Maple Ave
Bovey Tracey TQ13 . . . 180 C4
Torpoint PL11 . . . . . . 247 A3
Maple Cl
Brixham TQ5 . . . . 230 A2
Chudleigh Knighton
TQ13 . . . . 123 C4
Honiton EX14 . . . . . . 85 C2
Kingsteignton TQ12 . . 207 E6
Plymouth PL6 . . . . . . 245 E6
Seaton EX12 . . . . 192 A5
Tavistock PL19 . . . . . 171 C3
Willand EX15 . . . . 162 C4
Maple Ct
Paignton TQ4 . . . . . . 226 B2
Plymouth PL6 . . . . . . 255 F7
Mapledene Cl TQ9 . . . . 227 F8
Maple Dr EX8 . . . . 196 D3
Maple Gr
Barnstaple EX31 . . . . 154 C3
Plymouth, Mutley PL4 . 248 D4
Plymouth, Plympton PL7 . 250 B5
Tiverton EX16 . . . . . . 161 D4
Maple Rd
Brixham TQ5 . . . . 230 A2
Broadclyst EX5 . . . . . 175 D6
Exeter EX4 . . . . 177 A5
Maples Ct EX32 . . . . . . 154 F6
Mapleton Cl TQ12 . . . . 206 F4
Maple Way PL6 . . . . 245 E7
Maple Wlk TQ2 . . . . 219 C8
Marber Cross TQ7 . . . . . 144 F6
Marchant's Cross PL20 . . 127 C1
Marchant's Way PL20 . . 127 C2
March Ct EX2 . . . . 170 B5
Marcombe Rd TQ2 . . . . 219 E5
Marcom Cl EX11 . . . . . . 169 E3
Marcus Rd
Dunkeswell EX14 . . . . 67 B2
Exmouth EX8 . . . . . . 196 D1
Marder's Bequest DT7 . . 260 D3
Mardle Way TQ11 . . . . . 236 B5
Mardle Way Bsns Pk
TQ11 . . . . 236 B5
Mardon Cl PL6 . . . . 245 D4
Mardon Cross EX6 . . . . 112 C4
Mardon Hill EX4 . . . . . . 173 B1
Mare Hill EX17 . . . . 61 C5

Mare La
Beer EX12 . . . . 191 B5
Middle Marwood EX31 . . 9 B1
Marepark Cross TQ7 . . . 144 D3
Marepark Gate EX20 . . . 77 C7
Marett Rd PL5 . . . . 243 F3
Margaret Cl
East Ogwell TQ12 . . . . 206 F1
Kingsteignton TQ12 . . 207 E2
Margaret Gdns TQ12 . . 207 F2
Margaret Pk PL3 . . . . . 248 E8
Margaret Rd
East Ogwell TQ12 . . . . 206 F1
Exeter EX4 . . . . 173 E1
Kingsteignton TQ12 . . 207 E7
Margaret St EX8 . . . . . 202 A6
Margrove Terr EX32 . . . 154 F6
Marguerite Cl TQ12 . . . 206 F4
Marguerite Rd EX16 . . . 161 F6
Marguerite Way TQ12 . . 213 A4
Marhamchurch CE Prim Sch
EX23 . . . . 70 A6
Mariansleigh Cross EX36 . 30 E1
Marina Cl TQ5 . . . . 230 E5
Marina Ct
Brixham TQ5 . . . . 230 F6
Exmouth EX8 . . . . . . 202 B5
Teignmouth TQ14 . . . 210 C4
Marina Dr TQ5 . . . . 230 E5
Marina Rd
Brixham TQ5 . . . . 230 E4
Plymouth PL5 . . . . . . 243 F3
Marina Terr PL4 . . . . . . 248 F4
Marina Way EX16 . . . . . 64 D7
Marine Aquarium & Cobb
History The DT7 . . . . . 260 D2
Marine Cres EX12 . . . . . 192 A4
Marine Ct
Budleigh Salterton EX9 . 199 H2
Instow EX39 . . . . 15 B1
Torpoint PL11 . . . . . . 247 B2
Marine Dr
Bigbury-on-S TQ7 . . . . 142 E3
Heybrook Bay PL9 . . . 140 A7
Paignton TQ3 . . . . . . 226 C7
Torpoint PL11 . . . . . . 247 B2
Marine Gdns TQ3 . . . . . 226 C8
Marine Mount TQ1 . . . . 221 A3
Marine Pde
Appledore EX39 . . . . . 15 A1
Budleigh Salterton EX9 . 199 H2
Dawlish EX7 . . . . 204 E5
Instow EX39 . . . . 15 B1
Lyme Regis DT7 . . . . . 260 D2
Paignton TQ3 . . . . . . 226 D8
Teignmouth TQ14 . . . 210 B3
Marine Pk TQ3 . . . . 226 C7
Marine Pl
Ilfracombe EX34 . . . . 150 B6
Seaton EX12 . . . . 192 A4
Marine Rd PL9 . . . . 255 B7
Mariners Cl EX33 . . . . . 152 D5
Mariners Ct
Brixham TQ5 . . . . 230 D5
Plymouth PL1 . . . . . . 254 A1
Mariner's Way TQ3 . . . . 218 F1
Mariner's Way EX39 . . . 15 A1
Marine Terr TQ14 . . . . . 210 B4
Marine Way EX8 . . . . . . 202 A8
Marions Way EX8 . . . . . 196 D3
Maristow Ave
Exmouth EX8 . . . . . . 196 B2
Maristow Cl PL6 . . . . . . 244 F5
Marist Way EX32 . . . . . 155 C2
Marjery Cross PL21 . . . . 237 A2
Marjorie Kelly Way PL21 . 237 D4
Marjory Wlk EX14 . . . . . 88 B7
Markadon Cotts EX39 . . . 22 E4
Markers EX15 . . . . 66 A7
Markers Pk EX14 . . . . . . 84 C4
Markers Rd EX15 . . . . . . 66 A7
Marker Way EX14 . . . . . 166 C5
Market Ave PL1 . . . . . . 262 B3
Market Cl
Bampton EX16 . . . . . . 34 B1
Brushford EX22 . . . . . 33 E4
Buckfastleigh TQ11 . . . 236 B5
Plymouth PL1 . . . . . . 248 A1
Market Pl
Bideford EX39 . . . . . . 157 A2
Burlescombe EX16 . . . 51 B4
Colyton EX24 . . . . . . 103 A5
Sidmouth EX10 . . . . . 188 B3
Willand EX15 . . . . 162 C5
Market St
Plymouth PL7 . . . . . . 250 D5
Tavistock PL19 . . . . . 171 C5
Market St
Axminster EX13 . . . . . 167 D6
Dartmouth TQ6 . . . . . 233 F3
Ilfracombe EX34 . . . . 150 B6
Plymouth PL1 . . . . . . 262 B2
Market St
Appledore EX39 . . . . . 15 A1
Barnstaple EX31 . . . . 154 F5
Brixham TQ5 . . . . 230 C5
Buckfastleigh TQ11 . . . 236 B5
Cawsand PL10 . . . . . . 253 A2
Crediton EX17 . . . . . . 165 D5
Dartmouth TQ6 . . . . . 233 F3
Exeter EX1, EX4 . . . . 261 A3
Exmouth EX8 . . . . . . 202 A6
Hatherleigh EX20 . . . . 75 C7

Market St *continued*
Ilfracombe EX34 . . . . 150 B6
Lynton EX35 . . . . 151 C5
Newton Abbot TQ12 . . 207 B3
North Tawton EX20 . . . 77 C4
Okehampton EX20 . . . 170 B5
Plymouth PL1 . . . . . . 248 A1
Salcombe TQ8 . . . . . . 259 E5
South Molton EX36 . . . 158 C4
Torquay TQ1 . . . . 220 B5
Yealmpton PL8 . . . . . 257 F4
Market Terr EX16 . . . . . 161 C4
Market Way
Chudleigh TQ13 . . . . . 123 E6
Plymouth PL1 . . . . . . 262 C3
Market Wlk
Newton Abbot TQ12 . . 207 B3
Tiverton EX16 . . . . . . 161 D4
Markham Cross EX2 . . . 114 B8
Markham La
Exeter EX2 . . . . 181 B7
Ide EX2 . . . . 114 C8
Marland Cross EX8 . . . . 136 B1
Marland Sch EX38 . . . . . 56 B8
Marland Terr EX39 . . . . 156 F1
Marlborough Cl
Exmouth EX8 . . . . . . 196 E2
Ilfracombe EX34 . . . . 150 B5
Musbury EX13 . . . . . . 103 D5
Saltash PL12 . . . . 242 F1
Marlborough Cross EX5 . 179 D6
Marlborough Ct
Bideford EX39 . . . . . . 157 A3
Exeter, Alphington EX2 . 181 B8
Exeter, Heavitree EX2 . . 177 E5
Marlborough Dr EX2 . . . 178 D5
Marlborough Pk EX34 . . 150 B5
Marlborough Pl TQ12 . . 207 A4
Marlborough Prim Sch
PL1 . . . . 247 E2
Marlborough Rd
Exeter EX2 . . . . 261 C2
Ilfracombe EX34 . . . . 150 C5
Musbury EX13 . . . . . . 103 D5
Plymouth PL4 . . . . . . 263 A4
Marlborough Row PL1 . . 247 E2
Marlborough St EX31 . . 154 F5
Marlborough Terr TQ13 . 180 C7
Marlborough Way EX14 . 150 A4
Marlcombe Cross EX14 . . 85 A6
Marldon Ave TQ3 . . . . . 226 A6
Marldon CE Prim Sch
TQ3 . . . . 218 D3
Marldon Cl PL5 . . . . 244 B3
Marldon Cross TQ3 . . . 218 D3
Marldon Cross Hill TQ3 . 218 D3
Marldon Gr TQ3 . . . . . . 218 D3
Marldon La TQ3 . . . . . . 218 B4
Marldon Rd
Paignton TQ3 . . . . . . 225 F8
Torquay TQ2 . . . . 219 B7
Marldon Way TQ3 . . . . 218 E2
Marlen Ct EX39 . . . . 25 C4
Marles The EX8 . . . . 196 C5
Marley Dr EX8 . . . . 196 D5
Marley Head TQ10 . . . . 135 C3
Marley Rd EX8 . . . . 196 C3
Marlow Cres PL16 . . . . 106 D1
Marlow Ct EX39 . . . . . . 156 D7
Marlowe Cl EX2 . . . . . . 177 F4
Marlow Gdns PL9 . . . . . 255 F5
Marlpit Cl EX12 . . . . . . 191 F7
Marlpit Cross EX14 . . . . 87 A6
Marlpit La EX12 . . . . . . 192 A5
Marlpits La EX13 . . . . . 166 C5
Marl Pk
Harbertonford TQ9 . . . 139 C7
Holne TQ11 . . . . 130 A3
Marmora Terr EX12 . . . 191 D5
Marnham Rd TQ1 . . . . . 220 B7
Marpool Cres EX8 . . . . . 202 C8
Marpool Hill EX8 . . . . . 202 B7
Marpool Prim Sch EX8 . 202 C8
Marridge Cross PL21 . . . 137 F5
Marrowbone Slip PL4 . . 263 B2
Marryat Gdns PL5 . . . . 244 E1
Marshall Cl
Tavistock PL16 . . . . . 171 D2
Tiverton EX16 . . . . . . 161 F3
Marshall Est Nature Trail The
EX39 . . . . 38 D5
Marshall Rd
Plymouth PL7 . . . . . . 250 A5
Tavistock PL19 . . . . . 171 D2
Marshalls Field PL21 . . . 237 D5
Marshalls Mead EX19 . . . 42 D1
Marsh Barton La EX5 . . 172 D8
Marsh Barton Rd EX2 . . 177 B3
Marsh Barton Trad Est
EX2 . . . . 177 C2
Marshbridge Cross TA22 . 33 C7
Marsh Cl PL6 . . . . 245 D8
Marshclose Hill TA22 . . . 21 E2
Marsh Cross EX14 . . . . . 85 B1
Marsh Dro EX13 . . . . . . 87 B2
Marsh End EX17 . . . . . . 165 F5
Marsh Green La EX5 . . . 99 C5
Marsh Green Rd E EX2 . . 177 C2

Marsh Green Rd N EX2....177 C2
Marsh Green Rd W EX2....177 C2
Marsh Hill
  Cheriton Fitzpaine EX16....63 A4
  Dulverton TA22.............33 C8
Mars Hill Way EX35....151 C5
Marsh La
  Bow EX17......................78 B5
  Calstock PL18............125 D3
  Cheriton Fitzpaine EX16....63 A4
  Chudleigh TQ13............123 F8
  Clyst St George EX3....183 B6
  Crediton EX17.............165 E5
  Instow EX39..................15 B1
  Newton St Cyres EX5.......98 F8
  North Molton EX36.........30 E6
  Seaton EX12................192 B7
  South Molton EX36.......158 F7
  West Charleton TQ7....144 C1
Marsh La Cross TQ13....123 F8
Marsh Mill Ct EX5.......172 F2
Marsh Mills PL6.........249 F7
Marsh Mills Pk PL6....249 F7
Marsh Mills Rta Pk EX5...249 F7
Marsh Mills Sta Pk PL7...250 A7
Marsh Rd
  Crediton EX17.............165 E5
  Newton Abbot TQ12....207 C4
  Newton Abbot TQ12....207 C4
  Seaton EX12................192 B5
Marston Cl EX7.............204 F7
Martinhoe Cross EX31.....4 E3
Martin La
  Plymouth, Barbican PL4..263 A2
  Plymouth, Millbay PL1...262 B2
Martin Rd EX32.............155 B5
Martins Bldgs **4** TA21...160 D5
Martins Cl
  Great Torrington EX38...159 F5
  Wellington TA21.........160 D5
Martins La EX16..........161 D4
Martin's La EX1, EX4....261 B3
Martin Rd EX2.............196 E2
Martin St PL1...............262 B2
Martlesham Pl PL5......243 F4
Mart The EX20............170 B5
Marven Cl DT7...........260 B6
Marwell Cross EX5.......142 E6
Marwood Cross EX5......99 B3
Marwood Cross EX38....159 D5
Marwood Hill Gdns EX31...16 C8
Marwood La EX5...........99 C3
Marwood Pl EX14.........166 D6
Marwood Prim Sch EX31...9 D1
Marwood's Cross TQ10...134 C1
Mary Arches St EX4.....261 A3
Mary Cross PL21..........137 C3
Mary Dean Ave PL5....244 C7
Mary Dean Cl PL5.......244 C7
Mary Dean's CE Prim Sch
  PL5..............................244 C7
Maryfield Ave EX7.......177 D8
Mary La **10** EX16.........34 B1
Maryland Gdns PL2....247 E7
Mary Rose Ho
  1 Honnycok EX15........67 B8
  Torquay TQ1...............220 D7
Mary Seacole Rd PL1...262 A3
Mary St PL1................180 D8
Mary Tavy & Brentor Com
  Prim Sch PL19............117 E6
Marythorne Rd **15** PL20...125 E1
Masefield Ave EX31....154 F7
Masefield Gdns PL5...244 B1
Masefield Rd EX14......178 C8
Masey Rd EX8............202 D8
Mashford Ave TQ6.....233 C4
Masons Row PL18........125 C6
Masterman Rd PL2....247 F4
Matford Ave EX2.........177 E4
Matford La EX2...........261 C1
Matford Mews EX2......181 D7
Matford Park Rd EX2...181 D8
Matford Rd EX2...........177 E4
Mathew Ho **2** TQ1....219 F6
Mathews Cl EX14........166 B4
Mathill Cl TQ5............230 B3
Mathill Rd TQ5...........230 B3
Maton Cl PL21............237 D4
Matthews Cross EX15...163 C3
Matthews Ct EX4.........174 D2
Matthew's Cl EX15......163 C3
Matthews Pas TQ7....258 C5
Mattiscombe Cross TQ7...145 B1
Mattys Cross EX14.......168 A8
Maudlin Dr TQ14.........210 B8
Maudlin Rd TQ9..........223 C5
Maudlins La PL19........171 A5
Maunder's Hill EX9.....198 E7
Maunsell Cl PL2.........247 F7
Maurice Cl PL7...........250 F4
Mavisdale PL2............247 F6
Mawes Ct PL18...........125 A5
Maxstoke Ct **4** TQ1...220 D5
Maxwell Rd PL4..........255 B8
Maybank Rd PL4........263 C3
Maybrook Dr PL12......242 D2
May Bldgs PL19..........255 D6
Mayfair EX16..............64 E8
Mayfair Cres PL6........245 B1
Mayfair Ho PL4...........263 A3

Mayfair Rd TQ12.........211 D2
Mayfield PL21............237 A4
Mayfield Cres TQ12....206 F3
Mayfield Dr EX8.........202 D6
Mayfield Rd
  Exeter, Pinhoe EX4.....174 E1
  Exeter, Wonford EX2...178 A5
Mayfield Sch
  Paignton TQ3.............226 C2
  Torquay TQ2..............214 B3
Mayflower Ave
  Exeter EX4.................173 D2
  Newton Abbot TQ12....207 F2
Mayflower Cl
  6 Brixham TQ5.........230 C3
  Plymouth PL2.............248 B5
Mayflower St PL1........262 C3
Maynarde Cl PL7.........251 B5
Maynard Pk PL20........125 C1
Maynard Sch The EX1...261 C3
Mayne Cl EX39.............75 B7
Mayor's Ave TQ6.........233 F4
May St EX4................261 C4
May Terr
  Plymouth PL4.............263 B3
  Sidmouth EX10..........188 B4
Maytree Cl EX21...........73 D3
Mazard Tree Hill
  Ash Mill EX36..............31 C1
  South Molton EX36.......46 C8
Mazzard Cl **9** EX32....17 B2
Mead Cl
  Cullompton EX15........163 B2
  Ivybridge PL21...........237 A6
  Paignton TQ3.............226 C7
Mead Cnr EX39.............37 A4
Meadcombe Rd TQ7....143 A1
Mead Cotts EX8..........202 F7
Meadcourt TQ13.........226 C7
Mead Cross TQ13........131 B6
Mead Dr TQ7..............143 A1
Meadfoot Cl TQ1.........220 F4
Meadfoot La TQ1.........220 D3
Meadfoot Grange TQ1...220 D3
Meadfoot La TQ1.........220 D3
Meadfoot Sea Rd TQ1...220 D3
Meadfoot Terr **2** PL4...248 F5
Meadhurst Ct EX10.....188 A3
Mead La
  Paignton TQ3.............226 C7
  Thurlestone TQ7.........143 A1
Meadow Ave EX12.......192 A6
Meadow Bank EX13......87 D1
Meadow Brook
  Barnstaple EX31.........154 B2
  Tavistock PL19...........171 A4
  18 Totnes TQ9........223 F5
Meadowbrook Cl EX4...176 E8
Meadow Bsns Pk EX17...165 F5
Meadow Cl
  Bratton Fleming EX32....18 A8
  Budleigh Salterton EX9...197 F1
  Clyst St Mary EX5.......179 E3
  Harberton TQ9...........222 D2
  Ilfracombe EX34.........150 B4
  Kingskerswell TQ12....212 F6
  Landkey EX32..............17 C1
  Lympstone EX8...........195 F5
  Newton Ferrers PL8....141 A7
  Ottery St Mary EX11....169 E4
  Plymouth PL7.............251 D4
  Saltash PL12..............242 F3
  Totnes TQ9................223 F5
Meadow Cotts TQ6.....228 C2
Meadow Court Barns
  TQ7.........................145 B1
Meadow Cres EX8........203 A6
Meadowcroft Dr TQ13...123 C1
Meadow Dr
  Brixton PL8................257 A4
  Newton Poppleford EX10...186 F8
  Saltash PL12..............242 D4
Meadowfield Pl PL7....251 B3
Meadow Gdns EX17....165 D5
Meadow Halt TQ12.....207 A1
Meadow La
  Croyde EX33..................7 E2
  Cullompton EX15........163 C2
  Instow EX39.................15 B1
Meadowlands
  Newton St Cyres EX5...98 F8
  Plymouth PL6.............245 D7
Meadow Lea EX5...........82 B6
Meadow Park Dr..........43 F3
Meadow Pk
  Barnstaple EX31.........154 B2
  Bideford EX39.............25 D4
  Brixham TQ5.............230 B5
  Dawlish EX7..............204 C7
  Marldon TQ3.............218 D3
  Molland EX36..............31 E7
  Plymouth PL6.............255 C5
  Shebbear EX21.............55 E4
  South Molton EX36.....158 C3
  Willand EX15.............162 C4
Meadow Pk Cvn Site
  TQ13.......................236 D6
Meadow Rd
  Barnstaple EX31.........154 E7

Meadow Rd continued
  Budleigh Salterton EX9...197 F1
  Seaton EX12...............192 A5
  Torquay TQ2..............219 E3
Meadow Rise
  Dawlish EX7...............204 C7
  Plymouth PL7.............251 A4
  Spreyton EX17.............96 A7
  Teignmouth TQ14.......124 E1
Meadows Cres EX14....166 C5
Meadows Edge EX6......97 B4
Meadowside
  Ashford EX31...............16 B6
  Chillington TQ7..........145 A1
  Plymouth PL9.............255 F7
Meadow Side TQ12.....207 A3
Meadowside Rd EX17...80 B5
Meadow St EX8..........202 A7
Meadows The
  Beer EX12.................191 D5
  Kingsteignton TQ12....207 F6
  St Dominick PL12.......125 A2
  Torpoint PL11............246 E4
  Yeoford EX17..............79 C2
Meadowstone Cl EX38...40 F5
Meadowsweet La **3**
  EX31.......................154 B3
Meadowsweet Pk PL12...242 C2
Meadow Vale EX20.......57 A7
Meadow View
  2 Bampton EX16........34 B1
  Bishops Nympton EX36...30 F2
  East Ogwell TQ12.......206 F1
  Hartland EX39.............22 D3
  Holsworthy EX22........164 C6
  Lympstone EX8...........195 F5
  Rackenford EX16..........47 D5
  Uffculme EX15.............66 A7
Meadow View Cl EX10...188 C5
Meadowview Rd EX6...196 E2
Meadow View Rd PL7...250 D5
Meadowville Ct EX39...157 A3
Meadow View Rd EX39...157 A3
Meadow Way
  Colaton Raleigh EX10...186 D3
  Exeter EX2................177 F5
  Gunn EX32...................17 F4
  Plymouth PL7.............250 D7
Mead Park Cl EX31......16 A3
Mead Pk EX31..............16 A3
Mead Rd TQ2.............219 D2
Mead The
  Plymouth PL7.............250 D7
  Silverton EX5...............82 B5
Mead View Rd EX14....166 C5
Meadville TQ1.............220 D3
Meadway
  Newton Abbot TQ12....212 D8
  Saltash PL12..............242 E1
  Sidmouth EX10..........188 A4
Mead Way EX12...........192 A6
Meadwood TQ1...........220 D3
Mear Top EX31...........154 F7
Measbury Moor Cross
  EX18..........................45 C5
Meatherel Cl PL21......237 B4
Meavy Ave
  Plymouth PL5.............244 E2
  Torquay TQ2..............219 D7
Meavy Bourne PL20....127 A2
Meavy CE Prim Sch
  PL20.......................127 C2
Meavy La PL20............127 A2
Meavy Villas PL20.......127 A2
Meavy Way
  Plymouth PL5.............244 E2
  Tavistock PL19...........171 D5
Medard Ho **4** EX32....155 A5
Meddon Cross
  Edistone EX39.............37 F5
  Woolfardisworthy EX39...37 F4
Meddon St EX39.........157 A1
Mede The
  Exeter EX4.................178 B8
  Topsham EX3.............182 E5
Medland Cres PL6......254 E7
Medland Cross EX6......97 C6
Medley Ct EX4............176 E8
Medway Pl PL3...........249 D6
Medway Rd TQ2.........214 B2
Meerhay La EX13........104 F6
Meetford Cross EX6.....97 F7
Meethe Gate Cross EX36...29 D2
Meethe Hill EX36.........29 D1
Meeting La EX8...........195 E6
Meeting St
  Appledore EX39...........15 A1
  Exmouth EX8.............202 A7
Melbourne Cotts PL1...262 B3
Melbourne Ct
  10 Exeter EX2..........261 B2
  Torquay TQ1.............220 A6
Melbourne Pl **2** EX2...262 B3
Melbourne Rd
  Exeter EX2................261 B2
  Plymouth PL9.............262 B4
Melbourne St
  Exeter EX2................261 B2
  Tiverton EX16............161 B4
Melbury Rd EX39.........19 E8
Melcot Cl TQ12...........207 E7
Meldon La EX20...........93 E3
Meldon Quarry Sta EX20...93 E3
Meldon Rd TQ13........111 A6
Meldrum Cl EX7..........204 E6

Melhuish Pl EX16.........46 E1
Mellons TQ12.............206 D4
Mellons Wlk TQ12......206 D4
Mellowes Ct EX13.......167 D5
Mellowmead TQ13.....121 F7
Mellows Mdw TQ12....206 F3
Melrose Ave PL2.........248 C8
Melville La TQ1...........220 B4
Melville Pl **4** PL2.......248 A5
Melville Rd PL2...........248 A5
Melville St TQ1...........220 B4
Melville Terrace La PL2...248 A5
Memband Cl PL8.........141 C6
Membury Cl EX11.......178 D6
Membury Com Sch EX13...87 D6
Membury Rd EX13.......87 E3
Memory Cross TQ13....215 E8
Memory Cl EX7...........255 E7
Mena Park Cl
  Paignton TQ4............225 F2
  Plymouth PL9............256 B7
Mena Park Rd PL9......256 B7
Mendip Rd TQ2...........219 D3
Menors Pl EX22..........164 C5
Merafield Cl PL7.........250 B5
Merafield Dr PL7.........250 C4
Merafield Farm Cotts
  PL7..........................250 B4
Merafield Rd PL7.........250 B4
Merafield Rise PL7.....250 C4
Mercer St EX2.............178 A2
Merchants Cnr EX17.....61 C1
Merchant's Gdn TQ7...143 A1
Merchants House (Mus)
  PL1..........................262 C2
Meredith Rd PL2.........248 C6
Mere La **18** EX14......210 C5
Mereskye EX8............202 C6
Meriden TQ1..............220 B4
Meridian Ho PL4.........263 A3
Meridian Pl EX34........160 B6
Merivale PL20.............126 F2
Merivale Cl TQ14........210 C7
Merley Rd EX39..........156 B7
Merlin Bsns Pk EX5.....99 A4
Merlin Cl PL6.............245 E8
Merlin Cres EX4..........174 A1
Merlin Way TQ2..........213 D2
Mermaid Ct **6** EX1....261 A2
Mermaid Yd EX1.........261 A2
Merrifield Cross
  Bridgerule EX22...........70 E4
  Slapton TQ7..............145 C6
Merrifield Rd TQ11.....130 C1
Merrion Ave EX10.......202 D6
Merritt Flats **5** TQ3...226 A5
Merritt Rd TQ3...........226 A5
Merrivale Ct TQ2........214 B4
Merrivale Rd
  Exeter EX4................176 F4
  Okehampton EX20.......170 E6
  Plymouth, Ham PL2...248 B7
  Plymouth, Honicknowle
  PL5..........................244 B3
Merrivale View Rd PL20...127 B3
Merrow Down Dr EX21...191 F8
Merrydale Cres EX31.....27 D6
Merryfield La EX6.........95 F2
Merryfield Rd EX39.....157 C1
Merryn Cl PL21...........237 E6
Merrythorn Rd EX31...153 D5
Merrywood TQ12........206 F1
Mersey Cl PL3.............249 D6
Meshaw Cross Rds EX36...46 A5
Meshaw Moor Cross EX36...46 A5
Meshaw Rectory Cross
  EX36.........................46 A5
Metcombe Cross EX31...9 C2
Metcombe La EX31........9 B1
Metcombe Rise EX11...100 C2
Metcombe Vale EX11...100 C2
Meteor Wlk **8** EX2....155 B5
Metherell Ave TQ5......230 D3
Metherell Avenue Ind Est
  TQ5.........................230 C3
Metherell Cross EX21...91 F8
Metherell Rd EX39......156 F1
Metley Cross TQ12......131 E5
Mettaford Cross EX39...22 F3
Mews Ct **8** EX7........204 E6
Mews Gdns TQ6.........233 F3
Mews The
  1 Bittaford PL21......137 C8
  Dawlish EX7..............204 E6
  Exmouth EX8.............196 F3
  Plymouth, Devonport PL1...262 A3
  Plymouth, Stonehouse PL1...262 A3
  7 Teignmouth TQ14...210 B8
Mexico Ave PL9...........140 D8
Meyrick Rd TQ1..........220 C7
Michael Rd PL3...........249 A5
Michelcombe La TQ13...130 A4
Michigan Way
  Exeter EX4................173 C2
  Plymouth PL3............249 C6
Mid Churchway PL9...256 A7
Middle Blagdon La TQ3...225 B6
Middleborough La EX33...7 D3
Middle Budleigh Mdw
  PL11.........................206 F3

Middlecott Cross
  Holemoor EX22...........73 B8
  Virginstow EX21..........90 E4
Middlecott Hill EX32.....18 D3
Middlecott La EX17......60 F2
Middle Down Cl PL9...256 A5
Middlefield Rd PL6......244 D6
Middlefield Cl PL12......242 B2
Middle Green Rd TQ21...160 E3
Middle Leigh PL8........140 F7
Middle Lincombe Rd
  TQ1.........................220 D3
Middlemead Rd EX16...161 D5
Middle Mill La PL15.....163 C3
Middlemoor Cross EX37...43 C3
Middlemoor Police Training
  Coll EX2...................178 D5
Middle Park Terr TQ7...143 B1
Middle Ramshill La TQ3...225 C7
Middle Rd PL9............140 D8
Middle St
  Brixham TQ5.............230 C5
  East Budleigh EX9.......198 B6
  Teignmouth TQ14.......210 A3
Middleton Rd EX39......156 F3
Middleton Wlk PL15....243 D4
Middletown La EX9......198 B6
Middle Warberry Rd
  TQ1.........................220 D5
Middle Westerland Cross
  TQ3.........................218 D1
Middlewood EX6.........201 A5
Midella Rd PL20..........127 A2
Midlands Cvn Pk EX31...154 A8
Midvale Rd TQ4..........226 B5
Midway
  Exmouth EX8.............202 E8
  Kingskerswell TQ12....212 F6
Midway Cl EX2............177 A1
Midway Terr EX2..........177 A1
Miers Cl PL5..............247 C8
Miers Ct PL5..............247 C8
Miglo Ind Est TQ4.......225 E3
Milber Com Inf Sch
  TQ12.......................207 F3
Milber Com Jun Sch
  TQ12.......................207 F3
Milber La TQ12...........213 B6
Milber Trad Est TQ12...208 A1
Milbury Cl EX6...........182 B5
Milbury La EX6...........182 B4
Milch Pk PL12.............244 A3
Midmay Cl EX4...........176 F7
Mildmay St PL4...........263 A4
Mile End Rd TQ12......206 E5
Mile Gdns EX4............173 F2
Mile House Rd PL2......248 A5
Mile La EX4................174 A1
Milestone Cots PL6....245 C1
Milestone Cross TQ13...123 F8
Milestone La TQ13......123 F8
Milford Ave EX31........188 B4
Milford Cl TQ14..........210 A5
Milford Cotts EX6.......181 B2
Milford Cross EX39.......22 B1
Milford La PL5............244 B5
Milford Rd EX10.........188 B4
Military Rd
  Plymouth PL10...........252 C3
  Plymouth PL3.............249 E6
  Rame PL10................140 I2
Milizac Cl PL8.............257 E4
Milkaway La EX33..........7 E1
Milk Hill EX5...............81 B7
Milky Way Adventure Pk
  EX39.........................23 C1
Milland Cross EX20......75 D1
Millards Hill **10** EX39...15 B1
Millbarn Cross EX16.....61 F8
Millbay Rd PL1............262 A2
Mill Bottom La TQ12...209 A3
Mill Bridge PL1............262 A3
Millbrook Bsns Ctr PL1...110 D2
Millbrook CE Prim Sch
  PL10.......................252 E5
Millbrook Cross EX13...167 E6
Millbrook Dale EX13...167 E6
Millbrook La EX2.........177 F2
Millbrook Park Rd TQ2...219 E5
Millbrook Rd **2** TQ3...226 B6
Mill Cl
  Lee Mill PL21.............136 D6
  Newton Abbot TQ12....206 F4
Millcombe Cnr TQ9....139 E1
Millcombe La TQ9......224 C3
Mill Cotts
  Okehampton EX20......170 B5
  Stoke Canon EX5.......173 F7
Mill Cres TQ6.............233 D4
Millcroft EX11.............169 D3
Mill Cross
  Bickington TQ12.........131 F7
  Halwill EX21................73 C1
  Harberton TQ9...........222 C2
  Rattery TQ10.............135 D4
Milldale Cres EX14......166 B5
Mill Dr EX2................177 F1
Mill End **1** TQ12.......123 F1
Millen La TQ12...........209 C2
Millennium Way EX39...156 F2
Miller Cl EX2..............174 A2
Miller Cross EX31........155 A5
Miller Ct PL1..............262 A2
Millers Brook EX33........7 E1
Millers Way
  Honiton EX14.............166 B5
  Tedburn St Mary EX6...97 F4

Miller Way
Exminster EX6 . . . . .181 F5
Plymouth PL6 . . . . .245 E3
Milletts Cl EX6 . . . . .182 A4
Mill Ford Sch PL5 . . . . . .243 F4
Mill Gn DT7 . . . . .260 E3
Millgreen Ct DT7 . . . . . . .260 E3
Millgreen La EX13 . . . . . . .87 D1
Millham La TA22 . . . . .33 D6
Millhayes Cross EX14 . . . . .86 F6
Millhayes Rd EX14 . . . . . . .86 F6
Mill Head EX34 . . . . .150 C6
Millhead Rd EX14 . . . . . . .166 B5
Mill Hill
Barnstaple EX31 . . . . .16 A3
Fremington EX31 . . . . .153 F5
Stoke Gabriel TQ9 . . . . . . .227 F7
Witheridge EX16 . . . . .61 F7
Mill Hill Cotts PL19 . . . . .116 F1
Millhouse Pk PL11 . . . . . .247 A2
Mill La
Allington EX11 . . . . .84 F1
Aveton Gifford TQ7 . . . . . .143 C6
Axminster EX13 . . . . .88 F3
Barnstaple EX31 . . . . .154 E6
Barton Town EX31 . . . . .11 E3
Berrynarbor EX34 . . . . .2 D4
Bow EX17 . . . . .78 B4
Branscombe EX12 . . . . .190 D4
Brayford EX32 . . . . .18 F6
Brixham TQ5 . . . . .230 A1
Burrington EX37 . . . . .44 A2
Charmouth DT6 . . . . .104 F6
Cheriton Fitzpaine EX17 . . .62 E2
Clyst Honiton EX1 . . . . . . .175 C1
Croyde EX33 . . . . .7 E2
East Buckland EX32 . . . . . . .18 E2
East Ogwell TQ12 . . . . .206 D1
Exeter, Alphington EX2 . . . .177 B1
Exeter, Higher Wear EX2 . . .177 F1
Exton EX3 . . . . .183 D2
Galmpton TQ5 . . . . .229 A4
George Nympton EX36 . . . .30 A1
Loddiswell TQ7 . . . . .138 C7
Lower Loxhore EX31 . . . . . . .17 F8
Lyme Regis DT7 . . . . .260 E3
Meshaw EX36 . . . . .45 F7
Newton Poppleford EX10 . . .186 F6
North Tawton EX20 . . . . . . .77 B4
North Whilborough TQ12 . . .212 D2
Offwell EX14 . . . . .86 B1
4 Paignton TQ3 . . . . .226 B7
Sandford EX17 . . . . .80 B5
Stockland EX13 . . . . .87 B7
Stockland, Furley EX13 . . . .87 C7
Stoke Fleming TQ6 . . . . . . .146 A7
Teignmouth TQ14 . . . . .209 D7
Torpoint PL11 . . . . .247 A2
Torquay TQ2 . . . . .219 F5
Totnes TQ9 . . . . .223 D5
Uplyme DT7 . . . . .260 C5
Wambrook TA20 . . . . .69 F2
Woolacombe EX34 . . . . .7 F6
Wratton EX33 . . . . .152 F4
Mill Lane Cotts EX20 . . . . .77 B4
Mill Leat 14 EX15 . . . . . .67 B8
Mill Leat Cotts EX17 . . . . .57 B8
Mill-Leat Gdns EX32 . . . . .17 E2
Millmans Rd TQ3 . . . . . . .218 D3
Mill Mdw
Ashburton TQ13 . . . . .130 F5
16 Combe Martin EX34 . . .3 A3
Ivybridge PL21 . . . . .237 D5
Millmoor Cross EX37 . . . . .44 B2
Millmoor La EX10 . . . . . . .186 F8
Millmoor Vale EX10 . . . . . .186 F8
Mill-on-the-Mole Mobile
Home Pk EX36 . . . . .158 E4
Mill Park Ind Est EX5 . . . .184 E8
Mill Path TQ13 . . . . .130 F4
Mill Pk 2 TQ12 . . . . .123 E1
Millpool Head PL10 . . . . . .252 E4
Millpool Rd PL10 . . . . . . .253 A6
Mill Rd
Barnstaple EX31 . . . . .154 E5
Bradworthy EX22 . . . . .38 E1
Exeter EX2 . . . . .177 F1
Fremington EX31 . . . . .153 F5
High Bickington EX37 . . . . .43 B7
Landkey EX32 . . . . .17 B1
Millbrook PL10 . . . . .253 A5
Okehampton EX20 . . . . .170 B4
Totnes TQ9 . . . . .222 E8
Mill Rise EX14 . . . . .85 F8
Millsome La
Bondleigh EX18 . . . . .77 C8
North Tawton EX18 . . . . . . .59 D1
Mills Rd PL1 . . . . .247 F2
Mill St
Bideford EX39 . . . . .157 A2
Chagford TQ13 . . . . .110 F6
Crediton EX17 . . . . .165 D5
Great Torrington EX38 . . . .159 C4
Honiton EX14 . . . . .166 B5
Kingsbridge TQ7 . . . . .258 C5
Sidmouth St Mary EX11 . . .169 C3
Ottery St Mary EX11 . . . . .169 C3
South Molton EX36 . . . . . .158 D4
Uffculme EX15 . . . . .66 B7
Mill Steep
Brompton EX36 . . . . .31 C8
Twitchen EX36 . . . . .20 C1
Mill Stile EX33 . . . . .152 C5
Mill Stream Ct EX11 . . . . .169 D3
Mill Stream Gdns
Halberton EX16 . . . . .65 A7
Wellington TA21 . . . . .160 B7

Millstream Mdw 4 TQ13 . .123 F6
Mill Tail TQ9 . . . . .223 D5
Mill The EX2 . . . . .261 C1
Milltown Hill EX36 . . . . . .45 F7
Milltown La
Northlew EX20 . . . . .74 E2
Sidmouth EX10 . . . . .188 C6
Mill View 13 TQ13 . . . . . .123 F6
Mill View Gdns PL10 . . . . .252 F5
Mill View Rd PL10 . . . . . .252 F5
Millway
Bradninch EX5 . . . . .82 F6
8 Chudleigh TQ13 . . . . . .123 E6
Wambrook TA20 . . . . .69 F2
Millway Gdns EX5 . . . . . . .82 F6
Millway Pl PL9 . . . . .255 D8
Millway Ave EX13 . . . . . . .167 F7
Millway Ct EX13 . . . . .167 F7
Millwood
Millwood TQ3 . . . . .180 C4
Millwood Bsns Pk TQ12 . . .207 E3
Millwood Dr PL6 . . . . .245 E1
Millwood Terr EX37 . . . . . .28 C2
Mill Wood La
Branscombe EX12 . . . . .191 A7
Milsfords La EX5 . . . . .81 E5
Milsoms La EX5 . . . . .81 E5
Milton Abbot Sch PL19 . . .116 B5
Milton Cl
Brixham TQ5 . . . . .230 B2
Exmouth EX8 . . . . .196 C4
Plymouth PL5 . . . . .244 D2
Milton Cres
Brixham TQ5 . . . . .230 B2
Tavistock PL19 . . . . .171 D5
Milton Ct
3 Newton Abbot TQ12 . . .207 C2
Plymouth, Cattedown PL4 . .263 C2
Plymouth, Prince Rock PL4 . .249 B1
Milton Fields TQ5 . . . . . . .230 A2
Milton La TQ12 . . . . .233 C2
Milton Pk TQ5 . . . . .230 B2
Milton Pl EX39 . . . . .156 F1
Milton Rd
Exeter EX2 . . . . .177 F3
Newton Abbot TQ12 . . . . . .207 B4
Milton St TQ5 . . . . .230 A2
Milverton Rd TA21 . . . . . . .160 B8
Mimosa Cl 3 EX16 . . . . . .161 F6
Mimosa Ct EX4 . . . . .198 C1
Minacre La TQ12 . . . . .212 E1
Mincent Cl TQ2 . . . . .214 A3
Mincent Hill TQ2 . . . . . . .214 A3
Minchin La EX5 . . . . .99 D2
Minchin Orch EX5 . . . . . . .99 E2
Mincinglake Rd EX4 . . . . . .173 E1
Minden Rd 4 EX14 . . . . . .210 B5
Minehead La TQ12 . . . . . . .34 A7
Miners Cl 11 TQ13 . . . . . .131 A5
Minerva Cl PL7 . . . . .251 A6
Minerva Way TQ12 . . . . . . .207 E3
Mines Rd
Bideford EX39 . . . . .157 C1
Plymouth PL3 . . . . .248 E5
Minifie Rd EX14 . . . . .166 B6
Minniemoor Cross EX31 . . .4 B1
Minniemoor La EX31 . . . . . .4 C1
Minses Cl PL9 . . . . .256 C7
Minster Ct EX13 . . . . .167 C5
Minster Rd EX6 . . . . .182 B5
Mint Park Rd EX33 . . . . . .152 B7
Mint The EX4 . . . . .261 A3
Mirador Pl PL4 . . . . .248 F4
Miranda Rd TQ3 . . . . .225 F8
Mire La EX10 . . . . .189 B7
Mirey La EX5 . . . . .184 C3
Misdon Cotts EX20 . . . . . . .75 F1
Mission Ct EX1 . . . . .261 A2
Misterton Cl PL9 . . . . .256 B8
Mitchell Cl TQ13 . . . . .255 D5
Mitchell Ho EX4 . . . . .177 D8
Mitchell's Pool TA21 . . . . .160 E6
Mitchell St TA21 . . . . .160 C7
Mitre Cl
Bishopsteignton TQ14 . . . .208 E8
Tavistock PL19 . . . . .171 A3
Mitre La EX4 . . . . .261 A3
Moat Hill TQ9 . . . . .223 C4
Mockham Down Gate
EX32 . . . . .18 C7
Modbury Cl PL5 . . . . .244 B3
Modbury Cross PL21 . . . . . .136 E2
Modbury Ct 5 PL21 . . . . . .137 B2
Modbury Prim Sch PL21 . . .137 B2
Model Terr 2 EX39 . . . . . .157 A1
Modred Ct EX4 . . . . .174 A1
Modyford Wlk PL20 . . . . . .126 C3
Mogworthy La EX16 . . . . . .47 D3
Mohun's Cl PL9 . . . . .171 C4
Mohun's Pk PL9 . . . . .171 C3
Mole Bridge La EX36 . . . . .158 E4
Mole Ridge Way EX36 . . . . .158 C5
Moles Cotts EX6 . . . . .182 A4
Moles Cross TQ13 . . . . . . .218 E7
Moles La
Kingswell TQ12 . . . . .212 E1
Paignton TQ3 . . . . .218 E8
Molesworth Rd
Plymouth, Plympton PL7 . . .250 C6
Plymouth, Stoke PL1, PL3 . .248 A3
Molesworth Terr PL10 . . . . .252 F5
Molland Cross
Brayford EX36 . . . . .30 A6
Chulmleigh EX18 . . . . .45 E3
Molland Hill EX32, EX36 . . .19 A5
Mollison Rd PL5 . . . . .243 E2
Moll Tall's Cross PL7 . . . . .136 A8

Molyneaux Pl 10 PL1 . . . . .247 F3
Monastery Rd TQ3 . . . . . . .226 A6
Mondeville Way
8 Northam EX39 . . . . . . .156 F6
8 Northam EX39 . . . . . . .156 F7
Money Acre Cross EX34 . . .101 E7
Money Acre Rd EX24 . . . . .101 E7
Money Pit La EX13 . . . . . . .69 D1
Monica Wlk PL4 . . . . .263 B4
Monitor Cl EX2 . . . . .261 A1
Monkerton Ct EX1 . . . . . . .178 E8
Monkerton Dr EX1 . . . . . . .178 E8
Monkey La EX10 . . . . .186 E6
Monkleigh Mill La EX39 . . .40 D8
Monkleigh Prim Sch EX39 . .40 F7
Monkokehampton Cross
EX19 . . . . .76 A8
Monksbridge Rd TQ5 . . . . .230 B3
Monks Cl
Bideford EX39 . . . . .26 A4
Crediton EX17 . . . . .165 B6
Monks Hill PL15 . . . . .115 A4
Monkshead PL19 . . . . .171 A4
Monkstone Gdns EX13 . . . .167 E5
Monkston Point TQ8 . . . . . .259 D4
Monks Way TQ13 . . . . .180 C6
Monkswell Rd EX4 . . . . . . .177 E8
Monkton Rd EX14 . . . . . . .174 F7
Monkton Wyld Camping Site
DT6 . . . . .104 C7
Monkton Wyld Cross
DT6 . . . . .104 C7
Monkton Wyld La DT6 . . . .104 E7
Monmouth Ave EX4 . . . . . .182 F4
Monmouth Beach Chalets
DT7 . . . . .260 C2
Monmouth Gdns PL5 . . . . .244 C4
Monmouth Rd EX4 . . . . . . .182 F4
Monmouth St
Lyme Regis DT7 . . . . .260 E3
Topsham EX3 . . . . .182 F4
Monmouth Way EX14 . . . . .166 D5
Monro Mead 7 TQ12 . . . . .122 F1
Monshall EX31 . . . . .57 E3
Mons Terr 11 TQ10 . . . . . .114 F4
Montacute Ave PL5 . . . . . .244 B2
Montague Gdns EX9 . . . . . .197 E1
Montague Rise EX4 . . . . . . .261 B4
Montague Terr PL7 . . . . . . .132 F4
Montagu Rd TQ2 . . . . .258 C5
Monterey TQ4 . . . . .226 C1
Monterey Cl TQ2 . . . . .173 A4
Monterey Gdns EX4 . . . . . .173 E1
Montery Pl 8 EX22 . . . . . .155 B3
Montesson Cl TQ3 . . . . . . .225 D7
Montesson Rd TQ3 . . . . . . .225 D7
Montgomery Cl
Ivybridge PL21 . . . . .237 E5
Saltash PL12 . . . . .242 D3
Montgomery Comb Sch
EX4 . . . . .177 A5
Montgomery Rd 6 EX2 . . . .178 D5
Mont Le Grand EX1 . . . . . .177 E6
Montpelier Com Prim Sch
PL2 . . . . .248 B6
Montpelier Ct
Exeter EX4 . . . . .177 A7
Paignton TQ3 . . . . .219 B1
Montpelier Rd
Ilfracombe EX34 . . . . .150 C6
Plymouth PL2 . . . . .248 C7
Montpelier Terr 13 EX34 . .150 C6
Montpellier Rd
Exmouth EX8 . . . . .202 A6
Torquay TQ1 . . . . .220 B4
Montserrat Rise TQ2 . . . . . .213 E3
Monument Cl TA21 . . . . . . .160 E4
Monument La TA21 . . . . . . .160 D4
Monument St PL1 . . . . .247 E1
Moonhayes Cross EX14 . . . .68 C4
Moon Hill Cl EX7 . . . . .181 C8
Moon La
4 Modbury PL21 . . . . . . .137 B2
Plymouth PL4 . . . . .263 A3
Moonridge EX2 . . . . .182 C7
Moon's Cross EX20 . . . . . . .95 B6
Moon St PL4 . . . . .263 A3
Moorashes 17 TQ9 . . . . . . .223 C5
Moor Cl EX10 . . . . .210 C7
Moorcourt Cl EX10 . . . . . . .187 F3
Moorcox Cross EX13 . . . . . .86 E2
Moor Cres DT6 . . . . .128 A8
Moorcroft Cl
Okehampton EX20 . . . . .170 D5
Plymouth PL9 . . . . .256 A7
Moorcroft Cross EX20 . . . . .170 D5
Moor Cross EX22 . . . . .71 C3
Moor Ct EX10 . . . . .187 F3
Moore Cl EX17 . . . . .165 C6
Mooredge La EX5 . . . . .82 E1
Moor Farm Cotts TQ8 . . . . .148 F4
Moorfield Pl
Moorfield Ave 4 PL6 . . . . .249 C7
Moorfield Cl EX8 . . . . .202 C8
Moorfield Rd
Exmouth EX8 . . . . .202 C8
St Giles on t H PL15 . . . . . .90 C1
Moorfields
6 Bittaford EX37 . . . . . . .137 C8
8 Colyton EX24 . . . . .103 A4
Moorfoot Cross TQ12 . . . . .131 E3
Moor Gate EX20 . . . . .170 C1

Moorhaven EX9 . . . . .197 F2
Moorhayes TQ13 . . . . .180 D7
Moorhayes Bglws EX16 . . . .161 E5
Moorhayes Cross EX15 . . . .67 B6
Moorhayes Ct EX15 . . . . . . .84 A1
Moorhayne Cross TA3 . . . . .66 A2
Moorhouse La TA4 . . . . . . .35 A8
Moorings Reach TQ5 . . . . .230 D5
Moorings The
Braunton EX33 . . . . .152 D6
Exmouth EX8 . . . . .202 C5
Exmouth, The Point EX8 . . .201 E6
Kingsbridge TQ7 . . . . .258 D3
Plymouth PL1 . . . . .226 C5
Moor La
Bittadon EX31 . . . . .9 C5
Bovey Tracey TQ13 . . . . . .180 C5
Braunton EX33 . . . . .152 A5
Broadclyst EX5 . . . . .175 C8
Brushford TA22 . . . . .33 F4
Budlake EX5 . . . . .82 F8
Budleigh Salterton EX9 . . . .197 F2
Churchsford TA3 . . . . .68 D7
Croyde EX33 . . . . .7 D2
Exeter EX2 . . . . .178 F5
Hatherleigh EX20 . . . . .95 D3
Molland EX36 . . . . .31 E7
Newton Poppleford EX10 . . .100 C1
Plymouth PL5 . . . . .243 E1
Poltimore EX4 . . . . .174 F7
Sidmouth EX10 . . . . .187 F6
Staverton TQ9 . . . . .216 B5
Torquay TQ2 . . . . .214 B3
Yarnscombe EX31 . . . . .27 E2
Zeal Monachorum EX17 . . . .78 B8
Moorland Ave
Denbury TQ12 . . . . .211 A7
Plymouth PL7 . . . . .250 F6
Moorland Cl
4 Bittaford PL21 . . . . . . .137 C8
Yelverton PL20 . . . . .241 D8
Moorland Ct PL20 . . . . . . .126 F2
Moorland Dr PL7 . . . . .250 C6
Moorland Gate
Heathfield TQ12 . . . . .123 B2
Roborough EX19 . . . . .43 B3
Moorland Gdns PL7 . . . . . .250 F6
Moorland Pk TQ13 . . . . . . .180 D5
Moorland Rd PL7 . . . . .250 E5
Moorland Rise EX36 . . . . . .158 C4
Moorlands
Chagford TQ13 . . . . .110 F6
Tiverton EX16 . . . . .161 E6
West Hill EX11 . . . . .168 D5
Moorlands Cl TQ12 . . . . . . .207 F2
Moorlands La PL12 . . . . . . .242 C4
Moorlands Rd EX9 . . . . . . .197 F2
Moorlands Trad Est
PL12 . . . . .242 C4
Moorland Terr EX34 . . . . . .159 B5
Moorland View
Buckfastleigh TQ11 . . . . . .236 A5
Lapford EX17 . . . . .60 D3
Newton Abbot TQ12 . . . . . .208 A2
Plymouth, Derriford PL6 . . .245 A5
Plymouth, Plymstock PL9 . .256 F7
Princetown PL20 . . . . .241 F4
Saltash PL12 . . . . .242 F4
South Molton EX36 . . . . . .46 D8
Moorland Way
Exeter EX4 . . . . .176 F8
Gunnislake PL18 . . . . .125 C5
Moor Lane Cl EX7 . . . . .204 A6
Moor Lane Cross N EX36 . . .31 E8
Moor Lea EX33 . . . . .152 F5
Moormead EX9 . . . . .197 F1
Moorpark
Bittaford EX21 . . . . .137 C8
Exmouth EX8 . . . . .202 C6
Moor Park Cl EX33 . . . . . . .7 D2
Moor Park Rd TQ12 . . . . . .212 F6
Moor Pk
Chagford TQ13 . . . . .111 A6
Honiton EX14 . . . . .166 B3
Kingskerswell TQ12 . . . . . .212 F6
Moorplot La EX18 . . . . .59 D3
Moor Rd
Ipplepen TQ12 . . . . .211 C3
Staverton TQ9 . . . . .216 B5
Moorsend TQ12 . . . . .206 E4
Moor's End TQ12 . . . . .207 B6
Moorshead Cross
Buckfastleigh TQ11 . . . . . .135 B6
Yealmpton PL21 . . . . .149 A8
Moorside
Malborough TQ7 . . . . .147 E6
Mary Tavy PL19 . . . . .117 C6
Moors Pk TQ14 . . . . .208 F7
Moorstone Leat TQ4 . . . . . .226 C1
Moortown EX18 . . . . .59 F8
Moortown Cross
Chulmleigh EX18 . . . . .59 F8
Rackenford EX16 . . . . .47 B8
Moorview
Broadhempston TQ13 . . . . .131 B1
Marldon TQ3 . . . . .218 D2
Plymouth PL9 . . . . .256 F6
Payhembury EX14 . . . . .84 D3
Moor View
Bovey Tracey TQ13 . . . . . .180 C5
Chudleigh TQ13 . . . . .123 E6
Hatherleigh EX20 . . . . .95 B6
Mary Tavy PL19 . . . . .117 C6
Northlew EX20 . . . . .74 E2
Pennymoor EX16 . . . . .62 E6
Plymouth, Keyham PL2 . . . .247 F5
Plymouth, Laira PL3 . . . . . .249 C4

Moor View continued
Torpoint PL11 . . . . .247 B3
Moorview Cl EX4 . . . . .173 D1
Moor View Cl EX10 . . . . . . .187 F7
Moorview Ct PL6 . . . . .245 F5
Moorview Dr TQ14 . . . . . . .209 D8
Moor View Dr TQ4 . . . . . . .210 A6
Moorview End TQ3 . . . . . . .218 D2
Moor View Terr
9 Bittaford PL21 . . . . . . .137 C8
Plymouth PL4 . . . . .248 E4
Yelverton PL20 . . . . .127 A2
Moory Mdw EX34 . . . . .2 F4
Moothill Cross TQ9 . . . . . . .216 A6
Morchard Bishop CE Prim
Sch EX17 . . . . .61 B2
Morchard Road Sta EX17 . . .78 F8
Morecombe Cross EX21 . . . .73 A4
Moreton Ave
Bideford EX39 . . . . .156 E1
Plymouth PL6 . . . . .244 F1
Moreton Dr EX39 . . . . .156 E2
Moretonhampstead General
Hospl TQ13 . . . . .111 F5
Moretonhampstead Prim Sch
TQ13 . . . . .111 F5
Moreton Park Rd EX39 . . . .156 E1
Moreton Terr EX6 . . . . .112 F5
Morgan Ave TQ2 . . . . .220 A5
Morgan Ct EX34 . . . . .202 A6
Morganhayes Cross
EX24 . . . . .102 D4
Morgans Quay TQ14 . . . . . .210 B3
Morice Cl TQ12 . . . . .247 E2
Morice Sq PL1 . . . . .247 E2
Morice Terr EX22 . . . . .155 B3
Morice Town Prim Sch
PL2 . . . . .247 E4
Morin Rd TQ3 . . . . .226 C8
Morlaix Dr PL6 . . . . .245 B4
Morleigh Cl TQ9 . . . . .139 A3
Morleigh Gn TQ9 . . . . .139 A3
Morleigh Green Cross
TQ9 . . . . .139 A4
Morleigh Rd TQ9 . . . . .139 C6
Morley Cl PL7 . . . . .250 A5
Morley Ct PL1 . . . . .262 B3
Morley Dr PL20 . . . . .126 D2
Morley Rd EX4 . . . . .177 E8
Morley View Rd PL7 . . . . . .250 C6
Mornacott Cross EX36 . . . . .31 A4
Mornacott Rd EX36 . . . . . . .31 A4
Morningside
Dawlish EX7 . . . . .204 C4
Torquay TQ1 . . . . .220 E5
Mornington Pk TA21 . . . . . .160 E6
Morrell's Cross EX16 . . . . . .34 A4
Morrell's La EX16 . . . . .50 B6
Morris Cl PL5 . . . . .257 B7
Morrish Pk PL9 . . . . .255 F6
Morshead Rd PL6 . . . . .244 F2
Mortain Rd PL12 . . . . .242 D4
Mortehoe Cart Linhay Her
Ctr EX34 . . . . .7 F8
Mortehoe Station Rd EX34 . .1 B1
Mortimer Ave TQ3 . . . . . . .226 B8
Mortimer Ct EX2 . . . . .178 A2
Mortimer Ho EX1 . . . . .177 F6
Mortimers Cross EX15 . . . . .66 B4
Mortimore Ct PL2 . . . . .242 D2
Morton Cres EX8 . . . . .201 E6
Morton Crescent Mews
EX8 . . . . .201 F6
Morton Rd EX16 . . . . .201 F6
Morton Way EX13 . . . . .167 D4
Morven Dr EX39 . . . . .196 A2
Morwell Gdns PL3 . . . . .248 A6
Morwellham Quay PL19 . . . .125 E4
Morwenna Park Rd EX39 . . .156 F7
Morwenna Rd EX23 . . . . . . .37 A1
Morwenna Terr 2 EX39 . . . .156 F7
Moses Cl PL6 . . . . .244 E7
Mosshayne La EX1, EX5 . . . .175 B2
Mossop Cl EX11 . . . . .169 D3
Mostyn Ave PL4 . . . . .249 A4
Motehole Rd TQ12 . . . . . . .211 D2
Mote Pk PL12 . . . . .242 C3
Mothecombe Wlk PL6 . . . . .245 C1
Mott's Cross EX15 . . . . .84 A7
Motts La EX15 . . . . .84 A7
Moulton Cl PL7 . . . . .251 B5
Moulton Wlk PL7 . . . . .251 B4
Moult Rd TQ8 . . . . .259 D2
Mounson Hill EX6 . . . . .97 C5
Mountain Cl EX8 . . . . .202 F8
Mountain Hill EX8 . . . . . . .197 A1
Mountbatten Cl
Exmouth EX8 . . . . .196 D2
Plymouth PL9 . . . . .255 D6
Mountbatten Rd EX16 . . . . .161 C5
Mount Batten Waterside Pk
PL9 . . . . .256 A5
Mountbatten Way PL9 . . . . .255 E6
Mount Boone TQ6 . . . . .233 F4
Mount Boone Hill TQ6 . . . .233 F4
Mount Boone La TQ6 . . . . .233 F4
Mount Boone Way TQ6 . . . .233 F4
Mount Dinham EX4 . . . . . . .177 A6
Mount Edgcumbe Country Pk
PL10 . . . . .253 E6
Mounter's Hill TA20 . . . . . .69 E2

Mount Gould Ave PL4....249 B2
Mount Gould Cres PL4...249 B3
Mount Gould Hospl PL4..249 B3
Mount Gould Rd PL4.....249 B3
Mount Gould Way PL4....249 B3
Mount Hermon Rd TQ1....220 B6
Monthill Cotts TQ12....122 F1
Mounthill Cross EX24...103 B5
Mounthill La EX13......103 E5
Mount House Sch PL19...171 E7
Mounticombe Cross EX18..45 C1
Mounticombe La EX18....45 C1
Mount Pleasant
 Bideford, East-t-Wt EX39..157 C3
 Bideford, Littleham EX39...25 D2
 3 Bishop's Tawton EX32..16 E1
 14 Chudleigh TQ13....123 F6
 10 Crediton EX17.....165 C5
 Millbrook PL10.........252 E5
 Moretonhampstead TQ13..111 F4
 Plymouth PL5...........244 B2
Mount Pleasant Ave EX4.196 B3
Mount Pleasant Cl
 Kingsbridge TQ7........258 D6
 Kingskerswell TQ12....213 A3
Mount Pleasant Ct EX8..196 B2
Mount Pleasant La 7
 TQ14................210 A3
Mount Pleasant Mews
 TQ5.................230 C4
Mount Pleasant Rd
 Brixham TQ5...........230 C4
 Dawlish Warren EX7....201 B1
 Exeter EX4............177 E8
 Kingskerswell TQ12....213 A3
 Newton Abbot TQ12.....207 C7
 2 Torquay TQ1.......220 B6
Mount Radford Cres
 EX2.................261 C2
Mount Radford Sq EX2...261 C2
Mount Raleigh Ave EX39.156 F4
Mount Raleigh Dr EX39..156 F4
Mount Rd TQ5..........230 D5
Mount Ridley Rd TQ6....234 C3
Mount Rise EX6.........114 E4
Mount Sandford Rd
 EX32................155 D1
Mount St
 Plymouth, Mount Wise
  PL1...............247 E1
 Plymouth, Mutley PL4..263 A4
Mount Stone Rd PL1.....254 A8
Mount Street Prim Sch
 PL4.................263 A4
Mount Stuart Hospl TQ1.219 F7
Mount Tamar Cl PL5.....243 E2
Mount Tamar Sch PL5....243 E2
Mount Tavy Rd PL19.....171 E6
Mount The
 32 Appledore EX39....15 A1
 Brixham TQ5...........230 C6
 Teignmouth TQ14.......210 B6
 Torquay TQ2...........213 F4
 Totnes TQ9............223 C4
Mount View
 18 Colyton EX24......103 A4
 Feniton EX14...........84 E2
Mount View Cotts EX32..155 F2
Mount View Home Pk
 EX32................155 E2
Mount View Terr **2** TQ9.223 C5
Mount Wear Sq EX2......182 C8
Mount Wise Com Prim Sch
 PL1.................247 E1
Mount Wise Ct PL1......247 F1
Mourne Villas PL9......255 F8
Mouseberry Cross EX17..46 A4
Mouseberry La TQ13.....124 B4
Mousehole Cross EX14...84 D5
Mouse Hole La EX14.....84 C4
Mowbars Hayes EX13.....87 A3
Mowbray Ave EX4.......261 B4
Mowbray Cl EX2........178 A5
Mowhay Rd PL11........252 B8
Mowhay Rd
 Plymouth PL5..........243 F1
 Plymouth PL5..........244 A4
Mowlish La EX6.........200 B7
Mowstead Pk EX33......152 B7
Mowstead Rd EX33......152 B7
Moxeys Cl EX17.........62 E1
Moyses La EX20........170 B4
Moyses Mdw EX20.......170 F4
Mrs Ethelston's CE Prim Sch
 DT7.................260 A5
Mucky Duck EX20.......107 C2
Mucky La EX19..........57 D6
Mudbank La EX8........202 A8
Muddy La
 East Buckland EX32.....18 E2
 Ottery St Mary EX11...101 B7
Mudford Gate EX14......62 E7
Mudgate Cross EX36.....20 D3
Mudge La TQ12........217 E6
Mudges Terr PL18......125 D6
Mudge Way PL7........250 E5
Mudhouse Cross EX19....58 B7
Mudstone La TQ5.......230 E4
Mulberry Cl
 Exeter EX1............178 B6
 Paignton TQ3..........225 E6
 Plymouth PL6..........245 E7
 Willand EX15...........85 A3
Mulberry Gr PL19.......171 C2
Mulberry Rd PL12......242 E1

Mulberry St **3** TQ14....210 B4
Mulberry Way EX31......154 B2
Mulgrave St PL1........262 C2
Mullacott Cross EX34....1 E1
Mullacott Cross Ind Est
 EX34.................1 F1
Mullet Ave PL3........249 C4
Mullet Cl PL3.........249 C4
Mullet Rd PL3.........249 C4
Mullion Cl PL11.......246 F4
Munro Ave PL8.........141 B8
Munro Ho EX31.........155 B8
Muralto Ho PL19.......171 A4
Murchington Cross
 TQ13................110 E7
Murdock Rd PL11.......246 F3
Murley Cl EX17........165 A6
Murley Cres TQ14......208 E8
Murley Grange TQ14....208 E8
Musbury Prim Sch EX13.103 D5
Musbury Rd EX13.......167 C4
Museum Ct TQ7........258 C6
Museum Rd TQ1........220 C4
Musgrave Ho EX4......261 B3
Musgrave Row EX4.....261 B3
Musgraves TA22........33 E6
Mushroom Rd EX5.......99 A1
Musket Rd TQ12.......180 F2
Mutley Cl PL4.........263 A4
Mutley Plain PL4......248 E4
Mutley Plain La PL4....248 E4
Mutley Rd PL3.........248 A5
Muttersmoor Rd EX10..187 E5
Mutton La EX2.........181 C8
Muxworthy La EX32......19 A8
Mylor Cl PL2..........248 D8
Myra Ct EX39..........15 A1
Myrtle Cl
 Exeter EX2............177 B1
 Yelverton PL20........127 B3
Myrtle Cottage Rd EX39.157 B8
Myrtle Farm View EX13..157 A8
Myrtle Gdns EX39......157 A2
Myrtle Gr EX39........157 A2
Myrtle Hill TQ14......210 C5
Myrtle La TA21.........51 E7
Myrtle Rd EX4.........176 E4
Myrtle Row
 Exmouth EX8..........202 A6
 4 Torquay TQ2.......220 B5
Myrtles Ct PL12.......242 D4
Myrtle St **11** EX39.....15 A1
Myrtleville PL2.......248 A6

N

Nadder Bottom EX4.....176 B8
Nadder La
 Barnstaple EX4........176 B8
 South Molton EX36.....158 B4
Nadder Park Rd EX4....176 C6
Nadrid Cross EX36......30 A8
Nadrid East Cross EX36..30 A8
Naish's La EX13........87 B3
Nancarrows PL12.......242 C2
Napier St PL1.........247 F3
Napier Terr
 Exeter EX4............261 A3
 Plymouth PL4.........248 E4
Nap La EX18............44 C1
Napps Cvn & Camping Site
 EX34.................2 E4
Naps La EX10.........186 C5
Nap View EX14.........85 B4
Narfords La TA20.......69 F1
Narracott La
 Hollocombe EX18.......58 E7
 South Molton EX36.....158 A2
Narratons Rd EX20......93 E6
Narrow La
 Botusfleming PL12.....242 C7
 Copplestone EX17.......79 C4
 Tiverton EX16.........161 C2
Narrowmoor Cross TQ7..144 D4
Naseby Dr TQ12.......180 F2
Nash Cl PL7..........251 A5
Nash Gdns EX7........204 D4
Nash La DT6...........88 H2
Nasmith Cl EX8........196 D1
Natcott La EX39........22 F2
National Marine Aquarium
 PL4.................263 A2
Nats La
 Cornwood PL21........133 D1
 Sparkwell PL21.......136 C8
Natson Mill La EX17....78 B4
Natty Cross EX38.......43 A5
Nattadon Rd TQ13.....111 A6
Nautilus EX39........156 C7
Neadon La EX16.......112 F5
Neal Cl PL7..........251 B4
Neath Rd PL4.........263 C4
Needlewood Cl EX11...168 C3
Neet Way EX22........164 C6
Neilgate Cnr TQ13.....131 A3
Nelson Ave PL1.......247 F3

Nelson Rd
 Brixham TQ5...........230 C5
 Dartmouth TQ6.........233 C3
 Exeter EX4............177 A5
 Westward Ho! EX39.....156 C7
Nelson St PL4.........263 A4
Nelson Terr
 Plymouth PL6..........245 E6
 Westward Ho! EX39.....156 C7
Nelson Way **1** EX2.....178 D5
Neopardy Cross
 Yeoford, Neopardy EX17..79 D2
 Yeoford, Posbury EX17...79 D1
Nepean St **2** PL1......247 F3
Neptune Ct **3** EX1.....261 A2
Neptune Pk PL9.......255 B8
Ness Dr TQ14.........210 B2
Ness View Rd EX12.....210 C8
Neswick St PL1........262 B3
Neswick Street Ope PL1.262 A3
Nethercott Cross
 Ashwater EX21.........90 C7
 Oakford EX16..........48 C8
Nethercott Hill EX16...48 C7
Nethercott Rd EX33......8 A2
Netherham Cross EX33....8 A2
Netherhams Hill EX33....8 A3
Netherleigh Rd TQ1....220 B7
Nether Mdw TQ3.......218 D3
Netherton Cross EX34....3 A4
Netherton Hill EX6......96 D1
Netherton La EX34......3 A4
Netherton Rd TQ13....180 C4
Nettacott Cross EX5.....81 B2
Nettleford Hill EX16....46 F5
Nettlehayes PL9.......256 D7
Netton Cl PL3.........256 B6
Nevada Cl PL3........249 D6
Nevada Ct **10** EX12....192 A5
Neville Rd
 Newton Abbot TQ12....207 A4
 Okehampton EX20......170 C5
Newacott Cross EX22....70 E5
New Barn Cross EX5....172 A7
New Barn Hill PL7.....250 F3
New Barnstaple Rd EX34.150 E3
Newberry Cl EX34.......2 F4
Newberry Cotts EX33....8 A2
Newberry Cross EX37....44 B4
Newberry La EX34........2 F4
Newberry Rd
 Combe Martin EX34.....2 F4
 Georgeham EX33........8 A2
Newberry's Patch TA3...68 D7
Newberry Cl
 Axminster EX13.......167 E6
 Colyton EX24.........103 A4
Newberry Comm Ctr EX5..99 A4
New Bldgs
 3 Bampton EX16......34 C1
 8 Barnstaple EX32...155 A6
 Broadclyst EX5........175 C7
 Chittlehampton EX37....28 F3
 Doddiscombsleigh EX6..113 D5
 3 Exeter EX2........261 A2
 Fremington EX31......153 E5
 Thurlestone TQ7......143 C2
Newbridge Cl EX39.....157 B4
Newbridge Down
 Bishop's Tawton EX32...27 E7
 Cowley EX5............27 E7
New Bridge Hill
 Barnstaple EX32........27 E7
 EX32................27 E7
Newbridge Hill
 Cowley EX5...........172 E6
 Gunnislake PL18......125 D6
 Holne TQ13...........130 A6
 Witheridge EX16........46 D1
New Bridge St EX4.....261 A2
Newbuildings Cross EX17.79 D6
Newbuilding's Hill EX17..63 A3
Newbury Cl PL5........244 B5
Newbury Dr TQ13......180 E7
Newcastle Gdns PL5....244 B5
Newcombe Cross EX20..170 D5
Newcombes **5** EX17....165 C5
Newcombe St EX1......178 A6
Newcombe Street Gdns
 EX1.................178 A6
Newcombe Terr EX1.....177 F6
Newcomen Rd TQ6......233 F3
Newcot Cross EX15......8 C7
New Cotts EX5........202 F7
Newcourt Rd
 Silverton EX5..........82 B5
 Topsham EX5..........182 E7
New Cross
 Avonwick TQ10........135 C2
 Kingsteignton TQ12....123 E1
Newcross Pk **10** TQ12..123 E1
New Cswy **10** EX39.....156 F7
New Cut
 Beer EX12............191 D5
 Crediton EX17.........165 B5
New England Hill PL7...136 B5
New England Rd PL7....136 B5
New Esplanade Ct EX7..156 C7
New Est EX5...........81 A2
New Exeter St TQ13....123 E6
Newfoundland Cl EX4...173 C2
Newfoundland Way 13
 TQ12................207 B3
Newgate Cross TA22....33 D7
New George St PL1.....262 C3

New Rd continued
 Teignmouth TQ14......210 C7
 Totnes TQ9...........223 D6
 Uppottery EX14........68 B1
 Waterrow TA21.........35 F4
 Wilmington EX14.......86 D2
 Yealmpton PL8........136 A2
New Road Cl PL10......253 A2
New Road Cross
 Milton Damerel EX22...54 D3
 Okehampton EX20.......93 F5
 South Molton EX36.....46 D6
 Wilmington EX14.......86 D1
New Road Est EX20.....93 F8
New Road Gate EX5......6 D5
New Rd S EX39........157 A2
New Sch The EX6......182 A5
New Sidmouth Rd EX24..102 F4
New St
 6 Appledore EX39.....15 A1
 13 Bideford EX39.....157 A2
 Chagford TQ13........111 A6
 Chulmleigh EX18.......44 E1
 Cullompton EX15......163 B3
 Exmouth EX8..........202 A7
 Great Torrington EX38.159 C5
 Honiton EX14.........166 C6
 Millbrook PL10........252 E5
 Moretonhampstead TQ13.111 F5
 Ottery St Mary EX11...169 E4
 Paignton TQ3.........226 B6
 Plymouth PL1.........263 A2
 Sidmouth EX10........188 B3
Newtake Rd PL19......171 E2
Newtake Rise TQ12....207 F2
Newte's Hill EX16......64 D5
Newton Abbot & GWR Mus
 TQ12................207 C3
Newton Abbot Hospl
 TQ12................207 C3
Newton Abbot Sta TQ12.207 D3
Newton Ave PL5.......243 E2
Newton Cl PL8........141 A7
Newton Cross
 Blackawton TQ9.......145 B7
 Denbury TQ12.........211 B6
 Hartland EX39.........22 C2
 Zeal Monachorum EX17..77 F7
Newton Ct
 6 Bampton EX16.......34 B1
 Newton Ferrers PL8...140 F7
Newton Ferrers CE Prim Sch
 Newton Ferrers PL8...140 F7
 Newton Ferrers PL8...141 A7
New St
 Newton Ferrers PL8...140 F7
Newton Gdns PL5......243 F2
Newton Hall TQ12.....207 C2
Newton Hill
 Daccombe TQ12........213 F6
 Newton Ferrers PL8...140 F7
Newton Ho EX5.........86 F1
Newton La EX17........77 F7
Newton Poppleford Prim Sch
 EX10................186 F8
Newton Rd
 Bideford EX39.........157 A3
 Bishopsteignton TQ14..208 D7
 Bovey Tracey TQ13....180 C6
 Heathfield TQ13.......180 E3
 Kingskerswell TQ12....213 A5
 Kingsteignton TQ12....207 D5
 Salcombe TQ8.........259 D4
 Torquay TQ2..........213 D1
Newton Road Ret Pk
 TQ12................207 D6
Newton St Cyres Prim Sch
 TQ12................22 A8
Newton St Cyres Sta EX5.81 A1
Newton St Petrock Cross
 EX38.................40 B1
Newton School Cl EX5..55 C7
Newton Sq **8** EX16.....34 B1
Newton's Row PL7.....136 A8
Newtown
 Cornwood PL21........133 C2
 Sidmouth EX10........188 B4
Newtown Cl EX1.......261 C3
Newtown Cross EX36....31 A4
Newtown La EX16.......31 A4
Newtown Prim Sch EX1..261 C3
New Valley Rd EX4.....176 F7
New Village Cross EX17..59 F2
New Way EX5..........184 C6
New Way Est EX14......67 B2
New Wlk TQ9.........223 D5
New Wood Cl PL6......245 E8
New Zealand Ho PL3....248 B4
Nibbys Cross EX15......66 B5
Nicholas Cl TA22.......33 C4
Nicholas Mdw EX17.....125 D4
Nicholas Rd EX1.......178 A6
Nichols Nymett Cross
 EX20.................77 F4
Nichols Nymett La EX20.77 F5
Nichols Nymett Moors Cross
 EX20.................77 F5
Nicholson Rd
 Plymouth PL5..........244 E2
 Torquay TQ2..........213 D1
Nick Reed's La EX15....52 D1
Nightingale Cl
 Plymouth PL9.........256 C8
 Torquay TQ2..........213 E2
Nightingale Lawns EX15.163 A2
Nightingale Wlk EX2...176 D3
Nilgala Cl EX39.......156 E4
Nine Ash Cross EX16....49 D6

Nine Milestone Cross
PL21. . . . . 137 D7
Nine Oaks
Aylesbeare EX5. . . . . .99 C1
Dousland PL20. . . . . 127 C3
Nirvana PL21. . . . . 237 C5
Nirvana Cl PL21. . . . . 237 C5
Noelle Dr TQ12. . . . . 207 A4
Noland Pk TQ10. . . . . 135 A2
Nomansland Cross EX16 .62 B8
No Mans Chaple EX5. . . . .81 D3
Nomansland EX17. . . . . . . .80 D5
No Man's Land
Georgeham EX33. . . . . .8 B1
Whiddon EX13. . . . . .9 C1
Nook The PL19. . . . . 171 D6
No Place Hill TQ9. . . . . . 131 C4
Norah Bellot Ct [3] EX31. .154 F5
Norcombe Ct EX12. . . . . . 192 B4
Norden La TQ7. . . . . 258 B5
Nordon Cross TQ12. . . . . 131 F3
Norfolk Cl PL3. . . . . 249 C5
Norfolk Rd PL3. . . . . 249 C4
Norfolk Terr [25] EX32. . . 155 A4
Norleigh Cross EX20. . . . . .75 C3
Norley Rd EX33. . . . . .8 D1
Norman La
Exmouth EX8. . . . . 196 D2
Newton Abbot TQ12. . . . . . 206 E5
Norman Cres EX9. . . . . . . 198 A2
Norman Ct EX2. . . . . 177 C1
Norman Dr EX15. . . . . 163 C5
Normandy Cl EX8. . . . . . . 196 E1
Normandy Hill PL5. . . . . . 243 B2
Normandy Rd [1] EX1. . . . 177 F6
Normandy Way
Plymouth PL5. . . . . 243 C2
Salcombe TQ8. . . . . 259 E5
South Molton EX36. . . . . . . 158 B4
Norman Lockyer Observatory
EX10. . . . . 188 D5
Norman Rd TQ3. . . . . 226 C7
Normans Cleave EX35. . . 151 B5
Norman Terr EX39. . . . . . . 157 A7
Norns La TQ6. . . . . 145 F6
Norsworthy's Grave EX17 .97 E8
Northam Burrows Cntry Pk
EX39. . . . . .14 E1
Northam Ho EX39. . . . . . . 156 F6
Northampton Cl PL5. . . . . 244 B5
Northam Rd EX39. . . . . . . 156 F3
Northams Mdw EX20. . . . 170 A4
North Ave
Bideford EX39. . . . . 157 D1
Exeter EX1. . . . . 177 E6
Lyme Regis DT7. . . . . 260 D4
Northay Cross EX13. . . . . . .88 H3
Northay La
Axminster EX13. . . . . .88 G3
Northay TQ20. . . . . .69 E6
Northbeer Cross EX17. . . . .96 A8
Northbeer La EX17. . . . . . . .95 F8
North Boundary Rd TQ5 .230 B5
North Bridge Pl EX4. . . . . 261 A3
Northbrook Cl EX4. . . . . . 174 A1
North Buckland Mill EX33 .8 C3
North Castle Mews [8]
TQ9. . . . . 223 C6
Northclose Rd EX18. . . . . . .59 D8
North Combe Cross EX16 .48 A3
Northcombe La TA22. . . . . .33 E7
North Combe Rd EX14. . . . .86 C2
North Coombe La EX16. . . .47 A3
Northcote Cross EX37. . . . .43 E4
Northcote Hill EX14. . . . . 166 F7
Northcote La
Honiton. 166 B6
Pennymoor EX16. . . . . .62 F8
Northcote Rd EX14. . . . . . 166 E7
Northcott Gdns EX39. . . . 157 A2
Northcott Terr [8] EX32. . 164 C4
Northdene EX39. . . . . .59 A8
North Devon Coll EX31. . 154 E3
North Devon Cottage Rd
EX16. . . . . 161 B5
North Devon District Hospl
EX31. . . . . 155 A8
North Devon Farm Pk
EX32. . . . . .17 D1
North Devon Maritime Mus
EX39. . . . . .15 A1
North Dimson Cotts
PL18. . . . . 125 C6
North Down Cres PL2. . . . 247 F6
North Down Cross EX17. . .79 B1
Northdown Dr EX39. . . . . 156 F3
North Down Gdns PL2. . . 247 F6
Northdown La EX36. . . . . . .45 F6
Northdown Rd
Bideford EX39. . . . . 156 F2
Cadbury EX5. . . . . .81 F7
North Down Rd
Braunton EX33. . . . . 152 E6
Plymouth PL2. . . . . 248 B6
North East St EX39. . . . . . 157 A7
North Emb TQ6. . . . . 233 F4
North End Cl TQ12. . . . . . . 211 C2
Northernhay [17] TQ1. . . . 207 C3
Northernhay Pl EX4. . . . . 261 B3
Northernhay Sq EX4. . . . . 261 A3
Northernhay St EX4. . . . . 261 A3
Northern La
Branscombe EX12. . . . . 190 B5
Sidmouth EX10. . . . . 189 E8
Northesk St PL2. . . . . 248 A4
Northfield EX13. . . . . 103 D5
Northfield La EX31. . . . . . . 154 F7

Northfield Pk EX31. . . . . . . 154 F7
Northfield Rd
Bideford EX39. . . . . 157 C1
Georgeham EX33. . . . . .8 B2
Ilfracombe EX34. . . . . 150 B6
Okehampton EX20. . . . . . . 170 B5
Northfields Ind Est TQ5 .230 B5
Northfields La
Brixham TQ5. . . . . 230 B4
Brixham TQ5. . . . . 230 B5
Northfield Terr [1] EX34 .150 B6
North Ford Rd TQ6. . . . . . 233 F3
North Furzeham Rd TQ5 .230 C6
North Garron [3] EX32. . . 155 B5
Northgate EX39. . . . . .22 D3
North Gate Ct EX4. . . . . . . 261 A3
Northgate La EX14. . . . . . . .86 A3
North Gn [3] EX32. . . . . . . 155 B4
North Grange EX2. . . . . . . 178 D3
Northground La EX10. . . . 101 D1
North Hayne Cross EX36 ..31 B4
North Heasley Cross EX36 19 C4
North Hill PL4. . . . . 263 A4
North Hill TQ5. . . . . 230 B5
North Hill La
Morchard Bishop EX17. . . . . .61 B3
Stockland EX14. . . . . .86 F8
North Huish Cross TQ10 .138 B8
North Jaycroft EX15. . . . . 162 D5
North La
Ashford EX31. . . . . .16 A6
Barnstaple, Bickington
EX31. . . . . 154 A4
Challacombe EX31, TA24 . . .12 B4
Middle Marwood EX31. . . . . .9 B3
Whiddon EX31. . . . . .9 D2
Northland Cnr EX31. . . . . . .11 D2
Northland Cross EX36. . . . .19 A1
North Lawn Ct EX4. . . . . . 177 F6
Northleat Ave TQ3. . . . . . . 225 E5
Northleigh Cross
Chelfham EX32. . . . . .17 C6
Northleigh EX24. . . . . 102 B7
Northleigh Hill Rd
Honiton EX14. . . . . 166 E3
Offwell EX14. . . . . .86 A1
Northleigh Rd EX24. . . . . . 102 D6
**Northlew & Ashbury
Parochial CE Prim Sch**
EX20. . . . . .74 E2
Northlew Rd EX20. . . . . .93 D6
North Lodge Cl EX7. . . . . . 204 C5
North Molton Cross EX36 .30 B8
North Molton Sch EX36 . .30 B8
North Moor Cross EX22 . . .38 C3
Northmoor Rd EX22. . . . . . .33 D7
North Morte Rd EX34. . . . . .7 F8
Northmostown CE IO10 .187 A2
Northolt Ave PL5. . . . . 243 D4
North Park Almshouses
EX4. 261 C2
North Park Cnr TQ9. . . . . . 139 C6
North Park Rd
Exeter EX4. . . . . 173 B1
Tedburn St Mary EX6. . . . . . .97 F4
North Park Villas PL12 . . . 242 C4
North Prospect Prim Sch
PL2. 248 A7
North Prospect Rd PL2. . 248 A6
North Quay PL4. . . . . 263 A2
North Rd
Barnstaple EX31. . . . . 155 A7
Bideford EX39. . . . . 157 A2
Bradworthy EX22. . . . . .38 C1
Hartland EX39. . . . . .22 D3
High Bickington EX37. . . . . . .43 B7
Holsworthy EX22. . . . . 164 D5
Lee Mill PL21. . . . . 136 C7
Lifton PL16. . . . . 105 F4
Okehampton EX20. . . . . . . 170 C7
Saltash PL12. . . . . 242 F3
South Molton EX36. . . . . . . 158 C5
Torpoint PL11. . . . . 247 B3
Yelverton PL20. . . . . 126 F3
North Rd E PL4. . . . . 262 C4
North Rd W PL1. . . . . 262 B4
Northridge Cross EX5. . . . .98 E7
Northridge La EX5. . . . . . . .98 E7
North Rocks Rd TQ4. . . . . 229 C7
Northside TA21. . . . . 160 B5
North St
Ashburton TQ13. . . . . 130 F5
Axminster EX13. . . . . 167 D6
Braunton EX33. . . . . 152 D6
Chagford TQ13. . . . . 111 A6
Crediton EX17. . . . . 165 C5
Denbury TQ12. . . . . 211 A7
Dolton EX19. . . . . .57 F7
Exeter EX4. . . . . 261 A3
Exeter, Heavitree EX1 . . . . . 177 F6
Exmouth EX8. . . . . 202 A7
Hartland EX39. . . . . .22 D3
Ipplepen TQ12. . . . . 211 C2
Northam EX39. . . . . 157 A7
North Tawton EX20. . . . . . . .77 C4
Okehampton EX20. . . . . . . 170 B5
Ottery St Mary EX11. . . . . . 169 E4
Plymouth PL4. . . . . 263 A3
Sheepwash EX21. . . . . .56 C1
South Molton EX36. . . . . . . 158 C5
Tavistock PL19. . . . . 171 C5
Topsham EX3. . . . . 182 F4
Totnes TQ9. . . . . 223 C6
Wellington TA21. . . . . 160 D6
Witheridge EX16. . . . . .46 E1
North Tawton Prim Sch
EX20. . . . . .77 C4

North Terr EX31. . . . . 154 A4
North Thorne La EX31. . . . .11 A4
Northumberland Pl
TQ14. . . . . 210 B4
Northumberland St PL5 .247 E8
Northumberland Terr
PL1. 262 B1
North Upton Barns TQ7 .143 B3
North View EX21. . . . . .55 E4
North View EX39. . . . . 156 F3
North View Hill EX39. . . . 156 F3
Northview Rd EX9. . . . . . . 203 F8
North View Rd TQ5. . . . . . 230 D5
Northville Pk TQ7. . . . . . . 258 D6
Northville Rd TQ7. . . . . . . 258 D6
North Walk Hill EX35. . . . 151 C6
Northways La PL21. . . . . . 137 D7
North Weald Gdns PL5 . . 243 E5
North Wlk
Barnstaple EX31. . . . . 154 F5
Lynton EX35. . . . . 151 B6
Northwood Cross EX17. . . .61 B3
Northwood La
Buckfast TQ11. . . . . 236 C8
Buckland Brewer EX39. . . . . .40 C7
Morchard Bishop EX17. . . . . .61 B3
Northwoods TQ13. . . . . . . 180 C4
North Wyke Cotts EX20 . . .77 B1
Norton Ave PL4. . . . . 263 C4
Norton Cross TQ6. . . . . . . 233 A3
Norton Pk TQ6. . . . . 233 A3
Norton Pl EX8. . . . . 202 E8
Nortons Cross EX5. . . . . . . .81 A2
Norton View TQ6. . . . . 233 C3
Norwich Ave PL5. . . . . 244 B5
Norwich Rd EX34. . . . . 196 D4
Norwich Rd EX4. . . . . 174 F6
Norwood Ave EX2. . . . . . . 261 C1
Norwood Cl PL6. . . . . 261 B4
Norwood Rd EX4. . . . . 261 B4
Notre Dame Cl PL6. . . . . . 244 F5
Notre Dame Ho PL1. . . . . 262 B3
Notre Dame RC Sch PL6 .244 F5
Notte St PL1. . . . . 262 B2
Nottiston Cross EX31. . . . . .16 A1
Novorossisk Rd PL6. . . . . . 245 E2
Nower Rd EX13. . . . . .87 C3
Nowers La TA21. . . . . 160 C3

O

Oakapple Cl PL7. . . . . 250 B7
Oak Apple Cl PL12. . . . . . . 242 D4
Oakbank TQ13. . . . . 180 C4
Oak Cl
Dulford EX15. . . . . .84 B8
Exeter EX4. . . . . 174 E1
Kingsteignton TQ12. . . . . . . 207 F6
Ottery St Mary EX11. . . . . . 169 D3
Shillingford Abbot EX2. . . . . 181 A6
Silverton EX5. . . . . .82 C6
Tiverton EX16. . . . . 161 D5
Oakcliff Chalet Pk EX7. . . 201 B1
Oak Cliff Holiday Pk EX7 201 B1
Oak Cottage Cross EX22 . .72 E2
Oak Cres EX15. . . . . 162 C4
Oakcroft Rd PL2. . . . . 248 B6
Oak Cross
Bondleigh EX18. . . . . .77 D8
Inwardleigh EX20. . . . . .75 C1
Oak Ct
Holsworthy EX22. . . . . 164 C5
Lee Mill PL21. . . . . 136 D6
Oakdale Ave EX32. . . . . .17 E1
Oakdene Ct EX6. . . . . 114 F1
Oakdene Rise PL9. . . . . . . 255 F6
Oaken Hill
Great Torrington EX31. . . . . . .42 E8
Yarnscombe EX31. . . . . .27 D1
Oakery Cres PL20. . . . . . . 128 B8
Oakey Orch PL17. . . . . 125 A4
Oakfield Cl PL7. . . . . 251 C6
Oakfield Pk TA21. . . . . 160 E4

Oakfield Pl PL4. . . . . 249 B1
Oakfield Rd
Exeter EX4. . . . . 177 A5
Hatherleigh EX20. . . . . .75 C7
Plymouth PL7. . . . . 250 C6
Oakfields EX16. . . . . 161 D6
Oakfield St EX1. . . . . 177 F5
Oakfield Terr EX39. . . . . . . 157 A7
Oakfield Terrace Rd PL4. 249 B1
Oakford Cl PL7. . . . . 207 D7
Oakford Ct EX36. . . . . .30 D8
Oakford Cross
Kingsteignton TQ12. . . . . . . 207 D7
North Molton EX36. . . . . . . .30 C8
Oakford Villas EX36. . . . . . .30 D8
Oak Gdns PL21. . . . . 237 E5
Oakham Rd PL5. . . . . 244 B5
Oakhayes Rd EX5. . . . . 184 B3
Oakhays EX36. . . . . 158 D4
Oak Hill
Budleigh Salterton EX9. . . . 198 C6
Dawlish EX7. . . . . 204 C5
East Budleigh EX9. . . . . 198 B6
Oak Hill Cross Rd
Exeter EX7. . . . . 204 C4
Teignmouth TQ14. . . . . 210 D8
Oakhill Rd TQ1. . . . . 219 F6
Oakhill Rise [3] EX31. . . . 154 C3
Oak La
East Anstey TA22. . . . . .32 E6
Stockleigh Pomeroy EX17 . . .81 A4
Whitstone EX22. . . . . .70 E1
Oakland Ave EX31. . . . . . . 154 D4
Oakland Cl EX7. . . . . 204 D5
Oakland Pk EX31. . . . . 154 B4
Oakland Pk S EX31. . . . . . 154 B4
Oakland Rd TQ12. . . . . 207 F2
Oaklands
Bideford EX39. . . . . .25 D4
Petrockstow EX20. . . . . .56 F4
Tavistock PL19. . . . . 171 D2
Oaklands Cl
Buckfastleigh TQ11. . . . . . . 236 A5
Okehampton EX20. . . . . . . 170 B6
Saltash PL12. . . . . 242 C3
Oaklands Gdns EX31. . . . . 154 D4
Oaklands Gn PL12. . . . . . . 242 D3
Oaklands Park Sch EX7 .204 C5
Oaklands Pk
Buckfastleigh TQ11. . . . . . . 236 A5
Okehampton EX20. . . . . . . 170 B6
Oaklands Rd TQ11. . . . . . . 236 A6
Oaklands Wlk EX7. . . . . . . 204 D5
Oak Lawn TQ12. . . . . 207 C2
Oaklawn Ct TQ1. . . . . 219 F7
Oaklawn Terr TQ1. . . . . . . 219 F7
Oaklea
Honiton EX14. . . . . 166 B6
Tiverton EX16. . . . . 161 D6
Oaklea Cl TQ7. . . . . 258 C4
Oaklea Cres EX31. . . . . 153 D5
Oakleaf Cl EX21. . . . . .73 E2
Oakleaf Way EX32. . . . . .17 E4
Oaklea Pk TQ12. . . . . 123 A1
Oaklea EX15. . . . . .66 F3
Oakleigh Rd
Barnstaple EX32. . . . . 155 A4
Exmouth EX8. . . . . 202 B7
Oakley Cl
Exeter EX1. . . . . 174 E1
Teignmouth TQ14. . . . . 210 B7
Oakley Wlk EX5. . . . . 179 E3
Oak Mdw EX36. . . . . 158 B4
Oak Park Ave TQ2. . . . . . . 219 D8
Oak Park Cl TQ2. . . . . 219 D8
Oakpark Cross TQ12. . . . . 137 E6
Oakpark La EX7. . . . . 124 E6
Oak Park Rd
Dawlish EX7. . . . . 204 C5
Newton Abbot TQ12. . . . . . 206 F4
Oak Pl TQ12. . . . . 207 D3
Oak Rd
Exeter EX4. . . . . 176 F4
Okehampton EX20. . . . . . . 170 C6
Tavistock PL19. . . . . 171 C2
West Hill EX11. . . . . 168 C2
Oakridge TQ1. . . . . 220 C3
Oak Ridge
Exeter EX2. . . . . 181 A8
Lifton PL16. . . . . 105 E4
Oaks The
Bovey Tracey TQ13. . . . . . . 180 E7
[4] Hemyock EX15. . . . . .67 B8
Mary Tavy PL19. . . . . 117 E6
Yeoford EX17. . . . . .79 C1
Oaktree Cl
Broadclyst EX5. . . . . 175 D6
Exmouth EX8. . . . . 196 B3
Ivybridge PL21. . . . . 237 A5
Oak Tree Cl EX14. . . . . .68 C2
Oaktree Ct PL6. . . . . 244 F1
Oak Tree Dr
Barnstaple EX32. . . . . 155 E4
Newton Abbot TQ12. . . . . . 212 F8
Oak Tree Gdns EX34. . . . . 150 B5
Oak Tree Gr [6] TQ14. . . . 210 A3
Oak Tree La PL19. . . . . 171 C3
Oak Tree Pk
Plymouth PL6. . . . . 245 D6
Sticklepath EX20. . . . . .95 A5
Oak Tree Pl EX2. . . . . 181 C8
Oak Tree Villas EX10. . . . . 186 F8
Oak Units EX17. . . . . 165 F5

Oak View EX14. . . . . 166 A3
Oakwell Cl EX38. . . . . 159 E5
Oakwood Cl
Barnstaple EX31. . . . . 154 C2
Dartmouth TQ6. . . . . 233 C3
Plymouth PL6. . . . . 245 D7
Oakwood Ct EX36. . . . . . . 158 D4
Oakwood Gr EX39. . . . . . . 157 B3
Oakwood Pk TQ7. . . . . 143 E7
Oakwood Rise EX8. . . . . . 196 E3
Oakymead Pk TQ12. . . . . . 207 D6
Oates Rd PL2. . . . . 248 B5
Oatlands Ave EX32. . . . . . 155 A1
Oatlands Dr TQ4. . . . . 226 A4
Oberon Rd EX1. . . . . 178 E7
Occombe Cross TQ3. . . . . 218 F3
Occombe Valley Rd TQ3 .219 A2
Ocean Ct PL1. . . . . 253 F8
Ocean Pk EX39. . . . . 156 B7
Ocean St EX2. . . . . 247 E6
Ocean View Cres TQ5. . . . 230 A1
Ocean View Dr TQ5. . . . . . 230 A1
Ochil Cl EX39. . . . . .26 A4
Ockington Cl EX20. . . . . . 170 C5
Ockment Ct EX20. . . . . 170 B5
Octagon St PL1. . . . . 262 B3
Octagon The PL1. . . . . 262 B2
Octon Gr TQ1. . . . . 219 E7
Odam Cross EX36. . . . . .45 E5
Odam Moor Cross EX36 . .45 E5
Oddicombe Beach Hill
TQ1. 220 D8
Oddicombe Cliff Rly
TQ1. 220 D8
Odle Hill TQ12. . . . . 212 A6
Odlehill Gr TQ12. . . . . 212 A6
Odun Pl [34] EX39. . . . . .15 A1
Odun Rd [22] EX39. . . . . . . .15 A1
Offwell CE Prim Sch EX14 .86 D2
Offwell Turn EX14. . . . . . . 102 B8
Ogwell Cross TQ12. . . . . . 206 F2
Ogwell End Dr TQ12. . . . . 206 F2
Ogwell Mill Rd TQ12. . . . . 206 E3
Ogwell Rd TQ12. . . . . 206 F1
Oilmill Cross EX5. . . . . 179 C2
Oilmill La
Clyst St George EX5. . . . . . . 183 D8
Clyst St Mary EX5. . . . . 179 C1
Okefield Ave EX17. . . . . . . 165 C6
Okefield Rd EX17. . . . . 165 C6
Okefield Ridge EX17. . . . . 165 C6
Okehampton Castle
EX20. . . . . 170 A3
Okehampton Cl PL7. . . . . . 251 B4
Okehampton Coll EX20 . .170 B4
Okehampton Com Hospl
EX20. . . . . 170 C6
**Okehampton Mus of
Dartmoor Life** EX20 . . . .170 B5
Okehampton Pl [8] EX4 . . .177 A5
Okehampton Prim Sch
EX20. . . . . 170 B5
Okehampton Rd EX4. . . . . 177 A5
Okehampton St EX4. . . . . 177 A5
Okehampton Sta EX20 . . .170 C3
Okehampton Way PL21. . 237 D4
Oketor Cl EX20. . . . . 170 C3
Oke Tor Cl TQ3. . . . . 219 A2
Okewill Cross EX31. . . . . . . .10 A2
Okewood Ct EX8. . . . . 202 B5
Olands Rd TA21. . . . . 160 D6
Olchard La TQ12, TQ13 . . 124 A4
Old Abbey Ct EX2. . . . . 177 E2
Oldaway La EX5. . . . . 172 C7
Oldaway Tongue TQ7. . . . 143 E1
Old Bakery Cl EX39. . . . . . 156 F2
Old Bakery Cotts PL8 . . . . 257 F4
Old Bakery The EX8. . . . . . 202 B8
Old Barn Cl EX5. . . . . 173 F8
Oldbarn Cross EX12. . . . . 212 A7
Oldbarn La EX16. . . . . .33 D5
Oldberry La TA22. . . . . .33 D6
Old Barnstaple Rd
Bideford, East-t-W EX39 . . 157 C2
Bideford, Pillhead EX39. . . 157 D2
Braunton EX31. . . . . .15 F7
Ilfracombe EX34. . . . . 150 D2
Old Beer Rd EX12. . . . . 191 E6
Old Bell Hill EX16. . . . . .47 D5
Oldberry La TA22. . . . . .33 D6
Old Berrynarbor Rd
EX34. . . . . 154 F5
Old Bideford Rd EX31. . . . 154 C2
Old Blundell's EX16. . . . . . 161 D3
Oldborough Cross EX17 . . .61 B1
Oldborough La EX17. . . . . . .61 B1
Old Bridge Rd EX15. . . . . . .83 F6
Old Bridwell EX15. . . . . .65 F7
Old Butterleigh Rd EX5 . . .82 B6
Old Bystock Dr EX8. . . . . . 196 E3
Old Canal Cl EX23. . . . . .70 A6
Old Chapel Gdns EX19. . . .58 F3
Old Chapel Way PL10. . . . 252 F6
Old Chard Rd EX14. . . . . . . .86 C6
Old Cider Press The [3]
TQ4. 226 B5
Old Cider Works La
TQ12. . . . . 212 A7
Old Cider Works The
TQ12. . . . . 212 A7
Old Coach Rd EX5. . . . . . . 175 C6
Old Coastguard Cotts
PL9. 140 C2
Old Coastguard Sta
EX12. . . . . 192 D5
Old Coast Rd EX34. . . . . . . .2 E4

Old Cooperage The EX2..177 F5
Old Dairy The PL3 ....249 B6
Old Dawlish Rd EX6..... 181 C2
Old Ebford La EX3 ....183 C4
Old Eldorado Ct EX2.....164 C3
Oldenburg Pk TQ3 ....226 C7
Old English Ind Est PL20 .127 B3
Old Exeter Rd
  Bishop's Tawton EX32 ....16 E1
  Chudleigh TQ13 ....123 F8
  Chudleigh TQ13, EX6 ....114 A2
  Newton Abbot TQ12......207 B4
  Tavistock PL19 ....171 D7
Old Exeter St TQ13 ....123 E6
Old Farm Bglws EX10 ....188 B7
Old Farm Rd PL5 ....247 C8
Old Farm Way EX7 ....204 D4
Old Ferry Rd PL12 ....243 A3
Oldfields EX8............202 C6
Old Fore St EX10 ....188 B3
Old Foundry The PL19....171 D6
Old Gatehouse Rd EX7 ...204 E7
Old George St PL1.......262 C2
Old Greystone Hill PL15,
  PL19..................115 D6
Old Hayes 3 EX10 ....188 A4
Old Hazard Cotts TQ9 ...135 F2
Old Hill
  Bickington TQ12..........131 D7
  Cullompton EX15 ....135 D7
Old Home Farm DT7...193 E6
Oldhouse La TQ7 ....142 F7
Old Ide La EX2...........176 E2
Old Inn Mews EX38 .....159 D5
Old Jaycroft EX15........162 D4
Old Laira Rd PL3 ....249 C4
Oldlands Cl PL6 ....245 B6
Old Launceston Rd PL19 .171 B6
Old Laundry The PL1.....262 A3
Old Liverton Rd TQ12 ...180 D1
Old Lyme Hill DT6 ....104 F4
Old Lyme Rd DT6........104 F4
Old Manor Cl TQ13.......130 E5
Old Manor Ct 21 EX7....204 D6
Old Manor Gdns EX24....103 B3
Old Market Cl EX2 ....177 B3
Old Market Dr EX39......38 F8
Old Market Field EX16...46 E1
Old Market Field Ind Est
  EX16..................46 E1
Old Matford La EX6, EX2..181 E6
Old Mill Cl EX2 ....261 C1
Old Mill Ct PL7 ....250 E5
Old Mill Ind Est EX5 ....173 E7
Old Mill La TQ6..........233 C4
Old Mill Rd TQ2 ....226 C7
Old Mill The
  Culmstock EX15...........66 E8
  Harbertonford TQ9 ....139 B8
Old Mine La PL18.........125 B6
Old Newton Rd
  Bovey Tracey TQ13........180 E4
  Kingskerswell TQ12.......212 E5
Old Nursery Dr EX4 .....178 B8
Old Orchard TQ13........180 D7
Old Orchard Cl EX23.....70 A6
Old Orchard The EX20....74 E2
Old Paignton La TQ2.....219 D2
Old Paignton Rd TQ2....219 D3
Old Park Rd
  Exeter EX4.............261 B4
  Plymouth PL3 ....248 D6
Old Pavilion Cl EX7 .....178 C4
Old Pinn La EX1 ....174 E1
Old Plymouth Rd PL3 ...249 E5
Old Post Office Mews 19
  EX39..................157 A2
Old Printworks The TQ1..220 B4
Old Priory PL7...........250 D5
Old Priory Jun Sch PL7 ..250 D5
Old Quarry Rd PL20.....126 D3
Old Quay La 8 EX39......15 B1
Old Quay St TQ14........210 B4
Old Rd
  Brixton PL8 ....257 A5
  Galmpton TQ5 ....249 B8
  Harbertonford TQ9 ......139 C7
  Lutton PL21............133 B2
  Okehampton EX20 ....170 A4
  Stoke Fleming TQ6.......146 B7
  Tiverton EX16...........161 E4
Old Rectory Cl EX39 .....15 C2
Old Rectory Cross TQ13 .110 C7
Old Rectory Gdns
  Morchard Bishop EX17......61 B2
  Thurlestone TQ7 ....143 A2
Old Rectory La
  Ashwater EX21...........90 E6
  Bratton Fleming EX31.....18 A8
Oldridge Rd EX4.........98 B6
Oldridge View EX6.......97 F5
Old Rydon Cl EX2........178 E2
Old Rydon La EX2........178 D1
Old Rydon Ley EX2.......178 D2
Old Sawmills The EX37...28 B1
Old School Cl EX16 .....161 B4
Old School Ct
  6 Hemyock EX15..........67 B8
  6 Honiton EX14........166 C6
  Topsham EX3...........182 F5
Old School Ho The
  Kingsland PL10 ....253 A1
  North Tawton EX20.......77 C4
Old School La EX31.......153 E5

Old School Rd
  Barnstaple EX32 ....155 C2
  Plymouth PL5............247 C8
Old School The 5 EX16 .161 D4
Oldshute La TA22 ....33 C7
Old Sidmouth Rd EX24 ..103 A4
Old Smithy Cotts EX39 ...37 B4
Old Stables The
  15 Bideford EX39 ....157 A1
  Clyst St Mary EX5 ......179 A1
Old Station Rd
  Barnstaple EX32 ....155 B4
  Horrabridge PL20.......126 F4
Old Station The PL20....126 E4
Old Stickle Path
  EX31..................154 E3
Old Stone Cl EX39 ......156 B6
Oldstone Cross TQ9 .....139 F2
Old's View EX4 ....141 D1
Old Tannery Bsns Pk The 4
  PL4...................263 A4
Old Tannery The EX32 ...28 D8
Old Teignmouth Rd EX7 .204 D4
Old Tinhay PL16 ....105 F4
Old Tiverton Rd
  Bampton EX16...........34 C1
  Crediton EX17...........165 E6
  Exeter EX4.............177 D8
Old Torquay Rd TQ3 ....226 C8
Old Torrington Rd EX31 .154 D2
Old Torwood Rd TQ1 ...220 D4
Old Totnes Rd
  Ashburton TQ13.........130 F4
  Buckfastleigh TQ11 ......236 C5
  Newton Abbot TQ12......207 A1
Old Town EX33 ....157 A1
Old Town Hill TQ12,
  TQ13..................122 C2
Old Town St
  Dawlish EX7............204 D6
  Plymouth PL1...........262 C3
Old Vicarage Cl EX2 .....176 D1
Old Vicarage Gdn DT7...260 D3
Old Vicarage Rd EX2 ....177 A4
Old Vicarage The
  Sidmouth EX10 ....187 F3
  Wellington TA21.........160 E6
Old Walls Hill TQ1 ......124 D1
Old Warleigh La PL5 ....244 B7
Oldway TQ13 ....123 E6
Old Way
  Chipstable TA4...........35 D6
  Chudleigh TQ13 ....123 E6
Oldway Ho TA21 ....160 F4
Oldway Mansion TQ3....226 B8
Oldway Rd TA21.........160 F4
Oldway Rd
  East Anstey TA22........32 F5
  Paignton TQ3 ....226 B8
  Wellington TA21........160 E4
Old Weighbridge The 19
  EX8...................202 A6
Old Wharf The PL9......255 C7
Old Widdicombe La TQ3 225 D6
Old Widdicombe La TQ3 225 D7
Old Widdicombe La TQ3..225 C7
Old Woodlands Rd PL5...244 D3
Old Woods Hill TQ2......219 E7
Old Woods Trad Est TQ2.219 E8
Olga Terr EX8...........195 F5
Olive Gdns EX7..........201 B2
Olive Gr EX7............201 B2
Olive Rd EX32 ....155 B5
Olivia Ct PL4 ....263 B4
Omega Ctr The EX2 .....178 E5
Once Upon A Time
  (Childrens Theme Pk)
  EX34..................8 C6
One End St 4 EX39.......15 A1
One Fir EX15 ....83 C4
Onslow Rd
  Plymouth PL2............248 C7
  Sidcombe TQ8 ....259 D5
Ora Cl EX33 ....7 E2
Ora La EX33 ....7 E2
Orange Gr TQ2 ....214 A4
Orange Moor Cross EX18..44 F3
Ora Stone Pk EX33.......7 E1
Orchard Ave PL6.........249 B7
Orchard Cl
  Ashprington TQ9 ....139 F7
  Barnstaple EX31 ....154 C3
  Beesands TQ7 ....149 D7
  Braunton EX33..........152 C6
  Coldridge EX18..........59 C4
  Colyford EX24 ....103 B3
  6 Combe Martin EX34 ....3 A3
  Dawlish EX7............204 D6
  Denbury TQ12 ....211 A6
  East Budleigh EX9 ....198 B6
  East Ogwell TQ12 ....206 D1
  Exeter EX1.............174 F1
  Exmouth EX8 ....196 B1
  Exworth, Littleham EX8..203 A6
  Frogmore TQ7 ....144 E1
  Galmpton TQ5 ....229 C5
  Kingsteignton, Sandygate
    TQ12.................123 E2
  Kingsteignton TQ12 ....207 F7
  Lympstone EX8 ....195 E5
  Newton Poppleford EX10 .186 D8
  Okehampton EX20.......170 B4
  Ottery St Mary EX11....169 C3

Orchard Cl continued
  3 Plymouth PL7.........251 C5
  Rockwell Green TA21.....160 A5
  Sandford EX17..........80 A5
  Shaldon TQ14...........209 D5
  Sidford EX10 ....188 C8
  Sidmouth EX10 ....187 F3
  Talaton EX5 ....84 A2
  Tavistock PL19..........126 A8
  Uffculme EX15...........66 A7
  Upton Pyne EX5..........173 A7
  Whitford EX13...........103 B6
  Wilmington EX14........86 C2
  Woodbury EX5..........184 C3
  Yealmpton PL8..........257 F3
Orchard Cotts
  Holbeton PL8...........136 D1
  Lamerton PL19 ....116 F3
  Newton Tracey EX31......27 A6
Orchard Cres PL9.......255 C7
Orchard Cross EX17.....60 D3
Orchard Ct
  1 Crediton EX17 ....165 C5
  Exeter EX1.............178 E6
  Ivybridge PL21 ....237 B5
  Lamerton PL19 ....116 E3
  Newton St Cyres EX5.....81 A1
  North Tawton EX20.......77 C4
  Wellington TA21.........160 E6
  Whimple EX5............99 E8
Orchard Dr
  Ipplepen TQ12 ....211 D2
  Kingskerswell TQ12......212 F4
  Otterton EX9 ....198 E2
Orchard Farm EX14.....85 A3
Orchard Gate EX19......57 F7
Orchard Gdns
  Brixham TQ5 ....157 A4
  Broadclyst EX5 ....175 D6
  13 Dawlish EX7 ....204 D6
  Exeter EX4.............176 F4
  10 Teignmouth TQ14 ....210 C4
  West Buckland TA21.....52 F7
Orchard Gr
  Brixham TQ5 ....230 C3
  Croyde EX33 ....7 E1
Orchard Hill
  Bideford EX39 ....157 A4
  Exeter EX4.............176 F3
  Yealmpton PL8..........136 B3
Orchard Ho
  6 Chudleigh TQ13 ....123 E6
  1 Teignmouth TQ14 ....210 C4
  Torquay TQ1............220 C5
  Orchard Ind Est's TQ7...258 C5
Orchard La
  Plymouth PL7...........250 E6
  Silverton EX5...........82 B6
  Starcross EX6 ....201 A4
Orchard Leigh EX16.....161 C3
Orchard Mdw TQ13 .....111 A6
Orchardton La EX33.....8 B1
Orchard Pk
  Dartington TQ9 ....222 F8
  Dittisham TQ6 ....228 C3
  Ivybridge PL21 ....237 C4
Orchard Pl 3 TQ1 ......220 A7
Orchard Rd
  Ashburton TQ13.........130 F4
  Barnstaple EX32 ....155 B3
  2 Ilfracombe EX34 .....150 C5
  Knowle EX33...........8 D1
  Plymouth PL2...........248 B7
  4 Torquay, Ellacombe
    TQ1..................220 B6
  Torquay, Hele TQ2 ......213 F1
  Wrafton EX33...........152 E3
Orchard Rise EX39 .....157 A4
Orchardside EX10.......188 B7
Orchards The
  Galmpton TQ5 ....229 B5
  Landkey EX32 ....17 B2
  Swimbridge EX32 ....28 E8
Orchard Terr
  Abbotskerswell TQ12....212 B7
  Barnstaple EX32 ....155 B2
  3 Bovey Tracey TQ13 ...180 D8
  Buckfastleigh TQ11 ......236 B5
  Chagford TQ13 ....13 A6
  Crediton EX17 ....165 B5
  Kingskerswell TQ12......212 F5
  Kingswear TQ6..........234 B3
  Totnes TQ9 ....223 C5
  Tuckenhay TQ9 ....139 F6
Orchard The
  Abbotskerswell TQ12....212 B6
  Avonwick TQ10..........135 B1
  Barnstaple EX31 ....154 A3
  Bishopsteignton TQ14 ...208 F8
  Dunsford EX6...........112 F7
  Gunnislake PL18 ....125 D6
  Holcombe EX7...........210 E8
  Holywell Lake TA21......51 E7
  Honiton EX14...........166 B5
  Kilmington EX13.........87 D1
  Modbury PL21 ....152 A1
  Seaton EX12 ....192 A5
  Tipton St John EX10 .....100 D2
  Totnes TQ9 ....223 C5
  Whiddon Down EX20.....95 C1
Orchardton Terr 2 PL9 .255 F5
Orchard Vale Com Sch
  EX32..................155 A4
Orchard View
  Frogmore TQ7 ....144 E1
  Halberton EX16 ....65 B7

Orchard Way
  1 Bovey Tracey TQ13.....180 D8
  Chillington TQ7 ....145 A1
  Cullompton EX15 ....163 B2
  Honiton EX14...........166 D6
  Kenton EX6.............194 D3
  Lapford EX17...........60 D3
  Stoke Gabriel TQ9 ......227 F8
  Tiverton EX16...........161 B3
  Topsham EX3...........182 E5
  Uffculme EX15...........66 A7
  Willand EX15 ....162 D4
Orchard Waye TQ9......223 B5
Orchid Ave
  Ivybridge PL21 ....237 A6
  Kingsteignton TQ12......207 E7
Orchid Cl 7 EX16.......161 F6
Orchid Dr EX4..........176 E8
Orchid Vale 14 TQ12....123 F1
Orcombe Ct EX8 ....202 D8
Ordnance St PL1........247 E2
Orduff Rd PL19 ....171 A5
Oregon Way PL3.........249 D6
Orestone Cross TQ2.....213 D3
Orestone Dr TQ1 ....214 C6
Oreston Prim Sch PL9 ...255 C3
Oreston Rd PL9 ....255 C8
Orient Rd TQ3 ....220 B5
Oriole Dr EX4 ....173 D1
Orkney Cl TQ2 ....213 E2
Orkney Mews EX16 .....161 D6
Orleigh Ave TQ2 ....207 B5
Orleigh Cl EX39..........40 C7
Orleigh Ct EX39.........25 C1
Orleigh Pk TQ12 ....207 B5
Orley Rd TQ12 ....211 B2
Ormonde Ct EX36 ....158 D4
Orpington Ct EX16......65 B7
Orstone Cross EX32 .....18 E3
Orway Ash Cross EX15...56 B2
Orway Cross EX15 ....66 C1
Orwell Garth EX4 ....178 C8
Osbern Rd TQ3 ....219 A2
Osborn Cl TQ12.........211 D2
Osborn Dr EX39 ....156 D2
Osborne Cl TQ1.........262 C2
Osborne Ct PL1.........262 C2
Osborne La EX39 ....156 D2
Osborne Pl PL1.........262 C2
Osborne Rd
  Ilfracombe EX34 ....150 A5
  Plymouth PL3...........248 A3
Osborne St TQ2.........207 D3
Osborne Villas 2 PL3....248 A3
Osmond Lodge TQ4.....226 B4
Osmond's La 1 TQ14 ...210 B4
Osney Ave TQ4 ....226 B4
Osney Cres TQ4.........226 B4
Osney Gdns TQ4........226 B4
Osprey Dr TQ2 ....213 D3
Osprey Gdns PL9 ....256 C7
Osprey Ho TQ1 ....220 D7
Osprey Rd EX2..........178 F6
Oswald Browning Way 4
  EX31..................155 A7
Otterbourne Ct 4 EX39 .198 B1
Otter Cl
  Okehampton EX20 ....170 D6
  Tipton St John EX10 .....100 D3
  West Hill EX11..........168 D4
Otter Ct
  Bickington TQ12.........131 F8
  Budleigh Salterton EX9 ...198 C1
  Exeter EX2.............181 C8
Otter Estuary Nature Reserve
  EX9 ....198 D1
Otter Rd TQ2 ....219 C2
Otter Reach EX10.......186 F8
Otters The EX16 ....49 B2
Otterton CE Prim Sch
  EX9 ....198 E7
Otterton Mews EX14....167 F7
Otterton Mill EX9 ....198 D7
Otter Vale Ct EX14......68 C1
Ottervale Rd EX9 ....198 C1
Otter Way EX14.........155 D4
Ottery Cotts PL19.......116 E3
Ottery La EX10..........101 A1
Ottery Moor La EX14....166 A6
Ottery Park Ind Est PL19.116 E2
Ottery St Mary Hospl
  EX11..................169 C3
Ottery St Mary Prim Sch
  EX11..................169 C3
Ottery St & Ex EX19 ...198 F8
Our Lady & St Patrick's RC
  Prim Sch TQ4 ....210 A6
Our Lady's RC Prim Sch
  EX32..................155 B5
Oussaborough La EX34...8 C6
Outer Ting Tong EX9....197 B3
Outland Rd PL2.........248 A5
Oval Gn TQ2 ....178 C3
Overbeck's Mus & Gdn
  TQ8 ....259 B1
Overcliff EX7 ....204 D6
Overcliff Ct EX7 ....204 E7
Overclose TQ13 ....225 F8
Overcott La EX36........46 D8
Overdale Cl TQ2 ....213 F4
Overdale Rd PL2........248 B7
Overgang TQ5 ....230 D5
Overgang Rd TQ5 ......230 C6
Overland Ct EX4 ....174 E2
Overlands TQ12 ....142 C6
Overseas Est TQ6 ....146 B6
Overton Cl DT7..........260 E5

Overton Gdns 3 PL3....248 F5
Over Weir Cvn Site EX37..28 C3
Owen St TA21...........160 C6
Owlaborough La EX36...32 B2
Owlacombe Cross TQ12.131 A7
Oxenham Cross EX20...95 C5
Oxenham Gn TQ2 ....219 D6
Oxenpark Gate EX6 .....112 F5
Oxenpark La
  Bondleigh EX20..........77 C6
  Ilfracombe, Goosewell EX34..2 C3
  Ilfracombe, Two Pots EX34..2 C2
  Morchard Bishop EX17 ...61 F1
  Stockleigh Pomeroy EX17..80 F7
Oxford Ave PL3 ....248 E5
Oxford Cl EX8 ....196 E4
Oxford Cross EX33 ......8 A3
Oxford Ct TQ2 ....213 F1
Oxford Gdns PL3........248 E5
Oxford Gr EX34 ....150 B6
Oxford La TQ5 ....230 A4
Oxford Pk EX34 ....150 B5
Oxford Pl PL1 ....262 C3
Oxford Rd EX4..........261 C4
Oxford St
  Dartmouth TQ6 ....233 F3
  Exeter EX2.............177 A4
  Plymouth PL1...........262 B3
Oxford Terr
  Crediton EX17 ....165 D5
  4 Plymouth PL1 ....262 B3
  Sandford EX17..........80 A5
Oxham Cross EX36......45 D8
Ox Hill La EX24 ....102 F4
Oxlea Cl TQ1 ....220 E4
Oxlea Rd TQ1...........220 E4
Oxman's Cotts EX39.....157 E6
Oxmead EX5............99 D3
Oxmon's La EX39 ....157 A7
Oxton Ho EX6 ....114 E1
Oyster Bend TQ4 ....226 C2
Oyster Cl TQ4...........226 C2
Ozone Terr DT7 ....260 D2

P

Paccombe Pool La EX10 189 C7
Pacehayne La
  Dalwood EX13...........87 A1
  Shute EX13 ....103 A8
Packhall La TQ5 ....230 A2
Packhorse Cl EX10......188 D8
Packington St PL2.......248 A4
Packs Cl TQ9 ....139 C7
Padacre Rd TQ2 ....214 A4
Paddock Cl
  Plymouth PL9...........255 E5
  Saltash PL12 ....242 D4
  Seaton EX12 ....191 F7
Paddock Dr PL21 ....237 D4
Paddocks The
  Abbotskerswell TQ12....212 B7
  Dolton EX19............57 F7
  Honiton EX14...........166 A2
  Membury EX13 ....87 D6
  Totnes TQ9 ....223 D6
  Wellington TA21........160 E5
  Whimple EX5............99 E7
Paddock The
  Brixham TQ5 ....230 B4
  Dawlish EX7............204 E7
  Dulverton TA22 ....33 D6
  Torquay TQ1............214 B1
Paddons Coombe 9
  TQ12..................123 F1
Paddons La TQ14 ....210 A7
Pafford Ave TQ2 ....214 B2
Pafford Cl TQ2 ....214 A2
Page Ho TQ4 ....226 C6
Page's Cross EX16 ......62 F7
Paige Adams' Rd TQ9 ..223 B6
Paiges Farm PL9 ....255 C1
Paiges La 9 EX31 ....154 F5
Paignton Com & Sports Coll
  Paignton TQ3 ....225 C4
  Paignton TQ3 ....225 D4
Paignton & Dartmouth
  Steam Railway
  Galmpton TQ5 ....229 C5
  Kingswear TQ6..........234 A4
Paignton & Dartmouth
  Steam Rly TQ4 ....226 C2
Paignton & District Hospl
  TQ3...................226 B6
Paignton (Queen's Park) Sta
  TQ4...................226 B6
Paignton Rd TQ2 ....226 B8
Paignton Sta TQ4.......226 B6
Paignton Zoological &
  Botanical Gdns TQ4....225 F4
Pail Pk EX33.............8 D1
Painsford Cross TQ9 ....139 D7
Painter's Cross EX13....102 F7
Painters Ct EX2 ....261 A1
Painton Water EX37.....37 D8
Paizen La EX12 ....191 B6
Palace Ave TQ3 ....226 B6
Palace Cotts 10 EX8....202 A7
Palace Gate EX1 ....261 B2
Palace La EX21..........137 B7
Palace Mdw TQ13.......123 E6
Palace St PL1 ....262 A2
Palatine Ct TQ1 ....220 B5
Pale Gate Cl EX14 ......166 D7
Palegate Cross TQ7.....258 A8
Palermo 12 TQ1 ....220 B5

Palermo Rd TQ1 . . . . 220 C7
Palfrey's La EX16 . . . . 49 C5
Palk Cl TQ14 . . . . 209 D5
Palk St TQ2 . . . . 196 D3
Palm Cl EX8 . . . . 196 D3
Palm Gdns **1** PL21 . . . . . . 137 B2
Palm Ct EX7 . . . . 201 A2
Palmer Ct EX9 . . . . 198 A1
Palmers Cl EX33 . . . . 152 D5
Palmers Ct EX38 . . . . 159 E5
Palmer's La EX5 . . . . 99 E5
Palmerston Dr EX4 . . . . . . 176 E7
Palmerston Pk EX16 . . . . . . 161 B2
Palmerston St PL1 . . . . 262 A4
Palm Ho EX4 . . . . 176 E8
Palm Rd TQ2 . . . . 220 A5
Palms The **2** TQ1 . . . . . . 220 D4
Pamela Rd EX1 . . . . 177 F7
Pankhurst Cl EX8 . . . . 202 E7
Panney The EX4 . . . . 178 A7
Pannier Mkt
Great Torrington EX38 . . . . 159 D5
Tavistock PL19 . . . . 171 C5
Panorama TQ2 . . . . 219 E2
Panson Cross PL15 . . . . 90 B3
Papermakers La PL21 . . . . 237 E6
Parade
Chudleigh TQ13 . . . . 123 E6
Exmouth EX8 . . . . 202 A7
Plymouth PL1 . . . . 263 A2
Parade Bsns Pk **4** PL19 . 171 B4
Parade Ope PL1 . . . . 263 A2
Parade Pl PL5 . . . . 244 A3
Parade The
Chardstock EX13 . . . . 88 A7
Millbrook PL10 . . . . 252 E5
Milton Abbot PL19 . . . . . . 116 A6
Paradise Glen TQ14 . . . . . 210 B6
Paradise Lawn EX36 . . . . . 158 D4
Paradise Pk EX22 . . . . 70 E1
Paradise Pl
1 Brixham TQ5 . . . . 230 D5
Plymouth PL1 . . . . 248 A2
Paradise Rd
Plymouth PL1 . . . . 248 A2
Teignmouth TQ14 . . . . 210 C6
Paradise Wlk TQ4 . . . . 226 C4
Paragon EX34 . . . . 150 B6
Paramore Way EX36 . . . . . 158 C4
Parehayne La EX24 . . . . . . 102 E7
Parely Hill TQ13 . . . . 110 F6
Paris Rd TQ3 . . . . 226 C8
Paris St EX1 . . . . 261 B3
Park Ave
Barnstaple EX31 . . . . 154 C4
Bideford EX39 . . . . 157 A3
Brixham TQ5 . . . . 230 B3
Plymouth, Devonport PL1 . . 247 E3
Plymouth, Plymstock PL9 . . 255 D7
Westward Ho! EX39 . . . . . 156 C7
Park Bglws EX16 . . . . 51 B3
Park Cl
Clyst Hydon EX15 . . . . 83 D4
Fremington EX31 . . . . 153 E5
Holsworthy EX22 . . . . 164 C6
Ivybridge PL21 . . . . 237 C5
Plymouth PL7 . . . . 250 B7
Silverton EX5 . . . . 82 C5
Tiverton EX16 . . . . 161 D5
Woodbury EX5 . . . . 184 C2
Park Com Sch The EX32 . 155 A3
Park Cotts
Bigbury TQ7 . . . . 142 F5
Ugborough PL21 . . . . 137 D6
Park Cres
Combe Martin EX34 . . . . . . 3 A3
Plymouth PL9 . . . . 255 C7
Park Cross EX17 . . . . 62 C3
Park Ct
Brixham TQ5 . . . . 230 E5
Chillaton PL16 . . . . 106 D1
Honiton EX14 . . . . 85 C2
Ilfracombe EX34 . . . . 150 B4
Parkelands TQ13 . . . . 180 C7
Parker Cl
Plymouth PL7 . . . . 250 B5
Wellington TA21 . . . . 160 E6
Parker Rd
Bigbury-on-S TQ7 . . . . 142 E3
Plymouth PL2 . . . . 248 B6
Parkers Cl TQ9 . . . . 223 D4
Parkers Cross La EX1 . . . . 174 F2
Parkers Farm Holiday Pk
TQ13 . . . . 131 C6
Parker's Gn PL18 . . . . 125 C6
Parkers Hollow EX31 . . . . 154 B3
Parkes Rd EX4 . . . . 201 A8
Parkers Way TQ9 . . . . 223 D4
Parkes Rd EX38 . . . . 159 F5
Parkesway PL12 . . . . 242 D2
Parke Woodlands Walks
TQ13 . . . . 180 A8
Parkfield TQ7 . . . . 143 A2
Parkfield Cl
Marldon TQ3 . . . . 218 D3
Totnes TQ9 . . . . 223 F5
Parkfield Cross TQ13 . . . . 131 A3
Parkfield Dr PL6 . . . . 245 F1
Parkfield Rd
Topsham EX3 . . . . 182 F5
Torquay TQ1 . . . . 219 F7
Park Field Terr EX12 . . . . 190 D4
Parkfield Way EX3 . . . . . . 182 F5
Parkfield Wlk TQ7 . . . . . . 143 A2
Park Five Bsns Ctr EX2 . . 178 E4
Park Gate EX37 . . . . 28 D2
Park Gdns EX35 . . . . 151 B5
Park Hall TQ1 . . . . 220 B3

Parkham Cross EX39 . . . . . 24 F1
Parkham Glade TQ5 . . . . . 230 C4
Parkham La TQ5 . . . . 230 C4
Parkham Prim Sch EX39 . . 39 E8
Parkham Rd TQ5 . . . . 230 C4
Parkham Terr **5** TQ5 . . 230 C4
Parkham Twrs **6** TQ5 . . 230 C4
Parkhayes EX5 . . . . 184 C7
Park Hill
Teignmouth TQ14 . . . . 210 B5
Tiverton EX16 . . . . 161 C5
Parkhill Cotts PL21 . . . . . 136 F4
Parkhill Ho TQ12 . . . . 211 F3
Parkhill Rd TQ1 . . . . 220 C3
Park Hill Rd EX34 . . . . . . 150 B5
Parkhouse Rd EX2 . . . . . . 176 F3
Parkhurst Rd TQ1, TQ2 . . 219 F7
Park La
Barnstaple EX31 . . . . 155 A3
8 Bere Alston PL20 . . . 125 E1
Bideford EX39 . . . . 157 A3
Blackawton TQ9 . . . . 139 E1
Budleigh Salterton EX9 . . . 197 F1
Chittlehampton EX37 . . . . . 43 F8
Combe Martin EX34 . . . . . . 3 A3
Combe St Nicholas TA20 . . 69 F6
Exeter EX4 . . . . 174 C2
Fillleigh EX32 . . . . 18 D7
Madford EX14 . . . . 67 C4
Otterton EX9 . . . . 198 E6
Pennymoor EX16 . . . . 62 D6
Plymouth PL9 . . . . 255 C7
Sparkwell PL7 . . . . 132 C1
Torquay TQ1 . . . . 220 B3
West Buckland TA21 . . . . . . 52 E7
Whitford EX13 . . . . 103 B6
Parkland Dr EX2 . . . . 178 C3
Parklands
Barnstaple EX31 . . . . 154 C3
12 Hemyock EX15 . . . . . 67 B8
Okehampton EX20 . . . . . . 170 B3
9 Seaton EX12 . . . . . . 192 A5
South Molton EX36 . . . . . 158 B3
Totnes TQ9 . . . . 223 C6
Parklands Cl EX36 . . . . . . 158 B3
Parklands Rd TA21 . . . . . . 160 D7
Parklands Way TQ13 . . . . 180 C4
Park Lane Cotts EX32 . . . . 29 D7
Park Lodge EX9 . . . . 197 F1
Park Mews TQ5 . . . . 230 E5
Park Mill Cross EX17 . . . . . 59 F3
Park Mill La EX18 . . . . 59 F8
Park Pl
Exeter, Heavitree EX1 . . . . 177 F6
Exeter, Mount Radford
EX2 . . . . 261 C2
Winkleigh EX19 . . . . 58 F3
Park Place La **12** PL3 . . 248 A4
Park Rd
Beer EX12 . . . . 191 C5
Crediton EX17 . . . . 165 D4
Dartington TQ9 . . . . 216 B2
Dawlish EX7 . . . . 204 D6
Exeter EX1 . . . . 177 E7
Exmouth EX8 . . . . 202 A8
Hatherleigh EX20 . . . . 75 C7
Kingskerswell TQ12 . . . . . 212 F5
Lapford EX17 . . . . 60 D3
Lifton PL16 . . . . 105 E3
Plymouth PL3 . . . . 249 A6
Silverton EX5 . . . . 82 C5
St Dominick PL12 . . . . 125 A2
Tiverton EX16 . . . . 161 D5
Torpoint PL11 . . . . 247 B3
Torquay TQ1 . . . . 214 B1
Park Rise
Dawlish EX2 . . . . 204 D4
Salcombe TQ8 . . . . 259 C4
Park Row EX20 . . . . 170 B5
Park School TQ9 . . . . 216 C3
Parkside
Ivybridge PL21 . . . . 237 C5
Plymouth PL2 . . . . 247 F5
Salcombe TQ8 . . . . 259 D5
Parkside Com Tech Coll
PL1 . . . . 247 E3
Parkside Cres EX1 . . . . . . 174 F3
Parkside Ct EX2 . . . . 261 B2
Parkside Dr EX8 . . . . 196 E3
Parkside Rd
Exeter EX1 . . . . 174 F3
Paignton TQ4 . . . . 226 C6
Parkside Villas TQ1 . . . . . 220 C7
Park St
Crediton EX17 . . . . 165 D5
Ivybridge PL21 . . . . 237 C4
Lynton EX35 . . . . 151 B5
Plymouth PL3 . . . . 248 A4
Tiverton EX16 . . . . 161 D5
Willand EX15 . . . . 162 C5
Park Street Mews PL21 . . 237 C4
Park Street Ope PL3 . . . . 248 A4
Parks Villas EX33 . . . . 152 D5
Park Terr
22 Barnstaple EX32 . . . 155 A4
Ivybridge PL21 . . . . 237 C4
Tiverton EX16 . . . . 161 D5
Parkview EX17 . . . . 80 A5
Park View
Axminster EX13 . . . . 88 A3
Bedford EX19 . . . . 42 D1
Kenton EX6 . . . . 194 E3
Lifton PL16 . . . . 105 E4

Park View continued
Newton Abbot TQ12 . . . . . 212 F8
Plymouth PL4 . . . . 263 C3
Pyworthy EX22 . . . . 71 D5
Shute EX13 . . . . 103 A7
Park View Cl **21** EX34 . . 3 A3
Park View Cotts EX38 . . . . 42 B6
Park View Cvn Site EX31 . 155 A6
Park View Rd EX32 . . . . . 155 A6
Park View Terr
Kingston TQ7 . . . . 142 C6
Okehampton EX20 . . . . . . 170 C3
Westward Ho! EX39 . . . . . 156 C7
Park Villas EX32 . . . . 27 E8
Parkway
Exeter EX2 . . . . 176 F3
Ilfracombe EX34 . . . . 150 B3
Park Way
Exmouth EX8 . . . . 202 C8
Woodbury EX5 . . . . 184 C2
Parkway Ct PL6 . . . . 249 E7
Parkway Ind Est The
PL6 . . . . 249 E7
Parkway Rd TQ13 . . . . 123 C6
Parkway The PL3, PL5,
PL6 . . . . 244 B1
Parkwood Cl PL6 . . . . 241 B2
Parkwood Ct PL19 . . . . . . 171 D6
Parkwood Rd
Tavistock PL19 . . . . 171 D6
Tavistock PL19 . . . . 171 E7
Park Wood Rise PL16 . . . . 105 E4
Parkyns Cross EX19 . . . . . . 43 B4
Parliament **9** EX34 . . . . 150 C6
Parliament St EX17 . . . . . 165 C5
Parnell Cl PL6 . . . . 249 A8
Parracombe CE Prim Sch
EX31 . . . . 4 C1
Parracombe La EX31 . . . . . . 4 D2
Parracombe Lane Head
EX31 . . . . 4 D2
Parr Cl EX1 . . . . 261 C4
Parricks La EX13 . . . . 88 D3
Parr La PL4 . . . . 263 B2
Parrocks La TA20 . . . . 88 C8
Parr's La TQ13 . . . . 123 E6
Parr St
Exeter EX1 . . . . 261 C4
Plymouth PL4 . . . . 263 B2
Parsonage Cross
Chulmleigh EX18 . . . . 44 F2
Dartington TQ9 . . . . 215 F2
Germansweek EX21 . . . . . . 91 D5
Staverton TQ9 . . . . 216 B2
West Putford EX22 . . . . . . 39 B2
Woodbury EX5 . . . . 184 C3
Parsonage Ct PL16 . . . . . 105 E4
Parsonage Hill EX36 . . . . . 31 A3
Parsonage La
Awliscombe EX14 . . . . 85 C1
George Nympton EX36 . . . 29 F2
Hittisleigh EX6 . . . . 96 C6
Honiton EX14 . . . . 166 D5
Kentisbury EX31 . . . . 10 E5
Moreleigh TQ9 . . . . 139 A3
Silverton EX5 . . . . 82 B6
South Molton EX36 . . . . . 158 C5
Staverton TQ9 . . . . 216 E4
Ugborough PL21 . . . . 137 D6
Parsonage Lane Cross
EX32 . . . . 18 B2
Parsonage Lane End
PL21 . . . . 137 D6
Parsonage Rd PL8 . . . . . . 141 A7
Parsonage St EX5 . . . . 83 A7
Parsonage Way EX5 . . . . . 184 C4
Parson Cl EX8 . . . . 196 C2
Parsons Cl
Newton Poppleford
EX10 . . . . 186 D8
Plymouth PL9 . . . . 256 A4
Parson's Cl EX15 . . . . 66 A3
Parsons La EX5 . . . . 99 B5
Parson St TQ14 . . . . 210 B5
Parthia Pl EX8 . . . . 196 C1
Partridge Cross EX16 . . . . 63 A8
Partridge Hill EX36 . . . . . . 45 D7
Partridge La EX16 . . . . 63 A8
Partridge Rd EX8 . . . . 196 C2
Partwayes PL19 . . . . 116 E3
Pasley St E PL2 . . . . 247 F4
Pasley St PL2 . . . . 247 E4
Passage Rd PL8 . . . . 140 F6
Passmore Rd EX5 . . . . 82 F6
Pasture Cross TQ9 . . . . . . 144 F8
Pastures The EX20 . . . . . . 92 A2
Patchacott Cross
Bratton Clovelly EX21 . . . . 92 A8
Northlew EX21 . . . . 74 B1
Patchel Cross EX20 . . . . . . 56 F3
Patches Rd EX16 . . . . 161 B4
Paternoster La TQ12 . . . . 211 C2
Paternoster Row
10 Barnstaple EX31 . . . 154 F5
Ottery St Mary EX11 . . . . . 169 D4
Pathdown La EX33 . . . . 7 F2
Pathfield EX36 . . . . 159 F5
Pathfield Cl
Barnstaple EX31 . . . . 154 A3
Totnes TQ9 . . . . 223 D5
Path Field Cl EX32 . . . . . . 18 B2
Pathfield Lawn EX31 . . . . 154 E6
Pathfields
Croyde EX33 . . . . 7 E2
Totnes TQ9 . . . . 223 D5
Uffculme EX15 . . . . 66 A7
Pathfields Bsns Pk EX36 158 C6
Pathfield Sch EX31 . . . . . 154 E6

Pathfields Ind Est EX36 . 158 D6
Path The **22** EX39 . . . . . 15 A1
Pathworlands EX10 . . . . . . 188 A6
Patna Pl PL1 . . . . 262 B4
Pato Point PL11 . . . . 247 A5
Patricia Cl EX4 . . . . 173 C2
Pattard Cross EX39 . . . . . . 22 C4
Patterdale Cl PL6 . . . . . . 245 D3
Patterdale Wlk PL6 . . . . . 245 D3
Patterson's Cross EX11 . 169 D8
Patteson Cl EX1 . . . . 100 F8
Patteson Dr EX11 . . . . . . 169 F4
Pattinson Cl PL6 . . . . 245 E2
Pattinson Ct PL6 . . . . 245 E2
Pattinson Dr PL6 . . . . 245 F2
Paullet EX16 . . . . 50 C1
Paul St EX4 . . . . 261 A3
Pauntley Gdn EX10 . . . . . 187 F3
Paviland Grange **6** PL1 . 248 A3
Pavilion Ct PL21 . . . . 261 B2
Pavington Cross EX37 . . . 43 E3
Pavor Rd TQ2 . . . . 214 B2
Paws Rd EX37 . . . . 43 B7
Payne Ct EX4 . . . . 178 B8
Payne's Cotts EX14 . . . . . . 85 C3
Paynsford Mews TQ12 . . 207 B4
Paynsford Rd **1** TQ12 . 207 B4
Payton Rd
Holywell Lake TA21 . . . . . . 51 F7
Rockwell Green TA21 . . . . . 160 A5
Peacegate Cross EX20 . . . . 76 E4
Peacehay La TA21 . . . . 51 E4
Peacock Ave PL11 . . . . . . 247 A3
Peacock Cl PL7 . . . . 250 F7
Peacock La PL4 . . . . 263 A2
Peacocks Cl PL6 . . . . 201 A8
Peacocks Cl TA21 . . . . 52 F7
Peadhill La EX16 . . . . 49 D2
Peak Cnr EX16 . . . . 62 E7
Peak Cross TQ9 . . . . 222 F3
Peakfield Cross Ways
EX5 . . . . 82 E6
Peak Hill Rd EX10 . . . . . . 187 E3
Peak Tor Ave TQ1 . . . . . . 220 C2
Peamore Dr EX2 . . . . 182 D4
Peamore Ho **2** 207 C3
Pearmain Cl EX15 . . . . . . 162 D4
Pearn Cotts **2** PL3 . . . 248 E6
Pearn Gdns PL3 . . . . 249 A7
Pearn Rd PL3 . . . . 249 A7
Pearn Ridge PL3 . . . . 249 A7
Pearse Cl EX20 . . . . 75 B7
Pearson Ave **3** PL4 . . . 248 F4
Pearson Cl EX22 . . . . 164 C5
Pearson Rd PL4 . . . . 248 F4
Pear Tree Cl
Kenton EX6 . . . . 194 E3
Westleigh EX16 . . . . 51 A4
Pear Tree Cotts PL8 . . . . 257 A5
Peartree Cross
Ashburton TQ13 . . . . 130 E4
Denbury TQ12 . . . . 211 A7
Pear Tree Way **5** EX32 . . 17 B2
Peasedicth TQ13 . . . . 130 D3
Peasland Rd TQ2 . . . . 214 A4
Peaslands Rd EX10 . . . . . 188 A5
Peaspark Cross TQ7 . . . . . 144 D3
Peazen Flats EX12 . . . . . . 191 C6
Pebble Cl TQ4 . . . . 226 A4
Pebbleridge Rd EX39 . . . 156 C8
Pecorama Pleasure Gdns
EX12 . . . . 191 C5
Pedlerspool La EX17 . . . . 165 E7
Peek La PL21 . . . . 137 C8
Peek Mead DT7 . . . . 193 F7
Peek Moor Cross EX22 . . . 90 B4
Peeks Ave PL9 . . . . 255 F7
Peel Row **3** EX4 . . . . . 178 C8
Peel St PL1 . . . . 248 A1
Peep La **4** EX17 . . . . . . 165 D5
Pegasus Ct
Exeter EX1 . . . . 177 F6
Paignton TQ3 . . . . 226 B8
Pegwell La TQ14 . . . . 209 B3
Pelican Cl EX39 . . . . 156 B6
Pellew Ave **5** TQ14 . . . 210 B4
Pellew Ho **6** TQ14 . . . . 210 B4
Pellew Pl PL2 . . . . 247 F4
Pellew Way TQ14 . . . . 210 A7
Pellinore Rd EX4 . . . . 174 A1
Pembrey Wlk PL5 . . . . 243 E4
Pembroke La PL1 . . . . 248 A2
Pembroke Lodge **15**
EX34 . . . . 150 B5
Pembroke Pk TQ3 . . . . . . 218 D3
Pembroke Rd
Paignton TQ3 . . . . 225 E7
Torquay TQ1 . . . . 220 B5
Pembroke St
Plymouth PL1 . . . . 247 E1
Plymouth PL1 . . . . 247 F1
Pemros Rd PL5 . . . . 243 C1
Pencalenick Rd EX8 . . . . 202 A5
Pencair Ave PL1 . . . . 246 E2
Pencepool Cotts EX15 . . . 83 F6
Pencepool Orch EX15 . . . . 83 F6
Pencombe Rocks EX31 . . . 4 C1
Pencorse Rd TQ2 . . . . 219 C6
Pencreber Rd **3** PL20 . . 126 F4
Pencross View **1** EX15 . 62 B8
Pendarves TQ9 . . . . 222 D2
Pendeen Cl PL6 . . . . 244 F6
Pendeen Cres PL6 . . . . . . 245 A6
Pendeen Pk TQ7 . . . . 145 A1

Pendennis Cl
Plymouth PL3 . . . . 248 F8
Torpoint PL11 . . . . 246 F3
Pendennis Rd TQ2 . . . . . . 219 B8
Pendilly Ave PL11 . . . . . . 246 F2
Pendragon Rd EX4 . . . . . . 174 A2
Penfield Gdns **1** EX7 . . 204 D6
Pengelly Cl PL11 . . . . 246 F5
Pengelly Hill PL11 . . . . . . 247 A5
Pengelly Pk PL11 . . . . 246 F5
Pengilly Way EX39 . . . . . . 22 E3
Penhale Dr EX22 . . . . 164 B5
Penhayes Cl EX6 . . . . 194 E3
Penhayes Rd EX6 . . . . 194 E3
Penhill Chalets TQ6 . . . . 146 B7
Penhill Cross EX6 . . . . . . 113 F5
Penhill La TQ5 . . . . 234 E8
Peninsula Medical Sch
Exeter EX2 . . . . 177 F5
Plymouth PL6 . . . . 245 C3
Peninsular Pk PL12 . . . . . 242 C4
Penlee Cl EX9 . . . . 199 G2
Penlee Cotts PL10 . . . . . . 140 I2
Penlee Gdns PL3 . . . . 248 A4
Penlee Pk PL11 . . . . 246 A4
Penlee Pl **4** PL4 . . . . . 248 F4
Penlee Way PL3 . . . . 248 B4
Penleonard Cl EX2 . . . . . 177 E5
Pennant Ho EX8 . . . . 201 E6
Pennant Way PL21 . . . . . 136 D6
Pennball Cross TQ9 . . . . 217 B3
Penn Cross DT6 . . . . 260 F7
Penn Ho TQ12 . . . . 207 E2
Pennine Dr TQ4 . . . . 225 D4
Pennington Cl EX17 . . . . . 79 A5
Penn Inn Cl TQ12 . . . . . . 207 E2
Penn La TQ5 . . . . 230 D3
Penn Mdws TQ5 . . . . 230 D3
Penn Meadows Cl TQ5 . . 230 D3
Pennsland La TQ13 . . . . . 130 F7
Pennsylvania Cl EX4 . . . . 177 D8
Pennsylvania Cres EX4 . . 177 C8
Pennsylvania Pk EX4 . . . 173 D1
Pennsylvania Rd
Exeter EX1 . . . . 173 C3
Torquay TQ2 . . . . 220 B5
Penn Torr TQ8 . . . . 259 D4
Penn View TQ5 . . . . 230 D3
Pennyacre Rd TQ14 . . . . 210 C6
Penny Ct
Exminster EX6 . . . . 182 A4
Wellington TA21 . . . . 160 D7
Pennycomequick Hill PL1,
PL3 . . . . 262 B4
Pennycross Cl PL2 . . . . . 248 D8
Pennycross Park Rd PL2 248 C7
Pennycross Prim Sch
PL2 . . . . 248 C7
Penny Hill EX33 . . . . 7 E2
Penny Plot DT7 . . . . 260 C4
Penny's Hill TQ1 . . . . 219 F7
Penny's Terr EX13 . . . . . . 167 D5
Penny Thorn Cross EX4 . . 85 E7
Pennywell Ct TQ13 . . . . . 131 B1
Pennywell Farm & Wildlife
Ctr TQ11 . . . . 135 E6
Penpethy Cl TQ5 . . . . 230 B4
Penpethy Rd TQ5 . . . . . . 230 B5
Penrith Cl PL6 . . . . 245 D3
Penrith Gdns PL6 . . . . . . 245 D3
Penrith Wlk PL6 . . . . 245 D3
Penrose Almshouses **4**
EX32 . . . . 155 A4
Penrose St PL1 . . . . 262 B3
Penrose Terr EX22 . . . . . 164 C4
Penrose Terr **2** EX1 . . 261 A2
Penrose Villas **5** PL4 . . 248 F4
Penryn Pl **4** TQ14 . . . . 210 A2
Penscombe Cross PL15 . 115 A6
Penshurst Rd TQ12 . . . . . 207 B1
Pensilva Pk TQ5 . . . . 230 C2
Pens La EX15 . . . . 67 B7
Penson Cross EX20 . . . . . 59 B1
Penson La EX20 . . . . 77 B8
Penstone Barns EX5 . . . . . 82 E4
Penswell Cross TQ10 . . . 135 E4
Pentamar St PL2 . . . . 247 E4
Pentgrove Ct EX8 . . . . . . 202 D7
Pentice La EX34 . . . . 3 A3
Pentillie Cres PL4 . . . . . . 248 D4
Pentillie Rd
Bere Alston PL20 . . . . 125 E1
Plymouth PL4 . . . . 248 E4
Pentire Rd PL11 . . . . 246 F3
Pentland Cl PL6 . . . . 244 F7
Penton Cl EX17 . . . . 165 D6
Penton La EX17 . . . . 165 D5
Penton Rise EX17 . . . . . . 165 D6
Pentridge Ave TQ2 . . . . . 219 C2
Pentyre Ct PL4 . . . . 263 C4
Pentyre Terr PL4 . . . . 263 C4
Penwill Way TQ4 . . . . 226 A4
Pen-y-dre EX15 . . . . 67 A7
Peoples Park Rd EX17 . . 165 C5
Pepperdon Hall La TQ13 112 B3
Pepper La
Kingswear TQ6 . . . . 234 F7
Plymouth PL9 . . . . 256 D7
Pepper St PL19 . . . . 171 C6
Peppery La TQ14 . . . . 209 D5
Pepys Pl PL5 . . . . 244 E1
Perceval Rd EX4 . . . . 174 A2

Perches Cl PL8 .... 141 B7
Percy Cross EX14 .... 67 B2
Percy Rd EX2 .... 177 B3
Percy St PL5 .... 243 D1
Percy Terr PL4 .... 249 A4
Peregrine Cl TQ2 .... 213 D3
Perinville Cl TQ1 .... 220 E6
Perinville Rd TQ1 .... 220 D7
Perinwinkle Dr
 Barnstaple EX1 .... 154 B3
 Plymouth PL7 .... 251 C5
Perkins Cross EX5 ...... 99 C1
Perranporth Cl PL5 ..... 243 E4
Perriam's Pl EX9 .... 199 G2
Perridge Cl EX2 .... 176 E3
Perridge Cross EX6 ...... 98 E1
Perriman's Row EX8 ..... 202 A7
Perriton Cross EX5 ...... 99 E8
Perros Cl TQ14 .... 209 D8
Perry Cross TQ12 .... 206 D7
Perry Hill EX17 .... 80 E8
Perry La
 Doddiscombsleigh EX6 ... 113 D5
 Newton Abbot TQ12 ..... 206 D6
Perryman Cl PL7 .... 250 E7
Perryman's Hill EX17 .... 79 F7
Perry New Rd TA22 ...... 33 F4
Perry Rd EX4 .... 177 B8
Perrys Gdns EX11 .... 168 D4
Perry St TA20 .... 88 D8
Perseverance Cotts 1
 PL7 .... 250 E7
Perth Cl EX4 .... 173 E2
Peryam Cres EX2 .... 178 A4
Peryn Rd PL19 .... 171 A5
Peterborough Rd EX4 .... 176 E7
Peterclose Rd EX16 ...... 161 A6
Peter Hopper's Hill PL5. 240 C2
Peter's Cl PL9 .... 256 C7
Peters Cres TQ3 .... 218 D3
Petersfield Cl PL3 ...... 249 B6
Peter's Park Cl PL5 ..... 61 A1
Peter's Park La PL5 ..... 243 E1
Peter St EX5 .... 82 F7
Petertavy Cross PL19 ... 117 E3
Pethertons EX16 .... 65 A7
Pethick Cl PL6 .... 244 D6
Pethill Cl PL6 .... 245 F2
Pethybridge TQ13 ...... 122 B8
Petitor Mews TQ1 ...... 214 B1
Petitor Rd TQ1 .... 214 C1
Petit Well La TQ1 ...... 214 B1
Petrel Cl TQ2 .... 213 C3
Petroc Dr TQ12 .... 207 C4
Petticoat La EX13 ...... 167 A6
Petton Cross EX16 ...... 35 A3
Peverell Park Rd PL3 ... 248 D6
Peverell Terr PL3 ...... 248 D5
Pew Tor Cl
 Tavistock PL19 .... 171 E5
 3 Yelverton PL20 ...... 126 F3
Phear Ave EX8 .... 202 B7
Philham Cross EX39 ..... 22 D1
Philham La EX39 .... 22 D1
Philham Water EX39 ..... 22 D1
Philip Ave EX31 .... 154 D2
Philip Cl PL9 .... 256 A6
Philip Gdns PL9 .... 255 F6
Philip Ho EX1 .... 178 E6
Philip Rd EX4 .... 177 F8
Philips La 2 EX33 ...... 152 D5
Phillimore St 3 PL2 .... 247 F4
Phillipps Ave EX8 ...... 196 B1
Phillips Ct EX13 .... 167 D5
Phillips Sq EX14 .... 166 B6
Phoenix Bsns Pk PL6 ... 245 F4
Phoenix Cl 2 PL12 ..... 126 F4
Phoenix La EX16 .... 161 D3
Phoenix Pl
 Kingsbridge TQ7 .... 258 C5
 West Alvington TQ7 ..... 258 B4
Phoenix St PL1 .... 262 A2
Piazza Terracina EX2 ... 261 B1
Picket Head Hill TQ14 .. 210 A2
Pick Pie Dr PL6 .... 245 E8
Pidgeley Rd EX7 .... 204 F8
Pidgeon's La EX13 ..... 104 B7
Pidland La EX16 .... 47 F1
Pidsley Hill EX17 .... 79 F7
Pidsley La EX17 .... 79 F8
Piece Hill EX6 .... 97 E4
Piend La EX17 .... 62 B1
Pier Head EX8 .... 201 E6
Pier La PL10 .... 253 A1
Piermont Pl EX7 .... 204 E6
Pier St PL1 .... 262 B1
Piggy La EX39 .... 156 F7
Pig La EX13 .... 167 D6
Pigs Leg Cross EX20 ... 108 A8
Pigspark Cross TQ13 ... 131 A5
Pike Rd PL3 .... 249 D5
Pikes Hill EX16 .... 97 E3
Pike's Mead EX20 ...... 170 B4
Pilchers Field PL20 .... 126 E3
Pilemoor La EX16 .... 48 E3
Pilemore Cross EX16 .... 48 E4
Piley La TA21 .... 51 D8
Pilgrim Cl PL2 .... 248 B6
Pilgrim La 11 PL20 ..... 125 E1
Pilgrim Prim Sch PL2 .. 262 B3
Pilland Way EX31 ...... 154 D6
Pillar Ave TQ5 .... 230 B5
Pillar Cl TQ5 .... 230 B5

Pillar Cres TQ5 .... 230 B5
Pillar Ct TQ5 .... 230 B5
Pillar Flats TQ5 ...... 230 B5
Pillar Wlk PL6 .... 244 E7
Pillavins La EX36 ...... 158 F6
Pill Gdns EX33 .... 152 D5
Pill Ho EX32 .... 155 A2
Pilliven Cross EX16 ..... 46 F2
Pilliven La EX16 .... 47 A2
Pill La
 Barnstaple, Chestwood
  EX32 .... 155 A1
 Barnstaple EX32 ...... 155 A2
 Saltash PL12 .... 242 E4
Pill Lawn EX32 .... 155 A2
Pillmere Dr PL12 ...... 242 D4
Pillory Hill PL8 .... 140 F6
Pill Rd EX39 .... 157 A2
Pilmuir Ave TQ2 .... 219 E5
Pilton Com Coll EX31 ... 154 E7
Pilton Cswy EX32 ...... 154 F6
Pilton Inf Sch EX31 .... 154 F6
Pilton La EX1 .... 178 D8
Pilton Lawn EX31 ...... 154 F6
Pilton Quay EX31 ...... 154 F6
Pilton St EX31 .... 154 F6
Pilton the Bluecoat CE Jun
 Sch EX31 .... 154 F6
Pimlico TQ1 .... 220 B5
Pimm Rd TQ3 .... 225 E7
Pinaster Cl EX14 ...... 166 E5
Pinbridge Mews EX4 .... 174 D1
Pinbrook Mews EX4 .... 174 C2
Pinbrook Rd EX4 ...... 174 D1
Pinbrook Units EX4 .... 174 C1
Pinces Cotts EX2 ...... 177 A3
Pinces Gdns EX2 ...... 177 A3
Pinces Rd EX2 .... 177 A3
Pinch Hill EX23 .... 70 A7
Pincombe Cnr EX36 ..... 31 B3
Pinder Cl PL19 .... 171 B5
Pine Ave EX4 .... 176 F7
Pine Cl
 Brixham TQ5 .... 230 B2
 Ilfracombe EX34 ...... 150 E4
 Teignmouth TQ14 ..... 210 D7
 Tiverton EX16 .... 161 B4
Pine Ct TQ1 .... 220 D5
Pinefields Cl EX11 ..... 168 E3
Pine Gdns EX14 .... 166 D6
Pine Gr EX14 .... 166 D6
Pinehurst Way PL21 .... 237 A6
Pine Park Rd EX14 .... 166 D5
Pine Ridge DT7 .... 260 E5
Pineridge Cl EX14 ..... 166 D6
Pines Cl EX39 .... 22 E3
Pines Rd
 Exmouth EX8 .... 196 D3
 Paignton TQ3 .... 225 F8
Pines The
 Exeter EX4 .... 176 F7
 Honiton EX14 .... 166 D5
Pine Tree Cl EX7 ...... 201 B2
Pine View EX1 .... 178 C7
Pine View Ave TQ1 .... 220 C6
Pine View Cl
 Exmouth EX8 .... 196 F2
 Halwill Junction EX21 ... 73 E3
Pine View Gdns TQ1 .... 220 C6
Pine View Rd TQ1 ..... 220 C6
Pine Wlk DT7 .... 260 D2
Pinewood Cl
 Dawlish EX7 .... 205 A8
 Plymouth PL7 .... 250 F6
Pinewood Ct TQ4 ...... 226 C5
Pinewood Dr PL6 ...... 245 E7
Pinewood La EX4 ...... 174 B2
Pinewood Rd TQ12 ..... 207 B2
Pinhay Hollow DT7 ..... 104 B2
Pinhay La DT7 .... 104 B2
Pinhoe CE Prim Sch EX4 174 E1
Pinhoe Rd EX4 .... 178 B8
Pinhoe Sta EX1 .... 174 E1
Pinhoe Trad Est EX4 ... 174 D1
Pinkhams Cotts PL12 .. 242 B6
Pinksmoor La TA21 ..... 51 E7
Pinkworthy Cross EX16 .. 48 C8
Pinkworthy Hill EX16 .. 48 B7
Pinn La EX1 .... 263 A2
Pinnacle Quay PL4 ..... 263 B2
Pinnbridge Ct EX1 ..... 178 E8
Pinncourt La EX1 ...... 178 E8
Pinnex Moor Rd EX16 ... 161 E6
Pinn Hill EX1 .... 178 E7
Pinn La
 Exeter EX1 .... 178 F8
 Otterton EX10 .... 197 B2
Pinn Lane Cnr EX10 ... 187 A1
Pinn Valley Rd EX1 .... 174 F1
Pinslow Cross PL15 .... 105 B8
Pins Pk EX22 .... 164 C5
Pinwood La EX4 .... 174 B1
Pinwood Meadow Dr
 EX4 .... 174 B2
Pioneer Cotts EX12 ... 191 D5
Pioneer Terr TQ11 ..... 236 A5
Pipehouse La TQ13 .... 123 C4
Pipers Cross TQ7 ...... 142 C7
Pippins Pl EX14 ...... 68 C2
Pippin Cl EX1 .... 178 E6
Pippins EX23 .... 191 D5
Pippins Field EX15 .... 66 A7
Pipping The PL21 ..... 237 A5
Piscombe La EX9 ...... 198 F7
Pitcairn Cres TQ2 .... 213 E3
Pitchingstone Cross
 TQ7 .... 147 C7
Pitcombe La TA4 .... 35 B5

Pitfield Cl EX15....... 162 D3
Pitham La EX11........ 169 F7
Pit Hill EX34.......... 2 D4
Pitland Cnr PL19...... 117 B4
Pitland La TQ12........ 213 E6
Pitlands La EX15....... 67 A8
Pitley Cross TQ13..... 131 A5
Pitley Rd TQ13........ 131 B5
Pitman's La PL21...... 133 C2
Pitsham La TA4........ 34 E6
Pits La PL10.......... 140 E8
Piton La EX10......... 187 A5
Pitt Ave 12 EX39....... 15 A1
Pitt Cres TQ4......... 224 B7
Pitt Cross EX39....... 22 C4
Pitt Ct
 8 Appledore EX39..... 15 A1
 Loddiswell TQ7....... 143 F7
Pitt Hill
 8 Appledore EX39..... 157 B8
 Crediton EX17........ 79 F3
 Kenton EX6.......... 194 D3
 Shebbear EX21........ 55 D4
Pitt Hill Rd TQ12...... 206 F4
Pitt Ho TQ13......... 123 D5
Pitt La
 Bideford EX39........ 157 A2
 Bow EX17............ 78 B5
 Butterleigh EX15...... 64 C4
 Cadbury EX5......... 81 C8
 Chevithorne EX16..... 49 D2
 Huish Champflower TA4. 35 E8
 North Molton EX36.... 30 F8
 Thorverton EX5....... 81 F7
 Waterrow TA4........ 35 F5
Pitton Cross EX6...... 96 E5
Pitts Cnr EX16........ 63 A4
Pitts Ct EX2.......... 261 C1
Pixey Plain EX36...... 31 B3
Pixie Dell EX33....... 152 B7
Pixie La EX33......... 152 C6
Pixon La PL19......... 171 B4
Pixon Trad Ctr 2 PL19. 171 B4
Pixton Cross EX19..... 58 B2
Pixton Way TA22....... 33 E6
Place Cross
 Ashburton TQ13...... 131 A6
 Okehampton EX20..... 93 E5
Place de Brest PL1.... 262 C3
Place La TQ13........ 131 A5
Plainfield La EX16..... 63 C7
Plainmoor Rd 8 TQ1.. 220 B7
Plains The TQ9........ 223 D5
Plaistow Cl PL5....... 243 C2
Plaistow Cres PL5..... 243 E2
Plaistow Hill Inf Sch PL5 243 E2
Plantagenet Cl EX15... 163 C6
Plantagenet Wlk EX2.. 178 D4
Plantation Cl TQ12.... 207 F1
Plantation Terr EX7... 204 E6
Plantation Way
 Torquay TQ2......... 213 C2
 Totnes TQ9.......... 222 F6
Plant World Gdns TQ12. 213 C7
Plassey Cl EX4........ 173 D2
Plaston Gn EX6....... 112 D5
Platt Cl TQ8.......... 259 B4
Plat The TQ6......... 145 E5
Platway La TQ14...... 209 D5
Play Cross TQ13...... 130 A4
Playmoor Cotts EX14.. 87 F3
Playmoor Dr EX1...... 174 F1
Pleasant Terr 1 TQ3.. 226 A6
Pleasure Hill Cl PL9... 255 D8
Plintona View PL7..... 250 E7
Ploudal Rd EX15...... 163 B2
Plougastel Dr PL12.... 242 E3
Plough Gn PL12........ 242 C3
Ploughman Way PL8... 136 A2
Plover Rise PL21..... 237 B5
Plume of Feathers Cl
 EX15............... 163 C4
Plumer Rd PL6........ 244 F2
Plumper's Cross EX38.. 41 A7
Plumtree Dr EX2...... 178 B4
Plumtree La EX5....... 99 E2
Plym Bridge Gdns PL7. 250 C7
Plymbridge Gdns PL7.. 250 C7
Plymbridge La PL6.... 245 B4
Plymbridge Rd
 Plymouth, Estover PL6.. 245 E5
 Plymouth PL6........ 245 C1
 Plymouth, Plympton PL7. 250 C7
Plym Cl TQ2.......... 219 B7
Plym Cres PL19....... 171 D5
Plymouth City Airport
 PL6................ 245 C5
Plymouth Coll PL4.... 248 E4
Plymouth Coll Inf Sch
 PL3................ 248 F5
Plymouth Coll of Art &
 Design PL4.......... 263 A3
Plymouth Coll of Art &
 Design (Sutton Annexe)
 PL1................ 262 C2
Plymouth Coll of F Ed
 PL1................ 248 A2
Plymouth Coll of F Ed
 (Annexe) PL1........ 262 C4
Plymouth Coll Prep Sch
 PL3................ 248 E6
Plymouth Discovery Ctr
 EX2................ 249 F6
Plymouth Dome Discovery
 Ctr PL1............. 262 C1
Plymouth High Sch for Girls
 PL4................ 263 A4
Pope's La
 Lapford EX17......... 60 C3

Plymouth Medical & Tech Pk
 PL6................ 245 A3
Plymouth Nuffield Hospl The
 PL6................ 245 B4
Plymouth Pavilions PL1. 262 B2
Plymouth Rd
 Buckfastleigh, Lower Dean
  TQ11.............. 236 A3
 Buckfastleigh TQ11.... 236 B4
 Kingsbridge TQ7..... 258 C6
 Plymouth PL7........ 250 B6
 South Brent TQ10.... 134 F2
 Tavistock PL19...... 171 B4
 Totnes TQ9.......... 223 B5
Plymouth Road Ind Est
 PL19............... 171 C3
Plymouth Ski Ctr PL6.. 249 E7
Plymouth Sound Camping
 Site PL9............ 255 C1
Plympton Cross TQ7... 147 F5
Plympton Hill PL7..... 250 D5
Plympton Hospl PL7... 250 D5
Plympton St Mary CE Inf Sch
 PL7................ 250 D5
Plympton St Maurice Prim
 Sch PL7............. 250 F3
Plym St PL4.......... 263 A3
Plymstock Rd PL9..... 255 D7
Plymstock Sch PL9.... 255 C8
Plymtree CE Prim Sch
 EX15............... 83 F5
Plymtree Dr PL7...... 250 C7
Plym Valley Rly PL7... 250 A4
Plym View Prim Sch
 PL3................ 249 D6
Poadmarsh Cross EX36. 31 D1
Poadmarsh Hill
 Ash Mill EX36........ 31 D1
 Bishops Nympton EX36. 31 D1
Pocombe Hill EX2..... 176 D3
Pode Dr PL7.......... 251 B4
Pod La EX13.......... 87 F4
Point in View Cotts EX8. 196 B3
Point Terr EX8........ 201 E6
Polehouse La EX2..... 176 E1
Pole Rue La TA20..... 69 F6
Poles Hill EX31....... 154 D7
Poleshill La EX31..... 154 D7
Polhearne La TQ5..... 230 B3
Polhearne Way TQ5... 230 B3
Pollard Cl
 Plymouth PL9........ 255 B5
 Saltash PL12........ 242 E1
Pollard's La TA21..... 52 F7
Pollards The EX32.... 155 C3
Pollards Way PL12.... 242 E3
Pollyblank Rd 2 TQ12. 207 B3
Pollybrook EX5....... 184 C2
Polmer Mews EX9..... 199 G2
Polruan Terr PL1..... 262 A3
Polsham Pk TQ3...... 226 B7
Polsloe Bridge Halt Sta
 EX1................ 178 A6
Polsloe Rd EX1....... 177 E6
Polson Hill EX7....... 61 A2
Poltimore Cl EX36.... 158 D4
Poltimore Cross EX4.. 174 E6
Poltimore Cl EX4..... 174 F7
Poltimore Lawn EX32.. 155 B6
Poltimore Rd
 Farway EX24......... 101 F7
 Offwell EX14, EX24... 102 A8
 South Molton EX36.... 158 D4
Poltimore Sq EX4..... 261 B4
Polwhele Rd 14 EX16.. 64 D7
Polywell EX39........ 14 F1
Polzeath Gdns PL2.... 248 D8
Pomeroy Gdns PL2.... 248 D8
Pomeroy Pl 6 TQ12... 122 F1
Pomeroy Rd
 Newton Abbot TQ12... 207 B3
 Tiverton EX16....... 64 E8
Pomphlett Cl PL9..... 255 D8
Pomphlett Farm Ind Est
 PL9................ 255 E8
Pomphlett Gdns PL9... 255 D8
Pomphlett Prim Sch PL9 255 D8
Pondfield Rd PL12.... 242 B3
Pond Hill EX37....... 44 A4
Pond La TA21......... 51 D3
Ponsford Cross EX15.. 65 A2
Ponsford La EX15..... 65 A3
Ponsonby Rd PL3..... 248 B4
Pooks La TQ13........ 130 F5
Pool Anthony Dr EX16. 64 E8
Pool Cross EX20...... 107 F8
Poole Cross TQ12.... 211 A1
Poole Hill EX16...... 63 C1
Poole La EX31........ 11 A3
Poole Park Rd PL5.... 247 C8
Poole's Cl DT7....... 260 E3
Pooley Cross EX17.... 143 E4
Pool Hill
 Ashbittle TA21....... 35 E1
 Bridestowe EX20..... 107 F8
Pool La
 Burrington EX37...... 44 A4
 Chittlehampton EX37.. 29 A1
 Woolacombe EX34..... 1 B1
Poolmill Cross TQ13.. 143 E2
Pool Pk TQ10......... 135 A3
Pools Weir TQ12...... 214 B8
Popes EX17.......... 165 C6
Popes La EX24........ 103 A3
Pope's La

Pope's La continued
 Rockwell Green TA21.. 160 B4
Popham Cl EX16....... 161 F4
Popham Cross EX36... 19 A3
Popham Flats TA21... 160 D6
Popham La EX36...... 19 A3
Pop La EX13, TA20.... 88 B8
Poplar Cl
 Brixham TQ5......... 229 F2
 Exeter EX2.......... 177 A3
 Exmouth EX8........ 196 D3
 Newton Abbot TQ12... 213 A8
 Plymouth PL7........ 251 B5
Poplar Dr TQ7....... 258 C5
Poplar Mount EX13... 167 D6
Poplar Row EX9...... 199 H2
Poplars Dr TQ3...... 218 D2
Poplars The
 7 Chudleigh Knighton
  TQ13.............. 123 C4
 Exeter EX4......... 174 E2
Poplars Wlk EX5..... 179 E2
Poplar Terr
 High Bickington EX37.. 43 C7
 Ipplepen TQ12....... 211 D2
Poplar Tree Cnr EX12. 192 A8
Poplar Tree Dr EX12.. 192 A7
Porch Cotts EX16.... 160 A8
Poplar Dr EX7....... 201 A2
Porch EX13.......... 88 A3
Porch Cotts 15 EX10.. 101 B1
Pork Hill PL19....... 117 F1
Porlock Way TQ4..... 225 F2
Porsham Cl PL6...... 241 B1
Porsham La PL5...... 244 E8
Prospoder Pl PL10... 253 A2
Portal Pl PL21...... 237 B5
Portbridge Cross TQ9. 215 F8
Portchester Hts EX4.. 261 C4
Port Cross
 Bishops Nympton EX36. 31 C4
 Kentisbury EX31..... 10 F5
Porteous Cl PL1..... 247 F3
Porter's La EX8..... 195 E8
Porter Way PL12.... 242 C3
Portford Cross EX31. 27 E3
Portford La TQ10... 135 A2
Portgate Cross EX36. 30 B8
Port Hill EX31...... 10 F5
Port La
 Bishops Nympton EX36. 31 C4
 Bury EX22.......... 34 A5
 Chillington TQ7..... 145 A1
 Wotter PL7......... 132 C4
Portland Ave
 Exmouth EX8........ 202 B6
 Teignmouth TQ14.... 210 C7
Portland Bldgs 6 EX32 155 A4
Portland Cnr
 Kilmington EX13..... 103 C4
 Meavy PL20......... 127 D2
Portland Pk EX34... 150 C6
Portland Rd
 Plymouth PL1....... 247 F3
 Torquay TQ1........ 220 D7
Portland Sq PL4..... 262 C4
Portland St
 Barnstaple EX32..... 155 B3
 Exeter EX1......... 177 E6
 Ilfracombe EX34.... 150 C6
Portland Villas PL4.. 262 C4
Port Lane Cl TQ7.... 144 F1
Portledge Pl EX39... 25 A3
Portloe Way TQ7.... 147 E6
Portlemore Gdns TQ7. 147 E6
Portmarsh La EX32... 155 A4
Port Mer Cl EX8..... 196 E3
Port Rd EX6......... 200 D4
Portsmouth Arms Cross
 EX18............... 60 B7
Portsmouth Arms Sta
 EX18............... 66 C7
Portway EX15....... 66 C7
Portway Cl PL9...... 256 D7
Possession Cross EX37. 28 C7
Post Box Cross
 Bondleigh EX20..... 76 F6
 Cheriton Fitzpaine EX17. 63 A3
Post Cl TA21........ 160 C4
Post Cross EX15..... 65 F2
Post Cross Bsns Pk EX15. 65 F2
Post La
 Malmsmead EX35..... 6 C4
 Skilgate TA4........ 34 F3
Post Office La
 Cheriton Fitzpaine EX17. 62 F1
 Tatworth TA20...... 88 C8
Potacre St EX38..... 159 D5
Potemes Cross EX37.. 27 F1
Potshop Cross EX17.. 79 D2
Potters Cl PL11..... 168 D5
Potters Hill TQ1.... 220 B5
Potter's Cross TA4.. 35 C7
Potters Stile EX14.. 67 B1
Potters Way TQ5.... 250 D5
Potterswell EX31... 154 B3
Pottery Cl
 Bovey Tracey TQ13.. 180 C5
 Honiton EX14....... 166 D6
Pottery Ct TQ6...... 233 D4

Pottery Est PL10 . . . . 252 E6
Pottery La EX31 . . . . 153 A4
Pottery Mews TQ3 . . . . 218 D3
Pottery Rd
  Bovey Tracey TQ13 . . . . . . 180 C5
  Kingsteignton TQ12 . . . . . . 207 D6
  Plymouth PL1 . . . . 247 D3
Pottery Units TQ12 . . . . 207 D4
Pottington Bsns Pk
  EX31 . . . . 154 C6
Pottington Dr EX31 . . . . 154 E6
Pottington Ind Est EX31 . 154 D5
Pottington Rd EX31 . . . . . . 154 E6
Potties Cl EX6 . . . . 182 B3
Poultney Cl PL7 . . . . 251 A5
Pouncers Cross EX18 . . . . . .60 E6
Pound Cnr
  Clyst Honiton EX5 . . . . . . 179 E7
  Whitestone EX4 . . . . .98 C5
Pound Cross EX5 . . . . .99 B5
Pound Down Cnr EX4 . . . . . .98 D5
Pound Field TQ9 . . . . 227 F8
Poundfield Cl EX31 . . . . . . 153 F5
Pound Gate EX6 . . . . 112 F5
Pound Hill
  Axmouth EX12 . . . . 192 D7
  Holcombe Rogus TA21 . . . . .51 A5
Poundhouse Cross TQ6 .146 B8
Pound La
  Bridford EX6 . . . . 113 A4
  Buckland St Mary TA20 . . . .69 D8
  Colaton Raleigh EX10 . . . . 186 C5
  15 Combe Martin EX34 . . . .3 A3
  Exeter EX4 . . . . 196 C1
  High Bickington EX37 . . . . .43 C8
  Kingskerswell TQ12 . . . . . 212 F5
  Nadderwater EX4 . . . . .98 F4
  Raymond's Hill DT6 . . . . . 104 D8
  Shaldon TQ14 . . . . 209 C5
  5 Teignmouth TQ14 . . . 210 C4
  Topsham EX3 . . . . 182 E6
  Uplyme DT7 . . . . 260 B5
  Upottery EX14 . . . . .68 C1
  Woodbury EX5 . . . . 184 C3
  Yarcombe EX14 . . . . .69 B2
Pound Lane End EX37 . . . . . .43 D8
Pound Lane Trad Est
  EX8 . . . . 196 C1
Pound Mdw
  Great Torrington EX38 . . . . .42 B7
  Hatherleigh EX20 . . . . .75 C7
  Parkham EX39 . . . . .39 E8
Pound Pk EX20 . . . . 170 D6
Pound Pl
  Bovey Tracey TQ13 . . . . . . 180 D8
  19 Newton Abbot TQ12 . .207 B3
Pound Rd
  Axminster EX13 . . . . .88 F2
  Cragstone PL20 . . . . 126 E3
  Lyme Regis DT7 . . . . 260 D3
Poundsclose TA22 . . . . .33 E4
Pound's Cross PL6 . . . . 240 E5
Poundsgate Cl TQ5 . . . . . . 232 D4
Pounds Hill EX17 . . . . 165 D6
Poundshill Cross EX17 . . 165 D6
Poundsland EX5 . . . . 175 C6
Pounds Park Rd
  1 Bere Alston PL20 . . . . . 125 E1
  Plymouth PL3 . . . . 248 D7
Pounds Pk PL2 . . . . 242 F3
Pound Sq EX15 . . . . 163 C2
Pound St
  Exmouth EX8 . . . . 202 A6
  Lyme Regis DT7 . . . . 260 D3
  Moretonhampstead TQ13 . . 111 F4
  Plymouth PL1 . . . . 254 A8
Poundstone Ct TQ8 . . . . . . 259 D4
Pound Terr **3** TA21 . . . . . 160 D5
Poundwell Ho **8** PL21 . . 137 B2
Poundwell Mdws **7**
  PL21 . . . . 137 B2
Poundwell St **9** PL21 . .137 B2
Powderham Castle EX6 . 194 F4
Powderham Cl
  Newton Abbot TQ12 . . . . . 207 B2
  Topsham EX3 . . . . 182 E6
Powderham Cres EX4 . . . 177 D8
Powderham Ct
  20 Newton Abbot TQ12 . 207 B3
  21 Teignmouth TQ14 . . . 210 C4
Powderham Rd
  Exeter EX2 . . . . 177 A4
  Newton Abbot TQ12 . . . . . 207 B2
  Plymouth PL3 . . . . 248 F7
  Torquay TQ2 . . . . 213 F1
Powderham Terr
  Newton Abbot TQ12 . . . . . 207 B3
  Teignmouth TQ14 . . . . 210 C4
Powderham Wlk EX6 . . 181 F5
Powell Cl EX12 . . . . 192 A6
Powells Way EX14 . . . . . . .67 C1
Power of Water Mus
  EX35 . . . . 151 C5
Powis Gdns PL5 . . . . 244 B2
Powisland Dr PL6 . . . . 245 A5
Powlesland Rd EX4 . . . . . . 177 B1
Powys Ho EX10 . . . . 188 A4
Poyers EX33 . . . . 152 E4
Pratt's La TQ7 . . . . 143 B7
Precinct The TQ7 . . . . 258 D6
Premier Pl EX2 . . . . 261 C2

Prescot Rd EX4 . . . . 176 E5
Prescott Rd EX15 . . . . .51 D1
Prestbury Ct EX4 . . . . 176 D8
Prestbury Pk **4** TQ2 . . . 219 F5
Preston Barns TQ9 . . . . . . 222 D1
Prestonbury Cl PL6 . . . . . . 245 B7
Preston Cross
  Loddiswell TQ7 . . . . 138 C3
  West Alvington TQ7 . . . . . 143 E2
Preston Down Ave TQ3 . .219 B2
Preston Down Rd TQ3 . .219 B2
Preston Fork TQ9 . . . . 138 C2
Preston Gate EX31 . . . . . . .10 E6
Preston La EX14 . . . . .80 D7
Preston Prim Sch TQ2 . . 219 D2
Preston St EX1 . . . . 261 A2
Prestor EX13 . . . . 167 E5
Pretoria Rd EX1 . . . . 177 F7
Pretoria Terr EX34 . . . . . . 150 A3
Pretty Top
  Little Torrington EX38 . . . . .41 F1
  Petrockstow EX20 . . . . . . .56 F8
Priddis Cl EX8 . . . . 196 C3
Priddles La EX20 . . . . .69 F8
Prideaux Cl PL12 . . . . 242 C5
Prideaux Cres EX16 . . . . . 161 D6
Prideaux La TQ6 . . . . 145 F6
Prideaux Mdw EX38 . . . . . 159 F5
Prideaux Rd PL21 . . . . 237 E6
Pridham La PL2 . . . . 248 D7
Pridhams Way EX6 . . . . . . 182 A4
Priest Hill EX15 . . . . .66 A3
Priesthood Terr PL10 . . . . 252 E5
Priestley Ave
  Exeter EX4 . . . . 178 B8
  Plymouth PL5 . . . . 243 E2
Prigg Mdw TQ13 . . . . 130 F4
Primley Cross TQ3 . . . . . . 225 F5
Primley Ct TQ3 . . . . 225 E5
Primley Gdns EX10 . . . . . . 188 C7
Primley Mead EX10 . . . . . 188 C7
Primley Paddock EX10 . . 188 B7
Primley Pk TQ3 . . . . 225 F5
Primley Pk E TQ3 . . . . 226 A5
Primley Pk W EX10 . . . . . . 188 B7
Primrose Ave EX32 . . . . . . 155 E4
Primrose Cl
  Chillington TQ7 . . . . 144 F1
  Ivybridge PL21 . . . . 237 D5
  Kingsteignton TQ12 . . . . . 207 E7
  6 Tiverton EX16 . . . . . . 161 F6
  Torpoint PL11 . . . . 246 E4
Primrose Gdns PL19 . . . . 171 E4
Primrose La EX39 . . . . 157 B8
Primrose Lawn EX4 . . . . . . 176 D8
Primrose Mdw PL21 . . . . . 237 A6
Primrose Way
  Crediton EX17 . . . . 165 E6
  Kingskerswell TQ12 . . . . . 212 F6
  Seaton EX12 . . . . 192 B7
Primrose Wlk PL12 . . . . . . 242 D4
Prince Charles Cl EX8 . . 196 E1
Prince Charles Ct TQ2 . . 214 A3
Prince Charles Rd EX4 . . 177 F8
Prince Charles Way
  EX12 . . . . 192 A8
Prince Maurice Ct PL4 . . 263 B3
Prince Maurice Rd PL4 . . 248 F4
Prince Of Wales Dr
  Dartmouth TQ6 . . . . 233 F4
  Exmouth EX8 . . . . 196 E1
Prince Of Wales Rd
  Crediton EX17 . . . . 165 C6
  Exeter EX4 . . . . 177 B8
  Kingsbridge TQ7 . . . . 258 D5
Prince Rock Prim Sch
  PL4 . . . . 249 B2
Prince Rupert Way TQ12 .123 B2
Princes Cl **6** TQ1 . . . . . 220 B6
Princes Point TQ1 . . . . . . 220 C3
Princes Rd
  Plymouth PL5 . . . . 245 E6
  Torquay TQ1 . . . . 220 B5
Princes Rd E TQ1 . . . . 220 C5
Princes Rd W TQ1 . . . . 220 B5
Prince's St E EX2 . . . . 177 A3
Prince's St N EX2 . . . . 177 A3
Prince's St S EX2 . . . . 177 A3
Prince's St W EX2 . . . . 177 A3
Princess Alexandra Ct **8**
  EX4 . . . . 177 A5
Princess Ave
  Ilfracombe EX34 . . . . 150 C5
  Plymouth, Plymstock PL9 . . 255 A6
  Plymouth, West Park PL5 . . 244 A3
Princess Cotts TQ10 . . . . 213 C6
Princess Cres PL9 . . . . . . 255 A6
Princess Elizabeth Terr
  EX20 . . . . 107 F8
Prince's Sq EX2 . . . . 177 A3
Princess Rd
  Kingskerswell TQ12 . . . . . 213 A4
  Kingsteignton TQ12 . . . . . 207 D8
Princess St
  Barnstaple EX32 . . . . 155 A6
  Plymouth PL1 . . . . 262 C2
Princess Street Ope PL1 262 C2
Princes St
  10 Dawlish EX7 . . . . . . 204 D6
  2 Exmouth EX8 . . . . . . 202 A6
  Paignton TQ3 . . . . 226 B6
  Plymouth PL1 . . . . 247 E2
  Torquay TQ1 . . . . 220 B7
Princess Way PL1 . . . . . . 262 C2
Prince St TQ12 . . . . 207 C3
Princetown Prim Sch
  PL20 . . . . 128 A8

Prince William Ct **1**
  TQ5 . . . . 230 C4
Prince William Quay
  TQ5 . . . . 230 D5
Prings Ct **18** TQ5 . . . . 230 C5
Priorton Hill EX17 . . . . .80 B7
Priorton La EX17 . . . . .80 B7
Priory
  Bovey Tracey TQ13 . . . . . . 180 C8
  Wellington TA21 . . . . 160 E6
Priory Ave
  Kingskerswell TQ12 . . . . . 213 A5
  Totnes TQ9 . . . . 223 C6
Priory Cl
  Barnstaple EX31 . . . . 154 F7
  East Budleigh EX9 . . . . . . 198 B7
  Ivybridge PL21 . . . . 237 B5
  Tavistock PL19 . . . . 171 D3
Priory Ct
  3 Totnes TQ9 . . . . 223 C6
  Wellington TA21 . . . . 160 E7
Priory Dr
  Plymouth PL7 . . . . 250 D5
  Totnes TQ9 . . . . 223 C6
Priory Gdns
  Barnstaple EX31 . . . . 154 F7
  1 Dawlish EX7 . . . . . . 204 E6
  Exeter EX4 . . . . 261 A2
  Tavistock PL19 . . . . 171 D3
  Totnes TQ9 . . . . 223 C6
  Wellington TA21 . . . . 160 E6
Priory Gn EX4 . . . . 178 A7
Priory Hill
  2 Dawlish EX7 . . . . . . 204 E6
  Totnes TQ9 . . . . 223 C6
Priory La EX6 . . . . 113 A4
Priory Lawn Terr PL3 . . . 249 A6
Priory Mill PL7 . . . . 250 D5
Priory Park Rd **13** EX7 . 204 D6
Priory RC Prim Sch TQ1 220 B8
Priory Rd
  Abbotskerswell TQ12 . . . . 212 C7
  Barnstaple EX31 . . . . 154 F7
  Dawlish EX7 . . . . 204 E6
  Exeter EX4 . . . . 177 E8
  Plymouth PL3 . . . . 249 A6
  Tiverton EX16 . . . . 161 F6
  Torquay TQ1 . . . . 220 B8
Priory Ridge PL7 . . . . 250 D5
Priory St TQ6 . . . . 234 A2
Priory Terr **7** TQ9 . . . . 223 C6
Priory The
  Abbotskerswell TQ12 . . . . 212 C7
  3 Modbury PL21 . . . . . 137 B2
Priory View TQ9 . . . . 227 B4
Priory Wall Cross TQ5 . . .66 B2
Priswell La EX6 . . . . 112 F5
Prisam Lane Cross EX20 . .75 F2
Priscott Way TQ5 . . . . 207 E6
Prispen Dr EX5 . . . . .82 B6
Prispen Ho EX5 . . . . .82 B6
Prispen View EX5 . . . . .82 B6
Prixford EX31 . . . . .16 C7
Promenade
  Ilfracombe EX34 . . . . 150 B6
  Kingsbridge TQ7 . . . . 258 D5
  Paignton, Goodrington
    TQ4 . . . . 226 C4
  Paignton TQ3 . . . . 226 D8
Promenade The PL1 . . . . 262 C1
Prospect EX7 . . . . 204 E6
Prospect Cnr EX31 . . . . . . .27 A7
Prospect Cotts EX15 . . . . 151 B5
Prospect Cres EX15 . . . . . .66 A7
Prospect Gdns EX4 . . . . . . 177 E7
Prospect Hill
  Okehampton EX20 . . . . . . 170 B4
  Slapton TQ7 . . . . 145 C4
Prospect La PL12 . . . . 242 C3
Prospect Pk EX4 . . . . 177 D8
Prospect Pl
  Barnstaple EX32 . . . . 155 B3
  Exeter EX4 . . . . 177 A4
  Otter St Mary EX11 . . . . . 169 D3
  Plymouth PL1 . . . . 262 B2
  5 Tiverton EX16 . . . . . 161 B4
Prospect Rd **3** TQ5 . . . 230 C5
Prospect Row PL1 . . . . . . 247 E1
Prospect St PL4 . . . . 263 A3
Prospect Terr
  Gunnislake PL18 . . . . 125 D6
  Gunnislake, St Ann's Chapel
    PL18 . . . . 125 B5
  Newton Abbot TQ12 . . . . . 207 C3
Prospect Way EX17 . . . . . .60 D7
Prospect Wlk PL12 . . . . . . 242 C3
Prouse Cres EX2 . . . . 248 C8
Prouse Rise PL12 . . . . 242 E2
Providence Pl
  Calstock PL18 . . . . 125 D3
  Plymouth PL1 . . . . 248 A3
Providence Row **13**
  EX39 . . . . 157 A2
Providence St PL4 . . . . . . 263 A4
Prowse La
  East Village EX17 . . . . . . .80 C8
  Lapford EX17 . . . . .60 D3
Prowses EX15 . . . . .66 A7
Prowse's La EX14 . . . . .63 E1
Prynne Cl PL1 . . . . 262 B3
Puckridge Rd EX4 . . . . . . 174 D2
Puddavine Terr TQ9 . . . . . 223 A8
Pudleylake Rd
  Axminster EX13 . . . . 167 B1
  Musbury EX13 . . . . 103 E6
Puffin Ct EX39 . . . . 156 C6
Puffin Way EX2 . . . . 176 D3
Pugsley Rd **9** EX16 . . . .64 D7

Pulborough Farm Cvn Pk
  EX20 . . . . 107 F4
Pulchrass St **11** EX32 . 155 A4
Pullen's Row EX4 . . . . .46 E1
Pulleys Cl TQ7 . . . . 143 C6
Pulling Rd EX4 . . . . 174 D2
Pullins Terr **8** TQ13 . . 123 E6
Pulpit Wlk EX2 . . . . 181 C7
Pump La EX39 . . . . 156 A2
Pump St
  4 Brixham TQ5 . . . . . . 230 D5
  Newton St Cyres EX5 . . . . 172 A8
Punchards Down TQ9 . . 222 F6
Purbeck Ave TQ2 . . . . 219 D2
Purcell Cl EX2 . . . . 178 C5
Purcombe Cross TQ13 . .131 D3
Purlbridge Cross EX24 . .102 D6
Purzebrook Cl EX13 . . . . . 167 D5
Purzebrook Cotts EX13 . 167 D5
Pusehill Rd EX39 . . . . 156 B5
Putsborough Cl EX33 . . . . .8 A2
Putsborough Rd EX33 . . . .7 F3
Putshole La EX38 . . . . .40 E1
Putson Cross EX16 . . . . . . .64 E8
Putts Cnr EX10 . . . . 101 C7
Pye Cnr
  Brampford Speke EX5 . . . . .81 D1
  Cullompton EX15 . . . . . . 163 C3
  Kennford EX6 . . . . 181 B2
Pye La TQ20 . . . . .88 E8
Pykes Down PL21 . . . . . . 237 F4
Pyles Thorne TA21 . . . . . . 160 F4
Pyles Thorne Cl TA21 . . . 160 E5
Pyles Thorne Rd TA21 . . 160 E4
Pym St
  Plymouth PL1 . . . . 247 F3
  Tavistock PL19 . . . . 171 C6
Pyne Gdns EX5 . . . . 173 A7
Pyne Meadow Cross EX18 .44 D3
Pynes Cl
  Chenson Fitzpaine EX17 . . . .62 E1
  East Budleigh EX9 . . . . . . 198 B6
Pynes Ct EX4 . . . . .43 C7
Pynes Hill EX2 . . . . 178 C2
Pynes Hill Bsns Pk EX2 . 178 C3
Pynes Inf Sch EX39 . . . . . 156 F1
Pynes La EX39 . . . . .25 E4
Pynsent Ct **4** TQ13 . . . 123 E6
Pynes Wlk EX39 . . . . .25 E4
Pyrtle Ho EX3 . . . . 183 C7
Pyworthy CE Prim Sch
  EX22 . . . . .71 D5

Q

Quadrangle The EX4 . . . . 177 C8
Quadrant The EX2 . . . . . . 261 C2
Quagmire La EX22 . . . . . . 164 C7
Quantock Rd TA21 . . . . . . 160 D7
Quantocks EX33 . . . . 152 B6
Quantocks Rd TQ2 . . . . . 219 C3
Quant Pk PL19 . . . . 171 C6
Quarries La EX4 . . . . .43 C7
Quarries The EX4 . . . . . . 176 D4
Quarry Cl
  Bideford EX39 . . . . 156 E2
  Totnes TQ9 . . . . 222 F6
Quarry Cotts
  Beer EX12 . . . . 191 B5
  Plymouth, Honicknowle
    PL5 . . . . 244 B2
  Plymouth PL1 . . . . 262 A3
Quarryfields EX20 . . . . . . 170 C6
Quarry Foot Cross EX17 . .79 C4
Quarry Gdns TQ3 . . . . . . 226 A7
Quarry La
  Beer EX12 . . . . 191 B5
  Down St Mary EX17 . . . . . .78 F6
  Exeter EX2 . . . . 178 C4
  Gunnislake PL18 . . . . 125 C6
  Silverton EX5 . . . . .82 B5
Quarry Park Ave PL9 . . . 255 D7
Quarry Park Rd
  Exeter EX2 . . . . 178 C4
  Plymouth, Peverell PL3 . . . 248 D5
  Plymouth, Plymstock PL9 . . 255 D7
Quarry Rd EX7 . . . . .43 B7
Quarry St PL11 . . . . 247 C3
Quarterdeck The PL1 . . . 254 A8
Quarter Mile La EX5 . . . . .99 D3
Quartley Hill EX16 . . . . . . .34 E4
Quayfield Rd EX34 . . . . . . 150 C6
Quay Hill EX1, EX2 . . . . . 261 A2
Quay La
  Instow EX39 . . . . .15 B1
  Lympstone EX8 . . . . 195 D4
Quay Rd
  Newton Abbot TQ12 . . . . . 207 D3
  Plymouth PL1 . . . . 263 A2
  Teignmouth TQ14 . . . . . . 210 B4
Quayside **6** PL19 . . . . . 171 B5
Quay Terr **7** TQ12 . . . . 207 D3
Quay The
  Appledore EX39 . . . . .15 A1
  Ashprington TQ9 . . . . 139 F7
  Bideford EX39 . . . . 157 A2
  Brixham TQ5 . . . . 230 D5
  Dartmouth TQ6 . . . . 233 F3
  Dittisham TQ6 . . . . 228 D2
  Exeter EX2 . . . . 261 B2
  Ilfracombe EX34 . . . . 150 C6
  Salcombe TQ8 . . . . 259 C6
Queen Annes EX16 . . . . . 157 A2
Queen Annes Copse
  TQ12 . . . . 206 F1

Queen Anne's Ct **16** EX31 154 F5
Queen Anne's Mews **15**
  EX31 . . . . 154 F5
Queen Anne's Quay PL4 .263 B2
Queen Dart Cross EX16 . . .47 B4
Queen Dart Hill EX16 . . . . .47 B3
Queen Elizabeth Ave
  TQ6 . . . . 233 E4
Queen Elizabeth Ct
  EX39 . . . . 156 C6
Queen Elizabeth Dr
  Crediton EX17 . . . . 165 A6
  Paignton TQ3 . . . . 225 E6
Queen Elizabeth's Com Coll
  EX17 . . . . 165 B5
Queen Elizabeth's Lower Sch
  EX17 . . . . 165 B5
Queen La **8** EX4 . . . . . . 204 D6
Queen's Ave EX34 . . . . . . 150 C5
Queens Cl
  Kingsteignton TQ12 . . . . . 207 F8
  Plymouth PL6 . . . . 245 E6
Queen's Cres
  Brixham TQ5 . . . . 230 D3
  Exeter EX4 . . . . 261 B4
Queen's Ct **12** EX8 . . . . 202 A6
Queen's Dr EX8 . . . . 202 C5
Queen's Dr The EX4 . . . . . 177 B8
Queen's Gate
  Plymouth, Lipson PL4 . . . . 263 B4
  Plymouth, Stoke PL3 . . . . 262 A4
Queen's Gate Mews PL4 .263 B4
Queen's Gate Villas PL4 . 263 B4
Queen's Gate Villas Rd
  PL4 . . . . 263 B4
Queenshays EX20 . . . . . . .95 A5
Queen's Ho **8** EX32 . . . 155 A5
Queensland Dr EX4 . . . . . 173 E2
Queen's Park Rd TQ4 . . . 226 C6
Queen's Pk EX17 . . . . .80 C4
Queen's Pl EX22 . . . . .55 C1
Queen Sq EX15 . . . . 163 C3
Queens Rd
  Exeter EX4 . . . . 261 A1
  Plymouth PL5 . . . . 243 F3
  Wellington TA21 . . . . 160 E4
Queen's Rd
  Brixham TQ5 . . . . 230 D3
  Budleigh Salterton EX9 . . . 197 F2
  Moretonhampstead TQ13 . . 111 F5
  Paignton TQ4 . . . . 226 C6
  Plymouth PL4 . . . . 263 B4
Queen's Sq
  Broadclyst EX5 . . . . 175 C7
  2 Colyton EX24 . . . . . 103 A4
Queen St
  Barnstaple EX32 . . . . 155 A5
  Bideford EX39 . . . . 157 A2
  Budleigh Salterton EX9 . . . 199 G2
  9 Colyton EX24 . . . . . 103 A4
  Dawlish EX7 . . . . 204 D6
  Exeter EX4 . . . . 261 A3
  11 Exmouth EX8 . . . . . 202 A6
  Honiton EX14 . . . . 161 C5
  Lynton EX35 . . . . 151 C5
  Newton Abbot TQ12 . . . . . 207 D3
  Northlew EX20 . . . . .74 E2
  Plymouth PL1 . . . . 247 D2
  Seaton EX12 . . . . 192 A5
  South Molton EX36 . . . . . 158 C4
  12 Teignmouth TQ14 . . . 210 B4
  Torquay TQ1 . . . . 161 C3
  Torquay TQ2 . . . . 220 B5
  Winkleigh EX19 . . . . .58 F3
Queen's Terr
  Exeter EX4 . . . . 261 A4
  Great Torrington EX38 . . . 159 B5
  Stoke Canon EX5 . . . . . . .81 F1
  4 Totnes TQ9 . . . . 223 C6
Queensway
  Newton Abbot TQ12 . . . . . 207 E2
  Tiverton EX16 . . . . 161 F5
  Tiverton EX16 . . . . 161 F6
  Torquay TQ2 . . . . 219 D6
Queensway Cl TQ2 . . . . . 219 E2
Queensway Cres TQ2 . . . 219 E2
Queensway Ho TQ12 . . . 207 E2
Queensway RC Prim Sch
  TQ12 . . . . 219 D7
Queens Wlk DT7 . . . . 260 E4
Quentin Ave TQ5 . . . . 230 B2
Questant La EX10 . . . . . . 188 C6
Quicks Wlk EX8 . . . . 158 F5
Quilletts The TQ7 . . . . . . 147 E6
Quince Cross
  South Molton EX36 . . . . . .46 B8
  Spreyton EX17 . . . . .96 C7
Quince Hill EX36 . . . . .31 A7
Quince Honey Farm
  EX36 . . . . 158 C5
Quinnel Ho **7** TQ14 . . . 210 B5
Quinta Cl TQ1 . . . . 220 C4
Quinta Ct TQ1 . . . . 220 C4
Quinta Rd TQ1 . . . . 220 D6
Quintet Cl EX2 . . . . 178 C5
Quirk Hill EX16 . . . . .63 D7
Quoditch Cross EX21 . . . . .73 B1
Quoige Cross EX22 . . . . . .38 D3

R

Rackclose La EX4 . . . . . . 261 A2
Rackenford CE Prim Sch
  EX16 . . . . .47 D5

Rackenford Cross EX16 . . .47 D5
Rackenford Rd
  Tiverton EX16 . . . . 161 A6
  Witheridge EX15 . . . . .46 E1
Rackfield
  Rockwell Green TA21 . . . . . 160 A5
  5 Tiverton EX16 . . . . 161 C3
Rackfield Cotts EX4 . . . . . 176 F8
Rackfield Ct EX32 . . . . . . 154 F6
Rack Field Dr EX15 . . . . . .67 C8
Rackleigh La EX17 . . . . . . .46 A2
Rackmead EX37 . . . . .28 E4
Rack Park Ct EX38 . . . . . 159 C5
Rack Park Rd TQ7 . . . . . . 258 D5
Rack St EX1 . . . . 261 A2
Radcliffe Cl PL6 . . . . 244 E6
Radcliffe La EX33 . . . . . . 226 C7
Raddenstile Ct EX8 . . . . . 202 B6
Raddenstile La EX8 . . . . . 202 B6
Raddick La PL20 . . . . 127 F5
Raddicombe Cl TQ5 . . . . . 234 F8
Raddicombe Dr TQ5 . . . . . 234 F8
Raddicombe Farm TQ5 . . 234 F8
Raddon Cross EX17 . . . . . .81 A5
Raddon Down Cross EX17 79 D4
Raddon Hill EX17 . . . . .81 A6
Raddon Top EX17 . . . . .81 A6
Radford Ave PL4 . . . . 249 B1
Radford Ho TQ1 . . . . 214 A4
Radford La PL10 . . . . 252 D7
Radford Park Dr PL9 . . . . 255 D6
Radford Park Rd PL9 . . . . 255 D6
Radford Rd
  Exeter EX2 . . . . 261 C2
  Plymouth PL1 . . . . 262 B1
Radford Orch TQ9 . . . . . . 131 E1
Radford View PL9 . . . . . . 255 D6
Radford Way EX20 . . . . . 170 C6
Radiant Ho PL1 . . . . 262 B2
Radish La EX12 . . . . 102 A2
Radley Cross EX36 . . . . . . .30 D2
Radnidge La EX16 . . . . . . .32 D4
Radnor Hall PL4 . . . . 263 A3
Radnor Pl
  Exeter EX2 . . . . 261 C2
  Plymouth PL4 . . . . 263 A3
Radnor St PL4 . . . . 263 A3
Radnor Villa EX2 . . . . . . 261 C2
Radsbury La EX35 . . . . .5 B3
Radway EX10 . . . . 188 B4
Radway Gdns TQ14 . . . . . 209 A8
Radway Hill TQ14 . . . . . . 209 A8
Radway La EX9 . . . . 187 B1
Radway St TQ14 . . . . 209 A8
Ragged La EX18 . . . . .44 B1
Ragg La EX9 . . . . 199 G2
Rag La
  Aylesbeare EX5 . . . . .99 D4
  Colebrooke EX17 . . . . .79 A2
  Yarcombe EX14 . . . . .69 A2
Raglan Ct PL1 . . . . 247 F2
Raglan Gdns PL1 . . . . . . 247 F2
Raglan Rd PL1 . . . . 247 F2
Raglans EX2 . . . . 181 C8
Railway Cotts
  Holsworthy EX22 . . . . 164 C3
  6 Plymouth, Ford PL2 . . 247 F5
  Plymouth, Plymstock PL9 . 255 D7
  Tavistock PL19 . . . . 171 B6
Railway Terr
  8 Bideford EX39 . . . . . . 157 B1
  Broadclyst EX5 . . . . 175 E3
Rainbow Ct TQ2 . . . . 219 E2
Rainbow La TA3 . . . . .67 F8
Raisey La TA20 . . . . .69 F7
Rake Cnr TQ7 . . . . 143 F6
Rakeham Cotts EX38 . . . . .41 B6
Rakeham Hill EX38 . . . . . .41 B6
Rakelane Cross TQ7 . . . . 143 F6
Raleigh Ave TQ2 . . . . . . 219 D6
Raleigh Cl
  Dartmouth TQ6 . . . . 233 C3
  Sidmouth EX10 . . . . 188 B7
  South Molton EX36 . . . . . 158 C4
Raleigh Cotts 3 EX31 . . 155 A7
Raleigh Dr
  Budleigh Salterton EX9 . . . 198 B2
  Plymouth PL7 . . . . 251 B6
  Torquay TQ2 . . . . 219 D6
Raleigh Dr TQ4 . . . . 226 B2
Raleigh Hill
  Bideford, Raleigh Hill
    EX39 . . . . 156 E4
  Bideford, Silford EX39 . . . 156 D5
Raleigh Ho
  Exeter EX2 . . . . 261 C2
  Ottery St Mary EX11 . . . . . 169 D3
  Sidmouth EX10 . . . . 188 B7
Raleigh Hts EX31 . . . . . . 154 F7
Raleigh Lawn EX31 . . . . . 154 F7
Raleigh Mdw EX31 . . . . . 155 A7
Raleigh Mead EX36 . . . . . 158 C4
Raleigh Pk EX36 . . . . 158 C4
Raleigh Rd
  Barnstaple EX32 . . . . 154 F6
  Budleigh Salterton EX9 . . . 198 B2
  Dartmouth TQ6 . . . . 233 D4
  Exeter EX1 . . . . 261 A3
  Exmouth EX8 . . . . 202 A6
  Ivybridge PL21 . . . . 237 A6
  Newton Abbot TQ12 . . . . 207 F3
  Ottery St Mary EX11 . . . . . 169 E4
  Salcombe TQ8 . . . . 259 D4
  Teignmouth TQ14 . . . . . . 210 A8

Raleigh St PL1 . . . . 262 B3
Raleigh View EX39 . . . . . 157 A3
Raleigh Wk EX39 . . . . . . 157 A3
Raleigh Mead EX36 . . . . . 158 C4
Ralph Cl EX33 . . . . 152 B8
Ralph Rd EX33 . . . . 152 B6
Ralph's Cr PL19 . . . . 171 B5
Ramage Cl PL6 . . . . 245 F3
Ramehead Cotts PL10 . . . 140 H1
Ramehead La PL10 . . . . . 140 H2
Rame La
  Cawsand PL10 . . . . 252 F1
  Rame PL10 . . . . 140 H2
Ramillies Ave PL5 . . . . . . 244 A4
Ramsey Gdns PL5 . . . . . . 244 D1
Ramsey La
  Runnington TA21 . . . . .51 F8
  Sampford Courtenay EX20 . .76 F3
Ramshill Cross TQ3 . . . . . 225 E8
Ramshill Rd TQ3 . . . . 225 E8
Rance Dr EX8 . . . . 196 E3
Randolph Ct TQ12 . . . . . . 207 A4
Randwick Park Rd PL5 . . . 255 D7
Ranelagh Rd EX20 . . . . . 170 A5
Rangers Cl TQ11 . . . . 236 B4
Ranscombe Cl TQ5 . . . . . 230 E5
Ranscombe Cr 9 TQ5 . . . 230 D5
Ranscombe Rd TQ5 . . . . . 230 D5
Ransum Way PL19 . . . . . . 171 B4
Raphael Cl PL9 . . . . 256 B5
Raphael Dr PL9 . . . . 256 A6
Rapscott Cross EX36 . . . . .18 F1
Rapscott Hill EX36 . . . . . .18 F1
Rashleigh Ave
  Plymouth PL7 . . . . 250 F7
  Saltash PL12 . . . . 242 D1
Rashleigh La EX18 . . . . . . .59 D7
Ratcliffe Sch EX7 . . . . . . 204 C4
Rathlin TQ1 . . . . 220 C7
Rathmore Rd TQ2 . . . . . . 219 F4
Ratshole Gate EX24 . . . . 102 E5
Ratsloe Cross EX4 . . . . . 174 D8
Rattenbury Cotts EX12 . . 191 C6
Rattenbury Cross EX19 . . .76 A8
Rattle St TQ13 . . . . 113 D1
Ravelin Gdns 5 EX32 . . . 155 B5
Ravelin Manor Rd EX32 . . 155 B5
Raven Cl EX4 . . . . 173 C1
Ravensbourne La TQ6 . . . 146 B7
Ravensbury Dr TQ6 . . . . . 234 A2
Rawlin Cl PL6 . . . . 249 C8
Rawlyn Rd TQ2 . . . . 219 E4
Rawnsley La EX34 . . . . .7 F6
Rayer Rd 13 EX16 . . . . . . .64 D7
Raymond Way PL7 . . . . . 250 D6
Rayners EX6 . . . . 181 A1
Raynham Rd PL3 . . . . 248 B4
Rea Barn Cl TQ5 . . . . 230 D4
Rea Barn Rd TQ5 . . . . . . 230 D4
Read Cl EX8 . . . . 196 C1
Reading Wlk PL5 . . . . 244 C4
Rea Dr TQ5 . . . . 230 D5
Recreation Rd PL2 . . . . . 248 C7
Recreation Road Ind Est
  PL2 . . . . 248 C7
Rectory Cl
  Filleigh EX32 . . . . .29 B6
  9 Whimple EX5 . . . . .99 E8
  Willand EX15 . . . . 162 D4
  Wrafton EX33 . . . . 152 F4
Rectory Close Cross
  EX33 . . . . 152 F3
Rectory Cross TQ10 . . . . . 138 A7
Rectory Dr EX2 . . . . 181 B8
Rectory Hill
  Berrynarbor EX34 . . . . .2 D8
  Cheriton Fitzpaine EX17 . . .62 E1
Rectory La
  Parkham EX39 . . . . .39 E8
  Stoke Fleming TQ6 . . . . . 146 B7
  Yelland EX31 . . . . .15 C2
Rectory Pk EX39 . . . . 156 F2
Rectory Rd
  Ashbrittle TA21 . . . . .50 F8
  Bridestowe EX20 . . . . . . 107 F8
  Combe Martin EX34 . . . . . . .3 A3
  Dolton EX19 . . . . .57 F7
  East Ogwell TQ12 . . . . . . 211 E8
  Morchard Bishop EX17 . . . .61 A2
  Plymouth PL1 . . . . 248 A2
Rectory Rise TQ2 . . . . .56 F4
Redavon Rise TQ2 . . . . . . 219 B8
Red Brook Cl TQ4 . . . . . . 226 C1
Redburn Cl TQ3 . . . . 226 A7
Redburn Rd TQ3 . . . . 226 A7
Redcliff Ct EX9 . . . . 199 G2
Redcliffe Rd TQ1 . . . . . . 214 C1
Red Cross
  Colyton EX24 . . . . 102 F6
  Raymond's Hill EX13 . . . . . 104 C7
  Silverton EX5 . . . . .82 C5
Red Cross Hill EX17 . . . . 165 E6
Reddacleave Kiln Cross
  TQ11 . . . . 135 A6
Reddaway Dr EX6 . . . . . . 182 A4
Reddenhill Rd TQ1 . . . . . 220 C7
Red Devon Ct 10 PL21 . . 137 B2
Reddicliff Cl PL9 . . . . 255 E5
Reddicliffes The EX20 . . . 106 E5
Reddicliff Rd PL9 . . . . . . 255 D5
Reddington Rd PL3 . . . . . 249 B7
Redford Cross TQ7 . . . . . 258 A8
Redford Mdw TQ7 . . . . . . 258 C5
Redford Way TQ7 . . . . . . 258 C5
Red Gate
  King's Nympton EX37 . . . . . .44 E8
  Winkleigh EX19 . . . . .58 D2
Redgate Cl TQ1 . . . . 220 D6

Redhill Cl PL5 . . . . 243 E4
Redhill Cotts EX11 . . . . . 169 F6
Redhills
  Budleigh Salterton EX9 . . . 199 G2
  Exeter EX4 . . . . 176 E6
Redhills Cl EX4 . . . . 176 E6
Redhills Com Prim Sch
  EX4 . . . . 176 E6
Red Ho The EX7 . . . . 165 B5
Red House Cl 9 TQ13 . . . 123 C4
Red La
  Churchinford TA3 . . . . .68 C7
  Hatherleigh EX20 . . . . .75 C7
  Hemyock EX15 . . . . .52 E3
  Raymond's Hill EX13 . . . . . 104 C6
Redlake TQ9 . . . . 222 F8
Redlake Cross TQ9 . . . . . 222 F8
Redlake Trad Est PL21 . . . 137 B7
Redland Cross EX18 . . . . . .58 F7
Redlands
  Exeter EX4 . . . . 161 F4
  Exmouth EX8 . . . . 196 A1
Redlands Cl EX4 . . . . 178 A8
Redlands Cl TQ3 . . . . 225 F7
Redlands Rd EX31 . . . . . . 153 F5
Redlands The EX10 . . . . . 188 A3
Redlane Cross DT7 . . . . . 104 C6
Redlap Cross TQ6 . . . . . . 146 C8
Redlap Rd TQ6 . . . . 146 C8
Red Lion Hill PL8 . . . . 257 B5
Red Lion La EX1, EX4 . . . . 261 C4
Red Lion Pl EX7 . . . . 204 D6
Red Lion Yard EX20 . . . . . 170 B5
Redmoor Cl PL19 . . . . 171 A7
Redoubt Hill TQ6 . . . . . . 234 B3
Redpost Cross
  North Tawton EX20 . . . . . . .76 F5
  Sampford Courtenay EX20 . .76 E5
Red Post Cross
  Burrington EX37 . . . . .43 F4
  Totnes TQ9 . . . . 217 C4
Red Rock EX5 . . . . .81 E2
Red Rock Rd EX5 . . . . .81 D1
Redruth Cl PL5 . . . . 244 A5
Redside Terr EX5 . . . . 172 E5
Redstart Cl TQ12 . . . . 206 F1
Redvers Gr PL7 . . . . 250 E4
Redvers Ho 7 EX1 . . . . . 165 C5
Redvers Rd EX4 . . . . 177 A5
Redvers Way 5 EX16 . . . 161 E6
Redwalls Mdw TQ6 . . . . . 233 E4
Redwell La TQ3 . . . . 225 F8
Redwell Rd TQ3 . . . . 225 F8
Redwing Dr PL6 . . . . 245 D8
Redwood Cl
  Bovey Tracey TQ13 . . . . . . 180 C4
  Exmouth EX8 . . . . 196 D3
  10 Hemyock EX15 . . . . . .67 B8
  4 Honiton EX14 . . . . .85 C2
Redwood Dr PL7 . . . . 251 B5
Redwood Rd EX10 . . . . . . 188 C5
Redwoods TQ13 . . . . 180 C5
Redworth Terr TQ9 . . . . . 223 C6
Redyeates Cross EX17 . . . .63 A2
Reed Mdw EX20 . . . . .75 C7
Reed's Cross
  Ashill EX15 . . . . .66 C6
  Bittadon EX31 . . . . .9 E4
Reedsdown Cross EX17 . . .79 F6
Reeds Pl EX15 . . . . 163 C3
Red Vale TQ14 . . . . 210 A5
Reedy Hill EX6 . . . . 112 F8
Reeveacre Cross TQ9 . . . 216 D5
Reeves Cl 3 TQ9 . . . . . . 219 D5
Reeves Rd The TQ2 . . . . . 219 D5
Reform St 8 EX31 . . . . . 154 F6
Regal Ct PL12 . . . . 242 F7
Regency Cres EX8 . . . . . . 202 C6
Regency Ct 8 EX34 . . . . 150 B5
Regency Gate EX10 . . . . . 188 C5
Regent Cl
  Barnstaple EX31 . . . . 154 C2
  Fremington EX31 . . . . 153 F5
Regent Ct PL4 . . . . 263 A3
Regent Pl EX34 . . . . 150 B6
Regents Ct TQ4 . . . . 226 C5
Regents Gate EX8 . . . . . . 202 B6
Regents Gdns 6 TQ14 . . . 210 C4
Regent's Pk EX1 . . . . 177 E6
Regent's Sq EX1 . . . . 177 F5
Regent St
  Dawlish EX7 . . . . 204 D6
  Exeter EX2 . . . . 177 A3
  Plymouth PL4 . . . . 263 A3
  10 Teignmouth TQ14 . . . 210 C4
Regis Ct EX10 . . . . 188 C4
Reigate Rd PL9 . . . . 255 E8
Reme Dr EX14 . . . . .85 C2
Rena Hobson Ct EX16 . . . 161 B4
Rendells Mdw TQ13 . . . . 180 E7
Rendlesham Gdns PL6 . . . 245 E3
Rendle St PL1 . . . . 262 B3
Rennes Dr EX4 . . . . 173 C1
Rennes Ho EX1 . . . . 178 B7
Renney Rd
  Down Thomas PL9 . . . . . . 255 C1
  Heybrook Bay PL9 . . . . . . 140 B8
Rennie Ave PL5 . . . . 243 C1
Rennie Rd 12 EX16 . . . . . .64 D7
Renoir Cl PL9 . . . . 256 A6
Renown St PL2 . . . . 247 E6
Rensey La EX17 . . . . .60 C4
Renslade Ho EX4 . . . . 261 A2
Renton La TQ7 . . . . 142 E7
Research Way PL6 . . . . . . 245 C4
Reservoir Cres PL9 . . . . . 256 B7
Reservoir Cross PL16 . . . . .91 A4
Reservoir La 1 PL3 . . . . . 248 F6

Reservoir Rd
  Plymouth, Hartley PL3 . . . . 248 F6
  Plymouth, Plymstock PL9 . 256 B7
Reservoir Way PL3 . . . . . . 256 B7
Resolution Ho PL4 . . . . . . 263 B3
Rest Hill TQ12 . . . . 131 D7
Restland La EX20 . . . . .94 F7
Restormel Rd PL4 . . . . . . 262 C4
Restormel Terr PL4 . . . . . 262 C4
Retail Park Cl EX2 . . . . . . 177 B3
Retreat Cl TQ7 . . . . 258 C5
Retreat Dr The EX3 . . . . . 182 D6
Retreat Rd EX3 . . . . 182 E6
Retreat The
  Exmouth EX8 . . . . 202 D7
  Plymouth PL3 . . . . 249 B7
  Tiverton EX16 . . . . 161 D4
  Topsham EX3 . . . . 182 D6
Revell Park Rd PL7 . . . . . 250 D6
Revel Rd PL3 . . . . 249 A6
Revelstoke Rd PL8 . . . . . 140 F6
Revill Ind Units EX5 . . . . . .99 A4
Rew Cross
  Ashburton TQ13 . . . . 130 F5
  Newton St Cyres EX5 . . . . . .81 A2
Rewdown Cross TQ13 . . . 130 F6
Rewe Barton EX5 . . . . .82 A2
Rewe Cross EX5 . . . . .82 A2
Rewe Ct EX5 . . . . .82 B3
Rewe La EX5 . . . . .99 D6
Rewes Cross EX5 . . . . .82 F2
Rewlea Cotts TQ13 . . . . . 130 F5
Rewlea Cross TQ13 . . . . . 130 F5
Rew Rd TQ13 . . . . 130 F5
Rew's Cl EX14 . . . . .2 F4
Rews Cross EX36 . . . . .19 C2
Rews Mdw EX1 . . . . 174 F1
Rews Park Dr EX1 . . . . . . 174 F1
Rexona Cl EX2 . . . . 177 A2
Rexon Cross PL16 . . . . . . 106 B7
Reynell Ave TQ12 . . . . . . 207 F3
Reynell Rd TQ12 . . . . 211 F8
Reynolds Cl EX4 . . . . 174 D1
Reynolds Gr PL5 . . . . 247 C8
Reynolds Rd PL7 . . . . 250 C6
Rheola Gdns PL6 . . . . 245 D3
Rhodanthe Rd TQ3 . . . . . 219 B1
Rhode La DT7 . . . . 260 C6
Rhodes Cl PL7 . . . . 250 E7
Rhododendron Ave
  Barnstaple EX31 . . . . 154 D3
  Dunkeswell EX14 . . . . .67 B1
RHS Gardens Rosemoor
  EX38 . . . . .159 D2
Rhude Cross EX22 . . . . . . .53 D2
Rhydda Bank Cross EX31 . .4 A5
Rhyll Gate Cross TA22 . . . .32 E7
Ribble Gdns PL3 . . . . 249 D7
Ribston Ave EX1 . . . . 178 C6
Rices Mews EX2 . . . . 177 A4
Richard Cl EX39 . . . . .25 E4
Richard Ford Ct EX2 . . . . 177 F5
Richards Ct
  Dawlish EX7 . . . . 204 D5
  Exmouth EX8 . . . . 196 D2
  Wellington TA21 . . . . 160 C8
Richardson Dr PL8 . . . . . . 141 B8
Richards Row PL1 . . . . . . 248 F7
Richards Terr PL10 . . . . . 252 E5
Richmond Ave EX34 . . . . 150 A5
Richmond Cl
  Sampford Peverell EX16 . . . .50 D1
  Torquay TQ1 . . . . 221 A4
Richmond Ct
  14 Dawlish EX7 . . . . 204 E6
  Paignton TQ3 . . . . 226 B7
Richmond Gn EX39 . . . . . .14 F1
Richmond Hill TQ12 . . . . . 213 A5
Richmond Pk EX39 . . . . . 156 F7
Richmond Pl 18 EX7 . . . . 204 E6
Richmond Rd
  Appledore EX39 . . . . .15 A1
  Exeter EX4 . . . . 261 A3
  Exmouth EX8 . . . . 202 D7
  Ilfracombe EX34 . . . . 150 A4
  Plymouth PL6 . . . . 245 A4
Richmond St EX32 . . . . . 155 A5
Richmond Terr
  8 Appledore EX39 . . . . . .15 A1
  Buckland Monachorum
    PL20 . . . . 126 C3
  Kingsbridge TQ7 . . . . 258 D6
Richmond Villas EX34 . . . 150 A5
Richmond Wlk
  10 Barnstaple EX32 . . . . 155 A6
  Plymouth PL1 . . . . 247 F1
Rickards Gn EX39 . . . . . . 156 B2
Rickards Row EX39 . . . . . .40 B7
Rickham Cross TQ8 . . . . . 148 D4
Riddell Ave EX32 . . . . 154 F6
Riddistone Cross EX20 . . . .77 A8
Riddistone La EX20 . . . . . .77 A8
Ride The PL7, PL9 . . . . . . 249 D2
Ridge Cross
  Chillington TQ7 . . . . 149 B8
  Plymouth PL9 . . . . 256 A3
  Witheridge EX16 . . . . .46 E4
Ridge Hill
  Berrynarbor EX34 . . . . .2 E3
  Combe Martin EX34 . . . . . . .3 A2
  Dartmouth TQ6 . . . . 233 F4
Ridge Ho PL4 . . . . 249 A4
Ridge La
  Chudleigh TQ13 . . . . 124 B7
  Cornworthy TQ9 . . . . 139 F4
  Paignton TQ3 . . . . 218 F8
  Tiverton EX16 . . . . .63 F8
  Wilmington EX14 . . . . .86 C3

Ridge Lane Cross TQ9 . . . 139 E4
Ridgeleigh Ct 11 EX14 . . 166 C6
Ridgengaunt Cl TQ5 . . . . 230 E5
Ridge Park Ave PL4 . . . . . 248 D4
Ridge Park Rd PL7 . . . . . . 250 F5
Ridge Pk PL7 . . . . 250 E5
Ridge Rd
  Combeinteignhead TQ12 . . 208 D2
  Maidencombe TQ1, TQ12 . . 214 B7
  Modbury PL21 . . . . 137 B4
  Plymouth PL7 . . . . 250 C3
  Stokeinteignhead TQ12 . . 209 A1
  Ugborough PL21 . . . . 137 D7
  West Anstey TA22 . . . . . . .32 C7
Ridges The TQ6 . . . . 233 D1
Ridgeway
  Exeter EX14 . . . . 173 A3
  Honiton EX14 . . . . 166 B4
  Ottery St Mary EX11 . . . . . 169 E4
  Plymouth PL7 . . . . 250 D5
  Plymouth PL7 . . . . 250 F5
  Saltash PL12 . . . . 242 D1
  Sidbury EX10 . . . . 101 B2
Ridge Way PL6 . . . . 194 E2
Ridgeway Ave EX39 . . . . 156 E7
Ridgeway Cl
  Newton Abbot TQ12 . . . . 207 F1
  Sidbury EX10 . . . . 101 B2
  Westward Ho! EX39 . . . . . 156 D7
Ridgeway Ct EX39 . . . . . 156 D7
Ridgeway Dr EX39 . . . . . 156 D7
Ridgeway Gdns EX11 . . . . 169 E4
Ridgeway Gn EX37 . . . . . . .43 B7
Ridgeway Hill TQ13 . . . . 218 D6
Ridgeway Hts 17 TQ1 . . . 220 D4
Ridgeway La
  Awliscombe EX14 . . . . .85 A5
  Coffinswell TQ12 . . . . 213 D6
  Shillingford EX16 . . . . .34 C2
Ridgeway Mead EX10 . . . 187 F7
Ridgeway Rd
  Newton Abbot TQ12 . . . . 207 F1
  Torquay TQ1 . . . . 220 E4
Ridgeway Sch PL7 . . . . . 250 C5
Ridgeway's Cross EX17 . . .79 E6
Ridgewood Cross EX15 . . .67 D8
Ridgewood La EX15 . . . . . .67 D8
Ridgy Cross TQ13 . . . . . . 130 B4
Ridgway Cross EX36 . . . . .20 E1
Ridgway La EX24 . . . . 102 F4
Riding Cross EX37 . . . . . . .29 A4
Ridley The PL3 . . . . 183 C4
Ridleys Hill TQ6 . . . . 234 A3
Rifford Rd EX2 . . . . 178 B4
Rifton La EX16 . . . . .48 B4
Riga Terr PL3 . . . . 249 C4
Rigdale Cl PL6 . . . . 249 A7
Riggles Cross EX14 . . . . . .68 A3
Rigdale La EX9 . . . . 219 F6
Rill Cnr EX5 . . . . .99 D3
Rill La EX9 . . . . 199 H2
Ringdown La EX15 . . . . . . .52 F2
Ringhill Cross EX20 . . . . . .95 C5
Ringhill Cross EX14 . . . . . .68 A3
Ringmore Cl TQ14 . . . . . 209 D5
Ringmore Dr TQ7 . . . . . . 142 E3
Ringmore Rd
  Shaldon TQ14 . . . . 209 D5
  Teignmouth TQ14 . . . . . . 210 A3
Ringmore Way PL5 . . . . . 244 B3
Ringrona TQ8 . . . . 259 B2
Ringslade Cl TQ12 . . . . . 206 F5
Ringslade Rd TQ12 . . . . . 206 F5
Ringswell Ave EX1 . . . . . 178 C6
Ringswell Cross TQ9 . . . . 216 E6
Ringswell Pk EX2 . . . . . . 178 D5
Riphay Cross TA22 . . . . . .33 E3
Ripon Cl EX4 . . . . 176 E6
Rippon Cl
  Brixham TQ5 . . . . 229 F2
  17 Tiverton EX16 . . . . . . .64 D7
Riscombe Hill EX5 . . . . . . .98 F8
Risdon Ave PL4 . . . . 249 B1
Rising Sun EX13 . . . . .87 A3
Ritson La TQ9 . . . . 139 D3
Rivenford La EX5, EX17 . . .81 C4
Riverbank Cotts EX39 . . . 157 B4
River Cott EX5 . . . . 173 F8
River Ct
  Saltash PL12 . . . . 242 D5
  Tavistock PL19 . . . . 171 D6
Riverdale
  Harbertonford TQ9 . . . . . 139 C7
  Seaton EX12 . . . . 192 B7
Riverdale Cl EX12 . . . . . . 192 B7
River Dart Ctry Pk TQ13 . 130 D5
River Dr EX15 . . . . 163 D3
Riverford Cl PL6 . . . . 245 D7
River Front EX3 . . . . 183 C2
Riveria Ct TQ1 . . . . 220 C4
River Mdws EX2 . . . . 177 C3
Rivermead EX15 . . . . 163 C2
Rivermead Ave EX8 . . . . . 196 A3
Rivermead Cl EX4 . . . . . . 196 A3
Rivermead Rd EX2 . . . . . 177 C3
River Pk PL21 . . . . 137 A4
Rivers Cl PL21 . . . . 237 E5
Riversdale Ave EX34 . . . . 150 A6
Riverside
  Chillaton PL16 . . . . 116 D8
  Dawlish Warren EX7 . . . . . 201 A2
  Hemyock EX15 . . . . .67 C8
  Kingsbridge TQ7 . . . . 258 D4
  Teignmouth TQ14 . . . . . . 210 A3
  Totnes TQ9 . . . . 223 B7
  Wellington TA21 . . . . 160 B7

Riverside Apartments
EX36. . . . . .158 E4
Riverside Bsns Pk PL1 . .247 E3
Riverside Cl
Bideford EX39 . . . . .157 B4
Honiton EX14. . . . . .166 B6
1 Horrabridge PL20. . . . .126 F4
Riverside Cott PL12. . . . . .242 C1
Riverside Cross EX17 . . . . .62 A3
Riverside Ct
14 Barnstaple EX31 . . . . .154 F5
Bideford EX39 . . . . .157 B4
Dartmouth TQ6 . . . . .233 F3
Exeter EX2. . . . . .261 B2
Newton Abbot TQ12. . . . . .207 D4
Riverside Mews PL12 . . . .243 A3
Riverside Orch EX32 . . . . .192 B7
Riverside Pl PL1. . . . . .247 D2
Riverside Rd
Barnstaple EX31 . . . . .154 C6
Dittisham TQ6 . . . . .228 C3
Lynmouth EX35 . . . . .151 C6
Sidmouth EX10 . . . . .188 B3
Topsham EX3. . . . . .182 E6
Riverside Rd E PL8 . . . . . .140 F6
Riverside Rd W PL8. . . . . .140 F6
Riverside Terr TQ9 . . . . . .223 D5
Riverside Units EX31. . . . .154 C6
Riverside Valley Pk EX2 . .177 E2
Riverside View EX11 . . . .169 D3
Riverside Way EX12. . . . . .192 C5
River View
Barnstaple EX32 . . . . .155 C2
Exebridge TA22 . . . . .33 F3
Gunnislake PL18 . . . . .125 B5
Plymouth PL4. . . . . .249 B1
Saltash PL12 . . . . .242 F3
River View Cl
12 Chudleigh Knighton
TQ13. . . . . .123 C4
20 Colyton EX24 . . . . .103 A4
River View Commercial Ctr
EX31. . . . . .154 D6
Riverview Dr EX4 . . . . . . .176 F8
River View Dr **21** EX24. . .103 A4
River View La PL4. . . . . . .249 B1
Riverview Pl TQ7 . . . . .258 C5
River View Terr EX6 . . . . .182 B3
Riviera Terr
Dawlish EX7. . . . . .204 F7
Exminster EX6 . . . . .182 B3
Riviera The
Paignton TQ4 . . . . .226 B5
Torquay TQ1. . . . . .220 B7
Riviera Way TQ2 . . . . .213 D1
Rixafer Rd TQ13 . . . . .124 B3
Rixdale Rd TQ13 . . . . .124 C4
Rixey La EX7 . . . . .61 B2
Rixeypark Cnr TQ13 . . . . .123 D3
Roach Hill EX36 . . . . .31 F7
Roachill Cross EX36. . . . . .32 C1
Roach La EX5. . . . . .82 C6
Road Down Cross EX6. . . .96 F7
Road End Cross EX14 . . . . .87 A8
Roadford Lake Lakeside Wlks
EX20. . . . . .106 C8
Road Pk TQ13 . . . . .123 B7
Roadway Cnr EX34. . . . . . . .8 A5
Robartes Ct EX2 . . . . .261 C2
Robeclave Cl PL7. . . . . . . .251 C6
Robers Rd TQ12 . . . . .207 D8
Robert Adams Cl PL7. . . . .250 B5
Roberts Ave PL11. . . . . . . .247 B3
Roberts Cl
Cullompton EX15. . . . . . . .163 B2
Torquay TQ2. . . . . .214 B2
Roberts Rd
Exeter EX2. . . . . .261 B2
Plymouth PL5. . . . . .247 D8
Roberts Way TQ12 . . . . . . .96 F8
Robert Way EX10 . . . . .186 F8
Robin Cl EX15 . . . . .163 B2
Robin Dr PL15 . . . . .105 A2
Robins Cl EX16. . . . . .63 A6
Robins Field TQ7 . . . . .144 F1
Robins Hill EX39 . . . . .156 E4
Robinson's Row TQ8 . . . . .259 E4
Robins Way PL9 . . . . .255 E8
Roborough Ave PL6. . . . . .245 B5
Roborough Cl PL6. . . . . . . .245 B5
Roborough Down La PL6. .245 B5
Roborough Gdns 8
TQ13 . . . . .131 A5
Roborough La
Ashburton TQ13. . . . . .130 F5
Plymouth PL5. . . . . .244 D8
Roborough Rd EX31. . . . . .155 A8
Roborough Terr TQ13 . . . .130 F5
Robyns Cl PL7. . . . . .251 B5
Roche Gdn EX7 . . . . .182 A8
Rochester Rd **3** PL4. . . . .248 C4
Rochford Cres PL5. . . . . . .243 F5
Rock Ave
Barnstaple EX32 . . . . .155 A3
Lynton EX35. . . . . .151 C6
Rockbeare CE Prim Sch
EX5. . . . . .99 B5

Rockbeare Hill EX5 . . . . . .168 A5
Rock Cl TQ4 . . . . .229 C7
Rockcliffe Ct **1** EX34 . . . .150 C6
Rock Cotts TQ7 . . . . .142 C6
Rockerne Cl EX17 . . . . .97 B7
Rockdale Rd PL8 . . . . .136 A2
Rock End Ave TQ1 . . . . . . .220 C2
Rockerhayne Cross
EX24. . . . . .102 D7
Rockey La EX20. . . . . .74 E2
Rockfield Ave PL6 . . . . . . .244 F6
Rockfield Cl PL14. . . . . . . .210 D7
Rockfield Cotts TA21. . . . . .51 F7
Rockfield Rd EX34 . . . . .7 F7
Rock Gdns
Barnstaple EX32 . . . . .155 A3
Plymouth PL9. . . . . .249 D1
Rock Head EX37 . . . . .28 C2
Rock Hill
Aveton Gifford TQ7 . . . . . .143 C6
Berrynarbor EX34 . . . . .2 D3
Braunton EX33. . . . . .152 D6
Chulmleigh EX18. . . . . .59 E8
Georgeham EX33. . . . . .8 A2
Plymouth PL5. . . . . .244 C2
Umberleigh EX37. . . . . .28 C2
West Down EX34 . . . . .8 F4
Rock House La EX31 . . . . .214 C5
Rockingham Rd PL3 . . . . .249 A5
Rock La
Cheriton Bishop EX17 . . . . .97 B7
Chudleigh TQ13 . . . . .123 F8
16 Combe Martin EX34 . . . .3 A3
Offwell EX14. . . . . .86 C1
Rocklands TQ13 . . . . .123 E5
Rockley La EX32 . . . . .11 F1
Rock Lodge Pk EX35 . . . . .151 B5
Rockmount Terr 6
EX39. . . . . .157 A2
Rock Nursery The TQ13 . .123 E5
Rockpark Cross TQ13 . . . .131 A5
Rock Park Terr **24** EX32 . .155 A4
Rock Pk
4 Ashburton TQ13 . . . . . .131 A5
Dartmouth TQ6 . . . . .233 D4
Rock Rd
Chudleigh TQ13 . . . . .123 E5
Torquay TQ2. . . . . .220 B4
Rockshead Hill EX32. . . . . .18 F3
Rockside EX4. . . . . .177 A6
Rockstone The EX39. . . . . .156 B6
Rockstone The EX7 . . . . . .205 A7
Rock Terr PL7 . . . . .250 D4
Rock The EX31. . . . . .154 F7
Rock View EX16. . . . . .65 B7
Rock Villas PL16 . . . . .105 F4
Rockville Pk PL9. . . . . .255 E8
Rock Walk Hts TQ1 . . . . . .220 A4
Rockwell Gate TA21. . . . . .160 B5
Rockwell Green CE Prim Sch
TA21. . . . . .160 B5
Rocky Hill PL19. . . . . .171 B5
Rocky La
Abbotsham EX39 . . . . .156 A3
Buckfastleigh TQ11 . . . . . .236 A3
2 Combe Martin EX34 . . . .3 A4
Teignmouth TQ14. . . . . . . .210 A6
Rocky Park Ave PL9 . . . . . .255 E8
Rocky Park Rd PL9 . . . . . .255 E8
Rocombe Cl TQ2 . . . . .213 F4
Rocombe Cross
Daccombe TQ12. . . . . .213 F6
Raymond's Hill EX13 . . . . .104 C6
Rocombe Hill TQ12. . . . . .213 F7
Rodda Cl PL18. . . . . .125 D7
Roddick Way **8** PL7 . . . . .251 A4
Rodgements Cross EX18. . .59 E8
Rodgements Cross La EX18. .59 E8
Rodgemont's La EX18. . . . .59 E8
Rodgers Ind Est TQ4 . . . . .225 D3
Rodney Cl
Dartmouth TQ6 . . . . .233 D3
Exmouth EX8 . . . . .203 A7
Rodney St PL5. . . . . .247 D8
Rodsleigh La EX36 . . . . .31 C1
Rodsworthy La EX36. . . . . .31 C1
Rodway Cross EX14. . . . . . .87 A6
Roeselare Ave PL11. . . . . .247 A3
Roeselare Cl PL11 . . . . . . .247 A3
Rogada Ct TQ5 . . . . .230 D3
Rogate Dr PL6. . . . . .245 D4
Rogate Wlk PL6. . . . . .245 D4
Rogers Cl EX16. . . . . .161 E6
Rogers Dr PL12 . . . . .242 D4
Roland Bailey Gdns
PL19. . . . . .171 A6
Rolle Barton EX9 . . . . .198 D7
Rolle Cotts EX9 . . . . .197 E2
Rolle Ct EX38. . . . . .159 C5
Rolle Rd
Budleigh Salterton EX9 . . .199 G2
Exmouth EX8 . . . . .202 A6
Great Torrington EX38. . . .159 A5
Rolle's Quay EX31 . . . . . . .154 F5
Rolle St
Barnstaple EX31 . . . . .154 F6
Exmouth EX8 . . . . .202 A6
Rolle Terr EX39 . . . . .40 C7
Rollestone Cres EX4 . . . . .173 E2
Rolle The EX9 . . . . .199 G2
Rolle Villas EX8 . . . . .202 A6
Rollis Park Cl PL9 . . . . . . .255 C8
Rollis Park Rd PL9 . . . . . . .255 C8
Rolston Cl PL6. . . . . .244 D6
Romaleyn Gdns TQ4 . . . . .226 B4

Roman Rd
Feniton EX5. . . . . .84 C2
Kilmington EX13 . . . . .87 C1
Lyme Regis DT7. . . . . .260 D4
Plymouth PL5. . . . . .243 E2
Romansleigh Cross EX36. . .45 C7
Romansleigh Ridge EX18. . .45 C5
Romans Way EX16 . . . . . . .161 F6
Roman Way
Honiton EX14. . . . . .166 E7
Plymouth PL5. . . . . .243 E2
Seaton EX12 . . . . .192 A6
Romilly Gdns PL7. . . . . . . .250 B5
Romney Cl PL5 . . . . .244 B1
Romsey Dr EX2 . . . . .177 E5
Ronald Terr PL2 . . . . .247 F5
Roncombe Cnr EX24 . . . . .101 E5
Roncombe Gate EX24 . . . .101 E5
Roncombe Hill EX10 . . . . .101 E5
Ronsdale Cl PL9 . . . . .255 D8
Rookbear La EX31 . . . . .9 E2
Rookery Cvn Pk EX20 . . . . .77 F5
Rookery Hill EX16. . . . . . . .48 C8
Rookery La DT7. . . . . .260 C8
Rookery Terr TA21. . . . . . .160 C5
Rook La PL21. . . . . .133 C3
Rooklands **10** TQ12. . . . . .207 B3
Rooklands Ave TQ12. . . . . .219 E6
Rook Lane End PL21 . . . . .133 C3
Rooks Cl EX31. . . . . .154 B3
Rooks Cross EX31. . . . . . . .27 D3
Rooks Farm Rd EX31. . . . .153 A4
Rooks Nest EX31. . . . . . . .153 E5
Rooks Way EX16. . . . . . . .161 F6
Rookswood La EX5. . . . . . .99 C5
Rookwood Cl EX4 . . . . . . .166 B5
Rookwood Ho EX14 . . . . . .166 B6
Room Hill Rd TA24. . . . . . .21 D7
Roope Cl PL5. . . . . .247 C7
Rooty Cross EX31. . . . . . . .27 A7
Roper Ave PL9. . . . . .255 D8
Roperidge Cross PL21. . . .137 F6
Ropers Ct EX9 . . . . .198 E7
Roper's La EX9 . . . . .198 E7
Ropery Rd EX34 . . . . .150 C6
Ropewalk
Bideford EX39 . . . . .157 A2
Kingsbridge TQ7 . . . . .258 C4
Ropewalk Hill TQ5 . . . . . . .230 C5
Ropewalk Ho PL8. . . . . . . .201 E6
Rope Wlk
2 Teignmouth TQ14 . . . . .210 B5
Wellington TA21. . . . . .160 C4
Rorkes Cl PL5 . . . . .243 E2
Roscoff Cl EX38 . . . . .159 E5
Rosea Bridge La EX34. . . . .3 A4
Rose Acre Terr TQ5 . . . . . .230 D4
Rose And Crown Hill
EX17. . . . . .80 A5
Rosebank Cres EX4 . . . . . .173 E1
Rosebarn Ave EX4 . . . . . . .173 D1
Rosebarn La EX4 . . . . .173 E2
Rosebery Ave PL4 . . . . . . .263 C4
Rosebery La PL4 . . . . .263 C4
Rosebery Rd
Exeter EX4 . . . . .177 E8
Exmouth EX8 . . . . .202 A7
Plymouth PL4. . . . . .263 C4
Rose Cotts
Beer EX12 . . . . .191 D5
9 Bishop's Tawton EX32 . .16 E1
Frogmore TQ7 . . . . .144 E3
Rosedale Ave PL2. . . . . . . .248 D7
Rose Dene TQ2 . . . . .213 F2
Rosedown Ave PL2. . . . . . .248 A7
Rose Duryard EX4 . . . . . . .173 A1
Rose Gdns PL6. . . . . .245 E6
Rose Hill
Kingskerswell TQ12 . . . . . .212 F4
Wembury PL9 . . . . .140 D7
Rosehill Cl TQ12 . . . . .220 C5
Rose Hill Cl TQ12 . . . . . . .212 F4
Rosehill Gdns TQ12 . . . . . .212 F4
Rosehill Rd TQ1 . . . . .220 C5
Rose Hill Terr PL17. . . . . . .125 D3
Rosehip Cl PL6 . . . . .245 E7
Rose Ho TQ1 . . . . .220 D7
Rose La EX32 . . . . .155 C3
Roseland Ave EX1 . . . . . . .178 A6
Roseland Cres EX1. . . . . . .178 A6
Roseland Cross EX22. . . . . .54 C8
Roseland Dr EX1 . . . . .178 A5
Roselands EX10. . . . . .188 B6
Roselands Cotts EX24. . . .103 A5
Roselands Dr TQ4. . . . . . . .225 F2
Roseland Sq TQ12. . . . . . .207 E7
Rosemary Ave TQ12 . . . . .206 F4
Rosemary Cl PL7 . . . . .132 C4
Rosemary Ct TQ3 . . . . . . .226 C8
Rosemary Gdns TQ3 . . . . .225 F8
Rosemary La
Colyton EX24 . . . . .103 A5
Dulverton TA22 . . . . .33 D6
Holne TQ11 . . . . .130 A3
Musbury EX13 . . . . .103 D5
Rosemarylane Cross
EX15. . . . . .52 D1
Rosemary St EX4 . . . . .176 F5
Rosemary St La EX4 . . . . .176 F5
Rosemont Cl EX38 . . . . . . .159 E4
Rose Moor Rd EX38. . . . . .159 E5
Rosemount
Bideford EX39 . . . . .156 E4

Rosemount continued
Paignton TQ4 . . . . .226 C5
Rosemount Cl EX14. . . . . .166 B5
Rosemount Ct TQ8. . . . . . .259 D5
Rosemount La EX14. . . . . .166 B5
Rosery Rd TQ2. . . . . .219 E5
Rose Terr PL16. . . . . .105 E4
Rosevean Ct **8** PL3. . . . . .248 F6
Rosevean Gdns PL3. . . . . .248 F6
Rosevean Ho **7** PL3 . . . . .248 F6
Roseveare Cl PL9 . . . . .256 A8
Roseville St TQ6 . . . . .233 E2
Rosewarne Ave TQ12. . . . .207 F2
Roseway EX8 . . . . .202 F8
Rosewell Cl EX14 . . . . .166 D7
Rosewood Cl PL9 . . . . .255 F5
Rosewood Cres EX5. . . . . .179 E2
Rosewood Terr **5** EX4. . . .166 D7
Rospeath Cres PL2. . . . . . .248 D8
Rossall Dr TQ3. . . . . .226 A5
Ross Cl EX1 . . . . .174 F1
Rosse Rd EX16. . . . . .161 B5
Rosshayne La EX14 . . . . . . .68 F2
Rosslyn Park Rd PL3. . . . .248 B5
Rossyl Ave EX7 . . . . .204 C3
Rothbury Cl PL6. . . . . .245 D4
Rothbury Gdns PL6. . . . . .245 D4
Rotherfold TQ9 . . . . .223 B5
Rothesay Gdns PL5 . . . . . .244 D3
Rougemont Ave TQ2 . . . . .213 D1
Rougemont Cl PL3. . . . . . .249 B7
Rougemont Terr EX13 . . . .167 D5
Roundball Cl EX14 . . . . . . .166 B5
Roundball Cres EX14 . . . . .166 B5
Roundball La EX14 . . . . . . .166 B4
Round Berry Dr TQ8 . . . . .259 C4
Round Cross TQ11 . . . . . . .236 B6
Roundham Ave TQ4 . . . . . .226 D5
Roundham Cres TQ4 . . . . .226 D5
Roundham Gdns TQ4. . . . .226 D5
Roundham Ho TQ4 . . . . . . .226 C5
Roundham Rd TQ4. . . . . . .226 C5
Roundhead Rd TQ12 . . . . .180 F3
Roundhill Cl EX4 . . . . .161 B3
Roundhill La EX4 . . . . .173 A3
Roundhill Rd TQ2 . . . . . . .213 E2
Roundhouse La EX8. . . . . .196 B2
Roundings The TQ5 . . . . . .230 B5
Roundmoors Cl TQ12. . . . .213 A3
Roundsley La PL19. . . . . . .117 C6
Roundtable Meet EX4. . . . .174 B1
Roundway The TQ12 . . . . .212 F6
Rousdown Rd TQ2 . . . . . . .219 E4
Rowan Cl
East Ogwell TQ12 . . . . . . .206 F1
2 Honiton EX14 . . . . .85 C2
Plymouth PL7. . . . . .251 B5
Tavistock PL19. . . . . .171 C3
Tiverton EX16 . . . . .161 F5
Rowan Cl PL2 . . . . .242 C2
Rowan Dr EX12. . . . . .192 A8
Rowan Pk **2** EX3. . . . . . .154 C2
Rowans The PL16. . . . . . . .105 E4
Rowantree Rd TQ12 . . . . . .207 E1
Rowan Way
Brixham TQ5 . . . . .230 A2
Exeter EX4 . . . . .176 F7
Plymouth PL6. . . . . .245 E7
Rowbrook Cl TQ4 . . . . .225 E3
Rowcliffe Cotts TA21. . . . . .50 F8
Rowcroft Cl EX14. . . . . . . .166 B5
Rowcroft Rd TQ3 . . . . .226 C8
Rowden Cross
Salcombe TQ7 . . . . .148 A8
Teignmouth TQ14. . . . . . . .124 C1
Widecombe in the Moor
TQ13. . . . . .121 A3
Rowden Ct PL8. . . . . .201 A6
Rowdens Ho The TQ14 . . .210 D6
Rowdens Rd TQ2 . . . . .219 F5
Rowden St PL3 . . . . .248 E5
Rowdens The TQ14. . . . . . .210 C6
Rowdon Brook EX6 . . . . . .112 F5
Rowdown Cl PL7. . . . . .251 D4
Rowe Cl
Bideford EX39 . . . . .25 E4
Rockwell Green TA21. . . . .160 A4
Rowells Mead **4** TQ12 . .122 F1
Rowena EX39 . . . . .156 D6
Rowes Orchard EX15. . . . .162 C3
Rowe St PL11. . . . . .247 B3
Rowhorne Rd EX4 . . . . . . .176 C8
Row La PL5. . . . . .243 E2
Rowland Cl PL9. . . . . .255 E5
Rowley Cross EX31. . . . . . . .4 D1
Rowley Gate EX31. . . . . . . .11 B6
Rowley Rd TQ1 . . . . .214 C1
Rowlstone Cl EX4 . . . . . . .196 C3
Rowse Gdns PL18. . . . . . . .125 D3
Rowsell's La TQ9 . . . . .223 D5
Rows La
Bampton EX16. . . . . .34 A1
22 Combe Martin EX34 . . . .3 A3
Row The EX36 . . . . .30 A2
Row Tor Cl EX20 . . . . .170 D5
Rowtrey Cross EX20. . . . . . .74 E5
Royal Albert Memorial Mus
EX4 . . . . .261 A3
Royal Ave The EX8 . . . . . .201 F7
Royal Charter Pk EX18. . . . .44 E1
Royal Clarence Apts 4
EX12. . . . . .192 B4
Royal Clarence Apts 4
EX34. . . . . .150 B6
Royal Cres EX2 . . . . .178 D3

Royal Ct
Princetown PL20 . . . . .128 A8
Torquay TQ2. . . . . .220 D7
**Royal Devon & Exeter Hospl
(Heavitree)** EX1. . . . . . .177 E6
**Royal Devon & Exeter Hospl
(Wonford)** EX2 . . . . . . .177 F4
Royal Eye Infmy PL4. . . . .248 E4
Royal London Ct EX10. . . .188 B3
Royal Navy Ave PL2. . . . . .247 F6
Royal Oak Cotts EX20 . . . .107 F8
Royal Oak Cross EX14. . . . .86 E6
Royal Par PL1 . . . . .262 C2
Royal Pines TQ1 . . . . .220 E3
Royal Way PL6 . . . . .201 B8
**Royal West of England Sch
for the Deaf EX2** 261 C1
Royal William Rd PL1 . . . .254 A8
Royston Cl **4** EX1 . . . . . . .178 C8
Royston Rd
Bideford EX39 . . . . .156 F1
Churchinford TA3. . . . . .68 D7
Rozel TQ1 . . . . .220 D2
Rubby Cross EX6 . . . . .97 E5
Ruckamore Rd TQ2 . . . . . .219 E5
Ruckham La EX16. . . . . .62 F6
Rudds Bldgs **4** EX16. . . . .161 B4
Rudolf Steiner Sch TQ9 . .215 C3
Rudyard Way EX39 . . . . . .156 B6
Rudyerd Wlk PL3 . . . . .249 D6
Rue de Courseulles sur Mer
EX8. . . . . .202 C6
Rue St Pierre PL21. . . . . . .237 E5
Rufford Cl PL2. . . . . .248 A7
Rugby Rd EX4 . . . . .177 A4
Ruggadon La TQ12 . . . . . .123 D8
Ruggaton La EX34 . . . . .2 D2
Rule Cross EX23 . . . . .37 B2
Rull Cross EX16. . . . . .48 C5
Rull Hill
Oakford EX16. . . . . .48 C5
West Worlington EX17. . . . .61 B8
Rull La EX15. . . . . .163 B6
Rumbelow Rd EX16. . . . . .161 C6
Rumsam Cl EX32. . . . . . . .155 B2
Rumsam Gdns EX32. . . . . .155 B2
Rumsam Rd EX32. . . . . . . .155 B2
Rundle Rd TQ12 . . . . .207 C4
Runnacleave Rd EX34 . . . .150 B6
Runnymede EX6 . . . . .113 B4
Rupert Price Way TQ12 . . .123 B2
Rupertswood PL4. . . . . . . .244 C6
Rupertswood Terr **10**
EX34. . . . . .150 C6
Rus Cotts EX17 . . . . .165 A5
Rushcott Cl EX31 . . . . .153 A4
Rushcott Cross EX31. . . . . .27 B7
Rushforth Pl EX4 . . . . .176 E8
Rushlade Cl TQ4 . . . . .225 F2
Rush Park Terr PL18. . . . . .125 C7
Rush Way TQ9 . . . . .223 F5
Ruskin Cres PL5 . . . . .244 D2
Rusper Cl EX15 . . . . .83 F6
Russel Ct EX32. . . . . .17 C1
Russel La EX15 . . . . .65 A1
Russell Ave PL3. . . . . .248 F7
Russell Cl
East Budleigh EX9 . . . . . . .198 B6
Gunnislake PL18 . . . . .125 D7
Plymouth PL9. . . . . .256 B7
Saltash PL12 . . . . .242 C3
Russell Court Gdns PL19 .171 B6
Russell Ct
Plymouth PL1. . . . . .262 C2
Salcombe TQ8 . . . . .259 C5
Saltash PL12 . . . . .242 C3
Tavistock PL19 . . . . .171 B6
Russell Dr EX9 . . . . .198 B6
Russell Pl PL1 . . . . .262 B4
Russell St
Exeter EX1 . . . . .261 C3
Sidmouth EX10 . . . . .188 B3
Tavistock PL19 . . . . .171 C5
Russell Terr EX4 . . . . .261 A4
Russel Way EX3. . . . . .179 D2
Russet Ave EX1 . . . . .178 C6
Russet Cl EX15 . . . . .66 A7
Russets La TQ11 . . . . .236 A5
Russet Wood PL5 . . . . . . .243 F4
Ruston Hill EX17. . . . . .61 A6
Rutger Pl PL1 . . . . .262 A4
Rutherford St EX2 . . . . . . .178 A4
Rutland Rd PL4. . . . . .248 F4
Rutt's Cross EX14 . . . . .84 E2
Ruxhill La EX31 . . . . .10 D5
Ryall's Cnr
Beaford EX19. . . . . .42 A1
Merton EX20. . . . . .57 A8
Ryalls Ct EX12. . . . . .192 A5
Rydal Cl PL6 . . . . .245 D2
Rydal Mews EX4 . . . . .176 F5
Ryde Cl TQ2 . . . . .214 A2
Ryde Rd EX7. . . . . .204 E7
Ryder Cl **16** EX16 . . . . .64 D7
Ryder Rd PL2 . . . . .247 F4
Rydon Acres
Kingsteignton TQ12 . . . . . .207 E8
Stoke Gabriel TQ9 . . . . . . .227 F8
Rydon Ave TQ12 . . . . .207 E8
Rydonball Cross TQ12 . . . .211 F7
Rydon Cross
Denbury TQ12 . . . . .211 D6
Stoke Gabriel TQ9 . . . . . . .227 F8
Rydon Est TQ12 . . . . .207 E8
Rydon Ind Est TQ12 . . . . .207 D6

Rydon La
Abbotskerswell TQ12.....212 C6
Exeter EX2.............178 C3
Exton EX3, EX5........183 E2
Holsworthy EX22........71 E7
Payhembury EX14........84 B4
Rydon Pk Cvn Pk EX2..178 D3
Rydon Prim Sch TQ12..207 E8
Rydon Rd
Holsworthy EX22.......164 B5
Kingsteignton TQ12....207 E8
Rydons TQ5...........230 A4
Rye Hill PL12.........242 C2
Rye La TQ7...........144 B5
Ryeland Cl PL9.......140 D8
Ryelands Farm Ind Est
TA21.................160 B3
Rye Park Cl EX19......42 D1
Rye Pk
Beaford EX19..........42 D1
Monkton EX14..........86 C5
Ryll Cl EX8..........202 B7
Ryll Court Dr EX8....202 B7
Ryll Gr EX8..........202 B7

S

Sabre Cl TQ12........180 E3
Sabre Wlk 1 EX32....155 B5
Sackery TQ12.........208 D4
Sacred Heart RC Sch
TQ13.................226 B7
Saddlers Cl EX6.......96 F3
Saddlers Way EX20....170 D6
Saddle The TQ4.......226 C2
Sadler Cl EX8........202 E8
Saffron Cl TQ7.......258 D5
Saffron Pk TQ7.......258 D5
Sage Gr EX6..........161 F4
Sage Park Rd EX33....152 B7
Sages Lea EX5........184 C6
Sailmakers Ct EX8....201 E6
St Agnes La TQ2......219 E3
St Albans Cl EX4.....176 E6
St Albans La TQ1.....220 C7
St Albans Pk PL20....122 C2
St Albans Rd TQ1.....220 C7
St Andrew's CE Prim Sch
Buckland Monachorum
PL20.................126 C3
Plymouth PL1..........262 B2
St Andrew's CE Sch EX13 .88 A7
St Andrews
Ashburton TQ13........130 F4
12 Bere Alston PL20...125 E1
Cullompton EX15.......163 C3
Saltash PL12..........242 C2
Sutcombe EX22.........54 A6
St Andrew's Cl
Calstock PL18.........125 D3
Feniton EX14..........84 D2
Kennford EX6..........114 E4
Yarnscombe EX31.......27 E2
St Andrew's Cross 1
PL1..................263 A2
St Andrews Ct
3 Tiverton EX16.......161 E6
Torquay TQ2...........219 C8
St Andrews Dr EX13...167 F7
St Andrew's Est EX15..163 B4
St Andrews Ho EX8....201 F6
St Andrews Mdw DT7...260 D4
St Andrews Orch EX24..103 A5
St Andrew's Pl PL10...253 A1
St Andrews Prim Sch
EX15.................163 B3
St Andrews Rd
Cullompton EX15.......163 C3
Fremington EX31.......153 D6
Paignton TQ4.........226 C5
Tavistock PL19........171 D2
St Andrew's Rd
Cowley EX4............172 F2
Exmouth EX8...........201 F6
St Andrew's Sq EX24...103 A5
St Andrews St PL10....252 E6
St Andrew's St PL10...253 A1
St Andrew St
Plymouth PL1..........262 C2
Tiverton EX16.........161 C3
St Annes EX6..........194 D3
St Anne's Chapel Mus
EX31.................154 E7
St Annes Cl EX22......70 E1
St Annes Ct TQ12......207 B3
St Annes Pl EX5.......82 B5
St Anne's Rd
Exeter EX1............177 E7
Plymouth PL6..........245 D6
Saltash PL12..........242 E3
Torquay TQ1...........220 D7
St Annes Well Brewery
EX4..................261 A3
St Annes Well Mews
EX4..................261 A3
St Anthony's Cl EX11..169 E4
St Aubyn Ave PL2......247 F5
St Aubyn Rd PL1.......247 E3
St Aubyn's Cl EX5.....82 B5
St Aubyn's Villas EX16.161 F3
St Aubyn Terr PL7.....132 F4
St Augustines Cl TQ12.214 A3
St Austin Cl PL21.....237 B5
St Barnabas Ct PL1....262 A4

St Barnabas Hospl PL12..242 F2
St Barnabas Terr PL1.....262 A4
St Bartholomew Way
TQ12.................206 D1
St Bernard's Cl
Buckfast TQ11.........236 B7
Exeter EX2............261 C1
St Bernards Sch TQ12..207 C2
St Boniface Cl PL2....248 C7
St Boniface Dr PL2....248 C7
St Boniface Prim Sch
PL1..................262 B3
St Boniface Rd EX17...165 A5
St Boniface's RC Coll
PL5..................244 E1
St Brannock's Hill EX33.152 D7
St Brannock's Park Rd
EX4..................150 B4
St Brannock's Rd EX4..150 B4
St Brannock's Well Cl
EX33.................152 D7
St Briac Way EX8......196 E3
St Bridget Ave PL6....244 F1
St Budeaux Cl EX11....169 E3
St Budeaux Ferry Rd Sta
PL5..................247 D8
St Budeaux Foundation CE
Jun Sch PL5..........243 F2
St Budeaux Orch EX11..169 E3
St Budeaux Victoria Rd Sta
PL5..................243 D1
St Catherines Pk PL8..141 A7
St Catherine's Rd EX4.220 B8
St Christophers Sch TQ9 216 C5
St Clares Cl EX12.....192 B5
St Clements Ct TQ6....233 D4
St Clement's Terr TQ9.222 D2
St Columba Cl TQ12....207 E8
St Cuthbert Mayne Sch
TQ1..................214 A1
St Cyres Rd EX4.......166 B6
St Davids 12 EX39.....157 A1
St David's CE Prim Sch
EX4..................261 A3
St Davids Cl EX13.....167 F7
St David's Dr EX13....167 F7
St David's Hill EX4...177 A7
St David's Pl EX4.....177 A7
St Davids Rd TQ14.....210 C8
St David's Rd PL19....171 E5
St David's Terr EX4...261 A3
St Dominick CE Sch
PL12.................125 A2
St Dominic Pk PL17....125 A4
St Dominic's Cl TQ1...220 B8
St Dunstan's Abbey Plymouth
Coll Jun Sch PL1.....262 A3
St Dunstan's Rd TQ8..259 C4
St Dunstan's Terr PL4.263 C3
St Edmunds Rd TQ7....258 C6
St Edmund's Rd TQ12..192 B7
St Edmunds wlk TQ7..258 C6
St Edward Gdns PL6....245 B1
St Edward's CE Prim Sch
PL6..................245 C1
St Efride's Rd TQ2....259 B4
Ste Honorine Du Fay Cl
EX32.................28 E8
St Elizabeth Cl PL7...250 F3
St Elmo 8 EX12........192 A4
St Elmo Ct TQ8........259 C3
St Erth Rd PL2........248 D7
St Eval Pl PL5........243 E4
St Francis Ct PL5.....244 B3
St Gabriel's Ave PL3..248 D5
St Georges Ave EX13...167 F7
St George's Ave PL2...248 C7
St George's CE Inf Sch
EX39.................156 F8
St George's CE Prim Sch
PL1..................262 A1
St Georges Cl 15 PL21 137 B2
St Georges Cres TQ1..220 C7
St Georges Ct 1 PL2..247 F4
St Georges Hill DT7...260 C4
St Georges Rd PL12...242 D3
St George's Rd
Barnstaple EX32.......155 A6
Saltash PL12..........242 E3
Torquay TQ2...........220 C7
St George's Terr
1 Barnstaple EX32....155 A6
Plymouth PL2..........247 F4
Shillingford St George 114 C6
St George's View EX15..163 B4
St George's Way EX16..161 C3
St George's Well Ave
EX15.................163 B4
St German's Rd EX4....177 C8
St Giles on the Heath Prim
Sch PL15.............90 C1
St Gregorys Ct EX12...192 A6
St Helens EX39........156 A2
St Helen's CE Prim Sch
EX39.................156 A1
St Helen's Cl EX33....133 B7
St Helen's Ct EX10....187 F3
St Helen's Wlk PL5....244 C5
St Hilary Terr PL4....263 C3
St Hill Cl EX2........177 A2
St Ida's Cl EX2.......176 D1
St Ives Ct 5 TQ1......220 A6
St James Cl
Exeter EX4............261 C4
Landkey EX32..........17 C1
Parkham EX39..........39 E8
St James Ct
Exeter EX4............177 E8

St James Ct continued
Plymouth PL1..........262 B2
Torpoint PL11.........247 B3
St James High Sch EX4.174 B1
St James' Ho 16 TQ14..210 B5
St James Mews
Plymouth PL1..........262 B2
18 Teignmouth TQ14....210 B5
St James' Park (Exeter City
AFC) EX4.............261 C4
St James' Park Sta EX4.261 C4
St James Pl TQ1.......220 D7
St James' Pl E PL1....262 B2
St James' Pl W PL1....262 B2
St Jame's Prec 19 TQ14.210 B5
St James Rd
Torpoint PL11.........247 B2
Torquay TQ1...........220 A7
St James' Rd EX4......261 C4
St James St EX4.......150 C6
St James St EX20......170 B5
St James Terr EX4.....261 C4
St James Way 4 EX16..161 E6
St Joeseph's RC Prim Sch
TQ12.................207 A4
St Johns PL19.........171 C5
St Johns Ave PL19.....171 C5
St John's Bridge Rd PL4 263 B2
St John's CE Prim Sch
Totnes TQ9...........223 C5
Wellington TA21.......160 E6
St Johns Cl
16 Colyton EX24......103 A4
Plymouth PL6..........245 D4
Teignmouth TQ14......160 E6
St John's Cl
Bishopsteignton TQ14..208 F7
Bovey Tracey TQ13.....180 C6
Honiton EX14..........166 C6
Ivybridge PL21........237 B5
Millbrook PL10........252 E5
Skilgate TA4..........34 E6
St John's Cotts TQ13..180 C6
St Johns Ct EX22......53 E8
St John's Ct 3 TQ3....226 B6
St John's Dr
Bradworthy EX22.......53 E8
Plymouth PL6..........255 B6
St Johns La PL11......252 B8
St John's La
Bovey Tracey TQ13.....180 C7
Newton Abbot TQ12....207 B4
St Johns RC Prim Sch
St Johns Rd PL4.......263 C2
St John's Rd
Exeter EX1............177 E7
Exeter EX1............196 E2
Exmouth EX8...........196 F4
Horrabridge PL20......126 F4
Ivybridge PL21........237 B5
Millbrook PL10........252 F5
Plymouth PL4..........263 B2
Plymouth, Turnchapel PL9.255 A6
St John's Sch EX10....187 F3
St John's St TQ12.....207 C4
St John's St PL4......263 B2
St John's Terr TQ9....223 B6
St John's Villas EX4..177 F5
St John the Baptist RC Prim
Sch TQ6..............233 C2
St Joseph's Cl PL6....244 F1
St Joseph's RC Prim Sch
Exmouth EX8...........202 B7
Plymouth PL1..........247 E2
St Jude's Rd PL4......263 B2
St Julian's Cotts PL10.253 E7
St Katharine's Rd TQ2.219 E6
St Katherine's Cl EX31.153 A5
St Katherine's Mews 6
TQ9..................223 C5
St Katherines Rd EX4..178 A8
St Katherine's Way TQ9.223 C5
St Keverne Pl PL2.....248 D8
St Keyes Cl EX32......17 B2
St Kitts Cl TQ2.......213 F2
St Lawrence Cl 12 EX16.64 D7
St Lawrence Cres EX1..178 D6
St Lawrence Ct EX17...165 B5
St Lawrence La TQ13...130 F4
St Lawrence Mews PL4.263 A4
St Lawrence Rd PL4....263 A4
St Lawrence's Gn EX17.165 B5
St Leonard's Ave EX2..261 B1
St Leonard's CE Prim Sch
EX2..................261 C1
St Leonard's Cl 16 TQ12.207 B3
St Leonard's Pl EX2...261 C2
St Leonards Rd EX14...166 A5
St Leonard's Rd
Exeter EX2............261 C2
Newton Abbot TQ12....207 B3
Plymouth PL4..........263 C2
St Leo Pl PL2.........247 E4
St Levan Rd PL2.......247 F5
St Loye's Coll EX2....177 F2
St Loyes Rd EX2.......178 A4
St Loyes Rd EX2.......178 A5
St Loye's Terr EX2....178 A4
St Luke's Cl TQ12.....207 F1
Saint Luke's Coll EX1..177 E6
St Luke's Pk TQ2......220 A4
St Luke's Rd
Kingskerswell TQ12...212 E8
Torquay TQ2...........220 A4

St Luke's Rd N TQ2....220 B4
St Luke's Rd S TQ2....220 A4
St Luke's Sports & Science
Coll EX1.............178 D8
St Malo Cl EX8........196 E3
St Marco Gdns TQ2.....258 D6
St Margaret Clitherow RC
Prim Sch TQ2.........230 B3
St Margaret's Ave TQ2.220 B7
St Margaret's CE Jun Sch
EX39.................156 F7
St Margarets Cl EX15..67 B8
St Margarets Cl TQ1...220 B8
St Margarets Cl EX23..182 E5
St Margarets Ct 7 EX39 156 F7
St Margarets Gdn 1
EX31.................154 F6
St Margarets La TA20..88 C8
St Margaret's Prim Sch
TQ1..................220 B8
St Margarets Rd PL7...250 B7
St Margarets Rd TQ1...220 B8
St Margarets Sch EX2..177 E5
St Margarets Terr EX3.182 F5
St Margaret's View EX8.203 A7
St Mark's Rd 1 EX7....204 E6
St Marks Ave EX1......177 E7
St Mark's CE Prim Sch
EX23.................37 B2
St Marks Dr TQ1.......220 D3
St Marks Rd PL6.......245 D5
St Mark's Rd
Honiton EX14..........166 A4
Torquay TQ1...........220 D3
St Martin's Ave PL3...248 D7
St Martins Cl EX10....188 B6
St Martin's Cl EX17...78 C4
St Martin's Ct TQ2....213 F1
St Martin's La EX17...165 B6
St Martins Rd EX23....70 A8
St Marwenne Cl EX23..70 A6
St Marychurch CE Prim Sch
TQ1..................214 B1
St Marychurch Rd
Newton Abbot TQ12....207 F1
St Marychurch TQ1.....214 C1
Torquay, Plainmoor TQ1.220 B6
St Maryhaye PL19......171 A5
St Mary's CE Prim Sch
Bideford EX39.........157 A4
Brixton PL8...........257 A4
St Marys Cl
Axminster EX13........167 F5
Brixham TQ5...........230 B2
Great Torrington EX38.159 B4
St Mary's Cotts EX7...200 F4
St Marys Ct
Plymouth PL7..........250 C5
Teignmouth TQ14......210 C5
St Mary's Ct
4 Newton Abbot TQ12..207 B3
Paignton TQ2.........226 A6
Torquay TQ1...........220 A7
St Mary's Flats 7 EX39.157 A1
St Mary's La DT7......104 B6
St Marys Pk EX1.......169 F3
St Mary's Pk TQ4......225 C4
St Mary's RC Prim Sch
Axminster EX13........167 F5
Buckfast TQ11.........236 C7
St Mary's Rd
Barnstaple EX32.......155 A6
Brixham TQ5...........230 D2
Croyde EX33...........7 E2
Newton Abbot TQ12....250 C6
Plymouth PL7..........250 C6
Teignmouth TQ14......210 A7
St Mary St PL1........262 A2
St Mary Steps Terr 8
EX1..................261 A2
St Marys View
Silverton EX5.........82 B5
West Hill EX11........168 E5
St Matthews Cl EX1....177 E6
St Matthew's Rd TQ12..219 D4
St Matthews Wlk EX1...261 C3
St Matthias Church Rd
TQ1..................220 E5
St Maurice Mews PL7...250 E4
St Maurice Rd PL7.....250 F3
St Maurice View PL7...251 B4
St Mawes Dr TQ4......229 D8
St Mawes Terr 8 PL2..247 F5
St Michael Ave PL7....247 F5
St Michaels DT7.......260 E4
St Michael's Cl TQ2...219 E6
St Michael's Bsns Ctr
DT7..................260 E3
St Michael's CE Prim Sch
Exeter EX1............177 F6
Kingsteignton TQ12...207 D7
Lyme Regis DT7........260 E4
St Michaels Cl
Lawhitton PL15........105 B1
Otterton EX9..........198 C7
St Michael's Cl
Clyst Honiton EX5.....179 D8
Exeter EX1............177 B1
Plymouth PL1..........247 E3
Torquay TQ1...........219 E6
St Michael's Ct
Paignton TQ4.........226 A4
7 Plymouth PL1........247 F3

St Michael's Hill EX5..179 D8
St Michaels Ho 4 DT7..260 D3
St Michaels Rd
Kingsteignton TQ12...207 D6
Teignmouth TQ14......210 C7
St Michael's Rd
Newton Abbot TQ12....207 D1
Paignton TQ4.........226 B5
Torquay TQ1...........219 E7
St Michaels Sch EX31..27 D8
St Michaels Terr 5
TQ10.................134 F2
St Michael's Terr
8 Plymouth, Devonport
PL1..................247 F3
Plymouth PL4..........262 C4
6 Torquay TQ1.........220 B8
St Michaels View EX21..55 E4
St Modwen Rd PL6......249 F7
St Nazaire App PL1....247 F2
St Nazaire Cl PL1.....247 E2
St Nicholas CE Jun Sch
EX10.................188 A7
St Nicholas RC Prim Sch
EX2..................261 C1
St Olave's Cl EX4.....261 A3
St Olaves Mews EX4....261 A3
St Oswins TQ1.........220 B8
St Pancras Ave PL2....248 D8
St Patrick's Cl TQ14..210 A6
St Pauls Cl
Bovey Tracey TQ13.....180 D7
Plymouth PL3..........249 C5
St Paul's Cres TQ1....220 B7
St Paul's Ct 18 TQ12..207 C3
St Pauls Dr EX22......164 B5
St Pauls RC Prim Sch
PL5..................243 D1
St Paul's Rd
Honiton EX14..........166 A5
15 Newton Abbot TQ12.207 C3
Paignton TQ3.........219 D1
Torquay TQ1...........220 B7
St Paul's Sq EX16.....161 C3
St Paul St
Plymouth PL1..........254 A8
Tiverton EX16.........161 C4
St Peter Cl PL7.......250 F4
St Peter's Cath EX1...261 B3
St Peter's CE Jun Sch
PL19.................171 D5
St Peters CE Prim Sch
PL1..................262 B3
St Peter's CE Sch EX2.178 C5
St Peter's Church Sch
EX9..................197 F2
St Peters Cl
Shirwell EX31.........17 B8
Torquay TQ2...........219 D6
West Buckland EX32....18 B2
St Peter's Cl TQ13....180 E8
St Peters Ct
Plymouth PL1..........262 A3
Sidmouth EX10........188 B5
St Peter's Hill 5 TQ5.230 D5
St Peters Mount EX4...176 D7
St Peter's Quay TQ9...223 D4
St Peter's RC Prim Sch
PL5..................244 B5
St Peters Rd
Fremington EX31.......153 D5
Holsworthy EX22.......164 B5
Plymouth PL5..........244 C2
St Peter's Rd EX14....166 A5
St Peter's School EX8.196 A6
St Peter St EX16......161 C4
St Peter's Terr 11 EX3.150 C5
St Peter's Terr 11 EX3.154 C5
St Peters Way
Ivybridge PL21........237 E3
Ivybridge PL21........237 E5
St Peters Well La EX22.53 E8
St Petrock's Cl EX2...177 E4
St Phillips Ct EX4....176 F4
St Ronans 2 TQ1......220 D5
St Rumon's CE Inf Sch
PL19.................171 C6
St Saviours Ho 20 EX8.202 A6
St Saviours Rd EX11...169 D3
St Saviour's Way EX17.165 B5
St Scholastica's Abbey
TQ14.................210 D7
St Sevan Way EX8......196 E3
St Sidwell's Ave EX4..261 C4
St Sidwell's CE Prim Sch
EX4..................261 C4
St Sidwell's Ct EX4...261 B4
St Simon's La PL4.....249 B3
St Stephen Rd PL7.....250 F3
St Stephens Com Prim Sch
PL12.................242 E2
St Stephen's Hill PL12.242 C1
St Stephen's Pl PL7...250 F3
St Stephen's Rd PL12..242 E2
St Stephen St PL1.....247 F1
St Swithin's EX17.....80 A5
St Teresa Ho PL4......263 A3
St Teresa's Ct EX39...156 F7
St Teresa's Ct 9 EX39.156 F7
St Therese's Ct PL1...247 F2
St Thomas Cl
Bovey Tracey TQ13.....180 E7
Plymouth PL7..........250 F3
St Thomas Ct
Exeter EX4............177 A4
2 Tiverton EX16.......161 E6
St Thomas Prim Sch
EX2..................177 A4

St Thomas Sh Ctr EX4.... 177 A4
St Thomas Sta EX4....... 177 A4
St Vincent Ho TQ1 ...... 220 C3
St Vincent Cl TQ1 ....219 F6
St Vincent's Rd TQ1 .....219 F7
St Vincent St PL2 .... 247 E4
St Werburgh Cl PL9...... 140 D7
St Wilfrid's Sch EX4 ..... 261 A3
Salamanca St PL11 ...... 247 B3
Salcombe CE Prim Sch
  TQ8 .... 259 C5
Salcombe Ct EX10 ...... 188 C4
Salcombe Hill Cl EX10 .. 188 B4
Salcombe Hill Rd EX10.. 188 C4
Salcombe Lawn EX10 ... 188 B4
Salcombe Maritime &
  Local History Mus TQ8 ....259 E5
Salcombe Rd
  Malborough TQ7, TQ8 ....147 F6
  Plymouth PL4............ 263 C4
  Sidmouth EX10 .... 188 B4
Salcombe The TQ8 ...... 259 E4
Salem Almshouses **7**
  EX32.................... 155 A4
Salem Pl
  Exeter EX4............. 261 C4
  12 Newton Abbot TQ12... 207 B3
Salem St **8** EX32....... 155 A4
Salisbury Ave
  Feniton EX14 ....84 D2
  Torquay TQ2.............213 F1
Salisbury Cl EX14 ....84 D2
Salisbury Ope PL3 .... 248 B5
Salisbury Rd
  Exeter EX4............... 177 E8
  Exmouth EX8 .... 202 A7
  Newton Abbot TQ12.... 207 D4
  Plymouth PL4........... 263 C4
Salisbury Road Jun Sch
  PL4.................... 263 C3
Salisbury Terr
  Kilmington EX13 ....87 C1
  9 Teignmouth TQ14 .... 210 C5
Sallicombe Rd EX24 ..... 101 F6
Salmonhutch Cotts EX17 165 B3
Salmon Leap Cl TQ11 ... 236 C5
Salmonpool La EX2 ...... 177 E3
Salston Barton EX11 ..... 169 C2
Salston Ride EX11 .... 169 B2
Saltash Bsns Pk PL12 ... 242 C4
Saltash Com Sch PL12 .. 242 E1
Saltash Ind Est PL12 .... 242 D4
Saltash Parkway Ind Est
  PL12...................242 B4
Saltash Rd
  Plymouth, Keyham PL2 .. 247 E6
  Plymouth PL3........... 262 C4
Saltash Sta PL12 .... 243 A2
Saltburn Rd PL5.......... 243 C1
Salterne Mdws EX9 ..... 198 A2
Saltern Rd TQ4 .... 226 C1
Salterns Terr EX39 ...... 157 B2
Salter's Bldgs **4** EX16 .. 161 D4
Salter's Cross EX10 ..... 187 D6
Salters Ct EX2 .... 178 A4
Salter's La EX24 .... 103 A4
Salters Mdw EX10 ...... 188 B5
Salter's Rd EX2.......... 178 A4
Salterton Ct EX4.........202 F8
Salterton Rd
  Budleigh Salterton EX8,
  EX9....................197 B1
  Exmouth EX8 .... 202 C7
Salterton Workshops **1**
  EX9.................... 198 A1
Salting Hill EX9.......... 199 I2
Saltings The
  Seaton EX12 .... 192 B7
  Shaldon TQ14.......... 209 D5
Saltmer Cl EX34 .... 150 A2
Salt Mill PL12 .... 242 F4
Saltram House PL7 ..... 250 A4
Saltram Terr
  Lee Moor PL7 .... 132 F4
  Plymouth PL7........... 250 E5
Saltrens EX39........... 40 F8
Saltways La EX10 .... 100 F1
Salt Wood La EX34...... 2 F3
Salty La TQ14........... 209 D5
Salutary Mount EX1..... 177 F5
Salway Cl EX15......... 163 B2
Salway Gdns EX13 ..... 167 F5
Samara Bsns Pk TQ12 .. 180 F3
Sampford Arundel Com Prim
  Sch TA21............... 51 E1
Sampford Courtenay Sta
  EX20....................77 A2
Sampford Cross EX20 ...76 F3
Sampford Gdns PL20.... 127 A5
Sampford Peverell CE Prim
  Sch EX16...............50 C1
Sampford Terr **7** PL20 ..126 F5
Sampson Cl PL18 .... 125 A6
Sampson Cross EX37....44 E8
Sampson's Hill EX2 ..... 114 C6
Sampsons La EX1........ 177 E7
Sanctuary Cl EX32 ....16 E1
Sanctuary La
  Hatherleigh EX20........75 C7
  Woodbury Salterton EX5..185 B7
Sanctuary Rd EX22...... 164 C4
Sandaway La EX34 ..... 2 F4
Sandclose La EX36....... 31 D7
Sand Down La EX5...... 172 A8
Sanders Cl EX5 .... 175 D6
Sanders Cross EX22.....54 C8
Sandersfield EX13 ......83 F6
Sanders La **8** EX32......16 E1

Sanders' La EX22 .... 164 C5
Sanderspool Cross TQ10 135 A2
Sanders Rd
  Bow EX17 ....78 C4
  Brixham TQ5 .... 230 A5
  Exeter EX4............. 174 E1
Sandford Ash La EX17....79 A7
Sandford Cl EX32 .... 155 D1
Sandford Cross EX20.....77 E4
Sandford La EX17 ....77 C8
Sandford Orleigh TQ12...207 B5
Sandford Rd PL9......... 255 F8
Sandfords EX6........... 181 B1
Sandford Sch EX17 ......80 A5
Sandfords Gdns EX39 .. 159 B4
Sandford View TQ12.... 207 B4
Sandford Wlk EX1 ...... 261 C3
Sandgate La EX11 ...... 100 D4
Sandheap Cross TQ7 ... 143 C2
Sand Hill PL18.......... 125 D6
Sandhill Cross TQ13.....111 E5
Sand Hill Pk PL18....... 125 C6
Sandhills TQ8............ 259 C3
Sandhills Rd TQ8 .... 259 C3
Sandhill St EX11 .... 169 E4
Sandhole Cross EX39 ...37 A8
Sandick Cross EX32......17 F2
Sand La
  Calstock PL18 .... 125 D3
  Totnes TQ9............. 224 A8
Sandon Wlk PL6 .... 245 A1
Sandown Rd TQ4 .... 225 F2
Sandpark La EX31 ...... 10 D5
Sandpark Rd EX18 ...... 59 D2
Sandpath Rd TQ12 ..... 207 E6
Sandpiper Ct
  Exeter EX4............. 174 D1
  Woolacombe EX34....... 8 A6
Sandpiper Dr EX4....... 183 C2
Sandpiper Gn EX2 ..... 176 D3
Sandpiper Way TQ2 .... 213 C2
Sandpit Hill EX24 .... 101 E6
Sand Pit Hill La EX24 ... 102 F4
Sandquay Rd TQ6....... 233 F5
Sandringham Dr TQ3.... 219 B2
Sandringham Gdns TQ3 . 219 C1
Sandringham Rd TQ12 .. 207 E3
Sands Ct
  Paignton TQ4 .... 226 B5
  Seaton EX12 .... 191 F7
Sands Gate Cross TQ13...95 F1
Sands Rd
  Paignton TQ4 .... 226 C5
  Slapton TQ7 .... 145 D3
Sanduck Cross TQ13 ... 112 A2
Sandy Cross EX9........ 198 A8
Sandygate Bsns Pk TQ12 123 E1
Sandygate Mill TQ12 ... 123 E1
Sandy La
  Brampford Speke EX5 .... 81 E1
  Braunton EX33.......... 15 A6
  Broadclyst EX5 .... 175 D5
  Chittlehampton EX37.....29 A5
  Croyde EX33 .... 7 E2
  Ivybridge PL21 .... 237 D5
  Kingsbridge TQ7, TQ9 .. 144 B5
  Staverton TQ9 .... 216 A6
  Woolacombe EX34........ 1 A1
Sandylane Cross EX38 ...41 A2
Sandy Lane Ct EX34...... 7 F6
Sandy Lane End TQ9 ... 144 B6
Sandymere Rd EX39 ... 156 F7
Sandymoor Cross EX21 ..72 E1
Sandypark La EX32 ..... 163 E3
Sandy Rd PL7............ 251 C4
Sandy's La EX14 ....68 C2
Sandy Way EX33.........7 E1
Sandyway Cross EX36....20 D4
Sandyways Cross TQ13.. 111 C7
Sanford Rd TQ2......... 219 E5
Sango Ct PL10.......... 252 F6
Sango Rd PL11 .... 247 A2
Sannerville Way EX6.... 182 B5
San Remo Terr EX7 ..... 204 F7
Sanson Cl EX5.......... 173 F8
Sarah Cl PL20 .... 125 E1
Sargent Cl EX1 .... 178 C6
Sargents Mdw EX23.....37 A1
Sarlsdown Rd EX8 ...... 202 D7
Sarum Cl PL3........... 248 F7
Satterleigh Cross EX37...29 C1
Saturday's La TQ12 ..... 212 F1
Saundercroft Rd EX5.....99 F2
Saunders Way
  Cullompton EX15........ 163 E4
  West Charleton TQ7.... 144 C1
Saunders Wlk PL6 ...... 244 D6
Saunton Beach Villas
  EX33................... 14 E8
Saunton Cl EX33 .... 152 C6
Saunton Rd EX33 ...... 152 B6
Savage Rd PL5 .... 247 D7
Savery Cl PL21.......... 237 E6
Savery Terr PL4........ 249 A4
Savile Rd EX4 .... 176 F5
Savoy Hill EX4 .... 174 A2
Sawmill La EX9 .... 197 F7
Sawmills Way **3** EX14 .. 166 C5
Sawpit La TQ9.......... 222 F7
Sawrey St PL1 .... 262 A2
Sawyer Dr TQ14 .... 124 E1
Sawyers Mill EX16 ......34 E2
Saxon Ave EX4 .... 174 F2
Saxon Hts **2** TQ5 ..... 230 C4
Saxon Mdw TQ3 .... 225 C5
Saxon Rd EX4.......... 177 F6
Saxons Croft EX32 ..... 155 C3
Saxon Way EX15 .... 163 C6

Scabbacombe La TQ6 ... 235 A6
Scadsbury La EX20......75 A4
Scalders La PL21 .... 137 C2
Scalwell La EX12 .... 192 A7
Scalwell Mead EX12 .... 192 A7
Scalwell Pk EX12 .... 192 A7
Scarborough Pl TQ2 .... 219 F5
Scarborough Rd TQ2 ... 219 F5
Scarhill Cross EX20 ......95 D4
Scarsdale EX8........... 202 C5
Scattor View EX6 .... 112 F5
Scholars Wlk TQ7....... 258 D6
School Cl
  Bampton EX16 ....34 B1
  Fremington EX31....... 153 E5
  Plymouth PL7........... 250 D7
  Shobrooke EX17 ....80 E4
  Tavistock PL19......... 171 D5
School Cnr EX39..........22 E3
School Cotts TQ12 ..... 207 A8
School Cl TQ6 .... 233 D3
School Dr PL6........... 245 D7
School Hill
  Cockwood EX6.......... 201 B6
  7 Dawlish EX7....... 204 D6
  Lympstone EX8 .... 195 E5
  Stoke Gabriel TQ9 ..... 227 F7
School La
  7 Bishop's Tawton EX32 ..16 E1
  Blackawton TQ9........ 139 E1
  Broadclyst EX5 .... 175 C7
  Chilsworthy EX22 ....53 E1
  5 Colyton EX24 ..... 103 A4
  Exeter EX2.............. 178 A1
  Exmouth EX8 .... 196 C1
  Great Torrington EX38.. 159 C6
  Hartland EX39 ....22 E3
  Honiton EX14........... 166 C6
  Newton Poppleford EX10 .186 F8
  Plymouth PL7........... 250 D7
  Rousdon DT7........... 193 F7
  Tatworth TA20 ....88 C8
  Tedburn St Mary EX6.....97 F4
  3 Teignmouth TQ14 .. 210 A3
  Thorverton EX5 ....81 E4
  West Hill EX11.......... 168 E5
School Rd
  Ermington PL21........ 136 F4
  Exeter EX2.............. 177 A4
  Kingskerswell TQ12 .... 212 F4
  Lydford EX20 .... 107 F4
  Newton Abbot TQ12.... 207 C3
  Silverton EX5 ....82 B5
  Stoke Fleming TQ6..... 146 A7
  Tavistock PL19......... 171 D2
  Teigngrace TQ12 .... 206 F8
School St **9** EX10 ..... 188 B4
School Way EX20 .... 170 B5
Schooners Ct EX8 ...... 201 E6
Schumacher Coll TQ9....215 F2
Scobhill Rd EX35 .... 5 E3
Scoldens Cl **14** PL21 ... 137 B2
Sconner Rd PL11 .... 247 A3
Scoresby Cl TQ2........ 214 B3
Score View EX34........ 150 C3
Scorecheck EX5 ....99 D3
Scott Ave
  18 Appledore EX39 ....15 A1
  Exeter EX2.............. 177 F3
  Plymouth PL5........... 247 C8
Scott Bsns Pk PL2 ...... 248 A6
Scott Dr EX8 .... 196 B2
Scott Hospl PL2 .... 248 A6
Scottleigh TQ2.......... 219 F3
Scott Rd
  Plymouth PL2........... 248 A6
  Plymouth PL2........... 248 B6
Scott's Cl TQ7 .... 143 E4
Scott's Hill TA4 ....35 E8
Scott's La
  Raymond's Hill EX13 ... 104 C7
  Wellington TA21........ 160 E6
Scouse Cross EX13.......88 E2
Scous La EX13...........82 E3
Scrapton La TA20 ....69 F5
Scratchface La
  Bideford EX39 ....25 D4
  Bideford, Littleham EX39.. 25 F2
  Buckland Brewer EX39 ... 40 B6
  Stockleigh Pomeroy EX17 ..81 B6
Scratch Face La EX5 ....99 C4
Scratton Path TQ12 .... 211 F8
Screechers Hill TQ13 ... 130 F5
Scurfield Cl EX33 ...... 152 D7
Sea Birds Pk EX33 ...... 7 E1
Seabourne Ct TQ4 ..... 226 C4
Seabrook Ave EX2 ...... 182 C7
Seabrook Mews EX2 ... 182 C7
Seacliff TQ2............. 220 B4
Seacroft Rd PL5 .... 243 C2
Seafield Ave EX8 .... 196 A2
Seafield La EX10........ 188 A3
Seafield Rd
  Seaton EX12 .... 192 A5
  Sidmouth EX10 .... 188 A4
Seafields TQ4........... 226 C2
Seaforth Lodge EX12.... 191 F6
Sea Haven EX12 .... 192 B4
Sea Hill
  Beer EX12.............. 191 E5
  Seaton EX12 .... 192 A4
Sea Lawn Terr EX7...... 204 F7
Seale Cl EX6 .... 233 D4
Seale-Hayne (Univ of
  Plymouth) TQ12.......206 B7
Seapoint **16** TQ14 ..... 210 B4
Sea Point TQ4 .... 226 D5
Searle St EX17.......... 165 C5

Searle Terr EX39 .... 157 A7
Seashore Ctr TQ4....... 226 C4
Seaside Hill EX34........ 2 F4
Seasons The EX4 .... 178 C8
Seaton EX12............ 192 B5
Seaton and District Electric
  Tramway EX12......... 192 C7
Seaton Ave PL4......... 248 E4
Seaton Bsns Pk PL6 .... 245 B3
Seaton Burn EX10 ...... 187 F4
Seaton Cl TQ1 .... 220 D7
Seaton & District Hospl
  EX12.................... 192 A6
Seaton Down Cl EX12... 191 F8
Seaton Down Hill EX12.. 191 F8
Seaton Down Rd EX12 .. 192 A5
Seaton La PL4.......... 248 E4
Seaton Orch PL7........ 136 A8
Seaton Pl PL2 .... 247 F5
Seaton Prim Sch EX12 .. 192 A6
Seaton Rd
  Colyford EX24 .... 103 A3
  Farway EX10, EX24 ..... 101 E5
  Musbury EX13 .... 103 D5
  Seaton EX24 .... 192 B8
Seaton Way TQ2 .... 126 D2
Sea Trout Mews TQ9 ... 216 A5
Seaview TQ7............ 149 A3
Sea View
  Gunnislake PL18 .... 125 B5
  Ilfracombe EX34 .... 150 D4
Sea View Ave PL4...... 263 C4
Seaview Cres TQ3 ...... 219 C1
Sea View Dr **7** PL9 .... 140 D8
Sea View Gdns TQ7 .... 147 B7
Seaview Rd DT7 .... 104 B4
Sea View Rd
  Northam EX39 .... 156 F7
  Thurlestone TQ7 ...... 143 A2
Sea View Terr
  Beer EX12.............. 191 D5
  Brixham TQ5 .... 230 C6
  Plymouth PL4........... 263 B4
  Thurlestone TQ7 ...... 143 A2
  Thurlestone TQ10 ..... 188 A5
  Wellington TA21........ 143 A2
Seaward Cl EX12 .... 190 E4
Seaway Cl TQ2.......... 219 D3
Seaway Cres TQ3 ...... 226 D8
Seaway Ct TQ5 .... 230 B4
Seaway Gdns TQ3 ..... 226 D8
Seaway La
  Tipton St John EX10 ... 100 D2
  Torquay TQ2........... 219 E3
Seaway Rd TQ3 .... 226 D8
Seckerleigh Cross EX16..64 E5
Seckington Cross EX19...58 E4
Second Ave
  Axminster EX13......... 167 F7
  Dawlish EX7............ 204 C5
  Exeter, Countess Wear
    EX2................... 182 D7
  Exeter, Heavitree EX1... 177 F6
  Plymouth, Billacombe PL9. 250 A1
  Plymouth, Devonport PL1. 248 A2
  Plymouth, Weston Mill PL2. 247 E7
  Teignmouth TQ14 ..... 210 A5
  Torquay TQ1........... 220 A8
Second Dr
  Dawlish EX7............ 204 C5
  Teignmouth TQ14 ..... 210 D6
Second Field La EX33 ... 152 C6
Sector Hill EX13 .... 167 B4
Sector La EX13 .... 167 F5
Sedemuda Cl EX10 ..... 188 A8
Sedemuda Rd EX10 .... 187 F8
Sedge Cl PL21.......... 237 D4
Sedgeclaire Cl EX1 ..... 174 F1
Sedgewell Cross EX21 ...55 F4
Sedley Way PL5......... 244 D3
Sefton Ave PL4......... 249 B3
Sefton Cl PL4.......... 263 C4
Sefton Cl
  22 Dawlish EX7....... 204 E6
  Torquay TQ1........... 220 D7
Segrave Rd PL2........ 248 B6
Selcombe Cross TQ9 ... 144 E4
Seldons Cl PL21........ 137 D6
Selkirk Ho **5** PL9...... 255 F7
Selkirk Pl PL5 .... 247 E8
Sellbed Cross TA24 ..... 21 A8
Sellers Cl EX24 .... 103 B3
Seller's Grave EX24 .... 103 A4
Seller's Wood Hill EX12..190 E6
Sellick Ave TQ5 .... 230 D3
Selsden Cl EX9 .... 256 C6
Senate Ct EX8 .... 196 E1
Senate Way EX8 .... 196 E1
Sendall's Way PL6 ..... 244 E4
Sennen Cl PL11......... 246 F4
Sennen Pl PL2.......... 247 E5
Sentry Cnr EX39 .... 157 C1
Sentry Cross EX31......18 A8
Sentry La
  Bishop's Tawton EX32 ..16 F1
  Huntsham EX16......... 49 E6
Sentrys Orch EX6....... 182 B3
Sercombes Gdns EX6 .. 201 B8
Serge Ct EX2 .... 261 A2
Serpell Cl PL6.......... 244 E6
Serstone Cross EX17.....78 C5
Sessland La
  North Tawton EX17 .....77 E1
  Spreyton EX17 ....95 D8
Sett Cl TQ13 .... 180 D7
Seven Acre Cross EX36...31 E6

Seven Acre La
  Braunton EX33.......... 152 E5
  Bridford EX6 .... 112 F5
Seven Acres Pk EX33 ... 152 E5
Seven Ash Cross EX34 ...3 C1
Seven Brethren Ind Est
  EX31................... 154 F3
Seven Crosses EX16......63 F6
Seven Crosses Rd EX16. 161 A3
Seven Hills Ho TQ2 .... 220 A5
Seven Stars La PL5 ..... 244 C6
Seven Stones Cross TQ7 142 E8
Seven Thorns EX35.......6 D5
Seventh St **15** EX32 .. 154 F6
Seven Trees Ct PL4 .... 263 B4
Severn Pl PL3 .... 249 C5
Severn Rd TQ2......... 219 B7
Sewell Ct PL3 .... 248 E5
Sexton's Cross EX6 ..... 113 C6
Seymour Ave PL4 ...... 263 B4
Seymour Bglws EX34.... 1 A1
Seymour Ct
  Exmouth EX8 .... 196 B2
  9 Totnes TQ9 .... 223 D5
Seymour Dr
  Dartmouth TQ6 .... 233 C3
  Plymouth PL2........... 248 F5
  Torquay TQ2........... 214 B4
Seymour Mews PL4 .... 263 C4
Seymour Pk PL3 .... 249 A5
Seymour Pl
  Plymouth PL1........... 262 A4
  Totnes TQ9............. 223 D5
Seymour Rd
  Exmouth EX8 .... 196 B2
  Newton Abbot TQ12.... 207 C4
  Plymouth, Mannamead PL3 248 F5
  Plymouth, Plympton PL7. 250 C6
Seymour St
  Plymouth PL4........... 263 A3
  Wellington TA21........ 160 C6
Seymour Terr EX16...... 161 C4
Seymour Villas EX34 .... 1 A1
Shackel Cross TA3 ......67 E8
Shackhayes EX34 .... 3 A4
Shackleton Cl EX8 ..... 196 B2
Shackleton Ct PL1 ...... 262 A3
Shadrack Cross TQ9 .... 217 B3
Shadycombe Ct TQ8 ... 259 D5
Shadycombe Rd TQ8 .. 259 D5
Shady La TQ6.......... 146 B3
Shady Nook Pk TQ12 .. 207 E7
Shaftesbury Cl **2** EX7 . 204 E6
Shaftesbury Cotts PL4 . 263 A4
Shaftesbury Ct **3** PL4 . 263 A4
Shaftesbury Rd
  Exeter EX2.............. 177 A4
  7 Ilfracombe EX34 ... 150 C5
Shaftsborough La EX34 ...1 C1
Shaftsbury Pl **9** TQ9... 223 C5
Shakespeare Cl
  Exeter EX4............. 161 D6
  Torquay TQ2........... 219 D6
Shakespeare Rd
  Exeter EX2.............. 177 F3
  Plymouth PL5........... 244 C4
Shakespeare Way EX8 .. 196 C4
Shaldon Cres TQ5 ..... 224 B3
Shaldon Prim Sch TQ14 210 A3
Shaldon Rd
  Combeinteignhead TQ12 .208 F5
  Newton Abbot TQ12.... 207 F2
Shaldon Wildlife Trust
  TQ14................... 210 B2
Shalford Terr EX13...... 103 B8
Shallowford Cl PL6 ..... 249 C8
Shallowford Rd PL6 .... 249 C8
Shamble Way EX35 ..... 151 E2
Shamefaced La TQ13 ... 123 B7
Shamel's End EX16 ......64 C7
Shamples Dr EX17 ..... 78 C5
Shamrock Cl EX39 ..... 156 F7
Shamwickshire Cl EX39 . 157 C1
Shand Pk EX13 .... 167 C5
Shapcott La EX36........32 C2
Shapcott Wood Hill EX36..31 F2
Shapland Pl EX16 ...... 161 B3
Shapleys Gdns PL9 .... 256 A5
Shapley Tor Cl TQ5.... 230 A2
Shapley Way TQ12 .... 180 F3
Shapters Rd PL4........ 263 C2
Shapters Way PL4 ..... 255 B8
Shaptor Cross TQ13 ... 122 F8
Shaptor View TQ13 .... 180 B5
Sharland La EX17 ....78 F8
Sharland's La EX33 .... 152 C6
Sharlands Rd EX33......70 A6
Sharon Way PL6 .... 245 A5
Sharper La TQ14 ...... 209 C3
Sharpham Dr TQ9...... 223 D4
Sharpham Vineyard TQ9 . 222 F1
Sharpitor Cl EX39...... 218 F1
Sharpitor Row PL20.... 127 B4
Sharpland La EX33...... 7 F2
Sharp Rock EX34 ...... 7 E7
Sharps Cl TQ12 .... 123 B2
Sharps Crest TQ12 .... 123 B2
Sharps Ct EX8 .... 202 A6
Sharrose Rd PL9........ 255 B5
Shaugh Prior Prim Sch
  PL7.................... 132 C6
Shaw Way PL9 .... 255 B8
Sheafhayne Cross EX14 ..69 B4
Shearford La EX31...... 154 F8

Shearman Ct **10** EX2 . . . . . **261** A2
Shearwater Dr TQ2 . . . . **213** D3
Shearwood Cl PL7 . . . . . **250** C6
Shebbear Coll EX21 . . . .**55** E4
Shebbear Com Sch EX21 . .**55** E4
Shebbear Cross EX38 . . . .**41** A2
Shedden Hill Rd TQ2 . . . **220** A4
Sheepstor Rd PL6 . . . . . . **245** D1
Sheepwash Cross EX36 . . .**31** C6
Sheepwash Hill EX36 . . . . .**31** C6
Sheirs Orch EX9 . . . . **177** E8
Sheldon Cross EX14 . . . .**66** F2
Sheldon's La TA22 . . . .**33** A7
Shell Cl PL6 . . . . **245** E1
Shelley Ave
    Tavistock PL19 . . . . **171** D5
    Torquay TQ1 . . . . **220** B8
Shelley Cl EX2 . . . . **177** A2
Shelley Ct EX8 . . . . **201** E6
Shelley Way PL5 . . . . **243** D1
Shell La EX16 . . . .**47** F1
Shells La EX24 . . . . **103** A3
Shell's La TA20 . . . .**69** D3
Shelly Ct EX20 . . . .**95** B4
Shelly Rd
    Exmouth EX8 . . . . **201** E6
    South Zeal EX20 . . . .**95** B4
Shelly Reach EX8 . . . . . . **201** F6
Shelston Tor Dr TQ4 . . . . **225** F3
Shelton Pl EX1 . . . . **177** F6
Shepherd Cl TQ3 . . . . . . **225** E5
Shepherds La
    Colaton Raleigh EX10 . . . **186** E4
    Teignmouth TQ14 . . . . . . **124** E1
Shepherds Mdw
    Abbotsham EX39 . . . . . . **156** A2
    Beaford EX19 . . . .**42** D1
Sheplegh Ct TQ9 . . . . . . **145** B8
Sheppard Rd EX4 . . . . . . **173** D2
Sheppard's Knap EX13 . . . .**87** A2
Sheppard's Row EX2 . . . . **202** A7
Sheppaton La EX18, EX19,
    EX37 . . . .**43** B2
Sherborne Cl PL9 . . . . . . **256** C6
Sherborne La DT7 . . . . . . **260** E3
Sherborne Rd TQ12 . . . . . **207** B3
Sherbrook Cl EX9 . . . . . . **203** F8
Sherbrook Hill EX9 . . . . . **203** F8
Shercroft Cl EX5 . . . . **175** E2
Sherford Cres
    Plymouth, Elburton PL9 . . **256** C7
    Plymouth, West Park PL5 . . **244** A3
Sherford Cross TQ7 . . . . . **145** A3
Sherford Down Cross
    TQ7 . . . . **144** D3
Sherford Down Rd TQ7 . . **144** D3
Sherford Rd PL9 . . . . **256** D7
Sherford Wlk PL9 . . . . . . **256** E7
Sheridan Rd
    Exeter EX4 . . . . **178** C8
    Plymouth PL5 . . . . **244** C1
Sherman Ho EX11 . . . . . . **169** E3
Sherracombe Cross EX36 . .**19** C6
Sherratt's Oak EX31 . . . . . **155** B7
Sherrell Pk PL20 . . . . **125** E1
Sherrell Cl PL9 . . . . **255** F4
Sherwell Cl
    Dawlish Warren EX7 . . . . . **201** A4
    Staverton TQ9 . . . . **216** A5
Sherwell Ct TQ11 . . . . . . **236** B5
Sherwell Hill TQ2 . . . . . . **219** E5
Sherwell La
    Plymouth PL4 . . . . **263** A4
    Torquay TQ2 . . . . **219** E5
Sherwell Park Rd TQ2 . . . **219** E5
Sherwell Rise S TQ2 . . . . **219** E5
Sherwell Valley Prim Sch
    TQ2 . . . . **219** C7
Sherwell Valley Rd TQ2 . . **219** D6
Sherwill Cl PL21 . . . . **237** A6
Sherwill La TQ9 . . . . **216** A5
Sherwood DT7 . . . . **260** C4
Sherwood Cl EX2 . . . . **177** F5
Sherwood Dr TQ4 . . . .**84** D2
Sherwood Dr EX8 . . . . **196** E3
Sherwood Gn EX38 . . . .**42** E7
Shetland Cl TQ2 . . . . **213** E2
Shewte Cross TQ13 . . . . . **122** D5
Shields The EX14 . . . . **150** C4
Shieling Rd EX31 . . . .**16** A3
Shillands EX16 . . . . **161** B5
Shillingate Cl EX7 . . . . . . **204** C4
Shillingford La EX16 . . . . . **181** A3
Shillingford Rd EX16 . . . . **181** A7
Shilstone Cross EX32 . . . . . .**28** C5
Shilstone La TQ13 . . . . . . **113** C1
Shilston Gate PL21 . . . . . . **137** D4
Shindle Pk TQ7 . . . . **144** F1
Shinners Cotts TQ6 . . . . . **228** C2
Shiphay Ave TQ2 . . . . **219** D7
Shiphay Com Prim Sch
    TQ2 . . . . **219** C7
Shiphay La TQ2 . . . . **219** D7
Shiphay Manor Dr TQ2 . . **219** D7
Shiphay Park Rd TQ2 . . . **219** D7
Ship La EX5 . . . . **179** D8
Shipley Cl TQ10 . . . . **135** A3
Shipley Rd EX14 . . . . **166** E6
Shipley Wlk PL6 . . . . **245** A1
Shipney La TQ13 . . . . **124** A7
Shirburn Rd
    Plymouth PL6 . . . . **249** B8

Shirburn Rd continued
    Torquay TQ1 . . . . **220** A7
Shire Cl
    Honiton EX14 . . . . **166** A5
    Paignton TQ4 . . . . **229** B8
Shire Ct EX22 . . . .**70** E1
Shire La DT7 . . . . **260** B3
Shirley Cl EX8 . . . . **196** D4
Shirley Cnr EX17 . . . .**79** B5
Shirley Ct S TQ1 . . . . **220** D4
Shirley Gdns PL5 . . . . **244** C1
Shirley Towers TQ1 . . . . . **220** C3
Shirwell Com Prim Sch
    EX31 . . . .**17** B8
Shirwell Cross
    Barnstaple EX31 . . . .**16** E6
    Shirwell EX31 . . . .**17** B8
Shirwell Rd EX31 . . . .**17** A7
Shoalgate Cross EX20 . . . . .**94** F8
Shobbrook Hill TQ12 . . . . **206** E4
Shobrooke Cross EX17 . . . .**80** D4
Shobrook La EX17 . . . .**78** F7
Shoemaker's La PL12 . . . . **242** E2
Shooting La EX18 . . . .**60** B7
Shooting Marsh Stile
    EX2 . . . . **261** A1
Shoots Barn Cross EX14 . . .**84** D2
Shoot's La EX14 . . . .**67** A3
Shop Cotts PL7 . . . . **132** F4
Shore Head EX14 . . . .**86** F5
Shoreland Cross EX18 . . . . .**44** F5
Shorelands Rd EX31 . . . . . **154** D3
Shorelands Way EX31 . . . . **154** D3
Shoreland Way EX39 . . . . **154** D3
Shoresgate Cross EX19 . . . .**76** F8
Shoreside TQ14 . . . . **210** A3
Shorland Cl EX7 . . . . **204** F8
Shorneywell TQ7 . . . . **145** A1
Shortacombe Cnr EX31 . . . **103** A5
Shortacombe Dr EX33 . . . . **152** B7
Shorta Cross TQ7 . . . . **143** C7
Short Cl EX39 . . . . **156** D2
Short Cotts PL11 . . . . **247** A3
Short Cross TQ9 . . . . **139** B3
Short Cross TQ9 . . . . **135** D2
Short Furlong EX12 . . . . . . **191** D5
Short La
    Combe Martin EX34 . . . .**2** F1
    Halwell TQ7 . . . . **139** B3
    Shaldon TQ14 . . . . **209** C4
Shortlands
    Pyworthy EX22 . . . .**71** D5
    Yettington EX9 . . . . **197** F8
Shortlands La EX15 . . . . . . **163** B3
Shortlands Rd EX15 . . . . . **163** B3
Shortmoor Cross EX14 . . . . .**86** E6
Shorton Rd TQ3 . . . . **226** A8
Shorton Valley Rd TQ3 . . **219** A1
Short Park Rd PL3 . . . . . . **248** D5
Shortridge Cl
    Honiton EX14 . . . . **166** C4
    Witheridge EX16 . . . .**46** E1
Shortridge Mead **1**
    EX16 . . . . **161** B4
Shorts Way TQ9 . . . . **222** E6
Shortwood Cl EX9 . . . . . . **197** F2
Shortwood Cres PL9 . . . . . **256** A7
Shovelpiece La EX32 . . . . . .**19** A7
Shrewsbury Ave TQ2 . . . . **214** A1
Shrewsbury Rd PL5 . . . . . **244** C4
Shrinkhill La EX16 . . . . . . **161** D3
Shrubbery Cl EX32 . . . . . . **155** C3
Shrubbery La EX14 . . . .**86** E6
Shrubbery The
    Axminster EX13 . . . . **167** D5
    Exbourne EX20 . . . .**76** C5
Shute Cl PL21 . . . . **147** E6
Shute Barton EX13 . . . . . . **103** B8
Shute Cross
    Newton St Cyres EX17 . . . . .**81** B2
    South Brent TQ10 . . . . . . **134** E1
Shute Ct TQ14 . . . . **209** A8
Shute Hill
    Bishopsteignton TQ14 . . . **209** A8
    Malborough TQ7 . . . . **147** E6
    Teignmouth TQ14 . . . . . . **210** C5
Shute Hill Cres **10** EX10 . . **210** C5
Shute Ho EX13 . . . . **103** B7
Shute La
    Combe Martin EX34 . . . .**3** A4
    Denbury TQ12 . . . . **211** A6
    Huish Champflower TA4 . . . .**35** C8
    Moretonhampstead TQ13 . . **111** F5
    Winkleigh EX19 . . . .**58** F2
Shuteleigh TA21 . . . . **160** E6
Shute Meadow St 2
    EX8 . . . . **202** A7
Shute Park Rd PL9 . . . . . . **255** F6
Shute Pk TQ7 . . . . **147** E6
Shute Prim Sch EX13 . . . . **103** B8
Shute Rd
    Kilmington EX13 . . . .**87** C1
    Shute EX13 . . . . **103** A4
    Totnes TQ9 . . . . **223** D5
Shute Row TA21 . . . . **160** E5
Shutes Mead EX11 . . . . . . **169** E4
Shute Wood EX18 . . . .**58** F6
Shutscombe Hill EX32 . . . . .**18** E5
Shuttern Cl EX5 . . . . **172** A8
Shutterton Ind Est EX7 . . . **200** F1
Shutterton La EX7 . . . . **201** A3
Shutter Water Rd
    Westwood EX15 . . . .**83** C1
    Whimple EX5 . . . .**99** C8
Sicklemans Cl TQ7 . . . . . . **144** C1
Sidborough Hill EX17 . . . . . .**61** B1
Sidbury CE Prim Sch
    EX10 . . . . **101** C2

Sidcliffe EX10 . . . . **188** C6
Siddalls Gdns EX10 . . . . . **161** E5
Siddals Gdns EX16 . . . . . . **161** E4
Sideling Cl EX2 . . . . **114** A6
Sideling Fields EX16 . . . . . **161** F2
Side Wood La EX36 . . . .**32** A1
Sidford Cross **7** EX10 . . . **101** B1
Sidford Rd EX10 . . . . **188** B7
Sidgard Rd EX10 . . . . **188** C6
Sidholme Cotts EX10 . . . . **188** B5
Siding Cross TQ10 . . . . . . **137** E8
Sidings The
    Braunton EX33 . . . . **152** D6
    Kingsbridge TQ7 . . . . **258** C5
Sid La EX10 . . . . **188** C5
Sidlands EX10 . . . . **188** A4
Sidleigh EX10 . . . . **188** A4
Sidmount Gdns EX10 . . . . **188** A5
Sidmouth Coll EX10 . . . . . **188** C7
Sidmouth Inf Sch EX10 . . **188** B7
Sidmouth Jun Sch EX10 . . **188** B4
Sidmouth Junc Cross
    EX14 . . . .**84** D2
Sidmouth Rd
    Bradninch EX5 . . . .**83** B5
    Clyst St Mary EX2, EX5 . . **179** A3
    Colyton EX24 . . . . **103** A4
    Exeter EX2 . . . . **178** D5
    Exeter EX2 . . . . **178** E4
    Honiton EX14 . . . . **166** A3
    Lyme Regis DT7 . . . . **260** C3
    Ottery St Mary EX11 . . . . **169** E2
Sidney Cl **3** EX7 . . . . . . **204** D6
Sid Park Rd EX10 . . . . **188** B5
Sid Rd EX10 . . . . **188** C5
Sid Vale Cl **10** EX10 . . . . **101** B1
Sidvale Cl EX10 . . . . **101** B1
Sidvale Mews **10** EX10 . . **101** B1
Sidwell Ho EX1 . . . . **261** C3
Sidwell St EX4 . . . . **261** C4
Sigford Cross TQ13 . . . . . . **122** B2
Sigford Rd EX2 . . . . **181** D8
Signal Ct EX33 . . . . **152** D5
Signals The EX14 . . . .**84** D2
Signal Terr EX31 . . . . **154** F4
Sign of the Owl Cross
    TQ10 . . . . **137** E8
Signpost La EX17 . . . .**80** A7
Silbury Terr EX17 . . . . **165** C5
Silcombe Cross EX36 . . . . . .**30** F1
Silcombe Hill EX36 . . . .**30** E4
Silford Cross EX39 . . . . . . **156** C5
Silford Rd EX39 . . . . **156** C5
Silvan Dr EX33 . . . . **152** E7
Silver Birch Cl
    Exeter EX2 . . . . **178** A3
    Plymouth PL6 . . . . **245** C7
Silver Birch Ct **5** EX1 . . **154** C2
Silver Bridge Cl TQ4 . . . . **229** C8
Silverdale
    Exmouth EX8 . . . . **196** E3
    Silverton EX5 . . . .**82** B6
Silverdale Cl TA22 . . . .**33** E4
Silver Head Hill TQ9 . . . . . **216** F1
Silverhills Rd TQ12 . . . . . . **212** D8
Silverhills Rd TQ12 . . . . . . **212** D8
Silver La
    Exeter EX4 . . . . **261** C4
    Rockbeare EX5 . . . .**99** C5
Silver Lea EX13 . . . .**87** C1
Silver Pk EX15 . . . .**66** A3
Silver St
    3 Appledore EX39 . . . .**15** A1
    Axminster EX13 . . . . **167** D5
    11 Bampton EX16 . . . .**34** B1
    8 Barnstaple EX32 . . . . . **155** A5
    Bere Ferrers PL20 . . . . . . **240** A3
    Berrynarbor EX34 . . . .**2** E3
    Bideford EX39 . . . . **157** A1
    Braunton EX33 . . . . **152** D7
    Buckfastleigh TQ11 . . . . . **236** B5
    Colyton EX24 . . . . **103** A5
    Culmstock EX15 . . . .**66** D8
    Honiton EX14 . . . . **166** C6
    Ipplepen TQ12 . . . . **211** C1
    Kentisbeare EX15 . . . .**66** A3
    Kilmington EX13 . . . .**87** C1
    Lydford EX20 . . . . **107** F3
    Lyme Regis DT7 . . . . **260** D3
    Ottery St Mary EX11 . . . . **169** D4
    Saltash PL12 . . . . **243** A2
    Thorverton EX5 . . . .**81** E4
    Tiverton EX16 . . . . **161** D4
    West Buckland TA21 . . . . . .**52** F7
    Willand EX15 . . . . **162** D4
Silvers The EX3 . . . . **178** F2
Silver Stream Way PL8 . . . **257** B5
Silver Terr
    Exeter EX4 . . . . **261** A1
    Millbrook PL10 . . . . **253** A6
Silverton CE Prim Sch
    EX5 . . . .**82** B6
Silverton Rd EX2 . . . . **181** D8
Silverway EX17 . . . .**80** E4
Silverwell Pk PL12 . . . . . . **137** C2
Silverwood Ave TQ12 . . . . **207** E1
Silverwood Hts EX31 . . . . . **155** B6
Silworthy Cross EX22 . . . . . .**38** F2
Simcoe Cl EX4 . . . .**67** B8
Simcoe Way EX14 . . . .**67** B1
Simey Cl EX4 . . . . **176** F7
Simmonds Pl EX15 . . . . . . **163** E4
Simmons Cl EX20 . . . . **170** C5
Simmons Way EX20 . . . . . **170** D5
Simms Hill TQ12, TQ13 . . **122** C2
Simon Cl PL9 . . . . **255** E6
Simon Ct **5** TQ1 . . . . . . **220** B6

Simons Cross EX13 . . . .**87** E4
Simpson Barton
    Conservation Wlk EX22 . .**72** C7
Sims Terr PL18 . . . . **125** D6
Sinai Hill EX35 . . . . **151** C5
Singer Cl TQ3 . . . . **226** A5
Singmore Rd TQ12 . . . . . . **218** E2
Sing's La EX33 . . . . **152** D5
Sir Alex Wlk EX3 . . . . **182** E5
Sir John Hunt Com Coll
    (Southway Campus)
    PL5 . . . . **244** F6
Sir John Hunt Com Sports
    Coll PL5 . . . . **244** D4
Sir Robert's Path EX31 . . . . .**4** D5
Siskin Chase EX15 . . . . . . **163** A2
Sithney St PL5 . . . . **243** C1
Sivell Mews EX2 . . . . **177** F5
Sivell Pl EX2 . . . . **177** F5
Six Acre Cross EX35 . . . .**5** A4
Six Acre La EX35 . . . .**5** A5
Six Acres EX10 . . . .**98** C4
Six Mile Hill
    Dunsford EX6 . . . . **113** A8
    Tedburn St Mary EX6 . . . . .**98** A5
Skardale Gdns PL6 . . . . . . **249** D8
Skardon Pl PL4 . . . . **263** A4
Skelmersdale Cl TQ7 . . . . **258** D5
Skern Cl EX39 . . . . **156** E2
Skern Way EX39 . . . . **156** F8
Skerries Rd PL6 . . . . **244** F7
Skinnard La PL18 . . . . **125** C5
Skinner Cl **2** EX16 . . . . . **161** B4
Skirhead La EX34 . . . .**3** B3
Skye Cl TQ2 . . . . **213** E2
Skylark Rise PL6 . . . . **245** E8
Skylark Spinney **3** EX15 . **159** A4
Skyways Bsns Pk EX5 . . . . .**99** A2
Slade EX39 . . . . **156** E2
Slade Cl
    Ottery St Mary EX11 . . . . **169** F4
    Plymouth PL9 . . . . **256** A5
Slade Cross
    Kingsbridge TQ7 . . . . **144** B6
    Lustleigh TQ13 . . . . **122** D8
    North Tawton EX20 . . . .**77** D5
Slade La
    Abbotskerswell TQ12 . . . . **212** B6
    Combe Martin EX34 . . . .**3** E1
    Galmpton TQ5 . . . . **229** B5
    Hawkridge TA22 . . . .**21** D1
    Sidmouth EX10 . . . . **189** C7
    West Anstey EX36 . . . .**32** B6
Slade Lane Cross EX34 . . . .**3** E1
Slade Rd
    Ilfracombe EX34 . . . . **150** A3
    Ottery St Mary EX11 . . . . **169** F3
Slade Valley Rd EX34 . . . . **150** A3
Sladnor Park Rd TQ1 . . . . **214** C5
Sladnor Pk TQ1 . . . . **214** C5
Slanns Mdw TQ12 . . . . . . **207** E6
Slappers Hill TQ4, TQ5 . . **234** C2
Slapton Ley National Nature
    Reserve TQ7 . . . . **145** D2
Slatelands Cl PL7 . . . . **251** B3
Slattenslade La EX31 . . . . . .**4** D5
Sleap Hill EX9 . . . . **198** C7
Sleepy Hollow EX2 . . . . . . **177** A2
Sleepy La TQ3 . . . . **219** A1
Sletchcott Cross EX37 . . . . .**44** A4
Slew Hill EX14 . . . .**85** A6
Slewton Cres EX5 . . . .**99** E8
Slewton Cres EX5 . . . .**99** E8
Slipperstone TQ9 . . . . **139** A7
Slipperstone Cross TQ9 . . **216** C7
Slipper Stone Dr PL21 . . . **237** A6
Slipperstone La TQ9 . . . . . **216** C7
Slipway Quay PL12 . . . . . . **239** B2
Slittercombe La EX6 . . . . . **194** E3
Sloe La **4** EX32 . . . . **17** B2
Slough La
    Bishops Nympton EX36 . . . .**30** F8
    Upottery EX14 . . . .**68** C5
Smallack Cl PL6 . . . . **244** D7
Smallack Dr PL6 . . . . **244** F7
Smallacombe Dross
    TQ10 . . . . **135** D6
Smallacombe Hill EX16,
    EX36 . . . .**32** D4
Smallacombe La EX36 . . . . .**31** F8
Smallacombe Rd EX16 . . . . .**33** A1
Smallacott Hill EX31 . . . . . .**97** D3
Smallcombe Cross TQ3 . . **225** E8
Smallcombe Rd TQ3 . . . . . **225** E8
Smalldon La TQ2 . . . . **214** A4
Small La
    Broadclyst EX5 . . . . **175** D7
    Burlescombe EX16 . . . .**51** B2
    Rattery TQ10 . . . . **135** D3
Smallpark La TQ13 . . . . . . **111** C2
Smallridge Cl PL9 . . . . **255** F5
Smallridge Rd EX13 . . . .**87** E4
Small Sch The EX39 . . . . . **157** A2
Smallwell La
    Ashprington TQ9 . . . . **139** E7
    Marldon TQ3 . . . . **218** C3
Smardon Ave TQ5 . . . . . . **230** B4
Smardon Cl TQ5 . . . . **230** A5
Smeathy La EX15 . . . .**52** F1
Smeaton Sq PL3 . . . . **249** D6
Smiter's Pit La EX13 . . . .**87** A1
Smithay Mdws EX14 . . . . . **113** A4
Smithfield Dr PL12 . . . . . . **242** B3
Smith Field Rd EX2 . . . . . . **181** A8
Smithfields TQ9 . . . . **223** B6
Smith Hill EX10 . . . . **188** F8
Smiths Ct EX22 . . . . **261** A1

Smith's La
    Calverleigh EX16 . . . .**48** E4
    Hollocombe EX18 . . . .**58** E6
Smith St TQ6 . . . . **233** F3
Smiths Way PL12 . . . . **242** B3
Smithy Cl PL12 . . . . **242** C4
Smockpark La PL9 . . . . . . **140** B8
Smokey Cross TQ13 . . . . . **122** B3
Smugglers' La EX7 . . . . . . **210** F8
Smythen Cross EX34 . . . .**9** E6
Smythen St EX1, EX4 . . . . **261** A2
Smythes Cross PL5 . . . .**67** F7
Snell Dr PL12 . . . . **242** B3
Snodbrook Cross EX10 . . . **101** C1
Snowberry Cl TQ1 . . . . . . **219** F7
Snowdonia Cl TQ4 . . . . . . **225** D4
Snowdrop Cl **2** EX14 . . . **166** A4
Snowdrop Cres PL15 . . . . . **105** A2
Snowdrop Mews EX4 . . . . **176** D8
Snows EX17 . . . .**80** B5
Snydles La EX7 . . . .**44** B6
Sog's La EX10 . . . . **100** C2
Solar Cres EX17 . . . . **176** F4
Solland Cross EX20 . . . .**76** D4
Solland La EX20 . . . .**76** D4
Soloman Dr EX39 . . . . **157** A1
Solsbro Rd TQ2 . . . . **219** E4
Solways DT7 . . . . **260** E3
Somer Fields DT7 . . . . **260** B3
Somerlea EX15 . . . . **162** D5
Somerset Ave EX14 . . . . . . **176** E4
Somerset Cotts **10** PL3 . . **248** A4
Somerset Ct
    10 Brixham TQ5 . . . . . . **230** C5
    17 Totnes TQ9 . . . . **223** D5
Somerset Pl
    22 Barnstaple EX31 . . . . **154** F5
    Plymouth PL3 . . . . **248** A4
    11 Teignmouth TQ14 . . . **210** B4
    Totnes TQ9 . . . . **223** D5
Somerset Place La **11**
    PL3 . . . . **248** A4
Somers Rd DT7 . . . . **260** C3
Something La EX33 . . . .**7** E1
Somerville Cl
    Exmouth EX8 . . . . **196** D1
    Willand EX15 . . . . **162** C5
Somerville Pk EX15 . . . . . **162** C4
Somerville Rd EX15 . . . . . **162** C4
Sommers' Cres EX34 . . . . **150** C6
Soper Rd PL6 . . . . **210** A7
Soper's Hill PL5 . . . . **240** E1
Super Wlk TQ14 . . . . **210** A7
Sophia Way TQ2 . . . . **207** A2
Sorley Green Cross TQ7 . . **143** F5
Sorley La TQ7 . . . . **143** F5
Sorley Tunnel Adventure
    Farm TQ7 . . . . **143** F5
Sorrell Ct TQ12 . . . . **207** D7
Sorrento TQ1 . . . . **220** C5
South Ave
    Exeter EX1 . . . . **157** D1
    Exeter EX1 . . . . **177** E6
    Lyme Regis DT7 . . . . **260** D4
Southay Cross TA20 . . . .**69** D4
Southay La TA20 . . . .**69** C4
Southbank TQ12 . . . . **207** C4
South Bank Dr EX39 . . . . . **156** F2
South Brent Prim Sch
    TQ10 . . . . **135** A3
South Brent Rd TQ7 . . . . . **143** F7
Southbrook Cl **2** TQ13 . . **180** C8
Southbrook La
    Bovey Tracey TQ13 . . . . . **180** B8
    1 Bovey Tracey TQ13 . . **180** C8
    Otterton EX10 . . . . **187** B1
    Rockbeare EX5 . . . .**99** C7
Southbrook Rd
    Bovey Tracey TQ13 . . . . . **180** C8
    Exeter EX2 . . . . **178** A2
Southbrook Sch EX2 . . . . . **178** A2
South Burrow Rd **11**
    EX34 . . . . **150** B5
South Church La EX20 . . . **170** A4
Southcombe Cross
    Hittisleigh EX6 . . . .**96** F4
    Widecombe in the Moor
    TQ13 . . . . **121** B3
Southcombe Hill EX6 . . . . . .**96** F4
Southcombe St TQ13 . . . . **111** A6
South Common La EX13 . . . .**88** A5
Southcoombe Terr EX12 . . **192** E7
Southcote La EX14 . . . .**86** C4
Southcote Orch TQ9 . . . . . **223** C5
Southcott Cross
    Chawleigh EX18 . . . .**60** A6
    Langtree EX38 . . . .**40** F3
    Okehampton EX20 . . . .**93** C5
Southcott Rd EX34 . . . . . . **156** F4
South Dartmoor Com Coll
    TQ13 . . . . **131** A5
South Dean La EX31 . . . .**4** A5
South Dean La EX31 . . . .**4** A5
South Devon Coll
    Paignton TQ4 . . . . **219** F6
South Devon Rly
    Buckfastleigh TQ11 . . . . . **236** C4
    Staverton TQ9 . . . . **215** D4
Southdown Ave TQ5 . . . . **230** B2
Southdown Cl
    Beer EX12 . . . . **191** D5
    Brixham TQ5 . . . . **230** B2
Southdown Cotts EX10 . . **253** B6
Southdown Rd
    Brixham TQ5 . . . . **230** B1
    Burlescombe EX16 . . . .**51** B2
South Molton EX36 . . . .**46** A5

South Down Cross EX19....76 C7
South Down Farm TQ7...147 E5
Southdown Hill
  Brixham TQ5 ....230 B2
  Copplestone EX17.........79 D7
  Meshaw EX36 ....45 F6
Southdown Ho 🖸 TQ13 . 180 D8
Southdown La EX37......43 D3
South Down La EX36.....31 E6
Southdown Rd
  Beer EX12 ....191 D5
  Brixham TQ5 ....230 B1
  Millbrook PL10.........253 A6
South Down Rd PL7 ... 248 B6
South Downs Rd EX7 .. 204 D4
Southdown Terr PL10 .. 253 A6
South Dr EX38..........159 B5
Southella Rd PL20 ..... 127 A2
South Emb TQ6 ....233 F3
South End Cl 🖣 EX33 . 152 D5
Southern Cl
  Plymouth PL2..........247 F7
  Torquay TQ2...........214 A4
Southernhay
  Newton Abbot TQ12 .... 207 C2
  Winkleigh EX19 ....58 F2
Southernhay E EX1 .....261 B3
Southernhay Gdns EX1.. 261 B3
Southern Rd EX8 ....202 A8
Southern Cross EX13.... 103 D5
Southern Terr PL4 ..... 248 F4
Southernway PL9 ....256 A8
Southern Wood EX8 .... 196 E2
Southey Cres TQ12 ..... 213 A3
Southey Dr TQ12 ....213 A3
Southey La
  Kingskerswell TQ12 .... 213 A3
  Sampford Courtenay EX20 ..76 F3
South Farm Rd EX9 ..... 198 C3
Southfield
  Saltash PL12 ....242 C3
  🖪 Torquay TQ1 ....220 D4
  West Alvington TQ7 .... 258 A4
Southfield Ave TQ3 .... 226 A8
Southfield Cl TQ3......226 A8
Southfield Dr EX17 .... 165 B6
Southfield Rd
  Bideford EX39 ....157 C1
  Paignton TQ3 ....226 A7
Southfield Rise TQ3.. 226 A7
Southfields
  Bridgerule EX22........70 F5
  Totnes TQ9............224 B8
Southfield Way EX16... 161 B4
Southford La TQ9.......216 A4
South Ford Rd TQ6 ..... 233 F3
South Furzeham Rd TQ5 230 C5
Southgate EX2.........255 E4
Southgate Ave PL9..... 255 E4
Southgate Cl PL9 ...... 255 E4
Southgate Ct 🖣 EX2 .. 261 B2
South Gn 🖣 EX32.......155 B4
South Grange EX2 ..... 178 D3
South Hams Bsns Pk
  TQ7..................143 E4
South Hams Hospl TQ7. 258 C6
South Hayes Cross EX32...17 B2
South Hayne Cross EX36..31 B4
South Hele Cross EX16....35 C1
South Hill
  Plymouth, Hooe PL9 .... 255 C5
  Plymouth, Stoke PL1 .. 248 A3
South Hill Cotts EX22 ..... 38 C1
South Hill Rd TQ1....... 220 C4
South La
  Braunton EX33............15 E8
  Challacombe EX31.........11 F3
  Hartland EX39 ....22 E2
  Lynton EX35 ....5 F5
Southland Park Cres 🖪
  PL9..................140 D8
Southland Park Rd PL9 140 D8
Southlands
  🖪 Braunton EX33........152 D5
  Exeter EX1.............177 E6
  Wrafton EX33...........152 E4
Southlands Dr EX38......40 F2
Southlands Rd TQ2 ..... 220 A5
South Lawn
  Exeter EX2............261 C2
  Sidmouth EX10 ....188 C8
South Lawn Terr EX1.... 177 F6
Southlea EX39 ....156 E6
South Lea EX33.........152 E5
South Lea Cl EX33 ..... 152 E5
South Lee Cross EX36....30 B7
Southleigh Hill Cross
  EX24..................102 B3
South Ley Cross EX31 .... 3 D1
Southley Rd EX36 ...... 158 C4
Southmead Sch EX33 ... 152 E4
South Milton St PL4 ... 263 C2
South Molton Com Coll
  EX36..................158 C3
South Molton Com Hospl
  EX36..................158 C4
South Molton Inf Sch
  EX36..................158 C5
South Molton Mus EX36. 158 C4
South Molton Rd EX16....34 B1
South Molton St EX18....44 E1
South Molton United CE Jun
  Sch EX36 ....158 C5
South Moor La EX17 .....59 E1
South Par EX9..........199 H2
South Parks Rd TQ2 ... 213 F2

South Pk
  Barnstaple EX32........155 B3
  Braunton EX33.........152 F5
  Woolfardisworthy EX39....38 F7
Southport Ave EX4.....176 E5
South Quay TQ4 ....226 C5
South Rd
  🖪 Appledore EX39 .....15 A1
  Newton Abbot TQ12....207 B2
South Sands TQ4 ....226 C2
Southside EX17..........59 F2
Southside Ope 🖣 PL1 .. 263 A2
Southside St PL1.......263 A2
South Sq 🖪 EX24.......103 A4
South St
  Axminster EX13 ....167 D5
  Barnstaple EX32 ....155 B2
  Barnstaple EX32 ....155 B3
  Braunton EX33.........152 D5
  Colyton EX24...........103 A4
  Denbury TQ12 ....211 A6
  Dolton EX19 ....57 F7
  Exeter EX1............261 B2
  Exmouth EX8 ....202 A6
  Great Torrington EX38.. 159 C5
  Hatherleigh EX20........75 C7
  Hoicombe Rogus TA21....50 F5
  Sheepwash EX21.........56 C1
  South Molton EX36 .... 158 C4
  Torquay TQ2...........219 F6
  Totnes TQ9............223 C5
  Wellington TA21.......160 E5
  Winkleigh EX19 ....58 F3
  Woolacombe EX34........7 F6
South Tawton Prim Sch
  EX20..................95 B4
Southtown
  Dartmouth TQ6 ....233 F2
  Kenton EX6............194 F3
South Trelawny Prim Sch
  PL2 ....248 A8
Southview PL10.........253 A6
South View
  Abbotskerswell TQ12...212 B6
  Barnstaple EX31 ....154 D7
  Bideford EX39 ....156 F2
  Bovey Tracey TQ13....180 D7
  Bratton Fleming EX31....18 A8
  Braunton EX33.........152 D4
  🖪 Hemyock EX15.........67 B8
  🖽 Horrabridge PL20...126 F4
  Ilfracombe EX34 ....1 E3
  Lydford EX20 ....107 F4
  Mary Tavy PL19 ....117 E6
  Plymouth, Crownhill PL5 .244 E2
  Plymouth, Elburton PL9 . 256 B6
  Prixford EX31 ....16 C7
  Tiverton EX16 ....161 D4
  Westleigh EX16 ....51 A3
South View Cl
  Braunton EX33.........152 D4
  Plymouth PL7..........250 D7
  Willand EX15...........162 D5
South View Est EX15 ... 162 D5
South View Pk PL7..... 250 D7
Southview Rd TQ3 ..... 226 A7
South View Rd EX15.... 162 D5
South View Terr
  Exeter EX1............261 B3
  Exminster EX6 ....182 B4
  Plymouth PL4..........263 C3
  Sidmouth EX10 ....188 A5
Southville Gdns TQ7 .. 258 D3
Southway
  Sidmouth EX10 ....188 C4
  Tedburn St Mary EX6.....97 F4
Southway Ave TQ2 .....213 F1
Southway Dr PL6 ......244 E6
Southway La
  Plymouth, Southway PL6..245 B6
  Plymouth, Tamerton Foliot
  PL6 ....244 C6
Southway Prim Sch PL6..244 E1
Southwell Rd PL6.......244 E1
Southwood Cross EX5.....99 C4
Southwood Ct TQ1......220 C5
Southwood Dr EX39 .... 157 A3
Southwood Mdws EX20....40 C7
South Yeo Cross
  Northlew EX20 ....74 F2
  Poughill EX17 ....62 E3
South Yeo Hill EX17.....62 D3
Sovereign Cl EX8 ......196 E1
Sovereign Ct PL7 ......250 C5
Sovereign Mews TQ2...214 B2
Sowden La
  Barnstaple EX32 ....155 B5
  Lympstone EX8 ....195 E4
Sowden Pk EX32 ....155 B5
Sowton Cvn Site EX2...178 F6
Sowton Ind Est EX2....178 E5
Sowton La EX5 ....179 B6
Spa Ct TQ1 ....220 C4
Spanishlake Cross EX6..113 A4
Spanish Lane End TQ9 . 139 A5
Sparhanger Cross EX35...5 B3
Sparhanger La EX35 .....5 B3
Sparkatown La EX20.... 127 B3
Sparke Cl PL7 ....251 B4
Sparks Barn Rd EX4 ... 226 B4
Sparkwell All Saints Prim
  Sch PL7...............251 F8
Sparrow La EX34........21 C7
Sparrow Pk TQ7 ....147 F6
Sparrow Rd TQ7.......223 B5
Speakers Rd PL21......237 E5
Speares The PL12 .....242 B2

Spearfield Cl EX36......158 D4
Spears La TA21 ....35 F4
Speedwell Cl
  Barnstaple EX32 ....155 E3
  Bideford EX39 ....25 E4
  Brixham TQ5 ....230 C3
  Millbrook PL10.........252 F5
Speedwell Cres PL6.....249 B7
Speedwell Units EX2...233 C3
Speedwell Wlk PL6 .... 249 B7
Spekes Cross EX18.......59 C4
Spence Combe Cross
  EX17..................79 D4
Spence Cross EX14 ......84 D4
Spence La DT6 ....104 F7
Spencer Cl EX8.........196 E2
Spencer Ct EX11.........169 D3
Spencer Dr EX16 ....161 F3
Spencer Gdns PL12 .... 242 F1
Spencer Rd
  Newton Abbot TQ12.... 207 C2
  Paignton TQ3 ....225 E7
  Plymouth PL9..........255 E8
Spenser Ave EX2 ....177 F3
Speranza Gr 🖽 TQ14...210 B5
Spestos La EX17 ....78 C1
Spicer Cl EX15.........163 B2
Spicer Rd EX1 ....261 C3
Spicers Rd TQ13, EX6 . 194 A1
Spider's La EX8........196 C3
Spindlebury EX15 ......163 A2
Spindlewood Cl EX14 .. 166 C3
Spinnaker Quay PL9 ... 254 F7
Spinney Cl EX2.........178 C4
Spinney The
  Ivybridge PL21 ....237 A5
  Plymouth PL7..........251 A4
  Uffculme EX15 ....66 A8
Spinning Bath Gdns
  EX17..................165 C4
Spinning La EX13.......104 B8
Spire Ct PL3...........249 B5
Spire Hill Pk PL12 .... 242 C2
Spirelake EX36 ....30 F2
Spire Lake Cl EX36......30 F3
Spirelake Cross EX17....79 C8
Spirelake Hill EX17 .....79 C8
Spire's Cross EX20 ......77 A3
Spitfire Wlk EX32 ..... 155 C5
Spithead TQ6 ....233 F3
Spitlar Cross EX20 ......95 C6
Spittis Pk TQ6 ....234 B3
Spittle Cross EX18 ......44 D4
Spittles La DT7 ....260 E4
Spitup La EX10 ....122 A5
Splatford Dr EX15 ..... 163 C5
Splatts Cross EX19.......76 C7
Splitwell Cross EX17....62 B2
Spreacombe Gdns EX33....8 F4
Spreyton Cross EX17....96 A7
Spreyton Sch EX17......96 A7
Spring Cl
  Newton Abbot TQ12.... 206 E4
  Winkleigh EX19 ....58 E2
Springdale Cl TQ5 ..... 230 C2
Springfield
  Dunkeswell EX14.........67 C2
  🖽 Horrabridge PL20... 126 F4
  Membury EX13 ....87 D6
  Winkleigh EX19 ....58 E3
Spring Field EX39 ....22 D3
Springfield Ave
  Barnstaple EX32 ....155 B3
  Plymouth PL9..........256 B6
Springfield Cl PL9 ..... 256 B7
Springfield Cres
  Fremington EX31 ...... 153 F6
  Northam EX39 ....156 F7
Springfield Dr
  Kingsbridge TQ7 ......258 C5
  Plymouth PL3..........248 A4
  Tiverton EX16 ....161 B4
Springfield Gdns EX7 .. 200 F1
Springfield La PL9 ..... 256 B7
Springfield Pk
  Bridestowe EX20........107 F8
  Buckfastleigh TQ11 .... 236 D5
Springfield Rd
  Barnstaple EX31 ....154 B3
  Exeter EX4............177 D8
  Exmouth EX8 ....196 B1
  Honiton EX14..........166 F5
  Ilfracombe EX34 ....150 B6
  Offwell EX14 ....86 A3
  Plymouth PL9..........256 B6
  South Brent TQ10 .....134 F3
  Torquay TQ1...........220 B7
  Wellington TA21.......160 E6
  Woolacombe EX34........8 A6
Springfield Rise PL9... 256 B7
Springfields EX24......103 A3
Springfield Terr
  🖪 Bideford EX39 ......157 B1
  🖽 Combe Martin EX34.....3 A3
  🖪 Northam EX39 ......156 F7
  Tatworth TA20 ....75 F5
Springhead Cross EX13...87 C1
Springhead Cross EX13 193 A6
Springhead La EX13 ....87 C1
Spring Head Rd DT7 ... 260 B6
Spring Hill PL19 ....171 B5
Springhill Down Hill EX16 47 D4
Springhill Gdns DT7 .. 260 D4
Springhill Gn PL2 .....248 C8
Springhill Rd TQ1 .....223 E5
Spring Pk PL6..........245 E7

Spring Rd PL9 ....140 B8
Springwood Cl
  Ivybridge PL21 ....237 E5
  Plymouth PL7..........251 A3
Spruce Cl
  Exeter EX4............174 B2
  Exmouth EX8 ....196 D3
Spruce Gdns PL7 ....251 B5
Spruce Pk EX17 ....165 C4
Spruce Way TQ3 ....226 A8
Spry La PL16 ....106 A4
Sprys Shop Cross EX22...72 D2
Sprytown Cross PL16..106 B4
Sprywood Cross EX21....56 A1
Spur Cross EX39 ....32 E2
Spurfield Cotts EX6....182 A4
Spurway Gdns EX34......3 B3
Spurway Hill EX16 ......48 A3
Spurway Hill Cross EX16..48 A8
Spurway Rd EX16.......161 F3
Square's Quay TQ7..... 258 C4
Square The
  Ashreigney EX18.........58 E8
  Barnstaple EX12 ......154 F5
  Beer EX12 ....191 D5
  🖽 Bere Alston PL20....125 E1
  🖽 Bishop's Tawton EX32 ..16 E1
  Braunton EX33.........152 D6
  Bridestowe EX20.......107 F8
  Cawsand PL10.........253 A1
  Chagford TQ13 ....111 A6
  Chittlehampton EX37....28 F4
  Chulmleigh EX18 ....44 E1
  Ermington PL21........136 F4
  Exeter, Exwick EX4 ....177 A6
  🖪 Exeter, Middle Moor
  EX2 ....178 D5
  Fremington EX31 ......153 E5
  Gunnislake PL18 ......125 D6
  Gunnislake, St Ann's Chapel
  PL18 ....125 B5
  Hartland EX39 ....22 D3
  🖪 Holsworthy EX22....164 C4
  Inner Hope TQ7 ......147 B6
  Kingswear TQ6........234 A3
  Lutton PL21...........133 B2
  Moretonhampstead TQ13 .111 F5
  🖪 Northam EX39 ......156 F7
  North Molton EX36 .....30 D8
  North Tawton EX20.....77 C4
  Petrockstow EX20 ......56 F4
  Plymouth, Stonehouse PL1 248 A2
  Rockbeare EX5 ....99 C5
  Saltash PL12 ....242 C3
  Seaton EX12............80 A5
  🖽 Seaton EX12.........192 A5
  Shebbear EX21 ....55 D4
  Sheepwash EX21.........56 C1
  South Molton EX36 ....158 C4
  Uffculme EX15 ....66 A7
  Ugborough PL21 ....137 D6
  Whimple EX5 ....99 E8
  Witheridge EX16 ....46 E1
Squire's Ct EX32.......155 B2
Squires Cotts PL20.....128 B8
Squire's La EX12 ......192 C5
Squires' La
  Shebbear EX21 ....55 D6
  Shebbear EX21 ....55 D6
Squirrel Ct TA21 ......160 D5
Stabb Cl TQ4 ....226 A1
Stabb Dr TQ4 ....226 A1
Stabdon La EX19, EX20 ..59 C1
Stable Ctyd DT7 ....93 E6
Stable La TQ1 ....214 B1
Stables The TQ9 ....223 D6
Stabury Cross EX14......86 B5
Stadbury La EX14........86 C5
Staddens Lea La TQ2.. 219 C6
Staddiscombe Rd PL9...255 F4
Staddon Cl
  Barnstaple EX33.......152 C6
  Exeter EX4............178 B7
Staddon Court Cotts PL9 140 B8
Staddon Cres PL9......255 E6
Staddon Cross EX22.....72 C6
Staddon Gate EX20......77 D5
Staddon Gdns TQ2.....214 B2
Staddon Gn PL9........255 D6
Staddonhill Rd TA24....21 F8
Staddon La PL9........255 B4
Staddon Moor Cross
  EX20..................77 D5
Staddon Park Rd PL9...255 E6
Staddon Rd
  Appledore EX39 ....15 A1
  Holsworthy EX22.......164 F3
  Plymouth St Mary EX6...97 E2
Staddons View TQ13 .. 180 C8
Staddon Terrace La PL1 262 B4
Stadium Dr TQ12 ......213 A2
Stadium Way EX4......261 C4
Staffick Cl EX6.........194 E3
Stafford Cross EX24... 102 D2
Stafford Ct 🖽 TQ12....223 E5
Stafford Hill EX14......84 F8
Stafford La EX24.......103 A3
Stafford Rd
  Dolton EX19 ....57 F7
  Exeter EX4............176 F5
  Paignton TQ4 ....226 C5
Stafford Way EX17......57 F7
Stag Cnr EX15.........162 E1
Staggers La EX13 .....152 E3
Stag La
  Plymouth, Elburton PL9 . 256 B8
  Plymouth, Plympton PL9 . 250 B1
Stag Mill Cross EX16.....50 B3

Stag's Head EX32........29 D6
Stags Wood Dr EX21.....73 E2
Stakes Hill TQ7 ....143 A5
Stallards
  Braunton EX33.........152 C7
  Wellington TA21.......160 C3
Stamford Cl PL9 ....155 A6
Stamford Fort Cotts PL9 255 A6
Stamford La PL9........255 A6
Stammery Hill EX13......88 C1
Stamps Hill PL8 ....257 A6
Stamps The PL17 ....155 A6
Stanborough Cross PL9. 256 C7
Stanborough Ct TQ9 ... 139 A3
Stanborough Rd PL9...256 B7
Stanbridge Pk EX39... 156 D2
Stanbury Ave PL6......244 F1
Stanbury Cl PL15 ....90 C1
Stanbury Copse EX34 .. 150 A4
Stanbury Cross
  Holsworthy EX22 ......164 D6
  Morwenstow EX23.......36 F1
Stanbury Ct EX17 ..... 165 C5
Stanbury Rd
  Knowle EX33 ....8 D1
  Torquay TQ2...........219 C7
Stanburys Orch EX16.....96 F3
Stancombe Cross TQ7.. 144 F4
Standard Ct PL19......117 E6
Standarhay Cl PL9 .... 256 C7
Standarhay Villas PL9 . 256 C7
Stanfield TQ1..........220 E5
Stanford Rd EX2.......178 C5
Stang La EX34 ....8 F5
Stangray Ave PL4......248 D4
Stanhope Cl EX22......164 C5
Stanhope Dr EX10 .....188 B6
Stanhope Rd PL5 ......243 C1
Stanhope Sq 🖣 EX22 .. 164 C4
Stanhope Terr EX39....157 A3
Staniforth Dr PL21.....237 D4
Stanley Cotts EX24.....103 A3
Stanley Ct TQ1 ....220 C8
Stanley Gdns TQ3 .....226 A7
Stanley Mews EX9......198 A1
Stanley Pl PL4.........249 B2
Stanley Rd TQ1........220 C8
Stanley Sq EX3 ....182 F4
Stanley Wlk 🖽 TQ14...210 B4
Stanley Wlk EX8 ....196 D4
Stanmore Rise EX7.....204 E7
Stanmore Tor TQ3 ..... 226 A5
Stannary Bridge Rd
  PL19..................171 D6
Stannary Cl PL21 ......237 E5
Stannary Pl TQ13 ......111 A6
Stansfeld Ave TQ2 .....226 A6
Stantaway Hill TQ1.....219 F7
Stantaway Pk TQ1 .....219 F7
Stanton Ct TQ7 ....138 A1
Stanton La TQ3 ....218 F5
Stant Way TA20 ....69 F6
Stantyway Cross EX9.. 198 F6
Stantyway Ct EX9 .....198 F6
Stantyway Rd EX9 .....198 F5
Stanwell Dr EX39 ..... 156 C6
Stanwell Hill EX39 .... 156 C6
Stanwey EX1 ....178 A5
Staplake La EX6........201 A7
Staplake Rd EX6.......195 B1
Staplake Rise EX6......195 A1
Stapleback Cross EX19....57 E5
Staple Back La EX19....57 E5
Staple Cl PL6..........241 C1
Staple Cross EX19 ......57 F5
Stapledon Cotts EX22....72 E7
Stapledon La TQ13.....130 F5
Stapleford Gdns PL5 .. 243 F5
Staplegate EX17.........50 A3
Staplehill Rd
  Coldeast TQ12.........122 F1
  Newton Abbot TQ12... 206 B8
Staple Orch TQ9 ....222 F8
Staples Mdw TQ20 ......88 A7
Staples Mews 🖪 EX8 .. 202 A7
Staples Terr DT7.......260 E4
Stapleton Cl TQ4 ......225 E3
Star Barton La EX5.....172 D4
Starcombe La EX10.....101 D4
Star Cross EX13 ....87 E6
Starcross Prim Sch EX6..201 B8
Starcross Sta EX6......201 B8
Starkey Cl 🖽 EX16......57 C2
Starlings Roost EX15.. 163 A2
Starpitton Cross TQ12..214 B3
Starpitten La W TQ2 .. 214 A3
Star Pk PL18 ....125 D6
Starre Cl EX12.........192 A7
Start Ave
  Chillington TQ7 ....145 A1
  Teignmouth TQ14......210 C7
Start Bay Cvn Pk TQ6 . 145 E6
Start Bay Pk TQ6 ......145 C6
Start Cross TQ7 ....211 B7
Starved Oak Cross EX5...81 D1
Station App TQ10......134 F3
Station Bsns Pk TQ14 . 210 C5
Station Cl EX33 ....152 D5
Station Cotts
  Bittaford TQ12........137 E8
  Brandis Corner EX22....73 A5
Station Cross
  Bittaford TQ12........137 E8
  Crediton EX17.........165 E4
Station Ct TQ13 ....180 C7

Station Fields EX21....73 E2
Station Hill
　Bideford EX39........157 E1
　Bratton Fleming EX31....11 A1
　Brixham TQ5........230 C5
　Great Torrington EX38.159 A6
　Lynton EX35........151 B4
　Swimbridge EX32....17 E1
Station La
　Calstock PL18........125 D3
　Paignton TQ4........226 B5
Station Rd
　Bampton EX16........34 B1
　Barnstaple EX31......154 F4
　Bere Alston PL20....125 E2
　Bere Ferrers PL20....239 E3
　Bovey Tracey TQ13...180 C7
　Bow EX17........78 B3
　Bratton Fleming EX31...18 A8
　Braunton EX33........152 D5
　Bridestowe EX20....107 F7
　Broadclyst EX5........175 E3
　Buckfastleigh TQ11...236 C5
　Budleigh Salterton EX9.198 A1
　Burlescombe EX16.....51 B3
　Chard Junction TA20...88 D8
　Chulmleigh EX18......44 C3
　Colyton EX24........103 A5
　Cullompton EX15....163 C4
　17 Dawlish EX7........204 E6
　Exeter, Pinhoe EX1...174 E1
　Exeter, St David's EX4.177 A8
　Exminster EX6........182 D3
　Exton EX3........183 C1
　Feniton EX14........84 D2
　Gunnislake PL18.....125 C6
　Halwill Junction EX21...73 E2
　Hele EX5........82 F5
　Hemyock EX15........67 B8
　Holsworthy EX22....164 C4
　Horrabridge PL20...126 F4
　Ide EX2........176 D1
　Ilfracombe EX34....150 A4
　Ivybridge PL21......237 D6
　Lifton PL16........105 F4
　Lydford EX20........108 A6
　Mary Tavy PL19....117 C6
　Meeth EX20........57 C2
　Moretonhampstead TQ13.111 F4
　Newton Abbot TQ12...207 D3
　Newton Poppleford EX10.186 F8
　Newton St Cyres EX5...81 A1
　North Brentor PL19...117 C8
　Northlew EX20........74 E1
　Okehampton EX20....170 B4
　Plymouth, Elburton PL9.256 C7
　Plymouth, Keyham PL2.247 E5
　Plymouth, Plympton PL7.250 F5
　Plymouth, Tamerton Foliot
　　PL5........244 A6
　Princetown PL20....128 A8
　Saltash PL12........243 A2
　Sidmouth EX10........188 A4
　6 South Brent TQ10...134 F3
　3 Teignmouth TQ14...210 C4
　Tiverton EX16........161 D4
　Topsham EX3........182 F5
　Totnes TQ9........223 C6
　Wellington TA21......160 C7
　Willand EX15........162 C5
　Woolacombe EX34.....8 A6
　Yelverton PL20........127 A2
　Yeoford EX17........79 C1
Station Road Ind Est EX5.67 B8
Station View PL19......117 C8
Station Yard Ind Est
　TQ7........258 C5
Staverton Cotts TQ13...130 F4
Staverton Sta TQ9....215 E4
Stawley Prim Sch TA21...51 B8
Steamer Quay Rd TQ9...223 D4
Steamer Quay Wharf 11
　TQ9........223 D5
Steartfield Rd TQ3, TQ4.226 C7
Steddaford Ct EX20....95 A5
Stedhams Cl TA21....160 D7
Steed Cl TQ4........229 A8
Steel Cl EX14........166 D6
Steeperton Cl EX20....170 D5
Steep Head EX36......19 B1
Steep Hill TQ1........214 D6
Steep La
　Hartford TA22........34 C8
　Landkey EX32........17 D2
Steeple Cl PL9........255 F6
Steeple Dr EX2........181 B8
Steer Park Rd PL7...251 C5
Steer Point Cotts PL8...256 F2
Steer Point Rd PL8...257 A4
Stefan Cl PL9........255 B5
Stella Maris Ct EX39...157 E2
Stella Rd TQ3........219 A1
Stenlake Pl PL4......249 B2
Stenlake Terr PL4...249 B2
Stentaway Cl PL9....255 F8
Stentaway Dr PL9....256 A8
Stentaway La PL9....255 E7
Stentaway Rd PL9....255 F8
Stentiford Hill TQ7...258 D3
Stentiford Hill Rd TQ1...220 B5
Stentiford La TQ13...122 F1
Stepcote Hill EX1...261 A2
Steppes Mdw TQ12...207 A3
Steppingstone Cross EX33 .8 D1

Stepps Cross EX12........192 E7
Stepps Rd EX12, D17....193 B5
Steps Cl EX1........174 F1
Steps Cross TQ2........214 B3
Steps La TQ2........214 B3
Stepstone La EX33........8 D1
Steven's Cross EX10....188 D8
Steven's Cross Cl EX10..188 E8
Stevens La EX10........188 A7
Stevenstone Ct EX38....42 A6
Stevenstone Rd EX8....202 D7
Stewart Cl EX8........196 E1
Stewart Ct EX13........167 F7
Stewart Ho EX7........204 E7
Stibb La PL21........136 D7
Stickle Path EX16........35 C1
Sticklepath Com Sch
　EX31........154 C3
Sticklepath Cl EX31....154 E3
Sticklepath Hill EX31...154 E4
Sticklepath Terr EX31...154 F4
Stidson Cross TQ10....135 B3
Stidston La TQ10........135 A3
Stile Ct EX15........163 D4
Stile La D17........260 D3
Stile Orch TQ7........143 F7
Stillman Cl **7** PL4....263 A2
Stillman St PL4........263 A2
Stiniel Cross TQ13....111 A4
Stintway La EX10........187 E5
Stirling Cl PL5........243 C1
Stirling Rd PL5........243 C1
Stitchill Rd TQ1........220 C4
Stitworthy Cross EX39 ..23 C1
Stoat Pk EX32........155 D4
Stoats Cl EX36........158 C2
Stoats Mews EX20........77 C4
Stockadon Farm Barns
　PL12........238 B4
Stockadon La EX17........63 A1
Stocker Rd EX4........173 B1
Stockeydown La EX17...179 F7
Stockham Hill TQ12....33 E8
Stock Hill EX35........151 A1
Stock La EX12........192 E5
Stockland CE Prim Sch
　EX14........87 A7
Stockland Cross EX15...66 A3
Stockland Head Cross
　EX15........84 B7
Stockland Hill EX14....86 E6
Stockleigh Cross
　Cheriton Fitzpaine EX17...62 C1
　Stockleigh Pomeroy EX17.80 F6
Stockman La EX14........88 C7
Stockmeadow Gdns
　TQ14........209 A7
Stock Rd EX35........5 B3
Stockstyle La EX13........88 A8
Stockton Ave EX7........204 E6
Stockton Hill EX7........204 D6
Stockton La **9** EX7........204 D6
Stockton Rd EX7........204 D6
Stockwell Cross EX5....82 D5
Stoford Lane TA21........52 F7
Stoggy La PL7........251 A6
Stoke Beach Cvn Pk PL8.141 B5
Stoke Canon CE Prim Sch
　EX5........173 F8
Stoke Climsland Sch
　PL17........115 B1
Stoke Cross PL8........141 B5
Stoke Damerel Bsns Ctr 9
　PL3........248 A4
Stoke Damerel Com Coll
　PL3........248 B4
Stoke Damerel Prim Sch
　PL1........248 A3
Stoke Fleming Com Prim Sch
　TQ6........146 A7
Stoke Gabriel Prim Sch
　TQ9........227 F7
Stoke Gabriel Rd TQ5...229 A5
Stoke Hill
　Exeter EX4........173 E2
　Stoke Canon EX5........173 F6
　Stoke Gabriel TQ9........227 F7
Stoke Hill Cres EX4....173 E1
Stoke Hill Inf Sch EX4...173 E1
Stoke Hill Jun Sch EX4..173 E1
Stoke Hill La PL20....226 D2
Stoke House Gdns TQ6..146 B7
Stokeinteignhead Prim Sch
　TQ12........209 B1
Stokelake TQ13........123 D5
Stoke Lyne EX8........196 C1
Stoke Meadow Cl EX4...173 E2
Stokenham Area Prim Sch
　TQ7........145 B1
Stokenham Cross TQ7...145 B1
Stoke Rd
　Higher Gabwell TQ1,
　　TQ14........214 C2
　Noss Mayo PL8........141 A6
　Paignton, Higher Yalberton
　　TQ4........225 C3
　Paignton, Waddeton TQ5..228 F6
　Plymouth PL1........262 A3
　Stoke Canon EX4, EX5...173 D5
Stokesway Ave PL6....245 A5
Stokes La TQ3........126 C5
Stokes Mead EX5........184 D3
Stoke Valley Rd EX4...173 D2
Stoke Woods Forest Wlks EX4,
　EX5........173 B4
Stokingway Cl PL9....255 E5
Stoneacre Cl TQ5....230 C3
Stone Ash La EX17........61 C3

Stonebarrow La EX13....88 F2
Stonebarton Cl PL7...250 C6
Stonebarton Rd PL7...250 C6
Stoneborough Cnr EX9.198 B1
Stoneborough La EX9..198 B1
Stoneborough Ct EX9..198 B1
Stone Cl EX14........166 B4
Stonecombe Hill EX31...10 C6
Stone Cross
　Chagford TQ13........96 A1
　Lifton PL16........105 E5
　Meeth EX20........57 C4
　Molland EX36........31 F7
　North Tawton EX20....77 E4
　West Buckland EX32...18 A4
Stone Cross (Mus)
　　........121 B1
Stone Ct TQ2........213 D1
Stonehall Flats PL1...248 A1
Stonehanger TQ8........259 D4
Stonehanger Ct TQ8...259 D4
Stonehedge Cl PL21...237 D4
Stonehouse Bridge PL1.248 A1
Stonehouse St PL1...262 A2
Stone La
　Cadbury EX5........81 F7
　Lympstone EX8........195 E5
Stoneland Cross EX16...47 F4
Stoneland La EX16....47 F5
Stonelands Cotts EX7...204 C6
Stonelands Ct EX7...204 C6
Stonelands Mews EX7...204 C6
Stonelands Pk EX7...204 C6
Stonelands Terr EX7...204 C6
Stone Lane Gdns TQ13...96 A1
Stone Lane Ret Pk EX7.177 B3
Stoneleigh
　Sidmouth EX10........189 C7
　Wellington TA21........160 B8
Stoneleigh Cl TQ12....206 F4
Stoneleigh Dr TQ2....219 D3
Stoneman's Hill TQ12..212 B7
Stonemans La EX16....159 C5
Stone Moor Cross EX18...45 C1
Stonemoor La EX36....31 F7
Stonepark TQ13........130 F4
Stonepark Cres TQ13..130 F4
Stone Pk TQ4........229 D6
Stoneridge La TA4....35 D5
Stones Cl
　8 Kingsteignton TQ12..123 F1
　Modbury PL21........137 C2
Stone's Hill EX17........80 A7
Stoneshill Cross EX17...80 A7
Stonewall La EX17....165 C6
Stoneyford Pk EX9....198 B1
Stoneyhill TQ12........212 B3
Stonehouse La EX14....86 D1
Stoney La
　Bradninch EX5........82 F7
　Honiton EX14........166 D2
Stoneylands EX15........99 C5
Stoney Lane Cross EX16..50 B3
Stoney Lane Hill EX16...48 C2
Stoney Park La EX20...170 A4
Stoneywell **8** EX39......15 B1
Stoning Cross EX20....75 C7
Stonybridge Cross EX6..30 B8
Stonybridge Hill EX6...30 B8
Stony Close La EX12..192 E5
Stony Cnr EX5........3 D3
Stony Hill Cross EX36...31 A3
Stony La
　Axminster EX13........167 E6
　Gunnislake PL18........125 D6
　Hawkridge TA22........21 E3
　Landkey EX32........17 B1
　Lympstone EX8........195 F8
　Parracombe EX31........4 D1
　Swimbridge EX32........28 B8
　Woodbury Salterton EX5..184 C6
Stony Lane End EX32...17 B1
Stonypark La EX17....165 B5
Stoodleigh Cross
　Calverleigh EX16........48 B4
　West Buckland EX32...18 B2
Stoodleigh Moor Cross
　EX16........48 D6
Stoodley Knowle Convent
　Sch TQ1........220 F6
Stookes Cl EX15........83 C1
Stooks Ct EX5........81 E1
Stoop EX39........23 D3
Stoop Cross TQ7........131 E1
Stooper's Hill TA20....69 F6
Stopford Pl PL1........247 F3
Stopgate Cross
　Yarcombe EX14........68 F4
　Zeal Monachorum EX17...78 C8
Stormsdown Cotts TQ12.131 B7
Storridge La EX13........88 B6
Storrs Cl TQ13........180 C8
Stott Cl PL3........249 D5
Stour Cl PL3........249 D6
Stourscombe Wood
　PL15........105 A2
Stout Cross EX14........61 D1
Stovar Long La EX12..191 D6
Stover Ct EX4........261 C4
Stover Ctry Pk TQ12..123 B2
Stover Sch TQ12........123 B1
Stowe Gdns PL5........244 B2
Stowe La EX20........76 C4
Stowell La TQ20........88 D8
Stowford Bsns Pk EX20.237 D4
Stowford Cl PL20........127 B3

Stowford Cross
　Bradworthy EX22........53 C8
　Chittlehampton EX37....29 A5
　Cobbaton EX37........28 E5
　Halwill EX21........91 D8
　South Molton EX36........19 B2
　West Putford EX22........39 E2
Stowford Gate EX10....187 E8
Stowford Hill EX7........61 A7
Stowford Prim Sch PL21.237 E5
Stowford Rise EX10....187 F8
Straightway Head EX5 ..100 A7
Strand
　Teignmouth TQ14........210 A3
　Topsham EX3........182 F4
　Torquay TQ1........220 B4
Strand Cl EX31........16 B6
Strand Ct
　1 Bideford EX39........157 A2
　Topsham EX3........182 F4
Strand Hill EX7........204 E6
Strand La EX31........16 B6
Strand St PL1........254 A8
Strand The
　Barnstaple EX32........154 F5
　Bideford EX39........157 A2
　3 Brixham TQ5........230 D5
　Culmstock EX15........66 E8
　Dawlish EX7........204 E6
　Exmouth EX8........202 A6
　Ilfracombe EX34........150 C6
　Lympstone EX8........195 D5
　Shaldon TQ14........209 C5
　Starcross EX6........201 B7
　Topsham EX3........182 F4
Strand View EX3........182 F4
Strashleigh View PL21...136 D6
Stratford Ave EX4........178 C8
Strathculm Rd EX5........82 B5
Strathmore Ct EX39........25 E4
Stratton Wlk PL2........248 D8
Strawberry Ave EX2....181 C8
Strawberry Fields EX20...77 C4
Strawberry Hill EX8....195 F6
Strawberry La EX7....204 C3
Strawberry Terr TQ12..207 E8
Straypark Cnr EX35........5 E4
Stray Pk PL8........251 F4
Streamcombe La TA22...33 B5
Stream Ct EX2........261 A1
Streamers Mdws EX14..166 C5
Streams La EX31........9 B2
Stream The EX7........177 B8
Streatham Dr EX4........177 B8
Streatham Rise EX4....177 A8
Street Ash La TA20....69 F8
Street The
　Kilmington EX13........87 C1
　Musbury EX13........103 D5
Strete Gate Woodland Walk
　TQ6........145 E4
Strete Raleigh EX5....168 A8
Strode Rd
　Buckfastleigh TQ11....236 B4
　Plymouth PL7........250 F6
Stroma Cl PL6........244 F7
Strong Hill Cross EX21...73 F1
Stroud Park Rd PL2....248 C2
Stroxworthy Cross EX39..39 C4
Stuart Cres EX15........163 A8
Stuart Ct EX7........204 D4
Stuart Rd
　Exeter EX1........177 F6
　Plymouth, Pennycomequick
　　PL3........262 A4
Stuart Road Prim Sch
　PL1........262 A4
Stubbing Cross EX24...102 C5
Stubbins Cross TQ12...201 D2
Stubborn Cross EX16....62 C7
Stuckeridge Cross EX16..48 D8
Stucley Rd EX39........156 E1
Studd Dr EX32........209 A8
Studhayes Cross EX13...87 C1
Studhayes La EX13........87 B2
Studhayes Rd EX13........87 B2
Studley Ho **4** EX14....166 C5
Studley Rd TQ1........220 A7
Stumpy Cross
　Shobrooke EX17........80 F4
　Silverton EX5........82 B4
Stumpypost Cross TQ7..144 B6
Sturcombe Ave TQ4...225 E3
Sturdee Rd PL2........248 A5
Sturges Rd EX8........202 D8
Sturt Cotts EX17........78 E7
Sturtlebury La TA20...143 F5
Style Cl EX32........155 B2
Suddon's Cross EX14...102 B6
Suddon's La EX24........102 B6
Sugar Mill Bsns Pk PL9.249 C1
Sullivan Rd EX2........178 C5
Summer Cl
　Exeter EX4........178 B8
　Exmouth EX8........202 E8
　13 Hemyock EX15........67 B8
Summercourt Way TQ5..230 A2
Summerfield
　Sidmouth EX10........188 B8
　Woodbury EX5........184 C4
Summer Field EX15......99 C5
Summerfield Ave TA21...52 D8
Summerfield Cl
　Ivybridge PL21........237 A5
　Paignton TQ4........225 E3
Summerfield Rd TQ2...219 D8
Summerfields PL12....242 D1

Summerfield Way TA21...52 D8
Summerhayes EX7........204 D4
Summerhill Cl **18** TQ12...122 F1
Summerhill Cres 17
　TQ12........122 F1
Summerhill Cross TQ13.130 F4
Summerhill Ho TQ7....260 C4
Summerhill Rd
　16 Coldeast TQ12........122 F1
　Lyme Regis D17........260 C4
Summer La
　Alfington EX11........100 F8
　Bovey Tracey TQ13....123 C2
　Brixham TQ5........230 B2
　Exeter EX4........174 B1
　Exmouth EX8........96 B4
　Northlew EX20........74 F2
Summerland EX14........166 C5
Summerland Ave EX7...204 D7
Summerland Cl EX7....204 D6
Summerland Cotts
　Alfington EX11........100 F8
　5 Newton Abbot TQ12...207 C3
Summerland Ct **8** TQ12.207 C3
Summerland Pl **6** EX32.155 A4
Summerlands TQ12....123 A1
Summerlands Cl
　Brixham TQ5........230 A2
　Plymouth PL7........251 C5
Summerlands Ct
　Brixham TQ5........230 A2
　18 Coldeast TQ12........122 F1
　Exeter EX1........261 C3
Summerlands Gdns PL7.251 C5
Summerland St
　Barnstaple EX32........155 A5
　Exeter EX1........261 C3
Summermoor La EX37....28 E6
Summersby Cl EX12....192 A6
Summers Moor Cross
　EX19........58 F1
Summerville Cross EX39 .37 F6
Summerway EX4........178 C8
Summerwell La EX16....62 D4
Sumner Well La EX34.....9 A5
Sumner Rd **7** PL21....137 C7
Sunbury Rd TQ4........226 B5
Sunbury Terr **4** TQ4...220 A6
Suncrest Cl TQ2........213 F3
Sun Ct **9** TQ12........207 B3
Sunderland Cl PL9....255 A6
Sunflower Rd EX32....155 A5
Sunhill Ave PL3........182 F6
Sunhill La PL3........182 F6
Sunleigh TQ2........220 B4
Sunningbrook Rd EX16.161 E5
Sunningdale EX39....157 A3
Sunningdale Rd PL12...242 C2
Sunnybank
　Kenton EX6........194 E3
　Newton Abbot TQ12...207 B5
Sunny Bank EX32........155 B4
Sunny Cl **1** EX16........207 F3
Sunny Ct **11** EX16....161 D4
Sunnydale
　Beesands TQ7........149 E8
　13 Bittaford PL21....137 C8
Sunny Dene PL5........243 D1
Sunny Gdns TQ1........220 A6
Sunny Hill
　Ottery St Mary EX11...169 E4
　Torquay TQ1........220 C5
Sunnyhill Mews TQ1...220 C5
Sunny Hollow TQ12....211 D8
Sunnylands Cross EX13 ..87 A2
Sunnylands Way EX7...210 F8
Sunnymead EX17........79 B5
Sunnymead Terr **8** TQ9.223 C5
Sunnymoor Cl EX11...174 F7
Sunnyside
　Awliscombe EX14........85 C4
　9 Bideford EX39........157 B1
　3 Braunton EX33....152 D5
　Burlescombe EX16.....51 C2
　Combe Martin EX34........3 A3
　Cullompton EX15........163 C2
　St Giles in t W EX38....42 B5
　Thurlestone TQ7........143 C1
　Woolfardisworthy EX39...38 F8
Sunnyside Cotts **18** EX34..3 A3
Sunnyside Rd
　Kingskerswell TQ12...213 A4
　Plymouth PL4........249 B2
　Woolacombe EX34........7 F6
Sunnyside Terr EX35...151 B5
Sunny View EX19........58 F3
Sun Ray EX34........2 A2
Sunset Nb EX12........192 A4
Sunset Hts EX32........155 A5
Sun Valley Cl TQ5....230 C5
Sunway Cl PL19........171 A6
Sunwell La PL11........252 A8
Sunwine Pl EX8........202 B6
Surbiton Cres EX4........176 F4
Surf Bay Cvn Pk EX39...156 D8
Sussex Cl
　Exeter EX4........176 E4
　Torquay TQ2........214 A3
Sussex Pl PL1........262 C2
Sussex Rd PL2........247 F5
Sussex St PL1........262 C2
Sussex Terr **5** PL2....247 F5
Sutcliffe Cl TQ9........222 F7

Sutcombe Com Prim Sch
 EX22. . . . . .54 A6
Sutherland Cl TQ12 . . . . .212 F8
Sutherland Dr TQ2 . . . . . .214 B2
Sutherland Rd
 Plymouth PL4. . . . . .263 A4
 Torquay TQ1. . . . . .220 C5
Sutton Cl
 Dawlish EX7. . . . . .204 D7
 Torquay TQ2. . . . . .213 F4
Sutton Cross
 Moretonhampstead
 TQ13. . . . . .111 E5
 Thurlestone TQ7 . . . . . . .143 D1
Sutton Ct PL1 . . . . .247 F1
Sutton Mews 22 PL4 . . . . .263 A2
Sutton Pl PL4. . . . . .263 B2
Sutton Rd PL4. . . . . .263 B2
Suttons Cross EX14. . . . . . .86 D1
Sutton Wharf PL4. . . . . . . .263 A2
Swaddicott Cross EX21. . . . .56 C2
Swain Cl EX13. . . . . .167 D4
Swaindale Rd 3 PL3. . . . . .248 E6
Swains TA21. . . . . .160 D4
Swains Ct EX3. . . . . .182 E5
Swains La EX21. . . . . .160 D4
Swains Rd EX9 . . . . .198 B1
Swale Cl
 Plymouth PL3. . . . . .249 B6
 Torquay TQ2. . . . . .214 A3
Swallerton Gate TQ13 . . .121 D6
Swallow Cl EX32. . . . . . . .155 E4
Swallow Ct
 Exeter EX4. . . . . .176 F8
 Sampford Peverell EX16 . . . .50 F1
 Seaton EX12 . . . . .192 C4
Swallow Dr EX2 . . . . .176 D3
Swallow Field EX31. . . . . .154 A2
Swallowfield Rd EX2. . . . .178 B2
Swallowfield Rise TQ2 . . .213 C2
Swallowfields TQ9 . . . . . .223 B7
Swallows Acre EX7. . . . . .204 E7
Swallows End PL9 . . . . . . .255 E8
Swallowtree Cross EX6.. . . .96 C7
Swallow Units EX2. . . . . . .177 D1
Swallow Way EX15. . . . . .163 B2
Swanaford Rd EX6. . . . . . .112 F7
Swan Ave 1 EX16 . . . . . .161 E6
Swanborough Rd TQ12. . .208 A2
Swan Cl PL10. . . . . .253 A6
Swan Ct
 Dartmouth TQ6 . . . . .233 E3
 Exeter EX2. . . . . .261 B1
Swan Gdns PL7. . . . . .250 F5
Swan Hill Rd EX24 . . . . . .103 A3
Swan Maisonettes 10
 EX2. . . . . .177 A5
Swannaton La
 Crediton EX17. . . . . .79 E8
 Morchard Bishop EX17 . . . .61 E1
Swanpool Wlk TQ6 . . . . . .233 F1
Swannywell Hill EX17 . . . . .78 F8
Swan Rd EX6. . . . . .201 A8
Swanswood Gdns EX39 . .156 C6
Swan Units EX2. . . . . .178 E5
Swan Yd
 Exeter EX4. . . . . .177 A5
 12 Honiton EX14. . . . . . .166 C6
Swaynes Mews TQ1. . . . . .220 C6
Swedwell La TQ2. . . . . . . .214 A4
Swedwell Rd TQ2. . . . . . . .214 A4
Sweetbriar Cl EX7 . . . . . .204 C3
Sweetbriar La EX7. . . . . . .204 C3
Sweetbriar La EX11. . . . . .178 B6
Swiddacombe La EX36. . . . .32 C7
Swift Gdns PL5 . . . . .244 C2
Swift Ind Est TQ12 . . . . . .207 D6
Swimbridge CE Prim Sch
 EX32. . . . . .17 D1
Swinburne Gdns PL5. . . . .244 C1
Swincombe Dr TQ3 . . . . . .225 F6
Swincombe La EX31 . . . . . .11 F4
Swingate Cross EX22 . . . . .90 B8
Swing Gate EX6 . . . . .194 A4
Swing Gate Cross EX37 . . .29 A2
Swiss Cl EX8 . . . . .196 B3
Sycamore Ave
 Dawlish Warren EX7 . . . . .201 A2
 Plymouth PL4. . . . . .263 C2
 Tavistock PL19. . . . . .171 C2
Sycamore Cl
 Broadclyst EX5 . . . . .175 D6
 Exeter EX1. . . . . .178 E5
 Exmouth EX8 . . . . .196 E2
 Exmouth EX8 . . . . .196 F2
 Honiton EX14. . . . . .166 A4
 13 Instow EX39. . . . . .15 B1
 Paignton TQ4 . . . . .229 D7
 Willand EX15. . . . . .162 C4
Sycamore Dr
 Plymouth PL6. . . . . .245 C7
 Torpoint PL11 . . . . .247 A3
Sycamore Rd
 Saltash PL12 . . . . .242 B3
 Tiverton EX16 . . . . .161 E5
Sycamore Way
 Brixham TQ5 . . . . .230 A2
 6 Chudleigh TQ13 . . . . . .123 E6
 Plymouth PL6. . . . . .245 E6
Sydenham TQ1 . . . . .220 D4
Sydenham Cross PL19. . . .116 A2
Sydenham Ho EX4 . . . .-
Sydenham La EX16. . . . . . .47 E6
Sydney Cl PL7 . . . . .250 E4
Sydney Rd
 Exeter EX2. . . . . .177 A4
 Torpoint PL11 . . . . .247 B3
Sydney St PL1 . . . . .262 B4

Sylvan Ave EX4 . . . . .173 D1
Sylvan Cl EX8. . . . . .196 A2
Sylvan Ct
 Exmouth EX8 . . . . .196 A2
 Plymouth PL1. . . . . .248 A3
Sylvania Dr EX4 . . . . .173 E2
Sylvan Rd
 Exeter EX4. . . . . .173 D1
 Wellington TA21. . . . . . . .160 E5
Symons Rd PL1 . . . . .242 F2
Synagogue Pl EX4 . . . . . . .261 A3
Syncock's Cross EX39. . . .157 F3

T

Tabernacle Ct 8 EX1 . . . . .261 A2
Tackbear Rd EX22, EX23 . .70 D4
Tacket Ct TQ7. . . . . .258 C4
Taddiford Rd EX4 . . . . .177 A7
Taddiport EX38 . . . . .159 B4
Taddiforde Court Mans
 EX4. . . . . .177 A8
Taddyforde Ct EX4 . . . . . .177 A8
Taddyforde Est EX4 . . . . . .177 A8
Tadworthy Rd EX39 . . . . .156 E7
Tail Cnr EX17. . . . . .79 D7
Tailyour Rd PL6. . . . . .244 F2
Talbot Gdns PL5 . . . . .247 D7
Talbot Rd DT7 . . . . .260 D5
Tale Common Head Cross
 EX14. . . . . .84 B4
Taleford Cl EX11 . . . . .169 C7
Taleford Villas EX11. . . . . .169 C7
Talewater Cross EX5 . . . . . .84 C2
Tallow Wood Cl TQ13 . . . .225 E6
Tamar Ave
 Plymouth PL2. . . . . .247 E5
 Tavistock PL19. . . . . .171 D5
 Torquay TQ2. . . . . .219 B7
Tamar Bridge PL5 . . . . . . .243 A2
Tamar Bsns Units EX22. . .164 C6
Tamar Cl PL20. . . . . .125 E1
Tamar Cotts PL19 . . . . . . .116 A1
Tamar Ho PL1. . . . . .247 E1
Tamarind EX15. . . . . .162 C4
Tamarisk Cl EX4 . . . . .174 B2
Tamar Rd EX31 . . . . .15 E5
Tamar Science Pk PL6 . . .245 C4
Tamar's Dr EX15. . . . . . . .162 C4
Tamarside Com Coll PL5 .243 E1
Tamar St
 Plymouth PL1. . . . . .247 E3
 Saltash PL12 . . . . .243 A2
 Torpoint PL11 . . . . .247 C3
Tamar Terr
 Calstock PL17 . . . . .125 D3
 Horsebridge PL19 . . . . . .116 A1
 Saltash PL12 . . . . .243 A2
Tamar Valley Donkey Pk
 PL18. . . . . .125 A5
Tamar View
 Milton Abbot PL19. . . . . .116 A6
 St Dominick PL12. . . . . . .125 A2
Tamar View Ind Est
 PL12. . . . . .242 D5
Tamar Villas PL9 . . . . .255 D7
Tamar Way PL18. . . . . . . .125 D6
Tamar Wharf PL1. . . . . . . .247 D3
Tamerton Ave PL5. . . . . . .244 A6
Tamerton Cl PL5. . . . . .244 A6
Tamerton Foliot Rd PL6. .244 D5
Tamerton Rd PL6. . . . . . . .241 B2
Tamerton Vale Prim Sch
 PL6. . . . . .244 C6
Tamwny Cl TQ3 . . . . .226 C8
Tangmere Ave PL5. . . . . . .243 E5
Tan La EX2 . . . . .177 F4
Tanners Cl EX15. . . . . .163 B2
Tanner's Hill TA4 . . . . .35 E7
Tanners Mews EX15. . . . . .162 E5
Tanners Rd
 Landkey EX32 . . . . .17 C2
 Paignton TQ4 . . . . .226 C4
Tannery Flats 4 EX17. . . .165 C5
Tanpits Cross TQ7. . . . . . .145 A1
Tanpits Mdw TQ7. . . . . . . .145 A1
Tanworth Ho TQ7 . . . . . . .143 A1
Tanyard La TQ12 . . . . .217 F6
Tanyards Ct 7 EX12 . . . . .192 A5
Tape La EX14 . . . . .85 B3
Tapeley Park Gdns EX39. .157 F7
Tapfield Cross TQ7. . . . . . .142 F4
Tapley Gdns TQ14 . . . . . . .209 A8
Tappers Cl EX13 . . . . .87 C5
Tappers Knapp DT7 . . . . .260 B5
Tapp's La PL8 . . . . .257 B5
Taps Cl EX6 . . . . .182 B4
Tapson Dr PL9 . . . . .255 A6
Tarbet Ave EX1 . . . . .177 F7
Tarka Cl EX20. . . . . .170 D6
Tarn Wearfield Flats
 EX10. . . . . .188 B3
Tarraway Rd TQ3 . . . . .219 D1
Tarr Post TA22. . . . . .21 C1
Tarr's Ave TQ12. . . . . .207 E7
Tarrs End TQ12. . . . . .207 E7
Tarrs La TQ12. . . . . .207 E7
Tarr Steps TA22. . . . . .21 A3
Tatworth Prim Sch TA20. . .88 C8
Tatworth St TA20. . . . . .88 C8
Taunton Ave PL5. . . . . . . .244 B5
Taunton Cl EX2 . . . . .177 A3
Taunton Cross EX13. . . . . .87 A1
Taunton Ct 2 TQ9 . . . . . . .223 D5
Taunton Pl PL5. . . . . .244 B5
Taunton Rd TA21. . . . . . . .160 E7
Tavern Gdns EX39. . . . . . . .26 B1

Tavern Mews EX38. . . . . . .159 D5
Tavis Rd PL3. . . . . .225 F8
Tavistock Coll PL19 . . . . . .171 A3
Tavistock Com Prim Sch
 PL19. . . . . .171 B4
Tavistock Cross PL20. . . . .125 F2
Tavistock Hospl PL19 . . . .171 B5
Tavistock Mus PL19 . . . . .171 C6
Tavistock Pl
 Paignton TQ4 . . . . .229 B8
 Plymouth PL4. . . . . .263 A3
Tavistock Rd
 Exeter EX4. . . . . .177 A7
 Launceston PL15 . . . . . . .105 A2
 Okehampton EX20. . . . . . .93 E4
 Plymouth, Manadon PL5 .244 E1
 Plymouth PL6. . . . . .245 B5
 Princetown PL20. . . . . . . .128 A8
 Yelverton PL20. . . . . .126 F3
Tavy Ave TQ2 . . . . .219 B8
Tavy Pl PL4. . . . . .248 F4
Tavy Rd
 Saltash PL12 . . . . .243 A3
 Tavistock PL19. . . . . .171 D5
Taw Bridge Cross EX20. . . .77 B4
Taw Cl PL3 . . . . .249 D6
Taw Cres EX31. . . . . .15 B5
Taw Ct 10 EX32 . . . . .155 A4
Tawgreen Cross EX18. . . . .59 C1
Taw Green Cross EX20. . . .95 B7
Tawgreen La EX18 . . . . . . .59 C1
Tawgreen Rd EX20. . . . . . .59 C1
Taw Meadow Cres EX31 . .153 F6
Taw Mills Bsns Pk EX32 . .155 C4
Taw Mills La EX18 . . . . . . .59 C1
Tawmoor Cross EX20. . . . .95 C7
Taw Rd EX31. . . . . .15 E5
Tawton La EX20. . . . . .95 B4
Taw Trade Pk EX31. . . . . .154 E6
Taw Vale EX32 . . . . .154 F4
Taw Vale Ave EX20 . . . . . . .77 B4
Taw Vale Cl EX20. . . . . .77 B4
Taw View
 1 Bishop's Tawton EX32 . .16 E1
 Fremington EX31. . . . . . .153 F6
 Umberleigh EX37. . . . . . . .28 D3
Tay Gdns PL3 . . . . .249 D7
Taylor Cl
 Dawlish EX7. . . . . .204 D5
 Ottery St Mary EX11. . . . .169 B4
 Saltash PL12 . . . . .242 C3
Taylor Rd PL12 . . . . .242 C4
Taylor's Cross EX17. . . . . . .62 B1
Taylors Ct EX16. . . . . .161 E7
Taylors Field EX20 . . . . . . .77 C4
Taylor's Hill EX16, EX17 . . .62 E4
Taylor's La EX37 . . . . .43 D6
Taylors Newtake 2
 TQ12. . . . . .122 F1
Taylor Sq PL19. . . . . .171 B6
TDC Units EX22. . . . . .164 C6
Teachers Cl PL9 . . . . .255 F6
Teal Cl TQ2. . . . . .213 C2
Teats Hill Flats PL4 . . . . . .263 B1
Teats Hill Rd PL4 . . . . .263 B1
Teazle Ct EX2. . . . . .261 A2
Tedburn Rd EX4 . . . . .176 B5
Tedburn St Mary Sch EX6 .97 F5
Tedburrow La EX15 . . . . . . .67 A8
Tedders Cl 3 EX15 . . . . . . .67 B8
Tedstone Ho EX8 . . . . .196 A6
Tedstone La EX8 . . . . .196 A7
Teeds The EX5. . . . . .184 B2
Tees Cl PL3. . . . . .249 C7
Teignbridge Bsns Ctr
 TQ12. . . . . .180 F3
Teign Cl TQ14. . . . . .208 E8
Teigncombe EX6 . . . . .113 B4
Teign Ct
 Bishopsteignton TQ14 . . .209 A8
 Stokeinteignhead TQ12. . .209 B1
Teignharvey Rd TQ12. . . . .209 A3
Teignholt Cross EX6 . . . . . .96 D7
Teign La
 Chudleigh TQ13 . . . . .123 D7
 Trusham TQ13 . . . . .113 D1
Teignmouth Com Coll
 TQ14 . . . . .210 B5
Teignmouth Hill EX7. . . . .204 E5
Teignmouth Hospl TQ14 .210 A5
Teignmouth Mus TQ14 . . .210 C4
Teignmouth Rd
 Bishopsteignton TQ14. . . .209 B7
 Holcombe EX7, TQ14 . . . .210 E7
 Kingsteignton TQ12, TQ14 .208 B6
 Maidencombe TQ1 . . . . . .214 C6
 Shaldon TQ1, TQ14. . . . . .210 A1
 Torquay TQ1. . . . . .220 A8
Teignmouth Sta TQ14 . . .210 C5
Teign Rd
 Newton Abbot TQ12. . . . .207 D4
 Plymouth PL3. . . . . .249 B6
 Teignmouth TQ14 . . . . . .207 D8
Teign St TQ14 . . . . .210 C4
Teign Terr EX6. . . . . .113 B5
Teign View TQ13 . . . . .123 C4
Teign View Pl 14 TQ14. . .210 B4
Teignview Rd TQ14. . . . . . .208 F8
Teign Village TQ13 . . . . . .123 B7
Tekoa Units EX2 . . . . .177 C1
Telegraph Cross EX21. . . .136 D4
Telegraph Hill EX6. . . . . . .114 D2
Telegraph La EX5, EX11. .168 B6
Telegraph View TQ12. . . . .180 B1
Telegraph Wharf PL1 . . . .254 A8
Telford Cres PL5 . . . . .243 F2
Telford Rd EX4 . . . . .177 A7
Temeraire Rd PL5. . . . . . . .244 D2

Temperance Pl 6 TQ5. . . .230 D5
Temperance St TQ2. . . . . .220 A5
Templar Way TQ14 . . . . . .123 C1
Temple Cres EX16 . . . . . . .161 F4
Temple Gdns EX10. . . . . . .188 B5
Temple Mews EX10 . . . . . .188 B5
Temple Rd EX2 . . . . .261 B2
Templer Rd TQ3 . . . . .219 A3
Templers Rd TQ12 . . . . . . .207 D4
Temple's Way 11 TQ12 . . .123 E1
Temple's Wy 5 EX10 . . . . .188 B5
Templeton Cross EX16 . . . .48 A1
Templeton La EX16 . . . . . . .47 F1
Templetown EX8 . . . . .201 F6
Tenacott Hts EX39 . . . . . . .26 A4
Ten Acre Gate EX13 . . . . . .87 E7
Tenby Rd PL5. . . . . .243 C1
Tencery Orch EX14. . . . . . .67 C2
Tenerife TQ1. . . . . .220 C5
Tennacott La EX39. . . . . . . .26 B4
Tennyson Ave EX2 . . . . . . .177 F3
Tennyson Cl TQ1. . . . . .220 A8
Tennyson Gdns PL5 . . . . . .244 B1
Tennyson Way EX8. . . . . . .196 C4
Tern Gdns PL7. . . . . .250 F5
Terrace The
 Braunton EX33. . . . . .152 D6
 Harrowbarrow PL17 . . . . .125 A5
 Loddiswell TQ7. . . . . .143 E7
 Torquay TQ1. . . . . .220 B4
Terra Nova Gn PL2. . . . . . .248 A8
Terris Cross EX20 . . . . .76 A6
Tewkesbury Cl PL2. . . . . . .248 A8
Tews La
 Barnstaple, Bickington
 EX31. . . . . .154 A3
 Barnstaple, Roundswell
 EX31. . . . . .154 A2
Tewsley Cl EX31 . . . . .154 A3
Thackeray Gdns PL5 . . . . .244 B1
Thackeray Rd EX4 . . . . . . .178 C8
Thames Gdns PL3 . . . . . . .249 D5
Thanckes Cl PL11 . . . . . . .247 A3
Thanckes Dr PL11 . . . . . . .247 A4
Thatcher Ave TQ1. . . . . . . .221 A3
Thatcher Dr TQ12 . . . . . . .210 C8
Thatcher Hts TQ1. . . . . . . .220 F3
Thatcher's La EX5 . . . . .81 E6
Thatcher's Lane End EX5. . .81 E5
Thatches The PL21. . . . . . .137 C2
Theatre La 18 EX31 . . . . . .154 F5
Theatre Ope PL1 . . . . .247 F1
Theatre Royal Plymouth
 PL1. . . . . .262 C2
Thelbridge Cross EX17. . . .61 D6
Thelbridge Hill EX17 . . . . .61 C7
Therlow Rd PL3 . . . . .249 B6
Thetford Gdns PL6. . . . . . .249 D8
Third Ave
 Dawlish EX7. . . . . .204 D7
 Exeter, Countess Wear
 EX2. . . . . .182 C7
 Exeter, Heavitree EX1. . . .177 F6
 Plymouth, Billacombe PL9 .256 A6
 Plymouth, Camels Head
 PL2. . . . . .247 E7
 Plymouth, Stoke PL1 . . . .248 A2
 Teignmouth TQ14. . . . . . .210 A5
 Torquay TQ1. . . . . .220 A8
Third Dr TQ14 . . . . .210 B5
Thirlmere Gdns PL6. . . . . .244 F4
Thistle Cl PL6 . . . . .245 E7
Thomas Bassett Dr EX24 .103 A3
Thomas Cl EX8 . . . . .196 C4
Thomas La EX4 . . . . .177 A8
Thomas Newcomen Ct
 TQ6. . . . . .233 C3
Thomas's Cross EX6 . . . . .112 F8
Thompson Rd EX1 . . . . . . .178 A7
Thornberry Ave EX1. . . . . .177 B6
Thornbury Cross
 Sampford Courtenay EX20 . .76 E4
 Thornbury EX22 . . . . .55 A3
Thornbury Mill EX22. . . . . .55 A4
Thornbury Park Ave PL3 .248 D6
Thornbury Prim Sch
 PL6. . . . . .245 D4
Thornbury Rd PL6. . . . . . .245 E4
Thorn Cl
 Exeter EX1. . . . . .178 B6
 Newton Abbot TQ12. . . . .206 E4
Thorncliff Cl TQ1 . . . . .220 D5
Thorn Cnr EX18. . . . . .77 E8
Thorn Cotts
 Combeinteignhead TQ12 .208 E3
 Woodbury EX5. . . . . .184 C3
Thorn Cross
 Bovey Tracey TQ13. . . . . .180 C5
 Chagford TQ13. . . . . .110 E5
 Slapton TQ7. . . . . .145 C6
Thorndale Cts EX4 . . . . . .176 D8
Thorndon Cross EX22 . . . . .71 E5
Thorne Cotts EX11. . . . . . .169 B3
Thorne Cross EX6. . . . . .96 E4
Thorne Farm Way EX11. . .169 C3
Thorne La
 Bow EX17. . . . . .78 D3
 Spreyton EX17. . . . . .96 B8
Thorne Moor Cross EX6. . .96 E4
Thornemoor La EX17. . . . . .78 D2
Thorne Park Rd TQ2 . . . . .219 D5
Thorne Pk EX34 . . . . .8 F5
Thornes Cross EX16. . . . . . .64 E5
Thornes Mdw EX12 . . . . . .191 D5
Thornes Terr EX36. . . . . . .158 C4
Thorney Cross EX21. . . . . . .90 E7

Sut–Tim 311

Thornfield Cl
 Exmouth EX8 . . . . .196 A2
 Seaton EX12 . . . . .192 A7
Thornham Chapel Cross
 EX17. . . . . .46 B1
Thornham La EX17. . . . . . . .46 B1
Thornhedges Cross EX17. .80 B5
Thornhedges La EX17. . . . .80 B5
Thorn Hill EX16. . . . . .63 B6
Thornhillhead EX39. . . . . . .40 B3
Thornhill Rd PL3 . . . . .248 C6
Thornhill Way PL3 . . . . . . .248 E6
Thorning St TQ8 . . . . .259 E5
Thorn La
 Membury EX13 . . . . .87 D7
 Saltash PL12. . . . . .242 C3
Thornlea Ave EX31. . . . . . .153 D5
Thornlea (Univ of Exeter)
 EX4. . . . . .261 A4
Thornley Dr TQ14 . . . . . . .210 A5
Thorn Moor Cross PL15 .105 E7
Thorn Orch TQ12 . . . . .211 E2
Thornpark Cross EX32 . . . .18 C6
Thornpark Rise EX1. . . . . .178 C6
Thorns Cross PL13. . . . . . .111 C4
Thornton Ave PL4. . . . . . . .263 B4
Thornton Cl EX39 . . . . . . .156 E2
Thornton Hill EX4 . . . . . . .261 B4
Thorntree Bsns Units
 EX8. . . . . .196 F1
Thorn Villas TQ12 . . . . . . .208 E3
Thornville Terr PL9 . . . . . .255 C7
Thornville Cl PL9 . . . . .255 C8
Thornyville Dr PL9. . . . . . .255 D8
Thornyville Villas PL9 . . . .255 D8
Thorpe Ave EX8 . . . . .196 B3
Thorverton CE Prim Sch
 EX5. . . . . .81 A4
Three Ash Cross EX14. . . . .87 A5
Three Close La EX13. . . . . . .8 E2
Three Cnrs TQ12 . . . . .207 F8
Three Corner Cross EX36. .45 C5
Three Corner Pl EX2 . . . . .181 C8
Three Corners Cross
 EX14. . . . . .85 A6
Three Crossways
 Chulmleigh EX18 . . . . .44 E1
 Zeal Monachorum EX17. . .78 A6
Three Cross Ways EX19 . . .58 D2
Three Elms Cross EX15. . . .83 D3
Three Firs EX15. . . . . .83 D4
Threefoot Stool EX6 . . . . . .98 A3
Three Gate Cross
 Cheriton Bishop EX17 . . . .97 B6
 Yeoford EX17. . . . . .79 D2
Three Gates Cross
 Dulverton TA22 . . . . .33 C6
 Huntsham EX16. . . . . .49 C6
 Yarnscombe EX31 . . . . . . .27 D1
Three Gates Hill EX16. . . . .49 C6
Three Hammers Cross
 EX17. . . . . .61 B6
Three Lane End EX22 . . . . .38 E1
Three Limbed Oak EX5. . . .81 D3
Three Mariners Cross
 EX14. . . . . .86 C6
Three Sycamores Cross
 EX24. . . . . .102 F6
Three Tree La TQ14 . . . . . .124 C2
Three Ways EX31 . . . . .18 A8
Threshers EX17. . . . . .165 A5
Threwstones Cl EX16. . . . .161 E5
Thriverton Cross EX22 . . . .39 B1
Throgmorton Ho 1 TQ9 .223 D5
Throwcombe Cross EX16. .48 A6
Throwcombe La EX16. . . . .48 A6
Thrushel Cl TQ5 . . . . .230 A2
Thuborough Cross EX22.. .54 A4
Thurlescombe Cross
 EX16. . . . . .64 E6
Thurlestone All Saints CE
 Prim Sch TQ7 . . . . .143 A2
Thurlestone Beach Ho
 TQ7 . . . . .142 F8
Thurlestone Gdns TQ6 . . .233 E3
Thurlestone Rd 3 TQ2. . . .207 B8
Thurlestone Rock TQ7 . . .147 B8
Thurlestone Wlk TQ6. . . . .249 D8
Thurlow EX17. . . . . .165 A5
Thurlow Hill TQ1. . . . . .220 A6
Thurlow Pk TQ1 . . . . .220 A6
Thurlow Rd
 Exeter EX4. . . . . .177 E7
 Torquay TQ1. . . . . .220 A6
Tichfield Gdns TQ3 . . . . . .225 F7
Tick La EX6. . . . . .113 C5
Ticklemore St TQ9 . . . . . .223 D5
Tidcombe Cl 11 EX16. . . . .64 D7
Tidcombe La EX16. . . . . . . .64 D7
Tidderson Cross EX14. . . . .47 F4
Tidderson La EX16. . . . . . . .47 F3
Tiddly Brook Rd PL19 . . . .171 E2
Tiddy Cl PL19. . . . . .171 B3
Tideford Cross TQ9 . . . . . .227 A1
Tidlake La EX36. . . . . .45 C8
Tidwell Cross EX9 . . . . . . .198 A2
Tidwell La EX9 . . . . .198 B5
Tidwell Rd EX9 . . . . .198 B4
Tiery EX14. . . . . .69 A3
Tillard Cl PL7. . . . . .251 C5
Tilly Cl PL9. . . . . .255 F4
Timber Hill DT7 . . . . .260 E6

Timbers Cl TQ11 . . . . 236 A3
Timbers Rd TQ11 . . . . 236 A3
Timber Terr TQ12 . . . . 212 F4
Timber Vale Cvn Pk DT7 . .260 E5
Times Mews 15 TQ9 . . . . . . 223 C5
Timewell Hill EX16 . . . . .34 C4
Timridge La EX4 . . . . 113 E6
Tincombe PL12 . . . . .242 C2
Tinhay Cross PL16 . . . . .105 F4
Tinhay Mill Ind Est PL16 .105 F4
Tinker's Cross EX18 . . . . .59 A5
Tinkers Wood Cl 4 TQ5 .230 C4
Tinkley La TQ13 . . . . 123 C8
Tin La PL4 . . . . 263 A2
Tinpit Hill EX5 . . . . .98 F7
Tintagel Cl
  Exeter EX4 . . . . 174 A4
  Torquay TQ2 . . . . .219 F8
Tintagel Cres PL2 . . . . .248 C8
Tintern Ave PL4 . . . . .263 C2
Tip Hill EX11 . . . . 169 D3
Tipleyhill Cross TQ12 . . . . . 122 D2
Tipleyhill La TQ12, TQ13 . 122 D2
Tippacott La EX35 . . . . 6 A4
Tipple Cross EX11 . . . . .105 B6
Tipton La EX11 . . . . .168 E6
Tipton St John CE Prim Sch
  EX10 . . . . 100 C2
Tipton Vale EX11 . . . . 100 C3
Titchen's La
  Calverleigh EX16 . . . . .48 B1
  Tiverton EX16 . . . . .63 B8
Titching Park La EX34 . . . . . . 9 B5
Titham Hill EX14 . . . . .47 C6
Tithebarn Copse EX1 . . . . . 178 F8
Tithe Barn Cross EX15 . . . . . .51 D2
Tithebarn La EX1 . . . . 179 A8
Tithe Rd PL7 . . . . .250 B7
Titterton Cross EX20 . . . . . . .77 D7
Tiverton Bsns Pk EX16 . . . . .64 B8
Tiverton Castle EX16 . . . . . . 161 C4
Tiverton Cl PL6 . . . . .245 E7
Tiverton Clock Tower
  EX16 . . . . 161 D4
Tiverton & District Hospl
  EX16 . . . . 161 C5
Tiverton High Sch EX16 . . 161 C5
Tiverton Parkway Station
  EX16 . . . . .65 E8
Tiverton Rd
  Bampton EX16 . . . . .49 B8
  Cullompton EX15 . . . . .163 B3
  Silverton EX5 . . . . .82 B6
Tiverton Way EX16 . . . . 161 F5
Tiveton Mus of Mid Devon
  Life EX16 . . . . 161 C3
Tobruk Rd PL12 . . . . .242 F4
Toby Cross PL21 . . . . 137 D6
Toby La EX5 . . . . 184 E5
Tod Moor Cross PL21 . . . . . 237 A1
Todsworthy TQ9 . . . . .222 F8
Tolcis Cross EX13 . . . . .87 D3
Tollards Rd EX2 . . . . .178 B2
Tollbar Cl PL21 . . . . .237 F5
Tollbar Cross EX31 . . . . .17 E8
Toll Bar Cross EX18 . . . . .44 E3
Tolleys EX17 . . . . 165 E5
Tollit Gdn 12 TQ9 . . . . 223 D5
Tollox Pl PL3 . . . . .249 B4
Tolman Cres EX12 . . . . 192 B6
Tombstone La EX16 . . . . .63 D8
Tomhead Cross EX4 . . . . .98 B6
Tom Maddock Gdns
  PL21 .237 E4
Tomouth Cres 14 EX39 . . . . .15 A1
Tomouth Rd EX39 . . . . .15 A1
Tomouth Sq 15 EX39 . . . . . . .15 A1
Tom Sanders Cl EX34 . . . . . . .3 A3
Tomscclose La EX18 . . . . .59 C2
Tom's La EX39 . . . . .25 B3
Tonedale Bsns Pk TA21 . . .160 B8
Tonedale Ind Est TA21 . . .160 B8
Tone Hill TA21 . . . . .160 B8
Tongue End Cross EX20 . . . .94 E5
Tongue Gate EX36 . . . . .45 E7
Tongue La EX17 . . . . .45 E7
Tongue Lake La EX37 . . . . . . .44 E5
Tonyfield Wood Cross
  EX17 . . . . .60 B4
Top Cliff TQ14 . . . . .209 D5
Topcliff Rd TQ14 . . . . .209 D5
Top Of The Town Ctyd
  PL12 .242 F2
Topsham Mus EX3 . . . . 182 F4
Topsham Rd EX2 . . . . 178 A1
Topsham Sch The EX3 . . . . 182 E5
Topsham Sta EX3 . . . . 182 E5
Torbay Cl TQ5 . . . . 230 E5
Torbay Hospl TQ2 . . . . 219 D8
Torbay Hospl Annexe
  TQ2 . . . . 213 D1
Torbay Rd
  Paignton TQ4 . . . . .226 C6
  Torquay TQ2 . . . . .219 F3
Torbay Trad Est TQ5 . . . . . .230 C7
Torbridge Cl PL12 . . . . .242 D2
Torbridge Rd
  7 Horrabridge PL20 . . . .126 F4
  Plymouth PL7 . . . . .250 E6
Torbryan Cl PL6 . . . . .249 E6
Torbryan Hill TQ12 . . . . 211 A3
Torches Cnr EX19 . . . . .42 D1
Tor Church Rd TQ2 . . . . 220 A5

Tor Cl
  Exeter EX4 . . . . 174 A1
  Paignton TQ4 . . . . .229 B7
  Plymouth, Hartley PL3 . . .248 E7
Tor Cres PL3 . . . . 248 E7
Tor Dale Rd 3 TQ1 . . . . 220 A6
Tor Down EX20 . . . . .94 D5
Tordown Farm Nature Trail
  EX32 . . . . .17 F2
Tordown Gn EX32 . . . . .17 F2
Tor Gdns TQ12 . . . . .206 D1
Tor Haven TQ2 . . . . .220 B4
Tor Hill Rd TQ2 . . . . 220 A5
Tor La PL12 . . . . 242 B1
Torland Rd PL3 . . . . .248 E7
Torlands Ct PL20 . . . . .126 E2
Tor Lane End TQ9 . . . . 144 C7
Tor Mare Ct TQ2 . . . . .219 E4
Toronto Ho EX4 . . . . 177 E8
Toronto Rd EX4 . . . . 261 C4
Tor Park Rd
  Paignton TQ4 . . . . .225 D3
  Torquay TQ2 . . . . .219 F6
Torpeek Cross TQ9 . . . . 137 C7
Torpoint Com Sch PL11 . .247 A4
Torpoint Inf Sch PL11 . . . .247 B3
Torquay Boys' Grammar Sch
  TQ2 . . . . 219 F8
Torquay Com Coll TQ2 . . .219 F8
Torquay Grammar Sch for
  Girls TQ1 . . . . 219 D7
Torquay Mus TQ1 . . . . 220 C4
Torquay Rd
  Kingskerswell TQ12 . . . . . 213 A3
  Newton Abbot, Milber
    TQ12 . . . . 212 E8
  Newton Abbot TQ12 . . . . .207 C3
  Paignton TQ3 . . . . .226 C6
  Teignmouth TQ14 . . . . . . .210 A3
  Torquay TQ2 . . . . .219 F4
Torr Bridge Pk PL8 . . . . .136 A2
Tor Rd PL3 . . . . 248 E7
Torre Abbey TQ2 . . . . .219 F4
Torre CE Prim Sch TQ1 . .219 E7
Torre Cl PL21 . . . . .237 F5
Torr Cross TQ2 . . . . .219 E6
Torr Farm Cotts PL8 . . . . . . 136 A2
Torr Hill PL8 . . . . 257 F4
Torridge Ave TQ2 . . . . .219 B7
Torridge Cl
  12 Bideford EX39 . . . . . . .157 B1
  Plymouth PL7 . . . . .251 A6
Torridge Hill EX39 . . . . 157 A1
Torridge Ho 18 EX39 . . . . .157 A1
Torridge Mount EX39 . . . . . 157 B1
Torridge Pl 11 EX39 . . . . . .157 B1
Torridge Rd
  Appledore EX39 . . . . .15 A1
  Braunton EX31 . . . . .15 E5
  Plymouth PL7 . . . . .250 F6
Torridge St EX39 . . . . .157 B1
Torridge View EX38 . . . . 159 B5
Torridge View Bglws
  EX38 .159 B5
Torridge Way
  Holsworthy EX22 . . . . 164 C6
  Plymouth PL3 . . . . .249 C5
Torrington 1646 EX38 . . . . 159 C4
Torrington Cottage Hospl
  EX38 .159 D5
Torrington Cross EX37 . . . . . .29 C4
Torrington Heritage Mus
  EX38 .159 C5
Torrington La EX39 . . . . 157 B1
Torrington Pl EX6 . . . . .194 D3
Torrington Rd EX19 . . . . .58 E3
Torrington St 10 EX39 . . . .157 B1
Torr La
  East Allington TQ9 . . . . . . .144 B7
  Plymouth PL3 . . . . .248 E7
  Yealmpton PL8 . . . . .136 A2
Tor Royal La PL20 . . . . .128 B8
Tor Rd PL3 . . . . 248 E7
Torrs Pk EX34 . . . . .150 A5
Torrs Walk Ave EX34 . . . . . .150 A6
Tor View Ave PL3 . . . . 248 D7
Tor Sands 1 TQ4 . . . . .226 B5
Tors Pk EX35 . . . . .151 D5
Tor Square Ho 6 TQ2 . . . .219 F6
Tors Rd
  Lynmouth EX35 . . . . .151 D5
  Okehampton EX20 . . . . 170 B3
Tors The TQ12 . . . . .212 F4
Tors View EX16 . . . . .63 B8
Tor Vale TQ1 . . . . 219 F6
Torver Cl PL6 . . . . .245 D2
Tor View
  Buckfastleigh TQ11 . . . . . .236 A4
  8 Horrabridge PL20 . . . .126 F4
  Princetown PL20 . . . . 119 A1
Tor View Ave TQ12 . . . . .207 F2
Torview Flats 6 PL3 . . . . . .180 D8
Tor View Gdns TQ3 . . . . . . .226 A6
Torwood Cl TQ1 . . . . 220 C5
Torwood Ct TQ1 . . . . 220 C5
Torwood Gables TQ1 . . . . . 220 C3
Torwood Gardens Rd
  TQ1 . . . . 220 C4
Torwood Ho 4 TQ1 . . . . . . 220 A4
Torwood Mount 6 TQ1 . . .220 C4
Torwood St TQ1 . . . . 220 C4
Tory Brook Ave PL7 . . . . . . .250 E6
Tory Brook Ct PL7 . . . . 250 E6
Tory Way PL7 . . . . 250 D6
Tosberry Cross EX39 . . . . .37 E8
Tothill Ave PL4 . . . . .263 B3
Tothill Rd 2 TQ14 . . . . 210 A3

Tothill Rd PL4 . . . . .263 B3
Totnes Castle TQ9 . . . . 223 B6
Totnes Cl PL7 . . . . .251 A4
Totnes Com Hospl TQ9 . . .223 C6
Totnes Cross TQ9 . . . . 139 C3
Totnes Down Hill TQ9 . . . .223 D3
Totnes (Littlehempston) Sta
  TQ9 . . . . 223 C7
Totnes Mus TQ9 . . . . 223 C5
Totnes Rd
  Buckfastleigh TQ11 . . . . . .236 D5
  Ipplepen TQ12 . . . . .211 F5
  Marldon TQ3 . . . . .218 C1
  Paignton TQ3, TQ4 . . . . . . .225 F5
  10 South Brent TQ10 . . .134 F3
  Strete TQ6 . . . . 145 F5
  Torquay TQ2 . . . . .219 C4
Totnes Sta TQ9 . . . . 223 C6
Tottons Ct EX2 . . . . .181 A8
Touts Cl EX36 . . . . .158 D4
Tower La EX19 . . . . .42 D2
Tower Cross EX14 . . . . .86 A3
Tower Ct
  Dunchideock EX6 . . . . 114 A5
  Saltash PL12 . . . . .242 C2
Towerfield EX3 . . . . .182 E7
Towerfield Dr PL6 . . . . .245 C8
Tower Gdns EX17 . . . . 165 C6
Tower Hill
  Cheriton Fitzpaine EX17 . . .62 E1
  Holcombe Rogus TA21 . . . .50 D5
Tower Hill Cross EX17 . . . . . .62 E1
Tower Hill Rd PL15 . . . . .90 D1
Tower House Sch TQ4 . . . .226 B5
Tower La 2 EX21 . . . . .137 C8
Tower Moor EX37 . . . . .28 F6
Tower Pk EX36 . . . . .158 C3
Tower Rd
  Honiton EX14 . . . . .166 F4
  Offwell EX14 . . . . .86 A3
  Paignton TQ4 . . . . .226 B6
Towers Cl PL6 . . . . .245 F2
Tower St
  5 Bideford EX39 . . . . .157 A1
  13 Exmouth EX8 . . . . .202 A6
  Northam EX39 . . . . .156 F7
Tower View
  Broadclyst EX5 . . . . 175 C5
  Saltash PL12 . . . . .242 D1
Tower Way EX14 . . . . .67 B1
Tower Wlk EX2 . . . . .181 C8
Town Cl EX13 . . . . .87 A3
Town Ct EX13 . . . . .87 A3
Town End Cross EX20 . . . . . . .76 C5
Town Farm Bldgs EX14 . . . . .85 B1
Town Farm Cl
  6 Honiton EX14 . . . . .166 B6
  6 Horrabridge PL20 . . . .126 F4
Town Farm Cotts TQ9 . . . .139 C1
Town Farm Ct
  Braunton EX33 . . . . 152 C6
  Ideford TQ13 . . . . .124 B4
  Shirwell EX31 . . . . .17 B8
Town Farm La TQ13 . . . . 124 B4
Townfield EX6 . . . . .182 A4
Townfield Ave EX16 . . . . .61 A7
Town Hall Pl 4 TQ13 . . . . 180 D8
Town Hill
  Broadclyst EX5 . . . . 175 C7
  Culmstock EX15 . . . . .66 E8
  Ermington PL21 . . . . 136 F3
  Staverton TQ9 . . . . .216 A5
  West Anstey EX36 . . . . .32 C6
Town La
  Barton Town EX31 . . . . 11 E3
  Rackenford EX16 . . . . .47 D4
  Woodbury EX5 . . . . .184 C3
Townland Rise EX20 . . . . .56 F4
Townlands
  Bradninch EX5 . . . . .82 F6
  Willand EX15 . . . . .162 D3
Townliving Cross EX36 . . . . . .30 E1
Town Living Cross EX20 . . . .76 B5
Town Marsh TA21 . . . . .33 D7
Town Mdw
  Ilsington TQ13 . . . . 122 C3
  Little Torrington EX38 . . . . . .41 D3
Town Mdws EX39 . . . . .38 E8
Town Mill PL7 . . . . .260 E3
Town Mill Gdns PL19 . . . . . 171 C6
Town Mills EX7 . . . . .204 C6
Town Moor Cross EX17 . . . . .46 B1
Town Moor Hill EX17 . . . . . . .46 A1
Town Pk
  Crediton EX17 . . . . .165 B5
  Great Torrington EX38 . . . 159 C5
  West Alvington TQ7 . . . . . .143 E7
Town Rd TQ7 . . . . 148 F3
Townsend Ave EX12 . . . . . . 192 A6
Townsend Cl TQ7 . . . . 258 A4
Townsend Cross
  Malborough TQ7 . . . . 147 E6
  Winkleigh EX19 . . . . .58 E2
Town's End Cross TQ7 . . . . 145 C3
Townsend Hill EX12 . . . . . . 211 C3
Townsend Rd
  Seaton EX12 . . . . .192 A5
  West Alvington TQ7 . . . . . .258 A4
Townsend Terr PL4 . . . . .144 E7
Townshend Ave PL2 . . . . . . .247 E5
Town's La TQ7 . . . . .143 E7
Townstal Cres TQ6 . . . . .233 D3
Townstal Hill TQ6 . . . . .233 E3
Townstal Pathfields TQ6 .233 D3
Townstal Rd TQ6 . . . . .233 D3

Town Tree Hill 19 EX7 . . . .204 D6
Town View EX17 . . . . 165 C5
Tower View Rd EX32 . . . . . . 155 B4
Tracey Ct PL1 . . . . .262 B3
Traceys Ave EX12 . . . . 191 F8
Tracey Vale TQ13 . . . . 180 C6
Tracey View 2 EX14 . . . . . .166 B6
Trackfordmoor Cross
  TA22 . . . . .33 B3
Trafalgar Arc 20 EX34 . . . . . .3 A3
Trafalgar Cl
  Newton Abbot TQ12 . . . . .207 B5
  Plymouth PL5 . . . . .247 D8
Trafalgar Ct
  Topsham EX3 . . . . .182 E5
  Uffculme EX15 . . . . .66 A7
Trafalgar Dr EX38 . . . . 159 C6
Trafalgar Gdns EX32 . . . . . . 155 A3
Trafalgar Lawn EX32 . . . . . . 155 A3
Trafalgar Pl
  2 Bideford EX39 . . . . .156 F1
  Exeter EX4 . . . . 261 C4
  3 Plymouth PL1 . . . . .247 F3
Trafalgar Place La PL1 . . . .247 F3
Trafalgar Rd EX8 . . . . 195 E6
Trafalgar St 4 PL4 . . . . .263 A3
Trafalgar Terr TQ5 . . . . 230 C6
Trafford Mews EX2 . . . . 178 C3
Trago Mills 1 Pk TQ12 . . .123 A1
Trago Mills Cl PL4 . . . . .263 C3
Traine Brake PL9 . . . . .256 C1
Traine Rd PL9 . . . . 140 D8
Traine Terr PL21 . . . . 137 C2
Traine Villas PL21 . . . . .137 C3
Tramway Rd PL6 . . . . .245 E7
Tramways PL1 . . . . 220 B7
Transit Way PL5 . . . . 244 C3
Travellers Rest Cross
  EX37 . . . . .28 D6
Travershes Cl EX8 . . . . 196 B1
Traylane EX37 . . . . .28 B1
Treable La EX6 . . . . .96 B3
Treago Gdns PL6 . . . . .245 C8
Treasbeare La EX5 . . . . .99 A5
Trebblepark Rd TQ7 . . . . . . 258 C6
Treburley Cl PL15 . . . . 115 A4
Treburley Ind Est PL15 . . . 115 A4
Treby Rd PL7 . . . . .250 F4
Trecott Cross EX20 . . . . .76 F3
Tree Beech Rural Ent Pk
  EX32 . . . . .17 F4
Tree Cl EX32 . . . . .17 F4
Treefield EX31 . . . . .18 A8
Treefields TQ5 . . . . 230 B4
Treefield Wlk EX32 . . . . 155 D4
Trees Cl EX5 . . . . .182 E5
Treesdale Cl TQ3 . . . . .225 F6
Treetop Cl PL12 . . . . .242 D4
Trefusis Gdns PL3 . . . . .249 A4
Trefusis Pl EX8 . . . . .202 A5
Trefusis Terr
  Exmouth EX8 . . . . .202 A5
  Merton EX20 . . . . .57 A2
  Millbrook PL10 . . . . .252 E6
Trefusis Way EX19 . . . . 198 B6
Tregenna Cl PL7 . . . . .251 C4
Tregoning Rd PL12 . . . . .246 F2
Trehill Ho EX6 . . . . .114 D3
Trehill La PL10 . . . . .140 H2
Trehill Rd PL21 . . . . .237 E5
Trekenner Com Prim Sch
  PL15 .115 A5
Trelawney Ave PL5 . . . . .243 D1
Trelawney Cl PL11 . . . . .246 E3
Trelawney Ct EX39 . . . . .15 A7
Trelawney Pl PL5 . . . . .243 D1
Trelawney Rd
  Plymouth PL3 . . . . .248 D5
  Saltash PL12 . . . . .242 E2
Trelawney Rise PL11 . . . . . . .246 E3
Trelawney Way PL11 . . . . . . .246 E3
Trelawny Rd
  Plymouth PL7 . . . . .250 C6
  Tavistock PL19 . . . . .171 C6
Trelissick Cl TQ3 . . . . .225 D7
Trelissick Rd TQ3 . . . . .225 D7
Trelivan Cl EX8 . . . . .196 C3
Trelorrin Gdns PL3 . . . . .248 E5
Treloweth Cl PL2 . . . . .248 D8
Tremaine Cl EX14 . . . . .166 D6
Tremarran PL21 . . . . .236 E3
Trematon Ave TQ1 . . . . 220 A5
Trematon Cl PL11 . . . . .246 E4
Trematon Dr PL21 . . . . .237 E5
Trematon Terr PL4 . . . . .248 E4
Tremayne Rise PL19 . . . . . . .171 B5
Tremere Ct 22 EX32 . . . . . . 155 A4
Tremlett Gr TQ12 . . . . .211 D2
Tremletts Cl TQ6 . . . . .97 F5
Trencher La PL10 . . . . .252 D2
Trenchfirs Cnr TQ9 . . . . .139 C2
Trenchford Resr Woodland
  Wlk TQ13 . . . . 112 E1
Trendlewood Rd PL6 . . . . . .245 D7
Trengrouse Ave PL11 . . . . . .246 F3
Treninnow & Wiggle Chalets
  PL10 .252 C2
Trennaway Cross EX6 . . . . . . .96 C1
Trenode Ave EX34 . . . . .2 F4
Trentbridge Sq EX2 . . . . . . .178 C4
Trent Cl
  Bideford EX39 . . . . .26 A4
  Plymouth PL3 . . . . .249 B6
Trentham Cl
  Paignton TQ3 . . . . .225 E8
  Plymouth PL6 . . . . .245 B6
Trentishoe Hill EX31 . . . . .4 A5
Trentishoe La EX31 . . . . .4 A5
Trentworthy Cross EX22 . . . .38 B2

Trescote Way EX20 . . . . .92 F1
Tresillian Cotts EX3 . . . . . . .182 F3
Tresillian Gdns
  Exeter EX4 . . . . 177 E8
  Topsham EX3 . . . . .182 F4
Tresillian St 4 PL4 . . . . 263 C2
Tresluggan Rd PL5 . . . . 243 D1
Treston Cl EX7 . . . . .204 E7
Trethewey Gdns PL7 . . . . . . 132 D4
Tretower Cl PL6 . . . . .244 F5
Trevanna Rd TQ7 . . . . .258 C4
Trevannion Cl PL6 . . . . .249 A8
Trevelyan Rd EX12 . . . . 192 C4
Trevendon PL17 . . . . 115 B1
Treveneague Gdns PL2 . . .248 D8
Trevenn Dr TQ12 . . . . .213 A3
Treveor Gdns PL21 . . . . .137 B3
Treverbyn Cl PL7 . . . . .250 D6
Treverbyn Rd PL7 . . . . 250 D6
Trevethan Pk PL20 . . . . .239 F4
Trevithick Ave PL11 . . . . 246 F4
Trevithick Rd PL5 . . . . .243 E2
Trevol Bsns Pk PL11 . . . . . . .246 D3
Trevol Pl PL11 . . . . .246 E3
Trevol Rd PL11 . . . . .246 D3
Trevone Gdns PL2 . . . . .248 D8
Trevorder Cl PL11 . . . . .246 F2
Trevorder Rd PL11 . . . . .246 F2
Trevose Way PL3 . . . . 249 C6
Trewithy Ct PL6 . . . . .244 F1
Trewithy Dr PL6 . . . . .244 F1
Trews Weir Ct EX2 . . . . 261 C1
Trews Weir Reach EX2 . . . . 261 C1
Trewyn Pk EX22 . . . . .164 B5
Trewyn Rd EX22 . . . . .164 B6
Triangle Pl 18 TQ14 . . . . . .210 C4
Triangle The 19 TQ14 . . . . .210 C4
Trickey Cl EX16 . . . . 161 F5
Trick's Terr EX19 . . . . .42 D1
Tridley Foot Cross EX17 . . . .61 F4
Tridley Foot Hill EX17 . . . . . .61 F4
Trigger's Hill EX19 . . . . .42 D3
Trill Cross EX13 . . . . 103 E6
Trill La
  Axminster EX13 . . . . .167 C2
  Musbury EX13 . . . . .103 E6
Trimstone Cnr EX34 . . . . .8 F5
Trimstone Cross EX34 . . . . . . .8 E6
Trimstone La
  West Down EX34 . . . . .8 E5
  Woolacombe EX34 . . . . .8 D6
Trinfield Ave EX8 . . . . .196 B1
Trinity Cl
  Bere Alston PL20 . . . . 125 E1
  11 Teignmouth TQ14 . . .210 B6
  Wellington TQ21 . . . . .160 C5
Trinity Cross EX5 . . . . .82 F8
Trinity Cross EX5 . . . . .83 A8
Trinity Ct
  Sidmouth EX10 . . . . .188 B3
  Westward Ho! EX39 . . . . . .156 B6
Trinity Green EX34 . . . . 150 A5
Trinity Hill TQ1 . . . . 220 C3
Trinity Hill Rd
  Axminster EX13 . . . . .167 F1
  Raymond's Hill EX13 . . . . .104 B7
  Uplyme EX13 . . . . .104 B5
Trinity Mews TQ14 . . . . .210 B7
Trinity Pl 18 EX32 . . . . .155 A4
Trinity Rd EX8 . . . . .201 E6
Trinity Row TA21 . . . . .160 C5
Trinity Sq EX13 . . . . .167 D6
Trinity St EX32 . . . . .155 A4
Trinity Way PL19 . . . . 171 A4
Trinnaman Cl PL21 . . . . .237 D4
Trinnicks Orch PL21 . . . . . . .137 D6
Tristan Cl EX14 . . . . 174 A2
Tristford Cross TQ9 . . . . .223 A4
Tristford Rd TQ9 . . . . 222 D2
Trittencott Cross EX14 . . . . .46 A8
Troarn Way 21 TQ13 . . . . . .123 E6
Trobridge Cross EX17 . . . . . 165 D2
Trojan Ind Pk TQ4 . . . . 225 E3
Trood La EX2 . . . . 181 D6
Trough La TQ13 . . . . 123 A6
Trouville 16 EX32 . . . . .155 A5
Trowbridge Cl PL5 . . . . 244 C4
Trowell La TA4 . . . . .35 E4
Trow Hill EX10 . . . . .188 D8
Truckham La EX4 . . . . .3 D2
Trumans Ct EX4 . . . . .261 A2
Trumlands Rd TQ1 . . . . .214 B1
Trumpers Cl PL21 . . . . .237 A6
Trumps Cross EX16 . . . . .50 E3
Trumps Ct TQ12 . . . . .208 B3
Trumps Orch EX15 . . . . 163 A4
Truro Ave TQ2 . . . . 214 A1
Truro Dr
  Exeter EX4 . . . . 176 F7
  Exmouth EX8 . . . . .196 D4
  Plymouth PL5 . . . . .244 A5
Trusham Cross TQ13 . . . . . . 113 D1
Trusham Rd EX2 . . . . .177 C2
Tub Cnr EX5 . . . . .99 C7
Tucker Cl EX14 . . . . .166 C6
Tuckers Brook 12 PL21 . . .137 B2
Tuckers Cl EX17 . . . . .165 A5
Tucker's Hill EX13 . . . . .133 C1
Tucker's Hill Head PL21 . .133 C2
Tuckers Maltings TQ12 . . . 207 D4
Tuckers Mdw EX16 . . . . .161 C4
Tucker's Moor Cross EX16 32 F3
Tuckers Pk
  Bradworthy EX22 . . . . .38 E1
  Buckland Brewer EX39 . . . .40 B7

Tuckfield Cl EX2 . . . . 178 A4
Tucking Mill La EX36 . . . . 158 E3
Tuckmill Cross EX14 . . . . . .84 C4
Tudor Cl
  Lifton PL16 . . . . 105 E4
  Northam EX39 . . . . 156 F6
  Paignton TQ4 . . . . 226 A2
  Plymouth PL9 . . . . 255 E5
Tudor Ct
  Exeter EX4 . . . . 261 A2
  Saltash PL12 . . . . 243 A2
Tudor Dr EX31 . . . . 154 D2
Tudor Gr EX15 . . . . 163 C5
Tudor Rd TQ12 . . . . 207 B3
Tudor St EX4 . . . . 261 A2
Tuffery Ct EX4 . . . . 177 F8
Tugela Terr EX5 . . . . 179 A3
Tully Gdns EX10 . . . . 188 B7
Tuly St EX31 . . . . 154 F5
Tumbles The EX20 . . . . .76 C5
Tumbling Field La EX16 . 161 D3
Tumbling Fields EX16 . . 161 E3
Tumbly Hill TQ7 . . . . 258 D4
Tunnaford Cross TQ13. . .110 E4
Tunnel La EX14 . . . . 166 F8
Tuns La EX5 . . . . 82 B5
Tunworth Ct EX1 . . . . 261 A2
Tuplins TQ12 . . . . 207 E8
Turbill Gdns 4 PL7 . . . . . 251 B5
Turbury Cross EX4 . . . . 85 A8
Turkey La EX5 . . . . 99 E5
Turk's Head La EX14 . . . . 166 A6
Turlake Ho EX5 . . . . 172 F5
Turlake Mews EX5 . . . . . . 172 F5
Turner Ave EX8 . . . . 202 C7
Turner Cl EX10 . . . . 186 F7
Turners Cres EX39 . . . . 22 E3
Turner's La DT6 . . . . 288 H2
Turning Ways EX17 . . . . . . .61 A2
Turnpike
  Halberton EX16 . . . . .65 C8
  Honiton EX14 . . . . 166 D6
  Sampford Peverell EX16 . .50 C1
Turnpike Cl
  Clovelly EX39 . . . . .23 D3
  Whiddon Down EX20 . . . .95 F3
Turnpike Cross EX4 . . . . . . 8 C6
Turnpike Rd EX20 . . . . 95 F3
Turnquay PL9 . . . . 255 C2
Turret Gr PL4 . . . . 248 F4
Tute's La EX34 . . . . 3 B4
Tuxton Cl PL7 . . . . 251 C3
Tweed Cl EX14 . . . . 166 C4
Tweenaway Ct TQ4 . . . . . 225 E4
Tweenaways TQ11 . . . . . . 236 A4
Tweenaways Cross TQ4 . 225 E4
Tween Moor Cross EX17 . .60 F6
Tweenways TQ12. . . . . . . 207 D2
Twelve Acre Post TA22 . . .33 A4
Twelve Milestone Hill
  EX17. . . . . .79 D7
Twelve Oaks Cross EX18 .58 E6
Twickenham Rd TQ12 . . 208 A1
Twinaway La EX2 . . . . . . 114 B8
Twindle Beer TQ13. . . . . . 123 E6
Twiscombe Cnr EX4 . . . . . .98 C6
Twiscombe La EX4 . . . . . . .98 C6
Twisted Oak EX6 . . . . .97 D5
Twistgates La EX14 . . . . 168 A4
Twitchen Ball Cnr EX36 . .20 C3
Twitchen Cross
  Great Torrington EX38. . . .26 F2
  West Down EX34. . . . . 8 E6
Twitchen Gate EX31. . . . .11 F3
Twitchen Holiday Ctr EX34 .1 A1
Twitchen La
  Arlington EX31. . . . . .10 F4
  Burrington EX37 . . . . .43 F3
  Stowford EX31. . . . . .11 A3
Two Acre Cl TQ3 . . . . 225 E6
Twoacre Ct EX2 . . . . 181 A8
Two Bridges Rd
  Princetown PL20 . . . . . . 128 B8
  Sidford EX10 . . . . 101 B1
Two Crosses
  Dunsford EX6. . . . . 113 A8
  Yealmpton PL8 . . . . 136 A1
Two Gate Cross EX37 . . . .44 A4
Two Gates Cross EX16 . . .47 E5
Two Hills Pk PL12. . . . . . . 242 C2
Two Mile Oak Cross
  TQ12 . . . . .211 F5
Two Moors Prim Sch
  TQ16. . . . . 161 E5
Two Post Cross
  Pennymoor EX16 . . . . .62 E7
  Taw Green EX17 . . . . .95 D7
Two Post La EX17 . . . . .95 D7
Two Rivers Ind Est EX31.154 E6
Two Stone La EX6 . . . . . . 114 C5
Two Trees Rd EX31 . . . . . 153 D5
Twyford Pl
  Tiverton EX16 . . . . 161 D4
  Wellington TA21. . . . . . . 160 D5
Tyes Orch EX15 . . . . .83 F5
Tylney Cl PL6 . . . . 245 B6
Tyndale Cl PL5. . . . . 244 B1
Tyrrell Hosp (Private)
  EX34. . . . . 150 B5
Tyrrell Mead EX10 . . . . . 188 B7
Tyrrell Rd EX16 . . . . 161 A5
Tytheing Cl EX5. . . . . 172 A8
Tything Wlk 4 PL3 . . . . . 248 E6

U

Uffculme Ct EX15. . . . . . . .66 A7
Uffculme Prim Sch EX15 .66 A7
Uffculme Rd
  Culmstock EX15. . . . . .66 C5
  Uffculme EX15. . . . . .66 A7
  Willand EX15. . . . . 162 E6
Uffculme Sch EX15 . . . . . .66 A7
Ugborough Prim Sch
  PL21. . . . . 137 D6
Ugborough Rd PL21. . . . . 137 C7
Ugbrooke House & Gardens
  TQ13. . . . . 123 F5
Uggaton Cross EX14 . . . . .84 D5
Ullcombe La EX14 . . . . . . .68 C4
Ullswater Cres PL6 . . . . . 244 E4
Ullswater Ct EX4. . . . . . . 176 A3
Umber Cl EX34 . . . . 2 F4
Umberleigh Com Prim Sch
  EX37. . . . . .28 D2
Umberleigh Sta EX37 . . . .28 C2
Umberside 10 EX34 . . . . . . 3 A3
Undercliff TQ6. . . . . 233 F4
Undercliff Rd PL9. . . . . . . 255 B7
Underdown
  Clovelly EX39. . . . . .23 D3
  Kennford EX6. . . . . 114 A4
Underdown La EX20 . . . . . .76 D4
Underfleet The EX12 . . . . 192 B5
Underground Passages Mus
  EX4 . . . . 261 B3
Underhay PL8 . . . . 257 E4
Underheath 5 TQ1 . . . . . 220 D5
Underhill Cl EX8. . . . . 195 E5
Underhill Cl EX8 . . . . 195 E4
Underhill Cres EX8 . . . . . 195 E4
Underhill Rd
  Plymouth PL3. . . . . 248 A4
Underhill Terr EX14 . . . . 182 F5
Underhill Villas 1 PL3 . . 248 A4
Underidge Cl TQ3 . . . . . . 225 E6
Underidge Dr TQ3 . . . . . . 225 E6
Underidge Rd TQ3 . . . . . . 225 E6
Under La
  Bovey Tracey TQ13 . . . . . 180 A5
  Holsworthy EX22. . . . . . . 164 C3
  Sidbury EX10 . . . . 101 C1
Underlane
  Boyton PL15. . . . . .89 D3
  Marhamchurch EX23 . . . . .70 A6
  Plymouth, Plympton PL7 . 250 C5
  Plymouth, Plymstock PL9 . 255 E6
Underleat Cl 3 TQ13 . . . . 123 F6
Underleys EX8 . . . . 191 C5
Under Minnow Rd EX31 . 154 E7
Under Rd
  Bridgerule EX22. . . . . .70 F5
  Gunnislake PL18. . . . . . . 125 D6
Undertown PL21. . . . . 137 D6
Under Way TQ12 . . . . 213 A6
Underways PL20. . . . . 125 E1
Underwood Cl EX7 . . . . . . 204 D6
Underwood Cotts EX15. . .83 C4
Underwood Rd PL7 . . . . . 250 D4
Unicorn Cl PL7 . . . . 250 B6
Unicorn St EX12 . . . . 192 B5
Union Cl EX39. . . . . 156 F1
Union Hill EX17. . . . . .78 E7
Union La 9 TQ5. . . . . 230 C5
Union Pl PL1 . . . . 262 A2
Union Rd
  Crediton EX17 . . . . 165 C5
  Exeter EX4. . . . . 177 D8
  Sun Sq Sh Ctr TQ1. . . . . 220 B5
Union St
  Dartmouth TQ6 . . . . 233 F3
  Dulverton TA22 . . . . .33 D6
  Exeter EX2. . . . . 177 A4
  Newton Abbot TQ12. . . . 207 C3
  Plymouth PL1. . . . . 262 A2
  Salcombe TQ8 . . . . 259 E5
  Torquay TQ1, TQ2 . . . . . 220 A5
Union Terr
  Barnstaple, Bickington
    EX31. . . . . 154 A4
  Barnstaple EX32 . . . . . . 155 A4
  Crediton EX17 . . . . 165 C5
Unity Cl PL6. . . . . 245 D5
University of Plymouth
  Faculty of Arts & Education
    EX8. . . . . 202 B5
  Univ of Exeter EX4. . . . . 177 B6
  Univ of Plymouth PL1,
    PL4. . . . . 262 C3
  Univ of Plymouth Bsns Sch
    PL4. . . . . 262 C4
  Univ of Plymouth
    (Cookworthy Bldg)
    PL4. . . . . 263 A3
  Univ of Plymouth Faculty of
    Art & Education EX4. . . 261 A3
  Univ of Plymouth (Faculty of
    Art & Education) EX2. . .177 E2
  Univ of Plymouth The Hoe
    Ctr PL1. . . . . 262 C2
Upcott Ave EX31. . . . . . . 154 C6
Upcott Cross
  Cobbaton EX32 . . . . .28 C5
  Halwill EX21. . . . . .91 D8
  Holsworthy EX22. . . . . . . .72 D7
  Iddesleigh EX19 . . . . .57 F4
  St Giles on t H PL15. . . . . .90 E1
  Welcombe EX39. . . . . .37 C5
  West Buckland EX32 . . . . .18 C3

Upcott Gate EX18 . . . . .59 B3
Upcott Hill
  Barnstaple EX31 . . . . 154 D8
  Bideford EX39 . . . . .25 F4
  Okehampton EX20 . . . . . 170 A6
Upcott La
  Thorverton EX5 . . . . .81 E6
  West Buckland EX32 . . . . .18 C3
Upcott Mead Rd EX16 . . 161 B4
Upcott Valley EX20 . . . . . 170 A6
Upexe La EX5. . . . . .82 B5
Upham Cross EX17. . . . . . .63 A3
Upham La EX5. . . . . .99 C1
Uphay La EX13. . . . . 167 B8
Uphill Cl PL21 . . . . 237 E5
Upland Chase EX14 . . . . . 166 B3
Upland Dr PL6. . . . . 245 A5
Upland Gdns PL6 . . . . 140 D8
Uplands
  Saltash PL12 . . . . 242 E1
  Tavistock PL19 . . . . 171 A4
Uplands Dr EX4 . . . . 174 A1
Uplands Rd TQ3 . . . . 219 A2
Uplands Terr EX22 . . . . . 164 C3
Uplowman CE Prim Sch
  EX16. . . . . .50 B2
Uplowman Rd
  Chevithorne EX16 . . . . . . .49 F1
  Tiverton EX16 . . . . .64 E8
Uplyme Rd DT7 . . . . 260 C4
Uplyme Road Ind Est
  DT7. . . . . 260 C4
Upottery Prim Sch EX14 . .68 C2
Uppacott Cnr EX31. . . . . . .27 D8
Uppacott Cross
  Meshaw EX36. . . . . .45 F8
  Moretonhampstead TQ13 . 111 D7
Uppaton La PL21 . . . . 133 D1
Upper Braddons Hill Rd
  TQ1. . . . . 220 C4
Upper Church St 9 EX8 202 A6
Upper Churston Rise
  EX13. . . . . 191 E8
Upper Claypark CE Prim . . 7 F7
Upper Cloister Wlk EX6 .181 F5
Upper Cockington La
  TQ2 . . . . 219 C7
Upper Crooked Mdw
  EX20. . . . . 170 C5
Upper Headland Park Rd
  TQ3 . . . . 219 C1
Upper Hermosa Rd 1
  TQ14 . . . . 210 B5
Upper Highfield EX10 . . 188 A5
Upper Knollys Terrace La
  PL3. . . . . 248 C4
Upper Longlands EX7. . . 204 D7
Upper Manor Rd TQ3 . . 226 B8
Upper Morin Rd TQ3 . . . . 226 C7
Upper Paul St EX4 . . . . . . 261 A3
Upper Penns Rd TQ3 . . . . 219 C1
Upper Ridings PL7. . . . . . 251 B7
Upper Stoneborough La
  EX9. . . . . 198 A1
Upperton La PL6. . . . . 241 F3
Upperton Rd EX6 . . . . .97 D1
Upper Torrs EX34 . . . . .4 E3
Upper Westhill Rd DT7. . 260 C3
Upper West Terr EX5 . . . . 198 A1
Upper Wood La TQ6 . . . . 234 B3
Uppincott Hill EX17. . . . . .63 C1
Uppincott La
  Bickleigh EX5. . . . . .63 C1
  Cadbury EX5. . . . . .81 C8
Upright Villas 4 EX33. . . 152 D5
Upton Cross
  Payhembury EX14 . . . . . . .84 D5
  Thurlestone TQ7 . . . . . . 143 D2
Upton Cl 2 TQ1 . . . . 220 A6
Upton Hill TQ1. . . . . 220 A6
Upton Hill Rd TQ5 . . . . . . 230 C2
Upton Manor Ct TQ5 . . . 230 C2
Upton Manor Pk TQ5 . . . 230 C2
Upton Manor Rd TQ5 . . . 230 C2
Upton Pyne Cross EX5 . . 172 E4
Upton Pyne Hill EX5 . . . . 172 F6
Upton Rd
  Bideford EX39 . . . . 157 B1
  Torquay TQ1. . . . . 219 F6
Upton St James CE Prim Sch
  TQ1. . . . . 220 A7
Usticke La EX34 . . . . .3 B3
Uton Steep Cross EX17. .165 B1
Uxbridge Dr PL5 . . . . 243 E4

V

Vaagso Cl PL1. . . . . 247 E2
Vachell Cres EX2 . . . . 178 D5
Vale Cl
  Barnstaple EX32 . . . . . . 155 A6
  Galmpton TQ5 . . . . 229 B5
Vale Cl 17 EX10. . . . . 101 B1
Vale La EX33 . . . . 167 D6
Valentine Manor TQ11. . 236 C5
Valentines TA22 . . . . .33 E6
Vale Rd
  Exmouth EX8 . . . . 202 D7
  Kingskerswell TQ12. . . . . 213 A5
  Newton Abbot TQ12. . . . 207 D1
Vales Rd EX9 . . . . 198 B1
Valiant Ave PL5 . . . . 244 A4
Valiant Soldier Mus &
  Heritage Ctr The TQ11 . 236 C5
Valletort Flats PL1 . . . . . 248 A2
Valletort Ho PL1 . . . . 262 C3

Valletort La PL1 . . . . 248 A3
Valletort Pk TQ5 . . . . 230 A4
Valletort Pl PL1. . . . . 248 A2
Valletort Rd PL1, PL3 . . . 248 A3
Valletort Terr PL1 . . . . . . 262 A4
Valley La
  Barnstaple EX32 . . . . . . 155 B5
  Teignmouth TQ14 . . . . . 124 E1
Valley Park Cl PL9 . . . . . . 140 D8
Valley La 7 EX34. . . . . .3 A3
Valley of Rocks The EX35 . .5 A6
Valley Park Cl EX4 . . . . . . 173 D2
Valley Path TQ12 . . . . 206 E4
Valley Rd
  Clyst St Mary EX5 . . . . . 179 E3
  Exeter EX4. . . . . 176 F7
  Plymouth PL7 . . . . 250 B5
  Saltash PL12 . . . . 242 E2
Valleyside TQ7 . . . . 143 A2
Valley View
  Axminster EX13 . . . . 167 E5
  Bideford EX39 . . . . 156 D2
  Chagford TQ13. . . . . 111 A6
  Farway EX24 . . . . 101 F6
  Landkey EX32 . . . . .17 C1
  Millmoor EX15. . . . . .51 E1
  Morebath EX16 . . . . .34 B3
  Plymouth PL6. . . . . 245 D7
  Seaton EX12 . . . . 192 A6
  Shebbear EX21 . . . . .55 E4
Valley View Cl
  Plymouth PL3. . . . . 249 B6
  Seaton EX12 . . . . 192 B6
  Torquay TQ1. . . . . 219 F7
Valley View Rd PL3 . . . . . 249 B7
Valley Ways EX4 . . . . 196 E3
Valley Wlk PL6. . . . . 245 E6
Van Buren Pl EX2 . . . . . . 178 D3
Vanehill Rd TQ1 . . . . 220 C3
Vanguard Cl PL5. . . . . 244 D1
Van Post EX16 . . . . .49 D6
Vanpost Hill EX16. . . . . . . .49 D5
Vansittart Dr EX4. . . . . . . 196 C3
Vansittart Rd TQ2 . . . . . . 219 F6
Vapron Rd PL3. . . . . 248 F6
Varco Sq EX2 . . . . 178 C4
Varian Ct 4 TQ9. . . . . 223 E5
Varley Ct EX16 . . . . 161 E6
Vauban Pl PL2 . . . . 247 F4
Vaughan Cl PL2. . . . . 248 C7
Vaughan Par TQ2 . . . . . . 220 B4
Vaughan Rd
  Exeter EX1. . . . . 178 B6
  Torquay TQ2. . . . . 220 B4
Vaughan Rise EX1. . . . . . 178 B6
Vauxhall St 10 PL4 . . . . . 263 A2
Vauxhall St PL4 . . . . 263 A2
Vauxhall Street Flats 19
  PL4. . . . . 263 A2
Vavasours Slip TQ6 . . . . . 233 F4
Veale Cl EX20 . . . . .75 B6
Vealenia Terr TQ13 . . . . . 130 F4
Veales Rd TQ7 . . . . 258 C4
Veasypark PL9. . . . . 140 D8
Veille La TQ2 . . . . 219 C8
Veitch Gdns PL21 . . . . . . 181 B8
Velator Cl TQ3 . . . . 152 D4
Velator Dr EX33. . . . . 152 D5
Velator Lane Ave EX33 . . 152 D5
Velator Rd EX33 . . . . 152 D4
Vellacott La EX34 . . . . .3 C3
Vellaford Cross EX20 . . . . .75 E7
Velland Ave TQ2 . . . . 213 F4
Vellator Way EX33 . . . . . 152 D4
Velwell Rd EX4 . . . . 261 A4
Venborough Cl EX12 . . . . 191 F8
Venbridge Hill EX6 . . . . . .97 B4
Venford Ct TQ4 . . . . 229 B8
Venford Hill
  East Anstey TA22. . . . . . . .32 E8
  Hawkridge TA22. . . . . .47 C8
Venford Villas EX36 . . . . . .30 D4
Venhay Cross EX36. . . . . . .46 D6
Venlake Cl DT7. . . . . 260 A5
Venlake Ct DT7 . . . . 260 A5
Venlake End DT7 . . . . 260 A5
Venlake Mdw DT7 . . . . . . 260 A5
Venlock Cl EX4 . . . . 155 D4
Venmore Orch EX5. . . . . . 184 B2
Venn Bridge TQ10 . . . . . . 137 E8
Venn Cl
  Instow EX39 . . . . .15 C2
  6 Plymouth PL3 . . . . . . 248 C5
Venn Cotts EX39 . . . . .15 C2
Venn Cres PL3 . . . . 248 C5
Venn Cross
  Barnstaple EX32 . . . . . . 155 D1
  Broadhempston TQ12 . . 131 D4
  East Allington TQ9. . . . . . 144 C5
  Stoke Fleming TQ6. . . . . 146 B8
  Ugborough PL21. . . . . . . 137 C7
  Waterrow TA4 . . . . .35 D3
  West Putford EX22 . . . . . .39 D3
Venn Ct
  Brixton PL8 . . . . 257 F7
  Plymouth PL3 . . . . 248 C5
Venn Dr PL8 . . . . 257 F7
Venn Gdns PL3 . . . . 248 C5
Venn Gr PL3. . . . . 248 C5
Venn Hill
  Copplestone EX17 . . . . . . .79 B8
  Milton Abbot PL19 . . . . . 116 A6
Venn La
  Cheriton Fitzpaine EX17 . . .63 A1
  Dartmouth TQ6 . . . . 233 B1
  Plymouth PL2, PL5 . . . . . 248 C6
  Stoke Fleming TQ6. . . . . 146 A8

Venn Lane End EX2 . . . . . .17 B1
Venn Ottery Rd EX10. . . . 186 E8
Venn Pk TQ6. . . . . 146 B8
Venn Rd EX32 . . . . 155 C1
Venn Way
  Plymouth PL3. . . . . 248 E7
  Stoke Fleming TQ6. . . . . 146 B7
Venny Bridge EX4 . . . . . . 174 D1
Ventiford Cotts TQ12 . . . 123 C2
Vention La EX33 . . . . 7 E3
Vention Rd EX33 . . . . 7 E3
Venton Cross
  Highampton EX21 . . . . . . .74 E6
  Tigley TQ9 . . . . 135 F3
Venton Ct TQ9 . . . . 144 F5
Venton Dr EX39. . . . . 156 D7
Venture Ct TQ12 . . . . 207 A3
Verbena Terr TQ14 . . . . . 209 D5
Vermont Gdns PL2 . . . . . 247 F7
Verna Rd EX5 . . . . 243 E2
Verney St EX1 . . . . 261 C4
Vernon Cl PL7 . . . . 132 E3
Vernon Cl EX1. . . . . 220 C2
Vernon Ct TQ1. . . . . 220 A4
Vernon Rd EX4 . . . . 196 D2
Vernons La 25 EX39. . . . . .15 A1
Verona Ct 3 EX32 . . . . . . 155 A6
Verwill La EX34 . . . . .3 D3
Vestry Dr EX2. . . . . 181 B8
Viaduct View EX32 . . . . . 164 C4
Vial's Cnr EX16 . . . . .48 D5
Vicarage Ball TQ9 . . . . . . 222 C2
Vicarage Cl
  Brixham TQ5 . . . . 230 C5
  Hartland EX39 . . . . .22 D3
  Stoke Gabriel TQ9 . . . . . 227 F7
Vicarage Gdns
  Dawlish EX7 . . . . 204 C6
  Milton Abbot PL19 . . . . . 116 A6
  Plymouth PL5. . . . . 243 B1
Vicarage Gr TQ9 . . . . 227 F8
Vicarage Hill
  Brixham TQ5 . . . . 230 C5
  Cornwood PL21 . . . . 133 D3
  Dartmouth TQ6 . . . . 233 E3
  Dulverton TA22 . . . . .33 D6
  Rackenford EX16. . . . . . . .48 C6
  Kingsteignton TQ12 . . . . 207 F7
  Marldon TQ3 . . . . 218 E3
  Torquay TQ2. . . . . 219 D4
Vicarage La
  15 Cluddeigh TQ13 . . . . 123 E6
  Exeter EX4. . . . . 174 E2
  Longdown EX6. . . . . .98 E1
  South Tawton EX20 . . . . . .95 B5
Vicarage Lawn EX32 . . . . 155 A5
Vicarage Rd
  Abbotskerswell TQ12. . . . 212 B6
  Blackawton TQ9 . . . . 139 E1
  Brixham TQ5 . . . . 230 C2
  Cockwood EX6 . . . . 201 B6
  East Budleigh EX9 . . . . . 198 B6
  Landkey EX32 . . . . .17 B2
  Plymouth PL7 . . . . 250 C6
  Okehampton EX20 . . . . . 170 A5
  Plymouth PL7. . . . . 250 C6
  Sidmouth EX10 . . . . 188 B4
  South Brent TQ10 . . . . . 134 F3
  Stoke Gabriel TQ9 . . . . . 227 F8
  Torpoint PL11 . . . . 247 B2
  Totnes TQ9 . . . . 219 D4
Vicarage St
  Barnstaple EX32 . . . . . . 154 F5
  Colyton EX24 . . . . 103 A5
Vicary Cl TQ12 . . . . 207 A3
Vickers Ground EX39. . . . 156 F8
Vickery Cl EX5 . . . . 163 B3
Victor Cl EX1 . . . . 178 A5
Victoria Ave PL1 . . . . 262 A4
Victoria Ct
  7 Barnstaple EX32 . . . . 155 B4
  Kenton EX6 . . . . 194 D3
  Willand EX15 . . . . 162 D4
Victoria Cottage Hospl
  EX10. . . . . 188 B4
Victoria Cotts
  2 Holsworthy EX22. . . . . 164 C4
  Lee Mill PL21 . . . . 136 D6
  Plymouth PL6. . . . . .77 C4
  Plymouth PL6. . . . . 249 B8
Victoria Cres EX17 . . . . . 165 D6
Victoria Ct
  Dartmouth TQ6 . . . . 233 D4
  4 Totnes TQ9 . . . . 223 C5
Victoria Gdns 1 EX39 . . . 157 A1
Victoria Gr EX39. . . . . 157 A1
Victoria Ind Est EX32 . . . 164 C4
Victoria Hts TQ6 . . . . 233 D3
Victoria La PL12 . . . . 242 F2
Victoria Lawn EX32 . . . . . 155 B4
Victoria Par 7 TQ1 . . . . . 220 B3
Victoria Park Rd
  Exeter EX2. . . . . 177 C6
  Torquay TQ1. . . . . 220 B7
Victoria Pl
  Axminster EX13 . . . . 167 D6
  Brixham TQ5 . . . . 230 C6
  Budleigh Salterton EX9 . . 199 G2
  Chardstock EX13 . . . . .88 A7
  Dartmouth TQ6 . . . . 233 F3
  6 Exmouth EX8 . . . . . . 202 A6
  Kingsbridge TQ7 . . . . . . 258 D5
  Newton Abbot TQ12. . . . 207 C3

Victoria Pl continued
Plymouth, Devonport PL2 . .**247** F4
Plymouth PL1. . . . . **262** A2
Salcombe TQ8 . . . .**259** E5
Victoria Rd
Barnstaple EX32 . . . . **155** A4
Barnstaple EX32 . . . . **155** B4
Black Torrington EX21 . . . . . **74** A8
Brixham TQ5 . . . .**230** F6
Dartmouth TQ6 . . . .**233** E3
1 Exeter EX4 . . . .**177** D8
Exmouth EX8 . . . .**201** F6
Hatherleigh EX20. . . . .**75** C7
Ilfracombe EX34 . . . .**150** B5
Plymouth PL5. . . . .**243** D2
Saltash PL12 . . . .**242** F2
Sidmouth EX10 . . . .**188** B4
Topsham EX3. . . . .**182** F5
Torquay TQ1 . . . .**220** B6
Victoria Road Prim Sch
PL5. . . . .**243** D1
Victoria Sh Ctr TQ4 . . . . . **226** C6
Victoria Sq
3 Holsworthy EX22 . . . . . .**164** C4
Paignton TQ4 . . . .**226** C6
Victoria St
Barnstaple EX32 . . . .**155** B4
Combe Martin EX34. . . . .**3** B3
Exeter EX4. . . . .**177** D8
Holsworthy EX22 . . . .**164** C4
Okehampton EX20 . . . .**170** C5
Paignton TQ4 . . . .**226** B6
Torpoint PL11 . . . .**247** B3
Totnes TQ9. . . . .**223** C5
Wellington TA21. . . . .**160** D6
Victoria Terr
Barnstaple EX32 . . . .**155** A4
16 Bideford EX39 . . . .**157** A1
2 Bovey Tracey TQ13 . . . . .**180** D8
3 Brixham TQ5. . . . .**230** C4
Cullompton EX15 . . . .**163** C3
Honiton EX14. . . . .**166** B6
Kingsteignton TQ12 . . . .**207** E7
Ottery St Mary EX11 . . . . . .**169** C3
Plymouth PL4. . . . .**262** C4
Tiverton EX16. . . . .**161** B4
Victoria Way EX8 . . . .**201** F6
Victor La EX1. . . . .**178** A5
Victor St EX1 . . . .**178** A5
Victory Cl TQ12 . . . .**207** B5
Victory Rd
Dartmouth TQ6 . . . .**233** D3
North Tamerton EX22 . . . . . .**89** D8
Victory St PL2 . . . .**247** E6
Victory Way EX38 . . . .**159** C6
Vicus Cl EX9. . . . .**198** E7
View Rd DT7 . . . .**260** D3
Vigobridge Rd PL19 . . . . . .**171** C6
Vigo Mews PL19 . . . .**171** C6
Villa Capri TQ1 . . . .**220** D2
Villa Cli EX32. . . . .**155** B2
Village Cl EX8 . . . .**202** F7
Village Cross
Coldridge EX17 . . . .**59** F2
Loddiswell TQ7. . . . .**143** E7
Morchard Bishop EX17 . . . . . .**61** B2
Village Cross Rd TQ7 . . . . .**143** E7
Village Dr PL6. . . . .**241** C1
Village Farm Cl EX23. . . . . .**70** A6
Village La EX14 . . . .**86** B1
Village Rd
Christow EX6. . . . .**113** B3
Marldon TQ3 . . . .**218** D3
Woodbury Salterton EX5. . . . .**184** C6
Village St 10 EX32 . . . .**16** E1
Village The PL20 . . . .**126** C3
Village Way PL19 . . . .**117** F4
Villa Pardiso TQ1 . . . .**220** C5
Villa Rd EX38. . . . .**159** C5
Villas The TQ12 . . . .**123** E1
Villiers Ave TQ12. . . . .**207** F2
Villiers Cl PL9 . . . .**255** D7
Vincents Rd TQ7 . . . .**258** D5
Vincent Way PL12. . . . .**242** F2
Vine CE EX2. . . . .**261** C2
Vine Cres PL2 . . . .**248** B6
Vinegar Hill EX39 . . . .**157** B2
Vine Gdns PL2. . . . .**248** B6
Vine Passage EX14. . . . . . .**166** C6
Vine Rd TQ2 . . . .**219** F6
Vinery La PL7, PL9. . . . . . .**256** C1
Vinery The TQ1 . . . .**220** B4
Vine St EX19. . . . .**58** F2
Vineyard TQ9 . . . .**223** A8
Vineyard Hill TQ9 . . . .**223** A8
Vineyard La EX13 . . . .**167** C7
Vineyards The EX22 . . . . . .**164** C5
Vineyard Terr TQ14 . . . .**144** D7
Vineycroft La EX10. . . . . . .**188** F7
Viney Cross EX14 . . . .**86** B6
Viney La
Monkton EX14 . . . .**86** C7
Upottery EX14 . . . .**68** C1
Viney Lane Cross EX14 . . . .**86** B5
Vinivers Cross EX38 . . . . . .**148** F4
Vinnicombes Rd EX5. . . . . .**173** F8
Vinstone Way TQ5 . . . .**243** D1
Violet Dr PL6. . . . .**245** E8
Violet La PL19 . . . .**171** E6
Virginia Cl EX39 . . . .**153** A1
Virginia Gdns PL2. . . . .**247** F7
Virginia Lodge 14 TQ1. . . . .**220** D4
Vision Hill Rd EX9 . . . .**198** B2
Visitors Hill EX16 . . . .**63** D4
Vittery Cl TQ5 . . . .**230** B5

Vix Ct TQ5 . . . .**230** B5
Vixen Tor Cl
Okehampton EX20 . . . .**170** E5
Yelverton PL20. . . . .**126** F3
Vognacott Cross EX22. . . . . .**53** F3
Voscombe Cross EX31. . . . . .**26** F7
Voulsdon Cross EX20. . . . . .**92** A4
Voysey Hill EX17 . . . .**62** F1
Vuefield Hill EX2. . . . .**176** E3
Vulscombe Cross EX16. . . . .**63** A6
Vulscombe La EX16 . . . .**63** B6
Vyvyan Ct EX1 . . . .**178** A5

W

Wadbrook Cross EX13. . . . . .**88** C4
Waddens Cross EX24. . . . . .**102** D4
Wadderly Hill EX17 . . . .**79** F7
Waddeton Cl TQ4 . . . .**225** F1
Waddeton Ind Est TQ4 . . . .**225** F1
Waddeton Rd
Paignton TQ4 . . . .**225** F1
Stoke Gabriel TQ5 . . . .**228** C4
Waddington Cross EX36. . . . .**31** A3
Waddington La EX18. . . . . . .**45** A5
Waddles Down Cross EX4 . .**98** E5
Waddon Cl PL7 . . . .**250** E7
Waddons Cross TQ9. . . . . .**216** C6
Wadham Cl EX8 . . . .**202** E8
Wadham Cross
Knowstone EX36 . . . .**32** A2
West Anstey EX36. . . . .**32** A4
Wadham Hill EX36. . . . .**32** A2
Wadham Ho EX4. . . . .**173** A1
Wadham Terr 6 PL2. . . . . .**248** A5
Waggoners Way EX4 . . . . .**177** A8
Waggon Hill PL7 . . . .**251** A4
Waggs Plot EX13 . . . .**88** B4
Waie Cotts EX17 . . . .**78** C6
Waie Cross EX17. . . . .**78** B6
Wain La TQ12 . . . .**207** A4
Wain Pk PL7. . . . .**250** F4
Wakefield Ave PL5. . . . . . .**243** E1
Wakeham Ct EX33 . . . .**152** E4
Wakehams Cl PL21. . . . . . .**137** C2
Wake St PL4. . . . .**262** B4
Walcot Cl PL6 . . . .**245** E3
Walcott Way EX14 . . . .**67** C1
Walden Rd EX14. . . . .**67** C1
Waldon Cl PL7. . . . .**251** B6
Waldon Ct TQ2 . . . .**220** B4
Waldon Ho TQ2 . . . .**220** B4
Waldon Point TQ2 . . . .**220** B4
Waldons Cross EX19 . . . . . .**57** F1
Waldon Way EX22. . . . . . .**164** C6
Waldron's Cross TA21. . . . . .**35** E1
Walkers Gate TA21 . . . . . .**160** D5
Walker Terr PL1. . . . .**262** B1
Walkham Bsns Pk PL5 . . . . .**244** B1
Walkham Cl PL19 . . . .**171** D5
Walkham Mdws PL20 . . . . . .**126** C4
Walkham Rd PL20 . . . .**126** F4
Walkhampton Wlk PL6 . . . . .**245** E1
Walkham Rise TQ2. . . . . . .**219** B8
Walkham Terr 5 PL20 . . . . .**126** F5
Walk La EX36. . . . .**30** F6
Wallace Ave
Dawlish EX7. . . . .**204** E7
Exeter EX4. . . . .**178** B8
Torquay TQ2 . . . .**219** C8
Wallace La
Lynton EX35. . . . .**5** A3
West Alvington TQ7 . . . .**258** B3
Wallace Rd PL7. . . . .**251** A4
Wallaford Rd TQ11. . . . . . .**135** C8
Walland Cross EX32. . . . . . .**18** E3
Wallaton Cross TQ9 . . . . . .**145** A7
Walled Gdn The EX2 . . . . .**182** C7
Wallfield Rd TQ13. . . . .**180** B5
Wallingford Rd TQ7 . . . . . .**258** D6
Wallis Gr TQ14. . . . .**209** A8
Wallon Cross TQ13. . . . . . .**110** F7
Wallpark Cl PL7 . . . .**250** F7
Wall Park Cl TQ5 . . . .**230** E5
Wall Park Rd TQ5. . . . . . .**230** E5
Wall Pk TQ9 . . . .**222** F6
Walls Cl EX8. . . . .**196** D2
Walls Hill Rd TQ1 . . . .**220** D7
Walnut Cl
3 Chudleigh TQ13 . . . .**123** F6
Exminster EX6 . . . .**182** A4
Plymouth PL7 . . . .**251** B5
Totnes TQ9. . . . .**223** B6
Walnut Ct
Brixham TQ5 . . . .**230** C4
Torquay TQ2 . . . .**219** E4
Walnut Dr
Crediton EX17 . . . .**165** D6
Plymouth PL7 . . . .**251** C5
Tiverton EX16. . . . .**161** F5
Walnut Gdns PL7 . . . .**251** C5
Walnut Gr EX8. . . . .**202** C7
Walnut La TQ2 . . . .**219** E4
Walnut Rd
Exeter EX2. . . . .**177** F2
Honiton EX14. . . . .**166** A4
Torquay TQ2 . . . .**219** E4
Walnut Way EX32 . . . .**155** D4
Walpole Cl EX4 . . . .**174** C1
Walreddon Cl PL19 . . . .**171** B4
Walronds The EX16 . . . . . .**161** C2
Walshams EX14. . . . .**87** A7
Walson Cl PL7. . . . .**251** B6
Walson Cross EX17. . . . .**78** C4
Walson La EX19 . . . .**76** F7
Walson Rd EX17 . . . .**228** D3
Waltacre PL8 . . . .**257** F3

Walter Daw Fst Sch EX2 .**178** B4
Walters Orch EX15. . . . . . .**163** C3
Walters Rd PL5. . . . .**243** C2
Waltham Pl PL2 . . . .**248** A8
Waltham Rd TQ12. . . . . . .**207** A3
Waltham Way PL21. . . . . . .**237** E4
Walton Cres PL5. . . . .**244** C1
Walton Rd EX2 . . . .**178** C5
Walton Way EX32 . . . .**155** C5
Wandle Pl PL3. . . . .**249** D5
Wanstead Gr PL5 . . . .**244** A2
Wantage Gdns PL1. . . . . . .**262** A3
Warberry CE Prim Sch
TQ1. . . . .**220** C5
Warberry Rd W TQ1. . . . . .**220** B5
Warberry Vale 3 TQ1 . . . . .**220** B6
Warboro Terr EX6. . . . .**201** B8
Warborough Hill EX6 . . . . .**194** E3
Warborough Rd TQ5 . . . . . .**229** C6
Warbrightsleigh Hill EX16 .**48** A7
Warbro Ct 11 TQ1 . . . .**220** B7
Warbro Rd TQ1 . . . .**220** C7
Warburton Gdns PL5. . . . . .**243** C1
Warcombe La EX34 . . . .**1** B2
Wardens Cl EX37 . . . .**43** B7
Wardle La EX19. . . . .**59** A2
Wardleworth Way TA21. . . .**160** C7
Wardlow Cl PL6 . . . .**248** F8
Wardlow Gdns PL6. . . . . . .**248** F8
Wardour Wlk PL6. . . . .**245** B7
Ward Pl PL3 . . . .**249** B5
Wardrew Rd EX4. . . . .**176** F5
Wards Cross PL5 . . . .**99** C8
Ware Cl TQ12 . . . .**207** F7
Ware Cliff Chalets DT7. . . . .**260** D2
Warecroft Rd TQ12. . . . . . .**207** F7
Ware Cross
Kingsteignton TQ12 . . . .**207** F7
Ugborough PL21 . . . .**137** D6
Warecross Gdns TQ12. . . . .**207** F7
Warecross Way TQ3 . . . . . .**226** C7
Wareham Cross EX13 . . . . .**88** E1
Wareham Rd EX13 . . . .**88** E2
Ware La DT7 . . . .**260** B2
Waresfoot Dr EX17. . . . . . .**165** B6
Warfelton Cres PL12 . . . . . .**242** E2
Warfelton Gdns PL12 . . . . .**242** E2
Warfelton Terr PL12. . . . . . .**242** E2
Warfield Villas EX34 . . . . . .**150** C5
Warfleet Creek Rd TQ6. .**234** A1
Warfleet Rd TQ6. . . . .**234** A2
Waring Bowen Ct EX2. . . . .**177** F1
Warkleigh Rd PL6 . . . .**244** D7
Warkidons Way EX5. . . . . .**185** A5
Warleigh Ave PL2. . . . .**247** E5
Warleigh Cres PL6. . . . . . .**244** F5
Warleigh La PL2. . . . .**247** E5
Warm Hill TQ13. . . . .**123** B7
Warmwell Rd PL5. . . . .**243** E4
Warneford Gdns EX8. . . . . .**196** C2
Warne La PL19 . . . .**117** E6
Warnicombe La EX16 . . . . .**64** D6
Warran La PL19. . . . .**171** C3
Warraton Cl PL12. . . . .**242** D3
Warraton Gn PL12 . . . .**242** D3
Warraton Rd PL12 . . . .**242** D3
Warren Cl
Great Torrington EX38. . . . . .**159** C5
Wembury PL9 . . . .**140** D7
West Hill EX11. . . . .**168** D4
Warren Cross EX16 . . . . . .**161** B7
Warren Dr EX9 . . . .**198** B2
Warren Hill TQ2 . . . .**220** B4
Warren La
Dartington TQ9 . . . .**216** B3
Exeter EX4. . . . .**261** B4
Farway EX24 . . . .**102** A7
Great Torrington EX38. . . . . .**159** C5
Lee Mill PL21. . . . .**136** D6
Plymouth PL5. . . . .**244** A8
Wembury PL9 . . . .**140** E7
Warren Pk
Bigbury-on-S TQ7. . . . .**142** E3
Dawlish EX7. . . . .**205** A8
Kingsbridge TQ7 . . . .**258** E3
Mary Tavy PL19 . . . .**117** E6
Thurlestone TQ7 . . . .**143** A1
Torquay TQ2 . . . .**220** B4
Warrens Mead EX10 . . . . . .**188** D8
Warren St
Plymouth PL4. . . . .**263** A4
Plymouth, Stoke PL1 . . . . . .**248** A3
14 Teignmouth TQ14 . . . . . .**210** C4
Warren The EX16 . . . .**161** B7
Warren View EX39 . . . .**156** E2
Warspite Gdns PL5 . . . . . .**244** D2
Warton Cl PL5 . . . .**244** D3
Warwick Ave
Exeter EX1. . . . .**178** C5
Plymouth PL5. . . . .**244** D3
Warwick Cl
Feniton EX14. . . . .**84** E2
Honiton EX14. . . . .**166** D6
Warwick Orchard Cl PL5 .**244** B3
Warwick Rd PL5. . . . .**244** B3
Warwick Terr 8 EX32. . . . .**154** F6
Warwick Way EX4 . . . .**174** C8
Wasdale Cl PL6 . . . .**249** A8
Wasdale Gdns PL6. . . . . . .**249** A8
Washabrook La TQ7. . . . . .**258** E5
Washabrook Way TQ7. . . . .**258** E5

Washbourne Cl
Brixham TQ5 . . . .**230** E5
Plymouth PL1. . . . .**247** E3
Washbourne Cross TQ9 . .**139** D6
Washbrook View EX11. . . . .**169** E4
Wash Cross TQ11 . . . .**215** B8
Washfield La
Calverleigh EX16. . . . .**48** F2
Tiverton EX16 . . . .**161** B7
Washford Pyne Cross
EX17. . . . .**61** E4
Washford La TQ12 . . . .**219** B1
Washington Ho 6 EX12 .**192** A4
Wastor Cross PL21. . . . . . .**142** D7
Wastor Pk TQ7. . . . .**142** D7
Watching Place Cross
TQ13 . . . .**111** B3
Watch The TQ7 . . . .**143** A2
Watcombe Heights Rd
TQ1. . . . .**214** C4
Watcombe Prim Sch
TQ2. . . . .**214** B3
Waterbeer St EX4. . . . . . .**261** A3
Water Bridge Cross EX17 .**78** F6
Waterbridge Ct EX2. . . . . .**181** D8
Water Cotts TQ13 . . . .**121** F7
Waterdale Pk TQ12. . . . . . .**213** A4
Waterford La EX31 . . . .**16** A7
Waterford La EX13 . . . .**103** C5
Water Gate EX2. . . . .**262** C2
Watergate Cotts PL9 . . . . .**140** D8
Watergate Cross EX20 . . . .**107** G6
Waterhaynes La TA20 . . . . .**68** F8
Waterhead Cl TQ6 . . . .**234** B4
Waterhead Terr TQ6. . . . . .**234** B4
Waterhouse Cross EX17. . .**62** E1
Waterhouse Hill EX20 . . . . .**74** F1
Waterhouse La EX13, EX14 .**87** C6
Watering Ct EX37 . . . .**43** D7
Water La
Barnstaple EX32 . . . .**155** B3
Bow EX17. . . . .**78** C4
Combe Martin EX34. . . . .**3** A3
Cornworthy TQ9 . . . .**227** A3
Exeter EX2. . . . .**177** C3
Kingskerswell TQ12 . . . .**213** A4
Sidmouth EX10 . . . .**188** B5
Tiverton EX16 . . . .**161** D4
Torquay TQ2 . . . .**219** C8
Waterlake La EX31. . . . .**16** A7
Waterlake Rd TA20. . . . .**88** C8
Water Lane 2 EX32. . . . . .**155** B3
Water Lane Cotts 4
EX32. . . . .**155** B3
Water Lane End TQ9 . . . . .**215** B3
Waterlears Cross TQ7. . . . .**147** D8
Waterleat Ave
Honiton EX14. . . . .**166** D5
Paignton TQ4 . . . .**225** D5
Waterleat Cl TQ3 . . . .**225** F5
Waterleat Ct TQ3 . . . .**225** F5
Waterleat Rd TQ3 . . . .**225** E5
Waterloo Cl PL1. . . . .**248** A2
Waterloo Cotts EX15. . . . . .**65** F8
Waterloo Cross Cvn Pk
EX15. . . . .**65** F8
Waterloo Ct PL1. . . . .**248** A2
Waterloo Hill EX16. . . . .**47** B6
Waterloo Rd
Exeter EX2. . . . .**177** A3
Holsworthy EX22. . . . .**164** D5
Kingsbridge TQ7 . . . .**258** D6
Torquay TQ1. . . . .**220** A5
Wellington TA21. . . . .**160** C6
Waterloo St
Plymouth PL4. . . . .**263** A4
Plymouth, Stoke PL1 . . . . . .**248** A3
14 Teignmouth TQ14 . . . . . .**210** C4
Waterloo Yard Flats PL1. .**248** A2
Water Mdw EX15 . . . .**163** C2
Watermead TA20. . . . .**88** D8
Watermore Ct EX4. . . . . . .**177** E7
Watermouth Rd EX34 . . . . .**150** C6
Waterpark Cl EX10 . . . .**187** F4
Water Park Rd EX39 . . . . . .**156** D2
Water Parts TA21 . . . .**160** A5
Waterpool Rd TQ6 . . . .**233** E2
Waterside
Exeter EX2. . . . .**261** A1
Kingsbridge TQ7 . . . .**258** D5
Uplyme DT7. . . . .**260** B5
Waterside Ho
Paignton TQ4 . . . .**237** C4
10 Totnes TQ9. . . . .**223** C5
Waterside Holiday Pk
TQ4. . . . .**226** C1
Waterslade Dr PL21 . . . . . .**237** F4
Waterslade La PL5 . . . .**179** E8
Watersmeet EX35. . . . .**5** E1
Watersmeet House EX35 .**5** E1
Watersmeet Rd EX35. . . . .**151** E4
Waterstream Sq 13 TQ13 .**123** F6
Water Terr 11 EX34. . . . . . .**3** A4
Water Turn TQ13. . . . .**130** E5
Waterworks La TQ14 . . . . .**209** D4
Watery La
Axminster EX13 . . . .**88** A3
Beara EX31. . . . .**16** B8
Braunton EX33. . . . .**152** F5
Budlake EX5. . . . .**82** E3
Colyton EX13, EX24 . . . . . .**103** A6
Combe Martin EX34. . . . .**3** A3

Watery La continued
Croyde EX33 . . . .**7** E2
Great Torrington EX38. . . . . .**159** B4
Great Torrington EX38. . . . . .**159** E5
Milton Combe PL6 . . . .**240** D6
Stoke Canon EX5 . . . .**81** F3
Tiverton EX16 . . . .**161** E5
Whiddon EX31. . . . .**9** C1
Woodbury EX5. . . . .**184** B4
Watkins Way TQ3 . . . .**225** D7
Watson Gdns PL4. . . . . . .**263** B3
Watson Pl PL4. . . . .**263** B2
Watts Park Rd PL2. . . . . . .**248** C7
Watts Rd PL9 . . . .**171** B5
Watts' Rd PL4 . . . .**263** C3
Waveney Gdns PL5. . . . . .**244** C3
Waverley Ave EX4. . . . . . .**261** B4
Waverley Rd
Exmouth EX8 . . . .**202** A8
Newton Abbot TQ12. . . . . . .**207** B4
Plymouth PL5. . . . .**243** D2
Waverley Terr EX35 . . . . . .**151** B5
Wavish Pk PL11. . . . .**246** E3
Waybrook Cotts EX2. . . . .**181** B7
Waybrook Cres EX2 . . . . .**181** C8
Waybrook La EX2. . . . . . .**181** B6
Way Cnr EX16 . . . .**63** A5
Waycott Wlk PL6. . . . .**244** D6
Way Cross EX20 . . . .**107** D8
Way Down Cross TQ13 . . .**110** F8
Waye Cross TQ13 . . . .**110** F5
Wayfaring EX32. . . . .**155** D3
Way La EX6. . . . .**98** B5
Wayland Ave EX2 . . . .**261** C1
Waylands Rd EX16 . . . . . .**161** D6
Way Rd
Brixham TQ5 . . . .**230** A4
Ivybridge PL21 . . . .**237** C4
Wayside Cl TQ5 . . . .**230** A4
Wayside Cres EX1 . . . .**178** B7
Way's La EX15. . . . .**163** C2
Waytown Cross TQ9 . . . . .**131** D2
Wear Barton Rd EX2 . . . . .**182** B7
Wear Cl EX2. . . . .**182** C7
Wear Park Ct EX2. . . . . . .**182** C7
Weatherdon Dr PL21. . . . . .**237** F5
Weatherill Rd EX14 . . . . . .**166** C4
Weaver Cross EX15 . . . . . .**83** E6
Weaver La EX15. . . . .**83** E7
Weavers Ct EX2. . . . .**261** A2
Weaver's Reach TA21. . . . .**160** B7
Weavers Rd EX2 . . . .**261** A3
Weavers Wlk EX15. . . . . . .**163** B2
Webber Cl TQ12 . . . .**211** F8
Webbers CE Prim Sch
TA21. . . . .**50** F5
Webbers Cl
Wellington TA21. . . . .**160** E4
Whimple EX5 . . . .**99** E8
Webbers Way
Dartington TQ9 . . . .**222** F8
Willand EX15. . . . .**162** D4
Webbers Yard Est TQ9 . . . .**222** F8
Webberton Cross EX2. . . .**113** F6
Webbery Cross EX39 . . . . .**26** D4
Webbery Moor Cross
EX36. . . . .**31** A3
Webble Green Cross
EX15. . . . .**87** C8
Webland La TQ10 . . . .**135** C3
Webley Rd EX2 . . . .**176** F3
Weddicott Cross TQ13. . . .**111** A4
Wedding Well La EX33 . . . . .**8** F1
Wedgwood Ct TQ12 . . . . . .**207** A4
Wedlake Mews 22 EX7 . . .**204** D6
Weech Cl EX7 . . . .**204** C6
Weeches The EX16. . . . . . .**48** F2
Weech Rd EX7. . . . .**204** C6
Weekaborough Dr TQ3. . . .**218** D2
Weekaborough Oak Cross
TQ12. . . . .**217** E4
Week Cross
Bishop's Tawton EX31 . . . . . .**27** F6
Bradninch EX5 . . . .**82** F7
Burrington EX37. . . . .**43** C5
Chulmleigh EX18 . . . .**43** E6
Monkhampstead TQ13 . . . . .**111** C4
Puddington EX16 . . . .**62** D6
South Zeal EX20 . . . .**95** B3
Zeal Monachorum EX17. . . . . .**78** C7
Weeke Cross PL21 . . . . . .**137** D4
Weeke Hill TQ6. . . . .**146** C8
Weekes Mdw TA21 . . . .**51** E6
Week La
Dawlish Warren EX7 . . . . . .**201** A1
High Bickington EX37 . . . . . .**43** D5
Week Park Cross EX37 . . . .**43** C5
Weeksland Rd TQ12 . . . . . .**219** C6
Weeks Row PL18. . . . .**125** D6
Weir Cl PL6 . . . .**245** F2
Weirfield Rd EX2 . . . .**261** B1
Weirfields EX2 . . . .**261** A4
Weirfields TQ9 . . . .**223** C6
Weirford La EX20. . . . .**76** F4
Weir Gdns PL6. . . . .**245** F2
Weir Head Cotts TA22 . . . .**33** D7
Weir Pk TA22. . . . .**33** D6
Weirside Pl EX2 . . . .**182** D7
Weirside Way EX32. . . . . .**155** B6
Welbeck Ave PL4 . . . .**262** C4
Welch's La EX31 . . . .**15** C2
Welcombe Cross EX39. . . . .**37** E4
Welcome Family Holiday Pk
EX7. . . . .**201** B2

Welcome Holiday Pk
  EX7. . . . . .201 B2
Welcome St EX2. . . . . .261 A1
Weld Park Ave **1** EX34. . 150 D5
Welland Gdns PL9. . . . . . . 249 C5
Welland Cl EX15. . . . . 66 B7
Wellands Cross EX13. . . . . .87 D4
Wellbrook Gn EX16. . . . . . 161 B4
Wellbrook St EX16. . . . . . . 161 C4
Wellbrook Terr
  11 Bideford EX39. . . . . . 157 A1
  5 Tiverton EX16. . . . . . 161 B4
Wellclose Rd EX33. . . . . . . 152 D5
Well Cross PL21. . . . . 137 E6
Welle House Gdns TQ7. . 258 D6
Weller Rd EX13. . . . . .167 D4
Wellesley Park Prim Sch
  TA21. . . . . .160 E4
Wellesley Pk TA21. . . . . . . 160 D4
Wellesley Rd TQ1. . . . . . . 220 B6
Wellesley Way TA1. . . . . . . .68 D7
Wellfield Cl PL7. . . . . 251 C5
Wellfield Hill EX13, DT6. . . 88 H2
Well Gdns PL1. . . . . 262 B3
Wellhay Cl PL9. . . . . 256 C6
Well Hill TQ7. . . . . 147 E6
Well Hill Cl TQ7. . . . . 147 E6
Wellings Cl TA20. . . . . 88 C8
Wellington Cl **2** EX2. . . 178 D5
Wellington Cottage Hospl
  TA21. . . . . .160 D5
Wellington Hill TA21. . . . . 160 F2
Wellington Jun Sch
  TA21. . . . . .160 E6
Wellington Mus TA21. . . . . 160 E6
Wellington Pl **1** TQ1. . . 220 B6
Wellington Rd
  Exeter EX2. . . . . 177 A3
  Torquay TQ1. . . . . 220 B6
Wellington Sq EX1. . . . . . . 160 E5
Wellington Sq **16** TQ10. . 134 F3
Wellington St
  Plymouth PL4. . . . . 263 A4
  Plymouth, Stoke PL1. . . 248 A4
  13 Teignmouth TQ14. . . 210 C4
  Torpoint PL11. . . . . 247 B3
Well La EX39. . . . . .37 B5
Well Mead EX13. . . . . 87 C1
Well Oak Pk EX2. . . . . 177 F3
Wellpark Cl EX4. . . . . 176 E6
Well Park Flats EX38. . . . . 159 C5
Wellpark Rd PL18. . . . . 125 C5
Well Park Rd
  Great Torrington EX38. . . 159 D5
  Torpoint PL11. . . . . 247 B3
Well Pk EX22. . . . . .164 C5
Wells Ave EX13. . . . . .84 E2
Wellsbourne Pk PL3. . . . . 249 A6
Wells Cl EX8. . . . . 196 E4
Wells Ct PL10. . . . . 252 E4
Wellspring La EX20. . . . . . . 76 F3
Wells St EX32. . . . . 154 F5
Well St
  Exeter EX4. . . . . 261 C4
  Starcross EX6. . . . . 201 B8
Wells Terr EX17. . . . . 62 E1
Wellstones Cl PL21. . . . . . 237 C4
Wellswood Ave TQ1. . . . . . 220 D5
Wellswood Gdns
  Exeter EX4. . . . . 176 E5
  Torquay TQ1. . . . . 220 D5
Wellswood Manor **3**
  TQ1. . . . . 220 D5
Wellswood Path TQ1. . . . . 220 D5
Wellswood Pk TQ1. . . . . . . 220 D5
Well The TA21. . . . . 160 B5
Welman Rd PL6. . . . . 252 F6
Welsbere La EX17. . . . . 62 C3
Welsford Ave PL2. . . . . 247 F5
Welsh Cross TQ13. . . . . . . 130 E7
Wembury Dr TQ2. . . . . 214 A2
Wembury Marine Ctr
  PL9. . . . . 140 C7
Wembury Mdw **1** PL9. . 248 D8
Wembury Park Rd PL3. . . 248 D6
Wembury Prim Sch PL9. 140 D8
Wembury Rd
  Plymouth PL9. . . . . 256 A4
  Plymouth PL9. . . . . 140 E8
Wembworthy Down La
  EX18. . . . . .59 C4
Wendover Way EX2. . . . . . 178 B2
Wenlock Gdns PL2. . . . . . . 248 B8
Wensum Cl PL7. . . . . 251 A4
Wentwood Gdns PL6. . . . . 245 E3
Wentwood Pl PL6. . . . . . . 245 E3
Wentworth Gdns EX4. . . . 176 E4
Wentworth Pl PL4. . . . . . . 249 B2
Wentworth Rd TQ12. . . . . 180 F3
Wentworth Way PL12. . . . 242 C2
Wesley Ave PL8. . . . . 248 E5
Wesley Cl
  Exeter EX4. . . . . 177 A3
  3 Tiverton EX16. . . . . . 64 D7
  Torquay TQ1. . . . . 214 A3
Wesley Ct PL11. . . . . 247 C3
Wesley Mews TQ2. . . . . . . 214 A2
Wesley Pl
  Harberton TQ9. . . . . 222 D2
  Plymouth, Mutley PL3. . . 248 E5
  1 Plymouth, Stoke PL1. . 248 A4
Wesley Terr TQ12. . . . . . . 211 D2
Wesley View TQ12. . . . . . . 211 D2

Wesley Way EX2. . . . . 181 B8
Wessex Cl EX3. . . . . 182 D6
Wessex Est EX4. . . . . 177 A7
Wessex Ho **1** DT7. . . . . . 260 D3
Wessiters EX12. . . . . 192 A5
Westabrook Ave TQ13. . . . 130 F5
Westabrook Cl TQ13. . . . . 130 F5
Westabrook Dr TQ13. . . . . 130 F5
Westacombe EX31. . . . . .27 B8
Westacott Cross
  Inwardleigh EX20. . . . . . . 75 C3
  Meshaw EX36. . . . . 45 E8
  North Tawton EX20. . . . . . 77 E5
Westacott La
  Coldridge EX17. . . . . 59 E2
  East Buckland EX32. . . . . . 18 D2
  North Tawton EX20. . . . . . 77 E5
Westacott Mdw EX32. . . . 155 E3
Westacott Rd EX32. . . . . . 155 E4
West Acres EX12. . . . . 191 F7
West Alvington Butts
  TQ7. . . . . .143 E2
West Alvington CE Prim Sch
  TQ7. . . . . .258 A4
West Alvington Hill TQ7. 258 C5
West Anstey School Cross
  EX36. . . . . .32 C5
West Ave
  Barnstaple EX31. . . . . . . 154 D3
  Exeter EX4. . . . . 177 C8
  4 Tavistock PL19. . . . . . 171 B5
Westaway EX31. . . . . 153 E5
Westaway Cl EX31. . . . . . . 155 A7
Westaway Hts EX31. . . . . . 155 A8
Westaway Plain EX31. . . . 155 A8
Westaway Rd **6** EX24. . . 103 A4
West Ball Hill EX39. . . . . . . 22 D3
West Barton La EX20. . . . . . 76 E4
West Beckon Cl EX23. . . . . 37 A1
Westbourne Gr EX34. . . . . 150 A5
Westbourne Rd
  Plymouth PL3. . . . . 248 D5
  Torquay TQ1. . . . . 220 A7
Westbourne Terr
  Budleigh Salterton EX9. . 203 F8
  Saltash PL12. . . . . 242 F3
  Westward Ho! EX39. . . . 156 C7
Westbourne Villas EX34. . 150 B6
Westbridge Cl EX20. . . . . . 170 B5
Westbridge Cotts PL19. . . 171 B4
Westbridge Ind Est **3**
  PL19. . . . . .171 B4
Westbrook Ave TQ14. . . . . 210 A5
Westbrook Cl EX4. . . . . . . 178 B8
Westbrook Pl EX16. . . . . . 161 E4
West Brushford La EX18. . . 59 C2
West Buckeridge TQ14. . . 210 B6
West Buckland Com Prim
  Sch TA21. . . . . 52 F7
West Buckland Cross
  EX32. . . . . .18 B2
West Buckland Rd EX32. . . 18 C2
West Buckland Sch EX32. . 18 C2
West Burridge Cross
  EX18. . . . . .60 E7
Westbury Cl PL5. . . . . 244 B4
West Challacombe La EX34. 3 A3
West Charleton Ct TQ7. . 144 C1
West Cl EX13. . . . . 167 C5
West Cliff Cl EX7. . . . . 204 E6
West Cliff EX7. . . . . 204 E6
West Cliff Park Dr EX7. . 204 D5
Westcliff Rd DT6. . . . . 104 F4
West Cliff Rd EX7. . . . . . . 204 E6
Westcliff Sch EX7. . . . . . . 204 C5
West Cliff Terr **2** EX12. . 192 A4
Westclyst EX1. . . . . 175 A3
Westcombe EX2. . . . . 181 B8
Westcombe Cres PL9. . . . 255 D5
Westcombe La EX39. . . . . 156 F2
Westcombes EX13. . . . . 88 B7
West Coombe La TA4. . . . . 35 D8
Westcots Dr EX19. . . . . 58 F2
Westcott Cl PL6. . . . . 245 D7
Westcott Cross EX14. . . . . 66 F2
Westcott La
  Aylesbeare EX5. . . . . 99 D4
  Beara EX31. . . . . 9 A1
  Witheridge EX16. . . . . 61 E7
Westcott Way EX14. . . . . . . 64 D7
West Cotts TA24. . . . . 13 A2
Westcott Way EX16. . . . . . 166 D6
West Country Amb Trust HQ
  EX2. . . . . .178 F5
Westcountry Cl PL2. . . . . . 247 F7
Westcroft Ct **3** EX39. . . 156 F1
West Croft Jun Sch
  EX39. . . . . .156 F1
Westcroft Rd PL5. . . . . 243 D1
West Croft Rd EX22. . . . . . 164 B4
West Cross EX33. . . . . 152 D6
Westcroyde EX33. . . . . 14 D7
West Devon Bsns Pk
  PL19. . . . . .171 B3
West Down Hill EX33, EX34. . 8 F4
West Down La EX34. . . . . . 203 A6
West Down Rd PL2. . . . . . 248 B6
West Down Sch EX34. . . . . 8 F5
West Down Terr EX34. . . . 203 B6
West Efford La EX17. . . . . . 81 A4
Westella Rd PL20. . . . . 127 A2
West Emlett La EX17. . . . . . 61 E3
West End Cross EX16. . . . . 48 D5
West End La EX16. . . . . 48 D5

West End Rd
  Bradninch EX5. . . . . 82 F6
  Buckfastleigh TQ11. . . . . 236 B4
West End Terr
  Ashburton TQ13. . . . . . . 130 F4
  Denbury TQ12. . . . . 211 A6
  South Molton EX36. . . . . 158 C4
Westernmoot TQ7. . . . . . . 142 C6
Westeria Terr PL2. . . . . . . 248 C7
Westernoo **6** EX36. . . . . 234 B3
Westerland Gn TQ3. . . . . . 218 D2
Westerland La TQ3. . . . . . . 218 D2
Wester-Moor Dr EX31. . . 154 A2
Wester-Moor Way EX31. . 154 A2
Western App PL1. . . . . 262 B2
Western Ave
  Appledore EX39. . . . . 15 A1
  Exeter EX2. . . . . 182 D7
Western By-Pass TQ9. . . . 223 B5
Western College Rd PL4 . 248 F5
Western Cotts EX20. . . . . 107 E1
Western Ct EX10. . . . . 188 A3
Western Dr
  Newton Abbot TQ12. . . . 206 F4
  Plymouth PL3. . . . . 249 B4
  Starcross EX6. . . . . 201 B8
Western Field EX10. . . . . . 188 A3
Western Gardens Rd EX34. . 3 A3
Western Gr EX17. . . . . 204 E7
Westernlea EX14. . . . . 165 A5
Western Piece La EX31. . . . 9 D1
Western Pl **4** EX24. . . . . 103 A4
Western Rd
  Ashburton TQ13. . . . . . . 130 F4
  Crediton EX17. . . . . 165 A6
  Exeter EX4. . . . . 177 A5
  Holsworthy EX22. . . . . . 164 C4
  Ivybridge PL21. . . . . 237 C4
  Newton Abbot TQ12. . . . 207 C3
  Torquay TQ1. . . . . 214 B1
  Zeal Monachorum EX17. . 78 B6
Western Rise EX34. . . . . 8 A6
Western Terr
  Barnstaple EX31. . . . . . . 154 E5
  Ilfracombe EX34. . . . . . . 150 A4
  Totnes TQ9. . . . . 223 B6
  Totnes, Smith TQ13. . . . . 180 D5
Western Villas
  Crediton EX17. . . . . 165 B5
  Totnes TQ9. . . . . 223 B5
Western Way
  Exeter, Barnfield EX1,
    EX2. . . . . 261 C3
  Exeter, Friars' Green EX1 . 261 A2
Western Way Ind Est
  EX15. . . . . .163 C4
Western Wood Way PL7. . 251 D5
West Exe N EX16. . . . . 161 C4
West Exe S EX16. . . . . 161 C3
West Exe Tech Coll EX2. . 177 A2
Westfield
  Bradninch EX5. . . . . 82 F6
  Plymouth PL7. . . . . 251 A6
Westfield Ave
  Barnstaple EX31. . . . . . . 154 D4
  Plymouth PL9. . . . . 255 C6
Westfield Cl
  Brixham TQ5. . . . . 230 B3
  Budleigh Salterton EX9. . 198 A1
Westfield Rd
  Budleigh Salterton EX9 . 198 A1
  Tiverton EX16. . . . . 161 C3
West Field Rd EX6. . . . . . . 182 B3
Westfield Terr **8** EX16. . 161 C3
Westford Cl TA21. . . . . 160 A5
Westford Dr TA21. . . . . . . 160 A5
West Garth Ct EX4. . . . . . 172 F2
West Garth Rd EX4. . . . . . 173 A3
Westgate EX17. . . . . 60 A2
West Grove Rd EX2. . . . . . 261 C2
Westhampnett Pl PL5. . . . 243 F4
West Hartley TQ9. . . . . . . 139 E3
Westhay Cross EX13. . . . . . 88 F3
Westhayes Cvn Pk DT7. . 193 D8
Westhays Cl PL7. . . . . 255 F4
Westhead Rd PL10. . . . . . . 140 H2
West Hill
  Budleigh Salterton EX9 . 203 F8
  Heybrook Bay PL9. . . . . 140 A7
  Heybrook Bay PL9. . . . . 140 B7
West Hill Ave EX10. . . . . . 220 B7
Westhill Avenue Cl TQ1 . 220 B7
Westhill Cres TQ3. . . . . . . 226 B7
West Hill Ct EX9. . . . . 203 F8
West Hill Gdns EX9. . . . . 203 F8
West Hill La
  Braunton EX33. . . . . 152 C6
  Budleigh Salterton EX9 . 197 F1
  Parracombe EX31. . . . . . . 4 B2
  West Hill Prim Sch EX11 168 D4
Westhill Rd
  Paignton TQ3. . . . . 226 A7
  Torquay TQ1. . . . . 220 B8
West Hill Rd
  Lyme Regis DT7. . . . . . . 260 D3
  Plymouth PL4. . . . . 248 F4
  West Hill EX11. . . . . 168 D4
Westhill Terr TQ12. . . . . . 213 A4
West Ho PL13. . . . . 167 D5
West Hoe Rd PL1. . . . . . . 262 B1
Westholme TQ1. . . . . 220 C5
West La
  Challacombe EX31. . . . . . 11 D4
  Dolton EX19. . . . . 57 E6
  Knowle EX33. . . . . .8 C2

West La continued
  Lapford EX17. . . . . 60 C3
  Paignton TQ3. . . . . 225 A6
Westlake Cl PL11. . . . . 246 F3
Westlake Rd PL9. . . . . 140 A8
Westlake Rise PL9. . . . . . . 140 A8
Westland La EX16. . . . . 62 C6
Westlands
  Exmouth EX8. . . . . 202 C6
  Wrafton EX33. . . . . 152 E4
Westlands La TQ1. . . . . . . 220 B7
Westlands Sec Sch TQ1 . 220 C7
Westleat Ave TQ3. . . . . . . 225 F6
West Leigh Cross TQ9. . . 135 F1
Westleigh La EX44. . . . . 3 C2
West Lodge DT7. . . . . 193 D5
West Lyn Rd EX35. . . . . . . 151 C2
West Malling Ave PL5. . . 243 E5
West Manley La EX16. . . . 64 E7
Westmead Cl EX33. . . . . . 152 C6
West Meadow Cl EX33. . . 152 A7
West Meadow Rd EX33. . . 152 A7
West Mill Cross TQ11. . . . 236 B4
Westminster Cl
  Exmouth EX8. . . . . 196 D3
  Feniton EX14. . . . . 84 D1
Westminster Rd EX4. . . . . 176 E6
Westminster Villas EX34. . 150 D5
West Molland La EX36. . . . 31 D7
Westmoor Cl PL7. . . . . 251 C6
West Moor Cl EX39. . . . . . 156 E7
Westmoor Pk PL19. . . . . . 171 C4
West Moor Way EX39. . . . 156 F8
West Mount TQ12. . . . . . . 207 D1
West of England Sch for
  Children with Little or no
  Sight EX2. . . . . 178 B1
West Ogwell Cross TQ12 211 C8
Weston Cl
  Brixham TQ5. . . . . 230 C3
  Broadhembury EX14. . . . . 84 D7
Weston Cross
  Awliscombe EX14. . . . . . . 85 C3
  Sidmouth EX10. . . . . 189 D8
Westonfields TQ9. . . . . . . 223 E5
Weston La
  Awliscombe EX14. . . . . . . 85 B4
  Totnes TQ9. . . . . 223 E4
Weston Mill Com Prim Sch
  PL2. . . . . 247 E2
Weston Mill Dr PL5. . . . . 247 D2
Weston Mill Hill PL5. . . . 243 F1
Weston Mill La PL5. . . . . 244 A1
Weston Mill Rd PL5. . . . . 243 E1
Weston Park Rd PL3. . . . 248 D6
Weston Rd TQ9. . . . . 223 D5
Weston Terr EX11. . . . . . . 169 E4
Westover Cl
  Brixham TQ5. . . . . 230 D4
  Ivybridge PL21. . . . . 237 B5
Westover Hill DT6. . . . . . . 104 F5
Westover Ind Est PL21. . . 237 C4
Westover La PL21. . . . . . . 237 B5
Westown Rd EX2. . . . . 176 C1
West Pafford Ave TQ2. . . 214 B3
West Park Dr PL7. . . . . . . 251 C5
West Park Hill PL7. . . . . . 251 B7
West Park Prim Sch PL5 244 A2
West Park Rd EX10. . . . . . 188 A5
Westpark Villas **8** PL20 . 126 F5
West Pk
  Braunton EX33. . . . . 152 C6
  Outer Hope TQ7. . . . . . . 147 B7
  South Molton EX36. . . . . 158 B4
  Stoke Fleming TQ6. . . . . 146 B8
Westpoint (County
  Showground) EX5. . . . . 179 C3
West Pugsley Cross EX37. . 29 A2
West Rd
  Roborough EX19. . . . . . . 42 F4
  Sheepwash EX21. . . . . . . 56 C1
  Woolacombe EX34. . . . . . 7 F6
Westridge Cross EX16. . . . 63 C4
West Spurway La EX16. . . 48 A8
West St
  Ashburton TQ13. . . . . . . 130 F4
  Axminster EX13. . . . . . . 167 D5
  Bampton EX16. . . . . 34 B1
  Bishops Nympton EX36. . 30 F2
  Bishopsteignton TQ14. . . 208 F8
  Denbury TQ12. . . . . 211 A6
  Exeter EX1, EX4. . . . . . . 261 A2
  Hartland EX39. . . . . 22 D3
  Millbrook PL10. . . . . 252 E5
  Okehampton EX20. . . . . 170 B5
  South Molton EX36. . . . . 158 C4
  Tavistock PL19. . . . . 171 B5
  Witheridge EX16. . . . . . . 46 E1
West Terr
  Budleigh Salterton EX9 . 198 A1
  Churston Ferrers TQ5. . . 229 F4
  Exeter EX1. . . . . 177 F6
West Town Cross EX39. . . . 38 E8
West Town Mdw EX39. . . 208 E8
West Town Rd EX39. . . . . . 98 F8
West Ugworthy Cross
  EX22. . . . . .53 E3
West Underleys EX12. . . . 191 C5
West View
  Beer EX12. . . . . 191 D5
  Colyford EX24. . . . . 103 A3
  Holsworthy EX22. . . . . . 164 C5
  Tavistock PL19. . . . . 171 C2
West View Ave EX39. . . . . 157 B2
Westview Cl EX5. . . . . 99 E8
West View Cl TQ12. . . . . . 206 F1
West View Ct **1** EX32. . 155 B4

West View Rd
  5 Bere Alston PL20. . . 125 E1
  Marldon TQ3. . . . . 218 D2
  Okehampton EX20. . . . . 170 C5
West View Terr
  Exeter EX4. . . . . 261 A2
  3 Honiton EX14. . . . . . 166 B6
  Lympstone EX8. . . . . . . 195 F5
Westward Cl TQ2. . . . . 223 C5
Westward Dr EX8. . . . . . . 202 B7
Westward Ho! Beach Holiday
  Village EX39. . . . . 156 C7
Westward View TQ12. . . . 208 A2
Westwater Hill EX6. . . . . . 97 E5
West Waters La EX31. . . . . .4 D5
Westway PL9. . . . . 255 B5
Westway Cross EX16. . . . . . 61 F8
Westwood Ave PL6. . . . . . 245 C6
Westwood Cl EX17. . . . . . 165 A5
Westwood Cotts EX6. . . . . 98 E2
Westwood Hill EX6. . . . . . 201 A5
Westwood La EX16. . . . . . 176 B4
Westwood Rd
  Crediton EX17. . . . . 165 A5
  East Ogwell TQ12. . . . . . 212 A8
Westwoods EX16. . . . . 98 B4
Westwood Units EX2. . . . 177 D1
Westwood Way EX12. . . . 192 B7
Westworthy Cross EX20. . 77 E6
Westyard La EX18. . . . . 58 E8
West Yelland EX31. . . . . 15 C2
West Yeo Moor Hill EX16. 46 C3
Wetherell Cl EX16. . . . . . . 161 C3
Wet La
  Christow EX6. . . . . 113 B4
  3 Combe Martin EX34. . . 3 A3
Weycroft Ave EX13. . . . . . 167 F7
Weycroft Cl EX13. . . . . . . 178 D6
Weymouth Pk TQ7. . . . . . 147 B7
Whalley La DT7. . . . . 260 B4
Wharf Cotts TA21. . . . . . . 160 B8
Wharf Rd TQ12. . . . . 207 D4
Whatley La TA20. . . . . 69 A7
Wheadon Cross EX14. . . . . 66 B4
Wheal Betsy PL19. . . . . . . 117 C6
Wheal Maria Cotts PL19. . 116 B1
Wheal Rd PL19. . . . . 117 C6
Wheatclose Cross EX36. . . 20 D7
Wheatcombe Ct TQ2. . . . 214 B3
Wheatfield Cl EX15. . . . . . 163 B2
Wheatland Cross EX16. . . . 48 C6
Wheatland La EX16. . . . . . . 48 C6
Wheatland Rd TQ4. . . . . . 226 B4
Wheatley Cl EX4. . . . . 176 E5
Wheatley Ct **5** EX1. . . . 261 A2
Wheatley Cotts EX17. . . . . 78 C4
Wheat Pk TQ9. . . . . 138 D8
Wheatridge PL7. . . . . 250 B7
Wheatridge La TQ12. . . . . 219 E2
Wheatsheaf Way EX2. . . . 177 A1
Wheatsheaf Way EX15. . . 67 C8
Wheel Cross EX34. . . . . 2 F1
Wheelers Cross EX22. . . . . 39 E1
Wheel La EX34. . . . . 2 F1
Wheelwright Cl PL20. . . . 127 B4
Whelmstone Cross EX17 . 78 E3
Whetcombe Cross PL21. . 137 F6
Whey Cross EX37. . . . . 28 D3
Whiddborne Ave TQ1. . . . 221 A4
Whidborne Cl TQ1. . . . . . 220 F3
Whidborne Mews TQ14. . 124 D1
Whiddon Cross
  Abbotskerswell TQ12. . . 212 B4
  Whiddon PL5. . . . . 9 D1
Whiddon Dr EX32. . . . . . . 155 D3
Whiddon La
  Ide EX2. . . . . 114 A8
  Whiddon EX32. . . . . 9 D1
Whiddon Rd TQ12. . . . . . . 212 B2
Whiddon Valley Ind Est
  EX32. . . . . .155 D3
Whidley La EX16. . . . . 112 E8
Whilborough Rd TQ12. . . 212 E2
Whimble Hill EX22. . . . . . 164 D3
Whimple Prim Sch EX5. . 99 E8
Whimple St PL1. . . . . 262 C2
Whimple Sta EX5. . . . . 99 E8
Whin Bank Rd PL5. . . . . . 244 E2
Whippenscott Hill EX36. . 46 B8
Whipton Barton Rd **1** EX1. 178 B7
Whipton Barton Jun Sch
  EX1. . . . . .178 C7
Whipton Hospl EX1. . . . . 178 C7
Whipton Inf Sch EX1. . . . 178 B7
Whipton La EX1. . . . . 178 A6
Whipton Rd EX4. . . . . 178 A8
Whipton Village Rd EX1 . 178 B8
Whistley Down EX20. . . . 126 E2
Whistley Rd TQ13. . . . . . . 131 A4
Whistley Hill Cross TQ13 131 A4
Whitby Cres PL6. . . . . 245 A1
Whitby Rd PL6. . . . . 245 A1
Whitchurch Com Prim Sch
  PL19. . . . . .171 D2
Whitchurch Rd
  Horrabridge PL20. . . . . . 126 F5
  Tavistock PL19. . . . . 171 C3
Whitcott Hill EX36. . . . . . . 30 E5
Whiteabury Cross TQ13 . 111 C7
Whitear Cl TQ14. . . . . 124 E1

Whitear's Way TQ12 207 E7
White Ash La TA20 69 D5
Whitebeam Cl
 Exeter EX4 174 B2
 Paignton TQ3 225 E7
Whitebeam Gr EX14 67 B1
Whitebear Cross EX22 54 F6
Whiteborough La
 Chudleigh TQ13 123 D8
 Trusham TQ13 113 D1
Whitebridges
 Honiton EX14 166 B4
 Honiton EX14 166 C5
Whitebrook Terr TA21 50 F5
Whitechapel La EX36 30 F6
White Cl TQ3 219 B2
Whitecleave Cross EX37 43 F2
White Cliff ❶ EX12 192 B4
White Cross
 Aylesbeare EX5 99 C1
 Cheriton Fitzpaine EX17 62 F1
 Malborough TQ7 147 E6
 Ottery St Mary EX11 100 F3
White Cross Ct PL4 263 A3
White Cross Hill EX17 62 F1
White Cross Rd EX5 184 D6
White Cross Woodland Wk EX11 100 F4
White Ct ❶ EX7 204 E6
Whitedown Cross EX15 67 E4
White Down Cross EX16 64 E5
White Farm La EX11 168 D3
Whitefield EX14 86 C3
White field Cross EX36 32 D3
Whitefield Hill EX31 9 E2
Whitefield La EX32 19 A6
Whitefield Terr PL4 263 B4
Whiteford Rd PL3 288 E6
Whiterfurs La PL4 263 B3
White Gate EX24 102 E3
Whitegates EX34 2 F4
White Gates Cross TQ13 110 F7
Whitehall CE EX36 158 C3
Whitehall Dr
 ❾ Bere Alston PL20 125 E1
 Plymouth PL9 256 B7
Whitehall La EX3 182 F8
Whitehall Manor TQ7 143 E4
White Hart La TA21 160 D6
Whitehayes Cl
 Kilmington EX13 87 C1
 Kilmington EX13 87 D1
 Wilmington EX14 86 D2
Whiteheads Cross TQ11 135 C7
White Heather Terr TQ13 180 D8
Whitehill Cl TQ12 207 B5
Whitehill Cotts TQ12 206 F5
Whitehill Cross PL15 105 B6
White Hill Dro TA20 69 F5
Whitehill Gdns PL7 238 E4
Whitehill Rd TQ12 207 A5
Whitehouse Cl ❷❸ EX39 15 B1
Whitehouse Cross EX39 156 B3
Whitehouse La EX18 58 D5
White La PL1 263 A2
White Ladies TQ6 146 B7
White Lady Rd PL9 255 D5
White Lady Waterfall EX20 107 C2
Whiteland Head EX20 57 B8
Whiteley Ave TQ9 222 F6
Whiteley Cross PL21 137 B5
White Lodge EX9 198 B1
Whitemoor Cross PL8 142 A8
Whitemoor Hill EX32 16 E1
Whitemoor La EX5 81 C8
Whiteoxen Cross TQ10 135 C4
White Pk TQ9 157 A8
White Post EX36 20 F2
White Rock Prim Sch TQ4 229 A8
Whiterocks Pk PL18 125 A6
Whites Cotts EX20 95 B4
Whiteside Cl EX2 178 C4
Whites La EX31 154 F7
White's La EX38 159 C5
White St EX33 182 F4
Whitestaunton Cross TA20 69 E5
Whitestone Cross TQ7 145 C5
Whitestone Dr EX16 161 C6
Whitestone La EX33 8 D1
Whitestone Orch ❷ TQ4 226 B5
White Stones EX8 202 C6
Whitethorn Cl
 Honiton EX14 166 C4
 Sidmouth EX10 187 F8
Whitethorn Pk EX4 173 C3
White Tor Cl EX20 170 E5
Whitewater Ct PL7 250 E6
Whiteway Cl ❻ EX5 99 E8
Whiteway Dr EX1 178 B6
Whiteway La TQ12 214 D8
Whiteway Rd TQ12 207 D7
Whitford Rd EX13 103 C6
Whitham Pk PL19 171 C4
Whitleigh Ave PL5 244 C4
Whitleigh Com Prim Sch PL5 244 D4
Whitleigh Cotts PL5 244 D4
Whitleigh Ct PL5 244 D4
Whitleigh Gn PL5 244 C4
Whitleigh Villas PL5 244 E2
Whitleigh Way PL5 244 C4
Whitley Cross TQ7 143 C3
Whitley Rd
 Farway EX24 101 F7
 Paignton TQ4 226 A4
Whitley Rocks EX36 31 C7
Whitlocks Mews VL4 210 A6
Whitlow Copse EX2 178 C4
Whitman Cl EX8 196 C4
Whitmore La PL21 137 C4
Whitmore Way EX14 166 A4
Whitnage La EX16 50 C2
Whitnole Cross EX16 48 A5
Whitnole La EX16 48 A4
Whitsam Cross PL20 125 D1
Whitsley Cross EX39,EX38 42 C4
Whitson Cross PL5 244 C7
Whitsoncross La PL5 244 C7
Whitstone Com Prim Sch EX22 70 E1
Whitstone Head Sch EX22 70 E1
Whitstone La
 Bovey Tracey TQ13 180 C8
 Meshaw EX36 46 B5
Whitstone Rd TQ4 226 B5
Whittingham Rd
 Ilfracombe EX34 150 C5
 Yealmpton PL8 141 B8
Whittington St TQ1 262 B4
Whitton Ct EX10 187 F7
Whitton La EX33 103 A3
Whitycombe Way EX4 176 D8
Whitty Cross PL7 242 A4
Whympston Cross PL21 137 D1
Wicaford Cross EX36 31 A2
Wicaford La EX36 31 A2
Wick Cross EX14 85 F7
Wicket The EX2 178 C3
Wickington La EX20 95 B7
Widdicombe Cross
 Marldon TQ3 218 F5
 Paignton TQ3 218 E5
Widdicombe Dr PL21 237 D4
Widecombe in the Moor Prim Sch TQ13 131 B3
Widecombe Way EX4 173 E1
Widegate Nursery PL9 256 D8
Wiend Camping Pk TQ3 225 A8
Widepost La EX3 167 C5
Widewell La PL6 245 C7
Widewell Prim Sch PL6 245 B7
Widewell Rd PL6 245 B7
Widey Court Prim Sch PL6 244 F4
Widey Cross PL6 244 F1
Widey Ct PL6 244 F1
Widey Hill PL8 141 A7
Widey La PL6 244 F1
Widey View PL3 248 F6
Widgery Dr EX36 158 C4
Widgery Rd EX4 178 A8
Widworthy Ct EX14 86 C2
Wigford Cross TQ7 138 C1
Wigley Cross EX31 16 C8
Wigmore Barn Rd TQ3 226 C7
Wilburton Cross PL21 136 C3
Wilbury Way PL7 204 F7
Wilcocks Rd EX4 174 D1
Wilcombe Cross EX32 18 E4
Wilcombe Prim Sch EX16 161 F3
Wilcove La PL11 246 E5
Wilderness La EX14 84 D6
Wilderness Rd PL3 248 E5
Wilder Pk EX34 150 B5
Wilder Rd EX34 150 B6
Wildmoor La TA21 152 F6
Wildner Top EX35 4 F4
Wildwoods Cres TQ12 207 F4
Wilford Rd EX13 155 C4
Wilkinson Rd PL5 247 D8
Willake Rd TQ12 213 A5
Willand Cty Prim Sch EX15 162 D4
Willand Ind Est EX15 162 D5
Willand Moor Mews EX15 162 D4
Willand Moor Rd EX15 162 E5
Willand Old Village EX15 162 C3
Willand Rd
 Braunton EX33 152 C6
 Cullompton EX15 163 C4
Willas Rd PL16 105 E4
Willcocks Cl EX2 161 D5
Willet St ❸ EX39 157 A2
Willeys Ave EX2 261 A1
Willeys Ct EX2 261 A1
Willhayes Cross EX13 113 A6
Willhayes Hill EX13 167 D6
Willhay La EX13 167 D4
Willhays EX19 TQ12 123 F1
William Evans Cl PL7 88 A5
William Prance Rd PL6 245 A3
Williams Ave
 Exeter EX2 261 A1
 Plymouth PL4 249 B1
Williams Ct
 Barnstaple EX31 154 C4
Williams Ct continued
 Buckfastleigh TQ11 236 B5
Williamson Cl EX33 8 A2
Williamson Ho EX31 155 A8
Williamson Way EX36 158 C4
William St ❸ EX16 161 D4
Willicombe Rd TQ3 226 A5
Willingcott Cross EX34 8 C6
Willingcott Hill EX34 8 D4
Willingcott Valley Holiday Village EX34 8 C5
Willis Cross TQ10 135 F5
Willis Ct ❶ TQ1 220 A7
Willis's Cross TQ12 122 D2
Willmott Cl EX4 196 E1
Willoughby Cl EX8 196 C3
Willoughby Ho EX10 187 E2
Willoughby Rd TQ1 220 C6
Willow Ave
 Exmouth EX8 196 B3
 Torquay TQ2 214 A3
Willoway Cl EX33 152 C6
Willoway Gr EX33 152 C6
Willoway La EX33 152 C7
Willowbank Prim Sch EX15 163 B3
Willowbrook Sch EX4 174 B1
Willow Gdns PL20 127 A2
Willow Pk PL20 127 A2
Willow Cl
 Ilfracombe EX34 150 E4
 Newton Abbot TQ12 213 A8
 Plymouth PL3 249 E5
 Seaton EX12 192 A8
 Stoke Canon EX5 173 F8
Willow Cotts PL7 250 D4
Willow Ct
 Exeter EX2 178 A4
 Plymouth PL6 249 E7
Willowfield Cl ❶ EX4 166 B6
Willowfield EX33 152 C7
Willow Gdns EX5 175 C6
Willow Gn PL12 242 D2
Willow Gr
 Bideford EX39 25 D4
 Stibb Cross EX38 40 D2
Willow La
 Cornworthy TQ9 227 B3
 Hemyock EX15 52 F2
Willowpark La TQ12 213 C4
Willow Rd PL19 171 C3
Willows Cl TQ7 144 E1
Willow St ❷ TQ14 210 B4
Willows The
 Chilsworthy EX22 53 E1
 Shillingford St George EX2 114 D5
 Torquay TQ2 213 D2
Willow Tree Cl EX20 170 C5
Willow Tree Rd EX32 155 B2
Willow View Pk EX5 100 A7
Willow Way
 Dawlish Warren EX7 201 A2
 Exeter EX4 178 C8
Willow Wlk
 Crediton EX17 165 E6
 ❷ Exeter EX4 177 D8
 Plymouth PL6 166 B4
Wills Ave TQ3 219 C1
Wills Cl PL6 244 E7
Willsdown Rd EX2 181 C8
Willshere Rd EX32 155 C4
Willsland Cl EX4 194 D3
Willsworthy Cross EX20 8 C4
Wilminstone Ind Est PL19 171 E7
Wilmot Gdns PL5 243 D3
Wilncote Lodge ❻ PL1 220 A6
Wilsham Cross EX35 6 A5
Wilsham La EX35 5 F5
Wilson Cres PL2 248 B5
Wilsworthy La
 Rackenford EX16 47 B4
 Witheridge EX17 46 B1
Wilton Cl TQ12 212 B6
Wilton Rd
 Paignton TQ3 219 B2
 Plymouth PL1 248 A3
Wilton St TQ1 262 A4
Wilton Way
 Abbotskerswell TQ12 212 B6
 Exeter EX1 178 D6
Wiltown La EX15 52 F3
Wiltshire Cl
 Exeter EX4 176 E4
 Plymouth PL4 248 F4
Wilway La TQ2 33 C6
Wincanton Cross TQ12 164 D3
Winchester Ave
 Exeter EX4 176 F1
 Torquay TQ3 213 F1
Winchester Cl EX14 84 D2
Winchester Dr TQ3 196 D4
Winchester Gdns PL5 244 A5
Windabout Cross EX39 39 B7
Windall Terr EX20 86 A4
Windball Hill EX17 33 B7
Window La EX14 48 D3
Windeatt Sq ❹ TQ9 223 D5
Windermere Cl EX4 176 F6
Windermere Cres PL6 244 F4
Windermere Rd TQ1 220 C6
Windford Hill EX31 30 C3
Windjammer Ct EX8 201 E6
Windmilland Cross EX21 74 A6
Windmill TQ3 219 A1
Windmill Cl TQ5 230 D4
Windmill Cross EX31 27 A3
Windmill Ct ❾ TQ5 230 C4
Windmill Gdns TQ3 219 A1
Windmill Hill
 Brixham TQ5 230 D4
 Saltash PL12 242 E2
Windmill La
 Northam EX39 157 B7
 North Whilborough TQ12 212 D1
 Paignton TQ3 218 F1
 West Hill EX11 168 D5
Windmill Rd
 Brixham TQ5 230 D4
 Holsworthy EX22 164 D4
 Paignton TQ3 219 A1
Windout La EX6 97 E3
Windrush Rise EX11 169 D3
Windsor Ave TQ2 207 F3
Windsor Cl
 Cullompton EX15 163 C6
 Exeter EX4 177 A7
 Ivybridge PL21 237 E4
 Newton Abbot TQ12 207 C2
 Torquay TQ1 220 B6
Windsor Ct
 Ilfracombe EX34 150 B5
 Kingsbridge TQ7 258 C5
Windsor Ho EX7 200 E2
Windsor Ho EX8 202 B7
Windsor Mead EX10 101 A1
Windsor Pl PL1 242 C2
Windsor Rd
 Barnstaple EX31 154 E7
 Dartmouth TQ6 233 C3
 Kingsbridge TQ7 258 D5
 Northam EX39 156 F7
 Plymouth PL3 249 B7
 Torquay TQ1 220 C6
Windsor Terr DT7 260 D4
Windsor Villas PL1 262 C2
Windthorn Cross TQ12 128 A7
Windthorn La TQ3,TQ12 218 D7
Windward Ct EX8 201 E6
Windward La EX7 210 F8
Windward Rd TQ2 213 E3
Windway Hill TA4 34 D6
Windwhistle Cross EX5 81 C8
Wind Whistle Force EX15 66 C1
Windy Ash Cross EX32 16 F1
Windy Ash Hill EX32 155 C1
Windy Cnr TQ4 229 B6
Windy Cross
 Ashford EX31 16 A6
 Chulmleigh EX18 44 E1
 Doddiscombsleigh EX6 113 E7
 Great Torrington EX38 159 C5
 Holsworthy Beacon EX22 54 F2
Windypost Cross EX35 151 C2
Wingate La EX24 75 C7
Wingfield TQ7 143 A1
Wingfield Mans PL3 248 A3
Wingfield Pk PL3 248 A3
Wingfield Way PL1 262 A4
Winham La EX15 83 B6
Winifred Baker Ct ❺ PL4 263 A4
Winifred Cliff Ct ❶ EX16 34 B1
Winkleigh Cl EX2 177 A2
Winkleigh Moor Cross EX19 58 E2
Winkleigh Prim Sch EX19 58 F2
Winneford La EX14 85 C3
Winner Hill Rd TQ3 226 C5
Winner St TQ3 226 B5
Winnicott Cl PL6 244 E7
Winnings Way TQ2 220 D7
Winnow Cl PL9 255 F4
Winsbeer La
 Rackenford EX16 47 B4
 Witheridge EX17 46 B1
Winscott Cross
 Holsworthy EX22 72 A4
 Newton St Cyres EX5 81 B1
Winsford Rd TQ2 219 C3
Winsham Cross
 Knowle EX33 8 D1
 Knowle EX33 8 E2
Winsham Rd EX33 8 D1
Winsland La EX5 175 C5
Winslade Ct
 Ilfracombe EX34 144 E1
 Topsham EX3 179 B2
Winslade La TQ7 144 E1
Winslade Park Ave EX5 179 B2
Winslade Rd TQ7 144 E1
Winsland Mdw EX6 97 F4
Winsland Rd TQ9 222 E6
Winsor Cross EX37 29 A4
Winsor Cross PL8 136 C4
Winstanley Wlk PL6 249 D6
Winstitchen Cross TA24 13 C2
Winstitchen La TA24 13 C2
Winston Ave TQ3 214 A1
Winston Cl TQ12 207 D4
Winston Cotts PL8 257 B4
Winston La PL8 257 B4
Winstone Ave TQ2 214 A1
Winstone Cotts EX5 82 A5
Winstow Cross EX36 31 A2
Winston Ho EX36 158 C5
Winston Rd EX36 158 C5
Winston Rd EX8 196 E2
Winsu Ave TQ3 226 A8
Winswell Water EX38 56 D7
Winswood EX17 165 D4
Winsworthy EX39 23 D3
Winter Gdn TQ2 210 D5
Winterbourne Rd TQ14 210 C5
Winterland La EX22 164 D2
Winters Cross TA4 35 C8
Winter's La EX11 169 D3
Wiriga Way EX16 46 E1
Wishings Rd TQ5 230 D3
Wisteria DT TQ7 258 C5
Wistford Cross EX32 18 C4
Wistman's Wood Nature Reserve PL20 119 D4
Witch La EX14 86 F8
Witcombe La EX6 194 D3
Witham Gdns PL3 249 C5
Witheby EX10 187 F3
Withecombe Cross TQ13 110 F8
Withen Cross EX5 99 C1
Withen Cross EX5 99 C1
Witherdon Cross EX21 91 D5
Witheridge CE Prim Sch EX16 46 E1
Witheridge Mill Cross EX16 46 E1
Witheridge Moor Cross (East) EX16 47 E1
Witheridge Moor Cross (West) EX16 47 D1
Withey The EX5 99 E8
Withleigh Cross EX16 63 C8
Withleigh La EX16 63 D7
Withnoe La PL10 252 B6
Withy Bed La EX5 99 E3
Withy Cl EX14 166 C8
Withycombe Park Dr EX8 196 C2
Withycombe Raleigh CE Prim Sch EX8 196 C1
Withycombe Rd EX8 202 A8
Withy Cross EX38 42 E6
Withygate La EX32 19 A5
Withy La EX15 52 B1
Withypool Cross
 Hawkridge TA22 21 C2
 Twitchen EX36 20 E4
Withywell La EX33 34 C5
Withywine La TA22 34 C5
Wixenford Ct PL9 255 F8
Wixon Cross EX18 45 B3
Wixon La EX18 45 B3
Woburn Cl TQ3 213 D2
Woburn Terr PL9 255 C7
Wolborough CE Prim Sch TQ12 207 C3
Wolborough Cl TQ12 207 C2
Wolborough Gdns
 Brixham TQ5 230 B6
 Newton Abbot TQ12 207 B3
Wolford Cross TA4 85 B8
Wollaton Cross PL18 257 A6
Wollaton Gr PL5 244 D2
Wolrige Ave PL7 251 B5
Wolrige Way PL7 251 B5
Wolsdon Pl PL1 262 A3
Wolsdon St PL1 262 A3
Wolseley Bsns Pk ❷ PL2 248 A5
Wolseley Cl PL2 248 A5
Wolseley Rd
 Plymouth, Camels Head PL5 247 F8
 Plymouth, St Budeaux PL5 243 C1
Wolseley Road Flats PL5 247 E8
Wolston Cl TQ5 230 B6
Wolverstone Cross EX14 85 A7
Wolverton Cl PL2 247 D7
Wolverton Dr TQ12 207 D7
Wolverwood Cl PL7 251 C3
Wolverwood La PL7 251 B3
Wombwell Cres PL2 247 E7
Wonders Cnr EX38 40 D2
Wonford Hospl EX2 177 F4
Wonford Rd EX2 261 C2
Wonford St EX2 178 A4
Wonnacott's Rd EX20 170 C5
Wonton Cross TQ13 131 A1
Woodacott Cross EX22 54 E2
Wood Acre PL12 242 D4
Woodah Rd EX4 176 F5
Wooda Rd EX39 210 D4
Woodbine Cotts PL7 250 E4
Woodbine Pl ❽ TQ12 192 C4
Woodbine Terr EX4 261 A4
Woodbridge La
 Bondleigh EX18 77 D8
 Farway EX24 102 B6
 North Tawton EX17 77 C6
Woodbrook Rd TQ9 223 C5
Woodburn Cl PL21 237 B5
Woodbury CE Prim Sch EX5 184 C3
Woodbury Cross EX8 202 C6
Woodbury Gdns PL5 244 A3
Woodbury Hill Cross TA4 34 C5
Woodbury Pk EX13 167 C4
Woodbury Rd EX3,EX5 183 C5
Woodbury Water Cross EX16 32 F1

Woodbury Salterton CE Prim Sch EX5 ...... 184 C7
Woodbury View
Broadclyst EX5 ...... 175 D6
Exeter EX2 ...... 177 A2
Woodbury Way EX13 ...... 167 D4
Woodbury Wlk EX6 ...... 181 F5
Woodchurch PL20 ...... 126 E3
Wood Cl
Christow EX6 ...... 113 B4
Saltash PL12 ...... 242 B3
Wood Cnr EX6 ...... 97 C2
Woodcock Cl PL10 ...... 253 A6
Woodcock Way EX13 ...... 88 B7
Woodcote Ct EX5 ...... 184 C3
Wood Cotts TQ12 ...... 180 C1
Woodcourt Rd TQ9 ...... 139 C7
Woodcroft Cross EX19 ...... 76 D7
Woodcroft La EX19 ...... 76 D8
Woodcroft Mdws TA20 ...... 69 B7
Wood Cross EX14 ...... 86 C6
Woodend Rd
Plymouth PL6 ...... 245 D7
Torquay TQ1 ...... 220 D4
Wooder Wharf 13 EX39 ...... 157 A1
Wood Farm Cvn & Camping Pk DT6 ...... 104 F5
Woodfield Cl EX8 ...... 196 E2
Woodfield Cres PL21 ...... 237 E4
Woodfield Ct TQ1 ...... 220 D7
Woodfield Prim Sch PL5 244 C5
Woodfields EX12 ...... 192 A7
Woodford Ave PL7 ...... 250 A7
Woodford Cl PL7 ...... 250 A7
Woodford Cres PL7 ...... 250 A6
Woodford Gdns EX32 ...... 155 C2
Woodford Gn PL7 ...... 250 B6
Woodford Inf Sch PL7 ...... 250 B6
Woodford Jun Sch PL7 250 B7
Woodford Rd PL6 ...... 245 D6
Woodhaye Cl 2 TQ10 ...... 134 F2
Woodhaye Gdns 5 TQ1 220 D4
Woodhaye Terr 7 TQ10 134 F2
Woodhead Cross
Branscombe EX12 ...... 190 E7
Totnes TQ9 ...... 217 D4
Woodhead La
Cheriton Fitzpaine EX16 ...63 A7
Totnes TQ9 ...... 217 E4
Woodhey Rd PL2 ...... 248 A7
Woodhill View EX14 ...... 166 B4
Woodhouse Cl TQ7 ...... 258 C4
Woodhouse Cross TQ13 122 D3
Woodhouse Fields DT7 ...104 B4
Woodhouse La
Axminster EX13 ...... 88 D1
Uplyme DT7 ...... 104 B4
Woodhouse Rd EX13 ...... 88 D1
Woodhuish La TQ5, TQ6...235 B7
Wood La
Abbotskerswell TQ12 ...... 212 A5
Ashreigney EX18 ...... 43 D1
Broadhembury EX14 ...... 84 E7
Christow EX6 ...... 113 B4
Combe Martin EX34 ...... 3 B2
Exmouth EX8 ...... 196 D1
Kingswear TQ6 ...... 234 B3
Monkton EX14 ...... 86 B6
Morchard Bishop EX17 ...61 A2
Slapton TQ7 ...... 145 D4
Stockleigh Pomeroy EX17 ...81 A4
West Alvington TQ7 ...... 258 A4
West Down EX34 ...... 8 F4
Woodland Ave
Kingskerswell TQ12 ...... 212 F5
Plymouth PL9 ...... 256 A8
Teignmouth TQ14 ...... 210 D7
Woodland Bsns Pk TQ2 ...219 E8
Woodland Cl
Barnstaple EX32 ...... 155 E4
Denbury TQ12 ...... 131 F3
Gunnislake PL18 ...... 125 C6
Ivybridge PL21 ...... 237 B5
Staverton TQ9 ...... 216 A4
Torquay TQ2 ...... 219 E8
Woodland Cotts EX5 ... 175 D6
1 Paignton TQ3 ...... 226 B7
Woodland Ct
1 Barnstaple EX32 ...... 155 A4
Ivybridge PL21 ...... 237 A5
Paignton TQ3 ...... 226 B7
Woodland Dr
Brixton PL8 ...... 257 B5
Plymouth PL7 ...... 250 B4
Woodlandhead Cross EX17 ...... 97 B7
Woodland Hill TQ7 ...... 97 B8
Woodland La TQ9 ...... 227 D4
Woodland Mews
Broadclyst EX5 ...... 175 D6
1 Paignton TQ3 ...... 226 B7
Woodland Pk
Northam EX39 ...... 157 A5
Paignton TQ3 ...... 226 B7
Woodland Rd
Ashburton TQ13 ...... 130 F4
Broadclyst EX5 ...... 175 C6
Denbury TQ12 ...... 211 A6
Exeter EX4 ...... 178 D7
Harbertonford TQ9 ...... 139 C7
Ivybridge PL21 ...... 237 B5
Lee Mill PL21 ...... 136 D7
Plymouth PL7 ...... 250 C6
Torquay TQ12 ...... 219 E8
Woodlands
Budleigh Salterton EX9 ...203 E8
Churchstow TQ7 ...... 143 E4
Combe Martin EX34 ...... 2 F4

Woodlands *continued*
Dousland PL20 ...... 127 B3
Halwill EX21 ...... 73 D3
Kingsteignton TQ12 ...... 123 E2
Newton St Cyres EX5 ...... 98 F8
Plymouth PL9 ...... 255 F6
Sidmouth EX10 ...... 188 A4
Wellington TA21 ...... 160 F3
Whimple EX5 ...... 99 F8
Woodlands Bsns Pk EX16 51 C3
Woodlands Cl
Churchstow TQ7 ...... 143 E4
Offwell EX14 ...... 86 B7
Teignmouth TQ14 ...... 210 C5
Woodlands Ct
Exmouth EX8 ...... 196 B3
Plymouth PL5 ...... 244 A3
Woodlands Dr EX8 ...... 196 B3
Woodlands End PL6 ...... 245 D5
Woodlands Gdns 5 TQ12 ...... 207 F2
Woodlands La PL6 ...... 245 F1
Woodlands Leisure Pk TQ9 ...... 139 F3
Woodlands Park Prim Sch PL21 ...... 237 A5
Woodlands Rd EX6 ...... 98 B4
Woodlands Sch PL5 ...... 244 B4
Woodlands Way EX5 ...... 179 C3
Woodlands Wlk TQ13 ...... 180 C4
Woodland Terr
Ivybridge PL21 ...... 237 B4
Kingswear TQ6 ...... 234 A3
Plymouth PL4 ...... 263 B4
Woodland Terr La PL4...263 B4
Woodland View EX22 ...... 164 C3
Woodland Way
Gunnislake PL18 ...... 125 D6
Torpoint PL11 ...... 246 F3
Woodlark La 2 EX31 ...... 154 A2
Woodleigh Cl EX4 ...... 173 A3
Woodleigh Pk TQ14 ...... 210 A8
Woodleigh Rd TQ12 ...... 206 F3
Woodley Cross EX5 ...... 98 F8
Woodley La EX5 ...... 98 E8
Woodleys Dr EX10 ...... 186 D8
Woodleys Mdw TQ2 ...... 219 E2
Woodman's Cnr PL20 ...... 127 A3
Woodmans Cres 2 EX14 ...... 166 C5
Woodmans Orch EX5 ...... 84 A2
Woodmead Rd
Axminster EX13 ...... 167 C5
Lyme Regis DT7 ...... 260 D3
Woodmere Way TQ12 ...... 207 E6
Woodovis Cvn Pk PL19 116 D1
Woodpark Cross EX17...61 A8
Woodpark La
Midland EX36 ...... 31 E6
Paignton TQ3 ...... 218 E8
Wood Park La EX34 ...... 2 E3
Woodpecker Way EX6 ...97 B4
Wood Pk
Ivybridge PL21 ...... 237 D6
Plymouth PL6 ...... 132 A2
Woodplace La EX16 ...... 62 F7
Woodridge Cross EX31 ...51 D4
Wood Rock EX36 ...... 32 C5
Woodstock Rd EX2 ...... 178 A5
Woodvale EX3 2 TQ12 ... 207 B3
Wood View EX4 ...... 207 A3
Woodview Pk PL9 ...... 256 A6
Woodview Rd TQ4 ...... 225 E1
Wood View Terr PL21...136 F3
Woodville EX31 ...... 154 C3
Woodville Ave PL20 ...... 128 A8
Woodville Cl
Barnstaple EX31 ...... 154 C4
Plymouth PL2 ...... 247 F7
Woodville Cross EX31...36 F1
Woodville Rd
Exeter EX4 ...... 177 B3
Exmouth EX8 ...... 202 A8
Morwenstow EX23...36 A5
Torquay TQ1 ...... 220 C6
Woodward Rd EX16 ...... 161 B2
Woodwater La
Exeter EX4 ...... 178 B4
Exeter EX2 ...... 178 C3
Woodway PL9 ...... 256 A2
Wood Way EX5 ...... 6 D4
Woodway Cl TQ14 ...... 210 C7
Woodway Dr TQ14 ...... 210 C6
Woodway Rd TQ14 ...... 210 C6
Woodway St TQ13 ...... 123 E6
Woody Bay Sta EX31...4 F1
Woolacombe Cross PL20 125 F1
Woolacombe Ct EX34 ...... 8 A6

Woolacombe Rd PL20....125 F1
Woolacombe Rise EX34 .... 8 B6
Woolacombe Sands Cvn Pk EX34 ...... 8 A6
Woolacombe St EX34 ...... 8 A6
Woolacombe Station Rd EX34 ...... 8 B6
Wooloan Lawn EX32 ...... 155 D4
Woolbrook Cl EX10 ...... 188 A7
Woolbrook Mdws EX10 ... 188 A7
Woolbrook Mead EX10 ... 187 F7
Woolbrook Pk EX10 ...... 188 A7
Woolbrook Rd EX10 ...... 188 A7
Woolbrook Rise EX10 ... 188 A7
Woolcombe La
Ivybridge PL21 ...... 237 D4
Sidmouth EX10 ...... 188 B5
Woolcott Way EX15 ...... 163 B2
Woolfardisworthy Cross
Clovelly EX39 ...... 23 D2
Woolfardisworthy EX17...62 A3
Woolhanger's La EX34 ...... 2 F2
Woollcombe Ave PL7 ...... 250 F4
Woolleigh Cross EX19...42 B3
Woolms Mdw EX21 ...... 237 A4
Woolpit La TA24 ...... 21 B7
Woolsery Ave EX4 ...... 178 B8
Woolsery Cl EX4 ...... 178 B8
Woolsery Gr EX4 ...... 178 B8
Woolsery Sch EX39 ...... 38 F7
Woolster Ct 8 PL4 ...... 263 A2
Woolwell Cres PL6 ...... 245 C8
Woolwell Dr PL6 ...... 245 C7
Woolwell Rd PL6 ...... 245 D7
Wootton Cross EX13 ...... 88 F1
Worcester Cres EX15...162 D4
Worden Cross
Milton Damerel EX22...54 E6
Sutcombe EX22 ...... 54 C8
Wordland Cross EX17...80 F8
Wordsworth Ave EX31...154 F7
Wordsworth Cl
Exmouth EX8 ...... 196 C4
Torquay TQ2 ...... 219 E6
Wordsworth Cres PL2...247 F7
Wordsworth Dr EX8 ...... 196 D4
Worham's La EX13...86 F2
Works The EX16 ...... 161 C4
World of Country Life EX9 ...... 203 B6
Worlington Cross EX39...15 C1
Worlington Hill EX39...15 C1
Wormsworthy Hill EX16 ...48 D6
Worthele Cl PL21 ...... 237 A4
Worthele Cross PL21...237 B1
Worth La
Hele EX5 ...... 82 E5
Withypool TA22, TA24...21 C4
Worthy La EX16 ...... 47 C6
Wotton Cross TQ12 ...... 131 E4
Wotton La EX8 ...... 196 B5
Wotton Pound EX8 ...... 196 A5
Wotton Way TQ9 ...... 131 E1
Wrafton Rd EX33 ...... 152 E4
Wrangaton Rd PL21, TQ10 ...... 137 D8
Wrangcombe La TA21...52 A4
Wrangcombe Rd TA21...52 A4
Wrangway Rd EX15...52 A3
Wrangworthy Cross EX39 .39 E4
Wreford's Cl EX4 ...... 173 A3
Wreford's Dr EX4 ...... 173 A3
Wreford's La
Exeter EX4 ...... 173 A3
Exeter EX4 ...... 173 B3
Wreford's Link EX4 ...... 173 A3
Wren Cl
Honiton EX14 ...... 166 B4
Northam EX39 ...... 157 A6
Wren Cl 10 TQ5 ...... 230 C4
Wren Gdns PL7 ...... 250 C6
Wren Hill TQ5 ...... 230 C4
Wren Ret Pk TQ2 ...... 213 D2
Wrens Gate PL9 ...... 255 E8
Wrentham Bsns Ctr EX4. 177 D8
Wrentham Est EX4 ...... 177 D8
Wrenwell Cross TQ12...131 F3
Wressing View EX15...66 A3
Wrey Ave EX31 ...... 154 D4
Wright Cl PL1 ...... 247 E3
Wright Dr EX17 ...... 79 A5
Wrights La PL8 ...... 140 F7
Wright's La
Exmouth EX8 ...... 196 F6
Torquay TQ1 ...... 220 A7
Wrigwell Cross TQ12...211 E1
Wrigwell La TQ12 ...... 217 F8
Wrinkleberry La EX39...23 D3
Wroxall Grange TQ1 ...... 220 C4
Wulphere Cl EX14...67 B1
Wyatts La PL19 ...... 171 B6
Wychall Orch EX12...192 A6
Wychall Pk EX12 ...... 192 A7
Wych Cl EX13 ...... 88 E3
Wychwood Cl EX7...204 E7
Wycliffe Rd PL3 ...... 249 B4
Wye Gdns PL3 ...... 249 D7
Wyke Cross EX17 ...... 80 F2
Wykeham Dr PL2 ...... 248 A7
Wyke Hill EX17 ...... 80 F2
Wyke La EX13 ...... 167 D2
Wyke Moor Cross EX20...95 C8
Wyke Rd EX13 ...... 167 D3
Wykes Rd EX1 ...... 177 F2
Wylie Ho EX2 ...... 261 A1
Wynards EX2 ...... 261 B2

Wynards Cl EX9 ...... 198 B6
Wynards La 2 EX2 ...... 261 B2
Wynards Rd EX9 ...... 198 B6
Wyndham Ave EX1 ...... 177 F6
Wyndham La PL1 ...... 262 A3
Wyndham Mews PL1 ...... 262 A3
Wyndham PI PL1 ...... 262 A3
Wyndham Rd EX5...82 B6
Wyndham St E PL1 ...... 262 B3
Wyndham St W PL1 ...... 262 B3
Wyndham Sq PL1 ...... 262 A3
Wyndthorpe Gdns 17 EX34 ...... 150 C6
Wynford Rd EX4 ...... 173 F1
Wynstream Sch EX2 ...... 177 F3
Wyoming Cl PL3 ...... 249 C6
Wyre Cl TQ4 ...... 226 A2
Wytch Gn EX13 ...... 88 E3
Wythburn Gdns PL6 ...... 245 D3

Y

Yalberton Ind Est TQ4 ... 225 D3
Yalberton Ind Management Units TQ4 ...... 225 E3
Yalberton Rd TQ4 ...... 225 D3
Yalberton Tor Ind Est TQ4 ...... 225 D3
Yalland Cross TQ10 ...134 F5
Yallop Way EX14 ...... 166 B4
Yanhey Hill EX16 ...... 32 E4
Yannon Dr TQ14 ...... 210 B5
Yannon La TQ14 ...... 212 E5
Yannons The TQ14 ...... 210 B6
Yannon Terr TQ14 ...... 210 B6
Yapham Cross EX39...23 A4
Yarda Wlk PL8 ...... 257 A4
Yardbury Hill Rd EX24...102 E7
Yard Cross EX14 ...... 86 B7
Yard Down Cross EX36...19 C6
Yard Downs La EX5...82 C6
Yarde Cl EX10 ...... 188 B7
Yarde Cross EX38 ...... 41 D1
Yarde Cross EX36 ...... 18 A4
Yarde Gate Cross EX36...19 C6
Yarde Hill Orch EX36...188 B7
Yardelands Cl EX10 ...... 188 B7
Yardelands Cl EX10 ...... 188 B7
Yarde Mead EX10 ...... 188 B7
Yarde's Grave Cross TQ9 222 F7
Yard Hill TQ13 ...... 111 D2
Yard La EX36 ...... 46 B8
Yardleigh Cross EX13...88 D4
Yardley Gdns PL6 ...... 245 E3
Yards La TQ5 ...... 230 C2
Yardwells Cross EX36...19 B5
Yarmleigh La EX17...79 E7
Yarnacott Cnr EX32 ...... 17 E1
Yarnapitts Cross TQ13...110 F2
Yarner Wood Nature Trail TQ13 ...... 122 C5
Yarrow Mead PL9 ...... 256 D7
Yawl Cres DT7 ...... 104 B5
Yawl Cross DT7 ...... 104 B6
Yawl Hill DT7 ...... 104 C6
Yawl Hill La DT7 ...... 104 B5
Yealmbury Hill PL8 ...... 257 F4
Yealm Gr TQ2 ...... 219 C2
Yealm Pk PL8 ...... 257 E4
Yealmpstone Cl PL7...251 B4
Yealmpstone Dr PL7...251 B3
Yealmpstone Farm Prim Sch PL7 ...... 251 B3
Yealmpton Prim Sch PL8 ...... 257 E4
Yealm View Rd PL8 ...... 140 F6
Yearlstone Vineyard EX16 .63 F5
Yearnor Mill La TA24...... 6 F5
Yeats Cl PL5 ...... 244 C2
Yeatt Cross TQ12 ...... 131 F3
Yellaford Way 1 EX31...154 B3
Yelland Bglws TQ10 ...... 135 E5
Yelland Cross
Challacombe EX31 ...... 11 D4
Rattery TQ10 ...... 135 E5
Yelland EX31 ...... 153 A5
Yelland Rd EX31 ...... 153 C5
Yellands Pk TQ7 ...... 142 C6
Yellaton La EX34 ...... 3 B1
Yellow Tor Ct PL12 ...... 242 C7
Yellow Tor La EX17...67 B1
Yellow Tor Rd PL12 ...... 242 B2
Yelverton Bsns Pk PL20. 126 E2
Yelverton Cl PL5 ...... 243 E4
Yelverton Paperweight Mus PL20 ...... 126 E2
Yelverton Terr
Tavistock PL19 ...... 171 D6
Yelverton PL20 ...... 127 A2
Yendacott La EX17...81 B3
Yeo Cl PL3 ...... 249 B5
Yeo Cotts TQ12 ...... 133 D3
Yeo Dr 20 EX39 ...... 15 A1
Yeoford Com Prim Sch EX17 ...... 79 C1
Yeoford Mdws EX17...79 C1
Yeoford Sta EX17 ...... 79 C1
Yeoford Way EX2 ...... 181 D8
Yeo Gate EX36 ...... 31 C4
Yeo La
Molland EX36 ...... 31 C5
North Tawton EX20 ...... 77 B5
Yeoland Down PL20...126 F1
Yeoland La
Swimbridge EX32 ...... 17 F1
Yelverton PL20 ...... 126 F1

Yeoland Lane Cvn Pk PL20 ...... 126 F1
Yeolands The TQ9 ...... 227 F8
Yeoland La PL21 ...... 237 D5
Yeoland Pk PL21 ...... 237 E5
Yeomadon Cross EX22...71 D4
Yeomans Way PL7 ...... 251 A4
Yeo Mill Cross EX36...32 C5
Yeo Pk PL8 ...... 136 A3
Yeo Rd
Braunton EX31 ...... 15 E5
Zeal Monachorum EX17...78 D7
Yeotown Cross EX37...44 C8
Yeo Vale Cross EX17...60 C2
Yeo Vale Cross Ind Est EX17 ...... 60 C2
Yeo Vale Ho 5 EX32 ...... 154 F6
Yeo Vale Rd EX32 ...... 154 F6
Yeo Valley Prim Sch EX32 ...... 155 A6
Yeo View EX17...79 C1
Yerris Rd EX15...65 F3
Yetsonais Cross TQ9 ...... 144 D8
Yettington Rd EX9 ...... 198 A7
Yew Cl
Brixham TQ5 ...... 229 F4
Honiton EX14 ...... 166 A4
Yewdale Gdns PL6 ...... 245 D2
Yew Tree Cl
Exeter EX4 ...... 173 E1
Exmouth EX8 ...... 196 C3
Yew Tree Dr TQ12 ...... 207 E6
Yew Wood Cross EX15...66 A4
Yolhey La TQ12 ...... 212 C5
Yonder Cl EX11 ...... 169 E3
Yonder Cnr EX11...169 E3
Yonder Hill Cotts EX13...88 E7
Yonder Mdw TQ9 ...... 222 F8
Yonder Mount EX13 ...... 103 D5
Yonder St
Ottery St Mary EX11 ...... 169 E3
Plymouth PL9 ...... 255 B6
Yon St TQ12 ...... 212 F4
York Cl
Axminster EX13 ...... 167 E6
Exmouth EX8 ...... 196 E2
Exeter EX4 ...... 84 D2
York Cres
Feniton EX14 ...... 84 D2
Torquay TQ1 ...... 220 C8
Yorke Rd TQ6 ...... 233 D3
York Gdns TQ4 ...... 226 B4
York Mews TQ4 ...... 226 B5
York Pl
Bideford EX39 ...... 157 A3
Cullompton EX15 ...... 163 C5
Plymouth PL2 ...... 247 F4
York Rd
Exeter EX4 ...... 261 C4
Paignton TQ4 ...... 226 B4
Plymouth PL5 ...... 247 E8
Seaton EX12 ...... 192 A5
Torpoint PL11 ...... 247 B3
Torquay TQ1 ...... 220 C8
York St
Plymouth PL1 ...... 247 E2
Sidmouth EX10 ...... 188 B3
York Terr
Exeter EX4 ...... 261 C4
7 Paignton PL2 ...... 247 F5
Sidmouth EX10 ...... 188 B3
York Villas TQ1 ...... 220 C8
Youings Dr EX31 ...... 155 A7
Youlden La EX20...95 C7
Youldon Moor Cross EX22 53 E4
Youldons TQ9 ...... 139 C7
Youldon Way PL20...126 F4
Youlston Cl EX31...17 A7
Youltree Cross EX39...22 E4
Youngaton Rd EX39 ...... 156 C7
Young's Park La TQ4 ...... 226 C4
Young's Park Rd TQ4 ...... 226 C4

Z

Zeal Cross EX6 ...... 112 F8
Zealley Est TQ12 ...... 207 E6
Zeal Rd
Dunsford EX6 ...... 112 F8
Tedburn St Mary EX6...97 F1
Zempson Cross TQ10...135 B5
Zephyr Cres EX32 ...... 155 B5
Zeth Hill La PL21 ...... 136 D8
Zion Pl
Dartmouth TQ6 ...... 233 F4
Ivybridge PL21 ...... 237 C5
Zion Rd 3 TQ2 ...... 219 F5
Zion St PL1 ...... 262 C2

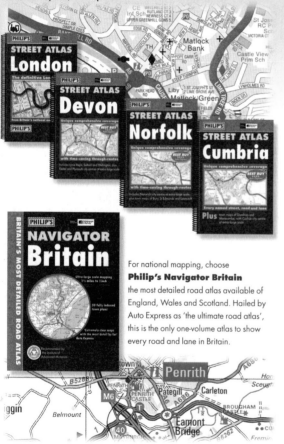